D0071329

Experiencing the Lifespan

Praise for *Experiencing the Lifespan!*

"I have never seen a textbook that covers the lifespan in such a clear and concise, but also detailed way as the Belsky text. The supplemental information embedded within the text is relatable to students and attracts their interest in the topic. To me this is the best lifespan development text on the market. This text also uses great real-world examples that students can relate to and encourages students to critically think about many questions and dilemmas that arise in development. I always say I will never change this text out. I haven't seen another textbook that adequately covers the lifespan as well as this text and does so in a thought-provoking and easy-to-understand way."

—*Heidi Beattie, Troy University*

"The greatest strength of this textbook is Janet Belsky's writing style. You feel as if she is talking to you, explaining things so well and telling you about her own life. It's a wonderful skill. My students tell me it is an easy book to read and it keeps their interest."

—*Suzy Horton, Mesa Community College*

"The Belsky text gives fundamental coverage to most of the major areas of developmental psychology very efficiently and effectively. Many of the features such as "Hot in Developmental Science" add a great deal to the coverage of material and understanding of the reader. Diversity is apparent throughout the text. I think that the book establishes a firm foundation to build a developmental course upon."

—*Ron Mulson, Hudson Valley Community College*

"I love the attachment section in Ch. 4. It is more thorough than in other texts I've used and it is such an important topic in development. I also love how Belsky presents different sides of some controversial topics in human development and invites the students to decide for themselves, and to use critical thinking skills based on research (such as co-sleeping, pros and cons of hospice care, etc.)"

—*Wendy Bianchini Morrison, Montana State University – Bozeman*

"The last several sentences of the final chapter are so touching and nicely wrap up the entire theme of the course that I often will read them word for word to the students. One student in conversation referred to the text as a perfect guide for life and another said reading it was like reading one of those popular press psychology magazines. The text and the way it is written is relevant to any major, not just psychology. Since selecting this book for the 2008 academic year, I have not looked at any other textbook for the course. Why change when the book is engaging, covers the needed material and does so in a thoughtful way that hits both the "science" and "humanness" of human psychology?

—*Chad Keller, Lewis and Clark Community College*

Experiencing the Lifespan

FIFTH EDITION

Janet Belsky

worth publishers
Macmillan Learning

New York

FOR DAVID AND SHELLY

Senior Vice President, Content Strategy: Charles Linsmeier
Program Director: Shani Fisher
Executive Program Manager: Christine M. Cardone
Developmental Editor: Elaine Epstein
Editorial Assistant: Dorothy Tomasini
Marketing Manager: Clay Bolton
Marketing Assistant: Chelsea Simens
Executive Media Editor: Laura Burden
Lead Media Project Manager: Eve Conte
Director, Content Management Enhancement: Tracey Kuehn
Senior Managing Editor: Lisa Kinne
Senior Content Project Manager: Vivien Weiss
Project Manager: Valerie Brandenburg, Lumina Datamatics, Inc.
Senior Photo Editor: Sheena Goldstein
Photo Researcher: Brittani Morgan
Director of Design, Content Management: Diana Blume
Design Services Manager: Natasha A. S. Wolfe
Cover Designer: John Callahan
Interior Designer: Lumina Datamatics
Senior Workflow Supervisor: Susan Wein
Production Supervisor: Lawrence Guerra
Art Manager: Matthew McAdams
Composition: Lumina Datamatics, Inc.
Printing and Binding: LSC Communications
Cover photo: Terry Vine/Blend Images/Getty Images
Chapter-closing photos: Sky View/DigitalVision/Getty Images, Monkey
    Business Images/Shutterstock.com, gregorydean/iStock/Getty Images,
    Joana Lopes/Shutterstock.com, Plush Studios/Bill Reitzel/Blend
    Images/Getty Images, Image Source/DigitalVision/Getty Images
Photo of brain icon: RENGraphic/DigitalVision Vectors/Getty Images
Photo of flame icon: rilora/iStock/Getty Images

Library of Congress Control Number: 2018945669

ISBN-13: 978-1-319-10701-7
ISBN-10: 1-319-10701-X

© 2019, 2016, 2013, 2010 by Worth Publishers
All rights reserved.

Printed in the United States of America

3 4 5 6 7   23 22 21 20 19

WORTH PUBLISHERS
One New York Plaza
Suite 4500
New York, NY
10004-1562

www.macmillanlearning.com

About the Author

Sheldon Gertzfeld

Born in New York City, Janet Belsky always wanted to be a writer but was also very interested in people. After receiving her undergraduate degree from the University of Pennsylvania, she deferred to her more practical and people-loving side and earned a Ph.D. in clinical psychology at the University of Chicago. Janet spent her thirties in New York City teaching at Lehman College, CUNY, and doing clinical work in hospitals and nursing homes. During this time, she wrote one trade book, *Here Tomorrow, Making the Most of Life After 50*, got married, adopted a child and, with the publication of the first undergraduate textbook in the psychology of aging, began what turned into a lifelong developmental science textbook writing career. In 1991, Janet moved to Tennessee with her family to write and teach undergraduate courses in psychology at Middle Tennessee State University. After her husband died in 2012, Janet enrolled in the Master's Program in Liberal Arts at the University of Chicago (a beginning graduate student after 45-plus years!). Still, she remains committed to her life passion—exciting readers in the marvelous human lifespan through this book.

Brief Contents

Contents

Image Source Plus/Alamy

PART VII
Endings 437

I got my Ph.D. in clinical psychology in my late twenties and began working as a practicing psychologist. But for me, that career didn't emotionally fit. When I had the chance to teach a new course called Lifespan Development to first-generation college students and then was asked to write a book in an emerging field called the Psychology of Aging, everything changed. I became hooked on textbook writing for life. At age 70, I'm even more passionate about writing than at age 29. The reason is simple: Textbooks have a unique ability to get students to think deeply about life.

Textbooks are unique because they are focused on the forest. Unlike Wikipedia entries or Ted Talks, they offer a panorama of an *entire* field. Textbooks put it all together: They organize a discipline; they make connections for students; they train readers to critically evaluate evidence and think in a rational, scientific way. As with my previous books, *Experiencing the Lifespan*, Fifth Edition, strives to present the latest research. I hope to entice students to enter our field. But I have special goals in writing this particular book. In an era when basic research facts may be questioned, I want to convince students of the power of the scientific worldview. In a digital age when students tend to be reluctant readers, I want to convey the power of the written word.

What Makes This Book Compelling?

- *Experiencing the Lifespan* **reads like a story.** My main strategy to excite students in science and reading is to adopt a storylike, conversational style. Each chapter begins with a vignette constructed to highlight the material I will be discussing. I've designed my narrative to flow from topic to topic. I've planned every chapter to connect. In this book, the main themes that underlie developmental science flow throughout the *whole* book. I believe that telling a coherent story and talking directly to readers makes learning come alive.

- *Experiencing the Lifespan* **highlights development.** A second mission that drives my writing is to show how the story of living unfolds. What *exactly* makes an 8-year-old different from a 4-year-old, or a 60-year-old different from a person of 85? In order to emphasize development during childhood, I've anchored my discussion in Erikson's and Piaget's landmark stages. How can we use these seminal theories to pull together the findings relating to expanding executive functions and explain why status and self-esteem issues become vital during elementary school?

In fact, I've designed this *whole* text to highlight development. I follow the characters in the chapter-opening vignettes throughout each book part. I've planned each section of the book to flow in a developmental way. In the first "Infancy" chapter, I begin with a discussion of newborn states. The second chapter in this sequence ends with a discussion of toddlerhood. The "Early and Middle Adulthood" book part starts with an exploration of emerging adulthood, then tackles marriage, parenthood, and career. It culminates with a chapter tracking personality and intelligence through

The fact that Latino grandchildren have such intense contact with their grandparents offers one reason for the "Hispanic paradox"—the statistic that, in spite of being far less affluent, Latino-heritage adults tend to live a surprisingly long time. The lesson: As a caring, involved grandchild of *any* cultural background, you might be "working" to help extend a beloved elderly family member's life!

midlife, and explores "older" family roles, such as parent care and grandparenthood. In Part VI, "Later Life," I begin with a chapter devoted to topics, such as retirement, that typically take place during the young-old years, then focus on physical aging because sensory-motor impairments, dementing diseases, and interventions for late-life frailty become crucial mainly in the eighties and beyond. Yes, this textbook does—for the most part—move through the lifespan stage by stage. But, because it highlights how we *change over time*, I believe my book captures the best features of the chronological and topical approaches.

- *Experiencing the Lifespan* **is both shorter and more in depth.** Adopting this integrative, development-focused approach makes for a more manageable teacher-friendly book. With 15 chapters and at fewer than 500 pages, my textbook *really* can be mastered in a one-semester course! And focusing on the lifespan "forest" makes for a more interesting text. Rather than attempting to superficially cover *everything*, I continually ask myself: What are the most important issues in developmental science? How can I get students to reflect on these core topics in a genuinely thoughtful way?

- *Experiencing the Lifespan* **fosters critical thinking.** Guiding students to reflect on what they are reading is center stage in my book. A great advantage of engaging readers in a conversation is that I can naturally embed critical thinking into the text. So, as I move from discussing Piaget's ideas on cognition to Vygotsky's theory, I point out the gaps in each perspective and highlight *why* each theorist offers a unique contribution to understanding children's intellectual growth. On a policy-oriented level, after discussing day care, teenage storm and stress, or physical aging, I ask readers to think critically about how to improve the way our culture cares for young families, treats teenagers, and can make life more user-friendly for the baby boomers now in their older years.

Could this have been you in high school, particularly toward the end of the week? Do you think we are making a mistake by resisting teenagers' biological clocks and insisting that the school day start at 8 A.M.?

- *Experiencing the Lifespan* **has a global and historical orientation.** Intrinsic to getting students to evaluate their own cultural practices is the need to high-light alternate perspectives on our developing life. Therefore, *Experiencing the Lifespan* is a firmly international book. I introduce this global orientation in the first chapter when I spell out the differences between collectivist and indi-vidualistic cultures and between the developed and developing worlds. When discussing topics from pregnancy to parenting, I provide the larger historical context. I'm passionate to spell out how our ideas about child-rearing and development have evolved over time. In the adulthood sections, "Setting the Context" heads, preceding the research, offer snapshots of love and marriage in other eras and places, discuss retirement around the world, and explore different societal practices and attitudes toward death. (In fact, "How do other groups handle this?" is a question that crops up when I talk about practically every topic in the book!)

This photo shows another landmark loosening of traditional Sharia law rules. In 2018, Saudi women were *finally* allowed to drive!

- *Experiencing the Lifespan* **highlights the multiple forces that shape develop-ment.** Given my emphasis on variations within our universal human experience, it should come as no surprise that the organizing spirit of my book is the ecological, developmental systems approach. Throughout the chapters, I explore the many influences that interact to predict life milestones from puberty to physical aging. Attachment theory, behavioral genetics, evolutionary theory, self-efficacy, and, especially, the importance of looking at nature and nurture and providing the best person–environment fit—all are concepts that I introduce in the first chapter and continue to stress as the book unfolds. Another theme that runs through this text is the impact of socioeconomic status on shaping everything from breast-feeding practices to the rate at which we age and die.

- *Experiencing the Lifespan* **is applications-oriented and focused on how to construct a satisfying life.** Because of my background as a clinical psychologist, my other passion is to concretely bring home how we can use the scientific findings to improve life. So most topics in this text end with **Interventions** sections that spell out practical implications of the research. From its varied childhood interventions, such as "Using Piaget's Theory at Home and at Work," or "Encouraging Less Stereotyped Play," to my detailed coverage of wisdom and happiness in the chapter on midlife, *Experiencing the Lifespan* is designed to show how research can make a difference in people's lives.

The fact that toddlers naturally take joy in giving suggests that giving is built into being human.

- *Experiencing the Lifespan* **is a person-centered, hands-on textbook.** This book is also designed to bring the experience of the lifespan home in a personal way. Therefore, in **Experiencing the Lifespan** boxes, I report on interviews I've conducted with people ranging from a 16-year-old (a student of mine) who was charged as an adult with second-degree murder to a 94-year-old psychotherapist still practicing his passion. To entice readers to empathize with the challenges of other life stages, I continually ask students to "imagine you are a toddler" or "a sleep-deprived mother" or "an 80-year-old struggling with the challenges of driving in later life."

  Another strategy I use to make the research vivid and personal is to devise creative questionnaires (often based on the chapter content) that get readers to think more deeply about their *own* lives: the checklist to identify your parenting priorities in Chapter 7; surveys for "evaluating your relationships" in Chapters 10 and 11; true/false quizzes at the beginning of my chapters on adolescence, adult roles, and later life that provide a hands-on preview of the content and entice students into reading the chapter so that they can assess the scientific accuracy of their ideas.

- *Experiencing the Lifespan* **is designed to get students to learn the material while they read.** The chapter-opening vignettes, the applications sections with their summary tables, the hands-on exercises, and the end-of-section questionnaires (such as "Evaluating Your Own Relationship: A Section Summary Checklist" in Chapter 10) are part of an overall pedagogical plan. As I explain in my introductory letter to students on page 2, I want this to be a textbook you don't have to struggle to decode — one that helps you *naturally* cement the concepts in mind. After beginning each major topic, with a few **Learning Outcomes** to help students guide their reading, the centerpiece of this effort is the end-of-section **Tying It All Together** quizzes. These mini-tests — involving multiple-choice, essay, and critical-thinking questions — allow students to test themselves on what they have absorbed. I've planned the photos in *Experiencing the Lifespan* to illustrate the major terms and concepts. As you page through the text, you may notice that the pictures and their captions feel organically connected to the writing. They visually bring the main text messages home. When it's important for students to learn a series of terms or related concepts, I provide a summary series of photos. You can see examples in the photographs illustrating the different infant and adult attachment styles on pages 111 and 312, and in Table 3.7 on page 94, highlighting Jean Piaget's infant circular reactions.

- *Experiencing the Lifespan* **actively teaches the *science* of development.** In addition to offering a panorama of the latest findings, I want to immerse readers in the joys and challenges of the research enterprise itself. To show students exactly how scientific questions translate into research, **How do we know . . . ?** boxes in most chapters describe how specific studies are carried out and planned; **Hot in Developmental Science** sections showcase cutting-edge topics, from the impact of communities on upward mobility to social media's influence on romance. My mission in each edition of *Experiencing the Lifespan* has been to transcend the standard focus on listing "what we know" and ask those critical questions: What are the most pressing current topics in developmental science? How exactly *do* we know what we know?

What will make this book excite students in science? How can I make my writing a joy to read? These are the questions I have been passionate to answer as I've been glued to my computer—often seven days a week. Above all, I want this textbook to enrich readers' lives.

If you can relate to this photo the next time you are tempted to text during that not-so-interesting class, keep this message in mind: *Divided-attention tasks* make memory worse!

What Makes Each Chapter Special?

Now that I've spelled out my general writing missions, what follows are two structural changes designed to improve this new edition, as well as a preview of the topics you will find in the chapters to come:

1. To improve the flow of this edition, I've organized each life stage into four predictable parts: physical development, cognitive development, emotional development, and social development.

2. To bring home the message that early and middle childhood are fundamentally different, I now discuss these two childhood stages in separate chapters.

Here are some highlights of each chapter and what's new.

PART I: The Foundation

CHAPTER 1: The People and the Field

- Outlines the basic contexts of development: social class, culture, ethnicity, and cohort.

- Traces the evolution of the lifespan over the centuries and explores the classic developmental science theories that have shaped our understanding of life.

- Spells out concepts, perspectives, research methods, and the research studies I will be exploring in each chapter of the book.

What's New?

- Showcases data relating to income inequalities and introduces the concept of upward mobility.

- Revises items in the Tying It All Together quizzes and updates figures to offer data on recent demographic trends. (I've made similar changes to the quiz items and relevant figures throughout the book.)

CHAPTER 2: Prenatal Development, Pregnancy, and Birth

- Discusses pregnancy rituals and superstitions around the world.

- Highlights the latest research on fetal brain development.

- Explores the experience of pregnancy from both the mother's and father's points of view, and discusses infertility.
- Looks at birth historically and discusses policy issues relating to pregnancy and birth in the United States and around the world.

What's New

- Discusses the career impact of informing a boss of one's pregnancy.
- Provides recent information on the impact of pregnancy stress on the fetus.
- Offers an international look at the emotional effects of infertility.
- Updates the material on c-sections, ART, and infant mortality.

PART II: Infancy and Toddlerhood

CHAPTER 3: Physical and Cognitive Development in Infants and Toddlers

- Covers the latest research on brain development.
- Focuses on basic infant states such as eating, crying, and sleep.
- Explores breast-feeding and scans global undernutrition.
- Provides a comprehensive, personal, and practice-oriented look at infant motor development, Piaget's sensorimotor stage, and beginning language.
- Explores the new findings on infant social cognition.

Consistently pointing with her right hand points to the fact that this adorable 8-month-old may have a world-class vocabulary at age 2 or 3.

What's New?

- Offers recent data on the challenges of breast-feeding for working women.
- Showcases the latest research on co-sleeping.
- Introduces the concept of fear bias and offers more information on how early face preferences evolve.
- Describes how right-hand pointing predicts early language.

CHAPTER 4: Emotional and Social Development in Infants and Toddlers

- Provides unusually detailed coverage of attachment theory.
- Offers an honest, comprehensive look at day care in the United States and discusses early childhood poverty.
- Highlights exuberant and shy toddler temperaments, explores research on the genetics of temperament, and stresses the need to promote the right temperament–environment fit for each child.

What's New?

- Updates research exploring the life paths of orphanage-reared babies.
- Discusses recent data on the percent of U.S. young children living in poverty and the widening socioeconomic gap in early childhood family enrichment activities.

- Expands the day-care discussion by focusing on how these programs are structured.

- Introduces a new study exploring the effectiveness of different discipline techniques when toddlers disobey.

PART III: **Childhood**

CHAPTER 5: **Early Childhood (Newly structured chapter!)**

- Focuses on what makes preschool (age 3–6) unique, by anchoring the research on this special life stage in Piaget's and Erikson's theories.

- Describes physical development and threats to preschool physical skills.

- Showcases Piaget's and Vygotsky's approaches to cognition—with examples that stress the practical implications of these landmark perspectives for parents and people who work with young children.

- Discusses theory of mind and autobiographical memory in depth.

- Explores the development of play and the emergence of gender roles.

- Concludes with a discussion of autism spectrum disorders, including research that dispels the misplaced idea that autism is caused by vaccines.

CHAPTER 6: **Middle Childhood (Newly structured chapter!)**

- Focuses on the challenges of elementary school, by anchoring the research findings in Piaget's concrete operational stage and Erikson's concept of industry.

- Describes frontal lobe development, how lack of exercise affects elementary school motor skills, and includes a table exploring facts about childhood obesity.

- Explores expanding memory, executive functions, and showcases the latest research on ADHD.

- Highlights the challenge of emotion regulation and focuses on internalizing and externalizing disorders.

- Discusses the development of self-understanding, prosocial behavior, aggression, friendships, and popularity.

- Covers the causes and consequences of bullying, including cyberbullying.

CHAPTER 7: **Settings for Development: Home, School, and Community**

- This final childhood chapter shifts from the process of development to the major settings *for* development—home, school, and community—and tackles important controversies in the field, such as the influence of parents versus peers versus genetics in shaping development and the pros and cons of intelligence testing.

- Offers extensive discussions of ethnic variations in parenting styles and describes the research on how to stimulate intrinsic motivation.

- Showcases schools that beat the odds and targets the core qualities involved in effective teaching.

Compare the activities of this kindergarten class of little scientists with rote learning and grades, and you will immediately understand why by about age 8, many children begin to say, "I hate school."

What's New?

- Expands this chapter to include the impact of the community on development, including spelling out two new terms: *collective efficacy* and *upward mobility*.

- Updates information on immigration, spanking, child maltreatment, and divorce, and stresses the impact of the community on child-abuse rates and immigrant adjustment.

- Showcases Raj Chetty's landmark research on the role a single elementary school teacher can play in promoting life success, as well as illustrating how upward mobility varies dramatically, depending on the U.S. community where poor children are raised.

What are the teens who avidly scan the photos on a social network site likely to do? The surprise is that girls may decide to post more assertive, sexually oriented comments than boys.

PART IV: Adolescence

CHAPTER 8: Physical Development in Adolescents

- Offers an in-depth look at puberty, including the multiple forces that program the timing of this life transition, and looks at historical and cultural variations in puberty timetables.

- Explores the emotional experience of puberty (an "insider's" view) and the emotional impact of maturing early for girls.

- Covers teenage body image issues, eating disorders, and emerging sexuality.

What's New?

- Presents a new "How do we know . . ." box that describes Tanner's classic research spelling out pubertal stages.

- Updates the research on eating disorders, teenage sexuality, and pregnancy rates and offers new information about unwanted sexual activity during the early teens.

- Describes interventions to teach teens about how to have romantic relationships.

CHAPTER 9: Cognitive, Emotional, and Social Development in Adolescents

- Covers teenage brain development and various facets of adolescent "storm and stress."

- Spells out the forces that enable adolescents to thrive and explains what society can do (and also may not be doing!) to promote optimal development in teens.

- Explores parent–child relationships and discusses teenage peer groups.

What's New?

- Updates the research on early teenage impulsiveness and offers information about the prevalence of adolescent suicidal thoughts.

- Discusses zero-tolerance school policies and the school-to-prison pipeline.

PART V: Early and Middle Adulthood

CHAPTER 10: Emerging into Adulthood

- Devotes a whole chapter to the concerns of emerging adulthood.

- Offers extensive coverage of diversity issues during this life stage, such as forming an ethnic and biracial identity, interracial dating, and issues related to being gay and transgender.

- Gives students tips for succeeding in college and spells out career issues for non-college emerging adults.

- Introduces career-relevant topics, such as the concept of "flow," and provides extensive coverage of the research relating to selecting a mate and adult attachment styles.

- Focuses on current social policy issues, such as the impact socioeconomic status makes on attending and completing college, and discusses "nest residing," given that so many twenty-somethings now live at home.

What's New?

- Discusses the decline in marriage in the United States.

- Presents facts about transgender adults and describes the issues that gay ethnic minorities face.

- Offers a *completely revised* social media section showcasing research that describes how people respond to different kinds of Facebook posts, and featuring more data relating to the nuances of on-line love.

CHAPTER 11: Social Development: Relationships and Roles

- Focuses directly on the core issues of adult life: work and family.

- Provides an extensive discussion of the research relating to how to have happy, enduring relationships; the challenges of parenting; and women's and men's work and family roles.

- Looks at marriage, parenthood, and work in their cultural and historical contexts.

- Offers research-based tips for having a satisfying marriage and career.

- Discusses job insecurity in our current economy.

Their caring facial expressions tip us off that this couple may be blissfully in love. But, specifically, how do happy couples communicate when they talk? The answers are listed in this chapter.

What's New?

- Expands on Middle Eastern marital practices.

- Presents a new section that evaluates whether being married is superior to cohabiting for life and provides more data on predictors of marital happiness and divorce.

- Offers an updated fatherhood section, discusses forces involved in being a hands-on dad, and showcases a study of stay-at-home fathers with working wives.

- Features a rewritten work section that explores the growth of the "gig" economy (including a new figure) and critiques this fundamental transformation in twenty-first-century careers.

- Introduces a new term, *work–life balance*, and features studies showing that employers continue to be biased against people—particularly women—who take family time.

CHAPTER 12: Midlife

- Describes the complexities of measuring adult personality development.

- Anchors the research on adult intellectual change (the fluid and crystallized distinctions) to lifespan changes in creativity and careers.

- Offers thorough coverage of the research on generativity and adult well-being.

- Provides research-based advice for attaining a fulfilling adult life.

- Covers age-related changes in sexuality, menopause, grandparenthood, and parent care.

What's New?

- Completely restructured chapter begins by spelling out core questions we have about how people change with age, and then discusses each topic in sequence, beginning with sexuality (Physical Development), moving to intelligence and wisdom (Cognitive Development), and finally to personality and happiness (Social and Emotional Development).

- New section focuses in depth on cutting-edge research on wisdom.

- Explores the latest findings on adult happiness.

- Updates the research on grandparenthood and parent care.

PART VI: Later Life

CHAPTER 13: Later Life: Cognitive, Emotional, and Social Development

- Offers an extensive discussion of Carstensen's socioemotional selectivity theory.

- Helps decode our contradictory stereotypes about later-life emotional states, the core qualities that make for a happy or unsatisfying old age, and offers a section on "aging optimally."

- Describes the research on aging memory, retirement, and widowhood.

- Discusses salient social issues such as new trends to leave the workforce later, age discrimination in hiring, and intergenerational equity.

- Looks at later life developmentally by tracing changes from the young-old to the old-old years.

What's New?

- Explores new neuroscience research on memory, and offers updated information on socioemotional selectivity theory.

- Includes information on the current trend to go back to work after retiring, and introduces a new term, *bridge job*.

- Rewritten widowhood section targets loneliness as the main issue and explores how widowed people cope with this concern. This section also describes a study suggesting that if a husband was warm and upbeat, women cope well with a partner's death.

CHAPTER 14: The Physical Challenges of Old Age

- Offers a clear developmental look at how normal aging shades into chronic disease and ADL impairments and looks at the impact of gender and socioeconomic forces on physical aging.

- Focuses on how to change the environment to compensate for sensorimotor declines.

- Provides an in-depth look at neurocognitive disorders, or dementia, accompanied by compelling firsthand descriptions of people's inner experience coping with Alzheimer's disease.

- Explores alternatives to institutionalization and provides a full description of nursing home care.

- Strives to provide a realistic, honest, and yet action-oriented and uplifting portrait of the physical frailties of advanced old age.

What's New?

- Discusses the ethics of living beyond the maximum lifespan and features a new "How do we know . . ." box describing a calorie restriction experiment.

- Introduces a new term, *health span*, and discusses the impact of neighborhoods on promoting good health practices and longevity.

- Updates sections on vision and hearing and driving, including advances in hearing aids.

- Discusses emerging tests that predict Alzheimer's disease and includes a new figure showing that resilient "dendritic spines" insulate people from developing symptoms, even when they have the brain changes emblematic of this disease.

- Expands on the nursing-home care research, including adding a table spelling out tips for evaluating these institutions.

PART VII: Endings

CHAPTER 15: Death and Dying

- Explores cross-cultural variations in dying and offers an historical look at death practices from the Middle Ages to today.

- Discusses the pros and cons of the hospice movement, with its focus on dying at home.

- Offers a look at the pros and cons of different types of advance directives and explores controversial topics such as physician-assisted suicide.

What's New?

- Greatly expands the discussion of parental bereavement.

- Critiques traditional hospital care by featuring studies in which patients and families and nurses describe their experience in hospitals.

- Offers worldwide statistics on the prevalence of palliative care and describes minorities' attitudes toward hospice.

- Updates the number of states permitting physician-assisted suicide, and features attitudes of clergy members toward "assisted dying."

Because they are the front-line professionals who spend hours with hospitalized patients, nurses are uniquely equipped to convey at these team meetings what treatments dying people and families desire.

Final Thoughts

In this short epilogue, I've decided to let readers enter my own textbook writer's mind. What steps went into writing and producing this edition of *Experiencing the Lifespan*? What topics did I find most compelling in surveying the latest research? *Why* has textbook writing been my passion for my entire adult life? What—in my view—is a key to feeling passionate about any career?

What Teaching and Learning Aids Support This Book?

When you decide to use this book, you're adopting far more than just this text. You have access to an incredible learning system—everything from tests to video clips that bring the material to life. The Worth team and several dozen dedicated instructors have worked to provide an array of supplements to my text to foster student learning and make this course memorable: Video clips convey the magic of prenatal development, clarify Piaget's tasks, highlight child undernutrition, and showcase the life stories of active and healthy people in their ninth and tenth decades of life. Lecture slides and clicker questions make class sessions more visual and interactive. My publisher has amassed a rich archive of developmental science materials. For additional information, please contact your Worth Publishers sales consultant or visit the Worth website at LaunchPadWorks.com. Here are descriptions of the on-line offerings.

LaunchPad with LearningCurve Quizzing and *Developing Lives*

A comprehensive Web resource for teaching and learning about human development, **LaunchPad** combines Worth Publishers' award-winning media with an innovative platform for easy navigation. For students, it is the ultimate on-line study guide, with rich interactive tutorials and videos, as well as an e-book and the **LearningCurve** adaptive quizzing system. For instructors, LaunchPad is a full-course space where class documents can be posted, quizzes easily assigned and graded, and students' progress assessed and recorded. LaunchPad for *Experiencing the Lifespan*, Fifth Edition, includes all the following resources:

- **LearningCurve** adaptive quizzing system is based on the latest findings from learning and memory research. It combines adaptive question selection, immediate and valuable feedback, and a gamelike interface to engage students in a learning experience that is unique to them. Each LearningCurve quiz is fully integrated with other resources in LaunchPad through the Personalized Study Plan, so students will be able to review using Worth's extensive library of videos and activities. And state-of-the-art question analysis reports allow instructors to track the progress of individual students, as well as their class as a whole.

- *Developing Lives* is a robust and sophisticated interactive experience in which each student "raises" a virtual child from sperm-and-egg to teenager—fully integrated into LaunchPad. With *Developing Lives*, each student creates a personal profile, selects a virtual partner (or chooses to be a single parent), and marks the arrival of his or her newborn (represented by a unique avatar based on the parents' characteristics). As the child grows, the student responds to events both planned and unforeseen, making important decisions (nutrition choices, doctor visits, sleeping location) and facing uncertain moments (illness, divorce, a new baby), with each choice affecting how the child grows. Throughout, *Developing Lives* deepens each student's attachment and understanding of key concepts in the field with immediate, customized feedback based on child development research. It integrates more than 200 videos and animations and includes quizzes and essay questions that are easy to assign and assess.

- **Immersive Learning Activities:** *Something to Consider* activities apply the research to everyday life and to possible future careers for students. Each activity concludes with a quiz to assess what students have learned.

- **Videos**—in collaboration with dozens of instructors and researchers, Worth has developed an extensive collection of video clips. The collection covers the full range of the course, from classic experiments (like the Strange Situation and Piaget's tasks) to investigations of children's play to adolescent risk-taking. Instructors can show these videos in class, assign them to students through LaunchPad, or choose one of the **video activities** that combine videos with short-answer and multiple-choice questions.

- **An interactive e-book** allows students to highlight, bookmark, and add their own notes on the e-book page, just as they would in a printed textbook.

- The *Scientific American* **News Feed** delivers weekly articles, podcasts, and news briefs on the very latest developments in psychology from the first name in popular science journalism.

NEW! Achieve Read & Practice

Achieve Read & Practice is the marriage of our LearningCurve adaptive quizzing and our mobile, accessible e-book in one easy-to-use and affordable product. The benefits of Read & Practice include:

- It is easy to get started.

- Students come to class having read the materials and are more prepared for discussion.

- Instructors are able to use analytics to help students as needed.

- Student course performance improves.

Assessment and Other Instructor's Resources

The Instructor's Resources are fully integrated with LaunchPad. This rich collection of resources includes learning objectives, springboard topics for discussion and debate, handouts for student projects, course-planning suggestions, ideas for term projects, and a guide to audiovisual and on-line materials.

Diploma Computerized Test Bank (for Windows and Macintosh) offers an easy-to-use test-generating system that guides you through the process of creating tests. The Diploma software allows you to add an unlimited number of questions; edit questions; format a test; scramble questions; and include pictures, equations, or multimedia links. The Diploma software will also allow you to export into a variety of formats that are compatible with many Internet-based testing products.

Lecture Slides are available in two slide sets for each chapter of *Experiencing the Lifespan*, Fifth Edition—one featuring a comprehensive chapter lecture and the other featuring all chapter art and illustrations.

Who Made This Book Possible?

This book was a collaborative endeavor engineered by the finest publishing company in the world: Worth (and not many authors can make that statement)! Firstly, again heartfelt thanks go to Elaine Epstein. Elaine, whom I have been fortunate to have as my developmental editor for several editions of this book, has been working more than full time on this edition for over a year. She meticulously pored over every sentence of this manuscript multiple times, helped prepare all the figures and tables, skillfully guided everything into production, and is shepherding this book into print as we speak. Elaine, as usual, is my real, unseen, full partner on this book.

The other collaborator working overtime on this book is my masterful hands-on editor, Program Manager Chris Cardone. After decades spent working with publishers, I can honestly say that in terms of attentiveness to authors, sensitivity to their needs, reliability, and genuine good smarts, Chris ranks in the top 1 percent. I've relied on Chris's second-to-none knowledge of the literature to suggest new topics for this edition. I regularly count on Chris's impeccable good sense—about how phrases might affect readers—to save me from making embarrassing gaffes!

Then there are the talented people who transformed this manuscript into print. Thanks go to my hardworking production staff, for helping ensure everything fit together, especially Vivien Weiss, our Senior Content Project Manager, for her attention to detail and to Valerie Brandenburg, Project Manager at Lumina. It's been my great fortune to have Beth Rosato as my eagle-eyed copyeditor check the manuscript for accuracy. Sheena Goldstein had the heroic task of helping select photos that embodied my thoughts. At the final stage of this process, proofreader Martha Ghent meticulously picked through the manuscript to place my commas correctly and make sure each sentence made grammatical sense. My thanks also go to editorial assistant Dorothy Tomasini for her careful reading of chapters during the production process.

Then there are the talented people who make *Experiencing the Lifespan* look like a breathtaking work of art. As you delight in looking at this fabulous design, you can thank Director of Design, Content Management Diana Blume, Design Services Manager Natasha Wolfe, and Art Manager Matthew McAdams. Thanks go to Laura Burden, Executive Media Editor, and to the accomplished supplements and media authors, too.

Without good marketing, no one would read this book. And, as usual, this arm of the Worth team gets my A+ rating. Clay Bolton, our Marketing Manager, does an outstanding job. Special kudos go to the sales reps who spend countless hours in the field advocating for my work. Although I may not meet many of you personally, I want to take this chance to thank you for working so hard to get "Belsky" out in the real world.

I am grateful for my accomplished reference checker, Sidney Reichin (congrats for getting into the Industrial/Organizational psychology Ph.D. program at Penn State!) and to the readers who took the time to personally e-mail and tell me, "You did a good job," or, "Dr. Belsky, I like it; but here's where you went wrong." These kinds of comments really make an author's day! This book has benefited from the insights of an incredible number of reviewers over the years. Here are the instructors who helped improve each edition of *Experiencing the Lifespan:*

Heather Adams, *Ball State University*

Daisuke Akiba, *Queens College*

Cecilia Alvarez, *San Antonio College*

Andrea S. Anastasiou, *Mary Baldwin College*

Emilie Aubert, *Marquette University*

Pamela Auburn, *University of Houston Downtown*

Tracy Babcock, *Montana State University*

Harriet Bachner, *Northeastern State University*

Carol Bailey, *Rochester Community and Technical College*

Thomas Bailey, *University of Baltimore*

Shelly Ball, *Western Kentucky University*

Mary Ballard, *Appalachian State University*

Lacy Barnes-Mileham, *Reedley College*

Kay Bartosz, *Eastern Kentucky University*

Laura Barwegen, *Wheaton College*

Jonathan Bates, *Hunter College, CUNY*

Don Beach, *Tarleton State University*

Lori Beasley, *University of Central Oklahoma*

Heidi Beattie, *Troy University*

Martha-Ann Bell, *Virginia Tech*

Daniel Bellack, *Trident Technical College*

Jennifer Bellingtier, *University of Northern Iowa*

Karen Bendersky, *Georgia College and State University*

Keisha Bentley, *University of La Verne*

Robert Billingham, *Indiana University*

Kathi J. Bivens, *Asheville-Buncombe Technical Community College*

Jim Blonsky, *University of Tulsa*

Cheryl Bluestone, *Queensborough Community College, CUNY*

Greg Bonanno, *Teachers College, Columbia University*

Aviva Bower, *College of St. Rose*

Marlys Bratteli, *North Dakota State University*

Bonnie Breitmayer, *University of Illinois, Chicago*

Jennifer Brennom, *Kirkwood Community College*

Tom Brian, *University of Tulsa*

Sabrina Brinson, *Missouri State University*

Adam Brown, *St. Bonaventure University*

Kimberly D. Brown, *Ball State University*

Donna Browning, *Mississippi State University*

Janine Buckner, *Seton Hall University*

Ted Bulling, *Nebraska Wesleyan University*

Holly Bunje, *University of Minnesota, Twin Cities*

Melinda Burgess, *Southwestern Oklahoma State University*

Barbara Burns, *University of Louisville*

Marilyn Burns, *Modesto Junior College*

Joni Caldwell, *Spalding University*

Norma Caltagirone, *Hillsborough Community College, Ybor City*

Lanthan Camblin, *University of Cincinnati*

Debb Campbell, *College of Sequoias*

Lee H. Campbell, *Edison Community College*

Robin Campbell, *Eastern Florida State College, Titusville*

Kathryn A. Canter, *Penn State Fayette*

Peter Carson, *South Florida Community College*

Michael Casey, *College of Wooster*

Kimberly Chapman, *Blue River Community College*

Tom Chiaromonte, *Fullerton College*

Yiling Chow, *North Island College, Port Albernia*

Toni Christopherson, *California State University, Dominguez Hills*

Wanda Clark, *South Plains College*

Judy Collmer, *Cedar Valley College*

David Conner, *Truman State University*

Deborah Conway, *University of Virginia*

Diana Cooper, *Purdue University*

Ellen Cotter, *Georgia Southwestern State University*

Deborah M. Cox, *Madisonville Community College*

Kim B. Cragin, *Snow College*

Charles P. Cummings, *Asheville-Buncombe Technical Community College*

Karen Curran, *Mt. San Antonio College*

Antonio Cutolo-Ring, *Kansas City (KS) Community College*

Ken Damstrom, *Valley Forge Christian College*

Leslie Daniels, *Florida State College at Jacksonville*

Nancy Darling, *Bard College*

Paul Dawson, *Weber State University*

Janet B. Dean, *Asbury University*

Lynda DeDee, *University of Wisconsin, Oshkosh*

David C. Devonis, *Graceland University*

Charles Dickel, *Creighton University*

Darryl Dietrich, *College of St. Scholastica*

Stephanie Ding, *Del Mar College*

Lugenia Dixon, *Bainbridge College*

Benjamin Dobrin, *Virginia Wesleyan College*

Delores Doench, *Southwestern Community College*

Melanie Domenech Rodriguez, *Utah State University*

Sundi Donovan, *Liberty University*

Lana Dryden, *Sir Sanford Fleming College*

Gwenden Dueker, *Grand Valley State University*

Bryan Duke, *University of Central Oklahoma*

Trisha M. Dunkel, *Loyola University, Chicago*

Robin Eliason, *Piedmont Virginia Community College*

Traci Elliot, *Alvin Community College*

Frank Ellis, *University of Maine, Augusta*

Kelley Eltzroth, *Mid Michigan Community College*

Marya Endriga, *California State University, Stanislaus*

Lena Ericksen, *Western Washington University*

Kathryn Fagan, *California Baptist University*

Daniel Fasko, *Bowling Green State University*

Nancy Feehan, *University of San Francisco*

Meredyth C. Fellows, *West Chester University of Pennsylvania*

Gary Felt, *City University of New York*

Martha Fewell, *Barat College*

Mark A. Fine, *University of Missouri*

Roseanne L. Flores, *Hunter College, CUNY*

John Foley, *Hagerstown Community College*

James Foster, *George Fox University*

Geri Fox, *University of Illinois, Chicago*

Thomas Francigetto, *Northampton Community College*

James Francis, *San Jacinto College*

Doug Friedrich, *University of West Florida*

Lynn Garrioch, *Colby-Sawyer College*

Bill Garris, *Cumberland College*

Caroline Gee, *Palomar College*

C. Ray Gentry, *Lenoir-Rhyne College*

Carol George, *Mills College*

Elizabeth Gersten, *Victor Valley College*

Linde Getahun, *Bethel University*

Afshin Gharib, *California State University, East Bay*

Nada Glick, *Yeshiva University*

Andrea Goldstein, *Kaplan University*

Arthur Gonchar, *University of La Verne*

Helen Gore-Laird, *University of Houston, University Park*

Tyhesha N. Goss, *University of Pennsylvania*

Dan Grangaard, *Austin Community College, Rio Grande*

Julie Graul, *St. Louis Community College, Florissant Valley*

Elizabeth Gray, *North Park University*

Stefanie Gray Greiner, *Mississippi University for Women*

Erinn L. Green, *Wilmington College*

Dale D. Grubb, *Baldwin-Wallace College*

Laura Gruntmeir, *Redlands Community College*

Lisa Hager, *Spring Hill College*

Michael Hall, *Iowa Western Community College*

Andre Halliburton, *Prairie State College*

Laura Hanish, *Arizona State University*

Robert Hansson, *University of Tulsa*

Richard Harland, *West Texas A&M University*

Gregory Harris, *Polk Community College*

Virginia Harvey, *University of Massachusetts, Boston*

Margaret Hellie Huyck, *Illinois Institute of Technology*

Janice L. Hendrix, *Missouri State University*

Gertrude Henry, *Hampton University*

Rod Hetzel, *Baylor University*

Heather Hill, *University of Texas, San Antonio*

Elaine Hogan, *University of North Carolina, Wilmington*

Judith Holland, *Hawaii Pacific University*

Debra Hollister, *Valencia Community College*

Heather Holmes-Lonergan, *Metropolitan State College of Denver*

Rosemary Hornak, *Meredith College*

Suzy Horton, *Mesa Community College*

Rebecca Hoss, *College of Saint Mary*

Cynthia Hudley, *University of California, Santa Barbara*

Alycia Hund, *Illinois State University*

David P. Hurford, *Pittsburgh State University*

Elaine Ironsmith, *East Carolina University*

Jessica Jablonski, *Richard Stockton College*

Katie Jacobs, *University of Central Missouri*

Sabra Jacobs, *Big Sandy Community and Technical College*

David Johnson, *John Brown University*

Emilie Johnson, *Lindenwood University*

Mary Johnson, *Loras College*

Mike Johnson, *Hawaii Pacific University*

Peggy Jordan, *Oklahoma City Community College*

Lisa Judd, *Western Wisconsin Technical College*

Tracy R. Juliao, *University of Michigan Flint*

Elaine Justice, *Old Dominion University*

Steve Kaatz, *Bethel University*

Jyotsna M. Kalavar, *Penn State New Kensington*

Chi-Ming Kam, *City College of New York, CUNY*

Richard Kandus, *Mt. San Jacinto College*

Skip Keith, *Delaware Technical and Community College*

Chad Keller, *Lewis and Clark Community College*

Michelle L. Kelley, *Old Dominion University*

Richie Kelley, *Baptist Bible College and Seminary*

Robert Kelley, *Mira Costa College*

Jeff Kellogg, *Marian College*

Colleen Kennedy, *Roosevelt University*

Sarah Kern, *The College of New Jersey*

Marcia Killien, *University of Washington*

Kenyon Knapp, *Troy State University*

Cynthia Koenig, *Mt. St. Mary's College of Maryland*

Steve Kohn, *Valdosta State University*

Holly Krogh, *Mississippi University for Women*

Martha Kuehn, *Central Lakes College*

Alvin Kuest, *Great Lakes Christian College*

Rich Lanthier, *George Washington University*

Peggy Lauria, *Central Connecticut State University*

Melisa Layne, *Danville Community College*

John LeChapitaine, *University of Wisconsin, River Falls*

Barbara Lehmann, *Augsburg College*

Rhinehart Lintonen, *Gateway Technical College*

Nancy Lobb, *Alvin Community College*

Martha V. Low, *Winston-Salem State University*

Carol Ludders, *University of St. Francis*

Dunja Lund Trunk, *Bloomfield College*

Vickie Luttrell, *Drury University*

Nina Lyon Jenkins, *University of Maryland, Eastern Shore*

Christine Malecki, *Northern Illinois University*

Marlowe Manger, *Stanly Community College*

Pamela Manners, *Troy State University*

Kathy Manuel, *Bossier Parish Community College*

Howard Markowitz, *Hawaii Pacific University*

Jayne D. B. Marsh, *University of Southern Maine, Lewiston-Auburn College*

Esther Martin, *California State University, Dominguez Hills*

Jan Mast, *Miami Dade College, North Campus*

Pan Maxson, *Duke University*

Nancy Mazurek, *Long Beach City College*

Christine McCormick, *Eastern Illinois University*

Jim McDonald, *California State University, Fresno*

Clark McKinney, *Southwest Tennessee Community College*

George Meyer, *Suffolk County Community College*

Barbara J. Miller, *Pasadena City College*

Christy Miller, *Coker College*

Mary Beth Miller, *Fresno City College*

Al Montgomery, *Our Lady of Holy Cross College*

Robin Montvilo, *Rhode Island College*

Peggy Moody, *St. Louis Community College*

Michelle Moriarty, *Johnson County Community College*

Wendy Bianchini Morrison, *Montana State University, Bozeman*

Ron Mulson, *Hudson Valley Community College*

Ken Mumm, *University of Nebraska, Kearney*

Joyce Munsch, *Texas Tech University*

Jeannette Murphey, *Meridian Community College*

Lori Myers, *Louisiana Tech University*

Lana Nenide, *University of Wisconsin, Madison*

Margaret Nettles, *Alliant University*

Gregory Newton, *Diablo Valley College*

Barbara Nicoll, *University of La Verne*

Nancy Nolan, *Nashville State Community College*

Harriett Nordstrom, *University of Michigan, Flint*

Wendy North-Ollendorf, *Northwestern Connecticut Community College*

Elizabeth O'Connor, *St. Mary's College*

Susan O'Donnell, *George Fox University*

Jane Ogden, *East Texas Baptist University*

Shirley Ogletree, *Texas State University*

Claudius Oni, *South Piedmont Community College*

Randall E. Osborne, *Texas State University, San Marcos*

Sandy Osborne, *Montana State University, Bozeman*

John Otey, *Southern Arkansas University*

Carol Ott, *University of Wisconsin, Milwaukee*

Patti Owen-Smith, *Oxford College*

Heidi Pasek, *Montana State University*

Margaret Patton, *University of North Carolina, Charlotte*

Julie Hicks Patrick, *West Virginia University*

Evelyn Payne, *Albany State University*

Ian E. Payton, *Bethune-Cookman University*

Carole Penner-Faje, *Molloy College*

Michelle L. Pilati, *Rio Hondo College*

Meril Posy, *Touro College, Brooklyn*

Shannon M. Pruden, *Temple University*

Ellery Pullman, *Briarcrest Bible College*

Samuel Putnam, *Bowdoin College*

Jeanne Quarles, *Oregon Coast Community College*

Mark Rafter, *College of the Canyons*

Cynthia Rand-Johnson, *Albany State University*

Janet Rangel, *Palo Alto College*

Jean Raniseski, *Alvin Community College*

Frances Raphael-Howell, *Montgomery College*

Celinda Reese, *Oklahoma State University*

Ethan Remmel, *Western Washington University*

Paul Rhoads, *Williams Baptist College*

Kerri A. Riggs, *Lourdes College*

Mark Rittman, *Cuyahoga Community College*

Jeanne Rivers, *Finger Lakes Community College*

Wendy Robertson, *Western Michigan University*

Richard Robins, *University of California, Davis*

Millie Roqueta, *Miami Dade College*

June Rosenberg, *Lyndon State College*

Christopher Rosnick, *University of South Florida*

Trisha Rossi, *Adelphi University*

Rodger Rossman, *College of the Albemarle*

Lisa Routh, *Pikes Peak Community College*

Stephanie Rowley, *University of Michigan, Ann Arbor*

Randall Russac, *University of North Florida*

Dawn Ella Rust, *Stephen F. Austin State University*

Tara Saathoff-Wells, *Central Michigan University*

Traci Sachteleben, *Southwestern Illinois College*

Douglas Sauber, *Arcadia University*

Chris Saxild, *Wisconsin Indianhead Technical College*

Barbara Schaudt, *California State University, Bakersfield*

Daniela E. Schreier, *Chicago School of Professional Psychology*

Pamela Schuetze, *SUNY College at Buffalo*

Donna Seagle, *Chattanooga State Technical Community College*

Bonnie Seegmiller, *Hunter College, CUNY*

Chris Seifert, *Montana State University*

Marianne Shablousky, *Community College of Allegheny County*

Susan Shapiro, *Indiana University, East*

Elliot Sharpe, *Maryville University*

Lawrence Shelton, *University of Vermont*

Shamani Shikwambi, *University of Northern Iowa*

Denise Simonsen, *Fort Lewis College*

Penny Skemp, *Mira Costa College*

Peggy Skinner, *South Plains College*

Barbara Smith, *Westminster College*

Valerie Smith, *Collin County Community College*

Edward Sofranko, *University of Rio Grande*

Joan Spiegel, *West Los Angeles College*

Jason S. Spiegelman, *Community College of Baltimore County*

Carolyn I. Spies, *Bloomfield College*

Scott Stein, *Southern Vermont College*

Stephanie Stein, *Central Washington University*

Sheila Steiner, *Jamestown College*

Jacqueline Stewart, *Seminole State College*

Robert Stewart, Jr., *Oakland University*

Cynthia Suarez, *Wofford College*

Joshua Susskind, *University of Northern Iowa*

Josephine Swalloway, *Curry College*

Jodi Swanson, *Arizona State University*

Emily Sweitzer, *California University of Pennsylvania*

Chuck Talor, *Valdosta State University*

Jamie Tanner, *South Georgia College*

Norma Tedder, *Edison Community College*

George Thatcher, *Texas Tech University*

Shannon Thomas, *Wallace Community College*

Donna Thompson, *Midland College*

Vicki Tinsley, *Brescia University*

Eugene Tootle, *Barry University*

David Tracer, *University of Colorado, Denver*

Stephen Truhon, *Austin Peay Centre, Fort Campbell*

Dana Van Abbema, *St. Mary's College of Maryland*

Mary Vandendorpe, *Lewis University*

Janice Vidic, *University of Rio Grande*

Steven Voss, *Moberly Area Community College*

William Walkup, *Southwest Baptist University*

Anne Weiher, *Metropolitan State College of Denver*

Robert Weis, *University of Wisconsin, Stevens Point*

Lori Werdenschlag, *Lyndon State College*

Noel Wescombe, *Whitworth College*

Andrea White, *Ithaca College*

Meade Whorton, *Louisiana Delta Community College*

Wanda A. Willard, *Monroe Community College*

Joylynne Wills, *Howard University*

Nancy A. Wilson, *Haywood Community College*

Steffen Wilson, *Eastern Kentucky University*

Bernadette Wise, *Iowa Lakes Community College*

Steve Wisecarver, *Lord Fairfax Community College*

Alex Wiseman, *University of Tulsa*

Rebecca Witt Stoffel, *West Liberty State College*

Nanci Woods, *Austin Peay State University*

Chrysalis L. Wright, *University of Central Florida*

Stephanie Wright, *Georgetown University*

David Yarbrough, *Texas State University*

Nikki Yonts, *Lyon College*

Ling-Yi Zhou, *University of St. Francis*

On the home front, I'm grateful to my baby, Thomas, for being born and giving my life such meaning, and who, now, at age 35, has become an accomplished, *mature* adult! But the real credit for this book belongs to Shelly Gertzfeld, my new life love since I moved to Chicago, and my late husband David, for putting this book and my happiness center stage and for giving me the best possible life.

Janet Belsky
May 2018

The Foundation

This two-chapter part offers you the foundations for understanding the lifespan.

Chapter 1—The People and the Field introduces *all* the major concepts and themes in this course. I'll describe our discipline's basic terminology, provide a bird's-eye view of the evolving lifespan, offer a framework for how to think about world cultures, and highlight some new twenty-first-century life stages. Most important, in this chapter you will learn about the themes, theories, and research strategies that have shaped our field. Bottom line: Chapter 1 gives you the tools you will need for understanding this book.

Chapter 2—Prenatal Development, Pregnancy, and Birth lays the foundation for our developing lives. Here, you will learn about how a baby develops from a tiny clump of cells, and gain insights into the experience of pregnancy from the point of view of mothers and fathers. This chapter describes pregnancy rituals in different cultures, discusses the impact of prenatal issues such as stress and infertility, and offers an in-depth look at the miracle of birth.

Application to Developing Lives Parenting Simulation: *Introduction and Prenatal Development*

In the Introduction module of *Developing Lives,* you will begin to customize the developmental journey of your child with information about your personality, cognitive abilities, and demographic characteristics. Below is a list of questions you will answer in the Prenatal simulation module. As you answer these questions, consider the impact your choice will have on the physical, cognitive, and social and emotional development of your baby.

Physical	Cognitive	Social and Emotional
• Will you modify your behaviors and diet during pregnancy? • Will you find out the sex of your baby prior to delivery? • What kind of delivery will you and your partner plan for (in the hospital with medication, at home with a doula, etc.)?	• Are you going to talk to your baby while he or she is in the womb? • How much does your baby understand during prenatal development?	• How will you and your partner's relationship change as a result of the pregnancy? • Will you begin bonding with your baby prior to birth?

Left: Terry Vine/Blend Images/Getty Images

CHAPTER 1

Dear Students,

Welcome to lifespan development! This course is about your parents and grandparents, friends and colleagues, the children you have or expect to have. If you plan to work with children, adults, or the elderly, this course will give you a good foundation for your career. Most important, this course is all about your *own* evolving life. This semester, starting with our first minutes in the womb, I'll provide a motion picture of development in the flesh.

As we travel through the lifespan, I urge you to look outward to the wider world. While reading the infancy sections, visit a relative with a baby. In the chapters on childhood and adolescence, pay attention to boys and girls at school, spend an afternoon with a 4-year-old, watch preteens at the mall. Then, interview a 20-something friend or a middle-aged relative. Talk to a 68-year-old about to retire or an 85-year-old coping with the physical challenges of old age. The purpose of this class is to widen your horizons, to enable you to look at each stage of life in a more empathic way.

How can you fully enjoy the scenery on this semester-long trip and still get a great grade in this course? Follow the principle that learning happens when we are emotionally engaged: Make it relevant; make it personal; see the concepts come alive in the world. To help you, I begin each chapter with a fictional life story. Enjoy the vignette. I've constructed it to alert you to some major chapter themes. To test your knowledge after reading each section, return to the introductory Learning Outcomes to guide your review. Look at each photo and chart. Concentrate on the section-end summary tables. Complete the Tying It All Together quizzes and other checklists. I planned these hands-on activities to enrich your self-understanding, plus help you effortlessly learn the material. My goal in writing this book is simple: I want you to share my passion for the marvelous human lifespan and to think more deeply about life. I want to prove that textbooks can be scholarly and a joy to read!

Now that you know my main agendas (stay tuned for the scholarly ones later), let's get started. In this chapter, I'll introduce the basic themes in the course. Let's begin by introducing the people you will meet in the introductory vignettes.

Janet Belsky

The People and the Field

Susan is having a party to celebrate Carl's wonderful life. Losing her husband was tough, but Susan takes comfort in the fact that during their 55-plus-year-long marriage, she and her husband amassed so many friends—people of every age, ethnicity, and social group. After Carl's death, everyone flooded Susan's Facebook page with expressions of love. But, being from a different era, Susan craves having her friends physically close, to hug and reminisce about Carl.

First to arrive were María and baby José, whom Susan and Carl met on a cross-country trip to Las Vegas five years ago. Then, Mathew and Jamila, the lovely couple from last year's Alaskan cruise, knocked on the door. For Susan, bonding with her new 50-something friends on that trip through the glaciers offered a lesson in how the world has changed. Susan and Carl married at age 21—at a time when middle-class women often stopped working after getting married, and gender roles were defined. Jamila waited to get married until she was 37 years old and had a stable career, met Matt on-line, and even selected a husband of a different race. How, with juggling step-kids and demanding jobs, have Matt and Jamila mastered the secret of staying in love for more than 15 years?

Finally, Kim, her husband Jeff, and baby Elissa drove up. Although Susan was devastated when this close neighborhood couple moved across the country, she had been thrilled to witness Elissa's transformations through video chats. Now, it's time to (finally) envelop that precious 1-year-old in her arms and hear, in person, about everyone else's lives!

At dinner, Kim reports that since Elissa began walking, she doesn't slow down for a minute. Actually, it's kind of depressing. Elissa used to go to Susan with a smile. Now, all she wants is Mom. Jose's transformation is astonishing. Now that he is 8, that precious child can talk to you like an adult!

Soon, the dinnertime talk turns to deeper issues: Kim shares her anxieties about putting Elissa in day care. Matt gushes about the joys of step-parenthood. María anguishes about balancing full-time work and motherhood, and opens up about the challenges of being an immigrant, a single mom, and an ethnic minority in the United States. Jamila informs the group that she wants to make a difference. She plans to return to school for a Ph.D. But can she make it academically at age 55?

Susan tells the group not to worry. The sixties and early seventies (until Carl's stroke) were the happiest time of their lives. Now, with her slowness, her progressing vision problems, and that frightening fall she took at the supermarket last week, the future looks bleaker. Susan knows that life is precious. She treasures every moment she has left. But the eighties aren't like the seventies. What will happen when she really gets old?

Left to right from top left photo: Petrol/Getty Images, KIYOKO FUKUDA/a.collectionRF/amana images RF/Getty Images, Karel Noppé/Alamy Stock Photo, Ryan McVay/Getty Images, Folio Images/Alamy, Rick Gomez/Getty Images, SpeedKingz/Shutterstock, Stockbyte/Getty Images, Juanmonino/E+/Getty Images, Jupiterimages/Getty Images, Johnny Greig/Getty Images, Gerardo Ricardo López/Getty Images

Is Susan right that the sixties and early seventies are life's happiest stage? If you met Susan at age 30 or 50, would she be the same upbeat person as today? Are Jamila's worries about her abilities realistic, and what *are* some secrets for staying passionately in love with your spouse? Why do 1-year-olds such as Elissa get clingy just as they begin walking, and what mental leaps make children at age 8, such as José, seem so grown up? How has single parenthood and the social media revolution transformed twenty-first-century life?

Developmentalists, also called **developmental scientists**—researchers who study the lifespan—are about to answer these questions and hundreds of others about our unfolding lives.

> **developmentalists (or developmental scientists)** Researchers and practitioners whose professional interest lies in the study of the human lifespan.

Who We Are and What We Study

- Describe developmental scientists' interests.

> **lifespan development** The scientific study of development through life.
>
> **child development** The scientific study of development from birth through adolescence.
>
> **gerontology** The scientific study of the aging process and older adults.
>
> **adult development** The scientific study of adult life.

Lifespan development, the scientific study of human growth throughout life, is a latecomer to psychology. Its roots lie in **child development,** the study of childhood and the teenage years. Child development traces its origins back more than a century. In the 1890s, a pioneering psychologist named G. Stanley Hall established the first institute in the United States devoted to research on the child. Child development began to take off between World Wars I and II (Lerner, 1998). It remains the passion of thousands of developmental scientists working in every corner of the globe.

Gerontology, the scientific study of aging—the other core discipline in lifespan development—had a slower start. Researchers began to really study the aging process only after World War II (Birren & Birren, 1990). Gerontology and its related field, **adult development,** underwent their phenomenal growth spurt during the final third of the twentieth century.

Lifespan development puts it all together, synthesizing what researchers know about how we grow and change. Who works in this mammoth mega-discipline, and what passions drive developmentalists?

- **Lifespan development is multidisciplinary.** It draws on fields as different as neuroscience, nursing, psychology, and social policy to understand human development. A biologically oriented developmentalist might examine toddlers' output of salivary cortisol (a stress hormone) during day care. An anthropologist might look at cultural values that shape the day-care choice. A social policy expert might explore the impact of offering universal government-funded day care in Finland and France. A biochemist who studies Alzheimer's disease might decode what produces the plaques and tangles that ravage the brain. A nurse might head an innovative Alzheimer's unit. A research-oriented psychologist might construct a scale to measure the impairments caused by this devastating disease.

A developmental scientist—like this young woman—might be passionate to decode the early signs of Alzheimer's disease.

- **Lifespan development explores the predictable milestones on our human journey,** from walking to working, to Elissa's sudden shyness and attachment to her mother. Are people right to worry about their learning abilities in their fifties? What is physical aging, or puberty, or menopause all about? Are there specific emotions we feel as we approach that final universal milestone, death?

- **Lifespan development focuses on the individual differences that give spice to human life.** Can we really see the person we will be at age 80, by age 50 or 30? How much does personality or intelligence change as we travel through life? Developmentalists want to understand what *causes* the striking differences between people in temperament, talents, and traits. They are interested in exploring individual differences in the timing of developmental milestones, too—examining, for instance, why people reach puberty earlier or later or age more quickly or slowly than their peers.

- **Lifespan development explores the impact of life transitions and practices.** It deals with **normative,** or predictable, **transitions,** such as retirement, becoming parents, or beginning middle school. It focuses on **non-normative,** or atypical, **transitions,** such as divorce or the death of a child. It explores life practices, such as smoking, spanking, or sleeping in the same bed with your baby.

Developmentalists realize that the life transitions we view as normative, such as retiring or starting middle school, are products of living in a particular time in history. They understand that practices such as smoking or sleeping in bed with a child vary, depending on our social class and cultural background. They know that several basic markers, or overall conditions of life, shape development from birth to old age.

Now it's time to introduce some **contexts of development,** or broad general influences, which I will be continually discussing throughout this book.

> **normative transitions** Predictable life changes that occur during development.
>
> **non-normative transitions** Unpredictable or atypical life changes that occur during development.
>
> **contexts of development** Fundamental markers, including cohort, socioeconomic status, culture, and gender, that shape how we develop throughout the lifespan.

Setting the Context

How does living in a particular historical time affect our lifespan? What about our social class, cultural background, or that basic biological difference, being born female or male?

The Impact of Cohort

Cohort refers to our birth group, the age group with whom we travel through life. In the vignette, you can immediately see the heavy role our cohort plays in influencing adult life. Susan reached adulthood in 1960, when women married in their early twenties and typically stayed married for life. Jamila came of age during the final decade of the twentieth century, when women began to feel they needed to get their careers together before finding a mate. As an interracial couple, Matt and Jamila are taking an atypical life path today! Because they are in their fifties, this couple is at an interesting place in history. They are traveling through life right after that huge explosion in the population called the *baby boom.*

The **baby boom cohort,** defined as people born from 1946 to 1964, has made an outsized impact on the Western world. The reason lies in size. When soldiers returned from World War II and got married, the average family ballooned to almost four children. When the baby boomers were growing up during the 1950s, gender roles were traditional, and the two-parent, stay-at-home-mother family was the national ideal. Then, as rebellious adolescents during the 1960s and 1970s, this mammoth cohort ushered in a radical transformation of these attitudes and roles (more about this life-style revolution soon). Society today, as we know, is experiencing an old-age explosion as the baby boomers flood into later life.

The cohorts living in the early twenty-first century are part of an endless march of cohorts stretching back thousands of years. Let's now take a brief historical tour to get a sense of the dramatic changes in childhood, old age, and adulthood during just the past few centuries, and pinpoint what our lifespan looks like today.

Changing Conceptions of Childhood

At age ten he began his work life helping . . . manufacture candles and soap. He . . . wanted to go to sea, but his father refused and apprenticed him to a master printer. At age 17 he ran away from Boston to Philadelphia to search for work.

LEARNING OUTCOMES

- Describe the major twentieth-century changes in childhood, adulthood, and later life.
- Explain how socioeconomic status, culture, and gender affect people's lives.
- Identify the core difference between developed and developing nations, as well as individualistic and collectivist cultural worldviews.
- Describe the impact of the social media revolution and increasing income inequalities in the United States.

> **cohort** The age group with whom we travel through life.
>
> **baby boom cohort** The huge age group born between 1946 and 1964.

His father died when he was 11, and he left school. At 17 he was appointed official surveyor for Culpepper County in Virginia. By age 20 he was in charge of managing his family's plantation.

(Mintz, 2004)

Who were these boys? Their names were Benjamin Franklin and George Washington.

Imagine being born in Colonial times. In addition to reaching adulthood at a much younger age, your chance of having *any* lifespan was far from secure. In seventeenth-century Paris, roughly 1 in every 3 babies died in early infancy (Ariès, 1962; Hrdy, 1999). As late as 1900, almost 1 in 5 U.S. children did not survive the first year of life (Gordon, 2015).

The incredible childhood mortality rates, plus poverty, may partly explain why child-rearing practices that we would label as abusive today used to be considered routine. Children were often beaten and, at their parents' whim, might be abandoned at birth (Konner, 2010; Pinker, 2011). In the early 1800s in Paris, about 1 in 5 newborns was "exposed"—placed in the doorways of churches, or simply left outside to die. In cities such as St. Petersburg, Russia, the statistic might have been as high as 1 in 2 (Ariès, 1962; Hrdy, 1999).

In addition, for most of history, people did not share our modern view that childhood is a special life stage (Ariès, 1962; Mintz, 2004). Children, as you saw above, began to work at a young age. During the early industrial revolution, poor boys and girls made up more than one-third of the labor force in British mills (Mintz, 2004).

In the nineteenth century, children as young as ages 5 and 6 worked in factories such as this cannery. Clearly, we have come a long way in our attitudes toward childhood.

In the seventeenth and eighteenth centuries, enlightenment philosophers such as John Locke and Jean Jacques Rousseau spelled out a different vision of childhood (Pinker, 2011). Locke believed that human beings are born a *tabula rasa*, a blank slate on which anything could be written, and that the way we treat children shapes their adult lives. Rousseau argued that babies enter life totally innocent; he felt we should shower these dependent creatures with love. However, this message could fully penetrate society only when the early-twentieth-century explosion of technological advances—from indoor toilets to washing machines, from refrigerators to cars—allowed us to enter our modern age (Gordon, 2015).

Twentieth-century technology ushered in a new, extended view of childhood. As daily living became less arduous, sons and daughters no longer needed to work from an early age to help their families. Moreover, education became far more important, as now people needed abstract skills for functioning competently in the world (such as understanding math or decoding complex written instructions).

Education sets the limits of childhood because as long as we are in school, we depend on our parents to provide care. As late as 1915, only 1 in 10 U.S. children attended high school (Gordon, 2015). Most boys and girls began their work lives right after puberty. Then during the Great Depression of the 1930s, when President Franklin Roosevelt signed a bill making high school attendance mandatory, adolescence became a standard life stage (Mintz, 2004). Rather than being universal, our famous teenage culture is less than a century old!

Now with the need for college and, sometimes, graduate school, developmentalists have identified an additional not-quite-adult stage (see Tanner & Arnett, 2010). **Emerging adulthood,** lasting from age 18 to roughly the late twenties, is devoted to exploring our place in the world. This more differentiated view of childhood was accompanied by a more elastic conception of old age.

Changing Conceptions of Later Life

Throughout history, a few people always lived to "old age." However, before the twentieth century, largely due to high rates of infant and childhood mortality, **average life expectancy,** our fifty-fifty chance at birth of living to a given age, was shockingly

emerging adulthood
The phase of life that begins after high school, lasts through the late twenties, and is devoted to constructing an adult life.

average life expectancy
A person's fifty-fifty chance at birth of living to a given age.

low. In Maryland during Colonial times, average life expectancy was only 20 years, for both masters and their slaves (Fischer, 1977).

Beginning in the late nineteenth century, life expectancy in the United States rapidly improved. By 1900, it was 46 years. Nowadays, it has shot up to 76.7 years—which means that, in the last century, life expectancy in North America and Western Europe has increased by almost 30 years! (Centers for Disease Control and Prevention [CDC], Health United States, 2007.)

The **twentieth-century life expectancy revolution** may qualify as the most important milestone in human history. The most dramatic increases in longevity occurred about 100 years ago, when public health improvements, such as pasteurized milk, allowed babies to survive past infancy (Gordon, 2015), and medical advances, such as antibiotics, wiped out deaths from many *infectious diseases*. Because these illnesses, such as mumps and malaria, killed both the young and old, conquering them has allowed us to live past midlife. In the last 50 years, our progress has been slower because the diseases we now die from, called *chronic diseases*—such as heart disease, cancer, and stroke—are tied to the aging process itself.

As you can see in Figure 1.1, the outcome is that today life expectancies have zoomed into the upper seventies in the United States, Western Europe, Israel, and Japan. A baby born in affluent parts of the world, especially if that child is female, now has a good chance of making it close to our **maximum lifespan,** the biological limit of human life (about age 105).

This extension of the lifespan has changed our ideas about *every* life stage. It helped to postpone the average age of marriage by almost a decade. Rather than taking place right after the teens, today young people agree that the "right" time to get married is after they have finished their education and found a secure, decently paying career (more about this transformation in Chapter 10). Grandparenthood, once a sign of being "old," has slid down to the middle of life. If you become a grandparent in your forties, expect to be called Grandma or Grandpa for half of your life. Most important, we have moved the beginning of old age to well beyond age 65.

Today, people in their sixties and early seventies are often active and relatively healthy. But as we approach the eighties, our chance of being disabled by disease increases dramatically. Developmentalists therefore make a distinction between two groups of older adults: The **young-old** are people in their sixties and seventies, who usually look and feel middle-aged and often reject the idea that they are old (Lachman, 2004); the **old-old** are people in their eighties, who seem in a different class. They are more likely to have physical and mental disabilities, and so are more prone to fit the stereotype of the frail, dependent older adult. In sum, Susan in the vignette was right: Today, the eighties are a different stage of life!

twentieth-century life expectancy revolution The dramatic increase in average life expectancy that occurred during the first half of the twentieth century in the developed world.

maximum lifespan The biological limit of human life (about 105 years).

young-old People in their sixties and seventies.

old-old People age 80 and older.

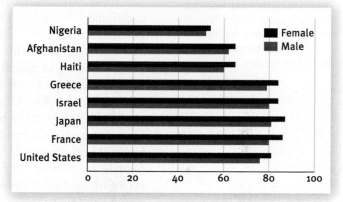

FIGURE **1.1: Average life expectancy of men and women in some selected nations, 2015:** Notice the gap in life expectancy between the rich and poor nations. Notice also the astonishingly high life expectancy women enjoy in France, Greece, Israel, and Japan. Although millions of females are now inching toward the maximum lifespan, unfortunately in 2015, the United States—with its already poor showing in the affluent world—reached an unhappy milestone. For the first time *ever,* average life expectancy slightly declined for women and men.

Data from World Bank, n.d.

The healthy, active couple in their sixties *(left)* have little in common with the disabled 90-year-old woman living in a nursing home *(right)*—which illustrates why developmentalists classify the elderly as either *young-old* or *old-old.*

AP Photo

The 1960s revolution, with its mantra of personal freedom and doing your own thing, upended our ideas about family life. Here you can see a landmark counterculture event, the 1969 Woodstock concert.

Changing Conceptions of Adult Life

If the health-care miracles of the early twentieth century allowed us to survive to old age, during the last third of that century, a revolution in lifestyles changed the way we live our adult lives. This transformation in the West, which has spread around the globe, began when the baby boomers entered their teenage years.

The 1960s "Decade of Protest" included the civil rights and women's movements, the sexual revolution, and the "counterculture" movement that emphasized liberation in every area of life (Bengtson, 1989). People could have sex without being married. Women could fulfill themselves in a career. We encouraged husbands to share the housework and child care equally with their wives. Divorce became an acceptable alternative to living in an unfulfilling marriage. To have a baby, women no longer needed to be married at all.

Today, with most married women in the labor force, a minority of couples fit the traditional 1950s roles of breadwinner husband and homemaker wife (U.S. Bureau of Labor Statistics, n.d.). With roughly 1 out of 2 U.S. marriages ending in divorce, we can no longer be confident of staying together for life. While divorce rates may have been declining in recent years, the Western trend toward having children without being married continues to rise. As of 2015, more than 1 in 3 U.S. babies were born to single moms (Kids Count Data Center, n.d.).

The timeline at the bottom of this page illustrates the twentieth-century shifts in life expectancy and family life, as well as charts the passage of the mammoth baby boom. Throughout this book, I'll pay special attention to the late-twentieth-century lifestyle revolution—highlighting the issues facing stepparents and single parents, exploring gay relationships, and shedding light on the changing family roles of women and men. While this text does divide development into its standard categories (infancy, childhood, adolescence, adulthood, and later life), I'll also devote a chapter to emerging adulthood—that life stage many of you are in right now. In the later-life section, I'll continually emphasize the distinction between the young-old and old-old (physically and mentally, being 60 is miles away from being 80 or 95) and focus on the challenges society faces as the baby boomers flood into their older years.

But, because history is always advancing, let's end this section by touching on two recent changes: (1) that global transformation, the Internet, and (2) an unwelcome economic development, especially in the United States.

Residing in Cyberspace

> Meet the Alvin family. . . . Sandra, a former journalist . . . has over 800 followers on twitter and keeps an elaborate . . . blog; their 16-year-old daughter Zara is a fanatic Facebook user—464 friends right now—and she also uses Pinterest for "pinning and sharing photos." . . .
>
> (quoted in Van Dijck, 2013, p. 3)

TIMELINE	Selected Twentieth-Century Milestones and the Progress of the Huge Baby Boom													
	1900	1910	1920	1930	1940	1950	1960	1970	1980	1990	2000	2010	2020	2030
MAJOR SOCIETAL CHANGE	**Life Expectancy Takes Off** Deaths shift from infectious to chronic diseases							**Lifestyle Revolution** Women's movement/rise in divorce and single parenthood/more lifestyle freedom						
BABY BOOM COHORT						Born		Teenagers				Young-old	→	Old-old

Julia, . . . a Sophomore at a . . . public high school turns texting into a kind of polling. After Julia sends out a text, she is uncomfortable until she gets one back: "I'm always looking for a text that says, "Oh I'm sorry" or "Oh that's great." Without this feedback, she says, "It's hard to calm down." Julia describes how painful it is to text about her feelings and get no response: "If . . . they don't answer me . . . I'll text them again "are you mad? . . . Is everything Ok?"

(adapted from Turkle, 2011, p. 175)

How many of you feel the urge to check some social media site or your smart phone as you are reading these lines? Perhaps, like Sandra, you avidly use Twitter, or can relate to Julia's anxiety when you text and don't get an immediate response.

Cell phones and texting instituted what one expert (Van Dijck, 2013) has labeled our twenty-first century "culture of connectivity," by tethering us to our significant others every moment of the day. Then that early-twentieth-century advance in technology, called Web 2.0, accelerated this revolution by allowing us to interact 24/7 with strangers around the globe (Van Dijck, 2013). In particular, Web 2.0 fostered the development of **social networking sites** that permit us to broadcast every feeling to an expanding array of "friends."

How are social network sites affecting romantic relationships? Does cyberbullying differ from in-person bullying? How is technology altering our career path? Stay tuned for subsequent chapters that showcase studies exploring how being on-line has transformed twenty-first-century life.

Rising Income Inequalities

After World War II, the United States was the producer for the world. Manufacturing jobs were plentiful. Incomes rose dramatically for workers at every economic rung. A working-class man could support a family with a stay-at-home wife. Then, starting around the 1970s, middle- and low-income wage growth began to stall. Bedrock U.S. sectors of the economy, such as the steel and auto industries, began relocating manufacturing jobs, first from the unionized North to the South, then to low-wage regions, like Mexico and Thailand. The fortunes of laborers and the well-off diverged. **Income inequalities**—the widening gaps between the richest fraction of citizens and everyone else—became the number one economic problem in the United States (Stone and others, 2017).

Figure 1.2a graphically shows this accelerating change. Notice that, while from 1980–2010 the bottom half of wage earners did gain a bit, the incomes of the top 1 percent soared. In 2016, as Figure 1.2b shows, this tiny fraction of Americans owned almost 40 percent of U.S. wealth!

social networking sites
Internet sites whose goal is to forge personal connections among users.

income inequality
The gap between the rich and poor within a nation; specifically, when income inequality is wide, a nation has few very affluent residents and a mass of disadvantaged citizens.

FIGURE **1.2: Snapshots of blossoming income inequalities: (A)** Percent change in U.S. real income at different economic levels from 1980–2010. Notice how, in recent decades, income gains of the top 1 percent of the population dwarfed those of other U.S. citizens, with the richest fraction of Americans becoming far richer, especially during the twenty-first century. **(B) Fraction of U.S. wealth held by the top 1 percent, 9 percent, and bottom 90 percent of U.S. families, in 2016.** This chart shows the astonishing concentration of wealth at the very top of the economic ladder—the top 1 percent now have a much higher fraction of U.S. wealth than the bottom 90 percent combined!

Data from Stone and others, 2017.

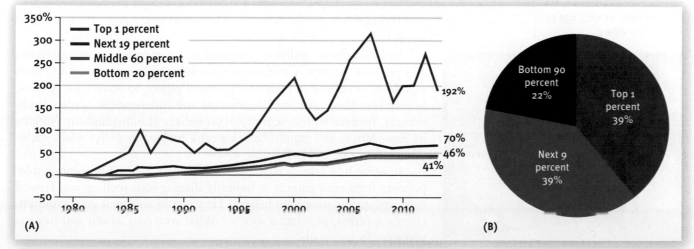

(A)

(B)

upward mobility Rising in social class and/or economic status from one's childhood.

socioeconomic status (SES) A basic marker referring to status on the educational and, especially, income rungs.

developed world The most affluent countries in the world.

developing world The more impoverished countries of the world.

collectivist cultures Societies that prize social harmony, obedience, and close family connectedness over individual achievement.

individualistic cultures Societies that prize independence, competition, and personal success.

Income inequalities erode every citizen's well-being. As you will learn later in the book, shared prosperity and a vital middle class is the defining characteristic of the "happiest nations" on Earth (Wilkinson & Pickett, 2009).

Income inequalities also erode the American dream—the basic faith that, by working hard, any young person can succeed. During the first half of the twentieth century, U.S. **upward mobility,** that is, a child's chance of rising in socioeconomic status compared to her parents, was virtually guaranteed. It's only an iffy fifty/fifty today (Chetty & Hendren, 2017; see Chapter 10). What exactly is *socioeconomic status,* and why is this marker vital in shaping our lives?

The Impact of Socioeconomic Status

Socioeconomic status (SES)—a term referring to our education and income—actually makes a major impact on development at every life stage. As you will see throughout this book, poverty in particular makes people vulnerable to a cascade of problems—from being born less healthy to attending lower-quality schools; from living in more dangerous neighborhoods to never getting married to dying at a younger age. Not only do developmentalists rank people by SES, but they rank nations that way, too.

Developed-world nations are defined by their wealth, or high median per-person incomes. In these countries, as you learned earlier, life expectancy is high, income inequality is not extreme, and each citizen has access to good education and modern medical care. Traditionally, the United States, Canada, Australia, New Zealand, and Japan, as well as every Western European nation, have been classified in this "most affluent" category, although its ranks *may* be expanding as the economies of nations such as China and India explode.

Developing-world countries stand in sharp contrast to these most affluent world regions. In the least-developed countries, people may not have indoor plumbing, clean running water, or access to education. They may die at a young age from "curable" infectious diseases. Babies born in the poorest regions of the globe face a twenty-first-century lifespan that has striking similarities to the one developed-world children faced more than a century ago.

The Impact of Culture and Ethnicity

Residents of developing nations often have shorter, more difficult lives. Still, if you visited these places, you might be struck by a sense of community we seldom see in the West. Can we categorize societies according to their values, apart from their wealth? Developmentalists who study culture answer yes.

Collectivist cultures place a premium on social harmony. The family generations expect to live together, even as adults. Children are taught to obey their elders, to suppress their feelings, to value being respectful, and to subordinate their personal needs to the good of the wider group.

For this grandmother, mother, and daughter, getting dressed up to visit this Shinto family shrine and pay their respects to their ancestors is an important ritual. It is one way that collectivist societies such as Japan teach children from an early age to honor their elders.

Individualistic cultures emphasize independence, competition, and personal success. Children are encouraged to openly express their emotions, to believe in their own personal power, to leave their parents, to stand on their own as self-sufficient and independent adults. Traditionally, Western nations score high on indices of individualism. Nations in Asia, Africa, and South America rank higher on collectivism scales (Hofstede, 1981, 2001; Triandis, 1995).

Imagine how your perspective on life might differ if becoming independent from your parents or honestly sharing your feelings was viewed as an inappropriate way to behave. How would you treat your children, choose a career, or select a spouse? What concerns would you have as you were facing death?

As we scan development around the world, I will regularly distinguish between collectivist and more individualistic societies. I'll highlight the issues families face when they move from these traditional cultures to the West, as well as explore research relating to the major U.S. ethnic groups listed in Figure 1.3.

As you read this information, keep in mind that what unites us as people outweighs any distinctions based on culture, ethnicity, or race. Moreover, making diversity generalizations is hazardous because of the diversity that exists *within* each nation and ethnic group. In the most individualistic country (no surprise, that's the United States), people have a mix of collectivist and individualistic worldviews. Due to globalization, traditionally collectivistic cultures, such as China and Japan, now fully embrace individualistic, Western worldviews.

If the census labels you as "Hispanic American," you also are probably aware that this label masks more than it reveals. As a third-generation Cuban American, do you really have much in common with an immigrant from Mexico or Belize? Given that people arrive in Western nations from hundreds of culturally different countries, does it make sense to lump people into a small number of ethnic groups? There is, however, one distinction that does clearly divide us at birth—being female or male.

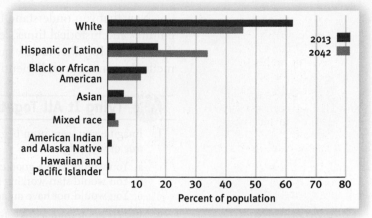

FIGURE **1.3: The major ethnic groups in the United States, their percentages in 2013, and a few mid-twenty-first-century projections:** By 2042, more than half of the U.S. population is projected to be made up of ethnic minorities. Notice in particular the huge increase in the proportion of Latino Americans.

Data from http://quickfacts.census.gov/qfd/states/00000.htm.

The Impact of Gender

As we are now well aware, sex chromosomes no longer define our lives—just listen to the transgender adults who feel liberated to live according to their inner gender identity, not their anatomy at birth. Then listen to a few revolutionary young people who refuse to be defined by the binary labels "male" or "female."

Still, as you saw in Figure 1.1, worldwide, there are basic differences in life expectancy based on sex. In *every* nation, women outlive men by at least two years (World Bank, n.d.). And statistically speaking, males and females *do* behave differently; we can see these gender differences early in life.

Are boys more aggressive than girls? Are male/female differences in caregiving, career interests, and childhood play styles mainly due to the environment (societal pressures or the way we are brought up) or to inborn, biological forces? Throughout this book, I'll examine these questions as we explore the scientific truth of our gender stereotypes and speculate about their causes. To introduce this conversation, you might want to take the "Is It Males or Females?" quiz in Table 1.1. Keep a copy. As we travel through the lifespan, you can check the accuracy of your ideas.

Table 1.1: Is It Males or Females?

1. Who are more likely to survive the hazards of prenatal development, male or female fetuses? (You will find the answer in Chapter 2.)

2. Who are more likely to be diagnosed with ADHD, girls or boys? (You will find the answer in Chapter 6.)

3. Who are more aggressive, boys or girls? (You will find the answer in Chapter 6.)

4. Who are more likely to be diagnosed with learning disabilities in school, boys or girls? (You will find the answer in Chapter 7.)

5. Who, when they reach puberty at an earlier-than-typical age, are more at risk of developing problems, boys or girls? (You will find the answer in Chapter 8.)

6. Who are more likely to get depressed as teens, girls or boys? (You will find the answer in Chapter 9.)

7. Who tend to earn more today, women or men? (You will find the answer in Chapter 11.)

8. Who are more at risk of committing suicide after being widowed, men or women? (You will find the answer in Chapter 13.)

9. Who are apt to live longer, sicker men or women? (You will find the answer in Chapter 14.)

10. Who cares more about being closely attached, males or females—or both sexes? (You will find the answer throughout this book.)

Now that you understand that our lifespan is a work in progress that varies across cultures and historical times, let's get to the science. After you complete this section's Tying It All Together review quiz below, I will introduce the main theories, research methods, concepts, and scientific terms in this book.

Tying It All Together

1. Imagine you were born before the twentieth century. Which statement would be *least true* of your life?
   a. You would have a good chance of dying during childhood.
   b. You would start working right after high school.
   c. You would not have an adolescence.

2. Rosa is 80; Ramona is 65. In a sentence, describe the major statistical difference between these two women, and then label each person's life stage.

3. Carlos is in his early twenties today; his grandfather was in his early twenties 50 years ago. In comparing their lives, plug in the statistically correct items: Carlos will enter the workforce at an *older/younger* age, get married *later/earlier*, be *more/less* likely to rise in socioeconomic status than his granddad.

4. Hakeem says, "I would never think of leaving my parents or living far from my brothers and sisters. A person must take care of his extended family before satisfying his own needs." Peter says, "My primary commitment is to my wife and children. A person needs, above all, to make an independent life." Hakeem has a(n) _____ worldview, while Peter's worldview is more _____.

5. Categorize your great-grandparents, grandparents, and parents by socioeconomic status (working class, middle class, upper middle class). Was upward mobility a defining characteristic of your family? Do you believe you will outpace your parents educationally and in your career?

Answers to the Tying It All Together questions can be found at the end of this chapter.

Theories: Lenses for Looking at the Lifespan

LEARNING OUTCOMES

- Summarize the theories scientists use to understand the lifespan.
- Describe the research strategy behavioral geneticists use.
- Explain how "nature" and "nurture" interact during development.

theory Any perspective explaining why people act the way they do; theories allow us to predict behavior and also suggest how to intervene to improve behavior.

nature Biological or genetic causes of development.

nurture Environmental causes of development.

During her twenties, Jamila was probably searching for her identity. Susan's sunny, people-oriented personality is genetic. If Elissa's mother gives her a lot of love during her first years of life, she will grow up to be a loving, secure adult. If any of these thoughts entered your mind while reading about the people in the chapter-opening vignette, you touched on a major theory that developmentalists use to understand human life.

Theories attempt to explain what causes us to act as we do. They may allow us to predict the future. Ideally, they give us information about how to improve the quality of life. Theories in developmental science may offer broad explanations of behavior that apply to people at every age, or describe changes that occur at particular ages. This section provides a preview of both kinds of theories.

Let's begin by outlining some theories (one is actually a research discipline) that offer general explanations of behavior. I've organized these theories somewhat chronologically—based on *when* they emerged during the twentieth century—but mainly according to their position on that core issue: Is it the environment, or the wider world, that determines how we develop? Are our personalities, talents, and traits shaped mainly by biological or genetic forces? This is the famous **nature** (biology) versus **nurture** (environment) question.

Behaviorism: The Original Blockbuster "Nurture" Theory

traditional behaviorism
The original behavioral worldview that focused on charting and modifying only "objective" visible behaviors.

> Give me a dozen healthy infants . . . and I'll guarantee to take any one at random and train him to be any specialist I might select—doctor, lawyer, artist, merchant-chief, and yes, even beggar man and thief.
>
> (Watson, 1930, p. 104)

So proclaimed the early-twentieth-century psychologist John Watson as he spelled out the nurture-is-all-important position of traditional behaviorism. Intoxicated by the scientific advances that were transforming society, Watson and his fellow behaviorist B. F. Skinner (1960, 1974) dreamed of a science of human behavior that would be as rigorous as physics. These theorists believed that we could not study feelings and thoughts because inner experiences could not be observed. It was vital to chart only measurable, observable responses. Moreover, according to these **traditional behaviorists,** a few general laws of learning explain behavior in every situation at every time of life.

Exploring Reinforcement

According to Skinner, the general law of learning that causes each voluntary action, from forming our first words to mastering higher math, is **operant conditioning.** Responses that we reward, or reinforce, are learned. Responses that are not reinforced go away, or are *extinguished*. So what accounts for Watson's beggar men and thieves, the out-of-control kids, all the marriages that start out so loving and then fall apart? According to Skinner, the reinforcements are operating as they should. The problem is that instead of reinforcing positive behavior, we often reinforce the wrong things.

One excellent place to see Skinner's point is to take a trip to your local market or a restaurant. Notice how, when children act up at the store, parents often buy them a toy to quiet them down. At that restaurant dinner, as long as a toddler is playing quietly, adults ignore her. When she starts to hurl objects off the table, they pick her up, kiss her, and take her outside. Then, they complain about their child's difficult personality, not realizing that their *own* reinforcements have produced these responses!

One of Skinner's most interesting concepts, derived from his work with pigeons, relates to *variable reinforcement schedules.* This is the type of reinforcement that typically occurs in daily life: We get reinforced unpredictably, so we keep responding, realizing that if we continue, *at some point* we will be reinforced. Readers with children will understand how difficult it is to follow the basic behavioral principle to be consistent or not let a negative variable schedule emerge. At Walmart, even though you vow, "I won't give in to bad behavior!" as your toddler's tantrums escalate, you cave in, simply to avoid other shoppers' disapproving stares ("What an out-of-control parent and bratty kid!"). Unfortunately, your child has learned, "If I keep whining, *eventually* I'll get what I want."

Reinforcement (and its opposite process, *extinction*) is a powerful force for both good and bad. It explains why a child who starts out succeeding early in elementary school (being reinforced by receiving A's) is apt to study more. If a kindergartner begins failing socially (i.e., does not get positive reinforcement from her peers), she is at risk for becoming incredibly shy or highly aggressive in third or fourth grade (see Chapter 6). If people did not reinforce your behavior, wouldn't you withdraw or act in socially inappropriate ways?

This photo shows B. F. Skinner with his favorite research subject for exploring operant conditioning—the pigeon. By charting how often pigeons pecked before being reinforced by food, Skinner was able to tell us how humans act.

operant conditioning
According to traditional behaviorists, the law of learning that determines any voluntary response.

reinforcement Behavioral term for reward.

Imagine wheeling this whining toddler through a Walmart grocery aisle. Wouldn't you be tempted to reinforce this unpleasant behavior by silencing the child with an enticing object on the shelf?

Behaviorism makes sense of why marriages that start out lovingly can end in divorce. As newlyweds, couples are continually reinforcing each other with expressions of love. Then, over time, husbands and wives tend to ignore the good parts of their partner and pay attention only when something is wrong.

The theory even offers an optimistic environmental explanation for the physical and mental impairments of old age. If you were in a nursing home and weren't being reinforced for remembering or walking, wouldn't your memory or physical abilities decline? The solution is simple to produce well-behaved children; enduring, loving marriages; and fewer old-age disabilities. According to traditional behaviorists, we need to reinforce the right things.

However, things are not that simple. Human beings *do* think and reason. People do not need to be personally reinforced to learn.

Taking a Different Perspective: Exploring Cognitions

Enter **cognitive behaviorism (social learning theory),** launched by Albert Bandura (1977, 1986) and his colleagues in the 1970s. Their studies demonstrated the power of **modeling,** or learning by watching and imitating what other people do.

Because we are a social species, modeling (both imitating other people and others reciprocally imitating us) is endemic in daily life. Given that we are always modeling everything from the latest hairstyle on, who are we most likely to *generally* model as children and adults?

Bandura (1986) finds that that we tend to model people who are nurturing, who relate to us in a caring way. (The good news here is that being a loving, hands-on parent is the best way to naturally embed your values and ideas.) We model people whom we categorize as being like us. At age 2, you probably modeled anything from the vacuum cleaner to the behavior of the family dog. As we grow older, we tailor our modeling selectively, based on our understanding of who we are.

Modeling similar people partly explains why, after children understand their gender label (girl or boy) at about age 2½, they separate into sex-segregated play groups and prefer to play with their "own group" (see Chapter 5). It also makes sense of why at-risk teenagers gravitate to the druggies group at school, and then model the leader who most embodies the group norms (see Chapter 9). While I will use modeling to explain behavior at several points in this book, another concept—also devised by Bandura—serves as a *genuine* foundation for the chapters to come: self-efficacy.

Self-efficacy refers to our belief in our competence, our sense that we can be successful at a given task. According to Bandura (1989, 1992, 1997), efficacy feelings determine the goals we set. They predict which activities we engage in as we travel through life. When self-efficacy is low, we decide not to tackle that difficult math problem. We choose not to ask a beautiful stranger for a date. When self-efficacy is high, we not only take action, but we also continue to act long after the traditional behavioral approach suggests that extinction should occur.

Let's imagine that your goal is to be a nurse, but you get an F on your first test in this course. If your academic self-efficacy is low, you might conclude: "I'm basically not smart." You might not put forth any effort on the next exam. You might even drop out of school. But if you have high self-efficacy, you will think: "I just need to work harder. I can do it. I'm *going* to get a good grade in this class!"

How do children develop low or high self-efficacy? Can efficacy feelings predict success decades later in a career? What role does self-efficacy play in happiness in old age? These are the kinds of questions we will explore throughout this book in examining efficacy feelings throughout life.

By now, you may be impressed with behaviorism's simple, action-oriented concepts. Be consistent. Don't reinforce negative behavior. Reinforce positive things (from traditional behaviorism). Draw on the principles of modeling and stimulate efficacy feelings to help children and adults succeed (from cognitive behaviorism).

cognitive behaviorism (social learning theory) A behavioral worldview that emphasizes that people learn by watching others and that our thoughts about the reinforcers determine our behavior. Cognitive behaviorists focus on charting and modifying people's thoughts.

modeling Learning by watching and imitating others.

self-efficacy According to cognitive behaviorism, an internal belief in our competence that predicts whether we initiate activities or persist in the face of failures, and predicts the goals we set.

Still, many developmentalists—even people who believe that nurture (or the environment) is important—find behaviorism unsatisfying. Aren't we more than just efficacy feelings or reinforced responses? Isn't there a basic core to personality, and aren't the lessons we learn in childhood vital in shaping our adult life? Notice that behaviorism doesn't address that core question: What *really* motivates us as people? To address these gaps, developmental scientists, particularly in the past, turned to the insights of that world-class genius, Sigmund Freud.

Psychoanalytic Theory: Focus on Early Childhood and Unconscious Motivations

Sigmund Freud's ideas are currently not in vogue in developmental science. However, no one can dispute the fact that Freud (1856–1939) transformed the way we think about human beings. Anytime you say, "I must have done that unconsciously" or "My problems are due to my childhood," you are quoting Freudian thought.

Freud, a Viennese Jewish physician, wrote more than 40 books and monographs in a burst of brilliance during the early twentieth century. His ideas revolutionized everything from anthropology to the arts, in addition to jump-starting the modern field of mental health. Freud's mission, however, was simple: to decode why his patients were in emotional pain.

Freud's theory is called *psychoanalytic* because it analyzes the psyche, or our inner life. By listening to his patients, Freud became convinced that our actions are dominated by feelings of which we are not aware. The roots of emotional problems lay in repressed (made unconscious) feelings from early childhood. Moreover, "mothering" during the first five years of life determines adult mental health.

Specifically, Freud posited three hypothetical structures. The *id*, present at birth, is the mass of instincts, needs, and feelings we have when we arrive in the world. During early childhood, the conscious, rational part of our personality—called the *ego*—emerges. Ego functions involve thinking, reasoning, planning, and fulfilling our id desires in realistic ways. Finally, a structure called the *superego*—the moral arm of our personality—exists in opposition to the id's desires.

According to Freud and his followers, if our parents are excellent caregivers, we will develop a strong ego, which sets us up to master the challenges of life. If our parents are insensitive or their caregiving is impaired, our behavior will be id driven, and our lives will be out of control. The purpose of his therapy, called *psychoanalysis*, was to enable his patients to become aware of the repressed early childhood experiences causing their symptoms and liberate them from the tyranny of the unconscious to live rational, productive lives. (As Freud famously put it, "where *id* there was, *ego* there will be.")

In sum, according to Freud: (1) Human beings are basically irrational; (2) lifelong mental health depends on our parents' caregiving during early life; and (3) self-understanding is the key to living a fulfilling adult life.

By now, many of you might be on a similar page as Freud. Where you are apt to part serious company with the theory relates to Freud's stages of sexuality. Freud argued that sexual feelings (which he called *libido*) drive human life, and he put forth the shocking idea—especially at that time—that babies are sexual human beings. As the infant develops, he argued, sexual feelings are centered on specific areas of the body called *erogenous zones*. During the first year of life, the erogenous zone is the mouth (the famous *oral stage*). Around age 2, with toilet training, sexual feelings center on elimination (the *anal stage*). Finally, around ages 3 and 4, sexual feelings shift to the genitals (the *phallic stage*). During that time, the child develops sexual fantasies relating to the parent of the opposite sex (the *Oedipus complex*), and the same-sex parent becomes a rival.

This man is clearly upbeat and ebullient. In Chapter 13, you will learn what health benefits result from having his efficacious sense of purpose in life.

Freud, pictured here in his robust middle age, alerted us to the power of childhood experiences and unconscious motivations in shaping human life.

attachment theory
Theory formulated
by John Bowlby
centering on the crucial
importance to our
species' survival of being
closely connected with
a caregiver during early
childhood and being
attached to a significant
other during all of life.

Then, sexuality is repressed, the child identifies with the same-sex parent, the superego is formed, and we enter *latency*—an asexual stage that lasts through elementary school.

Partly because Freud's sexual stages seem so foreign to our thinking, we tend to reject psychoanalytic theory as outdated—an artifact of a distant era. A deeper look suggests we might be wrong. Like Freud, contemporary developmentalists believe that self-understanding—the ability to reflect on and regulate our emotions—is the defining quality of being mature. Like Freud, developmental scientists are passionate to trace the roots of lifelong development to what happens in our earliest months and years of life. As you read through this book, perhaps you will agree with me that—despite its different terminology and approaches—our field owes a great philosophical debt to Freud. Moreover, psychoanalytic theory gave birth to that important modern perspective called *attachment theory*.

Attachment Theory: Focus on Nurture, Nature, and Love

British psychiatrist John Bowlby formulated **attachment theory** during the mid-twentieth century. Bowlby, like Freud, believed that our early experiences with caregivers shape our adult ability to love, but he focused on what he called the *attachment response*.

In observing young children separated from their mothers, Bowlby noticed that babies need to be physically close to a caregiver during the time when they are beginning to walk (Bowlby, 1969, 1973; Karen, 1998). Prolonged disruptions in this biologically programmed attachment response, he argued, might cause serious problems later in life. Moreover, our impulse to be close to a "significant other" is a basic human need during every stage of life.

How does the attachment response develop? Are Bowlby and Freud right that our early attachments determine adult mental health? How can we draw on attachment theory to understand everything from adult love relationships to our concerns as we approach death? Stay tuned for answers throughout this book as we explore this influential theory.

Why did Bowlby's ideas eclipse psychoanalytic theory? A main reason was that Bowlby agreed with a late-twentieth-century shift in the way developmentalists understood human motivations. Yes, Bowlby did believe in the power of caregiving (nurture), but he firmly anchored his theory in nature (genetics). Bowlby (1969, 1973, 1980) argued that the attachment response is genetically programmed into our species to promote survival. He was an early *evolutionary psychologist*.

Image Source/Getty Images

Bowlby believed that the intense, loving bond between this father and infant son will set the baby up for a fulfilling life. In Chapter 4, I will describe exactly how the attachment bond unfolds, and whether this core principle of Bowlby's theory is correct.

evolutionary psychology
Theory or worldview
highlighting the role
that inborn, species-
specific behaviors play
in human development
and life.

Evolutionary Psychology: Theorizing About the "Nature" of Human Similarities

Evolutionary psychologists are the mirror image of behaviorists. They look to nature, or inborn biological forces that have evolved to promote survival, to explain how we behave. Why do pregnant women develop morning sickness just as the fetal organs are being formed, and why do newborns prefer to look at attractive faces rather than ugly ones? (That's actually true!) According to evolutionary psychologists, these reactions cannot be changed by modifying the reinforcers. They are based in the human genetic code that we all share.

Evolutionary psychology lacks the practical, action-oriented approach of behaviorism, although it does alert us to the fact that we need to pay close attention to basic human needs. Still, as we look at how far-flung topics—from the timing of puberty (Chapter 8) to the purpose of grandparents (Chapter 12)—are viewed through an evolutionary psychology lens, you will realize just how influential this "look to the human genome" perspective has become in our field. What *first* convinced developmentalists that genetics is important in determining the person we become? A simple set of research techniques.

Behavioral Genetics: Scientifically Exploring the "Nature" of Human Differences

Behavioral genetics is the name for research strategies devoted to examining the genetic contribution to the *differences* we see between human beings. How genetic is the tendency to bite our nails, develop bipolar disorders, have specific attitudes about life? To answer these kinds of questions, scientists typically use twin and adoption studies.

In **twin studies,** researchers typically compare identical (monozygotic) twins and fraternal (dizygotic) twins on the trait the researchers are interested in (playing the oboe, obesity, and so on). Identical twins develop from the same fertilized egg (it splits soon after the one-cell stage) and are genetic clones. Fraternal twins, like any brother or sister, develop from two fertilized eggs and so, on average, share 50 percent of their genes. The idea is that if a given trait is highly influenced by genetics, identical twins should be much more alike in that quality than fraternal twins. Specifically, behavioral geneticists use a statistic called *heritability* (which ranges from 1 = totally genetic, to 0 = no genetic contribution) to summarize the extent to which a given behavior is shaped by genetic forces.

For instance, to conduct a twin study to determine the heritability of friendliness, you would select a large group of identical and fraternal twins. You would give both sets of twins various tests that measure outgoing attitudes, and then compare the strength of the relationships you found for each twin group. Let's say the identical twins' scores were incredibly similar—almost like the same person taking the tests twice—and the fraternal twins' test scores varied a great deal from one another. Your heritability statistic would be high, and you could conclude: "Friendliness is a mainly genetically determined trait."

In **adoption studies,** researchers compare adopted children with their biological and adoptive parents. Here, too, they evaluate the impact of heredity on a trait by looking at how closely these children resemble their birth parents (with whom they share only genes) and their adoptive parents (with whom they share only environments).

Twin studies of children growing up in the same family and adoption studies are fairly easy to carry out. The most powerful evidence for genetics comes from the rare **twin/adoption studies,** in which identical twins are separated in childhood and reunited in adult life. If Joe and James, who have exactly the same DNA, have similar abilities, traits, and personalities, even though they grow up in *different families*, this would be strong evidence that genetics plays a crucial role in who we are.

Consider, for instance, the Swedish Twin/Adoption Study of Aging. Researchers combed national registries to find identical and fraternal twins adopted into different

behavioral genetics Field devoted to scientifically determining the role that hereditary forces play in determining individual differences in behavior.

twin study Behavioral genetic research strategy, designed to determine the genetic contribution of a given trait, that involves comparing identical twins with fraternal twins (or with other people).

adoption study Behavioral genetic research strategy, designed to determine the genetic contribution to a given trait, that involves comparing adopted children with their biological and adoptive parents.

twin/adoption study Behavioral genetic research strategy that involves comparing the similarities of identical twin pairs adopted into different families, to determine the genetic contribution to a given trait.

How "genetic" are these children's friendly personalities? To answer this question, researchers compare identical twins, such as these two girls *(left)*, with fraternal twins, like this girl and boy *(right)*. If the identicals (who share exactly the same DNA) are much more similar to each other than the fraternals in their scores on friendliness tests, friendliness is defined as a highly heritable trait.

families in that country—where birth records of every adoptee are kept. Then they reunited these children in late middle age and gave the twins a battery of tests (Finkel & Pedersen, 2004; Kato & Pedersen, 2005).

While specific qualities varied in their heritability, you might be surprised to know that the most genetically determined quality was IQ (Pedersen, 1996). In fact, if one twin took the standard intelligence test, statistically speaking we could predict that the other twin would have an almost identical IQ despite living apart for almost an entire lifetime!

Behavioral genetic studies such as these have opened our eyes to the role of nature in shaping who we are (Turkheimer, 2004). Our tendencies to be religious, vote for conservative Republicans (Bouchard and others, 2004), drink to excess (Agrawal & Lynskey, 2008), or get divorced—qualities we thought *must* be due to how our parents raised us—are all somewhat shaped by genetic forces (Plomin and others, 2003).

These studies have given us tantalizing insights into nurture, too. It's tempting to assume that children growing up in the same family share the same nurture, or environment. But as you can see in the How Do We Know research box, that assumption is wrong. We inhabit different life spaces than our brothers and sisters do, even when we eat at the same dinner table and share the same room—environments that are influenced by our genes (Rowe, 2003).

HOW DO WE KNOW . . .
that our nature affects our upbringing?

For much of the twentieth century, developmentalists assumed that parents treated all their children the same way. We could classify mothers as either nurturing or rejecting, caring or cold. The Swedish Twin/Adoption Study turned these basic parenting assumptions upside down (Plomin & Bergeman, 1991).

Researchers asked middle-aged identical twins who had been adopted into different families as babies to rate their parents along dimensions such as caring, acceptance, and discipline styles. They were astonished to find similarities in the ratings, even though the twins were evaluating different families!

What was happening? The answer, the researchers concluded, was that the genetic similarities in the twins' personalities *created* similar family environments. If Joe and Jim were both easy, kind, and caring, they evoked more loving parenting. If they were temperamentally difficult, they caused their adoptive parents to react in more rejecting, less nurturant ways.

I vividly saw this *evocative,* child-shapes-parenting relationship in my own life. Because my adopted son Thomas has dyslexia and is very physically active, in our house we ended up doing active things like sports. Thomas didn't like to sit still for story time, so, if some psychologist had come into my home to rate how much I read to my child, I probably would have been described as a "less than optimally stimulating" parent.

And now, the plot thickens. When I met Thomas's biological mother Maureen, I found out that she also has dyslexia. She's energetic and peppy. It's one thing to see the impact of nature in my son, as his mother revealed. But I can't help wondering. . . . Maureen is a very different person than I am (although we have a terrific time together—traveling and doing active things). Would Thomas have had the *same* kind of upbringing (at least partly) if he had grown up with his biological mother instead of me?

The bottom line is that there is no such thing as nature *or* nurture. To understand human development, scientists need to explore how nature *and* nurture combine.

Nature and Nurture Combine: Where We Are Today

Let's now lay out two basic nature-plus-nurture principles, and then introduce cutting-edge developmental science research relating to how nature and nurture interact.

Principle 1: Our Nature (Genetic Tendencies) Shapes Our Nurture (Life Experiences)

Developmentalists understand that nature and nurture are not independent entities. Our genetic tendencies shape our wider-world experiences in two ways.

Evocative forces refer to the fact that our inborn talents and temperamental tendencies evoke, or produce, certain responses from the world. A joyous child elicits smiles from everyone. A child who is temperamentally irritable, hard to handle, or has trouble sitting still is unfortunately set up to get the kind of harsh parenting she least needs to succeed. Human relationships are **bidirectional.** Just as you get grumpy when with a grumpy person, fight with your difficult neighbor, or shy away from your colleague who is paralyzingly timid, who we are as people causes other people to react to us in specific ways, driving our development for the good and the bad.

Active forces refer to the fact that we *actively select* our environments based on our genetic tendencies. A child who is talented at reading gravitates toward devouring books and so becomes a better reader over time. His brother, who is well coordinated, may play baseball three hours a day and become a star athlete in his teenage years. Because we choose activities to fit our biologically based interests and skills, what start out as minor differences between people in early childhood snowball—ultimately producing huge gaps in talents and traits. The high heritabilities for intelligence test scores in the Swedish Twin/Adoption Study are lower in similar behavioral genetic studies conducted during childhood (Plomin & Spinath, 2004). The reason is that, like heat-seeking missiles, our nature causes us to gravitate toward specific life experiences, so we literally become *more like ourselves* genetically as we travel into adult life (Scarr, 1997).

Principle 2: We Need the Right Nurture (Life Experiences) to Fully Express Our Nature (Genetic Talents)

Developmentalists understand that even if a quality is mainly genetic, its expression can be 100 percent dependent on the outside world. Let's illustrate by returning to the high heritabilities for intelligence. If you lived in an impoverished developing country, were malnourished, and worked as a laborer in a field, having a genius-level IQ would be irrelevant, as there would be no chance to demonstrate your hereditary gifts.

The most fascinating example that a high-quality environment can bring out our human genetic potential relates specifically to intelligence. As you will see in Chapter 7, scores on the standard intelligence test have risen over the past century. The same correct items a twenty-first-century teenager needed to be ranked as "average" in intelligence would have boosted that same child into the top one-third of the population in 1950. A century ago, having the identical number of items correct would get that child labeled as gifted, in the top 2 percent of his peers (Pinker, 2011)!

What is causing this shift? Obviously, our "genetic" intellectual capacities can't have changed. It's just that as human beings have become better nourished, more educated, and more technologically adept, they perform better, especially on the kinds of abstract-reasoning items the IQ test measures (see Flynn, 2007; Pinker, 2011). So even when individual differences in IQ are "genetic," the environment makes a dramatic difference in how people perform.

This discussion brings home the fact that to promote our human potential, we need to provide the best possible environment. This is why a core goal of developmental science is to foster the correct **person–environment fit**—making the wider world bring out our human "best."

evocative forces The nature-interacts-with-nurture principle that our genetic temperamental tendencies produce certain responses from other people.

bidirectionality The principle that people affect one another, or that interpersonal influences flow in both directions.

active forces The nature-interacts-with-nurture principle that our genetic temperamental tendencies cause us to choose to put ourselves into specific environments.

Because this musically talented girl is choosing to spend hours playing the piano, she may become more gifted, showing that we actively shape the environment to fit our genetics.

person–environment fit The extent to which the environment is tailored to our biological tendencies and talents.

MedicalRF/Science Source

Due to an *epigenetic process,* this female fraternal twin fetus may be insulated from developing an eating disorder by being exposed to the testosterone her brother's body is giving off.

epigenetics Research field exploring how early life events alter the outer cover of our DNA, producing lifelong changes in health and behavior.

Erikson's psychosocial tasks In Erik Erikson's theory, each challenge that we face as we travel through the eight stages of the lifespan.

Ted Streshinsky/The LIFE Images Collection/Getty Images

With his powerful writings on identity and, especially, his concept of age-related psychosocial tasks, Erik Erikson (shown here with his wife, Joan) has become a father of our field.

Hot in Developmental Science: Environment-Sensitive Genes and Epigenetically Programmed Pathways

It's a no-brainer that we need to provide a superior environment for every child (and adult). But why does one child sail through traumas, such as poor parenting, while another breaks down under the slightest stress? What causes that same "genetically fragile" boy or girl to excel in a nurturing setting, such as high-quality day care, while his hardier peer seems immune to the gifts this exceptional environment provides? These questions are driving the hunt for genes that make people either more or less reactive to life events (see Belsky & Pluess, 2016). In the childhood chapters, I'll be outlining findings that suggest some of us are like cactuses, set up biologically to survive in less than nourishing environments; others seem similar to fragile orchids, capable of providing gorgeous flowers but only with special care. I'll also showcase exciting research suggesting that our genetics may be altered by early life events.

Epigenetics refers to the study of how our environment—often, but not exclusively, intrauterine and early childhood experiences—alters the outer cover of our DNA, causing effects that last throughout life. Can obesity, our tendency to develop gender atypical behavior, or even our predisposition to die at a younger age be partly programmed by events in the womb? Stay tuned for fascinating epigenetic hints in the chapters to come. 🔥

Emphasis on Age-Linked Theories

Now that I've highlighted this book's basic nature-combines-with-nurture message, it's time to explore the ideas of two psychologists who view human development as occurring in defined stages. Let's start with Erik Erikson.

Erik Erikson's Psychosocial Tasks

Born in Germany in 1904, Erik Erikson was an analyst who, like Bowlby, adhered to most tenets of psychoanalytic theory; but rather than emphasizing sexuality, Erikson (1963) believed that our basic motivations center on becoming an independent self and relating to others (which explains why Erikson's theory is called *psychosocial,* to distinguish it from Freud's psychosexual stages). Erikson, however, is often labeled as the father of lifespan development because, unlike Freud, he believed development occurs throughout life. He spelled out unique challenges we face at each life stage.

You can see these **psychosocial tasks,** or challenges, listed in Table 1.2. Erikson argued that each task builds on another because we cannot master the issue of a later stage unless we have accomplished the developmental milestones of the previous ones.

Table 1.2: Erikson's Psychosocial Stages

Life Stage	Primary Task
Infancy (birth to 1 year)	Basic trust versus mistrust
Toddlerhood (1 to 2 years)	Autonomy versus shame and doubt
Early childhood (3 to 6 years)	Initiative versus guilt
Middle childhood (7 to 12 years)	Industry versus inferiority
Adolescence to emerging adulthood (teens into twenties)	Identity versus role confusion
Early adulthood (twenties to early forties)	Intimacy versus isolation
Middle adulthood (forties to sixties)	Generativity versus stagnation
Late adulthood (late sixties and beyond)	Integrity versus despair

Notice how parents take incredible joy in satisfying their baby's needs and you will understand why Erikson believed that *basic trust* (the belief that the human world is caring) is our fundamental life task in the first year of life. Erikson's second psychosocial task, *autonomy*, makes sense of the infamous *"no stage"* and "terrible twos." It tells us that we need to *celebrate* this not-so-pleasant toddler behavior as the blossoming of a separate self! Think back to elementary school, and you may realize why Erikson used the term *industry*, or learning to work—at friendships, sports, academics—as our challenge from age 7 to 12. Erikson's adolescent task, the search for *identity*, has now become a household word.

How have developmentalists expanded on Erikson's ideas about identity? Is Erikson right that nurturing the next generation, or *generativity*, is the key to a fulfilling adult life? These are just two questions I'll be addressing as we draw on Erikson's theory to help us think more deeply about the challenges we face at each life stage.

Erikson offered a general emotional road map for our developing lives. But, in terms of brilliance and transformational thinking, there is only one human development rival to Freud: Jean Piaget.

Piaget's Cognitive Developmental Theory

A 3-year-old tells you "Mr. Sun goes to bed because it's time for me to go to sleep." A toddler is obsessed with flushing different-sized wads of paper down the toilet and can't resist touching everything she sees. Do you ever wish you could get into the heads of young children and understand how they view the world? If so, you share the passion of our foremost genius in child development, Jean Piaget.

Born in 1894 in Switzerland, Piaget was a child prodigy himself. As the teenaged author of several dozen articles on mollusks, he was already becoming well known in the field of biology (Flavell, 1963; Wadsworth, 1996). Piaget's interests shifted to studying children when he worked in the laboratory of a psychologist named Alfred Binet, who was devising the original intelligence test. Rather than ranking children according to how much they knew, Piaget became fascinated by children's *incorrect* responses. He spent the next 60 years meticulously devising tasks to map the minds of these mysterious creatures in our midst.

Piaget believed—in his **cognitive developmental theory**—that from birth through adolescence, children progress through *qualitatively different* stages of cognitive growth (see Table 1.3). The term *qualitative* means that rather than simply knowing less or more (on the kind of scale we can rank from 1 to 10), infants, preschoolers, elementary-school-age children, and teenagers think about the world in *completely* different ways. However, Piaget also believed that at every life stage human

Piaget's cognitive developmental theory Jean Piaget's principle that from infancy to adolescence, children progress through four qualitatively different stages of intellectual growth.

Table 1.3: Piaget's Stages of Development

Age	Name of Stage	Description
0–2	Sensorimotor	The baby manipulates objects to pin down the basics of physical reality. This stage, ending with the development of language, will be described in Chapter 3.
2–7	Preoperations	Children's perceptions are captured by their immediate appearances. "What they see is what is real." They believe, among other things, that inanimate objects are really alive and that if the appearance of a quantity of liquid changes (e.g., if it is poured from a short, wide glass into a tall, thin one), the amount actually becomes different. You will learn about all these perceptions in Chapter 5.
7–12	Concrete operations	Children have a realistic understanding of the world. Their thinking is really on the same wavelength as adults'. While they can reason conceptually about concrete objects, however, they cannot think abstractly in a scientific way.
12+	Formal operations	Reasoning is at its pinnacle: hypothetical, scientific, flexible, fully adult. The person's full cognitive human potential has been reached. We will explore this stage in Chapter 9.

assimilation In Jean Piaget's theory, the first step promoting mental growth, involving fitting environmental input to our existing mental capacities.

accommodation In Piaget's theory, enlarging our mental capacities to fit input from the wider world.

Jean Piaget, in his masterful studies spanning much of the twentieth century, transformed the way we think about children's thinking.

beings share a hunger to learn and mentally grow. Mental growth occurs through **assimilation:** We fit the world to our capacities or existing cognitive structures (which Piaget calls *schemas*). And then **accommodation** occurs. We change our thinking to fit the world (Piaget, 1971).

Let's illustrate by reflecting on your own thinking while you were reading the previous section. Before reading this chapter, you probably had certain ideas about heredity and environment. In Piaget's terminology, let's call them your "heredity/environment schemas." Perhaps you felt that if a trait is highly genetic, changing the environment doesn't matter; or you may have believed that genetics and environment were totally separate. While fitting (assimilating) your reading into these existing ideas, you entered a state of disequilibrium—"Hey, this contradicts what I've always believed"—and were forced to accommodate. The result was that your nature/nurture schemas became more complex and you developed a more advanced (intelligent) way of perceiving the world! Like a newborn who assimilates every new object to her small sucking schema, or a neuroscientist who incorporates each new finding into her huge knowledge-base, while assimilating each object or fact to what we already know, we must accommodate, and so—inch by inch—cognitively advance.

Piaget was a great advocate of hands-on experiences. He felt that we learn by acting in the world. Rather than using an adult-centered framework, he had the revolutionary idea that we need to understand how children experience life *from their point of view.* As we explore the science of lifespan development, I hope you will adopt this hands-on, person-centered perspective to understand the human experience from the perspective of 1-year-olds to people aged 101.

By now, you may be overwhelmed by theories and terms. But take heart. You have the basic concepts you need for understanding this semester well in hand! Now, let's conclude by exploring a worldview that says, "Let's embrace *all* these influences on development and explore how they interact." (For a summary of the theories, see Table 1.4.)

The Ecological, Developmental Systems Approach

An influential child psychologist named Urie Bronfenbrenner (1977) was among the earliest lifespan theorists to highlight the principle that real-world behavior has *many* different causes. As you can see in Figure 1.4, Bronfenbrenner viewed each of us being at the center of an expanding circle of environmental influences. At the inner

Table 1.4: Summary of the Major Current Theories in Lifespan Development

Theory	Nature vs. Nurture Emphasis and Ages of Interest	Representative Questions
Behaviorism	Nurture (all ages)	What reinforcers are shaping this behavior? Who is this person modeling? How can I stimulate self-efficacy?
Psychoanalytic theory	Nurture	What unconscious motives, stemming from early childhood, are motivating this person?
Attachment theory	Nature and nurture (infancy but also all ages)	How does the attachment response unfold in infancy? What conditions evoke this biologically programmed response at every life stage?
Evolutionary theory	Nature (all ages)	How might this behavior be built into the human genetic code?
Behavioral genetics	Nature (all ages)	To what degree are the differences I see in people due to genetics?
Erikson's theory	(all ages)	Is this baby experiencing basic trust? Where is this emerging adult in terms of identity? Has this middle-aged person reached generativity?
Piaget's theory	Children	How does this child understand the world? What is the child's thinking like?

Bill Anderson/Science Source

School System

Economic Patterns

Medical Institutions

Social Conditions

Cultural Values

Mass Media

Community

Family   Classroom

Religious   Peer
Class   Group

Red Chopsticks/Getty Images

FIGURE 1.4: Bronfenbrenner's ecological model: This set of embedded circles spells out the multiple forces that Bronfenbrenner believed shape development. First and foremost are the places that form the core of the child's daily life: family, church, peers, classroom (orange). What is the child's family, school, and religious life like? Who are her friends? How does the child interact with her siblings, parents, teacher, and peers? Although its influence is more indirect, development also depends on the broader milieu—the media, the school system, the community where the boy or girl lives (see blue circle). At the most macro or broadest level, we also need to consider the child's culture, the prevailing economic and social conditions of her society (green circle) and her cohort or the time in history in which she lives. Bottom line: Human behavior depends on multiple complex influences!

circle, development is shaped by the relationships between the child and people he relates to in his immediate setting, such as family, church, peers, and school. The next wider circles that indirectly feed back to affect the child lie in overarching influences, such as his community, the media environment, the health-care community, and the school system itself. At the broadest levels, as you saw earlier in the chapter, our culture, economic trends, and cohort crucially shape behavior, too. Bronfenbrenner's plea to examine the total *ecology*, or life situation, of the child forms the heart of a contemporary perspective called the **ecological, developmental systems approach** (Ford & Lerner, 1992; Lerner, 1998; Lerner, Dowling, & Roth, 2003). Specifically:

- **Ecological, developmental systems theorists stress the need to use many different approaches.** There are *many* valid ways of looking at behavior. Our actions *do* have many causes. To fully understand development, we need to draw on the principles of behaviorism, attachment theory, evolutionary psychology, and Piaget. At the widest societal level, to explain our actions, we need to look outward to our culture and cohort. At the molecular level, we need to look inward to our genes. We have to embrace the input of everyone—from nurses to neuroscientists, from anthropologists to molecular biologists—to make sense of each individual life.

- **Ecological, developmental systems theorists emphasize the need to look at how processes interact.** Bronfenbrenner pointed out that our genetic tendencies influence the cultures we construct; the cultures we live in affect the expression of our genes. In the same way that our body systems and processes are in constant communication, continual back-and-forth influences are what human development is all about (see Diamond, 2009).

ecological, developmental systems approach
An all-encompassing outlook on development that stresses the need to embrace a variety of approaches, and emphasizes the reality that many influences affect development.

For example, let's consider that basic marker: poverty. Growing up in poverty might affect your attachment relationships. You are less likely to get attention from your parents because they are under stress. You might not get adequate nutrition. Your neighborhood could be a frightening place. Each stress might overload your body, activating negative genetic tendencies and setting you up physiologically for emotional problems down the road.

But some children, because of their genetics, their cultural background, or their cohort, might be insulated from the negative effects of growing up poor. Others might thrive. In a classic study tracing the lives of children growing up during the Great Depression, researchers discovered that if this event occurred at the right time in the life cycle (adolescence, when the young person could take action to help support the family), it produced an enduring sense of self-efficacy (Elder & Caspi, 1988). During adulthood, as you will learn in Chapter 12, we may need to experience some life traumas in order to become wise! In sum, development occurs in surprising directions for good and for bad. Diversity of change processes and individual differences are the spice of human life.

Tying It All Together

1. Ricardo, a third grader, is having trouble sitting still and paying attention in class, so his parents consult developmentalists about Ricardo's problem. Pick which comments might be made by: (1) a traditional behaviorist; (2) a cognitive behaviorist; (3) a Freudian theorist; (4) an evolutionary psychologist; (5) a behavioral geneticist; (6) an Eriksonian; (7) an advocate of developmental systems theory.

   a. Ricardo has low academic self-efficacy. Let's improve his sense of competence at school.
   b. Ricardo, like other boys, is biologically programmed to run around. If the class had regular gym time, Ricardo's ability to focus in class would improve.
   c. Ricardo is being reinforced for this behavior by getting attention from the teacher and his classmates. Let's reward appropriate classroom behavior.
   d. Did you or your husband have trouble focusing in school? Perhaps your son's difficulties are hereditary.
   e. Ricardo's behavior may have many causes, from genetics, to the reinforcers at school, to growing up in our twenty-first-century Internet age. Let's use a variety of different approaches to help him.
   f. Ricardo is having trouble mastering the developmental task of industry. How can we promote the ability to work that is so important at this age?
   g. By refusing to pay attention in class, Ricardo may be unconsciously acting out his anger at the birth of his baby sister Heloise.

2. In the preceding question, which suggestion involves providing the right person–environment fit?

3. Dr. Im, a scientist, wants to determine how being born premature might alter our genetic propensity to develop chronic disease. The field Dr. Im is working in is called (pick one): *outergenetics/epigenetics.*

4. Billy, a 1-year-old, mouths everything—pencils, his favorite toy, DVDs—changing his mouthing to fit the object that he is "sampling." According to Piaget, the act of mouthing everything refers to _____, while changing the mouthing behavior to fit the different objects refers to _____.

5. Samantha, a behaviorist, is arguing for her worldview, while Sally is pointing out behaviorism's flaws. First, take Samantha's position, arguing for the virtues of behaviorism, and then discuss some limitations of the theory.

Answers to the Tying It All Together questions can be found at the end of this chapter.

Research Methods: The Tools of the Trade

Theories give us lenses for interpreting behavior. *Research* allows us to find the scientific truth. I already touched on the research technique designed to determine the genetic contributions to behavior. Now let's sketch out the general research strategies that developmental scientists use.

Two Standard Research Strategies: Correlations and Experiments

What impact does poverty have on relationships, personality, or physical health? What forces cause children to model certain people? Does a particular intervention to help improve self-efficacy really work? To answer any question about the impact one condition or entity (called a *variable*) has on another, developmentalists use two basic research designs: correlational studies and true experiments.

In a **correlational study,** researchers chart the relationships between the dimensions they are interested in exploring as they naturally occur. Let's say you want to test the hypothesis that parents who behave more lovingly have first graders with superior social skills. Your game plan is simple: Select a group of children by going to a class. Relate their interpersonal skills to the nurturing that parents provide.

Immediately, you will be faced with decisions related to choosing your participants. Are you going to explore the practices of mothers and fathers or of mothers alone? Confine yourself to a middle-class group? Consider two-parent versus one-parent families? Look at a mix of ethnicities or not? You would need to get permission from the school system. You must also get parents to volunteer. Are you choosing a **representative sample**—a group that reflects the characteristics of the population about whom you want to generalize?

Then you would face your most important challenge—accurately measuring your variables. Just as a broken thermometer can't tell us if we have a fever, without adequate indices of the concepts we are measuring, we can't conclude anything at all.

With regard to the parent dimension, one possibility might be to visit parents and children and observe how they relate. This technique, called **naturalistic observation,** is appealing because you are seeing the behavior as it occurs in "nature," or real life. However, this approach presents a huge practical challenge: the need to travel to each home to observe each family on many occasions. Plus, when we watch parent–child interactions, or any socially desirable activity, people try to act their best. Wouldn't you make an effort to act especially loving if a psychologist arrived at your house?

The most cost-effective strategy would be to give the parents a questionnaire with items such as: "Do you make an effort to kiss, hug, and praise your daughter? Is it important to avoid yelling at your child?" This **self-report strategy,** in which people evaluate their behavior anonymously, is the main approach researchers use with adults. Still, it has its own biases. Do you think that people can report accurately on their activities? Don't we have a natural tendency to magnify our positive behaviors and minimize our negative ones?

Now, turning to the child side of your question, one reasonable way to assess social skills would be to have teachers evaluate each student via a questionnaire: "Does this child make friends easily?"; "Does she relate to her peers in a mature way?" Or, we could ask children to rank their classmates by showing photos: "Does Calista or Cory get a smiley face?"; "Pick your three best friends." Evaluations from expert

LEARNING OUTCOMES

- List the main developmental science measurement techniques.
- Compare experiments and correlational studies.
- Contrast cross-sectional and longitudinal studies.
- Describe new advances in developmental science research.

correlational study
A research strategy that involves relating two or more variables.

representative sample
A group that reflects the characteristics of the overall population.

naturalistic observation A measurement strategy that involves directly watching and coding behaviors.

self-report strategy
A measurement having people report on their feelings and activities through questionnaires.

The deficiencies of self-reports were stunningly showcased in the U.S. 2016 presidential election when virtually no polls (which asked people to report their voting preferences) predicted Donald Trump would win!

Table 1.5: Common Strategies Developmentalists Use to Measure Specific Variables (Behaviors or Concepts of Interest)

Type	Strategy	Commonly Used Ages	Pluses and Minuses
Naturalistic observation	Observes behavior directly; codes actions, often by rating the behavior as either present or absent (either in real life or the lab)	Typically during childhood, but also used with impaired adults	**Pluses:** Offers a direct, unfiltered record of behavior **Minuses:** Very time intensive; people behave differently when watched
Self-reports	Questionnaires in which people report on their feelings, interests, attitudes, and thoughts	Adults and older children	**Pluses:** Easy to administer; quickly provides data **Minuses:** Subject to bias if the person is reporting on undesirable activities and behaviors
Observer reports	Knowledgeable person such as a parent, teacher, or trained observer completes scales evaluating the person; sometimes peers rank the children in their class.	Typically during childhood; also used during adulthood if the person is mentally or physically impaired	**Pluses:** Offers a structured look at the person's behavior **Minuses:** Observers—in particular teachers and parents—have their own biases

observers, such as teachers, and even peers, are often used to assess concepts such as popularity and personality during the childhood years.

Table 1.5 spells out the uses, and the pluses and minuses, of these frequently used ways of measuring concepts: naturalistic observation, self-reports, and observer evaluations. Now, returning to our study, suppose you found a relationship, that is, a correlation, between having nurturing parents and children's interpersonal skills. Could you infer that a loving home environment *causes* children to socially flower? The answer is no!

- **With correlations, we may be mixing up the result with the cause.** Given that parent–child relationships are bidirectional, does loving parenting really *cause* superior social skills, or do socially skilled children provoke parents to act in loving ways? ("My son is such an endearing person. You want to just love him up.") This evocative chicken-or-egg argument applies to far more than child–parent interactions. Does exercising promote health in later life, or are some older adults likely to become physically active because they are *already* in good health?

- **With correlations, there may be another variable that explains the results.** In view of our discussion of heritability, with regard to the social skills study, the immediate third force that comes to mind is genetics. Wouldn't parents who are genetically blessed with superior social skills provide a more caring home environment and genetically pass down these same positive personality traits to their sons and daughters? Wouldn't older adults who go to the gym or ski regularly also be likely to watch their diet and generally take better care of their health? Given that these other activities should naturally be associated with keeping physically fit, can we conclude that exercise *alone* accounts for the association we find?

true experiment The only research strategy that can determine that something causes something else; involves randomly assigning people to different treatments and then looking at the outcome.

To rule out these confounding forces, the solution is to conduct a **true experiment** (see Figure 1.5). Researchers isolate their variable of interest by manipulating that condition (called the *independent variable*), and then randomly assign people to either receive that treatment or another, *control* intervention. If we *randomly assign* people to different groups (by, say, tossing a coin), there can't be any preexisting differences between our participants that would bias our results. If the group does differ in the way we predict, we have to say that our intervention *caused* the particular result.

The problem is that we could never assign children to different kinds of parents! If, as Figure 1.5 suggests, developmentalists trained one group of mothers to relate in

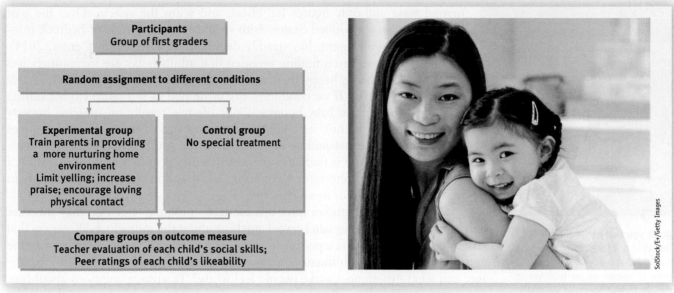

```
                    Participants
                 Group of first graders

            Random assignment to different conditions

    ┌──────────────────────────────┐   ┌──────────────────────────┐
    │      Experimental group      │   │       Control group      │
    │   Train parents in providing │   │     No special treatment │
    │    a more nurturing home     │   │                          │
    │        environment           │   │                          │
    │     Limit yelling; increase  │   │                          │
    │    praise; encourage loving  │   │                          │
    │        physical contact      │   │                          │
    └──────────────────────────────┘   └──────────────────────────┘

            Compare groups on outcome measure
       Teacher evaluation of each child's social skills;
          Peer ratings of each child's likeability
```

FIGURE 1.5: How an experiment looks: By randomly assigning children to different groups and then giving an intervention (this is called the *independent variable*), we know that our treatment (nurturing parents) *caused* better social skills (this outcome is called the *dependent variable*).

more caring ways and withheld this "intervention" from another group, the researchers would run into ethical problems. Would it be fair to deprive the control group of that treatment? In the name of science, can we take the risk of doing people harm? Experiments are ideal for determining what causes behavior. But to tackle the most compelling questions about human development, we *have* to conduct correlational research—and control as best we can for competing explanations that might bias our results.

Designs for Studying Development: Cross-Sectional and Longitudinal Studies

Experiments and correlational studies are standard, all-purpose research strategies. In studying development, however, we have a special interest: How do people change with age? To answer this question, scientists also use two research designs—cross-sectional and longitudinal studies.

cross-sectional study A developmental research strategy that involves testing different age groups at the same time.

Cross-Sectional Studies: Getting a One-Shot Snapshot of Groups

Because cross-sectional research is relatively easy to carry out, developmentalists typically use this strategy to explore changes over long periods of life (Hertzog, 1996). In a **cross-sectional study**, researchers compare *different age groups at the same time* on the trait or characteristic they are interested in, be it political attitudes, personality, or physical health. Consider an older study that (among other questions) explored this interesting issue: "How do our feelings about human nature change with age?"

Researchers gave 2,138 U.S. adults a questionnaire measuring their beliefs in a benevolent world (Poulin & Silver, 2008). Presented with items such as "Human nature is basically good," people ranging in age from 18 to 101 ranked each statement on a scale from "agree strongly" to "disagree." As you scan the findings in Figure 1.6, notice that the youngest age group has the most negative perceptions about humanity. The elderly feel most optimistic about people and the world. If you are in your early twenties, does this mean you can expect to grow less cynical as you age?

Not necessarily. Perhaps current younger cohorts have particular reasons to distrust human motivations. After all, today the media delights in documenting the

FIGURE 1.6: "Benevolence beliefs," or faith in humanity across different age groups in a decade-old study of U.S. adults: Notice that, while young people feel worst about human nature, the elderly have the most positive feelings about their fellow human beings.

Data from Poulin & Silver, 2008.

Don't you think that these innocent 1950s-era 20-somethings would have a more optimistic view of human nature than young people today? So could we really conclude from a cross-sectional study that "faith in humanity" grows with age?

longitudinal study
A developmental research strategy that involves testing an age group repeatedly over many years.

myriad ways authority figures lie, cheat, and scam the system. Over the past half-century in the United States, faith in the trustworthiness of bedrock institutions, like government, has steadily declined (Pew Research Center, 2014). One distressing research finding revealed that adults today are increasingly less likely to report being happy than were previous cohorts (Twenge, Sherman, & Lyubomirsky, 2016). If we conducted the same poll as in Figure 1.6 but during the 1950s (before the baby boomer 1960s lifestyle revolution stressing honesty exploded on the scene), we might find the opposite pattern: Positive feelings about human nature would be highest among the young and decline with age!

The bottom line is that cross-sectional studies give us a current snapshot of differences among cohorts (or age groups), but they don't necessarily tell us about real *changes that occur as we grow old*.

Cross-sectional studies have a more basic problem. Because they measure only *group differences*, they can't reveal anything about the individual differences that give spice to life. If you are a pessimistic emerging adult, will your worldview stay the same as you age? What influences make people feel better about humanity as they age, and what experiences make people feel worse? To answer questions about how *individuals* develop, as well as look at what makes for specific changes, it's best to be on the scene to measure what is going on. This means doing longitudinal research.

Longitudinal Studies: The Gold-Standard Developmental Science Research Design

In **longitudinal studies,** researchers typically select a group of a particular age and periodically test those people over many years (the descriptive word part here is *long*). Consider the Dunedin Multidisciplinary Health and Development Study: An international team of researchers descended on Dunedin, a city in New Zealand, to follow more than 1,000 children born between April 1972 and March 1973, examining them at two-year intervals during childhood and roughly every three years after that. At each evaluation, they examined participants' personalities and looked at parenting practices and life events. The scientists are now tracking these babies in their forties (Dunedin Multidisciplinary Health and Development Research Unit, 2014).

The outcome has been an incredible array of findings related to personality and psychological problems. Can we predict adult emotional difficulties as early as age 3? What teenage behaviors predict later substance abuse (Meier and others, 2016)? As you will learn in Chapter 12, scientists have discovered that a personality trait called *conscientiousness*, measured during emerging adulthood, powerfully predicts whether people follow good health habits—from not smoking to exercising to watching one's diet—as participants travel into middle age (Israel and others, 2014).

Moreover, because cutting-edge DNA technology is being used, this landmark research was the first to identify candidate genes that may make us more or less responsive to wider world stress. Plus, like other longitudinal research, the Dunedin Study offers a crystal ball into those questions at the heart of our field: How will I change as I get older? When should we worry about children, and when should we *not* be concerned?

Longitudinal studies are exciting, but they have their own problems. They require a tremendous amount of time, effort, and expense. Imagine the resources involved in planning this particular study. Think of the hassles involved in seeking out the participants and getting them to return again and again to take the tests. The researchers must fly the overseas Dunedin volunteers back and forth for each evaluation. They need to reimburse people for their time and lost wages. These logistical and financial problems become more significant the longer a study continues. For this reason, we have hundreds of studies covering infancy, childhood, or defined segments of adult life, such as the old-old years. Only a precious handful trace development from childhood to later life.

The difficulty with getting people to return for testing leads to an important bias in itself. People who stay in longitudinal studies, particularly during adulthood, tend to be highly motivated. Think of which classmates are going to attend your high school reunion. Aren't they apt to be the people who are successful versus those who have made a mess of their lives? Participants in longitudinal research comprise elite, better-than-average groups. While they offer us unparalleled information, these gold-standard studies have their biases, too.

Critiquing the Research

To summarize, when you are scanning the findings in our field, keep these concerns in mind:

- Consider the study's participants. How were they selected? Ask yourself, "Can I generalize from this particular group to the wider world?"

- Examine the study's measures. Are they accurate? What biases might they have?

- In looking at the *many* correlational studies in this book, be attuned to the fact that their findings might be due to other forces. What competing interpretations can you come up with to explain this researcher's results?

- With cross-sectional findings, beware of making assumptions that this is the way people *really* change with age.

- Look for longitudinal studies and welcome their insights. However, understand that these investigations, especially during adult life, are probably tracing the lives of the best and brightest people rather than the average adult.

Emerging Research Trends

Developmental scientists are attuned to these issues. In conducting correlational studies, they typically try to control for other influences that might explain their findings. They use different types of measures to assess their concepts. A current trend is the explosion of international research, as developmentalists from nations as different as Iran and Ireland or China and Cameroon offer their own perspectives into core topics in our field. Still, in addition to becoming more global, our research is getting up close and personal, too.

Quantitative research techniques—the strategies I have been describing, using groups of people and statistical tests—are the main approaches that researchers use to study human behavior. In order to make general predictions about people, we need to examine different individuals. We must pin down our concepts by using scales or ratings with numerical values that can be tallied and compared.

Developmentalists who conduct **qualitative research** are not interested in making numerical comparisons. They want to understand the unique lives of people by conducting in-depth interviews. In this book, I will be focusing mainly on quantitative research because that is how we find out the scientific "truth." But I also will pay special attention to qualitative studies, because stories and personal experiences—not numbers—best convey the magic of human life.

Some Concluding Introductory Thoughts

This discussion brings me back to the letter on page 2 and my promise to let you in on my other agendas in writing this text. Because I want to teach you to critically evaluate research, in the following pages I'll be analyzing individual studies and focusing on research-related issues in more depth, especially in the How Do We Know features that appear in many chapters. To bring home the personal experience of the lifespan and alert students to careers in our field, I've filled the chapters with quotations, and in the Experiencing the Lifespan boxes I occasionally interviewed people. To underscore the principle that our lifespan is a work in progress, I'll be starting many chapters by setting the historical and cultural context. To emphasize the power of research to

Ingram Publishing/Newscom

A 20-something street person would probably be too ashamed to return to his high school reunion—and drop out of a longitudinal study that began in childhood, making it impossible to conclude that most people get it together as they grow up.

quantitative research Standard developmental science data-collection strategy that involves testing groups of people and using numerical scales and statistics.

qualitative research Occasional developmental science data-collection strategy that involves personal interviews.

improve lives, I'll conclude most sections by spelling out interventions that improve the quality of life.

This book is designed to flow like a story, with later chapters building on concepts and terms mentioned in previous ones. It's structured to emphasize how our insights about earlier life stages relate to older ages. I will be discussing separately four major categories of human change—physical, cognitive, emotional, and social development. However, I'll be continually stressing how these aspects of who we are relate. After all, we are not just bodies, minds, and relationships, but whole human beings!

While I want you to share my excitement in the research, please don't read this book as "the final word." Science, like the lifespan, is always evolving. Moreover, with any research finding, take the phrase "it's all statistical" to heart. Yes, developmentalists are passionate to make general predictions about life; but, because human beings are incredibly complex, at bottom, each person's lifespan journey is a beautiful surprise.

Now, beginning with prenatal development and infancy (Chapters 2–4); then moving on to childhood (Chapters 5–7); adolescence (Chapters 8 and 9); early and middle adulthood (Chapters 10–12); later life (Chapters 13 and 14); and, finally, that last milestone, death (Chapter 15), welcome to the lifespan and to the rest of this book!

Tying It All Together

1. Four developmentalists are studying whether eating excessive sugar has detrimental effects on the body and mind. To test how the amount of sugar elementary schoolers eat at breakfast relates to aggression, Alicia goes to a playground and counts the frequency of hitting on selected days. Betty randomly assigns students in a high school class into two groups; she tells one group to eat a healthy diet and another to eat candy bars, and compares their grades on tests. Calista measures the sugar consumption of teens and then retests them periodically into their fifties. Farook constructs a questionnaire that explores sugar consumption and gives it to adults of different ages. For each of the following questions, link the appropriate person's name to the correct study.

   a. Who is conducting a cross-sectional study?
   b. Who is using naturalistic observation?
   c. Who is conducting a correlational study?
   d. Who can prove that eating a lot of sugar *causes* problems—but is doing an unethical study?
   e. Who is going to have a huge problem with dropouts?
   f. Who can tell you that if you are a sugar junkie in your twenties, you might still be eating an incredible amount of sugar (compared to everyone else) as you age?

2. Plan a longitudinal study to test a developmental science question. Describe how you would select your participants, how your study would proceed, what measures you would use, and what problems and biases your study would have.

Answers to the Tying It All Together questions can be found at the end of this chapter.

SUMMARY

Who We Are and What We Study

Lifespan development is a mega-discipline encompassing **child development, gerontology,** and **adult development. Developmental scientists,** or **developmentalists,** chart universal changes from birth to old age, explore individual differences in development, study the impact of **normative** and **non-normative** life transitions, and explore every other topic relevant to our unfolding lives.

Contexts of Development

Several major **contexts of development** shape our lives. The first is our **cohort,** or the time in history in which we live. The huge **baby boom cohort,** born in the years following World War II, has changed society as it passes through the lifespan. Cohorts of babies born before the twentieth century faced a shorter, harsher childhood, and many did not survive. During the twentieth century, modern technology extended the "in school" years and so produced a new life phase called *adolescence* and then, with the need for college and graduate school, **emerging adulthood.** Today, the starting date of full adulthood is often the late twenties.

The early-**twentieth-century life expectancy revolution,** with its dramatic advances in curing *infectious disease* shifted our major causes of death to age-related illnesses called *chronic illnesses,* thereby allowing most babies to survive to later life. **Average life expectancy** is now within striking distance of the **maximum lifespan** in affluent nations, and we distinguish between the healthy **young-old** (people in their sixties and seventies) and the frail **old-old** (people in their eighties and beyond). The second major twentieth-century change occurred in the 1960s with the lifestyle revolution, which has given us freedom to engineer our own adult path. During this current century, the Internet and **social networking sites** have transformed relationships, while widening **income inequalities** prevent many people from being able to fulfill the classic American dream of **upward mobility.**

Socioeconomic status (SES) greatly affects our lifespan—with poor people in each nation facing a harsher, more stressful, and shorter life. The gaps between **developed-world** countries and **developing-world** countries are even more dramatic, with the least developed countries lagging well behind in terms of health, wealth, and technology.

Our cultural and ethnic background also determines how we develop. Scientists distinguish between **collectivist cultures** (typically non-Western), which stress social harmony and extended-family relationships, and **individualistic cultures** (often Western), which value independence and personal achievement. We need to be aware, however, that residents living in all nations have a mix of individualistic and collectivist worldviews; the practice of lumping people into broad ethnic labels masks diversity within each group. Finally, our gender influences our travels through life. Women worldwide, for instance, outlive men by at least two years.

Theories: Lenses for Looking at the Lifespan

Theories offer explanations about what causes people to act the way they do. The main theories in developmental science that offer general explanations of behavior vary in their position on the **nature** versus **nurture** question. Behaviorists believe nurture is all-important. **Traditional behaviorists,** in particular B. F. Skinner, believe **operant conditioning** and **reinforcement** determine all voluntary behaviors. According to **cognitive behaviorism/ social learning theory, modeling**, and **self-efficacy**—our internal sense that we can competently perform given tasks—predict how we act.

Sigmund Freud, in his psychoanalytic theory, believed our adult personality is shaped by the way our parents treated us during the first five years of life. Freud also felt that human beings are dominated by unconscious drives, that mental health depends on self-awareness, and that sexuality (different erogenous zones) motivates behavior during the early childhood years. John Bowlby's **attachment theory** draws on the psychoanalytic principle that parenting during early life (or our attachment relationships) determines later mental health, but he believes that the attachment response is genetically built in to our species to

promote survival. **Evolutionary psychologists** adopt this nature perspective, seeing actions and traits as programmed into our DNA. **Behavioral genetic** research—in particular, **twin studies, adoption studies,** and occasionally **twin/adoption studies**—convinced developmental scientists of the power of nature, revealing genetic contributions to almost any way we differ from each other as human beings.

Developmental scientists today are exploring how nature *and* nurture combine. Due to **evocative** and **active forces,** we shape our environments to go along with our genetic tendencies, and human relationships are **bidirectional**—our temperamental qualities and actions influence others, just as their actions influence us. A basic developmental science challenge is to foster an appropriate **person–environment fit.** We need to match our genetically based talents and abilities to the right environment. New research suggests that people differ genetically in how responsive they are to environmental events, and that early life environments may alter our genome, producing long-lasting **epigenetic** effects.

Erik Erikson spelled out eight **psychosocial tasks** that we must master as we travel from birth to old age. According to Jean Piaget's **cognitive developmental theory,** children progress through four qualitatively different stages of intellectual development, and all learning occurs through **assimilation** and **accommodation.**

Most developmental scientists today adopt the **ecological, developmental systems approach.** They welcome input from every theory and realize that many interacting influences shape who we are. They understand that diversity among people and change processes is the essence of development.

Research Methods: The Tools of the Trade

The two main research strategies scientists use are **correlational studies,** which relate naturally occurring variations among people, and **true experiments,** in which researchers manipulate a variable (or give a specific treatment) and randomly assign people to receive that intervention or not. With correlational studies, there are always competing possibilities for the relationships we find. While experiments do allow us to prove causes, they are often unethical and impractical. In conducting research, it's best to strive for a **representative sample,** and it's essential to have accurate measures. **Naturalistic observation, self-reports,** and observer evaluations are three common measurement strategies developmental scientists use.

The two major designs for studying development are cross-sectional and longitudinal research. **Cross-sectional studies,** which involve testing people of different age groups at the same time, are very easy to carry out. However, they may confuse differences between age groups with true changes that occur as people age, and they can't tell us about individual differences in development.

Longitudinal studies can answer vital questions about how people develop. However, they involve following people over many years and may sample atypical, elite groups.

Quantitative research involves groups of participants and statistical tests, and it is still the standard way we learn the scientific truth. But developmentalists now occasionally conduct **qualitative research** by interviewing people in depth. Our research is getting genuinely global, too.

KEY TERMS

accommodation, p. 22

active forces, p. 19

adoption study, p. 17

adult development, p. 4

assimilation, p. 22

attachment theory, p. 16

average life expectancy, p. 6

baby boom cohort, p. 5

behavioral genetics, p. 17

bidirectionality, p. 19

child development, p. 4

cognitive behaviorism
(social learning theory),
p. 14

cohort, p. 5

collectivist cultures, p. 10

contexts of development,
p. 5

correlational study, p. 25

cross-sectional study, p. 27

developed world, p. 10

developing world, p. 10

developmentalists
(developmental scientists),
p. 4

ecological, developmental
systems approach, p. 23

emerging adulthood, p. 6

epigenetics, p. 20

Erikson's psychosocial tasks,
p. 20

evocative forces, p. 19

evolutionary psychology, p. 16

gerontology, p. 4

income inequality, p. 9

individualistic cultures, p. 10

lifespan development, p. 4

longitudinal study, p. 28

maximum lifespan, p. 7

modeling, p. 14

naturalistic observation, p. 25

nature, p. 12

non-normative transitions,
p. 5

normative transitions, p. 5

nurture, p. 12

old-old, p. 7

operant conditioning, p. 13

person–environment fit, p. 19

Piaget's cognitive
developmental theory,
p. 21

qualitative research, p. 29

quantitative research, p. 29

reinforcement, p. 13

representative sample, p. 25

self-efficacy, p. 14

self-report strategy, p. 25

social networking sites,
p. 9

socioeconomic status (SES),
p. 10

theory, p. 12

traditional behaviorism, p. 13

true experiment, p. 26

twentieth-century life
expectancy revolution,
p. 7

twin study, p. 17

twin/adoption study, p. 17

upward mobility, p. 10

young-old, p. 7

ANSWERS TO **Tying It All Together** QUIZZES

Setting the Context

1. b. There was no real high school before the twentieth century.

2. Rosa is more likely to be physically disabled than Ramona. Rosa is old-old; Ramona is young-old.

3. Carlos will enter the workforce at an *older* age, get married *later,* be *less* likely to rise in socioeconomic status than his granddad.

4. Hakeem has a collectivist worldview, whereas Peter's worldview is individualistic.

5. Your answers here will all vary.

Theories: Lenses for Looking at the Lifespan

1. (1) c; (2) a; (3) g; (4) b; (5) d; (6) f; (7) e

2. b. As Ricardo and other children need to run around, regular gym time would help to foster the best person–environment fit.

3. Dr. Im is working in a field called epigenetics.

4. assimilation; accommodation

5. Samantha might argue that behaviorism is an ideal approach to human development because it is simple, effective, and easy to carry out. Behaviorism's easily mastered, action-oriented concepts—be consistent, reinforce positive behavior, draw on principles of modeling, and stimulate efficacy feelings—can make dramatic improvements in the quality of life. Also, because behaviorism doesn't blame the person but locates problems in the learning environment, it has special appeal. Sally might argue that behaviorism's premise that nurture is all-important neglects the powerful impact genetic forces have in determining who we are. So the theory is far too limited—offering a wrongheaded view about development. We need the insights of attachment theory, evolutionary psychology, and behavioral genetics, plus Piaget's and Erikson's theories to fully understand what motivates human beings.

Research Methods: The Tools of the Trade

1. a. Farook; b. Alicia; c. Alicia; d. Betty; e. Calista; f. Calista

2. After coming up with your hypothesis, you would need to adequately measure your concepts—choosing the appropriate tests. Your next step would be to solicit a large representative sample of a particular age group, give them these measures, and retest these people at regular intervals over an extended period of time. In addition to the investment of time and money, it would be hard to keep track of your sample and entice participants to undergo subsequent evaluations. Because the most motivated fraction of your original group will probably continue, your results will tend to reflect how the "best people" behave and change over time (not the typical person).

CONNECT ONLINE:

 LaunchPad
macmillan learning

Check out our videos and additional resources located at:
www.macmillanlearning.com

CHAPTER 2

Prenatal Development, Pregnancy, and Birth

It's hard to explain, Kim told me. You are two people now. When you wake up, shop, or plan meals, this other person is always with you. You are always thinking, "What will be good for the baby? What will be best for the two of us?"

Feeling the first kick—like little feathers brushing inside me—was amazing. At first I felt like I could never explain this to my husband. But Jeff is wonderful. I think he gets it. So I feel lucky. I can't imagine what this experience would be like if I didn't have a loving partner to share my joy.

Now that it's the thirtieth week and my little girl can survive, there is another shift. I'm focused on the moment she will arrive: What will it be like to hold my baby? Will she be born healthy?

The downside is the fear that she will be born with some problem. Being an older mom, it took me two years to get pregnant. Now that I've gone through those exhausting procedures and they worked (hooray!), I'd never risk having an invasive genetic test. So, you eat right and never take a drink; but there are concerns. I worry about my career. How will my boss feel about my taking maternity leave? And, of course, I worry about labor and delivery. Suppose I have some problem during birth, or my baby has a serious genetic disease?

Another downside is that, until recently, I still felt tired. Some days, I could barely make it to work. (Everything they told you about morning sickness only lasting through the first trimester is wrong—at least for me!)

But nothing equals the thrill of having my little girl inside—fantasizing about her future, watching her grow into a marvelous adult. I also adore what happens when I'm at the mall. People light up and grin, wish me good luck, or give me advice. It's like the world is watching out for me, rooting for me, cherishing me.

Left: Petrol/Getty Images

LEARNING OUTCOME

- List the main pregnancy concerns in earlier eras worldwide.

Setting the Context

The joy and fear Kim is experiencing seem built into our humanity. Throughout history, societies have seen pregnancy as an exciting and frightening time of life. Cultures used to make heroic efforts to keep pregnant women calm and happy. Certain groups might use good luck charms to keep evil spirits away—such as a pregnancy girdle in medieval England, a garlic-filled sack in Guatemala (Aldred, 1997; Von Raffler-Engel, 1994), or a cotton pregnancy sash in Japan (Ito & Sharts-Hopko, 2002).

In the past, societies celebrated pregnancy milestones, too. In Bulgaria, the first kick was the signal for a woman to bake bread and take it to the church. In Bali, at the seventh month, a prayer ceremony took place to recognize that there was finally a person inside whom the spirits should protect from harm (Kitzinger, 2000; Von Raffler-Engel, 1994). This chapter draws on the miracle of twenty-first-century science to explore each pregnancy concern as I chart the marvelous milestones of prenatal development, pregnancy, and birth.

MATT YORK/AP Images

In this traditional southern Indian ceremony performed at the sixth or eighth month of pregnancy, family members and friends gather around to protect the woman and fetus from "the evil eyes." Rituals such as this one are common around the world and embody our fears about this special time of life.

The First Step: Fertilization

LEARNING OUTCOMES

- Identify the structures and process of fertilization.
- Describe what genetically happens when the sperm and ovum unite.

uterus The pear-shaped muscular organ in a woman's abdomen that houses the developing baby.

cervix The neck, or narrow lower portion, of the uterus.

fallopian tube One of a pair of slim, pipelike structures that connect the ovaries with the uterus.

ovary One of a pair of almond-shaped organs that contain a woman's ova, or eggs.

ovum An egg cell containing the genetic material contributed by the mother to the baby.

Before embarking on this journey, let's focus on the starting point. What structures are involved in reproduction? What physiological process is involved in conceiving a child? What happens at the genetic level when a sperm and an egg unite to form a human being?

The Reproductive Systems

The female and male reproductive systems are shown in Figure 2.1. Notice that the female system has several parts:

- Center stage is the **uterus,** the pear-shaped muscular organ that carries the baby to term. The uterus is lined with a velvety tissue, the *endometrium*, which thickens in preparation for pregnancy and, if that event does not occur, sheds during menstruation.

- The lower section of the uterus is the **cervix.** During pregnancy, this thick uterine neck must perform an amazing feat: Be strong enough to resist the pressure of the expanding uterus; be flexible enough to open fully at birth.

- Branching from the upper ends of the uterus are the **fallopian tubes.** These slim, pipelike structures serve as conduits to the uterus.

- The feathery ends of the fallopian tubes surround the **ovaries,** the almond-shaped organs where the **ova,** the mother's egg cells, reside.

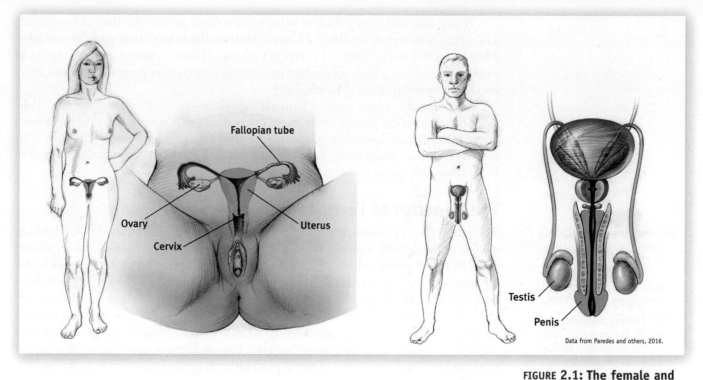

FIGURE **2.1: The female and male reproductive systems**

Data from Paredes and others, 2016.

The Process of Fertilization

The pathway that results in **fertilization**—the union of sperm and egg—begins at **ovulation.** This is the moment, typically around day 14 of a woman's cycle, when a mature ovum erupts from the ovary wall. At ovulation, a fallopian tube suctions the ovum in, and the tube begins vigorous contractions that propel the ovum on its three-day journey toward the uterus.

Now the male's contribution to forming a new life comes in. In contrast to females, whose ova are all mainly formed at birth, the **testes**—male structures comparable to the ovaries—are continually manufacturing sperm. An adult male typically produces several hundred million sperm a day. During sexual intercourse, these cells are expelled into the vagina, where a small proportion enter the uterus and wend their way up the fallopian tubes.

What happens now is a team assault. The sperm drill into the ovum, penetrating toward the center. Suddenly, one reaches the innermost part. Then the chemical composition of the ovum wall changes, shutting out the other sperm. The nuclei of the male and female cells move slowly together. When they meld into one cell, the landmark event called *fertilization* has occurred.

fertilization The union of sperm and egg.

ovulation The moment during a woman's monthly cycle when an ovum is expelled from the ovary.

testes Male organs that manufacture sperm.

The sperm surround the ovum.

One sperm burrows in (notice the large head).

The nuclei of the two cells fuse. The watershed event called fertilization has occurred.

To promote pregnancy, it's best to have intercourse around the time of ovulation. The ovum is receptive for about 24 hours while in the tube's outer part. Sperm take a few hours to journey from the cervix to the tube. However, sperm can live almost a week in the uterus, which means that intercourse several days prior to ovulation may also result in fertilization (Marieb, 2004).

Although the ovum emits chemical signals as to its location, the tiny tadpole-shaped travelers cannot easily make the perilous journey upward into the tubes. So, of the estimated several hundred million sperm expelled at ejaculation, only 200 to 300 reach their destination, find their target, and burrow in. What happens genetically when the sperm and egg combine?

The Genetics of Fertilization

The answer lies in looking at **chromosomes,** ropy structures composed of ladder-like strands of the genetic material **DNA.** Arrayed along each chromosome are segments of DNA called **genes,** which serve as templates for creating the proteins responsible for carrying out the physical processes of life (see Figure 2.2). Every cell in our body contains 46 chromosomes—except the sperm and ova, each of which has half this number, or 23. When the nuclei of these two cells, called *gametes,* combine at fertilization, their chromosomes align in pairs to again comprise 46. So nature has a marvelous mechanism to ensure that each human life has an identical number of chromosomes and every human being gets half of its genetic heritage from the parent of each sex.

You can see the 46 paired male chromosomes in Figure 2.3. Notice that each chromosome pair (one from our mother and one from our father) is a match, except for the sex chromosomes. The X is longer and heavier than the Y. Because each ovum carries an X chromosome, our father's contribution determines the baby's sex. If a lighter, faster-swimming, Y-carrying sperm fertilizes the ovum, we get a boy (XY). If the victor is a more resilient, slower-moving X, we get a girl (XX).

In the race to fertilization, the Y's are statistically more successful; scientists estimate that 20 percent more male than female babies are conceived. But the prenatal period is particularly hard on males. If a family member learns that she is pregnant, the odds still favor her having a boy; but because more males die in the uterus, only 5 percent more boys than girls make it to birth (Werth & Tsiaras, 2002).

chromosome A threadlike strand of DNA located in the nucleus of every cell that carries the genes, which transmit hereditary information.

DNA (deoxyribonucleic acid) The material that makes up genes, which bear our hereditary characteristics.

gene A segment of DNA that contains a chemical blueprint for manufacturing a particular protein.

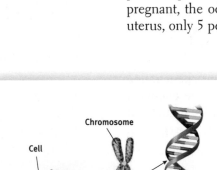

FIGURE 2.2: The human building blocks: The nucleus of every human cell contains chromosomes, each of which is made up of two strands of DNA connected in a double helix.

FIGURE 2.3: A map of human chromosomes: This magnified grid, called a karyotype, shows the 46 chromosomes in their matched pairs. The final pair, with its X and Y, shows that this person is a male. Also, notice the huge size of the X chromosome compared to the Y.

And during childhood, as I will describe, males are the less hardy sex. Boys are more susceptible to developing everything from autism (see Chapter 5) to ADHD (see Chapter 6).

⊕ Tying It All Together

1. In order, list the structures involved in "getting pregnant." Choose from the following: *uterus, fallopian tubes, ovaries.* Then name the structure in which fertilization occurs.

2. The _____ house the female's genetic material, while the _____ contain the sperm. (Identify the correct names)

3. Tiffany feels certain that if she has intercourse at the right time, she will get pregnant—but asks you, "What is the right time?" Give Tiffany your answer, referring to the text discussion.

4. If a fetus has the XX chromosomal configuration, *he/ she* is *more/ less* apt to survive the prenatal journey and is *more/ less* apt to be conceived.

Answers to the Tying It All Together questions can be found at the end of this chapter.

Prenatal Development

Now that we understand the starting point, let's chart prenatal development, tracing how the microscopic, fertilized ovum divides millions of times and differentiates into a living child. This miraculous transformation takes place in three stages.

First Two Weeks: The Germinal Stage

The first approximately two weeks after fertilization—when the cell mass has not fully attached to the uterine wall—is called the **germinal stage** (see Figure 2.4 on page 40). Within 36 hours, the fertilized ovum, now a single cell called the **zygote,** makes its first cell division. Then the tiny cluster of cells divides every 12 to 15 hours as it wends its way down the fallopian tube. When the cells enter the uterine cavity, they differentiate into layers—some destined to form the pregnancy support structures, others the child-to-be. Now called a **blastocyst,** this ball of roughly 100 cells faces the challenge called **implantation**—embedding into the uterine wall.

The blastocyst seeks a landing site on the upper uterus. Its outer layer develops projections and burrows in. From this landing zone, blood vessels proliferate to form the **placenta,** the lifeline that passes nutrients from the mother to the developing baby. Then, the next stage of prenatal development begins: the all-important embryonic phase.

Week 3 to Week 8: The Embryonic Stage

Although the **embryonic stage** lasts roughly only six weeks, it is the most fast-paced period of development. During this time, all the major organs are constructed. By the end of this stage, what began as a clump of cells looks like a recognizable human being!

One early task is to construct the conduit responsible for all development. After the baby hooks up to the maternal bloodstream—which will nourish its growth—nutrients must reach each rapidly differentiating cell. So by the third week after fertilization, the circulatory system (our body's transport system) forms, and its pump, the heart, starts to beat.

LEARNING OUTCOME

- Describe the stages of prenatal development.

germinal stage The first 14 days of prenatal development, from fertilization to full implantation.

zygote A fertilized ovum.

blastocyst The hollow sphere of cells formed during the germinal stage in preparation for implantation.

implantation The process in which a blastocyst becomes embedded in the uterine wall.

placenta The structure projecting from the wall of the uterus during pregnancy through which the developing baby absorbs nutrients.

embryonic stage The second stage of prenatal development, lasting from week 3 through week 8.

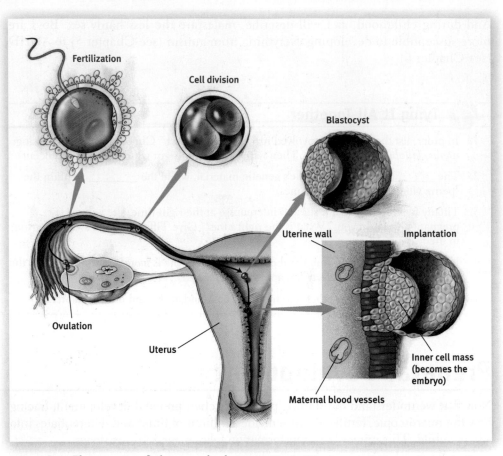

FIGURE 2.4: The events of the germinal stage: The fertilized ovum divides on its trip to the uterus, then becomes a hollow ball called a blastocyst, and finally fully implants in the wall of the uterus at about 14 days after fertilization.

At the same time, the rudiments of the nervous system appear. Between 20 and 24 days after fertilization, an indentation forms along the back of the embryo and closes up to form the **neural tube.** The upper part of this cylinder becomes the brain. Its lower part forms the spinal cord. Although it is possible to "grow" new brain cells throughout life, almost all of those remarkable branching structures, called **neurons,** which cause us to think, respond, and process information, originated in neural tube cells formed during our first months in the womb.

Meanwhile, the body is developing at an astounding rate. At day 26, arm buds form; by day 28, leg swellings erupt. At day 37, rudimentary feet start to develop. By day 41, elbows, wrist curves, and the precursors of fingers can be seen. Several days later, raylike structures that will become toes emerge. By about week 8, the internal organs are in place. What started out looking like a curved stalk, then an outer-space alien, now resembles a *human* being.

Principles of Prenatal Development

In scanning the photographs of the developing embryo on the next page, can you spell out three guiding principles related to the sequence of development just described?

- Notice that from a cylindrical shape, the arms and legs grow outward and then (not unexpectedly) the fingers and toes protrude. So growth follows the **proximodistal sequence,** from the most interior (proximal) part of the body to the outer (distal) sides.

- Notice that from a huge swelling that makes the embryo look like a mammoth head, the arms emerge and the legs sprout. So development takes place according

neural tube A cylindrical structure that forms along the back of the embryo and develops into the brain and spinal cord.

neuron A nerve cell.

proximodistal sequence The developmental principle that growth occurs from the most interior parts of the body outward.

cephalocaudal sequence The developmental principle that growth occurs in a sequence from head to toe.

mass-to-specific sequence The developmental principle that large structures (and movements) precede increasingly detailed refinements.

At about week 3, the embryo (the upside-down U across the top) looks like a curved stalk.

At week 4, you can see the indentations for eyes and the arms and legs beginning to sprout.

At week 9, the fetus has fingers, toes, and ears. All the major organs have developed, and the fetal stage has begun!

to the **cephalocaudal sequence,** meaning from top (*cephalo* = head) to bottom (*caudal* = tail).

- Finally, just as in constructing a sculpture, nature starts with the basic building blocks and then fills in the details. A head forms before eyes and ears; legs are constructed before feet and toes. So the **mass-to-specific sequence,** or gross (large, simple) structures before smaller (complex) refinements, is the third principle of body growth.

Keep these principles in mind. As I will describe in the next chapter, the same patterns apply to growth and motor skills *after* the baby leaves the womb.

Week 9 to Birth: The Fetal Stage

During the embryonic stage, body structures literally sprout. In the **fetal stage,** development occurs at a more leisurely pace. From the eyebrows, fingernails, and hair follicles that develop from weeks 9 to 12, to the cushion of fat that accumulates during the final weeks, it takes seven months to transform the embryo into a resilient baby ready to embrace life.

Why does our species require such a long refining period? One reason is to allow ample time for that masterpiece organ—the human brain—to form. Let's now look at this process of making a brain.

During the late embryonic stage, a mass of cells accumulates within the neural tube that will eventually produce the more than 100 billion neurons composing our brain (Stiles & Jernigan, 2010). From this zone, the neurons migrate to a region just under the top of the differentiating tube (see Figure 2.5). When the cells assemble in their "staging area," by the middle of the fetal period, they lengthen, develop branches, and interlink. This interconnecting process—responsible for every human thought and action—continues until almost our final day of life.

Figure 2.6 on page 42 shows the mushrooming brain. Notice that the brain almost doubles in size from month 4 to month 7. By now, the brain has the folded structure of an adult.

This massive growth has a profound effect. At around month 6, the fetus can hear (Crade & Lovett, 1988). By month 7, the fetus is probably able to see (Del Giudice, 2011). And by this time, with high-quality medical care, a few babies can survive.

Today, the **age of viability,** or earliest date at which a baby can be born and *possibly* live, has dropped to 22 to 23 weeks—almost halving the 38 weeks the fetus normally spends in the womb. By week 25, in affluent nations, the odds of survival are more than fifty-fifty (Lawn and others, 2011).

fetal stage The final phase of prenatal development, lasting seven months, characterized by physical refinements, massive growth, and the development of the brain.

age of viability The earliest point at which a baby can survive outside the womb.

FIGURE 2.5: Forming a brain: climbing neurons: Beginning in the earlier part of the fetal period, the neurons destined to make up the brain ascend these ladder-like filaments to reach the uppermost part of what had been the neural tube. Researchers had believed this migration was finished during mid-pregnancy, but they now realize neural migration continues well into the first year of life.

Data from Paredes and others, 2016.

FIGURE 2.6: The expanding brain: The brain grows dramatically month by month during the fetal period. During the final months, it develops its characteristic folds.

However, it is *vitally* important that the fetus stay in the uterus as long as possible. As I will describe later, being born too early (and too small) can have a lifelong impact on health.

Figure 2.7 shows the fetus during the final month of pregnancy, when its prenatal nest is cramped and birth looms on the horizon. Notice the baby's support structures: the placenta, projecting from the uterine wall, which supplies nutrients from the mother to the fetus; the **umbilical cord,** protruding from what will be the baby's bellybutton, the conduit through which nutrients flow; the **amniotic sac,** the fluid-filled chamber within which the baby floats. This encasing membrane provides insulation from infection and harm.

At this stage, parents may be running around, buying the crib or shopping for baby clothes. Couples may be marveling at the items their precious son or daughter "must have": a pacifier, a receiving blanket, a bassinet . . . and what else? What is happening during *all* nine months from the mother's—and father's—point of view?

umbilical cord The structure that attaches the placenta to the fetus, through which nutrients are passed and fetal wastes are removed.

amniotic sac A bag-shaped, fluid-filled membrane that contains and insulates the fetus.

FIGURE 2.7: Poised to be born: This diagram shows the fetus inside the woman's uterus late in pregnancy. Notice the placenta, amniotic sac, and umbilical cord.

Tying It All Together

1. In order, name the three stages of prenatal development. Then identify the stage in which the organs are formed.

2. A pregnant friend asks you, "How does my baby's brain develop?" Describe the process of neural migration—when it occurs, and when it is complete.

3. Match the following in utero descriptions to the correct names. (Choose from *cephalocaudal/ proximodistal/ mass-to-specific.*)
   a. The fingers form before the fingernails.
   b. The head forms first and the feet last.
   c. The neural tube develops and then the arms.

4. You are horrified to learn that your friend went into premature labor. Pick the minimum pregnancy age that she might be able to have a live birth: *around 12 weeks*; *around 22–23 weeks*; *around 30 weeks.*

Answers to the Tying It All Together questions can be found at the end of this chapter.

Pregnancy

LEARNING OUTCOMES

The 266- to 277-day **gestation** period (or pregnancy) is divided into three segments called **trimesters,** each lasting roughly three months. (Because it is difficult to know exactly when fertilization occurs, health-care professionals date the pregnancy from the woman's last menstrual period.)

Pregnancy differs, however, from the universally patterned process of prenatal development. Despite having classic symptoms, here individual differences are the *norm.*

- Summarize the woman's experience during each trimester of pregnancy.
- Describe how work and partner issues can impair the pregnancy experience.
- Outline the feelings of fathers-to-be.

Scanning the Trimesters

With the strong caution that the following symptoms vary—from person to person (and pregnancy to pregnancy)—let's now offer an in-the-flesh sense of how each trimester feels.

gestation The period of pregnancy.

trimester One of the 3-month-long segments into which pregnancy is divided.

First Trimester: Often Feeling Tired and Ill

After the blastocyst implants in the uterus—a few days before the woman first misses her period—pregnancy often signals its presence through unpleasant symptoms. Many women feel faint. (Yes, fainting can be a sign of pregnancy!) They may get headaches or have to urinate frequently. Like Kim in the introductory chapter vignette, they may feel incredibly tired. Their breasts become tender and painful to the touch. Therefore, many women do not need that tip-off—a missed menstrual period—to realize they are carrying a child.

Hormones, or chemicals that target certain tissues and cause them to change, trigger these symptoms. After implantation, the production of *progesterone* (literally *pro,* or "for," *gestation*)—the hormone responsible for maintaining the pregnancy—surges. The placenta produces its own unique hormone, *human chorionic gonadotropin (HCG),* thought to prevent the woman's body from rejecting the "foreign" embryo.

Given this hormonal onslaught, the tiredness, dizziness, and headaches make sense. What about that other early pregnancy sign—morning sickness?

Morning sickness—nausea and sometimes vomiting—affects at least two out of every three women during the first trimester (Beckmann and others, 2002). This well-known symptom is not confined to the morning, however. Many women feel queasy all day. And men sometimes develop morning sickness along with their wives! This phenomenon has its own special name: *couvade* (Munroe, 2010).

hormones Chemical substances released in the bloodstream that target and change organs and tissues.

But morning sickness seems senseless: Doesn't the embryo need all the nourishment it can get? Why, during the first months of pregnancy, might it be "good" to stop eating particular foods?

Consider these clues: The queasiness is at its height when the organs are forming, and, like magic, toward the end of the first trimester, it usually (but not always) disappears. Munching on bread products helps. Strong odors make many women gag. Evolutionary psychologists theorize that, before refrigeration, morning sickness prevented the mother from eating spoiled meat or toxic plants, which could be especially dangerous during the embryonic phase (Bjorklund & Pellegrini, 2002). If you have a friend struggling with morning sickness, you can give her this heartening information: Some research suggests that women with morning sickness are more likely to carry their babies to term.

This brings up that upsetting event: **miscarriage.** Roughly 1 in 10 pregnancies end in a first trimester fetal loss. For women in their late thirties, the chance of miscarrying during these weeks escalates to 1 in 5. Although early miscarriages are typically caused by problems in development incompatible with life, some women mistakenly blame themselves. When loved ones use platitudes like, "That's normal. Just try again," they minimize the grief that early miscarriage can cause (Markin, 2016).

> **miscarriage** The naturally occurring loss of a pregnancy and death of the fetus.

Second Trimester: Feeling Much Better and Connecting Emotionally

Morning sickness, the other unpleasant symptoms, and the relatively high chance of miscarrying make the first trimester less than an unmitigated joy. During the second trimester, the magic kicks in.

By week 14, the uterus dramatically grows, often creating a need to shop for maternity clothes. The wider world may notice the woman's expanding body: "Are you pregnant?" "How wonderful!" "Take my seat." Around week 18, an event called **quickening**—a sensation like bubbles that signals the baby kicking in the womb—occurs. The woman feels viscerally connected to a growing human being.

> **quickening** A pregnant woman's first feeling of the fetus moving inside her body.

Another landmark event that alters the emotional experience of pregnancy happens at the beginning of the third trimester, when the woman can give birth to a living child. This important late-pregnancy marker explains why some societies build in celebrations at month 6 or 7 to welcome the baby to the human community.

Third Trimester: Getting Very Large and Waiting for Birth

Look at a pregnant woman struggling up the stairs and you'll get a sense of her feelings during this final trimester: backaches (think of carrying a bowling ball); leg cramps; numbness and tingling as the uterus presses against the nerves of the lower limbs; heartburn, insomnia, and anxious anticipation as focus shifts to the birth ("When will this baby arrive?!"); irregular uterine contractions as the baby sinks into the birth canal and delivery draws very near.

Although women often do work up to the day of delivery, health-care workers advise taking time off to rest and relying on caring loved ones to help during the final months. Issues relating to working and having loving support loom large during all nine months!

Pregnancy Is Not a Solo Act

> I'm now almost five months and . . . with the right clothes I can easily hide it. By postponing making it public, . . . [my organization] will have less time to put me in this stigmatized hole of unproductive, useless, unprofessional future mom.
>
> (from a pregnant bank executive living in the Netherlands, quoted in Hennekam, 2016, p. 1776)

> All the happiness I would have in seeing the heartbeat, or feeling the first kick is erased by my rocky relationship with John. If only my partner accepted this pregnancy! Now I can't focus on the baby. I'm anxious and depressed.

Some women, such as Kim in the opening vignette, are in love with motherhood. Others slog through pregnancy, anxious, ambivalent, and depressed (Brenning, Soenens, & Vansteenkiste, 2015). Now, let's focus on two forces that shape women's emotions during this landmark time.

WORK WORRIES One influence destined to erode happiness is financial concerns. Couples struggling economically and, especially, low-income single parents worry, "Can we (or I) afford this child?" But the first quotation on the previous page shows that even women in high-powered jobs have fears: "Will I be passed over for a promotion, or demoted, because my employer believes mothers can't do a good job?"

This woman's happiness in getting pregnant may be affected by work worries: "Will I get that promotion if my boss knows I'm having a baby? How will having a child affect my job?"

These anxieties are legitimate. **Family–work conflict,** or being pulled between the demands of caregiving and career, is a major issue for working parents (see Belsky, 2016, for a review). Even in nations such as Sweden, where both sexes get equal paid time off after birth, mothers, not fathers, most often opt to take this family leave (Duvander, 2014). In fact, there is a striking gender difference here. Because society links fatherhood with career commitment ("Supporting a family settles men down"), U.S. statistics show that married men are apt to be rewarded with a *salary raise* after their wives give birth (Killewald, 2013)!

RELATIONSHIP ISSUES The main quality that colors the emotional experience of pregnancy, however, is illustrated in the second quotation on the previous page—the relationship. Research shows that couples are emotionally tethered as they confront this life change. If one person feels unhappy about the pregnancy, the other person feels distressed, too (Canário & Figueiredo, 2016). Moreover, these shared attitudes carry over after birth. Couples who are more ambivalent about the fetus during pregnancy tend to be more stressed out during their child's first two years of life (Edwards & Hans, 2016). So, rather than being an internal event, a woman's feelings about her expanding body depend on her relationships in the world.

> **family–work conflict**
> A common developed-world situation, in which parents are torn between the demands of family and a career.

What About Dads?

This brings up the emotions of the traditional pregnancy partner: dads. Given the attention we lavish on pregnant women, it should come as no surprise that fathers have been relatively ignored in the research exploring this transition of life. But fathers are also bonded to their babies-to-be (Vreeswijk and others, 2014). They can feel just as devastated when a pregnancy doesn't work out. Here are some comments about miscarriage from the male point of view:

> I keep thinking that my wife is still pregnant. Where is my little girl? I was so ready to spoil her and treat her like a princess . . . but now she is gone. I don't think I'll ever be the same again.
>
> (quoted in Jaffe & Diamond, 2011, p. 218)

> I had to be strong for Kate. I had to let her cry on me and then I would . . . drive up into the hills and cry to myself. I was trying to support her even though I felt my whole life had just caved in. . . .
>
> (quoted in McCreight, 2004, p. 337)

As you can see from the above quotations, men coping with this trauma have a double burden. They may feel compelled to put aside their feelings to focus on their wives (Jaffe & Diamond, 2011; Rinehart & Kiselica, 2010). Plus, because the loss of a baby is typically seen as a "woman's issue," the wider world tends to marginalize men's pain.

These examples remind us that husbands are "pregnant" in spirit along with their wives. We should *never* thrust their feelings aside.

Returning to the beginning of the chapter, we now know that the cultural practice of pampering pregnant women makes excellent psychological sense—for both the mother *and* her child. But we need to realize that expectant fathers need cherishing, too!

Table 2.1 summarizes these points in a brief "stress during pregnancy" questionnaire. Next, we return to the baby and tackle that common fear: "Will my child be healthy?"

Table 2.1: Measuring Stress in Mothers-to-Be: A Short Section Summary Questionnaire

1. Does this woman or couple have financial troubles?
2. Is this woman concerned that being pregnant will derail her career chances?
3. Is this woman having marital problems, and does her partner want this baby?

Tying It All Together

1. Samantha just entered her second trimester. Explain how she is likely to feel for the next few months. What symptoms was Samantha apt to describe during the first trimester, after learning she was pregnant?

2. Your cousin is a high-paid executive in a marketing firm. Based on this chapter, if she gets pregnant, describe in a sentence how she may feel about revealing the news to her boss.

3. As a clinic director, you are concerned that men are often left out of the pregnancy experience. Design a few innovative interventions to make your clinic responsive to the needs of fathers-to-be.

Answers to the Tying It All Together questions can be found at the end of this chapter.

- Name the main teratogenic threats during the first and second trimesters.
- Outline the impact of smoking, excessive alcohol, and prenatal stress on fetal development.
- Describe Down syndrome and several other single-gene disorders.
- Evaluate genetic counseling and the different prenatal diagnostic tests.
- Discuss infertility and assisted reproductive technologies.

birth defect A physical or neurological problem that occurs prenatally or at birth.

Threats to the Developing Baby

In this section, I'll explore the prenatal reasons for **birth defects,** or health problems at birth. I'll also discuss new research exploring how wider-world events while "in the womb" can potentially affect a fetus's lifelong health. In reading this catalogue of "things that can go wrong," keep these thoughts in mind: The vast majority of babies are born healthy. Many birth defects don't seriously impair a baby's ability to lead a fulfilling life. Often birth defects result from a complex nature-plus-nurture interaction. Fetal genetic vulnerabilities combine with environmental hazards in the womb. However, this section separates these conditions into two categories: toxins that flow through the placenta to impair development and genetic diseases.

Threats from Outside: Teratogens

The universal fears about the growing baby are expressed in cultural prohibitions: "Don't use scissors or your baby will have cut lips" (a cleft palate), Afghanistan; "Avoid looking at monkeys [Indonesia] or gossiping [China] or your baby will be deformed."

If you think these practices are strange, consider the standard mid-twentieth-century medical advice. Physicians routinely put U.S. women on a strict diet if they gained over 15 pounds. They encouraged mothers-to-be to smoke and drink to relax

(Von Raffler-Engel, 1994; Wertz & Wertz, 1989). Today, these pronouncements might qualify as fetal abuse! What *can* hurt the developing baby? When is damage most apt to occur?

A **teratogen** (from the Greek words *teras,* "monster," and *gen,* "creating") is the name for any substance that crosses the placenta to harm the fetus. A teratogen may be an infectious disease; a medication; a recreational drug; an environmental hazard, such as radiation or pollution; or, as you will see later, the hormones produced by a pregnant woman who is under extreme stress. Table 2.2 on page 48 describes potential teratogens in various categories.

> **teratogen** A substance that crosses the placenta and harms the fetus.

Basic Teratogenic Principles

Teratogens typically exert their damage during the **sensitive period**—the timeframe when a particular organ or system is coming "on line." For example, the infectious disease called *rubella* (German measles) often damaged a baby's heart or ears, depending on the week during the first trimester when a mother contracted the disease. The mild mosquito-borne virus, Zika, wreaks destruction during the late embryonic stage (see the photo below), when it prevents the immature cells from assembling in the neural tube.

> **sensitive period** The time when a body structure is most vulnerable to damage by a teratogen, typically when that organ or process is rapidly developing or coming "on line."

In general, with regard to teratogens, the following principles apply:

1. **Teratogens are most likely to cause major structural damage during the embryonic stage.** Before implantation, teratogens have an all-or-nothing impact. They either inhibit implantation and cause death, or they leave the not-yet-attached blastocyst unscathed. It is during organ formation (after implantation through week 8) that major body structures are most likely to be affected. This is why physicians advise forgoing any medications during the first trimester—that is, unless expectant mothers have a chronic disease that demands they continue their treatment (American Academy of Pediatrics [AAP], Committee on Drugs, 2000).

2. **Teratogens can affect the developing brain throughout pregnancy.** As you saw earlier, because the brain is forming during the second and third trimesters, the potential for neurological damage extends for all nine months. Typically, during the second and third trimesters, exposure to teratogens increases the risk of **developmental disorders.** This term refers to any condition that compromises normal development—from delays in reaching basic milestones, such as walking or talking, to learning problems and hyperactivity.

> **developmental disorders** Learning impairments and behavioral problems during infancy and childhood.

3. **Teratogens have a threshold level above which damage occurs.** For instance, women who drink more than four cups of coffee a day throughout pregnancy have a slightly higher risk of miscarriage; but having an occasional Diet Coke is fine (Gilbert-Barness, 2000).

4. **Teratogens exert their damage unpredictably, depending on fetal and maternal vulnerabilities.** Still, mothers-to-be metabolize toxins differently, and babies differ genetically in susceptibility. So the damaging effects of a particular teratogen can vary. On the plus side, you may know a child in your local school's gifted program whose mother drank heavily during pregnancy. On the negative side, we do not know where the teratogenic threshold lies in any particular case. Therefore, during pregnancy, it's best to err on the side of caution.

This Zika-exposed baby is a testament to the horrible damage teratogens can potentially cause during the first trimester, as he was born with the devastating condition called *microcephaly.*

Although the damaging impact of a teratogen may surface during infancy, it can also manifest itself years later. An unfortunate example of this teratogenic time bomb took place in my own life. My mother was given a drug called diethylstilbestrol (DES) while she was pregnant with me. (DES was prescribed routinely in the 1950s

Table 2.2: Examples of Known Teratogens and the Damage They Can Do

Teratogen	Consequences of Exposure
INFECTIOUS DISEASES	
Rubella (German measles)	If a pregnant woman contracts rubella during the embryonic stage, the consequences can be intellectual disability, blindness, or eye, ear, and heart abnormalities in the baby—depending on the week the virus enters the bloodstream. Luckily, women of childbearing age are now routinely immunized for this otherwise minor adult disease.
Cytomegalovirus	About 25% of babies infected with this virus develop vision or hearing loss; 10% develop neurological problems.
AIDS	HIV-infected women can transmit the virus to their babies prenatally during delivery (through the placenta) or after birth (through breast milk). Rates of transmission are much lower if infected mothers take the anti-AIDS drug AZT or if newborns are given a new drug that blocks the transmission of HIV at birth. If a mother takes these precautions, does not breastfeed, and delivers her baby by c-section (see page 62), the infection rate falls to less than 1%. While mother-to-child transmission of HIV has declined dramatically in the developed world, it remains a devastating problem in sub-Saharan Africa and other impoverished regions of the globe (AVERT, 2005).
Herpes	This familiar sexually transmitted disease can cause miscarriage, growth retardation, and eye abnormalities in affected fetuses. Doctors recommend that pregnant women with active genital herpes undergo c-sections to avoid infecting their babies during delivery.
Toxoplasmosis	This disease, caused by a parasite in raw meat and cat feces, can produce sensory and cognitive impairments in infants. Pregnant women should avoid handling raw meat and cat litter.
Zika virus	Pregnant women who contract this mild adult mosquito-borne illness during the first trimester are at high risk of miscarrying or giving birth to a baby with microcephaly (missing most of a brain). Women planning to get pregnant should avoid traveling to Zika-affected regions. Having sex with an infected partner can also transmit the virus.
MEDICATIONS	
Antibiotics	Streptomycin has been linked to hearing loss; tetracycline to stained infant tooth enamel.
Thalidomide	This drug, prescribed in the late 1950s in Europe to prevent nausea during the first trimester, prevented the baby's arms and legs from developing if taken during the embryonic period.
Anti-seizure drugs	These medications have been linked to developmental delays during infancy.
Anti-psychotic drugs	These drugs may slightly raise the risk of giving birth to a baby with heart problems.
Antidepressants	Although typically safe, third-trimester exposure to selective serotonin reuptake inhibitors and tricyclic antidepressants has been linked to temporary jitteriness, excessive crying, and eating and sleeping difficulties in newborns. Rarely, these drugs can produce seizures and dehydration in the baby, as well as miscarriage.
RECREATIONAL DRUGS	
Cocaine	This drug is linked to miscarriage, growth retardation, and learning and behavior problems.
Methamphetamine	This drug may cause miscarriage and growth retardation.
ENVIRONMENTAL TOXINS	
Radiation	Japanese children exposed to radiation from the atomic bomb during the second trimester had extremely high rates of severe intellectual disability. Miscarriages were virtually universal among pregnant women living within 5 miles of the blast. Pregnant women are also advised to avoid clinical doses of radiation such as those used in X-rays (and especially cancer treatment radiation).
Lead	Babies with high levels of lead in the umbilical cord may show impairments in cognitive functioning (Bellinger and others, 1987). Maternal exposure to lead is associated with miscarriage.
Mercury and PCBs	These pollutants are linked to learning and behavior problems.
VITAMIN DEFICIENCIES	In addition to eating a balanced diet, every woman of childbearing age should take folic acid supplements. This vitamin, part of the B complex, protects against the incomplete closure of the neural tube during the first month of development—an event that may produce *spina bifida* (paralysis in the body below the region of the spine that has not completely closed) or *anencephaly* (failure of the brain to develop—and certain death) if the gap occurs toward the top of the developing tube.

Data from Huttenlocher, 2002, and the references in this chapter.

and 1960s to prevent miscarriage.) During my early twenties, I developed cancerous cells in my cervix—and, after surgery, had three miscarriages before being blessed by adopting my son.

The Teratogenic Impact of Medicines and Recreational Drugs

The fact that some common medications are teratogenic presents dilemmas for women. Suppose you are among the estimated 1 in 10 U.S. women who enter into a pregnancy depressed (Tebeka, Le Strat, & Dubertret, 2016). You are alarmed at the research suggesting your mental state can impair your attachment to the baby (and feelings about your partner). But you also know that taking antidepressants slightly raises the risk of having a premature birth (Deligiannidis, Byatt, & Freeman, 2014; Huang and others, 2014; Jensen and others, 2013). What do you do? When it comes to medicines and pregnancy, sometimes there are no perfect choices.

With recreational drugs the choice is clear. Each substance is potentially teratogenic. So it's best to just say *no!*

Because tobacco and alcohol are woven into the fabric of daily life, let's now focus on these widely used teratogens. What *can* happen to the baby when pregnant women smoke and drink?

SMOKING Each time a pregnant woman reads the information on a cigarette pack, she is reminded that she may be doing her baby harm. Still, polls suggest that approximately 1 in 3 pregnant women—when they are young and poorly educated—smoke (Agency for Healthcare Research and Quality [AHRQ], 2014). Because this practice is such a "no, no," these surveys almost certainly underestimate the number of smoking mothers-to-be. When scientists in a national U.S. study measured blood levels of cotinine (a biological indicator of tobacco use), they discovered that roughly 1 in 4 pregnant smokers had earlier falsely reported: "Oh yes, I definitely quit!" (see Dietz and others, 2011).

The danger posed by smoking is giving birth to a smaller-than-normal, less healthy baby (Krstev and others, 2013). Nicotine constricts the mother's blood vessels, reducing blood flow to the fetus and preventing ample nutrients from reaching the child. Infants born to pregnant smokers are less able to regulate their behavior (Wiebe and others, 2015). Tobacco-exposed fetuses are more prone to develop antisocial behaviors during childhood and the teens (Huizink, 2015; Knopik and others, 2016; Liebschutz and others, 2015).

Heavy smoking (more than half a pack a day) is most poisonous for development (Huizink, 2015). And, because quitting is difficult, some women get mixed signals from health-care providers: "My doctor told me stopping would stress the baby . . . I'm continuing to smoke but not that much" (quoted in Naughton, Eborall, & Sutton, 2013, pp. 27, 28). How many cigarettes a day are dangerous? Let's keep this murky issue in mind as I turn to that other familiar teratogen: alcohol.

ALCOHOL As I mentioned earlier, it used to be standard practice to encourage pregnant women to have a nightcap to relieve stress. During the 1970s, as evidence mounted for a disorder called **fetal alcohol syndrome (FAS),** these prescriptions were quickly revised. Whenever you hear the word *syndrome*, it is a signal that the condition has a constellation of features that are present to varying degrees. The defining qualities of fetal alcohol syndrome include a smaller-than-normal birth weight and brain; facial abnormalities (such as a flattened face); and developmental disorders ranging from serious intellectual disability to seizures and hyperactivity (Dean & Davis, 2007; May and others, 2016; Roussotte, Soderberg, & Sowell, 2010).

Women who binge-drink (have more than four drinks at a sitting), or pregnant women who regularly consume several drinks nightly, are at highest risk of giving birth to a baby with fetal alcohol syndrome. Their children, at a minimum, may be

fetal alcohol syndrome (FAS) A cluster of birth defects caused by the mother's alcohol consumption during pregnancy.

As this woman downed her many drinks, she put her baby at risk for fetal alcohol syndrome—explaining why patrons at a bar who saw this scenario would get very upset!

born with a less severe syndrome called *fetal alcohol spectrum disorders,* characterized by deficits in learning and impaired mental health (Wedding and others, 2007). As alcohol crosses the placenta, it causes genetic changes that impair neural growth (Hashimoto-Torii and others, 2011).

Faced with these warnings, polls in New Zealand and Australia show most women reported that they stopped using alcohol after learning they were pregnant (Parackal, Parackal, & Harraway, 2013; Pettigrew and others, 2016). Surprisingly, however, a study in the Netherlands revealed that *well-educated,* expectant mothers were likely to still drink (Pfinder and others, 2014)!

This unexpected finding may reflect cultural norms. Every U.S. public health organization recommends no alcohol during pregnancy. In Europe, having a cocktail or a glass of wine is an expected practice during meals. This may explain why European physicians disagree with their U.S. counterparts: "One drink per day can't *possibly* do the fetus harm" (Paul, 2010; Royal College of Obstetricians and Gynaecologists [RCOG], 1999).

Measurement Issues

Why is there *any* debate about a "safe" amount of alcohol to drink? For answers, imagine the challenges you would face as a researcher exploring the impact of tobacco or alcohol on the developing child: The need to ask thousands of pregnant women to estimate how often they indulged in these "unacceptable" behaviors and then track the children for decades, looking for problems that might appear as late as adult life. Plus, because your study is *correlational,* the difficulties you find might be due to other confounding causes. Pregnant women who drink are more likely to smoke, to be depressed, to be under stress, and to take other drugs. They could be passing down behavior problems to their sons and daughters in their genes.

Drawing on research using sophisticated techniques to control for genetics, one expert (Huizink, 2015) concludes that light smoking and drinking won't affect the fetus. But don't take this pronouncement as a green light! With a biologically at-risk baby, who knows what damage five cigarettes a day or a single glass of wine each night could do?

🌀 Hot in Developmental Science: The Long Shadow of Prenatal Stress

---

Giving up wine and cigarettes for the sake of the baby is doable—and many women stop using social drugs when they are having a child. Implementing the cultural advice to keep pregnant women "calm and happy" can be impossible to carry out. What happens to the fetus when pregnant women are depressed or experience traumatic stresses?

The danger is that prenatal depression and severe emotional upheavals can impair fetal growth or provoke premature labor, and so produce smaller, less healthy babies (Lin and others, 2017). In fact, in one alarming study, elevated levels of the stress hormone **cortisol**, measured in women *prior to getting pregnant*, predicted giving birth to a tinier child (Guardino & Schetter, 2014). Cortisol, transferred via the placenta to the fetus, even has a direct physiological effect, making newborns irritable during the first months of life (Baibazarova and others, 2013).

While pregnancy stresses range from poverty to abusive partners, from job concerns to experiencing a loved one's death (Class and others, 2013), the most fascinating data relates to natural disasters. Women who were pregnant during

cortisol A hormone often measured in saliva by researchers as a biological marker of stress.

the 2011 earthquake in Japan had preschoolers with abnormally high rates of mental health problems (Sato and others, 2016). Months after the Red River in Fargo, North Dakota, crested in 2009, the prevalence of low-birth-weight babies in that city peaked. Women in their first trimester living close to the flood were most likely to have small newborns, suggesting again that early pregnancy is a time of maximum risk (Hilmert and others, 2016).

Imagine being this terrified refugee family escaping Aleppo, Syria, during the civil war. Horrific holocausts (and natural disasters) can have enduring consequences on development, even when a baby manages to survive.

Being born small casts a shadow over the *whole* span of life. During World War II, in 1944, the Germans cut off the food supply to Holland, putting that nation in a semi-starvation condition for a few months. As you might imagine, miscarriages and stillbirths were far more frequent during this "Hunger Winter." But the surviving babies also had enduring scars. Midlife heart disease rates were higher if a baby had been in the womb *specifically* during the Hunger Winter (Paul, 2010). Imagine what health concerns could affect babies who were born during the civil war in Aleppo, Syria, even if these newborns survived this human-made disaster that has stained humankind.

Why might deprivation in the womb be linked to premature, age-related disease? Speculations again center on being born too small. When fetuses are deprived of nutrients and/or exposed to intense maternal stress, researchers hypothesize the resulting impaired growth primes the baby to enter the world expecting "a state of deprivation" and to eat excessively or store fat. But while this strategy promotes survival when nutrition is scarce, it boomerangs—promoting obesity and a potentially shorter life—when a child arrives in the world in today's era of overabundant food.

Is obesity (and adult chronic disease) caused just by personal lifestyle choices or partly promoted by a poor body–environment fit at birth? These tantalizing questions are driving **fetal programming research**—studies that explore how intrauterine events may *epigenetically* change our genetic code (Belsky & Pluess, 2011).

Freud revolutionized the twentieth century by arguing that childhood experiences shape personality. Will twenty-first-century scientists trace the roots of human development to experiences in the womb?

Fetal programming research is action oriented. Ideally, interventions—such as therapy to ward off depression (Dimidjian and others, 2016) or prevent prenatal drinking (Parrish and others, 2016)—can have a long-term impact on a child's fate. With the conditions I discuss next, the problems are often more serious. They are frequently diagnosed at birth because the child's condition is "genetic." It was sealed at conception with the union of an egg and sperm.

fetal programming research New research discipline exploring the impact of traumatic pregnancy events and stress on producing low birth weight, obesity, and long-term physical problems.

Threats from Within: Chromosomal and Genetic Disorders

When a birth defect is genetic, there are two main causes. The child might have an unusual number of chromosomes, or the issue might be a faulty gene (or set of genes).

Chromosomal Problems

As we know, the normal human chromosomal complement is 46. However, sometimes a baby with a missing or extra chromosome is conceived. The vast majority of these fertilizations end in first-trimester miscarriages, as the cells cannot differentiate much past the blastocyst stage.

Still, babies can be born with an abnormal number of sex chromosomes (such as an extra X or two, an extra Y, or a single X) and survive. In this case, although the symptoms vary, the result is often learning impairments and sometimes infertility.

Down syndrome The most common chromosomal abnormality, causing intellectual disability, susceptibility to heart disease, other health problems, and distinctive physical characteristics including slanted eyes and a stocky build.

Survival is also possible when a child is born with an extra chromosome on a specific other pair. The most common example—happening in roughly 1 in every 700 births (National Down Syndrome Society [NDSS], n.d.)—produces a baby with Down syndrome.

Down syndrome typically occurs because a cell-division error, called *nondisjunction,* in the egg or sperm causes an extra chromosome or piece of that copy to adhere to chromosome pair 21. (Figure 2.3 on page 38 shows this is the smallest matching set, so the reason extra material adhering to chromosome 21 is not uniformly lethal is that this pair generally contains the fewest genes.) The child is born with 47 chromosomes instead of the normal 46.

This extra chromosome produces familiar physical features: a flat facial profile, an upward slant to the eyes, a stocky appearance, and an enlarged tongue. Babies born with Down syndrome are at high risk for having heart defects and childhood leukemia. Here, too, there is a lifespan time-bomb impact. During midlife, many adults with Down syndrome develop Alzheimer's disease (NDSS, n.d.). The most well-known problem with this familiar condition, however, is mild to moderate intellectual disability.

A century ago, Down syndrome children rarely lived to adulthood. They were shunted to institutions to live severely shortened lives. In the United States today, due to medical advances, these babies have an average life expectancy of 60 years (NDSS, n.d.). Ironically, this longevity gain can be a double-edged sword. Elderly parent caregivers may worry what will happen to their middle-aged child when they die or become physically impaired (Gath, 1993).

Lauren Shear/Science Source

Knowing a Down syndrome child has a powerful effect on every person. Will this older girl become a more caring, sensitive adult through having played with this much loved younger friend?

This is not to say that every Down syndrome baby is dependent on a caregiver's help. These children can sometimes learn to read and write. They can live independently, hold down jobs, marry and have children, and construct fulfilling lives. Do you know a child with Down syndrome like the toddler in this photo who is the light of her loving family and friends' lives?

Although women of any age can give birth to Down syndrome babies, the risk rises exponentially among older mothers. Over age 40, the chance of having a Down syndrome birth is 1 in 100; over age 45, it is 1 in 30 (NDSS, n.d.). The reason is that, with more time "in storage," older ova are more apt to develop chromosomal faults.

Down syndrome is typically caused by a spontaneous genetic mistake. Now let's look at a different category of genetic disorders—those passed down in the parents' DNA to potentially affect *every* child.

Genetic Disorders

Most illnesses—from cancer to heart disease to schizophrenia—are caused by complex nature-plus-nurture interactions. Several, often unknown, genes act in conjunction with murky environmental forces (Moore, 2015). A *single,* known gene causes these next disorders that often appear at birth.

single-gene disorder An illness caused by a single gene.

Single-gene disorders are passed down according to three modes of inheritance: They may be *dominant, recessive,* or *sex-linked.* To understand these patterns, you might want to look again at the paired arrangement of the chromosomes in Figure 2.3 (page 38) and remember that we get one copy of each gene from our mother and one from our father. Also, in understanding these illnesses, it is important to know that one member of each gene pair can be dominant. This means that the quality will always show up in real life. If both members of the gene pair are not dominant (that is, if they are recessive), the illness will manifest itself only if the child inherits two of the faulty genes.

Dominant disorders are in the first category. In this case, if one parent harbors the problem gene (and so has the illness), each child the couple gives birth to has a fifty-fifty chance of also getting ill.

Recessive disorders are in the second category. Unless a person gets two copies of the gene, one from the father and one from the mother, that child is disease free. In this case, the odds of a baby born to two carriers—that is, parents who each have one copy of that gene—having the illness are 1 in 4.

The mode of transmission for **sex-linked single-gene disorders** is more complicated. Most often, the woman is carrying a recessive (nonexpressed in real life) gene for the illness on *one* of her two X chromosomes. Since her daughters have another X from their father (who doesn't carry the illness), the female side of the family is typically disease free. Her sons, however, have a fifty-fifty chance of getting ill, depending on whether they get the normal or abnormal version of their mother's X.

Because their single X leaves them vulnerable, sex-linked disorders typically affect males. But as an intellectual exercise, you might want to figure out when females can get this condition. If you guessed that it's when the mother is a carrier (having one faulty X) and the dad has the disorder (having the gene on his single X), you are right!

Table 2.3 on page 54 visually decodes these modes of inheritance and describes a few of the best-known single-gene diseases. In scanning the first illness on the chart, Huntington's disease, imagine your emotional burden as a genetically at-risk child. People with Huntington's develop an incurable dementia in the prime of life. As a child you would probably have watched a beloved parent lose his memory and bodily functions, and then die. You would know that your odds of suffering the same fate are 1 in 2. (Although babies born with lethal dominant genetic disorders typically die before they can have children, Huntington's disease remained in the population because it, too, operates as an internal time bomb, showing up during the prime reproductive years.)

With the other illnesses in Table 2.3—programmed by recessive genes—the fears relate to bearing a child. If both you and your partner have the Tay-Sachs carrier gene, you may have seen a beloved baby die in infancy. With cystic fibrosis, your affected child would be subject to recurrent medical crises as his lungs filled up with fluid, and he would face a dramatically shortened life. Would you want to take the 1-in-4 chance of having this experience again?

The good news, as the table shows, is that the prognoses for some routinely fatal childhood single-gene disorders are no longer as dire. With hemophilia, the life-threatening episodes of bleeding can be avoided by supplying the missing blood factor through transfusions. While surviving to the teens with cystic fibrosis used to be rare, today these children can expect on average to live to their twenties and sometimes beyond (CysticFibrosis.com, n.d.). Still, with Tay-Sachs or Huntington's disease, there is *nothing* medically that can be done.

In sum, the answer to the question of whether single-gene disorders can be treated and cured is, "It depends." Although people still have the faulty gene—and so are not "cured" in the traditional sense—through advances in nurture (or changing the environment), we have made remarkable progress in treating what used to be uniformly fatal diseases.

Our most dramatic progress, however, lies in **genetic testing**. Through a simple blood test, people can find out whether they carry the gene for various illnesses.

These diagnostic breakthroughs bring up difficult issues. Would you want to know whether you have the gene for Huntington's disease? The inspiring story of Nancy Wexler, the psychologist who helped discover the Huntington's gene and

dominant disorder An illness that a child gets by inheriting one copy of the abnormal gene that causes the disorder.

recessive disorder An illness that a child gets by inheriting two copies of the abnormal gene that causes the disorder.

sex-linked single-gene disorder An illness, carried on the mother's X chromosome, that typically leaves the female offspring unaffected but has a fifty-fifty chance of striking each male child.

genetic testing A blood test to determine whether a person carries the gene for a given genetic disorder.

Table 2.3: Some Examples of Dominant, Recessive, and Sex-Linked Single-Gene Disorders

DOMINANT DISORDERS

- **Huntington's disease (HD)** This fatal nervous system disorder is characterized by uncontrollable jerky movements and irreversible intellectual impairment (dementia). Symptoms usually appear around age 35, although the illness can occasionally erupt in childhood and in old age. There is no treatment for this disease.

RECESSIVE DISORDERS

- **Cystic fibrosis (CF)** This most common single-gene disorder in the United States is typically identified at birth by the salty character of the sweat. The child's body produces mucus that clogs the lungs and pancreas, interfering with breathing and digestion and causing repeated medical crises. As the hairlike cells in the lungs are destroyed, these vital organs degenerate and eventually cause premature death. Advances in treatment have extended the average life expectancy for people with CF to their late twenties. One in 28 U.S. Caucasians is a carrier for this disease.*

- **Sickle cell anemia** This blood disorder takes its name from the characteristic sickle shape of the red blood cells. The blood cells collapse and clump together, causing oxygen deprivation and organ damage. The symptoms of sickle cell anemia are fatigue, pain, growth retardation, ulcers, stroke, and, ultimately, a shortened life. Treatments include transfusions and medications for infection and pain. One in 10 African Americans is a carrier of this disease.*

- **Tay-Sachs disease** In this universally fatal infant nervous system disorder, the child appears healthy at birth, but then fatty material accumulates in the neurons and, at 6 months, symptoms such as blindness, intellectual disability, and paralysis occur and the baby dies. Tay-Sachs is found most often among Jewish people of Eastern European ancestry. An estimated 1 in 25 U.S. Jews is a carrier.[†]

SEX-LINKED DISORDERS

- **Hemophilia** These blood-clotting disorders typically affect males. The most serious forms of hemophilia (A and B) produce severe episodes of uncontrolled joint bleeding and pain. In the past, these episodes often resulted in death during childhood. Today, with transfusions of the missing clotting factors, affected children can have a fairly normal life expectancy.

*Sickle cell anemia may have remained in the population because having the trait (one copy of the gene) conferred an evolutionary advantage: It protected against malaria in Africa. Scientists also speculate that the cystic fibrosis trait may have conferred immunity to typhoid fever.

[†]Due to a vigorous public awareness program in the Jewish community, potential carriers are routinely screened and the rate of Tay-Sachs disease has declined dramatically.

Father (has illness)   **Mother (unaffected)**

Child 1 (has illness)   **Child 2 (has illness)**   **Child 3 (unaffected)**   **Child 4 (unaffected)**

Here, the gene is dominant, and there is a 1-in-2 chance that each child of an affected parent will have the disease.

Father (carrier)   **Mother (carrier)**

Child 1 (carrier)   **Child 2 (unaffected)**   **Child 3 (has illness)**   **Child 4 (carrier)**

Here, both parents are carriers, and each child has a 1-in-4 chance of having the disease.

Father (unaffected)   **Mother (carrier)**

XY   XX

XY Son (unaffected)   **XY Son (has illness)**   **XX Daughter (unaffected)**   **XX Daughter (carrier)**

Here, the mother has the faulty gene on her X chromosome, so the daughters are typically disease-free, but each son has a 1-in-2 chance of getting ill.

whose mother died of the disease, is instructive here (see the How Do We Know box). While Nancy will not say whether she has been tested, her sister Alice refused to be screened because she felt not knowing was better for her emotionally than the anguish of living with a positive result.

HOW DO WE KNOW . . .
about the gene for Huntington's disease?

Nancy Wexler and her sister got the devastating news from their physician father, Milton: "Your mother has Huntington's disease. She will die of dementia in a horrible way. As a dominant single-gene disorder, your chance of getting ill is fifty-fifty. There is nothing we can do [see Table 2.3]. But that doesn't mean we are going to give up." In 1969, Milton Wexler established the Hereditary Disease Foundation, surrounded himself with scientists, and put his young daughter, Nancy, a clinical psychologist, in charge. The hunt was on for the Huntington's gene.

A breakthrough came in 1979, when Nancy learned that the world's largest group of people with Huntington's lived in a small, inbred community in Venezuela—descendants of a woman who harbored the gene mutation that caused the disease. After building a pedigree of 18,000 family members, collecting blood samples from thousands more, and carefully analyzing the DNA for differences, the researchers hit pay dirt. They isolated the Huntington's gene.

Having this diagnostic marker is the first step to eventually finding a cure. So far the cure is elusive, but the hunt continues. Nancy still serves as the head of the foundation, vigorously advocating for research on the illness that killed her mother. She works as a professor in Columbia University's Neurology and Psychiatry Department. But every year, she comes back to the village in Venezuela to counsel and just visit with her families— her relatives in blood.

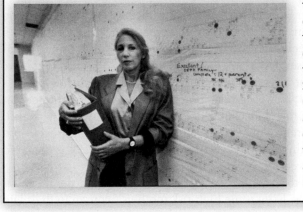

Acey Harper/The LIFE Images Collection/Getty Images

Interventions

The advantages of genetic testing are clearer when the issue relates to having a child. Let's imagine that you and your spouse know you are carriers of the cystic fibrosis gene. If you are contemplating having children, what should you do?

Sorting Out the Options: Genetic Counseling

Your first step would be to consult a **genetic counselor,** a professional skilled in both genetics and counseling, to help you think through your choices. In addition to laying out the odds of having an affected child, genetic counselors describe advances in treatment. For example, they inform couples who are carriers for cystic fibrosis about biological strategies on the horizon, such as gene therapy. They also highlight the interpersonal and economic costs of having a child with this disease. They explore the ambiguities of making this difficult decision in simple terms (Werner-Lin, McCoyd, & Bernhardt, 2016). But they are trained never to offer advice. Their goal is to permit couples to make a *mutual decision* on their own.

Now, suppose that armed with this information, you and your partner go ahead and conceive. Let's scan the major tests that are available to every woman carrying a child.

Tools of Discovery: Prenatal Tests

Blood tests performed during the first trimester can detect (with reasonable accuracy) various chromosomal conditions, such as Down syndrome. Brain scans (MRIs) offer a vivid prenatal window on the developing brain (Jokhi & Whitby, 2011). The standard fetal diagnostic test has been a staple for over 40 years: the **ultrasound.**

genetic counselor
A professional who counsels parents-to-be about their children's risk of developing genetic disorders and about available treatments.

ultrasound In pregnancy, an image of the fetus in the womb that helps to date the pregnancy, assess the fetus's growth, and identify abnormalities.

Due to the miracles of 3D ultrasound technology, when women visit their health-care provider, they can clearly see their baby's face. As they peer through this "window on the womb," doctors can get vital information about the health of this 26-week-old fetus, too.

chorionic villus sampling (CVS) A relatively risky first-trimester pregnancy test for fetal genetic disorders.

amniocentesis A second-trimester procedure that involves inserting a syringe into a woman's uterus to extract a sample of amniotic fluid, which is tested for genetic and chromosomal conditions.

Ultrasounds, which now provide a clear image of the fetus (see the accompanying photo), are used to date the pregnancy and assess in utero growth, in addition to revealing physical abnormalities. By making the baby visually real, ultrasound visits have become emotional landmarks on the pregnancy journey itself (Paul, 2010). Imagine the thrill of getting this vivid photo of your baby months before she is born!

Pregnant women embrace ultrasound technology and noninvasive genetic tests (Verweij and others, 2013). They tend to be more wary of the procedures described next, because those require entering the womb.

During the first trimester, **chorionic villus sampling (CVS)** can diagnose a variety of chromosomal and genetic conditions. A physician inserts a catheter into the woman's abdomen or vagina and withdraws a piece of the developing placenta for analysis. Knowing early on is the advantage of CVS; however, this test can be slightly dangerous, as it carries a risk of miscarriage and limb impairments (Karni, Leshno, & Rapaport, 2014).

During the second trimester, a safer test, called **amniocentesis,** can determine the fetus's fate. The doctor inserts a syringe into the woman's uterus and extracts a sample of amniotic fluid. The cells can reveal a host of genetic and chromosomal conditions, as well as the fetus's sex.

Amniocentesis is planned for a gestational age (typically week 14) when there is enough fluid to safely siphon out. However, it also carries a small chance of infection and miscarriage, depending on the skill of the doctor performing the test (Karni, Leshno, & Rapaport, 2014). Moreover, when the results arrive, a woman is well into her second trimester; and, as of this writing (2018), in some U.S. states, it is illegal to terminate a pregnancy after 20 weeks.

Will the political pressure to reverse *Roe v. Wade* make these procedures illegal in the United States? Not necessarily. Even some high-risk mothers (women in their late thirties or forties) who would never consider abortion might want to know in advance whether their baby has a genetic disease.

Yes, a diagnosis of serious fetal problems transforms pregnancy joy into pain (Fonseca, Nazaré, & Canavarro, 2014). But knowledge confers power. If you were pregnant and at high risk of having a child with some genetic disorder, would you decide to undergo these tests?

The summary timeline spanning these pages outlines these procedures and charts the landmark events of prenatal development and pregnancy. I cannot emphasize

TIMELINE	**Prenatal Development, Pregnancy, Prenatal Threats, Tools of Discovery**		
	Germinal stage (weeks 1 and 2)	**Embryonic stage** (weeks 3–8)	**Fetal stage** (weeks 9–38)
PRENATAL DEVELOPMENT	Zygote → blastocyst, which implants in uterus.	All major organs and structures form.	Massive growth and refinements; brain develops; live birth is possible at 22–24 weeks.
THREATS	At fertilization: chromosomal and single-gene diseases.	Teratogens can cause basic structural abnormalities.	Teratogens can impair growth, affect the brain, and so cause developmental disorders. They can also produce miscarriage or premature labor.

strongly enough that giving birth to a baby with serious birth defects is rare. That is not true, however, of the topic I turn to now—problems conceiving a child.

Infertility and New Reproductive Technologies

I feel incomplete and useless . . . all the other blessings are valueless unless you can have a child.

(from Nadia, a 35-year-old Pakistani woman,
quoted in an interview in Batool & de Visser, 2016, p. 184)

According to Psalm 127:3, "Children are a heritage unto the Lord and the fruit of his womb is His Reward." So why didn't I get this gift? I asked myself over and over if I was being punished.

(quoted in Ferland & Caron, 2013, p. 183)

The idea that being unable to give birth renders females useless (the often used, evocative word here is *barren*) begins in *Genesis*. When biblical patriarch Abraham's beloved wife Sarah couldn't get pregnant, he felt compelled to "procreate" with a substitute wife.

Infertility—the inability to conceive a child after a year of unprotected intercourse—is far from rare, affecting an estimated 1 in 5 couples. These rates have been rising, due to sexually transmitted diseases (in the developing world) and the fact that so many developed-world women today delay childbearing to their mid-thirties and beyond (Petraglia, Serour, & Chapron, 2013).

While infertility can affect women (and men) of every age, just as with miscarriage and Down syndrome—as we know from the standard phrase, "the ticking of the biological clock"—getting pregnant is far more difficult at older ages. Within the first six months of trying, roughly 3 out of 4 women in their twenties conceives. At age 40, only 1 out of 5 achieves that goal (Turkington & Alper, 2001). Because of their more complicated anatomy, we often assume infertility is usually a "female" problem. Not so! Male issues—which can vary from low sperm motility to varicose veins in the testicles—are *equally* likely to be involved (Turkington & Alper, 2001).

As the quotes at the beginning of this section suggest, infertility is apt to hit women hardest (Teskereci & Oncel, 2013). But males also feel pressured to prove their manhood by fathering a child (here, the revealing word is *impotent*). In one Danish questionnaire study, almost 1 in 3 patients at a male fertility clinic confessed that their condition affected their sense of masculinity and self-esteem (Mikkelsen, Madsen, & Humaidan, 2013).

In the Middle East, women coping with fertility problems may worry about being shunned by their family: Will my husband abandon me (Behboodi-Moghadam and others, 2013)? Will my in-laws kick me out of the house (see Batool & de Visser, 2016)?

In every nation, infertility isolates couples from relationships. Imagine going to dinner parties and needing to listen quietly as everyone at the table bonds around the joys and trials of having kids.

> **infertility** The inability to conceive after a year of unprotected sex. (Includes the inability to carry a child to term.)

	First trimester (month 1–month 3)	Second trimester (month 4–month 6)	Third trimester (month 7–month 9)
PREGNANCY	Morning sickness, tiredness, and other unpleasant symptoms may occur; miscarriage is a worry.	Woman looks pregnant. Quickening occurs (around week 18). Mother can feel intensely bonded to baby.	Woman gets very large and anxiously waits for birth.
TOOLS OF DISCOVERY	Ultrasound Blood tests Chorionic villus sampling (CVS) around week 10	Ultrasound Amniocentesis (around week 15)	Ultrasound

Then there are the painful reminders of what you are missing from life: "Going out shopping, everyone seems to be pregnant"; "Whenever I listen to the news of newborns around me, I can't just sleep . . ." (as reported in Batool & de Visser, 2016).

What helps people cope? Again, the key is having a collaborative, supportive mate (Darwiche and others, 2013; Ying & Loke, 2016), someone who loves you as *a person*, not a baby-making machine.

> When I told him (my second husband) when we were dating that I could not have children, he said, "If god wanted me to have kids, he would have made me fall in love with a woman who could have them."
>
> (quoted in Ferland & Caron, 2013, p. 186)

Today, having a caring collaborator is very important for any couple, gay or straight, as science offers so many options to help fulfill the quest to have a biological child.

INTERVENTIONS Exploring ART

For females, there are treatments to attack every problem on the reproductive chain (see the illustration in Figure 2.8)—from fertility drugs to stimulate ovulation, to hormonal supplements to foster implantation; from surgery to help clean out the uterus and the fallopian tubes, to artificial insemination (inserting the sperm into the woman's uterus through a syringe). Males may take medications or undergo surgery to increase the quality and motility of the sperm. Then there is that ultimate approach: **assisted reproductive technology (ART)**.

Assisted reproductive technology refers to any strategy in which the egg is fertilized outside the womb. The most widely used ART procedure is **in vitro fertilization (IVF)**. After the woman is given fertility drugs (which stimulate multiple ovulations), her eggs are harvested and placed in a laboratory dish, along with the partner's sperm, to be fertilized. A few days later, the fertilized eggs are inserted into the uterus. Then, the couple anxiously waits to find out if the cells have implanted in the uterine wall.

In vitro fertilization, initially developed to bypass blocked fallopian tubes, has spawned amazing variations. A sperm may be injected directly into the ovum if it cannot penetrate the surface on its own. The woman may use a donor egg—one from another woman—in order to conceive. Or, she may go to a sperm bank to utilize a donor sperm. The fertilized eggs may be inserted into a "carrier womb"—a surrogate mother, who carries the couple's genetic offspring to term. If both partners are female, one person may donate her eggs (be the genetic parent) while the other carries the

assisted reproductive technology (ART) Any infertility treatment in which the egg is fertilized outside the womb.

in vitro fertilization An infertility treatment in which conception occurs outside the womb.

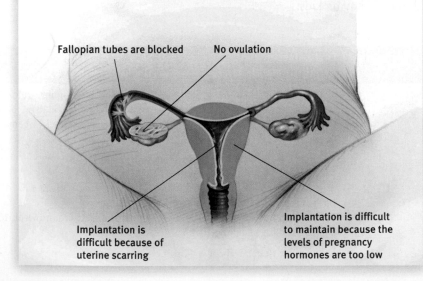

FIGURE 2.8: Some possible missteps on the path to reproduction: In this diagram, you can see some problems that may cause infertility in women. You can also use it to review the ovulation-to-implantation sequence.

Fallopian tubes are blocked   No ovulation

Implantation is difficult because of uterine scarring

Implantation is difficult to maintain because the levels of pregnancy hormones are too low baby (be the gestational mother) (Roache, 2016). If the same-sex couples are male, they search for a surrogate to carry their biological child.

In addition to the painful procedures—taking hormones, harvesting the eggs, waiting anxiously to see whether one or two will take—ART can be very expensive, especially when added "pregnancy players" are involved. As the cost of soliciting a donor egg can be as high as $30,000, and fees to the donor vary from $5,000 to $15,000, an investment can top $40,000—and that's before each roughly $12,000 round of treatment even begins! (See Jaffe & Diamond, 2011.)

The outcome is dicey. According to 2015 U.S. data, the odds of a woman under age 35 getting pregnant after a round of in vitro treatments was roughly fifty-fifty. Over age 44, success rates slid down to 1 in 12 (2015 Assisted Reproductive Technology, National Summary Report, n.d.).

Critics emphasize the headaches and heartaches involved in ART: the pain; the expense; the emotional cost of miscarrying; the risk of having fragile, small babies if two eggs are inserted and both come to term; and the issues attached to third-party arrangements ("Should I meet my egg or sperm donor?" "Do I tell my child this person exists?") (Johnson, 2013).

These criticisms ignore the life-changing blessing ART provides: "I could never have accomplished all of this myself," gushed one grateful Taiwanese woman. Another said: "I no longer felt pitiful. . . . My child represents the continuation of my life" (quoted in Lin, Tsai, & Lai, 2013, p. 194).

Now let's look at what happens when these wished-for pregnancies—or any pregnancies—reach the final step: exploring the miracle of birth.

Tying It All Together

1. Teratogen A caused limb malformations. Teratogen B caused developmental disorders. Teratogen A wreaked its damage during the _____ stage of prenatal development and was taken during the _____ trimester of pregnancy, while teratogen B probably did its damage during the _____ stage and was taken during the _____ trimester.

2. Seto's and Brandon's mothers each contracted rubella (German measles) during different weeks in their first trimester of pregnancy. Seto has heart problems; Brandon has hearing problems. Which teratogenic principle is illustrated here?

3. Monique is planning to become pregnant and asks her physician if it will be okay for her to have a glass of wine with dinner each night. What would her doctor answer if Monique lived in the United States? What might the doctor say if Monique lived in France?

4. Imagine that in 2021, a tornado hit Nashville, Tennessee. Based on the fetal programming research, which *two* predictions might you make about babies who were in utero during that time?
    a. They might be at higher risk of being born small.
    b. They might be at higher risk of developing premature heart disease.
    c. They might be at higher risk of being very thin throughout life.

5. Latasha gives birth to a child with Down syndrome, while Jennifer gives birth to a child with cystic fibrosis. Which woman should be more worried about having another child with that condition, and why?

6. To a friend who is thinking of choosing between chorionic villus sampling (CVS) and amniocentesis, mention the advantages and disadvantages of each procedure.

7. After years of unsuccessful fertility treatments, Jennifer and Brad are considering ART. First describe some pros and cons of this procedure. According to the text, what force is most critical in determining how well Jennifer has been coping with her troubles getting pregnant?

Answers to the Tying It All Together questions can be found at the end of this chapter.

Birth

LEARNING OUTCOMES

• List the three stages of birth.
• Contrast natural childbirth and c-sections.

During the last weeks of pregnancy, the fetus's head drops lower into the uterus. At their weekly visits to the health-care provider, women, such as Kim in the chapter-opening vignette, may be told, "It should be any minute now." The uterus begins to contract as it prepares for birth. The cervix thins out and softens under the weight of the child. Anticipation builds . . . and then—she waits!

> I am 39 weeks and desperate for some sign that labor is near, but so far NOTHING—no softening of the cervix, no contractions, and the baby has not dropped—the idea of two more weeks makes me want to SCREAM!!!

What sets off labor? One hypothesis is that the trigger is a hormonal signal that the fetus sends to the mother's brain. Once it's officially under way, labor proceeds through three stages.

Dilation

Crowning

Birth

FIGURE 2.9: Labor and childbirth: In the first stage of labor, the cervix dilates; in the second stage, the baby's head emerges and the baby is born.

Stage 1: Dilation and Effacement

This first stage of labor is the most arduous. The thick cervix, which has held in the expanding fetus for so long, has finished its job. Now it must *efface*, or thin out, and *dilate*, or widen from a tiny gap about the size of a dime to the width of a coffee mug or a medium-sized bowl of soup. This transformation is accomplished by *contractions*—muscular, wavelike batterings against the uterine floor. The uterus is far stronger than a boxer's biceps. Even at the beginning of labor, the contractions put about 30 pounds of pressure on the cervix to expand to its cuplike shape.

The contractions start out slowly, perhaps 20 to 30 minutes apart. They become more frequent and painful as the cervix more rapidly opens up. Sweating, nausea, and intense pain can accompany the final phase, as the closely spaced contractions reach a crescendo, and the baby is poised for the miracle of birth (see Figure 2.9).

Stage 2: Birth

The fetus descends through the uterus and enters the vagina, or birth canal. Then, as the baby's scalp appears (an event called *crowning*), parents get their first exciting glimpse of this new life. The shoulders rotate; the baby slowly slithers out, to be captured and cradled as it enters the world. The prenatal journey has ended; the journey of life is about to begin.

Stage 3: The Expulsion of the Placenta

In the ecstasy of the birth, the final event is almost unnoticed. The placenta and other supporting structures must be pushed out. Fully expelling these materials is essential to avoid infection and to help the uterus return to its pre-pregnant state.

Threats at Birth

Just as with pregnancy, a variety of missteps may happen during this landmark passage into life: problems with the contraction mechanism; the inability of the cervix to fully dilate; deviations from the normal head-down position as the fetus descends and positions itself for birth (this atypical positioning, with feet, buttocks, or knees first, is called a *breech birth*); difficulties stemming from the position of the placenta or the umbilical cord as the baby makes its way into the world. Today, these in-transit troubles are easily surmounted through obstetrical techniques. This was not the case in the past, however.

Birth Options, Past and Present

For most of human history, pregnancy was a grim nine-month march to an uncertain end (Kitzinger, 2000; Wertz & Wertz, 1989). The eighteenth-century New England preacher Cotton Mather captured the emotions of his era when, on learning that a parish woman was pregnant, he thundered, "Your death has entered into you!" Not only were there the hazards involved in getting the baby to emerge, but a raging infection called childbed fever could also set in and kill a new mother (and her child) within days.

This classic nineteenth-century illustration shows just why early doctors were clueless about how to help pregnant women. They could not view the relevant body parts!

Women had only one another or lay midwives to rely on during this frightening time. So birth was a social event. Friends and relatives flocked around, perhaps traveling miles to offer comfort when the woman's due date drew near. Doctors were of little help, because they could not view the female anatomy directly. In fact, due to their clumsiness (using primitive forceps to yank the baby out) and their tendency to spread childbed fever by failing to wash their hands, eighteenth- and nineteenth-century doctors often made the situation worse (Wertz & Wertz, 1989).

Techniques gradually improved toward the end of the nineteenth century, but few wealthy women dared enter hospitals to deliver, as these institutions were hotbeds of contagious disease. Then, with the early-twentieth-century conquest of many infectious diseases, it became fashionable for affluent middle-class women to have a "modern" hospital birth. By the late 1930s, the science of obstetrics gained the upper hand, fetal mortality plummeted, and birth became genuinely safe (Leavitt, 1986). By the turn of this century, in the developed world, this conquest was virtually complete. In 1997, there were only 329 pregnancy-related maternal deaths in the United States (Miniño and others, 2002).

This watershed medical victory was accompanied by discontent. The natural process of birth had become an impersonal event. Women protested the assembly-line hospital procedures and objected to being strapped down and sedated in order to give birth. They eagerly devoured books describing the new Lamaze technique, which taught controlled breathing, allowed partner involvement, and promised undrugged births. During the women's movement of the 1960s and early 1970s, the natural-childbirth movement arrived.

Natural Childbirth

Natural childbirth, a vague label for returning the birth experience to its "true" natural state, is now embedded in the labor and birth choices available to women today. To avoid the hospital experience, some women choose to deliver in homelike birthing centers. They may use certified midwives rather than doctors and draw on the help of a *doula*, a nonmedical pregnancy and labor coach. Women who are committed to the most natural experience may give birth in their own homes. (Table 2.4 on the next page describes some natural birth options, as well as some commonly used medical procedures.)

natural childbirth Labor and birth without medical interventions.

Table 2.4: The Major Players and Interventions in Labor and Birth

NATURAL-BIRTH PROVIDERS AND OPTIONS

Certified midwife: Certified by the American College of Nurse Midwives, this health-care professional is trained to handle *low-risk* deliveries, with obstetrical backup should complications arise.

- **Plus:** Offers a birth experience with fewer medical interventions and more humanistic care.
- **Minus:** If the delivery suddenly becomes high risk, an obstetrician may be needed on the scene.

Doula: Mirroring the "old-style" female experience, this person provides loving emotional and physical support during labor, offering massage and help in breathing and relaxation, but not performing actual health-care tasks, such as vaginal exams. (Doulas have no medical training.)

- **Plus:** Provides caring support from an advocate.
- **Minus:** Drives up the birth expense.

Lamaze method: Developed by the French physician Ferdinand Lamaze, this popular method prepares women for childbirth by teaching pain management through relaxation and breathing exercises.

- **Plus:** Offers a shared experience with a partner (who acts as the coach) and the sense of approaching the birth experience with greater control.
- **Minus:** Doesn't necessarily work for pain control "as advertised"!

Bradley method: Developed by Robert Bradley in the 1940s, this technique is designed for women interested in having a completely natural, nonmedicated birth. It stresses good diet and exercise, partner coaching, and deep relaxation.

- **Plus:** Tailored for women firmly committed to forgoing any medical interventions.
- **Minus:** May set women up for disappointment if things don't go as planned and they need those interventions.

MEDICAL INTERVENTIONS

Episiotomy: The cutting of the perineum or vagina to widen that opening and allow the fetus to emerge (not recommended unless there is a problem delivery).*

- **Plus:** May prevent a fistula, a vaginal tear into the rectal opening, which produces chronic incontinence and pain.
- **Minus:** May increase the risk of infection after delivery and hinder healing.

Epidural: This most popular type of anesthesia used during labor involves injecting a painkilling medication into a small space outside the spinal cord to numb the woman's body below the waist. Epidurals are now used during the active stage of labor—effectively dulling much of the pain—and during c-sections, so that the woman is awake to see her child during the first moments after birth.

- **Plus:** Combines optimum pain control with awareness; because the dose can be varied, the woman can see everything, and she has enough feeling to push during vaginal deliveries.
- **Minus:** Can slow the progress of labor in vaginal deliveries, can result in headaches, and is subject to errors if the needle is improperly inserted. Concerns also center on the fact that the newborn may emerge "groggy."

Electronic fetal monitor: This device is used to monitor the fetus's heart rate and alert the doctor to distress. With an external monitor, the woman wears two belts around her abdomen. With an internal monitor, an electrode is inserted through the cervix to record the baby's heart rate through the fetal scalp.

- **Plus:** Shown to be useful in high-risk pregnancies.
- **Minus:** Can give false readings, leading to a premature c-section. Also, its superiority over the lower-tech method of listening to the baby's heartbeat with a stethoscope has not been demonstrated.

C-section: The doctor makes an incision in the abdominal wall and the uterus and removes the fetus manually.

- **Plus:** Is life-saving to the mother and baby when a vaginal delivery cannot occur (as when the baby is too big to emerge or the placenta is obstructing the cervix). Also is needed when the mother has certain health problems or when the fetus is in serious distress.
- **Minus:** As a surgical procedure, it is more expensive than vaginal delivery and can lead to more discomfort after birth.

---

*Late-twentieth-century research has suggested that the once-common U.S. practice of routinely performing episiotomies had no advantages and actually hindered recovery from birth. Therefore, in recent decades, the episiotomy rate in the United States has declined.

At the medical end of the spectrum, as Table 2.4 shows, lies the arsenal of physician interventions designed to promote a less painful and safer birth. Let's now pause for a minute to look at the last procedure in the table: the cesarean section.

The Cesarean Section

cesarean section (c-section) Delivering a baby surgically by extracting the fetus through incisions in the abdominal wall and uterus.

A **cesarean section** (or **c-section**), in which a surgeon makes incisions in the woman's abdominal wall and enters the uterus to remove the baby manually, is the final solution for labor and delivery problems. This operation exploded in popularity during the 1970s. By 2015, c-sections accounted for an amazing 1 in 3 U.S. deliveries (CDC, 2016). In Shanghai, China, where the former one-child policy made women frantic to have a perfect child, the percentage tops 1 in 2 (Hellerstein, Feldman, & Duan, 2016).

C-sections may be planned because the physician knows in advance that there are dangers in a vaginal birth. But, as in China, it's now fashionable in many countries for some affluent women to choose this operation. Women opt for c-sections because they mistakenly assume this procedure is more hassle-free and safer (in fact, as with any surgery, this delivery method is more dangerous than a natural birth).

Many of these procedures, however, are provoked by problems once labor has begun. What fraction of emergency c-sections is due to doctors' fears of legal liability ("I might get sued unless I get this baby out")? We don't know. What we do know is that the best-laid birth plans may not work out, and some women can feel upset if they had counted on having a child "the natural way":

Today, women have a variety of birth choices in the developed world. The woman in this photo is having a water birth.

> "I sort of feel like I failed in the birthing arena," said one Australian woman. . . . "Logically, I knew that the c-section was necessary, but somehow I think if I was slim . . . and had not eaten as much ice cream that would not have happened."
>
> (quoted in Malacrida & Boulton, 2014, p. 18)

While some affluent women may bemoan their c-sections, the real tragedy is the horrifying lack of access to routine medical interventions in the least-developed regions of the world. Every day almost 900 women in impoverished regions of the world die of preventable pregnancy-related causes, such as postpartum hemorrhage, infections, or other complications that would prompt an immediate c-section in developed nations (World Health Organization [WHO], 2016). So let's keep in mind that billions of developing-world mothers-to-be still approach birth with a more basic concern than their Western counterparts. Their worries are not, "Should I *choose* a c-section?" It's not, "What birth method should I use?" Unfortunately, all too often, it's still: "Will I survive my baby's birth?" (Lester, Benfield, & Fathalla, 2010; Potts, Prata, & Sahin-Hodoglugil, 2010).

Tying It All Together

1. Melissa says that her contractions are coming every 10 minutes now. Sonia has just seen her baby's scalp emerge. In which stages of labor are Melissa and Sonia?

2. To a friend interested in having the most natural birth possible, spell out some of these options.

3. C-sections may sometimes be *overused/ underused* in the developed world; but life-saving medical interventions are *underutilized/ overutilized* in poor areas of the globe.

Answers to the Tying It All Together questions can be found at the end of this chapter.

The Newborn

Now that we have examined how the baby arrives in the world, let's focus on that tiny arrival. What happens after the baby is born? What dangers do babies face after birth?

Tools of Discovery: Testing Newborns

The first step after the newborn enters the world is to evaluate its health in the delivery room with a checklist called the *Apgar scale*. The child's heart rate, muscle tone, respiration, reflex response, and color are rated on a scale of 0 to 2 at one minute and

LEARNING OUTCOMES

- Describe the Apgar scale and the potential consequence(s) of low birth weight.

- Outline trends in infant mortality in the developed and developing worlds.

CHAPTER 2 Prenatal Development

Apgar scale A quick test used to assess a just-delivered baby's condition by measuring heart rate, muscle tone, respiration, reflex response, and color.

then again at five minutes after birth. Newborns with five-minute **Apgar** scores over 7 are usually in excellent shape. However, if the score stays below 7, the child must be monitored or resuscitated and kept in the hospital for awhile.

Threats to Development Just After Birth

After their babies have been checked out medically, most mothers and fathers eagerly take their robust, full-term baby home. But other parents hover at the hospital and anxiously wait. The reason, most often, is that their child has arrived in the world too small and/or too soon.

Born Too Small and Too Soon

low birth weight (LBW) A weight at birth of less than 5½ pounds.

In 2010, about 15 million babies were born *preterm,* or premature—they entered the world more than three weeks early (Chang and others, 2013). In the United States, about 1 in every 11 babies is categorized as **low birth weight (LBW).** They arrive in the world weighing less than 5½ pounds. Babies can be designated as low birth weight because they either arrived before their due date or did not grow sufficiently in the womb.

Earlier in this chapter, I highlighted smoking and maternal stress as risk factors for going into labor early and/or having a low-birth-weight baby. But uncontrollable influences—such as an infection that prematurely ruptures the amniotic sac, or a cervix that cannot withstand the pressure of the growing fetus's weight—also can cause this too-early or excessively small arrival into life.

You might assume that prematurity has declined in tandem with our pregnancy medical advances. Not so! Ironically, the same cutting-edge procedures discussed earlier, such as c-sections on demand and ART, boost the probability of a baby leaving the womb early and being more frail (Chang and others, 2013).

very low birth weight (VLBW) A weight at birth of less than 3¼ pounds.

neonatal intensive care unit (NICU) A special hospital unit that treats at-risk newborns, such as low-birth-weight and very-low-birth-weight babies.

Many early arrivals are fine. The vulnerable newborns are the 1.4 percent classified as **very low birth weight (VLBW),** who weigh less than 3¼ pounds. When these infants are delivered, often *very* prematurely, they are immediately rushed to a major medical center to enter a special hospital unit for frail newborns—the **neonatal intensive care unit.**

> At 24 weeks my water broke, and I was put in the hospital and given drugs. I hung on, and then, at week 26, gave birth. Peter was sent by ambulance to Children's Hospital. When I first saw my son, he had needles in every point of his body and was wrapped in plastic to keep his skin from drying out. Peter's intestines had a hole in them, and the doctor had to perform an emergency operation. But Peter made it! . . . Now it's four months later, and my husband and I are about to bring our miracle baby home.

Peter was lucky. He escaped the fate of the more than 1 million babies who die each year as a consequence of being very premature (Chang and others, 2013). Is this survival story purchased at the price of a life of pain? Enduring health problems are a serious risk with newborns such as Peter, born too soon and excessively small. Study after study suggests low birth weight can compromise brain development (Rose and others, 2014; P. Yang and others, 2014). It can limit intellectual and social skills throughout childhood (Murray and others, 2014) and the adolescent years (Healy and others, 2013; Saigal and others, 2016; Yang and others, 2014)—in addition, as you know, to possibly promoting overweight and early age-related disease. And what about the costs? Astronomical sums are required to keep frail babies such as Peter alive—expenses that can bankrupt families and are often borne by society as a whole (Caplan, Blank, & Merrick, 1992).

When a child is born at the cusp of viability—at around 22 weeks—doctors, not infrequently, refuse to vigorously intervene (Duffy & Reynolds, 2011; Ramsay & Santella, 2011). But survival rates vary, depending on the individual baby and—very important—that child's access to high-quality care (Sjörs, 2010). Plus, due to dramatic neonatal advances occurring

This baby has an excellent Apgar score. Notice his healthy, robust appearance.

Experiencing the Lifespan   Marcia's Story

The service elevator at Peck Hall takes forever to get there, then moves in extra-slow motion up to the third floor. If, as sometimes happens, it's out of service, you are out of luck. It's about a 30-minute drive from my dorm in the motorized wheelchair, including the ramps. When it rains, there's the muck—slowing you up—keeping you wet. So I try to leave at least an hour to get to class.

My goal is to be at least five minutes early so I don't disrupt everything as I move the chair, back and forth, back and forth, to be positioned right in front. Because my bad eye wanders to the side, you may not think I can read the board. That's no problem, although it takes me weeks to get through a chapter in your book! The CP [cerebral palsy], as you know, affects my vocal cords, making it hard to get a sentence out. But I won't be ashamed. I am determined to participate in class. I have my note-taker. I have my hearing amplifier turned up to catch every sound. My mind is on full alert. I'm set to go.

I usually can take about two courses each semester—sometimes one. I'm careful to screen my teachers to make sure they will work with me. I'm almost 30 and still only a junior, but I'm determined to get my degree. I'd like to be a counselor and work with CP kids. I know all about it—the troubles, the physical pain, what people are like.

I'm not sure exactly what week I was born, but it wasn't really all that early; maybe two months at the most. My problem was being incredibly small. They think my mom might have gotten an infection that caused me to be born weighing less than one pound. The doctors were sure I'd never make it. But I proved everyone wrong. Once I got out of the ICU and, at about eight months, went into convulsions, and then had a stroke, everyone thought that would be the end again. They were wrong. I want to keep proving them wrong as long as I live.

I've had tons of physical therapy, and a few surgeries; so I can get up from a chair and walk around a room. But it took me until about age five to begin to speak or take my first step. The worst time of my life was elementary school—the kids who make fun of you; call you a freak. In high school, and especially here at MTSU, things are much better. I've made close friends, both in the disability community and outside. Actually, I'm a well-known figure, especially since I've been here so long! Everyone on campus greets me with a smile as I scoot around.

In my future? I'd love to get married and adopt a kid. OK, I know that's going to be hard. Because of my speech problem, I know you're thinking it's going to be hard to be a counselor, too. But I'm determined to keep trying, and take every day as a blessing. Life is very special. I've always been living on borrowed time.

---

during the 1980s, many more small babies are now living to adulthood unimpaired (Baron & Rey-Casserly, 2010). I have vividly seen these statistics in operation when, in recent years, a student proudly informed our class: "I weighed less than 2 pounds at birth" or "I was born at the twenty-sixth week of life."

Even when they do have disabilities, these tiny babies can have a full life. Listen to my former student Marcia, whose 15-ounce body at birth would have easily fit in the palm of your hand—and whom no doctor believed was capable of surviving. Marcia, as the Experiencing the Lifespan box describes, is partially deaf, blind in one eye, and suffers from the disorder cerebral palsy. She was born with the sensory impairments that, as research shows, predict tiny babies will almost certainly have enduring difficulties functioning in the world (Saigal and others, 2016). But rarely have I met someone so upbeat, joyous, and fully engaged in life.

infant mortality Death during the first year of life.

The Unthinkable: Infant Mortality

In the developed world, prematurity is the primary cause of **infant mortality**—the term for deaths occurring within the first year of life. The good news is that in affluent nations, infant mortality is at a historic low (see Figure 2.10 on the next page). The bad news is the dismal standing of the United States compared to many other industrialized countries. Why does the United States rank a humiliating fifty-sixth in this basic marker of a society's health (Central Intelligence Agency [CIA], 2017)? The main cause lies in income inequalities, stress, poor health practices, and limited access to high-quality prenatal care.

This baby weighing less than one pound was incredibly lucky to make it out of the womb alive—but she is at high risk for having enduring problems as she travels through life.

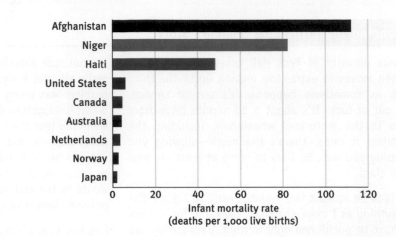

FIGURE 2.10: Deaths of infants under 1 year of age per 1,000 live births in selected countries (estimated data for 2016): Infant mortality rates vary tremendously around the globe. Notice the huge disparities between affluent and least-developed countries. Also notice that the United States has more than twice the infant mortality rate of Norway and Japan.

Data from Central Intelligence Agency, 2017.

The socioeconomic link to pregnancy and birth problems is particularly troubling. In every affluent nation—but especially the United States—poverty puts women at higher risk of delivering prematurely or having their baby die before age 1. So, sadly, I must end this chapter on a downbeat note. At this moment in history, our wealthiest nations are falling short of "cherishing" each woman during this landmark journey of life.

A Few Final Thoughts on Resilience

But I also can't leave you with the downbeat impression that what happens during pregnancy is destiny. Yes, researchers now believe events in utero play a role in how we develop. But a basic message of this book is that human beings are resilient. A quality environment matters greatly in shaping our life path. As discussed in Chapter 1, the environment can even epigenetically change our DNA (Belsky & Pluess, 2016; Moore, 2015).

Families come in many forms, and the love you have for *all* your adopted children is no different than if you personally gave birth. Take it from me as an adoptive mom!

Now that we are on the topic of DNA and genetics, I feel compelled to highlight a personal point, as an adoptive mom. In this chapter, you learned about the feelings of attachment (or mother–child bond) that often begin before birth. But I can assure you that to bond with a baby, you don't need to personally carry that child inside or share the same set of genes. So, just a reminder for later chapters when we scan the beautiful mosaic of families on our landscape today: The bottom-line blessing is being a parent, not being pregnant. Parenting is far different from personally giving birth!

The next two chapters turn directly to the joys of babyhood, as we catch up with Kim and her daughter Elissa, and track development during the first two years of life.

Tying It All Together

1. Baby David gets a two-minute Apgar score of 8; at five minutes, his score is 9. What does this mean?

2. Rates of premature births have *risen/ declined* due to ART, and low birth weight *always causes serious problems/ can produce problems/ has no effects* on later development.

3. Bill says, "Pregnancy and birth are very safe today." George says, "Hey, you are very wrong!" Who is right?
   a. Bill, because worldwide maternal mortality is now very low
   b. George, because birth is still unsafe around the world
   c. Both are partly correct: Birth is typically very safe in the developed world, but maternal and infant mortality remains unacceptably high in the poorest regions of the globe.

4. Sally brags about the U.S. infant mortality rate, while Samantha is horrified by it. First make Sally's case and then Samantha's, referring to the chapter points.

5. You want to set up a program to reduce prematurity and neonatal mortality among low-income women. List some steps that you might take.

Answers to the Tying It All Together questions can be found at the end of this chapter.

SUMMARY

The First Step: Fertilization

Every culture cherishes pregnant women. Some build in rituals to announce the baby after a certain point during pregnancy, and many use charms to ward off fetal harm. Pregnancy is a time of intense mixed emotions—joyous expectations coupled with uneasy fears.

The female reproductive system includes the **uterus** and its neck, the **cervix;** the **fallopian tubes;** and the **ovaries,** housing the **ova.** To promote **fertilization,** the optimum time for intercourse is when the egg is released. **Hormones** program **ovulation** and all of the events of pregnancy. At intercourse, hundreds of millions of sperm, produced in the **testes,** are ejaculated, but only a small fraction make their way to the fallopian tubes to reach the ovum. When the single victorious sperm penetrates the ovum, the two 23 **chromosome** pairs (composed of **DNA,** segmented into **genes**) unite to regain the normal complement of 46 that form our body's cells.

Prenatal Development

During the first stage of pregnancy, the two-week-long **germinal stage,** the rapidly dividing **zygote** travels to the uterus, becomes a **blastocyst,** and faces the next challenge—**implantation.** The second stage of pregnancy, the **embryonic stage,** begins after implantation with the formation of the **placenta,** and ends around week 8. During this time, the **neural tube** forms and the major body structures are created, according to the **proximodistal, cephalocaudal,** and **mass-to-specific** principles of development.

During the third stage of pregnancy, the **fetal stage,** development is slower paced. The hallmarks of this stage are enormous body growth and construction of the brain as the **neurons** migrate to the top of the tube and differentiate. Another defining landmark of this seven-month phase occurs around week 22, when the fetus can possibly be **viable,** that is, survive outside the womb if born.

Pregnancy

The nine months of **gestation,** or pregnancy, are divided into **trimesters.** The first trimester is often characterized by unpleasant symptoms, such as morning sickness, and a relatively high risk of **miscarriage.** The landmarks of the second trimester are looking clearly pregnant, experiencing **quickening,** and often feeling intensely emotionally connected to the child. During the third trimester, the woman's uterus gets very large, and she anxiously awaits the birth.

A woman's feelings about being pregnant can be affected by career concerns, and **family–work conflict** is common when working mothers (and fathers) have a child. The most critical force affecting the emotional quality of pregnancy, however, is having a supportive partner. Dads, the neglected pregnancy partners, also feel bonded to their babies.

Threats to the Developing Baby

Rarely, babies are born with a **birth defect.** One possible cause is **teratogens,** toxins from the outside that exert their damage during the **sensitive period** for the development of a particular body part. In general, the embryonic stage is the time of greatest vulnerability, although toxins can affect the developing brain during the second and third trimesters also, producing **developmental disorders.** While there is typically a threshold level beyond which damage can occur, teratogens have unpredictable effects. Damage may not show up until decades later.

Any recreational drug is potentially teratogenic. Smoking during pregnancy is a risk factor for having a smaller-than-optimal-size baby. Drinking excessively during pregnancy can produce **fetal alcohol syndrome,** or *fetal alcohol spectrum disorder.* Because it raises **cortisol** levels, depression and intense stress during pregnancy can produce premature labor and lead to smaller-than-normal babies. **Fetal programming research** suggests that natural (or human-made) disasters can have enduring epigenetic effects, because being born small may prime babies for obesity and premature, age-related chronic diseases.

The second major cause of prenatal problems is genuinely "genetic"—chromosomal problems and single-gene diseases. **Down syndrome** is one of the few disorders in which babies born with an abnormal number of chromosomes survive. Although Down syndrome, caused by having an extra chromosome on pair 21, produces intellectual disability and other health problems, babies with this condition do live fulfilling lives.

With **single-gene disorders,** a specific gene passed down from one's parents causes the disease. In **dominant disorders,** a person who harbors a single copy of the gene gets ill, and each child born to this couple (one of whom has the disease) has a fifty-fifty chance of developing the condition. If the disorder is **recessive,** both parents carry a single copy of the "problem gene" that is not expressed in real life, but they have a 1-in-4 chance of giving birth to a child with that disease (that is, a son or daughter with two copies of the gene). With **sex-linked disorders,** the problem gene is recessive and lies on the X chromosome. If a mother carries a single copy of the gene, her daughters are spared (because they have two Xs), but each male baby has a fifty-fifty risk of getting the disease. Through advances in genetic testing, couples (and individuals) can find out if they harbor the genes for many diseases. **Genetic testing** poses difficult issues with regard to whether people want to find out if they have incurable adult-onset diseases.

Couples at high risk for having a baby with a single-gene disorder (or any couple) may undergo **genetic counseling** to decide whether they should try to have a child. During pregnancy, tests, including the **ultrasound,** and more invasive procedures such as **chorionic villus sampling** (during the first trimester) and **amniocentesis** (during the second trimester) allow us to determine the baby's genetic fate.

Infertility can be emotionally traumatic and socially isolating, especially for women because of their historic imperative to bear children. Problems getting pregnant are far from rare today, especially at older ages. The most radical intervention, **assisted reproductive technologies (ART),** such as **in vitro fertilization (IVF),** in which the egg is fertilized outside of the womb, is emotionally and physically demanding, costly, and offers no guarantee of having a baby. However, this landmark procedure has given couples who could never have conceived the chance to have a biological child.

Birth

Labor and birth consist of three stages. During the first stage of labor, contractions cause the cervix to efface and fully dilate. During the second stage, birth, the baby emerges. During the third stage, the **placenta** and supporting structures are expelled.

For most of history, childbirth was life-threatening to both the mother and the child. During the first third of the twentieth century, birth became much safer. This victory set the stage for the later-twentieth-century **natural childbirth** movement. Today, women in the developed world can choose from a variety of birth options, including **cesarean sections.** Impoverished, developing-world women do not have this kind of access or luxury of choices. Their main concern is surviving the baby's birth.

The Newborn

After birth, the **Apgar scale** and other tests are used to assess the baby's health. While most babies are healthy, **low birth weight** can compromise development. **Very-low-birth-weight** infants are most apt to have enduring problems and need careful monitoring in the **neonatal intensive care unit** during their early weeks or months of life.

Infant mortality is a serious concern in the developing world. While rates of infant mortality are generally very low in developed-world countries, the United States has a comparatively dismal standing compared to other affluent countries on this basic health parameter. Even though the environment in the womb (stress during pregnancy) can affect the baby, providing a high-quality environment shapes development throughout childhood (and adult life).

KEY TERMS

age of viability, p. 41

amniocentesis, p. 56

amniotic sac, p. 42

Apgar scale, p. 64

assisted reproductive technology (ART), p. 58

birth defect, p. 46

blastocyst, p. 39

cephalocaudal sequence, p. 40

cervix, p. 36

cesarean section (c-section), p. 62

chorionic villus sampling (CVS), p. 56

chromosome, p. 38

cortisol, p. 50

developmental disorders, p. 47

DNA (deoxyribonucleic acid), p. 38

dominant disorder, p. 53

Down syndrome, p. 52

embryonic stage, p. 39

fallopian tube, p. 36

family–work conflict, p. 45

fertilization, p. 37

fetal alcohol syndrome (FAS), p. 49

fetal programming research, p. 51

fetal stage, p. 41

gene, p. 38

genetic counselor, p. 55

genetic testing, p. 53

germinal stage, p. 39

gestation, p. 43

hormones, p. 43

implantation, p. 39

in vitro fertilization (IVF), p. 58

infant mortality, p. 65

infertility, p. 57

low birth weight (LBW), p. 64

mass-to-specific sequence, p. 40

miscarriage, p. 44

natural childbirth, p. 61

neonatal intensive care unit (NICU), p. 64

neural tube, p. 40

neuron, p. 40

ovary, p. 36

ovulation, p. 37

ovum, p. 36

placenta, p. 39

proximodistal sequence, p. 40

quickening, p. 44

recessive disorder, p. 53

sensitive period, p. 47

sex-linked single-gene disorder, p. 53

single-gene disorder, p. 52

teratogen, p. 47

testes, p. 37

trimester, p. 43

ultrasound, p. 55

umbilical cord, p. 42

uterus, p. 36

very low birth weight (VLBW), p. 64

zygote, p. 39

ANSWERS TO **Tying It All Together** QUIZZES

The First Step: Fertilization

1. ovaries, fallopian tubes, uterus; fertilization occurs in the fallopian tubes

2. ovaries for female; testes for male

3. Tell Tiffany that the best time to have intercourse is around the time of ovulation.

4. *She* is *more* apt to survive and *less* apt to be conceived.

Prenatal Development

1. germinal; embryonic; fetal. Organs are formed during the embryonic stage.

2. From the neural tube, a mass of cells differentiates during the late embryonic phase. During the next few months, the cells ascend to the top of the neural tube, completing their migration by week 25. In the final months of pregnancy,

the neurons elongate and begin to assume their mature structure.

3. (a) mass-to-specific (b) cephalocaudal (c) proximodistal

4. around 22–23 weeks

Pregnancy

1. In this second trimester, she will feel better physically and perhaps experience an intense sense of emotional connectedness when she feels the baby move. During the first trimester she may have been very tired, perhaps felt faint, and had morning sickness.

2. Your cousin may be reluctant to tell her employer she is pregnant because she worries that the news may negatively affect her career.

3. You may come up with a host of interesting possibilities. Here are a few of mine: Include fathers in all pregnancy and birth educational materials the clinic provides; strongly encourage men to be present during prenatal exams; alert female patients about the need to be sensitive to their partners; set up a clinic-sponsored support group for fathers-to-be.

Threats to the Developing Baby

1. Teratogen A most likely caused damage during the *embryonic stage* of development and was taken during the *first trimester* of pregnancy. Teratogen B probably did its damage during the *fetal stage* and was taken during the *second or third trimesters*.

2. Teratogens exert damage during the sensitive period for the development of a particular organ.

3. A doctor in the United States would advocate no alcohol, while a physician in France might say a glass of wine is fine.

4. a and b. They might be at higher risk of being born small and of developing premature heart disease.

5. Jennifer. Down syndrome is typically caused by an unlikely, random event. With cystic fibrosis, that single-gene recessive disorder, the mom (in this case, Jennifer) has a 1-in-4 chance of giving birth to another child with that disease.

6. Tell your friend that the plus of chorionic villus sampling is finding out a child's genetic fate in the first trimester. However, this procedure is more dangerous, carrying a slight risk of limb malformations and, possibly, miscarriage. Amniocentesis is much safer and can show a fuller complement of genetic disorders but must be performed in the second trimester. And in some U.S. states, should a

woman decide to terminate the pregnancy at this point, it may be illegal.

7. *Cons:* ART is expensive, requires effort, and causes physical symptoms, and the chance per cycle of getting pregnant is small—especially for older women. *Pros:* ART gives women (and men) who could never have a biological child a chance to have a baby who is genetically theirs! The best predictor of Jennifer's coping well is having a supportive spouse.

Birth

1. Melissa is in stage 1, effacement and dilation of the cervix. Sonia is in stage 2, birth.

2. "You might want to forgo any labor medications, and/or give birth in a birthing center under a midwife's (and doula's) care. Look into new options such as water births, and, if you are especially daring, consider giving birth at home."

3. C-sections may sometimes be *overused* in the developed world. But they are seriously *underutilized* in poor areas of the globe.

The Newborn

1. Baby David is in excellent health.

2. Rates of premature births *have risen* due to ART; and low birth weight *can produce problems* in later development.

3. c. While birth is very safe in the developed world, maternal and infant mortality is a serious problem in the least-developed countries.

4. Sally: The United States—like other developed countries—has made tremendous strides in conquering infant mortality. Samantha: The fact that the United States has higher infant mortality rates than other developed countries is incredibly distressing.

5. You can come up with your own suggestions. Here are mine: Increase the number of nurse-practitioners and obstetrician-gynecologists in poor urban and rural areas. Provide monetary incentives to health-care providers to treat low-income women. Offer special "healthy baby" educational programs at schools, community centers, and local churches. Make it easier for low-wage workers to see a health-care provider by providing incentives to employers. Set up volunteer programs to visit isolated pregnant single mothers. Target nutrition programs to low-income mothers-to-be.

CONNECT ONLINE:

LaunchPad
macmillan learning | Check out our videos and additional resources located at:
www.macmillanlearning.com

Infancy and Toddlerhood

This two-chapter part is devoted to infancy and toddlerhood. How does a helpless newborn become a walking, talking, loving child?

Chapter 3—**Physical and Cognitive Development in Infants and Toddlers** starts by offering an overview of brain development, then explores those basic newborn states: feeding, crying, and sleeping. Next, I chart sensory and motor development: What do babies see? How do newborns develop from lying helplessly to being able to walk? What can caregivers do to keep babies safe as they travel into the world? Finally, I'll offer an overview of infants' blossoming cognition and their first steps toward language, the capacity that allows us to enter the human community.

Chapter 4—**Emotional and Social Development in Infants and Toddlers** looks at what makes us human: our relationships. First, I'll explore the attachment bond between caregiver and child, then examine poverty and day care. The final part of this chapter focuses on toddlerhood—from age 1 to 2½. Toddlers are intensely attached to their caregivers and passionate to be independent. During this watershed age, when children are walking and beginning to talk, we first learn the rules of the human world.

Application to Developing Lives Parenting Simulation: *Babies and Toddlers*

Below is a list of questions you will answer in the Babies and Toddlers simulation module. As you answer these questions, consider the impact your choice will have on the physical, cognitive, and social and emotional development of your child.

Physical	Cognitive	Social and Emotional
• Will you get your baby vaccinated?	• What kind of activities are you going to expose your baby to (music class, reading, educational videos)?	• How will you soothe your baby when he or she is crying?
• Will you breast-feed your baby? If so, for how long?	• What kind of activities will you do to promote language development?	• Can you identify your baby's temperament?
• What kind of foods will you feed your baby during the first year?	• What is your child's Piagetian stage of cognitive development?	• Can you identify your baby's attachment style?
• How will you encourage motor development?		• What kind of discipline will you use with your child?
• How does your baby's height and weight compare to national norms?		

Left: © Nicole Hill/RubberBall/Age Fotostock

CHAPTER 3

Physical and Cognitive Development in Infants and Toddlers

In Chapter 2, I talked to Kim at the beginning of the third trimester, anxiously waiting for her child's birth. Now, let's pay her a visit and meet Elissa, her baby girl.

She's been here for 5 months and 10 days, and I feel like she's been here forever. For me, it was love at first sight and, of course, the same for Jeff. But the thrill is watching a wonderful person emerge day by day. Take what's happening now. At first, she couldn't care less, but a month ago, it was like, "Wow, there's a world out there!" See that baby seat? Elissa can make the colored buttons flash by moving her legs. When I put her in it, she bats her legs like crazy. She can't get enough of the lights and sounds. Now that she is finally able to reach, notice her hunger to grab for everything and the way she looks at your face—like she can get into your soul. Sometimes, I think she understands what I'm feeling . . . but I know she must be way too young for this.

Elissa doesn't cry much—nothing like other babies during the first three months. Actually, I was worried. I asked the doctor whether there was something wrong. Crying is vital to communicating what you need! The same is true of sleeping. I'm almost embarrassed to tell you that I have the only baby in history who has been regularly giving her mother a good night's sleep since she was 2 months old.

Breast-feeding is indescribable. It feels like I am literally making her grow. But, here I also was concerned. Could I do this? What helped me persevere through the painful first week was my supportive husband—and most important, the fact that my boss gave me paid time off from work. I feel sad for my friend, Nora, who had to abandon this incredible experience when she needed to go back to her job right after her son's birth.

Pick her up. Feel what it's like to hold her—how she melts into you. But notice how she squirms to get away. It's as if she is saying, "Mom, my agenda is to get moving into the world." I plan to YouTube every step now that she's traveling into life.

At 5 months of age, Elissa has reached a milestone. She is poised to physically encounter life. This chapter charts the transformation from lying helplessly to moving into the world and the other amazing physical and cognitive changes that occur during infancy and toddlerhood—that remarkable first two years of life.

To set the context, I'll first spell out some brain changes (and principles) that program development. Then, I'll chart those basic newborn states—eating, crying, and sleeping—and track babies' emerging vision and motor skills. The final sections of this chapter tour cognition and language, the capacity that makes our species unique.

Left: KIYOKO FUKUDA/a.collectionRF/amana images RF/Getty Images

- Define synaptogenesis, neural pruning, myelination, and brain plasticity.

What does this young baby see and understand about the tremendous loving object he is facing? That is the mystery we will be exploring in this chapter.

cerebral cortex The outer, folded mantle of the brain, responsible for thinking, reasoning, perceiving, and all conscious responses.

axon A long nerve fiber that usually conducts impulses away from the cell body of a neuron.

dendrite A branching fiber that receives information and conducts impulses toward the cell body of a neuron.

synapse The gap between the dendrites of one neuron and the axon of another, over which impulses flow.

synaptogenesis Forming of connections between neurons at the synapses. This process, responsible for all perceptions, actions, and thoughts, is most intense during infancy and childhood but continues throughout life.

myelination Formation of a fatty layer encasing the axons of neurons. This process, which speeds the transmission of neural impulses, continues from birth to early adulthood.

Setting the Context

What causes the remarkable changes—from seeing to walking to speaking—that unfold during infancy and toddlerhood? Answers come from scanning development in that masterpiece structure—the human brain.

The Expanding Brain

The **cerebral cortex,** the outer, furrowed mantle of the brain, is the site of every conscious perception, action, and thought. With a surface area 10 times larger than the monkey's and 1,000 times larger than the rat's, the cortex is what makes human beings different from any other species on earth.

Because of our immense cortex, humans are also unique in the amount of brain growth that occurs outside the womb. During the first four years of life, brain volume quadruples (Stiles & Jernigan, 2010). It takes more than two decades for the brain to fully mature. Actually, the cortex only starts taking over behavior a few months *after* birth.

During the fetal period and first year of life, the cells composing the brain migrate to the top of the neural tube (Paredes and others, 2016). When they reach this staging area, they explode into their mature form. The cells form long **axons**—fibers that conduct impulses away from the cell body. They sprout **dendrites**—treelike, branching ends. As the dendrites proliferate at junctions, or **synapses,** the axons and dendrites interconnect (see Figure 3.1).

Synaptogenesis, the process of making myriad connections, programs every skill—from Elissa's vigorous push-ups to composing symphonies or solving problems in math. Another critical transformation is called **myelination:** The axons form a fatty layer around their core. Just as a stream of water prevents us from painfully bumping down a water park slide, the myelin sheath is the lubricant that permits the neural impulses to speedily flow. This insulating layer may also determine which cells thrive (Stiles & Jernigan, 2010).

Synaptogenesis and myelination occur at different rates in specific brain areas (Dean and others, 2014). In the visual cortex, the part of the brain responsible for interpreting visual stimuli, the axons are myelinated by about age 1. In the frontal lobes, the brain region involved in reasoning, the myelin sheath is still forming into our twenties.

This makes sense. Seeing is a skill we need soon after birth. Visual abilities, as you will learn in this chapter, develop rapidly during our first year of life. But we won't need the skills to compose symphonies, do higher math, or competently make our way in the world until we become adults. So there are parallels between our unfolding abilities and the way our brain matures.

Neural Pruning and Brain Plasticity

So far, you might imagine that more neural connections equal superior skills. Not so! Neural loss is critical to development, too. Following a phase of lavishly producing synapses, each cortical region undergoes synaptic pruning and neural death. This shedding timetable also reflects our expanding abilities. It begins around age 1 in the visual cortex. It starts during late childhood in the frontal lobes. Just as weeding is critical to sculpting a beautiful garden, we need to get rid of the unnecessary neurons to permit the essential cells to flower.

Why does the brain undergo this frantic overproduction, followed by cutting back? Clues come from research suggesting that during infancy, synaptic connections progressively strengthen in more distant areas of the brain (Damaraju and others, 2014). Perhaps having an oversupply of connections allows us to

Peter Correz/The Image Bank/Getty Images

"recruit" from this wider pool and redirect these extra neurons to perform other functions, should we have a major sensory deficit or brain insult early in life (Fox, Levitt, & Nelson, 2010; Stiles & Jernigan, 2010). Actually, our cortex is malleable, or **plastic** (able to be changed), particularly during infancy and the childhood years.

Using brain scans, which measure the brain's energy consumption, researchers find that among people blind from birth, activity in the visual cortex is intense while reading Braille and localizing sounds in space. This suggests that, without environmental stimulation from the eye, the neurons programmed for vision are captured, or taken over, to strengthen hearing and touch (Collignon and others, 2011; Fox, Levitt, & Nelson, 2010).

A similar process occurs with language, normally represented in the left hemisphere of the brain. If an infant has a left-hemisphere stroke, with intense verbal stimulation the right hemisphere takes over, and language develops normally (Rowe and others, 2009). Compare this to what happens when a person has a left-hemisphere stroke after language is located firmly in its appropriate places. The result can be devastating—a permanent loss in understanding speech or forming words.

So, brain plasticity highlights the basic nature-combines-with-nurture principle that governs human life. Yes, the blueprint for our cortex is laid out at conception. But environmental stimulation is vital in strengthening specific neural networks and determining which connections will be pruned (Fox, Levitt, & Nelson, 2010). Before the pruning phase, the brain is particularly malleable—permitting us to grow a somewhat different garden should disaster strike. Still, as synaptogenesis is a lifelong process, we continue to grow, to learn, to develop intellectually from age 1 to age 101.

plastic Malleable, or capable of being changed (refers to neural or cognitive development).

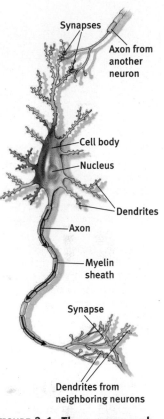

FIGURE 3.1: The neuron and synapses: Here is an illustration of the remarkable structure that programs every developing skill, perception, and thought. Notice the dendrites receiving information at the synapses and how impulses flow down the long axon to connect up with the dendrites of the adjoining cells.

This resilient baby has survived major surgeries in which large sections of his brain had to be removed. Remarkably—because the cortex is so *plastic* at this age—he is expected to be left with few, if any, impairments.

Table 3.1: Brain-Busting Facts to Wrap Your Head Around

- Our adult brain is composed of more than 100 billion neurons and, via synaptogenesis, makes roughly 60 trillion neural connections.

- As preschoolers, we have roughly double the number of synapses we have as adults—because, as our brain develops, roughly 40 percent of our synapses are ultimately pruned (see the text). So, ironically, the overall cortical thinning during elementary school and adolescence is a symptom of brain maturation.

- Specific abilities, such as language, that scientists had believed were localized in one part of the cortex are dependent on many brain regions. Moreover, the cortical indicators of "being advanced" in an ability shift in puzzling ways as a child gets older. For instance, while rapid myelination in the left frontal lobe predicts language abilities at age 1, by age 4 this relationship reverses, with linguistically advanced preschoolers showing more myelin in the right frontal lobe. Although there is a steeper-than-normal loss in cortical thickness when children show rapid IQ declines, boys and girls whose intelligence scores rise show no special cortical changes.

- Boys' brains, on average, are 10 percent larger than girls' brains, even during childhood, when both sexes are roughly the same size, body-wise.

- The most amazing finding relates to the surprising, dramatic variability in brain size from child to child. Two normal 10-year-old boys might have a twofold difference in brain volume, without having any difference in intellectual abilities!

Information from Dean and others, 2014; Giedd and others, 2010; Stiles & Jernigan, 2010.

Table 3.1 offers additional fascinating facts about neurons, synaptogenesis, and the pruning phase. Notice from the last item that, in the same way as the houses in your subdivision look different—although they may have had the same original plan (as each owner took charge of decorating his personal space)—scientists find remarkable variability in the brains of *normally* developing girls and boys (Giedd and others, 2010). And why should these variations be a surprise, given the diversity of interests and talents we develop in life!

Now keeping in mind the basic brain principles—(1) development unfolds "in its own neurological time" (you can't teach a baby a skill before the relevant part of the brain comes on-line); (2) stimulation sculpts neurons (our wider-world experiences physically change our brain); and (3) the brain is still "under construction" (and shaped by those same experiences) for as long as we live—let's explore how the expanding cortex works magic during the first years of life.

Tying It All Together

1. Cortez and Ashley are arguing about what makes our brain unique. Cortez says it's the size of our cortex. Ashley says it's the fact that we "grow" most of our brain after birth and that the cortex continues to mature for at least two decades. Who is right—Cortez, Ashley, or both students?

2. Latisha tells you that the myelin sheath speeds neural impulses and the more synaptic connections, the higher the level of development. Is Latisha totally correct? If not, describe how she is wrong.

3. When babies have a stroke, they may end up (choose one) *more/ less* impaired than they would be as adults, due to brain (choose one) *myelination/ plasticity*.

4. Which neural process is occurring in babies, mothers, and grandmas alike? (Choose one) *myelination/ synaptogenesis*

Answers to the Tying It All Together questions can be found at the end of this chapter.

Basic Newborn States

Visit a newborn and you will see simple activities: She eats, she cries, she sleeps. In this section, I'll spotlight each state.

Eating: The Basis of Living

Eating patterns undergo amazing changes during the first two years of life. Let's scan these transformations and then discuss nutritional topics that loom large in the first years of life.

Developmental Changes: From Newborn Reflexes to 2-Year-Old Food Cautions

Newborns seem to be eating even when sleeping—a fact vividly brought home to me by the loud smacking that erupted from my son's bassinet. The reason is that babies are born with a powerful **sucking reflex**—they suck virtually all the time. Newborns also are born with a **rooting reflex.** If *anything* touches their cheek, they turn their head in that direction and suck.

Reflexes are automatic activities. Because they do not depend on the cortex, they are not under conscious control. It is easy to see why the sucking and rooting reflexes are vital to surviving after we exit the womb. If newborns had to learn to suck, they might starve before mastering that skill. Without the rooting reflex, babies would have trouble finding the breast.

Sucking and rooting have clear functions. What about the other infant reflexes shown in Figure 3.2? Do you think the grasping reflex may have helped newborns survive during hunter-gatherer times? Can you think of why newborns, when adults stand them on a table, take little steps (the stepping reflex)? Whatever their value, these reflexes, and a few others, must be present at birth. They must disappear as the cortex grows.

As the cortex matures, voluntary processes replace these newborn reflexes. By month 4 or 5, babies no longer suck continually. Their sucking is governed by *operant conditioning.* When the breast draws near, they suck in anticipation of that delicious reinforcer: "Mealtime has arrived!" Still, Sigmund Freud named infancy the oral stage for good reason: During the first years of life, the theme is "Everything in the mouth."

This impulse to taste everything leads to scary moments as children crawl and walk. There is nothing like the sickening sensation of seeing a baby put a forgotten pin in his mouth or taste your possibly poisonous plant. My personal heart-stopping experience occurred when my son was almost 2. I'll never forget the frantic race to the emergency room after Thomas toddled in to joyously share a treasure, an open vial of pills!

LEARNING OUTCOMES

- Identify the purpose of newborn reflexes.
- Name two issues that limit breast-feeding.
- Describe the prevalence of undernutrition and food insecurity.
- List techniques to quiet a crying baby.
- Outline infant sleep changes and offer a strategy to promote baby sleep.
- Describe sudden infant death syndrome (SIDS).

sucking reflex The automatic, spontaneous sucking movements newborns produce, especially when anything touches their lips.

rooting reflex Newborns' automatic response to a touch on the cheek, involving turning toward that location and beginning to suck.

reflex A response or action that is automatic and programmed by noncortical brain centers.

Rooting Whenever something touches their cheek, newborns turn their head in that direction and make sucking movements.

Sucking Newborns are programmed to suck, especially when something enters their mouth.

Grasping Newborns automatically vigorously grasp anything that touches the palm of their hand. If the baby's brain is developing normally, each of these reflexes is present at birth and gradually disappears after the first few months of life.

FIGURE 3.2: Some newborn reflexes: In addition to the reflexes illustrated here, other newborn reflexes include the Babinski reflex (stroke a baby's foot and her toes turn outward), the stepping reflex (place a baby's feet on a hard surface and she takes small steps), and the swimming reflex (if placed under water, newborns can hold their breath and make swimming motions).

Luckily, a mechanism may protect toddlers from sampling every potentially lethal substance during their first travels into the world. Between ages 1½ and 2, children can revert to eating a few familiar foods, such as peanut butter sandwiches and apple juice. Evolutionary psychologists believe that, like morning sickness, this behavior is adaptive. Sticking to foods they know reduces the risk of children poisoning themselves when they begin to walk (Bjorklund & Pellegrini, 2002). Because this *2-year-old food caution* gives caregivers headaches, we need to reassure frantic parents: Picky eating can be *normal* during the second year of life (as long as a child eats a reasonable amount of food).

What is the best diet during a baby's first months? When is not having enough food a widespread problem? These questions bring up breast-feeding and global malnutrition.

Breast Milk: Nature's First Food

For most of human history, as I discussed in Chapter 1, babies faced perils right after birth. Infectious diseases and impure food and water ensured that many newborns did not survive beyond age 1 (Gordon, 2015). Before the early-twentieth-century public-health miracles, breast-feeding—for as long as possible—was a life-saving act (Preston, 1991).

Breast-feeding is a life-saver in poor nations today. In Southern Africa—Zambia, Zimbabwe, and Swaziland—mothers who nurse (without offering other liquids or foods) increase their infants' survival odds (Motsa, Ibisomi, & Odimegwu, 2016). In the developed world, exclusive breast-feeding is linked to widespread benefits, from making toddlers more resistant to the flu (McNiel, Labbok, & Abrahams, 2010) to accelerating myelin formation (Deoni and others, 2013) to producing 1-year-olds who are less reactive to stress (Beijers, Riksen-Walraven, & de Weerth, 2013). In one sophisticated longitudinal study, women who nursed for longer had kindergarteners with fewer disruptive behaviors—such as aggression and tantrums—if these children were genetically at-risk (Jackson, 2016).

But these findings involve correlations. And just because a relationship exists between two variables does not mean one *causes* the other. The research exploring breast milk's benefits does not control for maternal motivation (Sulaiman, Liamputtong, & Amir, 2016). In the study just mentioned, wouldn't a woman's passion to breast-feed a "fussy" infant suggest that she is generally a more committed mother (Chong and others, 2016)? Perhaps this intense commitment to caregiving mutes a child's temperamental tendency to misbehave.

The "correlation-is-not-causation" issue is especially problematic because, in the developed world, breast-feeding is *strongly* linked to social class. Women who nurse for months tend to be well-educated and affluent (Dennis and others, 2013). They spend more time in hands-on infant care (Smith & Ellwood, 2011). Is it really breast *milk* that promotes health, or the extra love that goes along with providing this natural food?

Exclusive breast-feeding for as long as possible is vital in nations where water and food are still impure. Breast-feeding remains an optimal choice in the developed world. Given these scientific realities, however, even the most motivated women may find it impossible to follow the six-month recommendation. What barriers can make exclusive breast-feeding for months an unusually difficult task?

This woman has the luxury of nursing her infant for months because she is affluent and doesn't need to return to work full-time after giving birth.

Work Demands

One reason for abandoning the breast-feeding advice—particularly in the United States—is the need to work (Flower and others, 2008; Vaughn and others, 2010). Women with paid-for maternity leave nurse their babies for longer (Mirkovic, Perrine, & Scanlon, 2016); work conflict dampens down the motivation to persist (Chong and others, 2016). In one striking comparison, U.S. mothers who returned to work full-time within three months after a child's birth breast-fed their babies an average 15 weeks *less* than their counterparts with part-time jobs (Lubold, 2016).

Imagine being a restaurant server or supermarket clerk who needs to work 40 or 50 hours per week to make ends meet (Guendelman and others, 2009). Would you have time to nurse your baby, no matter what the experts advised?

Physical Pain

But even when a woman has the luxury of breast-feeding for months, she can be let down by her body. This "natural" activity can be painful to carry out (Brown, Rance, & Bennett, 2016; M. A. Martin and others, 2016). As one new mother reported: "I never realized . . . that I would be reduced to tears every time I fed" (Sheehan, Schmied, & Barclay, 2013, p. 23). Another woman, forced to abandon the breast because of pain, anguished: "I felt so horrible . . . that I couldn't do this for my child" (quoted in Andrews & Knaak, 2013, p. 95).

Yes, exclusive breast-feeding for months can be ideal for all new mothers world-wide. But, because so many contemporary women cannot follow the six-month advice, it seems unfair to make mothers feel guilty when things don't work out. And rather than a person's milk delivery method, what's *really* important is the way a mother bonds with her child.

Malnutrition: A Serious Developing-World Concern

Breast-feeding gives *every* newborn a chance to thrive. However, there comes a time—at around 6 months of age—when babies need solid food. That's when the horrifying developing-world inequalities, described in the Experiencing the Lifespan box, hit (Caulfield and others, 2006).

How many young children suffer from **undernutrition**, having a serious lack of adequate food? For answers, epidemiologists measure **stunting**, the percentage of

> **undernutrition** A chronic lack of adequate food.
>
> **stunting** Excessively short stature in a child, caused by chronic lack of adequate nutrition.

Experiencing the Lifespan **A Passion to Eradicate Malnutrition: A Career in Public Health**

What is it like to battle malnutrition in the developing world? Listen to Richard Douglass describe his career:

I grew up on the South Side of Chicago—my radius was maybe 4 or 5 blocks in either direction. Then, I spent my junior year in college in Ethiopia, and it changed my life. I lived across the street from the hospital, and every morning I saw a flood of people standing in line. They would wait all day . . . , and eventually a cart would come and take away the dead. When I saw the lack of doctors, I realized I needed to get my master's and Ph.D. in public health.

In public health we focus on primary prevention, how to prevent diseases and save thousands of people from getting ill. My interest was in helping to eradicate Kwashiorkor in Ghana. What the name literally means is "the disease that happens when the second child is born." The first child is taken off the breast too soon and given a porridge that doesn't have amino acids, and so the musculature and the diaphragm break down. You get a bloated look (swollen stomach), and then you die. If a child does survive, he ends up stunted, and so looks maybe 5 years younger.

Once someone gets the disease, you can save their life. But it's a 36-month rehabilitation that requires taking that child to the clinic for treatment every week. In Ghana it can mean traveling a dozen miles by foot. So a

single mom with two or three kids is going to drop out of the program as soon as the child starts to look healthy. Because of male urban migration, the African family is in peril. If a family has a grandmother or great-auntie, the child can make it because this woman can take care of the children. So the presence of a grandma saves kids' lives.

Most malnutrition shows up after wars. In Ghana there is tons of food. So it's a problem of ignorance, not poverty. The issue is partly cultural. First, among some groups, the men eat, then women, then older children, then the babies get what is left. So the meat is gone, the fish is gone, and then you just have that porridge. We have been trying to impose a cultural norm that everyone sits around the dining table for meals, thereby ensuring that all the children get to eat. The other issue is just pure public health education—teaching families "just because your child looks fat doesn't mean that he is healthy."

I feel better on African soil than anywhere else. With poor people in the developing world who are used to being exploited, they are willing to write you off in a heartbeat if you give them a reason; but if you make a promise and follow through, then you are part of their lives. I keep going back to my college experience in Ethiopia . . . watching those people standing at the hospital, waiting to die. Making a difference for them is the reason why I was born.

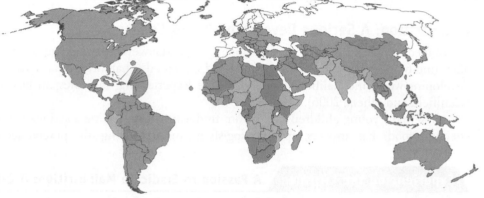

Latest country estimates of stunting in children aged: 0–5 years (☐, no data; ■, <20%; ■, 20–29.9%; ■, 30–39.9%; ■, ≥40%)

(B)

FIGURE 3.3: (A) Trends in stunting in different world regions, 1990–2020 (B) Stunting prevalence in different world regions today: The good news is that stunting has dramatically declined in Asia, Latin America, and the Caribbean (see chart A), although, as you can see on the map (B), this sign of severe malnutrition is still unacceptably high in Africa, Southeast Asia, and South Central Asia. Data from de Onis, Blössner, & Borghi, 2012.

micronutrient deficiency Chronically inadequate level of a specific nutrient important to development and disease prevention, such as vitamin A, zinc, and/or iron.

food insecurity According to U.S. Department of Agriculture surveys, the number of households that report needing to serve unbalanced meals, worrying about not having enough food at the end of the month, or having to go hungry due to lack of money (latter is *severe food insecurity*).

children under age 5 in a given region who rank below the fifth percentile in height, according to the norms for their age. This very short stature is a symptom of *chronic* inadequate nutrition, which compromises every aspect of development and activity of life (Abubakar and others, 2010; UNICEF, 2009).

The good news is that, as Figure 3.3A shows, stunting rates have dramatically declined in Asia, Latin America, and the Caribbean. The tragedy, as you can see in Figure 3.3B, is that in sub-Saharan Africa and South Asia, malnutrition still affects an alarming 2 in 5 girls and boys. In the developing world, **micronutrient deficiencies**—inadequate levels of nutrients such as iron, zinc, or vitamin A—are rampant. Disorders, such as Kwashiorkor (described in the Experiencing the Lifespan box on the previous page), can even strike when there is ample food.

How many young children are stunted or chronically hungry in the United States? In 2015, more than 1 in 6 (17 percent) of U.S. households with children was **food insecure.** Caregivers reported not having the money to provide a balanced diet, or being worried that their funds for food might run out. About 1 in 11 families reported *severe food insecurity.* They sometimes went hungry due to lack of money.

Table 3.2: Major U.S. Federal Nutrition Programs Serving Young Children[†]

Food Stamp Program (now called SNAP, Supplemental Nutrition Assistance Program): This mainstay federal nutrition program provides electronic cards that participants can use like a debit card to buy food. Families with young children make up the majority of food stamp recipients.

Special Supplemental Nutrition Program for Women, Infants, and Children (WIC): This federally funded grant program is specifically for low-income pregnant women and mothers with children under age 5. WIC offers a monthly package of supplements tailored to the family's unique nutritional needs (such as infant formula and baby cereals) plus nutrition education and breast-feeding support.

Child and Adult Care Food Program (CACFP): This program reimburses child-care facilities, day-care providers, after-school programs, and providers of various adult services for the cost of serving high-quality meals. Surveys show that children in participating programs have higher intakes of key nutrients and eat fewer servings of fats and sweets than those who attend facilities that do not participate.

Information from U.S. Department of Agriculture, Food and Nutrition Service, 2014.

[†]This information was correct as of 2018; however, as the new Congress may cut funding for these services, the status of some programs may have changed by the time you are reading this book.

While rates of U.S. food insecurity vary—from more than 1 in 3 families in an impoverished Mississippi County, to under 1 in 25 in an affluent Virginia suburb—as of this writing (2018), low-income children have access to the nutrition-related entitlement programs described in Table 3.2 (Hunger and Poverty Facts and Statistics, 2016). So—at least for now—in the United States, this developing-world scourge is rare.

Crying: The First Communication Signal

At 2 months, when Jason cried, I was clueless. I picked him up, rocked him, and kept a pacifier glued to his mouth; I called my mother, the doctor, even my local pharmacist, for advice. Since it put Jason to sleep, my husband and I took car rides at three in the morning—the only people on the road were teenagers and other new parents like us. Now that my little love is 10 months old, I know why he is crying, and those lonely countryside tours are long gone.

Crying, that vital way we communicate our feelings, reaches its lifetime peak at around one month after birth (St. James-Roberts, 2007). However, a distinctive change in crying occurs at about month 4. As the cortex blossoms, crying rates decline, and babies use this communication to express their needs.

It's tempting to think of crying as a negative state. However, because crying is as vital to survival as sucking, when babies cry too little, this can signal a neurological problem (Zeskind & Lester, 2001). When babies cry, we pick them up, rock them, and give them loving care. So, up to a point, crying cements the infant–parent bond.

Still, there is a limit. When a baby cries continually, she may have that bane of early infancy—**colic.** Despite what some "friends" (unhelpfully) tell new mothers, it's a myth that inept parents produce colicky babies. Colic is caused by an immature nervous system. After they exit the cozy womb, some babies get unusually distressed when bombarded by stimuli, such as being handled or fed (St. James-Roberts, 2007). So we need to back off from blaming stressed-out caregivers for this biological problem of early infant life.

Imagine having a baby with colic. You feel helpless. You cannot do anything to quiet the baby down. There are few things more damaging to parental self-efficacy than an infant's out-of-control crying (Keefe and others, 2006).

The good news is that colic is short-lived. Most parents find that around month 4, their baby suddenly becomes a new, pleasant person overnight. For this reason, there is only cause for concern when a baby cries excessively *after* this age (Schmid and others, 2010).

colic A baby's frantic, continual crying during the first three months of life; caused by an immature nervous system.

Because it promotes intense skin-to-skin bonding, kangaroo care is an effective baby-calming technique.

skin-to-skin contact An effective calming strategy that involves holding a young infant next to a caregiver's body.

kangaroo care Carrying a young baby in a sling close to the caregiver's body. This technique is most useful for soothing an infant.

FIGURE 3.4: Mean number of hours babies sleep during the day and night, at 2 weeks, 3 months, and 6 months of age: This chart shows that particularly during the first three months of life, babies shift their cycle to mainly nighttime slumber (but unfortunately, infants continue to wake up several times each night).

Data from Figueiredo and others, 2016.

INTERVENTIONS **What Quiets a Young Baby?**

What calms a crying newborn? The familiar answer: Pick up the baby, hold her, rock her, feed her, provide a pacifier or anything that satisfies the need to suck.

Skin-to-skin contact, holding a baby close, has a clear physiological effect. It reduces newborn's levels of the stress hormone *cortisol* (Beijers, Cillessen, & Zijlmans, 2016). The best real-world evidence comes from the !Kung San hunter-gatherers of Botswana. In this culture, where mothers strap infants to their chests and feed them on demand, the frequency of colic is dramatically reduced.

Kangaroo care, using a baby sling, can even help premature infants grow (World Health Organization [WHO], 2003). In one experiment, developmentalists had mothers with babies in an intensive care unit carry their infants in baby slings for one hour each day. At 6 months of age, compared to a group given standard care, the kangaroo-care babies scored higher on developmental tests. Their parents were rated as providing a more nurturing home environment, too (Feldman & Eidelman, 2003).

Imagine having your newborn whisked away to spend weeks with strangers. Now, think of being able to caress his tiny body, the sense of self-efficacy that would flow from helping him thrive. So it makes sense that any cuddling intervention can have an impact on the baby and the parent–child bond.

Another baby-calming strategy is infant massage. From helping premature infants gain weight to treating toddler (and adult) sleep problems, massage enhances well-being from the beginning to the end of life (Field, Diego, & Hernandez-Reif, 2007, 2011).

We all know the power of a cuddle or a relaxing massage to soothe our troubles. Can holding and stroking in early infancy generally insulate children against stress? Consider this study with rats.

Because rodent mothers (like humans) differ in the "hands-on" contact they give their babies, researchers classified rats who had just given birth into one of three groups: high licking and grooming, average licking and grooming, and low licking and grooming. As adults, the lavishly licked and groomed rats reacted in a more placid way when exposed to stress (Menard & Hakvoort, 2007). We need to be cautious about generalizing this finding to humans. Advocating for the !Kung San approach to caregiving might be asking too much of modern moms. Still, the implication is clear: During the first months of life (or, for as long as you can), keep touching and loving 'em up!

Cuddles calm us from day 1 to age 101. However, as children get older, the reasons for their crying undergo fascinating changes. The long car ride that magically quieted a 2-month-old evokes agony in a toddler who cannot stand to be confined. First, it's swaddling, then watching a mobile, then seeing Mom enter the room that has the power to soothe. In preschool, it's monsters that cause wailing; during elementary school and teenager-hood, it's failing or being rejected by our social group. As emerging adults, we weep for a lost job or love. Our crying shows just where we are emotionally as we travel from babyhood until adult life!

Sleeping: The Main Newborn State

If crying is a crucial baby (and adult) communication signal, sleep is the quintessential newborn state. Visit a relative who has recently given birth. Will her baby be crying or eating? No, she is almost certain to be asleep. Two-week-old babies typically sleep for almost 14 hours out of a 24-hour day (Figueiredo and others, 2016, see Figure 3.4). And there is a reason for the saying, "She sleeps like a baby." Perhaps because it mirrors the whooshing sound in the womb, noise helps newborns zone out. The problem for parents is that babies wake up and start wailing, like clockwork, every 3 to 4 hours.

FIGURE 3.5: Sleep brain waves and lifespan changes in sleep and wakefulness: In chart A, you can see the EEG patterns associated with the four stages of sleep that first appear during adolescence. After we fall asleep, our brain waves get progressively slower (these are the four stages of non-REM sleep) and then we enter the REM phase during which dreaming is intense. Now, notice in chart B the time young babies spend in REM. As REM sleep helps consolidate memory, is the incredible time babies spend in this phase crucial to absorbing the overwhelming amount of information that must be mastered during the first years of life?

Data from Roffwarg, Muzio, & Dement, 1966.

Developmental Changes: From Signaling to Self-Soothing to Shifts in REM Sleep

During the first year of life, infant sleep patterns adapt to the human world. Within the first three months of life, as Figure 3.4 shows, sleep shifts toward nighttime hours. Then, by about 6 months of age, there is a milestone. The typical baby sleeps for 6 hours a night. At age 1, the typical pattern is roughly 12 hours of sleep a night, with an additional morning and afternoon nap. During year 2, the caretaker's morning respite to do housework or rest is regretfully lost, as children give up the morning nap. Finally, by late preschool, sleep often (although not always) occurs only at night (Anders, Goodlin-Jones, & Zelenko, 1998).

In addition to its duration and on-again/off-again pattern, infant sleep differs physiologically from our adult pattern. When we fall asleep, we descend through four stages, involving progressively slower brain-wave frequencies, and then cycle back to **REM sleep**—a phase of rapid eye movement, when dreaming is intense and our brain-wave frequencies look virtually identical to when we are in the lightest sleep stage (see Figure 3.5). When infants fall asleep, they immediately enter REM and spend most of their time in this state. It is not until adolescence that we undergo the adult sleep cycle, with four distinct stages (Anders, Goodlin-Jones, & Zelenko, 1998).

Although parents are thrilled to say, "My child is sleeping through the night," this statement is false. Babies *never* sleep continuously through the night. However, by about 6 months of age, many have the skill to become **self-soothing.** They put themselves back to sleep when they wake up (Goodlin-Jones and others, 2001).

Imagine being a new parent. Your first challenge is to get your baby to develop the skill of nighttime self-soothing. Around age 1, because your child is now put into the crib while still awake, there may be issues getting your baby to *go* to sleep. During pre-school and elementary school, the sleep problem shifts again. Now, it concerns getting the child *into* bed: "Mommy, can't I stay up later? Do I *have* to turn off the lights?"

Although it may make them cranky, parents expect to be sleep-deprived with a young baby; but once a child has passed the 5- or 6-month milestone, parents get agitated if an infant has never permitted them a full night's sleep. Parents expect sleep problems when their child is ill or under stress, but not the zombielike irritability

REM sleep The phase of sleep involving rapid eye movements, when the EEG looks almost like it does during waking. REM sleep decreases as infants mature.

self-soothing Children's ability, usually beginning at about 6 months of age, to put themselves back to sleep when they wake up during the night.

that comes from being chronically sleep-deprived for years. There is a poisonous bidirectional effect here: Children with chronic sleep problems produce irritable, stressed-out parents. Irritable, stressed-out parents produce childhood problems with sleep (Goldberg and others, 2013).

There are interesting variations. Some women get unusually agitated when a 1-year-old wakes up repeatedly during the night. Other mothers don't seem to mind. Based on measuring pregnant mothers' sleep, researchers discovered that how a person reacts depends on her unique sleep style. Women who needed a lot of sleep while their baby was in utero tended to get unusually depressed when their toddler woke up frequently. Their counterparts who slept less during pregnancy felt more upset when a child slept *through the night* (Newland and others, 2016)!

So, with sleep, it's important to have the right *person–environment fit*—a baby's behavior should mesh with the wider world (in this case, the parent world). Still, I don't want to minimize the impact of enduring sleep issues. One longitudinal study suggested chronic sleep problems that continue into preschool put children at risk for having difficulties regulating their emotions in elementary school (Williams and others, 2016).

INTERVENTIONS What Helps a Baby Self-Soothe?

Returning to infancy, what should parents do when their baby signals (cries out) from the crib? At one end of the continuum stand the behaviorists: "Don't reinforce crying by responding—and be consistent. Never go in and comfort the baby lest you let a variable reinforcement schedule unfold, and the child will cry longer." At the other pole, we have John Bowlby with his emphasis on the attachment bond, or Erik Erikson with his concept of *basic trust* (see Table 3.3). During the first year of life, both Bowlby and Erikson imply that caregivers should sensitively respond when an infant cries. These contrasting points of view evoke passions among parents, too:

> I feel the basic lesson parents need to teach children is how to be independent, not to let your child rule your life, give him time to figure things out on his own, and not be attended to with every whimper.

> I am going with my instincts and trying to be a good, caring mommy. Putting a baby in his crib to "cry it out" seems cruel. There is no such thing as spoiling an infant!

Where do you stand on this "Teach 'em" versus "Give unconditional love" controversy? Given that in a young baby the cortex has not fully come on-line, the behavioral "teach 'em not to cry" doesn't work during early infancy (Douglas & Hill, 2013; Stremler and others, 2013). But, by about month 7 or 8, it may be better

---

Table 3.3: Erikson's Psychosocial Stages

Life Stage	Primary Task
Infancy (birth to 1 year)	**Basic trust versus mistrust**
Toddlerhood (1 to 2 years)	Autonomy versus shame and doubt
Early childhood (3 to 6 years)	Initiative versus guilt
Middle childhood (7 to 12 years)	Industry versus inferiority
Adolescence to emerging adulthood (teens into twenties)	Identity versus role confusion
Early adulthood (twenties)	Intimacy versus isolation
Middle adulthood (forties to sixties)	Generativity versus stagnation
Late adulthood (late sixties and beyond)	Integrity versus despair

According to Erikson, in the first year of life, our mission is to feel confident that the human world will lovingly satisfy our needs. Basic trust is the foundation for the challenges we face at every life stage.

to hang back a bit, as experts believe that parents who immediately respond to crying are more at risk for having infants with sleep issues during the first year (Byers & Simon, 2017; Sadeh and others, 2016). Again, however, the decision is up to you. Each baby is different. And your own sleep will suffer most if you feel very guilty by not quickly responding when your baby wakes up!

Vigorous "settling activities"—carrying a child around at bedtime, making a big deal of an infant's getting to sleep—are correlated with sleep difficulties at age 5 (Sheridan and others, 2013). Therefore, new parents might metaphorically err on the side of letting sleeping dogs lie, meaning not make excessive efforts to quiet the child. Still, this doesn't mean don't get involved!

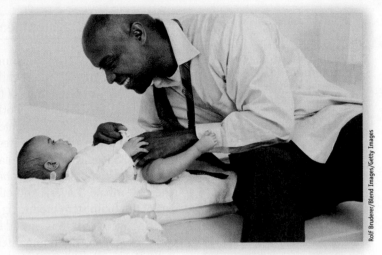

By lovingly preparing his baby for bed, this man is helping ensure a better night's sleep for *both* father and child. He also may be fostering basic trust—according to Erikson, the foundation for having a good life.

Research suggests that parents who use gentle, sensitive, and loving bedtime routines tend to have babies with fewer sleep problems (Teti and others, 2010). When caregivers spend ample time gently lulling infants to sleep, bedtime cortisol levels slide down (Philbrook & Teti, 2016). So, rather than any specific sleep strategy, the real key to promoting infant sleep is to put a child to bed with love.

And notice that when you feel disconnected from loved ones, you too may have trouble sleeping. To sleep soundly at *any age*, we need to feel cushioned by love.

The principle that love cushions sleep raises that controversial issue: Should parents have a baby regularly sleep with them in their bed?

To Co-Sleep or Not to Co-Sleep?

How do you feel about **co-sleeping,** or sharing a bed with a child? In the past, experts in individualistic societies strongly cautioned against co-sleeping (see Ferber, 1985). Behaviorists warned that bed sharing could produce "excessive dependency." Freudian theorists implied that co-sleeping might place a child at risk for sexual abuse. To ward off these evils, the standard practice was to place an infant's crib in a separate room.

co-sleeping The standard custom, in collectivist cultures, of having a child and parent share a bed.

In collectivist cultures, this solo sleep arrangement would qualify as infant abuse! (See Latz, Wolf, & Lozoff, 1999; Yang & Hahn, 2002.) Japanese parents, for instance, often separate to give each child a sleeping partner, because they believe co-sleeping is crucial to babies developing into caring, loving adults (Kitahara, 1989).

Who is right? As the research about co-sleeping is inconclusive (see Belsky, 2016, for a review), the key, again, is to arrange the right person–environment fit—that is, do what works best for you, but with this caution: In families where bed sharing is not part of the traditional culture, continual co-sleeping may be a symptom of marital distress. In one rural Pennsylvania survey, mothers who reported that they always had their babies share the family bed were more apt to report unhappy marriages, to (erroneously) see their babies as frequently waking up at night, and, ironically, were less emotionally available to their infants at bedtime than a comparison group whose babies slept alone (Teti and others, 2016).

What do U.S. parents do? National polls show most couples adopt a midway approach: They usually room share, but not bed share. They follow the professional advice that the best way to promote breast-feeding (and possibly guard against SIDS) is *not* to isolate infants in a separate room (Smith and others, 2016). What is *sudden infant death syndrome (SIDS)*?

studiomoment/iStock/Getty Images

This portable sleeping basket is user friendly around the world, but in the Maori culture, it qualifies as culture friendly, too.

sudden infant death syndrome (SIDS) The unexplained death of an apparently healthy infant, often while sleeping, during the first year of life.

🐾 Hot in Developmental Science: SIDS

Sudden infant death syndrome (SIDS) refers to the unexplained death of an apparently healthy infant, often while sleeping, during the first months of life. Although it strikes only about 1 in 1,000 U.S. babies, SIDS is a top-ranking cause of infant mortality in the developed world (Karns, 2001).

What causes SIDS? In autopsying infants who died during the peak risk zone for SIDS (about 1 to 10 months), researchers targeted abnormalities in a particular region of the brain. Specifically, SIDS infants had either too many or too few neurons in a section of the brain stem involved in coordinating tongue movements and maintaining the airway when we inhale (Lavezzi and others, 2010). SIDS has been linked to pathologies in the part of the brain stem producing cerebrospinal fluid, too (Lavezzi and others, 2013).

But even if SIDS is caused by biological pre-birth problems, this tragedy can have post-birth environmental causes. In particular, SIDS is linked to infants being inadvertently smothered, by being placed face down in a "fluffy" crib. During the early 1990s, this evidence prompted the American Academy of Pediatrics to urge parents to put infants to sleep on their backs. The "Back to Sleep" campaign worked, because from 1992 to 1997, there was a 43 percent reduction in SIDS deaths in the United States (Gore & DuBois, 1998).

Still, because placing babies on their backs requires that infants sleep separately in a crib, the "Back to Sleep" public health message contradicts the strong pro co-sleeping culture among non-Western groups. To circumvent this barrier, New Zealand scientists devised a strategy to permit Maori mothers to follow their traditional sleeping style and minimize the SIDS risk. They encouraged these women to return to another old-style practice—weaving a baby sleeping-basket. By placing this basket on parents' beds, co-sleeping has now become scientifically "correct" (Ball & Volpe, 2013)! 🐾

Table 3.4 offers a section summary in the form of practical tips for caregivers dealing with infants' eating, crying, and sleeping. Now it's time to move on to sensory development and moving into the world.

Table 3.4: Infants' Basic States: Summary Tips for Caregivers (and Others)

Eating

- Don't worry about continual newborn sucking and rooting. These are normal reflexes, and they disappear after the first months of life.

- As the baby becomes mobile, be alert to the child's tendency to put everything into the mouth and baby-proof the home (see the next section's discussion).

- Try to breast-feed, but if you need to work full-time or if nursing is too painful, don't berate yourself. The main benchmark of good motherhood is providing a child with loving care.

- Employers should make efforts to support nursing in the workplace. To really promote breast-feeding, *society* should offer mothers universal paid family leave!

- After the child is weaned, provide a balanced diet. But don't get frantic if a toddler limits her intake to a few "favorite foods" at around age 1½—this pickiness is normal and temporary.

Crying

- Appreciate that crying is crucial—it's the way babies communicate their needs—and realize that this behavior is at its peak during the first months of life. The frequency of crying declines and the reasons why a child is crying become clearer after early infancy.

- If a baby has colic, hang in there. This condition typically ends at month 4. Moreover, understand that colic has nothing to do with insensitive mothering.

- During the day, carry a young infant around in a "baby sling" as much as possible. In addition, employ infant massage to soothe the baby.

Sleeping

- Expect to be sleep-deprived for the first few months, until the typical infant learns to self-soothe; meanwhile, take regular naps. After that, expect periodic sleep problems and understand that children will give up their daytime nap at around age 2.

- After about 6 to 8 months of age, to promote self-soothing, don't pick up a sleeping infant at the first whimper. But the choice is really up to you—as the best way to promote sleep is to put a baby to bed with love.

- Co-sleeping is a personal decision; but the safest policy may be to room share, yet not routinely to have a baby sleep in a family bed.

- For sleep troubles occurring regularly into preschool, seek professional help.

Tying It All Together

1. You're a nurse in the obstetrics ward, and new parents often ask you why their babies turn their heads toward anything that touches their cheek and then suck. You say (pick two): *This is called the rooting reflex; This behavior is programmed by the lower brain centers to automatically occur at birth and disappear as the brain matures; This is a sign of early intelligence.*

2. Elaine tells you that breast-feeding is more difficult than medical authorities suggest. Make her argument, drawing on the points in this section.

3. Your sister and her husband are under enormous stress because of their 1-month-old's crying. Based on this section, give your relatives advice for soothing their child.

4. Jorge tells you that he's thrilled because last night his 6-month-old finally slept through the night. Is Jorge's child *ahead of schedule, behind schedule,* or *on time* for this milestone? Is Jorge right in saying, "My child is sleeping *through* the night"?

5. Poll your classmates, asking them if they believe in co-sleeping and whether they would immediately go in to quiet a crying infant. Do you find any differences in their answers by ethnicity, by gender, or by age?

Answers to the Tying It All Together questions can be found at the end of this chapter.

Sensory and Motor Development

Sleeping, eating, and crying are easy to observe; but suppose you could time-travel back to your first days of life. What would you experience through your senses?

One sense is operational before we leave the womb. Using ultrasound, researchers can see startle reactions in fetuses in response to noise, showing that rudimentary hearing capacities exist before birth. As I mentioned in the previous chapter, the basics of vision may also be in place by about the seventh month of fetal life.

Table 3.5 on page 88 lists other interesting facts about newborn senses. Now, let's focus on vision because the research in this area is so extensive, the findings are so astonishing, and the studies devised to get into babies' heads are so brilliantly planned.

What Do Newborns See?

Imagine you are a researcher who wants to figure out what a newborn can see. What do you do? You put the baby into an apparatus, present images, and watch his eyes move. Specifically, researchers use the **preferential-looking paradigm**—the principle

LEARNING OUTCOMES

- Explain how scientists find out what infants can see.
- Describe the face perception findings and the purpose of the visual cliff study.
- Name three core principles of motor development.
- Trace how motor development unfolds and its impact on caregivers.

preferential-looking paradigm A research technique to explore early infant sensory capacities and cognition, drawing on the principle that we are attracted to novelty and prefer to look at new things.

Table 3.5: Some Interesting Facts About Other Newborn Senses

Hearing: Fetuses can discriminate different tones in the womb (Lecanuet and others, 2000). Newborns prefer women's voices, as they are selectively sensitive to higher-pitched tones. At less than 1 week of age, babies recognize their mother's voice (DeCasper & Fifer, 1980). By 1 month of age, they tune in to infant-directed speech (described on page 100) communications tailored to them.

Smell: Newborns prefer the odor of breast milk to that of amniotic fluid (Marlier, Schaal, & Soussignan, 1998). Plus, smelling breast milk has a soothing effect; newborns cry more vigorously when facing a scentless breast (one covered with a transparent film) (Doucet and others, 2007).

Taste: Newborns are sensitive to basic tastes. When they taste a bitter, sour, or salty substance, they stop sucking and wrinkle their faces. They suck more avidly on a sweet solution, although they will stop if the substance grows too sweet. Having babies suck a sweet solution before a painful experience, such as an injection, reduces agitation and so is a helpful pain-management technique (Fernandez and others, 2003; Gibbins & Stevens, 2001).

habituation The predictable loss of interest that develops once a stimulus becomes familiar; used to explore infant sensory capacities and thinking.

that human beings are attracted to novelty and look selectively at new things. They draw on a process called **habituation**—the fact that we naturally lose interest in a new object after some time.

You can notice preferential looking and habituation in operation right now in your life. If you see or hear something new, you look up with interest. After a minute, you habituate and return to reading this book.

By showing newborns small- and large-striped patterns and measuring preferential looking, researchers find that at birth the ability to see clearly at distances is very poor. With a visual acuity score of roughly 20/400 (versus our ideal adult 20/20), a newborn would qualify as legally blind in many states (Kellman & Banks, 1998). But because the visual cortex matures quickly, vision improves rapidly, and by about age 1, infants see just like adults.

What visual capacities *do* we have at birth? A century ago, the first American psychologist, William James, described the inner life of the newborn as "one buzzing, blooming confusion." Studies exploring **face perception** (making sense of human faces) offer scientific data about the truth of James's ideas.

face-perception studies Research using preferential looking and habituation to explore what very young babies know about faces.

Focusing on Faces

Actually, when babies emerge from the womb, they selectively attend to the social world. When presented with the paired stimuli in Figure 3.6, newborns spend more time looking at the face pattern than at the scrambled pattern. They follow that facelike stimulus longer when it is moved from side to side (Farroni, Massaccesi, & Simion, 2002; Slater and others, 2010).

Newborns can make amazing distinctions. They prefer to look at a photo of their mother compared to one of a stranger (Bushnell, 1998). They also gravitate toward attractive-looking people!

Researchers selected photos of attractive and unattractive women, then took infants from the maternity ward and measured preferential looking. Babies looked at the attractive faces for significantly longer—61 percent of the time (Slater and others, 2010). Unhappily, our tendency to prefer people based on their looks seems somewhat biologically built in. (In case you are interested, more symmetrical faces tend to be rated as better-looking.)

Face preferences sharpen over time. Two-month-old infants preferentially look at speaking faces (those that move or make sounds) versus still faces (Bahrick and others, 2016). When researchers show photos of entrancing colored objects, 4-month-old babies gravitate to these visually captivating images rather than scanning a drabber face. But, no matter how exciting the competing stimulus, 8-month-olds prefer to gaze at a face (Kwon and others, 2016).

Face   Scrambled

FIGURE 3.6: Babies prefer faces: When shown these illustrations, newborns looked most at the facelike drawing. Might the fact that infants are biologically programmed to selectively look at faces be built into evolution to help ensure that adults give babies loving care?

At around the same age, an important lifelong pattern locks in. Infants selectively look at photos showing fearful expressions (versus happy or angry faces) (Grossman & Jessen, 2017). This **fear bias**—or hypersensitivity to facial expressions of fear, as you will learn in the next chapter—seems built into our species to keep us safe from harm.

A related, selective perception has not-so-nice effects. At approximately 9 months of age, infants around the world become less sensitive to facial differences in other ethnic groups (Kobayashi and others, 2016).

In a classic study demonstrating this visual narrowing, researchers tested European American babies at different points during the first year of life for their ability to discriminate between different faces within their own racial group and those belonging to other ethnicities (African American, Middle Eastern, and Chinese). While the 3-month-olds preferentially looked at "new faces" of every ethnicity, showing they could see the differences between individuals in each group, by 9 months of age, the babies could only discriminate between faces of their own ethnicity.

Why did this skill disappear? The cause, as you may have guessed, is cortical pruning—the fact that unneeded synapses in our visual system atrophy, or are lost (Slater and others, 2010). So if you have wondered why other races look more alike (compared to your own ethnic group, of course!), it's a misperception. You learned not to see these differences during your first year of life!

Is Prejudice Partly Prewired?

This tantalizing research suggests that spending our first years of life in a racially homogenous environment might promote prejudice because the resulting neural atrophy could blunt our ability to decode the emotions of other ethnic groups. Amazingly, in testing U.S. teens adopted from Eastern European or Asian orphanages (places where infants are only exposed to caregivers of their ethnicity), scientists discovered that this was true. The longer a child lived in an orphanage, the less sensitive that adolescent was at picking up facial expressions of people from other races. Moreover, brain scans showed an unusual spike in the amygdala (our brain's fear center) when these young people viewed "foreign" faces. Therefore, simply being born in a multicultural city, such as New York or Chicago, might make us more tolerant because that experience prewires us *visually* to be more sensitive to the feelings of other races (Telzer and others, 2013)!

The main conclusion, however, is that William James was wrong. Newborns don't experience the world as a "blooming, buzzing confusion." We arrive in life with built-in antennae to tune into the human world. But visual skills change as we mature, in sometimes surprising ways.

Now let's trace another visual capacity as it comes on-line—the ability to see and become frightened of heights.

Seeing Depth and Fearing Heights

Imagine you are a researcher facing a conundrum: How can I find out when babies develop **depth perception**—the ability to "see" variations in heights—without causing them harm? Elinor Gibson's ingenious solution was to develop an apparatus called the **visual cliff**. As Figure 3.7 shows, Gibson and her colleague placed infants on one end of a table with a checkerboard pattern while their mothers stood at the opposite end (Gibson & Walk, 1960). At the table's midpoint, the checkerboard design moved from table to floor level, so it appeared to the babies that if they crawled beyond that point, they would fall. Even when parents encouraged their children to venture beyond what appeared to be the drop-off, 8-month-old babies refused to move—showing that depth perception fully comes on-line, but only when infants begin to crawl.

Randy Faris/Corbis/VCG/Getty Images

While we might think this adorable 8-month-old child would be entranced by these paintings, her attention is apt to be riveted on the human (facial) scene.

fear bias The human tendency to be hypersensitive to fearful facial cues that, by alerting us to danger, may prevent us from getting injured or killed.

depth perception The ability to see (and fear) heights.

visual cliff A table that appears to "end" in a drop-off at its midpoint; used to test infant depth perception.

FIGURE 3.7: The visual cliff: Even though his mother is on the other side, this 8-month-old child gets anxious about venturing beyond what looks like the drop-off point in the table—demonstrating that by this age babies have depth perception.

In sum, the sick feeling we have when leaning over a balcony—"Wow, I'd better avoid falling into that space below"—emerged when we started moving into the world and needed that fear to protect us from getting hurt. How does mobility unfold?

Expanding Body Size

Our brain may expand dramatically after birth. Still, it's outpaced by the blossoming of the envelope in which we live. Our bodies grow to 21 times their newborn size by the time we reach adulthood (Slater, 2001). This growth is most dramatic during infancy, slows down during childhood, and speeds up again during the preadolescent years. Still, looking at overall height and weight statistics is not that revealing. This body sculpting occurs in a definite way.

Imagine taking time-lapse photographs of a baby's head from birth to adulthood and comparing your photos to snapshots of the body. While you would not see much change in the size and shape of the head, the body would elongate and thin out. Newborns start out with tiny "frog" legs timed to slowly straighten out by about month 6. Then comes the stocky, bowlegged toddler, followed by the slimmer child of kindergarten and elementary school. So during childhood, growth follows the same principle as inside the womb: Development, as Figure 3.8 suggests, proceeds according to the *cephalocaudal sequence*—from the head to the feet.

Now think of Mickey Mouse, Big Bird, and Elmo. They, too, have relatively large heads and small bodies. Might our favorite cartoon characters be enticing because they mimic the proportions of a baby? Did the deliciously rounded infant shape evolve to seduce adults into giving babies special care?

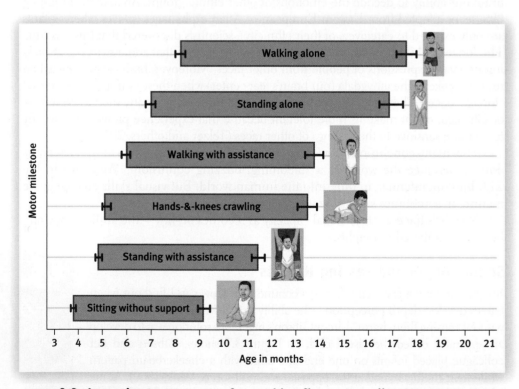

FIGURE 3.8: Approximate age ranges for reaching five motor milestones: Notice how motor development follows the cephalocaudal principle, and the remarkable age span in the times at which babies *normally* reach each skill.
Data from World Health Organization, 2006.

Mastering Motor Milestones

Actually, all three growth principles spelled out in the previous chapter—*cephalocaudal, proximodistal,* and *mass-to-specific*—apply to infant *motor milestones*, the exciting progression of physical abilities during the first year of life. First, babies lift their head, then pivot their upper body, then sit up without support, and finally stand (the cephalocaudal sequence). Infants have control of their shoulders before they can make their arms and fingers obey their commands (proximodistal sequence, from interior to outer parts).

But the most important principle in programming motor abilities throughout childhood is the *mass-to-specific* sequence (large before small and detailed). From the wobbly first step at age 1 to the home run out of the ballpark during the teenage years—as the neurons myelinate—big, uncoordinated movements are honed and perfected as children grow.

At 8 or 10 months of age, getting around is a challenge that babies approach in creative, unique ways.

moodboard-Mike Watson/Getty Images

Variations (and Joys) Related to Infant Mobility

Charting these milestones does not speak to the joy of witnessing them unfold—that landmark moment when your daughter masters turning over, after those practice "push-ups," or first connects with the bottle, grasps it, and awkwardly moves it to her mouth. I'll never forget when my son, after what seemed like years of cruising around holding onto the furniture, finally ventured (so gingerly) out into the air, flung up his hands, and, *yes, yes,* took his ecstatic first step!

The charts don't mention the hilarious glitches that happen when a skill is emerging—the first days of "creeping," when a baby can only move backward and you find him huddled in the corner in pursuit of objects that get farther way. Or when a child first pulls herself to a standing position in the crib, and her triumphant expression changes to bewilderment: "Whoops, now tell me, Mom, *how do I get down?*"

Actually, rather than viewing motor development in static stages, researchers stress the variability and ingenuity of babies' passion to get moving into life (Adolph, 2008). Consider the creeping or belly-crawling stage. Some babies scoot; others hunch over or launch themselves forward from their knees, roll from side to side, or scrape along with a cheek on the floor (Adolph & Berger, 2006). And can I *really* say that there was a day when my son mastered walking? When walking, or any other major motor skill, first occurs, children do not make steady progress (Adolph & Berger, 2006). They may take their first solo step on Monday and then revert to crawling for a week or so before trying, oh so tentatively, to tackle toddling again.

But suppose a child is behind schedule. Let's say your son is almost 15 months old and has yet to take his first solo step. And what about the fantasies that set in when an infant is ahead? "Only 8 months old, and he's walking. Perhaps my baby is special—a genius!"

What typically happens is that, within weeks, the worries become a memory and the fantasies about the future are shown to be completely wrong. Except in the case of children who have developmental disorders, the rate at which babies master motor milestones has no relation to their later intelligence. Since different regions of the cortex develop at different times, why should our walking or grasping-an-object timetable predict development in a complex function such as grasping the point of this book?

But even if a baby's early locomotion (physically getting around) does not mean he will end up an Einstein, each motor achievement provokes other advances.

Motor Milestones Have Widespread Effects

Consider, for instance, that landmark event: reaching. Because it allows babies to physically make contact with the world, the urge to grasp objects propels sitting, as a child will tolerate plopping over in her hunger to touch everything she can (Harbourne and others, 2013).

Now consider how crawling changes the parent–child bond (Campos and others, 2000). When infants crawl, parents see their children as more independent—people with a mind of their own. Many say this is the first time they discipline their child. So as babies get mobile, our basic child-rearing agenda emerges: Children's mission is to explore the world. Adults' job, for the next two decades, lies in limiting exploration—as well as giving love.

> **INTERVENTIONS** **Baby-Proofing, the First Person–Environment Fit**

baby-proofing Making the home safe for a newly mobile infant.

Motor development presents perils. Now safety issues become a concern. How can caretakers encourage these emerging skills and protect children from getting hurt? The answer is to strive for the right person–environment fit—that is, to **baby-proof** the house.

Get on the floor and look at life from the perspective of the child. Cover electrical outlets and put dangerous cleaning substances on the top shelf. Unplug countertop appliances. Take small objects off tables. Perhaps pad the furniture corners, too. The challenge is to anticipate possible dangers and stay one step ahead. There will come a day when that child can pry out those outlet covers or ascend to the top of the cleanser-laden cabinet. Unfortunately, those exciting motor milestones have a downside, too!

Tying It All Together

1. Your 3-month-old perks up when you start the vacuum cleaner, and then after a moment, loses interest. You are using a kind of _____ paradigm; and the scientific term for when your baby loses interest is _____.

2. Tania says, "Visual capacities improve dramatically during the first year of life." Thomas replies, "No, in some ways our vision gets worse." Who is correct: Tania, Thomas, or both students? Why?

3. One implication of the face perception studies is that the roots of adult prejudice begin (choose one) *at birth/ during the second 6 months of life/ after age 2.*

4. If Alicia's 8-month-old daughter is participating in a visual cliff study, when she approaches the drop-off, she should (choose one): *crawl over it/ be frightened.*

5. What steps would you take to baby-proof the room you are sitting in right now?

Answers to the Tying It All Together questions can be found at the end of this chapter.

LEARNING OUTCOMES

- Describe the purpose of Piaget's sensorimotor stage.
- Outline the development of objective permanence.
- List two critiques of Piaget's theory.
- Explain some findings relating to social cognition.

Cognition

Why *do* infants have an incredible hunger to explore, to reach, to touch, to get into every cleanser-laden cabinet and remove outlet plugs? For the same reason that, if you landed on a different planet, you would need to get the basics of reality down.

Imagine stepping out onto Mars. You would roam the new environment, exploring the rocks and the sand. While exercising your *walking schema*, or habitual way of physically navigating, you would need to make drastic changes. On Mars, with its minimal gravity, when you took your normal earthling stride, you would probably bounce up 20 feet. Just like a newly crawling infant, you would have to accommodate, and in the process reach a higher mental equilibrium, or a better understanding of

Table 3.6: Piaget's Stages: Focus on Infancy

Age (years)	Name of Stage	Description
0–2	Sensorimotor	The baby manipulates objects to pin down the basics of physical reality. This stage ends with the development of language.
2–7	Preoperations	Children's perceptions are captured by their immediate appearances. "What they see is what is real." They believe, among other things, that inanimate objects are really alive and that if a liquid looks visually different (for example, if it is poured from a short, wide glass into a tall, thin one), the amount actually becomes different.
7–12	Concrete operations	Children have a realistic understanding of the world. Their thinking is on the same wavelength as that of adults. While they can reason conceptually about concrete objects, however, they cannot think abstractly in a scientific way.
12+	Formal operations	Reasoning is at its pinnacle: hypothetical, scientific, flexible, fully adult. Children's full cognitive potential is reached.

life. Moreover, as a scientist, you would not be satisfied to perform each movement only once. The way to pin down the physics of this planet would be to repeat each action over and over again. Now you have the basic principles of Jean Piaget's **sensorimotor stage** (see Table 3.6).

Piaget's Sensorimotor Stage

Specifically, Piaget believed that during our first two years on this planet, our mission is to make sense of physical reality by exploring the world through our senses. Just as in the earlier Mars example, as infants *assimilate*, or fit the outer world to what they are capable of doing, they *accommodate* and so gradually mentally advance.

Let's take the "everything into the mouth" schema that figures so prominently during the first year of life. As babies mouth each new object—or, in Piaget's words, assimilate everything to their mouthing schema—they realize that objects have different characteristics. Some are soft or prickly. Others taste terrible or great. Through continual assimilation and accommodation, by age 2, babies make a dramatic mental leap—from relying on reflexes to reasoning and using symbolic thought.

Circular Reactions: Habits That Pin Down Reality

By observing his own children, Piaget discovered that driving all these advances were what he called **circular reactions**—habits, or action-oriented schemas, the child repeats again and again.

From the newborn reflexes, during months 1 to 4, **primary circular reactions** develop. These are repetitive actions centered on the child's body. A thumb randomly makes contact with his mouth, and a 2-month-old removes that interesting object, observes it, and moves it in and out. Waving her legs captivates a 3-month-old for hours.

At approximately 4 months of age, **secondary circular reactions** appear. As the cortex blossoms and the child begins to reach, action-oriented schemas become centered on the *outside* world. Here is how Piaget described his daughter Lucienne's first secondary circular reactions:

> Lucienne at 0:4 [4 months] is lying in her bassinet. I hang a doll over her feet which . . . sets in motion the schema of shakes. Her feet reach the doll . . . and give it a violent movement which Lucienne surveys with delight. . . . After the first shakes, Lucienne makes slow foot movements as though to grasp and explore. . . . When she tries to kick the doll, and misses . . . she begins again very slowly until she succeeds [without looking at her feet].
> (Piaget, 1950, p. 159 [as cited in Flavell, 1963, p. 103])

sensorimotor stage
Piaget's first stage of cognitive development, lasting from birth to age 2, when babies' agenda is to pin down the basics of physical reality.

circular reactions In Piaget's framework, repetitive action-oriented schemas (or habits) characteristic of babies during the sensorimotor stage.

primary circular reactions In Piaget's framework, the first infant habits during the sensorimotor stage, centered on the body.

secondary circular reactions In Piaget's framework, habits of the sensorimotor stage lasting from about 4 months of age to the baby's first birthday, centered on exploring the external world.

During the next few months, secondary circular reactions become better coordinated. By about 8 months of age, babies can simultaneously employ two circular reactions, using both grasping and kicking together to explore the world.

Then, around a baby's first birthday, **tertiary circular reactions** appear. Now, the child is not constrained by stereotyped schemas. He can operate like a real scientist, flexibly changing his behavior to make sense of the world. A toddler becomes captivated by the toilet, throwing toys and different types of paper into the bowl. At dinner, he gleefully spits his food out at varying velocities and hurls his bottle off the high chair in different directions to see where it lands.

How important are circular reactions in infancy? Spend time with a young baby, as she bats at her mobile or joyously pinwheels her legs. Try to prevent a 1-year-old from hurling plates from a high chair, flushing money down the toilet, or inserting bits of cookie into a USB slot. Then you will understand: Infancy is all about the insatiable drive to repeat interesting acts. (See Table 3.7 for a recap of the circular reactions, as well as a look at the sensorimotor substages.)

Piaget's concept of circular reactions offers a new perspective on those obsessions that drive adults crazy during what researchers call the **little-scientist phase** (and parents call the "getting into everything" phase). This is the time, around age 1, when the child begins experimenting with objects in a way that mimics how a scientist behaves: "Let me try this, then that, and see what happens." The reason you can't derail a 1-year-old from putting oatmeal into the computer, or

tertiary circular reactions In Piaget's framework, "little-scientist" activities of the sensorimotor stage, beginning around age 1, involving flexibly exploring the properties of objects.

little-scientist phase The time around age 1 when babies use tertiary circular reactions to actively explore the properties of objects, experimenting with them like scientists.

Table 3.7: The Circular Reactions: A Summary Table (with a Look at Piaget's Sensorimotor Substages)

PRIMARY CIRCULAR REACTIONS: 1–4 MONTHS

Description: Repetitive habits center around the child's own body.

Examples: Sucking toes; sucking thumb.

Rommel/Masterfile

SECONDARY CIRCULAR REACTIONS: 4 MONTHS–1 YEAR

Description: Child "wakes up to wider world." Habits center on environmental objects.

Examples: Grabbing for toys; batting mobiles; pushing one's body to activate the lights and sounds on a swing.

Substages: From 4 to 8 months, children use single secondary circular reactions such as those above; from 8 to 12 months, they employ two circular reactions in concert to attain a goal (that is, they may grab a toy in each hand, bat a mobile back and forth, coordinate the motions of toys).

© Christina Kennedy/PhotoEdit—All rights reserved.

TERTIARY CIRCULAR REACTIONS: 1–2 YEARS

Description: Child flexibly explores the properties of objects, like a "little scientist."

Examples: Exploring the various dimensions of a toy; throwing a bottle off the high chair in different directions; putting different kinds of food in the computer; flushing dollars down the toilet.

Substages: From 12 to 18 months, the child experiments with concrete objects; from 18 to 24 months, his little-scientist behavior transcends what is observable and involves using symbols to stand for something else. (I'll be describing the many advances ushered in by this ability to reason symbolically in later chapters.)

American Images Inc/Photodisc/Getty Images

clogging the toilet with your hard-earned wages (making a plumber a parent's new best friend) is that circular reactions allow infants to pin down the basic properties of the world.

Why do *specific* circular reactions, such as flushing dollar bills down the toilet, become irresistible during the little-scientist phase? This question brings me to Piaget's ideas about how babies progress from reflexes to the ability to think.

Tracking Early Thinking

How do we know when infants think? According to Piaget, one hallmark of thinking is deferred imitation—repeating an action that the baby witnessed at an earlier time. When Piaget saw Lucienne, at 16 months of age, mimic a tantrum she had seen another child have days earlier, he realized she had the mental skills to keep that image in her mind, mull it over, and translate it into action on her own. Another sign of reasoning is make-believe play. To pretend you are cleaning the house or talking on the phone like Mommy, babies must realize that something *signifies*, or stands for, something else.

But the most important sign of emerging reasoning is **means–end behavior**—when the child is able to perform a separate, or different, action to get to a goal. Pushing the toilet lever to make the water swirl down, manipulating a switch to turn on the light, screwing open a bottle to extract the juice—all are examples of "doing something different" to reach a particular end.

If you have access to a 1-year-old, you might try to construct your own means–end task. First, show the child something she wants, such as a cookie or a toy. Then, put the object in a place where the baby must perform a different action to get the treat. For instance, you might put the cookie in a clear container and cover the top with Saran Wrap. Will the baby ineffectively bang the side of the container, or will she figure out the *different* step (removing the cover) essential to retrieving what she wants? If you conduct your test by putting the cookie in an opaque container, the baby must have another basic understanding: She must realize that—although she doesn't see it—the cookie still exists.

Object Permanence: Believing in a Stable World

Object permanence refers to knowing that objects exist when we no longer see them—a perception that is, obviously, fundamental to our sense of living in a stable world. Suppose you felt that this book disappeared when you averted your eyes or that your house rematerialized out of nothing when you entered your driveway. Piaget believed that object permanence is not inborn. This perception develops gradually throughout the sensorimotor stage.

Piaget's observations suggested that during early infancy, life is a series of disappearing pictures. If an enticing image, such as her mother, passed her line of sight, Lucienne would stare at the place from which the image had vanished as if it would reappear out of thin air. (The relevant phrase here is "out of sight, out of mind.") Then, around month 5, when the *secondary circular reactions* are first flowering, there was

a milestone. An object dropped out of sight and Lucienne leaned over to look for it, suggesting that she knew it existed independently of her gaze. Still, this sense of a stable object was fragile. The baby quickly abandoned her search after Piaget covered that object with his hand.

Hunting for objects under covers becomes an absorbing game as children approach age 1. Still, around 9 or 10 months of age, children make a surprising mistake called the **A-not-B error:** Put an object in full view of a baby into one out-of-sight

Doug Goodman/Science Source

means–end behavior
In Piaget's framework, performing a different action to get to a goal—an ability that emerges in the sensorimotor stage as babies approach age 1.

object permanence In Piaget's framework, the understanding that objects continue to exist even when we can no longer see them, which gradually emerges during the sensorimotor stage.

A-not-B error In Piaget's framework, a classic mistake made by infants in the sensorimotor stage, whereby babies approaching age 1 go back to the original hiding place to look for an object even though they have seen it get hidden in a second place.

A minute ago, this 4-month-old girl was delightedly grabbing this little dog, but when this barrier blocked her vision, it was "out of sight, out of mind." If you have access to a young baby, can you perform this test to track the beginning of *object permanence*?

location, have the baby get it, and then move it to another place while the child is watching, and she will look for it in the initial place!

See if you can perform this classic test if you have access to a 10-month-old: Place an object, such as a toy, under a piece of paper (A). Then have the baby find it in that place a few times. Next, remove the toy as the infant watches and put it under a *different* piece of paper (B). What happens? Even though the child saw you put the toy in the new location, he will probably look under the A paper again, as if it had migrated unseen to its original place!

By their first birthday, children seem to master the basic principle. Move an object to a new hiding place and they look for it in the correct location. However, as Piaget found when he used this strategy but *covered* the object with his hand, object permanence does not fully emerge until children are almost 2 years old.

Emerging object permanence explains many puzzles about development. Why does peek-a-boo become a favorite activity at around 8 months? The reason is that a child now thinks there is *probably* still someone behind those hands, but doesn't know for sure.

Emerging object permanence offers a wonderful perspective on why younger babies are so laid back when you remove an interesting object, but then become possessive by their second year of life. Those toddler tantrums do not signal a new, awful personality trait called "the terrible twos." They simply show that children are smarter. They now have the cognitive skills to know that objects still exist when you take them away.

Finally, the concept of object permanence, or fascination with disappearing objects, plus means–end behavior makes sense of a 1-year-old's passion to flush dollar bills down the toilet or the compulsion to stick bits of cookie in a USB port. What could be more tantalizing during the little-scientist phase than taking a new action to get to a goal and causing things to disappear and possibly reappear? It also explains why you can't go wrong if you buy your toddler nephew a pop-up toy.

But during the first year of life, there is no need to arrive with any toy. Buy a toy for an infant and he will push it aside to play with the box. Your niece probably prefers fiddling with the TV remote to any object from Toys R Us. Toys only become interesting once we realize that they are different from real life. So a desire for dolls or action figures—or for anything that requires make-believe play—shows that a child is making the transition from the sensorimotor period to symbolic thought. With the concepts of circular reactions, emerging object permanence, and means–end behavior, Piaget masterfully made sense of the puzzling passions of infant life!

Critiquing Piaget

Piaget's insights transformed the way psychologists think about childhood. Research confirms the fact that children are, at heart, little scientists. The passion to decode the world is built into being human from our first months of life (Gopnik, 2010). However, Piaget's timing was seriously off. Piaget's trouble was that he had to rely on babies' actions (for instance, taking covers off hidden objects) to figure out what they knew. He did not have creative strategies, like preferential looking and habituation, to decode what babies understand before they can physically respond. Using these techniques, researchers realized that young infants know far more about life than this master theorist ever believed (Baillargeon, Scott, & Bian, 2016). Specifically, scientists now understand that:

- **Infants grasp the basics of physical reality well before age 1.** To demonstrate this point, developmentalist Renée Baillargeon (1993) presented young babies with physically impossible events, such as showing a traveling rabbit puppet that never appeared in a gap it had to pass through to reach its place on the other side (illustrated in Figure 3.9A). Even 5-month-olds looked astonished when they saw these impossible events. You could almost hear them thinking, "I know that's not the way objects should behave."

(A)   **(B)**

Impossible event   Impossible event

FIGURE 3.9: Two impossible events: At about 5 months of age, babies were surprised by the physically impossible sequence in part A—but they did not look surprised by the event in part B until about age 1. The bottom line: Infants understand the physical world far earlier than Piaget believed, but this knowledge occurs gradually.

Information from Baillargeon, 1993; Baillargeon & DeVos, 1991; Baillargeon & Graber, 1987.

information-processing approach A perspective on understanding cognition that divides thinking into specific steps and component processes, much like a computer.

social cognition Any skill related to understanding feelings and negotiating interpersonal interactions.

- **Infants' understanding of physical reality develops gradually.** For instance, while Baillargeon discovered that the impossible event of the traveling rabbit in the figure provoked astonishment around month 5, other research shows it takes until age 1 for babies to master fundamental realities, such as the fact that you cannot take a large rabbit out of a little container (shown in Figure 3.9B). (As an aside, that explains why "magic" suddenly becomes interesting around age 2 or 3.) Therefore, rather than viewing development in huge qualitative stages, contemporary researchers decode step by step how cognition *gradually* emerges.

Information-processing researchers use the metaphor of a computer with separate processing steps to decode children's (and adults') intellectual skills. For instance, instead of seeing means–end behavior as a capacity that suddenly emerges at age 1, a psychologist using this approach would isolate the talents involved in this milestone—memory, attention, the ability to inhibit one's immediate perceptions—and chart how each skill develops over time.

Table 3.8 on the next page showcases insights about babies' memories and mathematical capacities, derived from using this gradual, specific approach. In Chapter 6, I will describe how information-processing perspectives shed light on memory and thinking during elementary school. Now, it's time to tackle another question: What do babies understand about human minds?

Tackling the Core of What Makes Us Human: Infant Social Cognition

Social cognition refers to any skill related to managing and decoding people's emotions, and getting along with other human beings. One hallmark of being human is that we are always making inferences about people's feelings and goals, based on their actions. ("He's running, so he must be late"; "She slammed the door in my face, so she must be angry.") When do these judgments first occur? Piaget would say not before age 2 (or much later) because infants in the sensorimotor period can't think conceptually. Here, too, Piaget was incorrect. Babies make sophisticated judgments about intentions at an incredibly young age (Baillargeon, Scott, & Bian, 2016).

For this 1-year-old, pushing the buttons on the TV remote is utterly captivating. Information-processing researchers want to understand what specific skills made this boy capable of achieving this miraculous means–end feat.

LivingImages/istockphoto/Thinkstock/Getty Images

Table 3.8: Infant Memory and Conceptual Abilities: Some Interesting Findings

Memory: Researchers find that babies as young as 9 months of age can "remember" events from the previous day. Infants will push a button if they saw an adult performing that act 24 hours earlier. In another study, most 10-month-olds imitated an action they saw one month earlier. There even have been cases where babies this age saw an action and then remembered it a *year* later.*

Forming categories: By 7 to 9 months of age, babies are able to distinguish between animals and vehicles. They will feed an animal or put it to bed, but even if they watch an adult put a car to bed, they will not model her action. So the first classification babies make is between something that moves by itself or cannot move on its own. (Is it alive, like an animal, or inanimate?) Then, categorization abilities get more refined depending on familiarity. For example, 11-month-old infants can often distinguish between dogs and cats but not among dogs, rabbits, and fish.

Understanding numbers: By about 5 months of age, infants can make differentiations between different numbers—for instance, after seeing three dots on a screen, they will look preferentially at a subsequent screen showing four dots. Infants also have an implicit understanding of addition and subtraction. If they see someone add one doll to another, or take away a doll from a set, they look surprised when they see an image on a screen showing the incorrect number of dolls.

Information from Mandler, 2007.

*Because memory is central to cognition, a preverbal baby's skill in this area predicts the rapidity of language development and scores on intelligence tests.

After seeing this video sequence of events, even infants under 6 months of age preferentially reached for the "nice" tiger rather than the "mean" dog—showing that the fundamental human *social-cognitive* awareness that "he's acting mean or nice" emerges at a remarkably young age.

In one classic example, researchers first showed infants a video of a puppet or stuffed animal helping another puppet complete a challenging task (the nice puppet). In the next scene, another puppet hindered the stuffed animal from reaching his goal (the mean puppet). Then the experimenter offered the baby both puppets. And guess what? By the time they could reach (at about month 5), most infants grasped the "nice" stuffed animal rather than the puppet that acted "mean" (Hamlin & Wynn, 2011; Hamlin, 2013b).

This remarkable finding suggests we clue into motivations such as "She's not nice!" months before we begin to speak (Hamlin, 2013b). More astonishing, 8-month-old babies can make adult-like judgments about intentions. They preferentially reach for a stuffed animal that tries to help a puppet but fails. Here the reasoning may be: "He is a good guy. Even though he didn't succeed, he tried" (Hamlin, 2013a). Notice that these infants have intuitively mastered modern legal concepts we use in assessing criminal intent. Each system must determine: Was this an accident or did he mean it? He should only be punished if he *meant* to do harm.

But I cannot leave you with the sense that our species is primed to be mini-biblical King Solomons, behaving in a wise, ethical way. Some not-so-appealing human tendencies also erupt before age 1.

Using a similar procedure, the same research group found that 8-month-olds reach for a puppet they previously viewed hindering (acting mean) to another puppet if they view that puppet as different from themselves (Hamlin, 2013b; Hamlin and others, 2013). The principle here seems to be: "The enemy of my enemy is my friend." Or put more graphically: "I *like* people who are mean to people who are different than me." (In the next chapter, you will learn that a fear of anyone different—meaning, not a baby's primary caregiver—kicks in at exactly 8 months of age!)

In sum, during their second six months on this planet, babies can decode intentions—inferring underlying motivations from the way people behave. This mind-reading talent paves the way for that related human milestone: language, communicating our thoughts through words.

Tying It All Together

1. You are working at a child-care center, and you notice Darien repeatedly opening and closing a cabinet door. Then Jai comes over and pulls open the door. You decide to latch it. Jai—undeterred—pulls on the door and, when it doesn't open, begins jiggling the latch. And then he looks up, very pleased, as he manages to figure out how to open the latch. Finally, you give up and decide to play a game with Sam. You hide a stuffed bear in a toy box while Sam watches. Then Sam throws open the lid of the box and scoops out the bear. Link the appropriate Piagetian term to each child's behavior: *circular reaction; object permanence; means–end behavior.*

2. José, while an avid Piaget fan, has to admit that in important ways, this master theorist was wrong. José can legitimately make which two criticisms? (1) Cognition develops gradually, not in stages; (2) Infants understand human motivations; (3) Babies understand the basic properties of objects at birth.

3. Baby Sara watches her big brother hit the dog. Based on the research in this section, Sara might first understand her brother is being "mean" (choose one) *months before/ at/ months after age 1.*

Answers to the Tying It All Together questions can be found at the end of this chapter.

Language: The Endpoint of Infancy

Piaget believed that language signals the end of the sensorimotor period because this ability requires understanding that a symbol stands for something else. True, in order to master language, you must grasp the idea that the abstract word-symbol *textbook* refers to what you are reading now. But the miracle of language is that we string together words in novel, understandable ways. What causes us to master this feat, and how does language evolve?

LEARNING OUTCOMES

- Define the language acquisition device (LAD).
- List the stages of language development.
- Describe the function and features of infant-directed speech (IDS).

Nature, Nurture, and the Passion to Learn Language

The essential property of language is elasticity. How can I come up with this new sentence, and why can you understand its meaning, although you have never seen it before? Why does every language have a **grammar,** with nouns, verbs, and rules for organizing words into sentences? According to the linguist Noam Chomsky, the reason is that humans are biologically programmed to make "language," via what he labeled the **language acquisition device (LAD).**

Chomsky developed his nature-oriented concept of a uniquely human LAD in reaction to the behaviorist B. F. Skinner's nurture-oriented proposition that we learn to speak through being reinforced for producing specific words (for instance, Skinner argued that we learn to say "I want cookie" by being rewarded for producing those sounds by getting that treat). This pronouncement was another example of the traditional behaviorist principle that "all actions are driven by reinforcement" run amok (see Chapter 1). It defies common sense to suggest that we can generate billions of new sentences by having people reinforce us for every word!

Still, Skinner is correct in one respect. I speak English instead of Mandarin Chinese because I grew up in New York City, not Beijing. So the way our genetic program for making language gets expressed depends on our environment. Again, nature plus nurture work together to explain every activity of life.

Currently, developmentalists adopt a **social-interactionist perspective** on this core skill. They focus on the motivations that propel language (Hoff-Ginsberg, 1997). Babies are passionate to communicate. Adults are passionate to help babies learn to talk. How does the infant passion to communicate evolve?

grammar The rules and word-arranging systems that every human language employs to communicate meaning.

language acquisition device (LAD) Chomsky's term for a hypothetical brain structure that enables our species to learn and produce language.

social-interactionist perspective An approach to language development that emphasizes its social function, specifically that babies and adults have a mutual passion to communicate.

Table 3.9: Language Milestones from Birth to Age 2*

Age	Language Characteristic
2–4 months	*Cooing:* First sounds growing out of reflexes *Example:* "ooooh"
5–11 months	*Babbling:* Alternate vowel–consonant sounds *Examples:* "ba-ba-ba," "da-da-da"
12 months	*Holophrases:* First one-word sentences *Example:* "ja" ("I want juice.")
18 months–2 years	*Telegraphic speech:* Two-word combinations, often accompanied by an explosion in vocabulary *Example:* "Me juice"

*Babies vary a good deal in the ages at which they begin to combine words.

babbling The alternating vowel and consonant sounds that babies repeat with variations of intonation and pitch and that precede the first words.

holophrase First clear evidence of language, when babies use a single word to communicate a sentence or complete thought.

telegraphic speech First stage of combining words in which a toddler pares down a sentence to its essential words.

infant-directed speech (IDS) The simplified, exaggerated, high-pitched tones that adults and children use to speak to infants that function to help teach language.

Tracking Emerging Language

The pathway to producing language occurs in stages. Out of the reflexive crying of the newborn period comes *cooing* ("oooh" sounds) at about month 4. At around month 6, delightful vocal circular reactions called **babbling** emerge. Babbles are alternating consonant and vowel sounds, such as "da da da," that infants playfully repeat with variations of intonation and pitch.

The first word emerges out of the babble at around 11 months, although that exact landmark is difficult to define. There is little more reinforcing to paternal pride than when your 8-month-old genius repeats your name. But when does "da da da" really refer to Dad? In the first, **holophrase** stage of true speech, one word, accompanied by gestures, says it all. When your son says "ja" and points to the kitchen, you know he wants juice . . . or was it a jelly sandwich, or was he referring to his sister Jane?

Children accumulate their first 50 or so words, centering on the important items in their world (people, toys, and food), slowly (Nelson, 1974). Then, typically between ages 1½ and 2, there is a vocabulary explosion as the child begins to combine words. Because children pare down communication to its essentials, just like an old-style telegram ("Me juice"; "Mommy, no"), this first word-combining stage is called **telegraphic speech.** Table 3.9 summarizes these language landmarks and offers examples and the approximate time each milestone occurs.

Just as with the other infant achievements described in this chapter, developmentalists are passionate to trace language to its roots. It turns out that newborns are pre-wired to gravitate to the sounds of living things—as they suck longer when reinforced by hearing monkey and/or human vocalizations (versus pure tones). By 3 months of age, preferences get more selective. Now babies perk up *only* when they hear human speech (Vouloumanos and others, 2010).

By 8 months of age (notice the similarity to the visual-system atrophy research described earlier in this chapter), infants—like adults—lose their ability to hear sound tones in languages not their own (Gervain & Mehler, 2010). Simultaneously, a remarkable sharpening occurs. When language starts to explode, toddlers can hear the difference between similar sounds like "bih" and "dih" and link them to objects after *hearing this connection just once!*

Caregivers promote these achievements by continually talking to babies. Around the world, they train infants in language by using *infant-directed speech*. **Infant-directed speech (IDS)** (what you and I call *baby talk*) uses simple words, exaggerated tones, elongated vowels, and has a higher pitch than we use in speaking to adults (Hoff-Ginsberg, 1997). Although IDS sounds ridiculous ("Mooommy taaaaking baaaaby ooooout!" "Moommy looooves baaaaby!"), infants perk up when they hear this conversational style (Santesso, Schmidt, & Trainor, 2007). So we

FIGURE 3.10: **The relationship between gray matter (synaptogenesis) concentration in the cerebellum at 7 months of age and language comprehension at a child's first birthday:** This chart shows a close correlation between the quantity, or amount, of synaptogenesis in this particular brain region and a child's ability to understand language at age 1. The surprise is that this part of the brain—the cerebellum—does not qualify as a "higher brain center," as it programs balance and coordination.

Data from Deniz Can, Richards, & Kuhl, 2013.

naturally use infant-directed speech with babies, just as we are compelled to pick up and rock a child when she cries. Does IDS really help promote emerging language? The answer is yes.

Babies identify individual words better when they are uttered in exaggerated IDS tones (Thiessen, Hill, & Saffran, 2005). When adults are learning a new language, they benefit from the slow, repetitive IDS style. Therefore, rather than being just for babies, IDS is a strategy that teaches language across the board (Ratner, 2013). In fact, notice that when you are teaching a person *any* new skill you, too, are apt to automatically use IDS.

The close link between brain development at 7 months of age and children's speech understanding at age 1, shown in Figure 3.10, suggests that the neurological roots of language appear months before this capacity emerges (Deniz Can, Richards, & Kuhl, 2013; see also Dean and others, 2014). One surprising, observable sign of soon-to-emerge language is pointing with the right hand. Babies who demonstrate this pointing preference at an early age (let's say around 10 months of age) have larger later vocabularies because right-hand pointing is a general tip-off showing that the left-brain language centers are coming on-line (Mumford & Kita, 2016).

But even though our unique language timetable is genetically programmed (meaning due to biological differences), parents who use more IDS communications have babies who speak at a younger age (Ratner, 2013).

IDS is different from other talk. You don't hear this speech style on TV, at the dinner table, or on videos designed to produce 8-month-old Einsteins. IDS kicks in *only* when we communicate with babies one on one. So, if parents are passionate to accelerate language, investing millions in learning tools seems a distant second best to spending time *talking* to a child (Ratner, 2013).

Consistently pointing with her right hand points to the fact that this adorable 8-month-old may have a world-class vocabulary at age 2 or 3.

leungchopan/Shutterstock

A basic message of this chapter is that—from language to face perception to social cognition—our main agenda is to connect with the human world. The next chapter focuses on this number-one infant (and human) agenda by exploring attachment relationships during the first two years of life.

Tying It All Together

1. (a) "We learn to speak by getting reinforced for saying what we want." (b) "We are biologically programmed to learn language." (c) "Babies are passionate to communicate." Identify the theoretical perspective reflected in statements (a), (b), and (c): *Skinner's operant conditioning perspective; Chomsky's language acquisition device; a social-interactionist perspective on language.*

2. Baby Ginny is 4 months old; baby Jamal is about 7 months old; baby Sam is 1 year old; baby David is 2 years old. Identify each child's probable language stage by choosing from the following items: *babbling; cooing; telegraphic speech; holophrases.*

3. A friend makes fun of adults who use baby talk. Given the information in this section, is her teasing justified?

Answers to the Tying It All Together questions can be found at the end of this chapter.

SUMMARY

Setting the Context

Because our large **cerebral cortex** develops mainly after birth, during the first two years of life, the brain mushrooms. **Axons** elongate and develop a fatty cover called myelin. **Dendrites** sprout branches and at **synapses** link up with other cells. **Synaptogenesis** and **myelination** program every ability and human skill. Although the brain matures for decades, we do not simply "develop more synapses." Each region undergoes rapid synaptogenesis, followed by pruning (or cutting back). Before pruning, the brain is particularly **plastic**, allowing us to compensate for early brain insults—but synaptogenesis and learning occur throughout life.

Basic Newborn States

Eating patterns undergo dramatic changes during infancy. We emerge from the womb with **sucking** and **rooting reflexes,** which jump-start eating, as well as other **reflexes,** which disappear after the early months of life. Although the "everything into the mouth" phase of infancy can make life scary for caregivers, a 2-year-old's food caution can protect toddlers from poisoning themselves.

Breast-feeding is vital to survival in regions of the world without clean water and food. Although the link between nursing and infant health in developed nations can often be explained by confounding forces, such as greater maternal commitment and high social class, every public health organization advocates exclusive breast-feeding for the first 6 months of life. Most women, however, don't follow this advice. Breast-feeding is difficult when women need to work full-time or find nursing physically painful. The benchmark of being a good mother is unrelated to offering the breast; it's providing love.

Undernutrition, in particular **stunting** and **micronutrient deficiencies,** affect a significant fraction of young children in impoverished areas of the world. Although families with children in the United States may suffer from **food insecurity,** stunting is rare in the United States, thanks to government entitlement programs.

Crying is at its height during early infancy, and declines around month 4 as the cortex develops. **Colic,** excessive crying that disappears after early infancy, is basically a biological problem. Strategies for quieting babies include rocking, **skin-to-skin** contact, and massage. **Kangaroo care** helps at-risk premature babies grow.

Sleep is the basic newborn state, and from the 14-hour, waking-every-few hours newborn pattern, babies gradually adjust to sleeping through the night. **REM sleep** lessens and shifts to the end of the cycle. Babies, however, really do not ever sleep through the night. At about 6 months, many learn **self-soothing,** the ability to put themselves back to sleep when they wake up. The decision about whether to "let a baby cry it out" or respond immediately at night is personal, because the best way to foster sleep is to provide a caring bedtime routine. **Co-sleeping**—the norm in collectivist cultures—is controversial; and U.S. parents today typically room share, rather than share a bed.

Sudden infant death syndrome (SIDS)—when a young baby stops breathing, often at night, and dies—is a main cause of developed-world infant mortality. Although SIDS may be caused by impairments in the developing fetal brain, it tends to occur most often when babies sleep facedown. Therefore, a late-twentieth-century SIDS campaign urging parents to put babies to sleep on their backs (not stomachs) has been effective, although delivering this message is difficult in cultures that prize co-sleeping.

Sensory and Motor Development

The **preferential-looking paradigm** (exploring what objects babies look at) and **habituation** (the fact that we get less interested in looking at objects that are no longer "new") are used to determine what very young babies can see. Although at birth visual acuity is poor, it improves very rapidly. **Face-perception studies** show that newborns look at facelike stimuli, recognize their mothers, and even prefer good-looking people from the first weeks of life. At the same time as infants get more adept at reading facial cues and develop a **fear bias**, neural pruning causes babies to become less able to see facial variations in people of other races and ethnic groups. Sadly, this loss of sensitivity may promote prejudice against people outside of our ethnic group. **Depth perception** studies using the **visual cliff** show that babies get frightened of heights around the time they begin to crawl.

Infants' bodies lengthen and thin out as they grow. The cephalocaudal, proximodistal, and mass-to-specific principles apply to how the body changes and to emerging infant motor milestones. Although they do progress through stages when getting to walking, babies show incredible creativity and variability when they first attain various skills. Earlier-than-normal motor development does not predict advanced cognition; but as babies get more mobile, parents need to discipline their children and **baby-proof** their home.

Cognition

During Piaget's **sensorimotor stage**, babies master the basics of physical reality through their senses and begin to symbolize and think. **Circular reactions** (habits the baby repeats) help babies pin down the basics of the physical world. **Primary circular reactions**—body-centered habits, such as sucking one's toes—emerge first. **Secondary circular reactions**, habits centered on making interesting external stimuli last (for example, batting mobiles), begin around month 4. **Tertiary circular reactions**, also called **"little-scientist"** activities—like spitting food at different velocities just to see where the oatmeal lands—are the

hallmark of the toddler years. A major advance in reasoning that occurs around age 1 is **means–end behavior**—understanding the need to do something different to achieve a goal.

Piaget's most compelling concept is **object permanence**—knowing that objects exist when you no longer see them. According to Piaget, this understanding develops gradually during the first years of life. When this knowledge is developing, infants make the **A-not-B error,** looking for an object in the place where they first found it, even if it has been hidden in another location before their eyes.

Using preferential looking, and watching babies' expressions of surprise at impossible events, researchers now know that babies understand physical reality far earlier than Piaget believed. Because Piaget's stage model also does not fit the gradual way cognition unfolds, contemporary developmentalists may adopt an **information-processing approach,** breaking thinking into separate components and steps. Scientists studying **social cognition** find that babies understand people's motivations (and prefer people, based on judging their inner intentions) remarkably early in life.

Language: The Endpoint of Infancy

Language, specifically our use of **grammar** and our ability to form infinitely different sentences, sets us apart from any other animal. Although B. F. Skinner believed that we learn to speak through being reinforced, the more logical explanation is Chomsky's idea that we have a biologically built-in **language acquisition device (LAD). Social-interactionists** focus on the mutual passion of babies and adults to communicate.

First, babies coo, then **babble,** then use one-word **holophrases,** and finally, at age 1½ or 2, progress to two-word combinations called **telegraphic speech.** Caregivers naturally use **infant-directed speech (IDS);** exaggerated intonations and simpler phrases when they talk to babies. Talking to babies in IDS is better than any baby-genius tape in promoting this vital human skill.

KEY TERMS

ANSWERS TO **Tying It All Together** QUIZZES

Setting the Context

1. Both Cortez and Ashley are right. We are unique in our massive cerebral cortex, in growing most of our brain outside of the womb, and in the fact that the human cortex does not reach its adult form for more than two decades.

2. Latisha is only partly right. Synaptic loss and neural pruning are essential to fostering babies' emerging abilities.

3. When babies have a stroke, they may end up *less* impaired than during adulthood, due to *brain plasticity*.

4. *Synaptogenesis* is occurring in babies, mothers, and grandmas alike. *Myelination* (or formation of the myelin sheath) ends by the mid-twenties.

Basic Newborn States

1. You need to pick the first two statements: The rooting reflex is programmed by the lower brain centers to appear at birth and then go away as the cortex matures. Its appearance is definitely *not* a sign of early intelligence.

2. Elaine should say that breast-feeding is difficult if women need to work full-time. It also can be physically painful. This explains why many women don't follow the professional advice.

3. Tell your relatives to carry the child around in a baby sling (kangaroo care). Also, perhaps make heavy use of a pacifier and employ baby massage.

4. Jorge's child is right on schedule, but he's wrong to say his child is sleeping through the night. The baby has simply learned to self-soothe.

5. The answers here will depend on the class.

Sensory and Motor Development

1. You are using a kind of *preferential-looking* paradigm; the scientific term for when your baby loses interest is *habituation*.

2. Both Tania and Thomas are right. In support of Tania's "dramatic improvement" position, babies develop a remarkable sensitivity to facial nuances (such as their preference for good-looking people and the fear bias) early in life. Thomas is also correct that in some ways vision gets worse during infancy. He should mention the fact that by 9 months of age we have "unlearned" the ability to become as sensitive to facial distinctions in people of other ethnic groups.

3. The roots of adult prejudice may begin *during the second 6 months of life*.

4. The child should *be frightened* of the cliff.

5. Your answers might include installing electrical outlet covers; putting sharp, poisonous, and breakable objects out of a baby's reach; carpeting hard floor surfaces; padding furniture corners; installing latches on cabinet doors; and so on.

Cognition

1. Circular reaction = Darien; means–end behavior = Jai; object permanence = Sam.

2. Cognition develops gradually rather than in distinct stages; infants understand human motivations.

3. Baby Sara should pick up this idea *months before* age 1.

Language: The Endpoint of Infancy

1. (a) The idea that we learn language by getting reinforced reflects Skinner's operant conditioning perspective; (b) Chomsky hypothesized that we are biologically programmed to acquire language; (c) the social-interactionist perspective emphasizes the fact that babies and adults have a passion to communicate.

2. Baby Ginny is cooing; baby Jamal is babbling; baby Sam is speaking in holophrases (one-word stage); and baby David is using telegraphic speech.

3. No, your friend is wrong! Baby talk—or in developmental science terms, infant-directed speech (IDS)—helps promote early language.

CONNECT ONLINE:

 LaunchPad
macmillan learning | Check out our videos and additional resources located at:
www.macmillanlearning.com

CHAPTER 4

Emotional and Social Development in Infants and Toddlers

We've talked to Kim during pregnancy and visited when Elissa was a young baby. Now let's catch up with mother and daughter when Elissa is 15 months old.

Elissa had her first birthday in December. She's such a happy baby, but now if you take something away, it's like, "Why did you do that?" Pick her up. First everything is fine, and then she squirms and her arms go out toward me. She's busy walking, busy exploring, but she's always got an eye on me. When I make a motion to leave, she stops and races near. Elissa has a stronger connection to her dad now, because Jeff watches the baby some afternoons . . . but when she's tired or sick, it's still Mom.

It was difficult to go back to work. You hear terrible things about day care, stories of babies being neglected. I finally decided to send Elissa to a neighbor who watches a few toddlers in her home. I hated how my baby screamed the first week when I dropped her off. But it's obvious that she's happy now. Every morning she runs smiling to Ms. Marie's arms.

It's bittersweet to see my baby separating from me, running into the world, becoming her own person. The clashes are more frequent now that I'm turning up the discipline, expecting more from my "big girl." But mainly it's hard to be apart. I think about Elissa 50 million times a day. I speed home to see her. I can't wait to glimpse her glowing face in the window, how she jumps up, and we run to kiss and cuddle again.

Imagine being Kim, with your child the center of your life. Imagine being Elissa, wanting to be independent but needing your mother close. In this chapter, I'll focus on **attachment,** the powerful bond of love between caregiver and child.

My discussion of attachment starts a conversation that continues throughout this book. After exploring this core relationship, I'll turn to the wider world, first examining how that basic marker, socioeconomic status (SES), affects young children's development, then spotlighting day care, the setting where so many developed-world babies spend their days. The last section of this chapter focuses on the emotional challenges of **toddlerhood,** the famous time lasting roughly from age 1 to 2½ years. (Your tip-off that a child is a toddler is that endearing "toddling" gait that characterizes the second year of life.)

attachment The powerful bond of love between a caregiver and child (or between any two people).

toddlerhood The important transitional stage after babyhood, from roughly age 1 year to 2½.

Attachment: The Basic Life Bond

Perhaps you remember being intensely in love. You may be in that wonderful state right now. You cannot stop fantasizing about your significant other. Your moves blend with your partner's. You connect in a unique way. Knowing that this person is there gives you confidence. Your world depends on having your loved one close. Now you know how Elissa feels about her mother and the powerful emotions that flow from Kim to her child.

Setting the Context: How Developmentalists (Slowly) Got Attached to Attachment

During much of the twentieth century, U.S. psychologists seemed indifferent to this intense connection. At a time when psychology was dominated by behaviorism, studying love seemed unscientific. Behaviorists suggested that babies wanted to be close to their mothers because this "maternal reinforcement stimulus" provided food. Worse yet, the early behaviorist John Watson seemed *hostile* to mother love:

> When I hear a mother say "bless its little heart" when it falls down, I . . . have to walk a block or two to let off steam. . . . Can't she train herself to substitute a kindly word . . . for . . . the coddling? . . . Can't she learn to keep away from the child a large part of the day?
> (Watson, 1928/1972, pp. 82–83)

And then he made this memorable statement:

> I sometimes wish that we could live in a community of homes [where] . . . we could have the babies fed and bathed each week by a different nurse. (!)
> (Watson, 1928/1972, pp. 82–83)

European psychoanalysts felt differently. They believed that attachment was crucial to infant life.

Consider a heart-rending mid-twentieth-century film that featured babies living in orphanages (Blum, 2002; Karen, 1998). In these sterile, pristine institutions, behaviorists would predict that infants should thrive. So why did babies lie listless on cots—unable to eat, withering away?

Now consider that ethologists—the forerunners of today's evolutionary psychologists—noticed that *every* species had a biologically programmed attachment response (or drive to be physically close to their mothers) that appeared at a specific point soon after birth. When the famous ethologist Konrad Lorenz (1935) arranged to become a group of newly hatched goslings' attachment-eliciting stimulus, Lorenz became the adored Pied Piper the geese tried to follow to the ends of the earth.

However, it took a rebellious psychologist named Harry Harlow to convince U.S. psychologists that the behaviorist meal-dispenser model of mother love was wrong. In a classic study, Harlow (1958) separated newborn monkeys from their mothers and raised them in a cage with a wire-mesh "mother" (which offered food from a milk bottle attached to its chest) and a cloth "mother" (which was soft and provided contact comfort). The babies stayed glued to the cloth mother, making occasional trips to eat from the wire mom. In stressful situations, they scurried to the cloth mother for comfort. Love won, hands down, over getting fed!

Moreover, as adults, the motherless monkeys were unable to have sex; they were frightened of their peers. After being artificially inseminated and giving birth, the females became uncaring, abusive parents. One mauled her baby so badly that it later died (Harlow and others, 1966; C. M. Harlow, 1986).

Harlow Primate Laboratory, University of Wisconsin

In Harlow's landmark study, baby monkeys clung to the cloth-covered "mother" (which provided contact comfort) as they leaned over to feed from the wire-mesh "mother"—vividly refuting the behaviorist idea that infants become "attached" to the reinforcing stimulus that feeds them.

Then, in the late 1960s, John Bowlby put the evidence together—the orphanage findings, Lorenz's ethological studies, Harlow's research, his own clinical work with children who had been separated from their mothers during World War II (Hinde, 2005). In landmark books, Bowlby (1969, 1973, 1980) argued that there is no such thing as "excessive mother love." Having a **primary attachment figure** is crucial to development. It is essential to living fully at any age. By the final decades of the twentieth century, attachment moved to the front burner in developmental science. It remains front and center today.

Exploring the Attachment Response

Bowlby (1969, 1973) made his case for the crucial value of attachment based on evolutionary theory. Like other species, he argued, human beings have a critical period when the attachment response "comes out." As with Lorenz's geese, attachment is built into our genetics to allow us to survive. Although the attachment response is programmed to emerge during our first two years of life, **proximity-seeking behavior**—our need to make contact with an attachment figure—is activated when our survival is threatened at *any* age.

Bowlby believed that threats to survival come in two categories. First, they may be activated by our internal state. When a toddler clings only to her mom, you know she must be tired. When you have a fever or the flu, you immediately text your significant other.

Second, they are evoked by wider-world dangers. During preschool, a huge dog caused us to run into our parents' arms. As adults, a professor's nasty comment or a humiliating work experience provokes a frantic call to our primary attachment figure, be it our spouse, father, or best friend.

Although we all need to touch base with our significant others when we feel threatened, older children can be separated from their attachment figures for some time. During infancy and toddlerhood, simply being physically apart causes distress. Now, let's trace how attachment unfolds.

Attachment Milestones

Bowlby believed that, during their first three months of life, babies are in the **preattachment phase.** Remember that during this reflex-dominated time, infants have yet to wake up to the world. However, at around 2 months of age, a milestone occurs called the **social smile.** Bowlby believed that this first smile does not show true attachment. Because it pops up in response to any human face, it is an automatic reflex that evokes care from adults.

Still, a baby's eagerly awaited first smile can be an incredible experience for a parent. Suddenly, your relationship with your child is on a different plane. Now, I have a confession to make: During my first two months as a new mother, I was worried, as I did not feel anything for this beautiful child I had waited so long to adopt. I date Thomas's first endearing smile as the defining event in my lifelong attachment romance.

At roughly 4 months old, infants enter a transitional period, called **attachment in the making.** At this time, Piaget's environment-focused secondary circular reactions are unfolding. The cortex is coming on-line. Babies may show a slight preference for their primary caregiver. But still, a 4- or 5-month-old is the ultimate party person, thrilled to be cuddled by anyone—from grandma, to a neighbor, to a stranger at the mall.

By about 7 or 8 months of age, this changes. As I discussed in Chapter 3, babies can hunt for covered objects—showing that they have the cognitive skills to miss their caregivers. Now that they can crawl, or walk holding

primary attachment figure The closest person in a child's or adult's life.

proximity-seeking behavior Acting to maintain physical contact or to be close to an attachment figure.

preattachment phase The first phase of John Bowlby's developmental attachment sequence, during the first three months of life, when infants show no visible signs of attachment.

social smile The first real smile, occurring at about 2 months of age.

attachment in the making Second phase of Bowlby's attachment sequence, when, from 4 to 7 months of age, babies slightly prefer the primary caregiver.

A baby's first social smile, which appears at the sight of any face at about 2 to 3 months of age, is biologically programmed to delight adults and charm them into providing love and care.

A few weeks ago, this 7-month-old boy would have happily gone to his neighbor. But everything changes during the phase of clear-cut attachment when stranger anxiety emerges.

clear-cut (focused) attachment Critical attachment phase, from 7 months through toddlerhood, defined by the need to have a primary caregiver nearby.

separation anxiety When a baby gets upset as a primary caregiver departs.

stranger anxiety Beginning at about 7 months, when a baby grows wary of people other than a caregiver.

social referencing A baby's monitoring a caregiver for cues as to how to behave.

working model In Bowlby's theory, the mental representation of a caregiver that enables children over age 3 to be physically apart from the caregiver.

Strange Situation Procedure to measure attachment at age 1, involving separations and reunions with a caregiver.

onto furniture, children can get hurt. The stage is set for **clear-cut (or focused) attachment**—the beginning of the full-blown attachment response.

Separation anxiety signals this milestone. When a baby is about 7 or 8 months old, she suddenly gets uncomfortable if a caregiver leaves the room. Then, **stranger anxiety** appears. A child gets agitated when any unfamiliar person picks her up. So, as children approach age 1, the universal friendliness of early infancy is gone. While they may still joyously gurgle at the world from their caregiver's arms, it's normal for babies to forbid any "stranger"—a nice day-care worker or even a loving Grandma who flies in for a visit—to invade their space.

Between ages 1 and 2, the distress reaches a peak. A toddler clings and cries when Mom or Dad makes a motion to leave. It's as if an invisible string connects the caregiver and the child. In a classic study at a playground, 1-year-olds played within a certain distance from their mothers. Interestingly, this zone of optimum comfort (about 200 feet) was identical for both the parent and the child (Anderson, 1972).

To see these changes, pick up a young baby (such as a 4-month-old) and an older infant (perhaps a 10-month-old) and compare their reactions. Then, observe 1-year-olds at a park. Can you measure this attachment zone of comfort? Do you notice the busy, exploring toddlers periodically checking back to make sure a caregiver is there?

Social referencing, the scientific term for this regular checking-back, helps alert toddlers to which situations are dangerous and which are safe. ("Should I climb up this slide, Mommy?" "Does Daddy think this object is OK to explore?"). It explains why 8-month-old infants suddenly become sensitive to fearful faces (see Chapter 3). Our lifelong human *fear bias* is exquisitely timed to kick in when we first move into the world.

When does the need to be *physically* close to a caregiver go away? Although the marker is hazy, clear-cut attachment tapers off at about age 3. Children still care just as much about their primary caregiver. But now, according to Bowlby, they have the skills to carry a **working model,** or internal representation, of this number-one person in their minds (Bretherton, 2005).

The bottom line is that our human critical period for attachment unfolds during our most vulnerable time of life—when babies first become mobile and are most in danger of getting hurt. Moreover, what compensates parents for the frustrations of having a Piagetian "little scientist" is enormous gratification. Just when a toddler keeps messing up the house and saying "No!" parents know that their child's world revolves only around them.

Do children differ in the way they express this priceless connection? If so, what might these differences imply about the infant–parent bond?

Attachment Styles

Mary Ainsworth, Bowlby's colleague, answered these questions by devising a classic test of attachment—the **Strange Situation** (Ainsworth, 1967; Ainsworth and others, 1978).

The Strange Situation procedure begins when a mother and a 1-year-old enter a room full of toys. After the child has time to explore, an unfamiliar adult enters the room. Then the mother leaves the baby alone with the stranger and, a few minutes later, returns to comfort the child. Next, everyone leaves the baby alone in the room, and finally the mother returns (see Figure 4.1). By observing the child's reactions to these separations and reunions through a one-way mirror, developmentalists categorize infants as either *securely* or *insecurely attached.*

In kindergarten, this child can say goodbye with minimal separation anxiety because she is in the working-model phase of attachment.

Securely attached children use their mother as a secure base, or anchor, to explore the toys. When she leaves, they may or may not become highly distressed. Most important, when she returns, their eyes light up with joy. Their close relationship is apparent in the way they melt into their mothers' arms. **Insecurely attached** children react in one of three ways:

- **Avoidant** infants rarely show much emotion—positive or negative—when their attachment figure leaves and returns. They seem wooden, disengaged, without much feeling at all.

- Babies with an **anxious-ambivalent attachment** are at the opposite end of the spectrum—clingy, nervous, too frightened to explore the toys. Frantic when their attachment figure leaves, they are inconsolable when a parent comes back.

- Children showing a **disorganized attachment** behave in a bizarre manner. They freeze, run around erratically, or even look frightened when the caregiver returns.

Developmentalists point out that insecure attachments do not show a weakness in the *underlying* connection. Avoidant infants are just as bonded to their caregivers as babies who are categorized as secure. Anxious-ambivalent infants are not more closely attached even though they show intense separation distress. To take an analogy from adult life, when a person who cares deeply about you pretends to be indifferent, is this individual less in love? Is a lover who can't let his partner out of sight more attached than a person who allows his significant other to have an independent life? Unless they endure the grossly abnormal rearing conditions described later in this section, *every infant* is closely attached (Zeanah, Berlin, & Boris, 2011). Figure 4.2 on page 112 offers a visual summary of the different attachment styles.

secure attachment Ideal attachment response when a child responds with joy at being reunited with a primary caregiver.

insecure attachment Deviation from the normally joyful response of being reunited with a primary caregiver, signaling problems in the caregiver–child relationship.

avoidant attachment An insecure attachment style characterized by a child's indifference to a primary caregiver at being reunited after separation.

anxious-ambivalent attachment An insecure attachment style characterized by a child's intense distress when reunited with a primary caregiver after separation.

disorganized attachment An insecure attachment style characterized by responses such as freezing or fear when a child is reunited with the primary caregiver in the Strange Situation.

FIGURE 4.1: The Strange Situation: The classic Strange Situation, involving separations and reunions from a caregiver, can tell us whether this 1-year-old girl is securely or insecurely attached.

Worth Publishers

Secure Attachment: The child is thrilled to see the caregiver.

Avoidant Attachment: The child is unresponsive to the caregiver.

Anxious-Ambivalent Attachment: The child cannot be calmed by the caregiver.

Disorganized Attachment: The child seems frightened and behaves bizarrely when the caregiver arrives.

FIGURE 4.2: Secure and insecure attachments: A summary photo series

The Attachment Dance

Look at a baby and a caregiver and it is almost as if you are seeing a dance. The partners are alert to each other's signals. They know when to come on stronger and when to back off. They are absorbed and captivated, oblivious to the world. This blissful **synchrony,** or sense of being emotionally in tune, is what makes the infant–mother relationship our model for romantic love. Ainsworth and Bowlby believed that the parent's "dancing potential," or sensitivity to a baby's signals, produces secure attachments (Ainsworth and others, 1978). Were they correct?

synchrony The reciprocal aspect of the attachment relationship, with a caregiver and infant responding emotionally to each other in a sensitive, exquisitely attuned way.

The Caregiver

Decades of studies suggest that the answer is yes. From Peru to Peoria, sensitive caregivers have babies who are securely attached (Posada and others, 2016). Parents who misread their baby's signals or are rejecting, disengaged, or depressed are more apt to have infants who are categorized as insecure (see Behrens, Parker, & Haltigan, 2011; and Zeanah, Berlin, & Boris, 2011 for a review).

Moreover, an infant's attachment category, to some degree, mirrors that of his mom. Women who describe happy childhoods tend to have securely attached babies. Mothers who report dysfunctional early lives are more likely to have insecure 1-year-olds (Behrens, Haltigan, & Bahm, 2016; Verhage and others, 2016). With the caution that this correlation could be due to shared genetics, there is some intergenerational continuity to the attachment dance.

However, there can also be a tantalizing mismatch in infant–caregiver congruence (Behrens, Haltigan, & Bahm, 2016)—which suggests that some women, despite having unhappy childhoods, step up to the plate and offer their babies loving care. On the negative side, you may know a world-class caregiver with an insecurely attached child. The reason is that the attachment dance has *two partners.*

The blissful rapture, the sense of being totally engrossed with each other, is the reason why developmentalists use the word *synchrony* to describe parent–infant attachment.

The Child

Listen to a mother comparing her babies ("Sara was fussy; Matthew is easier to soothe") and you will realize that not all infants have the same dancing talent. The reason is that babies differ in **temperament**—characteristic, inborn behavioral styles of approaching the world.

In a pioneering study, developmentalists classified middle-class babies into three temperamental styles: *Easy* babies had rhythmic eating and sleeping patterns; they were happy and easily soothed. More wary babies were labeled *slow to warm up*. One in 10 infants were ranked as *difficult*—hypersensitive, unusually agitated, reactive to every sight and sound (Thomas & Chess, 1977; Thomas, Chess, & Birch, 1968). Here is an example:

> Everything bothers my 5-month-old little girl—a bright light, a rough blanket, a sudden noise—even, I'm ashamed to admit, sometimes my touch. I thought colic went away by month 3. I'm getting discouraged and depressed.

Think back to the stressful Strange Situation. Can you see why some developmentalists argue that temperamental reactivity, rather than the quality of caregiving, determines a child's attachment status at age 1? (See, for example, Kagan, 1984.)

Does a baby's biology (nature) evoke insensitive caregiving and then insecure infant attachments? As you might imagine—given the *bidirectional* nature of relationships—the answer is yes. Temperamentally fussy babies (infants who rarely smile and get agitated when adults pick them up) provoke less loving caregiving, especially when mothers are anxious and depressed (Nolvi and others, 2016). To use an analogy from real-life dancing, imagine waltzing with a partner who couldn't keep time with the music, or think of a time you tried to soothe a person who was too upset to relate. Even a world-class dancer, or someone with exceptional social skills, would feel inept.

The Caregiver's Other Significant Others

To continue the analogy, the attachment waltz has additional partners. As I discussed in Chapter 2, a woman's attachment to her baby depends in part on her partner's bonding style. If a couple has marital problems, or a caregiver's significant other feels ambivalent about the child, it's hard to relate to an infant in a loving way (Cowan, Cowan, & Mehta, 2009; Moss and others, 2005). For single parents, having other caring attachments—with family members, friends, and neighbors—is also crucial to providing sensitive care (see Chapter 7). A basic message of this book is that no parent is an island. The dance of attachment depends on having a supportive wider world.

Table 4.1 summarizes these messages in a questionnaire showing the different forces that predict caregiver-to-baby bonding. My discussion shows that by viewing mothers as solely responsible for promoting secure attachments, Bowlby and Ainsworth were taking an excessively limited view. What about the general theory? Is attachment to a primary caregiver universal? Do infants in different countries fall into the same categories of secure and insecure?

> **temperament** A person's characteristic, inborn style of dealing with the world.

Imagine the frustration of caring for this temperamentally frazzled baby—an infant who responded to every sight and sound with a frantic wail. Is it fair to blame this child's attachment issues on a parent's care?

Table 4.1: Predicting Caregiver-to-Baby Bonding: Four Section Summary Questions

1. Did this person have a happy childhood?

2. Is this baby temperamentally easy?

3. For couples: Is this relationship loving and are both partners excited about having a child?

4. For single parents: Does this caregiver have other close attachments?

Is Infant Attachment Universal?

From Chicago to Capetown, from Naples to New York, Bowlby's and Ainsworth's attachment ideas get high marks (van IJzendoorn & Sagi, 1999). Babies around the world get attached to a primary caregiver at roughly the same age. As Figure 4.3 shows, the percentages of infants categorized as secure in different countries are remarkably similar—roughly 60 to 70 percent (Sroufe, 2000; Tomlinson, Cooper, & Murray, 2005).

The most amazing validation of attachment theory comes from the Efé, a communal hunter-gatherer people living in Africa. Efé newborns nurse from any lactating woman, even when their own parent is around. They are dressed and cared for by the whole community. But Efé babies still develop a primary attachment to their mothers at the typical age! (See van IJzendoorn & Sagi, 1999.)

So far you might be thinking that during the phase of clear-cut attachment, babies are connected to one person. You would be incorrect. A toddler may be attached to her father and day-care provider, as well as her mom. And, just as you and I connect differently with each significant other, a baby can be securely attached to his father and insecurely attached to his mother.

Interestingly, when babies are upset, they run to the person who spends the most time with them even if they are insecurely attached to that adult. So the *amount* of hands-on caregiving, not its quality, evokes the biologically programmed, security-seeking response (Umemura and others, 2013). The good news is that if a child is securely attached *to one person*, then that may be all that matters for his life.

In a heartening longitudinal study, 15-month-olds labeled as "double insecure" (insecurely attached to both parents) were prone to have behavior problems in third grade. But children who were securely attached to only one parent were insulated

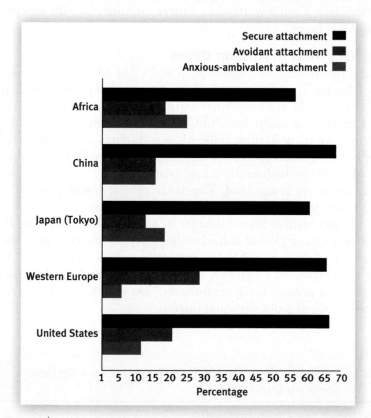

FIGURE 4.3: Snapshots of attachment security (and insecurity) around the world: Around the world, roughly 60 to 70 percent of 1-year-olds are classified as securely attached—although there are interesting differences in the percentages of babies falling into the different insecure categories.

Data from van IJzendoorn & Sagi, 1999, p. 729.

from poor mental health (Kochanska & Kim, 2013). Therefore, having *one* nurturing figure during infancy—a father, a grandma, an aunt—may be all we need to protect us from problems down the road. How *does* infant attachment relate to problems down the road?

Does Infant Attachment Predict Later Relationships and Mental Health?

Bowlby's argument, in his working-model concept, is that our attachment relationships during infancy determine how we relate to other people and feel about ourselves (Bretherton, 2005). A baby who acts avoidant with his parents will be aloof with his friends and teachers. An anxious-ambivalent infant will behave in a needy way in her relationships. A secure baby is set up to succeed socially.

Again, decades of research support Bowlby's prediction. Securely attached babies are more socially competent (McElwain and others, 2011; Rispoli and others, 2013). Insecure attachment foreshadows trouble managing one's emotions and interpersonal difficulties later on (Kochanska and others, 2010; Pasco Fearon and others, 2010; von der Lippe and others, 2010).

The most potent predictor of problems is the disorganized attachment style. This erratic, confused infant response is a risk factor for "acting-out issues" (aggression, disobedience, trouble controlling one's behavior) as children travel through elementary school (Bohlin and others, 2012; Pasco Fearon & Belsky, 2011).

Because this hands-on dad is caring for his infant son full time, he will be the loving attachment figure this young baby runs to during the toddler years.

However, the operative phrase here is *risk factor*. Programs that train mothers to be responsive caregivers can block the pathway from infant disorganized attachment to disruptive preschool behaviors (Mountain, Cahill, & Thorpe, 2017). Longitudinal studies that measure attachment at age 1 and then track babies into adulthood suggest that, while there normally is continuity, sensitive, loving relationships—at *every stage of childhood*—can transform a baby's "attachment status" from insecure to secure. Unfortunately, however, even the most blissful babyhood does not inoculate children from attachment traumas later on (Pinquart, Feubner, & Ahnert, 2013; Zayas and others, 2011).

Consider a boy named Tony who, in one major infant-to-adult attachment study, was categorized as securely attached at age 1. In preschool and early elementary school, Tony was popular, self-assured, and still securely attached; but as a teenager, he suffered devastating attachment blows. First, his parents went through a difficult divorce. Then his mother was killed in a car accident and his father moved to another state, leaving Tony with his aunt. It should come as no surprise that as an angry, depressed adolescent, Tony was classified as insecurely attached. But by age 26, Tony recovered. He met a wonderful woman and became a father. His status slowly returned to secure (Sroufe and others, 2005).

It seems logical that life experiences would change our attachment relationships for the better or the worse. But research—involving the "love hormone" oxytocin—suggests genetics is also involved.

Exploring the Genetics of Attachment Stability and Change

Oxytocin is known as the attachment hormone because this chemical elicits bonding, caregiving, and nurturing in other mammals and human beings (Rilling, 2013). When researchers in the infant-to-adult attachment study explored variations in a gene involved in producing oxytocin, they found that young people, like Tony, who changed in attachment status, showed one variant of this particular gene. Others, with a less environment-responsive genetic profile, were apt to stay stable in attachment from age 1. Therefore, some children seem genetically immune to less sensitive

oxytocin The hormone whose production is centrally involved in bonding, nurturing, and caregiving behaviors in our species and other mammals.

caregiving. Others vitally need a nurturing environment to thrive. (Stay tuned for more about environment-responsive infants later in this chapter.)

The bottom-line theme of *all* these studies, however, is that Bowlby's firm pronouncement was incomplete. We are not destined to have lifelong problems if we suffered from inadequate caregiving early in life. But what if a baby has experienced not just poor caregiving, but *no* caregiving at all?

Hot in Developmental Science: Experiencing Early Life's Worst Deprivation

"When I . . . walked into the . . . building (in 1990)," said a British school teacher . . . "what I saw was beyond belief . . . babies lay three and four to a bed, given no attention. . . . There were no medicines or washing facilities, . . . physical and sexual abuse were rife. . . . I particularly remember . . . the basement. There were kids there who hadn't seen natural light in years."

(McGeown, 2005, para. 4)

This scene was not from some horror movie. It was real. This woman had entered a Romanian orphanage, the bitter legacy of the dictator Ceausescu's decision to forbid contraception, which caused a flood of unwanted babies that destitute parents dumped on the state.

When the Iron Curtain fell and revealed these grisly Eastern European scenes, British and American families rushed in to adopt these children. But then parents began to report distressing symptoms—sons and daughters who displayed a strange, indiscriminate friendliness (see Kreppner and others, 2011). These responses did not qualify as insecure attachment. They showed a complete lack of *any* attachment response.

Which institution-reared babies are apt to show these deficits? Can children recover from this deprivation, and is there an age at which help comes too late?

Studies tracking the Romanian babies, as well as children adopted from orphanages in China and Russia, offer the following tantalizing conclusions (Julian, 2013).

First, babies adopted from the most negligent, worst-off institutions—such as in Romania—are most at risk for problems. In these places, damage is evident if adoption occurs after 6 months of age. In orphanages, like those in Russia that are classified as "socially depriving" but that satisfy infants' basic health needs, the cutoff point for having deficits is close to 18 months. Therefore, just as Bowlby would predict, the zone of attachment (7–18 months) is a sensitive period for receiving caregiving. But there is also a **dose–response effect**—meaning that the intensity (dose) of deprivation predicts the impact on (response of) a given child. The risk of having enduring problems depends on the length of time a child stays in an orphanage (Almas and others, 2016) and the care that institution provides (McCall and others, 2016).

What are these children's symptoms? A classic sign of this "institutionalization syndrome" is the indiscriminate friendliness I just described (this condition is called *reactive attachment disorder*). Another is deficits in children's ability to focus their attention (McLaughlin and others, 2010; Wiik and others, 2011) because lack of stimulation delays the maturation of the brain (McLaughlin and others, 2010).

Interestingly, boys are more vulnerable than girls to persistent attachment problems (McLaughlin and others, 2012). While a massive catch-up growth often occurs after moving to a new, loving home (Sheridan and others, 2013), the negative intellectual effects of institutional care linger into the adolescent years (Almas and others, 2016; see Figure 4.4). By exploring these grossly abnormal, worst-case scenarios, developmentalists are learning vital information about resilience, brain plasticity, and its limits in human beings.

dose–response effect
Term referring to the fact that the amount (dose) of a substance, in this case the depth and length of deprivation, determines its probable effect or impact on the person. (In the orphanage studies, the "response" is subsequent emotional and/or cognitive problems.)

Prolonged institutional care
Adopted by age 2½
Never institutionalized

FIGURE 4.4: Dose–response impact of institutional care on later intelligence: Notice that intelligence test scores are higher when Romanian orphanage infants are adopted into foster families before the end of toddlerhood (yellow versus red bars). But compared to being raised outside of an orphanage (green bar), spending any time in an institution still has marked, enduring, negative effects on cognition.

Data from Almas and others, 2016.

Wrapping Up Attachment

To summarize, the quality of attachment during infancy lays the foundation for healthy development in a variety of life realms. Still, attachment capacities (and human brains) are malleable, and negative paths can be altered, as long as the deprivation is not too profound and the wider world provides special help. How does the wider world affect development during infancy and beyond? To explore this question, let's now look at two important social contexts of early childhood: poverty and day care.

Tying It All Together

1. List an example of "proximity-seeking in distress" in your own life within the past few months.

2. Muriel is 1 month old, Janine is 5 months old, Ted is 1 year old, and Tania is age 4. List each child's phase of attachment.

3. Match the term to the correct definition: (1) social referencing; (2) working model; (3) synchrony; (4) Strange Situation.
   a. A researcher measures a child's attachment at age 1 after several separations and reunions with the mother.
   b. A toddler keeps looking back at the parent while exploring at a playground.
   c. An elementary school child keeps an image of her parent in mind to calm herself at school.
   d. A mother and baby relate to each other as if they are totally in tune.

4. Your cousin is the primary caregiver of her 1-year-old son. On a recent visit to her house, you notice that the baby shows no emotion when his mother leaves the room and—more important—seems indifferent when she returns. How might you classify this child's attachment style?

5. Manuel is arguing for the validity of attachment theory as spelled out by Bowlby and Ainsworth. Manuel should say (pick one, neither, or both): *Infants around the world get attached to a primary caregiver at roughly the same age/ a child's attachment status at age 1 never changes.*

6. Jasmine is adopting a 2-year-old from an orphanage in Haiti. List a few issues Jasmine might have to deal with, and then give Jasmine a piece of good attachment news.

Answers to the Tying It All Together questions can be found at the end of this chapter.

Settings for Development

What is the impact of living in poverty on children? And what about that crucial place where many young children spend their time—day care?

The Impact of Poverty in the United States

In Chapter 3, I examined the devastating physical and emotional effects of early-childhood poverty in developing nations. Now let's turn to research in the United States. What fraction of young U.S. children live in poverty? How does being poor during the earliest years of life affect later well-being?

How Common Is Early-Childhood Poverty?

As Figure 4.5 on page 118 shows, in 2014, almost 1 in 4 U.S. children under age 6 lived below the poverty line. If we include boys and girls in low-income families (those earning within 2 times the official poverty cutoff), the statistic is close to 1 in 2 (Jiang, Ekono, & Skinner, 2016)! Moreover, for the past 40 years, young children have been more likely to live in poverty than every other U.S. age group (Quinn & Cahill, 2016; see Chapter 13).

LEARNING OUTCOMES

- Discuss early-childhood poverty in the United States.

- Explore preschools and day care, making reference to what caregivers should look for in choosing a specific setting for a child.

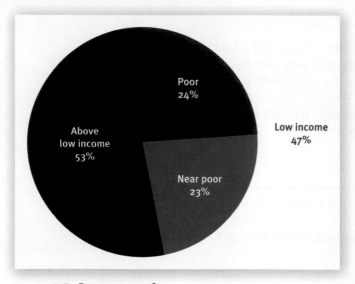

FIGURE 4.5: Percentage of U.S. children under 6 years old with different family incomes: This astonishing chart shows just how widespread economic disadvantage is among young U.S. children.

Data from Jiang, Ekono, & Skinner, 2016.

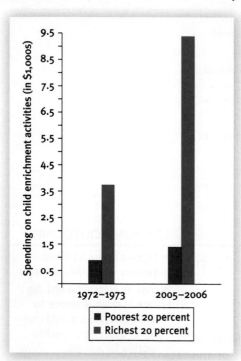

FIGURE 4.6: Family enrichment expenditures for children in the poorest 20 percent (red bars) and richest 20 percent (green bars) of U.S. families in 1972–1973 and 2005–2006: Low-income U.S. parents spend far less money on child enrichment activities, such as books and learning toys, than the richest 20 percent of families—an expenditure gap that has increased threefold since the early 1970s.

Data from Duncan, Magnuson, & Votruba-Drzal, 2017.

One cause is single motherhood. Imagine how difficult life is as a woman raising a baby alone. You need to work long hours, pay for child care, and still have enough money to feed and clothe your family. Now imagine how difficult it would be for *any* person to perform this feat with a job that pays less than $12 an hour. In 2013, more than 1 in 4 U.S. men age 25–34 had salaries below this amount. So it's no wonder that economic disadvantage is often the price of starting families during the very time young people are supposed to marry and give birth.

How Does Early-Childhood Poverty Affect Later Development?

Unfortunately, poverty affects children's physiology. Low-income toddlers and preschoolers have elevated levels of the stress hormone cortisol (Evans & Kim, 2013). One longitudinal study, measuring maternal salivary cortisol at different points during an infant's first two years of life, showed impoverished mothers also had high levels of this biological indicator of stress (Finegood and others, 2017).

Imagine arriving home exhausted from a low-wage job, or being unemployed, *food insecure*, and on the brink of getting evicted because you can't pay the rent. How would you deal with the kind of stressed-out, irritable infant discussed in the preceding section (Paulussen-Hoogeboom and others, 2007)? Although money cannot buy loving parents, it can buy any mother the economic luxury to relate sensitively to a child.

Poverty's most poisonous impact is on education. Being poor during the first four years of life dramatically lowers the odds of graduating from high school (Duncan, Magnuson, & Votruba-Drzal, 2017). With poverty and education, there is a clear dose–response effect: The depth of deprivation and its timing (during the earliest years of life) matter most. Why is poverty, before *entering* kindergarten, particularly detrimental to academic success?

Figure 4.6 offers one vivid answer. Low-income parents can't provide their infants and toddlers with the brain-stimulating activities that are the birthright of being born affluent in the contemporary United States: infant cognitive tools, baby gym visits, regular trips to museums. Moreover, notice that this gap in family "enrichment expenditures" has widened over the past 40 years. Technology combined with accelerating income inequalities means today's disadvantaged boys and girls face daunting intellectual hurdles even before they enter the classroom doors.

What amplifies these impediments is living in crowded, dilapidated housing (Leventhal & Newman, 2010) and perhaps having to move repeatedly (Miller, Sadegh-Nobari, & Lillie-Blanton, 2011)—chaotic conditions tailor-made to impair early childhood focusing skills (Blair, 2017; Hendry, Jones, & Charman, 2016). And if families live in high-crime neighborhoods, parents may be frightened to take their sons and daughters outside because the street is apt to be a dangerous place (Anakwenze & Zuberi, 2013).

Unfortunately, the cognitive impact of this chaos is evident before children even walk. When researchers explored how well 6-month-olds tracked visual stimuli, low-SES babies performed worse than the average child that age (Clearfield & Jedd, 2013).

Luckily, in wealthy world regions, low-income parents have government programs designed to help.

INTERVENTIONS Giving Disadvantaged Children an Intellectual and Social Boost

In the United States, the main government-sponsored early-childhood program is **Head Start.** This famous mainstay program, first established in 1965 by President Lyndon Johnson as part of his "Great Society" effort to reduce poverty, has the goal of offering the kind of learning experiences to make poverty-level preschoolers as ready for kindergarten as their middle-class peers.

Early Head Start extends this help to infants and toddlers. This federal program trains parents to be more effective caregivers, supporting low-income pregnant women by providing home visits and other services (Phillips & Lowenstein, 2011).

Do these interventions work? The answer *can be* yes. Programs that train poverty-level mothers to respond sensitively to their babies help promote secure attachment (Mountain, Cahill, & Thorpe, 2017). High-quality **preschools** (teaching-oriented programs that typically begin at age 3) make a difference in *every* child's life (Lee, 2016; Miller, Sadegh-Nobari, & Lillie-Blanton, 2011; Pölkki & Vornanen, 2016; Votruba-Drzal and others, 2013).

Day care (group settings for infants and toddlers) can be a lifeline for babies and toddlers who live in disorganized, chaotic homes (Berry and others, 2014; Phillips & Lowenstein, 2011). In one fascinating dose–response finding, researchers discovered that the more hours per week *poverty-level* 1-year-olds spent in day care, the lower their average cortisol rates (Berry, Blair, & Granger, 2016).

The problem is that here, too, money matters—especially in the United States. While social welfare states like Finland offer every child uniformly high-quality care, even as of early 2016, Head Start was seriously underfunded (Barnett & Friedman-Krauss, 2016). Because Head Start's budget depends on congressional approval, we don't know this classic U.S. program's future fate. Moreover, no one-shot intervention during early childhood can erase the impact of attending substandard elementary schools or being raised in a dysfunctional neighborhood where it is virtually impossible to construct a middle-class life (Chetty & Hendren, 2016; much more about this topic in Chapter 7).

But I can't end this discussion by leaving you with the stereotypical impression that *every* impoverished child's home life is deficient, or that *all* low-income neighborhoods blunt children's ability to learn. History is rife with examples of famous artists, scientists, and transformative public figures who grew up in families who could barely make ends meet—people who credit their parents for making them the successful people they became.

In one study, researchers found that if caregivers were securely attached to their own parents and had optimistic attitudes about life, they could put aside their problems and offer their children the ultimate in tender loving care (Kochanska and others, 2007). As a student of mine commented, "I don't see my family in your description of poverty. My mom is my hero. We grew up poor, but in terms of parenting, we were very rich."

Head Start A federal program offering high-quality day care at a center and other services to help preschoolers aged 3 to 5 from low-income families prepare for school.

Early Head Start A federal program that provides counseling and other services to low-income parents and children under age 3.

preschool A teaching-oriented group setting for children aged 3 to 5.

day care Less academically oriented group programs serving young children, most often infants and toddlers.

The Impact of Child Care

For affluent readers, this discussion of poverty can feel distant from your life. Child care affects every family, from millionaires to middle-class urban mothers and fathers to the rural poor. Almost 3 in 5 mothers in the United States returns to work during a baby's first year of life (U.S. Department of Labor Statistics, Fertility, 2017). Unlike in European nations, where free child care is a national birthright, in the United States, with average costs well over $1,000 per month, the expense of sending one child to day care is daunting, even to couples who are middle class. When we combine

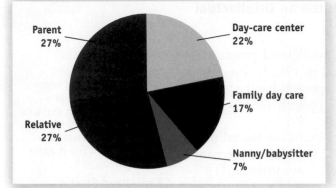

FIGURE 4.7: Day-care arrangements for infants and toddlers with employed mothers, late 1990s: Notice that, by the end of the twentieth century, while most infants and toddlers with working mothers were cared for by other family members, 1 in 5 attended licensed day-care centers.

Data from Shonkoff & Phillips, 2000, p. 304.

family day care A day-care arrangement in which a neighbor or relative cares for a small number of children in his or her home for a fee.

day-care center A day-care arrangement in which a large number of children are cared for at a licensed facility by paid providers.

these economic concerns ("This is taking up a huge chunk of my paycheck!") with anxieties about "leaving my baby with strangers," it makes sense that many new U.S. parents struggle to keep child care in the family. They may rely on grandma or juggle work schedules so that one spouse is always home (Phillips & Lowenstein, 2011).

People who use paid caregivers have several options. Well-off families often hire a nanny or babysitter. Parents who want a less expensive option often turn to **family day care,** in which a neighbor or local parent cares for a small group of children in her home.

The big change on the child-care landscape has been the dramatic increase in licensed **day-care centers**—larger settings that cater to children of different ages. By the late twentieth century, roughly 1 in 2 U.S. preschoolers attended these facilities. The comparable figure for infants and toddlers was more than 1 in 5 (see Figure 4.7).

Child Care and Development

Imagine you are the mother of a U.S. infant and must return to work. You probably have heard the media messages that link full-time day care with less than adequate mothering. So you are guilty, and perhaps feel compelled to explain your decision to disapproving family and friends (Fothergill, 2013). You may wonder, "Will my child be securely attached if I see her only a few hours a day?" You certainly worry about the quality of care your child would receive: "Will my baby get enough attention at the local day-care center?" "Am I *really* harming my child?"

To answer these kinds of questions, in 1989, developmentalists began the National Institute of Child Health and Human Development (NICHD) Study of Early Child Care. They selected more than 1,000 newborns in 10 regions of the United States and tracked the lives of these children, measuring everything from attachment to academic abilities, from mental health to mothers' caregiving skills. They looked at the hours each child spent in day care, and assessed the quality of each setting. The NICHD newborns are being followed as they travel into adult life (Vandell and others, 2010).

The good news is that putting a baby in day care does not weaken the attachment bond. Most infants attending day care are securely attached to their parents. The important force that promotes attachment is the *quality* of the dance—whether a parent is a sensitive caregiver—not whether she works (Nomaguchi and DeMaris, 2013; Phillips & Lowenstein, 2011). Moreover, what happens at home is the crucial influence affecting how young children develop, outweighing long hours spent in day care during the first years of life (Belsky and others, 2007b; Stein and others, 2013).

However, when we look at *just* the impact of spending those long hours, the findings are less upbeat. In contrast to the research with poverty-level infants, middle-class toddlers show *elevated* cortisol levels when they attend full-time day care (Berry, Blair, & Granger, 2016). Even worse, the NICHD follow-ups suggested that long hours spent in day care, beginning early in life, predict children's having a slightly higher risk of "acting-out issues" as late as in their teens (Vandell and others, 2010; see also Coley and others, 2013).

These results do not offer comfort to the millions of parents with babies who rely heavily on day care. Luckily, the correlations are weak (Vandell and others, 2010). Day care's negative effects apply mainly to children who attend large centers, not smaller family day care (Coley and others, 2013; Groeneveld and others, 2010).

What is the trouble with day-care centers? For hints, let's scan the general state of child care in the United States.

Exploring Child-Care Quality in the United States

Visit several facilities and you will immediately see that U.S. day care varies dramatically in quality. In some places, babies are warehoused and ignored. In others, every child is nurtured and loved.

The essence of quality day care again boils down to the dance—that is, the attachment relationship between caretakers and the children. Children develop intense attachments to their day-care providers. If a particular caregiver is sensitive, a child in her care tends to be securely attached (Ahnert, Pinquart, & Lamb, 2006; De Schipper, Tavecchio, & van IJzendoorn, 2008).

Child-care providers and parents agree: To be effective in this job, you need to be patient, caring, empathic, and child-centered (Berthelsen & Brownlee, 2007; Virmani & Ontai, 2010). You also need to work in a setting where you can relate to children in a one-to-one way. To demonstrate this point, researchers videotaped teachers at 64 Dutch preschools, either playing with three children or with five. Teachers acted more empathic in the three-child group. They were more likely to criticize and get angry with the group of five (De Schipper, Riksen-Walraven, & Geurts, 2006). These differences in teachers' tone and style were especially pronounced with younger children (the 3-year-olds). So group size matters; and the lower the child–teacher ratio, the better—especially earlier in life.

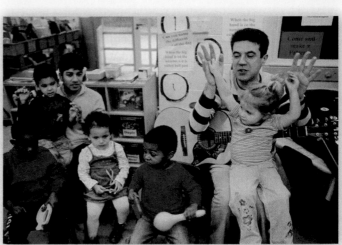

How will these male day-care workers feel about working at a nontraditional job? As the text shows, keys lie in whether they don't feel overwhelmed by caring for too many children, have enough money to meet their needs, and can use their creativity to arrange this class the way they want.

What other aspects of a program should parents look for, particularly with toddlers and 3-year-olds? The same qualities we crave from government, or workplace, or this class. We want to know exactly what to expect.

Excellent child-care facilities feature predictable, comforting routines: Children arrive and put their belongings in their own cubby; then play time, snack time, and rest time occur in a fixed sequence each day. Caregivers offer comfort through the *way* they interact (La Paro & Gloeckler, 2016). They stimulate children cognitively and socially. They balance consistent rules with lots of love (much more about this ideal child-rearing approach in Chapter 7).

It's also important for boys and girls to feel confident that a familiar person is providing care (Harrist, Thompson, & Norris, 2007). Forming an attachment takes time. Therefore, children are more apt to be securely attached to a caregiver when that person has been there a longer time (Ahnert, Pinquart, & Lamb, 2006).

However, partly because of the abysmal pay (in the United States, it's often close to the minimum wage), day-care workers are apt to quit. Surveys in Canada (Royer & Moreau, 2016) and Finland (Pölkki & Vornanen, 2016) show that most people in this field love their jobs. But no matter how much someone adores young children, that person must have enough money to survive. One U.S. comparison suggested that when teachers reported having *minimally adequate* wages and paid time-off, toddlers in that particular class were happier and better behaved (King and others, 2016).

Day-care providers also need to have the freedom to make their own choices about what activities to use and how to arrange the class day. In the Canadian survey I just mentioned, teachers cited work autonomy as the job feature most vital to their well-being.

In sum, now we know why day-care centers are at risk of providing inadequate care. Their culprit is lack of autonomy and less consistent care. Family day cares typically feature one stable caregiver who has considerable personal freedom (since the person is watching the children in her home). In large facilities, where directors or corporate bosses plan the day, staff is more apt to come and go (Ahnert, Pinquart, &

Lamb, 2006; Gerber, Whitebrook, & Weinstein, 2007; Groeneveld and others, 2010). Yes, children attending family day care are vulnerable because there is less oversight about what happens during the day. But, ideally, this more intimate setting can provide the nurturing, stable security very young children need.

INTERVENTIONS Choosing Child Care

Given these findings, what should parents do? The take-home message is not "avoid a day-care center," but rather "choose the best possible place." Look for low staff turnover; a predictable daily routine; caregivers who offer stimulation, empathy, and clear rules. Make sure that the staff members feel happy about their workplace as well.

Finally, here, too, consider a child's biology. While attending low-quality day cares are harmful for infants and toddlers with an environment-responsive genetic profile, these same children may flourish if a program is top notch (Belsky & Pluess, 2013). So, as we learn more about genetics, making blanket generalizations—such as "day care is bad (or good)"—may not be appropriate. It depends on the quality of the program, a child's home environment, and, now, the biology of a given child.

Table 4.2 draws on these messages in a checklist. And if you are a U.S. parent who relies heavily on day care, keep those guilty thoughts at bay. Your child may blossom at a high-quality day care. Moreover, *your* responsiveness matters most. You are your child's major teacher and the main force in making your child secure.

Table 4.2: Choosing a Day-Care Center: A Checklist

Overall Considerations

- Consider the caregiver(s). Are they nurturing? Do they feel that despite the low pay, they have enough money to live and the freedom to do what they want? Do they adore young children and especially enjoy working at *this place*?

- Ask about stability, or staff turnover. Have caregivers left in the last few months? Can infants have the same care provider when they move to the toddler room?

- Look for a low caregiver-to-baby ratio (and a small group of children overall). The ideal is one caregiver to every two or three babies.

- Look at the daily routine. Does a structured ritual flow through each day? Are activities clearly laid out, and do caregivers follow these plans? Do teachers stimulate cognition and behave in loving and predictable ways? (For toddlers and 3-year-olds it's also vital to have safe, age-appropriate play materials, such as blocks and books, as well as a dress-up corner, areas for painting near sinks, and places for children to congregate for group activities.)

Additional Suggestions

- For infants and toddlers in full-time care, limit exposure by having a child take occasional vacations or build in special time with the child every day.

- Consider the home environment. If a toddler's family life is chaotic or she lives in a dangerous neighborhood, it's better to spend the entire day at a stable, nurturing place.

- Consider a child's temperament. The kind of genetically responsive (highly environment-sensitive) babies I discussed earlier have special trouble coping with less than optimal care; but these same toddlers may flourish in a high-quality setting.

- And finally, for society: *Pay child-care workers decently and make day care more affordable for U.S. parents, too!*

Background information from the researchers cited in this section.

Now that we have examined attachment, poverty, and day care, it's time to turn to the topic I have been implicitly talking about all along—toddlerhood.

(◎) Tying It All Together

1. Hugo is telling your class which low-SES children are at highest risk of not graduating from high school. Pick the statement he should *not* make: *These children are poor during elementary school; these children are poor during the first four years of life.*

2. Sameera is anxious about her decision to put her 6-month-old in day care. Give a "good news" statement to ease Sameera's mind, and then be honest and give some "not such good news" statements about day care.

3. Imagine you are interviewing for a job at a local day-care center. What questions should you ask the director to better ensure that you will be satisfied at work?

Answers to the Tying It All Together questions can be found at the end of this chapter.

Toddlerhood: Age of Autonomy *and* Shame and Doubt

Imagine time-traveling back to when you were a toddler. Everything is entrancing—a bubble bath, the dishwasher soap box, the dirt and bugs in your backyard. You are just cracking the language barrier and thrilled to finally travel on your own two feet. Passionate to sail into life, you are also intensely connected to that number-one adult in your life. So, during our second year on this planet, the twin agendas that make us human first emerge: We need to be closely connected, and we want to be free, autonomous selves. This is why Erik Erikson (1950) used the descriptive word **autonomy** to describe children's challenge as they emerge from the cocoon of babyhood (see Table 4.3).

Autonomy involves everything from the thrill a 2-year-old feels when forming his first sentences, to the delight children have in dressing themselves. But it also involves those not-so-pleasant meltdowns we associate with the "terrible twos." In one study, while 1 in 3 parents labeled their child as having behavior problems that were "off the charts" (Schellinger & Talmi, 2013), this feeling may be a misperception. As you can see in Figure 4.8 on the next page, difficulties "listening" and angry outbursts (Barry & Kochanska, 2010) are *normal* during that magic age when children's passion is to explore the world (recall Piaget's little scientist behaviors).

Erikson used the words *shame* and *doubt* to refer to the situation in which a toddler's drive for autonomy is not fulfilled. But feeling shameful and doubtful is also vital to shedding babyhood and entering the human world. During their first year of life, infants show joy, fear, and anger. At age 2, more complicated, uniquely human emotions emerge: pride and shame. The appearance of these **self-conscious emotions** is a milestone—showing

LEARNING OUTCOMES

- Outline the emotional challenges of toddlerhood.
- Contrast exuberant and inhibited toddlers, and child-rearing strategies for each temperament.
- Summarize the caregiving advice in this section.

autonomy Erikson's second psychosocial task, when toddlers confront the challenge of understanding that they are separate individuals.

self-conscious emotions Feelings of pride, shame, or guilt, which first emerge around age 2 and show the capacity to reflect on the self.

Table 4.3: Erikson's Psychosocial Stages

Life Stage	Primary Task
Infancy (birth to 1 year)	Basic trust versus mistrust
Toddlerhood (1 to 2 years)	**Autonomy versus shame and doubt**
Early childhood (3 to 6 years)	Initiative versus guilt
Middle childhood (7 to 12 years)	Industry versus inferiority
Adolescence to emerging adulthood (teens into twenties)	Identity versus role confusion
Early adulthood (twenties to early forties)	Intimacy versus isolation
Middle adulthood (forties to sixties)	Generativity versus stagnation
Late adulthood (late sixties and beyond)	Integrity versus despair

that a child is becoming aware of having a self. The gift (and sometimes curse) of being human is that we are capable of self-reflection, able to get outside of our heads and observe our actions from an outsider's point of view. Children show signs of this uniquely human quality between ages 2 and 3, when they feel ashamed or are clearly proud of their actions for the first time (Kagan, 1984).

Socialization: The Challenge for 2-Year-Olds

Shame and pride are vital in another respect. They are essential to **socialization**—being taught to live in the human community.

When does the U.S. socialization pressure *heat up*? For answers, developmentalists surveyed middle-class parents about the rules they set for their 14-month-olds and when the children just turned 2 (Smetana, Kochanska, & Chuang, 2000). While rules for younger toddlers centered on safety issues ("Stay away from the stove!"), by age 2, parents were telling their children to "share," "sit at the table," and "don't disobey, bite, or hit." Therefore, we expect children to begin to act "like adults" around their second birthdays. No wonder 2-year-olds are infamous for those tantrums called the "terrible twos"!

Figure 4.8 illustrates just how difficult it is for toddlers to control themselves and to follow socialization rules when their parents are around. When can children follow unwanted directions when a parent *isn't* in the room? To answer this question related to early *conscience*—the ability to adopt internal standards for our behavior, or have that little voice inside us that says, "Even though I want to do this, it's wrong"—researchers devised an interesting procedure. Accompanied by their mothers, children enter a laboratory full of toys. Next, the parent gives an unwelcome instruction—telling the child either to clean up the toys or not to touch another easily reachable set of enticing toys. Then the mother leaves the room, and researchers watch the child through a one-way mirror.

Not unexpectedly, children's ability to "listen to a parent in their head" and stop doing what they want improves dramatically from age 2 to age 4 (Kochanska, Coy, & Murray, 2001). Who is better or worse at this feat of self-control?

As you might expect, the marked differences in self-control we see in young children have genetic roots (Gartstein and others, 2013; Wang & Saudino, 2013). Some of us are biologically better able to resist temptation at any age! Parenting matters, too. Caregivers who label a toddler's emotions ("You are really upset about that!") can help coach children to manage disappointment without immediately lashing out (Scrimgeour, Davis, &

socialization How children are taught to behave in socially appropriate ways.

SW Productions/Stockbyte/Getty Images

This toddler has reached a human milestone: She can feel shame, which shows that she is aware that she has a separate self.

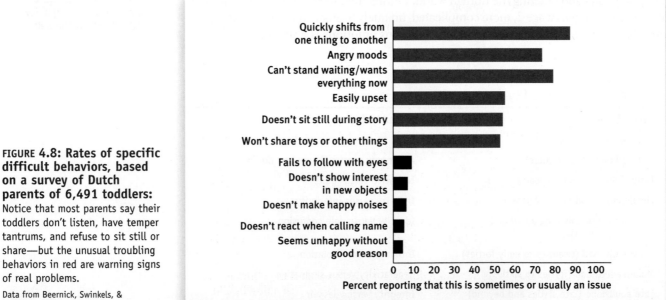

FIGURE 4.8: Rates of specific difficult behaviors, based on a survey of Dutch parents of 6,491 toddlers: Notice that most parents say their toddlers don't listen, have temper tantrums, and refuse to sit still or share—but the unusual troubling behaviors in red are warning signs of real problems.

Data from Beernick, Swinkels, & Buitelaar, 2007.

Buss, 2016). While mothers excel at this gentle coaching, a father's warmth weighs heavily in socializing children at older ages (Lickenbrock and others, 2013; Schueler & Prinz, 2013). So Dad's influence—at least in traditional two-parent families—is important, but mainly when children move beyond the clear-cut attachment zone.

What temperamental traits provoke early compliance? The answer comes as no surprise. Fearful toddlers are more obedient (Aksan & Kochanska, 2004; see also the How Do We Know box). Exuberant, joyful, fearless, intrepid toddler-explorers are especially hard to socialize! (See Kochanska & Knaack, 2003.)

HOW DO WE KNOW . . .
that shy and exuberant children differ dramatically in self-control?

How do researchers measure toddler temperaments? How do they test later self-control? Their first step is to design situations tailored to elicit fear, anger, and joy and then observe how toddlers act.

In the fear-eliciting "treatment," a child enters a room filled with frightening toy objects, such as a dinosaur with huge teeth or a black box covered with spider webs. The experimenter asks that boy or girl to perform a mildly risky act, such as putting a hand into the box. To measure anger, the researchers restrain a child in a car seat and then rate how frustrated the toddler gets. To tap into exuberance, the researchers entertain a child with a set of funny puppets. Will the toddler respond with gales of laughter or be more reserved?

Several years later, the researchers set up a situation provoking noncompliance by asking the same child, now age 4, to perform an impossible task (such as throwing Velcro balls at a target from a long distance without looking) to get a prize. Then they leave the room and watch through a one-way mirror to see if the boy or girl will cheat.

Toddlers at the high end of the fearless, joyous, and angry continuum show less "morality" at age 4. Without the strong inhibition of fear, their exuberant impulses to "get closer" are difficult to dampen down. So they succumb to temptation, sneak closer, and look directly at the target as they hurl the balls (Kochanska & Knaack, 2003).

Being Exuberant and Being Shy

Adam [was a vigorous, happy baby who] began walking at 9 months. From then on, it seemed as though he could never stop.

(10 months) Adam . . . refuses to be carried anywhere. . . . He trips over objects, falls down, bumps himself.

(12 months) The word *osside* appears. . . . Adam stands by the door, banging at it and repeating this magic word again and again.

(19 months) Adam begins attending a toddler group. . . . The first day, Adam climbs to the highest rung of the climbing structure and falls down. . . . The second day, Adam upturns a heavy wooden bench. . . . The fourth day, the teacher [devastates Adam's mother] when she says, "I think Adam is not ready for this."

(13 months) [Erin begins to talk in sentences the same week as she takes her first steps.] . . . Rather suddenly, Erin becomes quite shy. . . . She cries when her mother leaves the room, and insists on following her everywhere.

(15 months) Erin and her parents go to the birthday party of a little friend. . . . For the first half-hour, Erin stays very close to her mother, intermittently hiding her face on her mother's skirt.

(18 months) Erin's mother takes her to a toddlers' gym. Erin watches the children . . . with a "tight little face." . . . Her mother berates herself for raising such a timid child.

(Lieberman, 1993, pp. 83–87, 104–105)

My exuberant son—shown enjoying a sink bath at 9 months of age—began to have problems at 18 months, when his strong, joyous temperament collided with the need to "please sit still and listen, Thomas!"

Observe 1-year-olds and you will immediately pick out the Erins and the Adams. Some children are wary and shy. Others are whirlwinds of activity, constantly in motion, bouncing off the walls. I remember my own first toddler group at the local Y, when—just like Adam's mother—I first realized how different my exuberant son was from the other children his age. After enduring the horrified expressions of the other mothers as Thomas whirled gleefully around the room while everyone else sat obediently for a snack, I came home and cried. How was I to know that the qualities that made my outgoing, joyous, vital baby so charismatic during his first year of life might go along with his being so difficult to tame?

Psychologist Jerome Kagan carried out classic longitudinal studies following toddlers with shy temperaments. Kagan (1994; see also Degnan, Almas, & Fox, 2010) classifies about 1 in 5 middle-class European American toddlers as inhibited. Although they are comfortable in familiar situations, these 1-year-olds, like Erin, get nervous when confronted with anything new. Inhibited 13-month-olds shy away from approaching a toy robot, a clown, or an unfamiliar person. They take time to venture out in the Strange Situation, get agitated when the stranger enters, and cry bitterly when their parent leaves the room.

Intense shyness is also moderately "genetic" (Smith and others, 2012), and we can see clues to this temperament early in life. At 4 months of age, inhibited toddlers excessively fret and cry (Marysko and others, 2010; Moehler and others, 2008). At month 8 or 9, they have special trouble ignoring distracting stimuli such as flashing lights or background noise. Their attention wanders to any off-topic, irrelevant, unpleasant event (Pérez-Edgar and others, 2010a).

Inhibited toddlers tend to be fearful throughout childhood (Degnan, Almas, & Fox, 2010). They overfocus on threatening stimuli in their teens (Pérez-Edgar and others, 2010a). Using brain scans, Kagan's research team found that his inhibited toddlers, as young adults, showed more activity in the part of the brain that codes negative emotions when shown a stranger's face on a screen (Schwartz and others, 2003). So for all of you formerly very shy people (your author included) who think you have shed that childhood wariness, you still carry your physiology inside.

Still, if you think you have come a long way in conquering your *overpowering* childhood shyness, you are probably correct. Many anxious toddlers (and exuberant explorers) get less inhibited as they move into elementary school and their teens (Degnan, Almas, & Fox, 2010; Pérez-Edgar and others, 2010b).

INTERVENTIONS   ### Providing the Right Temperament–Socialization Fit

Faced with a temperamentally timid toddler such as Erin or an exuberant explorer like Adam or Thomas, what can parents do?

Socializing a Shy Baby

In dealing with fearful children, parents' impulse is to back off ("Erin is emotionally fragile, so I won't pressure her to go to day care or clean up her toys"). This "treat 'em like glass" approach is apt to backfire, provoking more wariness down the road (Natsuaki and others, 2013). With shy children, be caring but provide a gentle push. Exposing a shy toddler to *supportive* new social situations—such as family day care—helps teach that child to cope.

Raising a Rambunctious Toddler

power assertion An ineffective socialization strategy that involves yelling, screaming, or hitting a child.

When fearless explorers can't stop bouncing off the walls, it's natural for adults to get flooded with anxiety (Lorber, Mitnick, & Slep, 2016). Many parents resort to a harsh discipline strategy called **power assertion**—yelling, screaming, and hitting. Another response is to give up, abandoning any attempt to discipline a child.

Both reactions are counterproductive. Relying on power assertion alone strongly predicts behavior problems down the road (Brotman and others, 2009; Kochanska & Knaack, 2003; Leve and others, 2010). Disengaging from discipline robs the child of the tools to modify his behavior. Plus, it conveys the message, "You are out of control and there is nothing I can do."

While in interviews, mothers give screaming and hitting low marks; when these same people are observed interacting with their misbehaving toddlers, they often automatically resort to power assertion techniques (Passini, Pihet, & Favez, 2014). When dealing with toddler defiance, what kind of discipline works best?

The answer brings me to a fascinating study tracking the usefulness of different child-rearing strategies when toddlers act up (Larzelere & Knowles, 2015). If 2-year-olds whine, reasoning and emotion coaching are most effective. But for disruptive behavior, such as hitting or biting, the best response is to set firm limits, such as immediately putting the child in time-out.

The ultimate all-purpose socializer, however, is a secure attachment (Kochanska & Kim, 2013). As my husband insightfully commented, "Punishment doesn't matter much to Thomas. What he does, he does for your love."

Table 4.4 offers a summary of this discussion, listing these different toddler temperaments, their infant precursors, their pluses and potential later dangers, and lessons for socializing each kind of child. Now let's look at some general temperament-sensitive lessons for raising every child.

Table 4.4: Exuberant and Inhibited Toddler Temperaments: A Summary

Inhibited, Shy Toddler

- **Developmental precursor:** Responds with intense arousal to external stimulation in infancy.

- **Plus:** Easily socialized; shows early signs of conscience; not a discipline problem.

- **Minus:** Shy, fearful temperament can persist into adulthood, making social encounters painful.

- **Child-rearing advice:** Don't overprotect the child. Expose the baby to unfamiliar people and supportive new situations.

John Birdsall/Alamy Stock Photo

Exuberant Toddler

- **Developmental precursor:** Emotionally intense but unafraid of new stimuli.

- **Plus:** Joyous; fearless; outgoing; adventurous.

- **Minus:** Less easily socialized; potential problems with conscience development; at higher risk for later "acting-out" behavior problems.

- **Child-rearing advice:** While calm reasoning works best to quell whining, employ time-outs for defiant behavior. But, above all, use lots of love.

Picture Partners/Alamy Stock Photo

An Overall Strategy for Temperamentally Friendly Childrearing

In the classic study discussed earlier, in which developmentalists classified babies as easy, slow-to-warm-up, or difficult, researchers found that difficult infants were more likely to have problems with their teachers and peers (Thomas & Chess, 1977; Thomas, Chess, & Birch, 1968). However, some children learned to compensate for their biology and to shine. The key, the researchers discovered, lay in a parenting

goodness of fit An ideal parenting strategy that involves arranging children's environments to suit their temperaments, minimizing their vulnerabilities and accentuating their strengths.

strategy they labeled **goodness of fit.** Parents who carefully arranged their children's lives to minimize their vulnerabilities and accentuate their strengths had infants who later did well.

Understanding that their child was overwhelmed by stimuli, these parents kept the environment calm. They may have offered a quiet environment for studying and encouraged their child to do activities that took advantage of his talents. They went overboard to provide a placid, nurturing, low-stress milieu.

Here, too, emerging genetic studies suggest these parents were right. Again, researchers find that children are genetically predisposed to be highly responsive or relatively immune to environmental events (Ellis and others, 2011a). In typical settings, highly reactive babies may be categorized as difficult because they are wired to react negatively to changes. These same infants, however, may flourish when the environment is exceptionally calm (for review, see Belsky & Pluess, 2009). In fact, in one study, when environment-responsive children were put in a nurturing, placid environment, they performed *better* than their laid-back peers (Obradović, Burt, & Masten, 2010)!

The lesson again is that making assumptions about the enduring quality of infant attachment, seeing full-time day care as a universal stress, or, in this case, labeling a baby (or person) as "difficult" or "easy" is not appropriate. With the right person–environment fit, what looks like a liability might be a gift!

Some Concluding Thoughts: Giving Is Built into Being Human, Too

In this section, I've been emphasizing how confrontation comes on strongly during our second year on this planet. But I cannot leave you with the impression that angry independence is the sum-total of toddlers' emotional lives.

Two-year-olds will step in to help a researcher retrieve an out-of-reach object; they comfort that person when she bangs her finger and says, "Ouch!" (Dunfield & Kuhlmeier, 2013; Hepach, Vaish, & Tomasello, 2013; Thompson & Newton, 2013). Eighteen-month-olds even perform sharing acts that go beyond our adult norm, giving some of their own stickers to an experimenter when that person has acted selfishly in a previous trial (Sebastián-Enesco, Hernández-Lloreda, & Colmenares, 2013).

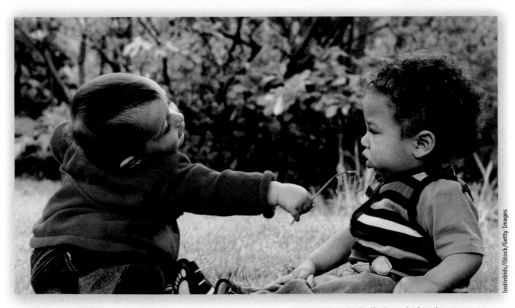

The fact that toddlers naturally take joy in giving suggests that giving is built into being human.

lostinbids/iStock/Getty Images

This impulse to help, comfort, and share, which blossoms during toddlerhood, appears in cultures worldwide (House and others, 2013). And doing good makes young children feel good. Toddlers look happier after giving a treat to another person than when they get that treat for themselves. They seem especially joyous when engaging in costly giving—giving up something they *wanted to get* (Aknin, Hamlin, & Dunn, 2012). So the principle that it feels better to give than to receive doesn't need to be vigorously instilled in us at a mosque, synagogue, or church. Caring is also baked into humanity, beginning before age 2 (Hepach, Vaisch, & Tomasello, 2013)!

How does sharing and kindness evolve during childhood, and how do infants' attachments to parents spread to peers? What happens to babies who are shy or exuberant, difficult or easy, as they journey into elementary school? Stay tuned for answers to these questions (and many more) as we enter the childhood years.

Tying It All Together

1. If Amanda is 2½, which prediction is FALSE? *Amanda wants to be independent, yet is closely attached. /Amanda can possibly feel shame. /Amanda's parents haven't begun to discipline her.*

2. To a colleague who confides that he's worried about his timid toddler, what comforting words can you offer?

3. Think back to your own childhood: Did you fit into either the shy or exuberant temperamental type? How did your parents cope with your personality style?

Answers to the Tying It All Together questions can be found at the end of this chapter.

SUMMARY

Attachment: The Basic Life Bond

For much of the twentieth century, behaviorists minimized the mother–child bond. European psychoanalysts such as John Bowlby were finding, however, that attachment was a basic human need. Harlow's primate studies convinced U.S. developmentalists of the importance of **attachment,** and Bowlby transformed developmental science by arguing that having a loving **primary attachment figure** is biologically built into our species, and crucial to development. Although threatening situations evoke **proximity-seeking behavior** at any age—during **toddlerhood**—just being physically apart from an attachment figure elicits distress.

According to Bowlby, life begins with a 3-month-long **preattachment phase,** characterized by the first **social smile.** After an intermediate phase called **attachment in the making,** at about 7 months of age, the landmark phase of **clear-cut attachment** begins, signaled by **separation anxiety** and **stranger anxiety.** During this period spanning toddlerhood, children need their caregiver to be physically close, and they rely on **social referencing** to monitor their behavior. After age 3, children can tolerate separations, as they develop an internal **working model** of their caregiver—which they carry into life.

To explore individual differences in attachment, Mary Ainsworth devised the **Strange Situation.** Using this test, which involves separations and reunions, developmentalists categorize 1-year-olds as **securely** or **insecurely attached.** Securely attached 1-year-olds use their primary attachment figure as a secure base for exploration and are delighted when she returns. **Avoidant** infants seem indifferent. **Anxious-ambivalent** children are overly frantic and inconsolable. Children with a **disorganized attachment** react in an erratic way and may show fear when their parent reenters the room.

Caregiver–child interactions are characterized by a beautiful **synchrony,** or attachment dance. Although a baby's attachment style can sometimes mirror the caregiver's own working model of attachment, attachment is also affected by the child's **temperament** and depends on the caregiver's other close relationships as well.

Cross-cultural studies support the idea that attachment to a primary caregiver is universal, with similar percentages of babies in various countries classified as securely attached. When distressed, babies run to the caregiver who spends the most time with them, but infants can be attached to several people, and having a secure attachment to only one caregiver may be all that infants need for optimal development.

As Bowlby predicted in his working-model concept, securely attached babies have superior mental health. Infants with insecure attachments (especially disorganized attachments) are at risk for later problems. However, the good-news/bad-news finding is that, when the caregiving environment changes, attachment security can change for the better or worse. A gene related to **oxytocin** production may make children more or less vulnerable to variations in caregiver sensitivity. Babies exposed to the worst-case attachment situation, living in an orphanage with virtually no caregiving, experience a **dose–response effect.** Although the chance of having enduring problems sets in during the "attachment zone," the chance of lifelong impairments depends on the depth of the deprivation and the age at which a child leaves that institution.

Settings for Development

Early-childhood poverty—widespread in the United States—affects children's physical health. It compromises caregiver sensitivity and—most important—has long-term effects on school success. **Head Start** and **Early Head Start** programs help impoverished young children in the United States. Poverty-level babies and toddlers benefit from full-time **day care. Preschool** has positive effects for every child. Despite their many daily challenges, low-income parents who are upbeat about life can give their children exceptional care.

It is common for parents to go back to work during a baby's first year of life, but due to the expense of day care and anxieties about leaving their baby with strangers, parents in the United States ideally prefer to keep infant care in the family. Paid child-care options include nannies (for affluent parents), **family day care** (in which a person cares for a small number of children in her home), and larger **day-care centers.**

The NICHD Study of Early Child Care showed that the best predictor of being securely attached at age 1 is having a sensitive parent. But middle-class children who attend day-care centers full time (versus family care) have elevated cortisol levels and a slightly higher risk of acting out as teens.

In choosing day care, search for loving teachers, low child-to-caregiver ratios, care-provider stability, and a predictable daily structure. Find out if the staff feels a sense of autonomy and believes their salary meets their basic needs. Because day-care workers are so poorly paid in the United States, staff turnover is a serious problem. This issue, plus the lack of freedom at larger, more institutional places, may explain why day-care centers can be problematic. Babies who are genetically prone to be environment-responsive are especially vulnerable to low-quality day care.

Toddlerhood: Age of Autonomy *and* Shame and Doubt

Erikson's **autonomy** captures the essence of toddlerhood, the landmark age when we shed babyhood, first observe the self, and enter the human world. **Self-conscious emotions** such as pride and shame emerge and are crucial to **socialization,** which begins in earnest at around age 2. Difficulties with focusing and obeying are normal during toddlerhood, but at this age, children differ in their ability to control themselves. Temperamentally fearful children show earlier signs of "conscience." Exuberant, active toddlers are especially hard to socialize.

As young babies, shy toddlers react with intense motor activity to stimuli. They are more inhibited in elementary school and adolescence and show neurological signs of social wariness as young adults. Still (with sensitive parenting), many shy toddlers and fearless explorers lose these extreme tendencies as they grow older.

To help an inhibited baby, don't overprotect the child. With exuberant toddlers, **power assertion** is a serious danger. For acts of defiance, like hitting, it is vital to set limits, as long as parents use discipline along with lots of love. Parents should promote **goodness of fit**—tailoring the environment to a child's temperament. Giving, helping, and sharing—not just confrontation—are built into toddlerhood, too.

KEY TERMS

anxious-ambivalent attachment, p. 111

attachment, p. 107

attachment in the making, p. 109

autonomy, p. 123

avoidant attachment, p. 111

clear-cut (focused) attachment, p. 110

day care, p. 119

day-care center, p. 120

disorganized attachment, p. 111

dose–response effect, p. 116

Early Head Start, p. 119

family day care, p. 120

goodness of fit, p. 128

Head Start, p. 119

insecure attachment, p. 111

oxytocin, p. 115

power assertion, p. 126

preattachment phase, p. 109

preschool, p. 119

primary attachment figure, p. 109

proximity-seeking behavior, p. 109

secure attachment, p. 111

self-conscious emotions, p. 123

separation anxiety, p. 110

social referencing, p. 110

social smile, p. 109

socialization, p. 124

Strange Situation, p. 110

stranger anxiety, p. 110

synchrony, p. 112

temperament, p. 113

toddlerhood, p. 107

working model, p. 110

ANSWERS TO **Tying It All Together** QUIZZES

Attachment: The Basic Life Bond

1. Your responses will differ, but any example you give, such as "I called Mom when that terrible thing happened at work," should show that under stress your impulse is to immediately contact your attachment figure.

2. Muriel = preattachment; Janine = attachment in the making; Ted = clear-cut attachment: Tania = working model.

3. (1) b; (2) c; (3) d; (4) a

4. The child has an avoidant attachment.

5. Manuel should say: Infants around the world get attached to a primary caregiver at roughly the same age.

6. Caution Jasmine that her baby may have difficulties focusing and may show indiscriminate friendliness; if she is adopting a boy, her child may have special trouble in developing a secure attachment. However, tell Jasmine that these problems can be muted with loving care.

Settings for Development

1. Children are at highest risk when their families are poor *during their first four years of life*.

2. The good news is that Sameera's parenting is the main force in determining her child's attachment (and emotional health). The bad news is that some day-care centers leave much to be desired, and long hours spent in these centers provoke spikes in cortisol levels, as well as a slightly elevated risk of later acting-out issues.

3. To supplement the critical question of how much the job pays, ask whether there is paid time off for planning the curricula, sick leave, and vacation days. Does this position encourage professional development time (attendance at conferences)? What are my chances for promotion? Will I have freedom to structure the day? How many babies and toddlers will be in the group (the fewer, the better)? If caring for infants, can I move up to the toddler room? How many staff members have left in the past few months? (This is a good clue as to how user-friendly this work place is.) Then linger and make your own observations by visiting different rooms and questioning staff members about their jobs.

Toddlerhood: Age of Autonomy *and* Shame and Doubt

1. Parents typically discipline their 2-year-olds (last alternative is wrong).

2. You might tell him that most children grow out of their shyness, even if they do not completely shed this temperamental tendency. But stress the advantages of being shy: His baby will be easier to socialize and may have a stronger conscience.

3. These answers will be totally your own.

CONNECT ONLINE:

LaunchPad
macmillan learning | Check out our videos and additional resources located at:
www.macmillanlearning.com

Childhood

In this three-chapter book part, the first two chapters trace children's development in stages. The final chapter explores the settings within which children develop: home, school, and community.

Chapter 5—**Early Childhood** focuses on preschool and kindergarten (ages 3 to 6). First, I'll explore young children's unfolding physical skills. Then, the heart of this chapter—cognition—decodes the strange ways preschoolers think, offers a framework for teaching, and shows how language develops. Next, I'll trace how children learn they have an enduring self and decode other people's mental states. The final section enters the world of preschool play and describes the unique mental challenges of children with those familiar conditions: autism spectrum disorders.

Chapter 6—**Middle Childhood** turns to elementary school (ages 7 to 12). After spelling out why two world-class psychologists target middle childhood as the first adult-like life stage, I'll describe the brain changes that make elementary school-aged children's thinking unique, and explore issues relating to health and motor skills. Then, I'll examine cognition and emotional states, tracking self-awareness (and self-esteem), caring acts, and aggression. The final parts explore friendships and popularity, then examine bullying.

Chapter 7—**Settings for Development: Home, School, and Community** first tackles children's family lives. Is there an ideal way of parenting? Why do some children thrive in spite of dysfunctional early lives? What is the impact of spanking, child abuse, and divorce on the child? Here you will learn about intelligence tests, what makes schools successful, and how teachers can make every child eager to learn. Throughout this chapter, I'll highlight the important role neighborhoods play in determining children's success.

Application to Developing Lives Parenting Simulation: Early and Middle Childhood

In the *Early Childhood* and *Middle Childhood* modules of *Developing Lives,* you will consider the impact your choices will have on the physical, cognitive, and social and emotional development of your child.

	Physical	Cognitive	Social and Emotional
Early Childhood & Middle Childhood modules	• What kinds of food will your child eat? • How much physical activity will you encourage? • Will you regulate your child's TV or video game time?	• What is your child's stage of Piagetian cognitive development? • What kind of school will you choose? • Will you put your child in tutoring if needed?	• What social environment will you place your child in? • How will you discipline your child? • Will you eat meals as a family or have a different routine?

Left: sanneberg/Shutterstock

CHAPTER 5

Early Childhood

As the 3-year-olds drift in to Learning Preschool, Ms. Angela fills me in:

"First, we have free play. Then, read a story. At 10:30, we have snack and go outside. We focus on stretching the children's capacities, but don't expect too much—no academics at this age. The goal is to get them to master the basics for school and life: listen; take turns; share; be respectful; talk about feelings; don't yell (use your inside voice). The room is arranged into activity centers to give the children plenty of room to explore."

At the kitchen center, Kanesha is pretending to scrub pots. "What is your name?" I ask. "You know!" says Kanesha, looking at me as if I'm totally dumb. Kanesha gives me a plate: "Let's have psghetti and Nadia makeacake." We are having a wonderful time talking as she loads me up with plastic food. The problem is that we aren't communicating. Who is Nadia, that great cook?

Then two girls and a boy run from the doll corner and things begin to escalate: "We are mommies and daddies. Our Barbies need food!" Sara and Tania grab plastic vegetables off the table; Mark commandeers Kanesha's pot. Then, Ms. Angela runs in: "What are you supposed to do?" The kids chant, "Listen; take turns; share," and everyone starts giggling and gives Kanesha hugs.

I move to the crafts table. "Hey!" Moriah yells as José cuts his sheet into pieces, "José has more than me!" Moriah is making beautiful circles with paste. José tries to copy her but can only make random lines. These children are so different in their physical abilities, even though they are the same age. But—oh no—here come the children from the kitchen corner, and things get out of control again! Luckily, it's story time.

Ms. Angela reads a book about a bear who takes honey from the community cave when no one is around. "What is Little Bear feeling?" she asks. One boy says, "Hungry!" Another says, "Sad." Then José proudly informs the class, "He's happy and scared because he is being bad." But—just when I conclude José is a psychological genius—Ms. Angela follows up: "When the bears return, will they know it's him?" José and everyone yell, "Yes!"

At the activity centers, the girls are already separating from the boys. During outdoor play, however, I notice (a bit sadly) that José abandons Moriah as the boys joyously wrestle and compete to jump as far as they can. As the wind starts gusting, everyone gets excited and these gender differences disappear: "Let's catch Mister Wind. . . . He ran away again!" And now (whew!) it's time for lunch and rest.

These 3-year-olds have amazing skills. They can cut, climb, and jump, follow directions (a bit), and tell me about their lives. But they are clearly on a different wavelength in the way they think about life. Why was the class certain that the other animals would know who took the honey even though no one saw the offending bear?

Why was Kanesha sure I *had* to know her name and why did Moriah assume José had more paper when he cut his sheet into pieces? What makes pretending compelling during preschool, and why do girls and boys separate into same-sex groups? This chapter offers answers as we immerse ourselves in the magical stage called **early childhood** (ages 3 to 6).

early childhood
The first phase of childhood, lasting from age 3 through kindergarten, or about age 6.

Left: Karel Noppé/Alamy Stock Photo

LEARNING OUTCOMES

- Describe what makes humanity special.
- Contrast Erikson's early-childhood and middle-childhood tasks.

middle childhood
The second phase of childhood, comprising the ages from roughly 7 to 12 years.

Michael Poliza/Getty Images

Imagine that these great apes could *really* share what insights they were having and understand what is in each other's minds. Wouldn't they be the species who has transformed the world?

initiative Erik Erikson's term for the early childhood psychosocial task that involves exuberantly testing skills.

industry Erik Erikson's term for the middle childhood psychosocial task involving bending to adult reality and needing to work for what we want.

Setting the Context

To introduce this special age, let's first step back. What makes human beings unique? What makes early childhood different from the next stage of development, called **middle childhood** (ages 7 to 12)?

Special "Mind Reading" Talents

The great apes in this photo are clearly enjoying life (Poirier & Smith, 1974). But why did this species stay in the savanna while human beings had the talent to construct cities and negotiate cyberspace?

The reason, according to evolutionary theorists, is that humans have a unique capacity—the complex ability to reflect on our actions and read each other's minds. Great apes do possess basic mindreading skills (see Buttelmann, Call, & Tomasello, 2009), yet because they lack language capacities, our primate cousins can't share each other's thoughts to transform the world. ("Oh, now I understand what you were trying to do. Let's work together to improve on that.")

In this chapter, you will learn how, during early childhood, the *social cognitive skills* that define humanity lock in. I'll also explain why early childhood is special compared to older ages. That master theorist, Erik Erikson, best captured the essential quality defining this unique stage of life.

Age of Exploration

Erikson, as you can see from Table 5.1, labeled the early childhood psychosocial task as **initiative**. From risking racing a tricycle in the street to scaling the school monkey bars, Erikson believed that our mission during preschool is to confidently exercise our bodies and minds.

In middle childhood (beginning approximately at age 7), this agenda shifts. Now our challenge is to develop **industry**, as we understand that succeeding in the world requires work. Therefore, the in-between interlude, when we have mastered walking and talking but haven't yet entered elementary school, is a time of vigorously testing our talents before we must bend to reality and curb our basic desires. Exploration (and initiative) is a vital prelude to confronting the demands of adult life.

Table 5.1: Erikson's Psychosocial Stages

Life Stage	Primary Task
Infancy (birth to 1 year)	Basic trust versus mistrust
Toddlerhood (1 to 2 years)	Autonomy versus shame and doubt
Early childhood (3 to 6 years)	**Initiative versus guilt**
Middle childhood (7 to 12 years)	Industry versus inferiority
Adolescence to emerging adulthood (teens into twenties)	Identity versus role confusion
Early adulthood (twenties to early forties)	Intimacy versus isolation
Middle adulthood (forties to sixties)	Generativity versus stagnation
Late adulthood (late sixties and beyond)	Integrity versus despair

Exuberantly taking off on your tricycle versus listening to the teacher and making sure you have finished your homework shows why early childhood is a magical time before we enter the adult world and must work.

Beginning with physical development, then moving to cognitive development, emotional development, and finally to play—the work of childhood—let's now track this age of exploration in the flesh.

Tying It All Together

1. In a sentence, explain what makes human beings different from other species.

2. When Steven played with his 4-year-old and 8-year-old sons, he realized that while the younger child was passionate to run, his older son was careful to follow the rules of the game. Use Erikson's distinction between initiative and industry to explain this difference between Steven's two sons.

3. Drawing on Erikson's preschool task, pick the stage of life most similar to early childhood.

Answers to the Tying It All Together questions can be found at the end of this chapter.

Physical Development

Compare preschoolers to older children and you will immediately see the *cephalocaudal principle* of physical growth discussed in Chapters 2 and 3. Three-year-olds have large heads and squat, rounded bodies. As children get older, their limbs lengthen and their bodies thin out. Because they grow at similar rates, boys and girls are roughly the same size until they reach the preadolescent years.

LEARNING OUTCOMES

-   Describe physical development.
-   Name two types of motor skills.
-   Outline threats to preschool physical skills.

The tip-off about the ages of the children in these two photographs relates to the *cephalocaudal principle* of development. We know that the children in the left photo are preschoolers because they have squat shapes and relatively large heads, whereas the longer bodies in the right photo are typical of the middle childhood years.

Table 5.2: Selected Motor Skill Milestones: Progression from Age 2 to Age 6

At age 2	At age 4
Walks unassisted, usually by 12 months	Cuts paper, approximates circle
Rolls a ball or flings it awkwardly	Walks down stairs, alternating feet
Picks up small objects with thumb and forefinger, feeds self with spoon	Catches and controls a large bounced ball across the body
At age 5	**At age 6**
Prints name	Copies two short words
Walks without holding on to railing	Hops on each foot for 1 meter but still holds railing
Tosses ball overhand with bent elbows	Catches and controls a 10-inch ball in both hands with arms in front of body

gross motor skills
Physical abilities that involve large muscle movements, such as running and jumping.

fine motor skills Physical abilities that involve small, coordinated movements, such as drawing and writing one's name.

Now visit a playground to see the *mass-to-specific* principle—the progression from clumsy to sure, swift movements from ages 2 to 6. Toddlers have trouble grasping markers; at age 6, they draw bodies and faces. Two-year-olds are just mastering spearing food; in first grade, they hurl balls down the alley and sometimes hit bowling pins. You can see the changes from mass to specific in a few skills from ages 2 to 6 in Table 5.2.

Two Types of Motor Talents

Developmentalists divide physical skills into two categories. **Gross motor skills** refer to large muscle movements, such as running, climbing, and hopping. **Fine motor skills** involve small, coordinated movements, such as drawing faces and writing one's name.

The stereotype that boys are better at gross motor abilities and girls at fine motor tasks is true—although often the differences are small. The largest sex difference in sports-related abilities occurs in throwing speed. During preschool, boys can typically hurl a ball much faster and farther than girls can (Geary, 1998; Thomas & French, 1985). Does this mean that girls can't compete with boys on teams? Not necessarily. The boys probably will be faster pitchers and more powerful hitters. But the female talent at connecting with the ball, which involves fine motor coordination, may even things out.

Imagine that a preschooler has exceptional physical abilities. Will that child be advanced at school? The answer is yes, provided we look at complex fine motor skills. Researchers asked 5-year-olds to copy images and then reproduce designs displayed on another page. Performance on this more difficult test (involving fine motor coordination and judging spatial dimensions) strongly predicted elementary school math and writing skills (Carlson, Rowe, & Curby, 2013; see also the next chapter).

These boys—being generally advanced in their gross motor skills—may be the victors when they compete with girls in this potato sack race. But this girl's exceptional fine motor talents set her up to do well in school.

This study suggests that, to improve their academic abilities, we might train young children to reproduce images. The problem is that pressuring (forcing) preschoolers to perform physical (and intellectual) tasks can be counterproductive. During early childhood, we should provide activities—such as cutting paper or scaling the monkey bars—that boys and girls naturally enjoy (Zaichkowsky & Larson, 1995). Allow young children to exercise their talents, but don't push, and provide the right *person–environment fit*.

Threats to Preschool Physical Skills

Now that we've scanned what normally happens, let's examine two forces that can limit children's growth and motor skills.

Lack of Outdoor Play

Anyone who is middle-aged or older can immediately identify one influence limiting physical initiative. When I was in preschool, children spent their days running outside. Today, a range of forces converge to limit the free-form physical explorations that have always defined early childhood, from adult anxieties ("If I let my child go to the park, he may be abducted or hurt") to living in dangerous neighborhoods ("With all that violence, I would never let my daughter out of the house") to the pressure to focus on academics at an early age ("Wouldn't my son be learning more by staying indoors and playing with that new computer device I just bought from Amazon?").

Today, the Internet coupled with tempting high-tech educational toys lure parents away from letting children play outdoors. In one longitudinal study, researchers measured mothers' use of "screen time" by asking how many hours per day pregnant women watched TV or spent on-line. Then they looked at their children's outdoor play during the first five years of life. As you might imagine, more parent screen time predicted less preschool time outdoors (Xu and others, 2016).

Learning tools can stimulate vital school-related skills, such as teaching children to ignore distracting information and focus their attention (Axelsson, Andersson, & Gulz, 2016). But wouldn't running around outside be equally effective at training children's minds? In one preschool study, children who engaged in "exercise play" (physically playing outside) were rated more well-liked by their peers (Lindsey, 2014).

Lack of Food

A telling example highlighting the social function of play relates to the problem discussed in Chapter 3: *undernutrition*. In addition to causing stunting, undernutrition impairs gross and fine motor skills because it compromises the development of our bones, muscles, and brain. Most important, when children don't have sufficient food, they are too tired to engage with the world.

During the 1980s, researchers observed how undernourished children in rural Nepal maximized their growth by cutting down on play (Anderson & Mitchell, 1984). Play, as you will learn later in this chapter, does more than exercise our bodies; it is crucial in promoting children's ability to compromise and understand other people's points of view. Therefore, it's important to understand that what happens physically during the first years of life affects all aspects of thinking—a topic I turn to now.

Imagine buying this device, guaranteed to propel your child into a kindergarten star. How would you like your child spending his time?

Tying It All Together

1. Darpreet has terrific gross motor skills but trouble with fine motor skills. Select the two sports from this list that Darpreet would be most likely to excel at: *long-distance running, tennis, water ballet, the high jump, bowling.*

2. Drawing on this section, which strategy would be *least helpful* in stimulating physical development during early childhood?

   a. Enrolling 4-year-olds in sports
   b. Encouraging pregnant women to reduce their Internet time
   c. Providing low-cost, safe spaces in the community for children to play (such as free local Y's)
   d. Ensuring that young children have enough food

Answers to the Tying It All Together questions can be found at the end of this chapter.

- Describe Piaget's preoperational stage, referring to specific terms and concepts.
- Compare Vygotsky's and Piaget's theories.
- Describe Vygotsky's ideas about language.
- Outline how language develops, making reference to its specific properties.

preoperational thinking In Piaget's theory, the type of cognition characteristic of children aged 2 to 7, marked by an inability to step back from one's immediate perceptions and think conceptually.

concrete operational thinking In Piaget's framework, the type of cognition characteristic of children aged 8 to 11, marked by the ability to reason about the world in logical, adult ways.

conservation tasks Piagetian tasks that involve changing the shape of substances to see whether children can go beyond the way that substance visually appears to understand that the amount remains the same.

Cognitive Development

How *does* a young child's cognition unfold? The genius who decoded this question (no surprise) was Jean Piaget.

Piaget's Preoperational Stage

As discussed in Chapter 1, Piaget believed that through assimilation (fitting new information into their existing cognitive structures) and accommodation (changing those cognitive slots to fit input from the world), children undergo qualitatively different stages of cognitive growth. In Chapter 3, I discussed Piaget's sensorimotor stage. Now, it's time to tackle Piaget's next stage: preoperations (see Table 5.3).

Just as with Erikson's stages, we can best understand preoperations in conjunction with Piaget's next stage of cognitive growth. **Preoperational thinking** is defined by what young children are missing—the ability to step back from their immediate perceptions. **Concrete operational thinking** is defined by what older children possess: the ability to reason about the world in a logical, adult-like way.

When children leave infancy and enter the stage of preoperational thought, they have made tremendous mental strides. Still, their thinking seems on a different planet from that of adults. The problem is that preoperational children are unable to look beyond the way objects immediately appear. By age 7 or 8 (during elementary school), children can mentally transcend what first catches their eye. They have entered the concrete operational stage.

Taking the World at Face Value

You saw vivid examples of this "from another planet" thinking in the chapter-opening vignette. Now let's enter the minds of young children and explore how they reason about physical substances and the social world.

Strange Ideas About Substances

The fact that preoperational children are locked into immediate appearances is illustrated by Piaget's (1965) famous **conservation tasks**. In Piaget's terminology, *conservation* refers to knowing that the amount of a given substance remains identical despite changes in its shape or form.

Table 5.3: Piaget's Stages: Focus on Childhood

Age (years)	Name of Stage	Description
0–2	Sensorimotor	The baby manipulates objects to pin down the basics of physical reality. This stage ends with the development of language.
2–7	Preoperations	Children's perceptions are captured by their immediate appearances: "What they see is what is real." They believe, among other things, that inanimate objects are really alive and that if the appearance of a quantity of liquid changes (for example, if it is poured from a short, wide glass into a tall, thin one), the amount of liquid itself changes.
7–12	Concrete operations	Children have a realistic understanding of the world. Their thinking is really on the same wavelength as that of adults. While they can reason conceptually about concrete objects, however, they cannot think abstractly in a scientific way.
12+	Formal operations	Reasoning is at its pinnacle: hypothetical, scientific, flexible, fully adult. Our full cognitive human potential has been reached.

In the conservation-of-mass task, an adult gives a child a round ball of clay and asks that boy or girl to make another ball "just as big and heavy." Then she reshapes the ball to look like a pancake and asks, "Is there still the same amount now?" In the conservation-of-liquid task, the procedure is similar: Present a child with identical glasses containing equal amounts of liquid. Make sure the child agrees, "Yes, they have the same amount of juice [or water]." Then pour the liquid into a tall, thin glass while the child watches and ask, "Is there more or less juice now, or is there the same amount?"

Typically, when children under age 7 are asked this final question, they give a peculiar answer: "Now there is more clay" or "The tall glass has more juice." Why? "Because now the pancake is bigger" or "The juice is taller." Then, after adults remold the clay into a ball or pour the liquid into the original glass, the children report: "Now it's the same again." The logical conflict in their statements doesn't bother them at all. Figure 5.1 illustrates these procedures, as well as additional Piagetian conservation tasks to perform with children you know.

Why can't young children conserve? One issue is that children don't grasp a concept called **reversibility.** This is the idea that an operation (or procedure) can be repeated in the opposite direction. Adults accept the fact that we can change substances, such as our hairstyle or our house decorations, and then reverse things to their original state. Young children lack this fundamental *schema*, or cognitive structure, for understanding the world.

reversibility In Piaget's conservation tasks, the concrete operational child's knowledge that a specific change in the way a given substance looks can be reversed.

Type of conservation	Initial step and question	Transformation and next question	Preoperational child's answer
Number	Two equal rows of pennies. "Are these two rows the same?" (Yes.)	Increase spacing of pennies in one line. "Now is the amount of money the same?"	"No, the longer row has more."
Mass	Two equal balls of clay. "Do these two balls have the same amount of clay?" (Yes.)	Squeeze one ball into a long pancake shape. "Now is the amount of clay the same?"	"No, the long, thin one has more clay."
Volume or liquid	Two glasses of the same size with liquid. "Do these glasses have the same amount of juice?" (Yes.)	Pour one into a taller, narrower glass. "Now do these glasses have the same amount of juice?"	"No, the taller glass has more juice."
Matter*	Two identical cubes of sugar. "Do these cubes have the same amount of sugar?" (Yes.)	Dissolve one cube in a glass of water. "Now is there the same amount of sugar?"	"No, because you made one piece of sugar disappear."

*That is, the idea that a substance such as sugar is "still there" even though it seems to have disappeared (by dissolving).

FIGURE 5.1: Four Piagetian conservation tasks: Can you perform these tasks with a child you know?

centering In Piaget's conservation tasks, the preoperational child's tendency to fix on the most visually striking feature of a substance and not take into account other dimensions.

decentering In Piaget's conservation tasks, the concrete operational child's ability to look at several dimensions of an object or substance.

class inclusion The understanding that a general category can encompass several subordinate elements.

identity constancy In Piaget's theory, the preoperational child's inability to grasp that a person's core "self" stays the same despite changes in external appearance.

A second problem lies in a perceptual style that Piaget calls **centering.** Young children interpret things according to what first catches their eye, rather than taking in the entire visual array. In the conservation-of-liquid task, children become captivated by the liquid's height. They don't notice that the width of the original glass makes up for the other container's increased height.

In concrete operations, children **decenter.** They can step back from a substance's immediate appearance and understand that an increase in one dimension makes up for a loss in the other one.

Centering—or fixating on immediate impressions—impairs **class inclusion.** This is the knowledge that a category can comprise subordinate elements. For example, spread 20 Skittles® and a few gummy bears in a dish and ask a 3-year-old: "Would you rather have the Skittles or the candy?" and she is almost certain to say, "The Skittles," even when you have determined beforehand that both types of candy have equal appeal. She gets mesmerized by the number of Skittles and does not notice that "candy" is the label for both.

This tendency to focus on immediate appearances explains why, in the opening chapter vignette, Moriah believed that José had more paper when he cut his sheet into sections. Her attention was captured by the spread-out pieces, and she believed that now there must be more paper than before.

The same idea that "bigger" automatically equals "more" extends to every aspect of preoperational thought. Ask a 3-year-old if he wants a nickel or a dime, and he will choose the first option. (This is a great source of pleasure to older siblings asked to equally share their funds.) Perhaps because greater height means "older" in their own lives, children even believe that a taller person has been on earth for a longer time:

I was substitute teaching with a group of kindergarten children—at the time I was about 22—and when I met a student's mother, she was shocked. "When I asked Ben about you," she said, "he told me you were much older than his regular teacher." This teacher was in her mid- to late fifties and looked it. However, then we figured out the difference. This woman was barely 5 feet tall, and I am 6 feet 2!

Peter Hvizdak/The Image Works

When this 4-year-old's dad puts on a mask, he suddenly becomes a scary monster because she has not grasped the principle of identity constancy.

Peculiar Perceptions About People

Young children's idea that "what catches my eye right now is real" explains why a 3-year-old thinks her mommy becomes a princess when she dresses up for Halloween, or cries after visiting the beauty salon because she is sure her short haircut has transformed her into a boy. It makes sense of why a favorite strategy of older sisters and brothers (to torture younger siblings) is to put on a mask and see the child run in horror from the room. As these examples show, young children lack **identity constancy.** They don't realize that people remain their essential selves despite changes in the way they visually appear.

I gained insight into this identity constancy deficit at my son's 5th birthday party, when I hired a "gorilla" to entertain the guests (some developmental psychologist!). As the hairy 6-foot figure rang the doorbell, mass hysteria ensued—requiring the gorilla to take off his head. After the children calmed down, and the gorilla put on his head again to enact his skit, guess what? Pure hysteria again!

Why did that huge animal cause pandemonium? The reason is that the children believed that the gorilla, even though a costumed figure, was alive.

Frank Gaglione/Getty Images

This 4-year-old boy's animistic thinking causes him to believe that his bear is going to enjoy the ride he is about to provide.

Experiencing the Lifespan   Animism and the Power of Stephen King

There was one shadow that would constantly cast itself on my bedroom wall. It looked just like a giant creeping towards me with a big knife in his hand.

I used to believe that Satan lived in my basement. The light switch was at the bottom of the steps, and whenever I switched off the light it was a mad dash to the top. I was so scared that Satan was going to stab my feet with knives.

Boy, do I remember the doll that sat on the top of my dresser. I called it "Chatty Kathy." This doll came to life every night. She would stare at me, no matter where I went.

My mother used to take me when she went to clean house for Mrs. Handler, a rich lady. Mrs. Handler had this huge, shiny black grand piano, and I thought it came alive when I was not looking at it. It was so enormous, dark, and quiet. I remember pressing one of the bass keys, which sounded really deep and loud and it terrified me.

I remember being scared that there was something alive under my bed. I must tell you I sometimes still get scared that someone is under my bed and that they are going to

grab me by my ankles. I don't think I will ever grow out of this, as I am 26.

Can you relate to any of these childhood memories collected from my students? Perhaps your enemy was that evil creature lurking in your basement; the scary stuffed animal on your dresser; a huge object (with teeth) such as that piano; or your local garbage truck.

Now you know where that master storyteller Stephen King gets his ideas. King's genius is that he taps into the preoperational thoughts that we have papered over, though not very well, as adults. When we read King's tale of a toy animal that clapped cymbals to signal someone's imminent death, or about Christine, the car with a mind of its own, or about the laundry-pressing machine that loved human blood—these stories fall on familiar childhood ground. Don't you still get a bit anxious when you enter a dark basement? Even today, at night, do you ever have an uneasy feeling that some strange monster might be lurking beneath your bed?

Animism refers to the problem young children have in sorting out what is alive. Specifically, preschoolers see inanimate objects—such as dolls or costumed figures— as having consciousness, too. Turn to the chapter-opening vignette to see examples of animistic thinking—for instance, the hungry Barbies or the wind that ran away. Now think back to when you were age 5 or 6. Do you remember being afraid the escalator might suck you in? Or perhaps you recall believing, as in the Experiencing the Lifespan box, that your dolls came alive at night.

Listen to young children talking about nature, and you'll hear delightful examples of animism: "The sun gets sleepy when I sleep." "The moon likes to follow me in the car." The practice of assigning human motivations to natural phenomena is not something we grow out of as adults. Think of the Greek thunder god Zeus, or the ancient Druids who worshiped the spirits that lived within trees. Throughout history, humans have regularly used animism to make sense of a frightening world.

A related concept is called **artificialism**. Young children believe that human beings make nature. Here is an example of this "daddy power" from Piaget's 3-year-old daughter, Laurent:

> L was in bed in the evening and it was still light: "Put the light out please" . . . (I switched the electric light off.) "It isn't dark"—"But I can't put the light out outside" . . . "Yes you can, you can make it dark." . . . "How?" . . . "You must turn it out very hard. It'll be dark and there will be little lights everywhere (stars)."
>
> (Piaget, 1951/1962, p. 248)

Animism and artificialism perfectly illustrate Piaget's concept of assimilation. The child knows that she is alive and so applies her "alive" schema to every object. Watching adults perform heroic physical feats, such as turning off lights, a 3-year-old generalizes the same "big people control things" schema to the universe. Imagine being a young child taking a family vacation. After visiting that gleaming construction called Las Vegas, wouldn't it make sense that people carved out the Grand Canyon and the Rocky Mountains, too?

The sun and moon examples illustrate another aspect of preoperational thought. According to Piaget, young children believe that they are the literal center of the

animism In Piaget's theory, the preoperational child's belief that inanimate objects are alive.

artificialism In Piaget's theory, the preoperational child's belief that human beings make everything in nature.

egocentrism In Piaget's theory, the preoperational child's inability to understand that other people have different points of view from one's own.

universe, the pivot around which everything else revolves. Their worldview is defined by **egocentrism**—the inability to understand that other people have different points of view.

By *egocentrism*, Piaget does not mean that young children are vain or uncaring—although they will tell you they are the smartest people on earth and the heavenly bodies are at their beck and call. There is nothing more loving than a 3-year-old offering a favorite "blankee" if he sees you upset. The child is egocentric, however, because he assumes that what comforts *him* will automatically comfort you.

You can see delightful examples of egocentrism when talking with a young child. Have you ever had a 3-year-old say to you, "Do you like my dress?" when you never saw that piece of clothing, or refer to a dream she had as if you already knew it because you were living in her head?

Piaget views egocentrism as a perfect example of centering in the human world. Young children are unable to decenter from their own mental processes. They don't realize that what is in their mind is not in everyone else's awareness, too.

Getting on the Adult Wavelength

Piaget discovered that the transition away from preoperations happens gradually. First, children are preoperational in every area. Then, between ages 5 and 7, their thinking gets less static, or "thaws out" (Flavell, 1963). In the conservation-of-liquid task, for instance, a 6-year-old might first say the taller glass had more liquid, but then, after seeing the liquid poured back into a wide glass, becomes unsure: "Is it bigger or not?" She has reached the tipping point where she is poised to reason on a higher cognitive plane.

By age 8, the child has reached this higher-level, concrete operational state: "Even though the second glass is taller, the first is wider" (showing decentering); "You can pour the liquid right back into the short glass and it would look the same" (illustrating reversibility). Now, she doesn't realize that she ever thought differently: "Are you silly? Of course it's the same!"

Piaget found that specific conservations appear at different ages. First, children master conservation of number and then mass and liquid. They may not figure out the most difficult conservations until age 11 or 12. Imagine the challenge of understanding the last task in Figure 5.1 (see page 141)—realizing that when sugar is dissolved in water and seems to disappear, it still exists, but in a different molecular form.

Still, according to Piaget, age 7 or 8 is a landmark for looking beyond immediate appearances, for understanding categories, for decentering in the physical and social worlds, for abandoning the tooth fairy and the idea that our stuffed animals are alive, and for entering the mental planet of adults.

Table 5.4 shows examples of different preoperational ideas. Now test yourself by seeing if you can classify each statement in Piagetian terms.

Table 5.4: Can You Identify the Type of Preoperational Thought from These Real-World Examples?

Here are your possible choices: (a) no identity constancy, (b) animism, (c) artificialism, (d) egocentrism, (e) no conservation, and (f) inability to use classification.

_____ 1. Heidi was watching her father fix lunch. After he cut her sandwich into quarters, Heidi said, "Oh, Daddy, I only wanted you to cut it in two pieces. I'm not hungry enough to eat four!" (Bjorklund & Bjorklund, 1992, p. 168).

_____ 2. My 2-year-old son and I were taking our yearly trip to visit Grandma in Florida. As the plane took off and gained altitude, Thomas looked out the window and said with a delighted grin, "Mommy, TOYS!"

_____ 3. Melanie watched as her father, a professional clown, put on his clown outfit and then began applying his makeup. Before he could finish, Melanie suddenly ran screaming from the room, terrified of the strange clown.

_____ 4. Your child can't understand that he could live in his town and in his state at the same time. He tells you angrily, "I live in Newark, not New Jersey."

_____ 5. As you cross the George Washington Bridge over the Hudson River to New Jersey, your child asks, "Did the same people who built the bridge also make the river?"

Answers: 1. (e) 2. (d) 3. (a) 4. (f) 5. (c)

INTERVENTIONS ⟨ **Using Piaget's Ideas at Home and at Work**

Piaget's concepts provide marvelous insights into young children's minds. For teachers, the theory explains why you need the same-sized cups at a kindergarten lunch table or an argument will erupt, even if you poured each drink from identical cans. Nurses understand that rationally explaining a medical procedure to a 4-year-old is less effective than providing a magic doll to help the child cope.

The theory makes sense of why organizing baseball is impossible with 4- or 5-year-olds. Grasping the rules of games requires abstract conceptualization—skills that preoperational children do not possess. It tells us why young children are terrified of the dark and scary amusement park clowns. So for parents who are uneasy about playing into children's fantasies when they provide "anti-monster spray" to calm bedtime fears, one justification is that, according to Piaget, when a child is ready, she naturally grows out of these ideas.

Piaget's concepts explain the power of pretending (more about this later) and the lure of that favorite childhood holiday, Halloween. When a 4-year-old child dresses up as Batman, he is grappling with understanding that you can look different, yet remain your essential self. The theory accounts for why fourth graders become captivated with soccer and can be avid collectors of baseball cards. Now that they understand rules and categories, concrete operational children are passionate to exercise their conceptual and classification skills.

Children take great pride in collecting, classifying, and trading items like Yu-Gi-Oh cards because they have reached concrete operations and are practicing their new skills.

The theory explains why "real school," the academic part, begins at about age 7. Before middle childhood, we don't have the intellectual tools to understand reversibility, a concept critical to mathematics (if 2 plus 4 is 6, then 6 minus 4 must equal 2). Even empathizing with the teacher's agenda is a concrete operational skill.

The fact that age 7 or 8 is a coming-of-age marker is represented in the classic movie *Home Alone*. The plot of this film would be unthinkable if its hero were 5, or even 6. If the star were 11, the movie would not be as interesting because, by this age, a child could competently take care of himself. Age 8 is when we make the transition to being "home alone." It is the time when we shift from worrying about imaginary threats such as monsters, to grappling with the realistic dangers we face during life.

Evaluating Piaget

Piaget clearly transformed our ideas about young children. Still, in important areas, Piaget was incorrect.

I described a major problem with Piaget's theory in Chapter 3: Just as he minimized what babies know, Piaget overstated young children's egocentrism. If babies can decode intentions, the awareness that we live in "different heads" must dawn on children at a far younger age than 8! (Much more about this mindreading ability soon.)

We might also disagree with Piaget that children abandon animism by age 7 or 8. Maybe he was giving us too *much* credit here. Do you have a good luck charm that keeps the plane from crashing, or a place you go for comfort where you can hear the trees whispering to you?

Children worldwide do learn to conserve (Dasen, 1977, 1984). But because nature interacts with nurture, the ages at which they master specific conservation tasks vary from place to place. An example comes from a village in Mexico, where weaving is the main occupation. Young children in this collectivist culture grasp conservation tasks involving spatial concepts earlier than age 7 or 8 because they have so much hands-on training in this skill (Maynard & Greenfield, 2003). This brings up the dimension Piaget's theory leaves out: how teaching promotes cognitive growth.

Because this girl growing up in Mexico gets so much practice at weaving, we might expect her to grasp concrete operational conservation tasks related to spatial concepts at a relatively early age.

zone of proximal development (ZPD) In Vygotsky's theory, the gap between a child's ability to solve a problem totally on his own and his potential knowledge if taught by a more accomplished person.

scaffolding The process of teaching new skills by entering a child's zone of proximal development and tailoring one's efforts to that person's competence level.

FIGURE 5.2: Vygotsky's zone of proximal development: These lines illustrate the ZPD— the gap between a child's current and potential intellectual ability. If a teacher sensitively teaches within this zone and employs scaffolding (see stepwise lines)— providing support, then backing off when help is no longer needed—students will reach their full intellectual potential.

Vygotsky's Zone of Proximal Development

Piaget implies that we can't convince preschoolers that their dolls are not alive or that the width of one glass makes up for the height of the other. Children naturally grow out of those ideas while manipulating objects on their own. The Russian psychologist Lev Vygotsky (1962, 1978) had a different perspective: People propel mental growth.

Vygotsky was born in the same year as Piaget. He showed as much brilliance at a young age, but—unlike Piaget, who lived to a ripe old age—he died of tuberculosis in his late thirties. Still, Vygotsky's writings have given him towering status in developmental science. One reason is that Vygotsky was an educator. He believed that adults make children mentally advance.

Vygotsky theorized that learning takes place within the **zone of proximal development (ZPD)**, which he defined as the difference between what the child can do by himself and his level of "potential development as determined through problem solving under adult guidance or in collaboration with more capable peers" (Vygotsky, 1978, p. 86; also, see the diagram in Figure 5.2). Teachers must tailor their instruction to a child's proximal zone. Then, as that child becomes more competent, adults should slowly back off and allow the student more responsibility for directing learning on his own. This sensitive pacing has a special name: **scaffolding** (Wood, Bruner, & Ross, 1976).

I gave an illustration of scaffolding in the Chapter 3 discussion of infant-directed speech (IDS). IDS, or baby talk, permits caregivers to penetrate a young child's zone of proximal development for language and so scaffolds emerging speech. In the opening vignette, you saw Ms. Angela draw on Vygotsky's ideas when she articulated the practices good teachers adopt: Encourage students to stretch their capacities, but operate within their proximal zones. Now let's explore scaffolding in operation as a mother teaches her 5-year-old daughter how to play her first board game, Chutes and Ladders:

> Tiffany threw the dice. . . . Her mother said, "How many is that?" . . . Tiffany . . . stared. Her mother counted the dots aloud, and then said . . . , "Now you count them," which Tiffany did. This was repeated for . . . five turns . . . On her sixth move, however, Tiffany. . . . threw the dice and counted the dots herself.
>
> (Bjorklund & Rosenblum, 2001)

This young girl in Thailand is learning to weave just by observing her mother—a strategy that we might find unusual in our teaching-oriented culture.

Notice that this mother was a superb scaffolder. By pacing her interventions to Tiffany's capacities, she paved the way for her child to master the game. But this process did not just flow from parent to child. Tiffany was also teaching her mother how to respond. Just as your professor is gaining new insights into children while teaching this class—or at this minute, as I struggle to write this page, I'm learning to better connect with Vygotsky's ideas—education is a *bidirectional*, mind-expanding duet (Scrimsher & Tudge, 2003).

In our teaching-oriented culture, we have definite ideas about good scaffolders: They actively instruct but are sensitive to a child's responses. However, in collectivist societies, such as among the Mayans living in Mexico's Yucatán Peninsula, children listen. They watch adults. They are not explicitly taught the skills for adult life (Rogoff and others, 2003). So the qualities our culture sees as vital to socializing children are not necessarily part of the ideology of good parenting around the globe.

INTERVENTIONS   **Becoming an Effective Scaffolder**

In our teaching-oriented society, what do superior scaffolders do? Let's list a few techniques:

- They foster a secure attachment, as nurturing, responsive interactions are a basic foundation for learning (Laible, 2004).

- They break a larger cognitive challenge, such as learning Chutes and Ladders, into manageable steps (Berk & Winsler, 1999).

- They continue helping until the child has fully mastered the concept before moving on, as Tiffany's mother did earlier.

Table 5.5 compares Vygotsky's and Piaget's ideas and summarizes these world-class geniuses' backgrounds (Vianna & Stetsenko, 2006). Although often described in opposing terms, these theories form an ideal pair. Piaget gave us insights into the structure of childhood cognition. Vygotsky offered us an engine to transform children's lives.

Table 5.5: Vygotskian (left) and Piagetian (right) Perspectives on Life and Learning

© 2016 Macmillan

Bill Anderson/Science Source

Biography	Russian, Jewish, communist (reached teenage years during the Russian Revolution), believed in Marx	Swiss, middle-class family
Basic interests	Education, literature, literary criticism, biology, mollusks	Wanted to know how to stimulate thinking and to trace the evolution of thought in stages
Overall orientation	Look at interpersonal processes and the role of society in cognition	Look for universal developmental processes
Basic ideas	1. We develop intellectually through social interactions.	1. We develop intellectually through physically acting on the world.
	2. Development is a collaborative endeavor.	2. Development takes place on our own inner timetable.
	3. People cause cognitive growth.	3. When we are internally ready, we reach a higher level of cognitive development.
Implications for education	Instruction is critical to development. Teachers should sensitively intervene within each child's zone of proximal development.	Provide ample materials to let children explore and learn on their own.

Language

So far, I have been discussing the mental milestones in this chapter as if they occurred in a vacuum. But language, that uniquely human cognitive skill, is the motor that helps scaffold everything we learn. Vygotsky (1978) actually put speaking front and center in children's ability to think.

According to Vygotsky, by talking to her image in the mirror "out loud," this girl is learning to monitor her behavior. Have you ever done the same thing when no one was watching?

inner speech In Vygotsky's theory, the way in which human beings learn to regulate their behavior and master cognitive challenges, through silently repeating information or talking to themselves.

phoneme The sound units that convey meaning in a given language—for example, in English, the c sound of *cat* and the b sound of *bat*.

morpheme The smallest unit of meaning in a particular language—for example, *boys* contains two morphemes: *boy* and the plural suffix *-s*.

mean length of utterance (MLU) The average number of morphemes per sentence.

syntax The system of grammatical rules in a particular language.

semantics The meaning system of a language—that is, what the words stand for.

overregularization An error in early language development, in which young children apply the rules for plurals and past tenses even to exceptions, so irregular forms sound like regular forms.

Inner Speech

According to Vygotsky, thinking happens when the words a child hears from parents and other scaffolders migrate inward to become talk directed at the self. Using the earlier Chutes and Ladders example, after listening to her mother say "Count them" a number of times, Tiffany learned the game by repeating "Count them" to herself. Thinking, according to Vygotsky, is really **inner speech.**

Support for this idea comes from listening to young children as they monitor their actions. A 3-year-old might say, "Don't touch!" as she moves near the stove; or reminds herself to be "a good girl" at preschool that day (Manfra & Winsler, 2006). We adults sometimes behave the same way. If something is *really important*—and if no one is listening—have you ever reminded yourself "Be sure to do X, Y, and Z" out loud?

Developing Speech

How does language *itself* unfold? Actually, during early childhood, language does more than unfold. It explodes.

By our second birthday, we are beginning to put together words (see Chapter 3). By kindergarten, we basically have adult language nailed down. Considering the challenges involved in mastering language, this achievement is remarkable. To speak like adults, children must articulate word sounds. They must string units of meaning together in sentences. They must produce sentences that are grammatically correct. They must understand the meanings of words.

The word sounds of language are called **phonemes.** When infants begin to speak, they produce single phonemes—for instance, they call their bottle *ba*. They repeat sounds that seem similar, such as calling their bottle *baba*, when they cannot form the next syllable of the word. By age 3, while children have made tremendous strides in producing phonemes, they still—as you saw in the chapter-opening vignette—have trouble pronouncing multisyllabic words (like *psghetti*). Then, early in elementary school, these articulation problems disappear—but not completely. Have you ever had a problem pronouncing a difficult word that you silently read on a page?

The meaning units of language are called **morphemes** (for example, the word *boys* has two units of meaning: *boy* and the plural suffix *-s*). As children get older, their average number of morphemes per sentence—called their **mean length of utterance (MLU)**—expands. A 2-year-old's telegraphic utterance of "Me juice" (2 MLUs) grows to "Me want juice" (3 MLUs) and then, at age 4, to "Please give me the juice" (5 MLUs). Also around age 3 or 4, children are fascinated by producing long, jumbled-together sentences strung together by *and* ("Give me juice and crackers and milk and cookies and . . .").

This brings up the steps to mastering grammar, or **syntax.** What's interesting here are the classic mistakes that young children make. As parents are well aware, one of the first words that children utter is *no*. First, children add this word to the beginning of a sentence ("No eat cheese" or "No go inside"). Then, they move the negative term inside the sentence, next to the main verb ("I no sing" or "He no do it"). A question starts out as a declarative sentence with a rising intonation: "I have a drink, Daddy?" Then it, too, is replaced by the correct word order: "Can I have a drink, Daddy?" Children typically produce grammatically correct sentences by the time they enter school.

The most amazing changes occur in **semantics**—understanding word meanings. Here, children go from three- or four-word vocabularies at age 1 to knowing about 10,000 words by age 6! (See Slobin, 1972; Smith, 1926.) While we have the other core abilities under our belts by the end of early childhood, our vocabularies continue to grow from age 2 to 102.

One mistake young children make while learning language is called **overregularization.** At approximately age 3 or 4, they adopt general rules for plurals or past tenses even to exceptions. A preschooler will say *runned, goed, teached, sawed, mouses, feets,* and *cup of sugars* rather than using the correct irregular form (Berko, 1958).

Table 5.6: Challenges on the Language Pathway: A Summary Table

Type of Challenge	Description	Example
Phonemes	Has trouble forming sounds	*Baba, psghetti*
Morphemes	Uses few meaning units per sentence	*Me go home*
Syntax (grammar)	Makes mistakes in applying rules for forming sentences	*Me come out*
Semantics	Has problems understanding word meanings	*Calls the family dog a horsey*
Overregularization	Puts irregular pasts and plurals into regular forms	*Foots; runned*
Over/underextension	Applies verbal labels too broadly/narrowly	*Calls every old man grandpa; tells another child he can't have a grandpa because grandpa is the name for his grandfather alone*

Another error lies in children's semantic mistakes. Also around age 3, children may use **overextensions**—extending a verbal label too broadly. In Piaget's terminology, they assimilate the word *horsey* to all four-legged creatures, such as dogs, cats, and lions in the zoo. Or they use **underextensions**—making name categories too narrow. A 3-year-old may insist that only her own pet is a dog and all the other neighborhood dogs must be called something else. As children get older, through continual assimilation and accommodation, they sort out these glitches.

Table 5.6 summarizes these challenges. Now you might want to have a conversation with a 3- or 4-year-old child. Can you pick out examples of overregularization, overextensions or underextensions, problems with syntax (grammar), or difficulties pronouncing phonemes (word sounds)? Can you figure out the child's MLU?

overextension An error in early language development in which young children apply verbal labels too broadly.

underextension An error in early language development in which young children apply verbal labels too narrowly.

Tying It All Together

1. While with your 3-year-old nephew Vincente, you observe many examples of preoperational thought. Give the Piagetian label—egocentrism, animism, no conservation, artificialism, identity constancy—for each of the following:
   a. Vincente tells you that the tree in the garden is watching him.
   b. When you stub your toe, Vincente gives you his stuffed animal.
   c. Vincente explains that his daddy made the sun.
   d. Vincente says, "There's more now," when you pour juice from a wide carton into a skinny glass.
   e. Vincente tells you that his sister turned into a princess yesterday when she put on a costume.

2. In a sentence, explain the basic mental difference between an 8-year-old in the concrete operational stage and a preoperational 4-year-old.

3. Four-year-old Christopher knows the alphabet and is sounding out words in books. Drawing on Vygotsky's theory, Chris's parents should (choose one): *buy alphabet books, because their son will easily recognize each word; buy "easy-to-read" books just above their son's skill level; challenge Chris by getting him books with complicated stories.*

4. Your 3-year-old cousin is talking out loud and making comments such as "Put the big piece here," while constructing a puzzle. What would Vygotsky say about this behavior?

5. You are listening to a preschooler named Joshua. Pick out the examples of overregularization and overextension from the following comments:
   a. When offered a piece of cheese, Joshua said, "I no eat cheese."
   b. Seeing a dog run away, Joshua said, "The doggie runned away."
   c. Taken to a petting zoo, Joshua pointed excitedly at a goat and said, "Horsey!"

Answers to the Tying It All Together questions can be found at the end of this chapter.

LEARNING OUTCOMES

- Explain autobiographical memory.
- Outline theory of mind, mentioning its importance and variations from child to child.

autobiographical memories Recollections of events and experiences that make up one's life history.

Emotional Development

Language makes us capable of the uniquely human talents described at the beginning of this chapter. We are the only species that reflects on our past (Fivush, 2011). The essence of being human is that we effortlessly transport ourselves into each other's heads, decoding what people are thinking from their own point of view. How do children learn to articulate their past experiences? When do we *fully* grasp that other people's perspectives are different from our own?

Constructing Our Personal Past

Autobiographical memories refer to reflecting on our life histories: from our earliest memories at age 3 or 4 to that incredible experience at work last week. Children's understanding that they have a personal autobiography is scaffolded through a specific kind of talk. Caregivers reminisce with young children: "Remember going on a train to visit Grandma?" "What did we do at the beach last week?" These *past-talk conversations* are teaching a lesson: "You have a past and future. You are an enduring self."

Past-talk conversations typically begin with parents doing the "remembering" when toddlers begin to speak (Harley & Reese, 1999). Then, during preschool, children become partners in these mutual stories and, at age 4 or 5, initiate past-talk conversations on their own (Nelson & Fivush, 2004). Listen to this vivid autobiographical memory produced by a 6-year-old:

INTERVIEWER: . . . [T]ell me about the ballet recital[.]

CHILD: I was . . . scared because . . . I couldn't see mom and dad. . . . Ummm, we were on a slippery surface and we . . . did "Where the Wild Things Are" and we . . . Mine had horns sticking out of it . . . And I had baggy pants.

(Nelson & Fivush, 2004)

As this girl reaches adolescence, she will link these memories to each other and construct a timeline of her life (Chen, McAnally, & Reese, 2013; Habermas, Negele, & Mayer, 2010). By about age 16, she will use these events to reflect on her enduring personality ("This is the kind of person I am, as shown by how I felt at age 4 or 5 or 9"). Then she will have achieved that Eriksonian milestone—an *identity* to carry through life (more about this topic in Chapter 10).

Caregivers can help stimulate autobiographical memory by sensitively asking questions about exciting experiences they shared with their child (Valentino and others, 2014). ("Wasn't the circus amazing? What did you like best?") By highlighting specific ways of thinking, past-talk conversations help scaffold the values a given society holds dear (Alea & Wang, 2015). But lecturing doesn't work. Parents must engage preschoolers in a loving, mutual, give-and-take talk (Salmon & Reese, 2015). Autobiographical memories are apt to be richer when children are securely attached (McDonnell and others, 2016). Therefore, the quality of these memories offers clues into a person's early life.

In one study, 8-year-olds with depressed mothers produced overly general autobiographical memories ("I went to the circus") rather than recalling specifics ("I remember how I went to the circus, and I'll never forget the cotton candy and lions") (Woody, Burkhouse, & Gibb, 2015). Traumatic childhood experiences produce stunted personal autobiographies, too (Salmon & Reese, 2015).

The most chilling example of this autobiographical memory failure (what Freud might call *repression*) occurred with children who were removed from an abusive home. If a boy or girl was insecurely attached, that child either made false statements about what took place that day or denied remembering anything about the traumatic event (Melinder and others, 2013).

When they get home, this mother can help her daughter construct her "personal autobiography" by starting a dialogue about their wonderful day at the beach.

Dan76/Shutterstock

The take-home message is that our personal autobiography (or full sense of self) is scaffolded through loving caregiver–child interactions. Relationships—as Vygotsky believed—teach us to be an independent self.

And at the same time as they understand their pasts, children begin to fully grasp that other people live in a different mental space.

Making Sense of Other People's Minds

Listen to 3-year-olds having a conversation, and it's as if you're hearing separate monologues, like mental ships passing in the night. Around age 4 or 5, children relate in a *give-and-take* way. They have reached that landmark called **theory of mind**, the understanding that other people have perspectives different from their own. Developmentalists use a creative procedure to demonstrate this milestone—*the false-belief task*.

With a friend and a young child, see if you can perform the classic theory-of-mind task illustrated on the next page in Figure 5.3 (Wimmer & Perner, 1983). Hide a toy somewhere (location A) while the child and your friend watch. Then have your friend leave the room. Once she is gone, move the toy to another hiding place (location B). Next, ask the child where *your friend* will look for the toy when she returns. If the child is under age 4, he will typically answer the second hiding place (location B), even though your friend could not know the toy has been moved. It's as if the child doesn't grasp the fact that what *he* observed can't be in your friend's head, too.

> **theory of mind**
> Children's first cognitive understanding, which appears at about age 4, that other people have different beliefs and perspectives from their own.

What Happens When Children Have a Theory of Mind?

Having a theory of mind is not only vital to having a real conversation, it is crucial to convincing someone to do what you say. Researchers asked children to persuade a puppet to do something aversive, such as eat broccoli or brush its teeth. Even controlling for verbal abilities, the number of arguments a given boy or girl made was linked to advanced theory of mind (Slaughter, Peterson, & Moore, 2013).

Theory of mind is essential to understanding that people may not have your best interests at heart. One developmentalist had children play a game with "Mean Monkey," a puppet the experimenter controlled (Peskin, 1992). Beforehand, the researcher had asked the children which sticker they wanted. Then, she had Mean Monkey pick each child's favorite choice. Most 4-year-olds figured out how to play the game and told Mean Monkey the opposite of what they wanted. Three-year-olds never caught on. They always pointed to their favorite sticker and got the "yucky" one instead.

A student brought home the real-world message of this research. She commented that her 4-year-old nephew had reached the stage where he was lying. Three-year-olds do impulsively tell lies. For example, after peeking at a forbidden toy while adults watched through a one-way mirror, many later report: "I did not look!" (See Ma and others, 2015.) But when children have a theory of mind, their lies become more strategic and sophisticated. So having the talent to lie effectively is a crucial life skill! (See Evans, Xu, & Lee, 2011.)

The false-belief studies, conducted during the last decades of the twentieth century, convinced developmentalists that Piaget's ideas about preoperational egocentrism were wrong. Although theory-of-mind abilities (and, of course, lying talents!) mature during elementary school (Hughes & Devine, 2015; Z. Wang and others, 2016) and into adulthood, even as young as preschool, children clearly grasp the principle that other people live in different heads.

Individual Differences in Theory of Mind

Boys and girls around the world typically pass false-belief tasks at around age 4 or 5. But perhaps because parents in nations such as Iran and China strongly socialize obedience, children in these collectivist cultures take longer to grasp the idea that people have conflicting opinions than do Western 4-year-olds (Shahaeian and others, 2011; see also Table 5.7 on page 153 for some fascinating neural findings related to theory of mind and the collectivist/individualistic distinction).

FIGURE 5.3: The false-belief task: In this classic test for *theory of mind,* children under age 4 are likely to say that Ms. X will look for the toy under the bed, even though Ms. X could not possibly know the toy was moved to this new location.

Data from Wimmer & Perner, 1983.

(1) Another adult and a young child watch while you hide a toy in a place like a desk drawer.

(2) The other adult [Ms. X] leaves the room.

(3) You hide the toy under the bed and then ask the child, "Where will Ms. X look for the toy?"

Conversely, because they have extensive hands-on experience colliding (that is, arguing) with opposing sibling perspectives—"Hey, I want that toy!" "No, I do!"—Western preschoolers who have older brothers and sisters tend to pass theory-of-mind tasks at somewhat earlier ages than only children do (McAlister & Peterson, 2013).

Bilingual preschoolers—because they must sensitively switch languages—and boys and girls with superior language skills also reach this social milestone earlier than the typical child (Adi-Japha, Berberich-Artzi, & Libnawi, 2010; Chertkow and others, 2010; Hughes & Devine, 2015). Preschoolers' ability to control themselves is particularly strongly

> **Table 5.7:** Brain-Imaging Theory-of-Mind and Autobiographical-Memory Findings to Wrap Your Head Around
>
> **Reflecting on the self and others' mental states is a frontal-lobe activity involving slightly different brain regions:** When Westerners are asked to recall autobiographical memories, a brain region called the *medial frontal cortex* lights up. When given theory-of-mind–type tasks, a slightly different area of the medial frontal cortex is activated. Therefore, thinking about ourselves and decoding other people's emotions involves distinctive (but closely aligned) brain areas.
>
> **Interesting cultural variation:** This classic neural separation, however, does not exist when Chinese adults think about themselves and their mothers. More astonishing, thinking about yourself and family members activates either the same or more separate brain regions, depending on whether you have a collectivist (interdependent) or individualistic (self-oriented) worldview.
>
> **Interesting variation from person to person:** When you judge the mental state of someone you view as similar, such as a good friend, a closely aligned brain region lights up as when you are asked to reflect on yourself (as if you are drawing on your feelings about how you would respond in interpreting this person's feelings). But, inferring the mental states of dissimilar others— people you view as very different—activates truly separate brain areas. Research also suggests that when people are asked to imagine the feelings of disliked out-group members (for example, a Palestinian is told to empathize with the perspective of a Jewish-Israeli West Bank settler), this instruction elicits reduced activity in the "social" brain!
>
> **Conclusion:** Our attitudes about the self in relationship to other human beings are mirrored in the physical architecture of our brain.
>
> Information from Abu-Akel & Shamay-Tsoory, 2011; Heatherton, 2011; Oddo and others, 2010; Rabin and others, 2010.

related to mastering false-belief tasks (Carlson, Claxton, & Moses, 2016; Duh and others, 2016; Z. Wang and others, 2016; more about this basic talent in the next chapter). Being early (or late) in developing theory of mind, in turn, has real-world effects.

In reviewing 20 studies, researchers found that children (especially girls) with superior theory-of-mind skills were more popular during preschool and early elementary school. Moreover, this advantage stayed stable with age, which suggests that the talent of understanding other people's mental states is an asset we carry through childhood and the adult years (Slaughter, Peterson, & Moore, 2013).

Theory-of-mind abilities are linked to sharing and helping—especially during elementary school (Imuta and others, 2016). Again, advanced theory of mind is more linked to behaving in a caring way for girls (Kuhnert and others, 2017).

The most poignant example of the critical value of having a theory of mind involves friendships. Even controlling for age, language skills, and popularity, researchers found that 5-year-old boys and girls with poor theory-of-mind abilities were more likely to travel friendless from kindergarten to second grade (Fink and others, 2015).

One reason that these best friends connected may be that both have developed a theory of mind.

INTERVENTIONS Stimulating Theory of Mind

Given its bedrock importance for relationships, here are some strategies adults can use to enhance children's theory of mind (Mori & Cigala, 2016):

- Continually train preschoolers in perspective-taking by pointing out other people's feelings, as Ms. Angela did throughout the chapter-opening vignette.

- When reading stories to young children, discuss what each protagonist is feeling. In one study, when researchers used this strategy at a preschool serving low-income children, the group trained in being alert to mental states showed better theory-of-mind abilities two months later when compared to children offered traditional story time (Tompkins, 2015).

- Embed false-belief tasks into games. For instance, leave a room and have the child hide a toy in a new place, then return and look for that toy where you think it should be. Open a chocolate box that is full of pencils, and then ask children to predict what an unfamiliar person will expect to find when she looks inside.

• Encourage dramatic play. Have children dress up in costumes and pretend.

Actually, dressing up in costumes and pretending does not need to be taught. As I will describe next, pretending is *basic* to the early childhood years.

Tying It All Together

1. Andrew said to Madison, his 3-year-old son, "Remember when we went to Grandma and Grandpa's last year? . . . It was your birthday, and what did Grandma make for you?" This _____ conversation will help scaffold Madison's _____.

2. Pick the statement that would *not* signify that a child has developed a full-fledged theory of mind:
   a. He's having a give-and-take conversation with you.
   b. He realizes that if you weren't there, you can't know what's gone on—and tries to explain what happened while you were absent.
   c. When he has done something he shouldn't do, he is likely to lie convincingly.
   d. He's learning to read.

3. What popular preschool game is implicitly tailored to teach theory of mind?

Answers to the Tying It All Together questions can be found at the end of this chapter.

Social Development

LEARNING OUTCOMES

• List the different play types.
• Outline the development and functions that pretending serves.
• Describe the characteristics and causes of gender-segregated play.
• List the symptoms, prevalence, and treatments for autism spectrum disorders.

Think back to your hours pretending to be a superhero or supermodel, or playing with battleships and Barbies with your friends. Why is pretend play a core preschool passion, and why do boys and girls play in different ways?

Play: The Work of Early Childhood

Developmentalists divide young children's play (the nonsports-oriented kind) into different categories. **Exercise play** involves the running and chasing behavior you saw in the opening vignette. **Rough-and-tumble play** refers to the excited shoving and wrestling that is most apparent with boys.

Actually, rough-and-tumble play is classically male behavior. Boys (but not girls) who engage in rough-and-tumble play *with their own sex* are especially popular with their peers (Lindsey, 2014). Rough-and-tumble play, evolutionary psychologists believe, is biologically built into being male (Bjorklund & Pellegrini, 2002; Flanders and others, 2013; Pellegrini, 2006).

Pretending

Fantasy play, or *pretending,* is different. Here, the child takes a stance apart from reality and makes up a scene, often with a toy or other prop. While fantasy play also can be intensely physical, this "as if" quality makes it unique. Children must pretend to be pirates or superheroes as they wrestle and chase.

THE DEVELOPMENT AND DECLINE OF PRETENDING Research suggests that the roots of pretending emerge in later infancy, and mothers scaffold this skill. In a classic study, developmentalists watched 1-year-olds with their mothers at home. Although toddlers often initiated a fantasy episode, they needed a parent to expand on the scene (Dunn, Wooding, & Hermann, 1977). For example, a child would pretend to make a phone call, and his mother would pick up the real phone and say, "Hello, this is Mommy. Should I come home now?"

rbsf_96/Photodisc/Getty Images

Rough-and-tumble play is not only tremendously exciting, but it seems to be genetically built into being "male."

At about age 3, children transfer pretending with mothers to pretending with peers. **Collaborative pretend play,** or fantasizing *together* with another child, gets going at about age 4 (Smolucha & Smolucha, 1998). Because they must work together to develop the scene, collaboratively pretending shows that preschoolers have a theory of mind. (You need to understand that your fellow playwright has a different script in his head.) Collaboratively pretending, in turn, helps teach young children to make better sense of other people's minds (Nicolopoulou and others, 2010).

Anyone with a child can see these changes firsthand. When a 2-year-old has his "best friend" over, they play in parallel orbits—if things go well. More likely, a titanic battle erupts, as each child exerts autonomy and initiative by attempting to gain possession of the toys. By age 4, children can play *together*. At age 5, they can often pretend together for hours—with only a few world-class fights that are usually resolved.

Although fantasy play can continue into early adolescence, when children reach concrete operations, their interest shifts to structured games (Bjorklund & Pellegrini, 2002). At age 3, a child pretends to bake in the kitchen corner; at 9, he wants to bake a cake. At age 4, you ran around playing pirates; at 9, you tried to hit the ball like the Pittsburgh Pirates do.

THE PURPOSES OF PRETENDING Interestingly, around the world, when children pretend, their play has similar plots. Let's eavesdrop at a U.S. preschool:

Boy 2: I don't want to be a kitty anymore.

Girl: You are a husband?

Boy 2: Yeah.

Boys 1 and 2: Husbands, husbands! *(Yell and run around the playhouse)*

Girl: Hold it, Bill, I can't have two husbands.

Boys 1 and 2: Two husbands! Two husbands!

Girl: We gonna marry ourselves, right?

(Corsaro, 1985, pp. 102–104)

Why do young children play "family," and assume the "correct" roles when they play mommy and daddy? For answers, let's turn to the insights of that genius, Lev Vygotsky, again.

Play allows children to practice adult roles. Vygotsky (1978) believed that pretending allows children to rehearse being adults. The reason girls pretend to be mommy and baby is that they immediately realize women are the main child-care providers around the world. Boys are pulled to play soldiers because this activity offers them built-in training for the wars they may face as adults (Pellegrini & Smith, 2005).

Play allows children a sense of control. As the following preschool conversation suggests, pretending has a deeper psychological function, too:

Girl 1: Yeah, and let's pretend when Mommy's out until later.

Girl 2: Ooooh. Well, I'm not the boss around here, though. 'Cause mommies are the bosses.

Girl 1: *(Doubtfully)* But maybe we won't know how to punish.

Girl 2: I will. I'll put my hand up and spank. That's what my mom does.

Girl 1: My mom does too.

(Corsaro, 1985, p. 96)

For these 4-year-old girls (aka women who have dressed up to go to a party), their collaborative pretend play is teaching them vital theory-of-mind skills.

exercise play Running and chasing play that exercises children's physical skills.

rough-and-tumble play Play that involves shoving, wrestling, and hitting, but in which no actual harm is intended; especially characteristic of boys.

fantasy play Pretend play in which a child makes up a scene, often with a toy or other prop.

collaborative pretend play Fantasy play in which children work together to develop and act out scenes.

Imagine that, like the supersized preschooler shown here (Professor William Corsaro), you could spend years going down slides, playing family, and bonding with 3- and 4-year-olds—and then get professional recognition for your academic work. What an incredible career!

While reading the preceding chapters, you may have been thinking that the supposedly carefree early childhood years are hardly free of stress. We expect 3- and 4-year-olds to "sit still," "share," and use their "inside voice" at the same age when, Erikson believes, their mission is to passionately explore life. We discipline preschoolers when they don't have the concrete operational talents to make sense of abstract adult rules. Vygotsky (1978) believed that, confronted by these continual frustrations, young children enter "an illusory role" in which they take control. In play, *you* can be the spanking mommy or the queen of the castle, even when you are small and sometimes feel insignificant.

To penetrate the inner world of preschool fantasy play, sociologist William Corsaro (1985, 1997) went undercover, entering a nursery school as a member of the class. (No problem. The children welcomed their new playmate, whom they called Big Bill, as a clumsy, enlarged version of themselves.) As Vygotsky would predict, Corsaro found that preschool play plots often centered on mastering upsetting events. There were separation/reunion scenarios ("Help! I'm lost in the forest." "I'll find you.") and danger/rescue plots ("Get in the house. It's gonna be a rainstorm!"). Sometimes, play scenarios centered on that ultimate frightening event, death:

Child 1: We are dead, we are dead! Help, we are dead! *(Puts animals on their sides)*

Child 2: You can't talk if you are dead.

Child 1: Oh, well, Leah's talked when she was dead, so mine have to talk when they are dead. Help, help, we are dead!

(Corsaro, 1985 p. 204)

Notice that these themes are basic to Disney movies and fairy tales. From *Finding Nemo*, *Bambi*, and *The Lion King* to—my personal favorite—*Dumbo*, there is nothing more heart-wrenching than being separated from your parent. From the greedy old witch in *Hansel and Gretel* to the jealous queen in *Snow White*, no scenario is as sweet as triumphing over evil and possible death.

Play furthers our understanding of social norms. Corsaro (1985) found that death was a touchy play topic. When children proposed these plots, their partners might try to change the script. This relates to Vygotsky's third insight about play: Although children's play looks unstructured, it has clear boundaries and rules. Plots involving dead animals waking up make children uncomfortable because they violate the conditions of life. Children get especially uneasy when a play partner proposes scenarios with gory themes, such as cutting off people's heads (Dunn & Hughes, 2001). Therefore, play teaches children how to act and how not to behave. Wouldn't you want to retreat if someone showed an intense interest in decapitation while having a conversation with you?

The idea that play teaches social norms brings me to that basic childhood play rule—girls and boys behave in different ways.

Girls' and Boys' Play Worlds

[Some] girls, all about five . . . years old, are looking through department store catalogues, . . . concentrating on what they call "girls' stuff" and referring to some of the other items as "yucky boys' stuff." . . . Shirley points to a picture of a couch . . . "All we want is the pretty stuff," says Ruth. Peggy now announces, "If you come to my birthday, every girl in the school is invited. I'm going to put a sign up that says, 'No boys allowed!'"

"Oh good, good, good," says Vickie. "I hate boys."

(Corsaro, 1997, p. 155)

gender-segregated play Play in which boys and girls associate only with members of their own gender—typical of childhood.

Does this conversation bring back memories of being age 5 or 6? How does **gender-segregated play** develop? What are the differences in boy versus girl play, and what causes the genders to separate into these different camps?

Exploring the Separate Societies

Visit a playground and observe children of different ages. Notice that toddlers show few signs of gender-segregated play. In preschool, children start to play in sex-segregated groups (Martin & Ruble, 2010). By approximately age 5 or 6, gender-segregated play is typical, although boys and girls do occasionally play in mixed-sex groups (Fabes, Martin, & Hanish, 2003).

Now, go back to the playground and look at the *way* boys and girls relate. Do you notice that boy and girl play differs in the following ways?

BOYS EXCITEDLY RUN AROUND; GIRLS CALMLY TALK Boys' play is more rambunctious. Even during physical games such as tag, girls play together in calmer, more subdued ways (Maccoby, 1998; Pellegrini, 2006). The difference in activity levels is striking if you have the pleasure of witnessing one sex playing with the other sex's toys. In one memorable episode, after my 4-year-old son and a friend invaded a girl's stash of dolls, they gleefully ran around the house bashing Barbie into Barbie and using their booty as swords.

A visit to this first grade lunchroom vividly brings home the fact that by middle childhood, gender segregation is entrenched.

BOYS COMPETE IN GROUPS; GIRLS PLAY COLLABORATIVELY, ONE-ON-ONE Their exuberant, rough-and-tumble play explains why boys tend to take over preschool playgrounds, running and yelling, filling most of the physical space. Another difference lies in playgroup *size*. Boys get together in packs. Girls play in smaller, more intimate groups (Maccoby, 1990, 1998; Ruble, Martin, & Berenbaum, 2006).

Boys and girls also differ in the *way* they relate. Boys try to establish dominance and compete to be the best. This competitive versus cooperative style spills over into children's talk. Girl-to-girl collaborative play really sounds collaborative ("I'll be the doctor, OK?"). Boys give each other bossy commands like "I'm doing the operation. Lie down, now!" (see Maccoby, 1998). Girl-to-girl fantasy play involves nurturing themes. Boys prefer the warrior, superhero mode.

The stereotypic quality of girls' fantasy play came as a shock when I spent three days playing with a visiting 5-year-old niece. We devoted day 1 to setting up a beauty shop, complete with nail polishes and shampoos. We had a table for massages and a makeover section featuring every cosmetic I owned. Then we opened for business with our relatives and (of course!)—by charging for our services—made money for toys. We spent the last day playing with a "pool party" Barbie combo my niece selected at Walmart that afternoon.

Boys' and girls' different play interests show why the kindergartners in the vignette at the beginning of this section came to hate those "yucky" boys. Another reason why girls sometimes turn off to the other gender is the unpleasant reception they get from the different camp. Researchers observing at a preschool found that, while active girls played with the boys early in the year, they eventually were rejected and forced to play with their own sex (Pellegrini and others, 2007). Therefore, boys first erect the barriers: "No girls allowed!" Moreover, the gender barriers are *generally* more rigid for males.

BOYS LIVE IN A MORE EXCLUSIONARY, SEPARATE WORLD My niece did choose to buy Barbies, but she also plays with trucks. She loves chasing and competing at jumping and running, not just doing her nails. So, even though they may dislike the other gender, girls cross the divide. Boys avoid that chasm—refusing to venture down the Barbie aisle or consider buying a toy labeled "girl." Therefore, boys live in a more roped-off gender world (Boyle, Marshall, & Robeson, 2003).

Now, you might be interested to know what happened during my final day pretending with the pool party toys. After my niece said, "Aunt Janet, let's pretend we are the popular girls," our Barbies tried on fancy dresses ("What shall I wear, Jane?") in preparation for a pool party, where the dolls met up to discuss—*guess what*—shopping and where they did their nails!

What Causes Gender-Stereotyped Play?

Why do children, such as my niece, play in gender-stereotyped ways? Answers come from exploring three forces: biology (nature), socialization (nurture), and cognitions (thoughts).

A BIOLOGICAL UNDERPINNING Ample evidence suggests that gender-segregated play is biologically built in. Children worldwide form separate play societies (Maccoby, 1998). Troops of juvenile rhesus monkeys behave *exactly* like human children. The males segregate into their own groups and engage in rough-and-tumble play (Pellegrini, 2006).

Actually, male gender-typed play is tied to hormone levels during the first months of life. Researchers looked at the naturally occurring amount of salivary testosterone in 3-month-old boys and girls (females also produce this classic male sex hormone). Remarkably, both sexes with high concentrations of testosterone displayed more male play behaviors at age 2 (Saenz & Alexander, 2013).

Moreover, female fetuses exposed to high levels of prenatal testosterone show more masculine interests as teens and emerging adults (Udry, 2000)! Therefore, in utero testosterone *epigenetically* programs a more "feminized" or "masculinized" brain.

THE AMPLIFYING EFFECT OF SOCIALIZATION The wider world solifies this split. From the images in preschool coloring books (Fitzpatrick & McPherson, 2010), to traditional parental gender-role attitudes (Halpern & Perry-Jenkins, 2016), to the color pink that screams "Just for girls" (see the How Do We Know box)—everything brings home the message: Males and females act in different ways.

Peers play a powerful role in this programming. When they play in mixed-gender groups, children act in less gender-stereotyped ways (Fabes and others, 2003). Therefore, splitting into separate play societies trains children to behave in ways typical of their own sex (Martin & Fabes, 2001).

Same-sex playmates reinforce one another for selecting gender-stereotyped activities ("Let's play with dolls." "Great!"). The pressure to toe the gender line is promoted by strong social sanctions. Children reject classmates who behave in "gender atypical ways" (such as girls who hit and boys who play with dolls) (Lee & Troop-Gordon, 2011; Smith, Rose, & Schwartz-Mette, 2010). In fact, in the study I mentioned earlier, while preschool boys who engaged in rough-and-tumble play with their own sex were popular, the class disliked children who used this play style with girls (Lindsey, 2014).

gender schema theory
Explanation for gender-stereotyped behavior that emphasizes the role of cognitions; specifically, once children know their gender label (girl or boy), they model their own sex.

THE IMPACT OF COGNITIONS A cognitive process reinforces these external messages. According to **gender schema theory** (Bem, 1981; Martin & Dinella, 2002), once children understand their category (girl or boy), they selectively attend to the activities of their own sex.

When do we first grasp our gender label and start this lifelong practice of modeling our group? The answer is at about age 2½ (Martin & Ruble, 2010)! Although they may not learn the real difference until much later, 3-year-olds can tell you that girls have long hair and cry a lot, whereas boys fight and play with trucks. At about age 5, when they are mastering the similar concept of identity constancy (the knowledge that your essential self doesn't change when you dress up in a gorilla costume), children grasp the idea that once you start out as a boy or girl, you typically stay that way for life (Kohlberg, 1966).

In sum, my niece's beauty-shop activities had a biological basis, although nurture forces greatly accelerated this process almost from birth.

Children embody gender schema theory by continually modeling their own sex.

Ariel Skelley/Getty Images

HOW DO WE KNOW . . .
that pink gives girls permission to act like boys?

While I was writing this chapter, the 2017 Women's March erupted around the globe. Witnessing the sea of pink-hued hats, I wondered: What power does the color pink have in women's lives? This research offered fascinating cues (Weisgram, Fulcher, & Dinella, 2014).

In two creative studies exploring the impact of color in gender toy preferences, developmentalists seated preschool boys and girls at tables featuring a variety of toys. The first study featured classic boy toys (such as guns and fighter jets) in traditionally masculine colors (like gray and black), as well as male-type toys painted in that classic female hue, pink. In a second study, the psychologists labeled unfamiliar objects, such as a nutcracker, as toys designed for either "boys" or "girls," and then painted these objects in either traditional or opposite-gender hues.

Boys, they discovered, gravitated to toys designated for "boys" no matter their color. But

if an object for boys was painted in pink, girls decided it was fine to play with that toy. Therefore, *pink* may give girls a green light to enjoy boy pleasures, such as fighter jets and guns, because that color signals, "That's okay for my sex."

This research suggests that pink becomes a defining symbol of womanhood during our earliest years of life. Moreover, donning this color during adulthood, I believe, may allow women to both embrace their gender identity and rebel at the same time. Wearing pink gives women full latitude to fight just like men!

Wearing pink boxing gloves may permit this woman to excel at her offbeat profession and prove her femininity at the same time.

INTERVENTIONS ◄ **Careers in Early Childhood: Encouraging Less Stereotyped Play**

Still, the rigid push to play in "girl" and "boy" ways collides with the real-world diversity in gender preferences. While an example is **transgender** teens and adults, people whose gender identity is different from their sex at birth, women do excel at classically male professions and men routinely act in gentle, nurturing ways. How can educators promote more diverse preschool play?

- Give children ample chances to interact in mixed-sex groups by carefully planning activities in which boys and girls must work together.

- Organize the classroom to foster mixed-gender play—no doll corner or truck corner, but dolls and trucks in *every* corner of the classroom.

- Showcase role models (in stories and posters) who behave in "non-standard" ways, such as female aerospace engineers and male nurses.

Hopefully, these techniques will mitigate the bullying that occurs when children are gay and transgender, described later, and permit every child to enjoy playing with dolls *and* trucks!

transgender people
People whose gender identity is different from their sex at birth. Transgender teens and adults may be attracted to same- or opposite-sex partners; they may or may not choose to undergo medical treatments to make their bodies congruent with their gender identity.

Throughout this chapter, I've been emphasizing how the ability to reflect on one's feelings and experiences, and to understand other people's perspectives, is fundamental to humanity. Therefore, it seems appropriate to conclude by describing the familiar condition when these basic human skills don't fully lock in—autism spectrum disorders.

Hot in Developmental Science: Autism Spectrum Disorders

autism spectrum disorders (ASDs)
Conditions characterized by persistent, severe, widespread social and conversational deficits; lack of interest in people and their feelings; and repetitive, restricted behavior patterns, such as rocking, ritualized behavior, hypersensitivity to sensory input, and a fixation on inanimate objects. A core characteristic of these disorders is impairments in theory of mind.

Autism spectrum disorders (ASDs) are syndromes that center on deficits in self-awareness and theory of mind—the inability to have normal back-and-forth conversations, to share feelings, and to connect with adults and friends. To qualify for this diagnosis, according to the most recent *Diagnostic and Statistical Manual (DSM-5)*, these severe social impairments need to be accompanied by restricted, stereotyped, repetitive behavior: rocking, flipping objects, being hypersensitive to sensory input, preferring the nonhuman world (American Psychiatric Association, 2013).

Autism spectrum disorders, often diagnosed in preschool, typically persist and so make life intensely challenging. Poor social referencing (or no social referencing) (Dequinzio and others, 2016) and delayed language (Kover, Edmunds, & Weismer, 2016) foreshadow this condition. Because autism has no cure, deteriorated thinking (Rosenthal and others, 2013) is an unfortunate path this disorder can take during the adult years.

The good news is that autism is still fairly rare, currently affecting roughly 1 in every 68 children in the United States (Ramsey and others, 2016). The problem is the alarming increase in this diagnosis over the past two decades. (See Figure 5.4 for an example from Denmark.) ASDs are several times more common in boys than girls (Volkmar and others, 2014).

What causes these devastating brain conditions? The fact that autism may run in families leads scientists to believe that this condition often has genetic causes (Fischbach and others, 2016). A puzzling array of environmental risk factors have been linked to this disorder, from air pollution (Volk and others, 2013) to maternal abusive relationships (Roberts and others, 2013); from prenatal medication use (Christensen and others, 2013) to—very important—being born extremely premature (Verhaeghe and others, 2016). Given its strong tie to prematurity and birth problems, it's no surprise that older parents are at higher risk of having a child with this condition. But astonishingly, one study traced the risk back a generation—to the advanced age of the granddad (see Frans and others, 2013)!

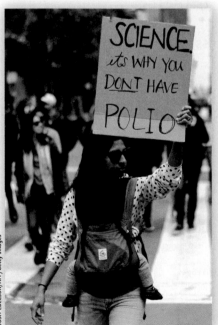

JOSH EDELSON/AFP/Getty Images

At the 2017 March for Science in San Francisco, people were passionate to point out the medical advances we take for granted today—in particular, the fact that vaccinations have wiped out many life-threatening childhood diseases, such as polio.

At this point, it's critical to set the record straight. Despite what some parents (and adults) still believe, vaccines do *not* cause autism (Fischbach and others, 2016). The initial small study suggesting this link was resoundingly discredited as methodologically flawed. Multiple careful and subsequent studies conducted over the past decade confirm that there is *no link* between autism spectrum disorders and vaccines (see Centers for Disease Control and Prevention, 2017).

Moreover, when parents succumb to misplaced fears and decide not to vaccinate their babies and toddlers, this practice puts *every* child at risk—because it exposes the whole population to illnesses such as measles, which vaccines now prevent. As I spelled out in Chapter 1, vaccinations qualify as a landmark twentieth-century medical magic bullet that helped vanquish child mortality and extend our lifespan well into the adult years. If we want to "blame" modern medicine for the recent rise in autism, the most reasonable culprit would be the (also landmark) advances in saving very tiny, at-risk babies, described in Chapter 2.

When a child is diagnosed with an autism spectrum disorder, what are the possible treatments? The classic intervention, developed about 40 years ago, involves operant conditioning. Children receive services from different professionals, while their parents get training in reinforcing adaptive behavior (Scahill and others, 2016). The interesting finding that having older siblings reduces the intensity of a child's social problems (Ben-Itzchak, Zukerman, & Zachor, 2016) suggests that school-based peer interventions also can be effective (Chang & Locke, 2016). And although medications don't touch the core symptoms, they can mute the emotional storms emblematic of this disorder, too. 🌀

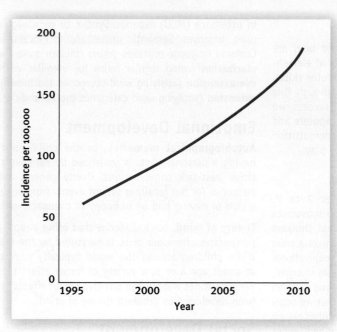

FIGURE 5.4: Time trends of autism spectrum diagnoses among children aged 4–6 in Denmark, 1995–2010: This chart vividly shows the rise in autism spectrum diagnoses among young children over the early twenty-first century in one representative Western nation (Denmark). Is this alarming increase partly due to the massive media attention focused on this condition? We do not know. But autism rates vary from place to place (Ramsey and others, 2016) partly because this condition is hard to distinguish from other developmental disorders, making illness statistics less than fully accurate (Hedley and others, 2016).

Data from Jensen, Steinhausen, & Lauritson, 2014.

Autism is a poster child for what happens when our uniquely human ability to understand other people's mental states is blocked. In the next chapter, I'll describe how children fully make sense of the adult world during that watershed age called middle childhood.

Tying It All Together

1. When Melanie and Miranda play, they love to make up pretend scenes together. Are these two girls likely to be about age 2, age 5, or age 9?

2. In watching 4-year-olds at a playground, which two observations are you likely to make?
   a. The boys are playing in larger groups.
   b. Both girls and boys love rough-and-tumble play.
   c. The girls are quieter and they are doing more negotiating.

3. Who may be more receptive to playing with toys of the other sex, 4-year-old Sara or 4-year-old Sam?

4. Mark argues that gender-typed behavior is biologically built in, whereas Martha believes that the environment shapes this behavior. Drawing on this chapter, make Mark's and then Martha's case.

5. Autism spectrum disorders are becoming *more/ less* prevalent, and scientists have *evidence/ no evidence* that these disorders are caused by vaccines.

Answers to the Tying It All Together questions can be found at the end of this chapter.

SUMMARY

Setting the Context

Childhood comprises two phases—**early** and **middle childhood.** During early childhood, we learn to decode other people's mental states, the talent that makes humanity special. At this age, Erikson believed, children's mission is **initiative**, exploring their emerging skills. During the elementary school years, our task is **industry**, the need to inhibit our desires and start to work.

Physical Development

Physical growth slows down after infancy. Girls and boys are roughly the same height during preschool and much of elementary school. Boys are a bit more competent at **gross motor skills.** Girls are slightly superior in **fine motor skills.** Although fine motor skills in preschool predict elementary school success, we need to be careful not to push young children. Computers and learning toys may discourage exercising outside. Undernutrition impairs development by making children too tired to play.

Cognitive Development

Piaget's preoperational stage lasts from about ages 3 to 7. **Preoperational thinkers** focus on the way objects and substances (and people) immediately appear. **Concrete operational thinkers** can step back from their visual perceptions and reason on a more conceptual plane. In Piaget's **conservation tasks,** preoperational children believe that when the shape of a substance has changed, the amount of it has changed. One reason is that young children lack the concept of **reversibility,** the understanding that an operation can be performed in the opposite direction. Another reason is that children **center** on what first captures their eye and cannot **decenter,** or focus on several dimensions at one time. Centering also affects **class inclusion** (understanding overarching categories). Preoperational children believe that if something *looks* bigger visually, it equals "more."

Preoperational children lack **identity constancy**—they don't understand that people are "the same" in spite of changes to their external appearance. Children's thinking is characterized by **animism** (the idea that inanimate objects are alive) and by **artificialism** (the belief that everything in nature was made by humans). They are **egocentric,** unable to understand that other people have different perspectives from their own. Although Piaget's ideas offer a wealth of insights into children's thinking, this premier theorist underestimated what young children know. Children in every culture do progress from preoperational to concrete operational thinking—but the learning demands of the particular society affect the ages at which specific conservations are attained.

Lev Vygotsky, with his concept of the **zone of proximal development,** suggested that learning occurs when adults tailor instruction to a child's capacities and then use **scaffolding** to gradually promote independent performance. Education, according to Vygotsky, is a collaborative, bidirectional learning experience.

Language makes every other childhood skill possible. Vygotsky believed that we learn everything through using **inner speech.** During early childhood, language abilities expand dramatically. **Phonemic** (sound articulation) abilities improve. As the number of **morphemes** in children's sentences increases, their **mean length of utterance (MLU)** expands. **Syntax,** or knowledge of grammatical rules, improves. **Semantic** understanding (vocabulary) shoots up. Common language mistakes young children make include **overregularization** (using regular forms for irregular verbs and nouns), **overextension** (applying word categories too broadly), and **underextension** (applying word categories too narrowly).

Emotional Development

Autobiographical memories, or the child's understanding of having a personal past, is socialized by caregivers through sensitive past-talk conversations. Overly general autobiographical memories (or not recalling salient events from one's past) may be a sign of having had an unhappy or traumatic early life.

Theory of mind, our knowledge that other people have different perspectives from our own, is measured by the false-belief task. While children around the world typically pass this milestone at about age 4 or 5, a variety of forces affect this critical skill. Because it has widespread positive social effects, strategies have been developed to promote theory of mind.

Social Development

Play, that defining activity of early childhood, comprises **exercise play** and **rough-and-tumble play** (play fighting and wrestling typical of boys). **Fantasy play** is jump-started by mothers when children are around age 1. The emergence of **collaborative play** at about age 4 signals that children can play together with peers. After reaching a peak in preschool, during concrete operations, pretending declines. Pretending may help children practice adult roles, offer young children a sense of control, and teach boys and girls appropriate social norms.

Gender-segregated play unfolds during preschool, when children begin to play mainly with their own sex. Boy-to-boy play is rambunctious, while girls play together in quiet, collaborative ways. Boys compete in groups; girls play one-to-one. Boys' play is more excluding of girls. Gender-stereotyped play seems to have a biological basis, as shown by the fact that high testosterone levels during babies' early months promote stereotypically male behaviors. In addition to being biologically built in, typical gender behavior is socialized by adults and by peers when children play together in same-sex groups. According to **gender schema theory,** once children understand that they are a boy or a girl, they attend to and model behaviors of their own sex.

Autism spectrum disorders (ASDs) are characterized by severely impaired social skills and abnormal, repetitive behaviors. These incurable conditions, which wreak havoc on development, are rising in prevalence and may have multiple causes—but research has proved that vaccination is definitely not one of them.

KEY TERMS

animism, p. 143

artificialism, p. 143

autism spectrum disorders (ASDs), p. 160

autobiographical memories, p. 150

centering, p. 142

class inclusion, p. 142

collaborative pretend play, p. 155

concrete operational thinking, p. 140

conservation tasks, p. 140

decentering, p. 142

early childhood, p. 135

egocentrism, p. 144

exercise play, p. 155

fantasy play, p. 155

fine motor skills, p. 138

gender schema theory, p. 158

gender-segregated play, p. 156

gross motor skills, p. 138

identity constancy, p. 142

industry, p. 136

initiative, p. 136

inner speech, p. 148

mean length of utterance (MLU), p. 148

middle childhood, p. 136

morpheme, p. 148

overextension, p. 149

overregularization, p. 148

phoneme, p. 148

preoperational thinking, p. 140

reversibility, p. 141

rough-and-tumble play, p. 155

scaffolding, p. 146

semantics, p. 148

syntax, p. 148

theory of mind, p. 151

transgender people, p. 159

underextension, p. 149

zone of proximal development (ZPD), p. 146

ANSWERS TO Tying It All Together QUIZZES

Setting the Context

1. Our mindreading ability is what makes us different from other animals.

2. Steven's younger son is showing initiative by pushing his body. His older son is displaying industry by carefully obeying the rules.

3. Adolescence is the other age of exploration.

Physical Development

1. Long-distance running and the high jump would be ideal for Darpreet, as these sports heavily tap into gross motor skills.

2. a. Based on the principle that we should not push preschoolers, enrolling 4-year-olds in sports would be counterproductive.

Cognitive Development

1. (a) animism; (b) egocentrism; (c) artificialism; (d) can't conserve; (e) (no) identity constancy

2. Children in concrete operations can step back from their current perceptions and think conceptually, whereas preoperational children can't go beyond how things immediately appear.

3. Buy Chris easy-to-read books that are just above his skill level.

4. Vygotsky would say it's normal—the way children learn to think through their actions and control their behavior.

5. (b) = overregularization; (c) = overextension

Emotional Development

1. This *past-talk* conversation will help stimulate Madison's *autobiographical memory*.

2. d

3. Hide and seek implicitly teaches theory of mind.

Social Development

1. The girls are about age 5.

2. a and c (Girls don't typically engage in rough-and-tumble play.)

3. Sara (The gender toy-line is more permeable for girls.)

4. Mark's evidence for biology: Girls and boys worldwide and young monkeys play (and behave) in gender-defined ways. Female testosterone levels, early in development, predict having more male occupational interests. Martha's case for the environment: Gender-defined behavior is drummed in from the media and parents and is solidified during preschool by children playing in same-sex groups. Pink permits girls to act like boys!

5. Autism spectrum disorders (ASDs) are becoming *more* prevalent, and scientists have *no* evidence they are caused by vaccines.

CONNECT ONLINE:

LaunchPad macmillan learning | Check out our videos and additional resources located at: **www.macmillanlearning.com**

CHAPTER 6

Middle Childhood

Ten-year-old José has a new best friend, Matt. The boys bonded over their love of soccer and their passion for chess. Although this offbeat obsession kept them far from the popular kids' group, their take-charge kindness has made them the go-to people when the class gets out of control. A perfect example happened last week when the fifth-grade boys decided to physically (!) play tag using a video game.

When he saw the kids jostling, filling up the recess area with joyous noise, Saul ran over and asked, "Can I play?"

Several kids closed ranks, jeering, "No fat kids allowed!"

Then Adam pushed in, as usual, disrupting the game, hogging the device the kids had renamed "the ball." A few minutes later, an anxious child named Jimmy worked up the guts to timidly enter the group.

"Get out!" erupted Adam, "You wuss. You girl!"

Adam bopped Jimmy over the head, did his standard imitation of Saul's lumbering walk and—as usual—a few boys smirked. Jimmy started to cry and began to slink away. But suddenly, José intervened.

"Cool it, guys," he said. "Man, are you all right? Come join us."

José comforted Jimmy and managed to tell the other boys to lay off Saul ("Hey guys, that's mean!"), while Matt did his best to keep Adam from disrupting the game. All of this earned these two good-guy heroes exuberant fist pumps from the teacher and the rest of the class!

Why are some children, such as José and Matt, unusually caring, while others, like Adam, are impulsive, aggressive, and rude? Why do social hierarchies blossom during late elementary school, and what makes bullying compelling at this age? What makes children bond as friends, and which mental skills allow some 10-year-olds, such as José and Matt, to master complex strategy games, such as chess? This chapter answers these questions and others, as we enter **middle childhood**, that landmark stage from approximately ages 7 to 12.

To introduce our discussion, let's first briefly summarize why both Piaget and Erikson view middle childhood as the tipping point when we first grasp "the adult world."

middle childhood
The second phase of childhood, comprising the ages from roughly 7 to 12 years.

Left: Ryan McVay/Getty Images

LEARNING OUTCOME

• Explain what makes middle childhood unique by referring to Piaget's and Erikson's theories.

Setting the Context

As I mentioned in the last chapter, Piaget believed that young children are tethered to their immediate perceptions. At age 7 or 8, we transcend appearances and think abstractly for the first time. Piaget offered a scientific explanation for why the Jesuits labeled year 7 as the age of "reason." During concrete operations (see Table 6.1), we first think logically about life.

Then Erikson fleshed out the implications of this mental advance. During middle childhood, we realize that succeeding in life requires *industry* (see Table 6.2). We need to control our impulses and work for what we want.

Table 6.1: Piaget's Stages: Focus on Childhood

Age (years)	Name of stage	Description
0–2	Sensorimotor	The baby manipulates objects to pin down the basics of physical reality. This stage ends with the development of language.
2–7	Preoperations	Children's perceptions are captured by their immediate appearances: "What they see is what is real." They believe, among other things, that inanimate objects are really alive and that if the appearance of a quantity of liquid changes (for example, if it is poured from a short, wide glass into a tall, thin one), the amount of liquid itself changes.
7–12	Concrete operations	Children have a realistic understanding of the world. Their thinking is really on the same wavelength as that of adults. While they can reason conceptually about concrete objects, however, they cannot think abstractly in a scientific way.
12+	Formal operations	Reasoning is at its pinnacle: hypothetical, scientific, flexible, fully adult. Our full cognitive human potential has been reached.

Table 6.2: Erikson's Psychosocial Stages

Life Stage	Primary Task
Infancy (birth to 1 year)	Basic trust versus mistrust
Toddlerhood (1 to 2 years)	Autonomy versus shame and doubt
Early childhood (3 to 6 years)	Initiative versus guilt
Middle childhood (7 to 12 years)	**Industry versus inferiority**
Adolescence to emerging adulthood (teens into twenties)	Identity versus role confusion
Early adulthood (twenties to early forties)	Intimacy versus isolation
Middle adulthood (forties to sixties)	Generativity versus stagnation
Late adulthood (late sixties and beyond)	Integrity versus despair

Tying It All Together

1. Drawing on Erikson's and Piaget's theories, name the qualities that make middle childhood (and human beings) special.

Answers to the Tying It All Together quizzes can be found at the end of this chapter.

Physical Development

Reaching Piaget's and Erikson's middle childhood landmarks depends on that human masterpiece structure, the frontal lobes.

Brain Development: Slow-Growing Frontal Lobes

In contrast to other species, our huge *cerebral cortex* actually takes more than two full decades to mature. The *myelin sheath*—the fatty neural cover—grows into our twenties. *Synaptogenesis* (making billions of connections between neurons) is on an extended blossoming and pruning timetable, too, especially in the brain region responsible for thinking through our actions and managing our emotions—the **frontal lobes**.

Figure 6.1, which compares the size of our cortex to that of other species, shows the huge frontal lobes at the top of the brain. During early childhood, the neurons in the visual and motor cortices are in their pruning phase, which explains why vision develops rapidly and why children master basic physical milestones, such as walking, at a young age. However, the frontal lobes are only beginning their synaptic blossoming when we start toddling around. Pruning in this part of the brain begins at about age 9.

Frontal lobe pruning explains why we have such high expectations for children during late elementary school. We expect fifth graders to grasp complex games such as chess, take responsibility for finishing their homework, and get along with their peers. These adult-like talents are accompanied by expanding motor skills.

Motor Skills, Obesity, and Health

In Chapter 5, I implied that lack of outdoor exercise might prevent preschoolers from fully developing their physical skills. Now let's delve into cutting-edge research relating to this issue during the middle childhood years.

Actually, studies from Britain to Germany and from Ireland to the United States confirm that today's elementary school children are less proficient physically than in the past (Burns and others, 2015; Gaul & Issartel, 2016; Lubans and others, 2010;

LEARNING OUTCOMES

- Outline how the frontal lobes develop.
- Describe recent changes in elementary motor skills.
- Explain what adults can do to promote children's physical development.
- List some facts about childhood obesity.

frontal lobes The area at the front uppermost part of the brain, responsible for reasoning and planning our actions.

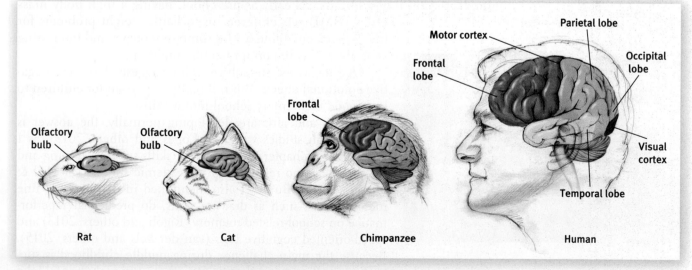

FIGURE 6.1: The human cortex and that of some other species: Notice the size of our cortex in comparison to other species. Our mammoth frontal lobes make humanity unlike any other animal on earth.

This scene would be typical just a few decades ago. Today, bike riding with friends in elementary school is becoming more rare.

Vandorpe and others, 2011). Yes, boys and girls do become stronger and more coordinated as they travel from first to sixth grade. But average scores on standard motor-skill tests are lower today than in previous cohorts, particularly as children advance to older grades.

The logical reason for this loss, as I suggested in the last chapter, is that children no longer regularly play outside (Lubans and others, 2010). When I was 7 or 8, after school I biked for hours around my town pretending to be a cowgirl (that's true!). In one recent German study, less than 1 in 2 second graders spent at least four days per week engaging in this kind of vigorous physical exercise (either indoors or outdoors) for a *single* hour (Kobel and others, 2015).

However, there are dramatic differences from child to child. Perhaps because peers and adults reinforce boys and girls who are skilled at "object control" ("Wow! This child is terrific at hitting or catching balls; let's have her on the team"), preschoolers with superior motor talents tend to be more physically active during middle childhood (Henrique and others, 2016). Skill at catching and throwing balls at age 10 predicts exercising more in high school (Barnett and others, 2009). But, interestingly, the correlation between physical coordination and fitness (aerobic exercise) decreases as children travel into their teens (Haga, Gísladóttír, & Sigmundsson, 2015). And when we see joggers running up the street, it's evident that adults can be exceptionally physically fit, without having much motor finesse!

Physically active parents have daughters and sons with better motor skills (Kobel and others, 2015), as we intuitively understand when we see 8- or 10-year-olds regularly shooting baskets or riding bikes with their moms and dads. Not being a micromanaging parent matters a good deal (Bradley and others, 2011). In one Danish survey, if mothers agreed with questionnaire items such as "I keep total tabs on my child's activities," elementary schoolers were apt to live more sedentary lives (Janssen, 2015). Therefore, to produce physically skilled children, caregivers should encourage outdoor activities but not micromanage or hover over a child.

childhood obesity A body mass index at or above the 95th percentile compared to the U.S. norms established for children in the 1970s.

body mass index (BMI) The ratio of a person's weight to height; the main indicator of overweight or underweight.

Longitudinal studies suggest that sports-oriented children tend to be more active as adults (L. Smith and others, 2015); but you may know a sedentary family member who became fit after falling in love with ballroom dancing or running marathons at age 30 or 55. Unfortunately, change is more difficult when struggling with **childhood obesity**. As early as preschool, having a high **body mass index (BMI)** sets children up to battle weight problems for life. (Check out Table 6.3 for some stereotypes and interesting facts about this important health condition.)

Obesity, as the stereotypes table suggests, has clear negative emotional effects. But is it really important for children to have good elementary school motor skills?

If boys and girls are developing normally, the answer is no. Although studies vary (see Lopes and others, 2013), as I suggested in Chapter 5, gross motor skills such as running and jumping have no relationship to academic success (Stöckel & Hughes, 2016). But, as I also mentioned in that chapter, fine motor talents, such as drawing skills, do predict later performance on school-related memory (Rigoli and others, 2013) and speed-oriented cognitive tests (van der Fels and others, 2015).

Because this kindergarten artist has such exceptional fine motor skills, he may be advanced in school.

Because the main challenge during middle childhood is succeeding in school and controlling our behavior, it is these uniquely frontal-lobe talents to which I now turn.

Table 6.3: Stereotypes and Research Facts About Child Obesity

Stereotype #1: Children become obese because they eat excessively and don't exercise.

Answer: False. The tendency to be overweight is epigenetically programmed, and a child's fate is shaped amazingly early in life. Excessive weight gain during the first year of life strongly predicts later obesity.

Stereotype #2: Parents are responsible for child obesity, because they overfeed their daughters and sons.

Answer: It's complicated. Pushing food on infants can unleash the epigenetic tendency to put on pounds, but parental feeding practices are less important in promoting child overweight at older ages.

Stereotype #3: School-based anti-obesity programs that measure children's BMI and inform families about this condition are effective.

Answer: False. These well-intended interventions are apt to backfire, making overweight children and their parents anxious and heightening children's strong tendency to stigmatize obese classmates.

Stereotype #4: Obese children tend to be bullied and suffer from psychological problems.

Answer: True, with interesting exceptions. Unfortunately, peers are apt to reject overweight classmates as early as preschool, and bullying, depression, and suicide are more common among obese teens. But in the African American community and in nations such as Korea, overweight children are less apt to be stigmatized.

Stereotype #5: Childhood obesity is increasing.

Answer: False! Child obesity rates escalated dramatically during the 1980s and rose more slowly until about a decade ago. Since about 2012, the good news is that the prevalence of this health problem has declined, particularly in preschool children.

Information from Barrera and others, 2016; Cheung and others, 2016; Faguy, 2016; Kim, Yun, & Kim, 2016; Nmyanzi, 2016; Puhl & Latner, 2007; Taveras, 2016; Vanderloo & Mandich, 2013.

Tying It All Together

1. When Steven played hide-and-seek with his 4-year-old nephew, he realized that while Ethan could run well, the child was having trouble not betraying his hiding place and understanding the rules of the game. The reason is that Ethan's _____ cortex is on an earlier developmental timetable than his _____ lobes.

2. Imagine transporting yourself to the 1950s and watching fourth graders in your neighborhood. Which observation is *false*?

    a. Children were better coordinated than they are today.
    b. Children were more physically active than they are today.
    c. Parents spent more time monitoring children's outdoor play than they do today.

3. Excellent motor skills are *crucially important/ not very important* in adult fitness, and preschool *gross motor skills/ fine motor skills* predict children's later academic abilities.

4. Obesity can be easily cured by diet and exercise. (*true/ false*)

Answers to the Tying It All Together quizzes can be found at the end of this chapter.

Cognitive Development

As I discussed in Chapter 5, Piaget and Vygotsky gave us terrific insights into how children think. But neither theorist explained *why* industry locks in. What skills are involved in managing our behavior and working for what we want? Parents might want to know if they can trust a 6-year-old to take care of a dog. Teachers might want tips for helping third graders memorize spelling words, or need strategies to intervene with students who have trouble sitting still in class. To get this information, everyone would gravitate toward the *information-processing approach*.

LEARNING OUTCOMES

- Outline the information-processing perspective on memory.
- List three examples of executive functions.
- Describe ADHD's features, causes, and treatments.

An Information-Processing Perspective on Intellectual Growth

Information-processing theorists, as I described in Chapter 3, divide thinking into steps. Let's illustrate this approach by examining memory, the basis of all thought.

Making Sense of Memory

Information-processing theorists believe that to become "a memory," information passes through different stages. First, we hold stimuli arriving from the outside world briefly in a sensory store. Then, features that we notice enter the most important store, called *working memory*.

working memory In information-processing theory, the limited-capacity gateway system, containing all the material that we can keep in awareness at a single time. The material in this system is either processed for more permanent storage or lost.

Working memory is where the "cognitive action" takes place. Here, we keep information in awareness and act to either process it or discard it. Working memory is made up of limited-capacity holding bins and an "executive processor," which allows us to mentally process material for permanent storage (Baddeley, 1992; Best & Miller, 2010).

To get a real-life example of the fleeting quality of working memory, you might try to challenge yourself to remember an address without relying on your smartphone. If you keep that information in your mind, notice that you are apt to succeed at this mental feat. But if you are interrupted by a text, the information evaporates. In fact, for adults, working memory bin capacity is roughly the size of a city and local street address: seven chunks of information.

Researchers find that working memory bin size dramatically enlarges during early elementary school (Cowan, 2016). The executive processor continues to mature well into the teens (Linares, Bajo, & Pelegrina, 2016). These achievements may explain why children reach concrete operations at roughly age 7 or 8 (Case, 1999). Now, children have the memory capacities to step back from their first impressions and remember that what they saw previously (for example, a wider glass in the conservation-of-liquid task) compensates for what they are seeing right now (a taller glass).

Expanding working memory explains why theory-of-mind capacities blossom during elementary school. In order to effortlessly relate to people or to lie effectively (Alloway and others, 2015), children must switch back and forth mentally from their own perspective to another person's point of view. Actually, working memory and theory of mind are both facets of a basic self-control skill critical to children succeeding in life.

Exploring Executive Functions

executive functions Abilities that allow us to plan and direct our thinking and control our immediate impulses.

Executive functions is a broad term that refers to every frontal lobe feat of self-control. Here are three school-related examples that show just how dramatically this talent at the core of being human blossoms as children travel into fourth and fifth grade.

Older Children Rehearse Information

rehearsal A learning strategy in which people repeat information to embed it in memory.

Rehearsal is a major way we learn. We repeat material to embed it in memory. In a classic study, developmentalists had kindergarteners and fifth graders memorize objects (such as a cat or a desk) pictured on cards (Flavell, Beach, & Chinsky, 1966). Prior to the testing, the researchers watched the children's lips to see if they were repeating the names of the objects to themselves. Eighty-five percent of the fifth graders used rehearsal; only 10 percent of the kindergarteners did. So, one reason why older children are superior learners is that they understand that they need to rehearse.

Older Children Understand How to Selectively Attend

selective attention A learning strategy in which people manage their awareness so as to attend only to what is relevant and to filter out unneeded information.

The ability to manage our awareness to focus on just what we need to know is called **selective attention**. In a classic study, researchers presented boys and girls of different ages with cards. On the top half of each card was an animal photo; on the bottom half was a picture of some household item (see Figure 6.2). The children were instructed to remember only the animals.

FIGURE 6.2: A selective attention study: In this study measuring selective attention, children were asked only to memorize the animals on the top half of the cards. Then researchers looked for age differences in the children's memory for the irrelevant household items.

As you might expect, older children were better at recalling the animal names. But when asked to remember the household items, both age groups performed equally well—suggesting that young children clog their memory bin space with irrelevant information (Bjorklund, 2005) because they cannot selectively attend as well.

Older Children Are Superior at Inhibition

To measure differences in inhibition, researchers ask children to perform some action that contradicts their immediate tendencies, such as saying, "Press a button as fast as you can each time you see an animal on the screen, but don't respond when you see a dog" (Pnevmatikos & Trikkaliotis, 2013). This "go, don't go" challenge is exemplified by the classic kindergarten game Simon Says.

Actually, fostering inhibition—that is, not doing what we feel like doing—is a continual *socialization* goal. From completing your assignments for this class rather than partying, to resisting the urge to check Facebook while you are reading this very page, inhibiting our responses can often be difficult even for most adults.

The childhood game of Simon Says is far from all fun and games—it's tailored to train executive functions by giving children practice in the vital skill of inhibiting their immediate responses.

INTERVENTIONS Using Information-Processing Theory at Home and at Work

So, returning to the beginning of this section, parents will need to regularly remind a 6-year-old child to feed the dog. Teachers *cannot* assume that third graders will automatically understand how to memorize spelling words. Scaffolding study skills (such as the need to rehearse) or teaching selective attention strategies (such as underlining important words for a test) should be an integral part of education in elementary school. And for everyone else, understand that while, over time, children's executive functions greatly improve, controlling and inhibiting our behavior takes effort *throughout* life. (See Table 6.4 on the next page for some information-processing tips to use with children.)

Now let's look at the insights information-processing theory offers for understanding and helping children with that well-known condition, attention-deficit/hyperactivity disorder, or ADHD.

Table 6.4: Information-Processing Guidelines for Teachers and Parents

General Principles for Younger (and Some Older) Children

1. Don't expect boys and girls to remember, without prompting, regular chores such as feeding a pet.

2. Expect most children to have a good deal of trouble in situations that involve inhibiting a strong "prepotent impulse"—such as not touching desirable toys, following unpleasant rules, or doing homework.

Throughout Middle Childhood

1. Actively teach the child study skills (such as rehearsing information) and selective attention strategies (such as underlining important points) for tests.

2. Scaffold organizational strategies for school and life. For example, get the child to use a notebook for each class assignment and keep important objects, such as pencils, in a specific place.

3. Expect situations that involve multiple tasks (such as getting ready for school) and activities that involve *ongoing* inhibition (such as refraining from watching TV before finishing homework) to be especially problematic. Build in a clear structure for mastering these difficult executive-functioning tasks: "At 8 or 9 P.M., it's time to get everything ready for school." "Homework must be completed by dinnertime, or immediately after you get home from school."

4. To promote selective attention (and inhibition), have a child do her homework, or any task that involves concentration, in a room away from tempting distractions such as the TV or Internet.

Hot in Developmental Science: Attention-Deficit/Hyperactivity Disorder

attention-deficit/ hyperactivity disorder (ADHD) The most common childhood learning disorder in the United States, disproportionately affecting boys; characterized by inattention and hyperactivity at home and at school.

Attention-deficit/hyperactivity disorder (ADHD)—defined by inattentiveness and hyperactivity/distractibility—is the most widely diagnosed childhood disorder in the United States, affecting roughly 1 in 10 children (CDC Attention deficit hyperactivity disorder, n.d.). While ADHD may sometimes be diagnosed in preschool, because sitting still and focusing are vital during elementary school, this label is typically applied to boys and girls during middle childhood. Actually, at *every* age, boys are several times more likely than girls to receive this label (CDC Attention deficit hyperactivity disorder, n.d.).

ADHD follows a bewildering array of paths: from first appearing in preschool to erupting during adulthood; from persisting for decades to fading after months (Sonuga-Barke & Halperin, 2010). Twin and adoption studies confirm that ADHD has primarily genetic causes (Thapar & Cooper, 2016). Epigenetic forces are also involved, from being exposed to prenatal maternal smoking to being born premature (Owens & Hinshaw, 2013; see Chapter 2).

Some scientists feel ADHD is caused by the delayed maturation of the frontal lobes. Others speculate that impairments in lower brain centers are to blame (Berger and others, 2013; Hoogman and others, 2013; Wang and others, 2013). Everyone agrees that ADHD is tied to a lower-than-normal output of dopamine, the neurotransmitter that modulates sensitivity to rewards (Silvetti and others, 2014).

The hallmark of ADHD, however, is executive function deficits (Halperin & Healey, 2011). These children have problems with working memory (Alderson and others, 2013) and especially inhibition (Barkley, 1998). When told, "Don't touch the toys," boys and girls diagnosed with ADHD have special trouble resisting this impulse.

These children have difficulties with selective attention. Researchers asked elementary schoolers to memorize a series of words. Some words were more valuable to remember (worth more points), and others less. Boys and girls with ADHD memorized an equal number of words as a comparison group; but like the younger children I described in the previous section, they got lower scores because they clogged their memory bins with less valuable words (Castel and others, 2010).

As you might imagine, performing tasks under time pressure, such as getting ready for school by 7:00 A.M., presents immense problems for boys and girls with ADHD. These children have more trouble estimating time (Gooch, Snowling, & Hulme, 2011). Moreover, perhaps because of their dopamine deficit, they seem less affected by punishments and rewards (Stark and others, 2011). So yelling or threatening simply may not work.

These issues explain why school is so problematic for boys and girls with ADHD. Working memory is critical to performing academic tasks. Focusing on a teacher demands inhibitory and selective attention skills. Taking tests can involve exceptional time-management talents, too.

Because the same difficulties with inhibition and time management spill over into problems at home, children with ADHD are more apt to be bullied by their siblings (Peasgood and others, 2016) and view their parents as over-controlling (Molina & Musich, 2015). Frustrated caregivers tend to resort to power-assertion disciplinary techniques (Wymbs & Pelham, 2010). They lash out at a 9-year-old who seems incapable of getting his things in order. They scream at, hit, and punish a daughter who can't "just sit still." Therefore, due to an evocative process, boys and girls with ADHD are least likely to get the sensitive parenting that they need. Their executive-function problems cause these children to routinely fail with their peers (Normand and others, 2013; Staikova and others, 2013). Given these dangers, what should caring adults do? 🐾

INTERVENTIONS   Helping Children with ADHD

The well-known treatment for ADHD is psycho-stimulant medications (Barkley & Murphy, 2006; Wender and others, 2011), often supplemented by parent (and sometimes teacher) training. Intervening with at-risk parents may be vital because, when adults have ADHD, their affected children tend to develop this condition at younger ages (Breaux, Brown, & Harvey, 2016).

Parent training often involves teaching caregivers to effectively use time outs and consistently reward appropriate behaviors (Ryan-Krause, 2011; Young & Amarasinghe, 2010). It's important not to pressure sons and daughters to complete demanding, time-based tasks. Children themselves may get practice in relaxing their minds via an EEG (which offers feedback about our brain waves) (Janssen and others, 2016).

Apart from consulting a health-care worker, what else should adults do? Because children with ADHD learn better in noisy environments, to help a fifth grader focus on homework, provide "white" background noise (Baijot and others, 2016). Give frequent small reinforcers for good behavior, rather than waiting for a big prize (10 minutes on the computer later today works better than promising a family trip to Disney World next month) (Scheres, Tontsch, & Lee Thoeny, 2013). As exercise mutes the impulse to uncontrollably run around, adults should build more physical activity into the day (Messler, Holmberg, & Sperlich, 2016). Presenting learning tasks in a gaming format is also especially beneficial for children with ADHD (Forster and others, 2014).

Students have told me that getting absorbed in games or sports was the treatment that "cured" a sibling's ADHD. Traditional, medication-oriented experts are listening (see Halperin & Healey, 2011). Scientists point out that medicines, even when they work, can have upsetting side effects. Once a person stops the treatment, symptoms sometimes return (Graham and others, 2011; Sonuga-Barke & Halperin, 2010). Might exercise, or even providing time for playing games, help mend a child's brain?

As of this writing (2018), scientists are poised to find physiological answers to these questions. A large-scale neuroimaging study is exploring brain changes as children with this condition travel from age 10 through the adolescent years (Silk and others, 2016).

But perhaps some brains don't need mending. ADHD symptoms appear on a continuum (Bell, 2011; Larsson and others, 2012). Where should we *really* put the cutoff point between normal childhood inattentiveness and a diagnosed "disease"?

Parent training will ideally help mothers and fathers feel more in control (and be far less angry and impatient) when dealing with this child who has ADHD.

Although he may regularly tune out in class, this boy clearly has no problem being riveted to this game. Therefore, it makes sense that providing high-intensity academics-related video games may help cure wandering school minds.

The dramatic early-twenty-first-century U.S. rise in the prevalence of ADHD (CDC, 2010b) is troubling. So is the male tilt to this diagnosis, as boys are more physically active than girls. Without denying that ADHD causes considerable heartache, what role might a poor elementary school child–environment fit play in this "disorder" at this moment in history?

So far I have been focusing on executive functions as they relate to school success. In the rest of this chapter, I'll turn to the emotional and the social sides of life.

🕐 Tying It All Together

1. Observe a 6-year-old for a day and list specific examples of failures in inhibition and selective attention.

2. Laura's son has been diagnosed with ADHD. Based on this section, list some environmental strategies she might use to help her child.

3. Bakari argues that ADHD is being overdiagnosed. Make Bakari's case, referring to the information in this section.

Answers to the Tying It All Together quizzes can be found at the end of this chapter.

LEARNING OUTCOMES

- Contrast internalizing and externalizing tendencies.
- Outline changes in self-awareness and self-esteem as children get older.
- Point out the perils of having excessively high or low self-esteem.
- Explain what promotes prosocial acts, referring to shame, guilt, induction, and moral disengagement.
- Compare the different types of aggression.
- List the two-step pathway to producing a highly aggressive child.

emotion regulation The capacity to manage one's emotional state.

externalizing tendencies A personality style that involves acting on one's immediate impulses and behaving disruptively and aggressively.

internalizing tendencies A personality style that involves intense fear, social inhibition, and often depression.

self-awareness The capacity to observe our abilities and actions from an outside frame of reference and to reflect on our inner state.

Emotional Development

Think of the overwhelming executive-function relationship challenges elementary school boys and girls face every single day. Children need to cool down their rage when they get a failing grade or are rejected by their peers. They must manage their terror and approach a scary teacher, or regularly work up the courage to join the daunting kind of social group I described in the introductory vignette. **Emotion regulation** is the term developmentalists use for the skills involved in controlling our feelings so that they don't get in the way of a productive life.

Children with **externalizing tendencies** have special trouble with this challenge. Like Adam in the chapter-opening vignette (or boys and girls with ADHD), they act on their immediate emotions and often behave disruptively and aggressively. Perhaps you know a child who bursts into every scene, fighting, bossing people around, wreaking havoc with his classmates and adults.

Children with **internalizing tendencies** have the opposite problem. Like Jimmy in the introductory vignette, they hang back in social situations. They are timid and self-conscious, frightened and depressed.

The beauty of being human is that we vary in our temperamental tendencies—to be shy or active, boisterous or reserved. But having serious trouble *controlling* one's aggression or anxiety puts children at a disadvantage around the world (Chen & Santo, 2016; Fu and others, 2016).

In Chapter 4, I discussed the temperaments that put toddlers at risk for having these emotion regulation issues—being exuberant or inhibited. Now, let's look at how these temperamental tendencies affect older children's emotional lives, beginning with their perceptions of themselves.

Observing and Evaluating the Self

How does **self-awareness**, or our perceptions about ourselves, change during middle childhood? To answer this question, Susan Harter (1999) asked children of different ages to describe themselves. Here are examples of the responses she found:

> I am 3 years old and I live in a big house. . . . I have blue eyes and a kitty that is orange. . . . I love my dog Skipper. . . . I'm always happy. I have brown hair. . . . I'm really strong.

I'm in fourth grade, and I'm pretty popular. . . . That's because I'm nice to people . . . , although if I get into a bad mood I sometimes say something that can be a little mean. At school I'm feeling pretty smart in . . . Language Arts and Social Studies. . . . But I'm feeling pretty dumb in Math and Science. . . .

(Harter, 1999, pp. 37, 48)

Notice that the 3-year-old talks about herself in terms of external facts. The fourth grader's descriptions are internal and psychological, anchored in her feelings, abilities, and traits. The 3-year-old describes herself in unrealistic, positive ways as "always happy." The fourth grader lists her deficiencies and strengths in different areas of life. Moreover, while the younger child talks about herself as if she were living in a bubble, the older child focuses on how she measures up to her classmates. So Harter believes that when children reach concrete operations, they realistically evaluate their abilities and decide whether they like or dislike the person they see. **Self-esteem** — the tendency to feel good or bad about ourselves — first becomes a *major issue* in elementary school.

Actually, worldwide, self-esteem tends to decline during early elementary school (Frey & Ruble, 1985, 1990; Super & Harkness, 2003). A mother may sadly notice this change when her 8-year-old daughter starts to make comments such as, "I am not pretty" or "I can't do math." ("What happened to that self-confident child who used to feel she was the most beautiful, intelligent kid in the world?") Caring teachers struggle with the same comparisons when their fourth graders are exquisitely sensitive to who is popular, which classmates are getting A's, and who needs special academic help.

Therefore, to expand on Erikson's theory, the price of entering the real world is both industry *and* inferiority. In fact, inferiority ("I'm jealous because he is better than me!") helps *propel* industry ("I need to work hard so I can be better than him!").

But luckily, most children avoid just feeling inferior, because reaching concrete operations produces another change. Notice how the fourth grader quoted above compares her abilities in different areas such as personality and school. So, as they get older, children's self-esteem doesn't hinge on one quality. Even if they are not doing well in a certain area, they take comfort in the places where they shine.

According to Harter, children draw on five areas to determine their self-esteem: *scholastic competence* (academic talents); *behavioral conduct* (obedience or being "good"); *athletic skills* (performance at sports); *peer likeability* (popularity); and *physical appearance* (looks). As you might expect, children who view themselves as failing in several competence realms often report low self-esteem. However, to really understand a given child's self-esteem, we need to know the priority that boy or girl puts on doing well in a particular area of life.

To understand this point, take a minute to rate yourself in your people skills, politeness or good manners, intellectual abilities, looks, and physical abilities. If you label yourself as "not so good" in an area you don't care about (for me, it would be motor skills), it won't make a dent in your self-esteem. If you care deeply about some skill where you feel deficient, you would get pretty depressed.

This discounting ("It doesn't matter if I'm not a scholar; I have great relationship skills") lets us gain self-esteem from the areas in which we excel. The problem is that children with externalizing issues take this discounting to an extreme — minimizing their problems in *essential* areas of life.

Two Kinds of Self-Esteem Distortions

Normally, we base our self-esteem on signals from the outside world: "Am I succeeding or not doing so well?" However, when children with externalizing problems *are* failing — for instance, being rejected in school — they may deny reality (Lynch and others, 2016) and impulsively blame others, to preserve their unrealistically high self-worth (Woltering & Shi, 2016). Perhaps you know an adult whose anger gets him into continual trouble but who copes by taking the position, "I'm wonderful. It's their fault." Because this person seems impervious to his flaws and has difficulty regulating his emotions, he cannot change his behavior and so ensures that he continues to fail.

self-esteem Evaluating oneself as either "good" or "bad" as a result of comparing the self to other people.

According to Susan Harter, even when children are failing in other areas of life, they can sometimes derive their self-esteem from the skills in which they shine. Do you think this girl can use this science prize to feel good about herself, even if she understands that she is not very popular with the other kids?

learned helplessness
A state that develops when a person feels incapable of affecting the outcome of events, and so gives up without trying.

Children with internalizing tendencies have the opposite problem. Their intense anxiety may cause them to read failure into benign events ("My teacher hates me because she looked at me the wrong way") (see Chen & Santo, 2016). They are at risk of developing **learned helplessness** (Abramson, Seligman, & Teasdale, 1978), feeling that they are powerless to affect their fate. They give up at the starting gate, assuming, "I'm going to fail, so why even try?"

So children with externalizing and internalizing tendencies face a similar danger—but for different reasons. When boys and girls minimize their difficulties or assume they are incompetent, they cut off the chance of working to change their behavior and ensure that they *will* fail.

Table 6.5 summarizes these self-esteem problems and their real-world consequences. Then, Table 6.6 offers a checklist, based on Harter's five dimensions, for evaluating yourself. Are there areas where you gloss over your deficiencies? Do you have pockets of learned helplessness that prevent you from living a full life?

Table 6.5: Externalizing and Internalizing Problems, Self-Esteem Distortions, and Consequences— A Summary Table

Description	Self-Esteem Distortion	Consequence
Children with externalizing problems act out "emotions," are impulsive, and are often aggressive.	May ignore real problems and have unrealistically high self-esteem.	Continue to fail because they don't see the need to improve.
Children with internalizing problems are intensely fearful.	Can read failure into everything and have overly low self-esteem.	Continue to fail because they decide that they cannot succeed and stop working.

Table 6.6: Identifying Your Self-Esteem Distortions: A Checklist Using Harter's Five Domains

You have externalizing issues if you regularly have thoughts like these:

1. **Academics:** "When I get poor grades, it's because my teachers don't give good tests or teach well"; "I have very little to learn from other people"; "I'm smarter than practically everyone else I know."

2. **Physical skills:** "When I play baseball, soccer, etc., and my team doesn't win, it's my teammates' fault, not mine"; "I believe it's OK to take physical risks, such as not wearing a seatbelt or running miles in the hot sun, because I know I won't get hurt"; "It's all statistics, so I shouldn't be concerned about smoking four packs a day or about drinking a six-pack of beer every night."

3. **Relationships:** "When I have trouble at work or with my family, it's typically my co-workers' or family's fault"; "My son (or mate, friend, mother) is the one causing the conflict between us."

4. **Physical appearance:** "I don't think I have to work to improve my appearance because I'm gorgeous."

5. **Conduct:** "I should be able to come to work late (or turn in papers after the end of the semester, talk in class, etc.)"; "Other people are too uptight. I have a right to behave any way I want to."

Diagnosis: You are purchasing high self-esteem at the price of denying reality. Try to look at the impact of your actions more realistically and take steps to change.

You have internalizing issues if you regularly have thoughts like these:

1. **Academics:** "I'm stupid"; "I can't do well on tests"; "My memory is poor"; "I'm bound to fail at science"; "I'm too dumb to get through college"; "I'll never be smart enough to get ahead in my career."

2. **Physical skills:** "I can't play basketball (or some other sport) because I'm uncoordinated or too slow"; "I'll never have the willpower to exercise regularly (or stick to a diet, stop smoking, stop drinking, or stop taking drugs)."

3. **Relationships:** "I don't have any people skills"; "I'm doomed to fail in my love life"; "I can't be a good mother (or spouse or friend)."

4. **Physical appearance:** "I'm unattractive"; "People are born either good-looking or not, and I fall into the *not* category"; "There is nothing I can do to improve my looks."

5. **Conduct:** "I'm incapable of being on time (or getting jobs done or stopping talking in class)"; "I can't change my tendency to rub people the wrong way."

Diagnosis: Your excessively low self-esteem is inhibiting your ability to succeed. Work on reducing your helpless and hopeless attitudes and try for change.

INTERVENTIONS: Promoting Realistic Self-Esteem

This discussion shows why school programs focused *just* on raising self-esteem—those devoted to instilling the message "You are a terrific kid"—are missing the boat (Baumeister and others, 2003; Swann, Chang-Schneider, & McClarty, 2007). True self-esteem is derived from industry—working for a goal. Therefore, when children are having trouble in a vital life domain, it's important to (1) enhance *self-efficacy,* or the feeling that "I can succeed if I work" (Miller & Daniel, 2007) and (2) promote *realistic* perceptions about the self. How might caring adults carry out this two-pronged approach?

ENHANCING SELF-EFFICACY As developmentalist Carol Dweck has demonstrated, one key to enhancing academic self-efficacy is to praise children for effort ("You are trying so hard!"), rather than making comments about basic ability ("You are incredibly smart!"). In her studies, elementary schoolers who were praised for being "very intelligent" after successfully completing problems later had *lower* self-efficacy. They were afraid to tackle other challenging tasks ("I'd better not try this or everyone might learn I'm dumb!") (Molden & Dweck, 2006; Mueller & Dweck, 1998).

Emphasizing effort is vital because, during concrete operations, children begin to categorize themselves according to fixed labels ("I'm the dumb kid" or "the poor kid in class"). Another downside of the concrete operational passion for categorizing everything described in Chapter 5 is succumbing to rigid racial or gender stereotypes, such as believing that women or African Americans can't do science or math.

But, when adults praise elementary schoolers for effort and show inspiring movies such as *Hidden Figures* (the untold story of how female African American scientists boosted the U.S. space program to success), they are implicitly teaching children the lesson: "You are not defined by a fixed criterion such as your gender or the color of your skin." Therefore, instilling the efficacious message that "working matters" *both* prevents prejudice and preserves self-esteem!

By complimenting her child for being such a hard worker, this mother is socializing her son not to succumb to negative stereotypes like "Black kids can't be scientists."

ENCOURAGING ACCURATE PERCEPTIONS Still, if a child—like Jimmy in the chapter-opening vignette—has internalizing tendencies, efficacy-enhancing interventions may not be enough. These children feel they are failing when they are not. Therefore, adults must continually provide accurate feedback: "The class doesn't hate you. Notice that Matt and José wanted you in the game." And, if an elementary schooler with externalizing tendencies discounts his failures at the price of preserving unrealistic self-esteem, gently point out reality, too (Thomaes, Stegge, & Olthof, 2007). Using the example of Adam in the vignette, you might say, "The kids don't like you when you barge in and take over those games, but I *know* you can control yourself if you try!"

So, returning to the beginning of this section, school programs (and adults) that value each child as a person, as well as foster self-efficacy ("You can succeed if you work hard"), promote *true* self-esteem (Miller & Daniel, 2007).

Doing Good: Morality and Prosocial Behavior

On September 11, 2001, the nation was riveted by the heroism of the firefighters who ran into the World Trade Center, risking almost certain death. We marveled at the "ordinary people" working in the Twin Towers, whose response to this emergency was to help others get out first.

What qualities made hundreds of New York City firefighters run into the burning Twin Towers on September 11, 2001, knowing that they might be facing death? This is the kind of question that developmentalists who study prosocial behavior want to answer.

prosocial behavior Sharing, helping, and caring actions.

empathy Feeling the exact emotion that another person is experiencing.

sympathy A state necessary for acting prosocially, involving feeling upset *for* a person who needs help.

Prosocial behavior is the term developmentalists use to describe such amazing acts of self-sacrifice, as well as the minor acts of helping, comforting, and sharing that we perform during daily life. Do we have to be taught to reach out in a caring way?

The answer is no. As I discussed in Chapters 3 and 4, the impulse to be prosocial and ethical blossoms during our first two years of life.

Individual and Gender Variations

However, as you saw in the vignette at the beginning of this chapter, children differ in this natural human propensity to be ethical and kind. Developmentalists visited preschool classrooms and looked at spontaneous sharing, the coming-from-the-heart giving that is different from being ordered to "Share!" When they tested these children in elementary school, during adolescence, and in emerging adulthood, the 3-year-olds who shared most readily were more prosocial at every age (Eisenberg and others, 2014). So, if your 8-year-old niece seems unusually generous (especially at cost to herself), she may grow up to be an unusually prosocial adult.

What about your 8-year-old nephew? Are females generally more prosocial than males? Studies suggest that girls are far more likely than boys to reach out and comfort a classmate who is being bullied (boys tend to actively confront the bully) (Duffy and others, 2016; Mulvey & Killen, 2016; Reijntjes and others, 2016). Females are more physiologically attuned to others' distress than males (Groen and others, 2013). The problem is that being sensitive to another person's emotional pain may not result in *acting* in a prosocial way.

Decoding Prosocial Behavior in a Deeper Way

Empathy is the term developmentalists use for directly feeling another person's emotions. For example, your daughter gets intensely anxious when she hears a teacher berating her best friend. She is overcome with horror when she sees a video of the Twin Towers crashing down.

Sympathy is the more muted feeling that we experience *for* another human being. Your daughter feels terrible *for* her friend. Her heart goes out to the people who lost their lives on 9/11, but she isn't overwhelmed with distress. Developmentalists believe that sympathy, rather than empathy, is related to behaving in a prosocial way (Eisenberg, 1992, 2003).

The reason is that experiencing another person's distress can provoke a variety of reactions, from being immobilized with fear to behaving in a far-from-caring way. We can vividly see this point when, out of embarrassment, we witness children (and even some adults) laugh hysterically as someone spills a lunchroom tray. So to be prosocial, children need to mute their empathic feelings into a sympathetic response (Eisenberg, 1992).

Actually, during middle childhood, acting prosocially requires sophisticated information-processing skills. Children must know *when* to be generous, which explains why 2-year-olds share with everyone, but, around age 5, we become selective, reaching out to people who are kind to us (Paulus & Moore, 2014). Older children also tailor their prosocial behavior to whether they can *effectively* offer aid. Preoperational preschoolers automatically offer you their blankee when you are upset, because they are egocentric and assume that everything that comforts them will comfort you. However, just as I would not run into a flaming building because I'm not a firefighter, the reasons elementary school children report for not acting prosocial are that they don't have the skills to help (Denham, 1998; Eisenberg & Fabes, 1998).

Returning to gender differences, this suggests we take a more nuanced approach to the idea that females are more prosocial than males. My earlier discussion suggests we have different styles of acting prosocially. Sometimes, being prosocial involves actively standing up to a bully (or running into a flaming building); at other times, it involves comforting and nurturing a person in pain.

So, do children get more prosocial with age? Unfortunately, the answer is no. During elementary school, other motivations override this basic caring sense (Visconti, Ladd, & Kochenderfer-Ladd, 2015). In one study exploring reactions to stories, while preschoolers were likely to say that a character who searched for prizes should "share things equally" with a helper, 8-year-olds tailored their giving to whether the other person had earned the gift. "If he was lazy, there is no reason to share" (Rizzo and others, 2016).

Therefore, the lifelong process of justifying uncaring actions locks in as children get older and grasp the complexities of the adult world: "Refugees are not like us—so we shouldn't let them into the United States"; "I refuse to give money to street people, because if human beings weren't lazy, everyone could succeed" (more about these serious limitations to self-efficacy in the next chapter). Given the universal human tendency to succumb to what Albert Bandura calls **moral disengagement** (rationalizing amoral, uncaring acts), what can adults do to promote moral behavior in a child?

> **moral disengagement** Rationalizing moral or ethical lapses by invoking justifications, such as "He deserved that."

INTERVENTIONS Socializing Moral Children

Provide the right socialization climate. Foster a secure, loving attachment (Pastorelli and others, 2016). Continually remind a boy or girl about fundamental ethical principles ("Hurting other people is wrong"). (See Visconti, Ladd, & Kochenderfer-Ladd, 2015.) Be attuned to children's caring acts and attribute that behavior to their personality—for instance, by saying, "You really are a caring person for doing that" instead of "That was a nice thing you did" (Eisenberg, 2003).

In a fascinating study, when researchers asked 8-year-olds to recall a time they acted in a generous way, their later behavior became more prosocial (Tasimi & Young, 2016). It was as if they mentally reminded themselves: "I remember how great I felt when I did that helpful thing. I *want* to feel that way again!"

Many studies of prosocial behavior focus on a socialization technique called **induction** (Hoffman, 1994, 2001). Caregivers who use induction point out the ethical issues when a child has performed a hurtful act. Now, imagine that classic situation when your 8-year-old daughter has invited everyone in class but Sara to her birthday party. Instead of punishing your child—or giving that other classic response, "Kids will be kids"—here's what you should say: "It's hurtful to leave Sara out. Think of how terrible she must feel!"

> **induction** The ideal discipline style for socializing prosocial behavior, which involves getting a child who has behaved hurtfully to empathize with the pain he has caused the other person.

Induction has several virtues: It offers children concrete feedback about exactly what they did wrong and moves them off of focusing on their own punishment ("Now, I'm really going to get it!") to the *other* child's distress ("Oh, gosh, she must feel hurt"). Induction also allows for reparations, the chance to make amends. Induction works because it stimulates guilt.

GUILT AND PROSOCIAL ACTS Think back to an event during childhood when you felt terrible about yourself. Perhaps it was the day you were caught cheating and sent to the principal. What you may remember was feeling so ashamed. Developmentalists, however, distinguish between feeling ashamed and experiencing guilt. **Shame** is the primitive feeling we have when we are *personally* humiliated. **Guilt** is the more sophisticated emotion we experience when we have violated a personal moral standard or hurt another human being.

> **shame** A feeling of being personally humiliated.
>
> **guilt** Feeling upset about having caused harm to a person or about having violated one's internal standard of behavior.

I believe that Erikson may have been alluding to this maturity difference when he labeled "shame" as the emotion we experience as toddlers, and reserved "guilt" for the feeling that arises during preschool, when our drive to master the world causes other people distress. While shame and guilt are both "self-conscious" emotions, they have opposing effects. Shame causes us to withdraw from people, to slink away, and

When parents use shame to discipline, a child's impulse is to get furious. But by pointing out how disappointed she is in her "good girl," this mother can induce guilt—and so ultimately have a more prosocial child.

aggression Any hostile or destructive act.

proactive aggression A hostile or destructive act initiated to achieve a goal.

reactive aggression A hostile or destructive act carried out in response to being frustrated or hurt.

crawl into a hole (Thomaes and others, 2007). We feel furious at being humiliated and want to strike back. Guilt connects us to people. We feel terrible about what we have done and try to make amends.

In a creative study charting the natural ebb and flow of 8-year-olds' angry feelings during the day, researchers found that a given child's scores on a measure of guilt (not the intensity of anger) best predicted that person's tendency to hold off from impulsively lashing out (Colasante, Zuffianó, & Malti, 2016). Did feeling guilty ever prevent you from retaliating when someone behaved insensitively? Did apologizing for acting insensitively ever make you feel closer to someone you love?

Table 6.7: How to Produce Prosocial Children: A Summary Table

- Praise a child effusively when she is being generous, and label her as a caring person. Give her many chances to act prosocially, and keep reminding her of situations when she acted in a caring way.

- When the child has hurt another person, clearly point out the moral issue and alert him to how the other person must feel.

- Avoid teasing and shaming. When the child has done something wrong, tell her you are disappointed and give her a chance to make amends.

- As moral disengagement tends to flare up during concrete operations, when children define certain people or groups as "less worthy," repeatedly emphasize basic moral precepts, such as the need to "help strangers" and "treat everyone with respect"—*and accompany these mantras by modeling these principles in your own life!*

Table 6.7 summarizes these section messages in four tips. Now that we have analyzed what makes us act morally (the angel side of personality), let's enter humanity's darker side, aggression.

Doing Harm: Aggression

Aggression refers to acts designed to cause harm, from shaming to shoving, from gossiping to starting wars. It should come as no surprise that physical aggression reaches its life peak at around age 2½ (Dodge, Coie, & Lynam, 2006; van Aken and others, 2008). Imagine being a toddler continually ordered by giants to do impossible things, such as sitting still. Because being frustrated provokes aggression, it makes perfect sense that hitting and having tantrums are normal during the "terrible twos."

As children get older and become skilled at regulating their emotions, rates of open aggression (yelling or hitting) dramatically decline (Dishion & Tipsord, 2011). During middle childhood, the reasons for aggression change. Preschool fights center on objects, such as toys. When children have a full-fledged sense of self-esteem, they strike out because they are wounded as human beings (Coie & Dodge, 1998). How do researchers categorize aggressive acts?

Types of Aggression

One way developmentalists classify aggression is by its motive. **Proactive aggression** refers to hurtful behavior that we initiate to achieve a goal. Johnny kicks José to gain possession of the block pile. Sally spreads a rumor about Moriah to replace her as Sara's best friend. **Reactive aggression** occurs in response to being hurt, threatened, or deprived. José, infuriated at Johnny, kicks him back.

Its self-determined nature gives proactive aggression a "cooler" emotional tone. When we behave aggressively to get something, we plan our behavior. We feel a sense of self-efficacy as we carry out the act. Reactive aggression involves white-hot, disorganized rage. When you hear that your best friend has betrayed you, or even have a minor frustrating experience such as being caught in traffic, you get furious and blindly lash out (Deater-Deckard and others, 2010).

This feeling is normal. According to a classic theory called the *frustration-aggression hypothesis*, when human beings are thwarted, we are biologically primed to strike back.

In addition to its motive—proactive or reactive—developmentalists distinguish between different *forms* of aggression. Hitting and yelling are direct forms of aggression. A more devious type of aggression is **relational aggression**, acts designed to hurt relationships. Not inviting Sara to a birthday party, spreading rumors, or tattling on a disliked classmate all qualify as relationally aggressive acts.

Because it targets self-esteem and involves more sophisticated social skills, relational aggression follows a different developmental path than openly aggressive acts. Just as rates of open aggression are declining, during middle childhood relational aggression rises. In fact, the overabundance of relational aggression during late elementary school and early adolescence (another intensely frustrating time) may explain why we label these ages as the "meanest" times of life.

Most of us assume relational aggression is more common in girls. But in research, this "obvious" relationship isn't always found. Yes, overt aggression is severely sanctioned in females, so girls make relational aggression their major mode (Ostrov & Godleski, 2010; Smith, Rose, & Schwartz-Mette, 2010). But as spreading rumors and talking trash about competitors is vital to dethroning adversaries and climbing the social ranks, one study showed that teenage boys were just as relationally aggressive as teenage girls (Mayeux & Cillessen, 2008)!

Table 6.8 summarizes the different types of aggression and gives examples from childhood and adult life. While scanning the table, notice that we all behave in

relational aggression
A hostile or destructive act designed to cause harm to a person's relationships.

Excluding someone from your group is a classic sign of *relational aggression*—which really gets going in middle childhood. Can you remember being the target of the behavior shown here when you were in fourth or fifth grade?

Table 6.8: Aggression: A Summary of the Types

What Motivated the Behavior?

Proactive aggression: Acts that are actively instigated to achieve a goal.

Examples: "I'll hit Tommy so I can get his toys"; "I'll cut off that car so I can get ahead of him"; "I want my boss's job, so I'll spread a rumor that he is having an affair."

Characteristics: Emotionally cool and more carefully planned.

Reactive aggression: Acts that occur in response to being frustrated or hurt.

Examples: "Jimmy took my toy, so I'm going to hit him"; "That guy shoved me to take my place in line, so I'm going to punch him out."

Characteristics: Furious, disorganized, impulsive response.

What Was Its Form?

Direct aggression: Everyone can see it.

Examples: Telling your boyfriend you hate his guts; beating up someone; screaming at your mother; having a tantrum; bopping a playmate over the head with a toy.

Characteristics: Peaks at about age 2 or 3; declines as children get older; more common in boys than in girls, especially physical aggression.

Relational aggression: Carried out indirectly, through damaging or destroying the victim's relationships.

Examples: "Sara got a better grade than me, so I'm going to tell the teacher that she cheated"; "Let's tell everyone not to let Sara play in our group"; "I want Sara's job, so I'll spread a rumor that she is stealing money from the company"; "I'm going to tell my best friend that her husband is cheating on her because I want to break up their marriage."

Characteristics: Occurs mainly during elementary school and may be at its peak during adolescence, although—as we all know—it's common *throughout* adulthood.

every aggressive way. Also, aggression is not "bad." Proactive aggression, particularly the relational kind, helps children climb the social ranks (more about this in the next section). Without reactive aggression (fighting back when attacked), our species would never survive. Still, this disorganized, rage-filled aggression doesn't work. Excessive reactive aggression *ensures* that children are apt to have problems getting along with people during life (White, Jarrett, & Ollendick, 2013).

Understanding Highly Aggressive Children

You just saw that, during elementary school, boys and girls typically get less physically aggressive. However, a percentage of children remain unusually aggressive. These boys and girls are labeled with externalizing disorders defined by high rates of aggression. They are classified as defiant, antisocial kids.

The Pathway to Producing Problematic Aggression

Longitudinal studies suggest that there may be a poisonous two-step, nature-plus-nurture pathway to being labeled as a highly aggressive child.

STEP 1: THE TODDLER'S EXUBERANT (OR DIFFICULT) TEMPERAMENT EVOKES HARSH DISCIPLINE When toddlers are impulsive and fearless, caregivers often react by using *power-assertion*. They may shame, scream, and hit: "Shut up! You are impossible. You'll get a beating from mom." But physically punishing a "difficult" toddler is apt to induce more rage (as I will describe in the next chapter's discussion of spanking); so, unfortunately, the very children who most need loving parenting often get the harshest, most punitive care.

STEP 2: THE CHILD IS REJECTED BY TEACHERS AND PEERS IN SCHOOL Typically, the transition to being an "antisocial child" occurs during late kindergarten or first grade. As impulsive, by now clearly aggressive, children travel outside the family, they get rejected by their classmates. Being socially excluded is a powerful stress that provokes reactive aggression (Ettekal & Ladd, 2015). Moreover, because these children *generally* may have executive function deficits (Cooley & Fite, 2016), during elementary school they are apt to start failing their classes (Romano and others, 2010). This amplifies the frustration ("I'm not making it in any area of life!") and compounds their tendency to lash out ("It's their fault, not mine!").

hostile attributional bias The tendency of highly aggressive children to see motives and actions as threatening when they are actually benign.

A Hostile Worldview

As I just implied, reactive-aggressive children also think differently in social situations. They may have a **hostile attributional bias** (Crick & Dodge, 1996). They see threat in benign social cues. A boy gets accidentally bumped at the lunch table, and he sees a deliberate provocation. A girl decides that you are her enemy when you look at her the wrong way. So the child's behavior provokes a more hostile world.

To summarize, let's enter the mind of a reactive-aggressive child, such as Adam in the chapter-opening vignette. During early childhood, your fearless temperament continually got you into trouble with your parents. You have been harshly disciplined for years. In school, your classmates shun you. So you never have a chance to interact with other children and improve your emotion regulation skills. In fact, your hostile attributional bias makes perfect sense. You are living in a "sea of negativity" (Jenson and others, 2004). And yes, the world *is* out to do you in!

If children shun a boy for his disruptive behavior, he may respond by developing a hostile attributional bias, feeling that his classmates are all against him.

INTERVENTIONS Taming Excessive Aggression

When an older child has an externalizing disorder, how should parents act? Avoid the punitive, shaming discipline style that exacerbates hostile attributional biases as boys travel into their teens (Yaros, Lochman, & Wells, 2015). Vigorously socialize prosocial behavior using the strategies in Table 6.7 (on page 180). Understand that the same sensation-seeking, risk-taking propensities that promote excessive childhood aggression can be potential life assets. In an amazing decades-long study, when researchers measured temperament during infancy and then looked at a person's personality during adulthood, the *one* quality that predicted being highly competent at age 40 was having been fearless during the first year of life (Blatney, Jelinek, & Osecka, 2007). So, with the right *person–environment fit*, a "difficult-to-tame" child may become a prosocial hero, like the firefighters on 9/11.

What was this incredibly brave prosocial soldier really like at age 1 or 2? Probably a fearless handful!

Why are peer relationships so vital during middle childhood, and how exactly do older children relate? This brings me to the final topic in this chapter—relationships.

Tying It All Together

1. You interviewed a 4-year-old and a fourth grader for your class project in child development, but mixed up your interview notes. Which statement was made by the 4-year-old?

    a. "My friend Megan is better at math than me."
    b. "Sometimes I get mad at my friends, but maybe it's because I'm too stubborn."
    c. "I have a cat named Kit, and I'm the smartest girl in the world."

2. Identify which of the following boys has internalizing or externalizing tendencies. Then, for one of these children, design an intervention using principles spelled out in this section: Ramon sees himself as wonderful, but he is having serious trouble getting along with his teachers and the other kids; Jared is a great student, but when he gets a B instead of an A, he decides that he's "dumb" and gets too depressed to work.

3. Carl, a fourth grader, is faced with the dilemma of whether to stand up for a bullied classmate. Which consideration does *not* predict he will reach out?

    a. Carl has the skills to help.
    b. Carl believes that the child deserves his help.
    c. Carl is incredibly sensitive to other people's emotions.

4. A teacher wants to intervene with a student who has been teasing a classmate. Identify which statement is guilt-producing, which is shame-producing, and which involves the use of induction. Then name which response(s) would promote prosocial behavior.

    a. "Think of how bad Johnny must feel."
    b. "If that's how you act, you can sit by yourself. You're not nice enough to be with the other kids."
    c. "I'm disappointed in you. You are usually such a good kid."

5. Alyssa wants to replace Brianna as Chloe's best friend, so she spreads horrible rumors about Brianna. Brianna overhears Alyssa dissing her and starts slapping Alyssa. Of the four types of aggression discussed in this section—*direct, proactive, reactive, relational*—which two describe Alyssa's behavior, and which two fit Brianna's actions?

6. Mario feels that everyone in the fifth grade is out to get him. What is the label for Mario's worldview?

Answers to the Tying It All Together quizzes can be found at the end of this chapter.

Social Development

What childhood talents foster peer success? Answers come from examining that core childhood relationship called friendship. Why do children choose specific friends, and what benefits do elementary school friendships provide?

Friendships: The Proving Ground for Relationships

The essence of friendship is similarity (Poulin & Chan, 2010). Children gravitate toward people who are "like them" in interests and activities (Dishion & Tipsord, 2011). In preschool, an active child will tend to make friends with a classmate who

LEARNING OUTCOMES

- Outline the different features of friendship and popularity.
- Explain which qualities make children "unpopular."
- Describe why some rejected children can succeed in adult life.
- Summarize the bullying research.

Although they don't realize it, these ten-year-old best buddies bonding over their secrets and plans may be training each other in the skills to be happily married for life!

likes to run around. In the vignette at the beginning of this chapter, José and Matt probably connected around their love of chess.

But, since they are in concrete operations, José and Matt probably gravitated toward each other for deeper reasons, such as shared morals ("I like José because we think the same way about what's right") (McDonald and others, 2014; Spencer and others, 2013), and especially loyalty ("I can trust José to stand up for me") (Hartup & Stevens, 1997; Newcomb & Bagwell, 1995). Listen to these fifth graders describing their best friend:

He is my very best friend because he tells me things and I tell him things.

Jessica has problems at home and with her religion and when something happens she always comes to me and talks about it. We've been through a lot together.

(quoted in Rose & Asher, 2000, p. 49)

These quotations would resonate with the ideas of personality theorist Harry Stack Sullivan. Sullivan (1953) believed that a chum (or best friend) fulfills the developmental need for self-validation and intimacy that emerges at around age 9. Sullivan also felt that best friends serve as a vital training ground for adult romance.

The Protecting and Teaching Functions of Friends

In addition to teaching us how to behave in adult love relationships, friends stimulate children's personal development in two important ways.

Friends Protect and Enhance the Developing Self

Perhaps you noticed this protective function in the quotation above in which the fifth grader spoke about how she helped her best friend when she had problems at home. In one fascinating study, although elementary schoolers who were bullied normally experienced cortisol spikes at school, a victimized boy or girl who had a best friend showed no change in this basic barometer of stress (Peters and others, 2011). Close friends can also mute children's genetic tendency toward developing depression (Reindl, Gniewosz, & Reinders, 2016) or help reduce the symptoms of ADHD (Becker, Fite, and others, 2013).

Friends Teach Us to Manage Our Emotions and Handle Conflicts

Friends offer on-the-job training in being our "best" (that is, prosocial) self. Your parents will love you no matter what you do, but the love of a friend is contingent. So, to keep a friendship, children must dampen down their immediate impulses and use their emotion regulation talents to yield to the other person's needs (Bukowski, 2001; Denham and others, 2003).

This is not to say that friends are always positive influences. They can bring out a child's worst self by encouraging relational aggression ("We are best friends, so Sara can't play with us") and dangerous behavior ("Let's walk together on these scary railroad tracks"). Best friends can promote an "us-against-them" mentality and promote a shared, hostile attributional worldview ("It's their fault you are getting into trouble. Only I can protect you from the outside world") (Spencer and others, 2013; more about these dark sides of friendship in Chapter 9). However, in general, Sullivan may be right: Friends *do* teach us how to relate as adults.

Popularity: Rising in the Peer Ranks

Friendship involves collaborating with a single person in a one-to-one way. Popularity involves competition. Children aggressively strive for dominance as they struggle to climb the social totem pole.

Although children differ in social status in preschool, we now understand why "Who is popular?" becomes an absorbing question during later elementary school.

Entering concrete operations makes children highly sensitive to making social comparisons. Moreover, during adulthood, popularity fades into the background because we select our own social circles. Children must make it on a daily basis in a classroom full of random peers.

Who Is Popular and Who Is Unpopular?

How do children vary in popularity during the socially stressful later elementary school years? Here are the categories researchers find when they ask third, fourth, or fifth graders to list the two or three classmates they really like and dislike:

- *Popular children* are frequently named in the most-liked category and never appear in the disliked group. They stand out as being really liked by everyone.

- *Average children* receive a few most-liked and perhaps one or two disliked nominations. They rank around the middle range of class status.

- *Rejected children* land in the disliked category often and never appear in the preferred list. They stand out among their classmates in a negative way.

What qualities make children popular? What gets elementary schoolers rejected by their peers?

Decoding Popularity

In elementary school, popular children are often friendly, outgoing, prosocial, and kind (Mayberry & Espelage, 2007). However, starting as early as third grade, popularity can also be linked to high levels of relational aggression (Ostrov and others, 2013; Rodkin & Roisman, 2010).

Figure 6.3, based on a study conducted in an inner city school, illustrates this unfortunate truth. Notice that relationally aggressive third to fifth graders were more apt to be rated as popular class leaders. But notice that the association between this poisonous kind of aggression and popularity was stronger for girls—which explains why we see relational aggression as mainly a female activity. Relational aggression earns females more social mileage than males.

Relational aggression is especially effective at propelling popularity during pre-adolescence, when rebellion is in flower and social status often becomes children's primary goal (Caravita & Cillessen, 2012; more about this change in Chapter 9). The good news is that the study described in Table 6.9 on the next page shows that being "popular" is different from being personally liked.

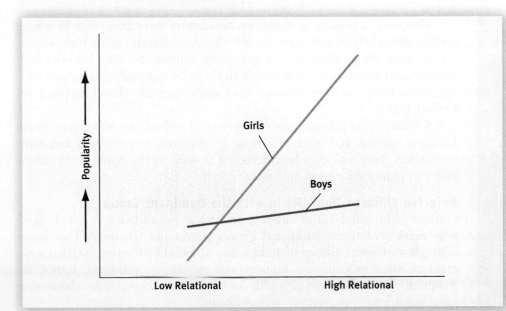

FIGURE 6.3: How relational aggression related to popularity among 227 elementary schoolers attending a low-income, urban school: In this city school, being relationally aggressive "worked" to make children—both males and females—more popular; but this type of aggression was far, far more often effective at promoting popularity among girls.
Data from Waasdorp and others, 2013, p. 269.

Table 6.9: Social Goals in Fifth Grade and How They Related to Peer Preferences a Year Later

1. I like it when I learn new ways to make a friend.

2. I try to figure out what makes for a good friend.

3. I try to get to know other kids better.

4. It's important to me that the other kids think I'm popular.

5. I want to be friendly with the popular kids.

6. It's important to me to have cool friends.

7. It's important to me that I don't embarrass myself around my friends.

8. When I am around other kids, I mostly just try not to goof up.

9. I try to avoid doing things that make me look foolish around other kids.

Researchers asked 980 fifth graders to fill out these questionnaire items and then charted their social rankings over the next year. Boys and girls who checked the green items were more likely to ascend the classroom social hierarchy (that was their goal); but children who checked the blue items were increasingly preferred as friends. Unfortunately, however, agreeing with the red items predicted that children would be increasingly disliked during the next year.

Information from Rodkin and others, 2013.

When researchers asked fifth graders questions such as those in the table above and then tracked their later social status, boys and girls whose agenda was being popular (those agreeing with the green items) did rise in the social ranks. But in sixth grade, the class preferred people with the blue agendas—children with prosocial goals. So reaching out in a caring way is important at every age if we look at what really matters: being liked as a human being.

Now let's focus on the fifth graders who checked the red items—children terrified about socially goofing up. This socially anxious group became *more* unpopular over time (Rodkin and others, 2013). Who exactly do peers reject?

Rejected Children Have Externalizing (and Often Internalizing) Problems

Actually, the traits that universally land a child into the rejected category are externalizing issues. Classmates shun boys and girls (like Adam in the chapter-opening vignette) who make reactive aggression a major life mode. Children with internalizing disorders may or may not be rejected. However, a child who is *socially anxious*— such as Jimmy in the introductory vignette or the fifth graders who agreed with the red items on the table—is apt to be avoided as early as first grade (Degnan, Almas, & Fox, 2010).

This child's behavior is tailor-made to set him up for being rejected in third grade, as he is violating the rigid elementary school gender norms.

Denise Hager, Catchlight Visual Services/AlamyStock Photo

Moreover, a poisonous nature-evokes-nurture interaction sets in when a child enters school extremely socially shy. As children realize that people are avoiding them, their shyness gets more intense. So they become less socially competent—and increasingly likely to be rejected (and, as you will see, victimized)—as they advance from grade to grade (Booth-LaForce & Oxford, 2008).

A *bidirectional* process is also occurring. The child's anxiety makes other children nervous and want to retreat. In response to your own awkward encounters, have you ever been tempted to walk in the opposite direction when you saw a shy person approaching in the hall?

Rejected Children Don't Fit in with the Dominant Group

Children who stand out as different are also at risk of being rejected: boys who don't conform to traditional gender stereotypes (Braun & Davidson, 2016); low-income children in middle-class schools (Zettergren, 2007); immigrant children in ethnically homogenous societies (Strohmeier, Kärnä, & Salmivalli, 2010); boys and girls with disabilities—any child whom classmates label as "different" or "weird," or "not like us."

Exploring the Fate of the Rejected

Is childhood rejection a prelude to poor adult mental health? The answer is sometimes. Highly physically aggressive children are at risk for getting into trouble—at home, in school, and with the law—during adolescence and in their adult years (also more about this pathway in Chapter 9). Being friendless during childhood predicts having psychological problems as a young adult (Sakyi and others, 2016).

Still, because some qualities (such as conformity and being mean) that gain children social mileage do not translate well into adult life, being rejected for being different can have surprising benefits. Consider an awkward little girl named Eleanor Roosevelt who was rejected at age 8 but ended her life as a worldwide role model for women (and all human beings). To understand the fleeting quality of childhood peer status, you might organize a reunion of your fifth- or sixth-grade class. You might be surprised at how many unpopular classmates flowered during their high school or college years.

Although she didn't fit in with her snobbish, patrician childhood group, by standing up for racial equality and pressuring her husband (the U.S. president) to admit Jewish refugees during the Holocaust, Eleanor Roosevelt, the U.S. post–World War II ambassador to the United Nations, became the social conscience of a nation.

Bullying: Moral Disengagement in Action

> You can get bullied because you are weak or annoying or because you are different. Kids with big ears get bullied. Dorks get bullied. . . . Teacher's pet gets bullied. If you say the right answer in class too many times, you can get bullied.
>
> (quoted in Guerra, Williams, & Sadek, 2011, p. 306)

Children who are different can triumph in the proving ground of life. This is not the case on the proving ground of the playground. As you just read, being different, weak, socially awkward, or even "too good" provokes **bullying**—being teased, made fun of, and verbally or physically abused by one's peers.

As I have implied, it's normal for children to be bullied as they strive for status. But the roughly 10 to 20 percent of children subject to chronic harassment fall into two categories. The first (less common) type are **bully-victims**. These children are highly aggressive boys and girls who bully, get harassed, then bully again in an escalating cycle of pain (Deater-Deckard and others, 2010; Waasdorp, Bradshaw, &, Duong, 2011). The classic victim, however, has internalizing issues (Crawford & Manassis, 2011). These children are anxious, shy, low on the social hierarchy, and unlikely to fight back (Cook and others, 2010; Degnan and others, 2010; Scholte, Sentse, & Granic, 2010; also, see my personal confession in the Experiencing the Lifespan box on the next page).

Home used to be a refuge for children who were being harassed at school. Not anymore! Social media, texting, and the Internet have made bullying a 24/7 concern.

Cyberbullying, aggressive behavior carried out via electronic media, is potentially more toxic than traditional bullying in several respects. Broadcasting demeaning comments on Instagram and Facebook ensures having a large, amorphous audience that multiplies the victim's distress. Sending a text anonymously can be scarier than confronting the person face to face. ("Who hates me this much?"; "Perhaps it's someone I trusted as a friend?") (See Sticca & Perren, 2013.)

Moreover, the temptation to bully on-line is easy emotionally, as it removes inner controls. Children can lash out free from immediate consequences (Runions, 2013), without experiencing the sympathy (and guilt) linked to seeing a victim's pained face.

Cyberbullying's ease, its relentless presence, and scary public nature explain why teens see this behavior as worse than traditional bullying (Bonanno & Hymel, 2013; Sticca & Perren, 2013). Still, the same motives propel each type of harassment: Kids bully for revenge (as reactive aggression, or to get back at someone). Kids bully for recreation (it's exciting and fun). Kids bully because this activity offers social rewards, or reinforcement from one's peers (Runions, 2013).

bullying A situation in which one or more children (or adults) harass or target a specific child for systematic abuse.

bully-victims Exceptionally aggressive children (with externalizing disorders) who repeatedly bully and get victimized.

cyberbullying Systematic harassment conducted through electronic media.

Experiencing the Lifespan **Middle-Aged Reflections on My Middle-Childhood Victimization**

It was a hot August afternoon when the birthday present arrived. As usual, I was playing alone that day, maybe reading or engaging in a favorite pastime, fantasizing that I was a princess while sitting in a backyard tree. The gift, addressed to Janet Kaplan, was beautifully wrapped—huge but surprisingly light. This is amazing! I must be special! Someone had gone to such trouble for me! When I opened the first box, I saw another carefully wrapped box, and then another, smaller box, and yet another, smaller one inside. Finally, surrounded by ribbons and wrapping paper, I eagerly got to the last box and saw a tiny matchbox—which contained a small burnt match.

Around that time, the doorbell rang, and Cathy, then Ruth, then Carol, bounded up. "Your mother called to tell us she was giving you a surprise birthday party. We had to come over right away and be sure to wear our best dresses!" But their excitement turned to disgust when they learned that no party had been arranged. My 9th birthday was really in mid-September—more than a month away. It turned out that Nancy and Marion—the two most popular girls in class—had masterminded this relational aggression plot directed against me.

Why was I selected as the victim among the other third-grade girls? I had never hurt Nancy or Marion. In fact, in confessing their role, they admitted to some puzzlement: "We really don't dislike Janet at all." Researching this

chapter has offered me insights into the reasons for this 60-year-old wound.

Although I did have friends, I was fairly low in the classroom hierarchy. Not only was I shy, but I was that unusual girl—a child who genuinely preferred to play alone. But most important, I was the perfect victim. I have always disliked competitive status situations. When taunted or teased, I don't fight back.

As an older woman, I still dislike status hierarchies and social snobberies. I'm not a group (or party) person. I far prefer talking one-to-one. I am happy to spend hours alone. Today, I consider these attributes a plus (after all, having no problem sitting by myself for many thousands of hours was a prime skill that allowed me to write this textbook!), but they caused me anguish in middle childhood. In fact, when I'm in status-oriented peer situations even today—as a widowed older woman—I still find myself occasionally getting teased by the group!

P.S. I can honestly tell you that what happened to me in third grade is irrelevant to my life. I can't help wondering, though. Suppose, as would be likely today, my classmates had been invited to my so-called birthday via social media: "Janet is having a party, and she is inviting X, Y, and Z." Could being targeted through this humiliating, public venue have caused more enduring emotional scars?

Actually, bullying—of any kind—often demands an appreciative audience. One person (or a few people) does the harassing, while everyone else eggs on the perpetrator by laughing, posting similar comments on-line, or passively standing by.

Therefore, children are less apt to bully when their classmates don't condone this behavior. Conversely, when the class norm supports relational aggression, elementary schoolers get more aggressive over time (Rohlf, Busching, & Krahé, 2016). In this situation, *everyone* is apt to bully regardless of whether or not they see this behavior as morally wrong (Scholte and others, 2010; Werner & Hill, 2010).

The fact that the nicest boys and girls bully when the atmospheric conditions are right (Mulvey & Killen, 2016) explains why programs to attack bullying focus on changing the peer-group norms.

INTERVENTIONS **Attacking Bullying and Helping Rejected Children**

In the classic, widely used Olweus Bully Prevention Program, administrators plan a school assembly to discuss bullying early in the year. Then they form a bullying-prevention committee composed of children from each grade. Teachers and students are on high alert for bullying in their classes. The goal is to develop a schoolwide norm to not tolerate peer abuse (Olweus, Limber, & Mihalic, 1999).

Do the many bullying-prevention programs now in operation work? The answer is: "Yes, to some extent" (Espelage & De La Rue, 2013). But, because bullying or relational aggression is such an effective way to gain status, this phenomenon, present at every age, is a bit like bad weather—not in our power to totally control.

That's why I'd like to end this section by commenting on the classic recipients of this unfortunate, universal human activity—children who are socially shy. How can we help these boys and girls succeed?

In following a group of shy 5-year-olds, researchers found that a child who developed friendships in kindergarten or first grade became less socially anxious over time (Gazelle & Ladd, 2003). So, to help a temperamentally anxious child, parents should connect their son or daughter with a playmate who might become a close friend. Friendships, again, are the gateway to well-being in elementary school (and life).

How do children choose friends in the teenage years? How do we change physically and emotionally as puberty unfolds? Stay tuned for Part IV of this book.

Tying It All Together

1. Best friends in elementary school (pick false statement): *Support each other/ have similar values/ encourage prosocial behavior.*

2. Describe in a sentence the core difference between being well liked and being popular.

3. Which child is *not* at risk of being rejected in late elementary school?

   a. Miguel, a shy boy
   b. Mathew, who likes to play with girls' toys
   c. Nicholas, who lashes out in rage at other kids
   d. Elaine, who is relationally aggressive

Answers to the Tying It All Together quizzes can be found at the end of this chapter.

SUMMARY

Setting the Context

Piaget and Erikson view **middle childhood** as the life stage when we first become adult. Concrete operations allows children to go beyond their immediate impressions and think abstractly. During middle childhood, we learn that the key to success lies in industry, managing our impulses, and working for what we want.

Physical Development

All the achievements of middle childhood are made possible by our mammoth, slow-growing **frontal lobes**. During this life stage, motor skills expand; but, because children no longer play outside, the average elementary schoolchild today is less physically competent than in the past. Children who are well coordinated tend to be more physically active. Parents can stimulate motor skills by sharing physical activities and not micromanaging their daughters and sons. Being fit is not dependent on being well coordinated as we travel into adult life, and only fine motor skills predict academic success. But, having a high preschool **BMI** predicts lifetime weight struggles, and **childhood obesity** sets boys and girls up for a more difficult life.

Cognitive Development

Information-processing theory allows us to understand how industry locks in. In this perspective, material is processed through **working memory** in order to be recalled at a subsequent time. As children get older, working memory bin capacity dramatically expands, which explains why children reach concrete operations at age 7 or 8. Our ability to keep other people's perspectives in mind explains why theory-of-mind capacities improve through adolescence.

Executive functions—the ability to think through our actions and manage our cognitions—dramatically improve during middle childhood. Children become adept at **rehearsal, selective attention,** and inhibiting their immediate responses. The research on executive functions provides a wealth of insights that parents and teachers can use in real life.

Attention-deficit/hyperactivity disorder (ADHD), the most common childhood disorder in the United States, causes widespread problems at home and school. This condition, usually diagnosed in elementary school (more often among boys), can have many pathways and causes. Treatments involve medication, training for parents and children, providing white noise, exercise, and high-intensity games. The dramatic rise in contemporary Western ADHD diagnoses could be partly a product of a poor child–environment fit.

Emotional Development

Emotion regulation, the ability to manage and control our feelings, is crucial to having a successful life. Children with **externalizing tendencies** often "act out" their emotions and behave aggressively. Children with **internalizing tendencies** have problems managing intense fear. Both temperamental tendencies, at their extreme, cause problems during childhood.

Self-awareness changes dramatically as children move into middle childhood. Concrete operational children think about themselves in psychological terms, accurately scan their abilities, and evaluate themselves in comparison with peers. These realistic self-perceptions explain why **self-esteem** normally declines during elementary school. Relationships, academics, behavior, sports, and looks are the five areas from which elementary schoolchildren derive their self-esteem.

Children with externalizing tendencies minimize their difficulties with other people and may have unrealistically high self-esteem. Children with internalizing tendencies may develop **learned helplessness,** the feeling that they are incapable of doing well. Because both attitudes keep children from improving their behavior, the key to helping every child is to enhance self-efficacy and promote realistic views of the self.

Prosocial behaviors and morality seem built into our human biology but differ from child to child. There also is consistency, with prosocial preschoolers tending to be prosocial later on. Girls are more apt to comfort victimized children, but females are not necessarily more prosocial than males. Each sex acts prosocially in its own distinctive way.

Behaving prosocially involves transforming one's **empathy** (directly experiencing another's feelings) into **sympathy** (feeling for another person), having the executive function talents to decide when to be prosocial, and feeling able to effectively provide aid. Unfortunately, during elementary school, other considerations—such as "Does this person deserve my help?"—promote **moral disengagement,** and so inhibit some prosocial acts. To encourage morality, define the child as "a good person," allow her to remember the joy of giving, and use **induction** (get a child who has behaved hurtfully to understand the other person's feelings). Induction helps stimulate prosocial behavior because it induces **guilt.** Child-rearing techniques involving **shame** (personal humiliation) backfire, making children angry and less likely to behave in prosocial ways.

Aggression, or hurtful behavior, is also basic to being human. Rates of overt aggression (hitting, yelling) decline as children get older and are replaced by less openly aggressive acts. **Proactive aggression** is hurtful behavior we initiate. **Reactive aggression** occurs in response to being frustrated or hurt. **Relational aggression** refers to acts designed to damage social relationships. Relational aggression increases during late elementary school and middle school and is present in girls and boys. High levels of reactive aggression provoke problems in children's relationships.

A two-step pathway may produce a highly aggressive child. When toddlers are very active (exuberant) and have trouble regulating their emotions, caregivers respond harshly and punitively—causing anger and aggression. Then, during school, the child's "bad" behavior provokes social rejection, which leads to more reactive aggression. Highly aggressive children may have a **hostile attributional bias.** This "the world is out to get me" outlook is understandable because aggressive children may have been living in a rejecting environment since their earliest years. To help highly aggressive elementary schoolers, avoid harsh punishment and cultivate morality. Understand that acting-out, risk-taking girls and boys can flourish if they find the right environment as adults.

Social Development

Friendships, those close one-to-one relationships, become vital during elementary school. In childhood (and adulthood), we select friends who are similar to ourselves and look for qualities such as loyalty and having similar moral worldviews. Friends provide emotional support and teach children how to have fulfilling love relationships during adult life.

Popularity is different from friendships because this activity involves competing to rise in the peer ranks. While relational aggression helps children climb the popularity totem pole, being kind causes children to be well-liked by their peers. Rejected children are disliked—either because of serious externalizing or internalizing problems, or because they are different from the group. Although unpopular, friendless children are at risk for later emotional problems; children who are rejected for being different may excel as adults.

Children who are unpopular—either aggressive **bully-victims** or, more typically, shy, anxious children—are vulnerable to chronic **bullying.** The anonymous, 24/7 public nature of **cyberbullying** makes this behavior more toxic than face-to-face harassment. Because bullying depends on peer reinforcement, school bully prevention programs try to change class norms favoring relational aggression. To help socially anxious children, connect timid kindergarteners with a friend. Understand that friendships, not social status, matter most during the childhood years.

KEY TERMS

aggression, p. 180

attention-deficit/hyperactivity disorder (ADHD), p. 172

body mass index (BMI), p. 168

bullying, p. 187

bully-victims, p. 187

childhood obesity, p. 168

cyberbullying, p. 187

emotion regulation, p. 174

empathy, p. 178

executive functions, p. 170

externalizing tendencies, p. 174

frontal lobes, p. 167

guilt, p. 179

hostile attributional bias, p. 182

induction, p. 179

internalizing tendencies, p. 174

learned helplessness, p. 176

middle childhood, p. 165

moral disengagement, p. 179

proactive aggression, p. 180

prosocial behavior, p. 178

reactive aggression, p. 180

rehearsal, p. 170

relational aggression, p. 181

selective attention, p. 170

self-awareness, p. 174

self-esteem, p. 175

shame, p. 179

sympathy, p. 178

working memory, p. 170

ANSWERS TO Tying It All Together QUIZZES

Setting the Context

1. Our ability to transcend immediate appearances and control our emotions to work for a goal make middle childhood (and humanity) special.

Physical Development

1. Ethan's *motor* cortex is on an earlier developmental timetable than his *frontal lobes*.

2. c (Parents used to be less micromanaging or heavily involved.)

3. Excellent motor skills are *not very important* to adult fitness and preschool; *fine motor* skills predict children's later academic abilities.

4. False; it's difficult to cure childhood obesity by diet and exercise.

Cognitive Development

1. Answers are up to the students, but examples should center on not being able to focus on something that requires careful attention, and reacting impulsively when a child should be able to inhibit her responses.

2. Don't put your son in demanding situations that involve time management. When he studies, provide "white" background noise. Use small immediate reinforcers, such as prizes for good behavior that day. Get your son involved in sports or playing exciting games. Avoid power assertion (yelling and screaming), and go out of your way to provide lots of love.

3. Bakari might mention the fact that boys are more often diagnosed with this disorder and that exercise mutes the symptoms of this condition. Each phenomenon suggests

that, rather than being an internal, biological "problem," ADHD results from a poor childhood–environment fit.

Emotional Development

1. c (This child has clearly not left the preoperational bubble.)

2. Ramon = externalizing tendencies. Jared = internalizing tendencies. *Suggested intervention for Ramon:* Point out his realistic problems ("You are having trouble in X, Y, Z areas."), but cushion criticisms with plenty of love. *Suggested intervention for Jared:* Continually point out reality ("No one can always get A's. In fact, you are a fabulous student."). Get Jared to identify his "hopeless and helpless" ways of thinking, and train him to substitute more accurate perceptions.

3. c (Being intensely sensitive to others' emotions does not predict behaving prosocially.)

4. a = induction; good for promoting prosocial behavior; b = shame; bad strategy; and c = guilt; good for promoting prosocial behavior

5. Alyssa = proactive, relational; Brianna = direct, reactive

6. Mario has a hostile attributional bias.

Social Development

1. The final choice is incorrect as best friends can encourage negative behavior.

2. Being popular demands being aggressive and competitive—qualities that may not make children be well-liked by peers.

3. d (Unfortunately, relationally aggressive children can be popular.)

CONNECT ONLINE:

LaunchPad macmillan learning | Check out our videos and additional resources located at: www.macmillanlearning.com

CHAPTER 7

best friends forever

Settings for Development: Home, School, and Community

José's parents migrated from Honduras to Las Vegas when he was a baby. Leaving their close, extended family was painful, but they knew their child would not have a future in their dangerous town.

At first, life was going well. They easily got green cards. Manuel joined the Culinary Workers' Union. María trained as a Spanish language computer tech. Liberated from the horrifying conditions in her country, where parents had to confine their children to the house to keep them safe, María was thrilled to lavish love on her child. Lavishing love was easy because José was such a sunny, talented boy. At age 5, José could put together puzzles that would stump children twice his age. He was picking up English beautifully, even though his parents, who spoke only Spanish at home, could not help him with school.

Then, when José was 6, Manuel was laid off. He started to drink. He came home late to regularly yell at his wife. María fell into a depression, agonizing over whether to break her family apart. After she had that difficult conversation—"Dad and I will be living separately"—her sweet boy cried for months. This painful talk couldn't have been more poorly planned. The next day, José was tested for the gifted program at school.

José's fluid reasoning score was off the charts. But growing up in a Spanish-speaking family was a handicap. José didn't make the gifted cutoff, because his verbal comprehension score was below the mean.

Now, three years later, life is going well. María found a job that allowed her to find a small (affordable!) apartment in the best school district in the state. José is returning to his old, delightful self. María sings the praises of her son's fifth-grade teacher for appreciating José's gifts and emphasizing collaboration in class. She adores her new, caring community and is grateful for the fact that shared custody is working because (to her shock) Manuel has become a loving, hands-on dad. The thorn in María's side is Grandma—or, to be exact, José's attitude toward Grandma. Having her mother in the house is a godsend. José doesn't have to stay home alone when María works 70-hour weeks. But José feels ashamed to bring his friends home to see that "old world" lady. He wants to be a regular American boy. The downside of seeing your baby blossom in this country is watching your heritage fade.

How do children, such as José, react after their parents get divorced? Given that we must succeed in the world, how important are the lessons we learn from our parents as opposed to our peers? What was that test José took, and what strategies can teachers use to make every child eager to learn? What role does the neighborhood play in children's success? Here, we tackle these questions, and others, as I explore the settings within which children develop: home, school, and community.

While my discussion focuses on children around the world, in this chapter, I'll pay special attention to boys and girls, such as José, whose families differ from the traditional two-parent, middle-class, European American norm. So let's begin by scanning the tapestry of families in the twenty-first-century United States.

Left: Julia Sjöberg/Folio Images/Alamy Stock Photo

Setting the Context

- Identify which type of U.S. family is most likely to be poor.
- Outline some immigration statistics.

Today, the *traditional nuclear family*—heterosexual married couples with biological children—has dwindled to less than half of U.S. households. Another 20 percent are *blended families*—spouses divorced and remarried—so children have stepparents and, often, stepsiblings. One and a half million never-married couples are raising children; two million boys and girls have gay or bisexual parents. Grandparents are bringing up a growing number of children (1.3 million), too (see Healthychildren.org, n.d.).

The most important distinction relates to the 1 in 4 U.S. children living in single-parent families (see Figure 7.1A). With an alarming *2 out of 3* one-parent households classified as low income, most people raising children alone in the United States can barely make ends meet (see Figure 7.1B).

On a brighter note, twenty-first-century Western children are being raised in the first truly global world. How long have you lived in Chicago or Cleveland, Canada or Sweden? Where were you born, and why did your parents move? (See Table 7.1 for interesting statistics relating to our world on the move.)

Brooke Slezak/Stone/Getty Images

First-generation immigrant grandmothers, such as this woman who is helping raise her grandchild, show that strong, loving families take many forms. What is this grandma doing right? This is the question we will explore in this next section.

FIGURE 7.1: Living arrangements of children in U.S. families: Chart A shows that the two-parent married couple family is still the most common one. Chart B shows the huge disparity in the proportion of two-parent families versus single parents earning less than $40,000 per year, the estimated earnings cutoff permitting a family of four to financially survive.

Data from healthychildren.org, n.d.; Yang, Granja, & Koball, 2017.

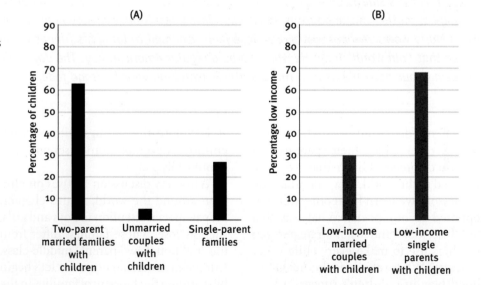

Table 7.1 A New World on the Move

- As of 2015, 1 in 30 people worldwide (a whopping 245 million adults!) lived outside of their nation of birth—a number that ballooned by more than 100 million people since the turn of this century.

- Luxemburg (42 percent), Israel (33 percent), and Switzerland (28 percent) rank as the top three nations in the percentage of foreign-born residents. But in absolute numbers, the United States still remains "a nation of immigrants." In 2015, 47 million people—almost 1 in 5 U.S. adults—were born in another country.

- With 60 million refugees at that time, 2015–2016 marked an historic march of humanity fleeing persecution. About 1.1 million people from the Middle East sought protection in Germany. In the United States, however, contrary to popular opinion, most refugees were not flooding in from the war-torn Middle East. They arrived from gang-ridden Central American nations, such as El Salvador, Honduras, and Guatemala.

- The *vast majority* of immigrants are not seeking refuge from oppression. They move in search of an economically secure future for themselves and their children, the classic reason why human beings migrated in the past!

Information from Bornstein, 2017.

Home

Can children thrive in every family? The answer is yes. The key lies in what parents do. We already know that parents need to promote a secure attachment and be sensitive to a child's temperamental needs. Is there a discipline style that works best? In landmark studies conducted a half century ago, developmentalist Diana Baumrind (1971) decided yes.

Parenting Styles

Think of a parent you admire. What is that mother or father doing right? Now think of parents who you feel are not fulfilling this job. Where are they falling short? Most likely, your list will center on two functions. Are these people nurturing? Do they provide discipline or rules? By classifying parents on these two dimensions—being caring and child-centered, and giving "structure"—Baumrind (1971) spelled out the following **parenting styles:**

- **Authoritative parents** rank high on nurturing and setting limits. They set clear standards but also provide some freedom and lots of love. In this house, there are specific bed and homework times. However, if a daughter wants to watch a favorite TV program, these parents might relax the rule that homework must be finished before dinner. They could let a son extend his regular 9:00 P.M. bedtime for a special event. Although authoritative parents firmly believe in structure, they understand that rules don't take precedence over human needs.

- **Authoritarian parents** are more inflexible. Their child-rearing motto is, "Do just what I say." In these families, rules are not negotiable. While authoritarian parents may love their children deeply, their child-rearing style can seem uncaring and cold.

- **Permissive parents** are at the opposite end of the spectrum from authoritarian parents. Their parenting mantra is, "Provide total freedom and unconditional love." In these households, there are no set bedtimes and no homework demands. Here, the child-rearing principle is that children's wishes rule.

- **Rejecting-neglecting parents** are the worst of both worlds—low on structure and on love. In these families, children are neglected, ignored, and emotionally abandoned. They are left to raise themselves (see Figure 7.2 on the next page for a recap).

LEARNING OUTCOMES

- Evaluate Baumrind's ideas.
- Identify resilient children's qualities.
- Outline collective efficacy issues for immigrant children.
- Contrast different ideas about the importance of parents.
- Summarize the research on corporal punishment, child abuse, and divorce.

parenting style In Diana Baumrind's framework, how parents align on love and discipline.

authoritative parents In the parenting-styles framework, the best child-rearing style, when parents provide ample love and family rules.

authoritarian parents In the parenting-styles framework, when parents provide many rules but rank low on love.

permissive parents In the parenting-styles framework, when parents provide few rules but lots of love.

rejecting-neglecting parents In the parenting-styles framework, the worst child-rearing approach, when parents provide little discipline or love.

Discipline (rules and structure)

	High	Low
High	Authoritative style	Permissive style
Low	Authoritarian style	Rejecting-neglecting style

Love (child-centered focus)

FIGURE 7.2: Parenting styles: A summary diagram
Information from Baumrind, 1971.

In relating the first three discipline studies to children's behavior (the fourth was added later), Baumrind found that children with authoritative parents were more academically successful, well-adjusted, and kind. Hundreds of studies worldwide have confirmed this finding. In a recent global example, "balanced parental discipline" (that is, love plus structure) was correlated with prosocial behavior among children living in Colombia, Italy, Jordan, Kenya, the Philippines, Thailand, and the United States (Pastorelli and others, 2016).

Decoding Parenting in a Deeper Way

These studies offer a beautiful blueprint for the right way to raise children: Provide clear rules and lots of love. However, if you classify your parents along these dimensions, you may find problems. Perhaps one parent was permissive and another authoritarian. Or maybe your families' rules randomly varied from authoritative to permissive over time.

One study suggested that the worst situation for a teenager's mental health occurred when families had inconsistent rules (Dwairy, 2010). Imagine how frustrated you would be if your parents sometimes came down very hard on you and, in other *similar situations*, seemed not to care!

But aren't there times when parenting styles should vary, that is, situations when children *need* a more authoritarian or permissive approach? These questions bring me to two classic critiques of Baumrind's parenting styles.

Critique 1: Parenting Styles Can Vary from Child to Child

Perhaps your parents came down harder on a brother or sister because that sibling needed more discipline, while your personality flourished with a permissive style. As I described earlier in this book, good parents *should* vary their childrearing, depending on the unique personality of a specific child.

Unfortunately, however, as I also stressed in earlier chapters, when children are "high maintenance" (difficult to raise), due to an evocative process, parenting styles may change for the worse. A mother might become excessively controlling (authoritarian) when her child has a chronic illness (Pinquart, 2013). She might yell, scream, and wall herself off emotionally from a son or daughter with ADHD.

So, again, parenting is far more bidirectional and child-evoked than Baumrind assumes. Does an authoritarian (or permissive) parenting style *ever* work best?

This mother's relaxed, totally accepting approach to parenting may get her ranked as "overly permissive."

Critique 2: Parenting Styles Can Vary Depending on One's Society

Critics point out that Baumrind's styles perspective reflects a Western middle-class perspective on childrearing. But new immigrants from Mexico who tend to avoid spanking their children (Lee & Altschul, 2015) may regard this parenting technique as too harsh (much more about spanking soon). Conversely, in collectivist cultures such as China, child-centered parenting may seem too lax.

This point was spelled out in a controversial book called *The Battle Hymn of the Tiger Mother* (2011). Amy Chua, a second-generation Chinese American parent, argued that, in contrast to our more laid-back style, more traditional Asian, rule-oriented "no back talk" childrearing was the best way to produce a Harvard-bound, high-achieving child (see Chua, 2011; Lui & Rollock, 2013).

Do Asian-heritage U.S. parents *typically* adopt a more authoritarian parenting style? Unless they are recent immigrants, the answer is no (Choi and others, 2013; Kim, Wang, and others, 2013).

If we want children to excel at school, should parents adopt Chua's rule-oriented child-rearing advice? Not really. From Japan (Uji and others, 2014) to Turkey (Cenk & Demir, 2016), from Indonesia (Abubakar and others, 2015) to Palestine (Alt, 2016), *authoritative parenting* is linked to academic achievement (and overall well-being).

In the past, adults were forced to act authoritarian because life was so dangerous (see Chapter 1). Even today, parents living in war-torn nations reluctantly report using authoritarian child-rearing techniques. As one mother in violence-wracked El Salvador anguished: ". . . I do not let my son go outside. . . . I think we have become overprotective against our will" (quoted in Rojas-Flores and others, 2013, p. 278). But in twenty-first-century Western nations, authoritarian parenting is a symptom of feeling less socially competent (Egeli & Rinaldi, 2016) and more stressed-out in the parenting role (Nomaguchi & House, 2013).

INTERVENTIONS   Lessons for Thinking About Parents

How can you use these insights to think about parents in a more empathic way?

- Understand that parenting styles don't operate in a vacuum. They vary depending on a family's unique life situation and child.

- Realize that while withdrawing emotionally is understandable when a child is "difficult," authoritarian parenting is not the best way to raise a child unless a family lives in a dangerous neighborhood or part of the world.

- Celebrate the fact that today we have the luxury to be child-centered, in the sense of listening empathically to our daughters and sons. Although specific discipline practices differ, most parents in our world village agree: "Give children limits, but above all offer lots of love!"

Table 7.2 gives you a chance to step back and list your own parenting priorities. Let's now consider that philosophical question: Is parenting critically important to how children turn out?

Table 7.2: Checklist for Identifying Your Parenting Priorities

Rank the following goals in order of their importance to you, from 1 (for highest priority) to 8 (for lowest priority). It's OK to use the same number twice if two goals are equally important to you.

_____ Producing an obedient, well-behaved child

_____ Producing a caring, prosocial child

_____ Producing an independent, self-sufficient child

_____ Producing a child who is extremely close to you

_____ Producing an intelligent, creative thinker

_____ Producing a well-rounded child

_____ Producing a happy, emotionally secure child

_____ Producing a spiritual (religious) child

What do your rankings reveal about the qualities you most admire in human beings?

How Much Do Parents Matter?

The most inspiring place to start is with those world-class role models who had terrible childhoods but succeeded brilliantly as adults.

🔥 Hot in Developmental Science: Resilient Children

Library of Congress [LC-US262-2280]

Abandoned by his father at age 9 and raised in a Kentucky shack without any chance to attend school, Abraham Lincoln grew up to become the most beloved U.S. president and perhaps the greatest man of the nineteenth century. What made this resilient child thrive? The answer: towering intellectual gifts, a remarkable drive to learn, optimism, self-efficacy, and a world-class talent for understanding human motivations and connecting with people in a caring, prosocial way.

resilient children
Children who rebound from serious early life traumas to construct successful adult lives.

acculturation Among immigrants, the tendency to become similar to the mainstream culture after time spent living in a new society.

His aristocratic parents spent their time gallivanting around Europe; they never appeared at the nursery doors. At age 7, he was wrenched from the only person who loved him—his nanny—and shipped off to boarding school. Insolent, angry, refusing to obey orders or sit still, he was regularly beaten by the headmaster and teased by the other boys. Although gifted at writing, he was incapable of rote memorization; he couldn't pass a test. When he graduated at the bottom of his boarding school class, his father informed him that he would never amount to anything. His name was Winston Churchill. He was the man who stood up to Hitler and carried England to victory in World War II.

Churchill's upbringing was a recipe for disaster. He had neglectful parents, behavior problems, and was a failure at school. But this dismal childhood produced the leader who saved the modern world.

Resilient children, like Churchill or Abraham Lincoln (in the photo), confront terrible conditions such as parental abuse, poverty, and war and go on to construct successful, loving lives. What qualities allow these children to thrive?

Developmentalists find that resilient children often have a special talent, such as Churchill's gift for writing, or Lincoln's towering intellect. They are adept at regulating their emotions. They have a high sense of self-efficacy and an optimistic worldview (Grych, Hamby, & Banyard, 2015). They possess a strong faith or sense of meaning in life (Wright & Masten, 2005).

Being resilient depends on inner resources—having good executive functions and intellectual and social skills. But the number of wider-world traumas matters (Panter-Brick and others, 2015). If you are exposed to a series of tragedies—for instance, your parents getting divorced after experiencing a disaster such as a hurricane—it's more difficult to preserve your efficacy feelings or rebound to construct a happy life (Becker-Blease, Turner, & Finkelhor, 2010; Kronenberg and others, 2010).

Most important, children who succeed against incredible odds typically have at least one close, caring relationship with a parent or another adult (such as Churchill's nanny). Like a plant that thrives in the desert, resilient children have the internal resources to extract love from their parched environment. But they cannot survive without any water at all.

The same qualities apply to immigrant children facing **acculturation**, the challenge of adapting to a different culture. But here, a family's fit to the new society looms large. Can this girl balance the need to preserve her cultural identity while embracing the norms of this new nation (Telzer and others, 2016)? Is this boy moving to a place that welcomes families from his region of the world (Bornstein, 2017; Pieloch, McCollough, & Marks, 2016)?

We marvel at the stamina of children who travel thousands of miles from war-torn nations and thrive. Might these survivors have resilience-promoting genes? As I mentioned in Chapter 4, some scientists believe a genetic profile may set certain newborns up to be relatively immune to stressful life events, but that this same "immunity" gene-form is a liability when the wider world is nurturing and calm. So, yes, some babies may arrive in this world biologically blessed to weather the biblical upheavals of human life.

Will these children succeed in their new home? In addition to having the classic attributes linked to resilience, it depends on whether their new community is a welcoming place and—very importantly—if they are genetically resistant to stress. 🐒

Making the Case That Parents Don't Matter

What matters more in how children develop, their parents or their genes? Twin and adoption studies, as I mentioned in Chapter 1, come down firmly on the "it's mainly genetic" side. Faced with this nature-oriented behavioral-genetic research message, one developmentalist famously concluded that it doesn't matter if you were raised in your particular family or the one down the street. Given adequate parenting, and a decent environment, children grow up to express their genetic fate (see Scarr, 1997; Scarr & Deater-Deckard, 1997).

Psychologist Judith Harris provided the most interesting twist on this "parents don't matter" argument. Harris (1995, 1998, 2002, 2006) believes that the environment has a dramatic impact on our development; but, rather than parents, our peer group socializes us to become adults.

Harris begins by taking aim at the principle underlying attachment theory—that the lessons we learn from our parents transfer to our other relationships. Learning, Harris believes, is context-specific. We cannot use the same *working model* with our mother and with the classroom bully, since we would never survive. Furthermore, because we live our lives in the wider world, she argues, the messages we absorb from the culture of our contemporaries must take precedence over the lessons we are taught at home.

Any parent can relate to Harris's peer-power principle when witnessing her 3-year-old pick up every bad habit from his preschool classmates. I outlined a chilling example of a similar group influence in the last chapter when I described how aggressive middle-school norms can evoke bullying in the "nicest kids."

An equally compelling argument lies in the pivotal role *adult peers*—meaning, the community—play in shaping children's lives. As I will emphasize throughout this chapter, parents become better caregivers—and children are more apt to thrive—in neighborhoods defined by high **collective efficacy,** places where community ties are close and neighbors bond around shared prosocial norms. To paraphrase that familiar African proverb: "It takes a village to raise children and successful parents, too!"

These arguments about the importance of genetics and living in caring communities alert us to the fact that when we see children acting out, we cannot leap to the assumption that "it's just the parents' fault." As Bronfenbrenner's *ecological developmental systems approach* predicts, many influences—from peer groups, to schools, to

collective efficacy
Communities defined by strong cohesion, a commitment to neighbor-to-neighbor helping, and shared prosocial values among residents.

Look at these exuberant boys, passionate to fit in with their friends. Then ask yourself whether these children are acting the same way they were taught to behave at home. Suddenly, doesn't Judith Harris's theory that "peer groups shape development" make a good deal of sense?

neighborhoods, to living in a particular nation—affect how children behave. But you may be thinking that the idea that parents are *not* important goes way too far.

Many experts agree. For children to realize their genetic potential, parents should provide the best possible environment (Ceci and others, 1997; Kagan, 1998; Maccoby, 2002). In fact, even in the most efficacious community, when children are biologically vulnerable, superior parenting is required.

Making the Case for Superior Parenting

Imagine, for instance, that your daughter is temperamentally "difficult." You know from reading this book that you may be tempted to disengage emotionally from your child. You understand that adopting this less responsive parenting style can make the situation worse. So you inhibit your use of *power assertion*. You provide lots of love. You arrange the environment to minimize your child's vulnerabilities and highlight her strengths.

Actually, when a child is biologically reactive, sensitive caregiving can make a critical difference. From the studies mentioned in Chapter 3 showing that loving touch helps premature infants grow to my suggestions for raising fearful or exuberant kids (discussed in Chapters 4 and 6), the message is the same: With vulnerable children, outstanding parenting matters most.

So let's celebrate the fact that resilient children can flower in the face of difficult life conditions. But when a baby needs special nurturing, high-quality nurturing is required.

INTERVENTIONS **Lessons for Readers Who Are Parents**

Now let's summarize by offering some concrete parenting advice.

There are no firm guidelines about how to be an effective parent—except to show lots of love, set consistent rules, and adapt your discipline to your unique child. You will face special challenges if you live in a dangerous environment or have a son or daughter who is "harder to raise" (where you may have to work harder to stay loving and attached). Your power is limited at best.

Try to see this message as liberating. Children cannot be massaged into having an idealized adult life. Your child's future does not totally depend on you. Focus on the quality of your relationship, and enjoy these wonderful years. And if your son or daughter is having difficulties, draw inspiration from Winston Churchill's history. Predictions from childhood to adult life can be hazy. Your struggling child may grow up to save the world!

Now that I've covered the general territory, let's turn to specifics. First, I'll examine the controversy surrounding spanking and then focus on the worst type of parenting, child abuse. Finally, I'll explore that common family event, divorce.

Spanking

corporal punishment The use of physical force to discipline a child.

Poll friends and family about **corporal punishment**—any discipline technique that involves physical measures such as spanking—and you are likely to get strong reactions. Some people adhere to the biblical principle, "Spare the rod and spoil the child." They may blame the decline in spanking for every social problem. Others blame corporal punishment for *creating* those social problems. They believe that parents who rely on "hitting" are implicitly teaching children that it is OK to respond in a violent way. To put these positions into perspective, let's take a tour of the total turnaround in corporal punishment attitudes in recent times.

Before the twentieth century, corporal punishment was standard practice. Flogging was routine in prisons (Gould & Pate, 2010), the military, and other places (Pinker, 2011). In the United States, it was legal for men to "physically chastise" their wives (Knox, 2010). Today, in Western democracies, these practices are universally condemned.

In fact, 24 nations—from Spain to Sweden and Croatia to Costa Rica—have passed laws banning child corporal punishment. Organizations from the American Academy of Pediatrics to the United Nations to the Methodist Church have also put forth resolutions that call spanking "inhumane" (Knox, 2010).

The United States is a dramatic exception. Although spanking is illegal at schools and day-care centers in most states, any U.S. senator proposing a bill to ban this behavior might be severely condemned. Not only is U.S. individualistic society wary about the government intruding into parental "freedom," but *many* parents do spank their daughters and sons (Barkin and others, 2007).

Still, with surveys showing that only 1 in 10 parents admit they "often spank," corporal punishment is not the preferred U.S. discipline mode. Today, the most frequent punishments parents report are removal of privileges and, to a lesser extent, getting sent to one's room (Barkin and others, 2007).

Who in the United States is most likely to spank? Corporal punishment is widely accepted in the African American community (Burchinal, Skinner, & Reznick, 2010; Lorber, O'Leary, & Smith Slep, 2011). As one Black woman reported: "I would rather me discipline them than (the police)" (quoted in Taylor, Hamvas, & Paris, 2011, p. 65). As you might imagine from the "spare the rod, spoil the child" injunction, people who believe this biblical pronouncement is literally true are apt to use this disciplinary technique (Rodriguez & Henderson, 2010).

Adults who were spanked as children see more value in this child-rearing approach (Simons & Wurtele, 2010). (In my classes, I often hear students report: "I was spanked and it helped; so I plan to do the same with my kids.") But if you feel that physical punishment got out of hand when you were a child, you are probably passionate about never hitting your own daughter or son (Gagne and others, 2007).

What do experts advise? Today, an overwhelming number of psychologists believe that spanking is *never* appropriate (Gershoff & Grogan-Kaylor, 2016). Hitting, as I mentioned earlier, models violence. Yes, spanking may produce immediate compliance. But it impairs prosocial behavior because it gets children to only focus on themselves (Andero & Stewart, 2002; Benjet & Kazdin, 2003; Knox, 2010).

A few mainstream developmentalists, such as Diana Baumrind, have a (slightly) different view (Baumrind, Larzelere, & Cowan, 2002). They believe that if we rule out corporal punishment completely, caregivers may resort to more damaging, shaming practices such as saying, "I hate you. You will never amount to anything." But even these psychologists have clear limits as to how and when physical discipline might be used:

- Never hit an infant. *Babies can't control their behavior. They don't know what they are doing wrong.* For a preschooler, a few light swats on the bottom can be a last resort disciplinary technique if a child is engaging in dangerous activities—such as running into the street—that need to be immediately stopped (Larzelere & Kuhn, 2005).

- This action, however, must be accompanied by a verbal explanation ("What you did was wrong because . . ."). Spanking should only be considered if other approaches fail.

The issue is that, with more than a hundred studies linking corporal punishment to mental health problems (see Gershoff & Grogan-Kaylor, 2016), we need to firmly dispel the misconception that spanking produces well-disciplined, obedient children. Because corporal punishment is rampant in neighborhoods low in collective efficacy, where daily life is frustrating and dangerous, its best to intervene by making communities more caring (Ma, 2016).

Frequent spanking promotes the very behavior it is supposed to cure. To take one example, researchers found that parents who believed strongly in spanking had sons and daughters who said that during disagreements with a playmate, hitting that other child was fine (Simons & Wurtele, 2010). Worse yet, what starts out as a "normal" spanking can escalate as a parent "gets into it," the child cries more, and soon we have that worst-case scenario: child abuse.

Child Abuse

child maltreatment
Any act that seriously endangers a child's physical or emotional well-being.

Child maltreatment—the term for actions that endanger children's physical or emotional well-being—comprises four categories. *Physical abuse* refers to bodily injury that leaves bruises. It encompasses everything from overzealous spanking to battering that may lead to a child's death. *Neglect* refers to caregivers' failure to provide adequate supervision and care. It might mean abandoning the child, not providing sufficient food, or failing to enroll a son or daughter in school. *Emotional abuse* refers to shaming, terrorizing, or exploiting a child. *Sexual abuse* covers the spectrum from rape and incest to fondling and exhibitionistic acts.

Everyone can identify serious forms of maltreatment, but there is a gray zone as to what activities cross the line (Cicchetti, 2016). Does every spanking that leaves bruises qualify as physical abuse? If a mother leaves her toddler in an 8-year-old sibling's care, is she neglectful? Are parents who walk around naked in the house guilty of sexual abuse? Emotional abuse is inherently murky to define, although this form of maltreatment may be the most common of all (Foster and others, 2010).

This labeling issue partly explains why maltreatment statistics vary, depending on who we ask. In one global summary (involving an incredible 150 studies and 10 million participants), scientists estimated that roughly 3 of 1,000 children worldwide were physically maltreated, using informants' (that is, other people's) reports. In polling adults themselves, the rates were 10 times higher (Stoltenborgh and others, 2013). In one study in Canada, a shocking 1 in 4 people reported being maltreated as a child (MacMillan and others, 2013).

Obviously, far more people will report that they were abused than the "objective" abuse-rate figures indicate. But, although some adults may err on the side of over-reporting (saying "I was abused" because they are chronically angry with their parents), reports to authorities probably qualify as the iceberg's tiny tip (Greenfield, 2010). Why is maltreatment still swept under the rug in our day and age? Before answering this question, let's look at what provokes this parenting pathology and probe its effects.

Exploring the Risk Factors

As ecological, developmental systems theory predicts, several categories of influence can spark child abuse (Wolfe, 2011).

Parents' Personality Problems Are Important

People who maltreat their children tend to suffer from psychological disorders such as depression and externalizing problems such as substance abuse (Plant, Donohue, & Holland, 2016). They may have hostile attributional biases (McCarthy & Lumley, 2012), assuming that a toddler is "bad" when she engages in benign activities like running around.

Life Stress Accompanied by Social Isolation Can Be Crucial

Abusive parents are often young and poorly educated (Cicchetti, 2016). They tend to be coping with an overload of upsetting life events, from domestic violence to severe poverty (Annerbäck, Svedin, & Gustafsson, 2010). They feel cut off from caring social contacts. Again, feeling isolated in neighborhoods low in collective efficacy can be the match that causes child abuse to flare up (Barnhart & Maguire-Jack, 2016).

Children's Vulnerabilities Play a Role

A child who is emotionally fragile can fan this fire—a baby who cries excessively (Reijneveld and others, 2004), has a medical problem (Svensson, Bornehag, & Janson, 2011), or is premature (Sieswerda-Hoogendoorn and others, 2013). Therefore, in a

A loving family life—and particularly, a caring relationship with one's spouse—can break the intergenerational cycle of abuse.

terrible irony, the very children that most need unusually loving care are apt to provoke an out-of-control caregiver's wrath. The fact that abusive parents may target just one child was brought home to me when I was working as a clinical psychologist at a city hospital in New York. A mother was referred for treatment for abusing her "spiteful" 10-year-old, although she never harmed his "sweet" 3-year-old brother. So disturbances in the attachment relationship are a core ingredient in the poisonous recipe for producing a battered child.

Exploring the Consequences

Maltreated children tend to suffer from internalizing and externalizing problems. They may have impaired theory of mind abilities and get rejected by their peers (Cicchetti, 2016). Just as with the orphanage-reared babies discussed earlier, neuro-imaging studies suggest child maltreatment may compromise the developing brain (Ahn and others, 2016).

Because traumatic childhood experiences prime the body to *epigenetically* break down (Danese & Baldwin, 2017), children who are maltreated have more physical problems during adult life (Cicchetti, 2016). They are at risk of getting embroiled in abusive love relationships (McCloskey, 2013); and yes, abused children are at higher risk of maltreating their own daughters and sons.

Still, most abused children become decent caring parents. Some are passionate to go in the opposite direction (Berlin, Appleyard, & Dodge, 2011). As one woman described: "I made a vow to protect my children. . . . It was almost like a mantra, that I'm never going to strike [my child]" (quoted in Hall, 2011, p. 38).

Adults who break the cycle of abuse tend to have good intellectual and coping skills (Hengartner and others, 2013). They are fortunate to have the DNA profile that I alluded to earlier, which makes them genetically more resistant to stress (Banducci and others, 2014). Having a loving marriage also offers potent insulation from repeating the trauma of abuse (Jaffee and others, 2013).

INTERVENTIONS   Taking Action Against Child Abuse

What should you do if you suspect child abuse? The law requires teachers, social workers, and health-care professionals to report the situation to child protective services. Children in imminent danger are removed from the home, and the cases are referred to juvenile court. Judges do not have the power to punish abusive parents, but they can place the children in foster care and limit or terminate parental rights.

Imagine you are a teacher who sees these suspicious burns on a student's hands. You know that unusual injuries like this can signal child abuse, but you aren't absolutely sure. Would you immediately report the situation to the authorities? Would you talk to the parents first? What exactly would you do?

In one Chinese survey, teenagers mentioned that having neighbors who spoke up helped prevent them from being physically abused (Cheung, 2016). But, even in the most efficacious neighborhood, adults have powerful temptations not to intervene. If you make a false report, you risk ruining a family's life. "Are those burns a sign of child abuse or a normal accident?" "If I do report the situation, will the authorities take action?"

This last fear seems justified. In one Swedish study, even in the face of accusations of severe abuse, only 1 percent of the cases actually went to trial (Otterman, Lainpelto, & Lindblad, 2013). This is unfortunate, because when parents have a history of abuse, the situation can get worse. In one study that tracked at-risk families, the home environment deteriorated from preschool to kindergarten, with mothers doing more yelling and hitting over time, especially with their sons (Haskett, Neupert, & Okado, 2014).

Divorce

Although it still occurs too often, child abuse is no longer common in this day and age (see Pinker, 2011). However, since the late-twentieth-century lifestyle revolution, children are more apt to face another unwelcome family change: divorce. How does divorce affect children, and what can adults do to help?

Let's start with the bad news. Studies worldwide comparing children of divorce with their counterparts in intact, married families show these boys and girls are at a disadvantage—academically, socially, and in terms of mental health (Al Gharaibeh, 2015; Lamela and others, 2016). One reason may be economic (see Weaver & Schofield, 2015). Divorce can propel a mother-headed household into poverty, even though that family had previously been middle class (Schramm and others, 2013; see also Figure 7.1B on page 194).

The good news is that children normally adjust to this life transition well, as long as their parents are authoritative and the divorce is fairly conflict free (Weaver & Schofield, 2015). Still, I don't want to minimize the guilt people feel when making this choice. One Israeli woman described a fairly common scenario when she lamented that for months her daughter's conversations started with the anxious phrase, "Soon, when Dad will come back home" (quoted in Cohen, Leichtentritt, & Volpin, 2014, p. 37).

In this qualitative study exploring the feelings of newly divorced Israeli mothers, women said their main agenda was to minimize their children's pain. So they struggled to put aside their vengeful feelings and not bad-mouth their former spouses. One mother helped her child cope with his father's painful absence by making it into a shared game: "I laugh. I tell him, 'OK you miss daddy. But where is he?' And he says, 'Far, far away'" (quoted in Cohen, Leichtentritt, & Volpin, 2014, p. 39).

Others vowed to avoid mentioning the gritty details: "I don't want to hurt him," said a woman named Trina. "I won't tell them that his father pointed a gun at his mother" (quoted in Cohen, Leichtentritt, & Volpin, 2014, p. 37).

This is not to say that **parental alienation**—poisoning children against ex-partners—is rare. Even years after separating, some people can't resist demonizing the other parent, especially after an acrimonious divorce (see van Lawick & Visser, 2015).

The temptation to engage in *relational aggression* (enlisting children against a former spouse) brings up issues related to custody and visitation. When the divorce is bitter (or labeled "high conflict"), should a child frequently see both a mother and father?

For almost the entire twentieth century, mothers were routinely given custody, based on the psychoanalytic principle that women are inherently superior nurturers—a practice that unfairly limited fathers from being fully involved in their children's lives. Today, Western nations have rectified this situation by passing laws encouraging joint custody (see Lavadera, Caravelli, & Togliatti, 2013). Spouses don't have to split living

parental alienation The practice among divorced parents of bad-mouthing a former spouse, with the goal of turning a child against that person.

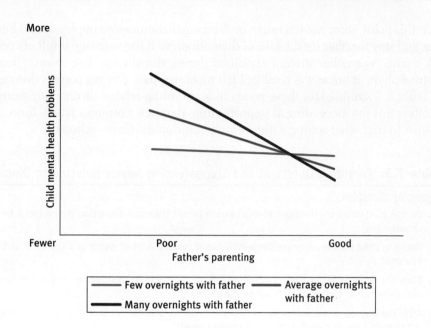

FIGURE **7.3: Child mental health problems as a function of father's parenting and whether the child spent many or few overnights at that parent's house:** Notice from the red line that staying over often at a divorced dad's house is good for children, *if* that man is a good parent. But frequent overnights with a father who has poor parenting skills are clearly detrimental to children's mental health.

Data from Sandler, Wheeler, & Braver, 2013.

arrangements 50-50. But even though the child lives mostly with a mother (or father), when parents share custody, the other partner can see a son or daughter any time.

Does shared custody help children cope? The answer hinges on the quality of care the other partner provides (Lamela and others, 2016). As the study summarized in Figure 7.3 illustrates, while more overnights with a dad who was a good parent promoted adjustment, when children spent time with an inadequate father, post-divorce child emotional problems escalated (Sandler, Wheeler, & Braver, 2013).

So with custody and visitation, we need to take a person-centered, *ecological, developmental systems approach.* Go for shared custody in the abstract, but if an ex-spouse is antisocial or the partners continually bad-mouth each other, limit access to mainly one caregiver to protect the child (see DeGarmo, 2010; Lessard and others, 2010).

After a divorce, it's normal for childrearing to get more disorganized, as parents cope with their upsetting feelings. But one study showed that it's important to guard against being too permissive, as having firm rules prevents children from acting out during this difficult time (Stallman & Ohan, 2016). The bottom line, however, is that what really matters is the ongoing parenting style. Children should spend their time with the parent (or parents) who parent the best (Weaver & Schofield, 2015).

Should older children be able to choose which custody arrangement they prefer? One study, comparing standard divorce mediation with approaches centered more on child wishes, suggested yes (Ballard and others, 2013).

Still, in another poll of divorced parents and their teens, everyone recoiled at the idea of putting *total* decision making on a child's shoulders (Cashmore & Parkinson, 2008). Imagine forcing a son or daughter to admit, "I prefer to live with Mom (or Dad)." And consider the coercion that might ensue from the parent side. During one semester's divorce discussion, a student poignantly described this scenario when she informed the class: "My daughter told the judge she wanted to live with her father, and then, years later said, 'Mom, I wanted you, but I was afraid to say so because I was frightened of Dad.'"

Do you think this girl should be testifying in court about whether to live with her Mom or Dad? Clearly, there are serious minuses here.

At this point, some readers might be thinking that unhappy couples should bite the bullet and stay together for the sake of their children. If the marriage is full of conflict, think again. As another student explained during this divorce discussion, "Because the atmosphere at home was terrible, I felt much happier after my parents divorced."

Table 7.3 summarizes these points in a parenting-related divorce questionnaire and offers tips for succeeding at stepparenting, that new common family form. Now let's turn to that other setting within which children develop—school.

Table 7.3: Parenting Questions and Stepparenting Advice Relating to Divorce

Parenting Questions

1. Do the ex-spouses continually bad-mouth each other? (Parental alienation is poisonous for children.)

2. Does the child see the ex-spouse frequently? (Joint custody is great, but only if the other partner is a good parent.)

3. Does the child have input into custody decisions? (This can be positive, as long as the total decision-making burden doesn't fall on the child.)

4. After the divorce, do the parent(s) set consistent rules? (Authoritative post-divorce childrearing is the main force that predicts how well children cope!)

Stepparenting Advice

1. Go slow in disciplining your new family. Understand that children naturally feel that their real parent is their "original" mom and/or dad.

2. Realize that, with authoritative parenting, attachments lock in over time. One study showed that children were more apt to view their stepdad as their "real" father the longer he lived in the house.

3. Strive for harmony in your childrearing. Agreeing on parenting styles is doubly important when raising a family the second time around!

Information from Kalmijn, 2013; Kinniburgh-White, Cartwright, & Seymour, 2010; and the references in this section.

Tying It All Together

1. Montana's parents set firm rules but value their children's input about family decisions. Pablo's parents have rules for everything and tolerate no *ifs*, *ands*, or *buts*. Sara's parents don't really have rules—at their house, it's always playtime. Which parenting style is being used by Montana's parents? By Pablo's parents? By Sara's parents?

2. Ahmid and his family moved to your town from a refugee relocation center in the Middle East. Based on this chapter, spell out some qualities that predict whether this traumatized child may be resilient, and summarize your community's main goal.

3. Melissa's son Jared, now in elementary school, was premature and has a difficult temperament. What might Judith Harris advise about fostering this child's development, and what might this chapter recommend?

4. Your sister is concerned about a friend who uses corporal punishment with her baby and her 4-year-old. She asks what the experts say. Pick which two statements developmentalists might make.
   a. Never spank children of any age.
   b. Mild spanking is OK for the infant.
   c. Corporal punishment is linked to some mental health problems.
   d. If the child has a difficult temperament, corporal punishment might help.

5. Ms. Ramirez is worried about an 8-year-old who meanders around the neighborhood at all hours of the night. Yesterday, she saw burn marks on the child's arms. Describe how Ms. Ramirez might feel about reporting this situation to the police, and what might happen if she accuses the parent of neglect.

6. Imagine you are a family court judge deciding to award joint custody. In a phrase, explain your main criterion for awarding unlimited overnights with a particular divorced dad.

Answers to the Tying It All Together questions can be found at the end of this chapter.

School

What was the test that José (in the chapter-opening vignette) took, and what does intelligence really mean? What makes for good teaching and superior schools? Before tackling these school-related topics, let's step back and, again, explore the impact of that basic marker—poverty—on young children's cognitive skills.

Unequal at the Starting Gate

Chapter 4 described the oversized negative impact early-childhood poverty has on high school success. Figure 7.4 reveals that devastation by offering sobering statistics relating to poor children's deficiencies at the brink of school. Notice that, while the vast majority of middle-class and affluent children score above the cutoff for doing kindergarten work, for boys and girls living in poverty, the percentage shrinks dramatically to less than 1 in 2 (Issacs, 2012; see also Duncan, Magnuson, & Votruba-Drzal, 2017).

You would think that when children start a race miles behind, they would get special help catching up. The reality, of course, is the reverse. From class size to the quality of teacher training, U.S. kindergartens serving poor children rank at the bottom of the educational heap.

Let's keep these mammoth disparities in school quality favoring financially well-off children in mind as we explore the controversial topic of intelligence tests.

Intelligence and IQ Tests

What does it mean to be intelligent? Ask people on the street this question, and they will probably mention both academic and "real life" skills (Sternberg, 2007; Sternberg, Grigorenko, & Kidd, 2005).

Traditional intelligence tests—called **intelligence quotient (or IQ)** tests—measure *only* academic abilities. These tests differ from **achievement tests,** the yearly evaluations children take to measure knowledge in various subjects. IQ tests are designed to predict general academic *potential*, or a child's ability to master any school-related task. Do the tests measure mainly genetic capacities and have any relevance beyond school? To approach these hot-button issues, let's examine the intelligence test that children typically take today: the WISC.

Examining the WISC

The **WISC (Wechsler Intelligence Scale for Children),** now in its fifth revision, was devised by David Wechsler and is the current standard intelligence test. As you can see in Table 7.4 on the next page, the WISC samples a child's performance in four basic areas. This means that, in addition to giving the child a single overall score, testers can look in a more detailed way at particular skills (see Cormier, Kennedy, & Aquilina, 2016).

Achievement tests are given to groups. The WISC is administered individually by a trained psychologist in about an hour of testing and concludes with a written report. If the child scores at the 50th percentile for his age group, his IQ is defined as 100. If that child's IQ is 130, he ranks at roughly the 98th percentile, or in the top 2 percent of children his age. If a child's score is 70, he is at the opposite end of the distribution, performing in the lowest 2 percent of children that age. This score distribution looks like a bell-shaped curve.

When do children take this test? The answer, most often, is during elementary school when there is a question about a child's classroom performance. School personnel then use the IQ score as one component of a multifaceted assessment—which includes achievement test scores, teachers' ratings, and parents' input—to determine whether a boy or girl needs special help (Sattler, 2001).

LEARNING OUTCOMES

- Describe the WISC and how psychologists use this test.
- Explore the controversial meaning of IQ.
- Contrast Sternberg and Gardner's ideas.
- Describe successful schools.
- Outline intrinsic motivation.

FIGURE 7.4: Percentage of U.S. 5-year-olds ready for school, by socioeconomic status: This chart shows the dramatic impact of family income on school readiness. According to national U.S. tests, less than half of all young children living in poverty scored as being "able to do kindergarten work."
Data from Isaacs, 2012, p. 3.

intelligence quotient (IQ) Measure designed to evaluate a child's overall cognitive ability, or general aptitude for mastering academic work.

achievement tests Measures that evaluate a child's knowledge in specific school-related areas.

WISC (Wechsler Intelligence Scale for Children) The standard intelligence test used in childhood, consisting of different subtests.

Table 7.4: The WISC-5 A Subtest Sampler

Subtest	Verbal Comprehension Index Sample (simulated) Item
Similarities (analogies)	Cat is to kitten as dog is to _____.
Vocabulary (defining words)	What is a table?
	Fluid Reasoning Index
Picture completion	Pick out what is missing in this picture.
Block design	Arrange these blocks to look like the photograph on the card within a time limit.
	Processing Speed Index
Coding	Using the key above, put each symbol in the correct space below.
	Working Memory Index
Digit span	Repeat these numbers forward. Now repeat these numbers backward.

intellectual disability The label for significantly impaired cognitive functioning, measured by deficits in behavior accompanied by having an IQ of 70 or below.

specific learning disorder The label for any impairment in language or any deficit related to listening, thinking, speaking, reading, writing, spelling, or understanding mathematics.

dyslexia A learning disorder that is characterized by reading difficulties, lack of fluency, and poor word recognition that is often genetic in origin.

gifted The label for superior intellectual functioning characterized by an IQ score of 130 or above, showing that a child ranks in the top 2 percent of his age group.

If a child's low score (below 70) and other behaviors warrant this designation, she may be classified as **intellectually disabled.** If a child's IQ is far higher than would be expected, compared to her performance on achievement tests, she is classified with a **specific learning disorder,** an umbrella term for any impairment in language or difficulties related to listening (such as ADHD), thinking, speaking, reading, spelling, or math.

Although children with learning disabilities often score in the average range on IQ tests, they have trouble with schoolwork. Many times, they have a debilitating impairment called **dyslexia** that undercuts every academic skill. Dyslexia, a catchall term that refers to any reading disorder, may have multiple causes (see Table 7.5). What's important is that, despite having good instruction and doing well on tests of intelligence, a dyslexic child is struggling to read (Shaywitz, Morris, & Shaywitz, 2008).

My son, for instance, has dyslexia, and our experience shows just how important having a measure of general intelligence can be. Because Thomas was falling behind in the third grade, my husband and I arranged to have our son tested. Thomas was defined as having a learning disability because his IQ score was above average, but his achievement scores were well below the norm for his grade. Although we were aware of our son's reading problems, the testing was vital in easing our anxieties. Thomas—just as we thought—was capable intellectually. Now we just had to get our son through school with his sense of self-efficacy intact!

Often, teachers and parents urge testing for a happier reason: They want to confirm that a child is intellectually advanced. If the child's IQ exceeds a certain number (typically 130), she is labeled as **gifted** (see Figure 7.5) and is eligible for

FIGURE 7.5: The bell curve snapshot of the gifted: As the bell curve illustrates, more than 2 out of 3 test takers have WISC scores clustering within 15 points of 100 (the 50th percentile). At an IQ of 130 or above, the child's score is gifted because that boy or girl performed at about the top 2 percent of all test takers that age.

Table 7.5: Some Interesting Facts About Dyslexia

- Reading difficulties are shockingly prevalent among U.S. children. According to one survey, more than 1 in 4 high school seniors were reading below the most basic levels. The figures were higher for fourth graders—over 1 in 3 had trouble grasping the basic points of a passage designed for their grade.

- Specific learning disabilities (including dyslexia) are a mainly male diagnosis—affecting roughly 3 times as many boys as girls worldwide.

- Dyslexia is inherited and "genetic" in origin. However, the condition has several genetic variants, and, as I mentioned in the text, difficulty in learning to read can be due to different causes.

- Late-appearing language (entering the word-combining phase of speech at an older-than-typical age, such as close to age 2½ [see Chapter 3]) and especially phonemic deficits (the inability to differentiate sounds [see Chapter 5]) are early predictors of dyslexia.

- Dyslexia can sometimes be diagnosed in the preschool pre-reading years by combining behavioral tests with brain scans. At-risk children can even be identified during their first weeks after birth—by looking at the pattern of their brain waves evoked by different sounds.

- Although many boys and girls with dyslexia eventually learn to read, this condition persists to some extent into adulthood. Early interventions—involving intensive instruction in teaching at-risk kindergartners and first graders to identify phonemes—can be effective, but special help may be needed throughout elementary school.

- Children with dyslexia unfortunately perform more poorly on general tests of executive functions. They are at higher risk of developing other mental health problems, such as depression and anxiety disorders. About 15 to 50 percent also have ADHD.

Information from Beneventi and others, 2010; Gooch, Snowling, & Hulme, 2011; Henry, Messer, & Nash, 2012; Hensler and others, 2010; Kraft and others, 2016; Landerl & Moll, 2010; Leppänen and others, 2010; Panicker & Chelliah, 2016; Shao and others, 2016; Shaywitz and others, 2008.

reliability In measurement terminology, a basic criterion for a test's accuracy that scores must be fairly similar when a person takes the same test more than once.

validity In measurement terminology, a basic criterion for a test's accuracy involving whether that measure reflects the real-world quality it is supposed to measure.

special programs. In U.S. public schools, the law mandates intelligence testing before children can be assigned to a gifted program or remedial class (Canter, 1997; Sattler, 2001).

Table 7.5 offers a fact sheet about dyslexia. The Experiencing the Lifespan box on page 210 provides a firsthand view of what it is like to triumph over this debilitating condition. Now that we have explored the measure and when it is used, let's turn to what the scores mean.

Decoding the Meaning of the IQ Test

The first question we need to grapple with in looking at the meaning of the test relates to a measurement criterion called **reliability.** When people take a test that is thought to measure a basic trait (such as IQ) more than once, their results should not vary. Imagine that your IQ score randomly shifted from gifted to average, year by year. Clearly, this test score would not tell us anything about a stable attribute called intelligence.

The good news is that, by elementary school, IQ test performance does typically remain stable (Ryan, Glass, & Bartels, 2010). In one amazing study, people's scores remained fairly similar when they first took the test in childhood and then were retested more than a half-century later (see Deary and others, 2000). Still, among individual children, IQ can change. Scores are most likely to shift when children have undergone life stresses.

This research tells us that we should never evaluate a child's IQ during a family crisis such as divorce. But being reliable is only the first requirement. The test must be **valid.** This means it must predict what it is supposed to be measuring. Is the WISC a valid test?

Ray Stott/The Image Works

When this second grader takes the WISC, her IQ is apt to be reliable, staying roughly the same at older ages, unless she undergoes severe stress. But what does this score mean? Stay tuned as I tackle this fascinating issue relating to validity, right below the Experiencing the Lifespan box on the next page!

Experiencing the Lifespan From Dyslexic Child to a Career Helping Dyslexic Boys and Girls

Aimee Holt, a colleague of mine who teaches our school's psychology students, is beautiful and intelligent, the kind of golden girl you might imagine would have been a great childhood success. When I sat down to chat with Aimee about her struggles with dyslexia and other learning disabilities, I found first impressions can be very misleading.

In first grade, the teachers at school said I was mentally retarded. I didn't notice the sounds that went along with letters. I walked into walls and fell down a lot. My parents refused to put me in a special school and finally got me accepted at a private school, contingent on getting a good deal of help. I spent my elementary school years being tutored for an hour before school, an hour afterwards, and all summer.

Socially, elementary school was a nightmare. . . . I remember kids laughing at me, calling me stupid. There was a small group of people that I was friendly with, but we were all misfits. One of my closest friends had an inoperable brain tumor. Because of my problems coordinating my vision with my motor skills, I couldn't participate in normal activities, such as sports or dance. By seventh grade, after years of working every day with my wonderful reading teacher, I was reading at almost grade level.

Then when we moved to Tennessee in my freshman year of high school, I felt like a new person. Nobody knew that I had learning difficulties. We moved to a rural community, so I got to be a top student, because I'd had the same classes in my Dallas private school the year before. In the tenth and eleventh grades, I was making A's and B's. I got a scholarship to college, where I was a straight-A student (with a GPA of 3.9).

My mom is the reason I've done well. She always believed in me, always felt I could make it; she never gave up. Plus, as I mentioned, I had an exceptional reading teacher. My goal was always to be an elementary school teacher, but, after teaching for years and realizing that a lot of the kids in my classes were not being accurately diagnosed, I decided to go to graduate school to get my Ph.D.

Today, in addition to teaching, I do private tutoring with children like me. First, I get kids to identify word sounds (phonemes) because children with dyslexia have a problem decoding the specific sounds of words. I'll have the children identify how many sounds they hear in a word. . . .

"Which sounds rhyme, which don't?" . . . "If I change the word from cat to hat, what sound changes?" Most children naturally pick up on these reading cues. Kids with dyslexia need to have these skills directly taught.

Many children I tutor are in fourth or even sixth grade and have had years of feeling like a failure. They develop an attitude of "Why try? I'm going to fail anyway." I can tell them that I've been there and that they can succeed. So I work on academic self-efficacy—teaching them to put forth effort. Most of these kids are intelligent, but as they progress through school, their IQ drops because they are not being exposed to written material at their grade level. I try to get them to stay in the regular classroom, with modifications such as books on tape and oral testing, to prevent that false drop in their knowledge base. I was so fortunate—with a wonderful mother, an exceptional reading teacher, getting the help I needed at exactly the right time—that I feel my mission is to give something back.

If our predictor is academic performance, the answer is yes. A child who gets an IQ score of 130 will tend to perform well in the gifted class. A child whose IQ is 80 will probably need remedial help. But now we turn to the controversial question: Does the test measure genetic learning potential or biological smarts?

Are the Tests a Good Measure of Genetic Gifts?

When evaluating children living in poverty (or boys and girls growing up in non-English-speaking families), logic tells us that the answer is *definitely* no. Look back at the items on the WISC verbal comprehension scale (Table 7.4 on page 208), and you will immediately see that if parents stimulate a child's vocabulary, she will be at a test-taking advantage. If, as I documented in Chapter 4, a family doesn't have the funds to buy preschoolers advanced learning toys, children will be handicapped on each part of the test.

Evidence that the environment weighs heavily in IQ comes from the fascinating fact that over the past century, IQ test scores have risen dramatically around the world (see Chapter 1)—a phenomenon called the **Flynn effect** (named for its discoverer James Flynn). More years of education have made twenty-first-century children and

Flynn effect Remarkable rise in overall performance on IQ tests that has been occurring around the world over the past century.

adults far better abstract thinkers than their parents and grandparents were at the same age (Must, Must, & Mikk, 2016). Incredibly, Flynn (2007) calculates that the average-scoring child taking the WISC in 1900 would rank as "mentally deficient" using today's IQ norms!

We now have compelling research showing that being poor *itself* artificially depresses test scores. For low-income children, the IQ score mainly reflects environmental forces. For upper-middle-class children, the test score is reflective of genetic gifts (Turkheimer and others, 2003). So if an elementary schooler comes from a poverty-level family and attends a low-quality school, then yes, his IQ predicts his current school performance. But that score can't reflect *true intellectual potential* unless the child has been exposed to the incredible learning advantages upper-middle-class life provides.

Now, imagine that you are an upper-middle-class child. You were regularly read to, visited museums, and attended the best schools. Your IQ score is only 95 or 100. Is your intellectual potential limited for life?

Do IQ Scores Predict Real-World Performance?

One student who approached me after this class lecture and proudly admitted that his IQ was 140 was not thinking of school learning. He assumed that his score measured a basic "smartness" that carried over to every life activity. In measurement terminology, this student would agree with Charles Spearman. Spearman believed that IQ test scores reflect a general underlying, all-encompassing intelligence factor called **g**.

Psychologists debate the existence of g. Many strongly believe that the IQ test *generally* predicts intellectual capacities. They argue that we can use the IQ as a summary measure of a person's cognitive potential for all life tasks (Herrnstein & Murray, 1994; Rushton & Jensen, 2005). Others believe that people have unique intellectual talents. There is no one-dimensional quality called g (Eisner, 2004; Schlinger, 2003; Sternberg, 2007). These critics believe it is inappropriate to rank people on a continuum from highly intelligent to not very smart (Gould, 1981; Sternberg, Grigorenko, & Kidd, 2005).

Tantalizing evidence for g lies in the fact that people differ in the speed with which they process information (Brody, 2006; Rushton & Jensen, 2005). Intelligence test scores also correlate with various indicators of life success, such as occupational status. However, the problem is that the gateway to high-status professions, such as law and medicine, is school performance, which is what the tests predict (Sternberg, 1997; Sternberg, Grigorenko, & Bundy, 2001).

One problem with believing that IQ tests offer a *total* X-ray into intellectual capacities is that people may carry around their test-score ranking as an inner wound. A psychologist supervisor once confessed to me that he was really not that intelligent because his IQ was only 105. He devalued the criterion his IQ was supposed to predict—his years of real-life success—by accepting what, in his case, was an invalid score!

A high test score can produce its own problems. Suppose the student who told me his IQ was 140 decided he was so intelligent he didn't have to open a book in my class. He might be in for a nasty surprise when he found out that what *really* matters is your ability to work. Or that student might worry, "I'd better not try in Dr. Belsky's class because, if I do put forth effort and *don't* get an A, I will discover that my astronomical IQ score was wrong." (As I suggested in Chapter 6, this type of interpretation isn't rare; as studies show that telling elementary schoolers they "are basically smart" makes them afraid to tackle challenging academic tasks.)

Even the firmest advocate of g would admit that people have specific intellectual talents. Some of us are marvelous mechanically yet miserable at math, wonderful socially but hopeless at taking tests.

g Charles Spearman's term for a general intelligence factor that he claimed underlies all cognitive activities.

Toward a Broader View of Intelligence

Because real-world intelligence involves such different abilities, perhaps we should go beyond the skills the IQ test measures and explore those talents in a truly broad way. Psychologists Robert Sternberg and Howard Gardner have devoted their careers to offering this broader view of what it means to be smart.

Sternberg's Successful Intelligence

Robert Sternberg (1984, 1996, 1997) has been a man on a mission. In hundreds of publications, this psychologist transformed the way we think about intelligence. Sternberg's passion comes from the heart. He began school with a problem himself:

> As an elementary school student, I failed miserably on the IQ tests. . . . My teachers . . . didn't expect much from me. . . . So I gave them what they expected. . . . Were the teachers disappointed? Not on your life. They were happy that I was giving them what they expected.
>
> (Sternberg, 1997, pp. 17–18)

Sternberg believes that traditional intelligence tests do damage in school. As I implied earlier, the relationship between IQ scores and schooling is somewhat bidirectional. Children who attend inferior schools or who miss months of classroom work due to illness perform more poorly on intelligence tests (Sternberg, 1997). Worse yet, Sternberg argues, when schools assign children to lower-track, less demanding classes based on their low test scores, the students' IQs gradually decline year by year.

Most importantly, Sternberg (1984) believes that conventional intelligence tests are too limited. Although they do measure one type of intelligence, they do not cover the whole terrain.

IQ tests, according to Sternberg, measure **analytic intelligence.** They test how well people can solve academic problems. They do not measure **creative intelligence,** the ability to "think outside the box" or to formulate problems in new ways. Nor do they measure a third type of intelligence called **practical intelligence,** common sense, or "street smarts."

Brazilian street children who make their living selling flowers show impressive levels of practical intelligence. They understand how to handle money in the real world. However, they do very poorly on measures of traditional IQ (Sternberg, 1984, 1997). Others, such as Winston Churchill, can be terrible scholars but flower after they leave their academic careers. Then there are people who excel at IQ test taking and traditional schooling but fail abysmally in life. Sternberg argues that to be **successfully intelligent** in life requires a balance of all three types of intelligence. (As a postscript, Sternberg later added a fourth type of intellectual gift—that rare attribute called *wisdom*; see Sternberg, 2010.)

analytic intelligence In Robert Sternberg's framework on successful intelligence, the facet of intelligence involved in performing well on academic problems.

creative intelligence In Robert Sternberg's framework on successful intelligence, the facet of intelligence involved in producing novel ideas or innovative work.

practical intelligence In Robert Sternberg's framework on successful intelligence, the facet of intelligence involved in knowing how to act competently in real-world situations.

successful intelligence In Robert Sternberg's framework, the optimal form of cognition, which involves striking the right balance of analytic, creative, and practical intelligence.

Being a math whiz (*analytic intelligence*) demands different skills from deftly snagging this fish (*practical intelligence*). That's why Robert Sternberg believes that IQ tests, which mainly measure school-type analytic skills, do not tap into many of the abilities that make people successful in the real world.

Gardner's Multiple Intelligences

Howard Gardner (1998) did not have Sternberg's problem with intelligence tests:

> As a child, I was a good student . . . but . . . music . . . and the arts were important [to me]. . . . Therefore, when I asked myself what optimal human development is, I became convinced that [we] had to . . . broaden the definition of intelligence. . . .
>
> (Gardner, 1998, p. 3)

Gardner is not passionately opposed to standard intelligence tests. Still, he believes that using the single IQ score is less informative than measuring children's unique gifts. (Gardner's motto is: "Ask not how *intelligent* you are, but *how* are you intelligent?") According to his **multiple intelligences theory,** human abilities come in eight, and possibly nine, distinctive forms (Gardner, 2004; Gardner & Moran, 2006).

In addition to the verbal and mathematical skills measured by traditional IQ tests, people may be gifted in *interpersonal intelligence,* or understanding other people. Their talents may lie in *intrapersonal intelligence,* the skill of understanding oneself. They may be gifted in *spatial intelligence,* grasping where objects are arranged in space. (You might rely on a friend who is gifted in spatial intelligence to beautifully arrange the furniture in your house.) Some people have high levels of *musical intelligence, kinesthetic intelligence* (the ability to use the body well), or *naturalist intelligence* (a gift for dealing with animals or plants and trees). There may even be an *existential (spiritual) intelligence,* too.

Being a world-class gymnast (*kinesthetic intelligence*) doesn't necessarily mean that you will also shine in reading or math. That's why Howard Gardner believes that schools need to broaden their focus to teach to the different kinds of intelligences that we all possess.

Evaluating the Theories

These perspectives on intelligence are exciting. Some readers may be thinking, "I'm gifted in practical or musical intelligence. I knew there was more to being smart than school success!" But let's use our practical intelligence to critique these approaches. Why did Gardner select these particular eight abilities and not others (Barnett, Ceci, & Williams, 2006; White, 2006)? Yes, parents may marvel at a 6-year-old's creative or kinesthetic intelligence, but it is analytic intelligence that will get this child into the school gifted program, not his artistic productions or how well his body moves (Eisner, 2004).

We can also criticize Sternberg's ideas. Is there a creative or practical intelligence apart from a particular field? Adopting the idea that there is a single "creative" intelligence might lead to the conclusion that Michelangelo would be a talented musician or that Mozart could beautifully paint the Sistine Chapel.

The bottom line is that neither Gardner nor Sternberg has developed replacements for our current IQ test. But this does not matter. Their mission is to transform the way schools teach (Gardner & Moran, 2006; Sternberg, 2010).

multiple intelligences theory In Howard Gardner's perspective on intelligence, the principle that there are eight separate kinds of intelligence—verbal, mathematical, interpersonal, intrapersonal, spatial, musical, kinesthetic, naturalist—plus a possible ninth type, called spiritual intelligence.

INTERVENTIONS ⟩ Lessons for Schools

Gardner's theory has been embraced by teachers who understand that intelligence involves more than traditional academic skills. However, to implement his ideas requires revolutionizing the way we structure education. Therefore, the main use of multiple intelligences theory has been in helping "nontraditional learners" succeed (Schirduan & Case, 2004). Here is how Mark, a dyslexic teenager, describes his use of spatial intelligence to cope with the maze of facts in history:

> I'll picture things; for example, if we are studying the French revolution . . . Louis the 16th . . . I'll have a picture of him in my mind [and I'll visualize] the castle and peasants to help me learn.
>
> (quoted in Schirduan & Case, 2004, p. 93)

Sternberg, being an experimentalist, has put his theory through rigorous tests. Does instruction tailored to each type of intelligence produce better achievement than teaching in the traditional way? Unfortunately, when Sternberg's research team carried out a massive intervention trial—assigning 7,702 fourth graders in 223 class-rooms to either be taught according to his theory or using several typical approaches—the outcome was inconsistent (Sternberg and others, 2014). So, while the concept of successful intelligence is intuitively appealing, it's not clear that Sternberg's ideas merit changing the way classrooms operate. How *do* classrooms operate?

Classroom Learning

The diversity of intelligences, cultures, and educational experiences at home is matched by the diversity of American schools. There are small rural schools and large urban schools, public and private schools, traditional schools where students wear uniforms, and schools that teach according to Gardner's intelligences. There are single-sex schools, charter schools, religious schools, magnet schools that cater to gifted students, and alternative schools for children with behavior problems or learning disabilities.

Can students thrive in every school? The answer is yes, provided schools have an intense commitment to student learning and teachers can excite students to learn. The rest of this chapter focuses on these challenges.

Examining Successful Schools

What qualities make a school successful? Insights come from surveying public elementary schools that are beating the odds. These schools, while serving high fractions of economically disadvantaged children, have students who are thriving.

In the Vista School, located on a Native American reservation, virtually all the children are eligible for a free lunch. However, Vista consistently boasts dramatic improvements on statewide reading and math tests. According to Ms. Thompson, the principal, "Our job is not to make excuses for students, but just to give them every possible opportunity. At Vista, teachers refuse to dumb down the curriculum. We offer tons of high-level conceptual work" (quoted in Borko and others, 2003, p. 177).

At Beacon Elementary School, in Washington State, 2 out of every 3 students exceed state-mandated writing standards despite coming from impoverished backgrounds. Here, Susie Murphy, the principal, comments: "You can . . . say, these kids are poor. You just need to love them. Or you can [say] . . . the best way to love them is to give them an education so they can make choices in their life" (quoted in Borko and others, 2003, p. 186). Beacon teachers, she continues, "are here . . . by choice. They are committed to proving that kids who live in poverty can learn every bit as well as other kids" (p. 192). At Beacon, the teachers' goal is to challenge all their students.

The school builds in opportunities for teachers to share ideas: "We have mini-workshops in geometry, or problem solving. Our whole staff talks about the general focus and where math is going" (p. 194).

Committed teachers, professional collaboration, and a mission to "deliver for *all* our kids" explains why a rural Florida elementary school, serving mainly low-income children, boosted the test scores of its most struggling students in a single year. Rather than isolating boys and girls with "learning differences," this school embedded every child into academic life. Before instituting their focus on inclusiveness, only 1 in 3 at-risk children ranked as proficient in math and language arts. At the year's end, these rates shot upward—to roughly 2 in 3 students.

In addition to attending a well-maintained school, having a genuinely inclusive mix of students is another defining feature of schools that "beat the odds."

FatCamera/E+/Getty Images

As Ms. Richards, the principal, explained: "We've got to . . . meet all [kids'] needs. . . . That's how we started . . . to make . . . everyone successful." A special education teacher named Ms. Wood summed up this school's teaching strategy best when she said, "We have ongoing conversations about challenging students . . . at our school . . . the meat of the curriculum is presented to everyone" (adapted from McLeskey, Waldron, & Redd, 2014, p. 63).

To summarize, successful schools set high standards. Teachers believe that every child can benefit from challenging, conceptual work. These schools excel in *collective efficacy*, reaching out to nurture each member of the teaching community. In Baumrind's *parenting-styles* framework, these schools are *authoritative* in their approach.

Now that we have the outlines for what is effective, let's tackle the challenge every teacher faces: getting students eager to learn.

Producing Eager Learners

But to go to school in a summer morn,

O! it drives all joy away;

Under a cruel eye outworn,

The little ones spend the day

In sighing and dismay.

—William Blake, from "The Schoolboy" (1794)

Jean Piaget believed that the hunger to learn is more important than food or drink. Why, then, do children over the centuries lament, "I hate school"? The reason is that learning loses its joy when it becomes a requirement instead of an activity we choose to engage in for ourselves.

The Problem: An Erosion of Intrinsic Motivation

Developmentalists divide motivation into two categories. **Intrinsic motivation** refers to self-generated actions, those that arise from our inner desires. When Piaget described our hunger to learn, he was referring to intrinsic motivation. **Extrinsic motivation** refers to activities that we undertake in order to get external reinforcers, such as praise or pay or a good grade.

Unfortunately, the learning activity you are currently engaged in falls into the extrinsic category. You know you will be tested on what you are reading. Worse yet, if you pick up this book for an intrinsic reason—because you wanted to learn about lifespan development—the fact that you might be graded would likely cause your basic interest to fade.

Numerous studies show that when adults give external reinforcers for activities that are intrinsically motivating, children are less likely to want to perform those activities for themselves (Patall, Cooper, & Robinson, 2008; Stipek, 1996). In one classic example, researchers selected preschoolers who were intrinsically interested in art. When they gave a "good player" award (an outside reinforcer) for the art projects, the children later showed a dramatic decline in their interest in doing art for fun (Lepper, Greene, & Nisbett, 1973). This research makes sense of the question you may have wondered about: "Why, after taking that literature class, am I *less* interested in reading on my own?"

Young children enter kindergarten brimming with intrinsic motivation. When does this love affair with school turn sour? Think back to your childhood, and you will realize that enchantment wanes during early elementary school, when teachers provide those external reinforcers—grades (Stipek, 1997). Moreover, during first or second grade, classroom learning often becomes abstract and removed from life. Rote activities, like filling in worksheets and memorizing multiplication tables, have replaced the creative hands-on projects of kindergarten. So ironically, school

intrinsic motivation The drive to act based on the pleasure of taking that action in itself, not for an external reinforcer or reward.

extrinsic motivation The drive to take an action because that activity offers external reinforcers such as praise, money, or a good grade.

Compare the activities of this kindergarten class of little scientists with rote learning and grades, and you will immediately understand why by about age 8, many children begin to say, "I hate school."

may be the very setting where Piaget's little-scientist activities are *least* likely to occur.

Then, as children enter concrete operations—at around age 8—and begin comparing their performance to that of their peers, this competitive orientation further erodes intrinsic motivation (Dweck, 1986; Self-Brown & Mathews, 2003). The focus shifts from "I want to improve for myself" to "I want to do *better* than my friends."

In sum, several forces explain why many children dislike school. School involves extrinsic reinforcers (grades). School learning, because it often involves rote memorization, is not intrinsically interesting. In school, children cannot set their own learning goals. Their performance is judged by how they measure up to the rest of the class.

Therefore, it is no wonder that studies in Western nations document an alarming decline in intrinsic motivation as children travel through school (Katz, Kaplan, & Gueta, 2010; Spinath & Steinmayr, 2008). Susan Harter (1981) asked children to choose between two statements: "Some kids work really hard to get good grades" (referring to extrinsic motivation) or "Some kids work really hard because they like to learn new things" (measuring intrinsic motives). When she gave these alternatives to hundreds of California public school children, intrinsic motivation declined from third to ninth grade.

Still, external reinforcers can be vital hooks that get us intrinsically involved. Have you ever reluctantly taken a required class (perhaps even this course in lifespan development) and found yourself captivated by the subject? Given that extrinsically motivating activities are basic to school and life, how can we make them work best?

The Solution: Making Extrinsic Learning Part of Us

To answer this question, Edward Deci and Richard Ryan (1985, 2000) make the point that we engage in some types of extrinsic learning unwillingly: "I have to take that terrible anatomy course because it is a requirement for graduation." We enthusiastically embrace other extrinsic tasks, which may not be inherently interesting, because we identify with their larger goal: "I want to memorize every bone of the body because that information is vital to my nursing career." In the first situation, the learning activity is irrelevant. In the second, the task has become intrinsic because it is connected to our inner self. Therefore, the key to transforming school learning from a chore into a pleasure is to make extrinsic learning relate to children's goals and desires.

The most boring tasks take on an intrinsic aura when they speak to children's passions. Imagine, for instance, how a first grader's motivation to sound out words might change if a teacher, knowing that student was captivated by dinosaurs, gave that boy the job of sounding out dinosaur names. Deci and Ryan believe that learning becomes intrinsic when it satisfies our basic need for relatedness (attachment). Finally, extrinsic tasks take on an intrinsic feeling when they foster autonomy, or offer us choices about how to do our work (Patall, Cooper, & Robinson, 2008; Ryan and others, 2006).

Studies around the globe suggest that when teachers and parents take away children's autonomy—by controlling, criticizing, or micromanaging learning tasks—they erode intrinsic motivation (see Jang, Reeve, & Deci, 2010; Soenens & Vansteenkiste, 2010). We can see this principle in our own lives. By continually denigrating our work, or hovering over every move, a controlling supervisor has the uncanny ability to turn us off to the most intrinsically interesting job.

Our need for autonomy explains why, as I suggested in the section on successful schools, assigning high-level conceptual learning tasks can be effective with every child. Conversely, the poisonous effects of taking away autonomy suggests why the U.S. practice of forcing teachers to follow a rigid set of learning requirements erodes satisfaction in this field ("I can't teach the way I want. I have to teach to the end-of-year tests, or I'll get fired").

But in a national experiment, when certain school districts gave staff the chance to *choose* between several new programs and provided *clear data* about their effectiveness, teachers did willingly embrace these options—and, after 4 years, students made impressive gains on standard reading tests (Slavin and others, 2013). Therefore, providing autonomy (giving choices) and fostering relevance (pointing out the importance of an activity to that person's goals) benefits *both* students and teachers!

Table 7.6 summarizes these messages for teachers: Focus on relevance, enhance relatedness, and provide autonomy. The table also pulls together other teaching tips based on Gardner's and Sternberg's perspectives on intelligence, our look at what makes schools successful, and research that shows how emphasizing collaborative learning can mute the uptick in bullying described in Chapter 6 (Choi, Johnson, & Johnson, 2011). Now let's conclude by tackling that interesting question: Can an exceptional elementary school teacher change students' lives?

Table 7.6: Lessons for Teachers: A Recap of This Chapter's Insights

General Principles

1. **Foster relevance.** For instance, in teaching reading, tailor the assigned books to fit the children's passions. And entice students to learn to read in other ways, such as energizing first and second graders by telling them they will be able to break a code used all over the world, just like a detective!

2. **Foster relatedness.** Develop a secure, loving attachment with every student. Continually tell each child how proud you are when that boy or girl tries hard or succeeds.

3. **Foster autonomy.** As much as possible, allow your students to select among several equivalent assignments (such as choosing which specific books to read). Don't give time limits, such as "It's 9:30 and this has to be done by 10:00," and don't hover, take over tasks, or make negative comments. Stand by to provide information and careful scaffolding (see Chapter 5) when students ask. Build in assignments that allow high-level thinking, such as writing essays instead of rote work such as copying sentences or filling out worksheets.

Teaching Tips Based on Gardner's and Sternberg's Theories

1. Offer balanced assignments that capitalize on students' different kinds of intelligence—creative work such as essays; practical-intelligence activities such as calculating numbers to make change at a store; single-answer analytic tasks (using Sternberg's framework); and classroom time devoted to music, dance, art, and caring for plants (capitalizing on Gardner's ideas).

2. Explicitly teach students to use their different intelligences in mastering classroom work.

Additional Teaching Tips

1. Don't rely on IQ test scores in assessing the abilities of low-income and ethnic-minority students; this number says little about children's true academic potential.

2. Avoid praising children for being "brilliant." Compliment them for hard work.

3. Go beyond academics to teach children interpersonal skills.

4. Strive for excellence. Expect all students to succeed.

5. Foster collaborative work. Grade competition is not only tailor-made to reduce intrinsic motivation, but it may also be a reason why relational aggression becomes rampant in later elementary school.

6. Minimize students' tendency to make grade-oriented comparisons (such as who got A's, B's, C's, and so on) by continually emphasizing that what matters is personal improvement.

Think back to your favorite teacher. Perhaps it was the talented woman who transformed a hated math class into a magical journey, or a middle-school teacher who believed in your gifts, even though you were struggling in class. You always felt this person made an enduring difference in your life. Now scientific data shows you were right!

In meticulous studies, economist Raj Chetty and his colleagues (Chetty, Friedman, & Rockoff, 2014) tracked the performance of two million students enrolled in an urban elementary school district as the children traveled into their twenties.

This beloved public school teacher may do far more than simply boost her students' scores on end-of-year achievement tests. She could help propel these third graders into a middle-class life.

The researchers identified what they called *value-added teachers*—educators whose students showed elevated bumps on end-of-year state tests, compared to the typical teacher a child would have in that grade. The economists were amazed to find that students who were taught by a value-added teacher for *one year* were more likely to attend college and less prone to have babies as teens. They earned more money than their classmates during emerging adulthood, too. Based on tax data at age 28, the researchers calculated that each student's boost in lifetime earnings as a result of having this exceptional teacher for a *single year* was roughly $40,000.

We talk about good educators being worth their weight in gold. This study shows that cliché is literally true. According to Chetty's calculations, a single value-added teacher can boost an entire class's lifetime earnings by over half a million dollars!

Hot in Developmental Science: Communities Matter in Children's Success

Throughout this chapter—from discussing the power of peers to living in neighborhoods high in collective efficacy to attending high-quality schools—I've been making the case that where children grow up makes a difference in their lives. Again, Raj Chetty's landmark research brings that message home.

Chetty's research team (Chetty & Hendren, 2017) calculated the odds of *upward mobility*—that is, rising in social status—for children growing up in *every county* in the United States. Even given equal family income, living in a "better community" made it more likely for poor children to make it into the middle class.

What is a "better community"? One answer comes as no surprise: Communities that promote upward mobility have less concentrated poverty, more high-ranked schools, a higher percentage of two-parent families, and less crime. But these places also stand out as special in far less obvious ways. In counties fostering upward mobility, income inequality is less dramatic—that is, there isn't such a huge gap between rich and poor. Moreover, in these communities, poor children's economic strides don't come at the expense of their relatively affluent peers. In upwardly mobile counties, Chetty's calculations showed, children whose families ranked at the 75th percentile of the income distribution rose in social status (though not as much).

Does decent housing cost more in these communities? Not necessarily. For instance, at that time in the New York City area, the researchers found that children being raised in Hudson County, New Jersey, had far higher rates of upward mobility than their age-mates in the New York City boroughs of Queens or the Bronx, even though the median rents in these areas were roughly the same.

Does moving to a better area during early childhood matter most? Here, the answer is yes. In fact, if families relocate to an upwardly mobile community when their children are young, and remain through high school, their sons and daughters benefit greatly. Twenty years spent in DuPage County, Illinois (ranked highest in upward mobility), versus low-ranked Baltimore, Maryland, statistically increased a given poverty-level child's annual income by one-third. Moreover, the researchers found that staying in deprived low-mobility communities was especially toxic for boys.

I believe the message here is that the U.S. mantra that, given sufficient industry, every poor child can succeed is incorrect. Having an efficacy-promoting *environment* is critically important in allowing talented, disadvantaged children to construct a middle-class life. And rather than retreating to isolated, gated communities, affluent parents might want to pay attention to this research, too. Healthy communities thrive on economic diversity. Income inequalities hinder everyone—both the rich and the poor.

In Chapter 9, I will vividly demonstrate exactly why low-efficacy communities—neighborhoods blighted by concentrated poverty—are so toxic for boys when I discuss teenage gangs. Then, in Chapter 10, I'll explore how the rise in income inequalities may be limiting the life chances of this cohort of U.S. emerging adults.

Tying It All Together

1. If Devin, from an upper-middle-class family, and Adam, from a low-income family, are starting kindergarten, predict which statement is most accurate:

   a. Both children will perform equally well on school readiness tests, but Adam will fall behind because he is likely to attend a poor-quality kindergarten.

   b. Devin will outperform Adam on school readiness tests, and the gap will probably widen because Adam will attend a poor-quality kindergarten.

2. Malik hasn't been doing well in school, and his achievement test scores have consistently been well below average for his grade. On the WISC, Malik gets an IQ score of 115. What is your conclusion?

3. You are telling a friend about the deficiencies of relying on a child's IQ score. Pick *two* arguments you might make.

   a. The tests are not reliable; children's scores typically change a lot during the elementary school years.

   b. The tests are not valid predictors of school performance.

   c. As people have different abilities, a single IQ score may not tell us much about a child's unique gifts.

   d. As poor children are at a disadvantage in taking the test, you should not use the IQ scores as an index of "genetic school-related talents" for low-income children.

4. Josh doesn't do well in reading or math, but he excels in music and dance, and he gets along with all kinds of children. According to Sternberg's theory of successful intelligence, Josh is not good in _____, but he is skilled in _____ and _____. According to Gardner's theory of _____, Josh is strong in which intelligences?

5. A school principal asks for tips to help her students with learning difficulties. Based on this section, you should advise (pick one): *making the material simple/putting these children together in a special class/providing high-level creative work and embedding these children in the life of the school.*

6. (a) Define intrinsic and extrinsic motivation. (b) Give an example of a task in your life right now being driven by each kind of motivation. (c) Based on your reading, can you come up with ways to make these unpleasant extrinsic tasks feel more intrinsic?

7. Your friend wants to move out of her dangerous Chicago neighborhood. But she is afraid that if she relocates to an economically diverse section of the city, her daughter will be classified as "the poor kid in the neighborhood," and be rejected by her classmates. Based on Chetty's research, what should you advise?

Answers to the Tying It All Together questions can be found at the end of this chapter.

SUMMARY

Home

Families vary, from never-divorced two-parent couples to blended families, from gay-parent families to unmarried couples or grandparents raising a child. The main distinction is that mother-headed families are far more likely to live in poverty than their two-parent counterparts. Today, developed-world children are growing up in the first genuinely global village. Children can thrive in any kind of family, depending on the care parents provide.

According to Diana Baumrind's **parenting styles** approach, based on setting rules and nurturing, parents are classified as **authoritative, authoritarian, permissive,** or **rejecting-neglecting.**

Although child-rearing approaches do vary in families, with at-risk children evoking poorer parenting, even Asian-heritage families, while often seen as authoritarian, also adopt a child-centered authoritative style. Today, being authoritarian, while necessary in dangerous environments, is a symptom of parenting distress.

Resilient children, boys and girls who do well in the face of traumatic life experiences, tend to have good executive functions; possess special talents; have one close, secure attachment; and are not faced with an overload of life blows. For immigrant children facing **acculturation,** it's important to have a welcoming community. A specific genetic profile may offer some remarkable survivor children resilience in the face of stress.

Behavioral-genetic researchers argue that children grow up to fulfill their genetic destiny, and adequate parenting is all that is necessary. Judith Harris believes that peer groups—not parents—are the main socializers in children's lives. Evidence for Harris's theory comes from the fact that in communities high in **collective efficacy,** both children and parents thrive. Exceptional parenting, however, is crucial when children are biologically and socially at risk. Parents need to be flexible, tailoring their childrearing to the environment and to their children's needs. They should also relax and enjoy these fleeting years.

Attitudes about **corporal punishment** have changed dramatically, with many nations now outlawing spanking. The United States is an outlier because, although spanking is not preferred, many U.S. parents do occasionally use this discipline. Hundreds of studies show corporal punishment is detrimental to children's well-being.

Child maltreatment—physical abuse, neglect, emotional abuse, or sexual abuse—can sometimes be hard to classify. Maltreatment statistics differ, depending on whether we ask adults to reflect on their childhoods or consider observers' reports. Parents' personality problems, severe life stress, low community support, and having an at-risk child are the main factors that can provoke abuse. Abused children often have problems that can persist into adult life. Although teachers and health-care professionals are required to report suspected abuse, it is difficult for people to speak up, and authorities often do not follow through on reports. So, unfortunately, the prevalence of reported child abuse underestimates the magnitude of this problem today.

Children of divorce are at risk for negative life outcomes, but most boys and girls adapt well to this common childhood event. Parents feel guilty when they divorce, and struggle not to bad-mouth an ex-spouse. Keys to making divorce less traumatic lie in minimizing **parental alienation,** giving children some say in custody arrangements, and promoting high-quality parenting. Shared custody is a common arrangement today, but it works well only if both partners are good parents.

School

Many children from low-income families enter kindergarten well behind their affluent counterparts in basic academic skills. These inequalities at the starting gate are magnified by the fact that poor children are likely to attend the poorest-quality kindergartens.

Achievement tests measure a child's knowledge. **Intelligence quotient (IQ)** tests measure a child's basic potential to succeed at school. The **Wechsler Intelligence Scale for Children (WISC)** is the main childhood IQ test, has specific parts, and is given individually to a child. If the IQ score is below 70—and if other indicators warrant this designation—a child may be labeled as **intellectually disabled.** If the child's score is much higher than his performance on achievement tests, he is classified as having a **specific learning disorder** such as **dyslexia.** If a child's IQ score

is at or above 130, she is considered **gifted** and is eligible to be placed in an accelerated class.

IQ scores satisfy the measurement criterion called **reliability,** meaning that people tend to get roughly the same score if they take the test more than once. However, stressful life experiences can artificially lower a child's score. The test is also **valid** if our benchmark is predicting school performance. Some psychologists believe that the test score reflects a single quality called **g** that predicts success in every area of life; others feel that intelligence involves multiple abilities and that it is inappropriate to rank people as intelligent or not based on a single IQ score. The remarkable **Flynn effect** (an increase in test performance over the last century due to improved environments) suggests that, for disadvantaged children, the IQ score does not accurately reflect a person's genetic gifts.

Robert Sternberg and Howard Gardner argue that we need to expand our measures of intelligence beyond traditional tests. Sternberg believes that there are three types of intelligence: **analytic intelligence** (academic abilities), **creative intelligence,** and **practical intelligence** (real-world abilities, or "street smarts"). **Successful intelligence** requires having a good balance among these three skills. Gardner, in his **multiple intelligences theory,** describes eight (or possibly nine) types of intelligences. Although neither of these psychologists has developed alternatives to conventional IQ tests, their ideas can lead to rethinking the way we teach.

Schools that serve disadvantaged students who flower academically share a mission to have every child succeed. They provide a challenging academic environment and assume that each student can do well at high-level work. Teachers support and mentor one another at these high collective-efficacy schools.

Why do many children dislike school? The reason is that classroom learning is based on **extrinsic motivation** (external reinforcers such as grades), which impairs **intrinsic motivation** (the desire to learn for the sake of learning). School learning is inherently less interesting because it often involves rote memorization. Being evaluated in comparison to the class also limits a child's interest in learning for learning's sake. Studies show a disturbing decline in intrinsic motivation as children progress through elementary school.

Teachers (and parents) can make extrinsic learning tasks more intrinsic by offering class material relevant to children's interests, fostering relatedness (or a close attachment), and giving students choices about how to do their work. Stimulating intrinsic motivation by offering more autonomy (providing choices) helps motivate teachers to adopt new effective teaching strategies. Rigorous statistical studies confirm that good teachers make an enduring difference in students' lives. Studies tracking upward mobility in every U.S. county show that the child's community matters, too. Being raised in an economically diverse community, with less income inequalities, benefits disadvantaged children and their relatively affluent counterparts.

KEY TERMS

acculturation, p. 198

achievement tests, p. 207

analytic intelligence, p. 212

authoritarian parents, p. 195

authoritative parents, p. 195

child maltreatment, p. 202

collective efficacy, p. 199

corporal punishment, p. 200

creative intelligence, p. 212

dyslexia, p. 208

extrinsic motivation, p. 215

Flynn effect, p. 210

g, p. 211

gifted, p. 208

intellectual disability, p. 208

intelligence quotient (IQ), p. 207

intrinsic motivation, p. 215

multiple intelligences theory, p. 213

parental alienation, p. 204

parenting style, p. 195

permissive parents, p. 195

practical intelligence, p. 212

rejecting-neglecting parents, p. 195

reliability, p. 209

resilient children, p. 198

specific learning disorder, p. 208

successful intelligence, p. 212

validity, p. 209

WISC (Wechsler Intelligence Scale for Children), p. 207

ANSWERS TO **Tying It All Together** QUIZZES

Home

1. Montana's parents = authoritative. Pablo's parents = authoritarian. Sara's parents = permissive.

2. Ahmid is more apt to be resilient if he has good social and intellectual skills, an optimistic worldview, at least one close secure attachment, and the right genetic profile. The goal of your community should be to go out of your way to warmly welcome this child and his family.

3. Judith Harris's advice: Get your son in the best possible peer group. This chapter's recommendation: Provide exceptionally sensitive parenting.

4. a and c

5. Ms. Ramirez might feel torn about reporting her observations because she is worried about making false accusations. Even if she does make a report, there is a good chance authorities will not investigate the situation.

6. The main criterion for awarding joint custody—or unlimited visits—should be whether the father is a good parent.

School

1. b

2. Malik has a learning disability.

3. c and d

4. Analytic intelligence; creative intelligence and practical intelligence; multiple intelligences; Josh's strengths are in musical, kinesthetic, and interpersonal intelligence.

5. You should advise giving these children high-level creative work and embed them in the life of the school.

6. (a) Intrinsic motivation is self-generated—we work at something simply because it gives us joy. Extrinsic motivation refers to activities propelled by external reinforcers like grades. (b) Ask yourself: Am I doing this because I love it or only because this activity results in an external reward? (c) 1. Make disliked, extrinsic tasks relevant to a larger personal goal. ("Cleaning the house will help me become a more organized person. Plus, it's great exercise, so I'll become healthier.") 2. Increase your sense of autonomy or feeling of having choices around this activity. ("I'll do my housecleaning at the time of day that feels least burdensome while I listen to my favorite CD.") 3. Enhance attachments. ("If my significant other comes home to a clean house, she'll feel wonderful!")

7. Go for it!

CONNECT ONLINE:

 LaunchPad | Check out our videos and additional resources located at:
macmillan learning | www.macmillanlearning.com

Adolescence

This two-chapter part devoted to adolescence progresses somewhat chronologically from puberty through the late teens.

Chapter 8—Physical Development in Adolescents covers puberty, that early teenage total body change. It also focuses on two other body-oriented topics: body image (and eating disorders) and adolescent sexuality.

Chapter 9—Cognitive, Emotional, and Social Development in Adolescents examines teenage minds and relationships. How do adolescents reason? Are teenagers more socially sensitive or emotionally disturbed than adults? What can parents, schools, and society do to help? How do adolescents separate from their parents and connect with their peers?

PART IV

Application to **Developing Lives Parenting Simulation:** *Adolescence*

Below is a list of questions you will answer in the Adolescence simulation module. As you answer these questions, consider the impact your choice will have on the physical, cognitive, and social and emotional development of your adolescent.

Physical	Cognitive	Social and Emotional
• Will your child experiment with smoking, drinking, or drugs during adolescence?	• What is your child's Piagetian stage of cognitive development?	• How will you respond if your child is struggling to fit in with peers?
• How will you respond if you learn your child is experimenting with drugs?	• What kind of path do you see your teenager pursuing after high school (college, military, work program)?	• How often do you think you and your teenager will have conflicts?
• How will you encourage your child to spend his or her free time after school (sports, part-time job)?		• How social will your child be during his or her teen years?
		• How much privacy will you grant your teenager?
		• How will you respond when your teenager starts dating?

Left: Indeed/Getty Images

CHAPTER 8

Physical Development in Adolescents

Samantha and her twin brother, Sam, were so much alike—in their physical features, their personalities, their academic talents. Except for the sex difference, they seemed like identical twins. Then, when Samantha was 10, she started to tower over Sam and the rest of the fifth-grade class.

Yes, there were downsides to developing first—needing to hide behind a locker when you dressed for gym; not having anyone to talk to when you got your period at age 10; being teased about your big, strange body. But what fun! Once a neglected, pudgy elementary school child, by sixth grade, Samantha was hanging out with the popular eighth-grade boys. At age 12, she was smoking and drinking. By 14, she regularly defied her helpless parents and often left the house at 2 A.M.

Samantha's parents were frantic, but their daughter couldn't have cared less. Everything else was irrelevant compared to exploring being an adult. It took a life-changing service learning trip and a pregnancy scare to get Samantha back on track. Samantha had abandoned Sara, her best friend since first grade, for her new "mature" friends. But when the two girls got close again on that memorable trip, Sara's calming influence woke Samantha up. Samantha credits comments like, "Why would you ruin your future by having unprotected sex?" with saving her life. Plus, Samantha's lifelong competition with her brother helped refocus her thoughts. Although Sam was also an early developer, when he shot up to 6 feet in the spring of seventh grade, he became stellar at sports and also a social star.

Now that Samantha is 33, married, and expecting her first child, it's interesting for the twins and Sara to get together and really talk (for the first time) about their early teens. Sam remembers getting much stronger and his first incredible feelings of being in love. Samantha recalls being excited about her changing body, but obsessively worrying about being too fat. Then, there is Sara, who says middle school was no problem because she didn't menstruate until age 14. Everyone goes through puberty, but why does everyone react in different ways?

Why did Samantha have trouble as an early-maturing girl, while Sam and Sara sailed through **puberty**? What is this landmark physical process of becoming adult *really* like? This chapter explores this question in depth, then tackles body image and sex. As you read the following pages, think back to when you were 10 or 12 or 14. How did you feel about your body during puberty? When did you begin dating and fantasizing about having sex?

puberty The hormonal and physical changes by which children become sexually mature human beings and reach their adult height.

LEARNING OUTCOMES

- Describe the secular trend.
- List the hormonal and physical changes of puberty.
- Outline gender and individual differences in puberty.
- Contrast the causes and consequences of maturing early in girls and boys.

Puberty

Compare photos of yourself in late elementary school and high school to get a vivid sense of how puberty physically catapults us into adulthood. From the size of our thighs to the shape of our nose, we become a different-looking person in under five years. Today, puberty is a pre-teen and early adolescent change (Archibald, Graber, & Brooks-Gunn, 2003; Herting & Sowell, 2017). Today, as you saw with Samantha, who started menstruating at age 10 and has just gotten pregnant at age 32, the gap between being physically able to have children and actually having children can be more than twice as long as infancy and childhood combined.

This lack of *person–environment fit*, when our body is passionately saying "have sex" while society is telling teenagers to "say no" to intercourse, explains why adolescent sexuality provokes such anxiety among Western adults. Our concerns are recent. They are a product of living in the contemporary developed world.

These photographs of fourth graders and high school juniors offer a vivid visual reminder of the total body transformation of puberty.

Setting the Context: Culture, History, and Puberty

> I am considered to be a woman, so I am ready to marry, have children, and assume adult privileges and responsibilities. My name is Telelia ole Mariani. I am 14 years old.
> (quoted in Wilson, Ngige, & Trollinger, 2003, p. 95)

Throughout history, and even now in some impoverished world regions (as the quotation above suggests), puberty was a young person's signal to get married and give birth (Schlegel, 1995; Schlegel & Barry, 1991). Today, society must downplay the body changes because sexuality (and parenthood) isn't supposed to happen for years. In other cultures, people could celebrate children's blossoming bodies in a coming-of-age ceremony called the *puberty rite*.

Celebrating Puberty

puberty rite A "coming of age" ritual held in traditional cultures to celebrate children's transition to adulthood.

Puberty rites were emotional events, carefully choreographed to teach adult gender roles. Often, children were removed from their families and forced to perform stressful tasks. There was anxiety ("Can I really do this thing?") and feelings of awe and self-efficacy, as the young person returned to joyfully enter the community as an adult (Feixa, 2011; Weisfeld, 1997).

In one Amazonian tribe, for instance, after proving their manhood by killing a large animal, boys would metaphorically "die"—by drinking a hallucinogen and spending time in isolation to "be born again" as adults. Among the Masai of Africa, young males had to stoically endure a painful circumcision, then master military maneuvers before proudly returning home to take wives (Feixa, 2011).

For girls, **menarche,** or first menstruation, was the signal for celebrating the entrance into womanhood. In the traditional Navajo Kinaalda ceremony, for instance, girls in their first or second menstrual cycle, guided by a female mentor, would perform the running ritual, pushing their bodies to sprint for miles. (Imagine your motivation to train for this event when your culture told you that the quality of your run symbolized how long you would live!) The female role model massaged the girl's body, painted her face, and supervised her as she prepared a huge corn cake (a symbol of fertility) to be served to the community during a joyous, all-night singalong. The Navajo believe that when females begin menstruating, they possess special spiritual powers, so everyone would gather around for the girl's blessings as they gave her a new adult name.

Today, however, many girls reach menarche at age 10 or even 9. At that age—in *any* society—could people be ready for adult life? The answer is no. In the past, we reached puberty at an older age.

This photo shows South African boys returning from an "initiation school" to welcome their entry into adulthood. As is classic, in this culture the puberty ritual involves separation from one's family and symbolically being "reborn" as a man.

menarche A girl's first menstruation.

secular trend in puberty A decline in the average age at which children reach puberty.

spermarche A boy's first ejaculation of live sperm.

The Declining Age of Puberty

This fascinating decline, called the **secular trend in puberty,** is illustrated in Figure 8.1. In the 1860s, the average age of menarche in northern Europe was over 17 (Tanner, 1978). In the 1960s, in the developed world, it dropped to under age 13 (Parent and others, 2003). Then, after a pause, about 20 years ago, the menarche marker began to slide downward again (Lee & Styne, 2013).

A century ago, many girls could not get pregnant until their late teens. Today, many girls can have babies *before* their teenage years!

Researchers typically use menarche as their benchmark for charting the secular trend because it is an obvious sign of being able to have a child. The male signal of fertility, **spermarche,** or first ejaculation of live sperm, is a hidden event.

In addition, because it reflects better nutrition, in the same way as with stunting (discussed in Chapter 3), we can use the secular trend in puberty as an index of a nation's economic development. In the United States, African American girls begin to menstruate at close to age 12. In impoverished African countries, such as Senegal, the comparable menarche age is over 16 (Parent and others, 2003)!

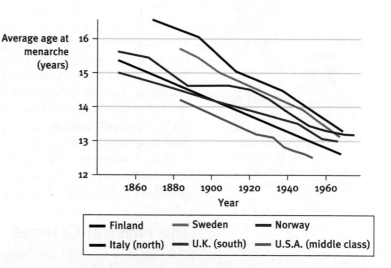

FIGURE 8.1: The secular trend in puberty: Notice that the average age of menarche dramatically declined in developed countries during the first half of the twentieth century. Why is this decline continuing? Stay tuned for surprising answers later in this chapter.

Data from Tanner 1978, p. 103.

For this rural, 15-year-old Vietnamese boy, reaching puberty means it's time to assume his adult responsibilities as a fisherman. The reason he now has the strength and stamina to wield this heavy net is that the all-important hormonal system programming the body changes of manhood (the HPG axis) has fully kicked in.

adrenal androgens
Hormones produced by the adrenal glands that program puberty.

HPG axis The main hormonal system that programs puberty; it involves a triggering hypothalamic hormone that causes the pituitary to secrete its hormones, which in turn cause the ovaries and testes to develop and secrete the hormones that produce the major body changes.

gonads The sex organs—the ovaries in girls and the testes in boys.

testosterone The hormone responsible for maturation of the male reproductive organs and other signs of puberty in men, and for hair and skin changes and sexual desire in both sexes.

primary sexual characteristics Physical changes of puberty that directly involve the reproductive organs, such as growth of the penis and onset of menstruation.

Given that nutrition is critical, what *exactly* sets puberty off? For answers, let's focus on the hormonal systems that program the physical changes.

The Hormonal Programmers

Puberty is programmed by two command centers. One system, located in the adrenal glands at the top of the kidneys, begins to release its hormones at about ages 6 to 8, several years before children show observable signs of puberty. The **adrenal androgens,** whose output increases to reach a peak in the early twenties, eventually produce (among other events) pubic hair development, skin changes, body odor, and, as you will read later in this chapter, our first feelings of sexual desire (Herting & Sowell, 2017).

About two years later, the most important command center kicks in. Called the **HPG axis**—because it involves the hypothalamus (in the brain), the pituitary (a gland at the base of the brain), and the **gonads** (the *ovaries* and the *testes*)—this system produces the major body changes (Plant, 2015).

As you can see in Figure 8.2, puberty is set off by a three-phase chain reaction. At about age 9 or 10, pulsating bursts of the hypothalamic hormone stimulate the pituitary gland to step up production of its hormones. This causes the ovaries and testes to secrete several closely related compounds called estrogens and the hormone called **testosterone** (Herting & Sowell, 2017).

As the blood concentrations of estrogens and testosterone float upward, these hormones unleash a physical transformation. Estrogens produce females' changing shape by causing the hips to widen and the uterus and breasts to enlarge. They set in motion the cycle of reproduction, stimulating the ovaries to produce eggs. Testosterone causes the penis to lengthen, promotes the growth of facial and body hair, and is responsible for a dramatic increase in muscle mass and other internal masculine changes.

Boys and girls *both* produce estrogens and testosterone. Testosterone and the adrenal androgens are responsible for sexual arousal in females and males. However, women produce mainly estrogens. The concentration of testosterone is roughly 8 times higher in boys after puberty than it is in girls; in fact, this classic "male" hormone is responsible for *all* the physical changes in boys.

Now, to return to our earlier question: What primes the triggering hypothalamic hormone? As Figure 8.2 illustrates, many forces help unleash the pulsating hormonal bursts—from genetics to exposure to light; from possible chemicals in our water and food to environmental stress (more about this fascinating force later). A threshold level of a hormone called *leptin*, tied to body fat, is essential. This explains why undernutrition delays puberty and why obesity might push the timer to a younger age (more about this later). These primers, in turn, unleash a cascade of body changes.

The Physical Changes

Puberty causes a total *psychological* and physical transformation. As the hormones flood the body, they affect specific brain regions, making teenagers more emotional, sensitive to social cues, and interested in taking risks (as you will read in Chapter 9). Scientists divide the physical changes into three categories:

- **Primary sexual characteristics** refer to the body changes directly involved in reproduction. The growth of the penis and menstruation are examples of primary sexual characteristics.

- **Secondary sexual characteristics** is the label for the hundreds of other changes that accompany puberty, such as breast development, the growth of pubic hair, voice changes, and alterations in the person's skin.

- The **growth spurt** merits its own special category. At puberty—as should come as no surprise—there is a dramatic increase in height and weight.

Health-care workers use a standard scale to plot the growth of the child's main secondary sexual characteristics in stages (see the How Do We Know box on page 230). Now let's offer a motion picture of all of the changes, first in girls and then in boys.

For Girls

The most dramatic early sign of puberty in girls is the growth spurt. First, girls' growth picks up speed, accelerates, and then begins to decrease (Herting & Sowell, 2017). During a visit to my 11-year-old niece, I got a vivid sense of this "peak velocity" phase of growth. Six months earlier, I had towered over her. Now, she insisted on standing back-to-back to demonstrate: "Look, Aunt Janet, I'm taller than you!"

About six months after the growth spurt begins, breasts and pubic hair become visible. On average, girls' breasts take about four years to grow to their adult form (Tanner, 1955, 1978).

FIGURE 8.2: The HPG axis: The three-phase hormonal sequence that triggers puberty: As you can see here, in response to various genetic and environmental influences, the hypothalamus releases a hormone that stimulates the pituitary gland to produce its own hormones, which cause the ovaries in girls and the testes in boys to grow and secrete estrogens and testosterone, producing the physical changes of puberty.

Menarche typically occurs in the middle to final stages of breast and pubic hair development, when girls' growth is winding down (Lee & Styne, 2013; Peper & Dahl, 2013). So you can tell your 12-year-old niece, who has just begun to menstruate, that, while her breasts are still "works in progress," she is probably about as tall today as she will be as an adult.

When they reach menarche, can girls get pregnant? Yes, but there is often a window of infertility until the system fully gears up. Does puberty unfold in the same way for every girl? The answer is no. Because the hormonal signals are complex, in some girls, pubic hair development (programmed by the adrenal androgens) is underway before the breasts begin to enlarge. Occasionally, a girl does grow much taller after she begins to menstruate.

The most fascinating variability relates to the *rate* of change. Some children are developmental "tortoises." Their progression through puberty is slow-paced. Others are "hares." They speed through the body changes. For instance, while breast development takes *an average* of four years, the entire process—from start to finish—can range from less than two to an incredible nine! (See Mendle and others, 2010.)

These external changes are accompanied by internal upheavals. During puberty, the uterus grows, the vagina lengthens, and the hips develop a cushion of fat. The vocal cords get longer, the heart gets bigger, and the red blood cells

secondary sexual characteristics Physical changes of puberty not directly involved in reproduction, such as female breast development and male facial hair.

growth spurt A dramatic increase in height and weight that occurs during puberty.

HOW DO WE KNOW . . .
how puberty progresses?

Imagine being a frantic parent concerned that your 8-year-old daughter is developing breasts. Your first step would be to visit your pediatrician, who would probably evaluate your child according to Tanner's five pubertal stages. What are the origins of this classic scale and what is it like? (See Roberts, 2016.)

During the early twentieth century, as the new science of pediatrics flourished, health-care workers needed benchmarks for evaluating their patients. Was a particular boy or girl growing normally? What exactly does growing "normally" mean? Then, during the late 1940s, James Tanner came to the rescue with landmark research tracking physical development in the flesh.

With a colleague, Tanner entered a London orphanage and began a mammoth study (as I mentioned when discussing Bowlby's research in Chapter 4, British orphanages were common during this era). The researchers photographed and measured children's bodies from ages 3 to 5 years, and then every 3 months during puberty. These meticulous assessments, converted into atlases, remain the gold standard that health-care workers use worldwide to chart pubertal growth.

Imagine the hurdles involved in conducting this research today. Now, caregivers must give informed consent for their children to be tested. It defies modern standards of ethics (and decency!) to have strangers regularly measure (and photograph) pre-teens' private parts. Tanner's sample—all white, probably somewhat malnourished, and perhaps subject to early abuse—was totally unrepresentative. But his stages remain the beacon that allowed adolescent research (and practice) to blossom for the past 50 years.

Tanner didn't formulate world-class theories. Still, his decades of dogged scientific work transformed our thinking about teenagers almost as much as Piaget's or Erikson's ideas. Below you can see how health-care workers would classify this 8-year-old girl's breast development, according to Tanner's five stages.

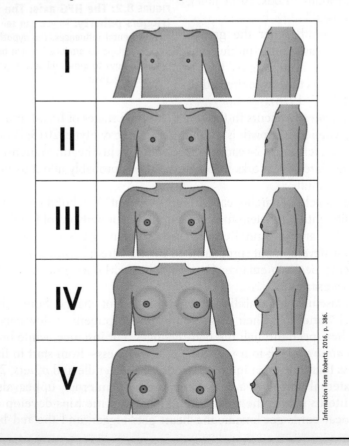

Information from Roberts, 2016, p. 386.

carry more oxygen. So, after puberty, girls become much stronger (Archibald, Graber, & Brooks-Gunn, 2003). The increases in strength, stamina, height, and weight are astonishing in boys.

For Boys

In boys, health-care workers also track the growth of the penis, testicles, and pubic hair by five Tanner stages. However, because these organs of reproduction begin developing first, boys still look like children to the outside world for a year or two after their bodies start changing. Voice deepening, the development of body hair, and that other visible sign of being a man—the need to shave—all take place after the growth of the testes and penis is underway (Tanner, 1978). Now, let's pause to look at the most obvious signals that a boy is becoming a man—the mammoth alterations in body size, shape, and strength.

In Chapter 5, I mentioned that elementary school boys and girls are roughly the same size. Then, during the puberty growth spurt, males shoot up an incredible average of 8 inches, compared to 4 inches for girls (Tanner, 1978). Boys also become far stronger than the other sex.

One cause is the tremendous increase in muscle mass. Another lies in the dramatic cardiovascular changes. At puberty, boys' hearts increase in weight by more than one-third. In particular, notice in Figure 8.3 that, compared to females, after puberty, males have many more red blood cells and a much greater capacity for carrying oxygen in their blood. The visible signs of these changes are a big chest, wide shoulders, and a muscular frame. The real-world outcome is that after puberty, males get a boost in gross motor skills that give them an edge in everything from soccer to sprinting and from cycling to carrying heavy loads.

Do you know any seventh- or eighth-grade boys? If so, you might notice that growth during puberty takes place in the opposite pattern to the one that occurs earlier in life. Rather than following the *cephalocaudal* and *proximodistal* sequences (from the head downward and from the middle of the body outward), at puberty, the person's hands, feet, and legs grow first. While this happens for both sexes, these changes are especially obvious in boys because their growth is so dramatic.

Their long legs and large feet explain why, in their early teens, boys look gawky. Add to that the crackly voice produced by the growing larynx, the wispy look of beginning

Because the landmark change of shaving occurs fairly late in the sequence of puberty, we can be sure that this 14-year-old boy has been looking like a man, for some time, in ways we can't see.

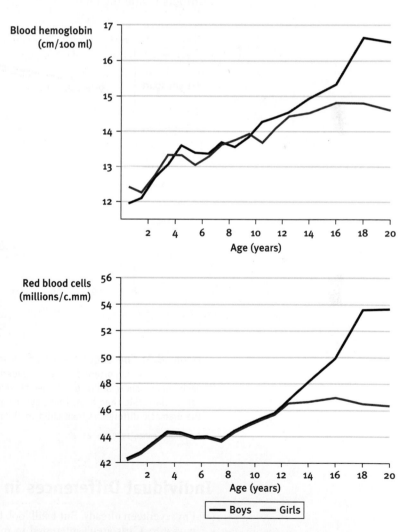

FIGURE 8.3: Changes in blood hemoglobin and red blood cells during puberty in males and females: At puberty, increases in hemoglobin and in the number of red blood cells cause children of both sexes to get far stronger. But notice that these changes are more pronounced in boys than in girls.

Data from Tanner, 1955, p. 103.

facial hair, and the fact that during puberty a boy's nose and ears grow before the rest of his face catches up. Plus, the increased activity of the sweat glands and enlarged pores leads to that familiar condition that produces such emotional agony: acne. Although girls also suffer from acne, boys are more vulnerable to this problem because testosterone, which males produce in abundance, causes changes in the hair and skin.

Are Boys on a Later Timetable? A Bit

Visit a middle school and you will be struck by the fact that boys, on average, appear to reach puberty two years later than girls. But appearances can be deceiving. In girls, as I mentioned earlier, the externally visible signs of puberty, such as the growth spurt and breast development, take place toward the beginning of the sequence. For boys, the hidden development—growth of the testes—occurs first (Huddleston & Ge, 2003; Lee & Styne, 2013).

If we look at the *real* sign of fertility, the sex differences are not that far apart. In one study, boys reported that spermarche occurred at roughly age 13, only about six months later than the average age of menarche (Stein & Reiser, 1994).

Figure 8.4 graphically summarizes some of these changes. Now, let's explore the numbers inside the chart. Why do children undergo puberty at such different ages?

FIGURE 8.4: The sequence of some major events of puberty: This chart shows the ages at which some important changes of puberty occur in the average boy and girl. The numbers below each change show the range of ages at which that event begins. Notice that girls are on a slightly earlier timetable than boys, that boys' height spurt occurs at a later point in their development, and the dramatic differences from child to child in pubertal timing.

Data from Tanner, 1978, pp. 23, 29.

Individual Differences in Puberty Timetables

> I'm seventeen already. But I still look like a kid. I get teased a lot, especially by the other guys. . . . Girls aren't interested in me, either, because most of them are taller than I am. When will I grow up?
>
> (adapted from an on-line chat room)

The sex difference in puberty timetables can cause anxiety. As an early-maturing girl, I vividly remember slumping to avoid the humiliation of having my partner's head encounter my chest in sixth-grade dancing class! But nature's cruelest blow may relate to the individual differences in timing. Why is there a five-year difference in puberty timetables between children living in the same environment? (See Parent and others, 2003.)

Not unexpectedly, genetics is important. Identical twins go through puberty at roughly the same ages (Lee & Styne, 2013; Silventoinen and others, 2008). Asian Americans tend to be slightly behind other U.S. children in puberty timetables (Sun and others, 2002). African American and Hispanic boys and girls are ahead of other North American groups (Lee & Styne, 2013; Rosenfield, Lipton, & Drum, 2009).

But remember that in impoverished African countries—where children are poorly nourished—girls begin to menstruate, on average, as late as age 16. During the past 30 years, obesity rates in the United States skyrocketed among African American elementary school girls and boys (Boonpleng and others, 2013). Given that body fat is intimately involved, and the secular trend has picked up steam, does being overweight predict when a boy or girl physically matures?

Look at female middle school friends—such as these girls getting ready for a dance— and you will be struck by the differences in puberty timetables. As the text shows, a variety of forces predict why children mature earlier or later than their peers.

Overweight and Early Puberty (It's All About Girls)

The answer is yes—if we consider female children *only*. Controlling for other forces, having a high BMI (body mass index) during elementary school does predict entering puberty earlier for girls (Lee & Styne, 2013; Rosenfield, Lipton, & Drum, 2009). Even more interestingly, rapid weight gain in the *first nine months of life* is strongly linked to menstruating at a younger age! (See Walvoord, 2010.)

This finding dovetails with the research I presented in Table 6.3 (page 169), suggesting that our overweight path is set in motion early in life. Now—in addition to foreshadowing later obesity—we know that weight gain during infancy may predict early puberty, too.

Interestingly, for boys the data is inconsistent. Some studies show obese boys mature early; others suggest these children develop later than their peers (see Lee & Styne, 2013).

Now let's turn to a more astonishing environmental influence predicting puberty, specifically in girls—the quality of a child's family life.

In Table 6.3, I suggested that overfeeding this adorable 8-month-old girl might program lifelong overweight. Now we know that excessive weight gain during infancy can have another negative epigenetic effect— priming this baby to reach puberty at an early age.

Family Stress and Early Puberty (Again, It's About Girls)

Drawing on an *evolutionary psychology perspective*, some developmentalists argue that when family stress is intense, a physiological mechanism kicks in to accelerate puberty and free a child from an inhospitable nest. Just as stress in the womb "instructs" the baby to store fat (as the fetal programming hypothesis described in Chapter 2 suggests), an unhappy childhood signals the body to expect a short life and pushes adult fertility to a younger age (Belsky and others, 2015).

I must emphasize that genetics is the most important force predicting a child's puberty timetable (the age when that person's parents developed). But, if a girl is temperamentally vulnerable, *controlling for every other influence* (genetics, body weight, and so on), her family life makes its small, tantalizing contribution (Ellis and others, 2011b). Early-maturing girls are more apt to grow up in mother-headed households (Graber, Nichols, & Brooks-Gunn, 2010; Neberich and others, 2010) and report intense childhood stress (Allison & Hyde, 2013; Ellis, 2004). In one longitudinal study, mothers' use of *power-assertive* discipline during preschool—yelling, shaming, rejecting—was associated with earlier menstruation (Belsky and others, 2007a;

Belsky, Houts, & Pasco Fearon, 2010). Even prenatal maternal stress may promote early menarche because, when women experience emotional upheavals during their pregnancies, these traumas can produce depression and so provoke more uncaring childrearing during a daughter's infant years (Belsky and others, 2015).

Why—specifically in girls—is the hypothalamic timer sensitive to body weight and family stress? We do not know. But these surprising findings emphasize the *ecological, developmental systems* message: *Many* influences—from genetics to sex, from physiology to parenting to everything else—affect how children grow.

Table 8.1 summarizes these points by spelling out questions that can predict a girl's chance of reaching puberty at a younger-than-average age. If you were an early maturer, how many—if any—of these forces applied to you?

Now that I've described the physical process, let's look at how children feel about three classic signs of puberty—breast development, menstruation, and first ejaculation. Then we'll explore the mental health impact of reaching puberty relatively early or late.

Table 8.1: Predicting a Girl's Chances of Early Puberty: Some Questions

1. Did this girl's parents reach puberty early?

2. Is this girl African American?

3. Is this girl overweight? Did she gain weight rapidly during her first year of life?

4. Has this girl's family life been stressful and unhappy? Were her caregivers angry and depressed during that child's first years of life?

An Insider's View of Puberty

Think back to how you felt about your body during puberty. You probably remember having mixed emotions: fear, pride, embarrassment, excitement. If a researcher asked you to describe your inner state, would you want to talk about how you *really* felt? The reluctance of pre-teens to discuss what is happening ("Yuck! Just don't go there!") explains why, to study reactions to puberty, psychologists often ask adults to remember this time of life. Or they may use indirect measures, such as having children tell stories about pictures, to reveal their inner concerns.

The Breasts

In a classic study, researchers used this indirect strategy to explore how girls feel in relation to their parents while undergoing that most visible sign of becoming a woman—breast development (Brooks-Gunn and others, 1994). They asked a group of girls to tell a story about the characters in a drawing that showed an adult female (the mother) taking a bra out of a shopping bag while an adolescent girl and an adult male (the father) watched. While girls often viewed mothers as being excited and happy, they typically described the teenager as humiliated by her father's presence in the room. Moreover, girls in the middle of puberty told the most negative stories about fathers, suggesting that body embarrassment is at its height while children are undergoing the physical changes.

Because society strongly values this symbol of being a woman (and our contemporary culture sees bigger as better!), other research suggests that U.S. girls feel proud of their developing breasts (Brooks-Gunn & Warren, 1988). However, among girls in ballet schools, where there are strong pressures

Imagine how these girls auditioning at a premier ballet academy in New York City will feel when they develop breasts and perhaps find that their womanly body shape interrupts their career dreams—and you will understand why children's reactions to puberty depend on their unique environment.

David Sacks/The Image Bank/Getty Images

to look prepubescent, breast development evokes distress (Brooks-Gunn & Warren, 1985). The principle that children's reactions to puberty depend on messages from the wider world holds true for menstruation, too.

Menstruation

Imagine being a Navajo girl and feeling that when you menstruate, you have entered a special spiritual state. Compare this with the less-than-glowing portrait most cultures paint about "that time of the month" (Brooks-Gunn & Ruble, 1982; Costos, Ackerman, & Paradis, 2002). From the advertisements for pills strong enough to handle *even* menstrual pain to its classic description as "the curse," it is no wonder that in the past girls approached this milestone with dread (Brooks-Gunn & Ruble, 1982).

Luckily, upper-middle-class mothers are trying to change these cultural scripts. When researchers asked 18- to 20-year-old students at Oregon State University to write about their "first period experiences," 3 out of 4 women recalled their moms as being thrilled ("She treated me like a princess"). One person wrote that the day after she told her mother, "I saw an expensive box of chocolates and a card addressed to me. It said 'Congrats on becoming a woman'" (quoted in Lee, 2008, p. 1332).

These positive responses matter. In one research summary, while low-income women in the United States recalled frequently feeling "gross, smelly and disgusting" at menarche (Herbert and others, 2016), about half of all middle-class young women described getting their period as "no big deal."

First Ejaculation

Daughters must confide in their mothers about menarche because this event demands specific coping techniques. Spermarche, in contrast, does not require instructions from the outside world. Who talks to male adolescents about first ejaculation? Read this memory from an 18-year-old boy:

> My mom, she knew I had them. It was all over my sheets . . . but she didn't . . . tease me. . . . She never asked if I wanted to talk about it—I'm glad. I never could have said anything to my mom.
>
> (quoted in Stein & Reiser, 1994, p. 377)

Most of these boys reported that they needed to be secretive. They didn't want to let *anyone* know. And notice—as you saw earlier with fathers and pre-teen girls—that boys also view their changing bodies as especially embarrassing around the parent of the other sex.

Is this tendency for children to hide the symptoms of puberty around the parent of the other sex programmed into evolution to help teenagers emotionally separate from their families? We do not know. We do have massive information, however, on the *emotional* impact of being early or late.

Maturing Early Can Be a Problem for Girls

Imagine being an early-maturing girl. How would you feel if you looked like an adult while everyone else in your classes still looked like a child? Now imagine being a late maturer and thinking, "What's wrong with my body? Will I *ever* grow up?"

Actually, the timing of development matters, but again the results differ for boys and girls. Early-maturing boys are more prone to abuse substances, particularly if these teens are low in impulse control (Castellanos-Ryan and others, 2013). They are at risk of developing depression if they have prior personality problems and an unhappy family life (Benoit, Lacourse, & Claes, 2013). But because males become so much stronger during puberty (and therefore are better at sports) and early-maturing boys are more in synch with the average girl, reaching puberty early boosts boys' popularity and self-esteem (Li and others, 2013).

While early-maturing girls may be prone to get into trouble, for these manlike seventh-grade boys, developing earlier can be a social plus, as they are right on time for the average girl in this class.

Unfortunately, the research is consistently downbeat for the other sex: *Hundreds of studies suggest that early-maturing girls can have widespread difficulties during their adolescent years.*

Early-Maturing Girls Are at Risk of Developing Externalizing Problems

Because we choose friends who are "like us," early-maturing girls may gravitate toward becoming friends with older girls and boys. So, around the world, they tend to get involved in "adult activities" such as smoking, drinking, and taking drugs at younger ages (Ren, Guo, & Chen, 2015). Maturing early heightens the tendency—described in the next chapter—for teens to make dangerous, impulsive decisions with their peers (Kretsch & Harden, 2014).

Because they are so busy testing the limits, one classic longitudinal Swedish study showed early-maturing girls tended to get worse grades than their classmates in the sixth and seventh grades (Simmons & Blyth, 1987). By their twenties, these girls were several times less likely to have graduated from high school than their later-developing peers (Stattin & Magnusson, 1990).

The main danger, of course, is having unprotected sex. Because they may not have the cognitive abilities to resist this social pressure and often have older boyfriends, early-maturing girls are more likely to have intercourse at a younger age (Graber, Nichols, & Brooks-Gunn, 2010). They are less apt to use contraception, making them more vulnerable to becoming pregnant as teens (Allison & Hyde, 2013). Imagine being a sixth- or seventh-grade girl thrilled to be pursued by the high school boys. Would you have the presence of mind to say no?

Early-Maturing Girls Are at Risk of Getting Anxious and Depressed

As if this were not enough, early-maturing girls, especially in affluent environments, are more likely to experience bouts of low self-worth (Mendle and others, 2016). In fourth or fifth grade, these girls are at risk of being bullied because they look so different from the other children in class (Allison & Hyde, 2013). Now, compound this with the shame attached to *generally* having a larger body size. Not only are early-maturing girls apt to be heavier during elementary school, but they also end up shorter and stockier because their height spurt occurs at an earlier point in their development (Adair, 2008; Must and others, 2005). Late-maturing girls are more likely to fit the tall ultra-slim model shape. Reaching puberty early sets girls up for having a poor body image and becoming depressed.

So far, I've been painting a dismal portrait of early-maturing girls. But, as with any aspect of development, it's important to look at the *whole* context of a person's life. Early maturation may not pose body-image problems in ethnic groups that have a healthier, more inclusive idea about the ideal female body (more about this later).

Most important, these negative effects happen mainly when there are other risk factors in a child's life. For example, if a girl is exposed to harsh parenting (Deardorff and others, 2013), then yes, early maturation can be the straw that breaks the camel's back (Lynne-Landsman, Graber, & Andrews, 2010). But if that child has *authoritative* parents (Ren and others, 2015), strong religious values—and doesn't gravitate to older "at-risk" friends—her puberty timetable will not matter (Stattin & Magnusson, 1990).

The dangers linked with maturing early also seem dependent on the nation in which a girl grows up. In one interesting international comparison, while early-maturing girls were more prone to act out against adult rules than late maturers, this was not true in Slovakia (see Figure 8.5). The reason, these researchers argue, is that Sweden is a permissive society that accepts adolescent sex, whereas Slovakia severely restricts these activities (Skoog and others, 2013). So, again, a structured, highly protective community can cushion a girl (or any child) from acting on the behavioral messages her body gives off.

This brings us to that critical setting: school. In classic studies, developmentalists found that early-maturing girls had special problems after moving to a large middle school versus staying in a smaller K–8 school (Simmons & Blyth, 1987). Therefore, based on this research, psychologists argued that it is a bad idea to compound the stressful changes of puberty by forcing pre-teens to change schools (see Eccles & Roeser, 2003).

But, because some middle schools offer superior nurturing (Farmer and others, 2011), it's important to go beyond a school's structure and ask more basic questions: Is this an author-itative environment (see Chapter 7)? Does this class have caring peer norms (see Chapter 6)? Moreover, imagine being locked into the calcified status hierarchies that can solidify, based on spending your whole childhood with the same group of peers. The advan-tage of middle school is that it offers you (and everyone else) a liberating new start!

FIGURE 8.5: The interaction between culture and pubertal timing in predicting girls' problem behavior in Sweden (red line) and Slovakia (blue line): Notice that in sexually permissive Sweden, maturing early has a huge impact on a girl's risk of getting into trouble (with drugs, ignoring curfews, being truant at school, and so on); but a girl's puberty timetable has comparatively little impact on her behavior if that child lives in Slovakia.

Data from Skoog and others, 2013.

Wrapping Up Puberty

Now let's summarize all these research messages:

- **Children's reactions to puberty depend on the environment in which they physically mature.** Negative feelings are more likely to occur when society looks down on a given sign of development (as with menstruation) or when the physical changes are not valued in a person's particular group (as with breast development in ballerinas). Living in a sexually permissive society or being in a non-nurturing school during puberty magnifies the stress of body changes.

- **With early-maturing girls, we should take special steps to arrange the right body–environment fit.** Having an adult body at a young age is dangerous for girls, but only when the changes happen in a high-risk milieu. Therefore, when a girl reaches puberty early, it's important for parents to closely monitor her activities (see Ren and others, 2015).

- **Communication about puberty should be improved—especially for boys.** While a few contemporary mothers may be doing a fine job discussing menstruation with their daughters, boys, in particular, seem to enter puberty without much guidance about what to expect (Omar, McElderry, & Zakharia, 2003).

INTERVENTIONS Minimizing Puberty Distress

Given these findings, what are the lessons for parents? What changes should society make?

Lessons for Parents

It's tempting for parents to avoid discussing puberty because children are so sensitive about their changing bodies (see Elliot, 2012; Hyde and others, 2013). This reluctance is a mistake. Developmentalists urge parents to discuss what is happening with a same-sex child. They advise beginning these discussions when the child is at an age when talking is emotionally easier, before the changes take place (Graber, Nichols, & Brooks-Gunn, 2010). Fathers, in particular, need to make special efforts to talk about puberty with their sons (Paikoff & Brooks-Gunn, 1991).

Finally, parents of early-maturing daughters should try to get their child involved in positive activities, especially with friends the same age and, if possible, carefully pick the best school or class.

Lessons for Society

No matter what a child's puberty timetable, the implicit message of this section is that schools matter *tremendously* at this gateway-to-adulthood age. Rather than viewing sixth or seventh grade as relatively unimportant (compared to, say, high school), caring schools are vital to setting young teens on the right path.

It also seems critical to provide adequate puberty education. Think back to what you wanted to know about your changing body ("My breasts don't look right"; "My penis has a strange shape"), and you will realize that offering a few fifth-grade health lectures is not enough. The good news is that, in recent years, Western nations have developed innovative school sex-education programs (American Teens' Sources of Sexual Health Education, 2016). But, since discussing sex is controversial (more about this inflammatory issue later), a declining fraction of U.S. middle schools even mention puberty (Lindberg, Maddow-Zimet, & Boonstra, 2016). Sex education is apt to begin in high school, after many children have finished developing (Centers for Disease Control and Prevention, 2015). (That's like locking the barn door after the horses have been stolen!)

UNESCO has global guidelines aimed at teaching young children (aged 5 to 8) to respect their bodies. But, with the exception of a few European nations, schools routinely ignore this document—offering "too little too late" alarmist-oriented talk focused on pubertal damage control: "Don't get pregnant," "Avoid STIs" (Goldman & Coleman, 2013).

Suppose our culture *celebrated* puberty, as the Navajo do? Perhaps we might really celebrate every body size.

Tying It All Together

1. In contrast to earlier times, give the main reason why our culture can't celebrate puberty today.

2. You notice that your 11-year-old cousin is starting to look more like a young woman. (a) Outline the three-phase hormonal sequence that is setting off the physical changes. (b) Name the three classes of hormones involved in puberty.

3. Kendra has recently begun to menstruate. Calista has just shot up in height. Carl is developing facial hair. Statistically speaking, which child is at the beginning of puberty?

4. Brianna, an overweight second grader, has harsh, rejecting parents. Based on this chapter, you might predict that Brianna should enter puberty *earlier/ later* than her peers.

5. Based simply on knowing a child's puberty timetable, spell out who is most at risk of getting into trouble (for example, with drugs or having unprotected sex) as a teen.

6. You are on a committee charged with developing programs to help children cope emotionally with puberty. What recommendations might you make?

Answers to the Tying It All Together questions can be found at the end of this chapter.

Body Image Issues

What do you daydream about?

Being skinny.

—Amanda (quoted in Martin, 1996, p. 36)

Puberty is a time of intense physical preoccupations, and there is hardly a teenager who isn't concerned about some body part. How important is it for young people to be *generally* satisfied with how they look?

Consider this finding: Susan Harter (1999) explored how feeling competent in each of her five "self-worth" dimensions—scholastic abilities, conduct, athletic skills, peer likeability, and appearance (discussed in Chapter 6)—related to teenagers' overall self-esteem. She found that being happy about one's looks outweighed *anything else* in determining whether adolescents generally felt good about themselves.

This finding is not just true of teenagers in the United States. It appears in surveys conducted in many countries among people at various stages of life. If we are happy with the way we look, we are likely to be happy with who we are as human beings.

Feeling physically appealing is important to everyone (Mellor and others, 2010). But, in a late-twentieth-century study, Harter found that, beginning in elementary school, girls in particular get increasingly distressed with their looks (see Figure 1.5 on page 27). One reason for this difference comes as no surprise—the intense cultural pressure for females to be thin.

The Differing Body Concerns of Girls and Boys

The distorting impact of the **thin ideal,** or pressure to be abnormally thin, was graphically suggested in an Irish survey. The researchers found that 3 out of 4 female teens with average BMIs felt they were too fat (Lawler & Nixon, 2011). More alarming, 2 out of 5 of the *underweight* girls in this poll also wanted to shed pounds (Lawler & Nixon, 2011). While some boys in this study (those who were genuinely heavy, for instance) also worried about their weight, males want to build up their muscles—and are at risk of spending excessive hours at the gym laboring to increase their body mass (Parent & Moradi, 2011; Smolak & Stein, 2010).

Body concerns are apt to take over children's lives at puberty because, during early adolescence, social sensitivities reach a peak (more about this in the next chapter). But new research suggests that the uniquely female weight obsession may

LEARNING OUTCOMES

- List several influences promoting teenage body distress.
- Contrast the different eating disorders.
- Evaluate eating disorder treatments.

thin ideal Media-driven cultural idea that females need to be abnormally thin.

When did our culture develop the idea that women should be unrealistically thin? Historians trace this change to the 1970s, when extremely slim actresses like Audrey Hepburn became our cultural ideal. More recently, as shown in the second photo, similar body pressures have infected the other sex, causing pubescent boys to struggle for the muscular male shape that is our contemporary cultural ideal.

Interestingly, due to an epigenetic process, this fraternal twin girl may be more insulated from developing an eating disorder as a teen by simply being exposed to the circulating testosterone her brother's body is giving off.

actually have pre-birth *epigenetic* roots. One group of scientists discovered that mothers exposed to intense stress during pregnancy were likely to have daughters with eating issues (Steigler & Thaler, 2016). In perhaps the most provocative study, scientists found that female twin pairs were more apt to develop unhealthy dieting practices at puberty than fraternal twin girls whose other twin was male. This fascinating finding suggests that testosterone (given off by the male twin's body) may dampen down a *biological* tendency for girls to become weight obsessed during their pubertal years (Culbert and others, 2013).

Still, even if the signal to "be supersensitive to weight" has biological roots, outer-world pressures prime the pump: Pre-teens love to tease one another about weight ("You are getting fat!!!") (Compian, Gowen, & Hayward, 2004; Jackson & Chen, 2008; Lawler & Nixon, 2011). As you will see soon, this teasing can activate unhealthy dieting practices that wreak havoc on vulnerable children's lives (Douglas & Varnado-Sullivan, 2016).

A primary culprit is the media, for its regular drumbeat advocating the female thin ideal. As early as preschool, one study showed, girls have internalized the message, "You need to be thin" (Harriger and others, 2010). Digitally altered images beamed from TV, the Internet, and magazines set body-size standards that are often impossible to attain (López-Guimerà and others, 2010). It's no wonder, then, that many hours spent watching media predicts body dissatisfaction in both ballet dancers and nonphysically active girls (Nerini, 2015).

Still, some children are less susceptible to the media messages. In Albert Bandura's social learning framework, for instance, African American and Latino girls should be more insulated from the thin ideal because their role models, such as Beyoncé, demonstrate that beauty comes in ample sizes. As one young African American woman in an interview study explained: "I feel like . . . for the woman of color . . . the look is like thick thighs, you know, fat butt . . . [men] like, like want you to have meat on your body" (quoted in Hesse-Biber and others, 2010, p. 704).

Does this mean that, unless they are obese, Latino and African American teens don't worry about their weight? Unfortunately, if an ethnic minority girl identifies with the mainstream Western thin ideal, she is just as likely to develop eating disorders as any other teen (Sabik, Cole, & Ward, 2010). What *exactly* are eating disorders like?

Eating Disorders

> In the morning I'll have a black coffee. At noon I have a mix of shredded lettuce, carrots and cabbage. At around dinnertime I have 9 mini whole-wheat crackers. On a bad day . . . I may have . . . black coffee and an egg white [for breakfast], . . .
> (adapted from Juarascio, Shoaib, & Timko, 2010, p. 402)

> Scales are evil! But I'm obsessed with them! I'm on the damn thing like 3 times a day!
> (adapted from Gavin, Rodham, & Poyer, 2008, pp. 327–328)

eating disorder A pathological obsession with getting and staying thin. The best-known eating disorders are *anorexia nervosa* and *bulimia nervosa*.

anorexia nervosa A potentially life-threatening eating disorder characterized by pathological dieting (resulting in severe weight loss and, in females, loss of menstruation) and by a distorted body image.

As these quotations from "pro-anorexia" social network sites show, **eating disorders** differ from "normal" dieting. Here, eating becomes a person's sole focus in life. Imagine waking up and planning each day around eating (or not eating). You monitor every morsel. You are obsessed with checking and rechecking your weight. Or you have the impulse to gorge every time you approach the refrigerator or buy a box of candy at the store. Let's now explore three classic forms these fixations take: anorexia, bulimia, and binge eating disorder.

Anorexia nervosa, the most serious eating disorder, is defined by self-starvation—specifically to the point of reaching 85 percent of one's ideal body weight or less. (This means that if a girl should weigh 110 pounds, she now weighs less than 95 pounds.)

Another common feature of this primarily female disorder is that leptin levels have become too low to support adult fertility and the girl stops menstruating. A hallmark of eating disorders—among both girls and boys—is a distorted body image (Espeset and others, 2011). Even when people look skeletal, they feel fat. They often compulsively exercise, running for hours and abandoning their other commitments to spend every day at the gym (Holland, Brown, & Keel, 2014).

People with eating disorders may be disconnected from reality, denying that their symptoms apply to them ("Oh no, I don't binge and purge") (Gratwick-Sarll and others, 2016). Sometimes they literally don't see their true body size: As a girl named Sarah commented: "I remember . . . passing an open door and saw myself in the mirror . . . and thought 'Oh gosh, she is thin!' But then when I understood that it was actually me, I didn't see me as thin anymore" (quoted in Espeset and others, 2011, p. 183).

Anorexia is a life-threatening disease. People who drop to two-thirds of their ideal weight or less need to be hospitalized and fed—intravenously, if necessary—to stave off death (Diamanti and others, 2008). A student of mine who now runs a self-help group for people with eating disorders provided a vivid reminder of the enduring physical toll anorexia can cause. Alicia informed the class that she had permanently damaged her heart muscle during her bout with this devastating disease.

Bulimia nervosa is typically not life threatening because the person's weight often stays within a normal range. However, because this disorder involves frequent binging (at least once weekly eating sprees in which thousands of calories may be consumed in a matter of hours) and either purging (getting rid of the food by vomiting or misusing laxatives and diuretics) or fasting, bulimia can seriously compromise health. In addition to producing deficiencies of basic nutrients, the purging episodes can cause mouth sores, ulcers in the esophagus, and the loss of tooth enamel due to being exposed to stomach acid.

Binge eating disorder, which first appeared in the *Diagnostic and Statistical Manual (DSM-5)* in 2013, involves recurrent out-of-control eating. The person wolfs down huge quantities of food and then may be wracked by feelings of disgust, guilt, and shame. This mental disorder was added to the *DSM-5* because (no surprise) it is intimately tied to obesity and so presents a serious threat to health (Myers & Wiman, 2014). Binge eating disorder, like anorexia and bulimia, can also wreak havoc on a person's life (Goldschmidt and others, 2014).

How common are these mainly female teenage and young-adult disorders? In one 8-year-long community survey, binge eating was most prevalent, affecting roughly 3 in 100 young women over that time; bulimia ranked second (at 2.6 in 100). Thankfully, the most serious condition, anorexia, struck only 8 out of 1,000 girls. The bad news is that subclinical (less severe) forms of eating disorders may affect an astonishing 18 million people in the United States at some point in their lives (Forbush & Hunt, 2014).

What causes these conditions? Twin studies strongly suggest anorexia and bulimia have a hereditary component (Striegel-Moore & Bulik, 2007). Whether due to shared genetic propensities to develop these disorders or parents with their own eating issues continually reinforcing the message ("There is *nothing* worse than being fat!"), these debilitating preoccupations tend to be passed down from parents to children (Lydecker & Grilo, 2016). One strong, nonspecific risk factor that provokes eating disorders involves internalizing issues—worrying excessively (Sala & Levinson, 2016), being depressed, and experiencing intense mood fluctuations (Lavender and others, 2016; Munch, Hunger, & Schweitzer, 2016). When temperamentally vulnerable children are teased about their weight and internalize the

bulimia nervosa
An eating disorder characterized by at least biweekly cycles of binging and purging in an obsessive attempt to lose weight.

binge eating disorder
A newly labeled eating disorder defined by recurrent, out-of-control binging.

What causes teenage girls to develop eating disorders? This condition is apt to be provoked by varying forces.

Jamie Grill/The Image Bank/Getty Images

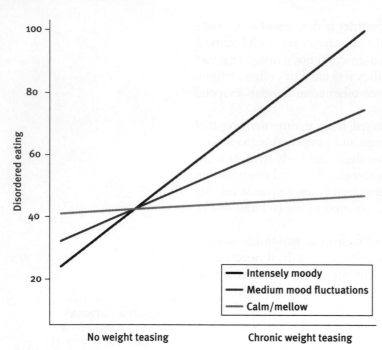

Intensely moody
Medium mood fluctuations
Calm/mellow

No weight teasing   Chronic weight teasing

FIGURE 8.6: The interaction between "mood fluctuations," weight teasing, and pathological eating among a sample of girls: This chart shows that when girls are intensely moody, being teased about weight is likely to escalate into eating disorder symptoms; but for mellow girls, weight-teasing has no impact on problematic eating.

Data from Douglas and Varnado-Sullivan, 2016, p. 171.

thin ideal, eating disorders can flare up (Douglas & Varnado-Sullivan, 2016; see Figure 8.6).

Researchers find that teens with eating disorders have other symptoms: insecure attachments (Munch, Hunger, & Schweitzer, 2016) and an extreme need for approval (Abbate-Daga and others, 2010). These children tend to be perfectionists (Lavender and others, 2016), prone to bouts of intensely low self-worth (Fairchild & Cooper, 2010). At bottom, teenagers with eating disorders have low *self-efficacy*—they feel out of control of their lives.

Table 8.2 offers a summary checklist for determining whether a teenager you love is at risk for developing an eating disorder. Still, if you know a young person who is struggling with this issue, there is brighter news. Most adolescents grow out of eating problems as they get older and construct a satisfying adult life (Keel and others, 2007). And, contrary to popular opinion, therapy for eating disorders works!

Table 8.2: Is a Teenager at Risk for an Eating Disorder? A Checklist

(Background influences: Has this child reached puberty? Is this child female?)

1. Does this teen have parents with eating issues?

2. Is she prone to worry, and does she have intense mood swings?

3. Does this girl have insecure attachments, set excessively high standards for her behavior, and have an overpowering need to be liked?

4. Does this child have very low self-efficacy?

5. Has this child been continually teased about her weight, and responded by vigorously internalizing the idea, "I *must* be thin"?

INTERVENTIONS Improving Teenagers' Body Image

Perhaps the best place to begin to treat young people with eating disorders is to examine how girls who embrace their bodies reason and think. These adolescents do not deny their "imperfections," but focus on their physical pluses. They care about their health—eating nutritious foods, appreciating what their bodies can do (Frisén & Holmqvist, 2010). They feel accepted for their bodies and avoid abusing cigarettes or alcohol (Andrew, Tiggemann, & Clark, 2016). They tend to be spiritually oriented (Boisvert & Harrell, 2013) and understand what *really* makes people beautiful in life. As one woman named Heather put it: "You have to remind yourself that even though [the thin ideal] is what [the media are all about] . . . promoting, self-esteem really looks the best" (Wood-Barcalow, Tylka, & Augustus-Horvath, 2010, p. 115).

Heather's remarks explain why a popular eating-disorder treatment (called *dialectic behavior therapy*) teaches meditation and strategies to promote self-efficacy (feeling in control of one's life) (Tanofsky-Kraff and others, 2015). Therapists have devised other creative approaches, such as repeatedly exposing women to video images of themselves, to train them to see their real body size (Trentowska, Svaldi, & Tuschen-Caffier, 2014).

One innovative treatment ignores *any* underlying psychological causes. Some therapists have had success by keeping the girl's body temperature warm and training her in the appropriate amount to eat via a scale under a plate that measures her intake (Bergh and others, 2013).

Although eating disorders have the reputation of being hard to cure, the reverse seems true. This may explain why therapists who treat these young people have lower burnout rates than do their colleagues (Thompson-Brenner, 2013; Warren and others, 2013) and find such personal meaning in this work (Zerbe, 2013).

The same upbeat message is typical of much (but not all) of the research relating to our final topic: teenage sex.

Tying It All Together

1. Mirai, an eleventh grader, tells you, "I am ugly," but knows she is terrific in sports and academics. According to Harter's studies, is Mirai likely to have high or low self-esteem?

2. Amy is regularly on a diet, trying for that Barbie-doll figure. Jasmine, who is far below her ideal body weight, is always exercising and has cut her food intake down to virtually nothing. Sophia, whose weight is normal, goes on eating sprees followed by purges every few days. Clara has regular, out-of-control eating sprees, after which she says she feels like a bloated "blimp." Identify which girls have an eating disorder, and name each person's specific problem.

3. Pick which three female teens seem protected from developing an eating disorder: *Cotonya, whose role model is Beyoncé; Caroline, who has high self-efficacy; Cora, who has a twin brother; Connie, who exercises for an hour every day.*

4. Eating disorders are very hard to treat—*true* or *false*?

Answers to the Tying It All Together questions can be found at the end of this chapter.

Sexuality

548: Immculate ros: Sex sex sex that all you think about?

559: Snowbunny: people who have sex at 16 r sick:

560: Twonky: I agree

564: 0Oo0CaFfEinNe; no sex until ur happily married—Thtz muh rule

566: Twonky: I agree with that too.

567: Snowbunny: me too caffine!

(quoted in Subrahmanyam, Greenfield, & Tynes, 2004, p. 658)

Sex is the elephant in the room of teenage life. Everyone knows it's a top-ranking issue, but the adult world often shies away from mentioning it. Celebrated in the media, minimized or ignored by parents ("If I talk about it, I'll encourage my child to do it") (see Elliot, 2012; Hyde and others, 2013), the issue of when and whether to have sex is left for teenagers to decide on their own as they filter through conflicting messages and—as you can see above—vigorously stake out their positions in on-line chats.

It is a minefield issue that contemporary young people negotiate in different ways. Poll your classmates. Some people, as with the teenagers quoted above, may advocate abstinence, believing that everyone should remain a virgin until marriage. Others probably feel that having sex within a loving relationship is fine. Some students, if they are being honest, will admit, "I want to try out the sexual possibilities, but I promise to use contraception!"

LEARNING OUTCOMES

- Outline recent trends in teenage sexuality.
- Explore forces influencing the transition to intercourse.
- Critique the sexual double standard and school-based sex education.

This increasing acceptability (within limits) of carving out our own sexual path was highlighted in sexual surveys polling U.S. high school seniors in 1950, 1972, and 2000 (Caron & Moskey, 2002). Over the years, the number of seniors who decided that it's OK for teenagers to have sex shot up from a minority to more than 70 percent. But in the final, turn-of-the-century poll, more teens agreed that a person could decide to not have sex and still be popular. Most felt confident they would use birth control when they were sexually active and could wait to have intercourse until they got married. How are these efficacious attitudes translated into action? Let's begin our exploration at the sexual starting gate—with desire.

Exploring Sexual Desire

David, age 14: Since a year or so ago, I just think about sex and masturbation ALL THE TIME! I mean I just think about having sex no matter where I am and I'm aroused all the time. Is that normal?

Expert's reply: Welcome to the raging hormones of adolescence!

(adapted from a teenage sexuality on-line advice forum)

At what age does sexual desire begin? Although scientists had long assumed that the answer was during puberty, when testosterone is pumping through the body, research with gay adults caused them to rethink this idea. When gay women and men were asked to recall a watershed event in their lives—the age when they first realized that they were physically attracted to a person of the same sex—their responses centered around age 10. At that age, the output of the adrenal androgens is rising but testosterone production has not yet fully geared up (McClintock & Herdt, 1996). So our first sexual feelings seem programmed by the adrenal androgens and appear before we undergo the visible changes of puberty, by about fourth grade!

How do sex hormone levels relate to teenagers' sexual desires? According to researchers, we need a threshold androgen level to prime our initial feelings of desire (Udry, 1990; Udry & Campbell, 1994). Then, signals from the environment feed back to heighten interest in sex. As children see their bodies changing, they think of themselves in a new, sexual way. Reaching puberty evokes a different set of signals from the outside world. A ninth-grade boy finds love notes in his locker. A seventh-grade girl notices men looking at her differently as she walks down the street. The physical changes of puberty and how outsiders react to those changes usher us into our lives as sexual human beings. Which young people act on those desires by having intercourse as teens?

Who Is Having Intercourse?

Today, the average age of first intercourse in the United States is 17.8 for women and 18 for men (Finer & Philbin, 2014). But about 1 in 8 children make a "sexual debut" by age 15 (Guttmacher Institute, 2014; see also Figure 8.7).

As ecological, developmental systems theory suggests, a variety of forces predict what researchers call an earlier *transition to intercourse*. One influence, for both boys and girls, is biological—being on an earlier puberty timetable. Ethnicity and socio-economic status (SES) also matter. African Americans and lower-income males are more apt to be sexually active at younger ages (Finer & Philbin, 2014; Moilanen and others, 2010; Zimmer-Gembeck & Helfand, 2008).

Personality makes a difference. Teens who are more impulsive—that is, those with externalizing tendencies—are apt to make the transition earlier (Moilanen and others, 2010). For European American girls, one study suggested that having a risk-taking personality and low social self-worth correlated with being advanced sexually—that is, engaging in pre-intercourse activities such as fondling at age 12 (Hipwell and others, 2010). Conversely, also for girls, having religious parents predicts staying a virgin because it makes it more likely that a teen will have close church friends who agree that abstinence is the way to go (Landor and others, 2011).

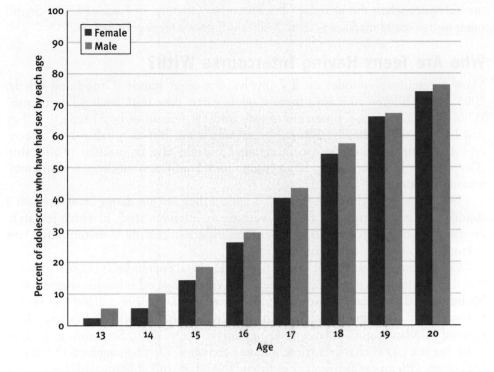

FIGURE 8.7: Percent of U.S. teens who have had intercourse, at different ages: This chart pinpoints late adolescence as the tipping point when most American teens have had sex. But it also shows (not unexpectedly) that intercourse rates rise dramatically with age.

Data from Guttmacher Institute, 2014.

This brings up the crucial role of peers. As I described in the discussion of early-maturing girls, we can predict a teenager's chance of having intercourse by looking at the company she (or he) chooses. Having an older boyfriend or girlfriend (no surprise) raises the chance of a child's becoming sexually active (Martin, 1996). In fact, scientists can make precise statistical calculations of a teen's intercourse odds based on the number of people in that child's social circle who have gone "all the way" (Ali & Dwyer, 2011). So, just as with other aspects of human behavior, to understand whether a teen is sexually active, look at the values and behaviors of his (or her) group.

You also might want to look at what a child watches on TV. In one fascinating study, researchers were able to predict which virgin boys and girls became sexually active from looking at their prior TV watching practices. Teens who reported watching a heavy diet of programs with sexually oriented talk, especially in mixed gender groups, were twice as likely to have intercourse in the next year as the children who did not watch such shows (Collins and others, 2004).

Since sexual experiences (affairs, and so on) are a common media theme, we might predict that simply watching a good deal of television would promote an earlier transition to intercourse. We would be wrong. With any media, it's the content that matters—whether a child prefers sex-laced cable channels (Bersamin and others, 2008), gravitates to Internet porn, or avidly consumes magazines like *Cosmo* rather than sticking to *Seventeen* (Walsh, 2008).

Should we blame *Cosmo* reports such as "101 Ways to Drive Him Wild in Bed" for *causing* teenagers to start having sex? A bidirectional influence is probably in operation here. If a teenager is *already* interested in sex, that boy or girl will gravitate toward media that fit this passion. For me, the tip-off was raiding my parents' library to read the steamy scenes in that forbidden book, D. H. Lawrence's *Lady Chatterley's Lover*. Today, parents know that their child has entered a different

Is my teenage daughter having intercourse? Researchers can now offer parents precise odds by determining how many people in this crowd of best buddies have gone "all the way."

skynesher/E+/Getty Images

mental space when she abandons the Discovery Channel in favor of MTV. Swimming in this sea of media sex, then, further inflames a teenager's desires.

Who Are Teens Having Intercourse With?

Many intercourse episodes on TV involve one-night stands (Grube and others, 2008). Are children imitating these models when they start having intercourse? With most U.S. teens (70 percent of girls and 56 percent of boys) reporting they first had sex with a steady partner, the answer is no. But as roughly 1 in 5 teens report making the transition to intercourse outside of a committed relationship (Guttmacher Institute, 2014), let's pause to look briefly at what these nonromantic encounters are like.

Do adolescents who have sex with a person they are not dating hook up with a stranger or a good friend? For answers, we have an interview study in which researchers asked high schoolers in Ohio about their experiences with "noncommitted" sex (Manning, Giordano, & Longmore, 2006).

Of the teens who admitted to a nonromantic sexual encounter, 3 out of 4 reported that their partner was a person they knew well. As one boy, who lost his virginity with his best friend described: "I wouldn't really consider dating her . . . but I've known her so long . . . anytime I feel down or she feels down, we just talk to each other" (quoted in Manning, Giordano, & Longmore, 2006, p. 469). Sometimes, the goal of having sex was to change a friendship to a romance. Or a teenager might fall into having sex with an ex-boyfriend or girlfriend: "Well, it kind of happened like towards the end when we were both friends" (quoted in Manning, Giordano, & Longmore, 2006, p. 470).

So far, I have painted a benign portrait of teenage dating and sexual relationships. Not true! According to national surveys, nearly 1 in 10 high school students reports having been physically hurt by a romantic partner in the past year. More than 1 in 3 middle schoolers say they have witnessed violence among their dating peers (Robert Wood Johnson Foundation, 2012). When we think of who perpetrates these aggressive acts, most people immediately put the blame on boys.

🔥 Hot in Developmental Science: Is There Still a Sexual Double Standard?

> It's different for boys, it's like . . . if they have sex with somebody and then they are rewarded . . . and all the guys are just like "That's great!" You have sex, and you're a girl and it's like "Slut." That's how it is . . .
>
> (quoted in Martin, 1996, p. 86)

sexual double standard
A cultural code that gives men greater sexual freedom than women. Specifically, society expects males to want to have intercourse and expects females to remain virgins until they marry and to be more interested in relationships than in having sex.

These complaints from a 16-year-old girl named Erin refer to the well-known **sexual double standard.** Boys are supposed to want sex; girls are supposed to resist. Teenage boys get reinforcement for "getting to home base." Intercourse is fraught with ambivalence and danger for girls: "Should I do it? Will he love me if I do it? Will he love me if I don't? Will I get pregnant? What will my friends and my parents think?"

Basic to the stereotype of the double standard is the idea that girls are looking for committed relationships and that boys mainly want sex. The Ohio study, discussed in the previous section, as well as more recent research conducted in South Africa (Bhana, 2016), offer different views. Feeling emotionally intimate, most teens report, is their main priority. And when a couple does have sex—often in a close relationship—the decision is frequently as difficult for guys as for girls. Read what a boy named Tim had to say:

> I really wanted to save it for marriage, but I was curious and um she was special enough to me. . . . She felt the same way . . . but we . . . [were] both curious . . . and so it just happened.
>
> (quoted in Giordano, Manning, & Longmore, 2010, p. 1007)

Moreover, when sex happens too quickly, as this next quotation shows, boys—as much as girls—were turned off:

> She was like . . . moving too fast . . . like she wanted to have sex with me in the car and I'm like "No" and then she starts touching me and I'm like "I'm cool, I'm cool; I got to go." . . . And I did that and I left. . . . I was just, I don't know; she wasn't the girl I wanted to have sex with. . . . She wasn't the right girl.
>
> (quoted in Giordano, Manning, & Longmore, 2010, p. 1002)

In this study, both male and female teens reported that the decision to have sex was mutual; no one was pressuring anyone else. Or, as another boy named Tim delightfully put it:

> So if a girl says yes and a boy says no; it's a maybe. If a guy doesn't know and a girl says yes, it's yes. . . . If a girl says yes and a guy says yes, it's yes. . . . So I think the women have more control because their opinion matters more in that situation.
>
> (quoted in Giordano, Manning, & Longmore, 2010, p. 1007)

Is it really true, as Tim implies, that females are the main initiators (aggressors) when it comes to sex? Consider this revealing evidence from the virtual world: When researchers analyzed the profile photo comments on a popular Belgian social network site, they found that girls' sexually oriented responses to boys' posted photos far outnumbered boys' comments to the photos posted by girls.

Here are a few enthusiastic female posts that a boy named Kendeman's photo evoked: "You are **** . . . beautiful!" "I just wanted to say this because I think you are wonderfuuuuuul. Nobody can compete with you!" (Quoted from De Ridder & Van Bauwell, 2013, p. 576.)

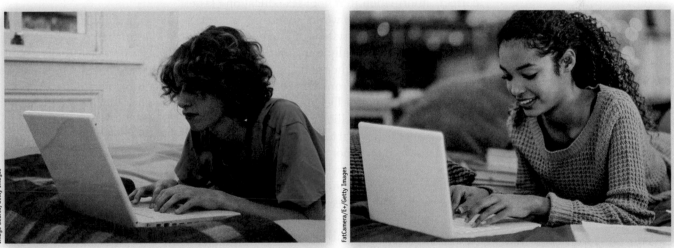

What are the teens who avidly scan the photos on a social network site likely to do? The surprise is that girls may decide to post more assertive, sexually oriented comments than boys.

So, even though the double standard seems firmly in operation, when we hear male teens brag about their exploits or listen to people make comments about "sluts and studs," the reality is complex. Boys want sex in a loving relationship—just like girls (Ott and others, 2006). In terms of making the first sexually oriented moves, either on-line or, sometimes, in the flesh—if anything, an anti-double standard can apply! 🐤

Wrapping Up Sexuality: Contemporary Trends

In summary, the news about teenage sexuality is good. Teenagers today feel more confident about charting their sexual path. Most sexual encounters occur in committed love relationships. The decision to have teenage sex is not typically taken lightly, but in a

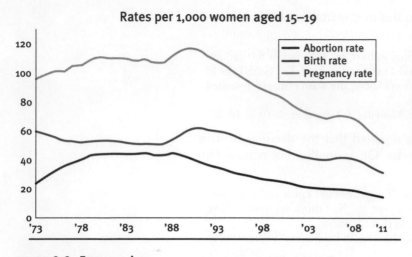

Rates per 1,000 women aged 15–19

— Abortion rate
— Birth rate
— Pregnancy rate

120

100

80

60

40

20

0

'73   '78   '83   '88   '93   '98   '03   '08 '11

FIGURE 8.8: Encouraging snapshots of twenty-first-century teenage sexuality in the United States: The news about adolescent pregnancy is good! For the past 30 years, teen abortion rates and especially adolescent pregnancies and births dramatically declined to reach historic lows in 2011.

Data from American Teens' Sources of Sexual Health Education, 2016.

Because teenagers are passionate for guidelines about how to have loving relationships, this high school couple might love romance education classes!

Ron Levine/Getty Images

climate of caring and mutual decision making for both girls and boys. Girls have far more control in the sexual arena than we think!

These changes are mirrored in the encouraging statistics in Figure 8.8: lower abortion rates and fewer U.S. teenage pregnancies and births. In fact, over the decade spanning the late 1990s to the early twenty-first century, teen pregnancy rates in the United States dipped from more than 5 to 4 per 1,000 girls.

Still, with regard to teenage pregnancy, the United States ranks near the pinnacle of the developed world. While European teens have comparable levels of sexual activity as U.S. adolescents, EU pregnancy rates put the United States to shame (Guttmacher Institute, 2014; McKay & Barrett, 2010). Compared to Western Europe, the prevalence of gonorrhea and chlamydia among U.S. adolescents is very high (Guttmacher Institute, 2011b).

INTERVENTIONS   **Toward Teenager-Friendly Sex Education**

These less-than-flattering statistics bring us back to the issue I alluded to in my discussion of puberty: sex education. Clearly, in its mission to prevent teenage pregnancy, the United States is falling short. Could *one* reason be that teens are not getting the "correct" information in school sex-education classes?

Actually, around the world, school sex education offers a patchwork of slip-shod strategies. Some school systems and countries teach only abstinence. Others discuss contraception and sexually transmitted infections (STIs). Some teach teens about gay and lesbian lives. Other nations have no school sex education at all. The reason comes as no surprise: From Canada to Australia (Goldman & Coleman, 2013) to South Africa (Francis & DePalma, 2014), parents are deeply divided about what to say to teens about sex (Elliot, 2012).

One classic fear is that teaching contraception might encourage teens to have intercourse. This we *know* is not true. Comprehensive sex education not only helps prevent pregnancy, but it can delay the transition to intercourse (UNFPA, 2015). When Irish researchers compared young people in that nation who had high school sex education versus a group who had received no instruction, girls and boys exposed to the classes became sexually active at an *older age* than their peers (Bourke and others, 2014).

Some of you reading this information might think, "OK, maybe that's true, but having my child's school discuss contraception violates my own moral principles because I believe abstinence is the only way to go." Perhaps everyone might agree with this next approach.

For decades, teens have complained that high school sex education is irrelevant to their lives. Adolescents say they are hungering for different information: "How can I develop a relationship?" "What does it mean to fall in love?" (See Martin, 1996.)

Therefore, controversies about whether to teach contraception are missing the point. To really speak to young people's passions, sex education should center on more than sex. We need romance education classes!

This imperative is incredibly timely because, as I'm writing this very page, *adult* sexual violence is center stage as the #MeToo movement has erupted around the globe. Moreover, as I pointed out earlier, while *both* boys and girls care deeply about having loving relationships, sexually abusive behavior can erupt as early as seventh and eighth grades.

The Start Strong program—sponsored by the Robert Wood Johnson Foundation and Blue Cross of California—tries to block the pathway to this adult dysfunction by teaching middle schoolers the skills to relate in a loving way (http://startstrong

.futureswithoutviolence.org/). Older teenage peer leaders facilitate workshops devoted to topics like "Dating Violence," "Healthy Relationships," and—very importantly—"Engaging in Healthy Breakups." Although the government no longer funds this model program, Start Strong embodies the kind of sensitive romance education preteens passionately desire.

Designing effective romance education classes depends on knowing how teenagers reason about life—the topic I will explore in the next chapter.

Tying It All Together

1. A mother asks you when her son will have his first sexual feelings. You answer: *around age 10, before the physical signs of puberty occur/ around age 13 or 14/ in the middle of puberty/ toward the end of puberty.*

2. A friend thinks her teenage daughter may be having sex. So she asks for your opinion. All the following questions are relevant for you to ask *except*:
   a. Are your daughter's friends having sex?
   b. Is your daughter watching a lot of TV?
   c. Is your daughter watching sexually explicit cable channels with her male friends and reading *Cosmo*?
   d. Does your daughter have an older boyfriend?

3. Tom is discussing trends in teenage sex and pregnancy. Which *two* statements should he make?
   a. Today, sex often happens in a committed relationship.
   b. Today, the United States has lower teenage pregnancy rates than other Western nations.
   c. In recent decades, rates of teenage births in the United States have declined.
   d. Today, boys are still the sexual initiators.

4. Imagine you are designing a "model" sex-education program. According to this section, you should focus on:
   a. encouraging abstinence.
   b. providing information about birth control and STIs.
   c. discussing how to have loving relationships.

Answers to the Tying It All Together questions can be found at the end of this chapter.

SUMMARY

Puberty

Today, the physical changes of **puberty** occur during early adolescence, and there can be more than a decade between the time children physically mature and when they enter adult life. Because in agrarian societies a person's changing body used to be the signal to get married, many cultures devised **puberty rites** to welcome the physical changes. The **secular trend in puberty** has magnified the separation between puberty and full adulthood, the fact that **menarche** (and **spermarche**) are occurring at much younger ages.

Two hormonal command centers program puberty. The adrenal glands produce **adrenal androgens** starting in middle childhood. The **HPG axis,** the main system that sets the bodily changes in motion, involves the hypothalamus, the pituitary, and the **gonads** (ovaries and testes), which produce estrogens and **testosterone** (found in both males and females). Leptin levels primed by a variety of environmental influences trigger the initial hypothalamic hormone.

The physical changes of puberty are divided into **primary sexual characteristics, secondary sexual characteristics,** and the **growth spurt.** Although in females puberty begins with the growth spurt and menarche occurs late in the process, the rate and sequence of this total body transformation varies from child to child. Because for males the externally visible changes of puberty occur later and the organs of reproduction are the first to start developing, the puberty timetables of the sexes are not as far apart as they appear.

The striking individual differences in pubertal timing are mainly genetically programmed. African American children tend to reach puberty at younger ages. For girls, being overweight and having stressful family relationships are tied to reaching puberty earlier. These "environmental events" push up the hypothalamic timer, but strangely, mainly for females.

How children feel about their changing bodies varies, depending on the social environment. Breast development often evokes positive emotions. Feelings about menstruation may be more positive among upper middle class girls because today's affluent mothers are more apt to celebrate this change. First ejaculation is rarely discussed. Children tend to be embarrassed about their changing bodies around their other sex parent.

Girls who mature early are at risk of getting into trouble as teens (for example, taking drugs, getting pregnant, or doing poorly in school)—but mainly if they reach puberty in a stressful environment, live in a permissive culture, and get involved with older friends. Because they often end up heavier and shorter, these girls tend to have a poor body image and are more prone to be anxious and depressed.

Based on early research, developmentalists argued against moving pre-teens to middle school; but in general, the key is to provide nurturing schools at this vulnerable age. Parents should discuss puberty with their children, especially their sons. We need to be alert to potential problems with early-maturing girls. We need to begin puberty education earlier and consider implementing global guidelines for elementary school children that focus on respecting one's body.

Body Image Issues

How children feel about their looks is closely tied to their overall self-esteem. Girls tend to feel worse about their looks than boys do, partly because society expects women to adhere to the **thin ideal.** Boys feel pressured to build up their muscles. The female impulse to be thin may have biological roots, but peer pressures and media images play an important role in this widespread passion.

The three **eating disorders** are **anorexia nervosa** (severe underweight resulting from obsessive dieting), **bulimia nervosa** (chronic binging and often purging), and **binge eating disorder** (binging alone). Family pressures, perfectionistic tendencies, mood swings, and low self-esteem put girls at special risk for these problems. Weight teasing can provoke eating disorders in vulnerable children. Eating-disorder interventions take varied forms, and treatments for these problems often do work.

Sexuality

Teenagers today feel freer to make their own decisions about whether and when to have intercourse. While sexual desire is triggered by the adrenal androgens and first switches on at around age 10, sexual signals from the outside world feed back to cause children to become interested in sex.

Factors that predict making the transition to intercourse include race, SES, family and peer influences, and gravitating to sex-laden media. Most teens have their first intercourse experience in a romantic relationship. Dating violence, however, is not very rare, even in the early teens. Still, even though the **sexual double standard** suggests that boys just want sex and girls are interested in relationships, both males and females are mainly interested in love. Ironically, our image of men as the sexual aggressors may operate in the opposite way in the "real world."

The good news about U.S teenage sexuality is that pregnancy rates are declining, although adolescent births are still markedly higher in the United States than in other Western nations. Rather than arguing about whether to teach contraception, some educators are now providing sex-education classes relevant to young people's real concerns: relationships and romance.

KEY TERMS

ANSWERS TO **Tying It All Together** QUIZZES

Puberty

1. Today, puberty occurs a decade or more before we can fully reach adult life.

2. (a) The initial hypothalamic hormone triggers the pituitary to produce its hormones, which cause the ovaries and testes to mature and produce their hormones, which, in turn, produce the body changes. (b) Estrogens, testosterone, and the adrenal androgens.

3. Calista

4. *earlier*

5. an early-maturing girl

6. *Possible recommendations:* Pay special attention to providing nurturing schools in sixth and seventh grade. Push for more adequate, "honest" puberty education at a younger age, possibly in a format—such as on-line—where children can talk anonymously about their concerns. Institute a public awareness program encouraging parents to talk about puberty with a same-sex child. Encourage mothers to speak positively about menstruation and have dads discuss events such as spermarche with sons. Make everyone alert to the dangers associated with being an early-maturing girl and develop formal interventions targeted to this at-risk group. Institute sensitive, school-based "respect your body" discussions—based on the UNESCO guidelines—for children beginning in the early elementary school years.

Body Image Issues

1. unfortunately, low self-esteem

2. Jasmine, Sophia, and Clara have eating disorders. Jasmine has the symptoms of anorexia nervosa; Sophia has the symptoms of bulimia nervosa. Clara has binge eating disorder.

3. Cotonya, Caroline, and Cora (We don't know about Connie— but, if she obsessively exercises just to stay thin, she might be at higher risk.)

4. False, as research suggests eating disorders are treatable.

Sexuality

1. around age 10, before the physical signs of puberty occur

2. b

3. a and c

4. c, discussing how to have loving relationships

CONNECT ONLINE:

 LaunchPad macmillan learning | Check out our videos and additional resources located at: www.macmillanlearning.com

CHAPTER 9

Cognitive, Emotional, and Social Development in Adolescents

Samantha's father began to worry when his daughter was in sixth grade. Suddenly, his sweet little princess was becoming so selfish, so moody, and so rude. She began to question everything, from her 10 o'clock curfew to why poverty exists. She had to buy clothes with the right designer label and immediately download the latest music. She wanted to be an individual, but her clique shaped every decision. She got hysterical if anyone looked at her the wrong way. Worse yet, Samantha was hanging out with the "popular" crowd—smoking, drinking, not doing her homework, cutting class.

Her twin brother, Sam, couldn't have been more different. Sam was obedient, an honor student, captain of the basketball team. He mellowly sailed into his teenage years. Actually, Sam defied the categories. He was smart and a jock. He volunteered to work with disabled children. He effortlessly moved among the brains, the popular kids, and the artsy groups at school. Still, this model child was passionate to vigorously test the limits. The most heart-stopping example happened when the police picked up Sam and a carload of buddies for drag racing. Sam's puzzled explanation: "Something just took over and I stopped thinking, Dad."

If you looked beneath the surface, however, both of his children were great. They were thoughtful, caring, and capable of having deep discussions about life. They just got caught up in the moment and lost their minds when they were with friends. What goes on in the teenage mind?

Think of our contradictory stereotypes about the teenage mind. Teenagers are idealistic, thoughtful, and introspective; concerned with larger issues; pondering life in deep ways; but also impulsive, moody, and out of control. Adolescents are the ultimate radicals, rejecting everything adults say, as well as the consummate conformists, dominated by the crowd and totally influenced by their peers.

These contradictory ideas are mirrored in confusing laws about when society views teens as "adults." In the United States, adolescents can sometimes be tried in adult courts at 14, an age when they are barred from seeing R-rated movies. Mature enough to vote at age 18, U.S. teens are unable to buy liquor until age 21. How is science shedding light on the teenage mind? That is the subject of the chapter you are about to read.

Left: SpeedKingz/Shutterstock.com

LEARNING OUTCOME

• Explain how teenagerhood evolved.

"storm and stress"
G. Stanley Hall's phrase for the intense moodiness, emotional sensitivity, and risk-taking tendencies that characterize the life stage he labeled adolescence.

Setting the Context

Youth are heated by nature as drunken men by wine.

(Aristotle, n.d.)

I would that there were no age between ten and twenty-three . . . , for there's nothing in between but getting wenches with child, wronging the ancientry, stealing, fighting. . . .
(William Shakespeare, *The Winter's Tale*, Act III)

As these quotations illustrate, throughout history, world-class geniuses viewed young people as being hot-headed and out of control. When, in 1904, G. Stanley Hall first identified a life stage characterized by **"storm and stress,"** which he called *adolescence*, he was only echoing these timeless ideas. Moreover, as a youth's mission is to view the world in fresh, new ways, it makes sense that most societies would naturally view each new generation in ambivalent terms—praising young people for their passion and energy; fearing them as a threat.

However, until recently, young people never had time to rebel against society because they took on adult responsibilities at an early age. As I described in Chapter 1, adolescence became a distinct stage of life in the United States only during the twentieth century, when—for most children—going to high school became routine (Mintz, 2004; Modell, 1989; Palladino, 1996).

Look into your family history and you may find a great-grandparent who finished high school or college. But a century ago, most U.S. children left school after sixth or seventh grade to find work (Mintz, 2004). Unfortunately, however, in the 1930s, during the Great Depression, there was little work to be found. Idle young people roamed the countryside, angry and depressed. Alarmed by this situation, the Roosevelt administration proposed laws to lure young people to school. The legislation worked. By 1939, 75 percent of all U.S. teenagers were attending high school.

High school boosted the intellectual skills of a whole cohort of Americans. But it produced a generation gap between young people and their less educated, often immigrant parents and encouraged adolescents to spend their days together in isolated, age-segregated groups. Then, during the 1950s, when entrepreneurs began to target products to this new, lucrative "teen" market, we developed our familiar adolescent culture with its distinctive music and dress (Mintz, 2004; Modell, 1989). The sense of young people bonded together (against their elders) peaked during the late 1960s and early 1970s. With "Never trust anyone over 30" as its slogan, the baby-boom cohort rejected the rules relating to marriage and gender roles, and transformed the way we live (see Chapter 1).

As illustrated in this famous 1930s photograph of a migrant family traveling across the arid Southwest to search for California jobs, during the Great Depression, there was no real adolescence because many children had to work from an early age to help support their families.

This chapter explores adolescence in the contemporary developed world—a time when we expect every teenager to finish high school and so insulate young people from adult responsibilities for almost a decade after they reach puberty. First, I'll examine cognition and teenage emotions, then I'll chart how teenagers separate from their parents and relate to each other in groups.

Before beginning your reading, you might want to take the "Stereotypes About Adolescence: True or False?" quiz in Table 9.1. In the following pages, I'll discuss why each stereotype is right or wrong.

Table 9.1: Stereotypes About Adolescence: True or False?

T/F	1. Adolescents think about life in deeper, more thoughtful ways than children do.
T/F	2. Adolescence is when we develop our personal moral code for living.
T/F	3. Adolescents are highly sensitive to what other people think.
T/F	4. Adolescents are unusually susceptible to peer influences.
T/F	5. Adolescents are highly emotional, compared to other age groups.
T/F	6. Adolescents are prone to taking risks.
T/F	7. Most adolescents are emotionally disturbed.
T/F	8. Rates of suicide are at their peak during adolescence.
T/F	9. Adolescents feel more stressed out with their parents than with their peers.
T/F	10. Getting in with a bad crowd makes it more likely for teenagers to "go down the wrong path."

(Answers: 1. T, 2. T, 3. T, 4. T, 5. T, 6. T, 7. F, 8. F, 9. T, 10. T)

Cognitive and Emotional Development: The Mysterious Teenage Mind

Thoughtful and introspective, but impulsive and out of control; peer-centered conformists and rebellious risk-takers; capable of making mature decisions, but needing to be sheltered from the world: Can teenagers *really* be all these things? In our search to explain these contradictions, let's look at three classic theories of teenage thinking, then explore the research related to teenage storm and stress.

Three Classic Theories of Teenage Thinking

Have a conversation with a 16-year-old and a 10-year-old and you will be struck by the incredible mental growth that occurs during adolescence. It's not so much that teenagers know more than fourth or fifth graders, but that adolescents *think* in a different way. With an elementary school child, you can have a rational conversation about daily life. With a teenager, you can have a rational talk about *ideas*. This ability to reason abstractly about concepts defines Jean Piaget's formal operational stage.

Formal Operational Thinking: Abstract Reasoning at Its Peak

Children in concrete operations look beyond the way objects immediately appear. They realize that when Mommy puts on a mask, she's still Mommy "inside." They understand that when you pour a glass of juice into a different-shaped glass, the amount of liquid remains the same. Piaget believed that during the **formal operational stage**, at around age 12, thinking takes a qualitative leap (see Table 9.2 on page 256). Specifically, according to Piaget, adolescents can think logically in the realm of pure thought.

LEARNING OUTCOMES

- Outline Piaget's, Kohlberg's, and Elkind's perspectives on adolescence.
- Explore adolescent brain development, teenage risk-taking, and storm and stress.
- Predict which teens are at risk for getting into serious trouble and which teens flourish.
- Evaluate how society and high schools can better fit the teenage mind.

formal operational stage Jean Piaget's fourth and final stage of cognitive development, reached at around age 12 and characterized by teenagers' ability to reason at an abstract, scientific level.

Table 9.2: Piaget's Stages: Focus on Adolescence

Age	Name of Stage	Description
0–2	Sensorimotor	The baby manipulates objects to pin down the basics of physical reality.
2–7	Preoperations	Children's perceptions are captured by their immediate appearances: "What they see is what is real." They believe, among other things, that inanimate objects are really alive and that if the appearance of a quantity of liquid changes (for example, if it is poured from a short, wide glass into a tall, thin one), the amount of liquid itself changes.
7–12	Concrete operations	Children have a realistic understanding of the world. Their thinking is really on the same wavelength as that of adults. While they can reason conceptually about concrete objects, however, they cannot think abstractly in a scientific way.
12+	Formal operations	Reasoning is at its pinnacle: hypothetical, scientific, flexible, fully adult. Our full cognitive human potential has been reached.

FIGURE 9.1: Piaget's pendulum apparatus: A task to assess whether children can reason scientifically: Piaget presents the child with the different weights and string lengths illustrated here and shows the child how to attach them to the pendulum (and to one another). Then he says, "Your task is to discover what makes the pendulum swing more or less rapidly from side to side—is it the length of the string, the heaviness of the weight, or the height (and force) from which you release the pendulum?" and watches to see what happens.

Adolescents Can Think Logically About Concepts and Hypothetical Possibilities

Ask fourth or fifth graders to put objects such as sticks in order from small to large, and they will effortlessly perform this concrete operational task. But present a similar verbal challenge—such as "Bob is taller than Sam, and Sam is taller than Bill. Who is the tallest?"—and children are lost. The reason is that only adolescents can logically manipulate concepts in their minds (Elkind, 1968; Flavell, 1963).

Moreover, if you give a concrete operational child a reasoning task that begins, "Suppose snow is blue," she will refuse to go further, saying, "That's not true!" Adolescents in formal operations have no problem tackling that question because, once our thinking is liberated from concrete objects, we can reason about concepts that may *not* be real.

Adolescents Can Think Like Real Scientists

When our thinking occurs on an abstract plane, we can approach problems in a systematic way, devising a strategy to scientifically prove that something is true.

Piaget designed an exercise to reveal this new scientific thought: He presented children with a pendulum apparatus and unattached strings and weights (see Figure 9.1). Notice that the strings differ in length and that the weights vary in size or heaviness. The children's task was to connect the weights to the strings, then attach them to the pendulum, to decide which influence determined how quickly the pendulum swung from side to side. Was it the length of the string, the heaviness of the weight, or the height from which the string was released?

Think about this problem, and you may realize that being systematic is essential in order to solve this task—keeping everything constant but the factor whose influence you want to assess. (This is the defining characteristic of the experimental method described in Chapter 1.) To test whether it's the heaviness of the weight, keep the string length and the height from which you drop it constant, varying only the weight; then isolate another variable, keeping everything else the same. When you vary just the length of the string, you will realize that string length alone determines how quickly the pendulum swings.

Elementary school children, Piaget discovered, approach these problems haphazardly. Only adolescents adopt a true "experimental" strategy to solve reasoning tasks (Flavell, 1963; Ginsburg & Opper, 1969).

How Does This Change in Thinking Apply to Real Life?

The ability to think hypothetically and scientifically explains why it's not until high school that we can thrill to a poetic metaphor or comprehend chemistry experiments (Kroger, 2000). It's only during high school that we can join the debate team and argue the case for and against teachers carrying guns in school, no matter what we *personally* believe. In fact, reaching the formal operational stage explains why teenagers are famous for debating *everything* in their lives. A 10-year-old who wants to stay up till 2 A.M. to watch a new movie will just keep saying, "I don't want to go to bed." A teenager will lay out his case point by point: "Mom, I got enough sleep last night. Besides, I only need six hours of sleep. I can go to bed after school tomorrow."

But do *all* adolescents reach formal operations? The answer is no. Rather than being universal, formal operational reasoning mainly occurs in scientifically oriented Western cultures. In fact, most people in *any* society don't make it to Piaget's final stage.

In one late-twentieth-century study, only a fraction of adults approached the pendulum problem scientifically. When asked to debate a controversial issue such as capital punishment, most people did not even realize that they needed to use logic to construct their case (Kuhn, 1989).

Does cognition *ever* change during adolescence in the way Piaget predicts? The answer is yes. Formal operational skills swing into operation when older teens plan their future lives.

Think back to the skills it took to get into college. You may have learned about your options from an adviser, researched possibilities on the Internet, visited campuses, and constructed different applications to showcase your talents. Then, when you got accepted, you needed to reflect on your future self again: "This school works financially, but is it too large? How will I feel about moving far from home?" Would you have been able to mentally weigh these different alternatives at age 10, 12, or 14?

The bottom line is that reaching concrete operations puts us on the same wavelength as adults. Formal operational thinking allows us to *behave* like adults.

Reaching formal operations enables undergraduates like this young man to be a research collaborator in his professor's chemistry lab.

Kohlberg's Stages of Moral Judgment: Developing Internalized Moral Values

This new ability to reflect on our future allows us to reflect on our values. Therefore, drawing on Piaget's theory, developmentalist Lawrence Kohlberg (1981, 1984) argued that, during adolescence, we can develop a moral code that guides our lives. To measure this moral code, Kohlberg constructed ethical dilemmas, had people reason about these scenarios, and asked raters to chart the responses according to the three levels of moral thought outlined in Table 9.3 on page 258. Before looking at the table, take a minute to respond to the "Heinz dilemma," the most famous problem on Kohlberg's moral judgment test:

Discussing your plans with an adviser and realistically assessing your interests and talents involve the future-oriented adult thinking that only becomes possible in late adolescence. So, even if they don't reason at the formal operational level on Piaget's laboratory tasks, these high school seniors are probably firmly formal operational in the way they think about their lives.

> A woman was near death from cancer. One drug might save her. The druggist was charging . . . ten times what the drug cost him to make. The . . . husband, Heinz, went to everyone he knew to borrow the money but he could only get together about half of what it cost. [He] asked the . . . druggist to sell it cheaper or let him pay later. But the druggist said NO! Heinz broke into the man's store to steal the drug. . . . Should he have done that? Why?
>
> (adapted from Reimer, Paolitto, & Hersh, 1983)

Table 9.3: Kohlberg's Three Levels of Moral Reasoning, with Sample Responses to the Heinz Dilemma

Preconventional Thought

Description: Person operates according to a "Will I be punished or rewarded?" mentality.

Reasons given for acting in a certain way: (1) To avoid getting into trouble or to get concrete benefits. (2) Person discusses what will best serve his own needs ("Will it be good for me?"), although he may also recognize that others may have different needs.

Examples: (1) Heinz shouldn't steal the drug because then the police will catch him and he will go to jail. (2) Heinz should steal the drug because his wife will love him more.

Conventional Thought

Description: Person's morality centers on the need to obey society's rules.

Reasons given for acting in a certain way: (1) To be thought of as a "good person." (2) The idea that it's vital to follow the rules to prevent a breakdown in society.

Examples: (1) Heinz should steal the drug because that's what "a good husband" does; or Heinz should not steal the drug because good citizens don't steal. (2) Heinz can't steal the drug—even though it might be best—because, if one person decides to steal, so will another and then another, and then the laws would all break down.

Postconventional Thought

Description: Person has a personal moral code that transcends society's rules.

Reasons given for acting in a certain way: (1) Talks about abstract concepts, such as taking care of all people. (2) Discusses the fact that universally valid moral principles transcend anything society says.

Examples: (1) Although it's wrong for Heinz to steal the drug, there are times when rules must be disobeyed to provide for people's welfare. (2) Heinz must steal the drug because saving a human life is more important than every other consideration.

Information from Reimer, Paolitto, & Hersh, 1983.

---

preconventional thought In Lawrence Kohlberg's theory, the lowest level of moral reasoning, in which people approach ethical issues by only considering the personal punishments or rewards of their actions.

conventional thought In Lawrence Kohlberg's theory, the intermediate level of moral reasoning, in which people respond to ethical issues by discussing the need to uphold social norms.

postconventional thought In Lawrence Kohlberg's theory, the highest level of moral reasoning, in which people respond to ethical issues by applying their own moral guidelines apart from society's rules.

If you thought in terms of whether Heinz would be personally punished or rewarded for his actions, you would be classified at the lowest moral level, **preconventional thought.** Responses such as "Heinz should not take the drug because he will go to jail" or "Heinz should take the drug because then his wife will treat him well" suggest that, because your focus is on external consequences (that is, whether Heinz will get in trouble or be praised), you are not demonstrating *any* moral sense.

If you made comments such as "Heinz shouldn't [or should] steal the drug because it's a person's duty to obey the law [or to stick up for his wife]" or "Yes, human life is sacred, but the rules must be obeyed," your response is classified as **conventional thought**—the moral level right where adults typically rank. This shows your morality centers around the need to uphold society's norms.

People who reason about this dilemma using their own moral guidelines *apart* from society's rules are operating at Kohlberg's highest moral level, **postconventional thought.** A response that shows postconventional reasoning might be "Heinz had to steal the drug because nothing outweighs the universal principle of saving a life."

When Kohlberg conducted studies with different age groups, he discovered that at age 13, preconventional answers were universal. By 15 or 16, most children around the world were reasoning at the conventional stage. Yet many of us stop right there. Although some of Kohlberg's adults did think postconventionally, using his *incredibly* demanding criteria, almost no person consistently made it to the highest moral stage (Reimer, Paolitto, & Hersh, 1983; Snarey, 1985).

How Does Kohlberg's Theory Apply to Real Life?

Kohlberg's categories get us to think deeply about our values. Do you have a moral code that guides your actions? Would you intervene, no matter what the costs, to save a person's life? These categories give us insights into other people's moral priorities, too. While reading about Kohlberg's preconventional level, you might have thought: "I know someone just like this. This person has no ethics. He only cares about whether or not he gets caught!"

However, Kohlberg's idea that children can't go beyond a punishment-and-reward mentality is fundamentally wrong. As I described in Chapter 3, our basic sense of ethics naturally kicks in before we begin to speak!

In a classic late-twentieth-century paper, psychologist Carol Gilligan offered a feminist critique of Kohlberg's ideas. Recall that postconventional thinking requires abstractly weighing ideals of justice. Women's morality, Gilligan believes, revolves around concrete, caring-oriented criteria: "Hurting others is wrong"; "Moral people reach out in a nurturing way" (Gilligan & Attanucci, 1988).

Is Kohlberg's scale *valid*? Does the way teenagers reason about artificial scenarios mirror their ethical actions in the real world? Not necessarily. When exceptionally prosocial teenagers (for example, community leaders who set up programs for the homeless) took Kohlberg's test, researchers rated their answers at the same conventional stage as nonprosocial teens! (See Reimer, 2003.)

Actually, it makes perfect sense that the way someone *talks* about morality doesn't necessarily reflect actual behavior. We all know adults who spout the highest ethical principles but act despicably—such as the minister who lectures his congregation about the sanctity of marriage while cheating on his wife, or the chairperson of an ethics committee who has been taking bribes for years.

Still, when Kohlberg describes changes in moral reasoning during adolescence, he makes an important point. Teenagers are famous for questioning society's rules, for seeing the world's injustice, and for getting involved in idealistic causes. Unfortunately, this ability to step back and see the world as it should be, but rarely is, may produce the emotional storm and stress of teenage life.

Elkind's Adolescent Egocentrism: Explaining Teenage Storms

This was David Elkind's (1978) conclusion when he drew on Piaget's concept of formal operations to make sense of teenagers' emotional states. Elkind argued that when children make the transition to formal operational thought at about age 12, they see beneath the surface of adult rules. A sixth-grader realizes that his 10 o'clock bedtime, rather than being carved in stone, is an arbitrary number capable of being contested and changed. A socially conscious 14-year-old becomes acutely aware of the difference between what adults *say* they do and how they act. The same parents and teachers who punish you for missing your curfew or being late to class can't get to the dinner table or arrive at meetings on time.

Taking to the streets to advocate for climate change is apt to be a life-changing experience for these teens. It also is a developmental landmark, as advances in moral reasoning make adolescents exquisitely sensitive to injustice.

According to Elkind, the realization that the emperor has no clothes ("Those god-like adults are no better than me") leads to anger, anxiety, and the impulse to rebel. From arguing with a ninth-grade English teacher over a grade to testing the limits by driving fast, teenagers are famous for protesting anything just because it's "a rule."

More tantalizing, Elkind draws on formal operational thinking to make sense of the classic behavior we observe in young teens—their incredible sensitivity to what other people think. According to Elkind, when children first become attuned to other people's flaws, the feeling turns inward to become an obsession with what others think about their *own* personal flaws. This produces **adolescent egocentrism**—the distorted feeling that one's own actions are at the center of everyone else's consciousness.

Therefore, 13-year-old Melody drives her parents crazy. She objects to everything from the way they dress to how they chew their food. When her mother picks her

adolescent egocentrism David Elkind's term for the tendency of young teenagers to feel that their actions are at the center of everyone else's consciousness.

Look at the worried expressions on the faces of these freshmen cheerleaders and you can almost hear them thinking, "If I make a mistake during the game, everyone will laugh at me for my whole life!" According to David Elkind, the imaginary audience makes daily life intensely humiliating for young teens.

up from school, she will not let this humiliating person leave the car: "Mom, I don't know you!" She does not spare herself from equally harsh critiques: A minuscule pimple is a monumental misery; stumbling and spilling her food on the school lunch line is a source of ultimate shame ("Everyone is laughing at me! My life is over!"). According to Elkind, a facet of adolescent egocentrism called the **imaginary audience** evokes this intense self-consciousness. Young teens, such as Melody, literally feel that they are on stage, with everyone watching everything they do.

A second component of adolescent egocentrism is the **personal fable.** Teenagers feel that they are invincible and that their own life experiences are unique. So Melody believes that no one has ever suffered as disgusting a blemish. She has the *most* embarrassing mother in the world.

These mental distortions explain the exaggerated emotional storms we laugh about during the early adolescent years. Unfortunately, the "It can't happen to me" component of the personal fable may lead to tragic acts. Boys put their lives at risk in drag racing contests because they believe they can never die. A girl does not use contraception when she has sex because, she reasons, "Yes, *other* girls can get pregnant, but not me. And, if I do get pregnant, I will be the center of attention, a real heroine."

imaginary audience
David Elkind's term for the tendency of young teenagers to feel that everyone is watching their every action; a component of adolescent egocentrism.

personal fable David Elkind's term for young teenagers' tendency to believe that their lives are special and heroic; a component of adolescent egocentrism.

Studying Three Aspects of Storm and Stress

Are teenagers unusually sensitive to other people's reactions? Is Elkind (like other observers, from Aristotle to Shakespeare to G. Stanley Hall) correct in saying that risk-taking is intrinsic to being a "hot-headed youth"? Are adolescents really highly emotional and/or likely to be emotionally disturbed? For answers, let's turn now to research that explores these three core aspects of teenage storm and stress.

Are Adolescents Exceptionally Socially Sensitive?

In the last chapter, I described that when they reach puberty, children—especially girls—become attuned to their bodies' flaws. In Chapter 6, I discussed how the passion to fit in socially (and target people who don't!) makes relational aggression explode around fifth or sixth grade. In one revealing study, when researchers asked middle schoolers to list their priorities, pre-teens ranked social success as their top concern. Being in the "popular crowd" was more important than being a scholar, being nice, or even having friends (see LaFontana & Cillessen, 2010)!

Moreover, as Elkind would predict, brain-imaging studies suggest that adolescents are unusually hypersensitive to other people's emotions (Monk and others, 2003). Young teens act impulsively, *specifically* in arousing situations involving their friends (Steinberg, 2016). This tendency—illustrated in the study described in the How Do We Know box—is mirrored in neural changes (Blakemore & Mills, 2014; Peake and others, 2013). Reward regions of the cortex spike when teens make risky decisions, but only when friends watch (A. R. Smith and others, 2015).

So the answer to the question of whether adolescents are more socially sensitive is absolutely yes, especially around the pubertal years!

Are Adolescents Risk-Takers?

> Doing something and getting away with it. . . . You are driving at 80 miles an hour and stop at a stop sign and a cop will turn around the corner and you start giggling. Or you are out drinking or maybe you smoked a joint, and you say "hi" to a police officer and he walks by. . . .
>
> (quoted in Lightfoot, 1997, p. 100)

HOW DO WE KNOW . . .
that adolescents make riskier decisions when they are with their peers?

Teenagers' heightened social sensitivity gives us strong evidence that they do more dangerous things in arousing situations with their friends. A classic, ingenious video study drove this point home scientifically. Researchers (Gardner & Steinberg, 2005) asked younger teenagers (aged 13 to 16), emerging adults (aged 18 to 22), and adults (aged 24 and over) to play a computer game in which they could earn extra points by taking risks, such as continuing to drive a car after a traffic light had turned yellow. They assigned the members of each age group to two conditions: Either play the game alone or in the presence of two friends.

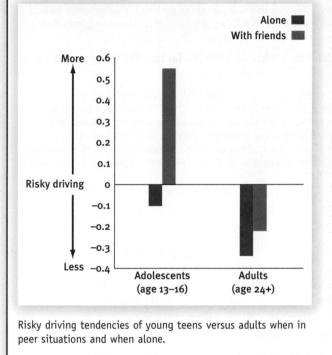

The chart shows the intriguingly different findings for younger teenagers and for people over age 24. Notice that, while being with other people had no impact on risky decision making in the adults, it had an enormous effect on young teens, who were much more likely to risk crashing the car by driving farther after the yellow light appeared when with friends. The bottom-line message: Watch for risky behavior when groups of teenagers are together—a fact to consider the next time you see a car full of adolescents barreling down the road with music playing full blast!

Risky driving tendencies of young teens versus adults when in peer situations and when alone.

The quotation from a teen at the bottom of the previous page, and the research in the previous section, suggest (no surprise) that the second storm-and-stress stereotype is *definitely true*. From the thrill of binge drinking to the lure of driving fast, risk-taking is a basic feature of teenage life (Duell and others, 2016; Steinberg, 2016). In laboratory gambling tasks, researchers pinpoint puberty as the age of maximum risky-decision making for both sexes (Icenogle and others, 2016); but, because of their later pubertal timetable (and, as you will see later, slower brain maturation), the male danger zone extends through the teens (Shulman and others, 2015).

Consider, for instance, yearly nationwide University of Michigan–sponsored polls that track U.S. young people's lives. In examining data spanning 1997 to 2008, researchers found that 1 in 6 mainly male teens had been arrested by age 18. By age 23, the arrest rate slid up to an astonishing almost 1 in 3! (See Brame and others, 2012.) In the 2010 survey, roughly 2 in 10 high school seniors admitted to binge drinking (defined as having five or more drinks at a time for males and four or more drinks in a row for females) (Johnston and others, 2011). (Table 9.4 on the next page showcases some interesting research facts related to alcohol and adolescents.)

Who is likely to risk betting all their chips on the off chance they might get a winning hand? All odds are on these teenage boys.

Table 9.4: Stereotypes and Surprising Research Facts About Alcohol and Teens

Stereotype #1: Teenagers who drink are prone to abuse alcohol later in life.

Research answer: "It depends on *when* you begin." Drinking during puberty is a risk factor for later alcohol problems (Blomeyer and others, 2013). However, during the late teens and early twenties, binge drinking—in Western societies—is often encouraged and then normally tends to decline when people assume adult roles such as marriage and parenthood (Gates, Corbin, & Fromme, 2016). So we can't predict from a person's consumption at these peak-use ages to the rest of adulthood.

Stereotype #2: Involvement in academics and/or athletics protects a teen from abusing alcohol.

Research answer: "It's complicated." While excelling at academics protects children at high genetic risk from drinking to excess as a teen (Benner and others, 2014), heavy athletic involvement is correlated with binge drinking for boys (Barnes and others, 2007; Peck, Vida, & Eccles, 2008). This research points (again) to the pivotal role of peers. Drinking (no surprise) is a prominent feature of the high school jock culture, and more of a "no-no" in the society of scholars, *specifically* during the high school years.

Stereotype #3: Middle childhood problems are risk factors for later excessive drinking.

Research answer: "Both true and surprisingly false." As you might expect, impulse control problems predict problem drinking (Lopez-Caneda and others, 2014). However, two longitudinal investigations—conducted in the United States and Great Britain—revealed that, for girls, high academic achievement was a risk factor for heavy drinking in the early twenties (Englund and others, 2008; Maggs, Patrick, & Feinstein, 2008)! To explain this uncomfortable finding, researchers suggest that girls who do well academically tend to go to college, where, again, the peer culture encourages drinking to excess.

The good news is that, in contrast to our images of rampant teenage substance abuse, most high school seniors do not report using *any* drugs, as you can see in Figure 9.2. A more recent 2016 University of Michigan poll found the *lowest* rates of teenage alcohol use since the survey was instituted four decades ago (Johnston and others, 2016)! The bad news is that—for an alarming fraction of young people in the United States—encounters with the criminal justice system are a depressing feature of modern life.

Younger children also rebel, disobey, and test the limits. But, if you have seen a group of teenage boys hanging from a speeding car, you know that the risks adolescents take can be life threatening. At the very age when they are most physically robust, teenagers—especially males—are most likely to die of preventable causes such as accidents (Dahl, 2004; Spear, 2008). So, yes, parents can worry about their children—particularly their sons—when they haven't made it home from a party and it's already 2 A.M.!

Are Adolescents More Emotional, More Emotionally Disturbed, or Both?

Given this information, it's no surprise that the third major storm-and-stress stereotype is also correct: Adolescents are more emotionally intense than adults. Developmentalists could not reach this conclusion by using surveys in which they asked young people to reflect on how they *generally* felt. They needed a method to chart the minute-to-minute ups and downs of teenagers' emotional lives.

Imagine that you could get inside the head of a 16-year-old as that person went about daily life. About 40 years ago, Mihaly Csikszentmihalyi and Reed Larson (1984) accomplished this feat by devising a procedure called the **experience-sampling technique.** The researchers asked students at a suburban Chicago high school to carry pagers programmed to emit a signal at random intervals during each day for a week.

experience-sampling technique A research procedure designed to capture moment-to-moment experiences by having people carry pagers and take notes describing their activities and emotions whenever the signal sounds.

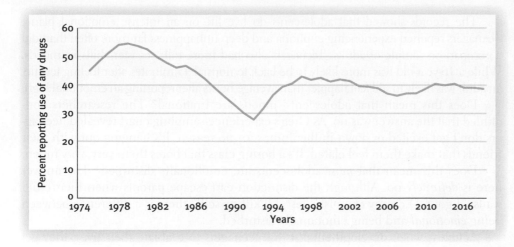

FIGURE 9.2: Trends in prevalence of illicit drug use, reported by U.S. high school seniors from the mid-1970s to 2016: Contrary to our stereotypes, only 2 in 5 U.S. high school seniors report using any illicit drugs (including alcohol) over the past year. Notice also that drug use was actually somewhat more common during the late 1970s and early 1980s—among the parents of today's teens, during their own adolescence.

Data from Johnston and others, 2016.

When the beeper went off, each teenager filled out a chart like the one shown in Figure 9.3. Notice that when you look at Greg's record, the experience-sampling procedure gives us insights into what experiences make teenagers (and people of other ages) feel joyous or distressed. Let's now look at what the charts revealed about the intensity of adolescents' moods.

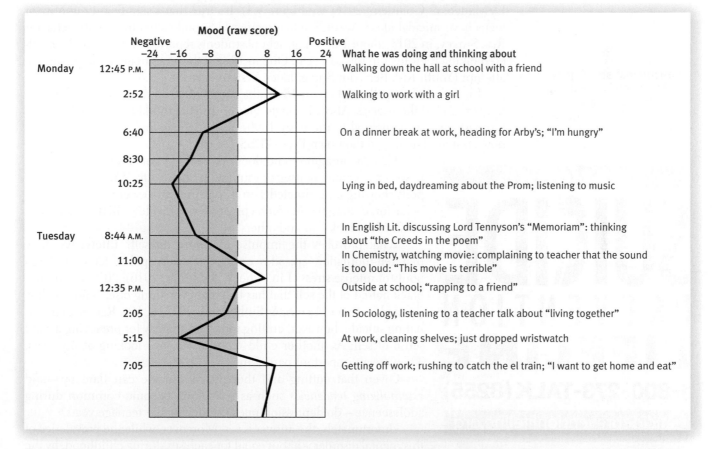

FIGURE 9.3: Two days in the life of Gregory Stone: An experience-sampling record: This chart is based on two days of self-reports by a teenager named Greg Stone, as he was randomly beeped and asked to rate his moods and what he was doing at that moment. By looking at Greg's mood, can you identify the kinds of activities that he really enjoys or dislikes? Now, as an exercise, you might want to monitor your own moods for a few days and see how they change in response to your own life experiences. What insights does your internal mental checklist reveal about which activities are most enjoyable for you?

Data from Csikszentmihalyi & Larson, 1984, p. 111.

The records showed that adolescents do live life on an intense emotional plane. Teenagers reported experiencing euphoria and deep unhappiness far more often than did a comparison sample of adults. Teenagers also had more roller-coaster shifts in moods. While a 16-year-old was more likely to be back to normal 45 minutes after feeling terrific, an adult was likely to still feel happier than average hours after reporting an emotional high.

Does this mean that adolescents' moods are irrational? The researchers concluded that the answer was no. As Greg's experience-sampling chart revealed, teenagers don't get excited or down in the dumps for no reason. It's hanging out with their friends that make them feel elated. It's a boring class that bores them very, very much.

Does this mean that *most* adolescents are emotionally disturbed? The answer here is *definitely* no. Although the distinction can escape parents when their child wails, "I got a D on my chemistry test; I'll kill myself!" there is a difference between being *emotional* and being emotionally disturbed.

Actually, when developmentalists ask teenagers to evaluate their lives, they get an upbeat picture of how young people generally feel. Most adolescents around the world are confident and hopeful about the future (Gilman and others, 2008; Lewin-Bizan and others, 2010). In one U.S. poll, researchers classified 4 out of 10 adolescents as "flourishing"—efficacious, zestful, connected to family and friends. Only 6 percent were "languishing," totally demoralized about life (Keys, 2007).

So the stereotype that most teenagers suffer from emotional problems is false. Still, the picture is far from rosy. Adolescents' risk-taking propensities make the late teens peak crime years (DeMatteo, Wolbransky, & LaDuke, 2016; Heilbrun, DeMatteo, & Goldstein, 2016; see Figure 9.4). It's true that a significant minority of teens have suicidal ideas. According to a regular U.S. poll called the Youth Behavior Risk Survey, in 2015, about 1 in 6 high school students reported that they had considered taking their lives in the past year. One in 12 said they had made a minor suicide attempt (Youth Risk Behavior Surveillance System [YRBSS], n.d).

I must emphasize that (at about 18 deaths per 100,000 teens) very, very few adolescents *do* kill themselves. Also, although rates of suicidal thinking rose slightly over the past 5 years, compared to the early 1990s, fewer twenty-first-century U.S. teens now contemplate taking their own lives (YRBSS, n.d).

nonsuicidal self-injury Acts of self-mutilation, such as cutting or burning one's body, to cope with stress.

Thankfully, a miniscule fraction of teens actually take their own lives, possibly in part due to the heroic efforts of organizations such as the one featured in this poster.

This encouraging trend does not apply to **nonsuicidal self-injury**, however, meaning cutting or mutilating one's body. With international polls showing an estimated 1 in 4 to 1 in 6 adolescents reporting this behavior, cutting has become epidemic worldwide (Giletta and others, 2012; Muehlenkamp and others, 2012).

What provokes the impulse to injure oneself? Interviews show that self-mutilation episodes erupt when susceptible teens undergo bouts of intense stress (Liu, Cheek, & Nestor, 2016): "It's due to pure black hatred of the self that has failed at everything else," said one boy (quoted in Breen, Lewis, & Sutherland, 2013, p. 59). Rather than signaling suicide, however, cutting may be a strategy for *preserving* a solid sense of self: As another child reported, "I love looking at my scars. They are an important part of me. . . ." (p. 60).

Given that cutting and thoughts of suicide can flare up—and *externalizing tendencies* such as risk-taking become common during adolescence—do depression rates rise during the teenage years?

Unfortunately, the answer is yes. Moreover, while the prevalence of this mental disorder is about equal for each sex during childhood, by the mid-teens, the adult gender pattern kicks in. Throughout life, women are roughly twice as susceptible to depression as are men. So, while they are worried about their acting out teenage sons, parents might be also concerned about their daughters becoming depressed during the adolescent years (see Oldehinkel & Bouma, 2011, for a review).

FIGURE 9.4: **Frequency of arrests by age in a California study of offenders:** This chart, although describing California statistics, reflects the standard pattern around the world. The peak years for law breaking are the late teens, after which criminal activity declines.

Data from Natsuaki, Ge, & Wenk, 2008.

Depression rates may escalate during adolescence because the hormonal changes of puberty make the teenage brain more sensitive to stress (Romeo, 2013). But why is depression a mainly female disorder? Are women biologically primed to internalize their problems when under stress? We do not know. What we do know is that if a child's fate is to battle *any* serious mental health disorder, from depression to schizophrenia, that condition often has its onset in late adolescence or the early emerging-adult years.

Moreover, I believe that the push to be socially successful (or popular) may explain *many* classic distressing symptoms during the early teens.

Hot in Developmental Science: A Potential Pubertal Problem—Popularity

Young teens' drive for social status, for instance, accounts for why academic motivation often takes a nosedive in middle school (LaFontana & Cillessen, 2010; Li & Lerner, 2011). Worse yet—because at this age it can be "cool" to rebel—for aggressive children, being in the "popular group" is a risk factor for failing in school (Troop-Gordon, Visconti, & Kuntz, 2011). Therefore, chasing popularity has academic costs. Moreover, young teens may be faced with a difficult choice: "Either be in the 'in crowd' or care about school" (Blakely-McClure & Ostrov, 2016; Wilson, Karimpour, & Rodkin, 2011).

Being part of the elite "in crowd" at school is probably a thrilling experience for these girls. But, they may develop some not-so-nice qualities as the price of being at the top of the class status rungs.

Making it into the in crowd has moral costs. Relational aggression, as I described in Chapter 6, helps propel pre-teens into the high-status group (Kiefer & Wang, 2016). As one Italian study showed, adolescents in the "cool" popular group were more apt than their classmates to view unethical behaviors, such as manipulating and deceiving people, as perfectly acceptable, too (Berger & Caravita, 2016).

Finally, because social standing is critical at this age (Molloy, Gest, & Rulison, 2011), feeling rejected by one's peers outweighs poor family relationships in producing teenage anxiety and depression (Haltigan and others, 2017). Therefore, the intense push to be popular may partly explain both the upsurge in *internalizing disorders* and the rise in moral disengagement during the early teens! 🕊

Different Teenage Pathways

So far, I seem to be stereotyping "adolescents" as a monolithic group. This is absolutely not true! Teenagers differ—in their passion to be popular, in their school connectedness, in their tendencies to take risks or get depressed. As diversity at this life stage is the norm, the critical question is, "Who gets derailed and who thrives during this landmark decade of life?"

Which Teens Get into Serious Trouble?

Without denying that serious adolescent difficulties can unpredictably erupt, here are three thunderclouds that foreshadow stormy weather ahead.

At-Risk Teens Tend to Have Prior Emotion Regulation Problems

It should come as no surprise that one thundercloud relates to elementary school externalizing tendencies (DeMatteo, Wolbransky, & LaDuke, 2016). Not only is the lure of getting into trouble overwhelming when children have problems regulating their behavior, but if children are rejected by the mainstream kids, they gravitate to antisocial friends (Ettekal & Ladd, 2015; more about this later).

Therefore, tests of *executive functions*—measures that chart whether girls and boys have difficulty thinking through their behavior—strongly predict adolescent storms. Moreover, getting into trouble at an atypically young age foreshadows delinquent behavior during the teenage years (DeMatteo, Wolbransky, & LaDuke, 2016).

At-Risk Teens Tend to Have Poor Family Relationships

Feeling alienated from one's parents can also be a warning sign of developing storms. When researchers explored the emotions of teens who self-injured, these children often anguished: "My parents are way too critical"; "I can't depend on my mom or dad" (Bureau and others, 2010; You, Lin, & Leung, 2013).

In essence, these young people were describing an insecure attachment. Teenagers want to be listened to and respected. They need to know they are unconditionally loved (Allen and others, 2007). So, to draw on my metaphor about dancing to describe infant attachment in Chapter 4, with adolescents, parents must be exceptionally skillful dancers. They should understand when to back off and when to stay close. In Chapter 7's terms, adolescents require an *authoritative* discipline style.

But since the attachment dance is *bidirectional*, when we see correlations between teenagers' reporting distant family relationships and having troubles, it's not *simply* parents who are at fault. Imagine that you are a 15-year-old who is having unprotected sex, taking drugs, or withdrawing from the world. Would you tell your parents about your life? And when you withdrew to your room or lied about your activities, wouldn't you feel even more alienated? "My family knows nothing about who I am" (Bradley & Coryn, 2013).

Yes, it's easy to *say* that being authoritative is vital in parenting teens. But take it from me (I've been there!), when your teenager is getting into trouble, confronting him about his activities is apt to backfire. So it can be difficult for frantic parents to understand how to *really* act authoritatively in a much-loved son's or daughter's life.

At-Risk Teens Live in a Risk-Taking Environment

Focusing on parent–child relationships neglects the role the social milieu plays in seeding teenage storms. If a child's adored older brother is taking drugs (Solmeyer,

McHale, & Crouter, 2014), and especially if a teen lives in a disorganized, low-efficacy community (Jennings and others, 2016), the chance of getting into trouble accelerates. As *ecological, developmental systems* theory spells out, to *really* help teenagers thrive, we need a nurturing wider world. Now, let's look at who thrives during their teens.

Which Teens Flourish?

> In high school, I connected with my lifelong love of music. I'll never forget that feeling when I got that special prize in band my senior year.

> At about age 15, I decided the best way to keep myself off the streets was to get involved in my church youth group. It was my best time of life.

Suppose this 16-year-old chess whiz had no adults to encourage and nurture his passion. He would probably never have a chance to express his talent and flourish during his teenage years.

As the quotations show, these attributes offer a mirror image of the qualities I just described: Teenagers thrive when they have superior executive functions (Gestsdottir and others, 2010; Urban, Lewin-Bizan, & Lerner, 2010). They flourish when parents reinforce their unique strengths ("You are terrific at the drums! I know you can succeed!") (Jach and others, 2017). A mentor or VIP (very important non-parental adult) can be vital: a caring adviser who spends time with a child and is on the same wavelength, in terms of personality (Futch Ehrlich and others, 2016).

Thriving does not mean staying out of trouble. Many adolescents who are flourishing also engage in considerable risk-taking during their early and middle teens (Lerner and others, 2010). Therefore, testing the limits is a *normal* adolescent experience even among the happiest, healthiest teens (Larson & Grisso, 2016).

And let's not give up on children who *do* get seriously derailed. Developmentalists make a distinction between **adolescence-limited turmoil** (antisocial behavior during the teenage years) and **life-course difficulties** (antisocial behaviors that continue into adult life) (Moffitt, 1993). Perhaps you have a friend who used to stay out all night partying and taking drugs, but later became a responsible parent. Or you may know a "troubled teen" who is succeeding incredibly well after finding the right *person–environment fit at* college or work. (For a compelling example, see the Experiencing the Lifespan feature on page 269.) If so, you understand a main message of the next chapter: We do get more mature during the emerging-adult years. (Table 9.5 offers a checklist so you can evaluate whether a child you love might have a stormy or sunny adolescence.)

adolescence-limited turmoil Antisocial behavior that, for most teens, is specific to adolescence and does not persist into adult life.

life-course difficulties Antisocial behavior that, for a fraction of adolescents, persists into adult life.

Table 9.5: Predicting Whether a Child Is Prone to Teenage Storms or to Flourish: A Section Summary Checklist

Threatening Thunderclouds

1. Does this child have emotion regulation difficulties and is he failing socially?

2. Does this child have distant or conflict-ridden family relationships?*

3. Does this child live in an environment where risk-taking is prized, or is this person being raised in a disorganized, low collective-efficacy neighborhood?

Sunny Signs

1. Does this child have good executive functions and a special talent?

2. Does this child have parents who encourage his or her gifts?

3. Does this boy or girl have an adult mentor?

Information from Masten (2004), p. 315, and the sources in this section.

*As I will describe later in this chapter, conflict (and distancing) from parents predictably occurs during early adolescence.

Wrapping Things Up: The Blossoming Teenage Brain

Now, let's put it all together: the mental growth, the morality, the emotionality, and the sensitivity to what others think. Give teenagers an intellectual problem and they can reason in mature ways. But younger teens tend to be captivated by popularity and get overwhelmed in arousing situations when they are with their friends.

According to Laurence Steinberg (2016), these qualities make sense when we look at the developing brain. Puberty heightens the output of certain neurotransmitters, which provokes the passion to take risks (Guerri & Pascual, 2010). At the same time, the insulating *myelin sheath* continues to grow until our twenties (see Table 9.6). As Steinberg explains, it's like starting the engine of adulthood with an unskilled driver. This heightened activation of the "socioemotional brain," with a cognitive control center still "under construction," makes adolescence a potentially dangerous time.

Studies around the world support Steinberg's dual-brain function explanation for teenage risk-taking (Shulman and others, 2015). From Kenya to China to Colombia, "sensation seeking" peaks during the early teens, while self-control steadily grows into the emerging-adult years (Steinberg, 2016). As I've highlighted in earlier chapters, it takes more than two decades for the *frontal lobes* to grow up.

Table 9.6: Teenage Brain-Imaging Questions and Findings

Question #1: How does the brain change during adolescence?

Answer: *Dramatically, in different ways.* Frontal lobe gray matter (the neurons and synapses) peaks right before puberty and then gradually declines due to pruning—that is, the cortex "gets thinner" over the teenage years. In contrast, white matter (the myelin sheath) steadily grows into the twenties.

Question #2: Are there gender differences in brain development?

Answer: *Yes.* Because girls reach puberty earlier, they are on a faster brain-development timetable than boys; their gray matter peaks at a younger age (10 for girls and 12 for boys), and white matter increases at an accelerated pace in the female brain. Do these gender differences explain why teenage boys are far more likely to get into trouble with the law? Many researchers believe the answer is yes.

Question #3: Do the brain-imaging findings mirror the behavioral research in this section?

Answer: *Not really.* Although the teen brain generally matures in the ways I've described, studies that explore differences in specific brain-activation patterns of deviant teens versus their more well-adjusted age mates have confusing results.

Conclusion: While we do have good general data on teenage brain development, we still have far to go in neuroscientifically mapping the teenage mind.

Information from Bava and others, 2010; Bjork & Pardini, 2015; Blakemore, Burnett, & Dahl, 2010; Bramen and others, 2011; Burnett and others, 2011; Herting & Sowell, 2017; Koolschijn & Crone, 2013; Lenroot & Giedd, 2010; Luciana, 2010; Moreno & Trainor, 2013; Negriff and others, 2011; Shulman and others, 2015.

But from an evolutionary standpoint, it is logical to start adolescence with an accelerated emotional engine. Teenagers' risk-taking tendencies propel them into the world. Their passion to bond with their peers is vital to leaving their parents and forming new attachments as adults. The teenage brain is beautifully tailored to help young people make the leap from childhood to adult life (Dahl, 2004; Steinberg, 2008).

INTERVENTIONS Making the World Fit the Teenage Mind

Table 9.7 summarizes these messages in a chart for parents. Now let's explore our discussion's ramifications for society.

Table 9.7: Tips for Parents of Teens

1. Understand that strong emotions may not have the same meaning for your teen as for you. So try not to take comments like "I hate myself" or "I'm the dumbest person in the world" very seriously. Also, during the early teen years, new research—discussed later in this chapter—suggests it's normal for your child to become secretive and rebellious. But just because your teen gets furious at you, don't think she doesn't love you.

2. Understand that, while sampling forbidden activities is normal, if your teen is getting involved in genuinely illegal activities or seems seriously depressed, you do need to be concerned.

3. Understand that your child's peer choices (and peer-group status) offer good hints about his behavior, and that striving to be in the "popular crowd"—while normal—can have unpleasant consequences.

4. Roll with the punches, encourage your child's passions, and enjoy your teenager!

Don't punish adolescents as if they were mentally just like adults. If the adolescent brain is a work in progress, it doesn't make sense to have the same legal sanctions for teenagers who commit crimes that we have for adults. Rather than locking adolescents up, it seems logical that at this young age the focus should be on rehabilitation. As Laurence Steinberg (2016; Shulman & Steinberg, 2016) and virtually every other adolescence expert suggests, with regard to the legal system, "less guilty by reason of adolescence" is the way to go.

Is the U.S. legal system listening to the adolescence specialists? The answer is "a bit." In 2005, the Supreme Court outlawed the death penalty for adolescents and, in 2012, eliminated life sentences without the possibility of parole for teens (Heilbrun, DeMatteo, & Goldstein, 2016). Still, today, as the Experiencing the Lifespan box suggests, judges and prosecutors can decide to transfer some children as young as age 13 (!) out of the juvenile justice system and then try them as adults (Larson & Grisso, 2016). Yes, as my amazing interview with Jason suggests, with luck and a resilient temperament, a shockingly punitive approach can help turn a person around. However, there is no evidence that condemning adolescents to the gulag of dysfunctional adult prisons deters later criminal acts (Fabian, 2011). Do you believe that it's *ever* acceptable to try teenagers as adults?

Experiencing the Lifespan   **Innocently Imprisoned at 16**

If you think the U.S. legal system protects 16-year-olds from adult jail and that citizens can't be falsely incarcerated without a trial, think again. Then, after reading Jason's story, you might link his horrific teenage years to the qualities involved in resilience (discussed in Chapter 7).

I grew up with crazy stuff. My mom was a drug dealer and my dad passed away so I was adopted by my grandparents. I was kicked out of four schools before ninth grade. By age 15, I was involved with a street gang and heavy gun trading in Birmingham, Alabama. I was in a car with some older guys during a drive-by shooting, got pulled over, and that was the last time I saw daylight for over 3 years.

The original charge was carrying a concealed weapon, and I was sent to a juvenile boot camp. Then, two days after

being discharged, detectives were knocking on my door with the full charges: three counts of attempted murder. The arresting officers decided to transfer me to county jail, where I ended up for 19 months. If you go to trial and lose, you get the maximum sentence, 20 years to life, so—even though I was innocent—avoiding trial is the thing you want to do. What happens is that your lawyers keep negotiating plea bargains. First, I was offered 20 to life, with the idea I'd be out in 10 years; then 15 years, then 10. Not very appealing for a 16-year-old kid! Finally, by incredible good luck, I got a lawyer who takes kids from prisons and puts them into rehab facilities, and he convinced the judge that was best for me. I quickly had to take what they offered—being sent to the Nashville Rescue Mission and then a halfway house for 2 years—because my trial date was coming up very soon.

Jail was unbelievable. The ninth floor of the Jefferson County Jail is well known because that's where they send criminals from the penitentiary who have committed the most violent crimes to await trial. My first cellmate had cut a guy's head off. Every time you get to know a group, the next week another group arrives in jail and you have to fight them. The guards were no better. If they didn't like a prisoner, they would persuade inmates to beat the living daylights out of that person.

What helped me cope were my dreams, because you are not in jail in your dreams. I wrote constantly, read all the

time. What ultimately helped was being sent out of state (so I couldn't get involved with my old friends) and, especially, my counselors at the mission. I never met guys so humble; such amazing people. Also, if I got into trouble again, I knew where I could be heading. Scared the heck out of me. Now, everything I do is dependent on being normal. I'm 22. I have good friends but I haven't told anyone anything about my past. I have a 3.5 average. I'm working two jobs. I'll be the first person in my family to graduate college. I want to go to grad school to get my psychology Ph.D.

Pass laws that are user-friendly to the teenage mind. Putting adolescents in adult prisons is counterproductive, simply because this practice exposes the most socially sensitive age group to adults who are apt to encourage criminal acts (Larson & Grisso, 2016). Therefore, it's best to craft legislation that takes teenagers' mental processes into account. One excellent example is graduated driving laws that limit young people from operating cars at night and while in groups. Since these U.S. rules were instituted in the late 1990s, teenage crash rates have declined dramatically, although adolescents still get into more accidents than adults (McCarty & Teoh, 2015). Another approach is to draw on adolescents' peer sensitivities in a positive way.

Provide group activities that capitalize on adolescents' strengths. How can we help teenagers forge growth-enhancing peer relationships and promote their inner development?

> **youth development program** Any after-school program or structured activity outside of the school day that is devoted to promoting flourishing in teenagers.

Youth development programs fulfill this mission. They give adolescents a safe place to explore their passions during the unstructured late afternoon hours, when teens are most prone to get into trouble while hanging out with friends (Hoeben and others, 2016). From 4-H clubs to church groups to high school plays, youth development programs ideally foster qualities that developmentalist Richard Lerner has named the five C's: *competence, confidence, character, caring,* and *connections.* They provide an environment that allows young people to thrive (Lerner, Dowling, & Anderson, 2003; Lerner and others, 2016; Tolan, 2016).

I wish I could say that every youth program fostered flourishing. But as anyone who has spent time at a girls' club or the local Y knows, these settings can also encourage group bullying and antisocial acts (Rorie and others, 2011). Therefore, after-school programs must be well structured and supervised. They have to promote the five C's. And, since youth development programs are voluntary and so tend to be utilized by teenagers who are already coping well, they don't help the very at-risk boys and girls most in need (Ciocanel and others, 2017).

Therefore, to really alter the adolescent experience, it seems more effective to embed enriching offerings into the place every child attends: school. In one heartening study, high schools that featured strong arts programs made students feel more engaged in *all* of their classes (Martin and others, 2013). Intense involvement in high school clubs in particular predicts work success years down the road (Gardner, Roth, & Brooks-Gunn, 2008; Linver, Roth, & Brooks-Gunn, 2009)—which brings me to another important issue. For the sake of *both* their present and future, how can we get *every* teenager connected to school?

Change high schools to provide a better adolescent–environment fit. Adolescents who feel embedded in nurturing schools tend to feel good about themselves (Hirschfield & Gasper, 2011; Lewis and others, 2011) and the world (Flanagan &

Stout, 2010). Just as with day care, as I described in Chapter 4, excellent high schools can offer at-risk teens a vital haven when they are having problems at home (Loukas, Roalson, & Herrera, 2010).

Unfortunately, however, in one disheartening international poll, although teenagers were generally upbeat about other aspects of their lives, they rated their high school experience as only "so-so" (Gilman and others, 2008). How can we turn this situation around?

In surveys, teenagers have said that they are yearning for the experiences that characterize high-quality elementary schools (described in Chapter 7)—autonomy-supporting work that encourages them to think, teachers who respect their abilities (LaRusso, Romer, & Selman, 2008), hands-on courses that are relevant to their lives (Wagner, 2000). Service-learning classes in particular can make an enduring impact on development (McIntosh, Metz, & Youniss, 2005). Here is what one young man had to say about volunteering at a soup kitchen: "I was on the brink of becoming one of those hoodlums the world so fears. This class was one of the major factors in my choosing the right path" (quoted in Yates & Youniss, 1998, p. 509).

These teens are taking great pleasure in serving meals to the homeless as part of their community-service project. Was a high school experience like this life-changing for you?

We also might rethink the school day to take into account teenagers' unique sleep requirements. During early adolescence, the sleep cycle is biologically pushed back (Colrain & Baker, 2011; Feinberg & Campbell, 2010). Because they tend to go to bed after 11 P.M. and must wake up for school at 6 or 7 A.M., the typical U.S. teen sleeps fewer than 7 hours each day (Colrain & Baker, 2011). Worse yet, children who strongly show this evening circadian shift are *generally* at risk for a stormy teenage life. They tend to have poorer family relationships (Díaz-Morales and others, 2014), are often lonely, and are less mentally tough (Brand and others, 2014; Doane & Thurston, 2014). Because sleep deprivation throws the cognitive and emotional systems more out of whack, these adolescents are apt to be impulsive (Peach & Gaultney, 2013) and engage in deviant acts (Telzer, Fuligni, and others, 2013), in addition to (no surprise) doing poorly in class. Might experimenting with starting high school at 10 A.M. promote a better body–school fit?

Could this have been you in high school, particularly toward the end of the week? Do you think we are making a mistake by resisting teenagers' biological clocks and insisting that the school day start at 8 A.M.?

Finally, it's past time to rethink **zero-tolerance policies,** high school rules mandating immediate suspension for any deviant act. This U.S. practice, which exploded during the 1990s, had laudable goals: protecting classmates from violent peers and deterring later criminal acting out. But studies show that being suspended from school *encourages* later delinquency. Schools that take a hard-core zero-tolerance approach make every student feel less connected to their teachers and classes (Daly and others, 2016).

Being expelled, sometimes for infractions as minor as smoking on school grounds, pathologizes normal teenage behavior. It prevents the most vulnerable teens from getting the caring attachment experiences they vitally require (see my discussions in Chapters 4 and 7). What developmentalists evocatively call the **school-to-prison pipeline**—meaning the transition from adolescence-limited turmoil to life-course criminal behavior—can be set in motion when an at-risk, frequently male, teenager is barred from the classroom doors (Daly and others, 2016).

zero-tolerance policies The practice in U.S. public high schools of suspending students after one rule infraction.

school-to-prison pipeline Term referring to the way school expulsion may provoke criminal behavior and incarceration for at-risk teens.

Think back to your high school days. What rules did you find problematic? What allowed you to thrive? How would you change your high school to help teenagers make the most of these special years?

Assuming adult responsibilities right after puberty, like fishing for a living, is what nature intended for our species (see Chapter 8). Therefore, Robert Epstein believes so-called teenage "dysfunction" is produced by a dysfunctional modern society.

Another Perspective on the Teenage Mind

Until now, I've been highlighting the mainstream developmental science message: "Because of their brain immaturity, teens need protection from the world." But might scientists be over-invoking biology to inappropriately label teenagers as out of control?

Consider, for instance, the fact that zero-tolerance school policies can collide with teenagers' natural impulse to sample *all of life.* Furthermore, is teenage risk-taking that dangerous compared to the impulsive activities we engage in *throughout* adulthood—from marrying multiple times, to making unaffordable investments, to starting unprovoked wars (see Willoughby and others, 2013)?

Drawing on these ideas, Robert Epstein has put forth an innovative critique of the immature adolescent brain. Epstein (2010) reminds us that adolescence is an artificial construction. Nature intended us to enter adulthood at puberty. Now young people must languish for a decade under the ill-fitting label "child." How many "predictable" teenage symptoms of storm and stress, Epstein argues, have little to do with faulty frontal lobes and everything to do with a poor contemporary body–environment fit? Do teenagers *really* have immature brains, or are adults to blame for shackling teenagers' minds?

Let's keep these thoughts in mind in the next section, as we turn to explore parent–teenager relationships in depth.

Tying It All Together

1. Katarina, a teacher, is about to transfer from fourth grade to the local high school, and she is excited by all the things that her older students will be able to do. Based on what you have learned about Piaget's formal operational stage and Kohlberg's theory of moral reasoning, pick which *two* new capacities Katarina may find among her students.

    a. The high schoolers will be able to memorize poems.
    b. The high schoolers will be able to summarize the plots of stories.
    c. The high schoolers will be able to debate different ideas even if they don't personally agree with them.
    d. The high schoolers will be able to develop their own moral principles.

2. Eric is a basketball coach. The year-end tournament is tomorrow, and the star forward has the flu and won't be able to play. Terry, last year's number one player, offers to fill in—even though this violates the conference rules. Eric agonizes about the ethical issue. Should he deprive his guys of their shot at the championship, or go against the regulations and put Terry in? How would you reason about this issue? Now, fit your responses into Kohlberg's categories of moral thought.

3. A 14-year-old worries that everyone is watching every mistake she makes; at the same time, she is fearless when her friends dare her to take life-threatening risks like bungee jumping off a cliff. According to Elkind, this feeling that everyone is watching her illustrates _____; the risk-taking is a sign of _____; and both are evidence of the process called _____.

4. Pick which symptom indicates your 15-year-old nephew has a genuine psychological problem: *intense mood swings and social sensitivities/ depression/ a tendency to engage in risky behavior with friends.*

5. Your child has made it into the popular kids' crowd at school. You should feel (pick one): *proud because that means he is able to get along with the kids/ worried because he is at risk for moral disengagement and acting-out behaviors.*

6. There has been a rise in teenage crimes in your town, and you are at the local high school to explore solutions. Given what you know about the teenage mind, which change should you *not* support?
    a. Vigorously implement zero-tolerance policies.
    b. Encourage the school to expand their menu of clubs and service-learning classes.
    c. Think about postponing the beginning of the school day to 10 A.M.

7. Imagine you are a college debater. Use your formal operational skills to argue first for and then against the proposition that society should try teens as adults.

Answers to the Tying It All Together questions can be found at the end of this chapter.

Social Development

LEARNING OUTCOMES

What are teenager–parent interactions like? Now it's time to tackle this question, as I focus on those twin adolescent agendas—separating from parents and connecting with peers.

- Outline how teenagers separate from parents and the special separation issues immigrant teens face.

- Describe cliques, crowds, and teenage peer groups.

- Explain the forces that promote delinquent peer groups, making special reference to gangs.

Separating from Parents

> When I'm with my dad fishing, or when my family is just joking around at dinner—it's times like these when I feel completely content, loved, the best about life and myself.

In their original experience-sampling study, Csikszentmihalyi and Larson (1984) discovered that teenagers' most uplifting experiences occurred when with their families—sharing a joke around the dinner table or having a close moment with Mom or Dad. Unfortunately, however, those moments were few and far between. In fact, while peer encounters were more apt to evoke passionate highs, when adolescents were with their families, unhappy emotions outweighed positive ones 10 to 1.

This tendency to lock horns with parents seems built into the universal adolescent experience, as shown in the global poll illustrated in Figure 9.5. Notice that, while the gap differs from nation to nation, teenagers typically rank stress with parents as more upsetting than stress with peers (Persike & Seiffge-Krenke, 2014).

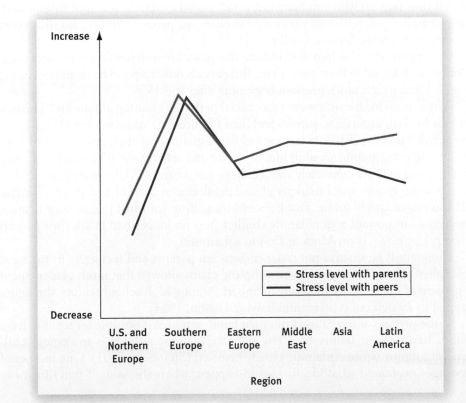

FIGURE 9.5: Mean of parent–child stress versus stress with peers, as reported by teens in various regions of the globe: This chart shows that with the exception of southern Europe, worldwide adolescent stress with parents is more intense than stress with peers.

Data from Persike & Seiffge-Krenke, 2014, p. 499.

The Issue: Pushing for Autonomy

Why does family life produce such teenage pain? As developmentalists point out, if our home life is good, our family is our loving cocoon. However, in addition to being a safe haven, parents are often a source of pain. The reason is that their job is both to love us and to limit us. When this parental limiting function gets into high gear, teenage distress becomes acute.

What do teenagers and their parents argue about? This global poll also offered for teens in every nation insights into specific cultural parenting priorities in different world regions (Persike & Seiffge-Krenke, 2014). In northern Europe and the United States, arguments around academic issues loom large ("I hate that pressure to get good grades!"). For Japanese and Chinese teens, these kinds of school-related conflicts outweigh everything else.

Perhaps because it's crucial in these societies to marry within "one's own group," in the Middle East, micromanaging peer relationships is a major stress ("My parents won't let me see the friends I want!"). In southern Europe, where children still live with their parents into their early thirties, dependency and general parent–child acrimony is a serious concern ("We fight all the time!" "They won't let me grow up!"). More about this in Chapter 10.

But the main issue for teens in *every nation* centers around is independence ("Why can't I do what I want? You have too many rules!"). Moreover, most clashes occur just when peer group pressures reach their peak—around the early teens (Daddis, 2011; De Goede, Branje, & Meeus, 2009).

The Process: Exploring the Dance of Autonomy

Actually, parent–adolescent conflict flares up while children are in the midst of puberty (Steinberg, 2005; Steinberg & Hill, 1978). From an evolutionary perspective, the hormonal surges of puberty may propel this struggle for autonomy ("You can't tell me what to do!"), which sets in motion the dance of separation intrinsic to becoming an independent adult.

How does the dance of autonomy unfold? Based on periodically asking teens questions—such as, "Do your parents know what you do in your free time?" or "Do you tell your parents who you hang out with?"—and exploring parental rules, Canadian researchers offered a motion picture of changing parent–child relationships over the teenage years (Keijsers & Poulin, 2013).

As it turns out, children first initiate the push for independence by becoming secretive and distant in their early teens. But parents only respond by steadily granting their children much more freedom beginning after age 15.

Why is mid- to later adolescence a crucial period of granting autonomy? The reason may be that, at this age, parents feel their children are more mature (Wray-Lake, Crouter, & McHale, 2010). As teens get closer to graduation, their priorities shift from rebelling to constructing an adult life. By junior and senior year, it's important to stop rebelling and to think concretely about college and a career (Malin and others, 2014).

Even the major social markers of independence at around age 16 or 17 eliminate sources of family strain. Think about how getting your first job, or your license, removed an important area of family conflict. You no longer had to ask your parents for every dime or rely on Mom or Dad to get around.

These adult landmarks put distance between parents and teenagers in the most basic, physical way. The experience-sampling charts showed that ninth-graders spent 25 percent of their time with family members. Among high school seniors, the figure dropped to 14 percent (Csikszentmihalyi & Larson, 1984).

So the process of separating from their families makes it possible for teens to have a more harmonious family life. The delicate task for parents is to respect children's autonomy while remaining closely involved (Steinberg, 2001). One mother of a teenager explained what ideally should happen, when she said: "I don't treat her like a young child anymore, but we're still very close. Sort of like a friendship, but not really, because I'm still in charge. She's my buddy" (quoted in Shearer, Crouter, & McHale, 2005, p. 674).

This quotation brings up a telling gender difference in the parent–child intimacy dance. The earlier Canadian study showed that boys maintained their new, distant pubertal communication pattern as they traveled into the late teens—not telling mothers much about their activities, avoiding sharing their lives. But girls, after becoming more secretive and distant as young teens, reached out to their mothers during mid- and later adolescence to reconnect.

Figure 9.6 illustrates the striking pubertal decline in family closeness in a national U.S. longitudinal study. Notice, as in the Canadian research I just described, the stark decline in parent–child attachment during the early teens, and how girls—but not boys—grow slightly more attached to their parents after ninth grade (Kim and others, 2015). Does this same dramatic dance of separation apply to immigrant teens from more collectivist regions of the world?

Passing a driving test and finally getting the keys to the car is a joyous late-teenage transition into adult liberation. It's almost the developed-world equivalent of a puberty rite!

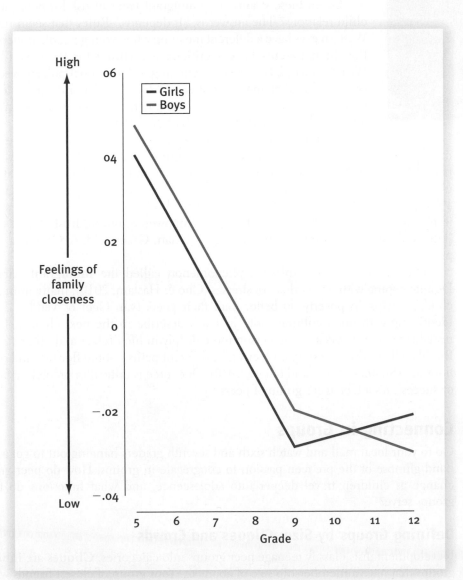

FIGURE 9.6: Changes in feelings of attachment to parents, reported among a sample of 4,407 children, tracked from fifth to twelfth grade: In this mammoth multi-site U.S study, notice how the pre-teen dance of separation from parents explodes during middle school. Notice also how girls but not boys become slightly more attached to their parents after ninth grade.

Data from Kim and others, 2015.

Cultural Variations on a Theme

My parents won't let me date anyone who isn't Hindi—or go to parties. They never tell me they love me. I have to be at home right after school to do the grocery shopping and take care of my parents. Why can't they just let me be a normal American kid?

As she translates an oath of naturalization to her non-English-speaking Iraqi mom, this daughter is engaging in a role reversal that, while distressing, offers a lifelong sense of empathy and self-efficacy.

immigrant paradox The fact that despite living in poverty, going to substandard schools, and not having parents who speak a nation's language, immigrant children do far better than we might expect at school.

In individualistic societies, we strive for parent–child adult relationships that are less hierarchical, more like friends. But, as the preceding quotation suggests, cultures that stress parental obedience above everything else have different ideas about how teenagers should behave.

Therefore, among immigrant adolescents, the impulse to separate from one's family can provoke intense conflicts relating to *acculturation.* Young people may face the wrenching dilemma of "choosing" between their parents' values and the norms of their new home (Kim & Park, 2011; Kim, Chen, and others, 2013; Park and others, 2010; Wu & Chao, 2011). Straddling two cultures, as described in the quotation above, can also upend the normal parent–child relationship because it catapults some second-generation children into becoming the family adults. As one teacher who worked with Chinese immigrants commented, "The kids may be doing the interpreting and translating . . . , they may be the de facto parents" (quoted in Lim and others, 2009).

Given these strains, are immigrant teens at risk for poor parent–child relations? The answer is, "It depends." Rules that seem rigid to Western eyes have a different meaning when young people understand that their parents have sacrificed everything for their well-being (Wu & Chao, 2011). As one touching, international poll showed, the core quality that makes adolescents feel loved *worldwide* is feeling their parents have gone out of their way to do things that are rare and emotionally hard (McNeely & Barber, 2010).

Therefore, knowing that one's parents made a rare sacrifice ("giving up their happiness and moving for my future") can create unusually close parent–child bonds. Helping a non-English-speaking mother or father negotiate this unfamiliar culture can promote *self-efficacy* and encourage empathy, too. As one 19-year-old revealingly commented: "My entire childhood, I was translating simple things day to day . . . [It made me feel] . . . empowered, proud, frustrated at times, [but] understanding of my parents' struggle" (Guan, Greenfield, & Orellana, 2014, p. 332).

This quotation may explain a phenomenon called the **immigrant paradox.** Despite coping with an overload of stresses (Cho & Haslam, 2010), many immigrant children living in poverty do better than their peers (van Geel & Vedder, 2011). Identifying with one's cultural roots, as I will describe in the next chapter, fosters resilience and anchors a young person more deeply in life (Telzer and others, 2016). But like all children, immigrant teens take different paths—some flourish and others flounder (Suárez-Orozco and others, 2010). One force is critical in predicting failure or success: it's a teenager's group of peers.

Connecting in Groups

Go to your local mall and watch sixth and seventh graders hanging out to get a first-hand glimpse of the pre-teen passion to congregate in groups. How do peer groups change as children travel deeper into adolescence, and what functions do these groups serve?

Defining Groups by Size: Cliques and Crowds

clique A small peer group composed of roughly six teenagers who have similar attitudes and who share activities.

Developmentalists classify teenage peer groups into categories. **Cliques** are intimate groups that have a membership size of about six. Your group of closest friends would constitute a clique. **Crowds** are larger groupings. Your crowd comprises both your best buddies and a more loose-knit set of people you get together with less regularly.

In a 1960s observational study in Sydney, Australia, one researcher found that these groups serve a crucial purpose: They are the vehicles that convey teenagers to relationships with the other sex (Dunphy, 1963).

As you can see in the photos in Figure 9.7, children enter their pre-teen years belonging to unisex cliques, close associations of same-sex best friends. Relationships start to change when cliques of boys and girls enter a public space and "accidentally" meet. At the mall, notice the bands of sixth- or seventh-grade girls who have supposedly arrived to check out the stores but who really have another agenda: They know that boy best buddies will be there. A major mode of interaction when these groups meet is loud teasing. When several cliques get together to walk around the stores, they have melded into that larger, first genuinely mixed-sex group called a *crowd* (Cotterell, 1996).

The crowd is an ideal medium to bridge the gap between the sexes because there is safety in numbers. Children can still be with their own sex while they are crossing into that "foreign" land. Gradually, out of these large-group experiences, small heterosexual cliques form. You may recall this stage during high school, when your dating activities occurred in a small group of girls *and* boys. Finally, at the end of adolescence, the structure collapses. It seems babyish to get together as a group. You want to be with your romantic partner alone.

You might be surprised to know that, although the tempo is slower today (see the next chapter's discussion), the same progression outlined in this 50-year-old research still rings true (Child Trends Data Bank, 2008): First, teenagers get together in large mixed-sex crowds; next, they align into smaller heterosexual groups; then, during their twenties, they get seriously romantically involved.

> **crowd** A relatively large teenage peer group.

| At entry to middle school: | Late middle school/ early high school: | High school: | Emerging adulthood: |
| Unisex cliques → | Crowds → | Mixed-sex cliques → | Romantic partners |

FIGURE 9.7: The steps from unisex elementary cliques to adult romantic relationships: A visual summary: Unisex cliques meld into large heterosexual crowds, then re-form as heterosexual cliques, and then break up into one-to-one dating relationships. Does this sequence match your own experience?

What Is the Purpose of Crowds?

Crowds have other critical functions. They allow teenagers to connect with people who share their values. Just as elementary school children select friends with similar attitudes (see Chapter 6), teenagers gravitate to the crowd that fits their interests. When a particular group's priorities are different from one's own, an adolescent disengages from that group. As one academically focused teenager lamented: "I see some of my friends changing. . . . They are getting into parties and alcohol. . . . We used to be good friends . . . and now, I can't really relate to them. . . . That's kind of sad" (quoted in Phelan, Davidson, & Yu, 1998, p. 60).

Crowds actually serve as a road map, allowing teens to connect with "my kind of people" in an overwhelming social world (Smetana, Campione-Barr, & Metzger, 2006). Today, adolescents can immediately find crowds that fit their interests by

As you pass this group of "punks" on the street, you may think, "Why do they dress in this crazy way?" But for this group, their outlandish hair and clothes are a message that "I'm very different, and I don't agree with what society says." Most importantly, they are a signal to attract fellow minds: "I'm like you. I'm safe. I have the same ideas about the world."

Bo Zaunders/Getty Images

going on-line. In fact, one great benefit of the social media revolution is that technology allows teenagers to instantly forge connections with compatible crowds (Xie, 2014).

In the real world, however, it's mainly in large high schools that young people need special help in sorting themselves into defined crowds. Therefore, one developmentalist suggested that a school's size plays a vital role in promoting defined teenage crowds (Cotterell, 1996). When your classes are filled with unfamiliar faces, it is helpful to develop a mechanism for finding a smaller set of people just like you. Teenagers adopt a specific look—like having weird hair and wearing ornament-studded jeans—to signal: "I'm your type of person. It's okay to be friends with me."

What Are the Different Kinds of Crowds?

In affluent societies, there is consistency in the major crowd categories. The intellectuals (also called brains and nerds), the popular kids, the deviants, and a residual type (such as Goths) appear in high schools throughout the West (Sussman and others, 2007).

How much mixing occurs between different crowds? Although teens do straddle different groups (Lonardo and others, 2009), adolescents tend to have friends in similar status crowds. So a popular boy associates with the popular kids. He shuns the socially more marginal groups, such as the deviants (bad kids) or nerdy brains. Moreover, because being brainy—and, especially, advertising that you work to get high grades—can go against the group norms, intellectuality does not gain teenagers kudos in the peer world in many U.S. public high schools today (Sussman and others, 2007).

A study tracking children's self-esteem as they moved from elementary school into high school documented how being brainy was transformed from a plus to more of a teenage liability during high school (Prinstein & La Greca, 2002). The researchers found that teenagers in the high-status jock crowd reported becoming more self-confident during adolescence. (These are the people who would tell you, "I wasn't very happy in elementary school, but high school was my best time of life.") The brainy group followed the opposite path—happiest during elementary school, less self-confident as teens.

Unfortunately, boys and girls who ended up in the high school deviant peer group were particularly unhappy in elementary school *as well as* during their adolescent years (see also Heaven, Ciarrochi, & Vialle, 2008). Recall that having prior *externalizing problems* and being rejected by the mainstream kids predict gravitating toward groups of "bad" peers. Now, let's explore why joining that bad crowd makes a teenager more likely to fail.

"Bad" Crowds

The classic defense that parents give for a teenager's delinquent behavior is, "My child got involved with a bad crowd." Without ignoring the principle of selection (birds of a feather flock together), there are powerful reasons why bad crowds *do* cause teenagers to do bad things.

As a group euphoria sets in and people start surging for the stage, these teenagers at an outdoor music festival might trample one another—and then later be horrified that they could ever have acted this way.

For one thing, as I've been highlighting, teenagers are incredibly swayed by their peers. Moreover, each group has a leader, the person who most embodies the group's goals. So, if a child joins the brains group, his academic performance is apt to improve because everyone is jockeying for status by competing for grades (Cook, Deng, & Morgano, 2007; Molloy, Gest, & Rulison, 2011). However, in delinquent peer groups, members model the most antisocial leader. This most acting-out girl or boy sets the standard for how others want to behave.

Therefore, just as you felt compelled to jump into the icy water at camp when the bravest of your bunkmates took the plunge, if one group member begins selling guns or drugs, the rest must follow the leader or risk being called "chicken." Moreover, when children compete for status by getting into trouble, this creates ever-wilder antisocial modeling and propels the group toward taking increasingly risky acts.

Combine this principle with the impact of just being in a group. When young people get together, a group high occurs. Talk gets louder and more outrageous. People act in ways that would be unthinkable if they were alone. From rioting at rock concerts to being in a car with your buddies during a drive-by shooting (recall the earlier Experiencing the Lifespan box), groups *do* cause people to act in dangerous ways (Cotterell, 1996).

By videotaping groups of boys, developmentalists have documented the **deviancy training,** or socialization into delinquency, that occurs as a function of simply talking with friends in a group (Dishion, McCord, & Poulin, 1999; Rorie and others, 2011). The researchers find that at-risk pre-teens forge friendships through specific kinds of conversations: They laugh, egg one another on, and reinforce one another as they discuss committing antisocial acts. So peer interactions in early adolescence are a medium by which problem behavior gets solidified, established, and entrenched.

The lure of entering an antisocial peer group is strong for at-risk kids because they are already feeling "it's me against the world" (Veenstra and others, 2010; see Chapter 6). Put yourself in the place of a child whose impulsive behavior is causing him to get rejected by the "regular" kids (Ettekal & Ladd, 2015). You need to connect with other children like yourself because you have failed at gaining entry anywhere else. Once in the group, your buddies reinforce your *hostile attributional bias*. Your friends tell you that it's fine to go against the system. You are finding acceptance in an unfriendly world.

In middle-class settings, popular kids sometimes get into trouble. "Self-identifying" as a jock is a risk factor for abusing alcohol or having unprotected sex (Cook, Deng, & Morgano, 2007). (At this point, any reader who has lived through adolescence is probably saying, "Duh!") But in affluent communities, children with prior problems tend to gravitate toward the druggy or delinquent groups. In economically

deviancy training
Socialization of a young teenager into delinquency through conversations centered on performing antisocial acts.

deprived neighborhoods, there may be *no* positive peer group. Flourishing is impossible because the whole community is a toxic place. The only major crowd may be the antisocial group called a *gang*.

Society's Nightmare Crowd: Teenage Gangs

gang A close-knit, delinquent peer group. Gangs form mainly in impoverished disorganized communities; they offer their members protection from harm and engage in a variety of criminal activities.

The **gang**, a close-knit, delinquent peer group, embodies society's worst nightmares. Gang members share a collective identity, which they often express by adopting specific symbols and claiming control over a certain turf (Jennings and others, 2016). This typically male group appears in different cultures and historical eras. However, with gangs, the socioeconomic context looms large: Adverse economic conditions, and especially living in communities low in collective efficacy, promote gangs (again, for a vivid example, turn back to the Experiencing the Lifespan box on page 269).

Gangs provide teenagers with status. They offer children physical protection in dangerous neighborhoods. Gangs give teenagers who are disconnected from their families the sense of belonging to a coherent (even far more caring!) group. When young people have few options for making it in the conventional way, gangs provide an avenue for making a living (for example, by selling drugs or stealing). So, a harsh, unfriendly environment can propel time-limited adolescent turmoil into life-course criminal careers.

A Note on Adolescence Worldwide

A kinder, gentler twentieth-century developed world propelled adolescence into a life stage. Adolescence still doesn't exist for the nearly 50 million children who have been displaced from their homes in war-torn, famine-ridden regions of the globe (United Nations Children's Fund, 2016). There is no adolescence for street children or females forced into the sex trade, or for African girls forced into unwanted marriages as early as age 13 (Erulkar, 2013).

There is no life stage called adolescence for the thousands of child soldiers compelled to take up arms in dysfunctional, failed-state civil wars. Many combatants in the poorest regions of the globe are teenage boys. Some are coerced into fighting as young as age 10 or 8 (Child Soldiers International, 2017).

Yes, many teenagers in the world are flourishing. But children in the least-developed countries may not have the chance to be adolescents or construct a decent adult life. Although critics, such as Robert Epstein, bemoan the shackles of Western teens, having an extra decade liberated from grown-up responsibilities can be critical to flourishing during adult life.

How do contemporary, developed-world young people construct an adult life? Stay tuned for answers in the next chapter of this book.

This 14-year-old soldier and devastated child bride in Africa offer a stark testament that, in some regions of the world, young people still are deprived of an adolescence.

ADAM BUTLER/AP Images

Marvi Lacar/Edit by Getty Images

Tying It All Together

1. Chris and her parents are arguing again. Based on this chapter, at what age might arguments between Chris and her parents be most intense? Around what age would Chris's parents have begun to seriously loosen their rules? Choose between ages *12, 16, and 19*.

2. Your niece Heather hangs around with a small group of girlfriends. You see them at the mall giggling at a group of boys. According to the standard pattern, what is the next step?

   a. Heather and her friends will begin going on dates with the boys.

   b. Heather and her clique will meld into a large heterosexual crowd.

   c. Heather and her clique will form another small clique composed of both girls and boys.

3. Mom #1 says, "Getting involved with the 'bad kids' makes teens get into trouble." Mom #2 disagrees: "It's the kid's personality that causes him to get into trouble." Mom #3 says, "You both are correct—but also partly wrong. The kid's personality causes him to gravitate toward the 'bad kids,' and then that peer group encourages antisocial acts." Which mother is right?

4. You want to intervene to help prevent at-risk pre-teens from becoming delinquents. First, devise a checklist to assess who might be appropriate for your program. Then, applying the principles in this chapter, offer suggestions for how you would turn potentially "troublemaking teens" around.

Answers to the Tying It All Together questions can be found at the end of this chapter.

SUMMARY

Cognitive and Emotional Development: The Mysterious Teenage Mind

Wise observers have described the "hot-headed" qualities of youth for millennia. However, adolescence, first identified by G. Stanley Hall in the early 1900s and characterized by **"storm and stress,"** became a life stage in the United States during the twentieth century, when high school became universal and brought teens together as a group.

Jean Piaget believes that when teenagers reach the **formal operational stage,** they can think abstractly about hypothetical possibilities and reason scientifically. Most adults can't reason like scientists, but older teenagers use the skills involved in formal operations to plan their futures.

According to Lawrence Kohlberg, reaching formal operations allows teenagers to develop moral values that guide their lives. By examining how they reason about ethical dilemmas, Kohlberg classified moral development as either **preconventional** (moral judgment in which only punishment and reward are important); **conventional** (moral judgment based on obeying social norms); or **postconventional** (the highest level of moral reasoning, based on having one's own moral ideals, apart from society's rules). Although Kohlberg's theory has serious flaws, children become attuned to society's injustices during adolescence.

According to David Elkind, this ability to evaluate the adult world produces **adolescent egocentrism.** The **imaginary audience** (the feeling that everyone is watching everything one does) and the **personal fable** (feeling invincible and utterly unique) are two components of this intense early-teenage sensitivity to what others think.

Many storm-and-stress stereotypes about teenagerhood are true. Adolescents are highly socially sensitive. In arousing peer situations, they are apt to take dangerous risks. This risk-taking (and sometimes law-breaking) tendency, especially with friends, makes adolescence a dangerous time. Research using the **experience-sampling technique** shows teens are more emotionally intense than adults. Contrary to our stereotypes, however, most adolescents are upbeat and happy. Still, **suicidal thinking and nonsuicidal self-injury** is not infrequent, and depression rates rise during adolescence—especially among females. The push to be popular may explain many unfortunate behaviors during the pubertal years.

The minority of teenagers who get into *serious* trouble tend to have prior emotional and social problems, feel distant from their families, and live in a risk-taking milieu. Having specific talents, good executive functions, and being connected to caring adults help teens thrive. However, even well-adjusted teenagers experiment with forbidden activities, and serious **adolescence-limited turmoil** may not lead to **life-course difficulties.** Many problem teens construct fulfilling adult lives.

The unique characteristics of the teenage brain make adolescence a relatively dangerous life stage. The frontal lobes are still maturing. Puberty heightens teenagers' social sensitivities and emotional states. The lessons for society are as follows: (1) Don't punish teenagers who break the law in the same ways that adult offenders are punished; (2) pass legislation that takes teenage sensitivities into account; and (3) channel teenage passions in a positive way through high-quality **youth development programs.** Make high schools more appealing, rethink punitive school **zero-tolerance policies** that promote the **school-to-prison pipeline,** and adjust the school day to fit adolescent sleep. While the "immature brain" conception of adolescence is in vogue, critics suggest that it minimizes teenagers' strengths.

Social Development

Teenagers' struggles with parents are most intense during puberty, and issues relating to independence loom large in these conflicts around the world (with cultural variations). After young teens distance themselves from their families, by mid- and later adolescence, parents respond by relaxing their rules. Eventually, young people develop a more friendlike (but still more distant) relationship with their parents. Immigrant adolescents face unique stresses, although the **immigrant paradox** suggests that caring for a non-English-speaking mother or father can make teens self-confident, empathic, and mature.

Cliques and **crowds** convey adolescents, in stages, toward romantic involvement. Crowds, such as the jocks or the brains, also give teenagers an easy way of finding people like themselves in large high schools. The jocks (in contrast to the lower-status brains) feel better about themselves in high school than during elementary school. Children who enter delinquent groups tend to be unhappy before high school and remain distressed during their teenage years.

Entering a "bad" crowd promotes antisocial behavior because group members model the most antisocial leader. **Deviancy training,** in which pre-teens egg one another on by talking about doing dangerous things, leads directly to delinquency as at-risk children travel into high school. **Gangs,** mainly male teenage peer groups that engage in criminal acts, may be the only social group available in disorganized, impoverished communities. In the least developed regions of the world, young people may still not have any adolescence at all.

KEY TERMS

adolescence-limited turmoil, p. 267

adolescent egocentrism, p. 259

clique, p. 276

conventional thought, p. 258

crowd, p. 277

deviancy training, p. 279

experience-sampling technique, p. 262

formal operational stage, p. 255

gang, p. 280

imaginary audience, p. 260

immigrant paradox, p. 276

life-course difficulties, p. 267

nonsuicidal self-injury, p. 264

personal fable, p. 260

postconventional thought, p. 258

preconventional thought, p. 258

school-to-prison pipeline, p. 271

"storm and stress," p. 254

youth development program, p. 270

zero-tolerance policies, p. 271

ANSWERS TO Tying It All Together QUIZZES

Cognitive and Emotional Development: The Mysterious Teenage Mind

1. c and d

2. If your arguments centered on getting punished or rewarded (the coach needs to put Terry in because that's his best shot at winning; or the coach can't put Terry in because if someone finds out, he will be in trouble), you are reasoning at the preconventional level. Comments such as "going against the rules is wrong" might be classified as conventional. If you argued, "Putting Terry in goes against my values, no matter what the team or the rules say," your response might qualify as postconventional.

3. the imaginary audience; the personal fable; adolescent egocentrism

4. depression

5. worried, because he is at risk for moral disengagement and acting-out behaviors

6. a

7. Trying teens as adults. Pro arguments: Kohlberg's theory clearly implies teens know right from wrong, so if teens knowingly do the crime, they should "do the time." Actually, the critical dimension in deciding on adult punishment should be a person's culpability—premeditation, seriousness of the infraction, and so on—not age. Con arguments:

The research in this chapter shows that teens are indeed biologically and behaviorally different, so it is cruel to judge their behavior by adult standards. Moreover, if the U.S. bars young people from voting or serving in the military until age 18, and won't let people buy alcohol until age 21, it's unfair to put teens in adult prisons.

Social Development

1. At age 12, the arguments would be most intense; by age 16, Chris's parents would be giving her much more freedom.

2. b

3. Mom #3 is correct.

4. Checklist: (1) Is this child unusually aggressive and does he have poor executive functions? (2) Is he being rejected by the mainstream kids? (3) Does this child have poor relationships with his parents? (4) Does he live in a dangerous, low-efficacy community or a risk-taking environment? Your possible program: Provide positive school activities that nurture the child's interests. Offer service-learning opportunities. Possibly institute group sessions with parents to solve problems around certain issues. Definitely try to get the child connected with caring mentors and a different set of (prosocial) friends.

CONNECT ONLINE:

 LaunchPad macmillan learning | Check out our videos and additional resources located at: www.macmillanlearning.com

Early and Middle Adulthood

This three-chapter book part spans the time from high school graduation until society labels us as senior citizens (our sixties)—a lifespan chunk that covers almost a half-century!

Chapter 10—Constructing an Adult Life tackles the challenge of making it to full adulthood. Here, among other topics, I'll discuss leaving home, finding an identity, negotiating college, choosing a career, and searching for love. If you are a traditional college student or adult in your twenties, this chapter is for you.

Chapter 11—Social Development: Relationships and Roles continues this focus on work and love by exploring marriage, parenthood, and careers. In the marriage section, I'll scan marriage ideas around the world, explore cohabiting couples, and offer a wealth of practical insights into how to make relationships work. Then you'll find out how becoming a parent changes couples, and learn what twenty-first-century motherhood and fatherhood is really like. The last section of the chapter tackles work: How have careers changed in recent decades? What makes for happiness in this vital role? How do men's and women's career attitudes and pathways differ today?

Chapter 12—Midlife covers the long life stage from the forties to the sixties. Here, my focus is "How do people change over adulthood?" As I survey the research on sexuality, on intellectual and emotional development, and wisdom and happiness, you'll gain a wealth of insights into what makes for a fulfilling adult life. The last sections of this chapter cover social roles specific to middle age: grandparenthood and caring for elderly parents.

Left: IMAGEMORE/AGE Fotostock

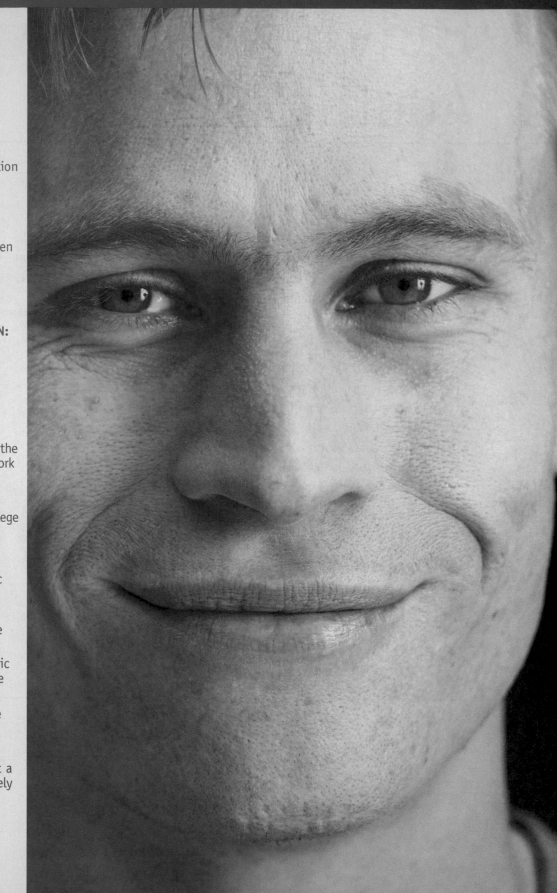

CHAPTER 10

Constructing an Adult Life

After graduating from high school, Matt looked forward to enjoying college. But his freshman year at State U was a nightmare. His courses felt irrelevant. He zoned out during lectures. Compared to high school, the work seemed impossibly hard. Most important, with his full-time job at the supermarket and five classes a semester, he lost his scholarship after the first year. The only rational solution was to drop out and move back in with his parents, so he could save money and then consider going back.

Six years later, Matt now has enough money to move out of the house. He was promoted to store supervisor (with health insurance!) and drives for a ride-sharing company on weekends. He met a terrific woman on Facebook named Clara. They just moved in together and plan to get married in a few years—if they both can get stable, well-paying jobs.

Clara and Matt share many values, even though, he must admit, she is more mature. He respects Clara's strong work ethic, and the fact that she helps care for her disabled sister while going to nursing school full time. Actually, Clara reminds him of his sister. She even physically resembles Samantha and his mom! Should Matt return to State U and get a business degree? Will having a B.A. allow him to support a family? At 28, it's crunch-time to get serious about life.

Can you identify with Matt's anxieties about finishing college? Perhaps, like Clara, you are trying to balance family demands while getting your degree. No matter what your situation, if you are in your twenties, you probably feel "in between." You are clearly not a child, but you haven't reached those classic adult goals—marriage, parenthood, embarking on your "real" career. You fit into that life stage Jeffrey Arnett (2004, 2007) labels **emerging adulthood.**

This chapter is devoted to this new life phase. It explores the decade lasting from age 18 to our late twenties, when we are constructing an adult life. First, I'll examine the features of emerging adulthood and describe the challenges we face during this pivotal, transitional life stage. Then I'll focus on three crucial emerging-adult concerns: career, college, and finding love.

emerging adulthood The phase of life that begins after high school, lasts through the late twenties, and is devoted to constructing an adult life.

Photo: Stockbyte/Getty Images

LEARNING OUTCOMES

- List the core emerging-adult challenges.
- Outline the historical forces that have shaped emerging adulthood, and how this life stage varies in southern Europe, Scandinavia, and the United States.
- Describe nest-leaving changes and social clock issues.

Setting the Context

Emerging adulthood is not a universal life stage. It occurs for the minority of young people living at this point in history in the developed world. Its goal is exploration—trying out options before committing to adult life. Although they often plan to get married (Willoughby and others, 2015; Willoughby & Hall, 2015), most emerging adults are not ready to settle down (Hall & Walls, 2015). They don't feel financially secure. They may move from job to job, enter and then exit college or a parent's home, and test out relationships before they get married and have children (Arnett, 2016).

Exploring different possibilities defines emerging adulthood. Its other core quality is exuberant optimism about what lies ahead (Tanner & Arnett, 2010; Silva, 2016). As Table 10.1 shows, emerging adults are at their physical peak. Their reasoning abilities are in top form. Still, the challenges young people face during this watershed age are more daunting than at any other life stage.

Table 10.1: A Twenty-Something Body at Its Physical Peak: A Brief Summary

The skeleton: Our height peaks at age 20 and then, due to the compression of the joint cartilage and bones, declines as we get older.

The muscles: The contracting skeletal muscle fibers allow us to perform physical tasks. During the late teens these fibers are at top capacity and then slowly atrophy and are replaced by fat.

The heart: During exercise, cardiac output (our heart's pumping capacity) dramatically increases—delivering more oxygen to the muscles. Cardiac function is at a high point during later adolescence, and then also gradually declines.

The lungs: The lungs are the bellows that deliver oxygen to the blood. Our ability to breathe in deeply and exhale forcefully (called *vital capacity*) peaks during youth and falls off year by year.

Information from Spense, 1989; Masoro, 1999.

FIGURE 10.1: Young men (blue bars) and women (pink bars) in the United States completing the classic "benchmarks of adulthood" at age 25, in 1960 and 2010: This chart documents the mammoth shift in the passage to adulthood that I will discuss in this chapter. In 1960, by their mid-twenties, most people had finished school, started a career, gotten married, and had children. Today, getting to these standard adult roles is rare by that age.

Data from Furstenberg, 2015.

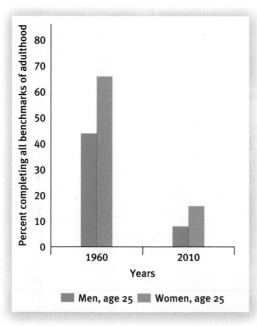

Percent completing all benchmarks of adulthood

■ Men, age 25 ■ Women, age 25

WE NEED TO RE-CENTER OUR LIVES Our parents protect us during adolescence. Now, our task is to take control of ourselves and act like "real adults" (Tanner, 2006; Tanner & Arnett, 2010). We used to count on marriage, parenthood, and supporting a family to make us feel adult. No more! Since only a tiny minority of contemporary U.S. young people have entered these adult roles by age 25 (see Figure 10.1), most people now view the criteria for reaching adulthood in internal terms: Adults accept responsibility for their actions; adults financially support themselves; adults make independent decisions about life (Arnett, 2016; Arnett & Padilla-Walker, 2015).

WE HAVE ENTERED AN UNSTRUCTURED, UNPREDICTABLE PATH During adolescence, high school organizes our days. We wake up, go to class; we are on an identical track. Then, at age 18, our lives diverge. Many of us go to college; others enter the world of work. Emerging adults live alone or with friends, stay with their parents or move far away. For some emerging adults, constructing an adult life takes decades. For people who have children and enter their work lives by age 18, there may be no emerging adulthood at all. So emerging adulthood is defined by variability—as we set sail on our own. Why did this structure-free stage emerge?

Culture and History

Our twentieth-century longevity gains made emerging adulthood possible. Imagine reaching adulthood a century ago. With an average life expectancy in the fifties (Gordon, 2015), you could not have the luxury of spending a decade constructing an adult life. Now, with life expectancy floating up to the late seventies and eighties in developed nations (Central Intelligence Agency, n.d.), putting off adult commitments until an older age makes excellent sense.

Education made emerging adulthood likely. A half-century ago, high school graduates could get high-paying jobs. Today, in the United States, we see college as crucial to career success (Danziger & Ratner, 2010; Silva, 2016). But, although most emerging adults enter college, it typically takes six years to get an undergraduate degree, especially because so many young people need to work to finance school. If we add in graduate school, constructing a career can take until the mid-twenties and beyond (Furstenberg, 2015).

Emerging adulthood was promoted by the fact that staying married and finding well-paying work can be elusive (Furstenberg, 2015; Willoughby & Hall, 2015). It took hold in a late-twentieth-century Western culture that stresses self-expression and "doing your own thing," in which people make dramatic changes *throughout* their adult years.

Longevity, education, and an uncertain modern life propelled emerging adulthood. Still, the forces that drive this life stage vary from place to place. For snapshots of this variability, let's travel to southern Europe, Scandinavia, and then enter the United States.

The Mediterranean Model: Living with Parents and Having Trouble Making the Leap to Adult Life

In southern Europe, the main barrier to reaching adulthood is alarmingly high youth unemployment rates (Crocetti & Tagliabue, 2016). In these nations, the social norms discourage **cohabitation,** or living together without being married. So young people in Portugal, Italy, Spain, and Greece typically spend their twenties and early thirties in their parents' house (Mendonça & Fontaine, 2013; Seiffge-Krenke, 2013). Unfortunately, as of this writing (2018), family traditions and financial constraints have seriously impeded young people's travels into an independent life.

> **cohabitation** Sharing a household in an unmarried romantic relationship.

The Scandinavian Plan: Living Independently with Government Help

> **nest-leaving** Moving out of a childhood home and living independently.

These barriers do not exist in Scandinavia, where jobs are more plentiful (again, as of 2018) and getting married is an optional choice (Wängqvist and others, 2016). In Norway, Sweden, and Denmark, the government funds university attendance. A strong social safety net provides free health care and other benefits to citizens of every age. So in these northern European countries, **nest-leaving**—moving out of a parent's home to live independently—often begins at the brink of the emerging-adult years (Furstenberg, 2010; Hendry & Kloep, 2010). In the Nordic nations, the twenties are more of a stress-free interlude—a time for exploring life before having children, and then *perhaps* deciding to marry a life love (Wängqvist & Frisén, 2016).

Klaus Vedfelt/Getty Images

The United States Route(s): Colliding Conceptions and Diverse, SES-Related Paths

Emerging adulthood in the United States has features of both Scandinavia and southern Europe. As in the Nordic nations, a high fraction of U.S. women now give birth without being married (Furstenberg, 2015). However, as the

Many Greek men in their late twenties and thirties still live with their families because they cannot afford to leave the nest and construct an adult life. How would you react in this situation?

If you visited this Scandinavian family, these parents might be happily cohabiting without feeling they needed a wedding ring. In the United States, families view a marriage ceremony as a pinnacle life event!

photos above show, like their southern European counterparts, U.S. young people view being married as an important life goal (Willoughby & Hall, 2015; Willoughby and others, 2015). The U.S. individualistic culture strongly encourages people to move out of a parent's home at age 18; but this same focus on self-reliance means that, unlike in Scandinavia, the government doesn't pay for college and emerging adults have trouble finding decently paying jobs.

The reality is that these colliding conceptions, combined with dramatic *income inequalities*, produce sharp social-class differences in how U.S. emerging adults construct an adult life. Because people are reluctant to get married until they can support a family, marriage in the United States has become a middle-class achievement. Low-income adults often travel through life without having a spouse (Furstenberg, 2015). And, unless they have fairly well-off parents, U.S. young people may have trouble immediately reaching the first classic benchmark of adult life—moving out of their parents' house (Settersten & Ray, 2010).

Beginning and End Points

This brings up an interesting issue: When *does* emerging adulthood begin and end?

Exploring the Traditional Entry Point: Nest-Leaving

Actually, in the United States and northern Europe, we traditionally see leaving the nest as an important rite of passage. It forces people to take that first important step toward independent adulthood—taking care of their needs on their own.

For this mother, being invited to her daughter's first apartment may be a thrilling experience: "My baby did grow up to become a responsible woman!"

It also causes a change in family relationships, as parents view their children in a different, adult way. Listen to this British mother gushing about her 20-year-old daughter: "I'm real proud of her. . . . I'd expected to be a laundry and maid service . . . , but fair play, she's done all [the] washing and cleaning" (quoted in Kloep & Hendry, 2010, p. 824).

This quotation hints at two benefits of leaving home: Moving out should produce more harmonious family relationships; it should force young people to "grow up."

Does Leaving Home Produce Better Parent–Child Relationships?

Here, U.S. research suggests that the answer is often yes. In several longitudinal studies, both young people and their parents reported less conflict when children left the nest (Morgan, Thorne, & Zubriggen, 2010; Whiteman, McHale, & Crouter, 2007). However, this is not true in Italy, where young people prize family closeness over friendships (Crocetti & Meeus, 2014) and, as I mentioned earlier, emerging adults typically live in their parents' home. In Portugal, one study showed that parents got more agitated when their children moved out of the house! (See Mendonça & Fontaine, 2013.)

I must emphasize that, even in the United States, physically leaving home does not mean having distant family relationships. Judging by the 24/7 texts that fly back and forth between my students and their parents, the impulse to stay closely connected to mothers and fathers is more intense among this cohort of twenty-somethings than when I was a college student decades ago (see Levine & Dean, 2012).

This twenty-first-century college student is more likely to openly share her feelings and rely on her mother's advice than her mother did when she was the girl's age.

Having close mother–child relationships and calling each other frequently is correlated with adjusting well to college and homing in on a satisfying career (Chih-Yuan, Bryan, & Lauren, 2016). Although they may not be making the meals or doing the laundry, mothers remain a vital support as young people leave the nest and travel into the wider world.

Does Leaving Home Make People More Adult?

Here, too, studies imply the answer is yes. When Belgian researchers compared young people in their early twenties who never left home with a same-aged group who moved out, the "nest residers" were less likely to be in a long-term relationship, felt more emotionally dependent on their parents, and were less satisfied with life (Kins & Beyers, 2010; see also Seiffge-Krenke, 2010). One emerging adult named Adam spelled out his feelings: "[It] is comparable to living in a hotel actually. I have no charges . . . my meals are prepared, my laundry is done" (quoted in Kins, de Mol, & Beyers, 2014, p. 104). Another British mother put it more graphically: "He is my . . . mummy's boy. . . . And 'cos he lives at home . . . I do his clothes, . . . , tidy his room . . . even still do packed lunch" (quoted in Kloep & Hendry, 2010, p. 826).

These quotations reinforce all of our negative images about emerging adults who stay in the nest: They are lazy, babyish, and unwilling to grow up. The problem is that we are confusing consequences with causes. Nest-leaving, as I've been suggesting, has an economic cause (Seiffge-Krenke, 2013). Young people often stay at home, or return to live with their parents, because they cannot afford to live on their own (Berzin & De Marco, 2010; Britton, 2013).

In addition to financial problems, there is another barrier to moving out for some immigrant and ethnic minority youth: values (Furstenberg, 2010; Kiang & Fuligni, 2009). If a young person's collectivist worldview says to put family first, children may stay in the nest for adult-centered reasons—to help with the finances and the chores. As one Latino 20-year-old explained: "I can't leave my mom by herself, she is a single mother. The only person she's got is me. . . ." (quoted in Sánchez and others, 2010, p. 872).

So, is nest-leaving still the beginning of emerging adulthood? Not really, anymore. Do young people *need* to live independently to act mature? The answer is

Table 10.2: Tips for Getting Along as Co-residing Adults

1. **For parents:** Don't micromanage or hover (for example, texting or calling) when your child comes home "late." Support your child's goals and encourage your son or daughter to make a financial contribution to the family, as subsidizing everything reinforces the impression that this young person is still a child (Nelson & Luster, 2016).

2. **For children:** Resist being babied (and totally subsidized), but lean on your parents for emotional support. If you have a sense of purpose, you are apt to feel "adult" and also close to your parents, even if you are living "at home" (see Hill, Burrow, & Sumner, 2016).

3. **For parents and children:** Talk openly about your concerns and set up shared rules: How will you divide household tasks? Is living together contingent on staying in school or searching for a job? Then vow to treat each other like loving adults.

social clock The concept that we regulate our passage through adulthood by an inner timetable that tells us which life activities are appropriate at certain ages.

age norms Cultural ideas about the appropriate ages for engaging in particular activities or life tasks.

on time Being on target in a culture's timetable for achieving adult life tasks.

off time Being too late or too early in a culture's timetable for achieving adult life tasks.

definitely no. Parents' task is to construct adult-to-adult relationships with their children no matter where the younger generation lives (see Table 10.2 for suggestions). And young people's challenge is to assemble the building blocks to construct a satisfying adult life. When should this constructing phase end and adulthood arrive? The answer brings up a classic concept in adult development.

Exploring the Fuzzy End Point: The Ticking of the Social Clock

Our feelings about when we should get our adult lives in order reflect our culture's **social clock** (Neugarten, 1972, 1979). This phrase refers to shared **age norms** that act as guideposts to what behaviors are appropriate at particular ages. If our passage matches up with the normal timetable in our society, we are defined as **on time**; if not, we are **off time**—either too early or too late for where we should be at a given age.

So in the twenty-first-century West, exploring different options is considered on time during our twenties, but these activities become off time if they extend well into the next decade of life. A parent whose 35-year-old son is "just dating" and shows no signs of deciding on a career or moves back home for the third or fourth time may become impatient: "Will my child ever grow up?" A woman traveling into her mid-thirties may get uneasy: "I'd better hurry up if I want a family," or "Do I still have time to go to medical school?" Although emerging adults *say* they view adulthood in internal terms, feeling seriously off time in the late direction can cause young people considerable distress (Nelson & Luster, 2016).

Society sets general social-clock guidelines. Today, with the average age of marriage in most European countries floating up to about the thirties (Shulman & Connolly, 2013), it's fine to date for more than a decade if you live in the West. But in China, where everyone is expected to get married and where the marriage age is lower now than in the past (Yeung & Hu, 2013), it can be embarrassing to be over age 30 without a mate: "The older generation cannot understand why I keep being single . . . ," said one woman. "Many people will think . . . I must have some mental or physical deficiencies" (quoted in Wang & Abbott, 2013, p. 226).

Personal preferences make a difference. In one survey, developmentalists found that they could predict a given undergraduate's social-clock timetable by asking a simple question: "Is having a family your main passion?" People who said that marriage was their top-ranking agenda or that they couldn't wait to be a mom or dad tended

When this not-so-young man in his forties finally proposed to his longtime, 38-year-old girlfriend, both their families were probably thrilled. Feeling "off time" in the late direction in your social-clock timetable can cause everyone considerable distress.

Volt Collection/Shutterstock

to get married and give birth at younger ages (Carroll and others, 2007). So, the limits of emerging adulthood are set both by our society and our personal goals (see Willoughby & Hall, 2015).

The problem, however, is that our social-clock agendas are not totally under control. People cannot "decide" to find the love of their life at a defined age (Sharon, 2015). This sense of being "out of control" may explain why emerging adulthood is both an exhilarating *and* emotionally challenging time. On the positive side, as I mentioned earlier, emerging adults are remarkably optimistic about their futures (Frye & Liem, 2011; Pryor and others, 2011; Silva, 2016). On the negative side, the twenties are the life stage when anxiety disorders reach their peak (Schwartz, 2016).

For some young people, the issue is failing to take responsibility. As one emerging adult anguished: "My life looks like a . . . gutter and effort to fight that gutter . . . then back in the gutter . . . I just don't have any control over myself" (quoted in Macek, Bejcek, & Vanickova, 2007, p. 466). For others, there may be romantic heartbreaks or understanding that one's career dreams can't be fulfilled (more about both issues soon). Or emerging adults may not have any sense of where they want to go in life: "We do have more possibilities . . . but that's why it's harder" . . . "You study and you wonder what it is good for" (quoted in Macek, Bejcek, & Vanickova, 2007, p. 468). The reason for this inner turmoil is that, during emerging adulthood, we undergo a mental makeover. We decide *who* to be as adults.

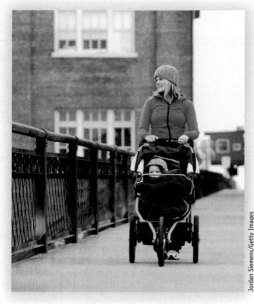

The fact that this young woman's passion since childhood was to be a mother could explain why she gave birth at the atypically young age of 24.

Tying It All Together

1. You are giving a toast at your friend Sarah's 20th birthday party, and you want to offer some predictions about what the next years might hold in store for her. Given your understanding of emerging adulthood, which would *not* be a safe prediction?

    a. Sarah may not reach the standard markers of adulthood for many years.

    b. Sarah will have graduated from college in four years.

    c. Sarah might need to move back into the nest or might still be living at home.

2. Which emerging adult is *least* likely to be in the nest?

    a. Manuel, who lives in Madrid

    b. Paula, whose parents live below the poverty line

    c. Silvia, who lives in Stockholm

3. Staying in the nest during the twenties today is a "symptom" of a child's refusing to grow up—*true* or *false*?

4. Which person is most apt to worry about a social-clock issue: Martha, age 50, who wants to apply to nursing school, or Lee, age 28, who has just become a father?

Answers to the Tying It All Together questions can be found at the end of this chapter.

Constructing an Identity

Erik Erikson was the theorist who highlighted the challenge of transforming our childhood self into the person we will be as adults. He named this process the search for **identity** (see Table 10.3 on page 294).

Time spent wandering through Europe to find himself sensitized Erikson to the difficulties young people face in constructing an adult self. Erikson's fascination with identity, however, crystallized when he worked in a psychiatric hospital for troubled

LEARNING OUTCOMES

*   Describe the different identity statuses.

*   Examine ethnic identity.

identity In Erikson's theory, the life task of deciding who to be as an adult.

Table 10.3: Erikson's Psychosocial Stages

Life Stage	Primary Task
Infancy (birth to 1 year)	Basic trust versus mistrust
Toddlerhood (1 to 2 years)	Autonomy versus shame and doubt
Early childhood (3 to 6 years)	Initiative versus guilt
Middle childhood (7 to 12 years)	Industry versus inferiority
Adolescence to emerging adulthood (teens into twenties)	**Identity versus role confusion**
Early adulthood (twenties to early forties)	Intimacy versus isolation
Middle adulthood (forties to sixties)	Generativity versus stagnation
Late adulthood (late sixties and beyond)	Integrity versus despair

role confusion Erikson's term for a failure in identity formation, marked by the lack of any sense of a future adult path.

teens. Erikson discovered that young patients suffered from a problem he labeled **role confusion.** They had no sense of any adult path:

> [The person feels as] if he were moving in molasses. It is hard . . . to go to bed and . . . to get up. . . .
>
> (quoted in Erikson, 1968, p. 169)

Some people felt a frightening sense of falseness: "If I tell a girl I like her, if I make a gesture . . . this third voice is at me all the time—'You're doing this for effect; you're a phony'" (p. 173). Others could not cope with having any future and planned to end their lives on a symbolic date.

This derailment, which Erikson called *role confusion*—an aimless drifting, or shutting down—differs from the active search process he labeled *moratorium* (1980). Taking time to explore different paths, Erikson argued, is crucial to forming a solid adult identity. Having witnessed Hitler's Holocaust, Erikson believed that young people must discover their *own* identities. He had seen a destructive process of identity formation firsthand. To cope with that nation's economic problems after World War I, German teenagers leaped into pathological identities by entering totalitarian organizations such as the Hitler Youth.

Can we categorize the ways people tackle the challenge of constructing an adult identity? Decades ago, James Marcia answered yes.

identity statuses Marcia's four categories of identity formation: identity diffusion, identity foreclosure, moratorium, and identity achievement.

identity diffusion According to James Marcia, an identity status in which the person is aimless or feels totally blocked, without any adult life path.

identity foreclosure According to James Marcia, an identity status in which the person decides on an adult life path (often one spelled out by an authority figure) without any thought or active search.

moratorium According to James Marcia, an identity status in which the person actively explores various possibilities to find a truly solid adult life path.

Marcia's Identity Statuses

Marcia (1966, 1987) devised four **identity statuses** to expand on Erikson's powerful ideas:

- **Identity diffusion** best fits Erikson's description of the most troubled teens—young people drifting aimlessly toward adulthood without any goals: "I don't know where I am going," "Nothing has any appeal."

- **Identity foreclosure** describes a person who adopts an identity without any self-exploration or thought. At its extreme, foreclosure might apply to a violent gang member or a teenager who becomes a terrorist. In general, however, researchers define young people as being in foreclosure when they adopt an identity handed down by some authority: "My parents want me to take over the family business, so that's what I will do."

- The person in **moratorium** is engaged in the exciting search for an adult self. While this internal process provokes anxiety because it involves wrestling with different philosophies and ideas, Marcia (and Erikson) believed it was critical to arriving at the final stage.

- **Identity achievement** is the end point: "I've weighed the options and I want to be a computer artist, no matter what my family says."

As the photo series shows, Marcia's categories offer a marvelous framework for pinpointing what is going wrong (or right) in a young person's life. Perhaps while reading these descriptions you were thinking, "I have a friend in diffusion. Now I understand exactly what this person's problem is!" How do these statuses play out in life?

This young woman may fit Marcia's category of *identity diffusion*. She seems listless and depressed.

This student, forced by his dad to get a degree in computer science in order to get a well-paying job, feels incredibly bored. People who follow their parents' career choices without exploring other possibilities are in *identity foreclosure*. (While Erikson and Marcia linked this status to poor mental health—as you will see on the next page—young people "in foreclosure" can also feel happy about this state.)

This young woman, who has accepted a company internship, is in *identity moratorium* because she wants to figure out if she likes working in this career. We don't know, however, if she is excitedly exploring her options or unproductively obsessing about her choices.

This delighted man is in *identity achievement* because he has discovered that his life passion lies in computer design.

> **identity achievement**
> A fully mature identity status in which the young person chooses a satisfying adult life path.

The Identity Statuses in Action

Marcia believed that as teenagers get older, they pass from diffusion to moratorium to achievement. Who thinks much about adulthood in ninth or tenth grade? At that age, your agenda is to cope with puberty. You test the limits. You sometimes act in ways that seem tailor-made to undermine your adult life (see Chapter 9). Then, older adolescents and emerging adults undertake a moratorium search as adulthood looms in full view. At some point during the twenties, people reach achievement, finding a secure adult identity.

However, in real life, people move back and forth across identity statuses *throughout* adulthood (Côté & Bynner, 2008; Schwartz and others, 2015; Waterman, 1999). A woman might enter college exploring different faiths, then become a committed Catholic, start questioning her choice again at 30, and finally settle on her spiritual identity in Bahai at age 45. As many older students are aware, you may have gone through moratorium and believed you were in identity achievement in your career, but then shifted back to moratorium when you realized, "I need a more fulfilling job."

This lifelong shift is appropriate. It's unrealistic to think we reach a final identity as emerging adults. The push to rethink our lives, to have plans and goals, is what makes us human. It is essential at any age. Moreover, revising our identity is vital to living fully since our lives are always being disrupted—as we change careers, become parents, are widowed, or adapt to our children leaving the nest (McAdams, 2013).

The bad news is that young people may get mired in unproductive identity statuses. In some studies, an alarming 1 in 4 undergraduates is locked in diffusion (Côté & Bynner, 2008). They don't have *any* career goals. Or, people may be sampling different paths, but without much Eriksonian moratorium joy. Is your friend who keeps changing his major and putting off graduating excitedly exploring his options, or is he afraid of entering the real world? Are the emerging adults who move from low-wage job to low-wage job really in moratorium or randomly drifting into adult life?

Actually, Erikson's and Marcia's assumptions that people need to sample *many* fields to construct a solid career identity is false. Having a career in mind from childhood, such as knowing you want to be a nurse from age 9 (the status Marcia dismisses as "foreclosure") can be fine. Anxiously obsessing about possibilities—that is, being locked in a state called **ruminative moratorium**—produces poor mental health (Beyers & Luyckx, 2016; Hatano, Sugimura, & Crocetti, 2016): "I don't know if I want to be an anesthesiologist or an actor, and that's driving me crazy."

There can even be problems with being identity achieved. Suppose that after searching various possibilities, you adopt a devalued identity ("Yes, I'll enter medical school, but I'm not convinced being a doctor is me"). It doesn't matter *how* we arrive at achievement. What's crucial is to make a commitment and *feel confident* that this decision expresses our inner self (see Schwartz and others, 2015, for reviews).

Ethnic Identity, a Minority Theme

The emotional advantages of feeling positive about our identity is underscored by **ethnic identity**, a person's sense of belonging to a defined ethnic category, such as Asian American. If you are a member of the dominant culture, you rarely think of your ethnicity. For minority children, categorizing oneself according to a defined label such as Latino or Asian occurs during concrete operations (see Chapter 6), although the salience of this perception waxes and wanes at different ages. For instance, a boy may be acutely aware of his Latino roots if he attends a mainly White high school (Douglass, Wang, & Yip, 2016). While bonding with friends who share her heritage, a girl may feel especially Korean or Vietnamese (Douglass, Mirpuri, & Yip, 2017).

Studies show that being proud of one's ethnic background offers young people a sense of meaning in life (Acevedo-Polakovich and others, 2014; Ajibade and others, 2016). Identifying with being Chinese or Cambodian buffers teenagers from becoming depressed or resorting to risk-taking (Polanco-Roman & Miranda, 2013; Toomey and others, 2013). Ethnic pride is even correlated with doing well in middle school (Santos & Collins, 2016). But it's important to reach out to the wider culture. Actually, firmly connecting with the mainstream culture ("I'm also proud of being American") is one sign that an ethnic minority young person has the skills to reach out fully in love.

ruminative moratorium When a young person is unable to decide between different identities, becoming emotionally paralyzed and highly anxious.

ethnic identity How people come to terms with who they are as people in relation to their unique ethnic or racial heritage.

Connecting with his ethnic identity can offer this young man an intense sense of life meaning.

The challenges for **biracial or multiracial** emerging adults—that is, people from mixed racial or ethnic backgrounds (like former President Barack Obama)—are particularly poignant. But here, too, reaching identity achievement has widespread benefits. Research suggests that having a biracial or bicultural background pushes people to think in more creative ways (Tadmor, Tetlock, & Peng, 2009). It also promotes resilience. As one biracial woman in her early thirties put it: "When I was younger I felt I didn't belong anywhere. But now I've just come to the conclusion that my home is inside myself" (quoted in Phinney, 2006, p. 128).

Making sense of one's "place in the world" as an ethnic minority is a minority identity theme. But every person grapples with choosing a career and finding love. The rest of this chapter tackles those agendas.

> **biracial or multiracial identity** How people of mixed racial backgrounds come to terms with who they are as people in relation to their heritage.

Tying It All Together

1. You overheard your psychology professor saying that his daughter Emma shows symptoms of Erikson's role confusion. Emma must be _____ (*drifting, actively searching for an identity*), which in Marcia's identity status framework is a sign of _____ (*diffusion, foreclosure, moratorium*).

2. Joe said, "I've wanted to be a lawyer since I was a little boy." Kayla replied, "I don't know what my career will be, and I've been obsessing about the possibilities day and night." Joe's identity status is _____ (*moratorium, foreclosure, diffusion, or achievement*), whereas Kayla's status is _____ (*moratorium, foreclosure, diffusion, or achievement*). According to the latest research, who is apt to have an emotional problem?

3. Your cousin Clara has enrolled in nursing school. To predict her feelings about this decision, pick the right question to ask: *Have you explored different career possibilities?/ Do you feel nursing expresses your inner self?*

4. Having a biracial or multiracial identity makes people think in more rigid ways about the world—*true* or *false*?

Answers to the Tying It All Together questions can be found at the end of this chapter.

Finding a Career

When asked to sum up the definition of ideal mental health, Sigmund Freud famously answered, "The ability to love and work." Let's now look at finding ourselves in the world of work.

When did you begin thinking about your career? What influences are drawing you to psychology, nursing, or business—a compelling class, a caring mentor, or the conviction that this field would fit your talents best? How do young people feel about their careers, their futures, and working itself?

To answer these questions, Mihaly Csikszentmihalyi and Barbara Schneider (2000) conducted a pioneering study of teenagers' career dreams. They selected 33 U.S. schools and interviewed students from sixth to twelfth grade. To chart how young people felt—when at home, with friends, when at school—they used the *experience-sampling method* (discussed in Chapter 9). Now let's touch on their insights and more recent studies as we track young people moving through their emerging adult years.

Entering with High (But Often Unrealistic) Career Goals

Almost every teenager dreams of going to college and having a high-paying career. This tendency to aim high appears regardless of gender or social class (Silva, 2016). Whether male or female, rich or poor, adolescents have lofty career goals. Moreover, I believe that the experts who view today's young people as overly coddled (Levine &

LEARNING OUTCOMES

- Describe self-esteem changes after young people enter college and emerging adult emotional growth.

- Outline the features and function of flow states.

- Explore higher education, making special reference to issues relating to completing college and the school-to-work transition.

- Summarize strategies for having a fulfilling college experience.

FIGURE 10.2: The fading chances of U.S. upward mobility: Basic to the "American dream" is having children who are more successful in terms of income (and of course education, too). But, while upward mobility was the birthright of American babies born during World War II (early 1940s) and, to a lesser extent, children born during the early baby boom (late 1940s to 1950), notice from the chart that by the mid-twentieth century, the odds of U.S. newborns earning more than their parents dramatically decreased.

Data from The Equality of Opportunity Project, n.d.

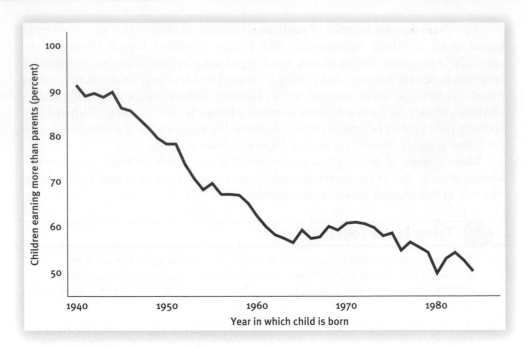

Dean, 2012), narcissistic (Twenge, 2006), and basically unmotivated are wrong. As you can see in Figure 10.2, emerging adults face a more difficult economy than their parents—and especially their grandparents—confronted at the same age. Therefore, it makes sense that in one survey of U.S. college freshmen, students reported being more driven to work hard than their counterparts in the past (Pryor and others, 2011).

The problem is that teenagers are (naturally) clueless about the objective barriers to reaching their dream careers. Can someone who "hates reading" spend a decade getting a psychology Ph.D.? What happens when my students learn they must earn a GPA close to 3.7 to enter my university's nursing program, or that they can't go to law school because of the astronomical costs? Career disappointment can lurk around the corner for young people as they enter college and confront the real world. How do people react?

Self-Esteem and Emotional Growth During College and Beyond

One U.S. survey showed that self-esteem dips dramatically during the first semester of college (Chung and others, 2014) and then gradually rises over the next few years (Higher Education Research Institute [HERI], 2013; see also Wagner and others, 2013). Because entering students inflate their academic abilities (Chung and others, 2014), it can be a shock when those disappointing first-semester grades arrive. Still, as the research described in Figure 10.3 shows, there is diversity, with some people

FIGURE 10.3: The ways depression changed in an economically diverse sample of over 1,000 young people traveling from age 18 to age 22: Notice from this chart that the vast majority of young people are happy both during their teens and as they emerge into their early twenties (red line). Teens with major depressive disorders are still battling their condition three years later (blue line). But a reasonable percentage of moderately depressed teens become happier as they make the transition to adult life (yellow line)—although, granted, some do become more depressed (black line).

Data from Frye & Liem, 2011.

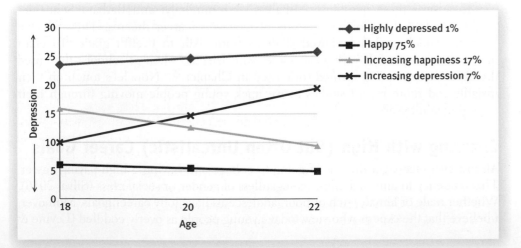

getting unhappier and others improving in mental health from age 18 to 22 (Frye & Liem, 2011).

Who thrives? The figure implies that personality matters. Young people who enter emerging adulthood upbeat and competent are set up to flourish when confronting the demands of college life. In their study, Csikszentmihalyi and Schneider (2000) called these efficacious teens "workers." They are the 16-year-olds who amaze you with their ability to balance band, a part-time job, and honors classes.

But even when teenagers don't qualify as workers, emerging adulthood can be a time of tremendous emotional growth (Alessandri and others, 2016; Syed & Seiffge-Krenke, 2015). Growth is most likely to occur in a personality dimension that psychologists call *conscientiousness*—becoming more reliable, developing self-control (see Cramer, 2008; Donnellan, Conger, & Burzette, 2007; Walton and others, 2013). Emerging adults tend to become more resilient (Zimmermann & Iwanski, 2014). They reason in more thoughtful ways (Labouvie-Vief, 2006; more about these changes in Chapter 12).

To explain this rise in *executive functions*, neuroscientists might look to the fully developed frontal lobes (Henin & Berman, 2016). But an equally plausible cause lies in the wider world. Finding a job that perfectly fits your talents (see the Experiencing the Lifespan box) can transform even troubled teens into workers (Dennissen, Asendorpf, & van Aken, 2008). Csikszentmihalyi argues that a powerful inner state can lock *anyone* into the right career.

Experiencing the Lifespan   A Surprising Path to Adult Success

Dyslexia caused him serious trouble in elementary school; then, at age 12, he began taking drugs. When, at 15, he took the family car and ran away for a weekend in New Orleans, his frantic father visited the local jail and begged the police to take their son in. Finally, his hysterical parents paid guards to take him to a wilderness program and then a school for troubled teens—where he spent his high school years. After dropping out of college his first semester, during his twenties, he drifted from job to job. He was incredibly talented with people but couldn't get along with his bosses.

At about age 30, he got into real estate—a profession for which you don't need a college degree, where what matters is hard work and world-class people skills. After taking the sales associate test eight times, he finally passed! Today, at age 35, he owns a management company and gets national performance awards. He is on track to out-earn his parents (who both graduated from Ivy League schools). His name is Thomas Belsky, and he is my son.

Am I sharing this story *just to* brag about my son and show that with incredible self-efficacy children can triumph against academic odds? I'll answer no. Suppose that Thomas had grown up with adults who weren't devoted to his well-being. Would he have fulfilled his natural gifts or even be alive today?

Finding Flow

Think back over the past week to the times you felt energized and alive. You might be surprised to discover that events you looked forward to—such as relaxing at home—do not come to mind. Many of life's most uplifting experiences occur when we connect deeply with people. Others take place when we are immersed in some compelling task. Csikszentmihalyi calls this intense task absorption **flow.**

Flow is different from "feeling happy." We enter this state during an activity that stretches our capacities, such as the challenge of decoding a difficult academic problem, or (hopefully) getting absorbed in mastering the material in this class. People also differ in the activities that cause flow. For some of us, it's hiking in the Himalayas that produces this feeling. For me, it has been writing this book. When we are in flow, we enter an altered state of consciousness in which we forget the outside world. Problems disappear. We lose a sense of time. The activity feels infinitely worth doing for its own sake. Flow makes us feel completely alive.

flow Csikszentmihalyi's term for feeling total absorption in a challenging, goal-oriented activity.

For this captivated graduate student, the hours may fly by. Challenging activities that fully draw on our talents and skills produce that marvelous inner state called flow.

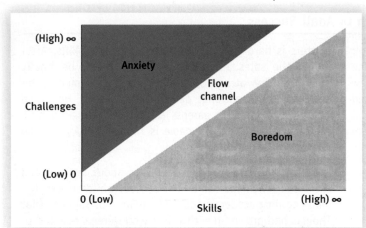

FIGURE 10.4: The zone of flow: Notice that the flow zone (white area) depends on a delicate matching of our abilities and the challenge involved in a particular real-world task. If the task is beyond our capacities, we land in the upper red area of the chart and become anxious. If the task is too easy, we land in the lower, gray area of the chart and become bored. Moreover, as our skills increase, the difficulty of the task must also increase to provide us with the sense of being in flow. Which theorist's ideas about teaching and what stimulates mental growth does this model remind you of? (Turn the page upside down for the answer.)

Data from Csikszentmihalyi, 1990.

Answer: Vygotsky

Csikszentmihalyi (1990), who has spent his career studying flow, finds that some people rarely experience this feeling. Others feel flow several times a day. If you feel flow only during a rare mountain-climbing experience or, worse yet, when robbing a bank, Csikszentmihalyi argues that it will be difficult to construct a satisfying life. The challenge is to find flow in ways related to a career.

Flow depends on being *intrinsically motivated.* We must be mesmerized by what we are doing right now for its own sake, not for an extrinsic reward. But there also is a future-oriented dimension to feeling flow. Flow, according to Csikszentmihalyi, happens when we are working toward a goal.

For example, the idea that this book will be published a year from now is pushing me to write this page. But what riveted me to my chair this morning is the actual process of writing. Getting into a flow state is often elusive. On the days when I can't construct a paragraph, I get anxious. But if I could not regularly find flow in my writing, I would never be writing this book.

Figure 10.4 shows exactly why finding flow can be difficult. That state depends on a delicate *person–environment fit.* When a task seems beyond our capacities, we become anxious. When an activity is too simple, we grow bored. Ideally, the activities that make us feel flow can alert us to our ideal careers. Think about some situation in which you recently felt in flow. If you are in ruminative moratorium or worry you may be in career diffusion, can you use this feeling to alert you to a particular field?

Drawing on flow, my discussion of identity, as well as economic concerns, let's now look at two career paths that emerging adults in the United States follow.

Emerging into Adulthood Without a College Degree (in the United States)

"I never want this kind of job for my kids." This comment, from a 40-year-old high-school graduate construction worker, sums up the general feeling in the United States that college is vital for having a good life (Arnett, 2016). Actually, more than 2 of every 3 U.S. high school graduates enroll in college right after high school. However, as time passes, the ranks thin. For students beginning at four-year institutions, the odds of graduating within the next six years are about 3 in 5 (National Center on Education Statistics, Fast Facts, n.d.). The graduation rates for their community-college counterparts are lower than this.

People in the United States who don't go to college or who never get their degree can have fulfilling careers. Some, like my son, excel at Robert Sternberg's practical intelligence (described in Chapter 7) but do not do well at academics. When they find their flow in the work world, they blossom.

However, I wouldn't rely on these unusual, anecdotal reports. As Figure 10.5 shows, in 2012, the median income of people aged 25 to 34 with master's degrees, who worked full time, was roughly $70,000 per year. Their counterparts, with only high school diplomas, earned less than one-half of that amount—$30,000 (National Center on Education Statistics, Fast Facts, n.d.). In 2013, in the 25 to 34 age group,

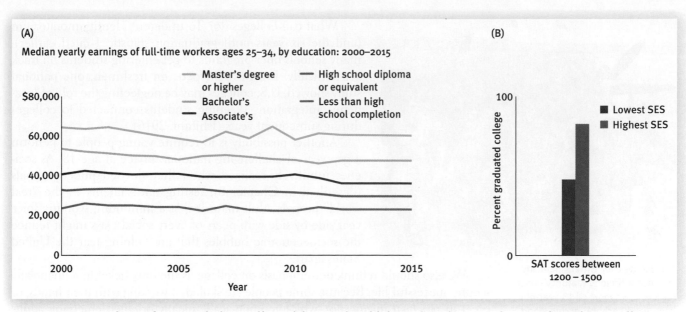

(A)

Median yearly earnings of full-time workers ages 25–34, by education: 2000–2015

Legend:
— Master's degree or higher
— Bachelor's
— Associate's
— High school diploma or equivalent
— Less than high school completion

(Y-axis: $80,000, 60,000, 40,000, 20,000, 0; X-axis: 2000, 2005, 2010, 2015 — Year)

(B)

(Y-axis: Percent graduated college, 0 to 100; X-axis: SAT scores between 1200–1500)

Legend:
■ Lowest SES
■ Highest SES

FIGURE 10.5: Snapshots of economic inequality, with regard to higher education, earnings, and getting a college degree: Chart (A) shows that the high school versus higher-education earnings gap has been pronounced during the twenty-first century, which underscores the fact that people without a college degree are "left behind" economically. Chart (B) shows that for intellectually talented young people, family income makes a huge difference in getting that degree. Bottom line: In the United States, finishing college is vital and low-income, high-ability students are at a severe disadvantage.

(A): Data from National Center on Education Statistics, n.d.; (B): Data from Carnevale & Strohl, 2010.

roughly 1 out of 10 non-college graduates were unemployed. The comparable statistic for young people with a B.A. or higher was 6 percent (National Center on Education Statistics, Fast Facts, n.d.).

Given these facts, why do many emerging adults drop out of school? Our first assumption is that these people are not "college material"—uninterested in academics, poorly prepared in high school, and/or can't do the work.

True, to succeed in college, academic aptitude is important (Ishitani, 2016). A U.S. public school student graduating high school with a C average has less than 1 in 5 odds of finishing a four-year degree (Engle, n.d.). But, as Figure 10.5B shows, economic considerations matter greatly. Academically talented, low-SES young people are far less likely to graduate from college than their affluent peers (Carnevale & Strohl, 2010; Silva, 2016).

When the Gates Foundation surveyed more than 600 twenty-first-century young adults ages 22 to 30 who had dropped out of college, they discovered the same message—money matters. Only 1 in 10 students said they left school because the courses were too difficult or they weren't interested in the work. The main reason was that they had to work full time to finance school, and the strain became too much (Silva, 2016).

The silver lining is that most of these people did plan to return. And, as many nontraditional student readers are aware, there can be emotional advantages to leaving and then coming back. In Sweden, the social clock for college is programmed to start ticking a few years after high school (Arnett, 2007). The reasoning is that time spent in the wider world helps people home in on what to study in school.

This twenty-something college student is at higher risk of dropping out simply because he has to work full time while going to school.

Photodisc/Getty Images

INTERVENTIONS ▸ **Smoothing the School Path and School-to-Work Transition**

Still, we can't let society off of the hook. The fact that financing college is so difficult for U.S. young people is a national shame (Arnett, 2016). The standard practice of taking out loans means that college graduates face frightening economic futures after earning their degrees (Gibson-Davis & Percheski, 2018; Silva, 2016). In 2012, more than 1 out of every 2 U.S. emerging adults left college owing the government and private lenders $20,000 or more (HERI, 2013).

Triumphing over Hitler's Germany provided a lifelong maturity boost for a whole cohort of 18-year-old boys—and because, during World War II, serving one's nation in the military was mandatory, these young soldiers were apt to develop strong lifelong bonds from sharing this pivotal experience that transcended social class.

school-to-work transition The change from the schooling phase of life to the work world.

What can colleges do? To undercut identity moratorium (and the six years until graduation statistic I cited earlier), many schools offer programs to get entering students on track academically. But in their focus on freshmen, one national study showed, U.S. colleges may be neglecting the role of "academic integration" (keeping students connected to college) during subsequent years (Ishitani, 2016).

Another possibility is to require young people to perform a gap year of challenging national service at age 18. As societies intuitively realized when they devised puberty rituals (described in Chapter 8), testing one's talents in the "real world" propels adult maturity. At a minimum, working for a year side by side with peers of every social class might reduce the socioeconomic bubbles that are helping tear the United States apart.

We also should rethink our emphasis on college as the only ticket to a financially secure, successful life. Because some people are skilled at working with their hands, or excel in *practical intelligence*, why force non-academically oriented emerging adults to endure a poor talent–environment fit? Can't we develop government-sponsored apprentice programs like the ones currently in operation in Germany? In that nation, employers partner with schools that offer on-the-job training. Graduates emerge with a *definite* position in that specific firm (see Buchanan, 2017).

Germany also has a youth unemployment problem. But because its apprenticeship programs offer young people careers outside of college, this nation helps undercut the unproductive ruminative-identity moratorium that produces such angst in the Western world. In one German national survey, having a job or being enrolled in an apprentice program predicted both identity achievement and occupational self-efficacy down the road (Seiffge-Krenke, Persike, & Luyckx, 2013).

How many young people are locked in diffusion or moratorium because the United States lacks a defined **school-to-work transition** (school-to-career path)? Rather than leaving the anxiety-ridden, post-education job-hunt to luck and putting the burden on the "inner" talents of kids, can't we devise strategies to help young people confront this crucial social-clock challenge of adult life?

Table 10.4 summarizes the main messages of this section, by offering suggestions for emerging adults and society. Now it's time to immerse ourselves in the undergraduate experience.

Table 10.4: Succeeding in College/Finding a Career Identity: Tips for Young People and Society

For Young People

1. Understand that when you enter college, you may overestimate your academic abilities. It takes time to get adjusted to the demands of this new life!

2. Focus on finding your flow in selecting a career. Avoid obsessing about different possibilities, but understand that it can take time to formulate a clear career plan.

3. If you need to drop out for some time, understand it's not the end of the world. Having a year or two off may help you home in on a career identity and be a better student.

For Colleges (and Society)

1. Provide support *throughout* college to help students succeed.

2. Reach out to low-income students and offer special services for parents or working adults.

3. Institute a national (ideally, mandatory) year of government service for all young people at age 18 and offer apprenticeship programs linked to jobs—ones that offer a conduit to careers without college.

4. Make negotiating young people's school-to-work transition a national priority!

Being in College

So far, I've been implying that the only purpose of college is to find a career. Thankfully, in surveys, most U.S. college graduates disagree. They report that the main value of being an undergraduate was to help them "grow intellectually and personally" (Hoover, 2011).

If you are a traditional college student, here are tips to make your college experience an inner-growth flow zone.

INTERVENTIONS Making College an Inner-Growth Flow Zone

GET THE BEST PROFESSORS (AND TALK TO THEM OUTSIDE OF CLASS!) It's a no-brainer that, just as in elementary school (see Chapter 7), an exciting college teacher can make an enduring difference in a young person's life (Komarraju, Musulkin, & Bhattacharya, 2010; Schreiner and others, 2011). Outstanding professors adore their subject and are committed to communicating their passion to students (Bane, 2004). So reach out and talk to your professors. Feeling listened to can be a peak experience in a person's academic life. As one community college student put it:

> You know . . . he really listens. I was . . . telling him . . . I was struggling. . . . He . . . let me talk . . . . It's like . . . he gives a damn.
>
> (quoted in Schreiner and others, 2011, p. 324)

CONNECT YOUR CLASSES TO POTENTIAL CAREERS Professors' mission is to excite you in their field. But classes can't provide the hands-on experience you need to find your zone of flow. So institute your personal school-to-work transition. Set up independent studies involving volunteer work. If you are interested in science, work in a professor's lab. If your passion is politics, do an internship with a local legislator. In one study, college seniors mentioned that the highlight of their undergraduate experience occurred during a mentored project in the real world (Light, 2001).

IMMERSE YOURSELF IN THE COLLEGE MILIEU Following this advice is easier if you attend a small residential school. At a large university, especially a commuter school, you'll need to make special efforts to get involved in campus life. Join a college organization—or two or three. Working for the college newspaper or becoming active in the drama club will not only provide you with a rich source of friends, but it can help promote your career identity, too.

CAPITALIZE ON THE DIVERSE HUMAN CONNECTIONS COLLEGE OFFERS As I've been highlighting, peer groups are vital in shaping children's development from preschool on. At college, it is tempting to find a single clique and then not reach out to other crowds. Resist this impulse. A major growth experience college provides is the chance to connect with people of different points of view (Hu & Kuh, 2003; see also Leung & Chiu, 2011). Here's what a Harvard undergraduate had to say:

> I have re-evaluated my beliefs. . . . At college, there are people of all different religions around me. . . . Living . . . with these people . . . has made me reconsider and ultimately reaffirm my faith.
>
> (quoted in Light, 2001, p. 163)

College is an ideal time to connect with people from different backgrounds. So go for it!

But this community college student summed it up best:

> When I . . . have all these great stories; they think college is . . . amazing . . . because of all the people I'm surrounded with.
>
> (quoted in Schreiner and others, 2011, p. 337)

Being surrounded by interesting people has another benefit: It promotes Erikson's other emerging adult task—finding love.

🌐 Tying It All Together

1. Your 17-year-old cousin is graduating from high school. Given what you learned in this section, you might predict that she has *overly high/overly low* expectations about her academic abilities and that she will become *more mature/remain exactly the same* as she travels through her twenties.

2. Ileara loves her server job. When the restaurant is hectic, time flies by. She feels like a multitasking whiz! Ileara is describing a _____ experience.

3. Josiah says the reason his classmates drop out of college is that they can't do the work. Jocasta says, "Sorry, it's the need to work incredible hours to pay for school." Make each person's case, using the information from this chapter.

4. Your cousin Juan, a new freshman, asks for tips about how to succeed in college. Based on this section, pick the advice you should *not* give:

   a. Get involved in campus activities.
   b. Select friends who have exactly the same ideas as you do.
   c. Get the best professors and reach out to make connections with them.

Answers to the Tying It All Together questions can be found at the end of this chapter.

Finding Love

LEARNING OUTCOMES

- Outline changes in the twenty-first-century search for love.

- Explain Murstein's theory, making reference to critiques of homogamy and the idea that mate selection progresses in defined stages.

- Survey Facebook romance and adult attachment theory.

- Summarize this section's tips for finding fulfilling relationships.

intimacy Erikson's first adult task, which involves connecting with a partner in a mutual loving relationship.

How do emerging adults negotiate Erikson's first task of adult life (see Table 10.5)—**intimacy**, the search for love? Let's first explore some cultural shifts in the ways we choose mates before turning to our main topic: finding fulfilling love.

Table 10.5: Erikson's Life Stages

Life Stage	Primary Task
Infancy (birth to 1 year)	Basic trust versus mistrust
Toddlerhood (1 to 2 years)	Autonomy versus shame and doubt
Early childhood (3 to 6 years)	Initiative versus guilt
Middle childhood (7 to 12 years)	Industry versus inferiority
Adolescence to emerging adulthood (teens into twenties)	Identity versus role confusion
Early adulthood (twenties to early forties)	**Intimacy versus isolation**
Middle adulthood (forties to sixties)	Generativity versus stagnation
Late adulthood (late sixties and beyond)	Integrity versus despair

Setting the Context: Seismic Shifts in Searching for Love

Daolin Yang lives in Hebie Province, China. . . . At age 15, he married his wife Yufen, then 13. . . . A matchmaker proposed the marriage on behalf of the Yang family. They have been married for 62 years. . . . He says that they married first and dated later. It is "cold at the start and hot in the end." The relationship gets better and better over the years.

(quoted in Xia & Zhou, 2003, p. 231)

I got married . . . to the woman . . . I met on Match a year ago. I met my wife . . . a week after setting up my profile, and we have been together ever since. . . . Thanks to the profiles, . . . I found the girl of my dreams.

(adapted from Top 10 Best Dating Sites, 2014)

Throughout history, parents chose a child's marital partner (often during puberty), and newlyweds hoped (if they were lucky) to later fall in love. Today, with the explosion of on-line dating, the Internet has globalized the search for love. By the second decade of the twenty-first century, an incredible 1 in 3 married couples in the United States had met on-line. Moreover, studies suggest that on-line marriages are more likely to be happy than those in which spouses meet in the traditional way! (See Cacioppo and others, 2013.)

Many More Partner Choices—with Cautions

The twentieth-century lifestyle revolution also produced a remarkable expansion in the *kind* of partners we choose. During the 1950s in the South, interracial marriages were against the law. By the turn of the twenty-first century, 1 in 3 European Americans reported getting romantically involved with someone of a different ethnicity or race (Yancey & Yancey, 2002). In one recent survey, 3 out of 4 students attending historically Black colleges said they were open to dating someone of a different race (Stackman, Reviere, & Medley, 2016).

However, there are limits to the global assumption that we live in a golden age of diverse partner choices. Yes, during the 1950s, young people risked being shunned by their parents (and society) for marrying outside of their race. But during that era of upward mobility, Americans were far more likely to select partners of a different social class than today. Escalating income inequalities mean that twenty-first-century U.S. children are increasingly likely to be raised in class-based social milieus. Therefore, research suggests that mate choices today are as stratified by income as during the early twentieth century (Gibson-Davis & Percheski, 2018; Mare, 2016)!

Still, one *total* transformation has occurred in the way we select mates: Same sex romance is clearly out of the closet in the Western world.

Hot in Developmental Science: Same-Sex Romance

In the 1990s, when I began teaching, I remember the students' uneasiness in the classroom when I mentioned **sexual orientation**—our sexual and romantic attraction other people. No more! Although the gay rights movement exploded in the late 1960s in New York City, its most amazing strides took place during the early twenty-first century. As one developmentalist put it, within a few years, the announcement "I'm gay" went from evoking shock to producing yawns—"So, what else is new?" (See Savin-Williams, 2001, 2008.) In an era in which emerging adults define themselves as "mostly straight," "sometimes gay," or "occasionally bisexual," limiting one's sexual identity to a defined category is becoming passé (see Morgan, 2013).

Homophobia, the fear and dislike of gay people, still is not rare. The fact that, as early as elementary school (see Chapter 6), peers reject boys who don't stick to

sexual orientation Our sexual and romantic attraction to other people.

homophobia Intense fear and dislike of gay people.

Table 10.6 Stereotypes and Scientific Realities Related to Being Transgender and Gay

Stereotype #1: Transgender people change their bodies to conform to their inner gender identity, and then select same-sex romantic partners.

Answer: False. Transgender teens and adults may decide to forego gender reassignment therapy. While hormonal and surgical interventions can be emotionally lifesaving, physically transitioning is not essential to having a fulfilling life. Moreover, because gender identity is unrelated to sexual orientation, a transgender man or woman may identify as gay (be attracted to same-sex partners only), heterosexual, bisexual, or asexual.

Stereotype #2: Overinvolved or distant parents cause children to be gay or transgender.

Answer: This statement is also false. Although a definite genetic/brain/biological cause has yet to be found, prenatal testosterone helps to program later sexual orientation and gender identity (see Chapter 5). In one compelling interview study, transgender participants reported that their parents had raised them in the *exact* same way as their siblings.

Stereotype #3: Gay and transgender couples have lower-quality relationships and pathological family interactions.

Answer: False, yet again. Same-sex and transgender romantic bonds vary in quality just like heterosexual relationships do. In fact, some research suggests that lesbian couples fight less and have superior child-rearing skills—hitting their children less frequently and engaging in less fantasy play.

Stereotype #4: Gay and transgender teens and emerging adults have high rates of mental health issues.

Answer: Unfortunately, this statement is accurate, with psychological problems such as depression and drug abuse common among sexual-minority youth. In one nationwide poll, 40 percent of gay teens had attempted suicide. One cause is the frequent bullying these young people typically experience beginning in childhood. Still, the massive social rejection that transgender and gay youth confronted in the past is less intense today in the West.

Information from: Diamond, 2013; Golombok and others, 2003; Harper & Wilson, 2017; Meuwly and others, 2013; National Center for Gender Equality, n.d.; Schuster, Reisner, & Onorato, 2016.

standard gender roles suggests that society still has serious qualms about accepting people who venture outside of the heterosexual norms.

Given this enduring social scorn, it makes sense that transgender and gay young people undergo considerable emotional turmoil during their teens (see Table 10.6 for data relating to this issue and the scientific facts about sexual-minority youth and adults). Because ethnic-minority families are more apt to strongly adhere to traditional gender conceptions, Black and Latino LGBTQ emerging adults frequently have the most difficulty coming out (Budge and others, 2016; Richter, Lindahl, & Malik, 2017). But in one U.S. survey of 165 bisexual and gay young people, the largest group (about 4 in 5 adolescents and emerging adults) was classified as identity achieved. These young people said they felt fully accepted by their families and comfortable with their sexual choices. The concern was the 1 in 5 respondents the researchers labeled as "struggling." While these young people "knew" their identity, they worried about disclosing this fact to disapproving parents and friends (Bregman and others, 2013).

The most at-risk group may be young people who are genuinely "identity questioning." When researchers explored the mental health of women who defined themselves as heterosexual but reported having mainly same-sex attractions, this group was as likely to be distressed as their counterparts who openly labeled themselves as bisexual or gay (Johns, Zimmerman, & Bauermeister, 2013). 🐢

Again, this research underscores the importance of being identity achieved in a positive way. Once you *embrace* your identity (or self)—whether as a gay or transgender person, or ethnic minority—there is a sense of self-efficacy and relief. But problems arise if your attachment figures dislike the person you "really" are (Velkoff and others, 2016), or when you languish untethered in moratorium for an extended time.

A More Erratic, Extended Dating Phase

Unfortunately, however, romantic moratorium is built into Western society because, as I've been highlighting, the untethered phase of mate selection lasts so long. In tracking over 500 economically diverse young people from age 18 to 25, U.S. researchers found that a fraction—about 1 in 4 respondents—did find an enduring, stable relationship soon after leaving their teens. The largest group—almost 1 in 3 people—had only sporadic relationships or no romantic involvements during their college careers (Rauer and others, 2013).

When emerging adults do find a partner, they may have on-again/off-again relationships, a process called **relationship churning.** In one U.S. survey, nearly 1 in 2 couples in their twenties who broke up had gotten back together again at some point. And, after ending the relationship, one-half continued to have sex with their ex (Halpern-Meekin and others, 2013).

In interviews, young people gamely frame their romantic disappointments as learning experiences: "Don't trust someone because they say they love you. Sometimes it's better to let things go" (quoted in Norona, Roberson, & Welsh, 2017, p. 168). But it's no surprise that, after these breakups, people are more likely to binge drink (Bowers, Segrin, & Joyce, 2016). Their health also declines (Barr and others, 2016). One longitudinal study suggested that, after a couple separates, the losses in self-esteem tend to last a full year (Luciano & Orth, 2017). Contrast this with the research suggesting that cohabiting and getting married increases young people's feelings of self-worth (Luciano & Orth, 2017; Mernitz & Dush, 2016)!

I believe that these studies validate Erikson's idea that finding intimacy is important during emerging adulthood. While it may make good sense to be wary about getting married, a high-quality love relationship can buffer young people from the ups and downs of the turbulent twenties (and of any age). How can people achieve this goal?

Similarity and Structured Relationship Stages: A Classic Model of Love and a Critique

Bernard Murstein's now-classic **stimulus-value-role theory** (1999) views finding satisfying love as a three-phase process. During the **stimulus phase,** we see a potential partner and make our first decision: "Could this be a good choice for me?" Since we know nothing about the person, our judgment is based on superficial signs, such as looks or the way the individual dresses. In this assessment, we compare our own reinforcement value to the other person's along a number of dimensions (Murstein, 1999): "True, I am not as good-looking, but she may find me desirable because I am better educated." If the person seems of equal value, we decide to go on a date.

When we start seeing each other, we enter the **value-comparison phase.** Here, our goal is to match up in attitudes: "Does this person share my interests and values?" If this partner seems "right," we enter the **role phase,** in which we work out our shared lives.

So, at a party, Aaron scans the room and rejects Sophia with the tattoos. If he is searching on eHarmony he might be put off by Georgette, who looks too gorgeous or has posted photos of her vacation in San Tropez. Aaron gravitates to Ashley because her profile suggests that she is more low maintenance and maybe—like him—a bit shy. When Aaron and Ashley begin seeing each other, they discover that they enjoy the same activities; they both love hiking; they have the same worldview. On their third or tenth date, there may be a revelation that "this person is too different." But, if things go smoothly, Aaron and Ashley plan their future. Should they cohabit or move to California when they graduate? When will they marry and have kids?

The *equal-reinforcement-value partner* aspect of Murstein's theory explains why we expect couples to be similar in "social value" as well as social class (Conroy-Beam & Buss, 2016). When we find serious value mismatches, we search for reasons to explain

Brocreative/Shutterstock

This once standard campus scene is less typical today, as more undergraduates are putting off romance until they have their careers in place. But, as I mention in the text, traveling through college (and the twenties) without a stable relationship has emotional downsides.

relationship churning
Having on-again/off-again romantic relationships in which couples repeatedly get together and then break up.

stimulus-value-role theory Murstein's mate-selection theory that suggests similar people pair up and that our path to commitment progresses through three phases (called the *stimulus, value-comparison,* and *role* phases).

stimulus phase In Murstein's theory, the initial mate-selection stage, in which we make judgments about a potential partner based on external characteristics such as appearance.

value-comparison phase In Murstein's theory, the second mate-selection stage, in which we make judgments about a partner on the basis of similar values and interests.

role phase In Murstein's theory, the final mate-selection stage, in which committed partners work out their future life together.

these discrepancies (Murstein, Reif, & Syracuse-Siewert, 2002): "That handsome young lawyer must have low self-esteem to have settled for that unattractive older woman"; "Perhaps he chose that person because she has millions in the bank."

Most important, Murstein's theory suggests that in love relationships, as in childhood friendships, **homogamy** (similarity) is the driving force. We want a soul mate, a person who matches us, not just in external status, but also in interests and attitudes about life.

> **homogamy** The principle that we select a mate who is similar to us.

Actually, because research suggests that identical twins (who have the same DNA) are more likely than fraternal twins to select partners with similar "bonding styles," humans may be biologically primed to gravitate to specific mates (Horwitz and others, 2016). Just like Lorenz's geese (described in Chapter 4), our species might even become attached to the way childhood caregivers *physically* appear. In one fascinating study, young people tended to choose partners who resembled their opposite sex parent—but only if they felt close to that person as a child (Kocsor and others, 2016). So if you have the uncanny sense you chose your lover partly because she looks like your beloved mother, you may be right!

Homogamy is enhanced by the fact that people with identical passions gravitate to similar zones of flow. Political junkies may discover the love of their life when working on election campaigns. Theater majors are apt to find the perfect mate when trying out for plays. Moreover, when couples connect though mutual interests ("I met my love at the theater"), they find an interesting side benefit: Sharing flow activities helps to keep passion alive (Reissman, Aron, & Bergin, 1993).

The Limits to Looking for a Similar Mate

Still, there are important exceptions to the rule that homogamy drives love. In examining happiness among long-married couples, researchers discovered that relationships worked best when one partner was more dominant and the other more submissive (Markey & Markey, 2007).

Logically, matching up two strong personalities might not promote romantic bliss (people would probably fight). Two passive partners might frustrate each other ("Why doesn't my lover take the lead?"). Yes, similarity is important (birds of a feather should flock together). But, as in the other familiar saying that opposites attract, couples get along best when they have a *few* carefully selected opposing personality preferences and styles.

Admiring each other's talents in their shared life passion predicts future happiness for this young couple. It also may make these actors feel as if they are becoming better performers just from being together—and it certainly helps if they inflate each other's talents, too ("My partner is sure to be the next Denzel Washington!").

Moreover, suppose a couple is very similar but in unpleasant traits, such as their tendency to fly off the handle or be pathologically shy. What really matters in happiness is not so much objective similarity, but believing that a significant other has terrific personality traits. People who see their partner as outgoing and emotionally stable ("He is a real people person, and open to new things") have better relationships over time (Furler, Gomez, & Grob, 2013; Furler, Gomez, & Grob, 2014).

The bottom-line message is that finding a soul mate does not mean selecting a clone. We don't want a reflection of our current self. We choose people who embody our "ideal self"—the person we would like to be. Moreover, one study showed that when people believe their partner embodies their best self ("I fell in love with him because he's a wonderful actor, and that's always been my goal"), they tend to grow emotionally as people, becoming more like their ideal (Rusbult and others, 2009).

Actually, rather than objectively matching up, happy couples see their mates through rose-colored glasses (Murray & Holmes, 1997). They inflate their partner's virtues (Murray and others, 2000). They overestimate the extent to which they and that person are alike in values and goals (Murray and others, 2002). So science confirms George Bernard Shaw's classic observation: "Love is a gross exaggeration of the difference between one person and everyone else."

The Limits to Charting Love in Stages

> As soon as I met R, . . . he was just so kind and thoughtful and he was considerate. So we started talking on email and . . . I got back from the trip, and he came over a month after the cruise. . . . I knew like right away. . . . It was just like kind of a confirmation that, I don't know, we were meant to be together.
>
> (quoted in Mackinnon and others, 2011, p. 607)

This quotation suggests that viewing mate selection in static stages minimizes the magical essence of romance. Couples may suddenly fall in love when they meet after months of emails. Or there may be an epiphany, at some point, when people decide, "This is the one."

In a classic study, researchers captured these ups and downs by asking dating couples to graph their chances (from 0 to 100 percent) of marrying their partner. They then had these student volunteers return each month, chart changes in their feelings of commitment, and explain the reasons for any dramatic relationship turning points (Surra & Hughes, 1997; Surra, Hughes, & Jacquet, 1999).

You can see examples of these turning points in Table 10.7. Notice that relationships do often hinge on homogamy issues ("This person is right for me"). Other causes are important, too—from the input of family and friends ("I really dislike that person") to the idea that I'm too young to get involved. Today, an important turning point in commitment is becoming Facebook official with a mate.

Table 10.7: Some Major Positive (+) and Negative (−) Turning Points in a Relationship

Personal Compatibility/Homogamy

We spent a lot of time together. +

We had a big fight. −

We had similar interests. +

Compatibility with Family and Friends

My friends kept saying that Sue was bad for me. −

I fit right in with his family. +

Her dad just hated me. −

Other Random Forces

I just turned 21, so I don't want to be tied down to anyone. −

The guy I used to date started calling me. −

Information from Surra, Hughes, & Jacquet, 1999.

 Hot in Developmental Science: Facebook Romance

As ground zero in our contemporary social life, Facebook (and other social media sites) is a research gold mine for exploring the nuances of modern love. Scroll through your daily feed and you will notice that some couples seem invisible on Facebook; others continually broadcast their love. Does Facebook homogamy (shared likes, profile similarities, mutual friends) reflect actual relationship closeness? By comparing couples' attitudes with these virtual love signs, researchers find the answer is yes. More Facebook similarity mirrors the depth of real world love (Castaneda, Wendel, & Crockett, 2015).

Monkey Business Images/Shutterstock

AJR_photo/Shutterstock

Would you rate the couple on the left as nicer human beings than the person on the right? If you are like most people, your answer would be yes.

Moreover, labeling oneself as "in a relationship" does reflect a major romantic turning point. In surveys, people who take this step report being more committed to their partners and less interested in searching for other mates (Lane, Piercy, & Carr, 2016).

Using simulated profiles, researchers find that posting loving photos of couples makes outsiders judge a given Facebook user as more likeable. On the other hand, putting gushy statements ("I love my sweet baby so much") on a partner's wall is a turnoff. This kind of behavior gets people fewer votes for being personally liked (Emery and others, 2015).

Normally, changing one's status from "single" to "in a relationship" evokes kudos like "Congrats!" But another study using simulated Facebook pages showed that what really matters are the comments *others* post. If friends make snide comments like, "Too bad," outsiders see the relationship as a negative, rather than as a plus (Ballantine, Lin, & Veer, 2015).

But the greatest danger happens when couples break up, and Facebook users feel compelled to broadcast their failure to the world by changing their on-line status to "it's complicated" or "single." To cope with their pain, people commonly use cleansing strategies such as deleting mutual photos and, sometimes, defriending a former mate (LeFebvre, Blackburn, & Brody, 2015). But the temptation can be overwhelming to monitor an ex by obsessively checking mutual friends' pages or engage in bouts of relational aggression on one's *own* Facebook page. As one young woman admitted (after breaking up), "I had a lot more status updates and pictures showing how much fun I was having" (quoted in LeFebvre, Blackburn, & Brody, 2015, p. 90).

This is why, in interviews, young people lambast Facebook as "a trap"; "It's a total . . . train wreck" (quoted in Fox, Osborn, & Warber, 2014, p. 531). Although it may not make or break a relationship, the social-media revolution makes love much "more complicated" in Facebook terms. (Check out Table 10.8 for some interesting additional research facts related to on-line romance.)

What concrete behaviors *really* predict whether a relationship will last? Without denying that couples have ups and downs, relationship churning erodes

Table 10.8: Fascinating Scientific FAQs About On-line Love

Question #1: Should I worry if there is a huge assortment of potentially competing romantic possibilities on my partner's Facebook friends list?

Research answer: No, but be concerned if your lover is adding *new* friends. In one study with college students, the sheer number of romantic possibilities on a person's friend list had nothing to do with the odds that a partner would stray; but a person who reported lower feelings of commitment was apt to solicit new Facebook friends (see Drouin, Miller, & Dibble, 2014). Furthermore, women in a relationship should never send winking emoticons to male friends because these implicit tips signal, "I'm interested in having sex" and, therefore, make male mates intensely jealous (Hudson and others, 2015).

Question #2: I must admit that I'm guilty of sexting my partner. Does that mean I'm a loose woman or have personality issues?

Research answer: Contrary to media alarm bells, sexting is not a symptom of mental health problems (Gordon-Messer and others, 2013). People sext for many reasons—such as for fun, as a joke, or to show off their bodies to friends (Burkett, 2015). Actually, the main correlate of sexting is being in a close romantic relationship (Delevi & Weisskirch, 2013; Samimi & Alderson, 2014). Still, among females, unwanted sexting is fairly common—with more than one-half of girls in one study reporting they engaged in this behavior to please their mates (Drouin & Tobin, 2014).

Question #3: My lover texts me millions of times every day. Does that mean he is anxious about my love and generally insecure?

Research answer: Not necessarily, but be alert to whether he prefers texting to contacting you in other ways. In measuring relationship satisfaction among 364 daters, and controlling for physical distance, one psychologist (Luo, 2014) found that the absolute number of texts per day didn't matter. However, overusing this communication mode, compared to calling or meeting face to face, predicted relationship distress. Other research suggests that texting at unusual hours, such as late at night, is symptomatic of being anxious about a relationship (Lepp, Li, & Barkley, 2016). So, when a lover's cyberspace messages pop up at inappropriate times and especially when these virtual communications replace "real life" interactions, your partner may feel uneasy about your love.

Question #4: I get intensely anxious if I haven't checked Facebook every hour. Is that a sign I have emotional problems?

Research answer: As one survey suggested, the average undergraduate spends two hours on social media; so, clearly, virtual reality has taken over young peoples' lives. But in this poll, students who reported getting very agitated when they didn't repeatedly check Facebook did report lower well-being than their peers (Satici & Uysal, 2015). Because face-to-face interactions evoke more happiness than spending time in solitary venues (such as being on-line) (Coccia & Darling, 2016), feeling *completely* tethered to Facebook can be incompatible with flourishing in life.

trust (Ogolsky, Surra, & Monk, 2016). Cycling through breaking up and getting back together signals that things are spiraling out of control (Vennum and others, 2015).

Why are some people prone to repeatedly having stormy, erratic relationships, while others know how to reach out in love? This brings me to the final piece of the puzzle relating to finding fulfilling love: Select someone who is securely attached!

Love Through the Lens of Attachment Theory

Chapter 4 discussed the different infant attachment styles. Mary Ainsworth (1973) found that *securely attached* babies run to their mother with hugs and kisses when she appears in the room. *Avoidant* infants act cold, aloof, and indifferent in the Strange Situation when the caregiver returns. *Anxious-ambivalent* babies are overly clingy, afraid to explore the toys, and angry and inconsolable when their caregiver arrives. Now, think of your own romantic relationships, or the relationships of family members or friends. Wouldn't these same attachment categories apply to adult romantic love? Cindy Hazan and Phillip Shaver (1987) had the same insight: Let's draw on Ainsworth's dimensions to classify people into different **adult attachment styles.**

adult attachment styles The different ways in which adults relate to romantic partners, based on Mary Ainsworth's infant attachment styles. (Adult attachment styles are classified as *secure, preoccupied/ambivalent insecure,* or *avoidant/ dismissive insecure.*)

preoccupied/ambivalent adult attachment An excessively clingy, needy style of relating to loved ones.

avoidant/dismissive adult attachment A standoffish, excessively disengaged style of relating to loved ones.

People with a **preoccupied/ambivalent** type of insecure attachment fall quickly and deeply in love (see the How Do We Know box). But, because they are engulfing and needy, they often end up being rejected or feeling unfulfilled. Adults with an **avoidant/dismissive** insecure attachment are at the opposite end of the spectrum—withholding, aloof, reluctant to engage. You may have dated this kind of person, someone whose mottos are "stay independent," "don't share," "avoid getting close" (Feeney, 1999).

HOW DO WE KNOW . . .
that a person is securely or insecurely attached?

How do developmentalists classify adults as either securely or insecurely attached? In the current relationship interview, researchers ask participants to describe their romantic relationships. Trained evaluators then code the responses.

People are labeled securely attached if they coherently describe the pluses and minuses of the relationship; if they talk freely about their desire for intimacy; and if they adopt an other-centered perspective, seeing nurturing the other person's development as a primary goal. People who describe their relationship in formal, stilted ways, emphasize "autonomy issues," or talk about the advantages of being together in non-intimate terms ("We are buying a house"; "We go places"), are classified as avoidant/dismissive. Those who express total dependence ("I can't function unless she is nearby"), anger about not being treated correctly, or anxiety about the partner leaving are classified as preoccupied/ambivalent.

This in-depth interview technique is time intensive. But many attachment researchers argue that it reveals a person's attachment style better than questionnaires in which people simply check "yes" or "no" to indicate whether items on a scale apply to them.

Westend61/Getty Images

Secure adult attachment

- **Definition:** Capable of genuine intimacy in relationships.
- **Signs:** Empathic, sensitive, able to reach out emotionally; balances own needs with those of partner; has affectionate, caring interactions; probably in a loving, long-term relationship.

Fuse/Corbis/Getty Images

Avoidant/dismissive adult attachment

- **Definition:** Unable to get close in relationships.
- **Signs:** Uncaring, aloof, emotionally distant; unresponsive to loving feelings; abruptly disengages at signs of involvement; unlikely to be in a long-term relationship.

Bill Aron/Photo edit

Preoccupied/ambivalent adult attachment

- **Definition:** Needy and engulfing in relationships.
- **Signs:** Excessively jealous, suffocating; needs continual reassurance of being totally loved; unlikely to be in a loving, long-term relationship.

Securely attached adults are fully open to love. They give their partners space to differentiate, yet are firmly committed. Like Ainsworth's secure infants, their faces light up when they talk about their partner: The joy in their love shines through.

Decades of research show that insecurely attached emerging adults have trouble with relationships (Lapsley & Woodbury, 2016). Securely attached people are more successful in love.

Securely attached adults have happier marriages. They report more satisfying romances (Mikulincer and others, 2002; Morgan & Shaver, 1999). Securely attached adults hang in there during difficult times. They freely support their partner in times of need. Using the metaphor of mother–infant attachment described in Chapter 4, people with secure attachments are wonderful dancers. They excel at being emotionally in tune.

In Chapter 4, I also discussed Bowlby and Ainsworth's idea that the dance of attachment between the caregiver and baby is the basis for feeling securely attached in infancy and for dancing well in other relationships. Listen to friends anguishing over their relationship problems, and you will hear similar ideas: "The reason I act clingy is that, during childhood, I felt unloved"; "It's hard for me to warm up because my mom was rejecting and cold." We know that attachment categories are malleable during childhood. Once we enter adulthood, how much can these styles change?

To answer this question, researchers measured the attachment styles of several hundred women at intervals over two years (Cozzarelli and others, 2003). They found that almost one-half of the women had changed categories over that time. So the good news is that we can change our attachment status from insecure to secure. And—as will come as no surprise—we can also move in the opposite direction, temporarily feeling insecurely attached after a terrible experience with love. The best way to understand attachment styles, then, is as *somewhat* enduring and consistent, arising, in part, from our experiences in love.

One reason attachment styles stay stable is that they operate as a self-fulfilling prophecy. A preoccupied, clingy person does tend to be rejected repeatedly. An avoidant individual remains isolated because piercing that armored shell takes such a heroic effort. A loving person gets more secure over time because his caring behavior evokes warm, loving responses (Davila & Kashy, 2009).

By now, you are probably impressed with the power of the attachment perspective to predict real-world love. But notice that these *correlational* findings have conceptual flaws. Suppose that a person labels his childhood as unhappy, has an insecure attachment style, and experiences relationship distress. It's tempting to say that "poor parenting" caused this insecure worldview, which then produced the current problems; but couldn't this connection operate in the opposite way? "I'm not getting along with my partner, so I believe love can't work out, and it must be my parents' fault." Or couldn't these *self-reports* be caused by a third force—such as being depressed? If you have a gloomy worldview, wouldn't you see both your childhood and current relationship as dissatisfying and also have an avoidant or preoccupied attachment style?

Still, as a framework for understanding people (and ourselves), the attachment-styles framework has great appeal. Who can't relate to having a lover (or friend or parent) with a dismissive or preoccupied attachment? Don't the defining qualities of secure attachment give us a beautiful road map for how we should relate to the significant others in our lives?

> **secure adult attachment** The genuine intimacy that is ideal in love relationships.

INTERVENTIONS Evaluating Your Own Relationship

How can you use *all* of these section insights to ensure smoother sailing in romance? Select someone who is similar in values and interests, but don't necessarily search for a partner with your exact personality traits. Find someone you respect as an individual, a person whose qualities embody the "self" you want to be—but it's best if you each differ on the need to take charge. Focus on the outstanding "special qualities" of your significant other, and to cement your passion, share arousing flow states. Expect bumps along the way, but be cautious if you repeatedly break up and get back together again. Look for someone who is securely attached.

Still, however, notice the other implicit message of Table 10.7 (page 309) describing relationship turning points: If things don't work out, it may have absolutely *nothing* to do with you, your partner, or any problem basic to how well you get along! If you want to evaluate your own relationship, you might take the questionnaire based on these chapter points in Table 10.9.

Table 10.9 Evaluating Your Own Relationship: A Section Summary Checklist

	No	Yes
1. Are you and your partner on the same wavelength in terms of values, and did you connect over similar passions or flow states?	☐	☐
You don't have to be clones, but having mutual passions and *regularly sharing* those interests is a key to keeping passion alive.*		
2. Do you believe that your partner embodies your ideal self?	☐	☐
Looking up to your partner as someone you want to be like predicts staying together happily, as well as growing emotionally toward your ideal.		
3. Do you see your partner as utterly terrific and unique?	☐	☐
Deciding that this person has no human flaws is not necessary—but seeing your partner as "unique and special" also predicts being happy together.		
4. Is your romance moving along steadily (versus being turbulent)?	☐	☐
If you experience minor ups and downs in your feelings of love, that's fine, but it's a bad sign if you repeatedly break up and get together again.		
5. Is your partner able to fully reach out in love, neither intensely jealous nor aloof?	☐	☐
Some jealousy or hesitation about commitment can be normal, but in general, your partner should be securely attached and able to love.		

If you checked "yes" for all five of these questions, your relationship is in excellent shape. If you checked "no" for every question, your "relationship" does not exist! One or two no's mixed in with yes's suggest areas that may need additional work.

*Recall that it may be best if one of you has a stronger, or more dominant, personality.

So far, I have just begun my exploration into those adult agendas: love and work. In the next chapter, we will focus directly on the core adult love relationship—marriage—and talk in more depth about careers.

Tying It All Together

1. Latoya is discussing how twenty-first-century relationships have changed. Which of the following statements is *incorrect?*

   a. Today, young people are more likely to marry outside of their social class.
   b. Today, same-sex relationships are much more acceptable.
   c. Today, homophobia no longer exists.

2. Today, *more/fewer* people are open to interracial dating, and people who meet on the Internet are *less/more* apt to be happily married than their counterparts who meet in traditional ways.

3. Natasha and Akbar met at a friend's New Year's Eve party and just started dating. They are about to find out whether they share similar interests, backgrounds, and worldviews. This couple is in Murstein's (choose one) *stimulus/value-comparison/role* phase of romantic relationships.

4. Catherine tells Kelly, "To have a happy relationship, find someone as similar to you as possible." Go back and review this section. Then list the ways in which Catherine is somewhat wrong.

5. Kita is clingy and always feels rejected. Rena runs away from intimate relationships. Sam is affectionate and loving. Match the attachment status of each person to one of the following alternatives: *secure*, *avoidant-dismissive*, or *preoccupied*.

Answers to the Tying It All Together questions can be found at the end of this chapter.

SUMMARY

Setting the Context

Psychologists have identified a new life phase called **emerging adulthood.** This in-between, not-quite-fully-adult time of life—which begins after high school and tapers off by the late twenties—involves testing out adult roles. Because young people haven't reached the standard benchmarks of adulthood—finding a career, getting married, becoming parents—for an extended time, we tend to see the essence of adulthood as taking responsibility for one's life. In southern Europe, young people typically live at home until they marry, and they have trouble becoming financially independent. In Scandinavia, **cohabitation** is widely accepted and marriage is optional. In the Nordic nations, better economies, an emphasis on independence, and government assistance make early **nest-leaving** the norm. In the United States, there are striking social-class differences. While most young people plan to marry, low-income adults have trouble making it to that state. Nest-leaving is also difficult when young people don't have the funds to leave home.

We think of the entry point of emerging adulthood as leaving the nest. Although parent–child relationships may improve after emerging adults move out, the idea that people *must* leave home to "act adult" is incorrect. Young people today often live with their parents because they cannot afford to live alone. Ethnic-minority youth, in particular, may stay in the nest as "full adults" to help their families.

Social-clock pressures, or **age norms,** set the boundaries of emerging adulthood. Exploring is **on time,** or appropriate, in the twenties, but **off time** if it extends well into the thirties. Although society sets the overall social-clock guidelines, people also have their own personal timetables for reaching adult markers. Social-clock pressures make emerging adulthood a time of special stress.

Constructing an Identity

Identity, or finding one's true adult self is, according to Erikson, the major challenge facing people on the brink of adulthood. Erikson believed that exploring various possibilities is critical to developing a solid identity. The alternative is **role confusion—** drifting and seeing no adult future.

James Marcia identified four **identity statuses: identity diffusion** (drifting aimlessly), **identity foreclosure** (leaping into an identity without any thought), **moratorium** (exploring different pathways), and **identity achievement** (settling on an identity).

In contrast to Marcia's idea that we progress through these stages and reach achievement in the twenties, people shift from status to status throughout life. Emerging adults may not need to sample different fields to develop a secure career identity. Being locked in **ruminative moratorium** produces special pain. In terms of identity—including one's **ethnic (biracial or multiracial) identity**—it's important to feel positive about who you are.

Finding a Career

Teenagers have lofty career goals. The downside is that, because many teens overinflate their abilities, self-esteem often drops when young people enter college. Emerging adults follow diverse emotional paths as they move through their early twenties. While people who enjoy mastering challenges ("workers") are set up to flourish during emerging adulthood, the twenties in general are a time of emotional growth. Troubled teens can be very successful if they find satisfying jobs.

Flow is a feeling of total absorption in a challenging task. The hours pass like minutes, intrinsic motivation is high, and skills are in balance with the demands of a given task. Flow states can alert people to their ideal careers.

Although higher education is important to constructing a middle-class life, and most young people in the United States enroll in college, many drop out before finishing. High-performing youths from low-income backgrounds are less apt to graduate than their affluent counterparts. We need to make it easier for financially strapped young people to get a B.A. and offer non-college alternatives that lead directly to jobs. The absence of a real **school-to-work transition** in the United States is a national crisis.

College should be a time of inner growth. Get the best professors, explore career-relevant work, become involved in campus activities, and reach out to students of different backgrounds.

Finding Love

Erikson's second emerging-adult task, **intimacy**—finding committed love—has changed dramatically in recent decades. People now find romance on-line and are far more likely to date outside their ethnicity, although partner choices are more stratified by income today. Despite enduring **homophobia,** Western gay and transgender teens feel more comfortable about coming out. The dating phase of life lasts longer, too, with many young people putting off serious romantic involvements until they establish a career.

Unfortunately, **relationship churning** has downsides, and romantic breakups take an emotional and physical toll. Having a loving partner is very helpful during the tumultuous emerging adult years.

Stimulus-value-role theory spells out a three-stage process leading to marriage. First, people select a potential partner who looks appropriate (the **stimulus phase**); then, during the *value-comparison phase,* they find out whether they have common interests. Finally, during the **role phase,** couples plan their lives together. **Homogamy,** people's tendency to choose similar partners and people of equivalent status and social value, is the main principle underlying this theory.

A variety of forces (such as genetic predispositions or connecting via similar flow states) make homogamy the underlying force driving romance. However, relationships flourish when people respect their partner's personality, and two very dominant (or submissive) personalities might not mesh. It helps to inflate a lover's virtues and view a partner as embodying one's "ideal self." While relationships can have dramatic turning points, too much turmoil is a bad sign. Social media sites such as Facebook provide a wealth of insights about modern love.

Researchers have spelled out three **adult attachment styles.** Adults ranked as insecurely attached—either **preoccupied/ambivalent** (overly clingy and engulfing) or **avoidant/dismissive** (overly aloof and detached)—have poorer-quality relationships. **Securely attached** adults tend to be successful in love and marriage. The attachment-styles framework offers additional fascinating insights into the qualities we should search for in finding fulfilling love.

KEY TERMS

adult attachment styles, p. 311

age norms, p. 292

avoidant/dismissive adult attachment, p. 312

biracial or multiracial identity, p. 297

cohabitation, p. 289

emerging adulthood, p. 287

ethnic identity, p. 296

flow, p. 299

homogamy, p. 308

homophobia, p. 305

identity, p. 293

identity achievement, p. 295

identity diffusion, p. 294

identity foreclosure, p. 294

identity statuses, p. 294

intimacy, p. 304

moratorium, p. 294

nest-leaving, p. 289

off time, p. 292

on time, p. 292

preoccupied/ambivalent adult attachment, p. 312

relationship churning, p. 307

role confusion, p. 294

role phase, p. 307

ruminative moratorium, p. 296

school-to-work transition, p. 302

secure adult attachment, p. 313

social clock, p. 292

stimulus phase, p. 307

stimulus-value-role theory, p. 307

value-comparison phase, p. 307

ANSWERS TO **Tying It All Together** QUIZZES

Setting the Context

1. b. Sarah is likely not to finish college within four years.

2. c. Silvia, who lives in Stockholm

3. false (There are many rational "adult reasons" people stay in the nest.)

4. Martha, who is starting a new career at age 50; she will be most worried about the ticking of the social clock.

Constructing an Identity

1. drifting; diffusion

2. foreclosure; moratorium. Kayla is most apt to have an emotional problem.

3. Do you feel nursing expresses your inner self?

4. false

Finding a Career

1. overly high; get more mature

2. flow

3. Josiah might argue that prior academic performance predicts college completion, with low odds of finishing for high school graduates with a C-average or below. Jocasta should reply that money is crucial because academically talented low-income kids are far less likely to finish college than their affluent peers, and dropouts cite "financial issues" as the main reason for leaving.

4. b

Finding Love

1. a and c

2. Today *more* people are open to interracial dating, and people who meet on the Internet are *more* apt to be happily married than their counterparts who meet in traditional ways.

3. value-comparison phase

4. Actually, people who have dominant personalities might be better off with more submissive mates (and vice versa). We gravitate to people with good personalities. Rather than searching for a clone, it's best to find a mate who is similar to one's ideal self. Overinflating that person's virtues helps tremendously, too!

5. Kita's status is preoccupied. Rena is avoidant/dismissing. Sam is securely attached.

CONNECT ONLINE:

LaunchPad
macmillan learning

Check out our videos and additional resources located at: **www.macmillanlearning.com**

CHAPTER II

Social Development: Relationships and Roles

Home at 3 A.M. from closing the restaurant and hopefully getting to bed by 4. Then, Jamila wakes up, gets the kids ready for school, and shuffles to the computer to begin her latest Web-design job.

Matt's first marriage to Clara ended in a disastrous divorce. He feels blessed to have a second chance for happiness at age 35. Matt and Jamila feel confident that this marriage will last. They are older and more mature. They have well-paying jobs. They understand that marriage involves sacrifice. They are committed to each other's emotional growth.

After struggling to connect with the twins, Matt finally feels that his stepchildren see him as their real dad—he knows he would give his life for these precious children. But supporting his family means being apart more than he (and the boys) would like. Matt wants to make enough money to give the kids a top-notch education and allow Jamila to enjoy motherhood, rather than enduring those exhausting weeks when she first gets an assignment, then goes crazy finishing that project at superhuman speed.

That's why Matt "supplements" his store manager position with driving for a ride-sharing company. Yes, the 70-plus-hour workweeks are exhausting, but Matt is thrilled. What a blessing to find the perfect combination—a rare, stable job offering health insurance (!) and a chance to earn money on the side. It's a 24/7 struggle, but this marriage must last for life!

Do you know someone like Matt who is trying to be a caring husband, a sensitive father, and support his family? Perhaps, like Jamila, you have a friend who feels overwhelmed by periodic bursts of high-stress work and wants to relax with her kids. If so, you know a twenty-first-century adult.

This chapter is devoted to the main social challenges involved in being adult. I'll build on our Chapter 10 discussion of emerging adult roles by focusing directly on marriage (and cohabitation), parenthood, and work during the long span of life from the thirties until the sixties. Before beginning your reading, you might want to take the family and work quiz in Table 11.1 on page 320. Soon you will learn why each stereotype is right or wrong.

Although I will discuss them separately, I must emphasize that we cannot look at marriage, parenthood, and career as separate. Having stable, well-paying jobs determines whether people choose to get married (as I mentioned in Chapter 10). Having children dramatically changes a couple's relationship and, as with Matt, shapes our career choices. As an *ecological, developmental systems approach* suggests, marriage, parenthood, and career are tri-directional, interlocking roles. Moreover, how we approach these core adult roles depends on the time in history and the society in which we live.

Left: Juanmonino/E+/Getty Images

Table 11.1: Stereotypes About Family and Work: A Quiz

Write "True" or "False" next to each of the following statements. To see how accurate your beliefs about family and work are, look at the correct answers, printed upside down below the table. As you read through the chapter, you'll find out exactly why each statement is true or false.

_____   1. Couples who choose to live together rather than get married have more fragile relationships, even if they are affluent and committed to each other.

_____   2. Poor people often don't get married because they are basically less interested in having a permanent commitment.

_____   3. People are happiest in the honeymoon phase of a marriage.

_____   4. Having children brings couples closer.

_____   5. People who don't have children are unhappy and narcissistic.

_____   6. Mothers used to spend more time with their children in the past than they do today.

_____   7. Most dads today share the childcare 50/50 with their wives.

_____   8. Technology has reduced the hours we spend at work.

_____   9. Being self-employed gives workers more control over their careers.

_____   10. Traditional gender roles have mainly disappeared in the world of work.

Answers: 1. F, 2. F, 3. T, 4. F, 5. F, 6. F, 7. F, 8. F, 9. F, 10. F

LEARNING OUTCOMES

- Compare historical changes in Western marriage with marital ideas in India and the Middle East.

- Evaluate under what conditions marriage is an ideal state.

- Outline changes in marriage over time and the forces that make for relationship satisfaction.

- Analyze divorce and step-parenthood.

deinstitutionalization of marriage The decline in marriage and the emergence of alternate family forms during the last third of the twentieth century.

Marriage

Ask young people to describe their ideal marriage and you may hear phrases such as "soul mates," "caring," and "mutual trust," (Amato, 2007; Lam and others, 2016). This vision of lovers for life is a luxury of living in our modern age.

Setting the Context: The Changing Landscape of Marriage

Throughout most of history, as I described in Chapter 1, life was short and harsh. Marriages were practical arrangements designed to cement family relationships, not fulfill a couple's inner needs. In fact, the typical marriage used to last only a decade or two before one partner died.

Then, with the health advances of the early twentieth century, Western nations developed the idea that people should get married in their twenties and be lovers for a half-century or more. The traditional 1950s marriage, with defined gender roles, reflected this vision of enduring love (Amato, 2007; Cherlin, 2004; Coontz, 1992).

In the last third of the twentieth century, Western ideas about marriage took another turn. The women's movement told us that women should have careers and that spouses should share the child care. As a result of the 1960s lifestyle revolution, which stressed personal fulfillment, we rejected the idea that people should stay in an unhappy marriage. We could get divorced, have babies without being married, and choose not to get married at all.

The outcome was a change that social scientists call the **deinstitutionalization of marriage** (Cherlin, 2004, 2010). This phrase means that marriage was transformed from the standard adult "institution" into an optional choice.

From the 1950s stay-at-home mom to the two-career marriage with fully engaged dads—over the last third of the twentieth century, a revolution occurred in our ideas about married life. How do you feel about these lifestyle changes?

Figure 11.1 shows one symptom of this transformation: a steady rise in cohabitation rates. When people born in the late 1950s and early 1960s (shown in the first bar of the figure) were in their twenties, only 1 in 3 women dared move in with a romantic partner without a wedding ring. (This was called "living in sin.") With the cohabitation odds now 2 in 3, living together before getting married is a normal event (Vespa, 2014).

The most revealing change relates to **serial cohabitation**—living unmarried with different partners during adult life. When emerging adults cohabit with only one person, they are more apt to see this arrangement as a prelude to engagement ("We want to see if we can make it as husband and wife"). Serial cohabiters are less likely to have *any* marriage goals (Vespa, 2014). They may join the millions of contemporary women who give birth without a spouse.

This brings up that controversial change: unmarried parenthood. During the 1950s, if a U.S. woman dared to have a baby without being married, her family

serial cohabitation
Living sequentially with different partners outside of marriage.

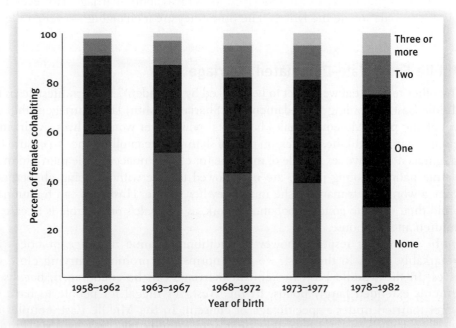

FIGURE 11.1 Percent of women who cohabited during emerging adulthood: This chart shows that cohabitation became a normal event for women in their twenties during the second decade of the twenty-first century (red, purple and gold bars). Also notice the increase in serial cohabitation—living together with different partners on the way to becoming an adult (purple and gold bars).

Data from Vespa, 2014, p. 211.

might ship her off to a home for unwed mothers or insist that she marry the dad (the infamously named "shotgun wedding"). In recent years, because only 11 percent of U.S. women without a college degree are married before giving birth (Gibson-Davis & Rackin, 2014), the disconnect between marriage and a baby carriage for less well-educated Americans is a predictable path (Furstenberg, 2015).

Acceptance of divorce, cohabitation, and unmarried motherhood varies in the West. In Scandinavia, as I mentioned in Chapter 10, people fully embrace these life-styles. In the United States, while we accept these nontraditional life-paths, marriage for life is the national ideal. What about world regions famous for their rigid marriage rules? For answers, let's travel to India and the Middle East.

If you visited this family, the mother would almost certainly have had an arranged marriage. There would be a good chance that the daughter would choose a mate on her own.

India: From Arranged Marriages to Eloping for Love

India stands in stark contrast to our Western search for soul mates because of its *arranged marriages*—unions in which parents choose their child's spouse. As late as 2005, most wives in India reported that their families had made the primary decision about whom they would wed, and many barely knew their husbands before their wedding day. However, with the younger generation now having veto power over parental choices, here, too, the rules have loosened a bit.

A radical change relates to what people in India call *elopements*—when young people run away and get engaged without their parents' consent. What typically happens is that the girl leaves home without telling her parents (or the boy and girl both leave home). Then the boy's family goes to the girl's family, informs them of her whereabouts, and gets consent for the marriage. A few months later, unless the girl's parents forbid the union, the couple formally weds (Allendorf, 2013).

What do people think about this change? For answers, researchers traveled to a rural area of India to conduct interviews. While believing that each type of marriage had its pluses and minuses, most residents were in favor of elopements. Well-educated people in particular used the terms "modern," "advanced," and "forward" to describe this trend.

India is still miles apart from the West in its ideas about marriage. However, here it is appropriate to cite the lyrics, "The times they are a changing"—ever so slightly at least.

Middle East: Male-Dominated Marriage

The other region that we expect to be shocked by "decadent" Western lifestyles is the Middle East. According to fundamentalist Sharia (Muslim) law, marriage is the *only* acceptable path. Moreover, males have total power over women's lives. A girl must remain a virgin until she marries, on pain of shaming the family name. To ensure that daughters don't have sex outside of marriage (or choose unacceptable men), in many Islamic nations, young people are not allowed to date without being chaperoned. Once a woman gets married, she must obey her spouse. Husbands can traditionally forbid their wives to go to school and to work, as a female's proper role is to care for children and the house.

In interesting respects, however, traditional Islamic marriage practices are remarkably open. In the West, we have norms that prohibit marrying close relatives. In the Middle East, first-cousin marriage can be encouraged, because it cements extended family bonds. In the West, it's illegal for people to have sex or get married under a specific age of consent. In the Middle East, couples are free to get married (and have sex) right after puberty takes place (Al-Hakami & McLaughlin, 2016).

Still, here, too, times are changing. Muslim women are becoming well educated. In Iran, more women enroll in universities than men (Aghajanian & Thompson, 2013). In Saudi Arabia, where fundamentalist Sharia law has its strongest hold, female activists are agitating against "child marriage" as well (Al-Hakami & McLaughlin, 2016).

The most dramatic crack in traditional Islamic marriage rules concerns divorce: Sharia law stipulates that only men can end a marriage. Ex-wives are barred from receiving alimony. Husbands automatically get custody of sons and daughters once the children are over a certain age.

Today, Iranian women are free to initiate divorce proceedings. They can draw up prenuptial agreements spelling out their right to work. They can insist on getting half the property if a couple splits up. In fact, over the past 15 years, divorce rates in this nation accelerated to outpace those in Catholic countries such as Ireland, Italy, and Spain (see Aghajanian & Thompson, 2013).

Still, one on-line poll of divorced women in Saudi Arabia shows just how differently Islam views this "normal" late-twentieth-century Western change. Many women anguished about being outcasts: "I don't belong to this society"; "I feel excluded"; "I'm treated as a criminal" (quoted in Saleh & Luppicini, 2017, p. 187). While Westerners react with sympathy when they hear a family member is getting divorced ("I'm so sorry!"), these women had the opposite experience: ". . . divorced women bring shame to their families" (p. 188); "It's agony, since I was treated with a lot of rebuke. . . ." (p. 189). Clearly, much of humanity is wedded to lifelong marriage. Do these people have a point?

This photo shows another landmark loosening of traditional Sharia law rules. In 2018, Saudi women were *finally* allowed to drive!

Is Being Married Better than Living Single?

Hundreds of U.S. comparisons suggest the answer is yes. Married couples are happier than the never married or divorced. Married couples are far richer (see Chapter 7). They live longer (Robles and others, 2014) and healthier into old age (Finkel, Simpson, & Eastwick, 2017; Slatcher & Selcuk, 2017; Zhang, Liu, & Yu, 2016).

Now consider the many life-enhancing advantages marriage provides—from offering economic security, to sharing parenting, to having a loving person take care of you in sickness (and health). As the consummate adult "secure base," marriage cradles us from the storms of life.

But wait a minute! These benefits apply to *happy* marriages—not relationships riddled with angst (Margelisch and others, 2017). Who wants to come home to an uncaring, avoidantly-attached spouse; someone who is chronically angry; a partner who minimizes your sense of self? In one typical comparison, people in miserable marriages were far less happy than their single counterparts (Chapman & Guven, 2016).

Moreover, contrasting married with unmarried adults is like comparing apples to oranges, because people who marry are already a self-selected group. Does marriage *itself* boost happiness and health, or are adults happier and healthier before they enter into this state?

Think about your requirements for getting married if you are single. Or, if you are married, think of the goals you had before you were wed. In addition to finding the right person, if you are like most people, you probably believe that making this commitment demands reaching a certain place in your development. It's important to have a solid sense of identity and to be financially secure (see Chapter 10). You want to avoid partners with debilitating emotional problems. You are looking for someone who can offer an economically secure life. Therefore, because we select mates according to *homogamy*, the marriage market for poverty-level women and men is dismal (Gibson-Davis, 2009; Gibson-Davis & Rackin, 2014). Even when couples are committed to each other, it can be difficult to move from living together to getting engaged.

Read what Candace, a 25-year-old, had to say about her marriage plans:

> Um, we have . . . things . . . to do before we get married. We both want very good jobs. . . . He's been looking out for jobs . . . we're trying. We . . . we gotta have everything before we say, "Let's get married."
>
> (quoted in Smock, Manning, & Porter, 2005, p. 690)

Is being married better than cohabiting for life?

Candace's heartfelt comment shows why comparing married to cohabiting couples is equally misplaced. Yes, cohabiting relationships are more fragile. These people are more likely to separate after stresses such as parenthood (Edin & Kefalas, 2005; Parham-Payne, Dickerson, & Everette, 2013). But is not having a wedding ring the issue, or is it the fact that U.S. couples who don't get married are far more likely to be poor?

This brings up an interesting question. Suppose you are in a long-term relationship and *could* get married. You and your significant other have terrific jobs. You feel committed to each other but don't believe in a wedding ring ("It's just a piece of paper"). Are you making a mistake?

A careful British study implies the answer is no. When researchers controlled for childhood influences such as poverty and compared long-term cohabiting couples with their counterparts who got married, they found no differences in midlife happiness (Perelli-Harris & Styrc, 2018). Fatherhood studies have the same theme: If a man is a committed dad, it doesn't matter if he is married to his children's mother or not (Nomaguchi, Brown, & Leyman, 2017; McClain & Brown, 2016).

The bottom line is that we should go beyond that formal marker (a wedding ceremony) to explore the quality of *any couple's* shared life. What makes for happy, enduring relationships? The rest of this section tackles this vital question.

The Main Marital Pathway: Downhill and Then Maybe Up

U-shaped curve of marital satisfaction The most common pathway of marital happiness in the West, in which satisfaction is highest at the honeymoon, declines during the child-rearing years, then rises after the children grow up.

Many of us enter marriage (or any romantic relationship) with blissful expectations. Then, disenchantment sets in. Decades of cross-sectional studies conducted in Western countries show that marital satisfaction is at its peak during the honeymoon and then decreases (Blood & Wolfe, 1960; Glenn, 1990; Lavner & Bradbury, 2010). This same downslide appears in longitudinal research: When psychologists followed married couples over 16 years, both husbands and wives reported more bickering and irritation as the years passed. While women generally had more marital complaints than men, the real red flag for divorce was a major uptick in *wives'* distress (Williamson and others, 2016). Perhaps because they are more sensitive to communication issues, women are often the bellwether signaling a marriage will end.

Do flashpoints that typically provoke divorce ("We can't talk to each other"; "He is incredibly insensitive") appear at the beginning of a marriage or emerge over time? A study tracking couples from engagement through the first years of marriage supports the "emerging distress" pattern (Burditt and others, 2017). On their wedding day, couples seem blissful and in tune; then cracks appear ("I never knew he was so pig-headed"; "Why didn't I realize she is pathologically attached to her mother, and periodically erupts in rage?"). As the downslide is deepest during the first four years, one group of researchers believes that if couples can survive the early years of a marriage, they are less likely to divorce (Bradbury & Karney, 2004).

Notice the interesting similarity to John Bowlby's ideas about the different attachment phases. In the first year or two of a relationship, couples are in the phase of clear-cut attachment, when they see their significant other as the center of life. As spouses move into their *working model* phase—developing more separate lives, getting involved in the wider world—they risk disconnecting from their mates.

The good news is that there can be a positive change to look forward to later on. According to the **U-shaped curve of marital satisfaction,** after it dips to a low point, couples can get happier at the empty nest phase, when the children leave the house and husbands and wives have the luxury of focusing on

The so-called "difficulties" of the empty nest are highly overrated. In fact, many couples find that, when the children leave, they can joyously rekindle marital love!

Andrew Olney/Masterfile

each other again (Glenn, 1990; White & Edwards, 1990). And, at retirement, the curve can swing up even more. Compared to middle-aged couples, elderly spouses fight less. They relate in kinder, less combative ways (Carstensen and others, 1996; Windsor & Butterworth, 2010).

Happy elderly couples actually embody many of the good love-relationship principles spelled out in Chapter 10. They idealize their partners ("Your grandma is the best woman in the world!"); and, you might be interested to know, men who rank themselves as disagreeable are especially likely to display this trait ("How did I deserve this woman? I married a saint!"). (See O'Rourke and others, 2010.) So, we are right to yearn to stay married "'til death do us part"—*if* our marriage is a happy one.

Still, perhaps you are fortunate to know a couple who bucks the U-shaped curve and grows happier as the years pass. For some newlyweds, marital happiness declines sharply during the first four years; for others, it wanes slightly. And even though it's hard to predict future problems, we can find clues into a relationship's fate by examining partners' general attitudes early on.

Virtually every couple who gets married is convinced the statistics don't apply to them: "We are going to live happily ever after. Our relationship will improve over time, and it certainly won't get worse." Ironically, in tracking newly married couples, researchers found that women who held these optimistic ideas to an extreme were at special risk of being disenchanted, or totally turned off, in the next few years (Lavner, Karney, & Bradbury, 2013).

Why might seeing one's *marriage*, in particular, as flawless promote distress? For answers, researchers made the interesting distinction between being a generally optimistic person and being optimistic about a marriage. They found that people who were generally upbeat were prone to constructively solve marital conflicts. But spouses who magically believed "We can't have problems" developed a shocked, learned-helplessness attitude when reality hit. Unprepared for disagreements, expecting romance to conquer all, they were blindsided when things didn't go as planned and so were poorly equipped to deal with the normal ups and downs of married life (Neff & Geers, 2013).

What does it mean to constructively handle conflicts, and what other attitudes help us stay together happily for life? To offer some perspective on these issues, let's first spell out a familiar psychologist's conceptualizations about love (that is, from his theory of intelligence, described in Chapter 7)—Robert Sternberg's *triangular theory*.

> **triangular theory of love** Robert Sternberg's categorization of love relationships into three facets: passion, intimacy, and commitment. When arranged at the points of a triangle, their combinations describe all the different kinds of adult love relationships.

The Triangular Theory Perspective on Happiness

According to Sternberg's (1986, 1988, 2004) **triangular theory of love,** we can break down adult love relationships into three components: passion (sexual arousal), intimacy (feelings of closeness), and commitment (typically marriage, but also exclusive, lifelong cohabiting relationships). When we arrange them on a triangle such as Figure 11.2, we get a portrait of the different kinds of relationships in life.

With passion alone, we have a crush—the fantasy obsession for the girl down the street or a handsome professor we don't really know. With intimacy alone, we have the caring that we feel for a best friend. *Romantic love* combines these two

FIGURE 11.2: Sternberg's triangle: The different types of love: The three facets of love form the points of this triangle. The relationships along the triangle's sides reflect combinations of the facets. At the center is the ideal relationship: consummate love.

qualities. Walk around your campus and you can see this relationship. Couples are passionate and clearly know each other well but have probably not made a commitment to form a lifelong bond.

On the marriage side of the triangle, commitment alone results in "empty marriages." In these emotionally barren, loveless marriages (luckily, fairly infrequent today), people stay together physically but live separate lives. Intimacy plus commitment produces *companionate marriages*, the best-friend relationships that long-married couples may have after passion fades. Finally, at the bottom of the diagram, a few married couples stay together because they share *sexual passion* and nothing else. The ideal in our culture is **consummate love**—a relationship that combines passion, intimacy, and commitment.

Why is consummate love fragile? One reason is that, with familiarity, passion dwindles. It's hard to keep lusting after your mate when you wake up together day after day for years (Klusmann, 2002). This sexual decline has an unfortunate hormonal basis. Married couples—both men and women—show lower testosterone levels than their single or divorced counterparts (Barrett and others, 2013; Gettler and others, 2013).

As couples enter into the working-model phase of their marriage and move out into the world, intimacy can also wane. You and your partner don't talk the way you used to. Work or the children are more absorbing. You may become "ships passing in the night."

Sternberg's theory beautifully alerts us to why marriages normally get less happy. But it does not offer clues as to how we can beat the odds and stay romantically connected for life. Actually, a fraction of couples (roughly 1 in 10 people) *do* stay passionate for decades (Acevedo & Aron, 2009). What are these relationship role models doing right? For answers, researchers decided to decode the experience of falling in love.

They discovered that when we fall in love, efficacy feelings are intense. We feel powerful, competent, capable of doing wonderful things (Aron and others, 2002). Given that romantic love causes a joyous feeling of self-expansion (and boosts testosterone!), couldn't we teach people to preserve passion and intimacy by encouraging couples to share exciting activities that expand the self?

To test this idea, the psychologists asked married volunteers to list their most exciting activities—the passions that gave them a sense of flow (see Chapter 10). Then they instructed one group of husbands and wives to engage in the stimulating activities *both* partners had picked out (for example, going to concerts or skiing) frequently over 10 weeks. As predicted, marital happiness rose among these couples compared to control groups who were told to engage in pleasant but not especially interesting activities (such as going out to dinner) or just to follow their normal routine (Reissman, Aron, & Bergen, 1993).

So, to stay passionate for decades, people may not need to take trips to Tahiti. The secret is to *continue* to engage in the flow-inducing activities that may have brought couples together in the first place. If you connected through your commitment to church, take mission trips with your mate. If you met through your passion for skateboarding, sharpen those skills with your spouse. The problem is that during the working-model phase of a relationship, arousing activities that expand the self tend to migrate outside of married life. When work does become more compelling (or flow-inducing), people may find their partner dull. Worse yet, they may fall in love with someone who is on the scene to promote their most efficacious, attractive self: "I feel so powerful and energized at my job. Hey, wait a second! It's my co-worker, not my wife, who brings out my best self!" Keeping "growth experiences" within a marriage helps keep marital (and sexual) passion alive.

consummate love In Robert Sternberg's triangular theory of love, the ideal form of love, in which a couple's relationship involves all three of the major facets of love: passion, intimacy, and commitment.

This couple is doing more than sharing a wonderful experience. They are actually "working" on their relationship. Engaging in mutually exciting activities helps preserve marital passion.

Peathegee Inc/Blend Images/Getty Images

Commitment, Sacrifice, and Compassion: Core Attitudes in Relationship Success

Still, sharing exciting activities may not be sufficient to keep couples glued to each other during the storms of daily life. People must be committed to a mate.

Researchers are passionate to identify the glue called *commitment*, the inner attitudes that keep couples cemented together over years. Committed couples, as you read in the chapter-opening vignette, are literally wedded to staying married. Their value system won't allow them to consider divorce (Epstein, Pandit, & Thakar, 2013). As one long-married African American man explained:

> I was committed to proving them [others' predictions] wrong . . . somewhere along in trying . . . to prove everyone wrong, I fell in love. I probably should have fallen in love before I said "I do" . . . but I wasn't you know . . . —it's amazing!
>
> (quoted in Hurt, 2013, p. 870)

But if you assume commitment means joylessly slogging through a relationship, you are wrong. Commitment involves immensely positive emotions, too.

Committed spouses are dedicated to a partner's "inner growth" (Finkel, Simpson, & Eastwick, 2017). So a person who prefers urban life may choose to move to a small town to further a partner's career. As in the chapter vignette, a husband may work 70-hour weeks so that his wife can spend more time with the kids. These decisions demand sacrifice, giving up one's desires to further the other person's joy. When people sacrifice for their loved one, they are also benefiting themselves. Drawing on our natural high from performing costly prosocial acts (discussed early in this book), there is no greater joy than performing personally difficult acts for the people we love (Kogan and others, 2010).

Imagine how this father-to-be feels when he pampers his wife and you will understand why the thrill of "sacrificing" for a loved one helps relationships lovingly survive.

Intrinsic to sacrifice is compassion, being devoted to the other person's well-being. In one study, older couples who checked items such as "I spend a lot of time concerned about my partner" were particularly likely to have happy married lives (Sabey, Rauer, & Jensen, 2014). Here, too, compassion benefited givers more than receivers. Feeling compassion *for* a spouse—not believing one's partner had that feeling—cemented one's attachment to a mate. These commitment attitudes translate into specific communication styles.

Couple Communications and Happiness

Watch happy couples, whether they are age 80 or 18, and you will be struck by the way they relate. Like mothers and babies enjoying the dance of attachment, loving couples share joyous experiences. They are playful, affectionate. They use humor to signal, "I love you," even when they disagree (Gottman & Gottman, 2017). During disagreements, women in happy relationships regulate their emotions. They dampen down angry feelings rather than letting the situation get out of hand (Bloch, Haase, & Levenson, 2014).

Their caring facial expressions tip us off that this couple may be blissfully in love. But, specifically, how do happy couples communicate when they talk? The answers are listed on the next page.

But have you ever spent an evening with friends and had the uneasy feeling, "This relationship isn't working out"? By listening to couples talk, psychologists John and Julie Gottman (2017) can tell, with uncanny accuracy, whether a marriage is becoming unglued. Here are four communication styles that distinguish thriving relationships from those with serious problems:

- **Happy couples engage in a high ratio of positive to negative comments.** People can fight a good deal and still have happy marriages. The key is to have caring comments *strongly* outweigh critical ones. In videotaping couples discussing problems in their "love lab," the Gottmans discovered that when the ratio of positive to negative interactions dips well below 5 to 1, the risk of getting divorced escalates.

- **Happy couples don't get personal when they disagree.** When happy couples fight, they confine themselves to the problem: "I don't like it when I come home and the house is messy. What can we do?" Unhappy couples personalize their conflicts: They use put-downs and sarcasm. They look disgusted. They roll their eyes. Expressions of contempt for a partner are poisonous to married life.

- **Happy couples are sensitive to a partner's need for "space."** Another classic way of interacting that signals a relationship is in trouble occurs when one person provides too much "support" (Brock & Lawrence, 2014). For instance, a husband gives his wife excessive advice about her clothes or raising the children; a wife intrusively micromanages her partner's life. You would not be surprised to learn that these actions don't qualify as compassion, even when a person says, "I'm doing this for your well-being." People who sensitively perform the dance of attachment—whether mothers with infants, or loving couples—know when to be close *and* when to back off (Feeney & Noller, 2002; Murray and others, 2003; Brock & Lawrence, 2014).

- **Happy couples listen nondefensively to complaints.** Relating lovingly also means not taking criticisms personally, being secure enough to step back and listen to a mate's point of view. In one fascinating intervention study, just being instructed to spend 20 minutes thinking about how to compromise during disagreements predicted marital happiness two years down the road! (See Finkel, Simpson, & Eastwick, 2017.)

Feeling listened-to has longer-term benefits. In one longitudinal study, when spouses reported that their partner "understands the way I feel about things," they felt more competent 10 years later (Selcuk and others, 2016). As Bowlby would predict, responsive attachment figures—people who sensitively listen—help promote development at any age!

INTERVENTIONS Staying Together Happily for Life

How can you draw on *all* of these insights to have an enduring, happy relationship? Understand the natural time course of love. Be fully committed to your partner. Act on that feeling by being devoted to the person's development and taking joy in sacrificing for your mate. Preserve intimacy and passion by sharing arousing, exciting activities. Be very, very positive after you get negative. Avoid getting personal when you fight. Be sensitive to your partner's need for space. Rather than lashing out during disagreements, take time to listen to your spouse! Table 11.2 offers a checklist based on these points to evaluate your current relationship or to keep on hand for the love relationships you will have as you travel through life.

Commitment, however, shouldn't occur in a vacuum. In one study, if a wife reported that her spouse didn't appreciate the times when she went that extra mile, marital satisfaction declined (Lin, Li, & Chen, 2016). If a relationship is totally one-sided—for example, one person is doing all the sacrificing or someone is being treated with a lack of compassion—it may be time to contemplate divorce.

Table 11.2: Evaluating Your Close Relationship: A Checklist

Answer these questions as honestly as you can. The more "yes" boxes you check, the stronger your relationship is likely to be.

	Yes	No
1. Do you have realistic expectations about your relationship—realizing that passion and intimacy don't magically last forever?	☐	☐
2. Do you engage in activities that your partner feels as passionate about as you do?	☐	☐
3. Does sacrificing your own needs to make your partner happy give you pleasure, and are you devoted to your mate's emotional growth?	☐	☐
4. Are you affectionate and positive with your partner?	☐	☐
5. Do you solve differences of opinion in a constructive way—and not get personal when you fight?	☐	☐
6. Do you give your partner space to make his or her own decisions and choices?	☐	☐
7. Do you listen to your lover's complaints without getting defensive?	☐	☐

Divorce

When people consider leaving a partner, they weigh the costs against the benefits (Allen & Hawkins, 2017). You and your mate are not getting along, but perhaps you should hang on. One deterrent is financial: "Can I afford the loss in income after a divorce?" But if the couple has children, money issues are trumped by a more critical concern: "How will divorce affect my parenting?" "Will this damage my daughter or son?" (See Poortman & Seltzer, 2007; see also Chapter 7.) At this stage, people may feel that they are on an emotional seesaw: "Every time I felt like the scales balanced in one direction (either for divorce or reconciliation), something would happen and the scales would tip. . . . It's been a . . . battle to keep the scales balanced" (quoted in Doherty & Harris, 2017, p. 111).

Once a couple separates, they experience an overload of changes: the need to move or perhaps find a better-paying job (Amato, 2010). Housework burdens rise, particularly for men (Hewitt, Haynes, & Baxter, 2013). There are the legal hassles, anxieties about the children, and telling loved ones ("How will my friends and family feel?").

Still, divorce can produce emotional growth and enhanced efficacy feelings as people learn they can make it on their own (Fahs, 2007; Hetherington & Kelly, 2002). And, of course, ending an unhappy marriage can come as a welcome relief. Perhaps aided by a burst of testosterone, some women rediscover their sexuality (Montemurro, 2014). Listen to a 58-year-old woman whose husband divorced her after years of an unfulfilling sexual relationship: "I've been like reborn almost . . . in the sexual realm. . . . It's like a renewal" (quoted on p. 83).

Who feels relieved or sexually energized after divorce? Insights come from considering why people separate. In one U.S. study tracking married couples, researchers categorized divorced couples into two groups: (1) spouses who had reported being miserable in their marriage, and (2) couples who divorced, even though they had previously judged their marital happiness as "fairly good" (Amato, 2010; Amato & Hohmann-Marriott, 2007).

People in very unhappy marriages did feel much happier after divorcing. But relatively satisfied couples who later divorced, perhaps thinking, "I just don't find our relationship fulfilling," reported subsequent declines in well-being! Given this finding, family expert Paul Amato (2007, 2010) suggests that perhaps our fantasy of finding a life soul mate (or the sense that something is missing if we don't

The fact that their marriage is so conflict ridden suggests that this couple may feel much better after they divorce—but simply splitting up because you find your relationship "somewhat unfulfilling" predicts feeling more depressed after a marriage breaks up.

automatically have intimacy and passion for life) lures people into leaving a marriage when they might be better off remaining with their spouse. And what happens to children when couples make this choice? If your house is a battleground, as I described in Chapter 7, it's better for the children if you divorce. But imagine being shocked to learn that your parents are separating when you always believed their marriage was perfectly fine. Then think of having to adjust to a new family when your mom or dad remarries.

Hot in Developmental Science: Marriage the Second or Third or "X" Time Around

---

This brings up that common sequel to divorce: remarriage. Today, about 1 in 4 U.S. marriages occur between previously divorced partners, and almost 1 in 2 involve a spouse who has been married at least once before (see Shafer & James, 2013). Are people correct that they might do better the second or third time around?

Before considering the issue, let's spell out some realities. One U.S. study showed that after a divorce, women have 60 percent lower odds of remarrying than men (Shafer & James, 2013). Wives who have custody of children have a particularly hard time finding new mates (Schnor, Pasteels, & Van Bavel, 2017).

Are remarried couples happier? Remarried people *say* they communicate better with their current spouse. Still, these reports go along with a gingerly approach to disagreements—more withholding and avoidance when couples talk (Mirecki, Brimhall, & Bramesfeld, 2013). Have these spouses decided "not to sweat the small stuff" or will this gun-shy approach to conflict cause them to harbor resentments down the road?

Whatever the answer, remarried couples face unique barriers. These spouses seem less committed, in the sense that they express more positive attitudes toward divorcing if they don't get along (Whitton and others, 2013). Bringing children into the marriage involves complications that go well beyond just relating to a husband or wife (Mirecki and others, 2013).

Stepchildren are a loose cannon in marriage because they naturally feel angry and resentful of a stepparent for "replacing" their real mom or dad. Therefore, it

sturti/Netta/Getty Images

Will this girl see this stepfather as a real dad? A good deal depends on whether this man is a caring father and how long he has been living with this child.

makes sense that some men might be wary about getting involved with women who have children, as stepchildren issues are one reason these relationships fail (DeLongis & Zwicker, 2017).

Still, there can be tremendous emotional benefits for people who take this step (Jensen, Shafer, & Larson, 2014). Stepfathers, as I mentioned in Chapter 7, are likely to be seen as "real fathers" the longer they live with children—provided they are caring and sensitive dads.

Most important, these new sons and daughters provide incredible joy: As one woman reported: "I don't look at her as a stepdaughter because that implies they are not . . . your child . . . she's my only child and I just accept the fact that she has another mother as well" (quoted in Whiting and others, 2007, p. 102). And a stepfather put it more bluntly: "I don't introduce her as my stepdaughter because I didn't step on her. I introduce her, 'This is my daughter.' . . . I'd go crazy if something happened to her" (quoted in Marsiglio, 2004, p. 32).

Now, let's explore the feelings these men and women are experiencing by turning to parenthood, that second important adult role.

Tying It All Together

1. Jared is describing marriage around the world today. Which *two* statements can he make?

   a. In Saudi Arabia, divorced women are still socially shunned.

   b. In the United States, we no longer believe in marriage.

   c. In India, traditional arranged marriages are in decline.

2. In describing marriage versus cohabitation, what should Sonia say? (a) *Couples who cohabit are more likely to be poor.* (b) *Being married is always a better way of ensuring a relationship will last.* (Choose both a and b, a only, or b only).

3. Three couples are celebrating their twenty-fifth anniversaries. Which relationship has followed the "classic" marital pathway?
   a. After being extremely happy with each other during the first three years, Ted and Elena now find that their marriage has gone steadily downhill.
   b. Stavros and Betty's marriage has had many unpredictable ups and downs over the years.
   c. Dave and Erika's marital satisfaction declined, especially during the first four years, but has dramatically improved now that their children have left home.

4. Describe the triangular theory to a friend and give an example of (a) romantic love, (b) consummate love, and (c) a companionate marriage. Can you think of couples who fit each category? At what stage of life are couples most likely to have companionate marriages?

5. Gina says, "I am trying to do exciting things with my spouse." Mark says, "I'm passionate about focusing on my wife's well-being." Explain in a sentence why each strategy promotes marital happiness.

6. Your best friend (who has children) is getting remarried. Without being excessively negative, explain frankly why her new relationship can be at risk.

Answers to the Tying It All Together questions can be found at the end of this chapter.

Parenthood

> I have never felt the joy that my daughter brings me when I wake up and see her . . . when you are laying there and . . . and feel this little hand tapping on your hand . . . that has been the most joyful thing I ever have experienced. . . . I've never been able to get that type of joy anywhere else.
>
> (quoted in Palkovitz, 2002, p. 96)

Setting the Context: More Parenting Possibilities, Fewer Children

Poll parents and you will hear similar comments: "The love and joy you have with children is impossible to describe." The great benefit of the 1960s lifestyle revolution is that more people than ever can participate in this life-changing experience, from stepparents to gay couples to never-married adults.

At the same time, people also have the freedom *not* to be parents—and more adults are making that choice. One sign of the times is a continuing decline in **fertility rates,** or the average number of births per woman, in many developed countries.

Are people who decide not to have children unfulfilled and narcissistic? (See Ashburn-Nardo, 2017.) The answer is no! (See Gerson, Posner, & Morris, 1991.) Childless adults—especially if they have freely chosen this path—are just as happy as parents (Nelson, Kushlev, & Lyubomirsky, 2014). Moreover, the stereotype that having children makes a relationship stronger (or that having a child saves an unhappy relationship) is equally false. How does having a baby change people's lives?

The Transition to Parenthood

To see how becoming parents can affect a marriage, researchers conduct longitudinal studies, selecting couples when the wife is pregnant, then tracking those families for a few years after the baby's birth. Understanding that parenthood arrives via many routes, social scientists have explored how having a child affects

LEARNING OUTCOMES

- Survey the transition to parenthood and its variations.
- Evaluate motherhood and fatherhood.

fertility rate The average number of children a woman in a given country has during her lifetime.

In the past, gay couples such as these women could never have hoped to be parents. They would have had to hide their relationship from the outside world. Today, they proudly can fulfill their life dream.

Rachel Epstein/Photo Edit, Inc.

the bond between gay partners (Goldberg, Smith, & Kashy, 2010), cohabiting couples (McClain & Brown, 2017; Ralph, 2016), and even parents of preterm infants (Porat-Zyman, Taubman-Ben-Ari, & Spielman, 2017). Here are the conclusions of these studies exploring the *transition to parenthood*:

- **Parenthood makes couples less intimate and happy.** Look back to the infancy chapters—especially the discussion of infant sleep in Chapter 3—and you will immediately see why a baby's birth is apt to change passion and intimacy for the worse. In fact, look at any couple struggling with an infant at a local restaurant and you will understand why researchers find that feelings about one's partner shift from lover to "fellow worker" after the baby arrives (Belsky, Lang, & Rovine, 1985).

- **If the couple is heterosexual, parenthood often produces more traditional (and potentially conflict-ridden) marital roles.** Among heterosexual partners, having children accentuates traditional gender roles (Ralph, 2016). Even when the man and woman have been sharing the household tasks fairly equally, women often take over most of the housework and child care after the baby arrives. Often this occurs because, as you will see later in this chapter, after having children, a woman may leave her job or reduce her hours at work. However, even when both spouses work full time, mothers tend to do far more diaper changing and household chores than dads do (Bureau of Labor Statistics, 2017). This change can provoke conflicts centered on **marital equity,** or feelings of unfairness: Women get angry with men for not doing their share around the house (Dew & Wilcox, 2011; Feeney and others, 2001).

marital equity Fairness in the "work" of a couple's life together. If a relationship lacks equity, with one partner doing significantly more than the other, the outcome is typically marital dissatisfaction.

What compounds the sense of over-sacrificing are clashes centered on differing parenting styles (discussed in Chapter 7). One unhappy wife described this kind of disagreement when she informed her husband: "What's really getting to me . . . is that we hardly ever agree on how to handle [the baby]. I think you are too rough, and you think I'm spoiling her, and none of us wants to change" (quoted in Cowan & Cowan, 1992, p. 112).

Will this young couple's relationship seriously deteriorate after the baby? Will it improve? To answer these questions, we need to look at what their marriage was like before having a child and this new father's hands-on parenting skills.

These examples show exactly why we can't expect that having a child will draw people closer together, whether the partners are gay or heterosexual, married or not. (Here the relevant saying may be, "Three is a crowd.") However, after becoming parents, a classic study revealed that about 1 in 3 spouses did report more love for a husband or wife (Belsky & Rovine, 1990). As one woman beautifully explained: "We feel more what the other is feeling . . . we understand each other more . . . It [the baby] is the icing on the cake of a relationship" (quoted in Klobucar, 2016, p. 1350).

Which couples are most likely to see a baby as the icing on their shared life cake? A classic study suggests the pre-baby attachment dance matters most. Was the couple able to relate well before the child arrived? (See Cowan & Cowan, 1992.) Recent research suggests the quality of a *man's* parenting looms large. As I mentioned early in this chapter, if a father is involved with the children—and a spouse respects his caregiving—relationships can thrive (Pedersen, 2017; McClain & Brown, 2017). What is parenthood *really* like from the point of view of mothers and fathers?

Exploring Motherhood

I've already talked about the love that mothers feel for their children, especially in the infancy section of this book. Drawing on the earlier chapter discussion, children are our prime vehicles for expressing compassion. They embody the joy we get from sacrificing for a beloved person's well-being.

Still, the downside of this 24/7 commitment—lack of sleep, financial strains, spending hours in less than fun (aka boring) activities, a messy house, dealing with tantrums, time taken away from being with your partner, and so on—can tip the balance from pleasure to pain. In surveys, mothers rank child care on an emotional par with housekeeping, and it's far less enjoyable than shopping and watching TV. Studies routinely show mothers are no happier (and sometimes far less happy) on a daily basis than their counterparts without children or people in the empty nest (Nelson, Kushlev, & Lyubomirsky, 2014). Actually, one mammoth statistical study showed that, while getting married tends to boost women's well-being, parenthood is apt to decrease a mother's feelings of self-esteem (Chen, Enright, & Tun, 2016). What produces these dips in self-worth? For answers, let's turn to a decades-old interview study exploring the motherhood experience in the flesh.

The Inner Motherhood Experience

This national survey suggested that motherhood is tailor-made to destroy cherished fantasies people have about how they expected to behave (Genevie & Margolies, 1987). One in two mothers in this poll admitted that they had trouble controlling their temper. Disobedience, disrespect, and even typical behaviors such as a child's whining might provoke reactions bordering on rage. When confronted with real-life children, these mothers found that their dream of being calm, empathetic, and always in control came tumbling down (Genevie & Margolies, 1987).

Given the *bidirectional* quality of the parent–child bond, it should come as no surprise that a main force that affected how closely a woman fit her motherhood image lay in her attachment with a given child. Children who were temperamentally difficult provoked more irritation and lowered a mother's self-esteem. An easy child evoked loving feelings and made that mother feel competent in her role. As one woman wrote:

> Lee Ann has been my godsend. My other two have given me so many problems and are rude and disrespectful. Not Lee Ann. . . . I disciplined her in the same way . . . except that she seemed to require less of it. Usually she just seemed to do the right thing. She is . . . my chance for supreme success after two devastating failures.
>
> (quoted in Genevie & Margolies, 1987, pp. 220–221)

These emotions destroy another motherhood ideal: Mothers love all their children equally. Many women in this study did admit they had favorites. Typically, a favorite child was "easy" and successful in the wider world. However, most important (again) was the attachment relationship, the feeling of being totally loved by a particular child. As one woman reported:

> There will always be a special closeness with Darrell. He likes to test my word. . . . There are times he makes me feel like pulling my hair out. . . . But when he comes to "talk" to mom, that's an important feeling to me.
>
> (quoted in Genevie & Margolies, 1987, p. 248)

Not only does the experience of motherhood vary dramatically from child to child, it shifts from minute to minute and day to day:

> Good days are getting hugs and kisses and hearing "I love you." The bad days are hearing "you are not my friend." Good days are not knowing the color of the refrigerator because of the paintings and drawings all over it. Bad days are seeing a new drawing on a just painted wall.
>
> (quoted in Genevie & Margolies, 1987, p. 412)

In sum, motherhood is *both* wonderful and terrible. It evokes the most uplifting emotions and offers painful insights into oneself. Now that we understand what makes motherhood challenging, let's explore how the wider world can amplify mothers' distress.

The blissful image of a mother and baby is nothing like contending with the reality of continual sleep deprivation and a screaming newborn—explaining why the idealized media images can make the first months of motherhood come as a total shock.

Expectations and Motherhood Stress

Society provides women with an airbrushed view of motherhood—from the movie stars who wax enthusiastic about the joys of having babies ("much better than that terrible old career") to the family members who gush at bleary-eyed, sleep-deprived new mothers: "How wonderful you must feel!" By portraying motherhood as total bliss, are we doing women a disservice when they realize that their own experience does not live up to this glorified image? (See Douglas & Michaels, 2004.)

What compounds the problem are unrealistic performance pressures. Good children, as you saw in the above quotation, make a mother feel competent. "Difficult" children can make a woman feel like a failure. Despite all we know about the crucial role of genetics, peers, and the wider society in affecting development, according to classic books, mothers still bear the responsibility for the way their children turn out (Coontz, 1992; Crittenden, 2001; Douglas & Michaels, 2004; Garey & Arendell, 2001).

Single mothers face the most intense pressures as they struggle with financial hurdles, working full time, plus trying to fulfill the "blissful" mom ideal. But *every* woman is subject to the intense pressures of contemporary motherhood: be patient; cram in reading; provide enriching lessons; produce a perfect child. To what degree is the so-called epidemic of micromanaging mothers a by-product of these intense demands, which compel women to go overboard in their hovering to prove that they are not slacking off in the motherhood role?

I'm sure you've heard that today's moms are not giving children the same attention as in "the good old days." Figure 11.3 proves this "obvious" assumption is wrong. Notice that twenty-first-century mothers spend more time with their children than their counterparts

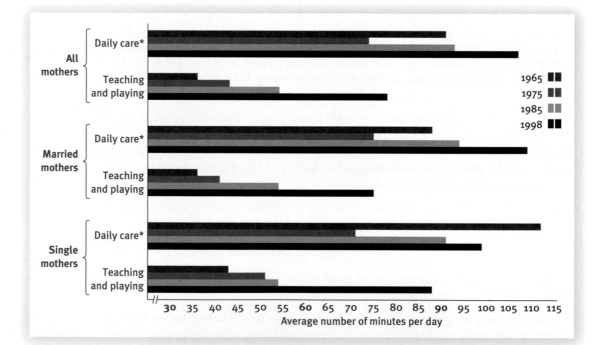

FIGURE 11.3 Minutes per day devoted to hands-on child care by U.S. mothers from diary studies during the last third of the twentieth century: Notice in particular that, in contrast to our myths, in more recent years, mothers are spending much more time teaching and playing with their children than in previous decades.

Data from Sayer, Bianchi, & Robinson, 2004.

*Refers to routine kinds of care, such as helping the child get dressed.

did a generation ago (Bianchi, Robinson, & Milkie, 2006). In particular, notice the dramatic increase in hours spent teaching and playing. This cohort of young mothers—including those remarkable single moms—is spending almost *twice as much time* engaging in child cognition-stimulating activities as their own mothers spent with them!

Where are fathers in his picture? Earlier, when I talked about equity issues during the transition to parenthood, I might have given the impression that many contemporary dads are slacking off. Not so! Today's fathers are often making valiant efforts to be involved parents, too.

This photograph shows the reality of motherhood today. Working mothers are spending much more time teaching their children than their own stay-at-home mothers did in the past!

Exploring Fatherhood

When women first entered the workforce in large numbers in the 1970s, it became a badge of honor for fathers, in addition to fulfilling the traditional **breadwinner role,** to change the diapers and to be deeply involved in caring for their children. From Slovakia (Švab & Humer, 2013) to Sweden (Björk, 2013) and from Australia (Thompson, Lee, & Adams, 2013) to Japan and the United States (Ito & Izumi-Taylor, 2013), the **nurturer father** has become one masculine ideal. Furthermore, according to psychologists, we expect fathers to be good sex-role models, giving children a road map for how men should ideally behave. Sometimes, we want them to be ultimate authority figures, people responsible for laying down the family rules (as in the old saying: "Wait until your father gets home!").

The lack of guidelines leaves fathers with contradictory demands. "Should I be strict or nurturing, sensitive or strong? Should I work full time to feed my family or reduce my hours at work and stay home to feed my child?" (Björk, 2013; McGill, 2014; Mooney and others, 2013). Given that there may be no "right" way to be a father, how do men carry out their role?

breadwinner role
Traditional concept that a man's job is to support a wife and children.

nurturer father Husband who actively participates in hands-on child care.

How Fathers Act

As you would expect from the principle that they should be good sex-role models, fathers, on average, spend more time with their sons than with their daughters (Bronstein, 1988). They play with their children in classically "male," rough-and-tumble ways. Fathers run, wrestle, and chase. They dangle infants upside down (Belsky & Volling, 1987). Although children adore this whirl-the-baby-around-by-the-feet play (in our house we called it "going to Six Flags"), it can give mothers palpitations as they wonder: "Help! Is my baby going to be hurt?"

How much hands-on nurturing do today's fathers perform? Diary studies show that, although in Western countries a genuine father-as-caregiver revolution occurred about 30 years ago, statistically speaking, contemporary child care remains primarily a female job. On average, as a 2016 national U.S. poll showed, women provide more than twice as much hands-on child care as men do in a typical week (Bureau of Labor Statistics, 2017).

Furthermore, these studies don't tell us which parent is taking bottom-line responsibility for the children—making that dentist appointment, arranging for a babysitter, planning the meals, and being on call when a child is sick. Having bottom-line responsibility may not translate into many hours spent physically with a daughter or son, but the weight and worry make this aspect of parenting a 24/7 job.

Think back to the thrilled expressions on the faces of the boys engaged in rough-and-tumble play in Chapter 5 and you can understand why this male "hang 'em upside down" play style is a compelling bonding experience for both fathers and their sons. It's also clear why "daddy play" is apt to give moms fits

Based on the earlier discussion of society's expectations, it seems likely that mothers typically continue to take bottom-line responsibility (Ralph, 2016). When we look at where the parenting buck stops, the gender dimension of being a parent is fully revealed (Lamb, 1997).

In sum, although today's fathers are doing far more hands-on child care than in the past, their involvement still is skewed toward play activities, particularly of the rough-and-tumble, "Six Flags" kind. Dads are often more involved with their sons than with their daughters. Mothers remain the caregivers of final resort.

Variations in Fathers' Involvement

If you look at the fathers you know, however, you will be struck by the variations in this profile. There are divorced men who never see their children, and traditional "I never touch a diaper" dads; there are househusbands who assume primary caregiving responsibilities, and single dads who have full custody of the kids. What statistical forces predict how involved a given father is likely to be?

A good deal depends on a man's attitudes. In one Israeli comparison of divorced fathers, men who could regulate their emotions and felt they got more care from their own fathers were most apt to take an active caregiving role (Finzi-Dottan & Cohen, 2017). Feeling efficacious at child care matters ("I'm a world-class diaper changer!") (Trahan, 2017), as does whether the pregnancy was wanted or not (Lindberg, Kost, & Maddow-Zimet, 2017). Fathers are more interested in being hands-on nurturers (no surprise) when they feel competent at nurturing and really wanted that child.

Physiological changes during pregnancy are a fascinating predictor of involved fatherhood. When researchers measured male prenatal salivary hormones, they found that men who showed greater declines in testosterone during their wives' pregnancy reported more satisfaction with being dads (Saxbe and others, 2017).

Who takes the ultimate hands-on nurturer step and chooses to be a stay-at-home father with a working wife? As the following quotations from a study that polled wives in this situation suggest, personality preferences loom large (Rushing & Sparks, 2017).

> He was more suited to being at home . . . like . . . he would manage . . . better than I would."
>
> (quoted on p. 1265)

Practical concerns also weigh heavily:

> The salary discrepancy was enormous. . . . I earn . . . 20 times what he was earning.
>
> (quoted on p. 1264)

> My husband worked crazy long hours . . . and we . . . made this choice. . . . So we are pretty thrilled.
>
> (quoted on p. 1265)

As I will describe in the next section on work, it can take courage to reject entrenched gender norms. Men—like women—complain that working long hours interferes with family time (Bryan, 2013). Children get upset when their dads miss important family occasions; they want their fathers to be more involved (Strazdins, Baxter, & Li, 2017). But in all of our talk about equal family roles, society remains wedded to the male breadwinner and female caregiver roles.

How are things *really* changing in the work world for women and men? First, let's sum up these section messages in Table 11.3, then explore this question as we turn to the third vital adult role: work.

Veronique Burger/Science Source

Contemporary fathers differ in how willing they are to change diapers. To explain this young man's behavior, we would predict that he is more mature, had an involved dad, feels competent as a caregiver—and interestingly, showed steeper declines in testosterone when his partner got pregnant!

Table 11.3: Advice for Parents: A Checklist

Coping with the Transition to Parenthood
- Don't expect your romantic feelings about each other to stay the same—they won't.
- Try to agree on who is going to do what around the house, but understand that you may fall into more traditional roles.
- Work on your communication skills before the baby arrives.

For Mothers
- Understand that you won't and can't be the perfect mother—in fact, sometimes you will be utterly terrible—and accept yourself for being human!
- Don't buy into the fantasy of producing a perfect child. Children cannot be micromanaged into being perfect. Focus on enjoying and loving your child as he or she is (see also Chapter 7).
- Don't listen to people who say that working full time automatically means that you can't be an involved mother. Remember the findings discussed in this section.

For Fathers
- Understand that your role is full of contradictions—and that there is no "perfect" way to be a dad.
- Be aware of your attitudes toward hands-on child-care, and clearly communicate these feelings to your partner.
- On the other hand, be a sensitive, loving dad! A strong message from the research is that if your partner feels you are a great father, your relationship is more likely to thrive after the baby arrives.

Tying It All Together

1. Jenna and Charlie, a married couple, are expecting their first child. According to the research, how might their marital satisfaction change after having the baby? What forces will predict coping well with this change?

2. Akisha, a new mother, is feeling unexpectedly stressed and unhappy. She and other mothers might cope better if they experienced which *two* of the following?
   a. had a less rosy, more accurate picture about motherhood from the media
   b. had more experts giving them parenting advice
   c. had less pressure placed on them from the outside world to "be perfect"

3. Your grandmother is complaining that children today don't get the attention from their parents that they got in the "good old days." How should you respond, based on this chapter? Be specific with regard to both mothers and fathers.

4. Construct a questionnaire to predict how heavily involved in child care a particular man is likely to be, and give it to some fathers you know.

Answers to the Tying It All Together questions can be found at the end of this chapter.

Work

Setting the Context: The Changing Landscape of Work

What is work like in the Western world, and how can you construct a fulfilling career life?

Let's begin our discussion by spelling out three dramatic changes in the developed-world career landscape. (I'll be discussing that other sea change, women in the work force, at the end of the chapter.)

LEARNING OUTCOMES
- List four major changes in the modern work world.
- Discuss the qualities that make for career happiness.
- Evaluate how work differs for women and for men.

traditional stable career
A career path in which people settle into their permanent life's work in their twenties and often stay with the same organization until they retire.

boundaryless career
Today's most common career path for Western workers, in which people change jobs or professions periodically during their working lives.

Having the flexibility to work at home is definitely a double-edged sword. Not only are you tempted to work on assignments when you should be paying attention to your child, but you are probably working far longer hours than if you had gone to the office.

More Career (and Job) Changes

During much of the twentieth century, work had a structured path. Right after high school or college, men found a job and often stayed in that same organization until they retired (Super, 1957). This **traditional stable career** is now atypical. People move from job to job, or change direction, starting new careers as they travel through life. Today, adults experience a shifting work pattern called **boundaryless careers** (DeFillippi & Arthur, 1994; Flecker, Fibich, & Kraemer, 2017; Korunka & Kubicek, 2017). This less defined career pathway is mirrored by less definition to work.

A Disappearing Barrier Between Work and Family

Work used to be separate from home life. You went to your job from 9 to 5 on Monday through Friday and spent weekends and evenings with your children and spouse. Today, working nonstandard hours has become common. In one U.S. survey, half of all workers worked at least some weekends or nights (Spreitzer, Cameron, & Garrett, 2017). At the same time, the Internet has moved work out of the office to permeate family life (Korunka & Kubicek, 2017).

The benefit of the on-line revolution is flexibility. People can telecommute from an office that is halfway around the world or, even if their office is around the corner, work on their own schedule at home. This melding of work and home time, however, is a double-edged sword. Yes, not having to go into the office allows you to take the kids to the dentist or pick them up from school, but you are potentially on the job 24 hours a day.

And it's not just that technology translates into working *longer hours*. Computers and cell phones accelerate the *pace* at which we must perform (Korunka & Kubicek, 2017; Paškvan & Kubicek, 2017). So, as the morning progresses, emails and texts multiply. A worker must respond to each communication ASAP. Ironically, people feel enslaved by the very devices that liberated them to work at home (Fleming, 2017)!

The Rise of Independent Contract, "Gig" Work

The same good-news-can-turn-into-bad-news issue applies to the most recent job transformation: People always worked for a specific employer. Now workers increasingly function as free agents, selling their skills to different companies for a limited time. The iconic example is Uber. But from Web designers to editors to per-diem nurses; from adjunct instructors at your university to textbook writers such as me, this new "gig" economy is metastasizing at a rapid pace. As Figure 11.4 shows, over the past 10 years, the fraction of U.S. jobholders who perform "alternative work" rose from 1 in 10 to almost 1 in 6 (Spreitzer, Cameron, & Garrett, 2017)!

Advocates tout the freedom of being your own boss. What could be better than choosing exactly *when* and where we work! Now we can explore *all* of our career passions rather than feeling forced to choose a single work identity as emerging adults: filling in as EMTs on Mondays and Wednesdays, designing logos on Friday, and starting an Internet baking business on the side.

Unfortunately, however, the liberation is heavily skewed to the employer's side. Companies who hire temporary workers don't have to pay health insurance or retirement benefits. They can hire and fire people just when they want to. They don't need to invest in training. They can demand that employees hit the ground running. Actually, British statistics show that when an industry shifts to more self-employed workers, the overall income of that profession declines (Fleming, 2017).

Is this new trend tailor-made to exacerbate income inequalities? Will it be a perilous step to promoting a huge underclass of drone workers scrambling for temporary jobs (see Fleming, 2017)? Will self-directed careers deprive twenty-first-century workers of the job security that is the bedrock of career happiness (see Punzo, Castellano, & Buonocore, 2017)? What *exactly* makes for career happiness and success?

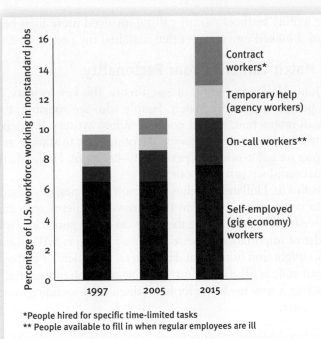

*People hired for specific time-limited tasks
** People available to fill in when regular employees are ill

FIGURE 11.4 **The fraction of the U.S. workforce working in nonstandard jobs in 1997, 2005, and 2015:** This chart shows how dramatically temporary work has mushroomed during the twenty-first century. It also lists the fraction of U.S. jobholders who are employed in different types of "nonpermanent jobs."

Data from Spreitzer, Cameron & Garrett, 2017, p. 474.

Exploring Career Happiness (and Success)

Suppose you wanted to predict which high school classmates would be successful at their careers. It's a no-brainer that you might bet on the class valedictorian or your friend from an affluent family. But some of you may know Harvard Ph.D.s or people with billionaire parents who are failing miserably to live up to their career potential. What are these people missing in life?

Clues come from the annual University of Michigan poll exploring health behaviors and attitudes in different cohorts of teens (discussed in Chapter 9). At their first evaluation, sampling high schoolers in 1979, the researchers measured what they called "core self-evaluations": whether a person had high self-esteem, was optimistic or depressed, and felt in control of his life. Among people who graduated college, this single evaluation from decades earlier predicted work success by early midlife! (See Judge & Hurst, 2007.)

Why do attitudes such as optimism and self-efficacy matter so much when we are on the college or graduate track? One reason is that people who generally feel good about themselves gravitate to more rewarding fields (Drago, 2011). So, given equal GPAs, your college classmates with high self-esteem will tend to "go for" a more fulfilling career.

Once at work, people who have high self-efficacy proactively shape their jobs. They seek realistic feedback from their supervisors and ask for the kind of support that will make them effective employees (L. Li and others, 2014; W. Li and others, 2014).

Other personality traits that go along with work success include (again) having the emotion-regulation talents to disengage from job stress (Hülsheger and others, 2014) and having a "worker oriented" temperament (Ilies and others, 2017). The goal is to see our job as a calling—perfectly expressing our identity, embodying our mission in life.

Are you blessed to see your work as a life calling? As I can tell you, there is no greater gratification than finding a career that you feel called to do. We might think that living a calling causes us to be committed to our work. One longitudinal study suggested the reverse. In a way similar to marriage, researchers found that developing this feeling grew out of time spent committed to a career (Duffy and others, 2014). So the reason I see writing textbooks as my life calling came from years spent making writing the center of my life.

But seeing writing textbooks as my calling involved more than being committed to working hard. I lucked into a career that matched my personality!

Strategy 1: Match Career to Your Personality

According to John Holland's (1997) classic theory, the key to work happiness is to find your best personality–career match. People who are sociable, those who crave continual human interaction, should not be textbook writers. If I needed to spend a lot of time outside, I would not be happy devoting days to staring at this computer screen. The closer we get to our ideal personality–career fit, Holland argues, the more satisfied and successful we can be at our jobs.

To promote this fit, Holland classifies six personality types, described in Table 11.4, and fits them to occupations. Based on their answers to items on a career inventory, people get a three-letter code, showing the three main categories into which they fit, in descending order of importance. A person whose ranking is SAE (social, artistic, and entrepreneurial) might find fulfillment directing an art gallery or managing a beautiful restaurant. If your code is SIE (social, investigative, and entrepreneurial), you might be better off marketing a new medicine for heart disease, or spending your work life as a practicing veterinarian.

Table 11.4: Holland's Six Personality Work Types

Realistic type: These people enjoy manipulating machinery or working with tools. They like physical activity and being outdoors. If you fit this profile, your ideal career might be in construction, appliance repair, or car repair.

Investigative type: These people like to find things out through doing research, analyzing information, and collecting data. If you fit this pattern, you might get special satisfaction in some scientific career.

Artistic type: These people are creative and nonconforming, and they love to freely express themselves in the arts. If this is your type, a career as a decorator, dancer, musician, or writer might be ideal.

Social type: These people enjoy helping others and come alive when they are interacting with other human beings. If this description fits you, a career as a bartender, practicing physician, or social worker might be right.

Entrepreneurial type: These people like to lead others, and they enjoy working on organizational goals. As this kind of person, you might find special joy as a company manager, in sales, or in starting your own business.

Conventional type: These people have a passion for manipulating data and getting things organized. If you fit this type, you would probably be very happy as an accountant, administrative assistant, or clerk.

Still, even when people have found work that fits their personality, there is no guarantee that they will be happy at a particular job. What if your gallery director job involves mountains of paperwork and little time exercising your creative or social skills? Suppose your gallery is in financial trouble, and you have a micromanaging owner in charge? To find work happiness, it's vital to consider the actual workplace, too.

Strategy 2: Find an Optimal Workplace

intrinsic career rewards Work that provides inner fulfillment and allows people to satisfy their needs for creativity, autonomy, and relatedness.

What constitutes an ideal workplace? Workers agree that jobs should give us autonomy to exercise our creativity and offer a sense of control over the conditions of our work (Levenson, 2017). They want organizations that are employee friendly and bosses who are fair and sensitive to their needs (Jiang & Men, 2017). As I mentioned in Chapter 7, these same qualities—autonomy, nurturing, and relatedness—define ideal school environments. Ideally, we are looking for **intrinsic career rewards**—work that is fulfilling in itself.

Extrinsic career rewards, or external reinforcers (such as salary), can also be crucial, depending on a person's situation. For instance, one longitudinal study showed intrinsic career rewards become less vital to work satisfaction as people (particularly men) moved beyond emerging adulthood and had families—again suggesting that the breadwinner role remains a priority for twenty-first-century married men (Porfeli & Mortimer, 2010). As people age, they feel freer to focus more on enjoying work in and of itself (Allen & Finkelstein, 2014; Kooij, Bal, & Kanfer, 2014). Moreover, while money does not make for happiness, below a certain salary, family income has a dramatic impact on well-being. So, for the many people struggling to make it from paycheck to paycheck, salary is a prime job concern. Unfortunately, having the luxury of viewing a job as an intrinsically gratifying, flow-inducing experience depends on having our "security needs" satisfied or knowing we can economically survive.

As I described in Chapter 10, flow states require that our skills match the demands of a given task. Therefore, it should come as no surprise that one poisonous job-related stress is "role ambiguity," or a lack of clear work demands (Gilboa and others, 2008). If you are unsure of what an employer expects, there is no chance of feeling "in flow." Good bosses (like good spouses) openly share information. There are no hidden agendas, such as a boss saying you get time off for family, and then punishing you for taking that time (more about this issue later) (Byrne & Canato, 2017; Jiang & Men, 2017). A huge problem, as I've been implying, is **role overload**—having way too much on your plate to do an effective job—or **role conflict**—being torn between competing life demands (such as family and career).

This brings up the topic of **work–life balance** (Fernadez-Crehuet, Gimenez-Nadal & Reyes Recio, 2016; Grawitch & Ballard, 2016; Jenkins, Bhanugopan, & Lockhart, 2016). Essential to adult happiness, organizational psychologists believe, is feeling happy at work and satisfied with one's nonwork life (Sirgy & Lee, 2016). Are you energized by your career and feel you have ample time to enjoy your hobbies, your children, your spouse? Idcally, a fulfilling job should *increase* the pleasure we get from family life (Babic and others, 2017; Ilies and others, 2017; Zhou & Buehler, 2016).

extrinsic career rewards Work that is performed for external reinforcers, such as pay.

role overload A job situation that places so many requirements or demands on workers that it becomes impossible to do a good job.

role conflict A situation in which a person is torn between two or more major responsibilities—for instance, parent and worker—and cannot do either job adequately.

work–life balance A situation in which people feel a perfect balance, energized and happy at work and fulfilled with other aspects of their lives.

Work satisfaction like this, experts now believe, comes from having a good work–life balance—meaning feeling satisfied with *all* aspects of one's life.

How do people behave when faced with the pulls of family and career? For answers, let's end this chapter with an exploration of the career issues women confront.

Hot in Developmental Science: Exploring the *Enduring* Difficulties Women Face at Work

With women now more likely than men to graduate from college in the United States and many other developed nations, we might expect females to overtake males in their careers. Still, the well-known gender differences in pay endure. In 2015, full-time working women in the United States made only 80 cents for every dollar earned by men (Institute for Women's Policy Research, 2017). Why?

- **Women (especially when they are married) have more erratic, less continuous "careers" than men.** One reason is that males are more apt to work continuously, while wives move in and out of the workforce to provide family care (Bianchi & Milkie, 2010). The first exit may occur early in adulthood. As one U.S. longitudinal survey showed, a pregnant woman is three times more likely to leave work than is her counterpart who is not planning to have a child (Shafer, 2011). Another hiatus may happen in midlife, when a female employee takes time off to care for her elderly parents as they become physically frail (see the next chapter for more information).

  Women, as you might expect, feel more distressed about their jobs taking precious time from their family life. And when you believe work is hampering your main priority (your children), you are more likely to want to reduce your hours or quit. As one mother concluded: "I feel distracted by work a lot of the time, which makes me feel guilty about spending less time with my kids. I feel like I can't win by working" (quoted in Borelli and others, 2017, p. 356).

- **Jobs are gender defined.** Another issue is the well-known reality that male-dominated professions such as astrophysics or working in the aerospace industry pay far better than typical female-type jobs such as secretary or home health aide. **Occupational segregation,** the fact that men and women gravitate to different kinds of jobs, ensures that gender pay gaps endure.

  Interestingly, however, the same salary gaps exist *within* comparable careers. So, as a U.S. female engineer, you can expect to earn considerably more than someone who majored in the arts; but you still will make, on average, a whopping $17,000 a year less than the typical male in that same field!

- **Work is still just for working (not family).** Actually, one revealing survey suggests that, even if some companies pay lip service to their workers having balanced lives, employers don't look kindly on people taking "family time" (see Byrne & Canato, 2017). In studying 30 corporate Web sites, one researcher found that firms did entice prospective employees by offering perks designed to foster work–life balance, but the benefits included health and wellness activities (nutritious snacks, exercise programs, walking trails). No mention was made of child care.

  As one (female) Human Resources director chillingly explained: "We . . . monitor absences so I can track and look for anything suspicious . . . letting employees know that we will be accommodating them . . . [but] also making sure that they are aware of their responsibilities to work and trying not to take advantage of anything" (quoted in Hari, 2016, p. 107).

  In fact, in another study exploring supervisor perceptions, if a boss felt a given employee—whether male or female—was conflicted between career and family, that manager was apt to give the person poorer job performance ratings, even when a given worker didn't report experiencing any family/work stress (Li, Bagger, & Cropanzano, 2017)!

occupational segregation
The separation of men and women into different kinds of jobs.

Imagine what it feels like to leave your screaming baby every morning and go to a job, and you will understand why working full time can be painful, in particular for new mothers.

Blend Images - Stretch Photography/Brand X Pictures/Getty Images

So, as I mentioned in Chapter 2, women are correct to worry that telling their bosses they are pregnant may result in their being demoted or even fired. Society's preconceived ideas about careers being far more important for men still endure. 🕸

How *can* people make wise choices about balancing work and family? What changes intellectually during adulthood, and what does "thinking wisely" mean? What is the key to happiness in life? The next chapter tackles these questions (and others) as we move on to midlife.

🎯 Tying It All Together

1. Michael, age 30, has just begun his career. Compared to his father, who entered his career in the 1990s, what *two* predictions can you make for Michael?
   a. Michael will be more likely than his dad to work from home.
   b. Michael will work fewer hours per week than his dad.
   c. Michael is more likely to be an independent contractor, selling his skills to different employers.

2. In a sentence or two, spell out one advantage and one serious disadvantage of being self-employed.

3. Vanessa, a bubbly, outgoing 30-year-old, has what her friends see as a perfect job: She's a researcher in a one-person office, with flexible hours; she has a large, quiet workspace; a boss who is often away; job security; and great pay. Yet Vanessa is unhappy with the job. According to Holland's theory, what is the problem?

4. Malia and her husband work full time. Statistically speaking, you can make two of the following predictions:
   a. Malia will probably take more time off from work for family caregiving.
   b. Malia will earn less than her spouse.
   c. Malia will be less well-educated than her spouse.

5. According to this chapter, with regard to family and work, traditional gender roles *still exist/ no longer exist*.

Answers to the Tying It All Together questions can be found at the end of this chapter.

SUMMARY

Marriage

Marriages used to be practical unions often arranged by families. In the early twentieth century, as life expectancy increased dramatically, we developed the idea that couples should be best friends and lovers for life. During the late twentieth century, with the women's movement, divorce, rising **serial cohabitation** rates, and the dramatic increase in unwed motherhood, marriage became **deinstitutionalized**—less of a standard path in the Western world.

Ideas about marriage differ around the globe. Marrying for love is becoming more common in India, although arranged marriages are the traditional norm. In the Middle East, marriage is male dominated, although women are acquiring more rights. In Islamic nations, divorced women are still subject to societal scorn.

Statistically speaking, married couples are happier and live longer than single adults. While cohabiting relationships are more fragile, when we compare people who have the resources to get married but decide to live together, the advantages to having a wedding ring disappear. Being unhappily married is worse than being single or divorced.

Especially during the first four years of marriage, couples can expect a decline in happiness; for people who stay together, there may be a **U-shaped curve of marital satisfaction,** with happiness rising at the empty-nest stage. Ironically, expecting one's relationship to be perfect may predict becoming especially disenchanted after the honeymoon phase.

According to Robert Sternberg's **triangular theory of love,** married couples start out with **consummate love,** but passion and intimacy can decline as partners construct separate lives. To preserve passion and intimacy, share exciting experiences with your mate, be committed to the marriage, feel devoted to a partner's well-being, and take joy in sacrificing for a mate. When communicating, happy couples make a high ratio of positive to negative comments, don't get personally hurtful or offer their partners excessive advice, and listen nondefensively to criticisms.

Divorce consists of an ambivalent decision-making phase followed by many stressful changes. Still, this common life event can result in greater well-being, especially if couples were very distressed (versus simply feeling "a bit" unfulfilled) with their mates. Although many people do remarry after divorcing, the odds of finding a new mate don't favor females (especially with children), and second marriages can be rockier, because it's hard for stepchildren to get attached to a "new" mom or dad. Stepchildren, however, give both men and women unparalleled joy.

Parenthood

Although many more people can become parents in our twenty-first-century society, declining **fertility rates** define the developed world. Despite our negative stereotypes, childless adults are not more self-centered or unhappy than parents.

The transition to parenthood tends to lessen romance and happiness. Among heterosexual couples, gender roles become more traditional. Conflicts that center on **marital equity** can arise. Still, some couples grow closer after the baby is born. Coping constructively with conflicts before becoming parents predicts how a relationship will fare. Competent, caring dads help make post-baby relationships thrive.

The emotional quality of motherhood is affected by a variety of forces, and this experience, although meaningful, is tailor-made to destroy women's images of how they thought they would behave as parents. Society conveys a sanitized view of motherhood. We tend to blame mothers for their children's "deficiencies," and we sometimes berate women who work for not spending enough time with their children. In contrast to our images of an epidemic of uninvolved mothers, twenty-first-century women spend much more time (especially teaching time) with their children than in the past. Contemporary mothers (and fathers) are giving their children unparalleled attention and love—even while they hold down jobs.

Today, we expect men to be **breadwinners** and **nurturer fathers,** as well as good sex-role models and, sometimes, disciplinarians. In recent decades, dads do far more hands-on caregiving, yet, statistically speaking, women typically still do much more. Fathers play with their children in traditionally male, active ways, and vary in their involvement, depending on various forces (including, interestingly, declining testosterone levels during a wife's pregnancy). Despite the rise in househusbands, traditional gender role attitudes endure.

Work

We used to have **traditional stable careers;** today, we often have **boundaryless careers.** The Internet revolution, while it offers flexibility with regard to physically being at an office, evokes more work intensity and a blurring of family and work time. The newest change in work, the rise in the gig economy, does offer more freedom, but it makes job insecurity endemic.

Among college graduates, high core self-evaluations, measured in high school, predict midlife career happiness and career success. People who have high self-efficacy and optimistic attitudes seek out challenging work and proactively shape their jobs. The ideal is to see our career as a calling, fully expressing our life mission.

Career happiness involves working hard at a job and, especially, finding an ideal personality–work fit. People want jobs that offer **intrinsic career rewards,** although **extrinsic career rewards** such as pay become salient when people need to support a family or need a paycheck to economically survive. **Role overload** (too much work to do) and **role conflict** (being pulled between family and career) is a major twenty-first-century stress. The ideal is **work–life balance**—feeling energized with one's career and having ample time for one's nonwork life.

Women still, on average, earn less than men even when they work full time. Females tend to periodically leave the workforce to provide family care and, due to **occupational segregation,** women work in lower-paying jobs (although a pay gap also exists within male-dominated industries). Even when companies give lip service to work–life balance, many corporations don't look favorably on workers who take time off for child care.

KEY TERMS

boundaryless career, p. 338

breadwinner role, p. 335

consummate love, p. 326

deinstitutionalization of marriage, p. 320

extrinsic career rewards, p. 341

fertility rate, p. 331

intrinsic career rewards, p. 340

marital equity, p. 332

nurturer father, p. 335

occupational segregation, p. 342

role conflict, p. 341

role overload, p. 341

serial cohabitation, p. 321

traditional stable career, p. 338

triangular theory of love, p. 325

U-shaped curve of marital satisfaction, p. 324

work–life balance, p. 341

ANSWERS TO **Tying It All Together** QUIZZES

Marriage

1. a and c

2. a only

3. c

4. According to Sternberg, by looking at three dimensions—passion, intimacy, and commitment—and exploring their combinations, we can get a portrait of all the partner love relationships that exist in life. By exploring how these facets change over time, we can also understand why marital happiness might naturally decline over the years. (a) This couple is extremely emotionally involved (has intimacy and passion) but has not decided to get married or enter a fully committed relationship. (b) This couple has it all: intimacy, passion, and commitment. Most likely, they are newlyweds. (c) This couple is best friends (intimate) and married (committed) but no longer passionate. Couples who have been married for decades are most likely to have companionate marriages.

5. Sharing mutually exciting activities cements passion. Commitment grows out of (and is embodied by) feeling devoted to a partner's well-being.

6. You may more quickly contemplate leaving your new spouse when you disagree. Your children are apt to feel threatened by your new relationship, and may place barriers to your getting along.

Parenthood

1. Statistically speaking, you would expect this couple's marital satisfaction to decline. This couple is most apt to cope well if Jenna and Charlie communicated well before the baby and if Charlie is an involved, caring dad.

2. a and c

3. Tell grandma that's not true! Parents are spending more time with their children than in the past. Moms do far more hands-on teaching—even when they have full-time jobs. And of course, fathers are also much more involved. Not only are dads spending more time playing, particularly with their sons, but depending on the person, they are even doing more routine care.

4. Possible questions: (1) Are you a mellow person? (2) What was your relationship like with your own father? (3) Do you feel competent (and happy) about providing hands-on child care? (4) Did you really want this child? (5) Very important: How committed are you to being the primary breadwinner?

Work

1. a and c

2. Theoretical advantage of the gig economy: being able to direct when and where you work; clear disadvantage: more job and economic insecurity.

3. Vanessa's isolated work environment doesn't fit her sociable personality. She needs ample chances to interact with people during the day.

4. a and b

5. still exist

CONNECT ONLINE:

 LaunchPad | Check out our videos and additional resources located at:
macmillan learning | www.macmillanlearning.com

CHAPTER 12

Midlife

At 20, I was so anxious about life. But there is nothing like 35 years of living to teach you who you really are. I mainly credit the life-changing experience of having twins for making me mature. Children lock you into the fact that you have a mission larger than the self. The downtimes strengthened me, too: raising my babies as a single mom before meeting Matt, taking care of Dad during his final years. At age 50, I have zero fears about physical aging. Getting through menopause was no problem; my sex life is better now than it was at 25! My anxiety relates to my mind. Now that the kids are grown, I'm passionate to make a difference in the world. I want to return to school to get a Ph.D. in public policy. But can I succeed in the classroom at my age? Am I too old to get a job?

Then there are anxieties about time. I'm watching my new grandbaby during the week, while my daughter is at work. Not only is day care expensive, I can't let Joshua spend his first year of life with strangers. Child care is a grandma's job!

Still, I'm up for these challenges, especially since I can rely on my life love, Matt, to cheer me on. In most ways, I'm the same person I was at 20—just as outgoing, caring—but much wiser, of course. And, it's now or never. I feel the clock ticking when I look around. My friend Charron recently died of cancer. My brother retired after having a stroke last year. I get my inspiration from Mom—at age 80, still the youth group director at church. Mom—well, she's supposed to be old, but she's really middle-aged.

When you think of middle age, what images come to mind? As is true of Jamila, you probably think of people at the peak of their powers: confident and mature. You might think of gaining wisdom, having a more balanced, less ego-involved perspective on life. You could imagine vigorous, happy grandparents, or daughters overburdened by caring for their parents in old age. You might worry about feeling more unattractive and not being interested in sex. In this chapter, devoted to the long life stage that psychologist Carl Jung (1933) poetically labeled "the afternoon of life," we'll explore these worries, joys, challenges, and changes.

Let's start by scanning the territory. When *are* people middle-aged? What are some classic ideas we have about this long life stage?

Setting the Context

Middle age is supposed to start at 40 and end at about 60 or 65 (Etaugh & Bridges, 2006; Lachman, 2004). But in U.S. surveys, roughly *half* of all people in their late sixties and early seventies call themselves middle-aged (Lachman, 2004). They may be right. While the leading 2016 U.S. presidential candidates clocked in at 69, 70, and an incredible 73 years old, can we pinpoint *any* age at which middle age ends?

Table 12.1 spells out common ideas we have about this remarkably long time of life. In these next sections, I will explore each question in depth. Let's begin with that nagging fear spelled out in item one: As we reach our forties and fifties, don't we feel less attractive and lose our passion for sex?

Table 12.1: Five Core Questions About Development in Middle Age

1. As I get older, will I feel worse about my looks and be less interested in sex?

2. As I get older, will I grow more intelligent?

3. As I get older, will I become wise?

4. As I get older, how will my personality change?

5. How can I be happy *throughout* the adult years?

Physical Development

LEARNING OUTCOMES

- Compare changes in sexual performance for aging females and males, making reference to the impact of menopause on women.

- List some keys to having a good body image and gratifying sex in middle and later life.

When Jung made his evocative statement, "We cannot live life's afternoon by the program of life's morning," he was alluding to the fact that, during the second half of adult life, we must abandon our quest for physical beauty in favor of deeper concerns. But do aging adults *really* care less about looking sexy and young?

Midlife Body Image

Given the mega billions we spend on Botox, hair replacements, body lifts, and anti-aging creams, the answer here is obviously no. In fact, as I mentioned in previous chapters, feeling physically appealing is centrally important to happiness at every age—and this is equally true among midlife women and men (Newton, Russell, & McAdams, 2017)!

The good news is that, perhaps because their reference point shifts upward ("How do I look compared to people my *own* age?"), female body dissatisfaction does not increase in middle age (see Rodgers & DuBois, 2016). The presence of so many 50-something sex symbols, such as Julia Roberts, suggests women don't have to give up their sexuality until well into life's afternoon.

Still, just as during adolescence (see Chapter 8), similar body-image issues plague vulnerable midlife women—feeling deficient by regularly comparing your appearance to the idealized images of "older" movie stars ("Why don't I look as sexy and youthful as Julia Roberts?"), subscribing to a 50-something version of the thin ideal ("I feel so wrinkled and overweight. Why can't I look like my 20-year-old self?") (See Hefner and others, 2014.) These negative attitudes (no surprise) impair sexual desire (Koch and others, 2005). How does *physical* sexual capacity change as men and women age?

Exploring the Physiological Sexual Changes

The age-related sexual findings for men and women are different. Older males need more time to develop an erection. They are more likely to lose an erection before ejaculation occurs. Their ejaculations become less intense. By their fifties, most men are not able to have another erection for 12 to 24 hours after having had sex (Masters & Johnson, 1966).

A 50-year-old man will probably feel just as attractive as he did in his twenties, provided he takes care of his body and doesn't expect to look exactly like his buff 20-year-old self!

Because their sexual apparatus does not critically depend on blood flow, females can be just as orgasmic at 80 as at age 20. Unfortunately, however, especially in late middle age, women are more apt to turn off to sex than men (D. M. Lee and others, 2016; Lindau and others, 2007). The reasons, as I implied earlier, are environmental: being without a partner (due to widowhood or divorce); having an older spouse with a chronic disease; not having people respond to you as a sexual human being. Menopause can indirectly affect sexuality, too.

Menopause typically occurs at about age 50, when estrogen production falls off dramatically and women stop ovulating. Specifically, the defining marker of menopause is not having menstruated for a year. As estrogen production declines, a woman's menstrual cycle becomes more irregular. During this sexual winding-down period (called *perimenopause*), as Table 12.2 shows, many people have other physical symptoms such as night sweats and hot flashes (sudden sensations of heat) (Lerner-Geva and others, 2010).

menopause The age-related process, occurring at about age 50, in which ovulation and menstruation stop due to the decline of estrogen.

Table 12.2: Stereotypes and Facts About Menopause

1. **The stereotype:** Women have terrible physical symptoms while going through menopause.

   The facts: Researchers find that an upsurge of minor physical complaints does occur during the few years preceding menopause: lack of energy, backaches, and joint stiffness. Many women experience hot flashes and some sleeplessness. Still, there is variability from person to person, and complaints vary from culture to culture. In one study, while fewer than half the women in a Scandinavian poll reported difficult symptoms, 2 out of 3 U.S. women did (Nappi & Kokot-Kierepa, 2010).

2. **The stereotype:** Women are very moody while going through menopause.

   The facts: Statistically speaking, women may show a minor rise in anxiety and depression as they approach menopause, when estrogen levels are waning (Avis and others, 2004). However, more recent research suggests menopause has no impact on mental health (Soares, 2013).

3. **The stereotype:** Women feel empty, "dried up," old, and asexual after menopause.

   The facts: Many women find menopause a relief. For instance, one-third of the women in Taiwan and almost half of all Australian women in a cross-cultural study said that they were happy not to have to deal with a period every month (Fu, Anderson, & Courtney, 2003). In another Danish study, at menopause, most women felt that they were entering a new, freer (and sexier!) stage of life (Hvas, 2001).

This estrogen loss produces changes in the reproductive tract. After menopause, the vaginal walls thin out and become more fragile. The vagina shortens, and its opening narrows. The size of the clitoris and labia shrinks and blood flow decreases. It takes longer after arousal for lubrication to begin (Masters & Johnson, 1966; Saxon, Etten, & Perkins, 2010). Women don't produce as much fluid as before. These changes can make having intercourse so painful that some women stop having sex.

Baring the *Real* Sexual Truth

By now readers might be sadly thinking, "I'd better enjoy my current sex life, because my sexual self will probably evaporate by my late fifties or when I'm 65." Not so fast!

Yes, statistically speaking, sexual desire does decline in women and men in late middle age (D. M. Lee and others, 2016; Sandberg, 2015; Waite and others, 2017). However, as you saw in Table 12.2, because they are liberated from anxieties about being pregnant, after menopause some women report that their sex lives improve. Their slower arousal-to-ejaculation tempo makes older males more physiologically in sync with women, as females generally require more time to become fully aroused (see Masters & Johnson, 1966).

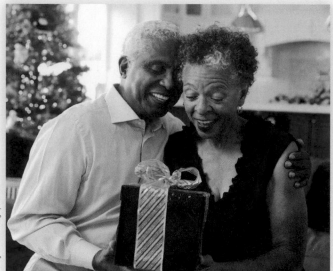

Monkey Business Images/Shutterstock

A 70-something couple may be just as passionate now as ever—if they have a more inclusive definition of intimacy.

And if you assume that marked male performance difficulties signal the death of sex, think again. In one survey, while admitting their problems were troubling, middle-aged and elderly men rejected the idea that erectile capacity defined their sexual selves (Thompson & Barnes, 2013). In an interview study, many reported becoming better lovers during life's afternoon (and evening). Eighty-four-year-old Owe shared this delightful under-the-covers account:

> [Sex is] more carefree . . . lying naked . . . caressing each other's bodies and saying tender words . . . fondling the genitals. . . . Back then it was . . . arousal and everything was over. . . . This is elongated; it can stretch over an entire . . . day.
>
> (quoted in Sandberg, 2013, p. 269)

This lovely description makes sense of why, in one survey, older couples described sex in similar ways: It's all about intimacy, communication, and authenticity. The only group who disagreed were sex therapists—who, by focusing on what goes wrong physically, believed that sex automatically becomes more dissatisfying with age.

Table 12.3 summarizes the male and female changes described in this section and offers advice for staying passionate about sex as you age. Now, let's look at the core question that first enticed researchers to study adult development. How do we change intellectually as we grow old?

Table 12.3: Staying Passionate About Sex with Age

FOR MEN

Problem	Solutions
Trouble maintaining or achieving an erection	1. Understand that physiological slowing down is normal, and do not be alarmed by problems performing. Sexual relations need to occur more slowly. Also understand that these changes may make you a more sensitive lover as you grow old.
	2. Stay healthy. Avoid sexually impairing conditions such as heart disease. If possible, avoid medications that have sexual side effects (such as antidepressants and blood pressure pills).
	3. If troubled by chronic problems performing, explore the many medical and surgical options that can help.

FOR WOMEN

Problem	Solutions
Possibly, poor body image; no sexual signals coming from the outside world	1. Stay sexy, be conscious of your physical appearance, but don't compare yourself to gorgeous midlife movie stars or your 20-year-old self.
	2. Find a partner (there may be many!) who appreciates you as a sexual human being.
	3. Consider hormone replacement therapy (but discuss this with your doctor).

Concluding advice for both sexes: Don't accept the stereotype that sexuality declines with age. Sex has the potential to become more emotionally gratifying (meaning, affection-centered) as people grow old.

Tying It All Together

1. In middle age, you will probably feel *worse/ the same* about your physical appearance as you did in your twenties, and you will probably *care less/ be just as interested* in how you look.

2. For the following age and sexuality statements, select the correct gender: *Males/ Females* decline the most physiologically. *Male/ Female* sexuality is most affected by social issues such as not having a partner.

3. Summarize in one sentence how lovemaking changes with age.

Answers to Tying It All Together questions can be found at the end of this chapter.

Cognitive Development

When do you think we reach our intellectual peak? Your answer will probably be at around age 50 rather than at 20 or 25 (Sternberg & Berg, 1992). But do we *really* get more intelligent with age? According to the Seattle Longitudinal Study, it depends (Schaie, Willis, & Caskie, 2004; Schaie & Zanjani, 2006).

Exploring the Lessons from Standard Intelligence Tests

The **Seattle Longitudinal Study,** carried out about 40 years ago, was a landmark in the blossoming field of adult development because it controlled for the contrasting biases of cross-sectional and longitudinal research. Since older people, especially in the late twentieth century, were less likely to go to college than younger cohorts, cross-sectional studies that compared different age groups at a single point in time greatly overestimated negative, age-related cognitive change. However, since only the most intellectually capable volunteers return to be tested over years, longitudinal studies were seriously skewed in a positive way (Baltes & Smith, 1997; see Chapter 1).

To compensate for these contrasting biases (cross-sectional research is too negative, longitudinal studies are overly positive), the researchers developed a brilliant solution: Conduct both kinds of studies simultaneously and compare their results to get a true picture of how intelligence changes with age. Moreover, the Seattle study was unusual because the researchers used an intelligence test measuring separate *kinds* of abilities, to get a panorama of how different intellectual skills change during adult life.

The psychologists first selected people enrolled in a Seattle health organization who were seven years apart in age, and then tested them and compared their scores. Next, they followed each group longitudinally, testing them at 7-year intervals. At each evaluation, the researchers selected another cross-sectional group, some of whom they also followed over time.

Figure 12.1 on the next page shows a few results. As we would predict, expect to reach your intellectual peak around the late forties or early fifties (Schaie, 1996; Schaie, Willis, & Caskie, 2004). But notice the differences from skill to skill. On tests measuring our knowledge base, such as vocabulary, scores improve into the sixties (Larsen, Hartmann, & Nyborg, 2007). But when a measure involves doing something new very fast (such as the word fluency measure in the chart), losses start as early as the forties (Ardila, 2007). Now let's look at a theory that puts this pattern into a larger perspective, and so tells us *exactly* how we behave intellectually in the real world.

Two Types of Intelligence: Crystallized and Fluid Skills

Psychologists divide intelligence into two categories. **Crystallized intelligence** refers to our knowledge base, the storehouse of information that we have accumulated over the years. **Fluid intelligence** involves our ability to reason quickly when facing new intellectual challenges.

LEARNING OUTCOMES

- Explain normal changes in intelligence during adulthood.
- List tips for keeping midlife intellectual capacities fine-tuned.
- Outline the defining features of wisdom.

Seattle Longitudinal Study The definitive study of the effect of aging on intelligence, involving simultaneously conducting and comparing the results of cross-sectional and longitudinal studies.

crystallized intelligence A basic facet of intelligence, consisting of a person's knowledge base, or storehouse, of accumulated information.

fluid intelligence A basic facet of intelligence, consisting of the ability to quickly master new intellectual activities.

FIGURE 12.1 Changes in two intellectual abilities over the decades in the Seattle Longitudinal Study: Notice that scores on a test demanding a heavier component of fluid skills (word fluency, which asks people to name as many words as they can starting with a letter such as A, within a time limit) decrease after the late forties, while scores on a totally crystallized test (vocabulary) stay stable into the sixties. But in general, intellectual abilities peak at about age 50 and decline in old age.

Data from Schaie, 1996.

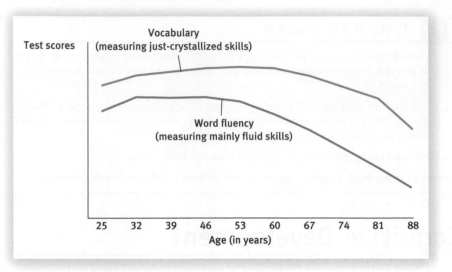

Because it depends on our nervous system being at its biological peak, fluid intelligence is at its high point during the twenties and then declines. Since crystallized intelligence measures the knowledge that we have amassed over years, this ability tends to increase well into late middle age. However, at some point (probably in the sixties), crystallized IQ declines, because our forgetting rate outpaces the new knowledge that we can absorb.

So, in any situation requiring quick performance and multitasking, people may notice their abilities declining at a relatively young age. In your late thirties, it seems harder to dribble a basketball while keeping your attention on the opposing team. At age 45, you have more trouble juggling cooking and conversing with guests at your dinner parties than at age 25. In old age, these steady fluid losses, as I will describe in Chapter 14, progress to the point where they truly interfere with daily life.

The distinction between fluid and crystallized intelligence accounts for why people in fast-paced jobs, such as air-traffic controllers, worry about being over the hill in their forties. It makes sense of why airline CEOs or professors reach their professional peak in their sixties (but not much beyond!). Anytime an activity depends heavily on quickness, being older presents problems. Whenever an intellectual challenge involves stored knowledge, people improve into their fifties and beyond.

As his passion demands speedy mental processing, this gaming guru may feel "old" in his thirties. But this 60-year-old professor will probably see his teaching as better today because his job depends almost exclusively on crystallized skills.

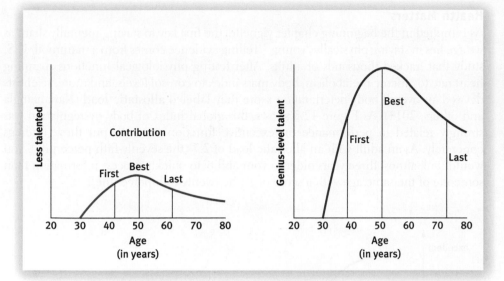

FIGURE 12.2: Age-related changes in the career paths of geniuses and of less eminent creators This chart shows that people reach their peak period of creativity in midlife. However, the most gifted geniuses stand head and shoulders above their contemporaries at every age. Data from Simonton, 1997.

Suppose you are an artist or a writer. When can you expect to do your finest work? Researchers find that when a creative activity is dependent on being totally original, such as dancing or writing poetry, people tend to perform best in their thirties (see Simonton, 2007). If the form of creativity depends just on crystallized skills, such as writing nonfiction or, in my case, producing college textbooks (yes!), people perform at their best in their sixties (Simonton, 1997, 2002). But in tracing the lives of people famous for their creative work, one researcher discovered that who we are *as people*, or our enduring abilities, outweighs the changes that occur with age. As Figure 12.2 shows, true geniuses outshine everyone else at any age (Simonton, 1997).

So, creatively or career-wise, expect to reach your peak in late middle age (in most fields). Still, expect to be the same person—to a large degree—as when you were younger. If you are exceptionally competent and creative at 30, you can stay exceptionally competent and creative at 70, or even 95.

Is a middle-aged fashion designer at his creative peak? According to the research, the answer is yes. How proficient is he, compared to his peers? For answers, we would want to look at this man's *enduring* creative talents from youth.

To illustrate this message, we can point to iconic actors who first wowed the world in their twenties and were still going strong in their seventies and beyond—such as Harrison Ford and Jane Fonda. We can cite writers, like John Grisham or Stephen King, whose new books continue to top the best-seller charts during their "older years." We even have inspiring people, like the actress Dame Judi Dench, who collected academy awards in her eighties, or the singer Mick Jagger, who still rocks the world in his seventies.

From Sigmund Freud to Toni Morrison, both of whom put forth masterpieces in old age, to Frank Lloyd Wright, who designed world-class buildings into his ninth decade of life, history is full of examples showing that creativity burns bright well into later life.

Staying IQ Smart

Returning to normally creative people, such as you and me, what qualities help *any* person stay cognitively sharp? What causes our intellectual capacities to decline at a younger-than-normal age?

Health Matters

As I implied in the beginning chapter vignette, the first key to staying mentally sharp as we age lies in staying physically "young." Telling evidence comes from a mammoth U.S. study that tracked thousands of adults. After testing physiological functions spanning heart rate to glucose metabolism, body mass index to cortisol levels, and more, scientists devised an overall body deterioration score they labeled **allostatic load** (Karlamangla and others, 2014). As Figure 12.3 shows, this global index of body dysregulation was strongly related to performance on executive function tests. To put these findings concretely: As an adult with an allostatic load of 2.7 (the seventy-fifth percentile), you would rank almost three years older in your ability to quickly process information than someone of the same age with a score of 1 (the twenty-fifth percentile)!

allostatic load An overall score of body deterioration, gained from summing how a person functions on multiple physiological indexes. Allostatic load predicts cognitive performance during adult life.

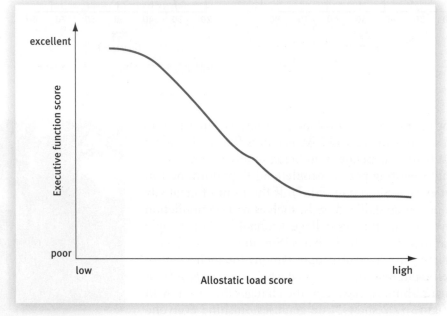

FIGURE 12.3 How allostatic load relates to scores on executive function tests in more than 1,000 U.S. adults with an average age in their late fifties: This chart shows concretely that body deterioration (measured by allostatic load) is intimately tied to cognitive functioning in midlife (not just over age 65). Data from Karlamangla and others, 2014, p. 391.

Obviously, Sue Semrau needs to take care of her health in order to coach the Florida State basketball team—but the interpersonal challenges involved in dealing with these young athletes will keep her "on her toes" intellectually during her older years.

The most compelling research relates to the connection between being physically fit (that is, exercising) and having a well-tuned mind. Physically fit older and midlife adults consistently perform better on cognitive tests (McAuley, Kramer, & Colcombe, 2004; Newson & Kemps, 2008). New research suggests that exercise physiologically changes the brain (Gourgouvelis, Yielder, & Murphy, 2017; P. Huang and others, 2016; Hwang, Castelli, and Gonzalez-Lima, 2017; Jonasson and others, 2017; Williams and others, 2017)!

Mental Stimulation (with People) May Matter

Because environmental stimulation promotes synaptogenesis (as I mentioned in Chapter 3), the second key to staying intelligent should be a no-brainer: Exercise your mental capacities.

People who work in complex, challenging jobs tend to become more mentally flexible with age (Schooler, 1999, 2001; Schooler, Mulatu, & Oates, 2004). Careers that involve people—from hosting a talk show to coaching college students—are most likely to keep midlife people mentally on their toes (Finkel and others, 2009). So one good intellectual insurance policy is to follow my advice in Chapters 10 and 11: Find a compelling, flow-inducing career!

But wait a second! Aren't adults with challenging jobs apt to be intelligent and well educated to begin with, and also younger health-wise than the average person their age? Couldn't these other forces account for why their abilities improve most with age? To *prove* that mental stimulation promotes cognitive growth, we might have to conduct an impossible (but fun) decades-long experiment: Assign young people to participate in a *Jeopardy!*-like quiz show, or to host National Public Radio's *All Things Considered*, then compare their IQs to those of a control group in later middle age.

The good news, however, is that while we can't carry out this study with our species, it's fine to experiment on rats. When researchers put a group of rats in a large cage with challenging wheels and swings and then compared their cortices with a control group of similar animals, this treatment produced thicker, heavier brains (Diamond, 1988, 1993). Let's tentatively accept the widespread idea, then, that just as intense physical exercise may change the brain, challenging life experiences promote resilient minds.

In sum, people in their forties and fifties are at the peak of their mental powers. But they will have more trouble mastering new cognitive challenges (those involving fluid skills) when under time pressure. To preserve their cognitive capacities as they age, adults need to take care of their health, become physically fit, and search out stimulating work. And you can tell any worried 50-year-old family member who is considering going back to school to go for it!

INTERVENTIONS   Keeping a Fine-Tuned Mind

Now let's look at the lessons the research offers for any person who wants to stay mentally sharp as the years pass.

- Take care of your physical health and exercise, exercise, exercise!

- Stay (or become) passionate about learning new things.

- As challenging interpersonal activities matter most, search out careers that involve people-oriented work, or try volunteer activities such as tutoring or serving on a community board.

- Understand that as you get older, new tasks involving complex information-processing will be difficult. To cope with these losses, you might adopt the following three-part strategy devised by developmentalist Paul Baltes, called **selective optimization with compensation.**

> **selective optimization with compensation**
> Paul Baltes's three principles for successful aging (and living): (1) focus on our most important activities; (2) work especially hard in these top ranking areas; and (3) rely on external aids when we cannot cope on our own.

As we move into later middle age and notice we cannot function as well as we used to, Baltes believed that we need to (1) *selectively* focus on our most important activities, shedding less important priorities; (2) *optimize*, or work harder, to perform at our best in these most important areas of life; and (3) *compensate*, or rely on external aids, when we cannot cope on our own (Baltes, 2003; Baltes & Carstensen, 2003; Krampe & Baltes, 2003).

Let's take Mr. Fernandez, whose hobby is gourmet cooking. In his fifties, he might decide to give up some less important interest such as tennis, to conserve his strength for the time he spends at the stove (*selection*). He would need to work harder to prepare difficult dishes demanding split-second timing, such as his prizewinning soufflés (*optimization*). He might put a chair in the kitchen rather than stand for hours, or give up preparing entire dinner party feasts and rely on his guests to bring an appetizer or dessert (*compensation*).

Although Baltes devised these guidelines to apply to successful aging, they are relevant to anyone striving for work–life balance: from parents struggling to handle careers and children, to students strategically selecting which courses need the most study time. And isn't finding the correct work–life balance critical to being wise?

As they age, men who delight in their cooking skills can still prepare gourmet feasts, provided they rely on some meal preparation help from their dinner guests.

Vico Collective/Alin Dragulin/Getty Images

Exploring Wisdom

Aristotle, the ancient philosopher whose ideas are the basis for much modern thinking about wisdom, believed one component of wise thinking is the ability to thoughtfully direct our lives. Wise people, one study showed, effectively tailor their responses to the situation. They work to change events they can control and face life's uncontrollable blows—be they accidents or fatal diseases—by modifying their attitudes (Haines and others, 2016). But wisdom involves more than competently directing the self—it demands a unique approach to life.

What qualities are involved in being wise? Although philosophers have mulled this question for millennia, psychologists only recently turned to scientifically studying wisdom. This oldest, most elevated human quest may be one of the youngest research topics in developmental science today!

As I implied in Chapter 7, traditional intelligence tests won't help us measure wisdom. Some of the finest test takers (that is, experts at analytic intelligence)—as Robert Sternberg pointed out—can make very unwise choices in life. One strategy has been to expand Piaget's stage theory of cognition beyond *formal operations* to spell out a unique form of intelligence called **postformal thought.** How does postformal thinking differ from Piaget's formal operations? Let's draw on these distinctions, and other ideas, to spell out four defining qualities of being wise. (I adapted these insights from Ardelt, 2016; Fowers, Richardson, & Slife, 2017; Grossman, 2017; Krause, 2016; Labouvie-Vief, 1992; Rybash, Hoyer, & Roodin, 1986; Sinnott, 2003; Sternberg, 2013; Wink and Staudinger, 2016.)

postformal thought A uniquely adult form of intelligence that involves being sensitive to different perspectives, making decisions based on one's inner feelings, and being interested in exploring new questions.

- **Wise thinkers embrace uncertainty.** As I described in Chapter 9, when adolescents reach formal operations, they can solve problems like real scientists. Wise adults realize that most real-world problems do not have "scientifically correct" answers. They understand that they need to flexibly weigh different possibilities in order to make the *best* decisions in the face of the complexity of life.

- **Wise thinkers are sensitive to other people's perspectives.** Wisdom requires a different skill set than solving Piaget's pendulum test. People who are wise are experts in empathy. They are attuned to relationships and adept at putting themselves in other people's shoes.

- **Wise thinking involves *self-transcendence*.** Adopting this empathic orientation means going beyond our own perspective. Rather than simply making decisions based on their personal needs ("Only I can come out on top!"), wise people distance themselves from their egos and select the best choices from everyone's point of view ("Let's compromise so we can *all* win!").

- **Wise thinking demands humility.** Striving for compromise requires understanding that we don't have all the answers to life. Rather than just saying, "What I believe is true" or "I'm the one that's always right," wise people are humble (Krause, 2016). They believe they *always* have more to learn about people and the world.

Now imagine that you are confronted with the kind of life challenge below. What is the wisest way to respond?

You get a frantic call from a college acquaintance. This person says that she has carefully hoarded several bottles of tranquilizers and plans to kill herself within the next week. What should you say, think, and do?

People who blurt out statements like: "This is ridiculous. . . . Life is not given to us or taken away . . . You must immediately stop!" are definitely not showing wisdom. In fact, in my view, this kind of impulsive moralizing might put a suicidal person over the edge!

Wise thinkers approach this problem in a more thoughtful, humble way:

"I don't believe in suicide, but I need to know more . . . What is causing these feelings? It seems . . . good . . . to bring the conversation . . . to . . . pleasant memories—but . . . everyone might respond differently. I'll . . . base my response on what I know about this friend.

(quoted in Wink & Staudinger, 2016, p. 310)

Clearly, if we were contemplating suicide, we would hope to have the second kind of friend! But again, we are faced with the issue relating to *validity* that I discussed in connection with Kohlberg's moral development scale in Chapter 9: Does wise thinking on artificial vignettes relate to acting wisely in life? It's one thing to behave like the ancient philosopher Socrates who pondered existence by retreating from the world, but what happens when you immerse yourself in the messy challenges of real life?

Are people *generally* wise, or does wise reasoning vary from life situation to life situation (Grossman, 2017)? To answer this question, researchers (Grossmann, Gerlach, & Denissen, 2016) asked volunteers to keep a diary listing the upsetting events they experienced within the past few days. When confronted with specific problems, how did the volunteers cope, think, and react?

The ancient philosopher Socrates became a universal model of wisdom when he withdrew from society to abstractly contemplate the world—but wise reasoning is far more difficult when people are emotionally involved in life.

As the researchers predicted, scores on self-transcendence and perspective-taking differed greatly, depending on how ego involving the situation became. For example, a person might be a model of maturity at reasoning out a friend's problems, but fly into a rage when that same friend starts to criticize her *own* life. It's easier to objectively present the pros and cons of gun control if you haven't lost a loved one to a drive-by shooting or lived through some horrific school massacre like the tragedy at Columbine or Parkland, Florida.

Yes, vignette-measured wisdom relates to a host of positive qualities—being well adjusted, prosocial, and especially being open to life (Wink & Staudinger, 2016). But, unfortunately, the more emotionally involved we are in a certain situation, the less likely we are apt to reason wisely.

INTERVENTIONS Teaching Wisdom

Can we train people to take a more self-transcendent perspective? The encouraging answer is yes. Researchers (Grossmann, Sahdra, & Cairrochi, 2016; Grossman, 2017) asked Australian volunteers to select a societal issue they cared about, such as climate change or educational funding. They instructed one group to "consider how this problem might evolve and focus on the situation as a third person might." Another group was encouraged to "put yourself in the situation and think of how you would respond." As you might expect, participants adopted a wiser framework when reflecting on social issues from a more distant, less ego-centered view.

If we can teach people to be wise, this suggests that the common idea that wisdom grows from years of living should be correct. Aristotle believed that only age brings wisdom, because the young don't have the experience to be able to gain perspective on the ebb and flow of events.

In polls, people specifically credit *stressful* life events as giving them a wiser perspective on living (Lilgendahl, Helson, & John, 2013): "Father's sudden death let me realize the importance of family"; "When I lost my home in the flood, I realized money isn't that important; only relationships matter in life."

Do life's traumas make us more mature? Or, as the philosopher Nietzsche famously said, "What does not kill me makes me stronger." How does personality *really* change during adult life? Stay tuned for answers in the next section.

🎯 Tying It All Together

1. Andrés is an air traffic controller, and Mick is a historian. Pick which man is likely to reach his career peak earlier, and explain the reasons why.

2. Your author (me) is writing another textbook on lifespan development. I am also learning a new video game. Identify each type of intellectual skill involved and describe how my abilities in each of these areas are likely to have changed now that I am 70 years old.

3. Rick says, "I've got too much on my plate. I can't do anything well." Identify the theory discussed in this chapter that would be most helpful in addressing this problem, and explain what this theory would advise.

4. Kayla is contemplating breaking up with her boyfriend, Tabil, because, she says, "He works too much. He doesn't give me the attention I need." Name the advice a wise thinker would *not* give to Kayla.

   a. "Leave the bum!"
   b. "Think of what is going on from Tabil's perspective—for instance, is he trying to make a life for you two? Can you compromise?"
   c. "There may be no 'right decision'; but whatever choice you make, look at all the angles."
   d. " I know this is incredibly upsetting, but if you do decide to end the relationship— consider this a learning experience. It will help you make better life choices in the future!"

5. Based specifically on this section, in a phrase, sum up a main prerequisite for thinking wisely.

Answers to the Tying It All Together questions can be found at the end of this chapter.

LEARNING OUTCOMES

- Classify the Big Five dimensions, making reference to conscientiousness in promoting adult success.
- Describe the attributes that foster generativity.
- Summarize the qualities involved in feeling happy and fulfilled during adulthood.

Big Five Five core psychological predispositions— neuroticism, extraversion, openness to experience, conscientiousness, and agreeableness—that underlie personality.

Emotional Development

Actually, we have *contradictory* views about how personality changes as we get older. One is that we don't change: "If Calista is irascible in college, she will be bitter in the nursing home." Another view is that entering new life stages and having life-changing experiences propels emotional growth: "Since getting married, I'm a more stable person"; "Coming close to death after my car accident transformed how I think about the world." Do people stay the same or grow as the years pass? Actually, they do both!

Exploring the Big Five

Today, the main way psychologists measure personality is by ranking people according to five basic temperamental qualities. As you read this list, take a minute to think of where you stand on these largely genetically determined dimensions, which Robert McCrae and Paul Costa (1990) have named the **Big Five**:

- *Neuroticism* refers to our general tendency toward mental health versus psychological disturbance. Are you resilient, stable, and well-adjusted—someone who bounces back after setbacks? Or are you hostile, high-strung, hysterical, and impulsive—a person whom others might label as psychologically disturbed? (Children with serious externalizing and internalizing tendencies, for instance, would rank high on neuroticism.)

- *Extraversion* describes outgoing attitudes, such as warmth, gregariousness, activity, and assertion. Are you sociable, friendly, a real "people person," someone who thrives on meeting new friends and going to parties? Or are you most comfortable curling up alone with a good book? Do you get antsy when you are by yourself, thinking "I've got to get out and be with people," or do you prefer living a reflective, solitary life?

- *Openness to experience* refers to our passion to seek out new experiences. Do you adore traveling the world, adopting different perspectives, having people shake up your preconceived ideas? Do you believe life should be a continual adventure and relish getting out of your comfort zone? Or are you cautious, rigid, risk-averse, and comfortable mainly with what you already know?

- *Conscientiousness* describes having the kind of efficacious, worker personality described in Chapters 10 and 11. Are you hardworking, self-disciplined, and reliable—someone others count on to take on demanding jobs and get things done? Or are you erratic and irresponsible, prone to renege on obligations and forget appointments—a person your friends and co-workers really can't trust?

- *Agreeableness* has to do with kindness, empathy, and the ability to compromise. Are you pleasant, loving, and easy to get along with; or stubborn, hot-tempered, someone who continually seems offended and gets into fights? (Agreeable people, for instance, have secure attachment styles.)

Hundreds of studies show that our Big Five rankings have consequences for our lives. Because extraverts are upbeat and happy, they have more fulfilling relationships (Butkovic, Brkovic, & Bratko, 2011; Cox and others, 2010). People high in neuroticism, being anxious and depressed, are more apt to suffer from chronic diseases (Sutin and others, 2013). As I implied in the last section, openness to experience is a core component of wise thinking (Wink & Staudinger, 2016). One longitudinal study even suggested that openness to experience and conscientiousness might help protect us against developing Alzheimer's disease (Duberstein and others, 2011).

Look at these exuberant women enjoying themselves at a party and you will understand why extraverts are generally happy (and also why simply being around a "people person" makes us feel more upbeat). How would you rank yourself on extraversion and each of the other Big Five traits I just described?

Without neglecting the role of each Big Five trait in constructing a successful life, let's now pause to look at the role conscientiousness plays in shaping our experiences as adults.

At the core of conscientiousness (and wise thinking) is having good *executive functions*—being able to think through our actions and modulate our emotions. Therefore, it makes sense that this Big Five trait is closely related to academic success (Sobowale and others, 2017; Song & Shi, 2017; Sorić, Penezić, & Burić, 2017). Actually, conscientiousness is related to most real-world achievements.

Conscientious adults have more stable marriages (Razeghi and others, 2011). They are less likely than their contemporaries to be unemployed during life (Egan and others, 2017). Study after study suggests conscientious people are healthier (Stoll and others, 2017) and live longer than their peers because they take such good care of their health (Hampson and others, 2013; Strickhouser, Zell, & Krizan, 2017; Sutin and others, 2013).

For example, let's take Sara, who ranked high on conscientiousness at age 10. Her hard-working personality ensured that she was accepted at a good college, graduated at the top of her class, and got an excellent first job. As she traveled through her career, Sara was praised for her industriousness, earned promotions, and eventually landed an executive position at a firm. Sara was committed to her marriage, had the emotion-regulation talents to communicate well with her mate and—because we match up by *homogamy*—selected a conscientious spouse. At age 55, Sara's life is a testament to the power of hard work in building a fulfilling life. Because Sara and her husband take care to exercise and eat right, this couple is on track to live healthy, wealthy, and happy, into old age.

Now, imagine Brett, your emerging-adult friend, who ranks low on this Big Five dimension. In his teens, Brett became ensnared in alcohol and drugs, so he never made it through school. Because Brett was so unreliable, he continually lost jobs and—over the decades—had several bitter divorces. His children rejected him for being an absent dad (Le Vigouroux and others, 2017). At age 60, Brett has serious health concerns and appears years older than his age. His decades of failure have left your friend penniless, lonely, and depressed.

These descriptions suggest that because our nature (or basic temperamental traits) shape specific life experiences, we should become more like ourselves as we age. Due to an *evocative and active* process, Sara's conscientious personality paved the way for her to outshine her contemporaries at each adult stage. Brett and Calista (mentioned earlier in this chapter) are set up to fail socially and work-wise, and become bitter over time. In addition to genetic and environmental forces that converge to promote consistency, we expect similar behaviors from people such as Sara, Brett, and Calista because we yearn for a stable world (Allemand, Steiger, & Hill, 2013). If you have ever been shocked when a family member acted totally "out of character," you know what I mean.

Therefore, what's astonishing is that twin studies show personality gets *less* heritable as we age and encounter the random ups and downs of life (Bleidorn, Kandler, & Caspi, 2014; Briley & Tucker-Drob, 2014; Specht and others, 2014). And, although the main theme is consistency (who you are as a person probably won't change on the most basic level), the good news is that during adulthood many of us *do* get wiser, in the sense of being more mature.

Making the Maturity (and Wisdom) Case

One early influence fostering maturity is confronting the normal challenges of adult life (see Hutteman and others, 2014). As I suggested in Chapters 9 and 10, after leaving the cocoon of our families, we need to emotionally grow up. And, although some research suggests there is also a tendency to become more agreeable as we move from youth to middle age, conscientiousness is the Big Five trait that increases most (Chopik & Kitayama, 2017).

A delightful example of the power of adult relationships to mold our character (meaning the Big Five trait of conscientiousness) comes from a German study exploring personality changes in relation to the living arrangements of emerging adults. While young people who cohabited with roommates did not increase much in conscientiousness over a 4-year period, moving in with a romantic partner was apt to be accompanied by a real boost in that core trait (Jonkmann and others, 2014). Bottom line: Close, adult encounters—especially of the romantic kind—force us to toe the maturity line.

But emotional growth doesn't just stop after we assume adult roles. Many people feel more in control of their lives and grow self-assured well into their older years (Specht and others, 2014).

Consider a cross-sectional study examining the prevalence of mature (resilient) personalities at different ages in huge samples of Australian and German adults. As Figure 12.4a shows, the percentages of women classified as resilient (people ranking high on the positive Big Five traits) floated upward from a low during emerging adulthood, to a high in old age (Specht, Luhmann, & Geiser, 2014). Now, scan the findings relating to self-criticism in Figure 12.4b. This chart comes from another thousand-plus person poll of Canadian adults. From a high point at age 19, notice that self-criticism scores decline for men and women at older ages (Kopala-Sibley, Mongrain, & Zuroff, 2013).

Moreover, this self-assured worldview does not signal narcissism. In creative studies conducted in Switzerland and the United States, researchers offered convincing evidence that midlife and older people have a less egocentric, more altruistic attitude toward life (Freund & Blanchard-Fields, 2014). When asked to imagine owning an apple orchard, older age groups were more prone to choose an ecology-friendly harvesting strategy over one that maximized profit. Midlife adults were more apt to donate what they earned from participating in the study to a social cause than were young people provided with the same choice (see Figure 12.4c). This greater generosity had nothing to do with older adults having more personal wealth, as it also appeared when controlling for people's income.

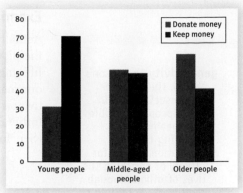

FIGURE 12.4a: In huge cross-sectional studies conducted in Germany and Australia, the percentage of resilient personalities floated upward in older groups: This chart, showing the findings for women, reveals that the probability of being classified as resilient increases dramatically, particularly during middle age.
Data from Specht, Luhmann, & Geiser, 2014.

FIGURE 12.4b: The relationship between age and self-criticism in over 300 Canadian adults ranging in age from 19 to 59, recruited from the Internet: In this study, when people of different ages were asked to respond to items such as "There is a big difference between how I am and how I want to be," far fewer people (especially men) gave self-critical ratings at each of the older ages.
Data from Kopala-Sibley, Mongrain, & Zuroff, 2013, p. 135.

FIGURE 12.4c: Donation behavior at different ages in several thousand Swiss and U.S. adults: When asked to either keep or donate the money from participating in this study to charity, notice, in particular, the dramatic rise in altruism (donating) among middle-aged and elderly people.
Data from Freund & Blanchard-Fields, 2014.

Obviously, these findings are averages. There are clearly many selfish, "out-of-control" 60-somethings. Perhaps you have a friend who peaked emotionally in adolescence and went on to have an unhappy life: the teenage football hero who descended into drug abuse, or your high school prom queen who now lives homeless, on the street.

Can we identify the core quality that makes for emotional growth (and happiness) during adult life? The answer is yes!

Generativity: The Key to a Happy Life

By now you should be impressed with the power of conscientiousness to predict life success. But while knowing where we stand on the Big Five can help reveal our journey's outcome, it tells us nothing about specifics of the journey itself. Think of several friends who rank high on conscientiousness. One person might be a full-time mother; another might be a company manager; yet another might have found the outlet for his conscientiousness through being a nurse. In order to really understand what makes human beings tick, we have to move in closer and interview people about their lives. This is the strategy that Dan McAdams has used to explore personality during the adult years. Let's eavesdrop on one of McAdams's interviews, with a woman reflecting on the traumatic event of witnessing her then 4-year-old son being hit by a car:

> When I got there, he [Jeff, who is now a healthy 18-year-old] was lying . . . unconscious. . . . That feeling of being helpless . . . while I was sure I was watching my son die was a turning point. I decided [to become] an E.M.T.
>
> (quoted in McAdams, de St. Aubin, & Logan, 1993, p. 228)

In listening to these stories, McAdams realized the power of random life events in shaping personality. Although this woman might have always ranked high in conscientiousness, the *specific* path her life took was altered by this pivotal experience. In McAdams's opinion, in order to really understand development, we need to get up close and personal and talk to people about their missions and goals.

Examining Generative Priorities

Actually, McAdams's professional mission has been to scientifically test the ideas of the pioneering theorist who *does* believe that our goals shift dramatically in different life stages: Erik Erikson. Does **generativity,** or nurturing the next generation, become our main agenda during midlife? Is Erikson (1969) correct that fulfilling our generativity is the key to feeling happy during "the afternoon" of life? When people in their forties or fifties don't feel generative, are they stagnant, demoralized, and depressed? (See Table 12.4.)

generativity In Erikson's theory, the seventh psychosocial task, in which people in midlife find meaning from nurturing the next generation, caring for others, or enriching the lives of others through their work. According to Erikson, when midlife adults have not achieved generativity, they feel stagnant, without a sense of purpose in life.

Table 12.4: Erikson's Psychosocial Stages

Life Stage	Primary Task
Infancy (birth to 1 year)	Basic trust versus mistrust
Toddlerhood (1 to 2 years)	Autonomy versus shame and doubt
Early childhood (3 to 6 years)	Initiative versus guilt
Middle childhood (7 to 12 years)	Industry versus inferiority
Adolescence to emerging adulthood (teens into twenties)	Identity versus role confusion
Early adulthood (twenties to early forties)	Intimacy versus isolation
Middle adulthood (forties to sixties)	**Generativity versus stagnation**
Late adulthood (late sixties and beyond)	Integrity versus despair

To capture Erikson's concept, McAdams's research team constructed a questionnaire to generally measure generative concerns (the first 10 items on this scale are listed in Table 12.5). The researchers also explored people's generative priorities by telling them to "list the top-ranking agendas in your life now" (see McAdams, 2001a).

Table 12.5: McAdams's Generative Concern Scale

True	False	
❑	❑	1. I try to pass along the knowledge I have gained through my experiences.
❑	❑	2. I do not feel that other people need me.
❑	❑	3. I think I would like the work of a teacher.
❑	❑	4. I feel as though I have made a difference to many people.
❑	❑	5. I do not volunteer to work for a charity.
❑	❑	6. I have made and created things that have had an impact on other people.
❑	❑	7. I try to be creative in most things that I do.
❑	❑	8. I think that I will be remembered for a long time after I die.
❑	❑	9. I believe that society cannot be responsible for providing food and shelter to all homeless people.
❑	❑	10. Others would say that I have made unique contributions to society.

Information from McAdams & de St. Aubin, 1992, pp. 1003–1015.

How do you score on this scale measuring overall generative motivations?

Answers: 1. T, 2. F, 3. T, 4. T, 5. F, 6. T, 7. T, 8. T, 9. F, 10. T

When these researchers gave their measures to young, middle-aged, and elderly people, they found few age differences in generative attitudes. People were just as likely to care about making a difference in the world at age 20 or 50 or 85. The researchers did discover age differences in generative *priorities*—with emerging adults ranking very low on this scale (McAdams, Hart, & Maruna, 1998). Young people's goals were centered on identity issues. A 20-year-old might say, "I want to make it through college and get a good job" or "My plan is to figure out what I want to do with my life." Midlife and older adults were more likely to report: "My mission is to help my teenage son," or "My goal is to work for justice and peace in the world."

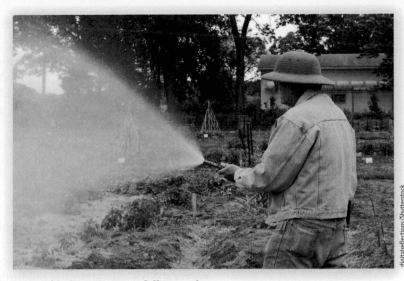

This makes sense. As I mentioned in Chapter 4, prosocial behaviors are in full swing by toddlerhood. There is no reason to think that our basic human drive to be nurturing changes at any life stage. But, just as Erikson would predict, we need to resolve issues related to our personal development before our primary concern shifts to giving to others in the world.

Is Erikson correct that generativity is the key to happiness during adult life? Here, the answer is yes, as long as we define happiness in the right way. If we imagine happiness as simply "feeling good" (**hedonic happiness**), generativity has nothing to do with living a happy life. But, if we consider this term in its richer sense, as having purpose and meaning (**eudaimonic happiness**), then yes, highly generative people do have exceptionally happy lives (Grossbaum & Bates, 2002; Versey, Stewart, & Duncan, 2013; Zucker, Ostrove, & Stewart, 2002).

When people don't have generative goals, do their lives lack meaning? Do these adults feel *stagnant*, as Erikson described—that is, purposeless and at loose ends? Read what one researcher had to say about Deborah, who, in her late forties, scored very low on generativity in his study of women's lives:

> In reference to the birth of her first child, Deborah wrote, "All actions automatic. No emotional involvement . . . ; totally self-preserving but very unpleasant."
> (quoted in Peterson, 1998, p. 12)

As this case history suggests, giving birth does not automatically evoke generativity. Conversely, some people who never have children, such as Mother Teresa, who took care of orphaned children in India, can be worldwide beacons of generativity. In fact, when we think of U.S. icons, such as Martin Luther King, the ultimate generative activity occurs when people change society in an enduring way.

Adults of every age derive great pleasure from engaging in generative activities. But now that he is in his fifties, cultivating a community garden to provide poor people with free vegetables qualifies as the generative center of a man's life.

hedonic happiness Well-being defined as pure pleasure.

eudaimonic happiness Well-being defined as having a sense of meaning and life purpose.

The lives of Martin Luther King, Jr. and Mother Teresa are a testament that exceptional generativity lies in making a difference in the world.

Examining the Childhood Memories of Generative Adults

Do the childhoods of people who commit their lives to changing society, such as those world-class generative role models Mother Teresa and Martin Luther King, differ from those of more typical adults? To answer this question, McAdams's research team selected community leaders who scored at the upper ends of their Generative Concern Scale (see page 362) and asked them to tell their life stories. Would these autobiographies differ from those of adults such as Deborah in my previous example, who ranked low on Erikson's midlife task?

The answer was yes. The life stories of highly generative adults had themes demonstrating what the researchers called a **commitment script.** They often described early memories of feeling "blessed": "I was my grandmother's favorite"; "I was a miracle child who should not have survived." They reported feeling sensitive to the suffering of others, from a young age. They talked about having an identity revolving around generative values that never wavered from their teenage years. A 50-year-old minister in one of McAdams's studies was a teenage prostitute, and then a con artist who spent two years in a federal prison; but throughout her life, she reported, "I was always doing ministry."

The most striking characteristic of generative adults' life stories was **redemption sequences**—examples of devastating events that turned out in a positive way (McAdams, 2006; McAdams & Bowman, 2001). For instance, in the example I just mentioned, the woman minister might view the humiliation of being sent to prison as the best thing that ever happened, the experience that turned her life around. According to McAdams (2006), early memories of feeling personally blessed, an enduring sensitivity to others' misfortunes, caring values, and, especially, being able to turn one's tragedies into growth experiences are the core ingredients of the commitment script and the main correlates of a generative adult life (see also Lilgendahl & McAdams, 2011).

What produces the kind of adult devoted to making a difference in the world? According to McAdams's interviews, one force may be the presence of caring adults in a person's past. When his research team asked people in their late fifties to pinpoint emotional turning points in their lives, adults high in generativity described critical incidents involving family members and teachers more frequently than did their less generative peers. Here is an example of a son's memory visiting his dying mother right before his high school graduation:

> The day before . . . mom died, . . . I shared [my senior photos]. . . . I could . . . tell . . . that she [was] real proud . . . she never saw me . . . [graduate], but . . . I . . . believe she was there in spirit. . . . That will always be a highlight of my life.
>
> (quoted in Jones & McAdams, 2013, p. 168)

If you think of your own generative role models—from a favorite teacher to, hopefully, your mom or dad—these special people are apt to be sprinkled in every ethnic group. But, interestingly, McAdams's studies consistently show that African American men and women are overrepresented in their samples of generative community-minded adults (Hart and others, 2001; Jones & McAdams, 2013; McAdams, 2006; Newton & Baltys, 2014). Does coping with discrimination—plus a strong grounding in religion—make African Americans unusually sensitive to human suffering and so prone to devote their lives to the greater good? In support of this possibility, themes stressing progress toward overcoming adversity are central in highly generative African Americans' autobiographies (McAdams & Bowman, 2001).

In sum, this powerful generativity research explains why raindrops—meaning upsetting experiences—might promote wisdom. It all depends on how we make meaning out of our personal storms. As one 61-year-old woman, who grew emotionally, in a

commitment script In Dan McAdams's research, a type of autobiography produced by highly generative adults that involves childhood memories of feeling special; being unusually sensitive to others' misfortunes; having a strong, enduring generative mission from adolescence; and redemption sequences.

redemption sequence In Dan McAdams's research, a characteristic theme of highly generative adults' autobiographies, in which they describe tragic events that turned out for the best.

study put it: "I do not regret the past, for it is the pain of my first 50 years that has brought me to where I am now" (quoted in Lilgendahl, Helson, & John, 2013, p. 413).

Hot in Developmental Science: Targeting Happiness

This discussion brings me full circle to wisdom and how this highest human quality relates to having a happy life. Wisdom is certainly not the same thing as feeling happy. In fact, wise thinkers might feel incredibly discouraged about the frailties of human beings ("Why do we continually have wars and pollute our beautiful planet?"). But wise reasoning is closely connected to being satisfied with life, especially in old age (Ardelt, 2016; Ardelt & Edwards, 2016; Krause, 2016; Wink & Staudinger, 2016). And isn't it vital to have a self-transcendent perspective as we confront that universal challenge of living—impending death? (I'll talk more about this in Chapter 15.)

What exactly makes people happy? Based on decades of social science studies examining this vital question, Table 12.6 (at the end of this section) showcases a few fascinating and surprising happiness stereotypes and scientific facts.

Now, let's offer three surprising, recent research tips for brightening your day:

TIP #1: Act in harmony with your inner self. We automatically assume that people are happiest when they feel upbeat. But we actually feel most fulilled when we are sad or angry—if these emotions are congruent with our "true" self. In one interesting cross-cultural study, people reported feeling best about themselves when they experienced the emotions they wanted to experience, a pattern that even applied to people who yearned to feel more pleasure in life (Tamir and others, 2017). The lesson: To be happy, strive to feel "right" (or connected to your real values) rather than simply striving for joy!

TIP # 2: You will get more happiness bang for your buck if you buy time and experiences rather than material things. We assume that our hard-earned funds are best spent when acquiring concrete objects such as a new car. But, *provided we have ample money to satisfy our basic needs*, that isn't necessarily true. If we want to use our money to make us feel joyful, it's best to purchase experiences, like cruising to the Bahamas, going to a concert (Gilovich, Kumar, & Jampol, 2015), or simply buying ourselves time to relax. In one experiment in which upper-middle-class adults were given $40 and asked to spend that money either on a material purchase or in some time-saving way, people reported feeling in a far, far better mood when they used the money to buy time—for instance, by hiring someone to prepare dinner that day (Whillans and others, 2017).

On a related note, adults who view happiness in terms of acquiring material objects (getting that new Mercedes) are less happy than their counterparts who link well-being to satisfying work (Muñiz-Velázquez, Gomez-Baya, & Lopez-Casquete, 2017). Worse yet, materialists, because they expect so much gratification from a Mercedes or Maserati, tend to be more let down when those coveted items arrive (Pandelaere, 2016). Bottom line: Science supports what your Sunday school teacher or grandpa advised. Getting and spending on "things" can be a false god!

TIP #3: Reach out to very different kinds of people. As Table 12.6 on the next page suggests, our personal happiness depends on the nation where we live. It's not just wars or poverty that make people miserable, but having a "tribal" (*us* versus *them*) worldview. In one international survey, nations with citizens prone to adopt this

A group project to restore the oldest Black Baptist church in South Carolina is typical in the African American experience, where a mission to be of service—especially in a caring community that revolves around the church—is standard.

bad group/ good group mentality—for instance being frightened of outsiders, such as immigrants—ranked at the low end of the happiness scale (Conzo and others, 2017).

So, one key to feeling better about your own life is to reach out and talk (meaning, share experiences, but don't argue) with groups you might otherwise avoid, such as the conservative next door if you are a committed liberal; or, if you are an Evangelical, the atheist down the street. Again, when we focus just on our *own* group winning, we all automatically lose! 🐚

Table 12.6 Happiness Stereotypes and Statistical Facts

"Youth is the happiest life stage."

Answer: *Wrong!* Emerging adulthood is the peak age for developing emotional problems. Many cross-sectional studies in Western nations agree: People are apt to be happiest in later life (more about this surprising finding in the next chapter)!

"Money can't buy happiness."

Answer: *That's true, but only once we are fairly comfortable economically.* Around the globe, poor people are significantly less happy than their more affluent counterparts. Once our basic survival needs are satisfied, the correlation between income and happiness becomes weaker—although it still exists. The main reason is probably not that getting more "things" matters, but that money can buy quality family and leisure time. And satisfying relationships (and experiences), as the text described, are highly related to reports of a happy life.

"I'll be happy when I get my career in order, become famous, and have the funds to eat at that five-star restaurant every night."

Answer: *Sorry, not really.* According to a phenomenon called the *hedonic treadmill,* when we win the lottery, graduate from college, or (in my case) get a book published, we are thrilled at first—but then we revert to our normal happiness set point ("So I got an Oscar last year. What's my next blockbuster film?"). Therefore, piling on kudos or engaging in pleasurable activities such as indulging in gourmet food no longer provide an emotional boost when these activities become routine. The good news, however, is that the hedonic treadmill also applies to negative events. We adjust and then, eventually, our "natural" happiness returns.

"You can't (1) measure happiness or (2) teach people to be happy."

Answer: *Point 1 is totally false; point 2 is probably false.* Research shows that we can concretely quantify what it takes to be happy. Once people get above a ratio of 2.9 positive to negative emotions, they generally feel good about life. Therefore, happiness experts (e.g., Seligman, 2011) have developed programs to teach people to savor the moment, count their blessings, or do gratitude exercises. Still, your author (me) believes the best strategy for achieving happiness is not to spend time monitoring that feeling. When we are generative and open to other people, a natural by-product is a happy life.

"Because happiness is an inner state, the nation we live in makes a minor impact on personal happiness."

Answer: *Wrong!* The nation we live in and its government greatly affect personal well-being. If you live in Finland or Denmark, for instance, you are probably very happy, with well-being scores topping the global charts at an average of 8 on a 10-point scale; in some African nations, the average person ranks fairly miserable (at below 4). Interestingly, nations such as in Scandinavia with low levels of income inequality, where people feel confident that their government will take care of all its citizens, rank at the top of the happiness charts. And, as I also discussed in the text, trusting one's fellow citizens is tied to high levels of well-being.

Information from Angelini and others, 2012; Bergsma & Ardelt, 2011; Conzo and others, 2017; George, 2010; Helson & Soto, 2005; Jorgensen, Jamieson, & Martin, 2010; Ladis, Daniels, & Kawachi, 2009; Windsor & Anstey, 2010.

Wrapping Up Flourishing in Middle Age

Now, let's summarize *all* of these chapter messages about how to flourish during midlife:

- Understand that you are apt to feel just as physically attractive at 50 as at 20—and that having a positive body image (which you can achieve by not having unrealistic expectations and making the most of your current self) is important to feeling upbeat during our older years.

- To keep your mind fine-tuned, exercise, take care of your physical health, and put yourself in mentally stimulating situations involving people.

- If you feel your life lacks balance, establish priorities, work hard in your most important areas, and rely on external aids to help you perform.

- Practice thinking wisely. Be open to different points of view, make decisions by taking everyone's perspective into account, and develop a humble attitude about what you don't know.

- Develop a generative mission. Feeling a sense of purpose, especially relating to making the world better, is the real key to happiness in life.

- And, finally, use the specific happiness tips I just suggested to brighten your daily life: Live in accordance with your values; prioritize experiences over material objects; and reach out to people who don't share your worldview.

Tying It All Together

1. Faruk is going to his 30th college reunion, and he can't wait to find out how his classmates have changed. Statistically speaking, which *two* changes might Faruk find in his former undergraduate friends?
   a. They will be more conscientious and self-confident.
   b. They will have different priorities, caring more about nurturing the next generation.
   c. They will care more deeply about making money.
   d. They will be more depressed and burned out.

2. You are giving your best friend tips about growing emotionally and feeling fulfilled and happy during midlife. Which item should be on your list?
   a. Live a calm, stress-free life.
   b. Live a generative life.
   c. Spend your wages acquiring luxurious objects.

3. Should your professor agree with this suggestion, write about a difficult life experience, and discuss how you coped with that event.

4. People are happiest when they *stick to their own group/ reach out to different kinds of people.*

Answers to the Tying It All Together questions can be found at the end of this chapter.

Social Development

As I mentioned at the beginning of this chapter, classic midlife events can be sources of joy and issues for concern. On the uplifting side, there is that terrific life experience called grandparenthood. The downside may be the need to care for disabled aged parents. Let's now look at these "aging phase of life" roles one by one.

Grandparenthood

> The (Lakota) grandparents always took . . . the first grandchild to raise. They think that . . . they're more mature , , and they could teach the children a lot more than the young parents. . . . I'm still trying to carry on that tradition because my grandmother raised me most of the time up until I was nine years old.
>
> (quoted in Weibel-Orlando, 1999, p. 187)

LEARNING OUTCOMES

- List the functions that grandparents serve in families.
- Summarize problems that contemporary grandparents may face.
- Survey situations that make parent care particularly stressful.

This comment from Mrs. Big Buffalo, a Native American grandmother, reminds us that every adult role, from spouse to worker to grandparent, is shaped by our culture. Native American grandparents—especially in rural areas—are more apt to see raising grandchildren as offering an opportunity to instill their traditional values (Dennis & Brewer, 2017; Henderson and others, 2017). In contrast, in our mainstream modern Western society, grandparents reluctantly take on this role when there is a problem in family life (Y. Lee & Blitz, 2016; more about this later).

Still, even in Western nations, at certain times, we want the older generation to be very hands-on. Isn't it better to have a loving grandma watching your baby than sending that precious child to day care while you work? Perhaps, this suggests, grandparents have a special evolutionary function.

Exploring the Grandparent Mission to Care

Because human beings are the only species with female bodies programmed to outlast the reproductive years, evolutionary theorists argue that menopause evolved to offer an extra layer of mothers, without their own child-rearing distractions, to care for the young (Coall & Hertwig, 2010). Put bluntly, grandmas function to help our species survive.

This lifesaving function is apparent in subsistence societies. As I mentioned in the Experiencing the Lifespan box in Chapter 3, in Ghana, a grandma often steps in to take care of the family so her daughter can make the weekly trek to the clinic to stave off death in a young, malnourished child. Therefore, in Africa, the presence of a grandmother reduces mortality rates during the early years of life (Gibson & Mace, 2005).

In our culture, grandparents do their lifesaving selectively. As **family watchdogs,** they step in during a crisis to help the younger family members cope (Dunifon, 2013). At these times, their true value shines through. Grandparents are the family's safety net (Troll, 1983).

Grandparents can function as mediators, helping parents and children resolve their differences (Kulik, 2007). Grandparents serve as cheerleaders and advocates (Dunifon, 2013) ("Wow, you got on the honor roll. Nana is SO proud of you!"). They can be the family cement, keeping cousins close. From Christmas get-togethers to Thanksgiving dinners, "Grandma's house" is often the focal meeting point—the place where cousins regularly reconnect. As one developmentalist put it:

> Grandparents serve as symbols of connectedness within and between lives; as people who can listen and have the time to do so; as reserves of time, help, and attention; as links to the unknown past; as people who are sufficiently varied, flexible, and complex to defy easy categories and . . . roles.

(quoted in Hagestad, 1985, p. 48)

You may notice this complexity and flexibility in your own family. One grandparent might be a shadowy figure; another may qualify as a second mother or best friend. Some grandmas love to jump on trampolines; others show their love in "baking cookies" ways. An intellectual grandparent may take you to lectures; a fishing grandpa may take you to the lake.

Which Grandparents Are More or Less Involved?

What forces determine how involved a particular grandparent is likely to be? Gender matters. Grandparenthood is typically a more joyous, emotionally central role for women than men (Danielsbacka & Tanskanen, 2016; Jang & Tang, 2016)—especially if they are upper middle class (Mahne & Huxhold, 2015). Becoming a grandma can change a woman's priorities in life. Women feel less committed to their careers if a daughter has given birth (Wiese, Burk & Jaeckel, 2016).

family watchdogs A basic role of grandparents, which involves monitoring the younger family member's well-being and intervening to provide help in a crisis.

Stockbroker/Superstock

Jose Luis Pelaez/Getty Images

From jumping on trampolines to taking the grandchildren to the local lake, grandparents fulfill this joyous life role in their own distinctive, personal ways.

Physical proximity makes a huge difference—whether those grandchildren live around the corner or many miles away (Hakoyama & MaloneBeach, 2013). As one grandfather sadly mentioned: "We rarely get to see her. And it hurts my heart."

Grandchildren's ages matter, too. Even when grandparents are very hands-on during childhood, teenagers naturally leave the grandparent orbit and prefer to be around their peers. As another man lamented: "We'll come for Thanksgiving and she'll . . . say, 'I gotta meet my friends' . . . ." (quoted in Bangerter & Waldron, 2014).

These quotations—from a study exploring grandparent–teenager closeness— suggest that technology *can* erode these barriers of distance and age. Here is how one woman described a video call with her 13-year-old granddaughter: "[I]t was like she and I were hanging . . . out" (quoted in Bangerter & Waldron, 2014, p. 93). And a side benefit of friending your grandchild on Facebook is that you can feel closely connected without having *any* conversation; you can just listen in and know what's going on: ". . . If I called they, would never tell me . . . anything."

Grandparent Problems

Grandparents take pride in the fact that they are free to "be there" to lovingly listen and leave the disciplining to Mom and Dad. But my discussion implies grandparents are really not free. For one thing, it's crucial to hold your tongue and not criticize your child's parenting, because your access to the grandchildren depends on having a good relationship with the generation in between (Lou and others, 2013; Sims & Rofail, 2013).

Now imagine your barriers if you are a paternal grandmother, the mother of a son. Because women are closer to their own mothers (versus their mothers-in-law), paternal grandparents are in danger of "not being there" as much as they would like.

Being in this situation created heartache for a friend of mine, when her daughter-in-law decided to move across the country to be close to her own mother in Seattle, rather than stay in New York City—transforming my friend into the distant grandma she never wanted to be.

The allegiance to one's family of origin can have devastating effects after a divorce. When the wife gets custody, and especially if she remarries and has other children, she can lock her ex-husband's parents out of the family's life (Sims & Rofail, 2013).

When people are robbed of seeing their grandchildren—whether due to a divorce, being a disliked paternal grandma, or because of disputes with a biological child—you might think the legal system would help. You would be wrong (Gair, 2017). Some ethicists argue that being a grandparent doesn't give people *any* intrinsic rights (Draper, 2013). Yes, many states have legislation allowing grandparent visitation depending on "the best interests of the child." But consider the situation in Florida (and Canada), where these statutes have been struck down as unconstitutional, in favor of the idea that parents alone are perfectly free to decide who their child sees (Beiner and others, 2014).

Then there is the opposite situation—feeling compelled to "be there" more than you want. Let's spell out a typical scenario: Your daughter (or son) wants you to watch the baby while she is at work. You don't want to disappoint your child, but you want your own life. You may be working full time, and need the income. Or you may feel resentful about being a caregiver again, because you love your job. The conflict is especially intense when grandparents assume the most demanding commitment— becoming full-time parents again.

Caregiving grandparents take full responsibility for raising their grandchildren. In recent decades, the ranks of these parenting grandparents have doubled in the United States. Concern about the stresses these grandparents face is increasing throughout the developed world (du Preez, Richmond, & Marquis, 2017; Tarrant and others, 2017).

For grandmas, spending the day with a grandson and her daughter-in-law is an absolute joy. Still, women must be careful not to criticize the younger generation's child-rearing skills or risk being cut off from future visits.

caregiving grandparents Grandparents who have taken on full responsibility for raising their grandchildren.

Caregiving grandparents must cope with a variety of burdens, from financial issues to fears that social service agencies want to send their grandchildren to foster care (Tarrant and others, 2017). But the main issue relates to devastating emotions—mourning the fact that their son or daughter cannot take on the parenting job, often because of drug issues, domestic violence (Sandberg, 2016), or mental health problems (Rubin, 2013).

How does being a full-time parent again feel? As you might expect, caregiving grandparents may feel angry at being forced into this "off-time" role. But they often feel a generative, "watchdog" responsibility to protect their flesh and blood (Hayslip & Patrick, 2003; Lee & Blitz, 2016). Here is what one woman had to say to the police after her drug-abusing daughter took off with a grandchild and stole her car:

> [They said], "Ma'am, . . . your grandson will be . . . in the [state protective services system]." I said, "I will fight" [this forever].
>
> (quoted in Climo, Terry, & Lay, 2002, p. 25)

And another woman summed up the general feeling of the grandmothers in this study when she blurted out: "Nobody is going to take [my grandson] away" (quoted in Climo, Terry, & Lay, 2002, p. 25).

These women, mainly in their late fifties, had mixed emotions about their situation: "Some days I feel . . . blessed . . . . [O]ther days I want to . . . cry" (quoted in Climo, Terry, & Lay, 2002, p. 23). They sometimes described redemption sequences: "God has given me this wonderful little boy. . . . How many people get the opportunity to do it a second time?" (p. 26).

Parent Care

parent care Adult children's care for their disabled elderly parents.

Ask friends and family members and they will tell you that becoming a grandparent is one of the joys of being middle-aged. Joyful feelings do not come to mind when we imagine caring for elderly parents. Researchers who study **parent care** use words like *burden, hassles,* and *strain* to describe this classic midlife role (Hunt, 2003; Son and others, 2007).

Caring for parents violates the basic principle in Western cultures that parents give to their children, not the reverse (Belsky, 1999). So it makes sense that, while elderly people may welcome help from siblings or a spouse, they prefer being the "givers" (or help providers) with an adult child. Moreover, as you might expect from the vow "in sickness and in health," elderly spouses find caregiving far less burdensome than daughters or sons do (Perrig-Chiello & Hutchison, 2010).

Actually, let me get personal and relate all of this to Chapter 11. When older people are happily married, sacrificing for a chronically ill spouse is *not* a burden, but a source of fulfillment. It's definitely a "labor of love."

Unfortunately, this is often not true with parent care. Because caring for an ill parent—like hands-on grandparenthood—is typically a woman's job, it can cause a daughter or daughter-in-law to cut back her work hours or leave her career (Naldini, Pavolini, & Solera, 2016). If, as is increasingly true, a caregiving child is in her sixties or seventies, parent care may put a damper in that child's retirement plans or interfere with the need to care for her frail, disabled spouse. More rarely, a woman is pulled between two intergenerational commitments, caring for her elderly parent and watching the grandchildren full time.

At this point, I need to set the record straight: The conflict traditionally called the "sandwich generation"—women pulled between caring for their *young* children and disabled *elderly* parents—is fairly rare. Since parent care typically occurs in the fifties, that job usually occurs during the empty nest, grandparent stage. Moreover, the stereotype that people have a predictable "midlife crisis" is another myth. The research facts show it doesn't exist for most adults.

Finally, the belief that in Asia children are "happy" to care for aging parents is also false (Freeman and others, 2010; Hashizume, 2010). China is in the midst of an eldercare crisis because adult children need to move to the cities for work (and now,

Chinese women have careers, too), leaving elderly parents alone in rural areas. One symptom of this problem is that, while money and physical help flow together in other nations when an elderly parent becomes disabled, in China, providing more funds to aging parents goes along with giving less hands-on care (Liu, Lu, & Feng, 2017)!

As I will discuss in more depth in Chapter 14, frail older people in China today are in special trouble because young generations can no longer obey their historic imperative to "care for one's elders," and no firm government-sponsored system of long-term care is in place. In Scandinavia, caregiving burdens on daughters are minimal because a strong social safety net offers all disabled elderly citizens paid-for care (Naldini, Pavolini, & Solera, 2016). Given that—again—the society we live in has a huge impact on caregiving burdens, how stressful, *personally*, is elder care?

The answer is "it varies" (Merz, Schulze, & Schuengel, 2010). If the older adult's needs are not that intense, a daughter is not working, and she has other female siblings available to share the burden (Grigoryeva, 2017), caring for an aged parent is not very burdensome (DiRosa and others, 2011). But coping with other stressful commitments such as working and caring for the grandchildren full time, and especially feeling that one's brothers and sisters are ungrateful (Amaro & Miller, 2016), is a recipe for depression and poor health.

The older person's personality also looms large. Parent care, as you will see in Chapter 14, poses particular challenges with Alzheimer's disease. According to one alarming study, if a caregiver perceived a parent as difficult and manipulative, the situation could escalate to that younger family member screaming, yelling, or threatening the aged person with a nursing home (Smith and others, 2011).

Still, caring for a disabled parent can have the opposite effect. It may offer its own *redemption sequence*, giving children the chance to repay a beloved mother or father for years of care (Kramer & Thompson, 2002). Moreover, as with other life stresses, productively confronting this challenge can help midlife children grow emotionally and become "wiser," especially about planning for their lives when they become old (Pope, 2013).

Balancing the need to respect a frail older parent's autonomy and knowing when to intervene (Funk, 2010); being generative with the grandchildren, but not intrusive: These are the kinds of complex relationship challenges that explain why, in Jung's words, experiencing the "afternoon of life" *may* teach us to be wise.

In the next part of this book—devoted to later life—I will describe a compelling theory offering another interesting perspective on why our attitude toward living may change for the better *specifically* in old age.

A middle-aged daughter may see caring for her aged mother as a redemption sequence, provided she has few other commitments, and feels this job gives her a chance to repay her beloved parent for a life of love.

🜨 Tying It All Together

1. Juanita, aged 4, has two grandmothers, Uma and Louisa. Grandma Uma is much more involved with Juanita than is Grandma Louisa. List two possible reasons why this might be. As Juanita gets older you might expect her to get *more/ less* involved with Grandma Uma.

2. Poll your class. Do most people report being closest to their maternal grandmother (or grandfather)? Does your class feel that technology is increasing their sense of connection to grandparents? (If so, perhaps they could give specific examples.)

3. Barbara is caring for her elderly mother, who just had a stroke. Each of the following should make Barbara's job feel easier *except*:

   a. Barbara views caregiving as an opportunity to repay her mom for years of love.
   b. Barbara's mom has a mellow personality.
   c. Barbara has several brothers.

Answers to the Tying It All Together questions can be found at the end of this chapter.

SUMMARY

Setting the Context

Although the boundaries of middle age span about age 40 to the early sixties, many older adults describe themselves as middle aged.

Physical Development

Feeling physically attractive is vitally important at every age, and, contrary to our stereotypes, most people do not feel worse about their looks in middle age. However, making unrealistic negative comparisons can promote female midlife body distress; marked age-related negative physical changes in erectile performance can affect males; and, for women, **menopause** has the side effect of making intercourse more painful. First-person accounts of old-age sexuality belie the standard gloom-and-doom decline message, suggesting that older people prioritize intimacy and that sexuality endures into later life.

Cognitive Development

The **Seattle Longitudinal Study**—the definitive research exploring age changes in IQ—showed that we reach our intellectual peak in midlife. However, on measures that require mastering new information quickly, declines start by the early forties; while on measures requiring stored knowledge, scores increase until the sixties. The reason is that there are two basic cognitive skills called fluid and crystallized intelligence.

Fluid intelligence, our capacity to master unfamiliar cognitive challenges quickly, is at its height early in adulthood and then declines. **Crystallized intelligence,** our knowledge base, rises until well into middle age. In professions that heavily depend on crystallized knowledge—versus fast information processing—people do well into their sixties. Creativity reaches its peak in midlife, although our basic talents predict our real-world performance (at any age) best.

Staying healthy, measured by having a low **allostatic load,** exercising, and searching out stimulating interpersonal jobs can slow age-related cognitive decline. Using **selective optimization with compensation** helps people successfully cope with age-related losses and have a better work–life balance at any life stage.

Psychological research on wisdom, perhaps our youngest topic in lifespan development, grew out of studies exploring an adult Piagetian stage of development called **postformal thought.** Wise thinkers search for the best answers in the face of real-world complexity. They are empathic and can make the best decisions from everyone's perspective; they also are humble, realizing that they don't have all the answers in life. Wise thinking in the real world varies, depending on how ego-involved we are in a particular situation. Because we can train people to adopt this self-transcendent view, the common idea that age and living through stressful life events teaches us to be wise may be correct.

Emotional Development

Personality both changes and doesn't change during adult life. Research on the **Big Five** shows personality is fairly stable as we age, and scores on basic traits such as extraversion, openness to experience, and the other core dimensions of personality predict a variety of life outcomes. In particular, conscientiousness sets us up to age healthier and to be successful in work and love. Still, people grow in conscientiousness as they assume adult roles and become less self-critical, and grow more altruistic as they move into middle age. Dan McAdams's research exploring Erikson's **generativity** shows that our priorities shift to "other-centered concerns" during midlife. Generativity, while not related to **hedonic happiness,** is at the core of **eudaimonic happiness**—living a meaningful, fulfilling adult life.

In their autobiographies, highly generative adults produce a **commitment script** and describe **redemption sequences**—negative events that turned out for the best. They also more often describe defining life events involving caring family members or teachers. The fact that African Americans may often be highly generative suggests that adversity—handled productively—may produce emotional growth.

Wise people are not necessarily happy, but having this larger, self-transcendent perspective is closely tied to well-being in later life (and may help us deal with approaching death). Research offers a wealth of fascinating insights about happiness and tips for feeling upbeat during our daily lives.

Social Development

Grandmotherhood may have evolved to help our species survive. In our society, grandparents act as **family watchdogs,** stepping in when the younger family members need help. Gender, physical proximity, the grandchildren's ages, and especially people's relationship with the parent generation determine people's involvement in this joyous but constrained life role. Because women tend to be closer to their own mothers, paternal grandmothers are at risk of being less involved with the grandchildren than they want. At its extreme, people may be cut off from seeing the grandchildren after a divorce or due to having alienated the parents. The opposite extreme, being forced to be too involved occurs with **caregiving grandparents,** who must become full time parents again.

Parent care is another family role that some middle-aged daughters may assume. A variety of forces affect how women feel when caring for a disabled parent, and this life role can sometimes promote emotional growth.

KEY TERMS

allostatic load, p. 354

Big Five, p. 358

caregiving grandparents, p. 369

commitment script, p. 364

crystallized intelligence, p. 351

eudaimonic happiness, p. 363

family watchdogs, p. 368

fluid intelligence, p. 351

generativity, p. 362

hedonic happiness, p. 363

menopause, p. 349

parent care, p. 370

postformal thought, p. 356

redemption sequence, p. 364

Seattle Longitudinal Study, p. 351

selective optimization with compensation, p. 355

ANSWERS TO **Tying It All Together** QUIZZES

Physical Development

1. You will feel *the same* about your physical appearance as you did in your twenties, and you will *probably be just as interested* in how you look.

2. *Males* decline the most physiologically. *Female* sexuality is most affected by social issues such as not having a partner.

3. Lovemaking becomes more leisurely, authentic, and centered on emotional intimacy.

Cognitive Development

1. Andres will reach his career peak far earlier than Mick because his job is heavily dependent on fluid skills. A historian's job depends almost exclusively on crystallized skills.

2. Textbook writing is a crystallized skill, so I should be almost as good at my career as when I was younger. Playing video games depends heavily on fluid skills, so I will be far worse now than when I was young.

3. The theory that applies to Rick's problem—"too much on his plate"—is Baltes's selective optimization with compensation: He needs to (1) prioritize and shed less

important jobs, (2) work harder in his top-ranking areas, and (3) use external aids to help him cope.

4. a

5. Having a less ego-involved, larger perspective on life.

Emotional Development

1. a and b

2. b

3. The answers here are up to you, but it would be best to confront and process that event in a way that might promote personal growth.

4. People are happiest when they reach out to different kinds of people.

Social Development

1. Uma may live closer to Juanita. Most likely, she is a maternal grandma. As Juanita gets older, you would expect her to be *less* involved with her grandma.

2. Answers here will vary.

3. a and b

CONNECT ONLINE:

 LaunchPad macmillan learning | Check out our videos and additional resources located at: www.macmillanlearning.com

Later Life

This two-chapter book part, devoted to life's last stage, highlights how we develop and change as we move through senior citizenhood (the sixties and beyond). Chapter 13 covers issues relevant to both the young-old and old-old years. Chapter 14 emphasizes concerns that become pressing priorities in advanced old age.

Chapter 13—Later Life: Cognitive, Emotional, and Social Development begins with an overview of the historic twenty-first-century age boom, then looks at how memory changes as we age. During this discussion, you will not only learn a wealth of information about memory and aging but also get insights into how to improve memory at any age. Then we turn to the emotional side of life. I'll outline a creative theory and research spelling out why old age might be the best life stage, and offer tips for living meaningfully at this pinnacle age. The second half of this chapter tackles those major social transitions: retirement and widowhood.

Chapter 14—The Physical Challenges of Old Age begins by describing the aging process and how it progresses into disease and disability. Then I'll explore late-life sensory and motor changes and offer a detailed look at that most feared old-age illness: Alzheimer's disease. At the end of this chapter, you will learn about the living arrangements and health-care options available to people when old-age frailties strike. This chapter will open your eyes to the challenges of age-related disabilities and, hopefully, sensitize you to the need to change the wider world to promote an ideal older adult–environment fit.

Left: Nick Daly/Getty Images.

CHAPTER 13

Later Life: Cognitive, Emotional, and Social Development

Ten years ago, at age 65, Susan and Carl retired. They were healthy (at the time) and, with Carl's investments and their pensions, well off. They were passionate to enjoy these final decades, to travel, to focus on the moment, to revel in this new phase of life. Carl and Susan never had children, but they had their nieces and nephews and many friends. In particular, Susan was close to her niece, Emma, who called her favorite aunt, "my adoptive mom."

For Susan and Carl, retirement meant spending time with their closest friends and family members, like Emma. It involved devoting weekdays to volunteering at church and taking those well-loved cruises to Mexico, the Mediterranean, and Marrakesh. Most of all, it meant having the joy of being together as a couple, free from the demands of work. Carl's heart disease—first diagnosed at age 64—lent poignancy to their shared life. As it turned out, their retirement years were priceless, but they were over too soon. After several bypass surgeries, and years of declining health, Carl died of a massive stroke.

After Carl's death, Susan felt numb. How can you go on without your high school sweetheart, your life love for more than 50 years? But she was astonished by her mixed emotions: the loneliness and sense of loss, even when surrounded by friends; the incredible joy (for the priceless relationship she and Carl had); the relief that Carl never had to suffer being bedridden; pride in her ability to go on.

Actually, Susan was amazed at her inner strength. Realizing that as an "old lady of 75" she needed to establish new routines, Susan enrolled in courses at the local college. She focused full-time on her passion to minister to the homeless, and took over coordinating the parish Monday meal. Susan was determined to avoid the conflict-ridden relationships she observed among other widows—the yearning to constantly visit younger family who had other priorities in life; foisting herself as an unwanted "fifth wheel" on married-couple friends. Susan credited Carl's upbeat personality for teaching her how to relate. After a joyous half-century marriage, you develop confidence that boosts you for life!

Susan's life changed dramatically from the time she and Carl retired until her husband got sick and died. These two chapters capture the developmental shifts people experience as they travel through the young-old (sixties and seventies) and old-old (over age 80) years. In the current chapter, I'll focus on cognition and emotional and social development. In Chapter 14, I'll be following Susan as she moves into her eighties and confronts the physical frailties of advanced old age.

Susan's life differs dramatically from many elderly widows around the globe—in her lifestyle and her upbeat, efficacious personality and in having the money to enjoy her older years. Still, in one way, her experience is similar to that of millions of other people her age. She is a foot soldier in an elderly army storming through the developed world.

Left: JohnnyGreig/Getty Images

LEARNING OUTCOMES

- Outline trends in the elderly population.
- Compare contradictory attitudes about later life.

median age The age at which 50 percent of a population is older and 50 percent is younger.

young-old People in their sixties and seventies.

old-old People age 80 and older.

MECKY/The Image Bank/Getty Images

Long life expectancies, declining fertility, the baby boomers reaching old age—all of these forces explain why the median age of the population is increasing and why, in the decades to come, more people will look closer in age to this elderly woman than her 22-year-old granddaughter.

Setting the Context

The well-known reason for this invasion is the baby boomers marching through their young-old years. Moreover, due to our twentieth-century advances in life expectancy, when people reach that magical sixty-fifth birthday, they can now expect, on average, to live for 18 more years (Adams & Rau, 2011).

Falling fertility is also causing this unique historic demographic change. When birth rates decline, the **median age** of a nation—the cutoff age at which half the population is older and half is younger—tends to rise. With childbearing rates dipping sharply in Europe and Asia in recent decades, the median age of the population in most developed countries is now well into middle age.

The baby boomers, longevity, and low fertility are converging to produce our new, old world. You can track this demographic storm shown in Figure 13.1 as it peaks in specific nations. By 2030 in Japan, where average life expectancy now tops age 81 and fertility rates are low, the median age of the population is projected to be roughly age 50. In Italy, 1 out of every 2 people will be at least 52. And in that same year, roughly 1 in every 5 Americans and 1 in 4 Europeans will be over age 65 (National Center for Health Statistics, 2008; Quinn & Cahill, 2016).

How will you feel about living in a nation where the people with walkers may outnumber the babies in strollers on your streets? For hints, you might visit a U.S. city where the age storm has struck. In Sarasota, Florida, where the 65-plus population tops 30 percent, residents view age 70 as "young." You aren't defined as elderly until you make it to age 80 and above (Fishman, 2010). In Sarasota, people understand: Statistically speaking, there is a world of difference between being healthy and **young-old** and having physical frailties (or depending on those walkers) during the **old-old** years.

The health (and wealth) differences between the young-old and old-old may explain our contradictory stereotypes about later life. We have the mental image of the vital, energetic widow returning to school and making a difference in life; and the vision of the lonely, aged person languishing in a nursing home; the portrait of affluent, retired married couples traveling the world; and the picture of depressed, institutionalized elders with dementing diseases.

FIGURE 13.1: Median age of the population, selected countries, in 2017 and 2030 projections: Today, the median age of the population—the point at which half the people are younger and half are older—is 45-plus in Italy, Germany, and Japan. Also, notice how high the median ages in these nations are projected to be in 2030. How do you think living in these "most-aged nations" will affect residents' daily lives?

Data from World Factbook CIA, 2017.

The expressions on the face of this joyous 65-year-old and this dour 90-year-old say it all. In terms of lifestyle, personality, memory, health, and everything else, there is a world of difference between being young-old and old-old.

But amid this diversity lies consensus about the negative qualities related to being old. Worldwide, people link old age with physical and mental decline. While residents in places like Sardinia, Italy—where the elderly have reputations for living healthy to the end of life—have upbeat attitudes (Bottiroli and others, 2013), if you ask most older adults to forecast their futures, you are apt to hear gloomy comments such as, "I won't be as happy in five years as I am today" (Lang and others, 2013).

The bottom line is that everyone—young and old—is guilty of **ageism**, intensely negative attitudes about old age. Moreover, as the Experiencing the Lifespan box shows, in contrast to our stereotypes, throughout history old age has also been feared as a time of unremitting loss. Luckily, we also gravitate to the elderly for classic positive traits.

ageism Stereotypic, intensely negative ideas about old age.

Experiencing the Lifespan   Ageism Through the Ages

The hair is gray. . . . The brows are gone, the eyes are blear . . . The nose is hooked and far from fair. . . . The ears are rough and pendulous. . . . The face is sallow, dead and drear. . . . The chin is purs'd . . . the lips hang loose. . . . Aye such is human beauty's lot! . . . Thus we mourn for the good old days . . . , wretched crones, huddled together by the blaze. . . .

(excerpted from an Old English poem called "Lament of the Fair Heaulmiere" [or Helmet-maker's girl], quoted in Minois, 1989, p. 230)

Many of us assume that people had better values and attitudes toward old age in "the good old days." Poems such as the one above show that we need to give that stereotype a closer look.

In ancient times, old age was seen as a miracle because it was so rare. Where there was no written language, older people were valued for their knowledge. However, this elevated status applied only to a few people—typically men—who were upper class. For slaves, servants, and women, old age was often a cruel time.

Moreover, just as today, cultures made a distinction between active, healthy older people and those who were disabled and ill. In many societies the same person who had been revered was subjected to barbaric treatment once he outlived his usefulness—that is, became decrepit or senile. Samoans killed their elderly in elaborate ceremonies in which the victim was required to participate. Other cultures left their older people to die of neglect. Michelangelo and Sophocles, revered as old men, stand as symbols of the age-friendly attitudes of the nations in which they lived. However, the images portrayed in their creative works celebrated youth and beauty. Even in Classical Greece and Renaissance Italy—societies known for being enlightened—people believed old age was the worst time of life.

As historian Georges Minois (1989) concluded in a survey of how Western cultures treated their elders, "It is the tendency of every society to live and go on living: it extols the strength and fecundity that are so closely linked to youth and it dreads the . . . decrepitude of old age. Since the dawn of history . . . young people have regretted the onset of old age. The fountain of youth has always constituted Western man's most irrational hope" (p. 303).

(The information in this box is taken from Minois, 1989, and Fischer, 1977.)

In one U.S. poll, adults agreed that a 75-year-old would be superior to a 20-something in calmly handling conflicts (Swift, Abrams, & Marques, 2013). When undergraduates were asked to discuss the personalities of audio recordings of speakers with "elderly" and "young" voices, students did judge the old voices as being less powerful. But they said they would gravitate to the elderly speakers for being gifted storytellers and being wise (Montepare, Kempler, & McLaughlin-Volpe, 2014).

In these next two chapters, I'll be giving you a wealth of scientific insights into our negative old-age stereotypes—as I chart the ways thinking and physical abilities decline in the older years. But as we enter the emotional lives of the elderly, I hope to give you a more positive image of your late-life future, too. Do older people really have a more balanced, wiser perspective on life? Before reading the research facts relating to this topic and others, you might want to explore your personal old-age stereotypes by taking the "Is It True About the Elderly?" questionnaire (Table 13.1).

Table 13.1: Is It True About the Elderly?

1. Memory stays stable through midlife, then declines in later life.

2. There is little that can be done to improve memory in old age.

3. Old age is the most unhappy life stage.

4. The typical retirement age is 65.

5. Older workers are more rigid.

6. Widowhood is always a devastating emotional blow.

7. Due to scientific advances, we will soon be able to live well beyond the maximum human lifespan.

8. Hearing losses in old age are "a piece of cake."

9. No one who has Alzheimer's disease can live a meaningful life.

10. About 50 percent of people over 65 live in nursing homes.

(I'll be discussing items 1–6 in this chapter and items 7–10 in Chapter 14.)

Answers: 1. F, 2. F, 3. F, 4. F, 5. F, 6. F, 7. F, 8. F, 9. F, 10. F

🔄 Tying It All Together

1. Our attitudes toward the elderly involve (choose one) *mainly negative traits/ a mixture of positive and negative traits/ positive traits alone*; and negative ideas about old age apply to the _____ years.

Answers to the Tying It All Together questions can be found at the end of this chapter.

LEARNING OUTCOMES

- Describe how memory changes with age, making reference to two major approaches to understanding memory.

- List interventions to improve memory.

- Outline socioemotional selectivity theory.

- Analyze why old age is the best and worst time of life.

- Evaluate what produces late-life happiness.

Cognitive and Emotional Development

Now, let's start our research tour, by first exploring how memory, that important component of thinking, changes during our older years, and then turning to the emotional quality of later life.

Memory

When we think of specific cognitive abilities as we get older, we can look forward to positive changes—expanding our crystallized skills, perhaps becoming wise (see Chapter 12). These upbeat feelings do not extend to memory. With memory, starting in midlife, we see only decline. (The familiar fifty-something phrase is, "Sorry, I'm having a senior moment!") Once people reach their late sixties and seventies, the wider world is on high alert for memory problems, too.

In a classic study, psychologists demonstrated this mindset by filming actors aged 20, 50, and 70 reading an identical speech. During the talk, each person made a few references to memory problems, such as "I forgot my keys." Volunteers then watched only the young, middle-aged, or older actor and wrote about what the person was like. Many people who saw the 70-year-old described him as forgetful. No one who heard the identical words read by the younger adults mentioned memory! (See Rodin & Langer, 1980.)

The reality is that when a young person forgets something we pass off the problem as due to external forces: "I was distracted"; "I had too much going on"; "It might be those four glasses of wine I had last night." When that same person is old, we have a more ominous interpretation: "Perhaps this is the beginning of Alzheimer's disease" (Erber & Prager, 1999). When you last were with an elderly family member and she forgot a name or appointment, did the idea that "Grandma is declining mentally" cross your mind?

Scanning the Facts

Are older people's memory abilities *really* much worse than those of younger adults? Unfortunately, the answer, based on thousands of studies, is yes. In testing everything from the ability to recall unfamiliar faces to the names of new places, from remembering the content of paragraphs to recalling where objects are located in space, the elderly perform more poorly than the young (see Dixon and others, 2007, for a review).

As a memory task gets more difficult, the performance gap between young and old people expands (see Klencklen and others, 2017; Moret-Tatay and others, 2017). When psychologists ask old people to recognize an item or word they have previously seen, they do almost as well as 20-year-olds (Danckert & Craik, 2013). The elderly score comparatively worse when they need to come up with that word or name completely on their own. (The distinction here is analogous to taking a multiple-choice exam versus a short-answer test.) Older people perform more dismally when they have to recall a face or name and link it to a specific context (Dennis and others, 2008; see also Craik, Luo, & Sakuta, 2010): "Yes, I recognize that guy . . . but was he the cable repairman or a guest at Claire's commencement party last month?"

While connecting names to places, or remembering exactly *where* we heard information, is difficult in old age, this task is not easy at any life stage. I'll never forget when a twenty-something student server blew me away with this comment: "I remember you very well, Dr. Belsky. I learned so much in your *English Literature class* three years ago."

The elderly do especially poorly on **divided-attention tasks**—situations in which they need to memorize material or perform an activity while monitoring something else. Remembering to keep checking the clock so that you don't miss your 3 P.M. class, texting, or spending time on Facebook while "listening" to a lecture—these multitasking activities impair memory performance at any age. *Warning:* This is a documented fact! But while young people can master these difficult divided-attention tasks, they are virtually impossible in old age (Gothe, Oberauer, & Kliegl, 2008).

If you can relate to this photo the next time you are tempted to text during that not-so-interesting class, keep this message in mind: *Divided-attention tasks* make memory worse!

More depressing, when researchers pile on the memory demands and add time pressures, deficits show up as early as the late twenties (Borella, Carretti, & De Beni, 2008). Returning to the preceding chapter, it makes sense that when people have to remember new, random bits of information very fast, losses take place soon after youth. These requirements are prime examples of *fluid intelligence* tasks.

What is going wrong with memory as we age? Let's get insights from examining two different ways of conceptualizing "a memory": the information-processing and memory-systems approaches.

divided-attention task
A difficult memory challenge involving memorizing material while simultaneously monitoring something else.

An Information-Processing Perspective on Memory Change

As I mentioned in Chapters 3 and 6, developmentalists who adopt an *information-processing approach* on cognition see memory as progressing through stages. The gateway system, which transforms information into more permanent storage, is called *working memory*.

Working memory contains a limited memory-bin space—the amount of information we can keep in our awareness. It includes an executive processor that controls our attention and transforms the contents of this temporary storage facility into material we can remember later on. As I discussed in Chapter 6, when the frontal lobes mature during childhood, working memory-bin capacity dramatically improves. Unfortunately, when we travel through adulthood, working memory works worse and worse (Febo & Foster, 2016; Klencklen and others, 2017).

What explains this decline? One cause is a loss of synaptic plasticity in the hippocampus, the brain region involved in encoding new memories (Febo & Foster, 2016). Another involves deficits with the executive processor, that hypothetical structure manipulating material into the permanent memory store. As people age, they have more problems focusing this master controller and so can't attend as well to what they need to learn (Müller-Oehring and others, 2013; Ofen & Shing, 2013). One symptom of this *executive function* deficit, as you just saw, is that older people have exceptional trouble mastering divided-attention tasks.

When we think of executive functions such as selective attention, a particular brain structure comes to mind. Later-life memory deficits, according to current thinking, in good part reflect deterioration in the frontal lobes (Febo & Foster, 2016). Neuroscientists can "see" this thinning by taking MRI images of varying cortical structures. Although they can't enter the brain to visualize individual cells, animal research combined with neuroimaging data confirm that neural loss is universal in the elderly brain (Febo & Foster, 2016).

How does the older brain adapt? Because brain-imaging techniques allow us to track activation patterns when adults are given memory tasks, they also offer fascinating information about this issue.

With easy memory challenges, such as remembering a few items, notice from Figure 13.2 that older adults show a broader pattern of frontal-lobe activity compared to young adults. But, as the task gets difficult, the older brain shifts to underactivation—suggesting that it totally maxed out! (See Febo & Foster, 2016; Park & McDonough, 2013; Reuter-Lorenz, 2013). Another study, measuring the activation patterns involved

Remembering the speaker's messages at this senior citizen center lecture is going to be especially hard because older people have special trouble screening out distracting conversations and focusing on what they need to learn.

FIGURE 13.2: Frontal lobe activation in young (left) and older (right) adults in a memory study: In this fMRI study, researchers measured activation in the frontal lobes when older and younger adults were given a relatively easy laboratory memory task. Notice in the left photo that, while regions of the left hemisphere alone are activated in young adults, the older brains (right image) are working harder to master this task—as here, activation occurs in both brain hemispheres.

Data from Reuter-Lorenz & Cappell, 2008.

in memorizing happy and upset faces, showed that, while older people must "recruit" distinctive neural networks to remember these different categories of emotion, young adults rely on a single system for encoding both cues (Ziaei, Salami, & Persson, 2017).

These findings are depressing. Does the aging brain have to go on overdrive and then ultimately "give up" (neurologically speaking) in confronting memory tasks? Luckily, the answer is no. Some memories are more indelibly carved in our mind.

A Memory-Systems Perspective on Change

Think of the amazing resilience of some memories and the incredible vulnerability of others. Why do you automatically remember how to hold a tennis racquet even though you have not been on a court for years? Why is "George Washington," the name of the first president, locked in your mind while you are incapable of remembering what you had for dinner three days ago? These kinds of memories differ in ways that go beyond how *much* effort went into embedding them into our minds. They seem qualitatively different in a fundamental way.

According to the **memory-systems perspective** (Craik, 2000; Tulving, 1985), there are three basic types of memory.

- **Procedural memory** refers to information that we automatically remember, without conscious thought. A real-life example involves physical skills. Once we have learned a complex motor activity, such as how to ride a bike, we automatically remember how to perform that skill once we are in that situation again.

- **Semantic memory** is our fund of basic facts. Remembering that George Washington was the first president and knowing what a bike is are examples of the information in this well-learned, crystallized database.

- **Episodic memory** refers to the ongoing events of daily life. When you remember going bike riding last Thursday or what you had for dinner last night, you are drawing on episodic memory.

As you can see in these examples and those described in Table 13.2, episodic memory is the most fragile system. A year from now you will still remember who

memory-systems perspective A framework that divides memory into three types: procedural, semantic, and episodic memory.

procedural memory In the memory-systems perspective, the most resilient (longest-lasting) type of memory; refers to material, such as well-learned physical skills, that we automatically recall without conscious awareness.

semantic memory In the memory-systems perspective, a moderately resilient (long-lasting) type of memory; refers to our ability to recall basic facts.

episodic memory In the memory-systems perspective, the most fragile type of memory, involving the recall of the ongoing events of daily life.

Table 13.2: Examples of the Differences Among Procedural, Semantic, and Episodic Memory

Procedural Memory	Semantic Memory	Episodic Memory
You get into your blue Toyota and automatically know how to drive.	You know that you have a blue Toyota.	You memorize where you left your blue Toyota in the parking lot of the amusement park.
You automatically find yourself singing the words to "Jingle Bells" when the melody comes on the radio.	You remember that "Jingle Bells" is a song.	You remember the last time you heard "Jingle Bells."
You begin to get excited as you approach your college campus for fall semester.	You know that you are a student at X University and that you are a psychology major.	You memorize the room number of this class during the first week of the new semester.*
I unconsciously find the letters I am typing now on my computer.	I know that I am writing a book called *Experiencing the Lifespan*.	I remember that today I must go to the library and scan an article on memory that I will need in preparing this chapter.

*Now that it's late in the semester, the location of this class has migrated into procedural memory; so, although you automatically walk to the door, if a friend says, "I'll meet you at class. Just tell me the room number," you are apt to draw a blank!

George Washington is (semantic memory). You will recall how to get on the bike and use the gears to pace your speed (procedural memory). However, even a few days after the event, you are likely to forget what you had for dinner on a particular night. Remembering isolated events—from what day we last went bike riding, to what we ate last Tuesday, to the paragraph you are reading now—are especially vulnerable to time.

The good news is that on tests of semantic memory, older people may do as well as the young (Dixon and others, 2007). Procedural memory is amazingly long-lasting, as we know when we get on a bike after not having ridden for decades, and take off down the road. The real age-related loss occurs in episodic memory—remembering the details of daily life.

This decline in episodic memory is what people notice when they realize they are having more trouble remembering the name of a person at a party or where they parked the car. Our databank of semantic memories stays intact until well into later life (Ofen & Shing, 2013)—explaining why we expect older people to outperform the young at crystallized verbal challenges such as crossword puzzles. People with Alzheimer's disease can retain procedural memories after the other memory systems are largely gone. They can walk, dress themselves, and even remember (to the horror of caregivers) how to turn on the ignition and drive after losing their ability to recall basic facts, such as where they live.

Why can an elegant 85-year-old pianist still beautifully entertain you, even though she is forgetting basic facts about her life? Because her talents have migrated into procedural memory—the final memory system to go.

The incredible resilience of procedural memory explains why your 85-year-old aunt, who was a musician, can still play the piano beautifully, even though she is now incapable of remembering family members' names. Why is this system the last to go? The reason, according to neuropsychologists, is that the information in procedural memory resides in a different region of the brain. When we first learn a complex motor skill, such as driving or playing an instrument, our frontal lobes are heavily involved. Then, after we have thoroughly learned that activity, this knowledge becomes automatic and migrates to a lower brain center, which frees up our frontal cortex for mastering other higher-level thinking tasks (Friedman, 2003).

Actually, this is good. If I had to focus on remembering how to type these words on my computer, would I be able to simultaneously do the complicated mental work of figuring out how to describe the concepts I am explaining now?

In sum, the message with regard to age and memory is both worse and also far better than we have thought: As we get older, we do not have to worry much about remembering basic facts. Our storehouse of crystallized knowledge is "really there." However, we will have more trouble memorizing bits of new information, and these losses in episodic memory show up at a surprisingly early age.

INTERVENTIONS Keeping Memory Fine-Tuned

What should people do when they notice that their ability to remember life's ongoing details is getting worse? Let's look at three approaches.

USE SELECTIVE OPTIMIZATION WITH COMPENSATION. The first strategy is to use Baltes's three-step process, spelled out in Chapter 12: (1) Selectively focus on what you want to remember—that is, don't clog your working memory bins with irrelevant thoughts; (2) optimize, or work hard, to manipulate material in this system into permanent memory; (3) use compensation, or external memory aids.

For example, to remember where you parked at the airport: (1) Focus on *where* you are parking when you slide your car into the spot. Don't daydream or get distracted by the need to catch the plane. (2) Work hard to encode that specific location in your brain. (3) Take a photo on your smartphone so you won't have to remember that place all on your own.

At this point, readers might be thinking: Why not just bypass those difficult executive-function challenges (selecting and optimizing) and skip to compensation, by using your phone? The problem is that over-relying on environmental supports has a negative side (Lindenberger & Mayr, 2014). If older people—or any person— depend excessively on external cues, they are destined for problems when those supports malfunction. Put concretely, if your smartphone goes on the fritz, without a recent backup, you may have lost your whole life. Moreover, no technology can eliminate our need to memorize everyday episodic facts, such as linking names to faces, remembering when we took Dr. Belsky's class, or recalling where we might have misplaced our keys. So let's turn to optimization (Baltes's step 2), by spelling out strategies for effortlessly sliding information into our memory bins.

USE MNEMONIC TECHNIQUES. Have you ever noticed that some episodic events are locked in memory (such as your wedding day or the time you and your significant other had that terrible fight), while others fade? Everyone—both old and young— remembers emotional stimuli best (see Ziaei, Salami, & Persson, 2017) because, as I suggested in the infancy chapters, we are biologically primed to be acutely sensitive to social cues. Therefore, the key to memorizing isolated bits of information is to make material stand out emotionally.

Mnemonic techniques are strategies to make information emotionally vivid. These approaches range from using the acronym OCEAN to help you recall the name of each Big Five trait in studying for the Chapter 12 test to thinking, when introduced to the elderly woman in the photo, "I'll remember her name is Mrs. Silver because of her hair."

The fact that we learn emotionally salient information without effort may explain why our memories vary in puzzling ways in real life. A history buff soaks up every detail about the Civil War but remains clueless about where he left his socks. Because your passion is developmental science, you do well with very little studying in this course, but it takes you hours to memorize a single page in your biology text.

Actually, the principle that emotional events are locked more firmly in our brain may partly account for our impression that the elderly remember past experiences best. In fact, when researchers asked adults to recall self-defining events in their personal autobiographies ("the day I got accepted into graduate school"; "when I hit that car on Lakeshore drive in November of 1982"), the elderly did perform better than the young! (See Martinelli and others, 2013.)

WORK ON THE PERSON'S MENTAL STATE. This brings up the thought that standard laboratory memory tests are unfair to older adults. These tests require remembering random bits of episodic information, so they showcase the very memory skill that dramatically declines with age. Wouldn't the elderly do comparatively better when asked to remember emotionally salient information they need in their daily lives?

Now compound this bias with the poisonous impact of self-doubt. If you were 70 or 80, imagine how you would feel when asked to participate in a memory study. Wouldn't you be frightened, thinking, "This test might show I have Alzheimer's disease!"

Actually, just being told, "I'm giving you a memory test," makes older people feel years older (Hughes, Geraci, & De Forrest, 2013). Moreover, labeling a test as "measuring memory" impairs an older person's performance on *any* cognitive test. In one scary study, after being informed that they'd be taking a memory test, 70 percent of older adults scored below the clinical cut-off for Alzheimer's disease on a classic diagnostic test, compared to less than 1 in 5 people not given that information! Conversely, when researchers said a given IQ scale tapped wisdom, older people's performance improved— even though that test really measured a fluid skill (Hehman & Bugental, 2013).

> **mnemonic technique**
> A strategy for aiding memory, often by using imagery or enhancing the emotional meaning of what needs to be learned.

Although his main goal is to greet this woman in a warm, personal way, in order to remember his new friend's name, an elderly man might want to step back and use the mnemonic strategy of forming a mental image, thinking, "I'll remember it's Mrs. Silver because of her hair."

Moreover, while new research shows subjective memory complaints ("I'm having terrible trouble remembering") have a clear relationship to brain deterioration (Chen and others, 2018), what also predicts cognitive loss is having a pessimistic view of aging (Chopik, Kim, & Smith, 2015) and feeling unhappy with one's current life (Goveas and others, 2014).

So, to take a family example, when my 90-year-old mother complained, "I can't remember anything," we children were wrong to *automatically* assume that she was developing Alzheimer's disease. And, after taking action to improve my mom's emotional state by moving her to a continuing care community (described in the next chapter), her memory greatly improved.

Actually, in contrast to the image of late-life memory loss as caused by a brain "condition," teaching the elderly memory improvement techniques does work (see, for instance, Borella and others, 2014). In recent years, these strategies have proliferated, with scientists training older adults on everything from video games (designed to heighten selective attention) (Toril, Reales, & Ballesteros, 2014) to mastering the demands of daily life (Brom & Kliegel, 2014; Burkard and others, 2014; McDaniel and others, 2014). Still, we run into the problem of motivation. People tend to "get lazy" (meaning not follow through) because optimization strategies demand serious mental work! (See Burkard and others, 2014.)

socioemotional selectivity theory A theory of aging (and the lifespan) put forth by Laura Carstensen, describing how the time we have left to live affects our priorities and social relationships. Specifically, in later life people focus on the present and prioritize being with their closest attachment figures.

Emotional Priorities (and Well-Being)

Everyone believes that memory declines with age. But as I mentioned earlier, we have more positive ideas about our emotional lives. Does old age really bring serenity and emotional balance? Laura Carstensen believes it does.

Focusing on Time Left to Live: Socioemotional Selectivity Theory

Imagine that you are elderly and aware of your limited time left to live. How might your goals change? The idea that our place on the lifespan changes our agendas is the premise of Carstensen's **socioemotional selectivity theory.**

According to Carstensen (1995), during the first half of adult life, our push is to look to the future. We are eager to make it in the wider world. We want to reach a better place at some later date. As we grow older and realize that our future is limited, we refocus our priorities. We want to make the most of our present life.

Carstensen believes that this focus on making the most of every moment explains why late life is potentially the happiest life stage. When our agenda lies in the future, we often forgo our immediate desires in the service of a later goal. Instead of telling off the boss who insults us, we hold our tongue because this authority figure holds the key to getting ahead. We are nice to that nasty person, or go to that dinner party we would rather pass up, in order to advance socially or in our career. We accept the anxiety-ridden months when we first move to an unfamiliar city because we expect to feel better than ever in a year or two.

In later life, we are less interested in where we *will* be going. So we refuse to waste time with unpleasant people or to enter anxiety-provoking situations because they may have a payoff at some later point. Almost unconsciously, we decide, "I don't have that long to live. I have to spend my time doing what makes me feel good emotionally *right now.*"

Furthermore, when our passion lies in making the most of the present, Carstensen argues, our social priorities shift. During childhood, adolescence, and emerging adulthood our mission is to leave our attachment figures. We want to expand our social horizons, form new

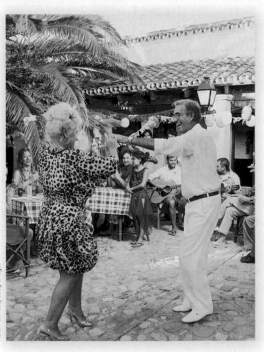

Martin Barraud/Getty Images

Socioemotional selectivity theory's principle that in old age we make the most of every moment shows why, at celebrations, older adults are often the life of the party.

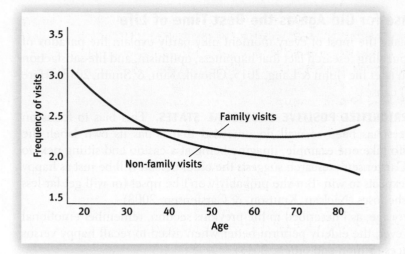

FIGURE 13.3: Non-family and family visiting throughout adulthood in a national German study: In this mammoth 36,000-plus person poll, researchers charted the visiting patterns of people aged 17–85 longitudinally for 15 years and then estimated how these trends applied through life. Notice that while visits to friends and acquaintances decline particularly sharply during emerging adulthood and continue to fall off into advanced old age, family encounters remain stable and even increase a bit during the old-old years.
Data from Sander, Schupp, & Richter, 2017, p. 1581.

close relationships, and connect with exciting new people who can teach us new things. Once we have achieved our life goals, we are less interested in developing new attachments. We already have our family and network of caring friends. So we center our lives on our spouse, our best friends, and our children—the people we love the most.

Actually, as Figure 13.3 suggests, *throughout* adulthood, people pare down visits with neighbors and acquaintances, but not family members (Sander, Schupp, & Richter, 2017). This bias to focus on family is paralleled in the virtual world. Older people (not unexpectedly) have many fewer Facebook friends on average than the young, and their networks are composed of many more real friends (Chang and others, 2015). (You might be interested to know this research showed that having a higher ratio of "real" to total Facebook friends related to feeling less lonely at every age. Rather than demonstrating world-class connectedness, accumulating 1,000-plus random Facebook acquaintances may signal feeling isolated and alone!)

This passion to center on close relationships applies to media preferences. Older people (also not unexpectedly) avoid the high-tech car chases and galactic, gore-filled battles beloved by the young; they relish movies with emotionally laden, family-oriented themes—especially those that are poignant and warm (Mares, Bartsch, & Bonus, 2016).

When Do We Prioritize the Present Regardless of Our Life Stage?

But is this change in priorities *simply* a function of being old? The answer is no. Adults with fatal illnesses also voted to spend an evening with a familiar close person. So did people who were asked to imagine that they were about to move across the country alone. According to Carstensen, whenever we see our future as limited, we pare down our social contacts and spend time with the people we care about the most.

Although normally you may be content to live a continent away, socioemotional selectivity theory explains why when you are in danger of losing a loved one you want to be physically close. So you fly in to spend time with your beloved grandma when she is seriously ill. You insist on spending a weekend with your high school friend in the military who is moving to a dangerous region of the world.

The theory accounts for the choices my cousin Clinton made when he was diagnosed with lymphoma in his twenties. An exceptionally gifted architect, Clinton gave up his promising career and retired to rural New Hampshire to build houses, hike, and ski for what turned out to be another quarter-century of life. Clinton's funeral, at age 50, was an unforgettable celebration—a testament to a person who, although his life was shorter than most, lived fully for longer than many people who survive to twice this age. Have you ever seen the principles of socioemotional selectivity theory in operation in your life?

It seems like a no-brainer that elderly people might gravitate to films with poignant relationship-oriented themes. Now we know that socioemotional selectivity explains why heartwarming family dramas are particularly appealing to the old.

Jose Luis Pelaez Inc/Getty Images

Making the Case for Old Age as the Best Time of Life

paradox of well-being The fact that despite their physical and mental losses, the elderly report being just as happy and often happier than the young.

This passion to make the most of every moment may partly explain the **paradox of well-being**—the puzzling research fact that happiness, optimism, and life-satisfaction take an upswing in later life (John & Lang, 2015; Chopik, Kim, & Smith, 2015). Here are three (related) causes.

OLDER PEOPLE PRIORITIZE POSITIVE EMOTIONAL STATES. This bias to focus on positive experiences has been so well documented that it has its own label: the **positivity effect**. To take one example, imagine being at a casino and sitting next to an elderly adult. Carstensen's research suggests the older person will be just as happy as you when she expects to win. But she probably won't be upset (or will get far less disturbed) when she loses (Nielsen, Knutson, & Carstensen, 2008).

positivity effect The tendency for older people to focus on positive experiences and screen out negative events.

People of every age, as I described in the previous section, remember emotional stimuli best. However, the elderly perform better when asked to recall happy versus sad images and faces (Simon and others, 2013).

In one compelling experiment, developmentalists tied this motivational impulse to feeling one's future was limited *at any life stage*. Researchers asked young and elderly volunteers to write about how they would spend their days if (1) they only had 6 months to live or (2) their life expectancy was extended to age 120. Then the researchers measured both groups' recall of happy and distressed faces. At each age, people primed to expect a limited future remembered a higher fraction of happy faces (Barber and others, 2016)!

SEEING TIME AS SLIPPING BY (CAN) STIMULATE FLOW. Feeling life's hourglass rapidly dwindling may propel people to take meaningful action in the world. Another group of psychologists asked different age groups, "How fast did yesterday go by?" As they expected, the elderly, compared to the young, felt time flew by faster. But interestingly, this subjective sense was only true during productive activities (such as caring for others or learning something new) versus eating or watching TV (John & Lang, 2015). Therefore, in contrast to our stereotypes, boredom—that bane of the human condition—should be *less common in old age*, because older people are motivated to engage in the challenging flow states that make us happiest in life.

Having help from a young woman is likely to be a new life experience for an elderly man. How would you feel about "the goodness of humanity" if people treated you in this unusually caring way?

OLDER PEOPLE LIVE LESS STRESSFUL LIVES. Now combine this passion to make each minute count with the external reasons why old age should be a happy life stage: no longer having the hassles of raising children or the gut-churning pressures to perform at work. Older people report fewer daily stresses than the young (Charles & Almeida, 2007; Charles and others, 2010; von Hippel, Henry, & Matovic, 2008). An added bonus is that the outside world treats you with special care (Luong, Charles, & Fingerman, 2010).

In one study, when researchers asked adults how they would react in a difficult interpersonal situation, people said they would be prone to hold off confronting someone if that individual was old (Fingerman, Miller, & Charles, 2008). An elderly speaker alerted my class to this perk when he mentioned, "The best thing about being 88 is that everyone is incredibly nice!" If strangers opened doors for you, people forgave your foibles, and everyone made a special effort to be kind, wouldn't you feel better about humanity and your fellow man (and woman)?

So knowing your life will end soon provides surprising emotional bonuses. Moreover, in old age, people have more luxury to do what they want, and the outside world bothers them less!

What Can Make Old Age the Unhappiest Time of Life?

But at this point, many of you may think, "Something is wrong with this picture." What about the miserable elderly people whom the world doesn't treat kindly—older adults left to languish, lonely and impoverished, in their so-called golden years? When I gave talks on successful aging at local senior centers in my thirties (some gall!), I vividly recall one 89-year-old woman who put me in my place: "Wait till you are my age, young lady. Then you will *really* know how terrible it is to be old!"

The erosion of U.S. retirement as a life stage (described in the next section) is destined to impair the emotional quality of old age. As "social connectedness" is critical to human happiness, widowhood and outliving friends *must* take a psychological toll. Now, combine this with the physical losses of old age, and it should come as no surprise that, while happiness peaks in the late sixties, well-being takes a nosedive during the old-old years (Chopik, Kim, & Smith, 2015; Rothermund & Brandstädter, 2003).

So, the paradox of well-being extends only so far. When people are physically impaired, robbed by death of their close attachments, and *cannot* act productively (the extreme image here is languishing in a nursing home), life can lose all purpose and joy. As one formerly ideally aging man wrote: "I was still driving, walking . . . and feeling pretty confident . . . at age 87; now after three more years of age-related decline, I've almost had enough . . . living without the people and possessions that shaped my life" (adapted from Crum, 2014, p. 6).

Still, let's not stereotype all ninety-somethings as living in a dismal holding pattern, waiting for death. As my inspiring interview with Jules in the Experiencing the Lifespan box shows, some people live exceptionally gratifying lives at the uppermost limits of life.

Experiencing the Lifespan   Jules: Committed to a Career at Age 94

It was a hot August morning at Vanderbilt University as friends, colleagues, and students gathered to celebrate the publication of his book. Their voices often cracked with emotion as they rose to testify: "You changed my life. You are an inspiration—the best therapist and supervisor I've ever had." Frail, bent over, beginning to doze—suddenly, 94-year-old Jules came to life. "My book traces the development of my ideas about ideal mental health. It's been a 60-year journey to identify the 'fully functioning person' that I'm still trying to get right today." Who is this revered role model? What made Jules the person he is, and what is his philosophy about aging and life? Let's read this interview.

My parents left Europe right before the First World War. So in 1915, I was lucky enough to arrive in this world [or be born]. Growing up in Baltimore, my brothers and I were incredibly close because, as the only Jewish family in our Christian immigrant neighborhood, we were living in an alien world. I remember the neighborhood kids regularly taunting us as Jesus killers as we walked to school. So we learned from an early age that the world can be a dangerous place. What this experience did was to take us in the opposite direction . . . to see every person as precious, to develop attitudes that were worldwide.

When I was a teenager, and asked myself, "What is important in life?" the answer was "relationships," . . . to have a fundamental faith in people. It was clear that human beings had a long way to go to reach maturity, but you need to act ethically and lovingly. I also looked to the Bible for guidance, asking myself, "What do the ancient prophets tell us about living an ethical life?" During the Second World War, my brothers and I were conscientious objectors. I knew I could never kill another human being.

I started out my work life as a public school teacher in Baltimore. I had no desire to get a Ph.D., but when I read a paper by Carl Rogers* in 1948, who was developing his client-centered therapy, I was electrified: Understand the person from his own framework; don't be judgmental; look beyond the diagnosis to the real human being. By listening empathically and relating unconditionally, you can guide a person toward health. Those decades collaborating with Carl ended up defining my life work.

I'm still the same person, the same adolescent hiding in the body of a 94-year-old man—but with much more experience in living! The difference is that, physically, I am handicapped [with congestive heart failure] and so I use a shorter horizon. Instead of thinking a year ahead, I might think about a week. . . . I am well aware that I could die any time. But it's unthinkable to me not to do therapy. I'm incomplete if I am not expressing my passion in life.

It's important never to put life in the past tense. There is no such thing as "aging" or "retirement." You are always learning and developing. When I was younger and looked to the Bible for guidance, I gravitated to the prophet Micah. Micah sums up my philosophy for living in this one sentence: "What doeth the lord require of me but to do justly, to love mercy, and to walk humbly with thy god."

*Rogers was one of the premier twentieth-century psychologists.

Decoding Some Keys to Happiness in Old Age

Do you have an old-age role model such as Jules, someone who believes he is developing at age 90 or 94? What makes these people stand out? For one thing, Jules demonstrates the openness to other people's feelings, self-efficacy, and big-picture view of life that defines being wise (see Chapter 12). Most striking is this master therapist's generativity, and the fact that Jules has reached Erikson's milestone of *integrity* (see Table 13.3). Jules knows he has lived according to the prophetic guidelines that he views at the core of having a meaningful life.

integrity Erik Erikson's eighth psychosocial stage, in which elderly people decide that their life missions have been fulfilled and so accept impending death.

Table 13.3: Erikson's Psychosocial Stages

Life Stage	Primary Task
Infancy (birth to 1 year)	Basic trust versus mistrust
Toddlerhood (1 to 2 years)	Autonomy versus shame and doubt
Early childhood (3 to 6 years)	Initiative versus guilt
Middle childhood (7 to 12 years)	Industry versus inferiority
Adolescence to emerging adulthood (teens into twenties)	Identity versus role confusion
Early adulthood (twenties to early forties)	Intimacy versus isolation
Middle adulthood (forties to sixties)	Generativity versus stagnation
Late adulthood (late sixties and beyond)	**Integrity versus despair**

According to Erikson, our task in later adulthood is to look back over our life to see if we accomplished what we set out to do. Older people who know they have lived fully are not afraid to die. But older adults who have serious regrets about their lives may be terrified of death and feel a sense of despair.

Notice this man's sense of pleasure at helping his friend. Now we know that being productive and having a sense of purpose may extend older people's lives.

Erikson believed that to reach **integrity** older people must review their lives and make peace with what they have previously done. But happiness in old age does not involve dwelling on the past. As with Jules, it involves finding purpose and meaning in your present life (Burr, Santo, & Pushkar, 2011).

Living a purposeful, meaningful life has an additional bonus. It makes people more likely to survive to Jules's age! In summarizing more than 60 longitudinal studies, researchers found that adults who agreed with questionnaire items such as, "My life is fulfilling" or "I feel I am making a difference" decades earlier, died at older ages than their peers (Martin-Maria and others, 2017). Having an optimistic view of aging—or like Jules, seeing later life as a time of development—can also operate as a self-fulfilling prophesy, predicting superior health down the road (Laditka & Laditka, 2017; Wurm and others, 2017).

Bottom line: Be positive, live a generative life, be open to other people, remain lovingly attached, see aging as a time of growth—these are some keys to living happily into advanced old age (and living happily during any stage of adult life!).

INTERVENTIONS: Using the Research to Help Older Adults

Now, let's summarize all of these messages. How can we help older people improve their memory skills? How should you think about the relationship priorities of older loved ones, and when should you worry about their emotional states? Here are some suggestions:

- As late-life memory difficulties show up in situations where there is "a lot going on," give older people ample time to learn material and provide them with a nondistracting environment (more about this environmental engineering in Chapter 14).

- Don't stereotype older adults as having a "bad" memory. Remember that semantic memory stays stable with age, and that teaching mnemonic strategies works. Help older people develop their memory skills by suggesting this chapter's tips. Also, however, be realistic. Tell the older person, "If you notice a decline in your ability to attend to life's details (episodic memory), that's normal. It does NOT mean you have Alzheimer's disease" (Dixon and others, 2007).

- Encourage older loved ones—even those with disabilities—to maintain a personal passion. Being "efficaciously" engaged or in flow not only helps slide information through our memory bins but makes for a happy life.

- Using the insights that socioemotional selectivity theory offers, don't expect older people to automatically want to make new friends. When an elderly person says, "I don't want to go to the senior citizen center. All I care about is my family," she may be making an age-appropriate response.

- Don't imagine that older people are unhappy. Actually, assume the reverse is true. However, be alert to depression in someone who is physically frail and socially isolated. Again, the key to warding off depression in old age is the same as at any age: being productive, feeling closely attached, having a sense of meaning in life.

Tying It All Together

1. Dwayne is planning to teach lifespan development at the senior center. He's excited; but since, until now, he's taught only younger people, he's worried about how memory changes in his older students might affect their enjoyment of his class. Based on your understanding of which memory situations give older people trouble, suggest changes Dwayne might make in his teaching.

2. Classify each of the following memory challenges as involving episodic memory, semantic memory, or procedural memory.

   a. Someone asks you for your street address.
   b. Someone asks you what you just read in this chapter.
   c. You go bike riding.

3. Which abilities in the previous question (a) will an older loved one retain the longest if she gets Alzheimer's disease, and (b) will start to decline early in life?

4. As you study this section, come up with a vivid image to embed the major terms in your mind. (For instance, to remember *working memory*, think of a brain on a treadmill; to recall *episodic memory*, think of an episode of your favorite TV show.) Do you agree that this optimization technique, while helpful, demands mental effort?

5. You are eavesdropping on three elderly friends as they discuss life. According to socioemotional selectivity theory, which two comments might you overhear?

   a. Shanthi says, "Now that I'm older, I want to meet as many new people as possible."
   b. Allen reports, "I'm enjoying life more than ever today. I'm savoring every moment—and what a pleasure it is to do just what I want!"
   c. Milly mentions, "I've been spending as much time as possible with my family, the people who matter the most."

6. Based on this chapter, give four reasons why happiness should peak in later life.

Answers to the Tying It All Together questions can be found at the end of this chapter.

LEARNING OUTCOMES

• Compare retirement trends worldwide, making reference to Germany and the United States.

• Analyze U.S. issues, patterns, and happiness during retirement.

• Explain widowhood challenges.

Social Development

Now let's look at how people find meaning as they confront the transitions of retirement and widowhood.

Retirement

When we imagine the U.S. retirement age, we immediately think of 65. But you might be surprised to know that the age for collecting full Social Security benefits is now 66 (and for people born after 1960, it will be 67) (Quinn & Cahill, 2016). When we think of being retired, we imagine a short life stage before death. But if you leave work in your early sixties—particularly if you are female—expect to be retired for about a quarter of your total life! (See Adams & Rau, 2011.)

What caused retirement to take up such a huge chunk of the lifespan, and what is happening to this life stage in the United States today? Stay tuned as I scan the global economic retirement scene and then offer a synopsis of current U.S. retirement trends.

Setting the Context: Differing Financial Retirement Cushions

If you are like many U.S. young people, you probably aren't sure whether retirement will continue to exist once you reach later life. Actually, there are places where retirement doesn't exist today. In Bangladesh, Jamaica, and Mexico, where more than half of all people over 65 are in the labor force, the elderly must work until they get seriously ill (Kinsella & Velkoff, 2001). The reason is that these nations lack the government-financed programs that propelled developed-world retirement into a full life stage.

By the late twentieth century, government-sponsored programs, sometimes allowing retirement as young as the late fifties—were a fixture in more than 160 nations (Kinsella & Velkoff, 2001). But even in Europe, which has universal old-age government supports, retirement anxieties differ from place to place. In Scandinavia, with its shared national goal to "help everyone cradle to grave," residents feel secure that they will be helped in old age. In Central Europe, where the gaps between rich and poor are wide and economic hardship is common earlier in life, people are intensely worried about their retirement years (Hershey, Henkins, & van Dalen, 2010).

What retirement programs can affluent nations provide? For answers, let's compare Germany and the United States.

GERMANY: MERCEDES MODEL OF GOVERNMENT SUPPORT. Germans currently do worry more about retirement because they live in a rapidly aging nation where the government may need to cut back on the funds citizens have long enjoyed—comfortable old-age income for life. Retirement in Germany is mainly financed by employee and employer payroll taxes similar to the system in the United States. However, unlike in the United States, in Germany, the philosophy has been to keep people well off during their older years. When the typical German worker retires, the government has replaced roughly three-fourths of that person's working income for life. Until recently, Germans have had no worries about falling into poverty in old age. Remarkably, German retirees had *more* spending power as they traveled further into old age (Hungerford, 2003).

THE UNITED STATES: GOING IT ALONE WITH MODEST GOVERNMENT HELP. If Germany offers a Mercedes-like model, government-funded U.S. retirement is more like an old used car; it allows people to barely make it, but in no comfort. The reason is that the famous, guaranteed old-age insurance program called Social Security functions as a safety net to keep people from being destitute in old age.

Social Security, the landmark government program instituted by President Franklin D. Roosevelt in 1935 at the height of the Great Depression, gets its financing from current workers. Employees and employers pay into this program to fund today's retirees; then, when it is their turn to retire, adults get a lifelong stipend financed by the current working population.

Social Security The U.S. government's national retirement support program.

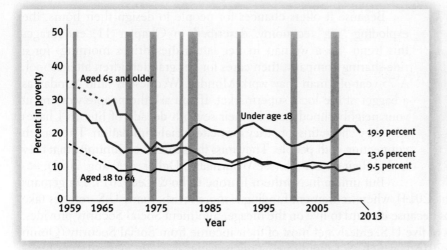

FIGURE 13.4: Poverty trends in the United States by age, from 1950 to 2013: In the mid-twentieth century, older adults were the most disadvantaged segment of Americans. Then, 40 years ago, expansions in Social Security and Medicare dramatically cut these rates, meaning that in more recent decades, children (orange bar) are much more likely to live in poverty than are people over age 65 (blue bar).
Data from Quinn & Cahill, 2016, p. 323.

As Figure 13.4 shows, Social Security, which was dramatically expanded in the 1970s, along with Medicare, represented an economic miracle for U.S. older adults. From not being able to financially survive, people over 65 today are less likely to live under the poverty line than any other U.S. age group.

Private pensions (and assets like personal savings) are the other supports floating retirement. Workers put aside a portion of each paycheck, and these funds, often matched by employer contributions, go into a tax-free account that accumulates equity. Then, at retirement, the person gets regular payouts, or a lump sum, on which to live (Johnson, 2009).

The central role of private pensions in financing retirement reflects the priority that the United States places on individual initiative. People are leery about the welfare-state implications of a federal government plan, preferring to provide tax incentives that encourage workers to plan for retirement on their own.

private pensions
The major source of nongovernmental income support for U.S. retirees, in which the individual worker and employer put a portion of each paycheck into an account to help finance retirement.

Hot in Developmental Science: New Bridges to U.S. Retirement

With an average retirement nest egg of $127,000, the problem is that most baby boomers haven't come close to amassing the pension cushion (at least 10 times that amount) to support a decent lifestyle for 15 or so years (Collinson, 2014; Leicht & Fitzgerald, 2014; see also Polivka & Baozhen, 2015; Quinn & Cahill, 2016). This reality has changed the landscape of U.S. retirement in two major ways. What are the *real, on the ground* retirement realities in the United States?

PEOPLE TRY TO WORK LONGER. During the late-twentieth century, people planned to retire happily as soon as they could. In fact, in the 1970s and 1980s, the average age of U.S. retirement was closer to 60 than 65 (Quinn & Cahill, 2016). During this century, there has been a dramatic shift. In 2016, almost 2 in 5 U.S adults *over age 65* reported they were still working, a full 6 percent more than in a comparable turn-of-the-century poll (Desilver, 2016)!

PEOPLE GO BACK TO WORK AFTER THEY RETIRE. Actually, rather than being an either/or transition, retirement today is often a fuzzy life change. Some fortunate people continue working for the same employer at reduced, flexible hours But the most important trend *after* retiring is to return to work part time (Lytle, Foley, & Cantor, 2015; Wang & Shi, 2014). More than half of all U.S. retirees take what are called **bridge jobs**—they work in another occupation to supplement their retirement funds (Quinn & Cahill, 2016).

bridge job When a retiree takes new work, often part-time, after retiring from a career job.

Elderly people may *say* they relish the human contact at a bridge job, but the reality is they often can use a paycheck to cobble together a decent life.

Because it offers chances for people to design their hours, the exploding "gig" economy, described in Chapter 11, encourages this trend. So a woman in her late sixties drives mornings for a ride-sharing company, then cares for her grandchildren after school. A 75-year-old man may work Monday, Wednesday, and Sunday as a bagger at the local supermarket. If you ask the people working at your neighborhood store in their seventh decade of life (as I have) why they chose this job, they may cite social stimulation. They relish connecting with people. They miss the sense of community that they had at their career job (see Wöhrmann, Deller, & Wang, 2013).

But unlike in Northern Europe (Cho & Lee, 2014; Dingemans & Henkens, 2014), where retirement funding is more lavish, many U.S. retirees take bridge jobs because it's hard to live on the meager allotment Social Security provides. Three out of five U.S. elderly get most of their income from Social Security (Quinn & Cahill, 2016)—which, as I mentioned, only provides the bare necessities of life.

Where do women and minorities fit into this picture? As you might imagine, their less continuous work histories and lower-wage jobs (discussed in Chapter 11) make it hard for single women in particular to amass pensions and other assets ("How can I save for old age when I need my income to live?") (Quinn & Cahill, 2016; Wang & Shi, 2014). While upper-middle-class married women entering retirement are better off, they are vulnerable to spending their nest eggs and ending their lives dependent on Social Security alone. In fact, the impressive government strides at cutting old-age poverty obscure the fact that a significant chunk of today's elderly is still teetering at the cusp of barely making ends meet (Quinn & Cahill, 2016). 🐵

The bottom-line message is that, yes, U.S. retirement is becoming a shorter, more fragile phase of life. Moreover, the income inequalities highlighted throughout this book persist into the older years. Just as being single and female predicts earlier adult poverty, the same forces spell financial trouble in later life. But even formerly upper-middle-class people are vulnerable to struggling financially if they live to the uppermost ends of life.

Now that we understand the U.S. landscape, let's explore other influences that go into the decision to leave work.

Exploring the Complex Push/Pull Retirement Decision

Imagine that you are in your sixties and considering leaving your job. Clearly, your primary consideration is economic: "Do I have enough money?" However, a second force that comes into play in Western nations is health: "Can I physically continue at work?" (De Preter, Van Looy, & Mortelmans, 2013; Wang & Shi, 2014). There may be another, insidious influence prompting your decision: age discrimination.

age discrimination
Illegally laying off workers or failing to hire or promote them on the basis of age.

THE IMPACT OF AGE DISCRIMINATION. Age discrimination in the United States is illegal. People cannot get fired for being "too old." But because it's acceptable to get rid of more expensive workers—who tend to be older—for "business reasons," it's difficult to prove that "age" was the reason why a fifty-something worker got laid off (Rothenberg & Gardner, 2011).

Encouraging retirement via a special buyout is a positive route employers use to entice Western workers to "go gently" into their retirement years (Ekerdt, 2010). But workers also disengage emotionally from their jobs when they identify with the negative stereotypes attached to "older workers" and feel discriminated against at work (MacDonald & Levy, 2016; Voss, Wolff, & Rothermund, 2017). Ironically, in one Finnish study, feeling age-related job discrimination predicted taking more sick days—perpetuating the very illness stereotype we associate with older employees (Viitasalo & Nätti, 2015)!

Older workers are also supposed to be rigid, make more mental mistakes, be fearful of technology, and less adaptable (McCann & Keaton, 2013). The problem is that these images are false! In one Swedish study, age made people *more* flexible at work (Kunze, Boehm, & Bruch, 2013). Research in the United States suggested that older workers are more compliant and, amazingly, *less likely* to take time off for being sick, in addition to being more reliable than younger employees (Newman, 2011)!

Still, these facts don't matter much when a laid-off worker of age 50 or 60 bumps up against age discrimination when looking for a new job (van Selm & Van der Heijden, 2013). It's impossible to prove that "too old" is the reason for a given applicant being consigned to the "won't hire" pile (Neumark, 2009). However, studies suggest that given hypothetical older and younger job seekers, employers routinely go for the younger adult (Ekerdt, 2010; Rothenberg & Gardner, 2011).

THE IMPACT OF WANTING TO WORK LONGER. So far, I've been focusing on the dismal forces that affect retirement: Financial problems keep people in the labor force unwillingly; health issues and age discrimination push people to retire. I've been neglecting the fact that retiring or working is a *positive* choice. Many baby boomers say they want to keep working after age 66 because they love their jobs (Adams & Rau, 2011; Galinsky, 2007). People may retire in order to enter an exciting, new phase of life (Duffy and others, 2017).

Who is passionate to stay in the labor force until their mid-seventies or up to age 85? As I implied earlier, these older adults are often healthy and highly educated—people like Jules in the Experiencing the Lifespan box on page 389, who feel tremendous flow in their careers (Adams & Rau, 2011; Boveda & Metz, 2016; Wang & Shi, 2014). What about adults who permanently retire? Are they depressed or thrilled after taking this step?

Life as a Retiree

The answer is "it depends." For educated workers, retirement may boost health (Smeaton, Barnes, & Vegeris, 2017; Wetzel, Huxhold, & Tesch-Romer, 2016) ("Now I am liberated to exercise and take good care of myself!"). But leaving work early and feeling forced out of the workforce does negatively affect people's emotional and physical well-being (Dingemans & Henkens, 2014; Zantinge and others, 2014).

Actually, the qualities that make for retirement happiness are identical to those that make for a satisfying adult life: Be open to experience and be conscientious, agreeable, and extraverted, but not neurotic (Henning, Lindwall, & Johansson, 2016); be healthy, happily married, and have the economic resources to enjoy life (Pinquart & Schindler, 2007).

One important predictor is entering retirement with a "calling" (see Chapter 11), meaning a flow-inducing life plan. In one survey exploring these passions, people's callings varied from exploring new artistic talents to developing the self ("I want to become wise"); but most often, people wanted to make a generative difference for others (Duffy and others, 2017). In fact, you can predict whether a just-retired relative will flourish by answering these questions: Is this person healthy, wealthy, and did he voluntarily leave work? (See Potocnik, Torera, & Peiro, 2013.) Does she have a life passion? What is she like as a human being? (See Table 13.4 for a summary of these forces.)

Table 13.4: Questions to Ask to Predict If a Relative Will Be Happy as a Retiree: A Section Summary

1. Did this person want to retire, or was he forced out of the workforce?

2. Is this person relying just on Social Security and/or compelled to take a post-retirement job to make ends meet?

3. Is this person generally happy and well adjusted?

4. Is this person married (happily!) and in good health?

5. Does this person have an absorbing calling or fulfilling retirement passions?

These older people, enrolled in an English class in a special senior citizens college in Japan, show that the human passion to learn burns bright in old age, and explains why educational programs for the elderly are flourishing in nations around the world.

How can you expect your relative to spend these years? Because "personality endures," one key is to look to her passions now (Atchley, 1989; Pushkar and others, 2010). So, a social activist joins the Peace Corps. A business executive volunteers at SCORE (Senior Corps of Retired Executives) advising young people about setting up small businesses. Others decide to take up new "bucket list" goals such as hiking the Himalayas or getting a history Ph.D. Many people open to experience might retire to pack in as much new learning as they possibly can.

A dazzling menu of options are available to older adults passionate to expand their minds—from reduced fees at colleges to older-adult institutes to senior citizen center classes. Readers might be interested to know that, in the spirit of mind expansion (not credential collection!), I'm currently getting a master's degree in Liberal Arts myself.

As my goal and the agendas of millions of baby boomers reveal, in the Western world, we see the older years as a time to vigorously connect to the world (Ekerdt, 1986). However, there is a different cultural model of retirement. In the traditional Hindu perspective, later life is a time to disengage from worldly concerns. Ideally, people become wandering ascetics, renouncing their connections to loved ones and earthly pleasures in preparation for death (Savishinsky, 2004). Although this plan is rarely followed in practice (after all, our need to be closely attached is a basic human drive!), let's not assume that our "do not go gently into the sunset," keep-active retirement ideal applies around the world.

Summing Things Up: Social Policy Retirement Issues

Now let's summarize these section messages by focusing on some critical social issues with regard to retirement.

old-age dependency ratio The fraction of people over age 60 compared to younger, working-age adults (ages 15 to 59). This ratio is expected to rise dramatically as the baby boomers retire.

- **Retirement is an at-risk life stage.** In the United States, the lack of pension income and other assets is the immediate threat to retiring. But the other issue is future cutbacks in Social Security (perhaps an increase until age 70 for receiving full benefits, or declining support levels). In 1950, there were about 16 workers for every U.S. retiree. Soon, the **old-age dependency ratio,** or proportion of working adults to retirees, will decline to almost 2 to 1 (Johnson, 2009). Social Security was never intended to finance a stage of life. It was instituted during an era when life expectancy was far shorter, and health issues made it impossible to work. Because the Social Security trust fund is set to run out around 2030, virtually ensuring retrenchments, millennials need to increase their savings now! (See Quinn & Cahill, 2016.)

- **Older workers are (currently) an at-risk group.** From being offered incentives to retire early, to not hiring older workers—age discrimination at work is clearly alive and well (Ekerdt, 2010; Neumark, 2009). But the situation is changing. Anxious about their shrinking labor force, European employers are taking steps to reverse their decades-long practice of enticing older people to leave work via pension perks (van Selm & Van der Heijden, 2013). While the United States still has ample young workers to float its economy, this may not be true when the mammoth baby boom cohort has all retired. At that time, will U.S. employers reverse their negative attitudes toward hiring older employees?

- **Many older people are more at risk of being poor.** During the 1960s and 1970s, as you saw earlier, the United States took the landmark step of dramatically reducing poverty among older adults. Still, as I mentioned, swaths of older Americans remain seriously left behind—men and women in low-wage jobs without pensions; single women; anyone who must stretch their retirement nest eggs into the nineties. Classic retirement supports like IRAs (Individual Retirement Accounts), pensions, and other assets depend on having traditional company-based middle-class jobs. Given the current explosion of the gig economy (which doesn't offer retirement perks), will economic pain again be the *dominant* old-age fate as this century unfolds?

Finally, I can't leave the topic of old-age poverty without touching on the topic of **intergenerational equity**—balancing the needs of the young and the old. Given that the U.S. elderly get Medicare and Social Security, and citizens in many other Western nations receive even more lavish old-age aid, it's easy for social critics to argue that affluent societies are over-funding older people at the expense of the young. But abandoning these programs leaves people dependent on their families. That hurts everyone, young and old (Binstock, 2010). Suppose you had to choose between helping your children and supporting your grandmother, and destitute older people roamed the streets? Again, we are in this together. Life is not a zero-sum game.

> **intergenerational equity**
> Balancing the needs of the young and old. Specifically, often referred to as the idea that U.S. government entitlements, such as Medicare and Social Security, "over-benefit" the elderly at the expense of other age groups.

Widowhood

Although we worry about its future, most of us associate retirement with joy. That emotion does not apply to widowhood. In a classic study of life stress, researchers ranked the death of a spouse as life's most traumatic change (Holmes & Rahe, 1967). What multiplies the pain is that today, widowhood still may strike a pre-baby-boom cohort who married in their early twenties and never lived alone.

Imagine losing your life partner after 60 years. You are unmoored and adrift, cut off from your main attachment figure. Tasks that may have been foreign, such as understanding the finances or fixing the food, fall on you alone. You must remake an identity whose central focus has been "married person" for all of adult life. Decades ago, British psychiatrist Colin Parkes (1987) beautifully described how the world tilts: "Even when words remain the same, their meaning changes. The family is no longer the same as it was. Neither is home or a marriage" (p. 93).

How do people mourn this loss? Who has special trouble with this trauma, and how can we help people cope? Let's look at these questions one by one.

Exploring Mourning

During the first months after a loved one dies, one classic study showed, people are often obsessed with the events surrounding the final event (Lindemann, 1944). Especially if the death was sudden, husbands and wives report repeatedly going over a spouse's final days or hours. They may feel the impulse to search for their beloved, even though they know intellectually that they are being irrational. Notice that these responses have similarities to those of a toddler who frantically searches for a caregiver when she leaves the room. With widowhood—as the poignant comments of the women in the Experiencing the Lifespan box show—John Bowlby's clear-cut attachment response reemerges at full force.

Experiencing the Lifespan | **Widows' Loneliness and a Widowhood Group**

What is it like to lose your mate? What are some of the hardest things to endure in the first year after a spouse dies? Here are the responses I got when I visited a local support group for widowed people and asked the women these kinds of questions:

"I've noticed that even when I'm with other people, I feel lonely."

"I find the weekends and evenings hard, especially now that it gets dark so early."

"Sundays are my worst. You sit in church by yourself. People avoid you when you are a widow."

"I think the hardest thing is when you had a handyman and then you lose your handyman. You would be amazed at how much fixing there is that you didn't know about. My hardest jobs were George's jobs. For instance, every time I have a car problem I break down and cry."

"I was married to a handyman and a cook. He spoiled me rotten. You don't realize it until they are gone."

"For me, it's the incessant doctors' bills. I got one yesterday. It's that continual painful reminder of the death."

"And you get all this stuff from Medicare, from Social Security. This year will be the last I file with him."

"You just don't know what to do. I didn't know anything, didn't know how much money we had . . . didn't know

about the insurance. . . . My family would help me out but, you know, it's funny—you don't ask."

"You have friends, but you can't really talk to them. You don't bring him up, and neither does anyone else."

"The thing that upsets me is that I'm scared that no one but me will remember that he was alive."

Experts dislike using the word *recovery* to describe bereavement, as this implies that mourning, a normal life process, is a pathological state (Sandler, Wolchik, & Ayers, 2008). Moreover, when people lose a spouse, they do not simply "get better." They emerge as different, hopefully more resilient human beings (Balk, 2008a, 2008b; Tedeschi & Calhoun, 2008). Still, after about a year, we expect widowed people to "improve" in the sense of remaking a satisfying new life. People still care deeply about their spouses. However, this mental image is incorporated into the survivor's evolving identity as the widowed person continues to travel through life.

Now, let's survey the messages we get from tracking people's feelings as they move from early bereavement into what attachment theorists might label the *working model*—or constructing an independent life—phase of widowhood.

WIDOWHOOD INVOLVES FLUCTUATING EMOTIONS. Interestingly (and in contrast to the image of unremitting pain), one conclusion of these studies is that widowhood evokes contradictory emotions. In following widowed people, psychologists typically chart a regular decline in depressive symptoms over time (Davies, Crowe, & Whitehead, 2016; Tiedt, Saito, & Crimmins, 2016). However, in one study, life satisfaction scores showed a different pattern, dipping to a low at the first-year anniversary and then rising during the second year (Powers, Bisconti, & Bergeman, 2014). Other researchers, following a huge national sample of Australian adults, found that after widowhood well-being rose (Anusic, Yap, & Lucas, 2014)!

What could explain this strange finding? One possibility is that, as you saw in the introductory chapter vignette, even people in the happiest long-term marriages may not realize how well they can cope on their own. When you discover that, yes, you can prepare the taxes or fix the faucet, and you do not fall apart when finding yourself single after 50 or 60 years, you have a tremendous sense of self-efficacy. As the Chinese proverb puts it: Within the worst crisis lies an opportunity (or, in the last chapter's terminology, a potential *redemption sequence*). As I described in Chapter 12, life traumas do promote emotional growth.

This is not to minimize the negative consequences of widowhood. From Switzerland (Perrig-Chiello and others, 2016) to Korea (Ha and others, 2016), from Africa (Ude & Njoku, 2017) to China and Japan (Tiedt, Saito, & Crimmins, 2016; Zhou & Hearst, 2016), compared to married adults, the widowed have higher depression rates and a poorer quality of life. The most powerful example comes from the **widowhood mortality effect**—a markedly higher risk of dying for the surviving spouse after a partner dies (Sullivan & Fenelon, 2014).

Now let's take a more detailed look at these challenges. What is the *main* issue widowed people face, and what steps should (and "do") they take to cope?

LONELINESS REMAINS THE NUMBER-ONE ISSUE. To get an in-the-flesh picture of what gives people pain, researchers asked volunteers whose partner died about a year ago to keep a diary for a week charting each stressful experience. What were the events, how intense was each experience, and when did each event occur (Ryckebosch-Dayez and others, 2016)?

While distressing feelings ran the gamut from emotions set off by external cues (being in bed alone, passing a place the former spouse had enjoyed), to regrets about being unkind to a former partner, to problems with practical concerns (cooking or repairing

widowhood mortality effect The elevated risk of death among surviving spouses after being widowed.

things at home), the *most* acute pain was loneliness—feeling deprived of the person who most loved you in life. A friend, widowed for three years, beautifully captured this anguish when she made this comment: "People like me, but they don't love me."

REACHING OUT TO ESTABLISH NEW ROUTINES IS KEY. Given that the primary issue is feeling disconnected, what is the cure? Another narrative study exploring people widowed for a longer period (on average, four years) suggested the solution is forcing yourself to establish regular routines (Davies, Crowe, & Whitehead, 2016). As one widower explained, "I go to a club now. . . . I didn't like it at the start. . . . It took me three or four visits before I started to settle in. . . . It takes your mind off things" (p. 536).

FRIENDS ARE MOST IMPORTANT IN DETERMINING HOW PEOPLE ADJUST. Intense family support, or moving in with children, can ease loneliness for widowed people living in collectivist cultures such as China and Japan (Tiedt, Saito, & Crimmins, 2016; Zhou & Hearst, 2016). But, because sons and daughters have their own lives, in affluent nations, children may need to move on ("Now that it's been three months, I don't need to visit Mom every day. I have to take care of my own husband and kids"). Therefore, to cope effectively over the long term, widows need to reach out to friends (Ha & Ingersoll-Dayton, 2008). The vital role friends play in widowhood well-being was showcased in this German finding: While satisfying "family attachments" predicted happiness among married elderly women, if a female was single, her happiness depended on having good friends (Albert, Labs, & Trommsdorff, 2010).

These widows enjoying a visit to a local nature preserve illustrate just why friends seem especially important after people lose a spouse.

The virtue of friends is that, not only are they companions to share activities, they allow you to more openly discuss your distress. This tendency to clam up (that is, not embarrass people by discussing your pain) may explain why widows report feeling lonely even when in a group (recall the Experiencing the Lifespan Box on pages 397–398). And, in another study measuring loneliness, researchers found the best cure for this number-one condition lay in making a *new widowed* friend (Utz and others, 2014).

At this point, readers may be tempted to urge everyone who has lost a spouse to join a widowed person's group. This is a mistake. An underlying message of my previous discussion is that most widowed people are resilient. We do them a disservice by assuming they are incompetent and totally in need of help. Actually, support groups for widowed people, psychologists find, are useful mainly for people who are having unusual trouble coping with this life event (Bonanno & Lilienfeld, 2008; Onrust and others, 2010). Who has special trouble coping with widowhood?

Predicting Which Widowed Adults Are Most at Risk

We might imagine that men should be most vulnerable to having serious problems after their spouse dies. Women are more emotionally embedded in relationships. They can use their close, enduring connections with friends to construct new lives. Imagine losing your only attachment figure and you will understand why, for elderly widowers living alone, suicide is a major concern (Stroebe, Schut, & Stroebe, 2007).

Are men more vulnerable than women to being widowed? The answer is mixed. For women, financial concerns can weigh heavily. For men, loneliness may be most intense (Perrig-Chiello and others, 2016; Tiedt, Saito, & Crimmins, 2016).

Chuck Franklin/Alamy

Lost in loneliness, spending your days staring out at sea, this classic image of the elderly widower says it all. Men—when they haven't found a new mate—can be at high risk for suicide in the older years.

Britta Pedersen/dpa/Alamy Live News

In the past, we expected widowed women to be locked in mourning. Today, the fact that we encourage widows to stay active in the world is epitomized by Katie Couric's life story. After her beloved husband Jay died of colon cancer in l998, the famed journalist and media icon became a passionate advocate for cancer screening and was universally praised for her resilient commitment to living fully after her devastating loss.

Still, men have one great advantage over women in overcoming the isolation odds—their higher chance of finding a new partner. To give just one example, 9 out of 10 men in a study that explored dating after widowhood were in new relationships. But only 1 of 9 women who said they were interested in dating was able to find a new mate (Carr & Boerner, 2013). Attend any U.S. boomer event at your local church (or older adult institute) and, like me, you might be struck by this strange thought: Have aliens swooped down and abducted the men?

However, rather than making generalizations based on gender in predicting reactions to widowhood, we must again adopt an *ecological, developmental systems approach*—that is, consider many forces. How emotionally resilient is the widowed person? Does that individual have a life passion or calling to cushion the blow? Is the person doubly burdened by dealing with a debilitating chronic disease? Is that woman or man generally securely attached? As one group of researchers concluded, widowed people who are insecurely attached are primed to feel unsupported by even the most caring children and friends (Karantzas & Gillath, 2017).

Interestingly, we may be able to predict a spouse's adjustment to widowhood by looking at the *deceased partner's* quality of life! In tracking a subset of married couples who later lost a spouse, researchers were astonished to discover that if a widow's husband or wife had been upbeat, happy, and highly satisfied with life about four years earlier (presumably before getting ill), the surviving spouse was resilient after that person died (Bourassa and others, 2016). Having an uplifting, loving mate carries over to emotionally float a survivor for life!

The overall environment makes a difference. In one study, researchers found that if older adults were living in an area with a high concentration of widowed people, their odds of dying after being widowed were reduced (Subramanian, Elwert, & Christakis, 2008). So moving as a couple to a senior citizen community with all those supportive widows and widowers has a survivor bonus in later life!

For women, it's important to live in a supportive culture. In one comparative study, scientists found that Swiss women widowed in 2011 reported fewer social and financial problems than their counterparts in 1979, an era when women had fewer life options and less lavish government financial supports (Perrig-Chiello and others, 2016). In fact, while we now expect widowed people to emotionally recover after a spouse dies, traditionally, widows were supposed to mourn for life!

Table 13.5 pulls together the main points of my discussion in guidelines for helping a widowed family member. As a final comment, if you lost your mother or father, please allow your widowed parent to develop a new romantic attachment! You might think that new relationships run into headwinds from children mainly after parents divorce (see Chapter 11). But, in the late-life dating study I alluded to earlier, when father–child bonds were somewhat ambivalent, daughters in particular were apt to get very angry when their widowed dad had a new life love (Carr & Boerner, 2013). My experience when I found a new partner after my husband's death confirms this result. Why do you think some children (both daughters and sons) react so negatively when their widowed parent finds someone new to love?

Table 13.5: Guidelines for Helping a Family Member Survive Widowhood

1. Expect your widowed relative to experience different emotions, and don't decide this person is uncaring for having positive feelings such as pride and a sense of relief.

2. Be alert that loneliness is the major issue, and encourage social connections. For women, the key may be finding a good, widowed friend. Among elderly widowers who don't find another mate, suicide is a serious concern.

3. Understand that the challenge is to establish new routines, ideally involving groups of people; and perhaps encourage your relative to join a widowed person's group, but only if this person seems especially isolated and distressed. Also understand that if your relative is insecurely attached, or had an unhappy marital life, being widowed can hit especially hard.

4. Advise seeking professional help if *any* widowed family member stays seriously depressed for over a year.

In the next chapter, I'll continue this discussion by offering tips about how to sensitively treat loved ones coping with that other major loss of later life: declining health.

Tying It All Together

1. Joe, a baby boomer, is approaching an age when he might retire from his public school teaching job. Compared to a colleague who retired a decade ago, Joe (*pick the false statement*):

   a. will probably retire at an older age.
   b. may go back to work after he does retire.
   c. will be unhappy if he devotes retirement to volunteering with at-risk kids.

2. Social Security provides a *lavish/ meager* income that is *guaranteed by the government/ depends on personal investments*.

3. To preserve Social Security, U.S. readers are apt to hear discussions about increasing the age of eligibility for getting full benefits to age 70. Discuss the pros and cons of this controversial idea.

4. If your favorite aunt's husband recently died, you can expect (*choose one*): *mixed feelings of loss and self-efficacy/ just sadness*. Now based on this chapter, spell out some forces that will predict your aunt should cope well.

Answers to the Tying It All Together questions can be found at the end of this chapter.

SUMMARY

Setting the Context

The **median age** of the population is rising due to declining fertility, longer life expectancies, and, of course, the baby boom. While **ageism** (negative stereotypes about the elderly) is universal, we also gravitate to the elderly for positive traits, and have contradictory old-age images partly because there are dramatic differences between being **young-old** and **old-old**.

Cognitive and Emotional Development

Everyone believes that as people get older, memory declines. Elderly people do perform less well than the young on most memory tasks. Memory challenges that are more difficult—such as linking faces to specific situations, remembering bits of information quickly, and especially **divided-attention tasks**—produce the most severe deficits, and losses here begin at a surprisingly young age.

Using the information-processing approach, researchers find that as people age, working memory declines because hypothalamic synaptic plasticity and frontal lobe executive functions are impaired. Using the **memory-systems perspective**, studies reveal few age-related losses in **semantic memory** or **procedural memory** but dramatic declines in **episodic memory**. To improve memory in old age (or at any age), use selective optimization with compensation, employ **mnemonic techniques**, and work on improving the person's mental state. Also, understand that when tests are labeled as "for memory," older people may get too anxious to perform well, and that late-life memory complaints may not predict scores on objective memory tests.

Socioemotional selectivity theory suggests that in old age (or at any age), when people see their future as limited, they focus on maximizing the quality of their current life and prefer to spend time with their closest attachment figures. This emphasis on enjoying the present, plus the late-life **positivity effect,**

the perception of time passing quickly, as well as lower daily stress, explain the **paradox of well-being,** the fact that older people report high levels of happiness. Still, depression does become a serious risk when people are old-old, physically frail, unable to act efficaciously, and have lost their attachment figures. Reaching **integrity,** feeling generative, and having a sense of purpose in life are keys to being happy in old age.

Social Development

Until recently, most people retired in their early sixties and lived in that stage for a large chunk of adult life. The reason was the explosion of government sponsored old-age programs offering many developed-world older citizens income for life. Germany has historically been a model of the ultimate in guaranteed, comfortable government support.

In the United States, our main sources of retirement income are **Social Security, private pensions,** and savings. However, unlike in Germany, Social Security only provides a meager guaranteed income. Today, because most U.S. baby boomers don't have the funds to fully float retirement, people are working until older ages, and may take **bridge jobs** after they formally retire. Cutting old-age poverty was a remarkable late-twentieth-century U.S. success story; but minorities, single women, and females who live into advanced old age often suffer serious economic distress.

Older workers base their retirement decisions mainly on financial considerations, but poor health can also force people to leave work. **Age discrimination,** although illegal, also propels older people to retire. Even though most negative stereotypes about older workers are false, employers are reluctant to hire older employees. Still, the decision to retire (or keep working) is a positive choice. People who choose to work into their seventies or eighties are typically healthy and well-educated, with flow-inducing jobs.

Retirees are happy when they have freely chosen to leave work, have few health and money worries, positive personality traits, and compelling leisure passions. People use these years to further a life calling, to pursue other "bucket list" goals, and to learn. Baby boomers' inadequate pension and savings, looming cuts to Social Security (partly due to the rising **old-age dependency ratio**), and age discrimination in the workforce remain serious threats. **Intergenerational equity** issues (especially over-benefiting the elderly) are a concern in nations where older people enjoy special government perks.

Widowhood is a top-ranking life stress, especially when it strikes old-old people who have been married for their entire adult lives. The early symptoms of bereavement have much in common with the separation response of an infant whose caregiver leaves the room. Rather than being an unmitigated trauma, however, losing a spouse evokes many different emotions. Still, loneliness is a major issue, and the **widowhood mortality effect** suggests that this life loss can take a dramatic toll.

While women who lose a spouse seem more burdened by financial issues, loneliness—the most important issue for both sexes—seems especially potent for widowed men unless they find a new partner. People adapt by establishing new social routines and, for women in particular, by connecting with friends. Being securely attached and having had an upbeat, loving spouse make adjusting easier. Personality resilience, following a life passion, socioeconomic status, health, and cultural forces shape the experience of widowhood, too. Children need to allow widowed parents to develop new romantic attachments after a mother or father has died.

KEY TERMS

age discrimination, p. 394

ageism, p. 379

bridge job, p. 393

divided-attention task, p. 381

episodic memory, p. 383

integrity, p. 390

intergenerational equity, p. 397

median age, p. 378

memory-systems perspective, p. 383

mnemonic technique, p. 385

old-age dependency ratio, p. 396

old-old, p. 378

paradox of well-being, p. 388

positivity effect, p. 388

private pensions, p. 393

procedural memory, p. 383

semantic memory, p. 383

Social Security, p. 392

socioemotional selectivity theory, p. 386

widowhood mortality effect, p. 398

young-old, p. 378

ANSWERS TO **Tying It All Together** QUIZZES

Setting the Context

1. a mixture of positive and negative traits; the old-old

Cognitive and Emotional Development

1. Dwayne should present concepts more slowly (but not talk down to his audience) and refrain from presenting a good deal of information in a single session. He should tie the course content to older adults' established knowledge base and strive to make the material relevant personally. He might offer tips on using mnemonic techniques. He should continually work on reducing memory fears: "With your life experience, learning this stuff should be a piece of cake!"

2. a. semantic memory
   b. episodic memory
   c. procedural memory

3. a. Bike riding, that automatic skill, is "in" procedural memory, so it can be maintained even into Alzheimer's disease.
   b. Remembering the material in this chapter, since it is in the most fragile system (episodic memory), is apt to decline at a relatively young age.

4. The answers here are up to you.

5. b and c

6. Older people (1) focus on enjoying the present, (2) selectively screen out negativity, (3) prioritize productive activities, and (4) live less stressful lives.

Social Development

1. c

2. meager/guaranteed by the government

3. *Pros:* Raising the retirement age to 70 will keep Social Security solvent, encourage older people to be productive for longer, and get society used to the fact that people can function competently well into later life. *Cons:* Depriving people of this money will add to the pressure forcing older people to unwillingly keep working; for the millions of workers who don't have other retirement nest eggs and must deal with health problems, it will have the *devastating* consequence of making people penniless in later life. Keeping older people in the labor force longer will make it more difficult for young people to get jobs or advance at work.

4. You can expect mixed feelings of loss and self-efficacy. Forces predicting coping: having compelling interests, a loving marriage and upbeat spouse, and developing close friendships, especially with new widows. It also is important to establish new routines.

CONNECT ONLINE:

 LaunchPad | Check out our videos and additional resources located at:
macmillan learning | **www.macmillanlearning.com**

CHAPTER 14

The Physical Challenges
of Old Age

At age 76, Susan was vigorous and fit. She walked 3 miles each day. As the community college's star pupil, she took classes two days a week. But Susan was finding it hard to hear her professors because those young students made so much noise! Her vision troubles made it scary to drive home from school, especially during the dark winter months.

Susan's doctor worried about her atherosclerosis. But it was the vision and bone problems that haunted Susan's thoughts. What if she fell when walking to class, or had an accident on those curving highway exit ramps? When Susan almost backed into a truck on Main Street—in broad daylight!—she realized she had to quit school and consider giving up her car.

Four years later, at age 80, Susan was having trouble cooking and cleaning. She began to worry: "What will happen when I can't take care of myself?" Her beloved niece, Emma, now 50 (and single), urged Susan to move in with her: "I'm buying a condo in this terrific planned community where you don't need to drive. It has no stairs; I'll put grab bars in the bathroom. I'd consider it a privilege to help care for you."

Susan politely said no. She was determined to plan for a future that did not involve burdening loved ones with her care. It was time to check out that beautiful assisted living facility that was advertised as being at the forefront of geriatric care. But after going on the Shady Acres Web site, Susan almost had a heart attack. The average rates ($6,000 a month) were higher than at a four-star hotel! Thank the Lord for Carl's IRA and the long-term care insurance her husband had urged her to buy at the impossibly young age of 63. Susan put her name on the waiting list—and none too soon. Six months later, she fell, breaking her hip, and could no longer live at home.

Today, Susan uses a walker. It's hard to get dressed and use the toilet. However, when I visited her, she was surprisingly upbeat. True, life at 83 can be difficult—not just because of a person's physical state. Still, the facility is wonderful. She loves the activities. Old people can hang onto their passions, too. The monthly lectures— covering everything from great books to politics, taught by her former community college professors—are a real joy!

What enemy is Susan battling? How does physical aging turn into disease, disability, and sometimes the need for a nursing home? This chapter offers answers to these questions and many more.

In the following pages, I'll explore problems that some gerontologists (Rowe & Kahn, 1998) label as "unsuccessful aging," describing what goes physically wrong during the old-old years. By now, you should realize that equating "successful aging" with walking for miles at age 90 is wrong. Successful aging means drawing on what gives your life meaning to live fully, no matter how your body behaves. It is epitomized by 94-year-old Jules, described on page 389, who—although he can barely take a step without stumbling—is sensitively doing therapy and writing books.

Aging successfully means having Jules's sense of purpose and generative mission. But successful aging also depends on whether the wider world offers older people the support they need to function at their best. The issue in later life is not so much being ill, but living fully in the face of chronic disease. The way elderly people function depends on their personal capacities (or nature) combined with nurture—having the right person–environment fit.

How can we engineer the best person–environment fit for older loved ones? Let's begin our search for answers by charting the aging process itself.

Left: Gerardo Ricardo López/Getty Images

Tracing Physical Aging

- Describe how physical aging occurs, and list its variations by gender and socioeconomic status.
- Outline tips for living healthier into old age.
- Analyze why extending the maximum lifespan is an unrealistic goal.

normal aging changes
The universal, often progressive signs, of physical deterioration intrinsic to the aging process.

ADL (activities of daily living) problems
Difficulty in performing everyday tasks that are required for living independently. ADLs are classified as either *basic* or *instrumental*.

instrumental ADL problems Difficulty in performing everyday household tasks, such as cooking and cleaning.

basic ADL problems
Difficulty in performing essential self-care activities, such as rising from a chair, eating, and getting to the toilet.

Susan has atherosclerosis, or fatty deposits on her artery walls. Her fragile bones and vision and hearing problems are also classic signs of **normal aging**—body deterioration that advances gradually over many years. Over time, normal aging shades into disease, then disability (Seals, Justice, & La Rocca, 2016), and, finally—by a specific barrier age—death.

PRINCIPLE #1: CHRONIC DISEASE IS OFTEN NORMAL AGING "AT THE EXTREME."
Many physical losses, when they occur to a moderate degree, are called normal. When these changes become extreme, they have a different label: chronic disease. Susan's bone loss and atherosclerosis are perfect examples. These changes, as they progress, produce those familiar later-life illnesses—osteoporosis and heart disease.

The National Health Interview Survey (NHIS), an annual government poll of health conditions among the U.S. population, tells us other interesting illness facts. As you can see in Figure 14.1, arthritis is the top-ranking chronic illness in later life (Centers for Disease Control and Prevention [CDC], n.d.). As we get older, our chance of having a variety of illnesses increases. Like arthritis, many age-related diseases are not fatal. They interfere with the ability to function in the world. So the outcome of chronic illness is not just death, but **ADL (activities of daily living) problems**—difficulties physically handling life.

PRINCIPLE #2: ADL IMPAIRMENTS ARE A SERIOUS RISK DURING THE OLD-OLD YEARS. ADL limitations come in two categories. **Instrumental ADL problems** refer to troubles performing tasks important for living independently, such as cooking and cleaning. **Basic ADL limitations** refer to problems with fundamental self-care activities, such as standing or getting to the bathroom or feeding oneself. When people have these severe disabilities, they typically need full-time caregiving help.

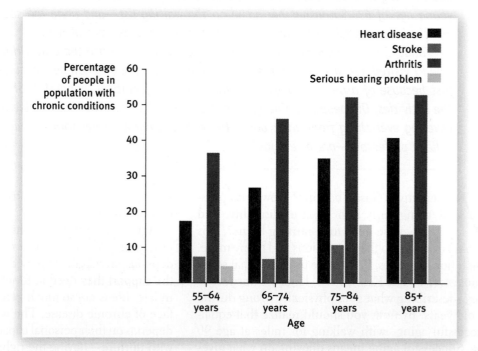

FIGURE 14.1: Prevalence of selected chronic health conditions among U.S. adults in middle and later life (percentages): As people travel into their seventies and eighties, the rates of common age-related chronic diseases rise. Although every chronic illness can impair the ability to fully enjoy life, many common chronic diseases don't actually result in death.
Data from CDC; National Center for Health Statistics (2015).

Although ADL problems can happen at any age, notice from Figure 14.2 that the old-old years are when these problems really strike. Half of all U.S. adults over 85 *living in their homes* have instrumental ADL difficulties. Basic ADL limitations, or impairments such as walking to the toilet or dressing, affect 1 in 6 of the oldest old (CDC, 2009). These statistics minimize the true rate of problems because older adults with basic ADL impairments often have to enter a nursing home.

So, yes, people can arrive at age 85 or 90 disability free. But as we travel further into later life, problems physically coping become a serious risk.

PRINCIPLE #3: THE HUMAN LIFESPAN HAS A DEFINED LIMIT. A final fact about aging is that it has a fixed end. More people than ever are surviving past a century. But a miniscule fraction live beyond that barrier age. In August 2014, worldwide, there were roughly 75 documented "super-centenarians"— people who lived until 110 and beyond (Gerontology Research Group, n.d.). Unless scientists can tamper with our built-in, species-specific *maximum lifespan*, soon after a century on this planet, we are all fated to die.

Here, you can see the real enemy in old age: It's ADL impairments. Moreover, if over the years, these problems walking progress to being unable to stand or get out of bed, a person might be forced to enter a nursing home.

FIGURE 14.2: Percentages of people needing assistance with instrumental ADLs and basic ADLs in the young-old years and over age 75: Although in the sixties and early seventies, the fraction of people with ADL difficulties is relatively small, the risk of having these problems escalates dramatically over age 75. (Over age 85, roughly 1 in 6 people living outside of nursing homes have a basic ADL problem.)

Data from U.S. Department of Health and Human Services, 2009.

Can We Live to 200?

At this point, you might be thinking that many babies will soon make it to be super-centenarians. Due to scientific breakthroughs in extending the lifespan, we may even be poised for the arrival of 200-year-old human beings (as reported in Carnes, Olshansky, & Hayflick, 2013).

These futuristic forecasts fall on fertile ground because one life-extension strategy has been known for almost 100 years. By underfeeding rats, researchers can increase the animals' maximum lifespan by up to 60 percent. The key is what one biologist calls "undernutrition without malnutrition." The animals are restricted to less food but given a nutritionally rich diet. They are allowed few empty calories (see Seals, Justice, & La Rocca, 2016; Bertozzi, Tosti, & Fontana, 2017 for reviews).

Calorie restriction is actually an all-purpose anti-ager, enhancing everything from glucose metabolism (Fok and others, 2013) to cardiac function (Csiszar and others, 2013; see the "How Do We Know" box). These research findings make excellent sense because obesity, especially via its side effect of diabetes (impaired sugar metabolism), causes every organ—from our eyes, to our heart, to our kidneys—to prematurely break down.

HOW DO WE KNOW. . .
that calorie restriction may extend the human lifespan?

Calorie restriction has remarkable longevity-enhancing effects in rats. But imagine the challenges of testing this strategy with human beings: Scientists must get volunteers to severely limit their calorie intake for many decades (ideally, this study should begin in early adulthood). People must give up sweets, fats, and coffee and never deviate from this difficult regimen. Then researchers must wait 80 or 90 years for answers, meaning they would need to live well beyond their own lifespans!

Is there any evidence that calorie restriction *might* extend human life? Consider this ambitious experiment: First, researchers selected a group of several hundred highly motivated young and middle-aged volunteers. The enrollees underwent an intensive screening. They had to be free of psychiatric problems, in good physical health, and of normal weight; they could not smoke or be pregnant. The scientists then divided these participants into two groups: The control group continued with their normal diet; the experimental group committed to reducing their intake by 25 percent for the next two years. During this time, everyone was tested at regular intervals.

Here are the results. The calorie-restricted group lost an average of about 10 pounds during the first six months—after which their weight stabilized. They showed an impressive array of physiological advantages: lower triglyceride and blood pressure levels, rising good cholesterol; improvements in glucose and thyroid function. Moreover—very importantly—participants reported no adverse mental health changes. The catch was that the volunteers did not quite reach the 25 percent mark—on average, they reduced their intake by about 11 percent.

We cannot say that these results apply to "normal people," as these volunteers were carefully selected to be in exceptional health. Still, the findings are fascinating. Even if it doesn't extend our life, calorie restriction can push back many risk factors for chronic disease! Would any of you reading this want to give calorie restriction a try?

Source: Information from Ravussin and others, 2015.

Without denying that it's important to watch your diet, however, restricting your intake *just* to live to age 200 is a mistake. The life extension findings have mainly been carried out with rats. Although we now know from the study above that calorie restriction can slow many risk factors for chronic disease, it's unclear if this regimen can push back the *biological limit* of human life.

Let's listen to the foremost experts in the biology of aging explain why extending the maximum lifespan in the near future is an unrealistic dream (Carnes, Olshansky, & Hayflick, 2013):

- The body breakdown involved in aging has complex causes, from multiple genetic timers to random insults that happen as cells do their metabolic work. There can't be a single magic-bullet intervention that stops aging and extends life. Even if a breakthrough technology such as stem-cell research fulfills its promise to regenerate cells lost to Parkinson's disease (Kim, Lee, & Kim, 2013), a few years later some other age-related illness, like cancer, is going to crop up. The best analogy to our aging bodies is an old car. Replacing each defective part only puts off the day when so much goes wrong that the system reaches its expiration date and everything stops.

• Our body's evolutionary expiration date is naturally set well below a century, because natural selection promotes, at best, living through the grandparent years (as I mentioned in Chapter 12). Therefore, even in the most affluent nations, the probability of a twenty-first-century newborn living to 100 remains low. (It's about 4.5 percent in Japan.) So let's celebrate our remarkable progress at allowing most babies born in the developed world to survive close to our expiration date. But let's also realize that extending the maximum lifespan is going to be far harder than the breakthroughs that allowed us to make it to later life.

At this point, many readers may feel relieved because—in addition to producing overpopulation—life extension has ethical problems: Will these strategies be available only to the wealthy? If so, imagine being financially sentenced to die at a normal age. And what if you *chose to* live a normal lifespan rather than extend your life (see Davis, 2016)? As socioemotional selectivity theory beautifully points out, knowing our life is near its end motivates us to savor every moment. Wouldn't being locked into living produce boredom, making *surviving* less sweet?

Religious young people, researchers find, reject life extension on spiritual grounds: Only God has the power to give and take away life (see Ballinger and others, 2017). And would you vote to live longer if the price was suffering for decades from the kinds of ADL impairments that make it hard to walk or get to the toilet on your own?

Who makes it close to our *current* maximum lifespan, and what are our odds of living with ADL impairments as we approach the end of life? Answers come from examining those familiar markers that shape development at every age: socioeconomic status and gender.

Socioeconomic Status, Aging, and Disease

The fact that socioeconomic status predicts how long we live comes from scanning the huge life expectancy gaps in the developed and developing worlds: Babies born in impoverished Malawi can expect on average to survive to age 61 (Central Intelligence Agency [CIA], 2018a). Infants lucky to emerge from the womb in Monaco have a 50/50 chance of living almost 30 years longer—to age 89.5 (CIA, 2018b).

These snapshots visually show why babies born in the affluent kingdom of Monaco (right photo) statistically out-survive newborns in Malawi (left photo) by a remarkable 30 years.

socioeconomic health gap The worldwide disparity between the health of the rich and poor.

This mammoth global difference is mirrored by a **socieoeconomic health gap**. In every nation, affluent and well-educated people live healthier lives and survive for a longer time (Choi, Kim, & Park, 2016; Hu, Wang, & Lee, 2017). In the United States, in 2014, this gap between the most impoverished (lowest 5 percent) and richest (top 5 percent) of adults was a decade for women. For men, it was almost 15 years (Chetty and others, 2017)!

Did this split widen as twenty-first-century income inequalities dramatically increased (see Chapter 1)? Raj Chetty's meticulous research (described earlier in this book) shows the unfortunate answer is yes. Between 2001 and 2014, life expectancy rose by close to three years for the richest 5 percent of Americans, while barely budging the bottom 5 percent (Chetty and others, 2017). And the news gets worse. In 2015, for the first time in U.S. history, life expectancy at birth declined (National Center for Health Statistics, 2016)!

What caused this troubling change? Researchers calculate that the reasons are different for women and men. For females, the longevity loss comes mainly from earlier deaths due to classic age-related diseases, such as heart attacks. For men, the declines are mainly driven by an uptick in what experts label as diseases of despair—poisonings, homicides, and accidents—and the reductions in life expectancy occur mainly during middle age (Acciai & Firebaugh, 2017).

FIGURE 14.3: Percentage of affluent and low-income people in their fifties with disabilities living in the United Kingdom: This chart shows the link between poverty and premature aging, as 2 in 5 low-income British citizens have an "old-age disease causing disability" during their fifties.
Data from Rahman, Kahn, & Hafford-Letchfield, 2016.

This brings up the fact that social-class differences in aging appear well before old age arrives. Notice how, by the late thirties, people show clear differences in their aging rates—developing weathered skin, perhaps having more trouble moving around. Although there are many exceptions, notice also that low-income adults are apt to look physically older than their wealthy counterparts. In fact, as the study illustrated in Figure 14.3 highlights, for disadvantaged adults, so-called old-age limitations often appear in midlife (Rahman, Kahn, & Hafford-Letchfield, 2016).

How far back can we trace this accelerated aging path? Based on the *fetal programming* hypothesis, its roots might emerge in the womb. As I mentioned in Chapter 2, *low birth weight*—which is linked to poverty—is epigenetically associated with premature heart disease and earlier death. Therefore, it's no wonder that childhood adversity (and poverty) is linked to midlife ADL problems as well as premature death (Anderson and others, 2017; Henretta & McCrory, 2016).

Now, compound this with the life-shortening adult lifestyle forces linked to poverty—from social-class differences in health practices, such as smoking and obesity (Boykin and others, 2011); to lack of exercise (who has time to work out if you are working two jobs in order to survive?); to the health consequences of being unemployed (Laditka & Laditka, 2016).

So far, I've spelled out a dismal scenario. But Chetty's research offers tantalizing qualifications. Life expectancy varies from place to place for poverty-level adults! If low-income people in their sixties live in an area with higher average home values—and especially a place boasting a higher fraction of college graduates—they tend to live longer than we might expect. It's not that these neighborhoods offer more access to health care, but that good health behaviors are infectious. In places with highly educated people, a social norm may develop that implicitly beams out the message: "You should watch your diet and exercise."

Just seeing runners pass by on the street may inspire people to be more fit—and there are more runners passing by on streets where more college graduates live.

Interestingly, our level of education in itself predicts how quickly we age (Rahman, Kahn, & Hafford-Letchfield, 2016) and die (Todd, Shkolnikov, & Goldman, 2016). Fascinating evidence involves telomeres, DNA sequences at the end of our chromosomes. Telomere shortening is an overall benchmark of body aging, as it shows that a particular cell has reached senescence and can no longer divide. Among a huge group of U.S. older adults, researchers found that high school graduates had shorter telomeres than people who attended college, a difference that was particularly striking among Black men (Adler and others, 2013; Mazzotti, Tufik, & Andersen, 2013). Therefore, in addition to (or due to) its other benefits, college can extend our lives!

Another life extender is nurturing close relationships, which can be even more important than good health practices in predicting how long we survive (Berkman & Breslow, 1983; Seals, Justice, & La Rocca, 2016).

Having caring, extended families may partly explain "the Hispanic paradox," the fact that, despite being far more likely to live in poverty, recent U.S. statistics showed that Latinos outlived whites by 2.6 years (Arias, Kochanek, & Anderson, 2015). It accounts for why loving marriages are strongly correlated with longevity, too (see Chapter 11). While attachment figures do everything from encouraging us to eat well (Friedman, 2014) to insisting we go to the doctor when we are ill, love stimulates oxytocin production, which, in itself, mutes the anxiety response to stress (Myers and others, 2014).

The fact that Latino grandchildren have such intense contact with their grandparents offers one reason for the "Hispanic paradox"—the statistic that, in spite of being far less affluent, Latino-heritage adults tend to live a surprisingly long time. The lesson: As a caring, involved grandchild of *any* cultural background, you might be "working" to help extend a beloved elderly family member's life!

Gender, Aging, and Disease

Their wider web of social connections could be one reason why women outlive men, sometimes by an incredible decade or more (OECD, 2014; see Chapter 1). Still, the main reason for women's superior survival is biological. Having an extra X chromosome makes females physically hardier at every stage of life.

During adulthood, the main reason for this gap can be summed up in one phrase: fewer early heart attacks. Illnesses of the cardiovascular system (the arteries and their pump, the heart) are the top-ranking killers for both women and men. In 2016, cardiac arrests accounted for roughly 1 in 4 U.S. deaths (Centers for Disease Control, 2017). However, because estrogen helps to slow the process by which fat deposits clog the arteries, men are roughly twice as likely as women to die of a heart attack in midlife (American Heart Association, 2001).

Their biological susceptibility to early heart attacks means that men tend to "die quicker and sooner." For women, the worldwide pattern is "surviving longer but being more frail" (OECD, 2014; Onadja and others, 2013; Rohlfsen & Kronenfeld, 2014; Tareque, Begum, & Saito, 2013).

It makes sense that disability is the price of traveling to the lifespan train's final stops. However, the phrase "living sicker" applies to women *throughout* adult life. During their twenties, thirties, and forties, only women experience the physical ailments related to pregnancy and menstruation. As they age, females have higher rates of arthritis, vision impairments, and obesity—illnesses that produce ADL problems but (except in the case of obesity) don't lead to death (Whitson and others, 2010).

This male/female disability distinction brings me to a concept called the **health span**—the age at which we can expect to survive without ADL limitations. Many gerontologists argue that rather than focusing on how long we live we need to extend *our healthy* years.

health span The number of years people can expect to live without ADL problems.

What can we do to live longer in health? The familiar answers are to exercise and eat right. But my discussion suggests we should adopt a broader lifespan approach.

 INTERVENTIONS Close Communities, Childhood, and Combating Chronic Disease

Specifically, we should:

- **Focus on children.** As I've been stressing throughout this book, it's important to prevent premature births and to make inroads in child poverty, as the seeds of poor health emerge during our earliest years. Now we understand that encouraging teens to enroll in and finish college can also have health benefits in middle and later life!

- **Focus on constructing caring communities.** Chetty's research underlines the powerful social effects of living in an area where the norm is to exercise and eat right. Chapter 7 showed that communities differ in *collective efficacy*, providing neighbor-to-neighbor help. So let's encourage each family to reach out to the people on their block or down the street (via neighborhood parties for instance), since we now understand that feeling connected to your community can literally extend life. And draw inspiration from the Hispanic paradox: Having loving, extended-family members is longevity-enhancing, too.

Finally, let's appreciate the realities. Without minimizing the value of extending the health span, as you saw in scanning Figure 14.1 on page 406, the normal price of living to the upper ends of the lifespan is disease. Given that running for miles at age 90 is unrealistic, and we are decades from tampering with our DNA, let's use our ingenuity to make the world user-friendly for normally aging people marching into later life. With this goal in mind, it's time to confront the main conditions causing ADL problems in the flesh—sensory-motor declines and dementia.

Tying It All Together

1. When she was in her late fifties, Edna's doctor found considerable bone erosion and atherosclerosis during a checkup. At 70, Edna's been diagnosed with osteoporosis and heart disease. Did Edna:

   a. suddenly develop these diseases?
   b. have normal aging changes that slowly progressed into these chronic diseases?
   c. undergo both events above?

2. Marjorie has problems cooking and cleaning the house. Sara cannot dress herself or get out of bed without someone's help. Marjorie has _____ problems, and Sara has _____ problems.

3. Anya brags that her newborn is likely to live to 200. Using the points in this section, convince Anya that she is wrong.

4. Nico and Hiromi are arguing about men's versus women's health. Nico says that women are basically "healthier"; Hiromi thinks that it's men. Explain why both Nico and Hiromi are partly correct.

5. Sonia wants to devise a scale to predict how long newborns will live. Based on *this section's points*, what items might she include?

Answers to the Tying It All Together questions can be found at the end of this chapter.

Sensory-Motor Changes

What happens to vision, hearing, and motor abilities as we grow old, and how can we minimize sensory-motor declines?

Our Windows on the World: Vision

One way aging affects our sight becomes evident during midlife. By the late forties and fifties, people have trouble seeing close objects. The year I turned 50, this change struck like clockwork, and I had to buy reading glasses.

Presbyopia, the term for age-related difficulties with seeing close objects, is one of those classic signs, like gray hair, that people are no longer young. When I squint to make out sentences, the fact of my age crosses my consciousness. I imagine students have this same thought ("Dr. Belsky is older") when they see me struggle with this challenge in class.

Other age-related changes in vision progress gradually. Older people have particular trouble seeing in dim light. They are more bothered by glare, a direct beam of light hitting the eye. They cannot distinguish certain colors as clearly or see visual stimuli as distinctly as before.

What is it like to be undergoing this progression? It can be annoying to ask the server what the impossibly faint restaurant bill comes to or to fumble your way past a neighbor's seat in a darkened movie theater. For me, the most hair-raising experiences relate to driving at night. Last week, a curve of the highway exit ramp loomed out of the dark and I was inches from death. But apart from worries about night driving, these problems have little effect on my life.

Unfortunately, this may not be true a decade from now. As Figure 14.4 illustrates, seeing in glare-filled environments such as a lighted medicine cabinet, or even making out the print on a white page, can be a real challenge during the old-old years.

These signs of normal aging—presbyopia, problems seeing in the dark, and increased sensitivity to glare—are mainly caused by changes in a structure toward the front of the eye called the **lens** (see Figure 14.5 on the next page). The disk-shaped lens allows us to see close objects by curving outward. As people reach midlife, the transparent lens thickens, develops impurities and so can no longer bend. This clouding and thickening not only produces presbyopia but limits vision in dimly lit places where people need as much light as possible to see.

LEARNING OUTCOMES

- List changes in vision, hearing, and motor abilities that occur with age.
- Identify strategies for minimizing sensory-motor losses.
- Critique age-related driving issues.

presbyopia Age-related midlife difficulty with near vision, caused by the inability of the lens to bend.

lens A transparent, disk-shaped structure in the eye, which bends to allow us to see close objects.

FIGURE 14.4: How an 85-year-old might see the world: Age-related visual losses, such as sensitivity to glare, make the world look fuzzier at age 80 or 85. So, as these images show, everything from finding a bottle of pills in the medicine cabinet to reading the print in books such as this text can be a difficult task.

Image Source/Getty Images

MayaCom/iStock/Getty Images

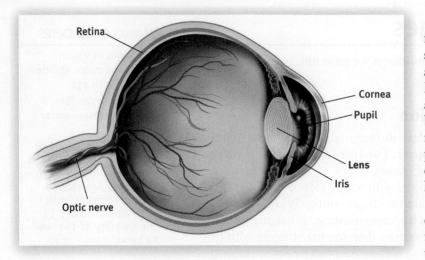

Retina
Cornea
Pupil
Lens
Iris
Optic nerve

FIGURE 14.5: The human eye: Deterioration in many structures of the eye contributes to older adults' poor vision. However, changes in the lens, shown here, are responsible for presbyopia and also contribute greatly to impaired dark vision and sensitivity to glare—the classic signs of "aging vision."

These changes also make older adults more sensitive to glare. Notice how, when sunlight hits a dirty window, the rays scatter and it becomes impossible for you to see out. Because older people view the world through a cloudier lens, they see far less well when a beam of light shines in their eye. When this normal, age-related lens clouding becomes so pronounced that the person's vision is seriously impaired, the outcome is that familiar late-life chronic condition—a *cataract.*

The good news is that cataracts are completely curable. The physician simply removes the defective lens and inserts a contact lens. The bad news is that the other three top-ranking old-age vision conditions—*macular degeneration* (deterioration of the receptors promoting central vision), *glaucoma* (a buildup of pressure that can damage the visual receptors), and *diabetic retinopathy* (a leakage from the blood vessels of the retina into the body of the eye)—can *sometimes* permanently impair sight.

INTERVENTIONS Clarifying Sight

To lessen the impact of the normal vision losses basic to getting old, again, the key is to modify the wider world. People should make sure their homes are well lit but avoid overhead light fixtures, especially fluorescent bulbs, shining down directly on a bare floor, as these produce glare. They should buy appliances with nonreflective materials and adjustable lighting. Putting enlarged letters and numbers on appliances will make the stove and computer keyboard easier to use.

Vision problems are a prime cause of ADL impairments because they make everything, from working to walking, a challenging task (Wahl and others, 2013). Poor vision is a risk factor for falling, which, as you will see later, is a frightening event in later life (Ambrose, Paul, & Hausdorff, 2013; Källstrand-Eriksson and others, 2013).

This brings up the emotional consequences of seriously limited sight: not leaving the house because you are afraid of falling; suffering the pain of depending on loved ones for jobs you used to do: "I feel so embarrassed . . . ," said one man; ". . . I can't even change a fuse, and it's embarrassing, belittling" (quoted in Girdler, Packer, & Boldy, 2008, p. 113); being "overprotected" (meaning infantilized) by well-meaning friends and family.

Given these dangers, how can loved ones help? Encourage the person to visit a low-vision center for rehabilitation, because these programs work (Smallfield, Clem, & Myers, 2013). Consider Jim Vlock, a retired executive whose eyes were literally opened when he (reluctantly) visited a center for the visually impaired. After an evaluation, Mr. Vlock emerged laden with devices, from a talking watch, to specialized glasses for different tasks, to a computer with an enlarged screen that can "read for him." As one center director put it, "Too often we get patients who . . . have lost their jobs, their wives, their home. . . . Our philosophy is to get patients to do things for themselves so they can feel fulfilled" (see Brody, 2010).

Actually, offering these aids at a younger age is vital, because impaired vision— more than poor hearing and having trouble getting around—limits life satisfaction in the very old (Liu and others, 2016). Even at age 60, vision impairments and hearing difficulties are a toxic double whammy provoking depression as people travel into later life (Cosh and others, 2017). How common is hearing loss as we age, and how does this condition affect daily life?

Our Bridge to Others: Hearing

It's natural to worry most about losing our sight in old age. But untreated hearing problems can also wreak havoc on people's well-being (Manrique-Huarte and others, 2016). Even among otherwise healthy older people, hearing loss predicts later physical decline (Kimiko and others, 2015). The reason is simple: Poor hearing robs us of understanding language, our bridge to other minds. So it is the human world we are deprived from fully entering when we lose the ability to hear.

Unfortunately, hearing difficulties are common in later life. They affect 1 in 3 people in their sixties. During the next decade, the statistics double to 2 in 3 (Bainbridge & Wallhagen, 2014). The figures are particularly alarming for men. Around the world, males are several times more likely than women to develop hearing losses in midlife (Belsky, 1999).

One reason is that age-related hearing loss has an environmental cause: exposure to noise. Men are more likely to be construction workers, ride motorcycles, and go to NASCAR races. Any person—male or female—who spends decades working in a noisy occupation is virtually destined to have hearing losses after age 65 (Hong, Chin, & Kerr, 2015). Government regulations mandate hearing protection devices in high-noise jobs, which may explain why U.S. hearing loss rates have stabilized in recent years (Bainbridge & Wallhagen, 2014). Still, from exposing ourselves to the roar of rock concerts to embedding an iPod in our ear, these statistics are apt to stay stubbornly high as today's emerging adults travel into later life.

Presbycusis—the characteristic age-related hearing loss—is caused by the atrophy or loss of the hearing receptors, located in the inner ear (Yamasoba and others, 2013; see Figure 14.6). This irreversible change, compounded by the neural declines discussed in the previous chapter, affect people's ability to quickly process speech. The receptors coding high-pitched tones are most vulnerable. This means older people have special difficulties hearing consonants, for instance mistaking the word *time* for *dime*, because these sounds are delivered at a higher pitch (Bainbridge & Wallhagen, 2014).

Put yourself in the place of someone with presbycusis. Because of your speech decoding difficulties, listening to conversations feels like hearing a radio filled with static. (That's why older people complain: "I can hear you, but I can't understand you.")

presbycusis Age-related difficulty in hearing, particularly high-pitched tones, caused by the atrophy of the hearing receptors located in the inner ear.

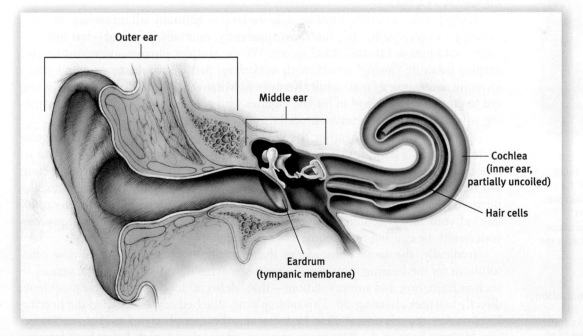

FIGURE 14.6: The human ear: Presbycusis is caused by the selective loss of the hearing receptors in the inner ear, called hair cells, that allow us to hear high-pitched tones. These changes are permanent.

Hearing problems like this may evoke marital misunderstandings in addition to isolating a couple from their friends.

Even if an aged woman is a Shakespeare scholar, a young person may be tempted to automatically adopt elderspeak. Have you ever used this patronizing talk with someone in her eighties just because she *looked* impaired?

elderspeak Communication style used when an older person looks frail and impaired, involving talking loudly and slowly, as if with a baby.

Because your impairment has been progressing gradually, you may not be sure you *have* a problem, thinking, "Other people talk too softly." After all, you can hear fairly well in quiet situations. It's only when it gets noisy that you can't hear at all.

Think of the pitch of the background noises surrounding you now: the hum of a computer, the sound of a car motor starting up. These sounds are lower in pitch than speech. This explains why hearing-impaired people complain about "all that noise." Background sounds overpower the higher-pitched conversations they need to understand.

Imagine having a conversation with a relative who cannot hear well—having to repeat your sentences, needing to shout to make yourself understood. Although you love your grandpa dearly, you automatically cringe when he enters the room. Now, imagine that you are a hearing-impaired person who must continually say, "Please repeat that," and you will understand why this ailment can provoke loneliness (Sung and others, 2015). Hearing losses, as I just suggested, impair our ability to lovingly connect.

INTERVENTIONS **Aiding Hearing in the Twenty-First Century**

Because background noise limits how well older people hear, one solution is to choose your social settings with care. Don't go to a noisy restaurant. Avoid places with low ceilings or bare floors, as they magnify sound. Install wall-to-wall carpeting in the house to help absorb background noise. Get rid of noisy appliances, such as a rattling air conditioner or fan. If a loved one is receptive, you might mention that assistive devices such as flashing phones might improve his life.

When talking to a hearing-impaired older adult, speak clearly and slowly. Face the person. Perhaps use gestures so the person can take advantage of multiple sensory cues (Diederich, Colonius, & Schomburg, 2008). But avoid *elderspeak*, the tendency to talk more in exaggerated tones ("HOW *ARE YOU, DARLING?* WHAT IS FOR *DINNER* TODAY?").

Elderspeak—a communication style we tend to naturally fall into when an older person looks physically, and, therefore apparently, mentally impaired—has unfortunate similarities to *infant-directed speech*. We use simpler phrases and grammar and employ infantile "loving" words, such as *darling*, that we would never adopt when formally addressing a "real" adult (Kemper & Mitzner, 2001). I'll never forget going out to dinner with a friend in his late eighties who needed to use a walker, and wincing when the 18-year-old server treated this intellectual man like a 2-year-old!

For your own future hearing, the message rings loud and clear. *Avoid high-noise environments and cover your ears when you pass by noisy places.* Why do we hear so much about the need to exercise, but there is a deafening silence about protecting our hearing? How many of you religiously work out to prevent health problems like heart attacks but attend rock concerts without a second thought? Think of the noise level at your fitness center. Could the same place where you are going to improve your health be causing this common age-related disease?

Ironically, the same noisy places that contribute to hearing losses now offer solutions for the hearing impaired. An assistive device is available in public venues—such as train, bus, and subway stations—that "delivers" loudspeaker announcements directly to a user's hearing aid. This microphone-attached advance, called the hearing loop, makes speech crystal clear by bypassing the cacophony of background noise (see Hearing Loop, n.d.). Because so many intellectual, older arts-lovers have hearing handicaps, notice how written messages now are often beamed from screens when you attend a big city lecture or play.

The huge domed ceilings are awe-inspiring, but, combined with bare floors and the clatter of commuters, they make New York City's Grand Central Station an acoustic nightmare. However, thanks to the miracle of the hearing loop, people can now bypass that background noise via loudspeaker train announcements beamed directly to their hearing aids.

Still, none of these external aids can supplant that simple device, the hearing aid. So what makes many people, even when they notice they're having problems, so averse to getting a hearing aid (Eckert, Matthews, & Dubno, 2017)?

As someone in that category right now, let me be honest. First, there is foot dragging—I know my hearing is worse, but it really isn't that bad. I've got so much to do; I'll go next week. All I need to do is avoid noisy restaurants. I'm fine having people to dinner at my house. If I get a hearing aid, won't it be cumbersome, expensive, and difficult to adjust? (See Kelly and others, 2013; McCormack & Fortnum, 2013.) But beneath these rationalizations is the concern I share with most people my age (David, Zoizner, & Werner, 2018): Won't I look old and ugly with this thing dangling from my ear?

Actually, I'm wrong. Advances in hearing aid technology have eliminated the old style bulky boxes I recall from my youth. Devices now selectively screen out background noise; tiny objects can be invisibly nestled within the ear. Still, as I suggested earlier, the best hearing aid can't completely compensate for age-related problems decoding fast-paced speech (Hoppe and others, 2016). The reason, as I described in Chapter 12, is that age makes us slower in *every* area of life.

Motor Performances

This overall slowness puts older people out of sync with the physical world. It can make driving or getting across the street a challenging feat. It causes missteps in relationships, too. If you find yourself behind an elderly person at the supermarket checkout counter or an older driver going 40 in a 65-mile-per-hour zone, notice that your reaction is to get annoyed. Therefore, age-related slowing alone may help explain why our time-oriented society has such negative prejudices against the old.

The slowness that is emblematic of old age is mainly caused by the loss in information-processing speed that starts decades earlier, in young adulthood (described in Chapters 12 and 13). This slowed **reaction time**—or decline in the ability to respond quickly to sensory input—affects every action, from accelerating when the traffic light turns green, to focusing on what the person across the table is saying, to performing well on a fluid IQ test.

Age changes in the skeletal structures propelling action compound the slowness: With *osteoarthritis*, the joint cartilage wears away, making everything from opening a jar to running for the bus an endurance test. With **osteoporosis**, the bones become porous, brittle, and fragile, and so are prone to break. Although men can also develop

reaction time The speed at which a person can respond to a stimulus.

osteoporosis An age-related chronic disease in which the bones become porous, fragile, and more likely to break. Osteoporosis is most common in thin women, and so most common in females of European and Asian descent.

osteoporosis, women, as is well known, are more susceptible to this disease. The main reason is that females—particularly slender women—have frailer, smaller bones. With this illness, the fragile bones break at the slightest pressure and cannot knit themselves back together. Hip fractures are a special danger. They are a primary reason for needing to enter a nursing home (Jette and others, 1998).

From Latin America (Smith and others, 2017) to China (Wu & Ouyang, 2017) to everywhere else, falling is a fear that older adults universally share. And, not unexpectedly, the chance of falling multiplies among women who are old-old. The cost of fall-related injuries in hospitalizations and nursing home placement is enough to knock society off its feet—representing at least 0.1 percent of health-care expenditures in the United States and the European Union (Ambrose, Paul, & Hausdorff, 2013).

INTERVENTIONS: Modifying Motor Problems, New and Older Techniques

The main risk factor for falling is frailty—having trouble competently walking around (Lin and others, 2017). Although normally, we can effortlessly walk while talking or checking the Internet on our smartphone or chewing gum, when people have problems with this automatic function, every step must be consciously planned. Falls can easily occur in situations demanding *divided attention*, such as when people are crossing the street and their phone rings (Liebherr and others, 2016).

Many studies demonstrate that exercise can improve later life mobility (see, for instance, Oh and others, 2017). The problem is adherence—following through on what, for some adults, might be a boring activity. Therefore, the most interesting new strategy is to entice older people to play video games. Computer games, you might be interested to know, improve reaction time and help improve balance and lower-limb strength (Neri and others, 2017). Also, video games are fun!

Older people should also take steps to modify their homes: Use high-quality indirect lighting (as I mentioned earlier) and low-pile, wall-to-wall carpeting to prevent tripping. Put grab bars in places such as in the bathtub, where falls are likely to occur. Install cabinet doors that open to the touch, and place shelves within easy reach. If a relative is worried about living independently, urge her to check out body sensors that signal health-care providers if she falls.

Actually, lower body impairments—because they limit mobility—are the number-one barrier to living independently in later life (Pressler & Ferraro, 2010). Suppose you needed help standing, and getting to the toilet was a scary balancing act? But I know a man who cannot walk—and should be in a nursing home—whose life was transformed by that simple assistive device: the medical scooter. The scooter has permitted him to stay in his own home (with a lot of loving family support) and given him wheels to travel. It has also kept him active and fully enjoying life!

Table 14.1 summarizes the main points of this sensory-motor section, with special emphasis on what older adults and their loved ones can do to produce the right person–environment fit at home.

Table 14.1 Age-Related Sensory-Motor Changes and Interventions: A Summary

Changes	Interventions
VISION	
Problems with seeing in dimly lit places, sensitivity to glare	• Use strong, indirect light and avoid using fluorescent bulbs. • Buy appliances with large letters, nonreflective surfaces, and adjustable lighting. • Consider giving up driving at night and in the rain.

Changes	Interventions
HEARING	
Loss of hearing for high-pitched tones	• Reduce background noise.
	• Speak distinctly while facing the person, but avoid elderspeak.
	• Install wall-to-wall carpeting and double-paned windows in a home.
	• Don't be wary about checking out hearing-aid technology. You can still look just as young—and feel much more connected to the world—with a device nestled in your ear.
MOTOR ABILITIES	
Slower reaction time	• Be careful in speed-oriented situations.
Osteoporosis and osteoarthritis	• Search out exercise programs and try to follow through.
Gait problems	• Install low-pile carpeting to prevent tripping, grab bars, and other assistive devices at home. (The lighting interventions suggested above will also help prevent falls.)
	• Regularly play video games!

How do the elderly handle that environmental challenge so important to staying independent: driving?

Hot in Developmental Science: Later-Life Driving Issues and Potential Solutions

Imagine that you are an elderly person whose vision problems or lower-body impairments are making driving dangerous. You first stop driving during rush hour. For years, you have been uncomfortable driving at night and in the rain. But even though you are aware of having problems, if you are like many older people, you cannot imagine giving up your car. Abandoning driving means confronting the loss of independent selfhood that you first gained when you got your license as a teen. Now, think of the *physical* consequences of feeling more imprisoned in your house because you need to ask loved ones to drive you around, and you will understand why, in one mammoth Japanese study, giving up driving strongly predicted later ADL declines (Shimada and others, 2016).

Actually, driving in later life is problematic because it involves *many* sensory and motor skills. In addition to demanding adequate vision, driving is affected by hearing losses because we become alert to the location of other cars and emergency vehicles partly by their sound (Jemaa and others, 2017). To drive well demands having the muscle strength to push down the pedals, and the joint flexibility to turn the wheel. And, as anyone behind an older driver when the light turns green knows, driving is especially sensitive to slowed reaction time (Salvia and others, 2016).

The good news is that vehicle anti-crash features, such as backup cameras and lane departure warnings, make driving more secure for older adults. As Cheryl, age 72, gushed: "It saves your life. Particularly the warning of a car coming up. [Because] I drive a lot . . . on the highway" (quoted in Gish and others, 2017 p. 501). The bad news is that a fancy menu of dashboard displays can multiply the distraction (what button do I push now?) and none of these innovations was designed with older eyes in mind (Young, Koppel, & Charlton, 2017). Nothing can mitigate the reaction-time errors the elderly make when they must decode complex traffic signals (Salvia and others, 2016)

Vision problems, hearing difficulties, and especially slowed reaction time—all combine to make 80-year-olds more dangerous drivers. But if we rob people of their cars, how will this affect their mental and physical health?

Jose Luis Pelaez Inc./Getty Images

FIGURE 14.7: Accident rates in U.S. urban areas, by age and gender during the late twentieth century: Driving is especially dangerous for drivers age 75 and over. Notice that, if we look at per-person miles driven, old-old drivers have accident rates that outpace those in the other highest-risk group—teenagers and emerging adults.

Data from Stamatiadis, 1996.

or quickly swerve to avoid pedestrians or bicycles. Therefore, it is no wonder that twenty-first-century statistics reinforce the findings in Figure 14.7. Driving *is* more risky during the old-old years.

What should society do? Our first thought would be to require yearly license renewals, accompanied by vision tests for people over 75. But international surveys show driving requirements are far more lax. No nation prevents people with mild dementia from driving (You Joung and others, 2017). In Florida, even over age 80, people need to renew their license (by mail) only every six years (Department of Motor Vehicles, 2018)!

Moreover, because operating a car demands so many abilities, to really weed out incompetent drivers requires a multidisciplinary evaluation involving input from physicians, neuropsychologists, and ophthalmologists, as well as data from road tests (Aksan and others, 2017). Should we rely on relatives or ask physicians to report impaired older drivers? Would you have the courage to rob your uncle of his adult status by taking away his keys?

None of these interventions speaks to the larger issue: "If I can't drive, I may be confined to my home." We need to redesign the driving environment by putting adequate lighting on road signs, streets, highways, and, especially, exit ramps. We should encourage logo exit signs that are simpler and easier to read (Zahabi and others, 2017). Although the explosion in low-cost car-sharing services should make giving up driving easier for middle-class older adults, a company's cell phone app may be daunting to learn. So only that technological breakthrough on the horizon—self-driving cars—will make the anxieties in this section obsolete. 🐾

At that time, let's hope a medical breakthrough has eliminated the *real* number one anxiety we all have when traveling the highway of later life: dementia.

🐾 Tying It All Together

1. Roy, who is 55, is having trouble seeing in the dark and in glare-filled environments. Roy's problem is caused by the clouding of his *cornea/ iris/ lens.* At age 80, when Roy's condition has progressed to the point where he can't see much at all, he will have *a cataract/ diabetic retinopathy/ macular degeneration,* a condition that *can/ cannot* be cured by surgery.

2. Dr. Kapur has just given a 45-year-old a diagnosis of presbycusis. All of the following predictions about this patient are accurate except (pick out the false statement):

    a. The patient is more likely to be a male.
    b. The patient has probably been exposed to high levels of noise.
    c. The patient is at risk for becoming isolated and depressed.
    d. The patient will hear best in noisy environments.

3. Your 80-year-old grandmother asks for advice about how to remodel her home to make it safer. Which modifications should you suggest?

    a. Install low-pile carpeting, and put grab bars in the bathroom.
    b. Put fluorescent lights in the ceilings.
    c. Buy appliances with larger numerals and nonreflective surfaces.
    d. Put a skylight in the bathroom that allows direct sunlight to shine down on the medicine cabinet.
    e. Get rid of noisy air conditioners and fans.

4. Andres is horrified that nations don't pass stricter laws limiting later-life driving. Explain the main reason why it's incredibly hard to take this step.

Answers to the Tying It All Together questions can be found at the end of this chapter.

Neurocognitive Disorders (NCDs, Popularly Called *Dementia*)

Major neurocognitive disorder (typically called **dementia**) is the general label for any illness that produces serious, progressive cognitive losses that compromise a person's ability to live independently. (While this title was changed to neurocognitive disorders in the current American Psychiatric Association's *Diagnostic and Statistical Manual, DSM-5*, the name dementia is still widely used around the world.) The DSM framers distinguish between a minor and major NCD; with the minor form, thinking problems, while significant, don't prevent living independently.

These devastating losses produce the total erosion of our personhood, the complete unraveling of the self. Younger people can also develop a neurocognitive disorder if they have a brain injury or an illness. However, as you will see later, these symptoms are typically produced by two conditions that strike in later life.

What is this cognitive decline like? As you can poignantly see in the Experiencing the Lifespan box, in the earlier stages, people forget basic *semantic information*. They cannot recall core facts about their lives, such as the name of their town or how to get home. Impairments in *executive functions* are prominent. A conscientious person behaves erratically. An extravert withdraws from the world.

LEARNING OUTCOMES

- List the major causes of neurocognitive disorders.
- Describe the characteristics of Alzheimer's disease.
- Critique Alzheimer's research and interventions.

major neurocognitive disorder (NCD, dementia) The general term for any illness involving serious, progressive cognitive decline that interferes with a person's ability to live independently. (A *minor neurocognitive disorder* is the label for a less severe impairment in memory, reasoning, and thinking which does not compromise independent living.)

Experiencing the Lifespan | An Insider Describes His Unraveling Mind

Hal is handsome and elegant, a young-looking 69. He warmly welcomes me into his apartment at the assisted-living facility. Copies of National Geographic *and* Scientific American *are laid out in stacks. Index cards list his daughters' names and phone numbers, and provide reminders about the city and the state where he lives. Hal taught university chemistry for years. When his mind began to unravel, he learned that he had the illness whose symptoms he graciously describes:*

I first noticed that I had a problem giving short speeches. You have a blank and like . . . what do I put in there. . . .

I can speak. You are listening to me and you don't hear any pauses, but if you get me into something. . . . I just had one of these little pauses. I knew what I wanted to say and I couldn't get into it, so I think a little bit and wait and try to get around to it. I know it's there . . . but where do I use it? . . . It's ups and downs; and then one day you are in a deep valley. You can't get tied up in the hills and valleys because they just lead you around and it makes you more frustrated than ever. . . . If I can't get things, I just give up and then try to calm down and come back to it. Like, when I read, I get confused; but then I just stop and try again a month later. Or the people here: I know them by face, by sight, but I cannot get that focus down to memorize any names. I remember things from when I was 5. It's what's happening now that doesn't make a lot of sense.

As we walk to my car after this interview, Hal's daughter fills me in:

My father seems a lot happier now that he is here. The problem is the frustration, when he tries to explain things and I can't understand and neither of us connects.

Then he gets angry, and I get angry. My father has always been a very intellectual person, so feeling out of control is overwhelming for him. . . . He has days where he gets paranoid, decides that there is a conspiracy out for him. It's tiny things. A letter came to the wrong place and he went down and exploded at the people at the desk. For me the worst thing is remembering how my father was. You expect a certain response from him and you get this strange response. It's like there's a different person inside.

As the symptoms progress, every aspect of thinking is affected. Abstract reasoning becomes difficult. People can no longer think through options when making decisions. Their language abilities are compromised. People cannot name common objects, such as a shoe or a bed. Judgment is gone. Older adults may act inappropriately—undressing in public, running out in traffic. They may wander aimlessly and behave recklessly, unaware that they are endangering their lives.

When these diseases reach their later stages, people may be unable to speak or move. Ultimately, they are bedridden, unable to remember how to eat or swallow. At this point, complications such as infections or pneumonia often lead to death.

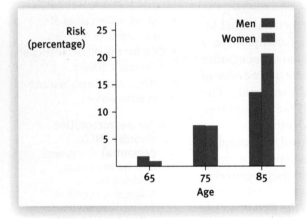

FIGURE 14.8: Estimated risks for major neurocognitive disorder (dementia) in a major U.S. study, by age and sex: The good news is that our chance of getting a major neurocognitive disorder by age 65 is low. The bad news is that by age 85—especially for females—the risk accelerates.

Data from Alzheimer's Association, 2016, Alzheimer's Disease Facts.

vascular neurocognitive disorder (vascular dementia) A type of age-related cognitive disorder caused by multiple small strokes.

Alzheimer's disease A type of age-related cognitive disorder characterized by neural atrophy and abnormal by-products of that atrophy, such as senile plaques and neurofibrillary tangles.

The Dimensions of These Disorders

How long does this devastating decline take? As I will describe soon, there is a precursor period between experiencing minor memory problems and having full-blown symptoms (Dubois and others, 2016). So it's sometimes hard to clearly define when a major neurocognitive disorder begins. The deterioration progresses at different rates from person to person and varies depending on the specific disease. But in general, these illnesses deserve the label *chronic disease*. On average, the time from diagnosis until death is approximately 4 to 10 years (Brodaty, 2018; Rabins, 2011; Theis & Bleiler, 2011).

The good news is that these devastating mental impairments are typically illnesses of *advanced* old age. Among the young-old, the prevalence of these diseases is in the single digits. Over age 85, 1 in 3 people are destined to develop memory problems this severe (see Figure 14.8). While these statistics are alarming, notice the small silver lining here: Most older adults do survive sound in mind well into the oldest years.

The Main Causes of Neurocognitive Disorders

What conditions produce these terrible symptoms? Although there are a host of rarer late life diseases, typically the older person will be diagnosed with *Alzheimer's disease, vascular neurocognitive disorder*, or some combination of those two illnesses.

Vascular neurocognitive disorder (typically called **vascular dementia**) involves impairments in the vascular (blood) system, or network of arteries feeding the brain. Here, the person's cognitive problems are caused by multiple small strokes.

Alzheimer's disease directly attacks the core structure of human consciousness, our neurons. With this illness, the neurons wither away and are replaced by strange wavy structures called **neurofibrillary tangles,** and, as you can see in the photo below, thick, bullet-shaped bodies of protein called **senile plaques.**

Vascular problems—because they limit the brain's blood supply—promote this neural loss (Strand and others, 2013). So, when an 85- or 90-year-old person develops this condition, small strokes plus Alzheimer's changes may work together to produce the mental decline.

As you just saw, the number-one risk factor for developing these conditions is being old-old (Dubois and others, 2016). But there are several genetic markers that raise the chances of getting Alzheimer's at a younger age (Bressler and others, 2017). The most important is having two copies of the APOE-4 marker. Instead of getting ill in the late eighties, adults with this unfortunate configuration have a 50/50 chance of getting full-blown symptoms at age 68! (See Bue, 2018; Dubois and others, 2016).

Suppose your parent developed Alzheimer's at this tragically young age. You feel as though you are living under a genetic cloud. Would you want to be tested for the APOE marker and other Alzheimer's genes? One issue—as a friend in that situation explained—relates to the fear of being denied health-care coverage if an insurance company learns the results. Moreover, while tests offer good insights into what is *more likely* to occur, a percentage of people at high risk genetically don't actually get a dementing disease (Hohman and others, 2017; more about this interesting fact later).

Now imagine you decide to be tested and find out you harbor this genetic time bomb. Can you take steps to ward off the blow? Where *are* we in terms of preventing Alzheimer's disease?

neurofibrillary tangles Long, wavy filaments that replace normal neurons and are characteristic of Alzheimer's disease.

senile plaques Thick, bullet-like amyloid-laden structures that replace normal neurons and are characteristic of Alzheimer's disease.

This magnified slice of the brain showing senile plaques (dark circles) provides a disturbing window into the ravages of Alzheimer's disease.

Targeting the Beginnings: The Quest to Nip Alzheimer's in the Bud

The main front in the war to prevent Alzheimer's centers on a protein called *amyloid,* a fatty substance that is the basic constituent of the senile plaques. According to current scientific thinking, the accumulation of a toxic form of amyloid produces a compound called *tau (tau-p)* that internally sets off the tangles and neural decay (Dubois and others, 2016; Sperling and others, 2018). Efforts to dissolve the amyloid plaques in Alzheimer's patients have not worked. The challenge is to limit this buildup while people are healthy but on the path to developing the disease.

This means it's vital to find reliable biomarkers (or precursors) of Alzheimer's. The effort has been remarkably successful. Measuring amyloid and tau-p levels in the cerebrospinal fluid of cognitively normal older people is an excellent predictor of later symptoms (Dubois and others, 2016); MRIs assessing the brain's gray matter and volume add to the accuracy of a subsequent diagnosis (Hohman and others, 2017). Scientists are also exploring how blood tests to measure proteins involved in the immune response to inflammation may eventually help in diagnosing the disease (Varma and others, 2017). Actually, as diagnosing this disorder now requires having a series of neuropsychological evaluations over time (Alzheimer's Association, 2016), it would be great to have a *simple* blood test, like the one for diabetes, that would foreshadow Alzheimer's disease.

Adults diagnosed with *subjective cognitive decline* and *mild cognitive impairment* are centrally important in this effort. These people either believe they have suffered dramatic memory changes or, in mild cognitive impairment, show significant learning problems on neuropsychological tests (Jack, 2018). Not everyone classified with these early stage diagnoses makes the transition to Alzheimer's. In fact, some people—those open to experience, with cognitively enriching lifestyles—can improve

(Karen and others, 2013). However, more than half of all people with mild cognitive impairment develop Alzheimer's within the next few years.

Is there anything you and I can do to slow this path? Although Alzheimer's is an equal-opportunity illness, affecting everyone from scholars to inventors to artists, being well educated offers adults a cognitive reserve to buffer the onset of symptoms. But, unfortunately, highly educated people decline faster once they have the disease (Soldan and others, 2017).

Actually, about 1 in 3 people who show clear signs of Alzheimer's pathology (plaques and tangles) at autopsy never show symptoms of the illness in life. And we now have a small study suggesting that these resilient people may possess a built-in neural reserve.

As you can see in Figure 14.9, cognitively normal people who show brain changes characteristic of Alzheimer's have neurons with a spine density very similar to people without the disease (Boros and others, 2017). We already know that the *only proven strategy* for stimulating neural growth is putting rats on running wheels. Could exercise be an antidote to Alzheimer's?

| Cognitively normal group | Cognitively normal group with Alzheimer's pathology | Alzheimer's disease |

FIGURE 14.9: Illustrations of the dendrites of a cognitively normal group; a group with Alzheimer's pathology who showed no clinical signs of the disease during life; and a group who died with Alzheimer's disease: Amazingly, resilient "dendrite spines" (see the middle illustration) may protect people who should get Alzheimer's from developing the memory changes characteristic of the disease.
Information from Boros and others, 2017, Annals of Neurology, 82: 602-614.

The seventy-something dancers in the photo are not only likely to see themselves as young, but their favorite activity may actually help grow the kind of resilient dendritic spines illustrated in Figure 14.9!

This tantalizing idea is hard to test experimentally because it's difficult to ask a random group of people to exercise for years and then compare them to control groups (Machado and others, 2017). Still, based on its cognition-stimulating effects discussed in Chapter 12, my number-one candidate for an anti-Alzheimer's strategy is exercise. Even if it doesn't help us construct new brain cells, at a minimum, going to the gym or walking will help with the vascular component of this illness (and, of course, help prevent the lower-body problems that are such a threat to independent living in later life).

INTERVENTIONS **Dealing with These Devastating Diseases**

What about those Alzheimer's drugs we see advertised on TV? Unfortunately, their effects, put charitably, are minor (see Bressler and others, 2017). With this illness, the main interventions are environmental. They involve providing the best disease–environment fit for the person and helping caregivers—the other casualties of these devastating diseases.

FOR THE ILL PERSON: USING EXTERNAL AIDS AND MAKING LIFE PREDICTABLE AND SAFE. Creative external aids such as using note cards can jog memory when people are in the earlier stages of Alzheimer's. It helps to put shoes right next to socks or the coffee pot by the cup, to visually remind the person what to do. A prime concern is safety. To prevent people from wandering off (or driving off!), double-lock or put buzzers on doors. Deactivate dangerous appliances, such as the stove, and put toxic substances, such as household cleaners, out of reach. Many nursing homes feature specialized "memory units," with living environments designed to promote cognitive capacities and staff skilled in dealing with this disease. At every stage of the illness, the goals are to (1) protect people and keep them functioning as well as possible for as long as possible and (2) be caring and offer loving support.

So far, I have mainly discussed what others can do for these devastating impairments—as if the diseases had magically evaporated a human being. This assumption is wrong. The real profiles in courage are the people in the early stages of Alzheimer's who get together to problem-solve and offer each other support. What does it feel like to be losing your inner self? We already got insights from Hal in the Experiencing the Lifespan box on page 421. Now let's read what other people with early Alzheimer's have to say:

Well, its pure terror—of incontinence, being a baby, not knowing who you are.

Outsiders can compound this anguish when they develop their own memory problem—centering on the label and forgetting the human being. A woman named Bea vividly described this situation when she was first told her diagnosis:

He [the neurologist] . . . just said it was going to get worse. . . . Why can't doctors be a *bit* caring and kind?

(quoted in Snyder, 1999, pp. 17–18)

Can people use their late-life *positivity* skills to act efficaciously in the face of their disease? Read what a determined man named Ed had to say:

I am alive and I'm going to live life to the best I can.

(quoted in MacRae, 2008, p. 401)

Another man named Gorman went even further:

This . . . diagnosis has given me time to enjoy . . . life . . . . : A beautiful sunset, . . . , the rising sun. Yes, having Alzheimer's has changed my life; it has made me appreciate life more.

(quoted in MacRae, 2008, p. 401)

Can older adults with Alzheimer's give us other insights into what it means to be wise? Judge for yourself, as you read what a loving dad named Booker said about the cycle of life:

I . . . have a wonderful daughter. I sent her to . . . school . . . and now she takes care of . . . my business. . . . I'm in my baby phase now. . . . So I call her "my mumma." . . . [Booker smiled appreciatively.] . . . She's such a blessing to me.

(quoted in Snyder, 1999, p. 103)

FOR THE CAREGIVER: COPING WITH LIFE TURNED UPSIDE DOWN. Imagine your beloved father or spouse has dementia. You know that this major neurocognitive disorder is permanent. You helplessly witness your loved one deteriorate. As the disease progresses to its middle stage, you must deal with a human being who has turned alien, where the tools used in normal encounters no longer apply. The person might be physically and verbally abusive and wake and wander in the night. When the 24/7 symptoms produce total role overload (Infurna, Gerstorf, & Zarit, 2013), you face the guilt of putting your loved one in a nursing home (Graneheim, Johansson, & Lindgren, 2014). Or you decide to put your own life on hold for years and care for the person every minute of the day.

What strategies do people use to cope? One study involving African American caregivers revealed that people rely on their faith for solace (Dilworth-Anderson,

Boswell, & Cohen, 2007): "All my strength comes from God" (p. 365). Others turn to the Alzheimer's caregiver support groups and Internet chat rooms for advice: "She seems to get worse during the night." . . . "What works for you?" . . . "My husband hit me the other day, and I was devastated." . . . "Keep telling yourself it's the illness. People with these illnesses can't help how they act."

Another key lies in relishing the precious moments together you have left:

> [Tom and Jane, married for 63 years] . . . shared smiles and giggles. . . . Although the stories Jane told did not . . . make sense, her eyes lit up whenever a question was asked about her marriage.
>
> (quoted in Daniels, Lamson, & Hodgson, 2007, p. 167)

Yes, dealing with a loved one with these disorders can be embarrassing (Montoro-Rodriguez and others, 2009). It's stressful and depressing, too. But this life experience offers its own *redemption sequence*. One woman summed up her journey of self-awareness like this: "What it's done for me, Alzheimer's, is . . . to give me a whole new life" (quoted in Peacock and others, 2010, p. 648). (Table 14.2 summarizes these messages in a list of caregiving tips.)

Table 14.2 Tips for Helping People with Cognitive Disorders

1. Provide clear cues to alert the person to his surroundings, such as using note cards and labeling rooms and objects around the home (e.g., use a picture of the toilet and tub at the door to the bathroom); use strong, contrasting colors to highlight the difference between different rooms in the house.

2. Protect the person from getting injured by double-locking the doors, turning off the stove, and taking away the car keys.

3. Offer a highly predictable, structured daily routine.

4. Don't take insulting comments personally. Try to understand that "it's the disease talking."

5. Remember that there is a real person in there. *Respect the individual's personhood*.

6. Try to see the silver lining; this is a time to understand what's really important in life, to grow as a person and show your love.

7. Definitely join a caregiver support group—and contact the Alzheimer's Association http://www.alz.org.

Up to this point, I've been exploring how older people and their loved ones can personally take action to promote the best person–environment fit when old-age frailties strike. Now, let's look at what society is doing to help.

Tying It All Together

1. Your grandmother has just been diagnosed with a major neurocognitive disorder. Describe the two disease processes that typically cause this condition.

2. Mary, age 50, is terrified of getting Alzheimer's. Which statement can you make that is both accurate and comforting? *(Pick one.)*
   a. Don't worry. These conditions are typically illnesses of the "old-old" years.
   b. Don't worry. Scientists can cure these conditions when the illnesses are caught at their earliest stages.

3. You are giving a status report to a senate committee on biomedical strides in preventing Alzheimer's disease. First, target the main focus of these efforts. Then offer a tip to the worried senators about a strategy that *might* help ward off the illness.

4. Mrs. Chen has just been diagnosed with early Alzheimer's disease. Her relatives might help by:

a. taking steps to keep her safe in her home.
b. encouraging her to attend an Alzheimer's patient support group.
c. treating her like a human being.
d. doing all of the above.

Answers to the Tying It All Together questions can be found at the end of this chapter.

Options and Services for the Frail Elderly

Imagine you are in your eighties, and cooking and cleaning are difficult. You have trouble walking to the mailbox or getting from your car to the store. You start out by using *selection* and *optimization*. You focus on your most essential activities. You spend more time on each important life task. You are determined to live independently for as long as possible. But you know that the time is coming when you will enter Baltes's full-fledged *compensation* mode. You will need to depend on other people for your daily needs. Where can you turn?

Setting the Context: Scanning the Global Elder-Care Scene

For most of human history, older people would never confront this challenge. Families lived in multigenerational households. When the oldest generation needed help, caregivers were right on the scene.

Today, however, this support network has frayed in some of the collectivist countries historically most committed to family care (Qu, 2014). In Japan, nursing home care has become common. In China, because younger people need to leave the oldest generation behind as they move from the villages to the cities to find work, older people in rural areas have nowhere to turn when they need ongoing ADL help (see Chapter 12). Therefore, the East is turning to the West for models of societal elderly care.

The Scandinavian countries offer our best examples of the elder care that advanced Western societies provide (Rodrigues & Schmidt, 2010). In Sweden, Norway, and Denmark, government-funded home health services swing into operation to help impaired older people "age in place"—meaning stay in their own homes. Innovative elderly housing alternatives dot the countryside—from multigenerational villages with a central community center providing health care, to small nursing facilities with attractive private rooms (Johri, Beland, & Bergman, 2003). Because their care is free and government funded, Scandinavian older adults don't need to face that anxiety-ridden question of "can I afford to get help?"

Alternatives to Institutions in the United States

In the United States, we have these worries. The reason is that **Medicare**, the U.S. health insurance system for the elderly, pays only for services defined as cure-oriented. It does not cover help with activities of daily living—the very services such as cooking or cleaning or bathing that might keep people out of a nursing home when they are having trouble functioning in life.

What choices do older people in the United States and other developed nations have instead of going to a nursing home? Here are the main **alternatives to institutionalization** that exist today:

LEARNING OUTCOMES

- Outline services for the frail elderly, making special reference to the United States.
- Evaluate nursing home care.
- Critique care for later-life disabilities.

Medicare The U.S. government's program of health insurance for elderly people.

alternatives to institutionalization Services and settings designed to keep older people who are experiencing age-related disabilities that don't merit intense 24-hour care from having to enter nursing homes.

continuing-care retirement community Elderly housing option characterized by different levels of care. People enter in relatively good health and then move to sections providing more intense help when they grow more disabled.

assisted-living facility Elderly housing option providing care for people with disabilities that, while significant, do not require a nursing home.

day-care program Center offering activities and a safe place to go during the day for impaired older adults living with relatives.

home health services Nursing-oriented help provided in the home of an impaired adult.

- A **continuing-care retirement community** is a residential complex that provides different levels of services, from independent apartments to nursing home care. Continuing care provides the ultimate person–environment fit. Residents arrive in relatively good health and get the appropriate type of care as their physical needs change. With this type of housing, older adults are purchasing a lifestyle focused on health. Plus, they are paying for peace of mind, knowing where they will be going when they need nursing home care.

- An **assisted-living facility** is designed for people who have ADL limitations, but not impairments that require full-time, 24-hour care. Assisted living—which has mushroomed in popularity—also offers care in a less medicalized, more homey setting. Residents have private rooms; they can keep the cherished mementos that allow them to live a dignified life (Nord, 2013). Here, too, the focus is on maximizing personal control (Koehn, Mahmood, & Stott-Eveneshen, 2016; Pirhonen & Pietilä, 2016) in a much safer environment than living at home (Speller & Stolee, 2015).

- **Day-care programs** are specifically for older people who live with their families. Much like its namesake for children, adult day care provides activities and a place for an impaired older person to go when family members work. Because this service allows relatives to care for a frail parent at home without having to give up their other responsibilities—day care puts off the need for a nursing home (Cho, Zarit, & Chiriboga, 2009).

- **Home health services** help people age "in place" (at home). Paid caregivers come to the house to cook, clean, and help the older adult with personal care activities such as bathing.

With their enriching activities and social contacts, assisted-living and continuing-care facilities can be wonderful settings in which to spend the final years of your life. ("It's like permanently living on a cruise ship," gushed a friend). Still, many affluent older people, even with those with marked ADL impairments, resist moving to these places (Koenig and others, 2014). Why?

Its tempting menus can make continuing care delicious places for wealthy older adults to spend their last years of life—provided you can tolerate the social "risk" of not being invited to sit at this dinner table.

One reason is that, for many older adults, entering these settings (like buying hearing aids) may symbolize, "I've landed in the territory of the old." Assisted living, in particular, limits the freedom people have in "real life." Yes, you won't have to struggle to make it alone, but you must bend to the group rules. (As one woman complained, "Well . . . you can't really have a family gathering. If the kids want to . . . play . . . and they are making noise . . . it's going to disturb everything" (quoted in Koehn, Mahmood, & Stott-Eveneshen, 2016, p. 527). Suppose your new peer group doesn't share your interests, or you confront the same poisonous group-status hierarchies you had to deal with during your preteen years (Ayalon & Green, 2013; Schafer, 2013). (Unfortunately, human nature doesn't change!)

Most importantly, in the United States, people only have the option of selecting continuing care (and often, assisted living) if they are *wealthy*—not even middle class! Can't we devise innovative, low-cost, elder-care alternatives that help people who have some ADL problems, but don't require that ultimate setting—the nursing home?

Nursing Home Care

Nursing homes, or long-term-care facilities, provide shelter and services to people with basic ADL problems—individuals who do require 24-hour caregiving help. Although adults of every age live in nursing homes, it should come as no surprise that the main risk factor for entering these institutions is being very old. The average nursing home resident is in his—or, I should say, her—late eighties (O'Shea Carney & Norris, 2017). Because, as we know, females live sicker into advanced old age, women make up the vast majority of residents in long-term care.

What causes people to enter nursing homes? Often, a person arrives after some incapacitating event, such as a broken hip or stroke. Given that these illnesses require such daunting 24/7 care, roughly half of all nursing home residents have some dementing disease (O'Shea Carney & Norris, 2017; Rist and others, 2016).

In predicting who ends up in a nursing home, both nature and nurture forces are involved. Yes, the person's biology (or physical state) does matter. But so does the environment: specifically, whether a network of attachment figures is available to provide care. Does the older adult have several family members and/or a friend willing to take the person in? The more places (and people) a frail person has "in reserve" to provide help, the lower the risk of that individual's landing in long-term care (Kasper, Pezzin, & Rice, 2010).

Just as the routes by which people arrive differ, residents take different paths once they enter nursing homes. Sometimes, a nursing home is a short stop for rehabilitation. Or, as these places provide hospice services, it may be a short interlude before death. Some residents live for years in long-term care (O'Shea Carney, & Norris, 2017).

You might be surprised to learn who is paying for these residents' care in the United States. Because people begin by paying the costs out of their own pockets and "spend down" until they are impoverished, *Medicaid,* the U.S. government health-care program specifically for the poor, finances our nation's nursing homes.

> **nursing home/long-term-care facility**
> A residential institution that provides shelter and intensive caregiving, primarily to older people who need help with basic ADLs.

The simple act of going down stairs can be an ordeal when you have osteoporosis (see left insert) and know that any misstep might land you in a nursing home.

Evaluating Nursing Homes

Nursing homes are often viewed as dumping grounds where residents are abused or left to languish unattended until they die. How accurate are these stereotypes?

Many times, the generalizations are unfair. Nursing homes may offer perks from beauty parlors to private rooms. A strong movement is afoot to make nursing homes homey and "person centered," and offer loving care (Barbosa and others, 2017; Kane & Cutler, 2015).

We still have far to go. Experts bemoan the excessive emphasis on safety that limits people from having a sliver of an autonomous life (Kane and Cutler, 2015). Nursing home residents are barred from leaving the facility unless relatives check them out; they are subject to random checks from caregivers. They do not have input into when to eat (or what to eat). They can't just decide to lie in bed or refuse to take a medicine. Their every action—from moving to a chair to being taken to the toilet—is dependent on the workers providing care. As one frustrated new resident named Luis put it: "I would say to my friends, don't go there. Go to jail instead" (quoted in Johnson & Bibbo, 2014, p. 60).

Having to share a room with a stranger is the worst insult. In the United States, normally, only married couples share rooms. The Medicaid standard is two people to every room (Kane & Cutler, 2015). Moreover, particularly if your roommate has a cognitive impairment, she may sit up moaning all night or be physically abusive. In one U.S. survey, one-third of nursing home workers reported witnessing an incident of resident-to-resident aggression within the past two weeks (Rosen and others, 2016).

Working in a nursing home can be hazardous to caregivers. In one poll in a Swiss nursing home, 2 in 3 staff members reported being the target of a resident's verbal aggression within the previous two weeks; almost half of these workers had to fend off a physically aggressive act. Again, difficult behaviors are most prone to erupt in Alzheimer's units because of the unfortunate personality changes this illness provokes. However, abuse from residents was also frequent in places where people felt emotionally exhausted because they had too much work to do (Stutte and others, 2017).

This brings me to the front-line nursing home caregivers—the **certified nurse assistant or aide.** Just as during life's early years, caregiving at the upper end of the lifespan is low-status work. Nursing home aides, like their counterparts in day-care centers, make poverty-level wages. Although in Europe, workers are more apt to say they have the resources to give adequate care (Backhaus and others, 2017; Zúñiga and others, 2015), U.S. nursing homes are chronically understaffed (O'Shea Carney & Norris, 2017). Even when an aide loves what she does, the job conditions can make it difficult to provide adequate care. Having worked in long-term care, I can testify that residents are sometimes left lying in urine for hours. They wait an inordinately long time for help getting fed. One reason is that it can take workers hours to feed the eight or so people in their care when dinner arrives!

Still, despite these problems, people can get enormous gratification from this low-status work. In focus group studies conducted at Arkansas nursing homes, aides said they relished the chance to make a difference: "I didn't want to become an LPN or RN. I wanted to be a CNA to be hands-on" (quoted in Gray and others, 2016, p. 247). They took pride in their stamina and skills: "You have to have a knack for it. I don't do it for the money" (p. 247). They felt incredibly close to the older people: "You go home and dream about the residents" (p. 247).

Jayson—a mellow, 6-foot-tall, 200-pound man, who worked in a Philadelphia nursing home—may have put it best:

> If you . . . say, ". . . I'm just doing my job," . . . you're in the wrong field. . . . When somebody . . . dies . . . , we . . . . go to their funerals. . . . I . . . spoke at . . . the funerals. . . . I say how much this person meant to me.
>
> (quoted in Black & Rubinstein, 2005, pp. S-4–6)

Jayson, who after being shot and lingering near death, reported seeing an angel visit him in the form of a little old man, believes his career is a calling from God. He is flourishing in this consummately generative job. What about nursing home residents? Can people get it together within this most unlikely setting? For uplifting answers, see the Experiencing the Lifespan box.

certified nurse assistant or aide The main hands-on care provider in a nursing home who helps elderly residents with basic ADL problems.

Experiencing the Lifespan \ Flourishing in a Nursing Home: A Psychologist Describes Her Career

A few years ago, I attended an unforgettable memorial service at a Florida nursing home. Person after person rose to eulogize this woman, a passionate advocate who had worked with immense self-efficacy to make a difference in her fellow residents' lives. Then

Mrs. Alonzo's son told his story. He said that he had never really known his mother. When he was young, she became schizophrenic and was shunted to an institution. Then, at age 68, Mrs. Alonzo entered the nursing home to await death. It was only in this place, where life is supposed to end, that she blossomed as a human being.

If you think this story of emotional growth is unique, read about a psychologist friend of mine who, like Jayson, finds her generativity in nursing home work.

My most amazing success entered treatment two years ago. This severely depressed resident had had an abusive marriage and suffered from enduring feelings of powerlessness and low self-esteem. I think that being sent to our institution allowed this woman to make the internal changes that she had been incapable of before. She began to look at her past and see how her experiences had shaped her poor sense of self and then to see her inner strengths. She and I formed a very close relationship.

So then she decided to work on becoming closer to her children. She had been aloof as a mother, and she told me that once her younger child had asked her to say that she loved her and she couldn't get the words out. Now, at age 89, she called this daughter, told her that she did love her and that she was sorry she couldn't say it before. Her daughters said that I had presented them with a miracle, the loving mother they always wanted. My patient made friends on the floor and became active in the residents' council. In the time we saw one another she used to tell me, "I never believed I could change at this age."

As she finished her story, my friend's eyes filled with tears: "My patient died a few months ago, and I still miss her so much."

Table 14.3 amplifies this section's messages by offering tips for choosing a nursing home. (Notice the similarities to the day-care suggestions Table 4.2 on page 122!) Now, let's offer a few wrap-up thoughts.

Table 14.3 Choosing a Nursing Home: A Checklist*

The General Milieu

- Is the setting appealing, with user-friendly features that take into account sensory and motor disabilities (e.g., carpeting on floors to prevent falling; adequate indirect lighting; dining areas that don't magnify hearing problems; no long hallways; clear differentiation between corridors)?

- Can the person have her own room, and is privacy allowed? Are there pleasant outdoor areas? Have residents decorated their living spaces?

- How many residents live here? Studies agree that smaller facilities provide better care.

- Are there good rehab facilities and enriching activities?

The Staff

- Now spend time observing and talking to the aides. Is the staff nurturing? Do they feel committed to this work? Do they feel they have too much to do? Are they happy with this organization?

- Ask about staff turnover: How many people have left within the last few months? More stability may signal better quality care.

The Residents

- If possible, interview a resident and/or a family member. What are the negatives and positives of this place?

- Is there a residents' council? Do consumers have input into how this place is run? Do older people here feel comfortable lodging complaints?

- And, if you are contemplating entering continuing care, spend a few nights living at your prospective home. Apart from everything else, it's imperative to know: *Will I fit in socially here?*

*I'm basing these suggestions on the studies I've surveyed and on my experience working in a state-of-the-art, research-based facility when I was younger. However, in evaluating any nursing home, your first step *must be* to consult the Web site sponsored by the U.S. Department of Health and Human Services, which offers a five-star ranking system evaluating each nursing home's quality of care.

Wrapping Up Age-Related Physical Decline

Dealing with ADL impairments is a vital social challenge facing our rapidly aging world. As we know, we can't count on science to magically cure the disabilities inherent to surviving beyond our "expiration date." We must prepare for the onslaught of frail elderly *now*.

A strong lesson of this chapter is to avoid the natural temptation to infantilize people when they develop old-age frailties. Autonomy—that basic human drive—is just as critical at age 92 as it is at age 2!

And just like in our youngest years, a second lesson is that the United States has a long way to go in providing optimal environments to people approaching the upper end of life. The wider world is not designed with older adults in mind. Assisted living and continuing care, like excellent child day care, is available only to well-off people. Medicaid reimbursements for nursing home care are dreadfully low (O'Shea Carney & Norris, 2017). Do we really want to honor our aged mothers and fathers by letting them suffer dismal care, just when their ranks are exploding and they need us most?

On a positive note, the story of the nursing home resident who got it together emotionally shows just how much growth can occur in the final years of life. It also enriches Erikson's masterful ideas that have guided our lifespan tour: It's never too late to accomplish developmental tasks that we may have missed. People can find their real identity (or authentic self), fulfill their generativity, and so reach integrity in their final months of life!

In the next chapter, I'll continue this theme of inner development and also stress the crucial importance of self-efficacy and control as I focus directly on life's endpoint—death.

Tying It All Together

1. You are a geriatric counselor, and an 85-year-old woman and her family come to your office for advice about the best arrangement for her care. Match the letter of each item below with the number of the suggestion that would be most appropriate if this elderly client:

   a. is affluent, worried about living alone, and has no ADL problems.
   b. has ADL impairments and is living with her family—who want to continue to care for her at home.
   c. has instrumental ADL impairments (but can perform basic self-care activities), can no longer live alone, and has a good amount of money.
   d. has basic ADL impairments.
   e. is beginning to have ADL impairments, lives alone, and has very little money (but does not qualify for Medicaid).

      (1.) a continuing-care retirement facility
      (2.) an assisted-living facility
      (3.) a day-care program
      (4.) a nursing home
      (5.) There are no good alternatives you can suggest; people in this situation must struggle to cope at home.

2. Joey and Jonelle realize that their mother needs to go to a nursing home. Which two likely comments can you make about this mother's situation—and nursing homes in general?

   a. No one in the family can take her in.
   b. Medicare will completely cover her expenses.
   c. The quality of the facilities available to her may vary greatly.
   d. The staff at her nursing home will hate their jobs.

3. Devise some creative strategies to care for the frail elderly in their homes.

Answers to the Tying It All Together questions can be found at the end of this chapter.

SUMMARY

Tracing Physical Aging

Normal aging changes progress into **chronic disease** and ultimately, during the old-old years, may result in **activities of daily living (ADL) problems,** either less incapacitating **instrumental ADL problems** or **basic ADL problems** (troubles with basic self-care).

Some gurus predict that we are about to extend our maximum human lifespan (currently about a century), especially because underfeeding can extend the maximum lifespan of rats. But gerontologists believe this goal is unlikely, because the cascade of faults involved in human aging ensure that our bodies must give out at about the century mark. Pushing the normal lifespan beyond our maximum lifespan can have unwanted effects.

Socioeconomic status predicts how quickly we age and die, as shown by the wide life expectancy differences between the developed and developing worlds. The **socioeconomic health gap** refers to the fact that, within each nation, people who are affluent live healthier for a longer time. Increasing income inequalities have exacerbated this gap in the United States, although low-income people live longer in communities when they have more well-educated neighbors. A variety of negative socioeconomic forces, starting from birth, work in tandem to promote early disability and death. In contrast, close attachments and being well educated enhances longevity and health.

Gender also affects aging. Men tend to die quickly at younger ages of heart attacks and women survive longer but live more disabled. Gerontologists are now focused on improving the **health span,** our years of healthy life. Although physical problems are the predictable price of living far into old age, improving children's lives and constructing caring communities may have dramatic health payoffs during the last half of life.

Sensory-Motor Changes

The classic age-related vision problems—**presbyopia** (impairments in near vision), difficulties seeing in dim light, and problems with glare—are caused by a rigid, cloudier lens. Modifying lighting can help compensate for these losses. Cataracts, the endpoint of a cloudy lens, can be easily treated, although other major age-related vision impairments can cause a more permanent loss of sight. Don't overprotect visually impaired loved ones. Encourage people to visit a low-vision center for help.

The common old-age hearing impairment **presbycusis** limits a person's contact with the human world. As exposure to noise promotes this selective loss for high-pitched tones, men are at higher risk of having hearing handicaps, especially at younger ages. To help a hearing-impaired person, limit low-pitched background noise and speak distinctly—but avoid **elderspeak,** the impulse to talk to the older person like a baby. For your own future hearing, protect yourself against excessive noise. While hearing aids have improved dramatically, older people are still often reluctant to get this simple device because it symbolizes old age.

"Slowness" in later life is due to age-related changes in **reaction time** and skeletal conditions such as osteoarthritis and **osteoporosis** (thin, fragile bones). Osteoporosis is a special concern because falling and breaking a hip is a major reason for entering a nursing home. As mobility is crucial to late-life independence, older people should modify their homes to reduce the risk of falls.

Although the elderly drive less often, accident rates rise sharply among drivers over age 75. While operating cars demands many sensory and motor skills, older people are reluctant to give up their cars, and governments are equally averse to spell out driver age limits because driving signals a dramatic loss of independence. Modifying the driving environment and, especially, developing a driver-free society is critical today.

Neurocognitive Disorders (NCDs, Popularly Called *Dementia*)

Major neurocognitive disorder, or **dementia,** is the label for any illness involving serious declines in cognitive functioning. The two illnesses that cause these symptoms are **Alzheimer's disease,** defined by neural atrophy accompanied by **senile plaques** and **neurofibrillary tangles,** and **vascular neurocognitive disorder,** or **vascular dementia,** caused by small strokes. These diseases typically erupt during the old-old years and progress gradually, ultimately causing the person to lose all functions. Several genetic configurations, especially the APOE-4 marker, predict developing Alzheimer's disease at a relatively young age.

To prevent the accumulation of the plaques (and thereby ward off the illness before it sets in), scientists have uncovered biomarkers predicting later Alzheimer's. Today, Alzheimer's cannot be prevented or cured, although exercise may delay its onset. The key is to make environmental modifications to keep the person safe—and understand that older adults with these problems are still people. Caregivers' accounts and the testaments of people in Alzheimer's early stages offer profiles in human courage.

Options and Services for the Frail Elderly

Although, traditionally, older people lived in multigenerational households, with a built-in family support network for when they became frail, even societies historically most committed to family care (such as China and Japan) now need Western options for dealing with disabled older adults. In the United States, the major **alternatives to institutionalization—continuing-care retirement communities, assisted-living facilities, day-care programs,** and **home health services**—are typically costly and not covered by **Medicare.** We need services to help people with disabilities who are not wealthy and do not need the intense care of a nursing home.

Being female, very old, and not having loved ones to take the person in are the main risk factors for entering **nursing homes,** or **long-term-care facilities.** While nursing homes vary in quality, even the best institutions severely limit an autonomous life. Although the **certified nursing assistant or aide,** the main caregiver, is poorly paid, people can find tremendous gratification in nursing home work. Preserving autonomy in the face of ADL impairments and providing better services for frail elders is a critical U.S. need. People can develop as human beings even in a nursing home, and, during their final years—or months—of life, reach Eriksonian milestones they may have missed earlier in life.

KEY TERMS

ADL (activities of daily living) problems, p. 406

alternatives to institutionalization, p. 427

Alzheimer's disease, p. 422

assisted-living facility, p. 428

basic ADL limitations, p. 406

certified nurse assistant or aide, p. 430

continuing-care retirement community, p. 428

day-care program, p. 428

elderspeak, p. 416

health span, p. 411

home health services, p. 428

instrumental ADL problem, p. 406

lens, p. 413

major neurocognitive disorder (NCD, dementia), p. 421

Medicare, p. 427

neurofibrillary tangles, p. 423

normal aging changes, p. 406

nursing home/long-term-care facility, p. 429

osteoporosis, p. 417

presbyopia, p. 413

presbycusis, p. 415

reaction time, p. 417

senile plaques, p. 423

socioeconomic health gap, p. 410

vascular neurocognitive disorder (vascular dementia), p. 422

ANSWERS TO **Tying It All Together** QUIZZES

Tracing Physical Aging

1. b

2. Marjorie has *instrumental ADL* problems, and Sara has *basic ADL* problems.

3. Tell Anya that physical aging has such complex causes that finding any single life-extension intervention will be virtually impossible. Moreover, even if we can replace individual body parts, such as our heart, other vital organs such as our kidneys are programmed to wear out. The fact that only a tiny percentage of twenty-first-century babies are projected to live to 100 makes it unlikely that her child—or any child—can live to 200.

4. Nico and Hiromi are both correct, because although women live longer (meaning that they must be healthier), they also live "sicker" (meaning that they are more apt to be ill) throughout adulthood.

5. Sonia would ask about the following: the person's gender; current SES, in particular, years of school; close attachments; the educational makeup of her community; being born premature and living in poverty during the first years of life; whether that individual is Latino.

Sensory-Motor Changes

1. lens; cataract; can

2. d

3. a., c., and e. (Suggestions b. and d. will make grandma's eyesight worse.)

4. Tell Andres that depriving older people of the chance to drive robs them of their independence; therefore, it can cause depression and provoke later functional declines.

Neurocognitive Disorders (NCDs, Popularly Called *Dementia*)

1. The illnesses are Alzheimer's disease, involving the deterioration of the neurons and their replacement with senile plaques and tangles, and vascular neurocognitive disorder, which

involves small strokes. (Grandma, not infrequently, may have both illnesses.)

2. a.

3. The main problem scientists face is diagnosing cognitive problems before they progress to the disease stage—so that we can develop treatments to ward off the illness. Tell the worried senators that they should start a fitness regimen now! While we don't have definitive evidence, exercise may help stave off Alzheimer's disease.

4. d.

Options and Services for the Frail Elderly

1. a., 1; b., 3; c., 2; d., 4; e., 5

2. a. and c

3. Here, you can use your own creativity. My suggestions: (1) Institute a program whereby people get cash incentives to care for frail elders in their homes. (2) Build small, intergenerational living communities, with a centrally located home option specifically for the frail elderly. Residents who buy houses here would commit to taking care of the older adults in their midst. (3) Set up a Web site, matching older people who have a spare room with area college students in need. Young people would live rent-free in exchange for helping the older person with cooking and shopping. (4) Establish a national scholarship program (perhaps called the "Belsky Grant"!) that would pay your tuition and living expenses if you commit to caring for frail elders in the community.

Endings

Now that we have reached the end of our lifespan journey, it's time to focus on life's final chapter (death) and reflect on what we've learned.

Chapter 15—**Death and Dying** is actually a perfect finale to this lifespan tour because, not only does this milestone end our personal lives, but death is the one milestone that occurs at every life stage. How have death attitudes and practices changed throughout history, and what do people (and their grieving loved ones) feel as they deal with this final "act"? How has the health-care system approached the terminally ill, and what can we do to make dying more humane? These concerns lead into that ethical issue: strategies for taking control of when we die.

In **Final Thoughts**, I'll reflect on my own passions, as I explain what has made textbook writing the finest person–environment fit for me.

Left: Image Source Plus/Alamy

CHAPTER 15

Death and Dying

I was getting in the car to drive to work when my wife, Amy, screamed, "Stewart! Come listen to the news!" We figured out quickly that it rammed into the Twin Towers right about the floor where Mom worked, the 96th. When the first building came down, we knew for sure that she had died. With a normal death, you prepare for the grieving process. This kind of death leaves you in total shock. I keep mentally playing back the events. Mom (typical, for her) had gone into work early so she could leave for a dentist appointment. If she'd been a less responsible person, she would not have been at her desk at 8:46. The other weird thing is that the whole country feels they own pieces of this tragedy and need to constantly remind you about it. So it doesn't go away.

My mom didn't have young children, but she was looking forward to retirement, to being a grandmother, and so she was cheated of all those things. Not only did she die in this horrible way—she died at an unacceptably early age.

. . .

In his seventies, my father seemed immortal. While he often joked about being an "old man," he had no major infirmities. At age 81, mortality hit. For a few months, Dad had been listless—not his old self, looking old. Then came the unforgettable call: "The doctor says that it's cancer of the liver. Jan, I'm going to die."

Because medicine never admits defeat, the plan was three rounds of chemotherapy, punctuated by "recovery" at home. The doctor said, "Maybe we can lick this thing," but the treatments were agonizing. Worse yet, recovery never happened. My father got weaker. After a few months, he could barely walk. Then, before going into the hospital for the third round, my mother called: "Last night we cried together and decided not to continue. We're calling in hospice. I think it's time for you to come down." My father had two more weeks to live.

A day or two before you die, you slip into a coma. It's the preceding week or two that seems to last for years. Everyone has been summoned to bustle around a train that cannot be derailed. Yes, you can talk, but what do you say? My father was never a verbal man. Then, as if on cue, the disease picks up speed. From the wheelchair to becoming bedridden, the voice that mutates into a whisper, followed by waiting . . . for what? You force yourself to be at the bedside when the breathing gets slow and rattled, but you are terrified. You have never seen a person die. You don't know how things will go. Above all, you hope that things go quickly. You can't stand to see your father suffer anymore.

My father died in the "normal" late-twentieth-century way. Although we knew nothing about how people die, we had plenty of time to plan for the event. Dad's death came at the "right" time, at the end of a long life. The kind of death Stewart's mother faced on September 11, 2001, was horrifying, unexpected—outside the norm. How does death *really* happen today, compared to dying in centuries past?

Left to right from top left photo: Petrol/Getty Images, KIYOKO FUKUDA/a.collectionRF/amana images RF/Getty Images, Karel Noppé/Alamy Stock Photo, Ryan McVay/Getty Images, Julia Sjöberg/Folio Images/Alamy Stock Photo, Rick Gomez/Getty Images, SpeedKingz/Shutterstock, Stockbyte/Getty Images, Juanmonino/E+/Getty Images, Jupiterimages/Getty Images, Johnny Greig/Getty Images, Gerardo Ricardo López/Getty Images

LEARNING OUTCOMES

- List three pathways to death.
- Describe changes throughout history in attitudes about dying.
- Compare the Hmong approach to contemporary Western death practices.

Pathway 1: Death occurs suddenly
Examples: heart attack in a person who seems healthy, any accidental death

Pathway 2: Death occurs after steady decline
Examples: cancer diagnosed in an advanced stage

Pathway 3: Dying is a long and erratic process
Examples: congestive heart failure, cancer that repeatedly goes into remission and comes back

TIME

FIGURE 15.1: Three pathways to death: Although some people die suddenly, the pattern in blue and especially that in yellow are the most common pathways by which people die today.

For most of human history, death was ever present—"up close and personal"—and occurred in the midst of normal life. Here is an eighteenth-century painting entitled "The Dying Request," in which a dying young woman is offering her final words to her spouse.

Setting the Context

Today, as Figure 15.1 suggests, our pathways to death take different forms (Field, 2009). As happened most dramatically in the World Trade Center tragedy, roughly 1 out of every 6 or 7 people in developed nations dies without warning—due to accidents or, more often, from a sudden, fatal, age-related event such as a heart attack or stroke (Enck, 2003; see the red line in Figure 15.1). My father's death fit the pattern when illnesses such as cancer are discovered at an advanced stage. Here, as the blue line shows, a person is diagnosed with a fatal disease and steadily declines.

The prolonged, erratic pattern, shown in yellow, is by far the most common dying pathway in our age of extended chronic disease. After developing cancer—or, like my husband, congestive heart failure (see the Experiencing the Lifespan Box on page 444)—people battle that condition for years, helped by medical technology, until death occurs.

So today, deaths in affluent countries occur slowly. They are dominated by medicine. They have a protracted, uncertain course (Burg, 2018; Field, 2009; Harris and others, 2013). For most of history, people died in a different way.

A Short History of Death

She contracted a summer cholera. After four days she asked to see the village priest, who came and waited to give her the last rites. "Not yet, M. le Curé, I'll let you know when the time comes." Two days later: "Go . . . tell M. le Curé to bring . . . Extreme Unction."

(reported in Walter, 2003, p. 213)

As you can see in this nineteenth-century description of the death of a French peasant woman, before modern medicine, death arrived quickly. People let nature take its course. There was nothing they could do. Dying was familiar, predictable, and normal. It was embedded in daily life (Wood & Williamson, 2003).

According to the historian Philippe Ariès (1974, 1981), while life in the Middle Ages was horrid and "wild," death was often "tame." Famine, childbirth, and infectious disease ensured that death was an expected presence throughout the lifespan. People died, as they lived, in view of the community and were buried in the churchyard in the center of town.

During the eighteenth and nineteenth centuries, death began to move off center stage when—because of fears about disease—villagers relocated burial sites to cemeteries outside of town (Kastenbaum, 2004). Then a more dramatic change took place during the early twentieth century, when medical science successfully waged war against disease. The conquest of many infectious illnesses moved dying toward the end of the lifespan, relocating it to old age (Zaman and others, 2017).

As modern medicine took over, the scene of death shifted to hospitals and nursing homes. So the act of dying was disconnected from life. Because hospitals billed themselves as places of recovery, death became a symptom of scientific failure. When people took their last breaths, embedded in the recesses of intensive care, health-care workers quickly erased all signs of death's presence, as they shrouded the body and shipped it to be spruced up in the funeral home (Kastenbaum, 2004). According to one social critic, by the mid-twentieth century, death had become disgusting, abnormal, never discussed (Gorer, 1965).

About 40 years ago, society shifted course (Zaman and others, 2017). First, doctors did a total turnaround from the practice of concealing a devastating diagnosis—never mentioning, for instance, the "C word"—in favor of telling people, "Yes, it's cancer, and there is not much we can do." (Now that we meticulously track each symptom on the Internet, physicians foolish enough not to be upfront about a patient's illness could be charged with malpractice or worse!) Then, our health-care system fully confronted the reality that "yes, people die," by developing structures to ease our passage through the terminal phase of life. We urge everyone to do their part, by documenting in writing how they want their final act to proceed.

Cultural Variations on a Theme

While mainstream society stresses full disclosure and planning for our "final act," death attitudes differ from group to group even in the developed world. To demonstrate this point, let's scan the practices of a culture for whom dying remains up close and personal, but where death is never openly discussed: the Hmong.

The Hmong, persecuted for centuries in China and Southeast Asia, migrated to North America after the Vietnam War and number close to a million U.S. residents today. According to Hmong tradition, the mere mention of dying "will unlock the gate of evil spirits," so when a person enters the terminal phase of life, no one is permitted to discuss that fact. However, when death is imminent, the family becomes intimately involved. Relatives flock around and dress the ill person in the traditional burial garment—a black robe or suit. After death arrives, they lovingly wash and groom the corpse, preparing it to be viewed.

If, contrary to Hmong custom, the person dies in a hospital, it's crucial that the body *not* be immediately sent to the morgue. The family congregates at the bedside to wail and caress the corpse for hours. Then, after a lavish four-day funeral ceremony, during which the body remains in view, the deceased is lovingly dressed in warm clothing to guard against the cold, and the feet are encased in special blue shoes for the journey to the next world. At the gravesite, the coffin is reopened for a final viewing before being permanently closed (Gerdner and others, 2007). Could you participate in these activities, by giving your relative the hands-on care that the Hmong and other societies routinely provided throughout history to prepare loved ones for the grave?

In this chapter, I'll explore what dying is like in the twenty-first-century developed world—an age of open communications, extended chronic disease, and intense attention to the need to provide quality end-of-life care (Zaman and others, 2017). First, I'll examine the feelings of the dying person; then, I'll turn to the health-care system and, finally, return to the person to tackle those touchy issues related to controlling the timing of when we die. As you just saw with the Hmong, however, it's crucial to remember that—just as dying pathways differ—with death and dying *in general*, diversity is the main theme. We all bring unique, *equally* valid perspectives to that ultimate event of human life.

Even today, small pockets of the U.S. population adopt an intensely hands-on approach to death. Here, you can see phase one in the carefully orchestrated days-long Hmong funeral ceremony—the body, dressed in its traditional garments, being caressed by distraught family members.

Darren Hauck/Getty Images

Tying It All Together

1. Imagine that you were born in the seventeenth or eighteenth century. Which statement about your dying pathway would be *false*?

   a. You would probably have died quickly of an infectious disease.
   b. You would have died in a hospital.
   c. You would have seen death all around you from a young age.
   d. You would probably have died at a relatively young age.

2. If you follow the typical twenty-first-century pattern, as you approach death, you can expect to decline (*quickly/ slowly and erratically*) due to (*an accident/ an age-related chronic disease*).

3. Ella says today we live in a death-denying society. Amanda argues, "That's not true. We are paying far more attention to the experience of dying than in the past." Who is most correct, and why?

Answers to the Tying It All Together questions can be found at the end of this chapter.

Answers to the Tying It All Together questions can be found at the end of this chapter.

LEARNING OUTCOMES

- Critique Kübler-Ross's theory.
- Outline the qualities involved in having a good death.
- Describe feelings, issues, and helpful coping strategies when a child dies.

Kübler-Ross's stage theory of dying
The landmark theory, developed by psychiatrist Elisabeth Kübler-Ross, that people who are terminally ill progress through five stages in confronting death: denial, anger, bargaining, depression, and acceptance.

The Dying Person

How do people react when they are diagnosed with a fatal illness? What are their emotions as they struggle with this devastating news? The first person to scientifically study these topics was a young psychiatrist named Elisabeth Kübler-Ross.

Kübler-Ross's Stages of Dying: Description and Critique

While working as a consultant at a Chicago hospital during the 1960s, Kübler-Ross became convinced that the health-care system was neglecting the emotional needs of the terminally ill. As part of a seminar, she got permission to interview dying patients. Many people, she found, were relieved to talk about their diagnosis and knew that their condition was terminal, even though the medical staff and family members had tried to conceal that fact. Kübler-Ross published her discovery that open communication was important to dying people in a slim best-seller called *On Death and Dying*, which ushered in a revolution in the care of the terminally ill.

Kübler-Ross (1969), in her **stage theory of dying,** originally proposed that we progress through five emotions in coming to terms with death: *denial, anger, bargaining, depression,* and *acceptance.* Let's now look at each emotional state.

When first given some terrible diagnosis, such as "You have advanced lung cancer," a person's immediate reaction is denial. She thinks, "There must be a mistake" and consults doctor after doctor, searching for a more favorable set of tests. When these efforts fail, denial gives way to anger.

In the anger stage, the person lashes out, bemoaning her fate, railing at other people. One patient might get enraged at a physician: "He should have picked up my illness earlier on!" Others direct their fury at a friend or family member: "Why did I get lung cancer at 50, while my brother, who has smoked a pack of cigarettes a day since he was 20, remains in perfect health?"

Eventually, this emotion yields to a more calculating one: bargaining. Now, the person pleads for more time, promising to be good if she can put off death for a bit longer. Kübler-Ross (1969) gives this example of a woman who begged God to let her live long enough to attend the marriage of her oldest son:

> The day preceding the wedding she left the hospital as an elegant lady . . . I wondered what her reaction would be when the time was up for which she had bargained. . . . the moment she returned to the hospital . . . [she] said, "Now don't forget I have another son."

(quoted on p. 83)

Then, once reality sinks in, the person gets depressed and, ultimately, reaches acceptance. By this time, the individual is quite weak and no longer feels upset, angry, or depressed. She may even look forward to the end.

Kübler-Ross deserves credit for alerting us to the fact that there is a living, breathing person inside the diagnosis "terminal cancer" or "end-stage heart disease." The problem is that her ideas were embraced in a rigid, simplistic way. Here are three reasons why we *cannot* take this theory as the final word about death.

Terminally Ill Patients Often *Don't* Want to Fully Discuss Their Situation

Many people read into Kübler-Ross's theory the idea that all ill people want to talk about impending death. This is not true! Research universally shows that both loved ones and patients have qualms about broaching this topic (Burg, 2018; Eun and others, 2017; Schulz and others, 2017). While it's easier to discuss death in the abstract—spelling out burial and funeral plans—mentioning the nitty gritty of dying risks bringing the end way too near: "When I asked my mother whether she'd want a breathing tube," one daughter commented, "mom looked horrified; and then she quickly blurted out, 'Your brother is coming to visit at 1 P.M today.'"

Patients shy away from bringing up their feelings to protect loved ones: "I've got as much as I can cope with. So I can't get her [my sister] upset . . . and then have . . . to calm her down" (quoted in McGrath, 2004, pp. 837, 839). They avoid these discussions to protect themselves: "The reason that I don't talk to anyone about my situation is that I need to have a little hope. . . . Ah, I would just like to have hope I can extend it" (quoted in Eun and others, 2017, p. 1013).

Therefore, death discussions operate like a delicate kabuki dance. *Everyone* tries to protect everyone else. And the hope that "honest," final conversations will cure festering, lifelong wounds ("Now I can tell Mom *exactly* how I felt about her preferring my brother!") doesn't pan out—and for good reason. As one daughter pointed out: "I was very torn at the end between wanting to get things off my chest and not wanting to upset him further, and ultimately decided not to say things" (quoted in Generous & Keeley, 2017, p. 167).

This makes sense: Preserving our attachment relationships is a paramount agenda when we die, just as during life.

Having loved ones pray by a bedside can offer solace and a sense of connection during a person's final days. But to be really sensitive, family members would also need to tread very gently, as many terminally ill people might not want to openly discuss impending death.

Terminally Ill Patients May Not Want to Know "The Full Truth"

Honesty from medical providers is over-rated, too. People *say* they want full disclosure: "Information is important," said one Swedish woman with cancer. "Even if you have a short time left, you have to plan this time" (quoted in Saeteren, Lindström, & Nåden, 2010, p. 814). But many patients shy away from hearing very bad news. And sensitive doctors pick up on these messages:

> "If I get a signal from a patient . . . that they are not ready to talk about it, I back off. . . . If . . . they don't want to hear about that, . . . well, I'm going to go where the patient is at."
> (quoted in Schulz and others, 2017, p. 640)

Kübler-Ross stressed full disclosure because she was railing against a late-twentieth-century death-denying culture. Now we have a more nuanced view: Yes, truth may be a *better* policy; but, above all, avoid causing people pain.

People Do Not Pass Through Stages in Adjusting to Death

The main problem, however, is that Kübler-Ross was wrong! People facing death do *not* progress emotionally in a stage-to-stage, cookie-cutter way. In fact, uncritically accepting Kübler-Ross's stages can be dangerous if it encourages us to distance ourselves from dying loved ones (Kastenbaum, 2004). Instead of understanding that becoming depressed is a reasonable reaction when facing a life-threatening illness, if friends and family see this feeling as "a phase," they might view this response as somehow not real. It's perfectly understandable for an ill person to get angry when others respond insensitively or don't call; but if we view this response through the lens of stage theory, we might dismiss these natural feelings of hurt as "predictable" signs of the anger stage.

Therefore, experts view Kübler-Ross's contributions with mixed emotions. Yes, she pioneered an important topic. But her theory encouraged its own insensitivity to the terminally ill (Kastenbaum, 2004).

The More Realistic View: Many Different Emotions; Wanting Life to Go On

People who are dying *do* get angry, bargain, deny their illness, and become depressed. However, as one psychiatrist argues, it's more appropriate to view these feelings as "a complicated clustering of intellectual and affective states, some fleeting, lasting for a moment, or a day" (quoted in Schneidman, 1976, p. 6).

Even when people "know" their illness is terminal, the awareness of "I am dying" may not penetrate in a definitive way (Groopman, 2004; Saeteren, Lindström, & Nåden, 2010). This emotional state, called **middle knowledge,** is highlighted in a description of Rachel, a 17-year-old who knew she had end-stage cystic fibrosis:

> Rachel said . . . that when she . . . die(s), she wanted to be here [the hospice] . . . , surrounded by family. . . . And then she said "but I have another way that I'd like to die . . . sitting in a rocking chair and my husband holding my hand."
>
> (quoted in Liben, Papadatou, & Wolfe, 2008, p. 858)

middle knowledge The idea that terminally ill people can know that they are dying yet at the same time not completely grasp or come to terms emotionally with that fact.

Moreover, as Rachel's final heart-wrenching comment and my earlier discussion implies, when people realize that they are close to death, an emotion that often burns strong is hope (Eun and others, 2017; Groopman, 2004; Schulz and others, 2017). If people are religious, their hope may hinge on divine intervention: "God will provide a miraculous cure." Others pin their hopes on meditation, emerging new therapies, or exercise. Another source of hope—as Kübler-Ross suggested—is the idea that the medical predictions can be wrong: "True, I have that diagnosis, but I know of cases where a doctor told a person with my illness she had six months left and she has been living for 10 years."

Hope, as you can see in the Experiencing the Lifespan box, doesn't mean hoping for a cure. It may mean wishing you survive through the summer, or live to see your wife's book published and not be bedridden before you die. It can mean hoping that your love lives on in your family, or that your life work will make a difference in the world. (Remember, that's what being generative is all about.) Contrary to what Kübler-Ross implies, even reaching acceptance has nothing to do with abandoning hope. People can understand "I'm dying" and still have future goals and plans.

Experiencing the Lifespan   Hospice Hopes

It started on a trip to Washington, David's favorite city. "Something is different with my body. I got out of breath when I took a walk around the mall." Then came the diagnosis: "You have congestive heart failure. Because your heart muscle is enlarged, fluid is accumulating around your lungs and legs. But with our medicines, you can almost certainly live—with restrictions—for some time."

During the next few years, when my husband's body became badly bloated, we periodically entered the hospital, to drain off the fluid and accumulate another cocktail of pills. Then, in May 2012, due to a side effect of the medicine, my husband went into kidney failure, and we rushed to the hospital again. Just as the frantic staff was poised to transfer David to endure another heroic intervention, our cardiologist entered the room: "I'm referring your husband to hospice," he tersely stated. "There is

nothing more we can do." We left the hospital that beautiful late spring afternoon to await death.

Those last few days turned into more than 9 months. With the help of just one pill to control his symptoms, David got much better. He was able to spend that summer and most of the fall walking around on his own. On the December day we finally needed to order a hospital bed, I served chili and chocolate chip cookies for dinner. Then, David just closed his eyes and died.

My husband's hope in hospice had been to live through the summer, enjoying nature and spending time sitting with me by the pool. He wanted to be alive to hold the third edition of this book, due in November, in his hands. He hated the idea of being bedridden during his final days. Hospice granted David all three of his final wishes.

Heart failure epitomizes that common twenty-first-century pathway to death. Patients have good days and bad days. They live for years in the shadow of death. Although extended, ultimately fatal, chronic illnesses can strike at any age (recall, for instance, the earlier quote relating to cystic fibrosis), most often, as with my husband, they occur *on time* in terms of our social clock, in our older years.

Drawing on Erik Erikson's theory, we might predict that facing death in our teens or early adult life is uniquely difficult. How can you reach integrity, or the sense that you have fulfilled your life goals, if you have not found your identity, mastered intimacy, or discovered your generative path? Because death is so appropriate at their life stage, older people don't show the classic avoidance to death-related words and phrases apparent even during middle age (De Raedt, Koster, & Ryckewaert, 2013). What do we mean by having an appropriate death?

Deprived of life as a husband and father at an off-time age seems totally "against" nature and unfair, which makes this man's death in his thirties impossibly hard.

In Search of a Good Death

Insights come from turning to religious sources. From the Old Testament (Spronk, 2004) to Hindu traditions (Gupta, 2011), religions agree that death should be celebrated after a long life. Death should be peaceful, which explains why violent deaths, like suicides or murders, are especially repellent—and why people universally reject the idea of being "tortured" by medical technology at the end of life (Enguidanos, Yonashiro-Cho, & Cote, 2013). Death is "best" when it occurs in the "homeland" (not far away), accounting for why—around the globe—people prefer to die surrounded by loved ones and reject the sanitized, impersonal dying that takes place in intensive care (Prevost & Wallace, 2009; Shih and others, 2009; Zaman and others, 2017).

A good death came to my grandmother, one beautiful summer day. Grandma, at age 98, was just beginning to get frail. One afternoon, before preparing dinner for her visiting great-grandchildren (which she insisted on doing), she got in her car to drive to the hairdresser and—on leaving the driveway—was hit by an oncoming car. Of the eight people involved in the accident, no one was hurt but Grandma, who was killed instantly. They said she never felt any pain.

Given that our chance of being killed at our doorstep, without frailties at the limit of human life, are almost nil, how can we expand on the previous criteria to spell out specific dimensions of a good death? Decades ago, one psychologist offered these guidelines (Corr, 1991–1992):

The principle that a good death must occur "near the homeland" is embedded in many religious traditions. This nineteenth-century depiction shows a Hindu funeral ceremony, with the deceased making his final passage surrounded by loving community members while being carried ceremoniously to the grave.

1. We want to minimize our physical distress, to be as free as possible from debilitating pain.

2. We want to maximize our psychological security, reduce fear and anxiety, and feel in control of how we die.

3. We want to enhance our relationships and be close emotionally to the people we care about.

4. We want to foster our spirituality and believe there was integrity and purpose to our lives.

Minimize pain and fear; be close to loved ones; enhance spirituality; feel that life has meaning—these are the themes from the studies that poll caregivers about the qualities involved in a loved one's "good death" (Downey and others, 2010; Karlsson & Berggren, 2011; Leung and others, 2010; Shih and others, 2009). Yes, a strong religious faith can offer people peace in their final days (Braam, Klinkenberg, & Deeg, 2011). But it's not necessary to believe in an afterlife or any religion. Actually, in one study, the main dimension that was related to feeling comfortable about dying was having a sense of purpose in life (Ardelt & Koenig, 2006).

So again, Erikson seems right in saying that the key to accepting death is fulfilling our life tasks and, especially, our generative missions. And in Erikson's (1963) poetic words, appreciating that one's "individual life is the accidental coincidence of . . . one lifecycle within . . . history" (p. 268) can be important in embracing death, too:

> Barbara [who had a day to live] turned on the lamp.... "Are you afraid?" I asked. "You know, . . . I have . . . comforting thoughts. . . . When fear starts to creep up . . . , I conjure up the idea that millions of people passed away before me. . . . if they . . . did it, so can I."

> (quoted in Groopman, 2004, pp. 137–138)

What are your priorities for a good death? Table 15.1 offers an expanded checklist based on the principles in this section, to help you evaluate your top-ranking death goals.

Table 15.1: Evaluating Your Priorities for a Good Death: A Checklist

When you think about dying, rank how important each of these criteria are as: (1) of utmost importance; (2) important, but not primary; or (3) relatively unimportant.

_____ 1. Not being a burden to my family.

_____ 2. Being at peace with death—that is, not being anxious about dying.

_____ 3. Not being in physical pain.

_____ 4. Having control over where I die—that is, being able to choose whether to die at home or in the hospital.

_____ 5. Having control over *how* I die—that is, being able to choose whether to be kept alive through medical interventions, or end my life if I am terminally ill and in great pain.

_____ 6. Feeling close to loved ones.

_____ 7. Feeling close to God.

_____ 8. Feeling that I have fulfilled my mission on earth or made a difference in the world.

Do your top-ranking priorities for dying tell you anything about your priorities for living?

Hot in Developmental Science: Evolving Ideas About Grieving

Death is just the first chapter in the survivor's ongoing life story. Although I discussed bereavement in the widowhood section of Chapter 13, let's now focus on how both psychologists and the public expect that universal experience to proceed (see Jordan & Litz, 2014; Penman and others, 2014).

In the first months after a loved one dies, people are absorbed in mourning, crying, perhaps having trouble eating and sleeping. They might be ruminating about their loved one, carrying around reminders, sharing stories, browsing photos, focusing on the person's last days. Some people literally sense their loved one's physical presence in the room (Keen, Murray, & Payne, 2013). Then, after about six months, we expect mourners to recover in the sense of reconnecting to the world (Jordan & Litz, 2014). People still care deeply about their loved one. The person's memory can be evoked at special times such as anniversaries. But this mental image becomes incorporated into the mourner's identity as that person travels through life.

Grief patterns, however, are shaped by each culture's unique norms (Neimeyer, Klass, & Dennis, 2014). In previous eras, as I suggested in Chapter 13, we expected widows to mourn for life. There are surprising variations in normal grieving today. Sometimes, people do their mourning *before* a person's death, such as when the doctor refers a loved one to hospice or after a diagnosis of Alzheimer's disease. While we are tempted to accuse these people of being callous ("She went to that party right after her mother died! She hasn't even cried much!"), you might be surprised to know many bereaved adults don't feel intense distress even during the first few months after a loved one dies (Boerner, Mancini, & Bonanno, 2013).

But suppose it's been more than a year and your relative still cries continually, feels life is meaningless, and seems incapable of constructing a new life. Can grieving last *overly* long?

Very cautiously, the framers of the American Psychiatric Association's *Diagnostic and Statistical Manual* answer yes. When the person's symptoms continue unabated or become more intense after six months to a year, and that individual shows no signs of reconnecting with the world, mental-health workers can diagnose a condition labeled **persistent complex bereavement-related disorder.**

This diagnosis is controversial, in part because it risks reclassifying that normal event of mourning as a pathological state. Furthermore, aren't some deaths so "bad" that prolonged grief is normal—for instance, if a loved one died violently, or you face the tragedy of outliving your child? 🕮

persistent complex bereavement-related disorder Controversial new diagnosis, appearing in the most recent of the American Psychiatric Association's *Diagnostic and Statistical Manual,* in which the bereaved person still shows intense symptoms of mourning, or an increase in symptoms six months to a year after a loved one's death.

Mourning a Child

When I worked in a nursing home, I realized that a child's death can be more upsetting than any other loss. Even if parents eventually construct a fulfilling life, after a child dies, people feel they enter an altered state of being (Denhup, 2017). Listen to Joan, 13 years after her losing her son:

> There is . . . line zero . . . before Joshua died . . . and [after]. . . . There is nothing that . . . hasn't changed.
>
> (p. 352)

And Emma, whose daughter was killed 41 years ago, summed up why parental bereavement never fully ends:

> I'm always thinking . . ."if she were here we would do this or this" . . . you never go back to . . . normal.
>
> (p. 353)

A child's death may evoke powerful feelings of survivor guilt: "Why am I still alive?" If the death occurred suddenly due to accident, there is disbelief and possibly guilt at having failed in one's mission as a parent: "I couldn't protect my baby!" (See Cole & Singg, 1998.) If the death was expected—for instance, a child died of cancer—parents have still lost their futures. They must cope with their anger that an innocent son or daughter had to suffer, unfairly robbed of life. The problem is that a child's death can never be really "good," because this *off-time* event shakes our worldview of the universe as predictable and fair (Neimeyer, Klass, & Dennis, 2014). What helps to mute the pain?

Researchers find that parents are more apt to get (partial) closure if they discuss what is happening with their child during the final weeks—but only if a son or daughter is older and able to understand death (Kreicbergs and others, 2004). In contrast, avoiding that topic is apt to produce enduring regrets:

> I wish I had him back so that we could hug and kiss and say goodbye [said one anguished mother]. We never said good-bye . . . there was no ending, no finish. . . . Yet he never took the lead . . . he never said, "Ma, I'm dying."
>
> (quoted in Wells-di Gregorio, 2009, p. 252)

Moreover, now we know that, when a child dies, the simplistic (so-called) helpful advice to "just move on" can't work. Adjusting may *depend* on mentally keeping a son or daughter alive (Albuquerque, 2017).

> I talk to her . . . every night. . . . I just say . . . mommy is so proud of you.
>
> I'd . . . get his ashes. . . . I'll . . . kiss his little container and say good night . . . before I go to bed.
>
> (quoted in Foster and others, 2011, pp. 427, 428, 429, 432)

> I went to the hospital to give encouragement to a mother whose son was dying. . . . This is the way I honor Matais . . . I immortalized him by working as a volunteer. Matais is immortalized in the things I do, in the good, in the beautiful things.
>
> (adapted from Vega, Rivera, & González, 2014, p. 171)

Actually, recovering from terribly unfair deaths depends on finding new meaning in one's disrupted life story, and so restoring the idea that the universe is predictable and fair (Neimeyer, Klass, & Dennis, 2014). Grieving parents report they turned the corner when they used their tragedy as a *redemption sequence*. Some families find solace in donating their child's organs to help others survive, or they may adopt that person's life passions, for instance by advocating for environmental change. As in the example above, parents may devote their lives to counseling families with an ill child (Vega, Rivera, & González, 2014). People transform bad deaths into love by working at suicide hotlines or rallying against gun violence. As one nationwide study tracking bereaved parents showed, the main predictor of adapting well is becoming active in the world (Infurna & Luthar, 2017). But acting in the world doesn't mean leaving a beloved child behind.

If a mother can get comfort from her spouse, and advocate for a cure for her baby's disease, she may come to terms with this unfair, tragic death.

The other important predictor of adjusting, this research revealed, was "social support"; specifically, having someone who understands how you feel (Infurna & Luthar, 2017)— which may explain why, in interviews, many couples report that this tragedy strengthened their marital bond (Albuquerque, 2017; Dyregrov & Dyregov, 2017): As one grieving mother pointed out: "There is one thing we have together. . . . I . . . understand his pain just like he . . . understands mine" (quoted in Albuquerque, 2017, p. 1822).

Understanding doesn't mean talking about one's loss, but connecting in deeper ways. One wife reported that she and her husband both spent hours sitting in their deceased child's room, but doing their own things:

> "We often understand each other without saying one word."
>
> (quoted in Hooghe, Rosenblatt, & Rober, 2017, p. 7)

Because grief comes in waves, spouses use their better days to support a mate.

> "Since my daughter died . . . we have never been down-hearted at the same time. There is always one of us who is . . . better and can pull the other up."
>
> (quoted in Albuquerque and others, 2017, p. 1821)

Clearly, a child's death can break a marriage and life apart. But these quotations offer lessons for how to adjust to any loss: Keep your connection to loved ones strong. Realize that sometimes the best comfort comes from not talking, but showing you care in other ways. Draw on your memories to enrich other people's lives.

Design Pics/Leah Warkentin/Getty Images

Table 15.2 expands on the topic of bad deaths by exploring another off-time loss—children's grief.

Table 15.2: Bereavement at an Off-Time Age: Tips for Understanding Mourning During Childhood

Tip 1: Look to the child's developmental stage. Infants and toddlers cannot grasp the concept of death, but losing a primary caregiver at this age can disrupt the attachment response. While some 5- and 6-year-olds may master the principle that death is permanent, this understanding is fragile, and most preoperational children still believe that the dead can be revived. Temper tantrums, sleep disturbances, and regressing to more babyish behavior are common responses to experiencing a caregiver's death at this age. After reaching concrete operations—around age 9—children are capable of grasping all facets of death: It's irreversible; it's universal; all bodily functions and mental processes cease. During older childhood, and especially adolescence, complicated bereavement responses center around acting-out behaviors and internalizing symptoms such as non-suicidal self-injury and depression.

Tip 2: Look to the child's life situation. Most children are resilient, coping with the death of a loved one without showing *any* signs of prolonged grief. But symptoms of complicated bereavement are more likely when the death is sudden or violent, the child is already emotionally fragile, and the person's family life is unstable. The risk of long-term problems also accelerates when the young person has experienced multiple life losses. Moreover, because at this age upsetting feelings cannot be channeled into a redemption sequence, especially after losing a parent during childhood, mourning may occur in extended fits and starts, with fresh waves of grief appearing during milestone events years later, such as when the person graduates from college, gets married, or becomes a parent.

Tip 3: Interventions should involve a multifaceted, community-centered approach. In helping children mourn in a healthy way, everyone—from teachers to siblings to peers—can play a vital role. The keys are to listen sensitively, offer emotional support, and, rather than "ignoring" the trauma, allow the child to discuss and process his feelings of loss.

Information is from Baker & Sedney, 1996; Barnard, Moreland, and Nagy, 1999; Christ, 2000; Humphrey & Zimpfer, 2007; McCarthy & Jessop, 2005; Panagiotaki and others, 2018; Sungeun & Soyeon, 2017.

The next section explores what the health-care system is doing to provide the best possible death.

⊕ Tying It All Together

1. Sarika is arguing that Kübler-Ross's conceptions about dying are "fatally flawed." Pick out the argument she should *not* use to make her case (that is, identify the false alternative):
   a. People who are dying may not want to discuss death.
   b. People who are dying do not go through "stages" in adjusting to impending death.
   c. People who are dying simply accept that fact.

2. If your uncle has recently been diagnosed with advanced lung cancer, he should feel (*many different emotions/ only depressed/ only angry*), but in general, he should have (*hope/ a lot of anger*).

3. Pablo says he feels comforted that his beloved uncle had a good death. Which statement is *least* likely to apply to this man?
   a. Pablo's uncle died peacefully after a long life.
   b. Pablo's uncle was religious.
   c. Pablo's uncle died surrounded by loving attachment figures.
   d. Pablo's uncle felt he had achieved his missions in life.

4. Imagine you are a psychologist, and a bereaved mother or father comes to your office. Based on this section, describe your main treatment goals.

Answers to the Tying It All Together questions can be found at the end of this chapter.

The Health-Care System

- List problems with traditional hospital care for the dying.
- Describe end-of-life instruction and hospital-based palliative care.
- Outline the characteristics and concerns with hospice care.

How does the health-care system deal with death? Let's first take a critical look at two problems with hospital terminal care and then explore new options designed to confront twenty-first-century death.

What's Wrong with Traditional Hospital Care for the Dying?

To understand exactly why hospitals are apt to treat dying patients poorly, let's first turn the clock back 50 years to a study in which sociologists entered these institutions and observed how the medical staff organized "the work" of terminal care (Glaser & Strauss, 1968).

The researchers found that, when a person was admitted to the hospital, nurses and doctors set up predictions about what pattern that individual's dying was likely to follow. This implicit **dying trajectory** then governed how the staff acted.

dying trajectory The fact that hospital personnel make projections about the particular pathway to death that a seriously ill patient will take and organize their care according to that assumption.

The problem was that dying trajectories could not be predicted. When someone mistakenly categorized as "having months to live" was moved to a unit in the hospital where he was not carefully monitored, this mislabeling tended, not infrequently, to hasten death. An interesting situation happened when someone was expected to die soon and then lived on. Doctors might call loved ones to the bedside to say goodbye, only to find that the person began to improve. This "final goodbye" scenario could play out time and time again. The paradox was that if dying was "off schedule," *living* might be transformed into a negative event!

> One patient who was expected to die [quickly] had no money, but started to linger indefinitely [being paid for as a charity patient in the hospital]. . . . The . . . doctor continually had to reassure [everyone] . . . that the patient [who lived for six weeks more] would soon die.
> (quoted in Glaser & Straus, 1968, pp. 11–12)

The bottom line is that deaths don't occur according to a programmed timetable. The health-care system is structured according to the assumption that they do. This brings up the first built-in problem with hospital terminal care.

DYING IS UNPREDICTABLE. Actually, just like forecasting the weather, with death, uncertainty is built in. In one study spanning 1996 to 2010, the odds of health-care workers accurately predicting the date of a patient's dying were only fifty-fifty (Phillips, Halcomb, & Davidson, 2011). So families and health-care providers still suffer the trauma of being caught "off guard" when faced with that event (Wells-di Gregorio, 2009). When dying proceeds as expected, health-care personnel classify the death as "good." As one resident reported: "I felt good that he died in a comfortable way. . . . I just knew it would happen in 24 hours so it doesn't come as a shock" (quoted in Good and others, 2004, p. 944). In contrast, unexpected trajectories cause special pain: (Well-di Gregorio, 2009) "She came in for a bone marrow transplant to cure her [cancer] and got pulmonary toxicity and died" (p. 945).

But there is a more critical problem endemic to traditional hospital care. To understand this issue, let's explore a recent study (Virdun and others, 2017) that synthesized focus group findings in which patients and caregivers discussed what they liked and disliked about hospital care.

People who spend days in the hospital appreciate the small things: to sit at a table for meals, to have their hair shampooed. They expect staff members to respond quickly to critical physical needs: "I hate . . . [when you are in pain and] pressing the button and they do not come" (quoted in Virdun and others, 2017, p. 593).

Patients pick up on the fact when they are being treated as a number: "I can see [the staff] thinking, . . . 'Is he costing . . . too much[?]'" (p. 595).

Above all, they want to be respected as dignified human beings:

> "What . . . made the difference is that [the nurse] treated me with . . . dignity and dignity was what made it go above and beyond."
> (p. 595)

Family members echo these themes: They yearn for caring, respectful nurses and aides, health-care workers who greet loved ones rather than ignoring relatives in the room. Instead of having physicians randomly look in at unpredictable times ("Oh, sorry. You missed the doctor. He was here at 8 A.M."), families want doctors to spell out ball-park times when they will be on the floor and so are available to talk.

Institutions should devise rules that make sense: No limits on visiting dying patients; give loved ones a bit of time to mourn after the person dies in the ICU: "Well they just came in [after he died] and said to move. And I left. I didn't know what else to do"(p. 598).

Are hospitals equipped to fulfill these emotional needs? The answer is probably no, for one reason: A physician's main mission is to keep the physical body alive!

In order to provide sensitive hospital care to the dying, doctors should let frantic family members know *when* they will be making these visits, so they can spell out a patient's prognosis and treatment plan.

MEDICINE'S GOAL IS TO CURE, NOT TO PROVIDE SENSITIVE COMFORT-CARE. Today, medicine has remarkable tools to preserve life when a body wants to die. Physicians can offer nutrition to people through a tube into the stomach, bypassing the normal signal to stop eating in preparation for death. They can put patients on ventilators, machines that breathe for the person, after the lungs have given out. Caring doctors agonize about using these heroic measures (Liben, Papadatou, & Wolfe, 2008), but their mission to cure can make it difficult to resist the lure of the machines:

> We were realizing that we were going to hurt him [a 40-year-old lung cancer patient who had had multiple surgeries and several strokes] if we . . . kept trying to keep a body alive. . . . And everyone figured "give it a shot."
>
> (quoted in Good and others, 2004, p. 945)

Physicians have other pressures to persist with painful, futile treatments. They may feel "What right do I have to give up, when the family wants everything to be done?" As one study in Iran suggested, doctors may feel compelled to keep treating dying patients on religious grounds.

> "According to Islamic principles . . . , sustaining a patient's life . . . gives the opportunity of showing repentance. Suffering disease-related torments may help patients wash away . . . sins."
>
> (quoted in Aghabarary & Nayeri, 2017, p. 38)

The bottom line is that abandoning the war against death collides with the imperative to preserve life (Chapple, 1999). Therefore, to shift from the standard cure-at-all-costs approach, the health-care system needs special help.

INTERVENTIONS ❭ **Exploring the New Health-Care Specialty Called Palliative Care**

Palliative care refers to any strategy designed to promote dignified dying. Palliative care includes educating health-care personnel about how to deal with dying patients, modifying the hospital structure, or that well-known alternative to dying in a hospital: hospice care. Let's scan these first two options—those located within the traditional health-care system—one by one.

Educating Health-Care Providers

End-of-life care instruction has become a common component of medical and nursing training. By the second decade of the twenty-first century, 9 in 10 medical schools offered instruction on this topic (Dickinson, 2017). Courses cover everything from the best drugs to control pain without "knocking the person out" to the ethics of withdrawing treatment. Instruction may involve having medical students visit terminally ill patients (Gadoud and others, 2013) or workshops in which student nurses personally imagine what it is like to die (Liu and others, 2011). Classes are shifting to the site of much contemporary dying, nursing homes (Kataoka-Yahiro and others, 2017).

palliative care Any intervention designed not to cure illness but to promote dignified dying.

end-of-life care instruction Courses in medical and nursing schools devoted to teaching health-care workers how to provide the best palliative care to the dying.

Because they are the front-line professionals who spend hours with hospitalized patients, nurses are uniquely equipped to convey at these team meetings what treatments dying people and families desire.

palliative-care service
A service or unit in a hospital that is devoted to end-of-life care.

We need to do more. In one survey evaluating an academic course, nursing students reported that they craved more hands-on experiences with dying patients (Glover and others, 2017). Nurses take pride in their role as advocates, the one member of the health team who best understands patients' needs. But they, too, chafe at insensitive institutional norms: "It's like can't we keep that room vacant for just a little while [after my patients] die . . . it hurts my heart that we are not allowed to grieve" (quoted in Montgomery, Sawin, & Hendricks-Ferguson, 2017, p. 51).

Medical students report that watching doctors deal with dying patients is vital. As one person said:

"I observed an attending breaking bad news about a patient who was going to die. He was very sincere and compassionate. . . . I will carry this pearl with me as my education continues."

(quoted in Cripe and others, 2017, p. 81)

Fortunately, rather than relying on random experiences, we now have a whole health-care discipline specifically devoted to providing good deaths.

Changing Hospital Care: Palliative-Care Services

A **palliative-care service** is a hospital-based unit or program that offers sensitive end-of-life care. Here, certain groups of inpatients—for instance, old-old people with multiple chronic illnesses and people with advanced cancer—have their treatment managed by specially trained health-care workers. Patients enrolled in palliative care are not denied cure-oriented interventions (Bonebrake and others, 2010). However, as their illness becomes terminal, the vigor of life-prolonging treatments shifts to providing the best possible "comfort care."

Palliative-care workers, such as this nurse—caring for a patient who has just had a stroke—find their jobs tremendously fulfilling. In fact, health-care workers who provide palliative care rank their job satisfaction highest of all.

Families give palliative care high marks, compared to traditional end-of-life care (García-Pérez and others, 2009). Doctors who work in this new medical specialty are more apt to feel their job is a calling than do their peers in standard medical fields (Yoon and others, 2017). And, unlike what some readers may fear, having this unit at a hospital doesn't make death more likely when patients enter that institution (Cassel and others, 2010). Therefore, by the first decade of the twenty-first century, most major medical centers in the developed world provided palliative care (Dobbins, 2007).

Still, there is a compelling need: Although the percentages vary from nation to nation, an estimated one- to two-thirds of the approximately 55 million people who die each year can benefit from palliative care (Zaman and others, 2017). Moreover, virtually all of this care takes place in affluent nations. Even in Canada, one study suggested that only about 1 in 2 people who needed palliative care had access to this service before they died (Tanuseputro and others, 2017).

The most damning evidence relates to global inequities in pain control. High-income nations consume 9 in 10 morphine prescriptions—leaving out 85 percent of the world's citizens (Zaman and others, 2017). The dismal fact is that, as we move well into the twenty-first century, much of humanity will almost certainly continue to die in agony even though we have simple tools to control people's pain (Clark, 2007).

hospice movement
A movement, which became widespread in recent decades, focused on providing palliative care to dying patients outside of hospitals and especially on giving families the support they need to care for the terminally ill at home.

Still, even with the best hospital-based palliative care, patients and families don't have ultimate control. They must rely on that third party—health-care workers—to manage dying. So perhaps the best way to promote dignified deaths might be to totally remove medicine from that event.

Unhooking Death from Doctors and Hospitals: Hospice Care

This is the philosophy underlying the **hospice movement**, which gained momentum in the 1970s, along with the natural childbirth movement. Like birth, hospice activists argue, death is a natural process. We need to let this process occur in the most pain-free, natural way (Corr, 2007).

Hospice workers are skilled in techniques to minimize patients' physical discomfort. They are trained in providing a humanistic, supportive psychological environment—one that assures patients and family members that they will not be abandoned in the face of approaching death (Monroe and others, 2008).

In many developed nations, hospice care is mainly delivered in a freestanding facility called a *hospice*. The main focus of the U.S. hospice movement is on providing backup care that allows people to die with dignity at home. As occurred with my husband, and as you can read in the Experiencing the Lifespan box, multidisciplinary hospice teams go into the person's home, offering care on a part-time, scheduled, or daily basis. They provide 24-hour help in a crisis, giving family caregivers the support they need to allow a relative to spend his final days at home. Their commitment does not end after the person dies: An important component of hospice care is bereavement counseling.

Experiencing the Lifespan   Hospice Care: An Incredibly Meaningful Career

What is hospice care really like? For answers, here are some excerpts from an interview I conducted with the team (nurse, social worker, and volunteer coordinator) who manages our local hospice.

Usually, we get referrals from physicians. People may have a wide community support system or be new to the area. Even when there are many people involved, there is almost always one primary caregiver, typically a spouse or adult child.

We see our role as empowering families, giving them the support to care for their loved ones at home. We go into the home as a team to make our initial assessment: What services does the family need? We provide families training in pain control, in making beds, in bathing. A critical component of our program is respite services. Volunteers come in for part of each day. They may take the children out for pizza, or give the primary caregiver time off, or just stay there to listen.

Families will say initially, "I don't think I can stand to do this." They are anxious because it's a new experience they have never been through. At the beginning, they call a lot. Then, you watch them gain confidence in themselves. We see them at the funeral and they thank us for helping

them give their loved one this experience. Sometimes, the primary caregiver can't bear to keep the person at home to the end. We respect that, too.

The whole thing about hospice is choice. Some people want to talk about dying. Others just want you to visit, ask about their garden, talk about current affairs. We take people to see the autumn leaves, to see Santa Claus. Our main focus is: What are your priorities? We try to pick up on that. We had a farmer whose goal was to go to his farm one last time and say goodbye to his tractor. We got together a big tank of oxygen, and carried him down to his farm. We have one volunteer who takes a client to the mall.

We keep in close touch with the families for a year after, providing them counseling or referring them to bereavement groups in the community. Some families keep in contact with notes for years. We run a camp each summer for children who have lost a parent.

We have an unusually good support system among the staff. In addition to being with the families at 3 A.M., we call one another at all times of the night. Most of us have been working here for years. We feel we have the most meaningful job in the world.

Entering a U.S. hospice program is simple. It requires a physician to certify that the person is within six months of death. Home hospice care is far less expensive than hospital-based palliative care (Brick and others, 2017). Because Medicare fully covers this service, U.S. hospice is available to people on every economic rung (Sengupta and others, 2014).

As you can see in Figure 15.2 on the next page, about three decades ago the hospice movement took off. By 2009, roughly 2 in 5 U.S. deaths occurred in hospice care. What is the hospice experience like?

Charting the U.S. Hospice Experience

Imagine that your doctor has just made the pronouncement: "I'm referring your spouse or parent to hospice. There is nothing more we can do." You must deal with the shock of grieving and embark on a difficult, uncharted path. Passionate to offer your loved one this final demonstration of love, you are anxious about what lies ahead. What can you expect about the person's pathway to death?

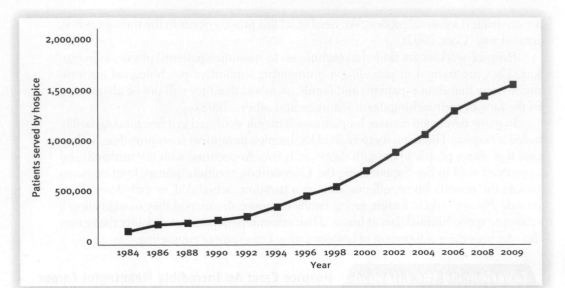

FIGURE 15.2: Patients served by hospice in the United States, 1984–2009: Notice that the number of people enrolling in hospice grew exponentially, especially during the first decade of the twenty-first century.

Data from National Hospice and Palliative Care Organization, 2011.

Although caregiving wives wouldn't have it any other way, deciding on home hospice care is likely to evoke scary feelings: Will I be able to control my beloved husband's pain?

The answer depends on the illness. If the disease is cancer, expect a more precipitous decline. With congestive heart failure or pulmonary disease, the transition to serious ADL problems is apt to be slower during the next days and weeks. Some people enter hospice bedridden and spend their final days comatose. Others, like my husband, are alert and able to perform basic ADL activities until their last moments of life (Harris and others, 2013). This variation partly explains why, although the average hospice stay is roughly two weeks, 1 in 10 U.S. patients spends close to a year in hospice care (Sengupta and others, 2014; National Hospice and Palliative Care Organization, 2018).

The uncertainty is scary, but your main fear is seeing your loved one suffer. The box full of medications you just got from the hospice team is frightening. Without nursing training, will you be able to control your family member's pain?

Actually, issues relating to pain control rank among hospice caregivers' primary concerns: Family members worry about getting their loved one addicted (Chi & Demiris, 2017), or they fear that the final powerful opioid dose hastened death (Kelley and others, 2013; Oliver and others, 2013). As one family caregiver reported: "She had chronic pain. The morphine was in an unusual bottle and I was afraid to give her too much or too little and the dropper wasn't working. It was very scary" (quoted in Kelley and others, 2013, p. 679).

These worries are realistic. In one survey, 2 out of 3 U.S. hospice providers cited medication management as their most problematic issue. One in three reported frequently encountering problems in this area as they struggled to help families provide care (Joyce & Lau, 2013).

Charting the Barriers to Hospice

This discussion brings up the hurdles to hospice. As I mentioned earlier, hope is the main emotion people feel when facing a terminal disease. Entering hospice means confronting the reality, "I am going to die." Family members (and patients) are naturally reluctant to contemplate hospice, because there may be exciting new treatments around the corner. (And they may be right! Breakthrough advances such as immunotherapy can now transform some previous death-sentence diagnoses into curable diseases.)

The same reluctance applies to the hospice gatekeeper—the physician. Doctors overwhelmingly tout the value of hospice (Prochaska and others, 2017). But, for the reasons discussed earlier, they find it difficult to initiate timely end-of-life discussions (Nedjat-Haiem and others, 2017) even though it's best to bring up this topic when a person is first hospitalized (Gieniusz and others, 2017).

Another issue relates to misconceptions about hospice. People are not aware that patients can still receive curative interventions after entering hospice, or survive for months in hospice with a fairly good quality of life (see the Experiencing the Lifespan box on page 444).

African Americans may be afraid that hospice will hasten death, due to a lifelong fear that traditional medicine has done them wrong (Rhodes and others, 2017). In one focus group study exploring these concerns, participants expressed fears of spending their final hours with people who do not share their spiritual needs: "If I am transitioning, I am transitioning to my God. . . . And someone who doesn't believe in the living God . . . cannot go through that experience with me" (quoted in Townsend, March, & Kimball, 2017, p. 35).

Most important, hospice depends on family care. Even when patients are aware that their illness is fatal, they may be less than thrilled to have loved ones care for them during their final weeks of life. Imagine being totally taken care of by your family when you have a terminal disease. You don't have any privacy. Loved ones must bathe you and dress you; they must care for your every need. You may be embarrassed about being seen naked and incontinent; you may want time alone to vent your anguish and pain. In a hospital (or inpatient hospice), care is impersonal. At home, there is the humiliation of having to depend on the people you love most for each intimate bodily act.

Care by strangers also equals care that is free from guilt. As I described earlier in this chapter, when people are approaching death, they often want to emotionally protect their loved ones—to shield them from pain. Witnessing the toll that your disease is taking on your family may multiply the pain of dying itself.

This explains why, in a rare interview study conducted with people receiving inpatient hospice care in Australia, patients' main worries centered around loved ones. Yes, people said, moving to hospice signaled a depressing step closer to death. But they were relieved to no longer be burdening their families: "My husband is . . . quiet. . . . If he feels he cannot cope, I would rather . . . give him a chance to come here, spend . . . time and then go home and get his head together," reported one woman (quoted in Broom & Kirby, 2013, p. 504). A man appreciated the privacy involved in getting care from strangers. "It's going with a little bit of dignity . . . and not in a mess" (p. 504).

This need to preserve dignity (or save face) with one's family may explain why U.S. hospice programs are rejected among the very cultural group historically most committed to family care. When researchers polled Chinese heritage older adults living in San Francisco, people reacted with horror when they learned hospice involves care at home. One woman summed up the general feelings when she said, "If I am dying I become very grumpy; it's a good idea to send me to a nursing home" (quoted in Enguidanos, Yonashiro-Cho, & Cote, 2013, p. 996).

Table 15.3 summarizes these section points in "a pros and cons of home care" chart. Now that I have surveyed the health-care options, it's time to continue our search for a "good" twenty-first-century death by returning to the dying person.

Table 15.3: Home Deaths: Pros and Cons

The case against dying at home

1. No worries about family members not being able to control your pain.
2. No fear of burdening your family with your care.
3. Privacy to vent your feelings, without family members around.
4. Avoiding the embarrassment of depending on loved ones for help with your intimate body functions.

The case in favor of dying at home

1. Avoiding having life-prolonging machines used on you.
2. Spending your final days surrounded by the people you care about most.
3. Spending your final days in the physical setting you love best.

Given these considerations, would you prefer to meet death at home?

Tying It All Together

1. List two features of traditional hospitals that interfere with providing humane terminal care.

2. Based on this section, which statement most accurately reflects physicians' approach to dying patients in traditional health care settings? (*Pick one.*) (a) Doctors give up too soon on using modern medical technologies. (b) Doctors may feel forced to use modern technologies that just "prolong" death.

3. Carol's husband has just been referred to hospice. If this couple lives in the United States (*pick FALSE statement*):

    a. Carol will be caring for her spouse at home.
    b. If Carol's spouse has heart disease, he may decline more slowly than if he has cancer.
    c. Carol may be terribly worried about her ability to control her husband's pain.
    d. Carol will spend a good deal of money on hospice care.

4. Feema is arguing that there's no way she will die in a hospital. She wants to end her life at home, surrounded by her husband and children. Using the information in this section, convince Feema of the downside to spending her final days at home.

Answers to the Tying It All Together questions can be found at the end of this chapter.

The Dying Person: Taking Control of How We Die

LEARNING OUTCOMES

- Compare different advance directives.
- Evaluate active euthanasia and physician-assisted suicide.
- Outline the principles of age-based rationing of care.

In this section, I'll explore two strategies people can use to control their final passage and so promote a "good death." The first is an option that our society strongly encourages: People should make their wishes known, in writing, about their treatment preferences should they become mentally incapacitated. The second approach is controversial: People should be allowed to get help if they want to end their lives.

Giving Instructions: Advance Directives

advance directive Any written document spelling out instructions with regard to life-prolonging treatment if individuals become irretrievably ill and cannot communicate their wishes.

living will A type of advance directive in which people spell out their wishes for life-sustaining treatment in case they become permanently incapacitated and unable to communicate.

durable power of attorney for health care A type of advance directive in which people designate a specific surrogate to make health-care decisions if they become incapacitated and are unable to make their wishes known.

An **advance directive** is any written document spelling out instructions with regard to life-prolonging treatment when people are irretrievably ill and cannot communicate their wishes. There are four types of advance directives: two that the individual drafts and two that other people, called *surrogates*, fill out when the ill person is seriously mentally impaired.

- In the **living will,** mentally competent individuals leave instructions about their treatment wishes for life-prolonging strategies should they become comatose or permanently incapacitated. Although people typically fill out living wills in order to refuse aggressive medical interventions, it is important to point out that this document can also specify that heroic measures be carried out.

- In a **durable power of attorney for health care,** individuals designate a specific person, such as a spouse or a child, to make end-of-life decisions "in their spirit" when they are incapable of making those choices known.

- A **Do Not Resuscitate (DNR) order** is filled out when the sick person is already mentally impaired, usually by the doctor in consultation with family members. This document, most often placed in a nursing home or hospital chart, stipulates that if a cardiac arrest takes place health-care professionals should not try to revive the patient.

- A **Do Not Hospitalize (DNH) order** is specific to nursing homes. It indicates that during a medical crisis a mentally impaired resident should not be transferred to a hospital for emergency care.

Advance directives have an admirable goal. Ideally, the healthy person offers a road map so that family members and doctors are not forced to guess what care that individual *might* want if he is permanently incapacitated. However, these documents can be problematic too.

One difficulty is, as I mentioned earlier, that people are naturally reluctant to contemplate death (Kermel-Schiffman & Werner, 2017). Do you or your parents have an advance directive? In the Netherlands, where people can choose to take their own lives, fewer than 1 in 10 people does (as reported in van Wijmen and others, 2014).

Interestingly, due to a vigorous public health push, polls show that most U.S. adults have some familiarity with advance directives (Kermel-Schiffman & Werner, 2017). An astonishing fraction (2 in 3) of U.S. elderly have taken the step of filling out this kind of document. But, even though they generally suffer from poorer health (Jang and others, 2017; Noh and others, 2018), elderly Puerto Ricans and Dominicans are less likely to consider advance care planning, reasoning that they will trust their future to family and rely on their faith (Boucher, 2017).

There are also serious problems with the most well-known advance directive, the living will. Because living wills are vague, these documents are subject to misinterpretations (Cicirelli, 2007): Does "no aggressive treatments" mean not putting in the feeding tube that has allowed my aunt to survive for 7 years after brain surgery? When your grandma wrote she wanted "No heroic measures," what *exactly* did she mean?

While we might think the solution would be to come up with specific checklists ("I don't want to be on a ventilator, but I do want a feeding tube"), can we expect people to make these detailed decisions? How many of you *really* know what being on a ventilator or having a feeding tube entails? Moreover, while you might say "no heroic measures" if you are healthy, your decisions might turn out to be different when you are battling a fatal disease. Therefore, the ideal strategy is to have a series of discussions with loved ones, and choose a specific family member who, in consultation with the physician, makes the final choice (see McMahan and others, 2013; van Wijmen & others, 2014).

This means the best advance directive is a durable power of attorney for health care. Granted, deciding on a single family member to carry out one's wishes can evoke jealousy ("Why did Mom choose my brother and not me?"). It doesn't ensure mistakes won't occur. Suppose after giving your so-called reliable daughter power of attorney, she elopes with a money-grubbing third husband and you realize that you made the wrong choice? Still, having a defined proxy—but making sure to sit down and regularly discuss your wishes with the family—can reduce the conflicts when you believe that Mom's suffering should not be prolonged, while your brother insists that treatment continue at all costs. These sibling disagreements are tailor-made to poison family relationships for years (or for life).

By now, some readers may be feeling uneasy—not about keeping people alive too long, but about the opposite problem: letting them die too soon. Let's ratchet up the anxiety as we move to the next step in the search for death with dignity: helping people take their own lives.

Deciding When to Die: Active Euthanasia and Physician-Assisted Suicide

> Mrs. Boyles was terminally ill, in excruciating pain and begged Dr. Cox to end her life. . . . As an act of compassion, he injected potassium chloride (a fatal drug). . . . Told to "disregard the doctor's motives" a jury . . . convicted Dr. Cox."
>
> (as reported in Begley, 2008; quotes are from pp. 436 and 438)

How do you feel about this doctor's decision and the jury's judgment? If you were like many people in Great Britain, you would have been outraged, believing that Dr. Cox was a hero because he acted on his mission to relieve human suffering rather than follow an unjust law.

Do Not Resuscitate (DNR) order A type of advance directive filled out by surrogates (usually a doctor in consultation with family members) for impaired individuals, specifying that if they go into cardiac arrest efforts should not be made to revive them.

Do Not Hospitalize (DNH) order A type of advance directive inserted in the charts of impaired nursing home residents, specifying that in a medical crisis patients should not be transferred to a hospital for emergency care.

Experts advise older people to regularly have frank conversations with family when they prepare a durable power of attorney for health care.

passive euthanasia
Withholding potentially life-saving interventions that might keep a terminally ill or permanently comatose patient alive.

active euthanasia A deliberate health-care intervention that helps a patient die.

physician-assisted suicide A type of active euthanasia in which a physician prescribes a lethal medication to a terminally ill person who wants to die.

Let's first make some distinctions. **Passive euthanasia**, or withdrawing potentially life-saving interventions, such as a feeding tube, is perfectly legal. (That's what advance directives specify.) But Dr. Cox's response qualified as **active euthanasia**— taking *action* to help a person die. Active euthanasia is illegal in every nation except Belgium, Luxembourg, and the Netherlands. However, as of this writing (2018), a variation on active euthanasia called **physician-assisted suicide** is legal in Switzerland, Germany, Canada, Oregon, Montana, Vermont, California, and Washington. Under strict conditions, at a terminally ill patient's request, physicians can prescribe a medication the individual can personally take to induce death.

As the judge in the above trial spelled out, the distinction between the two types of euthanasia lies in intentions (Dickens, Boyle, &Ganzini, 2008). When we withdraw some heroic measure, we don't specifically wish for death. When doctors give a patient a lethal dose of a drug or prescribe that medicine, they *want* the individual to die.

Although active euthanasia is typically against the law, surveys suggest practices that hasten death do routinely occur (Chambaere and others, 2011; Seale, 2009). To take a classic example, doctors may sedate a dying patient beyond the point required for pain control, and so "accelerate" that person's death (Cellarius, 2011). Polls show widespread public acceptance of assisted suicide in Western Europe and the United States (Braverman and others, 2017). But this is not true among clergy members who universally reject this option (Mason and others, 2017), and in Central Europe, where most citizens still believe terminating a life is *never* justified (Cohen and others, 2013). Why?

One reason is that killing violates the religious dictum that only God can give or take a life. Therefore, the fact that people in nations like Poland and Hungary are more apt to be highly religious may partly explain this attitude split. Apart from religious considerations, there are other reasons to be leery about taking this step.

Critics fear that legalizing euthanasia will allow families to "pull the plug" on people who are elderly and impaired. This argument may explain why, in 2015, the U.K. parliament voted down an Assisted Dying Bill (Monteverde, 2017). Even when someone requests help to end his life, a patient might be pressured into making that decision by unscrupulous relatives who are anxious to get an inheritance. Governments might be tempted to push through euthanasia legislation to spare the expense of treating seriously disabled citizens—offering another reason why residents in authoritarian Central European nations are apt to reject assisted death (Cohen and others, 2013).

Older people are apt to be against physician-assisted dying, based on upsetting personal encounters: "She [my niece] thought that I should be euthanized," reported one horrified woman. "And she actually said to me [when I was ill], 'If you were my dog, I would shoot you to put you out of your misery'" (quoted in Malpas and others, 2014, p. 356).

Another issue relates to where to draw the line. Should we allow people to kill themselves when they have a painful chronic condition, but may not be fatally ill? Suppose the person is simply chronically depressed (Blikshavn, Husum, & Magelssen, 2017)? Can permitting suicide *ever* be an ethically acceptable choice?

There are excellent arguments on the other side. Should patients be forced to unwillingly endure the pain and humiliation of dying when physicians have the tools to mercifully end life? Knowing the agony that terminal disease can cause, is it humane to stand by and let nature take its course? Do you believe that legalizing active euthanasia or physician-assisted suicide is a true advance in caring for the dying, or the beginning of a "slippery slope" that might end in sanctioning killing anyone whose quality of life is impaired?

A Looming Social Issue: Age-Based Rationing of Care

There obviously is an age component to the "slippery slope" of withholding care. As I suggested earlier, people with DNR or DNH orders in their charts are typically elderly, near the end of their natural lives. We already use passive euthanasia at the upper end of the lifespan, holding off from giving aggressive treatments to people we deem "too frail." Should we formally adopt the principle "don't use death-defying strategies" for everyone after they reach a certain age?

Daniel Callahan (1988), a prominent biomedical ethicist, argues that the answer must be yes. According to Callahan, there is a time when "the never-to-be-finished fight against death" must stop. Let's now read Callahan's two arguments in favor of **age-based rationing of care:**

> 1. *After a person has lived out a natural lifespan, medical care should no longer be oriented to resisting death.* While stressing that no precise cutoff age can be set, Callahan puts this marker at around the eighties. This does not mean that life at this age has no value, but rather that when people reach their old-old years, death in the near future is inevitable and this process cannot be vigorously defied.
>
> 2. The existence of medical technologies capable of extending the lives of elderly persons who have lived out a natural lifespan creates no presumption that the technologies must be used for that purpose. Callahan believes that the proper goal of medicine is to stave off premature death. We should not become slaves to our death-defying technology by blindly using each intervention on every person, no matter what that individual's age.

Age-based rationing of health care is poised to become an important developed-world issue as the baby boomers enter advanced old age, and governments grapple with the astronomical health-care costs involved in keeping impaired elderly citizens alive for years. As I mentioned in Chapter 14, we cannot count on medical miracles to cure the physical problems that are the downside to living to our eighties and beyond.

Do you think Callahan is "telling it like it should be" from a logical, rational point of view, or do his proposals make you cringe? Should we rely on markers such as life expectancy or quality of life to allocate who does or doesn't receive medical care?

Whatever your answer, notice that as we approach death, our life comes full circle, and we care only about what mattered during our first years of life—being connected to the people we most love. True, self-efficacy is important. But, when we come right down to it, attachment outweighs everything else!

age-based rationing of care The controversial idea that society should not use expensive life-sustaining technologies on people in their old-old years.

Tying It All Together

1. Your mother asks you whether she should fill out an advance directive. Given what you know about these documents, what should your answer be?
   a. Go for it! But fill out a living will.
   b. Go for it! But you need to regularly discuss your preferences with each of us and complete a durable power of attorney.
   c. Avoid advance directives like the plague because your preferences will never be fulfilled.

2. Latoya and Jamal are arguing about legalizing physician-assisted suicide. Jamal is furious that this practice is not legal and feels that "people should have the right to die." Latoya is terribly worried about formally institutionalizing this practice. Using the points in this section, first make Jamal's case, and then support Latoya's argument.

3. Poll your class: How would your fellow students vote if they were on the jury deciding Dr. Cox's case (see page 457)? If you were the ward nurse, would you have reported this doctor's decision to the police?

Answers to the Tying It All Together questions can be found at the end of this chapter.

SUMMARY

Setting the Context

Today, we have three major pathways to death: (1) People die suddenly, without warning; (2) they steadily decline after being diagnosed with a fatal disease; or (3) most often, they battle an ultimately fatal, chronic condition for a prolonged time. Before modern medicine, people died quickly and everyone had hands-on experience with death. Then, during most of the twentieth century, medical science relocated dying to hospitals, and people avoided talking or thinking about death.

During the past 40 years, Western attitudes changed. Doctors now openly discuss potentially fatal diagnoses, and society has health-care alternatives devoted to easing people's passage to death. We also urge everyone to discuss their end-of-life preferences, although mentioning death is still forbidden in some cultural groups.

The Dying Person

Elisabeth Kübler-Ross, in her **stage theory of dying,** proposed that people pass through *denial, anger, bargaining, depression*, and *acceptance* when learning they have a fatal disease. However, we cannot take this landmark theory as the final truth. Patients often shy away from discussing death. They may not want doctors to be totally honest about their prognosis. Dying people feel many different emotions—especially hope. Rather than emotionally approaching death in "stages," people may experience a state called **middle knowledge,** both knowing and not fully comprehending their fate. Even when they accept death, terminally ill people still have life goals.

Biblical accounts showcase the defining qualities of good deaths: It's best to die at peace after a long life, surrounded by our loved ones. Specifically, people want to die relatively free of pain and anxiety, want to feel in control of how they die, and end their lives feeling close to their attachment figures. Believing that we have fulfilled our purpose in living and appreciating that death is part of the universal human cycle of life is also important in accepting death.

Our culture has clear conceptions about normal mourning. After an initial period spent absorbed with their loss, we expect people to recover emotionally after about a year. Mourners who still show intense symptoms after this time are diagnosed with a controversial mental health condition called **persistent complex bereavement-related disorder.** However, prolonged grief may be normal when parents face the death of a child. In this traumatic situation, it helps to openly discuss dying (if that child understands what is happening) and to keep the child mentally "alive." Transforming the death into a redemption sequence allows grieving parents to restore a sense of life as predictable and fair. Marriages can become closer as couples seek comfort from the one person who can understand their pain: their spouse.

The Health-Care System

A classic study of **dying trajectories** showed that, since dying doesn't proceed according to a "schedule"—but medical personnel assume it does—the way hospitals manage death leaves much to be desired. Because traditional medicine is focused on cure-at-all-costs, the pressure to use futile heroic measures also impairs humane **palliative care.** Remedies include: (1) offering **end-of-life care instruction** to health-care personnel; (2) establishing hospital-based **palliative-care services;** and (3) removing the scene of dying from hospitals to the hospice.

The U.S. **hospice movement** offers backup services that allow families to let their loved ones spend their final months dying naturally, at home. Family caregivers can expect different trajectories to death depending on the person's illness. They confront scary issues relating to pain control. It may be hard for doctors and families to label patients as dying; also, minorities may have unique hospice concerns. Home deaths may not be the best choice when attachment-related issues, such as not wanting to burden loved ones, matter most to people facing a fatal disease.

The Dying Person: Taking Control of How We Die

Advance directives—the **living will** and **durable power of attorney for health care,** filled out by the individual in health, and the **Do Not Resuscitate (DNR)** and **Do Not Hospitalize (DNH)** orders, filled out by surrogates when the person is mentally impaired—provide information about whether to use heroic measures when individuals can no longer make their treatment wishes known. The best advance directive is the durable power of attorney, in which a person gives a specific family member decision-making power to determine end-of life care.

With **active euthanasia** and **physician-assisted suicide,** physicians move beyond **passive euthanasia** (withdrawing treatments) to actively promote the deaths of fatally ill people who want to end their lives. Paramount among the objections to legalizing active euthanasia is the idea that we may open the door to killing people who don't really want to die.

A related issue is **age-based rationing of care,** whether to hold off on using expensive death-defying technologies with people who are old-old. At this moment, age-based rationing of care is poised to move center stage in Western nations, as the massive baby boom cohort moves through their elderly years. The timeless message of this chapter—and the book—is that love (or, in developmental science terminology, our attachments) is at the core of human life.

KEY TERMS

active euthanasia, p. 458

advance directive, p. 456

age-based rationing of care, p. 459

Do Not Hospitalize (DNH) order, p. 457

Do Not Resuscitate (DNR) order, p. 457

durable power of attorney for health care, p. 456

dying trajectory, p. 450

end-of-life care instruction, p. 451

hospice movement, p. 452

Kübler-Ross's stage theory of dying, p. 442

living will, p. 456

middle knowledge, p. 444

palliative care, p. 451

palliative-care service, p. 452

passive euthanasia, p. 458

persistent complex bereavement-related disorder, p. 447

physician-assisted suicide, p. 458

ANSWERS TO Tying It All Together QUIZZES

Setting the Context

1. b

2. slowly and erratically; an age-related chronic disease

3. Amanda, because today we openly discuss death and are making efforts to promote dignified dying

The Dying Person

1. c

2. many different emotions; hope

3. b

4. Your goal is to restore the person's sense of meaning in life, ideally by helping that individual transform her loss into a redemption sequence; also, you might want to get the person to lean on a spouse for comfort, although partners don't need to openly discuss their mutual pain.

The Health-Care System

1. We cannot predict when people die, even though hospitals are structured as if we could. Medicine is focused on preserving life, so doctors are under pressure to persist with futile treatments, rather than focusing on providing the best comfort care.

2. b

3. d

4. Here's what you might say to Feema: Would you feel comfortable about burdening your family 24/7 with nursing you for months or having them manage the health crises that would occur? How would you feel about having loved ones see you naked and incontinent—would you want that to be their last memory of you? Wouldn't it be better to be in a setting where trained professionals could competently manage your physical pain?

The Dying Person: Taking Control of How We Die

1. b

2. *Jamal's case:* We are free to make decisions about how to live our lives, so it doesn't make logical sense that we can't decide when our lives should end. Plus, it's cruel to torture fatally ill people, forcing them to suffer fruitless, unwanted pain when we can easily provide a merciful death. *Latoya's argument:* I'm worried that greedy relatives might pressure ill people into deciding to die "for the good of the family" (that is, to save the family money). I believe that legalizing physician-assisted suicide leaves the door open to governments deciding to kill people when they think the quality of their life is not good. Furthermore, only God can take a life!

3. Here your answers may vary in interesting ways. Enjoy the discussion!

CONNECT ONLINE:

 LaunchPad macmillan learning | Check out our videos and additional resources located at: www.macmillanlearning.com

Final Thoughts

Left to right from top left photo: Petrol/Getty Images, KIYOKO FUKUDA/a.collectionRF/amana images RF/Getty Images, Karel Noppé/Alamy Stock Photo, Ryan McVay/Getty Images, Folio Images/Alamy, Rick Gomez/Getty Images, SpeedKingz/Shutterstock, Stockbyte/Getty Images, Juanmonino/E+/Getty Images, Jupiterimages/Getty Images, Johnny Greig/Getty Images, Gerardo Ricardo López/Getty Images

We're done! When I finish a book, I can't wait to relax; but first I'd like to take a few minutes to offer you an insider's view of *how* I wrote this edition, and explain *why* I write these books.

As the first step in preparing the Fifth Edition of *Experiencing the Lifespan*, I spend hundreds of hours surveying the literature—scanning research published from 2016 to 2018 on subjects from breast-feeding to bullying. Is there important new advice about improving adolescence and ADL abilities? Which cutting-edge research am I passionate to describe?

After writing this material, my editors and I pore over each topic. Do my words accurately convey their intended meaning? Are there better ways this information can be integrated and expressed?

We don't stop there. Each chapter in *Experiencing the Lifespan* goes through several rounds of reviews by professors who teach developmental psychology, and at least five rounds of word-by-word critiques by different editors, before it enters what we call "production"— the initial PDF stage before finalizing the book for print. Then, aided by a new team of designers and artists, we make additional changes to ensure the figures, tables, and photo captions align just right. By the time the chapters arrive in their final form, I have been working full time on this edition for more than a year.

So given this laborious effort (which happens every two years!), why do I continue to write these books? For the same reason that people are passionate about dancing, or decorating, or writing poetry. Each edition gives me a chance to express my creativity and love for our field. I want to produce the best possible work of art. And just like readers who want to make a difference as lawyers, or nurses, or teachers, or engineers, my mission is to improve people's lives.

In writing this edition, I've been especially captivated by Raj Chetty's research relating to U.S. upward mobility. His studies show how complex statistical calculations involving millions of people offer path-breaking insights about how to improve individual lives. I've been thrilled to share the blossoming studies relating to wisdom, an area in which psychologists, ethicists, and religious scholars are collaborating to articulate the core features of this fundamental facet of life. It's been a pleasure to describe the emerging research on happiness and studies spelling out the vital impact communities make on people's well-being.

Chetty's economic analyses, the new efforts to decode happiness and healthy communities, and the innovative speculations relating to wisdom epitomize why lifespan development is a thriving field. Developmental scientists embrace *all* ways of knowing to enhance our understanding of human beings.

I hope you will take inspiration from this edition by using your own creativity and generativity to make a difference for humanity in your own chosen field!

Janet Belsky

Glossary

accommodation In Piaget's theory, enlarging our mental capacities to fit input from the wider world.

acculturation Among immigrants, the tendency to become similar to the mainstream culture after time spent living in a new society.

achievement tests Measures that evaluate a child's knowledge in specific school-related areas.

active euthanasia A deliberate health-care intervention that helps a patient die.

active forces The nature-interacts-with-nurture principle that our genetic temperamental tendencies cause us to choose to put ourselves into specific environments.

ADL (activities of daily living) problems Difficulty in performing everyday tasks that are required for living independently. ADLs are classified as either *basic* or *instrumental.*

adolescence-limited turmoil Antisocial behavior that, for most teens, is specific to adolescence and does not persist into adult life.

adolescent egocentrism David Elkind's term for the tendency of young teenagers to feel that their actions are at the center of everyone else's consciousness.

adoption study Behavioral genetic research strategy, designed to determine the genetic contribution to a given trait, that involves comparing adopted children with their biological and adoptive parents.

adrenal androgens Hormones produced by the adrenal glands that program puberty.

adult attachment styles The different ways in which adults relate to romantic partners, based on Mary Ainsworth's infant attachment styles. (Adult attachment styles are classified as *secure, preoccupied/ ambivalent insecure,* or *avoidant/ dismissive insecure.*)

adult development The scientific study of adult life.

advance directive Any written document spelling out instructions with regard to life-prolonging treatment if individuals become irretrievably ill and cannot communicate their wishes.

age discrimination Illegally laying off workers or failing to hire or promote them on the basis of age.

age norms Cultural ideas about the appropriate ages for engaging in particular activities or life tasks.

age of viability The earliest point at which a baby can survive outside the womb.

age-based rationing of care The controversial idea that society should not use expensive life-sustaining technologies on people in their old-old years.

ageism Stereotypic, intensely negative ideas about old age.

aggression Any hostile or destructive act.

allostatic load An overall score of body deterioration, gained from summing how a person functions on multiple physiological indexes. Allostatic load predicts cognitive performance during adult life.

alternatives to institutionalization Services and settings designed to keep older people who are experiencing age-related disabilities that don't merit intense 24-hour care from having to enter nursing homes.

Alzheimer's disease A type of age-related cognitive disorder characterized by neural atrophy and abnormal by-products of that atrophy, such as senile plaques and neurofibrillary tangles.

amniocentesis A second-trimester procedure that involves inserting a syringe into a woman's uterus to extract a sample of amniotic fluid, which is tested for genetic and chromosomal conditions.

amniotic sac A bag-shaped, fluid-filled membrane that contains and insulates the fetus.

analytic intelligence In Robert Sternberg's framework on successful intelligence, the facet of intelligence involved in performing well on academic problems.

animism In Piaget's theory, the preoperational child's belief that inanimate objects are alive.

anorexia nervosa A potentially life-threatening eating disorder characterized by pathological dieting (resulting in severe weight loss and, in females, loss of menstruation) and by a distorted body image.

A-not-B error In Piaget's framework, a classic mistake made by infants in the sensorimotor stage, whereby babies approaching age 1 go back to the original hiding place to look for an object even though they have seen it get hidden in a second place.

anxious-ambivalent attachment An insecure attachment style characterized by a child's intense distress when reunited with a primary caregiver after separation.

Apgar scale A quick test used to assess a just-delivered baby's condition by measuring heart rate, muscle tone, respiration, reflex response, and color.

artificialism In Piaget's theory, the preoperational child's belief that human beings make everything in nature.

assimilation In Jean Piaget's theory, the first step promoting mental growth, involving fitting environmental input to our existing mental capacities.

assisted reproductive technology (ART) Any infertility treatment in which the egg is fertilized outside the womb.

assisted-living facility Elderly housing option providing care for people with disabilities that, while significant, do not require a nursing home.

attachment The powerful bond of love between a caregiver and child (or between any two people).

attachment in the making Second phase of Bowlby's attachment sequence, when, from 4 to 7 months of age, babies slightly prefer the primary caregiver.

attachment theory Theory formulated by John Bowlby centering on the crucial importance to our species' survival of being closely connected with a caregiver during early childhood and being attached to a significant other during all of life.

attention-deficit/hyperactivity disorder (ADHD) The most common childhood learning disorder in the United States, disproportionately affecting boys; characterized by inattention and hyperactivity at home and at school.

authoritarian parents In the parenting-styles framework, when parents provide many rules but rank low on love.

authoritative parents In the parenting-styles framework, the best child-rearing style, when parents provide ample love and family rules.

autism spectrum disorders (ASDs) Conditions characterized by persistent, severe, widespread social and conversational deficits; lack of interest in people and their feelings; and repetitive, restricted behavior patterns, such as rocking, ritualized behavior, hypersensitivity to sensory input, and a fixation on inanimate objects. A core characteristic of these disorders is impairments in theory of mind.

autobiographical memories Recollections of events and experiences that make up one's life history.

autonomy Erikson's second psychosocial task, when toddlers confront the challenge of understanding that they are separate individuals.

average life expectancy A person's fifty-fifty chance at birth of living to a given age.

avoidant attachment An insecure attachment style characterized by a child's indifference to a primary caregiver at being reunited after separation.

avoidant/dismissive adult attachment A standoffish, excessively disengaged style of relating to loved ones.

axon A long nerve fiber that usually conducts impulses away from the cell body of a neuron.

B

babbling The alternating vowel and consonant sounds that babies repeat with variations of intonation and pitch and that precede the first words.

baby boom cohort The huge age group born between 1946 and 1964.

baby-proofing Making the home safe for a newly mobile infant.

basic ADL problems Difficulty in performing essential self-care activities, such as rising from a chair, eating, and getting to the toilet.

behavioral genetics Field devoted to scientifically determining the role that hereditary forces play in determining individual differences in behavior.

bidirectionality The principle that people affect one another, or that interpersonal influences flow in both directions.

Big Five Five core psychological predispositions—neuroticism, extraversion, openness to experience, conscientiousness, and agreeableness—that underlie personality.

binge eating disorder A newly labeled eating disorder defined by recurrent, out-of-control binging.

biracial or multiracial identity How people of mixed racial backgrounds come to terms with who they are as people in relation to their heritage.

birth defect A physical or neurological problem that occurs prenatally or at birth.

blastocyst The hollow sphere of cells formed during the germinal stage in preparation for implantation.

body mass index (BMI) The ratio of a person's weight to height; the main indicator of overweight or underweight.

boundaryless career Today's most common career path for Western workers, in which people change jobs or professions periodically during their working lives.

breadwinner role Traditional concept that a man's job is to support a wife and children.

bridge job When a retiree takes new work, often part-time, after retiring from a career job.

bulimia nervosa An eating disorder characterized by at least biweekly cycles of binging and purging in an obsessive attempt to lose weight.

bullying A situation in which one or more children (or adults) harass or target a specific child for systematic abuse.

bully-victims Exceptionally aggressive children (with externalizing disorders) who repeatedly bully and get victimized.

C

caregiving grandparents Grandparents who have taken on full responsibility for raising their grandchildren.

centering In Piaget's conservation tasks, the preoperational child's tendency to fix on the most visually striking feature of a substance and not take into account other dimensions.

cephalocaudal sequence The developmental principle that growth occurs in a sequence from head to toe.

cerebral cortex The outer, folded mantle of the brain, responsible for thinking, reasoning, perceiving, and all conscious responses.

certified nurse assistant or aide The main hands-on care provider in a nursing home who helps elderly residents with basic ADL problems.

cervix The neck, or narrow lower portion, of the uterus.

cesarean section (c-section) Delivering a baby surgically by extracting the fetus through incisions in the abdominal wall and uterus.

child development The scientific study of development from birth through adolescence.

child maltreatment Any act that seriously endangers a child's physical or emotional well-being.

childhood obesity A body mass index at or above the 95th percentile compared to the U.S. norms established for children in the 1970s.

chorionic villus sampling (CVS) A relatively risky first-trimester pregnancy test for fetal genetic disorders.

chromosome A threadlike strand of DNA located in the nucleus of every cell that carries the genes, which transmit hereditary information.

circular reactions In Piaget's framework, repetitive action-oriented schemas (or habits) characteristic of babies during the sensorimotor stage.

class inclusion The understanding that a general category can encompass several subordinate elements.

clear-cut (focused) attachment Critical attachment phase, from 7 months through toddlerhood, defined by the need to have a primary caregiver nearby.

clique A small peer group composed of roughly six teenagers who have similar attitudes and who share activities.

cognitive behaviorism (social learning theory) A behavioral worldview that emphasizes that people learn by watching others and that our thoughts about the reinforcers determine our behavior. Cognitive behaviorists focus on charting and modifying people's thoughts.

cohabitation Sharing a household in an unmarried romantic relationship.

cohort The age group with whom we travel through life.

colic A baby's frantic, continual crying during the first three months of life; caused by an immature nervous system.

collaborative pretend play Fantasy play in which children work together to develop and act out scenes.

collective efficacy Communities defined by strong cohesion, a commitment to neighbor-to-neighbor helping, and shared prosocial values among residents.

collectivist cultures Societies that prize social harmony, obedience, and close family connectedness over individual achievement.

commitment script In Dan McAdams's research, a type of autobiography produced by highly generative adults that involves childhood memories of feeling special; being unusually sensitive to others' misfortunes; having a strong, enduring generative mission from adolescence; and redemption sequences.

concrete operational thinking In Piaget's framework, the type of cognition characteristic of children aged 8 to 11, marked by the ability to reason about the world in logical, adult ways.

conservation tasks Piagetian tasks that involve changing the shape of substances to see whether children can go beyond the way that substance visually appears to understand that the amount remains the same.

consummate love In Robert Sternberg's triangular theory of love, the ideal form of love, in which a couple's relationship involves all three of the major facets of love: passion, intimacy, and commitment.

contexts of development Fundamental markers, including cohort, socioeconomic status, culture, and gender, that shape how we develop throughout the lifespan.

continuing-care retirement community Elderly housing option characterized by different levels of care. People enter in relatively good health and then move to sections providing more intense help when they grow more disabled.

conventional thought In Lawrence Kohlberg's theory, the intermediate level of moral reasoning, in which people respond to ethical issues by discussing the need to uphold social norms.

corporal punishment The use of physical force to discipline a child.

correlational study A research strategy that involves relating two or more variables.

cortisol A hormone often measured in saliva by researchers as a biological marker of stress.

co-sleeping The standard custom, in collectivist cultures, of having a child and parent share a bed.

creative intelligence In Robert Sternberg's framework on successful intelligence, the facet of intelligence involved in producing novel ideas or innovative work.

cross-sectional study A developmental research strategy that involves testing different age groups at the same time.

crowd A relatively large teenage peer group.

crystallized intelligence A basic facet of intelligence, consisting of a person's knowledge base, or storehouse, of accumulated information.

cyberbullying Systematic harassment conducted through electronic media.

D

day care Less academically oriented group programs serving young children, most often infants and toddlers.

day-care center A day-care arrangement in which a large number of children are cared for at a licensed facility by paid providers.

day-care program Center offering activities and a safe place to go during the day for impaired older adults living with relatives.

decentering In Piaget's conservation tasks, the concrete operational child's ability to look at several dimensions of an object or substance.

deinstitutionalization of marriage The decline in marriage and the emergence of alternate family forms during the last third of the twentieth century.

dendrite A branching fiber that receives information and conducts impulses toward the cell body of a neuron.

depth perception The ability to see (and fear) heights.

developed world The most affluent countries in the world.

developing world The more impoverished countries of the world.

developmental disorders Learning impairments and behavioral problems during infancy and childhood.

developmentalists (or developmental scientists) Researchers and practitioners whose professional interest lies in the study of the human lifespan.

deviancy training Socialization of a young teenager into delinquency through conversations centered on performing antisocial acts.

disorganized attachment An insecure attachment style characterized by responses such as freezing or fear when a child is reunited with the primary caregiver in the Strange Situation.

divided-attention task A difficult memory challenge involving memorizing material while simultaneously monitoring something else.

DNA (deoxyribonucleic acid) The material that makes up genes, which bear our hereditary characteristics.

Do Not Hospitalize (DNH) order A type of advance directive inserted in the charts of impaired nursing home residents, specifying that in a medical crisis patients should not be transferred to a hospital for emergency care.

Do Not Resuscitate (DNR) order A type of advance directive filled out by surrogates (usually a doctor in consultation with family members) for impaired individuals, specifying that if they go into cardiac arrest efforts should not be made to revive them.

dominant disorder An illness that a child gets by inheriting one copy of the abnormal gene that causes the disorder.

dose–response effect Term referring to the fact that the amount (dose) of a substance, in this case the depth and length of deprivation, determines its probable effect or impact on the person. (In the orphanage studies, the "response" is subsequent emotional and/or cognitive problems.)

Down syndrome The most common chromosomal abnormality, causing intellectual disability, susceptibility to heart disease, other health problems, and distinctive physical characteristics including slanted eyes and a stocky build.

durable power of attorney for health care A type of advance directive in which people designate a specific surrogate to make health-care decisions if they become incapacitated and are unable to make their wishes known.

dying trajectory The fact that hospital personnel make projections about the particular pathway to death that a seriously ill patient will take and organize their care according to that assumption.

dyslexia A learning disorder that is characterized by reading difficulties, lack of fluency, and poor word recognition that is often genetic in origin.

E

early childhood The first phase of childhood, lasting from age 3 through kindergarten, or about age 6.

Early Head Start A federal program that provides counseling and other services to low-income parents and children under age 3.

eating disorder A pathological obsession with getting and staying thin. The best-known eating disorders are *anorexia nervosa* and *bulimia nervosa*.

ecological, developmental systems approach An all-encompassing outlook on development that stresses the need to embrace a variety of approaches, and emphasizes the reality that many influences affect development.

egocentrism In Piaget's theory, the preoperational child's inability to understand that other people have different points of view from one's own.

elderspeak Communication style used when an older person looks frail and impaired, involving talking loudly and slowly, as if with a baby.

embryonic stage The second stage of prenatal development, lasting from week 3 through week 8.

emerging adulthood The phase of life that begins after high school, lasts through the late twenties, and is devoted to constructing an adult life.

emotion regulation The capacity to manage one's emotional state.

empathy Feeling the exact emotion that another person is experiencing.

end-of-life care instruction Courses in medical and nursing schools devoted to teaching health-care workers how to provide the best palliative care to the dying.

epigenetics Research field exploring how early life events alter the outer cover of our DNA, producing lifelong changes in health and behavior.

episodic memory In the memory-systems perspective, the most fragile type of memory, involving the recall of the ongoing events of daily life.

Erikson's psychosocial tasks In Erik Erikson's theory, each challenge that we face as we travel through the eight stages of the lifespan.

ethnic identity How people come to terms with who they are as people in relation to their unique ethnic or racial heritage.

eudaimonic happiness Well-being defined as having a sense of meaning and life purpose.

evocative forces The nature-interacts-with-nurture principle that our genetic temperamental tendencies produce certain responses from other people.

evolutionary psychology Theory or worldview highlighting the role that inborn, species-specific behaviors play in human development and life.

executive functions Abilities that allow us to plan and direct our thinking and control our immediate impulses.

exercise play Running and chasing play that exercises children's physical skills.

experience-sampling technique A research procedure designed to capture moment-to-moment experiences by having people carry pagers and take notes describing their activities and emotions whenever the signal sounds.

externalizing tendencies A personality style that involves acting on one's immediate impulses and behaving disruptively and aggressively.

extrinsic career rewards Work that is performed for external reinforcers, such as pay.

extrinsic motivation The drive to take an action because that activity offers external reinforcers such as praise, money, or a good grade.

F

face-perception studies Research using preferential looking and habituation to explore what very young babies know about faces.

fallopian tube One of a pair of slim, pipelike structures that connect the ovaries with the uterus.

family day care A day-care arrangement in which a neighbor or relative cares for a small number of children in his or her home for a fee.

family watchdogs A basic role of grandparents, which involves monitoring the younger family member's well-being and intervening to provide help in a crisis.

family–work conflict A common developed-world situation, in which parents are torn between the demands of family and a career.

fantasy play Pretend play in which a child makes up a scene, often with a toy or other prop.

fear bias The human tendency to be hypersensitive to fearful facial cues that, by alerting us to danger,

may prevent us from getting injured or killed.

fertility rate The average number of children a woman in a given country has during her lifetime.

fertilization The union of sperm and egg.

fetal alcohol syndrome (FAS) A cluster of birth defects caused by the mother's alcohol consumption during pregnancy.

fetal programming research New research discipline exploring the impact of traumatic pregnancy events and stress on producing low birth weight, obesity, and long-term physical problems.

fetal stage The final phase of prenatal development, lasting seven months, characterized by physical refinements, massive growth, and the development of the brain.

fine motor skills Physical abilities that involve small, coordinated movements, such as drawing and writing one's name.

flow Csikszentmihalyi's term for feeling total absorption in a challenging, goal-oriented activity.

fluid intelligence A basic facet of intelligence, consisting of the ability to quickly master new intellectual activities.

Flynn effect Remarkable rise in overall performance on IQ tests that has been occurring around the world over the past century.

food insecurity According to U.S. Department of Agriculture surveys, the number of households that report needing to serve unbalanced meals, worrying about not having enough food at the end of the month, or having to go hungry due to lack of money (latter is *severe food insecurity*).

formal operational stage Jean Piaget's fourth and final stage of cognitive development, reached at around age 12 and characterized by teenagers' ability to reason at an abstract, scientific level.

frontal lobes The area at the front uppermost part of the brain, responsible for reasoning and planning our actions.

G

g Charles Spearman's term for a general intelligence factor that he claimed underlies all cognitive activities.

gang A close-knit, delinquent peer group. Gangs form mainly in impoverished disorganized communities; they offer their members protection from harm and engage in a variety of criminal activities.

gender schema theory Explanation for gender-stereotyped behavior that emphasizes the role of cognitions; specifically, once children know their gender label (girl or boy), they model their own sex.

gender-segregated play Play in which boys and girls associate only with members of their own gender—typical of childhood.

gene A segment of DNA that contains a chemical blueprint for manufacturing a particular protein.

generativity In Erikson's theory, the seventh psychosocial task, in which people in midlife find meaning from nurturing the next generation, caring for others, or enriching the lives of others through their work. According to Erikson, when midlife adults have not achieved generativity, they feel stagnant, without a sense of purpose in life.

genetic counselor A professional who counsels parents-to-be about their children's risk of developing genetic disorders and about available treatments.

genetic testing A blood test to determine whether a person carries the gene for a given genetic disorder.

germinal stage The first 14 days of prenatal development, from fertilization to full implantation.

gerontology The scientific study of the aging process and older adults.

gestation The period of pregnancy.

gifted The label for superior intellectual functioning characterized by an IQ score of 130 or above, showing that a child ranks in the top 2 percent of his age group.

gonads The sex organs—the ovaries in girls and the testes in boys.

goodness of fit An ideal parenting strategy that involves arranging children's environments to suit their temperaments, minimizing their vulnerabilities and accentuating their strengths.

grammar The rules and word-arranging systems that every human language employs to communicate meaning.

gross motor skills Physical abilities that involve large muscle movements, such as running and jumping.

growth spurt A dramatic increase in height and weight that occurs during puberty.

guilt Feeling upset about having caused harm to a person or about having violated one's internal standard of behavior.

H

habituation The predictable loss of interest that develops once a stimulus becomes familiar; used to explore infant sensory capacities and thinking.

Head Start A federal program offering high-quality day care at a center and other services to help preschoolers aged 3 to 5 from low-income families prepare for school.

health span The number of years people can expect to live without ADL problems.

hedonic happiness Well-being defined as pure pleasure.

holophrase First clear evidence of language, when babies use a single word to communicate a sentence or complete thought.

home health services Nursing-oriented help provided in the home of an impaired adult.

homogamy The principle that we select a mate who is similar to us.

homophobia Intense fear and dislike of gay people.

hormones Chemical substances released in the bloodstream that target and change organs and tissues.

hospice movement A movement, which became widespread in recent decades, focused on providing palliative care to dying patients outside of hospitals and especially on giving families the support they need to care for the terminally ill at home.

hostile attributional bias The tendency of highly aggressive children to see motives and actions as threatening when they are actually benign.

HPG axis The main hormonal system that programs puberty; it involves a triggering hypothalamic hormone that causes the pituitary to secrete its hormones, which in turn cause the ovaries and testes to develop and secrete the hormones that produce the major body changes.

I

identity In Erikson's theory, the life task of deciding who to be as an adult.

identity achievement A fully mature identity status in which the young person chooses a satisfying adult life path.

identity constancy In Piaget's theory, the preoperational child's inability to grasp that a person's core "self" stays the same despite changes in external appearance.

identity diffusion According to James Marcia, an identity status in which the person is aimless or feels totally blocked, without any adult life path.

identity foreclosure According to James Marcia, an identity status in which the person decides on an adult life path (often one spelled out by an authority figure) without any thought or active search.

identity statuses Marcia's four categories of identity formation: identity diffusion, identity foreclosure, moratorium, and identity achievement.

imaginary audience David Elkind's term for the tendency of young teenagers to feel that everyone is watching their every action; a component of adolescent egocentrism.

immigrant paradox The fact that despite living in poverty, going to substandard schools, and not having parents who speak a nation's language, immigrant children do far better than we might expect at school.

implantation The process in which a blastocyst becomes embedded in the uterine wall.

in vitro fertilization An infertility treatment in which conception occurs outside the womb.

income inequality The gap between the rich and poor within a nation; specifically, when income inequality is wide, a nation has few very affluent residents and a mass of disadvantaged citizens.

individualistic cultures Societies that prize independence, competition, and personal success.

induction The ideal discipline style for socializing prosocial behavior, which involves getting a child who has behaved hurtfully to empathize with the pain he has caused the other person.

industry Erik Erikson's term for the middle childhood psychosocial task involving bending to adult reality and needing to work for what we want.

infant mortality Death during the first year of life.

infant-directed speech (IDS) The simplified, exaggerated, high-pitched tones that adults and children use to speak to infants that function to help teach language.

infertility The inability to conceive after a year of unprotected sex. (Includes the inability to carry a child to term.)

information-processing approach A perspective on understanding cognition that divides thinking into specific steps and component processes, much like a computer.

initiative Erik Erikson's term for the early childhood psychosocial task that involves exuberantly testing skills.

inner speech In Vygotsky's theory, the way in which human beings learn to regulate their behavior and master cognitive challenges, through silently repeating information or talking to themselves.

insecure attachment Deviation from the normally joyful response of being reunited with a primary caregiver, signaling problems in the caregiver–child relationship.

instrumental ADL problems Difficulty in performing everyday household tasks, such as cooking and cleaning.

integrity Erik Erikson's eighth psychosocial stage, in which elderly people decide that their life missions have been fulfilled and so accept impending death.

intellectual disability The label for significantly impaired cognitive functioning, measured by deficits in behavior accompanied by having an IQ of 70 or below.

intelligence quotient (IQ) Measure designed to evaluate a child's overall cognitive ability, or general aptitude for mastering academic work.

intergenerational equity Balancing the needs of the young and old. Specifically, often referred to as

the idea that U.S. government entitlements, such as Medicare and Social Security, "over-benefit" the elderly at the expense of other age groups.

internalizing tendencies A personality style that involves intense fear, social inhibition, and often depression.

intimacy Erikson's first adult task, which involves connecting with a partner in a mutual loving relationship.

intrinsic career rewards Work that provides inner fulfillment and allows people to satisfy their needs for creativity, autonomy, and relatedness.

intrinsic motivation The drive to act based on the pleasure of taking that action in itself, not for an external reinforcer or reward.

K

kangaroo care Carrying a young baby in a sling close to the caregiver's body. This technique is most useful for soothing an infant.

Kübler-Ross's stage theory of dying The landmark theory, developed by psychiatrist Elisabeth Kübler-Ross, that people who are terminally ill progress through five stages in confronting death: denial, anger, bargaining, depression, and acceptance.

L

language acquisition device (LAD) Chomsky's term for a hypothetical brain structure that enables our species to learn and produce language.

learned helplessness A state that develops when a person feels incapable of affecting the outcome of events, and so gives up without trying.

lens A transparent, disk-shaped structure in the eye, which bends to allow us to see close objects.

life-course difficulties Antisocial behavior that, for a fraction of adolescents, persists into adult life.

lifespan development The scientific study of development through life.

little-scientist phase The time around age 1 when babies use tertiary circular reactions to actively explore the properties of objects, experimenting with them like scientists.

living will A type of advance directive in which people spell out their wishes for life-sustaining treatment in case they become permanently incapacitated and unable to communicate.

longitudinal study A developmental research strategy that involves testing an age group repeatedly over many years.

low birth weight (LBW) A weight at birth of less than 5½ pounds.

M

major neurocognitive disorder (NCD, dementia) The general term for any illness involving serious, progressive cognitive decline that interferes with a person's ability to live independently. (A *minor neurocognitive disorder* is the label for a less severe impairment in memory, reasoning, and thinking which does not compromise independent living.)

marital equity Fairness in the "work" of a couple's life together. If a relationship lacks equity, with one partner doing significantly more than the other, the outcome is typically marital dissatisfaction.

mass-to-specific sequence The developmental principle that large structures (and movements) precede increasingly detailed refinements.

maximum lifespan The biological limit of human life (about 105 years).

mean length of utterance (MLU) The average number of morphemes per sentence.

means–end behavior In Piaget's framework, performing a different action to get to a goal—an ability that emerges in the sensorimotor stage as babies approach age 1.

median age The age at which 50 percent of a population is older and 50 percent is younger.

Medicare The U.S. government's program of health insurance for elderly people.

memory-systems perspective A framework that divides memory into three types: procedural, semantic, and episodic memory.

menarche A girl's first menstruation.

menopause The age-related process, occurring at about age 50, in which ovulation and menstruation stop due to the decline of estrogen.

micronutrient deficiency Chronically inadequate level of a specific nutrient important to development and disease prevention, such as vitamin A, zinc, and/or iron.

middle childhood The second phase of childhood, comprising the ages from roughly 7 to 12 years.

middle knowledge The idea that terminally ill people can know that they are dying yet at the same time not completely grasp or come to terms emotionally with that fact.

miscarriage The naturally occurring loss of a pregnancy and death of the fetus.

mnemonic technique A strategy for aiding memory, often by using imagery or enhancing the emotional meaning of what needs to be learned.

modeling Learning by watching and imitating others.

moral disengagement Rationalizing moral or ethical lapses by invoking justifications, such as "He deserved that."

moratorium According to James Marcia, an identity status in which the person actively explores various possibilities to find a truly solid adult life path.

morpheme The smallest unit of meaning in a particular language—for example, *boys* contains two morphemes: *boy* and the plural suffix - *s*.

multiple intelligences theory In Howard Gardner's perspective on intelligence, the principle that there are eight separate kinds of intelligence—verbal, mathematical, interpersonal, intrapersonal, spatial, musical, kinesthetic, naturalist—plus a possible ninth type, called spiritual intelligence.

myelination Formation of a fatty layer encasing the axons of neurons. This process, which speeds the transmission of neural impulses, continues from birth to early adulthood.

N

natural childbirth Labor and birth without medical interventions.

naturalistic observation A measurement strategy that involves directly watching and coding behaviors.

nature Biological or genetic causes of development.

neonatal intensive care unit (NICU) A special hospital unit that treats at-risk newborns, such as low-birth-weight and very-low-birth-weight babies.

nest-leaving Moving out of a childhood home and living independently.

neural tube A cylindrical structure that forms along the back of the embryo and develops into the brain and spinal cord.

neurofibrillary tangles Long, wavy filaments that replace normal neurons and are characteristic of Alzheimer's disease.

neuron A nerve cell.

non-normative transitions Unpredictable or atypical life changes that occur during development.

nonsuicidal self-injury Acts of self-mutilation, such as cutting or burning one's body, to cope with stress.

normal aging changes The universal, often progressive signs, of physical deterioration intrinsic to the aging process.

normative transitions Predictable life changes that occur during development.

nursing home/long-term-care facility A residential institution that provides shelter and intensive caregiving, primarily to older people who need help with basic ADLs.

nurture Environmental causes of development.

nurturer father Husband who actively participates in hands-on child care.

O

object permanence In Piaget's framework, the understanding that objects continue to exist even when we can no longer see them, which gradually emerges during the sensorimotor stage.

occupational segregation The separation of men and women into different kinds of jobs.

off time Being too late or too early in a culture's timetable for achieving adult life tasks.

old-age dependency ratio The fraction of people over age 60 compared to younger, working-age adults (ages 15 to 59). This ratio is expected to rise dramatically as the baby boomers retire.

old-old People age 80 and older.

on time Being on target in a culture's timetable for achieving adult life tasks.

operant conditioning According to traditional behaviorists, the law of learning that determines any voluntary response.

osteoporosis An age-related chronic disease in which the bones become porous, fragile, and more likely to break. Osteoporosis is most common in thin women, and so most common in females of European and Asian descent.

ovary One of a pair of almond-shaped organs that contain a woman's ova, or eggs.

overextension An error in early language development in which young children apply verbal labels too broadly.

overregularization An error in early language development, in which young children apply the rules for plurals and past tenses even to exceptions, so irregular forms sound like regular forms.

ovulation The moment during a woman's monthly cycle when an ovum is expelled from the ovary.

ovum An egg cell containing the genetic material contributed by the mother to the baby.

oxytocin The hormone whose production is centrally involved in bonding, nurturing, and caregiving behaviors in our species and other mammals.

P

palliative care Any intervention designed not to cure illness but to promote dignified dying.

palliative-care service A service or unit in a hospital that is devoted to end-of-life care.

paradox of well-being The fact that despite their physical and mental losses, the elderly report being just as happy and often happier than the young.

parent care Adult children's care for their disabled elderly parents.

parental alienation The practice among divorced parents of bad-mouthing a former spouse, with the goal of turning a child against that person.

parenting style In Diana Baumrind's framework, how parents align on love and discipline.

passive euthanasia Withholding potentially life-saving interventions that might keep a terminally ill or permanently comatose patient alive.

permissive parents In the parenting-styles framework, when parents provide few rules but lots of love.

persistent complex bereavement-related disorder Controversial new diagnosis, appearing in the most recent versions of the American Psychiatric Association's *Diagnostic and Statistical Manual*, in which the bereaved person still shows intense symptoms of mourning, or an increase in symptoms six months to a year after a loved one's death.

personal fable David Elkind's term for young teenagers' tendency to believe that their lives are special and heroic; a component of adolescent egocentrism.

person–environment fit The extent to which the environment is tailored to our biological tendencies and talents.

phoneme The sound units that convey meaning in a given language—for example, in English, the *c* sound of *cat* and the *b* sound of *bat*.

physician-assisted suicide A type of active euthanasia in which a physician prescribes a lethal medication to a terminally ill person who wants to die.

Piaget's cognitive developmental theory Jean Piaget's principle that from infancy to adolescence, children progress through four qualitatively different stages of intellectual growth.

placenta The structure projecting from the wall of the uterus during pregnancy through which the developing baby absorbs nutrients.

plastic Malleable, or capable of being changed (refers to neural or cognitive development).

positivity effect The tendency for older people to focus on positive experiences and screen out negative events.

postconventional thought In Lawrence Kohlberg's theory, the highest level of moral reasoning, in which people respond to ethical issues by applying their own moral guidelines apart from society's rules.

postformal thought A uniquely adult form of intelligence that involves being sensitive to different perspectives, making decisions based on one's inner feelings, and being interested in exploring new questions.

power assertion An ineffective socialization strategy that involves yelling, screaming, or hitting a child.

practical intelligence In Robert Sternberg's framework on successful intelligence, the facet of intelligence involved in knowing how to act competently in real-world situations.

preattachment phase The first phase of John Bowlby's developmental attachment sequence, during the first three months of life, when infants show no visible signs of attachment.

preconventional thought In Lawrence Kohlberg's theory, the lowest level of moral reasoning, in which people approach ethical issues by only considering the personal punishments or rewards of their actions.

preferential-looking paradigm A research technique to explore early infant sensory capacities and cognition, drawing on the principle that we are attracted to novelty and prefer to look at new things.

preoccupied/ambivalent adult attachment An excessively clingy, needy style of relating to loved ones.

preoperational thinking In Piaget's theory, the type of cognition characteristic of children aged 2 to 7, marked by an inability to step back from one's immediate perceptions and think conceptually.

presbycusis Age-related difficulty in hearing, particularly high-pitched tones, caused by the atrophy of the hearing receptors located in the inner ear.

presbyopia Age-related midlife difficulty with near vision, caused by the inability of the lens to bend.

preschool A teaching-oriented group setting for children aged 3 to 5.

primary attachment figure The closest person in a child's or adult's life.

primary circular reactions In Piaget's framework, the first infant habits during the sensorimotor stage, centered on the body.

primary sexual characteristics Physical changes of puberty that directly involve the reproductive organs, such as growth of the penis and onset of menstruation.

private pensions The major source of nongovernmental income support for U.S. retirees, in which the individual worker and employer put a portion of each paycheck into an account to help finance retirement.

proactive aggression A hostile or destructive act initiated to achieve a goal.

procedural memory In the memory-systems perspective, the most resilient (longest-lasting) type of memory; refers to material, such as well-learned physical skills, that we automatically recall without conscious awareness.

prosocial behavior Sharing, helping, and caring actions.

proximity-seeking behavior Acting to maintain physical contact or to be close to an attachment figure.

proximodistal sequence The developmental principle that growth occurs from the most interior parts of the body outward.

puberty The hormonal and physical changes by which children become sexually mature human beings and reach their adult height.

puberty rite A "coming of age" ritual held in traditional cultures to celebrate children's transition to adulthood.

Q

qualitative research Occasional developmental science data-collection strategy that involves personal interviews.

quantitative research Standard developmental science data-collection strategy that involves testing groups of people and using numerical scales and statistics.

quickening A pregnant woman's first feeling of the fetus moving inside her body.

R

reaction time The speed at which a person can respond to a stimulus.

reactive aggression A hostile or destructive act carried out in response to being frustrated or hurt.

recessive disorder An illness that a child gets by inheriting two copies of the abnormal gene that causes the disorder.

redemption sequence In Dan McAdams's research, a characteristic theme of highly generative adults' autobiographies, in which they describe tragic events that turned out for the best.

reflex A response or action that is automatic and programmed by noncortical brain centers.

rehearsal A learning strategy in which people repeat information to embed it in memory.

reinforcement Behavioral term for reward.

rejecting-neglecting parents In the parenting-styles framework, the worst child-rearing approach, when parents provide little discipline or love.

relational aggression A hostile or destructive act designed to cause harm to a person's relationships.

relationship churning Having on-again/off-again romantic relationships in which couples repeatedly get together and then break up.

reliability In measurement terminology, a basic criterion for a test's accuracy that scores must be fairly similar when a person takes the same test more than once.

REM sleep The phase of sleep involving rapid eye movements, when the EEG looks almost like it does during waking. REM sleep decreases as infants mature.

representative sample A group that reflects the characteristics of the overall population.

resilient children Children who rebound from serious early life traumas to construct successful adult lives.

reversibility In Piaget's conservation tasks, the concrete operational child's knowledge that a specific change in the way a given substance looks can be reversed.

role conflict A situation in which a person is torn between two or more major responsibilities—for instance, parent and worker—and cannot do either job adequately.

role confusion Erikson's term for a failure in identity formation, marked by the lack of any sense of a future adult path.

role overload A job situation that places so many requirements or demands on workers that it becomes impossible to do a good job.

role phase In Murstein's theory, the final mate-selection stage, in which committed partners work out their future life together.

rooting reflex Newborns' automatic response to a touch on the cheek, involving turning toward that location and beginning to suck.

rough-and-tumble play Play that involves shoving, wrestling, and hitting, but in which no actual harm is intended; especially characteristic of boys.

ruminative moratorium When a young person is unable to decide between different identities, becoming emotionally paralyzed and highly anxious.

S

scaffolding The process of teaching new skills by entering a child's zone of proximal development and tailoring one's efforts to that person's competence level.

school-to-prison pipeline Term referring to the way school expulsion may provoke criminal behavior and incarceration for at-risk teens.

school-to-work transition The change from the schooling phase of life to the work world.

Seattle Longitudinal Study The definitive study of the effect of aging on intelligence, involving simultaneously conducting and comparing the results of cross-sectional and longitudinal studies.

secondary circular reactions In Piaget's framework, habits of the sensorimotor stage lasting from about 4 months of age to the baby's first birthday, centered on exploring the external world.

secondary sexual characteristics Physical changes of puberty not directly involved in reproduction, such as female breast development and male facial hair.

secular trend in puberty A decline in the average age at which children reach puberty.

secure adult attachment The genuine intimacy that is ideal in love relationships.

secure attachment Ideal attachment response when a child responds with joy at being reunited with a primary caregiver.

selective attention A learning strategy in which people manage their awareness so as to attend only to what is relevant and to filter out unneeded information.

selective optimization with compensation Paul Baltes's three principles for successful aging (and living): (1) focus on our most important activities; (2) work especially hard in these top ranking areas; and (3) rely on external aids when we cannot cope on our own.

self-awareness The capacity to observe our abilities and actions from an outside frame of reference and to reflect on our inner state.

self-conscious emotions Feelings of pride, shame, or guilt, which first emerge around age 2 and show the capacity to reflect on the self.

self-efficacy According to cognitive behaviorism, an internal belief in our competence that predicts whether we initiate activities or persist in the face of failures, and predicts the goals we set.

self-esteem Evaluating oneself as either "good" or "bad" as a result of comparing the self to other people.

self-report strategy A measurement having people report on their feelings and activities through questionnaires.

self-soothing Children's ability, usually beginning at about 6 months of age, to put themselves back to sleep when they wake up during the night.

semantic memory In the memory-systems perspective, a moderately resilient (long-lasting) type of memory; refers to our ability to recall basic facts.

semantics The meaning system of a language—that is, what the words stand for.

senile plaques Thick, bullet-like amyloid-laden structures that replace normal neurons and are characteristic of Alzheimer's disease.

sensitive period The time when a body structure is most vulnerable to damage by a teratogen, typically when that organ or process is rapidly developing or coming "on line."

sensorimotor stage Piaget's first stage of cognitive development, lasting from birth to age 2, when babies' agenda is to pin down the basics of physical reality.

separation anxiety When a baby gets upset as a primary caregiver departs.

serial cohabitation Living sequentially with different partners outside of marriage.

sex-linked single-gene disorder An illness, carried on the mother's X chromosome, that typically leaves the female offspring unaffected but has a fifty-fifty chance of striking each male child.

sexual double standard A cultural code that gives men greater sexual freedom than women. Specifically, society expects males to want to have intercourse and expects females to remain virgins until they marry and to be more interested in relationships than in having sex.

sexual orientation Our sexual and romantic attraction to other people.

shame A feeling of being personally humiliated.

single-gene disorder An illness caused by a single gene.

skin-to-skin contact An effective calming strategy that involves holding a young infant next to a caregiver's body.

social clock The concept that we regulate our passage through adulthood by an inner timetable that tells us which life activities are appropriate at certain ages.

social cognition Any skill related to understanding feelings and negotiating interpersonal interactions.

social networking sites Internet sites whose goal is to forge personal connections among users.

social referencing A baby's monitoring a caregiver for cues as to how to behave.

Social Security The U.S. government's national retirement support program.

social smile The first real smile, occurring at about 2 months of age.

social-interactionist perspective An approach to language development that emphasizes its social function, specifically that babies and adults have a mutual passion to communicate.

socialization How children are taught to behave in socially appropriate ways.

socioeconomic health gap The worldwide disparity between the health of the rich and poor.

socioeconomic status (SES) A basic marker referring to status on the educational and, especially, income rungs.

socioemotional selectivity theory A theory of aging (and the lifespan) put forth by Laura Carstensen, describing how the time we have left to live affects our priorities and social relationships. Specifically, in later life people focus on the present and prioritize being with their closest attachment figures.

specific learning disorder The label for any impairment in language or any deficit related to listening, thinking, speaking, reading, writing, spelling, or understanding mathematics.

spermarche A boy's first ejaculation of live sperm.

stimulus phase In Murstein's theory, the initial mate-selection stage, in which we make judgments about a potential partner based on external characteristics such as appearance.

stimulus-value-role theory Murstein's mate-selection theory that suggests similar people pair up and that our path to commitment progresses through three phases (called the *stimulus*, *value-comparison*, and *role* phases).

Strange Situation Procedure to measure attachment at age 1, involving separations and reunions with a caregiver.

stranger anxiety Beginning at about 7 months, when a baby grows wary of people other than a caregiver.

"storm and stress" G. Stanley Hall's phrase for the intense moodiness, emotional sensitivity, and risk-taking tendencies that characterize the life stage he labeled adolescence.

stunting Excessively short stature in a child, caused by chronic lack of adequate nutrition.

successful intelligence In Robert Sternberg's framework, the optimal form of cognition, which involves striking the right balance of analytic, creative, and practical intelligence.

sucking reflex The automatic, spontaneous sucking movements newborns produce, especially when anything touches their lips.

sudden infant death syndrome (SIDS) The unexplained death of an apparently healthy infant, often while sleeping, during the first year of life.

sympathy A state necessary for acting prosocially, involving feeling upset *for* a person who needs help.

synapse The gap between the dendrites of one neuron and the axon of another, over which impulses flow.

synaptogenesis Forming of connections between neurons at the synapses. This process, responsible for all perceptions, actions, and thoughts, is most intense during infancy and childhood but continues throughout life.

synchrony The reciprocal aspect of the attachment relationship, with a caregiver and infant responding emotionally to each other in a sensitive, exquisitely attuned way.

syntax The system of grammatical rules in a particular language.

T

telegraphic speech First stage of combining words in which a toddler pares down a sentence to its essential words.

temperament A person's characteristic, inborn style of dealing with the world.

teratogen A substance that crosses the placenta and harms the fetus.

tertiary circular reactions In Piaget's framework, "little-scientist" activities of the sensorimotor stage, beginning around age 1, involving flexibly exploring the properties of objects.

testes Male organs that manufacture sperm.

testosterone The hormone responsible for maturation of the male reproductive organs and other signs of puberty in men, and for hair and skin changes and sexual desire in both sexes.

theory Any perspective explaining why people act the way they do; theories allow us to predict behavior and also suggest how to intervene to improve behavior.

theory of mind Children's first cognitive understanding, which appears at about age 4, that other people have different beliefs and perspectives from their own.

thin ideal Media-driven cultural idea that females need to be abnormally thin.

toddlerhood The important transitional stage after babyhood, from roughly age 1 year to 2½.

traditional behaviorism The original behavioral worldview that focused on charting and modifying only "objective" visible behaviors.

traditional stable career A career path in which people settle into their permanent life's work in their twenties and often stay with the same organization until they retire.

transgender people People whose gender identity is different from their sex at birth. Transgender teens and adults may be attracted to same- or opposite-sex partners; they may or may not choose to undergo medical treatments to make their bodies congruent with their gender identity.

triangular theory of love Robert Sternberg's categorization of love relationships into three facets: passion, intimacy, and commitment. When arranged at the points of a triangle, their combinations describe all the different kinds of adult love relationships.

trimester One of the 3-month-long segments into which pregnancy is divided.

true experiment The only research strategy that can determine that something causes something else; involves randomly assigning people to different treatments and then looking at the outcome.

twentieth-century life expectancy revolution The dramatic increase in average life expectancy that occurred during the first half of the twentieth century in the developed world.

twin study Behavioral genetic research strategy, designed to determine the genetic contribution of a given trait, that involves comparing identical twins with fraternal twins (or with other people).

twin/adoption study Behavioral genetic research strategy that involves comparing the similarities of identical twin pairs adopted into different families, to determine the genetic contribution to a given trait.

U

ultrasound In pregnancy, an image of the fetus in the womb that helps to date the pregnancy, assess the fetus's growth, and identify abnormalities.

umbilical cord The structure that attaches the placenta to the fetus, through which nutrients are passed and fetal wastes are removed.

underextension An error in early language development in which young children apply verbal labels too narrowly.

undernutrition A chronic lack of adequate food.

upward mobility Rising in social class and/or economic status from one's childhood.

U-shaped curve of marital satisfaction The most common pathway of marital happiness in the West, in which satisfaction is highest at the honeymoon, declines during the child-rearing years, then rises after the children grow up.

uterus The pear-shaped muscular organ in a woman's abdomen that houses the developing baby.

V

validity In measurement terminology, a basic criterion for a test's accuracy involving whether that measure reflects the real-world quality it is supposed to measure.

value-comparison phase In Murstein's theory, the second mate-selection stage, in which we make judgments about a partner on the basis of similar values and interests.

vascular neurocognitive disorder (vascular dementia) A type of age-related cognitive disorder caused by multiple small strokes.

very low birth weight (VLBW) A weight at birth of less than 3¼ pounds.

visual cliff A table that appears to "end" in a drop-off at its midpoint; used to test infant depth perception.

W

widowhood mortality effect The elevated risk of death among surviving spouses after being widowed.

WISC (Wechsler Intelligence Scale for Children) The standard intelligence test used in childhood, consisting of different subtests.

working memory In information-processing theory, the limited-capacity gateway system, containing all the material that we can keep in awareness at a single time. The material in this system is either processed for more permanent storage or lost.

working model In Bowlby's theory, the mental representation of a caregiver that enables children over age 3 to be physically apart from the caregiver.

work–life balance A situation in which people feel a perfect balance, energized and happy at work and fulfilled with other aspects of their lives.

Y

young-old People in their sixties and seventies.

youth development program Any afterschool program or structured activity outside of the school day that is devoted to promoting flourishing in teenagers.

Z

zero-tolerance policies The practice in U.S. public high schools of suspending students after one rule infraction.

zone of proximal development (ZPD) In Vygotsky's theory, the gap between a child's ability to solve a problem totally on his own and his potential knowledge if taught by a more accomplished person.

zygote A fertilized ovum.

References

2015 Assisted Reproductive Technology, National Summary Report. (n.d.). Retrieved from https://www.cdc.gov/art/pdf/2015-report/ART-2015-National-Summary-Report.pdf

Abbate-Daga, G., Gramaglia, C., Amianto, F., Marzola, E., & Fassino, S. (2010). Attachment insecurity, personality, and body dissatisfaction in eating disorders. *The Journal of Nervous and Mental Disease, 198*(7), 520–524.

Abramson, L. Y., Seligman, M. E., & Teasdale, J. D. (1978). Learned helplessness in humans: Critique and reformulation. *Journal of Abnormal Psychology, 87*, 49–74.

Abu-Akel, A., & Shamay-Tsoory, S. (2011). Neuroanatomical and neurochemical bases of theory of mind. *Neuropsychologia, 49*, 2971–2984.

Abubakar, A., Holding, P., Vijver, F. J. R., Newton, C., & Baar, A. V. (2010). Children at risk for developmental delay can be recognised by stunting, being underweight, ill health, little maternal schooling or high gravity. *Journal of Child Psychology and Psychiatry, 51*(6), 652–659.

Abubakar, A. A., Vijver, F., Suryani, A., Handayani, P., & Pandia, W. (2015). Perceptions of parenting styles and their associations with mental health and life satisfaction among urban Indonesian adolescents. *Journal of Child & Family Studies, 24*(9), 2680–2692. doi:10.1007/s10826-014-0070-x

Acciai, F., & Firebaugh, G. (2017). Why did life expectancy decline in the United States in 2015? A gender-specific analysis. *Social Science and Medicine, 190*, 174–180. doi:10.1016/j.socscimed.2017.08.004

Acevedo, B. P., & Aron, A. (2009). Does long-term relationships kill romantic love? *Review of General Psychology, 13*, 59–65.

Acevedo-Polakovich, I. D., Cousineau, J. R., Quirk, K. M., Gerhart, J. I., Bell, K. M., & Adomako, M. S. (2014). Toward an asset orientation in the study of U.S. Latina youth: Biculturalism, ethnic identity, and positive youth development. *Counseling Psychologist, 42*(2), 201–222.

Adair, L. S. (2008). Child and adolescent obesity: Epidemiology and developmental perspectives. *Physiology & Behavior, 94*, 8–16.

Adams, G. A., & Rau, B. (2011). Putting off tomorrow to do what you want today: Planning for retirement. *American Psychologist, 66*(3), 180–192.

Adi-Japha, E., Berberich-Artzi, J., & Libnawi, A. (2010). Cognitive flexibility in drawings of bilingual children. *Child Development, 81*(5), 1356–1366.

Adler, N., Pantell, M. S., O'Donovan, A., Blackburn, E., Cawthon, R., Koster, A., . . . Epel, E. (2013). Educational attainment and late life telomere length in the health, aging and body composition study. *Brain, Behavior, and Immunity, 27*, 15–21.

Adolph, K., & Berger, S. E. (2006). Motor development. In D. Kuhn, R. S. Siegler, W. Damon, & R. M. Lerner (Eds.), *Handbook of child psychology: Vol. 2, Cognition, perception, and language* (6th ed., pp. 161–213). Hoboken, NJ: Wiley.

Adolph, K. E. (2008). Learning to move. *Current Directions in Psychological Science, 17*(3), 213–218.

Agency for Healthcare Research and Quality. (2014). Evidence report/technology assessment Number 214: Smoking cessation interventions in pregnancy and postpartum care executive summary. Effective Health Care Program, Rockville, MD: Author.

Aghabarary, M., & Nayeri, N. D. (2017). Reasons behind providing futile medical treatments in Iran: A qualitative study. *Nursing Ethics, 24*(1), 33–45. doi:10.1177/0969733016638142

Aghajanian, A., & Thompson, V. (2013). Recent divorce trend in Iran. *Journal of Divorce & Remarriage, 54*(2), 112–125.

Agrawal, A., & Lynskey, M. T. (2008). Are there genetic influences on addiction: Evidence from family, adoption, and twin studies. *Addiction, 103*, 1069–1081.

Ahn, S. J., Kyeong, S., Suh, S. H., Kim, J., Chung, T., & Seok, J. (2016). What is the impact of child abuse on gray matter abnormalities in individuals with major depressive disorder: A case control study. *BMC Psychiatry, 16*, 161–167. doi:10.1186/s12888-016-1116-y

Ahnert, L., Pinquart, M., & Lamb, M. (2006). Security of children's relationships with nonparental care providers: A meta-analysis. *Child Development, 74*(3), 664–679.

Ainsworth, M. D. S. (1967). *Infancy in Uganda: Infant care and the growth of love.* Baltimore, MD: Johns Hopkins Press.

Ainsworth, M. D. S. (1973). The development of infant–mother attachment. In B. M. Caldwell & H. N. Ricciuti (Eds.), *Review of child development research* (Vol. 3, pp. 1–94). Chicago, IL: University of Chicago Press.

Ainsworth, M. D. S., Blehar, M. C., Waters, E., & Wall, S. (1978). *Patterns of attachment: A psychological study of the strange situation.* Hillsdale, NJ: Erlbaum.

Ajibade, A., Hook, J. N., Utsey, S. O., Davis, D. E., & Tongeren, D. V. (2016). Racial/ethnic identity, religious commitment, and well-being in African Americans. *Journal of Black Psychology, 42*(3), 244–258.

Aknin, L. B., Hamlin, J. K., & Dunn, E. W. (2012). Giving leads to happiness in young children. *Plos ONE, 7*(6).

Aksan, N., & Kochanska, G. (2004). Links between systems of inhibition from infancy to preschool years. *Child Development, 75*(5), 1477–1490.

Aksan, N., Sager, L., Hacker, S., Lester, B., Dawson, J., Rizzo, M., & Foley, J. (2017). Individual differences in cognitive functioning predict effectiveness of a heads-up lane departure warning for younger and older drivers. *Accident Analysis and Prevention, 99*(Part A), 171–183. doi:10.1016/j.aap.2016.11.003

Al Gharaibeh, F. (2015). The effects of divorce on children: Mothers' perspectives in UAE. *Journal of Divorce and Remarriage, 56*(5), 347–368. doi:10.1080/10502556.2015.1046800

Albert, I., Labs, K., & Trommsdorff, G. (2010). Are older adult German women satisfied with their lives? On the role of life domains, partnership status, and self-control. *GeroPsych, 23*(1), 39–49.

Albuquerque, S., Ferreira, L. C., Narciso, I., & Pereira, M. (2017). Parents' positive interpersonal coping after a child's death. *Journal of Child and Family Studies, 26*(7), 1817–1830.

Alderson, R. M., Hudec, K. L., Patros, C. G., & Kasper, L. J. (2013). Working memory deficits in adults with attention-deficit/hyperactivity disorder (ADHD): An examination of central executive and storage/rehearsal processes. *Journal of Abnormal Psychology, 122*(2), 532–541.

Aldred, H. E. (1997). *Pregnancy and birth sourcebook: Basic information about planning for pregnancy, maternal health, fetal growth and development.* Detroit, MI: Omnigraphics.

Alea, N., & Wang, Q. (2015). Going global: The functions of autobiographical memory in cultural context. *Memory, 23*(1), 1–10. doi:10.1080/09658211.2014.972416

Alessandri, G., Eisenberg, N., Vecchione, M., Caprara, G. V., & Milioni, M. (2016). Ego-resiliency development from late adolescence to emerging adulthood: A ten-year longitudinal study. *Journal of Adolescence, 50,* 91–102.

Al-Hakami, H., & McLaughlin, K. (2016). Debatable marriages: Marriage and child marriage in Saudi Arabia. *Marriage & Family Review, 52*(7), 654. doi:10.1080/01494929.2016.1157119

Ali, M. M., & Dwyer, D. S. (2011). Estimating peer effects in sexual behavior among adolescents. *Journal of Adolescence, 34,* 183–190.

Allemand, M., Steiger, A. E., & Hill, P. L. (2013). Stability of personality traits in adulthood: Mechanisms and implications. *Geropsych: The Journal of Gerontopsychology and Geriatric Psychiatry, 26*(1), 5–13.

Allen, J. P., Porter, M., McFarland, C., McElhaney, K. B., & Marsh, P. (2007). The relation of attachment security to adolescents' paternal and peer relationships, depression, and externalizing behavior. *Child Development, 78*(4), 1222–1239.

Allen, S., & Hawkins, A. J. (2017). Theorizing the decision-making process for divorce or reconciliation. *Journal of Family Theory & Review, 9*(1), 50–68. doi:10.1111/jftr.12176

Allen, T. D., & Finkelstein, L. M. (2014). Work–family conflict among members of full-time dual-earner couples: An examination of family life stage, gender, and age. *Journal of Occupational Health Psychology, 19*(3), 376–384.

Allendorf, K. (2013). Schemas of marital change: From arranged marriages to eloping for love. *Journal of Marriage and Family, 75*(2), 453–469.

Allison, C. M., & Hyde, J. S. (2013). Early menarche: Confluence of biological and contextual factors. *Sex Roles, 68* (1–2), 55–64.

Alloway, T. P., McCallum, F., Alloway, R. G., & Hoicka, E. (2015). Liar, liar, working memory on fire: Investigating the role of working memory in childhood verbal deception. *Journal of Experimental Child Psychology, 137,* 30–38. doi:10.1016/j.jecp.2015.03.013

Almas, A. N., Degnan, K. A., Nelson, C. A., Zeanah, C. H., & Fox, N. A. (2016). IQ at age 12 following a history of institutional care: Findings from the Bucharest Early Intervention Project. *Developmental Psychology, 52*(11), 1858–1866.

Alt, D. (2016). Using structural equation modeling and multidimensional scaling to assess female college students' academic adjustment as a function of perceived parenting styles. *Current Psychology: A Journal for Diverse Perspectives on Diverse Psychological Issues, 35*(4), 549–561. doi:10.1007/s12144-015-9320-3

Alzheimer's Association. (2016). *2016 Alzheimer's Disease Facts and Figures:* Chicago, IL: National Office.

Amaro, L. M., & Miller, K. I. (2016). Discussion of care, contribution, and perceived (in)gratitude in the family caregiver and sibling relationship. *Personal Relationships, 23,* 98–110. doi.org/10.1111/pere.12113

Amato, P. R. (2007). Transformative processes in marriage: Some thoughts from a sociologist. *Journal of Marriage and Family, 69*(2), 305–309.

Amato, P. R. (2010). Research on divorce: Continuing trends and new developments. *Journal of Marriage and Family, 72,* 650–666.

Amato, P. R., & Hohmann-Marriott, B. (2007). A comparison of high- and low-distress marriages that end in divorce. *Journal of Marriage and Family, 69*(3), 621–638.

Ambrose, A. F., Paul, G., & Hausdorff, J. M. (2013). Risk factors for falls among older adults: A review of the literature. *Maturitas, 75*(1), 51–61.

American Academy of Pediatrics, Committee on Drugs. (2000). Use of psychoactive medication during pregnancy and possible effects on the fetus and newborn. *Pediatrics, 105,* 880–887.

American Heart Association. (2001). *2002 heart and stroke statistical update.* Dallas, TX: American Heart Association.

American Psychiatric Association. (2013). *Diagnostic and statistical manual of mental disorders* (5th ed.). Arlington, VA: American Psychiatric Publishing.

American Teens' Sources of Sexual Health Education. (2016, October 27). Retrieved from https://www.guttmacher.org/fact-sheet/facts-american-teens-sources-informationabout-sex

Anakwenze, U., & Zuberi, D. (2013). Mental health and poverty in the inner city. *Health & Social Work, 38*(3), 147–157.

Andero, A. A., & Stewart, A. (2002). Issue of corporal punishment: Re-examined. *Journal of Instructional Psychology, 29,* 90–96.

Anders, T., Goodlin-Jones, B. L., & Zelenko, M. (1998). Infant regulation and sleep–wake state development. *Zero to Three, 19*(2), 9–14.

Anderson, D. R., Roubinov, D. S., Turner, A. P., Williams, R. M., Norvell, D. C., & Czerniecki, J. M. (2017). Perceived social support moderates the relationship between activities of daily living and depression after lower limb loss. *Rehabilitation Psychology, 62*(2), 214–220. doi:10.1037/rep0000133

Anderson, J. W. (1972). Attachment behavior out of doors. In N. Blurton Jones (Ed.), *Ethological studies of child behaviour* (pp. 199–215). London, England: Cambridge University Press.

Anderson, R., & Mitchell, E. M. (1984). Children's health and play in rural Nepal. *Social Science & Medicine, 19,* 735–740.

Andrew, R., Tiggemann, M., & Clark, L. (2016). Predictors and health-related outcomes of positive body image in adolescent girls: A prospective study. *Developmental Psychology, 52*(3), 463–474. doi:10.1037/dev0000095

Andrews, T., & Knaak, S. (2013). Medicalized mothering: Experiences with breastfeeding in Canada and Norway. *The Sociological Review, 61*(1), 88–110.

Angelini, V., Cavapozzi, D., Corazzini, L., & Paccagnella, O. (2012). Age, health and life satisfaction among older Europeans. *Social Indicators Research, 105*(2), 293–308.

Annerbäck, E.-M., Svedin, C.-G., & Gustafsson, P. A. (2010). Characteristic features of severe child physical abuse—A multi-informant approach. *Journal of Family Violence, 25,* 165–172.

Anusic, I., Yap, S. Y., & Lucas, R. E. (2014). Does personality moderate reaction and adaptation to major life events? Analysis of life satisfaction and affect in an Australian national sample. *Journal of Research in Personality, 51,* 69–77.

Archibald, A. B., Graber, J. A., & Brooks-Gunn, J. (2003). Pubertal processes and physiological growth in adolescence. In G. R. Adams & M. D. Berzonsky (Eds.), *Blackwell handbook of adolescence* (pp. 24–47). Malden, MA: Blackwell.

Ardelt, M. (2016). Disentangling the relations between wisdom and different types of well-being in old age: Findings from a short-term longitudinal study. *Journal of Happiness Studies, 17*(5), 1963–1984. doi.org/10.1007/s10902-015-9680-2

Ardelt, M., & Edwards, C. A. (2016). Wisdom at the end of life: An analysis of mediating and moderating relations between wisdom and subjective well-being. *Journals of Gerontology: Series B, 71*(3), 502–513. doi.org/10.1093/geronb/gbv051

Ardelt, M., & Koenig, C. S. (2006). The role of religion for hospice patients and relatively healthy older adults. *Research on Aging, 28,* 184–215.

Ardila, A. (2007). Normal aging increases cognitive heterogeneity: Analysis of dispersion in WAIS-III scores across age. *Archives of Clinical Neuropsychology, 22,* 1003–1011.

Arias E., Kochanek, K. D., & Anderson R. N. (2015). *How does cause of death contribute to the Hispanic mortality advantage in the United States?* NCHS data brief, no 221. Hyattsville, MD: National Center for Health Statistics.

Ariès, P. (1962). *Centuries of childhood: A social history of family life.* New York, NY: Knopf.

Ariès, P. (1974). *Western attitudes toward death: From the Middle Ages to the present* (P. M. Ranum, Trans.). Baltimore, MD: Johns Hopkins University Press.

Ariès, P. (1981). *The hour of our death* (H. Weaver, Trans.). New York, NY: Knopf.

Arnett, J. J. (2004). *Emerging adulthood: The winding road from the late teens through the twenties.* New York, NY: Oxford University Press.

Arnett, J. J. (2007). The long and leisurely route: Coming of age in Europe today. *Current History: A Journal of Contemporary Affairs, 106,* 130–136.

Arnett, J. J. (2016). Does emerging adulthood theory apply across social classes? National data on a persistent question. *Emerging Adulthood, 4*(4), 227–235.

Arnett, J. J., & Padilla-Walker, L. M. (2015). Brief report: Danish emerging adults' conceptions of adulthood. *Journal of Adolescence, 38,* 39–44.

Aron, A., Norman, C. C., Aron, E. N., & Lewandowski, G. (2002). Shared participation in self-expanding activities: Positive effects on experienced marital quality. In P. Noller & J. A. Feeney (Eds.), *Understanding marriage: Developments in the study of couple interaction* (pp. 177–194). New York, NY: Cambridge University Press.

Ashburn-Nardo, L. (2017). Parenthood as a moral imperative? Moral outrage and the stigmatization of voluntarily childfree women and men. *Sex Roles: A Journal of Research, 5 6,* 393. doi:10.1007/s11199-016-0606-1

Atchley, R. (1989). A continuity theory of normal aging. *The Gerontologist, 29*(2), 183–190.

AVERT. (2005). *AIDS and HIV statistics for sub-Saharan Africa.* Retrieved from http://www.avert.org/subadults.htm,

Avis, N. E., Assmann, S. F., Kravitz, H. M., Ganz, P. A., & Ory, M. (2004). Quality of life in diverse groups of midlife women: Assessing the influence of menopause, health status and psychosocial and demographic factors. *Quality of Life Research, 13,* 933–946.

Axelsson, A., Andersson, R., & Gulz, A. (2016). Scaffolding executive function capabilities via play-&-learn software for preschoolers. *Journal of Educational Psychology, 108*(7), 969–981. doi:10.1037/edu0000099

Ayalon, L., & Green, V. (2013). Social ties in the context of the continuing care retirement community. *Qualitative Health Research, 23*(3), 396–406.

Babic, A., Hansez, I., Stinglhamber, F., & Bertrand, F. (2017). Work–home interface and well-being: A cross-lagged analysis. *Journal of Personnel Psychology, 16*(1), 46–55.

Backhaus, R., Van Rossum, E., Verbeek, H., Halfens, R. J., Tan, F. E., Capezuti, E., & Hamers, J. P. (2017). Work environment characteristics associated with quality of care in Dutch nursing homes: A cross-sectional study. *International Journal of Nursing Studies, 66,* 15– 22. doi:10.1016/j.ijnurstu.2016.12.001

Baddeley, A. D. (1992). Working memory: The interface between memory and cognition. *Journal of Cognitive Neuroscience, 4,* 281–288.

Bahrick, L. B., Todd, J. T., Castellanos, I., & Sorondo, B. M. (2016). Enhanced attention to speaking faces versus other event types emerges gradually across infancy. *Developmental Psychology, 52*(11), 1705–1720. doi:10.1037/dev0000157

Baibazarova, E., van de Beek, C., Cohen-Kettenis, P. T., Buitelaar, J., Shelton, K. H., & van Goozen, S. M. (2013). Influence of prenatal maternal stress, maternal plasma cortisol and cortisol in the amniotic fluid on birth outcomes and child temperament at 3 months. *Psychoneuroendocrinology, 38*(6), 907–915.

Baijot, S., Slama, H., Soderlund, G., Ban, B., Colin, C., Deitnre, P., & Deconnick, N. (2016). Neuropsychological and neurophysiological benefits in children without and with ADHD. *Behavioral Brain Function, 12*(11).

Baillargeon, R. (1993). The object concept revisited: New direction in the investigation of infants' physical knowledge. In C. Granrud (Ed.), *Visual perception and cognition in infancy* (pp. 265–315). Hillsdale, NJ: Erlbaum.

Baillargeon, R., & DeVos, J. (1991). Object permanence in young infants: Further evidence. *Child Development, 62,* 1227–1246.

Baillargeon, R., & Graber, M. (1987). Where's the rabbit? 5.5-month-old infants' representation of the height of a hidden object. *Cognitive Development, 2,* 375–392.

Baillargeon, R., Scott, R. M., & Bian, L. (2016). Psychological reasoning in infancy. *Annual Review of Psychology, 67*(1), 159–186. doi:10.1146/annurev-psych-010213-115033

Bainbridge, K. E., & Wallhagen, M. I. (2014). Hearing loss in an aging American population: Extent, impact, and management. *Annual Review of Public Health, 35,* 139–152.

Baker, J. E., & Sedney, M. A. (1996). How bereaved children cope with loss: An overview. In C. A. Corr & D. Corr (Eds.), *Handbook of childhood death and bereavement* (pp. 109–129). New York, NY: Springer.

Balk, D. E. (2008a). A modest proposal about bereavement and recovery. *Death Studies, 32,* 84–93.

Balk, D. E. (2008b). Special issue on bereavement, outcomes, and recovery: Guest editor's opening remarks. *Death Studies, 32,* 1–5.

Ball, H. L., & Volpe, L. E. (2013). Sudden Infant Death Syndrome (SIDS) risk reduction and infant sleep location— Moving the discussion forward. *Social Science & Medicine, 79,* 84–91.

Ballantine, P. W., Lin, Y., & Veer, E. (2015). The influence of user comments on perceptions of Facebook relationship status updates. *Computers in Human Behavior, 49,* 50–55.

Ballard, R. H., Holtzworth-Munroe, A., Applegate, A. G., D'Onofrio, B. M., & Bates, J. E. (2013). A randomized controlled trial of child-informed mediation. *Psychology, Public Policy, and Law, 19*(3), 271–281.

Ballinger, S., Tisdale, T., Sellen, D., & Martin, L. (2017). Slowing down time: An exploration of personal life extension desirability as it relates to religiosity and specific religious beliefs. *Journal of Religion & Health, 56*(1), 171–187. doi:10.1007/s10943-016-0218-7

Baltes, M. M., & Carstensen, L. L. (2003). The process of successful aging: Selection, optimization and compensation. In U. M. Staudinger & U. Lindenberger (Eds.), *Understanding human development: Dialogues with lifespan psychology* (pp. 81–104). Dordrecht, Netherlands: Kluwer Academic.

Baltes, P. B. (2003). On the incomplete architecture of human ontogeny: Selection, optimization, and compensation as foundation of developmental theory. In U. M. Staudinger & U. Lindenberger (Eds.), *Understanding human development: Dialogues with lifespan psychology* (pp. 17–43). Boston, MA: Kluwer Academic.

Baltes, P. B., & Smith, J. (1997). A systemic-holistic view of psychological functioning in very old age: Introduction to a collection of articles from the Berlin Aging Study. *Psychology and Aging, 12*, 395–409.

Banducci, A. N., Gomes, M., MacPherson, L., Lejuez, C. W., Potenza, M. N., Gelernter, J., & Amstadter, A. B. (2014). A preliminary examination of the relationship between the 5-HTTLPR and childhood emotional abuse on depressive symptoms in 10–12-year-old youth. *Psychological Trauma: Theory, Research, Practice, and Policy, 6*(1), 1–7.

Bandura, A. (1977). *Social learning theory.* Englewood Cliffs, NJ: Prentice Hall.

Bandura, A. (1986). *Social foundations of thought and action: A social cognitive theory.* Englewood Cliffs, NJ: Prentice-Hall.

Bandura, A. (1989). Human agency in social cognitive theory. *American Psychologist, 44*, 1175–1184.

Bandura, A. (1992). Exercise of personal agency through the self-efficacy mechanism. In R. Schwarzer (Ed.), *Self-efficacy: Thought control of action* (pp. 3–38). Washington, DC: Hemisphere.

Bandura, A. (1997). *Self-efficacy: The exercise of control.* New York, NY: Freeman.

Bane, K. (2004). *What the best college teachers do.* Cambridge, MA: President and Fellows of Harvard College.

Bangerter, L. R., & Waldron, V. R. (2014). Turning points in long distance grandparent–grandchild relationships. *Journal of Aging Studies, 29*, 88–97.

Barber, S. J., Opitz, P. C., Martins, B., Sakaki, M., & Mather, M. (2016). Thinking about a limited future enhances the positivity of younger and older adults' recall: Support for socioemotional selectivity theory. *Memory & Cognition, 44*(6), 869–882. doi:10.3758/s13421-016-0612-0

Barbosa, A., Nolan, M., Sousa, L., & Figueiredo, D. (2017). Person-centeredness in direct care workers caring for residents with dementia: Effects of a psycho-educational intervention. *Dementia: The International Journal of Social Research and Practice, 16*(2), 192–203. doi:10.1177/1471301215585667

Barkin, S., Scheindlin, B., Ip, E. H., Richardson, I., & Finch, S. (2007). Determinants of parental discipline practices: A national sample from primary care practices. *Clinical Pediatrics, 46*(1), 64–69.

Barkley, R. A. (1998). *Attention-deficit hyperactivity disorder: A handbook for diagnosis and treatment* (2nd ed.). New York, NY: Guilford Press.

Barkley, R. A., & Murphy, K. R. (2006). *Attention-deficit hyperactivity disorder: A clinical workbook* (3rd ed.). New York, NY: Guilford Press.

Barnard, P., Moreland, I., & Nagy, J. (1999). *Children, bereavement and trauma: Nurturing resilience.* London, England: Jessica Kingsley.

Barnes, G. M., Hoffman, J. H., Welte, J. W., Farrell, M. P., & Dintcheff, B. A. (2007). Adolescents' time use: Effects on substance use, delinquency and sexual activity. *Journal of Youth and Adolescence, 36*, 697–710.

Barnett, L. M., van Beurden, E., Morgan, P. J., Brooks, L. O., & Beard, J. R. (2009). Childhood motor skill proficiency as a predictor of adolescent physical activity. *Journal of Adolescent Health, 44*, 252–259.

Barnett, S. M., Ceci, S. J., & Williams, W. M. (2006). Is the ability to make a bacon sandwich a mark of intelligence? And other issues: Some reflections on Gardner's theory of multiple intelligences. In J. A. Schaler (Ed.), *Howard Gardner under fire: The rebel psychologist faces his critics* (pp. 95–114). Chicago, IL: Open Court.

Barnett, W. S., & Friedman-Krauss, A. H. (2016). *State(s) of Head Start.* New Brunswick, NJ: National Institute for Early Education Research.

Barnhart, S., & Maguire-Jack, K. (2016). Single mothers in their communities: The mediating role of parenting stress and depression between social cohesion, social control and child maltreatment. *Children & Youth Services Review, 70*, 37–45. doi:10.1016/j.childyouth.2016.09.003

Baron, I. S., & Rey-Casserly, C. (2010). Extremely preterm birth outcome: A review of four decades of cognitive research. *Neuropsychology Review, 20*(4), 430–425.

Barr, A. B., Lorenz, F. O., Sutton, T. E., Gordon Simons, L., Wickrama, K. S., & Simons, L. G. (2016). Romantic relationship transitions and changes in health among rural, White young adults. *Journal of Family Psychology, 30*(7), 832–842.

Barrera, C. M., Perrine, C. G., Li, R., & Scanlon, K. S. (2016). Age at introduction to solid foods and child obesity at 6 years. *Childhood Obesity, 12*(3), 188–192.

Barrett, E. S., Tran, V., Thurston, S., Jasienska, G., Furberg, A., Ellison, P. T., & Thune, I. (2013). Marriage and motherhood are associated with lower testosterone concentrations in women. *Hormones and Behavior, 63*(1), 72–79.

Barry, R. A., & Kochanska, G. (2010). A longitudinal investigation of the affective environment in families with young children: From infancy to early school age. *Emotion, 10*(2), 237–249.

Batool, S. S., & de Visser, R. O. (2016). Experiences of infertility in British and Pakistani women: A cross-cultural qualitative analysis. *Health Care for Women International, 37*(2), 180–196.

Baumeister, R. F., Campbell, J. D., Krueger, J. I., & Vohs, K. D. (2003). Does high self-esteem cause better performance, interpersonal success, happiness, or healthier lifestyles? *Psychological Science in the Public Interest, 4*(1), 1–44.

Baumrind, D. (1971). Current patterns of parental authority. *Developmental Psychology, 4*(1, Pt. 2), 1–103.

Baumrind, D., Larzelere, R. E., & Cowan, P. A. (2002). Ordinary physical punishment: Is it harmful? Comment on Gershoff. *Psychological Bulletin, 128*, 580–589.

Bava, S., Thayer, R., Jacobus, J., Ward, M., Jernigan, T. L., & Tapert, S. F. (2010). Longitudinal characterization of white matter maturation during adolescence. *Brain Research, 1327*, 38–46.

Becker, S. P., Fite, P. J., Luebbe, A. M., Stoppelbein, L., & Greening, L. (2013). Friendship intimacy exchange buffers the relation between ADHD symptoms and later social problems among children attending an afterschool care program. *Journal of Psychopathology and Behavioral Assessment, 35*(2), 142–152.

Becker-Blease, K. A., Turner, H. A., & Finkelhor, D. (2010). Disasters, victimization, and children's mental health. *Child Development, 81*(4), 1040–1052.

Beckmann, C. R. B., Ling, F. W., Laube, D. W., Smith, R. P., Barzansky, B. M., & Herbert, W. N. P. (2002). *Obstetrics and gynecology* (4th ed.). Baltimore, MD: Lippincott Williams & Wilkins.

Beernick, A. C. E., Swinkels, S. H. N., & Buitelaar, J. K. (2007). Problem behavior in a community sample of 14- and 19-month-old children. *European Child and Adolescent Psychiatry, 16,* 271–280.

Begley, A. M. (2008). Guilty but good: Defending voluntary active euthanasia from a virtue perspective. *Nursing Ethics, 15*(4), 434–445.

Behboodi-Moghadam, Z., Salsali, M., Eftekhar- Ardabily, H., Vaismoradi, M., & Ramezanzadeh, F. (2013). Experiences of infertility through the lens of Iranian infertile women: A qualitative study. *Japan Journal of Nursing Science, 10*(1), 41–46.

Behrens, K. Y., Haltigan, J. D., & Bahm, N. I. (2016). Infant attachment, adult attachment, and maternal sensitivity: Revisiting the intergenerational transmission gap. *Attachment & Human Development, 18*(4), 337–353. doi:10.1080/14616734.2016.1167095

Behrens, K. Y., Parker, A. C., & Haltigan, J. D. (2011). Maternal sensitivity assessed during the Strange Situation Procedure predicts child's attachment quality and reunion behaviors. *Infant Behavior and Development, 34*(2), 378–381.

Beijers, R., Cillessen, L., & Zijlmans, M. A. (2016). An experimental study on mother–infant skin-to-skin contact in full-terms. *Infant Behavior and Development, 43,* 58–65. doi:10.1016/j.infbeh.2016.01.001

Beijers, R., Riksen-Walraven, J. M., & deWeerth, C. (2013). Cortisol regulation in 12-month-old human infants: Associations with the infants' early history of breastfeeding and co-sleeping. *Stress: The International Journal on the Biology of Stress, 16*(3), 267–277.

Beiner, S. F., Lowenstein, L., Worenklein, A., & Sauber, S. R. (2014). Grandparents' rights: Psychological and legal perspectives. *American Journal of Family Therapy, 42*(2), 114–126.

Bell, A. S. (2011). A critical review of ADHD diagnostic criteria: What to address in the *DSM-V. Journal of Attention Disorders, 15*(1), 3–10.

Bellinger, D., Leviton, A., Waternaux, C., Needleman, H., & Rabinowitz, M. (1987). Longitudinal analyses of prenatal and postnatal lead exposure and early cognitive development. *New England Journal of Medicine, 316,* 1037–1043.

Belsky, J. (2016). Experiencing the lifespan (4th ed.). New York, NY: Worth.

Belsky, J. K. (1999). *The psychology of aging: Theory, research, and interventions* (3rd ed.). Pacific Grove, CA: Brooks/Cole.

Belsky, J., Houts, R. M., & Pasco Fearon, R. M. (2010). Infant attachment security and the timing of puberty: Testing an evolutionary hypothesis. *Psychological Science, 21,* 1195–1201.

Belsky, J., Lang, M. E., & Rovine, M. (1985). Stability and change in marriage across the transition to parenthood: A second study. *Journal of Marriage and the Family, 47,* 855–865.

Belsky, J., & Pluess, M. (2009). Beyond diathesis stress: Differential susceptibility to environmental influences. *Psychological Bulletin, 135*(6), 885–908.

Belsky, J., & Pluess, M. (2011). Beyond adversity, vulnerability, and resilience: Individual differences in developmental plasticity. In D. Cicchetti & G. I. Roisman (Eds.), *The origins and organization of adaptation and maladaptation* (pp. 379–422). Hoboken, NJ: Wiley.

Belsky, J., & Pluess, M. (2013). Genetic moderation of early child-care effects on social functioning across childhood: A developmental analysis. *Child Development, 84*(4), 1209–1225.

Belsky, J., & Pluess, M. (2016). Differential susceptibility to environmental influences. In D. Cicchetti (Ed.), *Developmental psychopathology* (3rd ed.). New York, NY: Wiley.

Belsky, J., & Rovine, M. (1990). Patterns of marital change across the transition to parenthood: Pregnancy to three years postpartum. *Journal of Marriage & the Family, 52,* 5–19.

Belsky, J., Ruttle, P. L., Boyce, W. T., Armstrong, J. M., & Essex, M. J. (2015). Early adversity, elevated stress physiology, accelerated sexual maturation, and poor health in females. *Developmental Psychology, 51*(6), 816–822. doi:10.1037/dev0000017

Belsky, J., Steinberg, L. D., Houts, R. M., Friedman, S. L., DeHart, G., Cauffman, E., . . . Susman, E. (2007a). Family rearing antecedents of pubertal timing. *Child Development, 78*(4), 1302–1321.

Belsky, J., Vandell, D. L., Burchinal, M., Clarke-Stewart, K. A., McCartney, K., Owen, M. T., & The NICHD Early Child Care Research Network. (2007b). Are there long-term effects of early child care? *Child Development, 78*(2), 681–701.

Belsky, J., & Volling, B. L. (1987). Mothering, fathering, and marital interaction in the family triad during infancy: Exploring family systems processes. In P. W. Berman & F. A. Pedersen (Eds.), *Men's transitions to parenthood: Longitudinal studies of early family experience* (pp. 37–63). Hillsdale, NJ: Erlbaum.

Bem, S. L. (1981). Gender schema theory: A cognitive account of sex typing. *Psychological Review, 88,* 354–364.

Beneventi, H., Tonnessen, F. E., Ersland, L., & Hugdahl, K. (2010). Working memory deficit in dyslexia: Behavioral and fMRI evidence. *International Journal of Neuroscience, 120,* 51–59.

Bengtson, V. L. (1989). The problem of generations: Age group contrasts, continuities, and social change. In V. L. Bengtson & K. W. Schaie (Eds.), *The course of later life: Research and reflections* (pp. 25–54). New York, NY: Springer.

Ben-Itzchak, E., Zukerman, G., & Zachor, D. A. (2016). Having older siblings is associated with less severe social communication symptoms in young children with autism spectrum disorder. *Journal of Abnormal Child Psychology, 44*(8), 1613–1620. doi:10.1007/s10802-016-0133-0

Benjet, C., & Kazdin, A. E. (2003). Spanking children: The controversies, findings and new directions. *Clinical Psychology Review, 23,* 197–224.

Benner, A. D., Kretsch, N., Harden, P., & Crosnoe, R. (2014). Academic achievement as a moderator of genetic influences on alcohol use in adolescence. *Developmental Psychology, 50*(4), 1170–1178.

Benoit, A., Lacourse, E., & Claes, M. (2013). Pubertal timing and depressive symptoms in late adolescence: The moderating role of individual, peer, and parental factors. *Development and Psychopathology, 25*(2), 455–471.

Berger, A., Alyagon, U., Hadaya, H., Atzaba-Poria, N., & Auerbach, J. G. (2013). Response inhibition in preschoolers at familial risk for attention deficit hyperactivity disorder: A behavioral and electrophysiological stop signal study. *Child Development, 84*(5), 1616–1632.

Berger, C., & Caravita, S. C. (2016). Why do early adolescents bully? Exploring the influence of prestige norms on social and psychological motives to bully. *Journal of Adolescence, 46,* 45–56.

Bergh, C., Callmar, M., Danemar, S., Holcke, M., Isberg, S., Leon, M., . . . Sodersten, P. (2013). Effective treatment of eating disorders: Results at multiple sites. *Behavioral Neuroscience, 127*(6), 878–889.

Bergsma, A., & Ardelt, M. (2011). Self-reported wisdom and happiness: An empirical investigation. *Journal of Happiness Studies, 37*(2), 1–19.

Berk, L. E., & Winsler, A. (1999). *NAEYC research into practice series: Vol. 7. Scaffolding children's learning: Vygotsky and early childhood education.* Washington, DC: National Association for the Education of Young Children.

Berkman, L., & Breslow, L. (1983). *Health and ways of living: The Alameda County study.* New York, NY: Oxford University Press.

Berko, J. (1958). The child's learning of English morphology. *Word, 14,* 150–177.

Berlin, L. J., Appleyard, K., & Dodge, K. (2011). Intergenerational continuity in child maltreatment: Mediating mechanisms and implications for prevention. *Child Development, 82*(1), 162–176.

Berry, D., Blair, C., & Granger, D. A. (2016). Child care and cortisol across infancy and toddlerhood: Poverty, peers, and developmental timing. *Family Relations, 65*(1), 51–72. doi:10.1111/fare.12184

Berry, D., Blair, C., Ursache, A., Willoughby, M. T., & Granger, D. A. (2014). Early childcare, executive functioning, and the moderating role of early stress physiology. *Developmental Psychology, 50*(4), 1250–1261.

Bersamin, M., Bourdeau, B., Fisher, D. A., Hill, D. L., Walker, S., Grube, J. W., & Grube, E. L. (2008). *Casual partnerships: Media exposure and relationship status at last oral sex and vaginal intercourse.* Paper presented at the Biennial Meeting of the Society for Research in Adolescence, Chicago, 2008.

Berthelsen, D., & Brownlee, J. (2007). Working with toddlers in child care: Practitioners' beliefs about their role. *Early Childhood Research Quarterly, 22,* 347–362.

Bertozzi, B., Tosti, V., & Fontana, L. (2017). Beyond calories: An integrated approach to promote health, longevity, and well-being. *Gerontology, 63*(1), 13–19.

Berzin, S. C., & De Marco, A. C. (2010). Understanding the impact of poverty on critical events in emerging adulthood. *Youth & Society, 43*(2), 278–300.

Best, J. R., & Miller, P. H. (2010). A developmental perspective on executive function. *Child Development, 81*(6), 1641–1660.

Beyers, W., & Luyckx, K. (2016). Ruminative exploration and reconsideration of commitment as risk factors for suboptimal identity development in adolescence and emerging adulthood. *Journal of Adolescence, 47,* 169–178.

Bhana, D. (2016). "Sex isn't better than love": Exploring South African Indian teenage male and female desires beyond danger. *Childhood, 23*(3), 362–377. doi:10.1177/0907568216642828

Bianchi, S. M., & Milkie, M. A. (2010). Work and family research in the first decade of the 21st century. *Journal of Marriage and Family, 72,* 705–725.

Bianchi, S., Robinson, J. R., & Milkie, M. A. (2006). *Changing rhythms of American family life.* New York, NY: Russell Sage Foundation.

Binstock, R. H. (2010). From compassionate ageism to intergenerational conflict? *The Gerontologist, 50*(5), 574–585.

Birren, J. E., & Birren, B. A. (1990). The concepts, models, and history of the psychology of aging. In J. E. Birren & K. W. Schaie (Eds.), *Handbook of the psychology of aging* (3rd ed., pp. 3–20). San Diego, CA: Academic Press.

Bjork, J. M., & Pardini, D. A. (2015). Who are those "risk-taking adolescents"? Individual differences in developmental neuroimaging research. *Developmental Cognitive Neuroscience, 11* (Proceedings from the inaugural Flux Congress; towards an integrative developmental cognitive neuroscience), 56–64.

Björk, S. (2013). Doing morally intelligible fatherhood: Swedish fathers' accounts of their parental part-time work choices. *Fathering, 11*(2), 221–237.

Bjorklund, D. F. (2005). *Children's thinking: Cognitive development and individual differences* (4th ed.). Belmont, CA: Wadsworth.

Bjorklund, D. F., & Bjorklund, B. R. (1992). *Looking at children: An introduction to child development.* Monterey, CA: Brooks-Cole.

Bjorklund, D. F., & Pellegrini, A. D. (2002). *The origins of human nature: Evolutionary developmental psychology.* Washington, DC: American Psychological Association.

Bjorklund, D. F., & Rosenblum, K. E. (2001). Children's use of multiple and variable addition strategies in a game context. *Developmental Science, 4,* 184–194.

Black, H. K., & Rubinstein, R. L. (2005). Direct care workers' response to dying and death in the nursing home: A case study. *Journals of Gerontology: Psychological Sciences, 60B,* S3–S10.

Blair, C. (2017). Educating executive function. Wiley Interdisciplinary Reviews. *Cognitive Science, 8*(1–2). doi:10.1002/wcs.1403

Blakely-McClure, S., & Ostrov, J. (2016). Relational aggression, victimization and self-concept: Testing pathways from middle childhood to adolescence. *Journal of Youth & Adolescence, 45*(2), 376–390.

Blakemore, S.-J., Burnett, S., & Dahl, R. E. (2010). The role of puberty in the developing adolescent brain. *Human Brain Mapping, 31,* 926–933.

Blakemore, S., & Mills, K. L. (2014). Is adolescence a sensitive period for sociocultural processing? *Annual Review of Psychology, 65,* 187–207.

Blatney, M., Jelinek, M., & Osecka, T. (2007). Assertive toddler, self-efficacious adult: Child temperament predicts personality over forty years. *Personality and Individual Differences, 43,* 2127–2136.

Bleidorn, W., Kandler, C., & Caspi, A. (2014). The behavioural genetics of personality development in adulthood—Classic, contemporary, and future trends. *European Journal of Personality, 28*(3), 244–255.

Blikshavn, T., Husum, T. L., & Magelssen, M. (2017). Four reasons why assisted dying should not be offered for depression. *Journal of Bioethical Inquiry, 14*(1), 151. doi:10.1007/s11673-016-9759-4

Bloch, L., Haase, C. M., & Levenson, R. W. (2014). Emotion regulation predicts marital satisfaction: More than a wives' tale. *Emotion, 14*(1), 130–144.

Blomeyer, D., Friemel, C. M., Buchmann, A. F., Banaschewski, T., Laucht, M., & Schneider, M. (2013). Impact of pubertal stage at first drink on adult drinking behavior. *Alcoholism: Clinical and Experimental Research, 37*(10), 1804–1811.

Blood, R. O., & Wolfe, D. M. (1960). *Husbands and wives: The dynamics of family living.* Oxford, England: Free Press Glencoe.

Blum, D. (2002). *Love at Goon Park: Harry Harlow and the science of affection*. Cambridge, MA: Perseus.

Boerner, K., Mancini, A. D., & Bonanno, G. (2013). On the nature and prevalence of uncomplicated and complicated patterns of grief. In M. Stroebe, H. Schut, & J. van den Bout (Eds.), *Complicated grief: Scientific foundations for health care professionals* (pp. 55–67). New York, NY: Routledge/Taylor & Francis Group.

Bohlin, G., Eninger, L., Brocki, K. C., & Thorell, L. B. (2012). Disorganized attachment and inhibitory capacity: Predicting externalizing problem behaviors. *Journal of Abnormal Child Psychology, 40*(3), 449–458.

Boisvert, J. A., & Harrell, W. A. (2013). The impact of spirituality on eating disorder symptomatology in ethnically diverse Canadian women. *International Journal of Social Psychiatry, 59*(8), 729–738.

Bonanno, G. A., & Lilienfeld, S. O. (2008). Let's be realistic: When grief counseling is effective and when it's not. *Professional Psychology: Research and Practice, 39*(3), 377–380.

Bonanno, R. A., & Hymel, S. (2013). Cyberbullying and internalizing difficulties: Above and beyond the impact of traditional forms of bullying. *Journal of Youth and Adolescence, 42*(5), 685–697.

Bonebrake, D., Culver, C., Call, K., & Ward-Smith, P. (2010). Clinically differentiating palliative care and hospice. *Clinical Journal of Oncology Nursing, 14*(3), 273–275.

Boonpleng, W., Park, C. G., Gallo, A. M., Corte, C., McCreary, L., & Bergren, M. D. (2013). Ecological influences of early childhood obesity: A multilevel analysis. *Western Journal of Nursing Research, 35*(6), 742–759.

Booth-LaForce, C., & Oxford, M. L. (2008). Trajectories of social withdrawal from grades 1 to 6: Prediction from early parenting, attachment, and temperament. *Developmental Psychology, 44*, 1298–1313.

Borella, E., Carretti, B., Cantarella, A., Riboldi, F., Zavagnin, M., & De Beni, R. (2014). Benefits of training visuospatial working memory in young–old and old–old. *Developmental Psychology, 50*(3), 714–727.

Borella, E., Carretti, B., & De Beni, R. (2008). Working memory and inhibition across the adult life-span. *Acta Psychologica, 128*, 33–44.

Borelli, J., Nelson, S., River, L., Birken, S., & Moss-Racusin, C. (2017). Gender differences in work–family guilt in parents of young children. *Sex Roles, 76*(5/6), 356. doi:10.1007/s11199-016-0579-0

Borko, H., Wolf, S. A., Simone, G., & Uchiyama, K. P. (2003). Schools in transition: Reform efforts and school capacity in Washington state. *Educational Evaluation and Policy Analysis, 25*, 171–201.

Bornstein, M. (2017). The specificity principle in Acculturation Science. *Perspectives on Psychological Science, 12*(1), 3–45.

Boros, B. D., Greathouse, K. M., Gentry, E. G., Curtis, K. A., Birchall, E. L., Gearing, M., & Herskowitz, J. H. (2017). Dendritic spines provide cognitive resilience against Alzheimer's disease. *Annals of Neurology, 82*(4), 602–614. doi:10.1002/ana.25049

Bottiroli, S., Cavallini, E., Fastame, M. C., & Hertzog, C. (2013). Cultural differences in rated typicality and perceived causes of memory changes in adulthood. *Archives of Gerontology and Geriatrics, 57*(3), 271–281.

Bouchard, T. J., Segal, N. L., Tellegen, A., McGue, M., Keyes, M., & Kruger, R. (2004). Genetic influences on social attitudes: Another challenge to psychology from behavior genetics. In L. F. DiLalla (Ed.), *Behavior genetics principles: Perspectives in development, personality, and psychopathology*. Washington, DC: American Psychological Association Press.

Boucher, N. A. (2017). Faith, family, filiality, and fate: Dominican and Puerto Rican elders' perspectives on end-of-life decisions. *Journal of Applied Gerontology, 36*(3), 351–372. doi:10.1177/0733464815627958

Bourassa, K. J., Knowles, L. M., Sbarra, D. A., & O'Connor, M. (2016). Absent but not gone: Interdependence in couples' quality of life persists after a partner's death. *Psychological Science, 27*(2), 270–281. doi:10.1177/0956797615618968

Bourke, A., Boduszek, D., Kelleher, C., McBride, O., & Morgan, K. (2014). Sex education, first sex and sexual health outcomes in adulthood: Findings from a nationally representative sexual health survey. *Sex Education, 14*(3), 299–309.

Boveda, I., & Metz, A. (2016). Predicting end-of-career transitions for baby boomers nearing retirement age. *Career Development Quarterly, 64*(2), 153–168. doi:10.1002/cdq.12048

Bowers, J. R., Segrin, C., & Joyce, N. (2016). The role of transitional instability, psychological distress, and dysfunctional drinking in emerging adults' involvement in risky sex. *Journal of Social & Personal Relationships, 33*(8), 1097–1119.

Bowlby, J. (1969). *Attachment and loss: Vol. 1. Attachment*. New York, NY: Basic Books.

Bowlby, J. (1973). *Attachment and loss: Vol. 2. Separation: Anxiety and anger*. New York, NY: Basic Books.

Bowlby, J. (1980). *Attachment and loss: Vol. 3. Loss: Sadness and depression*. New York, NY: Basic Books.

Boykin., S., Diez-Roux, A. V., Carnethon, M., Shrager, S., Ni, H., & Whitt-Glover, M. (2011). Racial/ethnic heterogeneity in the socioeconomic patterning of CVD risk factors in the United States: The multi-ethnic study of atherosclerosis. *Journal of Health Care for the Poor and Underserved, 22*, 111–127.

Boyle, D. E., Marshall, N. L., & Robeson, W. W. (2003). Gender at play: Fourth grade girls and boys on the playground. *American Behavioral Scientist, 46*, 1326–1345.

Braam, A. W., Klinkenberg, M., & Deeg, D. J. H. (2011). Religiousness and mood in the last week of life: An explorative approach based on after-death proxy interviews. *Journal of Palliative Medicine, 14*(1), 31–37.

Bradbury, T. N., & Karney, B. R. (2004). Understanding and altering the longitudinal course of marriage. *Journal of Marriage and Family, 66*, 862–879.

Bradley, R. H., & Coryn, R. (2013). From parent to child to parent . . . : Paths in and out of problem behavior. *Journal of Abnormal Child Psychology, 41*(4), 515–529.

Bradley, R. H., McRitchie, S., Houts, R. M., Nader, P., & O'Brien, M. (2011). Parenting and the decline of physical activity from age 9 to 15. *The International Journal of Behavioral Nutrition and Physical Activity, 8*, ArtID: 33.

Brame, R., Turner, M. C., Paternoster, R., & Bushway, S. (2012). Cumulative prevalence of arrest from ages 8 to 23 in a national sample. *Pediatrics, 129*(1), 21–27.

Bramen, J. E., Hranilovich, J. A., Dahl, R. E., Forbes, E. E., Chen, J., Toga, A. W., . . . Sowell, E. R. (2011). Puberty influences medial temporal lobe and cortical gray matter maturation differently in boys than girls matched for sexual maturity. *Cerebral Cortex, 21*(3), 636–646.

Brand, S., Gerber, M., Kalak, N., Kirov, R., Lemola, S., Clough, P. J., . . . Holsboer-Trachsler, E. (2014). Adolescents with greater mental toughness show higher sleep efficiency, more deep sleep and fewer awakenings after sleep onset. *Journal of Adolescent Health, 54*(1), 109–113.

Braun, S. S., & Davidson, A. J. (2016). Gender nonconformity in middle childhood: A mixed methods approach to understanding gender-typed behavior, friendship and peer preference. *Sex Roles, 44*, 1–14.

Braverman, D. W., Marcus, B. S., Wakim, P. G., Mercurio, M. R., & Kopf, G. S. (2017). Health care professionals' attitudes about physician-assisted death: An analysis of their justifications and the roles of terminology and patient competency. *Journal of Pain & Symptom Management,54*(4), 538–545.e3. doi:10.1016/j.jpainsymman.2017.07.024

Breaux, R. P., Brown, H. R., & Harvey, E. A. (2016). Mediators and moderators of the relation between parental ADHD symptomatology and the early development of child ADHD and ODD symptoms. *Journal of Abnormal Child Psychology.* doi:10.1007/s10802-016-0213-1

Breen, A. V., Lewis, S. P., & Sutherland, O. (2013). Brief report: Non-suicidal self-injury in the context of self and identity development. *Journal of Adult Development, 20*(1), 57–62.

Bregman, H. R., Malik, N. M., Page, M. L., Makynen, E., & Lindahl, K. M. (2013). Identity profiles in lesbian, gay, and bisexual youth: The role of family influences. *Journal of Youth and Adolescence, 42*(3), 417–430.

Brenning, K., Soenens, B., & Vansteenkiste, M. (2015). What's your motivation to be pregnant? Relations between motives for parenthood and women's prenatal functioning. *Journal of Family Psychology, 29*(5), 755–765.

Bressler, J., Mosley, T. H., Penman, A., Gottesman, R. F., Windham, B. G., Knopman, D. S., & Boerwinkle, E. (2017). Genetic variants associated with risk of Alzheimer's disease contribute to cognitive change in midlife: The atherosclerosis risk in communities study. *American Journal of Medical Genetics Part B: Neuropsychiatric Genetics, 174*(3), 269–282. doi:10.1002/ajmg.b.32509

Bretherton, I. (2005). In pursuit of the internal working model construct and its relevance to attachment relationships. In K. E. Grossmann, K. Grossmann, & E. Waters (Eds.), *Attachment from infancy to adulthood: The major longitudinal studies* (pp. 13–47). New York, NY: Guilford Press.

Brick, A., Smith, S., Normand, C., O'Hara, S., Droog, E., Tyrrell, E., . . . Johnston, B. (2017). Costs of formal and informal care in the last year of life for patients in receipt of specialist palliative care. *Palliative Medicine, 31*(4), 356–368. doi:10.1177/0269216316686277

Briley, D. A., & Tucker-Drob, E. M. (2014). Genetic and environmental continuity in personality development: A meta-analysis. *Psychological Bulletin, 140*(5), 1303–1331.

Britton, M. L. (2013). Race/ethnicity, attitudes, and living with parents during young adulthood. *Journal of Marriage and Family, 75*(4), 995–1013.

Brock, R. L., & Lawrence, E. (2014). Intrapersonal, interpersonal, and contextual risk factors for overprovision of partner support in marriage. *Journal of Family Psychology, 28*(1), 54–64.

Brodaty, H. (2018). Psychosocial research in dementia: Past, present, and future. Paper delivered for the AAIC Lifetime Achievement Award, Alzheimer's Association International Conference. Chicago, Illinois, July 24, 2018.

Brody, J. E. (2010, December 27). Just because one's vision is waning, hope doesn't have to. *The New York Times*, p. D2.

Brody, N. (2006). Geocentric theory: A valid alternative to Gardner's theory of intelligence. In J. A. Schaler (Ed.), *Howard Gardner under fire: The rebel psychologist faces his critics* (pp. 73–94). Chicago, IL: Open Court.

Brom, S. S., & Kliegel, M. (2014). Improving everyday prospective memory performance in older adults: Comparing cognitive process and strategy training. *Psychology and Aging, 29*(3), 744–755.

Bronfenbrenner, U. (1977). Toward an experimental ecology of human development. *American Psychologist, 32*, 513–531.

Bronstein, P. (1988). Father–child interaction: Implications for gender-role socialization. In P. Bronstein & C. P. Cowan (Eds.), *Fatherhood today: Men's changing role in the family* (pp. 107–124). Oxford, England: Wiley.

Brooks-Gunn, J., Newman, D. L., Holderness, C. C., & Warren, M. P. (1994). The experience of breast development and girls' stories about the purchase of a bra. *Journal of Youth and Adolescence, 23*, 539–565.

Brooks-Gunn, J., & Ruble, D. N. (1982). The development of menstrual-related beliefs and behaviors during early adolescence. *Child Development, 53*, 1567–1577.

Brooks-Gunn, J., & Warren, M. P. (1985). The effects of delayed menarche in different contexts: Dance and nondance students. *Journal of Youth and Adolescence, 14*, 285–300.

Brooks-Gunn, J., & Warren, M. P. (1988). The psychological significance of secondary sexual characteristics in nine- to eleven-year-old girls. *Child Development, 59*, 1061–1069.

Broom, A., & Kirby, E. (2013). The end of life and the family: Hospice patients' views on dying as relational. *Sociology of Health & Illness, 35*(4), 499–513.

Brotman, L. M., O'Neal, C. R., Huang, K., Gouley, K. K., Rosenfelt, A., & Shrout, P. E. (2009). An experimental test of parenting practices as a mediator of early childhood physical aggression. *Journal of Child Psychology and Psychiatry, 50*(3), 235–245.

Brown, A., Rance, J., & Bennett, P. (2016). Understanding the relationship between breastfeeding and postnatal depression: The role of pain and physical difficulties. *Journal of Advanced Nursing, 72*(2), 273–282. doi:10.1111/jan.12832

Bryan, D. M. (2013). To parent or provide? The effect of the provider role on low-income men's decisions about fatherhood and paternal engagement. *Fathering, 11*(1), 71–89.

Buchanan, C. (2017). What U.S. companies can learn from Germany's apprenticeship program, INC. Retrieved from www.inc.com

Budge, S. L., Thai, J. L., Tebbe, E. A., & Howard, K. S. (2016). The intersection of race, sexual orientation, socioeconomic status, trans identity, and mental health outcomes. *Counseling Psychologist, 47*(3), 404–433.

Bue, H. (2018). Pathobiology of APOE in Alzheimer's disease. Paper delivered for the plenary session, Alzheimer's Association International Conference, July 25, 2018, Chicago, Illinois.

Bukowski, W. M. (2001). Friendship and the worlds of childhood. In D. W. Nangle & C. A. Erdley (Eds.), *New directions for child and adolescent development*: No. 91. *The role of friendship in psychological adjustment* (pp. 93–105). San Francisco, CA: Jossey-Bass.

Burchinal, M., Skinner, D., & Reznick, J. S. (2010). European American and African American mothers' beliefs about parenting and disciplining infants: A mixed-method analysis. *Parenting: Science and Practice, 10*, 79–96.

Burditt, K., Wan, W., Orbuch, T. I., & Antonucci, T. C. (2017). The development of marital tension: Implications for divorce among married couples. *Developmental Psychology*, 379, 1–12.

Bureau, J.-F., Martin, J., Freynet, N., Poirier, A. A., Lafontaine, M.-F., & Cloutier, P. (2010). Perceived dimensions of parenting and non-suicidal self-injury in young adults. *Journal of Youth and Adolescence*, 39, 484–494.

Bureau of Labor Statistics. (2017, June 27). American Time Use Survey – 2016 Results [Press release]. Retrieved from https://www.bls.gov/news.release/archives/atus_06272017.pdf

Burg, M. M. (2018). *Psychological treatment of cardiac patients* (pp. 137–146). Washington, DC: American Psychological Association. doi:10.1037/0000070-010

Burkard, C., Rochat, L., Blum, A., Emmenegger, J., Van der Linden, A. J., & Van der Linden, M. (2014). A daily-life-oriented intervention to improve prospective memory and goal-directed behaviour in ageing: A pilot study. *Neuropsychological Rehabilitation*, 24(2), 266–295.

Burkett, M. (2015). Sex(t) talk: A qualitative analysis of young adults' negotiations of the pleasures and perils of sexting. *Sexuality & Culture*, 19(4), 835–863.

Burnett, S., Thompson, S., Bird, G., & Blakemore, S. (2011). Pubertal development of the understanding of social emotions: Implications for education. *Learning and Individual Differences*, 21(6), 681–689.

Burns, R., Brusseau, T., Fu, Y., & Hannon, J. (2015). Predictors and trends of gross motor skill performance in at-risk elementary school-aged children. *Perceptual and Motor Skills*, 121(1), 284–299.

Burr, A., Santo, J. B., & Pushkar, D. (2011). Affective well-being in retirement: The influence of values, money, and mental health across three years. *Journal of Happiness Studies*, 12, 17–40.

Bushnell, I. W. R. (1998). The origins of face perception. In F. Simion & G. Butterworth (Eds.), *The development of sensory, motor and cognitive capacities in early infancy: From perception to cognition* (pp. 69–88). Hove, England: Psychology Press.

Butkovic, A., Brkovic, I., & Bratko, D. (2011). Predicting well-being from personality in adolescents and older

adults. *Journal of Happiness Studies*, 21, 1–13.

Buttelmann, D., Call, J., & Tomasello, M. (2009). Do great apes use emotional expressions to infer desires? *Developmental Science*, 12(5), 688–698.

Byers, K. C., & Simon, S. L. (2017). American Academy of Pediatrics 2016 safe sleep practices: Implications for pediatric behavioral sleep medicine. *Behavioral Sleep Medicine*, 15, 175–179.

Byrne, J., & Canato, A. (2017). It's been a hard day's night: Work family interface and employee engagement. *Organizational Dynamics*, 46(2), 104–112. doi:10.1016/j.orgdyn.2017.04.006

Cacioppo, J. T., Cacioppo, S., Gonzaga, G. C., Ogburn, E. L., & Vander Weele, T. J. (2013). Marital satisfaction and break-ups differ across on-line and offline meeting venues. *PNAS Proceedings of the National Academy of Sciences of the United States of America*, 110(25), 10135–10140.

Callahan, D. (1988). *Setting limits: Medical goals in an aging society*. New York, NY: Simon & Schuster.

Campos, J. J., Anderson, D. I., Barbu-Roth, M. A., Hubbard, E. M., Hertenstein, M. J., & Witherington, D. (2000). Travel broadens the mind. *Infancy*, 1, 149–219.

Canário, C., & Figueiredo, B. (2016). Partner relationship from early pregnancy to 30 months postpartum: Gender and parity effects. *Couple and Family Psychology: Research and Practice*, 5(4), 226–239.

Canter, A. S. (1997). The future of intelligence testing in the schools. *School Psychology Review*, 26, 255–261.

Caplan, A. L., Blank, R. H., & Merrick, J. C. (Eds.). (1992). *Compelled compassion: Government intervention in the treatment of critically ill newborns*. Totowa, NJ: Humana Press.

Caravita, S. C., & Cillessen, A. H. (2012). Agentic or communal? Associations between interpersonal goals, popularity, and bullying in middle childhood and early adolescence. *Social Development*, 21(2), 376–395. doi:10.1111/j.1467-9507.2011.00632.x

Carlson, A. G., Rowe, E., & Curby, T. W. (2013). Disentangling fine motor skills' relations to academic achievement: The relative contributions of visual-spatial integration and visual-motor coordination. *The Journal of Genetic Psychology: Research and Theory on Human Development*, 174(5), 514–533.

Carlson, S. M., Claxton, L. J., & Moses, L. J. (2016). The relation between

executive function and theory of mind is more than skin deep. *Journal of Cognition and Development*, 16(1), 186–197.

Carnes, B., Olshansky, S., & Hayflick, L. (2013). Can human biology allow most of us to become centenarians? *Journals of Gerontology Series A: Biological Sciences and Medical Sciences*, 68(2), 136–142.

Carnevale, A., & Strohl, J. (2010). How increasing college access is increasing inequality and what to do about it. In R. D. Kahlenberg (Ed.), *Rewarding strivers: Helping low-income students succeed in college*. New York, NY: The Century Foundation Press.

Caron, S. L., & Moskey, E. G. (2002). Changes over time in teenage sexual relationships: Comparing the high school class of 1950, 1975, and 2000. *Adolescence*, 37, 515–526.

Carr, D., & Boerner, K. (2013). Dating after late-life spousal loss: Does it compromise relationships with adult children? *Journal of Aging Studies*, 27(4), 487–498.

Carroll, J. S., Willoughby, B., Badger, S., Nelson, L. J., Barry, C. M., & Madsen, S. D. (2007). So close, yet so far away: The impact of varying marital horizons on emerging adulthood. *Journal of Adolescent Research*, 22(3), 219–247.

Carstensen, L. L. (1995). Evidence for a life-span theory of socioemotional selectivity. *Current Directions in Psychological Science*, 4, 151–156.

Carstensen, L. L., Graff, J., Levenson, R. W., & Gottman, J. M. (1996). Affect in intimate relationships: The developmental course of marriage. In C. Magai & S. H. McFadden (Eds.), *Handbook of emotion, adult development, and aging* (pp. 227–247). San Diego, CA: Academic Press.

Case, R. (1999). Conceptual development. In M. Bennett (Ed.), *Developmental psychology: Achievements and prospects* (pp. 36–54). New York, NY: Psychology Press.

Cashmore, J., & Parkinson, P. (2008). Children's and parents' perceptions on children's participation in decision making after parental separation and divorce. *Family Court Review*, 46(1), 91–104.

Cassel, J. B., Hager, M. A., Clark, R. R., Retchin, S. M., Dimartino, J., Coyne, P. J., . . . Smith, T. J. (2010). Concentrating hospital-wide deaths in a palliative care unit: The effect of place on death and system-wide mortality. *Journal of Palliative Medicine*, 13(4), 371–374.

Castaneda, A. M., Wendel, M. L., & Crockett, E. E. (2015). Overlap in Facebook profiles reflects relationship closeness. *Journal of Social Psychology*, 155(4), 395–401.

Castel, A. D., Lee, S. S., Humphreys, K. L., & Moore, A. N. (2010). Memory capacity, selective control, and value-directed remembering in children with and without attention-deficit/hyperactivity disorder (ADHD). *Neuropsychology*, 25(1), 15–24.

Castellanos-Ryan, N., Parent, S., Vitaro, F., Tremblay, R. E., & Seguin, J. R. (2013). Pubertal development, personality, and substance use: A 10-year longitudinal study from childhood to adolescence. *Journal of Abnormal Psychology*, 122(3), 782–796.

Caulfield, L., Richard, S. A., Rivera, J. A., Musgrove, P., & Black, R. E. (2006). *Disease control priorities in developing countries* (2nd ed.). New York, NY: Oxford University Press.

Ceci, S. J., Rosenblum, T., de Bruyn, E., & Lee, D. Y. (1997). A bio-ecological model of intellectual development: Moving beyond h-sup-2. In R. J. Sternberg & E. L. Grigorenko (Eds.), *Intelligence, heredity, and environment* (pp. 303–322). New York, NY: Cambridge University Press.

Cellarius, V. (2011). 'Early terminal sedation' is a distinct entity. *Bioethics*, 25(1), 46–54.

Cenk, D. S., & Demir, A. (2016). The relationship between parenting style, gender and academic achievement with optimism among Turkish adolescents. *Current Psychology: A Journal for Diverse Perspectives on Diverse Psychological Issues*, 35(4), 720–728. doi:10.1007/s12144-015-9375-1

Centers for Disease Control. (2017). *Heart Disease Facts* [Fact sheet]. Retrieved from https://www.cdc.gov/heartdisease/facts.htm

Centers for Disease Control. (n. d.). Retrieved from https://www.cdc.gov/arthritis/data_statistics/national-statistics.html

Centers for Disease Control and Prevention. (2007). *Infant mortality statistics from the 2004 period: Linked birth/infant death data.* Retrieved from http://www.cdc.gov/nchs/data/nvsr/nvsr55/nvsr55_14.pdf

Centers for Disease Control and Prevention. (2009). *Health data interactive.* Retrieved from http://www.cdc.gov/nchs/hdi.htm

Centers for Disease Control and Prevention. (2010b). Increasing prevalence of parent-reported attention-deficit/hyperactivity disorder among children: United States, 2003–2007. *Morbidity and Mortality Weekly Report (MMWR)*, 59(44). Retrieved from http://www.ncbi.nlm.nih.gov/pubmed/21063274

Centers for Disease Control and Prevention. (2016). Fast Stats: Births—Method of delivery. Retrieved from http/www.cdc.

Centers for Disease Control and Prevention. (2017). Vaccines do not cause autism. Retrieved from https://www.cdc.gov/vaccinesafety/concerns/autism.html

Centers for Disease Control and Prevention. (n.d.). *Attention deficit hyperactivity disorder*. In *CDC Fast Stats*. Retrieved from http://www.cdc.gov/nchs/fastats/adhd.htm

Centers for Disease Control and Prevention (CDC), U.S. Department of Health and Human Services. (2015). *Results from the school health policies and practices study 2014.* Retrieved from https://www.cdc.gov/healthyyouth/data/shpps/pdf/shpps-508-final_101315.pdf

Central Intelligence Agency. (2017). The World Factbook, Infant mortality rate. Retrieved from https://www.cia.gov//library/publications/

Central Intelligence Agency. (2018a). Malawi. In *The world factbook*. Retrieved from https://www.cia.gov/library/publications/the-world-factbook/geos/mi.html

Central Intelligence Agency. (2018b). Monaco. In *The world factbook*. Retrieved from https://www.cia.gov/library/publications/the-world-factbook/geos/mn.html

Central Intelligence Agency. (n.d.). World Factbook, Life Expectancy at Birth, https://www.cia.gov/library/publications/the-world-factbook/rankorder/2102rank.html

Chambaere, K., Bilsen, J., Cohen, J., Onwuteaka-Philipsen, B. D., Mortier, F., & Deliens, L. (2011). Trends in medical end-of-life decision making in Flanders, Belgium 1998–2001–2007. *Medical Decision Making*, 31(3), 500–510.

Chang, H. H., Larson, J., Blencowe, H., Spong, C. Y., Howson, C. P., Cairns-Smith, S., . . . Lawn, J. E. (2013). Preventing preterm births: Analysis of trends and potential reductions with interventions in 39 countries with very high human development index. *The Lancet*, 381(9862), 223–234.

Chang, P. F., Choi, Y. H., Bazarova, N. N., & Löckenhoff, C. E. (2015). Age differences in online social networking: Extending socioemotional selectivity theory to social network sites. *Journal of Broadcasting & Electronic Media*, 59(2), 221–239.

Chang, Y., & Locke, J. (2016). A systematic review of peer-mediated interventions for children with autism spectrum disorder. *Research in Autism Spectrum Disorders*, 27, 1–10. doi:10.1016/j.rasd.2016.03.010

Chapman, B., & Guven, C. (2016). Revisiting the relationship between marriage and wellbeing: Does marriage quality matter? *Journal of Happiness Studies*, 17(2), 533–551. doi:10.1007/s10902-014-9607-3

Chapple, H. S. (1999). Changing the game in the intensive care unit: Letting nature take its course. *Critical Care Nurse*, 19, 25–34.

Charles, S. T., & Almeida, D. M. (2007). Genetic and environmental effects on daily life stressors: More evidence for greater variation in later life. *Psychology and Aging*, 22(2), 331–340.

Charles, S. T., Luong, G., Almeida, D. M., Ryff, C., Sturm, M., & Love, G. (2010). Fewer ups and downs: Daily stressors mediate age differences in negative affect. *Journals of Gerontology: Psychological Sciences*, 65B(3), 279–286.

Chen, B., & Santo, J. B. (2016). The relationships between shyness and unsociability and peer difficulties. *International Journal of Behavioral Development*, 40(4), 346–358. doi:10.1177/0165025415587726

Chen, E. Y.-J., Enright, R. D., & Tun, E. Y.-L. (2016). The influence of family unions and parenthood transitions on self-development. *Journal of Family Psychology*, 30(3), 341–352.

Chen X., Jingting, Z., Farrell, M., & Park, D. (2018). Subjective memory complaints reflect functional deterioration in the hippocampus and elevated amyloid burden in cognitively normal adults. Paper delivered at the Alzheimer's Association International Conference, Chicago, Illinois, July 23, 2018.

Chen, Y., McAnally, H. M., & Reese, E. (2013). Development in the organization of episodic memories in middle childhood and adolescence. *Frontiers in Behavioral Neuroscience*, 7, 84.

Cherlin, A. J. (2004). The deinstitutionalization of American marriage. *Journal of Marriage and Family*, 66, 848–861.

Cherlin, A. J. (2010). Demographic trends in the United States: A review of research in the 2000s. *Journal of Marriage and Family*, 72(3), 403–419.

Chertkow, H., Whitehead, V., Phillips, N., Wolfson, C., Atherton, J., & Bergman, H. (2010). Multilingualism (but not always bilingualism) delays the onset of Alzheimer disease: Evidence from a bilingual community. *Alzheimer Disease and Associated Disorders, 24*(2), 118–125.

Chetty, R., & Hendren, N. (2016). The impacts of neighborhoods on intergenerational mobility I: Childhood exposure effects. Working paper.

Chetty, R., & Hendren, N. (2017). The impacts of neighborhoods on intergenerational mobility ii: County-level estimates. NBER Working Papers, 1, p. 20.

Chetty, R., Friedman, J. N., & Rockoff, J. E. (2014). Measuring the impacts of teachers ii: Teacher value-added and student outcomes in adulthood. *American Economic Review, 104*(9), 2633–2679. doi:10.1257/aer.104.9.2633

Chetty, R., Grusky, D., Hell, M., Hendren, N., Manduca, R., & Narang, J. (2017). The fading American dream: Trends in absolute income mobility since 1940. *Science, 356*(6336), 398–406. doi:10.1126/science.aal4617

Cheung, C. (2016). Preventing physical child abuse by legal punishment and neighbor help. *Children and Youth Services Review, 71*, 545–557.

Cheung, P. C., Cunningham, S. A., Narayan, K. V., & Kramer, M. R. (2016). Childhood obesity incidence in the United States: A systematic review. *Childhood Obesity, 12*(1), 1–11. doi:10.1089/chi.2015.0055

Chi, N., & Demiris, G. (2017). Family caregivers' pain management in end-of-life care: A systematic review. *American Journal of Hospice & Palliative Medicine, 34*(5), 470–485. doi:10.1177/1049909116637359

Chih-Yuan, S. L., Bryan, J. D., & Lauren, A. B. (2016). Intergenerational solidarity and individual adjustment during emerging adulthood. *Journal of Family Issues, 37*(10), 1412–1432.

Child Soldiers International. (2017, April 01). Central African Republic. Retrieved from https://www.child-soldiers.org/central-african-republic

Child Trends Data Bank. (2008). Retrieved from http://www.childtrends.org/databank/

Cho, J., & Lee, A. (2014). Life satisfaction of the aged in the retirement process: A comparative study of South Korea with Germany and Switzerland, *Applied Research in Quality of Life, 9*(2), 179–195.

Cho, S., Zarit, S. H., & Chiriboga, D. A. (2009). Wives and daughters: The differential role of day care use in the nursing home placement of cognitively impaired family members. *The Gerontologist, 49*(1), 57–67.

Cho, Y., & Haslam, N. (2010). Suicidal ideation and distress among immigrant adolescents: The role of acculturation, life stress, and social support. *Journal of Youth and Adolescence, 39*(4), 370–379.

Choi, J., Johnson, D. W., & Johnson, R. (2011). The roots of social dominance: Aggression, prosocial behavior, and social interdependence. *Journal of Educational Research, 104*(6), 442–454.

Choi, Y., Kim, J., & Park, E. (2016). The impact of differences between subjective and objective social class on life satisfaction among the Korean population in early old age: Analysis of Korean longitudinal study on aging. *Archives of Gerontology & Geriatrics, 67*, 98–105. doi:10.1016/j.archger.2016.07.006

Choi, Y., Kim, Y. S., Kim, S. Y., & Park, I. K. (2013). Is Asian American parenting controlling and harsh? Empirical testing of relationships between Korean American and Western parenting measures. *Asian American Journal of Psychology, 4*(1), 19–29.

Chong, A., Biehle, S. N., Kooiman, L. Y., & Mickelson, K. D. (2016). Postnatal depression: The role of breastfeeding efficacy, breastfeeding duration, and family–work conflict. *Psychology of Women Quarterly, 40*(4), 518–531. doi:10.1177/0361684316658263

Chopik, W. J., Kim, E. S., & Smith, J. (2015). Changes in optimism are associated with changes in health over time among older adults. *Social Psychological and Personality Science, 6*(7), 814–822. doi:10.1177/1948550615590199

Chopik, W. J., & Kitayama, S. (2017). Personality change across the life span: Insights from a cross-cultural, longitudinal study. *Journal of Personality.* Advance online publication. doi.org/10.1111/jopy.12332

Christ, G. H. (2000). *Healing children's grief.* New York, NY: Oxford University Press.

Christensen, J., Gronborg, T. K., Sorensen, M. J., Schendel, D., Parner, E. T., Pedersen, L. H., & Vestergaard, M. (2013). Prenatal valproate exposure and risk of autism spectrum disorders and childhood autism. *Journal of the American Medical Association, 309*(16), 1696–1703.

Chua, A. (2011). *Battle hymn of the tiger mother.* New York, NY: Penguin Press.

Chung, J. M., Robins, R. W., Trzesniewski, K. H., Noftle, E. E., Roberts, B. W., &

Widaman, K. F. (2014). Continuity and change in self-esteem during emerging adulthood. *Journal of Personality and Social Psychology, 106*(3), 469–483.

Cicchetti, D. (2016). Socioemotional, personality, and biological development: Illustrations from a multilevel developmental psychopathology perspective on child maltreatment. *Annual Review of Psychology, 67*(1), 187–211. doi:10.1146/annurev-psych-122414-033259

Cicirelli, V. G. (2007). End of life decisions: Research findings and implications. In A. Tomer, P. T. Wong, & G. Eliason (Eds.), *Existential and spiritual issues in death attitudes* (pp. 115–138). Hillsdale, NJ: Erlbaum.

Ciocanel, O., Power, K., Eriksen, A., & Gillings, K. (2017). Effectiveness of positive youth development interventions: A meta-analysis of randomized controlled trials. *Journal of Youth & Adolescence, 46*(3), 483–504. doi:10.1007/s10964-016-0555-6

Clark, D. (2007). End-of-life care around the world: Achievements to date and challenges remaining. *Omega, 56*(1), 101–110.

Class, Q. A., Khashan, A. S., Lichtenstein, P., Langstrom, N., & D'Onofrio, B. M. (2013). Maternal stress and infant mortality: The importance of the preconception period. *Psychological Science, 24*(7), 1309–1316.

Clearfield, M. W., & Jedd, K. E. (2013). The effects of socio-economic status on infant attention. *Infant and Child Development, 22*(1), 53–67.

Climo, J. J., Terry, P., & Lay, K. (2002). Using the double bind to interpret the experience of custodial grandparents. *Journal of Aging Studies, 16*, 19–35.

Coall, D. A., & Hertwig, R. (2010). Grandparental investment: Past, present, and future. *Behavioral and Brain Sciences, 33*, 1–59.

Coccia, C., & Darling, C. A. (2016). Having the time of their life: College student stress, dating and satisfaction with life. *Stress & Health: Journal of the International Society for the Investigation of Stress, 32*(1), 28–35.

Cohen, J., Van Landeghem, P., Carpentier, N., & Deliens, L. (2013). Different trends in euthanasia acceptance across Europe. A study of 13 western and 10 central and eastern European countries, 1981–2008. *European Journal of Public Health, 23*(3), 378–380.

Cohen, O., Leichtentritt, R. D., & Volpin, N. (2014). Divorced mothers' self-perception of their divorce-related communication with their children. *Child & Family Social Work, 19*(1), 34–43.

Coie, J. D., & Dodge, K. A. (1998). Aggression and antisocial behavior. In W. Damon (Series Ed.) & N. Eisenberg (Vol. Ed.), *Handbook of child psychology: Vol. 3. Social, emotional, and personality development* (5th ed., pp. 779–862). Hoboken, NJ: Wiley.

Colasante, T., Zuffianó, A., & Malti, T. (2016). Daily deviations in anger, guilt, and sympathy: A developmental diary study of aggression. *Journal of Abnormal Child Psychology, 44*(8), 1515–1526. doi:10.1007/s10802-016-0143-y

Cole, B., & Singg, S. (1998). *Relationship between parental bereavement reaction factors and selected psychosocial variables.* Paper presented at the Annual Meeting of the American Psychological Society, Washington, DC.

Coley, R. L., Votruba-Drzal, E., Miller, P. L., & Koury, A. (2013). Timing, extent, and type of child care and children's behavioral functioning in kindergarten. *Developmental Psychology, 49*(10), 1859–1873.

Collignon, O., Vandewalle, G., Voss, P., Albouy, G., Charbonneau, G., Lassonde, M., & Lepore, F. (2011). Functional specialization for auditory-spatial processing in the occipital cortex of congenitally blind humans. *Proceedings of the National Academy of Sciences of the United States of America, 108*(11), 4435–4440.

Collins, R. L., Elliott, M. N., Berry, S. H., Kanouse, D. E., Kunkel, D., Hunter, S. B., & Miu, A. (2004). Watching sex on television predicts adolescent initiation of sexual behavior. *Pediatrics, 114,* e280–e289.

Collinson, C. (2014, September-October). Baby boomers will trailblaze new retirement models (they have to). *Aging Today, 35*(5), 1, 7.

Colrain, I. M., & Baker, F. C. (2011). Changes in sleep as a function of adolescent development. *Neuropsychology Review, 21,* 5–21.

Compian, L., Gowen, L. K., & Hayward, C. (2004). Peripubertal girls' romantic and platonic involvement with boys: Associations with body image and depression symptoms. *Journal of Research on Adolescence, 14,* 23–47.

Conroy-Beam, D., & Buss, D. M. (2016). How are mate preferences linked with actual mate selection? Tests of mate preference integration algorithms using computer simulations and actual mating couples. *Plos ONE, 6.*

Conzo, P., Aassve, A., Fuochi, G., & Mencarini, L. (2017). The cultural foundations of happiness. *Journal of Economic Psychology, 62,* 268–283. doi. org/10.1016/j.joep.2017.08.001

Cook, C. R., Williams, K. R., Guerra, N. G., Kim, T. E., & Sadek, S. (2010). Predictors of bullying and victimization in childhood and adolescence: A meta-analytic investigation. *School Psychology Quarterly, 25*(2), 65–83.

Cook, T. D., Deng, Y., & Morgano, E. (2007). Friendship influences during early adolescence: The special role of friends' grade point average. *Journal of Research on Adolescence, 17*(2), 325–356.

Cooley, J. L., & Fite, P. J. (2016). Peer victimization and forms of aggression during middle childhood: The role of emotion regulation. *Journal of Abnormal Child Psychology, 44*(3), 535–546. doi:10.1007/s10802-015-0051-6

Coontz, S. (1992). *The way we never were: American families and the nostalgia trap.* New York, NY: Basic Books.

Cormier, D. C., Kennedy, K. E., & Aquilina, A. M. (2016). Test review: "Wechsler Intelligence Scale for Children, Fifth Edition: Canadian 322 (WISC-VCDN) by D. Wechsler." *Canadian Journal of School Psychology, 31*(4), 322–334.

Corr, C. A. (1991–1992). A task-based approach to coping with dying. *Omega, 24,* 81–94.

Corr, C. A. (2007). Hospice: Achievements, legacies, and challenges. *Omega, 56*(1), 111–120.

Corsaro, W. A. (1985). *Friendship and peer culture in the early years.* Norwood, NJ: Ablex.

Corsaro, W. A. (1997). *The sociology of childhood.* Thousand Oaks, CA: Pine Forge Press/Sage.

Cosh, S., Hanno, T., Helmer, C., Bertelsen, G., Delcourt, C., & Schirmer, H. (2017). The association amongst visual, hearing, and dual sensory loss with depression and anxiety over 6 years: The tromsø study. *International Journal of Geriatric Psychiatry, 33*(4), 598–605. doi:10.1002/gps.4827

Costos, D., Ackerman, R., & Paradis, L. (2002). Recollections of menarche: Communication between mothers and daughters regarding menstruation. *Sex Roles, 46,* 49–59.

Côté, J., & Bynner, J. M. (2008). Changes in the transition to adulthood in the UK and Canada: The role of structure and agency in emerging adulthood. *Journal of Youth Studies, 11,* 251–268.

Cotterell, J. (1996). *Social networks and social influences in adolescence.* New York, NY: Routledge.

Cowan, C. P., & Cowan, P. A. (1992). *When partners become parents: The big life change for couples.* New York, NY: Basic Books.

Cowan, N. (2016). Exploring the possible and necessary in working memory development. *Monographs of the Society for Research in Child Development, 81*(3), 149–158. doi:10.1111/mono.12257

Cowan, P. A., Cowan, C. P., & Mehta, N. (2009). Adult attachment, couple attachment, and children's adaptation to school: An integrated attachment template and family risk model. *Attachment & Human Development, 11*(1), 29–46.

Cox, K. S., Wilt, J., Olson, B., & McAdams, D. P. (2010). Generativity, the big five, and psychosocial adaptation in midlife adults. *Journal of Personality, 78*(4), 1185–1208.

Cozzarelli, C., Karafa, J. A., Collins, N. L., & Tagler, M. J. (2003). Stability and change in adult attachment styles: Associations with personal vulnerabilities, life events, and global construals of self and others. *Journal of Social & Clinical Psychology, 22,* 315–346.

Crade, M., & Lovett, S. (1988). Fetal response to sound stimulation: Preliminary report exploring use of sound stimulation in routine obstetrical ultrasound examinations. *Journal of Ultrasound in Medicine, 7,* 499–503.

Craik, F. I. M. (2000). Age-related changes in human memory. In D. C. Park & N. Schwarz (Eds.), *Cognitive aging: A primer* (pp. 75–92). New York, NY: Psychology Press.

Craik, F. I. M., Luo, L., & Sakuta, Y. (2010). Effects of aging and divided attention on memory for items and their contexts. *Psychology and Aging, 25*(4), 968–979.

Cramer, P. (2008). Identification and the development of competence: A 44-year longitudinal study from late adolescence to late middle age. *Psychology and Aging, 23,* 410–421.

Crawford, A. M., & Manassis, K. (2011). Anxiety, social skills, friendship quality, and peer victimization: An integrated model. *Journal of Anxiety Disorders, 25*(7), 924–937.

Crick, N. R., & Dodge, K. A. (1996). Social information-processing mechanisms on reactive and proactive aggression. *Child Development, 67,* 993–1002.

Cripe, L. D., Hedrick, D. G., Rand, K. L., Burns, D., Banno, D., Cottingham, A., . . . Frankel, R. M. (2017). Medical students' professionalism narratives reveal that experiences with death, dying, or palliative care are more positive than other experiences during their internal medicine clerkship. *American Journal of Hospice & Palliative Medicine, 34*(1), 79. doi:10.1177/1049909115609296

Crittenden, A. (2001). *The price of motherhood: Why the most important job in the world is still the least valued.* New York, NY: Metropolitan Books.

Crocetti, E., & Meeus, W. (2014). "Family comes first!" Relationships with family and friends in Italian emerging adults. *Journal of Adolescence, 371*, 463–1473.

Crocetti, E., & Tagliabue, S. (2016). Are being responsible, having a stable job, and caring for the family important for adulthood? Examining the importance of different criteria for adulthood in Italian emerging adults. In R. Žukauskienė (Ed.), *Emerging adulthood in a European context* (pp. 33–53). New York, NY: Routledge/Taylor & Francis Group.

Crum, M. (2014, September-October). On frailty and facing death. *Aging Today, 35*(5), 6.

Csikszentmihalyi, M. (1990). *Flow: The psychology of optimal experience.* New York, NY: Harper & Row.

Csikszentmihalyi, M., & Larson, R. (1984). *Being adolescent: Conflict and growth in the teenage years.* New York, NY: Basic Books.

Csikszentmihalyi, M., & Schneider, B. L. (2000). *Becoming adult: How teenagers prepare for the world of work.* New York, NY: Basic Books.

Csiszar, A., Sosnowska, D., Tucsek, Z., Gautam, T., Toth, P., Losonczy, G., . . . Ungvari, Z. (2013). Circulating factors induced by caloric restriction in the nonhuman primate *macaca mulatta* activate angiogenic processes in endothelial cells. *Journals of Gerontology Series A: Biological Sciences and Medical Sciences, 68*(3), 235–249.

Culbert, K. M., Breedlove, S. M., Sisk, C. L., Burt, S. A., & Klump, K. L. (2013). The emergence of sex differences in risk for disordered eating attitudes during puberty: A role for prenatal testosterone exposure. *Journal of Abnormal Psychology, 122*(2), 420–432.

CysticFibrosis.com. (n.d.). Retrieved from http://www.cysticfibrosis.com/home/

Daddis, C. (2011). Desire for increased autonomy and adolescents' perceptions of peer autonomy: "Everyone else can; why can't I?" *Child Development, 82*(4), 1310–1326.

Dahl, R. E. (2004). Adolescent brain development: A period of vulnerabilities and opportunities. In R. E. Dahl & L. P. Spear (Eds.), *Adolescent brain development: Vulnerabilities and opportunities, Volume 1021* (pp. 1–22). New York, NY: Academy of Sciences.

Daly, B. P., Hildenbrand, A. K., Haney-Caron, E., Goldstein, N. S., Galloway, M., & DeMatteo, D. (2016). Disrupting the school-to-prison pipeline: Strategies to reduce the risk of school-based zero tolerance policies resulting in juvenile justice involvement. In K. Heilbrun, D. DeMatteo, & N. S. Goldstein (Eds.), *APA handbook of psychology and juvenile justice* (pp. 257–275). Washington, DC: American Psychological Association. doi:10.1037/14643-012

Damaraju, E., Caprihan, A., Lowe, J. R., Allen, E. A., Calhoun, V. D., & Phillips, J. P. (2014). Functional connectivity in the developing brain: A longitudinal study from 4 to 9 months of age. *NeuroImage, 84*, 169–180.

Danckert, S. L., & Craik, F. M. (2013). Does aging affect recall more than recognition memory? *Psychology and Aging, 28*(4), 902–909.

Danese, A., & Baldwin, J. R. (2017). Hidden wounds? Inflammatory links between childhood trauma and psychopathology. *Annual Review of Psychology, 68*(1), 517–544. doi:10.1146/annurev-psych-010416-044208

Daniels, K. J., Lamson, A. L., & Hodgson, J. (2007). An exploration of the marital relationship and Alzheimer's disease: One couple's story. *Families, Systems, & Health, 25*(2), 162–177.

Danielsbacka, M., & Tanskanen, A. O. (2016). The association between grandparental investment and grandparents' happiness in Finland. *Personal Relationships, 23*(4), 787–800. doi.org/10.1111/pere.12160

Danziger, S., & Ratner, D. (2010). Labor market outcomes and the transition to adulthood. *The Future of Children, 20*, 1–24. Retrieved from http://www.futureofchildren.org/publications/journals/article/index.xml?journalid=72&articleid=524

Darwiche, J., Favez, N., Maillard, F., Germond, M., Guex, P., Despland, J., & deRoten, Y. (2013). Couples' resolution of an infertility diagnosis before undergoing in vitro fertilization. *Swiss Journal of Psychology, 72*(2), 91–102.

Dasen, P. R. (1977). *Piagetian psychology: Cross-cultural contributions.* New York, NY: Gardner Press.

Dasen, P. R. (1984). The cross-cultural study of intelligence: Piaget and the Baoule. *International Journal of Psychology, 19*, 407–434.

David, D., Zoizner, G., & Werner, P. (2018). Self-stigma and age-related hearing loss: A qualitative study of stigma formation and dimensions. *American Journal of Audiology, 27*(1), 126–136. doi:10.1044/2017_AJA-17-0050

Davies, N., Crowe, M., & Whitehead, L. (2016). Establishing routines to cope with the loneliness associated with widowhood: A narrative analysis. *Journal of Psychiatric & Mental Health Nursing, 23*(8), 532–539. doi:10.1111/jpm.12339

Davila, J., & Kashy, D. A. (2009). Secure base processes in couples: Daily associations between support experiences and attachment security. *Journal of Family Psychology, 23*, 76–88.

Davis, J. K. (2016). Four ways life extension will change our relationship with death. *Bioethics, 30*(3), 165–172.

De Goede, I. H. D., Branje, S. J. T., & Meeus, W. H. J. (2009). Developmental changes in adolescents' perceptions of relationships with their parents. *Journal of Youth and Adolescence, 38*, 75–88.

de Onis, M., Blossner, M., & Borghi, E. (2012). Prevalence and trends of stunting among preschool children, 1990–2020. *Public Health Nutrition, 15*, 142–148.

De Preter, H., Van Looy, D., & Mortelmans, D. (2013). Individual and institutional push and pull factors as predictors of retirement timing in Europe: A multilevel analysis. *Journal of Aging Studies, 27*(4), 299–307.

De Raedt, R., Koster, E. W., & Ryckewaert, R. (2013). Aging and attentional bias for death related and general threat-related information: Less avoidance in older as compared with middle-aged adults. *Journals of Gerontology Series B: Psychological Sciences and Social Sciences, 68B*(1), 41–48.

De Ridder, S., & Van Bauwel, S. (2013). Commenting on pictures: Teens negotiating gender and sexualities on social networking sites. *Sexualities, 16*(5–6), 565–586.

De Schipper, E. J., Riksen-Walraven, J. M., & Geurts, S. A. E. (2006). Effects of child–caregiver ratio on the interactions between caregivers and children in child-care centers: An experimental study. *Child Development, 77*(4), 861–874.

De Schipper, J. C., Tavecchio, L. W. C., & van IJzendoorn, M. H. (2008). Children's attachment relationships with day care caregivers: Associations with positive caregiving and the child's temperament. *Social Development, 17*(3), 454–470.

Dean, D. C., O'Muircheartaigh, J., Dirks, H., Waskiewicz, N., Walker, L., Doernberg, E., . . . Deoni, S. L. (2014). Characterizing longitudinal white matter development during early childhood. *Brain Structure & Function, 220*(4), 1921–1933.

Dean, R. S., & Davis, A. S. (2007). Relative risk of perinatal complications in common childhood disorders. *School Psychology Quarterly, 22*(1), 13–23.

Deardorff, J., Cham, H., Gonzales, N. A., White, R. B., Tein, J., Wong, J. J., & Roosa, M. W. (2013). Pubertal timing and Mexican-origin girls' internalizing and externalizing symptoms: The influence of harsh parenting. *Developmental Psychology, 49*(9), 1790–1804.

Deary, I. J., Whalley, L. J., Lemmon, H., Crawford, J. R., & Starr, J. M. (2000). The stability of individual differences in mental ability from childhood to old age: Follow-up of the 1932 Scottish Mental Survey. *Intelligence, 28,* 49–55.

Deater-Deckard, K., Beekman, C., Wang, Z., Kim, J., Petrill, S., Thompson, L., & DeThorne, L. (2010). Approach/positive anticipation, frustration/anger, and overt aggression in childhood. *Journal of Personality, 78*(3), 991–1010.

DeCasper, A. J., & Fifer, W. P. (1980, June 6). Of human bonding: Newborns prefer their mothers' voices. *Science, 208,* 1174–1176.

Deci, E. L., & Ryan, R. M. (1985). The general causality orientations scale: Self-determination in personality. *Journal of Research in Personality, 19,* 109–134.

Deci, E. L., & Ryan, R. M. (2000). The "what" and "why" of goal pursuits: Human needs and the self-determination of behavior. *Psychological Inquiry, 11,* 227–268.

DeFillippi, R. J., & Arthur, M. B. (1994). The boundary-less career: A competency-based perspective. *Journal of Organizational Behavior, 15,* 307–324.

DeGarmo, D. S. (2010). Coercive and prosocial fathering, antisocial personality, and growth in children's post-divorce noncompliance. *Child Development, 81*(2), 503–516.

Degnan, K. A., Almas, A. N., & Fox, N. A. (2010). Temperament and the environment in the etiology of childhood anxiety. *Journal of Child Psychology and Psychiatry, 51*(4), 497–517.

Del Giudice, M. (2011). Alone in the dark? Modeling the conditions for visual experience in human fetuses. *Developmental Psychobiology, 53*(2), 214–219.

Delevi, R., & Weisskirch, R. S. (2013). Personality factors as predictors of sexting. *Computers in Human Behavior, 29*(6), 2589–2594.

Deligiannidis, K. M., Byatt, N., & Freeman, M. P. (2014). Pharmacotherapy for mood disorders in pregnancy: A review of pharmacokinetic changes and clinical recommendations for therapeutic drug monitoring. *Journal of Clinical Psychopharmacology, 34*(2), 244–255. doi:10.1097/JCP.0000000000000087

DeLongis, A., & Zwicker, A. (2017). Marital satisfaction and divorce in couples in stepfamilies. *Current Opinion in Psychology, 13,* 158–161. doi:10.1016/j.copsyc.2016.11.003

DeMatteo, D., Wolbransky, M., & LaDuke, C. (2016). Risk assessment with juveniles. In K. Heilbrun, D. DeMatteo, & N. S. Goldstein (Eds.), *APA handbook of psychology and juvenile justice* (pp. 365–384). Washington, DC: American Psychological Association.

Denham, S. A. (1998). *Emotional development in young children.* New York, NY: Guilford Press.

Denham, S. A., Blair, K. A., DeMulder, E., Levitas, J., Sawyer, K., Auerbach-Major, S., & Queenan, P. (2003). Preschool emotional competence: Pathway to social competence. *Child Development, 74,* 238–256.

Denhup, C. Y. (2017).The lived experience of parental bereavement: A new state of being. *Omega: Journal of Death and Dying, 74*(3), 345–360.

Deniz Can, D., Richards, T., & Kuhl, P. K. (2013). Early gray-matter and white-matter concentration in infancy predict later language skills: A whole brain vowel-based morphometry study. *Brain and Language, 124*(1), 34–44.

Dennis, C., Gagnon, A., Van Hulst, A., Dougherty, G., & Wahoush, O. (2013). Prediction of duration of breastfeeding among migrant and Canadian-born women: Results from a multi-center study. *Journal of Pediatrics, 162*(1), 72–79.

Dennis, M. K., & Brewer, J. P. (2017). Rearing generations: Lakota grandparents' commitment to family and community. *Journal of Cross-Cultural Gerontology, 32*(1), 95–113. doi.org/10.1007/s10823-016-9299-8

Dennis, N. A., Hayes, S. M., Prince, S. E., Madden, D. J., Huettel, S. A., & Cabeza, R. (2008). Effects of aging on the neural correlates of successful item and source memory encoding. *Journal of Experimental Psychology: Learning, Memory, and Cognition, 34*(4), 791–808.

Dennissen, J. J. A., Asendorpf, J. B., & van Aken, M. A. G. (2008). Childhood personality predicts long-term trajectories of shyness and aggressiveness in the context of demographic transitions in emerging adulthood. *Journal of Personality, 76*(1), 67–99.

Deoni, S. L., Dean, D. I., Piryatinsky, I., O'Muircheartaigh, J., Waskiewicz, N., Lehman, K., . . . Dirks, H. (2013). Breastfeeding and early white matter development: A cross-sectional study. *Neuro Image, 82,* 77–86.

Department of Motor Vehicles. (2018). *Senior drivers in Florida.* Retrieved from https://www.dmv.com/fl/florida/senior-drivers

Dequinzio, J. A., Poulson, C. L., Townsend, D. B., & Taylor, B. A. (2016). Social referencing and children with autism. *The Behavior Analyst, 39*(2), 319–331. doi:10.1007/s40614-015-0046-1

Desilver, D. (2016). More older Americans are working, and working more, than they used to. Retrieved from http://www.pewresearch.org/fact-tank/2016/06/20/more-older-americans-are-working-and-working-more-than-they-used-to/

Dew, J., & Wilcox, W. B. (2011). If momma ain't happy: Explaining declines in marital satisfaction among new mothers. *Journal of Marriage and Family, 73,* 1–12.

Diamanti, A., Basso, M. S., Castro, M., Bianco, G., Ciacco, E., Calce, A., . . . Gambarara, M. (2008). Clinical efficacy and safety of parental nutrition in adolescent girls with anorexia nervosa. *Journal of Adolescent Health, 42,* 111–118.

Diamond, A. (2009). The interplay of biology and the environment broadly defined. *Developmental Psychology, 45,* 1–8.

Diamond, M. (2013). Transsexuality among twins: Identity concordance, transition, rearing and orientation. *International Journal of Transgenderism, 14*(1), 24–36.

Diamond, M. C. (1988). *Enriching heredity: The impact of the environment on the anatomy of the brain.* New York, NY: Free Press.

Diamond, M. C. (1993). An optimistic view of the aging brain. *Generations, 17*(1), 31–33.

Díaz-Morales, J. F., Escribano, C., Jankowski, K. S., Vollmer, C., & Randler, C. (2014). Evening adolescents: The role of family relationships and pubertal development. *Journal of Adolescence, 37*(4), 425–432.

Dickens, B. M., Boyle, J. M., & Ganzini, L. (2008). Euthanasia and assisted suicide. In P. A. Singer & A. M. Viens (Eds.), *The Cambridge textbook of bioethics* (pp. 72–77). New York, NY: Cambridge University Press.

Dickinson, G. E. (2017). A 40-year history of end-of-life offerings in U.S. medical schools: 1975–2015. *American Journal of Hospice & Palliative Medicine, 34*(6), 559–565.

Diederich, A., Colonius, H., & Schomburg, A. (2008). Assessing age-related multisensory enhancement with the time-window-of-integration model. *Neuropsychologia, 46,* 2556–2562.

Dietz, P. M., Homa, D., England, L. J., Burley, K., Tong, V. T., Dube, S. R., & Bernert, J. T. (2011). Estimates of nondisclosure of cigarette smoking among pregnant and nonpregnant women of reproductive age in the United States. *American Journal of Epidemiology, 173*(3), 355–359.

Dilworth-Anderson, P., Boswell, G., & Cohen, M. D. (2007). Spiritual and religious coping values and beliefs among African American caregivers: A qualitative study. *Journal of Applied Gerontology, 26*(4), 355–369.

Dimidjian, S., Goodman, S. H., Felder, J. N., Gallop, R., Brown, A. P., & Beck, A. (2016). Staying well during pregnancy and the postpartum: A pilot randomized trial of mindfulness-based cognitive therapy for the prevention of depressive relapse/recurrence. *Journal of Consulting and Clinical Psychology, 84*(2), 134–145. doi:10-1037/ccp0000068

Dingemans, E., & Henkens, K. (2014). Involuntary retirement, bridge employment, and satisfaction with life: A longitudinal investigation. *Journal of Organizational Behavior, 35*(4), 575–591.

DiRosa, M., Kofahl, C., McKee, K., Bién, B., Lamura, G., Prouskas, C., . . . Mnich, E. (2011). A typology of caregiving situations and service use in family carers of older people in six European countries. *GeroPsych, 24*(1), 5–18.

Dishion, T. J., & Tipsord, J. M. (2011). Peer contagion in child and adolescent social and emotional development. *Annual Review of Psychology, 62,* 189–214.

Dishion, T. J., McCord, J., & Poulin, F. (1999). When interventions harm: Peer groups and problem behavior. *American Psychologist, 54,* 755–764.

Dixon, R. A., Rust, T. B., Feltmate, S. E., & See, S. K. (2007). Memory and aging: Selected research directions and application issues. *Canadian Psychology, 48*(2), 67–76.

Doane, L. D., & Thurston, E. C. (2014). Associations among sleep, daily experiences, and loneliness in adolescence: Evidence of moderating and bidirectional pathways. *Journal of Adolescence, 37*(2), 145–154.

Dobbins, E. H. (2007). End-of-life decisions: Influence of advance directives on patient care. *Journal of Gerontological Nursing, 33,* 50–56.

Dodge, K. A., Coie, J. D., & Lynam, D. (2006). Aggression and antisocial behavior in youth. In N. Eisenberg, W. Damon, & R. M. Lerner (Eds.), *Handbook of child psychology: Vol. 3. Social, emotional, and personality development* (6th ed., pp. 719–788). Hoboken, NJ: Wiley.

Doherty, W. J., & Harris, S. M. (2017). Discernment counseling for troubled relationships. In W. Doherty & S. Harris (Eds.), *Helping couples on the brink of divorce* (pp. 197–202). Washington: American Psychological Association.

Donnellan, M. B., Conger, R. D., & Burzette, R. G. (2007). Personality development from late adolescence to young adulthood: Differential stability, normative maturity, and evidence for the maturity-stability hypothesis. *Journal of Personality, 75*(2), 237–263.

Doucet, S., Soussignan, R., Sagot, P., & Schaal, B. (2007). The "smellscape" of mother's breast: Effects of odor masking and selective unmasking on neonatal arousal, oral and visual responses. *Developmental Psychobiology, 49,* 129–138.

Douglas, P. S., & Hill, P. S. (2013). Behavioral sleep interventions in the first six months of life do not improve outcomes for mothers or infants: A systematic review. *Journal of Developmental and Behavioral Pediatrics, 34*(7), 497–507.

Douglas, S. J., & Michaels, M. W. (2004). *The mommy myth: The idealization of motherhood and how it has undermined women.* New York, NY: Free Press.

Douglas, V., & Varnado-Sullivan, P. (2016). Weight stigmatization, internalization, and eating disorder symptoms: The role of emotion dysregulation. *Stigma and Health, 1*(3), 166–175. doi:10.1037/sah0000029

Douglass, S., Mirpuri, S., & Yip, T. (2017). Considering friends within the context of peers in school for the development of ethnic/racial identity. *Journal of Youth and Adolescence, 46*(2), 300–316.

Douglass, S., Wang, Y., & Yip, T. (2016). The everyday implications of ethnic-racial identity processes: Exploring variability in ethnic-racial identity salience across situations. *Journal of Youth & Adolescence, 45*(7), 1396–1414.

Downey, L., Curtis, J. R., Lafferty, W. E., Herting, J. R., & Engelberg, R. A. (2010). The quality of dying and death questionnaire (QODD): Empirical domains and theoretical perspectives. *Journal of Pain and Symptom Management, 39*(1), 9–22.

Drago, F. (2011). Self-esteem and earnings. *Journal of Economic Psychology, 32,* 480–488.

Draper, H. (2013). Grandparents' entitlements and obligations. *Bioethics, 27*(6), 309–316.

Drouin, M., Miller, D. A., & Dibble, J. L. (2014). Ignore your partners' current Facebook friends; beware the ones they add! *Computers in Human Behavior, 35,* 483–488.

Drouin, M., & Tobin, E. (2014). Unwanted but consensual sexting among young adults: Relations with attachment and sexual motivations. *Computers in Human Behavior, 31,* 412–418.

du Preez, J., Richmond, J., & Marquis, R. (2017). Issues affecting Australian grandparents who are primary caregivers of grandchildren: A review. *Journal of Family Studies, 23*(1), 142–159. doi.org/10.1080/13229400.2015.1086406

Duberstein, P. R., Chapman, B. P., Sink, K. M., Tindle, H. A., Bamonti, P., Robbins, J., . . . Franks, P. (2011). Personality and risk for Alzheimer's disease in adults 72 years of age and older: A 6-year follow-up. *Psychology and Aging, 26*(2), 351–362.

Dubois, B., Padovani, A., Scheltens, P., Rossi, A., & Dell'Agnello, G. (2016). Timely diagnosis for Alzheimer's disease: A literature review on benefits and challenges. *Journal of Alzheimer's Disease, 49*(3), 617–631. doi:10.3233/JAD-150692

Duell, N., Chein, J., Bacchini, D., Chaudhary, N., Dodge, K. A., Lansford, J. E., . . . Pena Alampay, L. (2016). Interaction of reward seeking and self-regulation in the prediction of risk taking: A cross-national test of the dual systems model. *Developmental Psychology, 52*(10), 1593–1605.

Duffy, A. L., Penn, S., Nesdale, D., & Zimmer-Gembeck, M. J. (2016). Popularity: Does it magnify associations between popularity prioritization and the bullying and defending behavior of early adolescent boys and girls? *Social Development, 26*(2), 263–277. doi:10.1111/sode.12206

Duffy, D., & Reynolds, P. (2011). Babies born at the threshold of viability: Attitudes of paediatric consultants and trainees in South East England. *Acta Paediatrica, 100*, 42–46.

Duffy, R. D., Allan, B. A., Autin, K. L., & Douglass, R. P. (2014). Living a calling and work well-being: A longitudinal study. *Journal of Counseling Psychology, 61*(4), 605–615.

Duffy, R. D., England, J., Torrey, C. L., & Tebbe, E. A. (2017). Calling in retirement: A mixed methods study. *Journal of Positive Psychology, 12*(4), 399–413. doi:10.1080/17439760.2016.1187201

Duh, S., Paik, J. H., Miller, P. H., Glick, S. C., Li, H., & Himmelfarb, I. (2016). Theory of mind and executive function in Chinese children. *Developmental Psychology, 52*(4), 582–591.

Duncan, G. J., Magnuson, K., & Votruba-Drzal, E. (2017). Moving beyond correlations in assessing the consequences of poverty. *Annual Review of Psychology, 68*(1), 413–434. doi:10.1146/annurev-psych-010416-044224

Dunedin Multidisciplinary Health and Development Research Unit. (2014). *The Dunedin multidisciplinary health & development study.* Retrieved from http://www.dunedinstudy.otago.ac.nz/

Dunfield, K. A., & Kuhlmeier, V. A. (2013). Evidence for partner choice in toddlers: Considering the breadth of other oriented behaviors. *Behavioral and Brain Sciences, 36*(1), 88–89.

Dunifon, R. (2013). The influence of grandparents on the lives of children and adolescents. *Child Development Perspectives, 7*(1), 55–60.

Dunn, J., & Hughes, C. (2001). "I got some swords and you're dead!" Violent fantasy, antisocial behavior, friendship, and moral sensibility in young children. *Child Development, 72*, 491–505.

Dunn, J., Wooding, C., & Hermann, J. (1977). Mothers' speech to young children: Variation in context. *Developmental Medicine & Child Neurology, 19*, 629–638.

Dunphy, D. C. (1963). The social structure of urban adolescent peer groups. *Sociometry, 26*, 230–246.

Duvander, A. (2014). How long should parental leave be? Attitudes to gender equality, family, and work as determinants of women's and men's parental leave in Sweden. *Journal of Family Issues, 35*(7), 909–926.

Dwairy, M. (2010). Parental inconsistency: A third cross-cultural research on parenting and psychological adjustment of children. *Journal of Child and Family Studies, 19*, 23–29.

Dweck, C. S. (1986). Motivational processes affecting learning. *American Psychologist, 41*, 1040–1048.

Dyregrov, A., & Dyregrov, K. (2017). Parents' perception of their relationship following the loss of a child. *Omega: Journal of Death & Dying, 76*(1), 35–52. doi:10.1177/0030222815590728

Eccles, J. S., & Roeser, R. W. (2003). Schools as developmental contexts. In G. R. Adams & M. D. Berzonsky (Eds.), *Blackwell handbook of adolescence* (pp. 129–148). Malden, MA: Blackwell.

Eckert, M. A., Matthews, L. J., & Dubno, J. R. (2017). Self-assessed hearing handicap in older adults with poorer-than-predicted speech recognition in noise. *Journal of Speech, Language, and Hearing Research, 60*(1), 251–263. doi:10.1044/2016_JSLHR-H-16-0011

Edin, K., & Kefalas, M. (2005). *Promises I can keep: Why poor women put motherhood before marriage.* Berkeley, CA: University of California Press.

Edwards, R. C., & Hans, S. L. (2016). Prenatal depressive symptoms and toddler behavior problems: The role of maternal sensitivity and child sex. *Child Psychiatry and Human Development, 47*(5), 696–707.

Egan, M., Daly, M., Delaney, L., Boyce, C. J., & Wood, A. M. (2017). Adolescent conscientiousness predicts lower lifetime unemployment. *Journal of Applied Psychology, 102*(4), 700–709. doi.org/10.1037/apl0000167

Egeli, N., & Rinaldi, C. (2016). Facets of adult social competence as predictors of parenting style. *Journal of Child & Family Studies, 25*(11), 3430–3439. doi:10.1007/s10826-016-0484-8

Eisenberg, N. (1992). *The caring child.* Cambridge, MA: Harvard University Press.

Eisenberg, N. (2003). Prosocial behavior, empathy, and sympathy. In M. H. Bornstein, L. Davidson, C. L. M. Keyes, & K. A. Moore (Eds.), *Well-being: Positive development across the life course* (pp. 253–265). Mahwah, NJ: Erlbaum.

Eisenberg, N., & Fabes, R. A. (1998). Prosocial development. In W. Damon (Series Ed.) & N. Eisenberg (Vol. Ed.), *Handbook of child psychology: Vol 3. Social, emotional, and personality development* (5th ed., pp. 701–778). Hoboken, NJ: Wiley.

Eisenberg, N., Hofer, C., Sulik, M. J., & Liew, J. (2014). The development of prosocial moral reasoning and a prosocial orientation in young adulthood: Concurrent and longitudinal correlates. *Developmental Psychology, 50*(1), 58–70.

Eisner, E. W. (2004). Multiple intelligences: Its tensions and possibilities. *Teachers College Record, 106*, 31–39.

Ekerdt, D. J. (1986). The busy ethic: Moral continuity between work and retirement. *The Gerontologist, 26*, 239–244.

Ekerdt, D. J. (2010). Frontiers of research on work and retirement. *Journals of Gerontology: Social Sciences, 65B*(1), 69–80.

Elder, G. H., & Caspi, A. (1988). Economic stress in lives: Developmental perspectives. *Journal of Social Issues, 44*, 25–45.

Elkind, D. (1968). Cognitive development in adolescence. In J. F. Adams (Ed.), *Understanding adolescence* (pp. 128–158). Boston, MA: Allyn and Bacon.

Elkind, D. (1978). Understanding the young adolescent. *Adolescence, 13*, 127–134.

Elliot, S. (2012). *Not my kid: What parents believe about the sex lives of their teenagers.* New York, NY: University Press.

Ellis, B. J. (2004). Timing of pubertal maturation in girls: An integrated life history approach. *Psychological Bulletin, 130*, 920–958.

Ellis, B. J., Boyce, W. T., Belsky, J., Bakermans-Kranenburg, M. J., & van IJzendoorn, M. H. (2011a). Differential susceptibility to the environment: An evolutionary-neurodevelopmental theory. *Development and Psychopathology, 23*(1), 7–28.

Ellis, B. J., Shirtcliff, E. A., Boyce, W., Deardorff, J., & Essex, M. J. (2011b). Quality of early family relationships and the timing and tempo of puberty: Effects depend on biological sensitivity to context. *Development and Psychopathology, 23*(1), 85–99.

Emery, L. F., Muise, A., Alpert, E., & Le, B. (2015). Do we look happy? Perceptions of romantic relationship quality on Facebook. *Personal Relationships, 22*(1), 1–7.

Enck, G. E. (2003). The dying process. In C. D. Bryant (Ed.), *Handbook of death & dying* (pp. 57–467). Thousand Oaks, CA: Sage.

Englund, M. M., Egeland, B., Olivia, E. M., & Collins, W. A. (2008). Childhood and adolescent predictors of heavy drinking and alcohol use disorders in early adulthood: A longitudinal development analysis. *Addiction, 103* (Suppl. 1), 23–35.

Enguidanos, S., Yonashiro-Cho, J., & Cote, S. (2013). Knowledge and perceptions of hospice care of Chinese older adults. *Journal of the American Geriatrics Society, 61*(6), 993–998.

Epstein, R. (2010). *Teen 2.0: Saving our children and families from the torment of adolescence.* New York, NY: Linton.

Epstein, R., Pandit, M., & Thakar, M. (2013). How love emerges in arranged marriages: Two cross-cultural studies. *Journal of Comparative Family Studies, 44*(3), 341–360.

Erber, J. T., & Prager, I. G. (1999). Age and memory: Perceptions of forgetful young and older adults. In T. M. Hess & F. Blanchard-Fields (Eds.), *Social cognition and aging* (pp. 197–217). San Diego, CA: Academic Press.

Erikson, E. H. (1950). *Childhood and society.* Oxford, England: Norton.

Erikson, E. H. (1963). *Childhood and society* (2nd ed.). New York, NY: Norton.

Erikson, E. H. (1968). *Identity: Youth and crisis.* New York, NY: Norton.

Erikson, E. H. (1969). *Gandhi's truth: On the origins of militant nonviolence.* New York, NY: Norton.

Erikson, E. H. (1980). *Identity and the life cycle.* New York, NY: Norton.

Erulkar, A. (2013). Adolescence lost: The realities of child marriage. *Journal of Adolescent Health, 52*(5), 513–514.

Espelage, D. L., & De La Rue, L. (2013). School bullying: Its nature and ecology. In J. C. Srabstein & J. Merrick (Eds.),

Bullying: A public health concern (pp. 23–37). Hauppauge, NY: Nova Science.

Espeset, E. M. S., Nordbo, R. H. S., Gulliksen, K. S., Skarderud, F., Geller, J., & Holte, A. (2011). The concept of body image disturbance in anorexia nervosa: An empirical inquiry utilizing patients' subjective experiences. *Eating Disorders, 19*(2), 175–193.

Etaugh, C. A., & Bridges, J. S. (2006). Midlife transitions. In J. Worell & C. D. Goodheart (Eds.), *Handbook of girls' and women's psychological health: Gender and well-being across the lifespan* (pp. 359–367). New York, NY: Oxford University Press.

Ettekal, I., & Ladd, G. W. (2015). Developmental pathways from childhood aggression-disruptiveness, chronic peer rejection, and deviant friendships to early-adolescent rule breaking. *Child Development, 86*(2), 614–631. doi:10.1111/cdev.12321

Eun, Y., Hong, I., Bruera, E., & Kang, J. H. (2017). Qualitative study on the perceptions of terminally ill cancer patients and their family members regarding end-of-life experiences focusing on palliative sedation. *Journal of Pain & Symptom Management, 53*(6), 1010–1016. doi:10.1016/j.jpainsymman.2016.12.353

Evans, A. D., Xu, F., & Lee, K. (2011). When all signs point to you: Lies told in the face of evidence. *Developmental Psychology, 47*(1), 39–49.

Evans, G. W., & Kim, P. (2013). Childhood poverty, chronic stress, self-regulation, and coping. *Child Development Perspectives, 7*(1), 43–48.

Fabes, R. A., Martin, C. L., & Hanish, L. D. (2003). Young children's play qualities in same-, other-, and mixed-sex peer groups. *Child Development, 74,* 921–932.

Fabian, J. (2011). Applying Roper v. Simmons in juvenile transfer and waiver proceedings: A legal and neuroscientific inquiry. *International Journal of Offender Therapy and Comparative Criminology, 55*(5), 732–755.

Faguy, K. (2016). Obesity in children and adolescents: Health effects and imaging implications. *Radiologic Technology, 87*(3), 279–302.

Fahs, B. (2007). Second shifts and political awakenings: Divorce and the political socialization of middle-aged women. *Journal of Divorce & Remarriage, 47*(3/4), 43–64.

Fairchild, H., & Cooper, M. (2010). A multidimensional measure of core beliefs relevant to eating disorders:

Preliminary development and validation. *Eating Behaviors, 11,* 239–246.

Farmer, T. W., Hamm, J. V., Leung, M., Lambert, K., & Gravelle, M. (2011). Early adolescent peer ecologies in rural communities: Bullying in schools that do and do not have a transition during the middle grades. *Journal of Youth and Adolescence, 40*(9), 1106–1117.

Farroni, T., Massaccesi, S., & Simion, F. (2002). La direzione dello sguardo di un'altra persona puo dirigere l'attenzione del neonato? [Can the direction of the gaze of another person shift the attention of a neonate?] *Giornale Italiano di Psicologia, 29,* 857–864.

Febo, M., & Foster, T. (2016). Preclinical magnetic resonance imaging and spectroscopy studies of memory, aging, and cognitive decline. *Frontiers in Aging Neuroscience, 8*(JUN). doi:10.3389/fnagi.2016.00158

Feeney, J. A. (1999). Adult romantic attachment and couple relationships. In J. Cassidy & P. R. Shaver (Eds.), *Handbook of attachment: Theory, research, and clinical applications* (pp. 355–377). New York, NY: Guilford Press.

Feeney, J. A., Hohaus, L., Noller, P., & Alexander, R. P. (2001). *Becoming parents: Exploring the bonds between mothers, fathers, and their infants.* New York, NY: Cambridge University Press.

Feeney, J. A., & Noller, P. (2002). Allocation and performance of household tasks: A comparison of new parents and childless couples. In P. Noller & J. A. Feeney (Eds.), *Understanding marriage: Developments in the study of couple interaction* (pp. 411–436). New York, NY: Cambridge University Press.

Feinberg, I., & Campbell, I. G. (2010). Sleep EEG changes during adolescence: An index of a fundamental brain reorganization. *Brain and Cognition, 72,* 56–65.

Feixa, C. (2011). Past and present of adolescence in society: The "teen brain" debate in perspective. *Neuroscience and Biobehavioral Reviews, 35*(8), 1634–1643.

Feldman, R., & Eidelman, A. I. (2003). Skin-to-skin contact (kangaroo care) accelerates autonomic and neurobehavioural maturation in preterm infants. *Developmental Medicine & Child Neurology, 45,* 274–281.

Ferber, R. (1985). Sleep, sleeplessness, and sleep disruptions in infants and young children. *Annals of Clinical Research, 17*(5). Special issue: Sleep research and its clinical implications, 227–234.

Ferland, P., & Caron, S. L. (2013). Exploring the long-term impact of female infertility: A qualitative analysis of interviews with postmenopausal women who remained childless. *The Family Journal, 21*(2), 180–188.

Fernandez, M., Blass, E. M., Hernandez-Reif, M., Field, T., Diego, M., & Sanders, C. (2003). Sucrose attenuates a negative electroencephalographic response to an aversive stimulus for newborns. *Journal of Developmental & Behavioral Pediatrics, 24*, 261–266.

Fernandez-Crehuet, J. M., Gimenez-Nadal, J. I., & Reyes Recio, L. E. (2016). The National Work–Life Balance Index[c]: The European case. *Social Indicators Research, 1*, 341. doi:10.1007/s11205-015-1034-2

Field, M. J. (2009). How people die in the United States. In J. L. Werth Jr. and D. Blevins (Eds.), *Decision making near the end of life: Issues, developments, and future directions* (pp. 63–75). New York, NY: Routledge.

Field, T., Diego, M., & Hernandez-Reif, M. (2007). Massage therapy research. *Developmental Review, 27*, 75–89.

Field, T., Diego, M., & Hernandez-Reif, M. (2011). Potential underlying mechanisms for greater weight gain in massaged preterm infants. *Infant Behavior and Development, 34*(3), 383–389.

Figueiredo, B., Dias, C. C., Pinto, T. M., & Field, T. (2016). Infant sleep–wake behaviors at two weeks, three and six months. *Infant Behavior and Development, 44*, 169–178. doi:10.1016/j.infbeh.2016.06.011

Finegood, E. D., Wyman, C., O'Connor, T. G., & Blair, C. B. (2017). Salivary cortisol and cognitive development in infants from low-income communities. *Stress: The International Journal on the Biology of Stress, 20*(1), 112–121. doi:10.1080/10253890.2017.1286325

Finer, L. B., & Philbin, J. M. (2014). Trends in ages at key reproductive transitions in the United States, 1951–2010. *Women's Health Issues 24*(3), 1–9.

Fingerman, K. L., Miller, L., & Charles, S. (2008). Saving the best for last: How adults treat social partners of different ages. *Psychology and Aging, 23*(2), 399–409.

Fink, E., Begeer, S., Peterson, C. C., Slaughter, V., & Rosnay, M. D. (2015). Friendlessness and theory of mind: A prospective longitudinal study. *British Journal of Developmental Psychology, 33*(1), 1–17. doi:10.1111/bjdp.12060

Finkel, D., Andel, R., Gatz, M., & Pedersen, N. (2009). The role of occupational complexity in trajectories of cognitive aging before and after retirement. *Psychology and Aging, 24*(3), 563–573.

Finkel, D., & Pedersen, N. L. (2004). Processing speed and longitudinal trajectories of change for cognitive abilities: The Swedish Adoption/Twin Study of Aging. *Aging, Neuropsychology, and Cognition, 11*, 325–345.

Finkel, E., Simpson, J., & Eastwick, P. (2017). The psychology of close relationships: Fourteen core principles. *Annual Reviews Inc.* doi:10.1146/annurev-psych-010416-044038

Finzi-Dottan, R., & Cohen, O. (2017). Fatherhood: Comparison between divorced custodial fathers, married fathers, and divorced non-custodial fathers in Israel. *Marriage and Family Review, 53*(4), 320–346. doi:10.1080/01494929.2016.1158220

Fischbach, R. L., Harris, M. J., Ballan, M. S., Fischbach, G. D., & Link, B. G. (2016). Is there concordance in attitudes and beliefs between parents and scientists about autism spectrum disorder? *Autism, 20*(3), 353–363. doi:10.1177/1362361315585310

Fischer, D. H. (1977). *Growing old in America.* New York, NY: Oxford University Press.

Fishman, T. (2010). *Shock of gray: The aging of the world's population and how it pits young against old, child against parent, worker against boss, company against rival, and nation against nation.* New York, NY: Scribner.

Fitzpatrick, M. J., & McPherson, B. J. (2010). Coloring within the lines: Gender stereotypes in contemporary coloring books. *Sex Roles, 62*, 127–137.

Fivush, R. (2011). The development of autobiographical memory. *Annual Review of Psychology, 62*, 559–582.

Flanagan, C. A., & Stout, M. (2010). Developmental patterns of social trust between early and late adolescence: Age and school climate effects. *Journal of Research on Adolescence, 20*(3), 748–773.

Flanders, J., Herman, L., Kahalisa, N., & Paquette, D. (2013). Rough-and-tumble play and the cooperation–competition dilemma. In D. Navaez, J. Panksepp, A. Schore, & T. Gleason (Eds.), *Evolution, early experience and human development: From research to practice* (pp. 371–387). New York, NY: Oxford University Press.

Flavell, J. H. (1963). *The developmental psychology of Jean Piaget.* New York, NY: Van Nostrand.

Flavell, J. H., Beach, D. R., & Chinsky, J. M. (1966). Spontaneous verbal rehearsal in a memory task as a function of age. *Child Development, 37*, 283–299.

Flecker, J., Fibich, T., & Kraemer, K. (2017). Socio-economic changes and the reorganization of work. In C. Korunka & B. Kubicek (Eds.), *Job demands in a changing world of work: Impact on workers' health and performance and implications for research and practice* (pp. 7–24). Cham, Switzerland: Springer International Publishing. doi:10.1007/978-3-319-54678-0_2

Fleming, P. (2017). The human capital hoax: Work, debt and insecurity in the era of uberization. *Organization Studies, 38*(5), 691–709.

Flower, K. B., Willoughby, M., Cadigan, R. J., Perrin, E. M., & Randolph, G. (2008). Understanding breastfeeding initiation and continuation in rural communities: A combined qualitative/quantitative approach. *Maternal and Child Health Journal, 12*(3), 402–414.

Flynn, J. R. (2007). *What is intelligence? Beyond the Flynn effect.* New York, NY: Cambridge University Press.

Fok, W., Zhang, Y., Salmon, A., Bhattacharya, A., Gunda, R., Jones, D., . . . Pérez, V. (2013). Short-term treatment with rapamycin and dietary restriction have overlapping and distinctive effects in young mice. *Journals of Gerontology Series A: Biological Sciences and Medical Sciences, 68*(2), 108–116.

Fonseca, A., Nazare, B., & Canavarro, M. C. (2014). Parenting an infant with a congenital anomaly: An exploratory study on patterns of adjustment from diagnosis to six months post birth. *Journal of Child Health Care, 18*(2), 111–122.

Forbush, K. T., & Hunt, T. K. (2014). Characterization of eating patterns among individuals with eating disorders: What is the state of the plate? *Physiology & Behavior, 134*, 92–109.

Ford, D. H., & Lerner, R. M. (1992). *Developmental systems theory: An integrative approach.* Newbury Park, CA: Sage.

Forster, S., Robertson, D. J., Jennings, A., Asherson, P., & Lavie, N. (2014). Plugging the attention deficit: Perceptual load counters increased distraction in ADHD. *Neuropsychology, 28*(1), 91–97.

Foster, R. E., Stone, F. P., Linkh, D. J., Besetsny, L. K., Collins, P. S., Saha, T., . . . Milner, J. S. (2010). Substantiation of spouse and child maltreatment reports as a function of referral source and maltreatment type. *Military Medicine, 175*(8), 560–566.

Foster, T. L., Gilmer, M. J., Davies, B., Dietrich, M. S., Barrera, M., . . . Gerhardt, C. A. (2011). Comparison of continuing bonds reported by parents and siblings after a child's death from cancer. *Death Studies, 35,* 420–440.

Fothergill, A. (2013). Managing childcare: The experiences of mothers and childcare workers. *Sociological Inquiry, 83*(3), 421–447.

Fowers, B. J., Richardson, F. C., & Slife, B. D. (2017). *Frailty, suffering, and vice: Flourishing in the face of human limitations.* Washington, DC: American Psychological Association. dx.doi.org/10.1037/0000035-000

Fox, J., Osborn, J. L., & Warber, K. M. (2014). Relational dialectics and social networking sites: The role of Facebook in romantic relationship escalation, maintenance, conflict, and dissolution. *Computers in Human Behavior, 35,* 527–534.

Fox, S. E., Levitt, P., & Nelson, C. A. (2010). How the timing and quality of early experiences influence the development of brain architecture. *Child Development, 81*(1), 28–40.

Francis, D. A., & DePalma, R. (2014). Teacher perspectives on abstinence and safe sex education in South Africa. *Sex Education, 14*(1), 81–94.

Frans, E. M., Sandin, S., Reichenberg, A., Langstrom, N., Lichtenstein, P., McGrath, J. J., & Hultman, C. M. (2013). Autism risk across generations: A population-based study of advancing grandpaternal and paternal age. *JAMA Psychiatry, 70*(5), 516–521.

Freeman, S., Kurosawa, H., Ebihara, S., & Kohzuki, M. (2010). Caregiving burden for the oldest old: A population based study of centenarian caregivers in Northern Japan. *Archives of Gerontology and Geriatrics, 50,* 282–291.

Freund, A. M., & Blanchard-Fields, F. (2014). Age-related differences in altruism across adulthood: Making personal financial gain versus contributing to the public good. *Developmental Psychology, 50*(4), 1125–1136.

Frey, K. S., & Ruble, D. N. (1985). What children say when the teacher is not around: Conflicting goals in social comparison and performance assessment in the classroom. *Journal of Personality and Social Psychology, 48,* 550–562.

Frey, K. S., & Ruble, D. N. (1990). Strategies for comparative evaluation: Maintaining a sense of competence across the life span. In R. J. Sternberg & J. Kolligian, Jr. (Eds.), *Competence considered* (pp. 167–189). New Haven, CT: Yale University Press.

Friedman, D. (2003). Cognition and aging: A highly selective overview of event-related potential (ERP) data. *Journal of Clinical and Experimental Neuropsychology, 25,* 702–720.

Friedman, E. M. (2014). Good friends, good food . . . what more could we want? Assessing the links between social relationships and dietary behaviors. A commentary on Conklin et al. *Social Science & Medicine, 100,* 176–177.

Frisén, A., & Holmqvist, K. (2010). What characterizes early adolescents with a positive body image? A qualitative investigation of Swedish girls and boys. *Body Image, 7,* 205–212.

Frye, A. A., & Liem, J. H. (2011). Diverse patterns in the development of depressive symptoms among emerging adults. *Journal of Adolescent Research, 26*(5), 570–590.

Fu, R., Chen, X., Wang, L., & Yang, F. (2016). Developmental trajectories of academic achievement in Chinese children: Contributions of early social-behavioral functioning. *Journal of Educational Psychology, 108*(7), 1001–1012. doi:10.1037/edu0000100

Fu, S.-Y., Anderson, D., & Courtney, M. (2003). Cross-cultural menopausal experience: Comparison of Australian and Taiwanese women. *Nursing & Health Sciences, 5,* 77–84.

Funk, L. M. (2010). Prioritizing parental autonomy: Adult children's accounts of feeling responsible and supporting aging parents. *Journal of Aging Studies, 24*(1), 57–64.

Furler, K., Gomez, V., & Grob, A. (2013). Personality similarity and life satisfaction in couples. *Journal of Research in Personality, 47*(4), 369–375.

Furler, K., Gomez, V., & Grob, A. (2014). Personality perceptions and relationship satisfaction in couples. *Journal of Research in Personality, 50,* 33–41.

Furstenberg, F. F. Jr. (2010). On a new schedule: Transitions to adulthood and family change. *The Future of Children, 20,* 67–87. Retrieved from http://www.futureofchildren/futureofchildren/publications/docs/20_01_04.pdf

Furstenberg, F. F. Jr. (2015). Becoming adults: Challenges in the transition to adult roles. *American Journal of Orthopsychiatry, Special Issue: Generations in Conflict: Responding to Sociocultural and Socioeconomic Trends, 85*(5), S14–S21.

Futch Ehrlich, V. A., Deutsch, N. L., Fox, C. V., Johnson, H. E., & Varga, S. M. (2016). Leveraging relational assets for adolescent development: A qualitative investigation of youth–adult "connection" in positive youth development. *Qualitative Psychology, 3*(1), 59–78. doi:10.1037/qup0000046

Gadoud, A., Adcock, Y., Jones, L., Koon, S., & Johnson, M. (2013). "It's not all doom and gloom": Perceptions of medical students talking to hospice patients. *Journal of Palliative Medicine, 16*(9), 1125–1129.

Gagne, M. H., Tourigny, M., Joly, J., & Pouliot-Lapointe, J. (2007). Predictors of adult attitudes toward corporal punishment of children. *Journal of Interpersonal Violence, 22*(10), 1285–1304.

Gair, S. (2017). Missing grandchildren: Grandparents' lost contact and implications for social work. *Australian Social Work, 70*(3), 263–275. doi.org/10.1080/0312407X.2016.1173714

Galinsky, E. (2007). The changing landscape of work. *Generations, 31*(1), 16–22.

García-Pérez, L., Linertová, R., Martín-Olivera, P., Serrano-Aguilar, P., & Benítez-Rosario, M. P. (2009). A systematic review of specialised palliative care for terminal patients: Which model is better? *Palliative Medicine, 23*(1), 17–22.

Gardner, H. (1998). A multiplicity of intelligences. *Scientific American Presents, 9*(4), 18–23.

Gardner, H. (2004). *Frames of mind: The theory of multiple intelligences.* New York, NY: Basic Books.

Gardner, H., & Moran, S. (2006). The science of multiple intelligences theory: A response to Lynn Waterhouse. *Educational Psychologist, 41*(4), 227–232.

Gardner, M., Roth, J., & Brooks-Gunn, J. (2008). Adolescents' participation in organized activities and developmental success 2 and 8 years after high school: Do sponsorship, duration, and intensity matter? *Developmental Psychology, 44,* 814–830.

Gardner, M., & Steinberg, L. (2005). Peer influence on risk taking, risk preference and risky decision-making in adolescence and adulthood: An experimental study. *Developmental Psychology, 41,* 625–635.

Garey, A. I., & Arendell, T. (2001). Children, work, and family: Some thoughts on "mother blame." In R. Hertz & N. L. Marshall (Eds.), *Working families: The transformation of the American home* (pp. 293–303). Berkeley, CA: University of California Press.

Gartstein, M. A., Bridgett, D. J., Young, B. N., Panksepp, J., & Power, T. (2013). Origins of effortful control: Infant and parent contributions. *Infancy, 18*(2), 149–183.

Gates, J. R., Corbin, W. R., & Fromme, K. (2016). Emerging adult identity development, alcohol use, and alcohol-related problems during the transition out of college. *Psychology of Addictive Behaviors, 30*(3), 345–355. doi:10.1037/adb0000179

Gath, A. (1993). Changes that occur in families as children with intellectual disability grow up. *International Journal of Disability, Development and Education, 40*, 167–174.

Gaul, D., & Issartel, J. (2016). Fine motor skill proficiency in typically developing children: On or off the maturation track? *Human Movement Science, 46*, 78–85.

Gavin, J., Rodham, K., & Poyer, H. (2008). The presentation of "pro-anorexia" in online group interactions. *Qualitative Health Research, 18*(3), 325–333.

Gazelle, H., & Ladd, G. W. (2003). Anxious solitude and peer exclusion: A diathesis-stress model of internalizing trajectories in childhood. *Child Development, 74*, 257–278.

Geary, D. C. (1998). *Male, female: The evolution of human sex differences.* Washington, DC: American Psychological Association.

Generous, M. A., & Keeley, M. (2017). Wished for and avoided conversations with terminally ill individuals during final conversations. *Death Studies, 41*(3), 162–172. doi:10.1080/07481187.2016.1236850

Genevie, L. E., & Margolies, E. (1987). *The motherhood report: How women feel about being mothers.* New York, NY: Macmillan.

George, L. K. (2010). Still happy after all these years: Research frontiers in subjective well-being in later life. *Journals of Gerontology: Social Sciences, 65B*(3), 331–339.

Gerber, E. B., Whitebook, M., & Weinstein, R. S. (2007). At the heart of child care: Predictors of teacher sensitivity in center-based child care. *Early Childhood Research Quarterly, 22*, 327–346.

Gerdner, L. A., Cha, D., Yang, D., & Tripp-Reimer, T. (2007). The circle of life: End-of-life care and death rituals for Hmong-American elders. *Journal of Gerontological Nursing, 33*(5), 20–29.

Gerontology Research Group. (n.d.). Retrieved from http://www.grg.org

Gershoff, E. T., & Grogan-Kaylor, A. (2016). Race as a moderator of associations between spanking and child outcomes. *Family Relations, 3*, 490. doi:10.1111/fare.12205

Gerson, M.-J., Posner, J.-A., & Morris, A. M. (1991). The wish for a child in couples eager, disinterested, and conflicted about having children. *American Journal of Family Therapy, 19*, 334–343.

Gervain, J., & Mehler, J. (2010). Speech perception and language acquisition in the first year of life. *Annual Review of Psychology, 61*, 191–218.

Gestsdottir, S., Bowers, E., von Eye, A., Napolitano, C. M., & Lerner, R. M. (2010). Intentional self-regulation in middle adolescence: The emerging role of loss-based selection in positive youth development. *Journal of Youth and Adolescence, 39*, 764–782.

Gettler, L. T., McDade, T. W., Agustin, S. S., Feranil, A. B., & Kuzawa, C. W. (2013). Do testosterone declines during the transition to marriage and fatherhood relate to men's sexual behavior? Evidence from the Philippines. *Hormones and Behavior, 64*(5), 755–763.

Gibbins, S., & Stevens, B. (2001). Mechanisms of sucrose and nonnutritive sucking in procedural pain management in infants. *Pain Research & Management, 6*, 21–28.

Gibson, E. J., & Walk, R. D. (1960). The "visual cliff." *Scientific American, 202*(4), 64–71.

Gibson, M. A., & Mace, R. (2005). Helpful grandmothers in rural Ethiopia: A study of the effect of kin on child survival and growth. *Evolution and Human Behavior, 26*, 469–482.

Gibson-Davis, C. M. (2009). Money, marriage, and children: Testing the financial expectations and family formation theory. *Journal of Marriage and Family, 71*, 146–160.

Gibson-Davis, C., & Percheski, C. (2018, May 18). Why the wealth gap hits families the hardest. *The New York Times.* Retrieved from http://www.nytimes.com

Gibson-Davis, C., & Rackin, H. (2014). Marriage or carriage? Trends in union context and birth type by education. *Journal of Marriage and Family, 76*(3), 506–519.

Giedd, J. N., Stockman, M., Weddle, C., Liverpool, M., Alexander-Bloch, A., Wallace, G. L., & Lenroot, R. K. (2010). Anatomic magnetic resonance imaging of the developing child and adolescent brain and effects of genetic variation. *Neuropsychology Review, 20*(4), 349–361.

Gieniusz, M., Kozikowski, A., Williams, M., Sinvani, L., Pekmezaris, R., Nouryan, C. N., . . . Kohn, N. (n.d.). PEG tubes in patients with advanced dementia: Are we "choosing wisely?" *Journal of the American Geriatrics Society, 65*, S77.

Gilbert-Barness, E. (2000). Maternal caffeine and its effect on the fetus. *American Journal of Medical Genetics, 93*, 253.

Gilboa, S., Shirom, A., Fried, Y., & Cooper, C. (2008). A meta-analysis of work demand stressors and job performance: Examining main and moderating effects. *Personnel Psychology, 61*(2), 227–272.

Giletta, M., Scholte, R. J., Engels, R. E., Ciairano, S., & Prinstein, M. J. (2012). Adolescent non-suicidal self-injury: A cross-national study of community samples from Italy, the Netherlands and the United States. *Psychiatry Research, 197*(1–2), 66–72.

Gilligan, C., & Attanucci, J. (1988). Two moral orientations: Gender differences and similarities. *Merrill-Palmer Quarterly: Journal of Developmental Psychology, 34*(3), 223–237.

Gilman, R., Huebner, E. S., Tian, L., Park, N., O'Byrne, J., Schiff, M., . . . Langknecht, H. (2008). Cross-national adolescent multidimensional life satisfaction reports: Analysis of mean scores and response style differences. *Journal of Youth and Adolescence, 37*, 142–154.

Gilovich, T., Kumar, A., & Jampol, L. (2015). A wonderful life: Experiential consumption and the pursuit of happiness. *Journal of Consumer Psychology, 25*(1), 152–165. doi.org/10.1016/j.jcps.2014.08.004

Ginsburg, H., & Opper, S. (1969). *Piaget's theory of intellectual development: An introduction.* Englewood Cliffs, NJ: Prentice-Hall.

Giordano, P. C., Manning, W. D., & Longmore, M. A. (2010). Affairs of the heart: Qualities of adolescent romantic relationships and sexual behavior. *Journal of Research on Adolescence, 20*(4), 983–1013.

Girdler, S., Packer, T. L., & Boldy, D. (2008). The impact of age-related vision loss. *OTJR: Occupation, Participation, and Health*, 28, 110–120.

Gish, J., Vrkljan, B., Grenier, A., & Van Miltenburg, B. (2017). Driving with advanced vehicle technology: A qualitative investigation of older drivers' perceptions and motivations for use. *Accident Analysis and Prevention*, 106, 498–504. doi:10.1016/j.aap.2016.06.027

Glaser, B. G., & Strauss, A. L. (1968). *Time for dying*. Chicago, IL: Aldine.

Glenn, N. (1990). Quantitative research on marital quality in the 1980s: A critical review. *Journal of Marriage and the Family*, 52, 818–831.

Glover, T. L., Garvan, C., Nealis, R. M., Citty, S. W., & Derrico, D. J. (2017). Improving end-of-life care knowledge among senior baccalaureate nursing students. *American Journal of Hospice & Palliative Medicine*, 34(10), 938–945. doi:10.1177/1049909117693214

Goldberg, A., Smith, J., & Kashy, D. A. (2010). Preadoptive factors predicting lesbian, gay, and heterosexual couples' relationship quality across the transition to adoptive parenthood. *Journal of Family Psychology*, 24(3), 221–232.

Goldberg, W. A., Lucas-Thompson, R. G., Germo, G. R., Keller, M. A., Davis, E. P., & Sandman, C. A. (2013). Eye of the beholder? Maternal mental health and the quality of infant sleep. *Social Science & Medicine*, 79, 101–108.

Goldman, J. G., & Coleman, S. J. (2013). Primary school puberty/sexuality education: Student-teachers' past learning, present professional education, and intention to teach these subjects. *Sex Education*, 13(3), 276–290.

Goldschmidt, A. B., Wall, M. M., Loth, K. A., Bucchianeri, M. M., & Neumark-Sztainer, D. (2014). The course of binge eating from adolescence to young adulthood. *Health Psychology*, 33(5), 457–460.

Golombok, S., Perry, B., Burston, A., Murray, C., Mooney-Somers, J., Stevens, M., & Golding, J. (2003). Children with lesbian parents: A community study. *Developmental Psychology*, 39, 20–33.

Gooch, D., Snowling, M., & Hulme, C. (2011). Time perception, phonological skills and executive function in children with dyslexia and/or ADHD symptoms. *Journal of Child Psychology and Psychiatry*, 52(2), 195–203.

Good, M.-J. D., Gadmer, N. M., Ruopp, P., Lakoma, M., Sullivan, A. M., Redinbaugh, E., Arnold, R. M., & Block, S. D. (2004). Narrative nuances on good and bad deaths: Internists' tales from high-technology work places. *Social Science & Medicine*, 58, 939–953.

Goodlin-Jones, B. L., Burnham, M. M., Gaylor, E. E., & Anders, T. F. (2001). Night waking, sleep–wake organization, and self-soothing in the first year of life. *Journal of Developmental and Behavioral Pediatrics*, 22(4), 226–233.

Gopnik, A. (2010). How babies think: Even the youngest children know, experience and learn far more than scientists ever thought possible. *Scientific American*, 303, 76–81.

Gordon, R. J. (2015). *The rise and fall of American growth*. Princeton, NJ: Princeton University Press.

Gordon-Messer, D., Bauermeister, J. A., Grodzinski, A., & Zimmerman, M. (2013). Sexting among young adults. *Journal of Adolescent Health*, 52(3), 301–306.

Gore, T., & Dubois, R. (1998). The "Back to Sleep" campaign. *Zero to Three*, 19(2), 22–23.

Gorer, G. (1965). *Death, grief, and mourning in contemporary Britain*. London, England: Cresset Press.

Gothe, K., Oberauer, K., & Kliegl, R. (2008). Age differences in dual-task performance after practice. *Psychology and Aging*, 22(3), 596–606.

Gottman, J., & Gottman, J. (2017). The natural principles of love. *Journal of Family Theory & Review*, 9, 7–26.

Gould, L. A., & Pate, M. (2010). Discipline, docility, and disparity: A study of inequality and corporal punishment. *British Journal of Criminology*, 50, 185–205.

Gould, S. J. (1981). *The mismeasure of man*. New York, NY: Norton.

Gourgouvelis, J., Yielder, P., & Murphy, B. (2017). Exercise promotes neuroplasticity in both healthy and depressed brains: An fMRI pilot study. *Neural Plasticity*, 2017(2017), 1–13. doi.org/10.1155/2017/8305287

Goveas, J. S., Espeland, M. A., Hogan, P. E., Tindle, H. A., Shih, R. A., Kotchen, J. M., . . . Resnick, S. M. (2014). Depressive symptoms and longitudinal changes in cognition: Women's health initiative study of cognitive aging. *Journal of Geriatric Psychiatry and Neurology*, 27(2), 94–102.

Graber, J. A., Nichols, T. R., & Brooks-Gunn, J. (2010). Putting pubertal timing in developmental context: Implications for prevention. *Developmental Psychobiology*, 52(3), 254–262.

Graham, J., Banaschewski, T., Buitelaar, J., Coghill, D., Danckaerts, M., Dittmann, R. W., . . . Taylor, E. (2011). European guidelines on managing adverse effects of medication for ADHD. *European Child & Adolescent Psychiatry*, 20, 17–37.

Graneheim, U. H., Johansson, A., & Lindgren, B. (2014). Family caregivers' experiences of relinquishing the care of a person with dementia to a nursing home: Insights from a meta-ethnographic study. *Scandinavian Journal of Caring Sciences*, 28(2), 215–224.

Gratwick-Sarll, K., Bentley, C., Harrison, C., & Mond, J. (2016). Poor self-recognition of disordered eating among girls with bulimic-type eating disorders: Cause for concern? *Early Intervention in Psychiatry*, 10(4), 316–333.

Grawitch, M. J., & Ballard, D. W. (2016). The psychologically healthy workplace: Building a win–win environment for organizations and employees. Washington, DC: American Psychological Association.

Gray, M., Shadden, B., Henry, J., Di Brezzo, R., Ferguson, A., & Fort, I. (2016). Meaning making in long-term care: What do certified nursing assistants think? *Nursing Inquiry*, 23(3), 244–252. doi:10.1111/nin.12137

Greenfield, E. A. (2010). Child abuse as a life-course social determinant of adult health. *Maturitas*, 66, 51–55.

Grigoryeva, A. (2017). Own gender, sibling's gender, parent's gender. *The Division of Elderly Parent Care among Adult Children*, 82(1), 116–146. doi.org/10.1177/0003122416686521

Groen, Y., Wijers, A. A., Tucha, O., & Althaus, M. (2013). Are there sex differences in ERPs related to processing empathy-evoking pictures? *Neuropsychologia*, 51(1), 142–155.

Groeneveld, M. G., Vermeer, H. J., van IJzendoorn, M. H., & Linting, M. (2010). Children's well-being and cortisol levels in home-based and center-based childcare. *Early Childhood Research Quarterly*, 25(4), 502–514.

Groopman, J. E. (2004). *The anatomy of hope: How patients prevail in the face of illness*. New York, NY: Random House.

Grossbaum, M. F., & Bates, G. W. (2002). Correlates of psychological well-being at midlife: The role of generativity, agency and communion, and narrative themes. *International Journal of Behavioral Development, 26,* 120–127.

Grossman, T., & Jessen, S. (2017). When in infancy does the "fear bias" develop? *Journal of Experimental Child Psychology, 153,* 149–154.

Grossmann, I. (2017). Wisdom and how to cultivate it: Review of emerging evidence for a constructivist model of wise thinking. *European Psychologist, 22*(4), 233–246. doi. org/10.1027/1016-9040/a000302

Grossmann, I., Gerlach, T. M., & Denissen, J. J. A. (2016). Wise reasoning in the face of everyday life challenges. *Social Psychological and Personality Science, 7*(7), 611–622. doi. org/10.1177/1948550616652206

Grossmann, I., Sahdra, B., & Ciarrochi, J. (2016). A heart and a mind: Self-distancing facilitates the association between heart rate variability, and wise reasoning. *Frontiers in Behavioral Neuroscience, 10*(68), 1–10. doi. org/10.3389/fnbeh.2016.00068

Grube, J. W., Bourdeau, B., Fisher, D. A., & Bersamin, M. (2008). *Television exposure and sexuality among adolescents: A longitudinal survey study.* Paper presented at the Biennial Meeting of the Society for Research in Adolescence: Chicago, IL.

Grych, J., Hamby, S., & Banyard, V. (2015). The resilience portfolio model: Understanding healthy adaptation in victims of violence. *Psychology of Violence, 5*(4), 343–354. doi:10.1037/ a0039671

Guan, S. A., Greenfield, P. M., & Orellana, M. F. (2014). Translating into understanding: Language brokering and prosocial development in emerging adults from immigrant families. *Journal of Adolescent Research, 29*(3), 331–355.

Guardino, C. M., & Schetter, C. D. (2014). Coping during pregnancy: A systematic review and recommendations. *Health Psychology Review, 8*(1), 70–94.

Guendelman, S., Kosa, J. L., Pearl, M., Graham, S., Goodman, J., & Kharrazi, M. (2009). Juggling work and breastfeeding: Effects of maternity leave and occupational characteristics. *Pediatrics, 123,* e38–e46.

Guerra, N. G., Williams, K. R., & Sadek, S. (2011). Understanding bullying and victimization during childhood and adolescence: A mixed methods study. *Child Development, 82*(1), 295–310.

Guerri, C., & Pascual, M. (2010). Mechanisms involved in the neurotoxic, cognitive, and neurobehavioral effects of alcohol consumption during adolescence. *Alcohol, 44*(1), 15–26.

Gupta, R. (2011). Death beliefs and practices from an Asian Indian American Hindu perspective. *Death Studies, 35,* 244–266.

Guttmacher Institute. (2011b). *In brief: Facts on American teens' sexual and reproductive health.* New York, NY: Guttmacher Institute.

Guttmacher Institute. (2014). *Contraceptive use in the United States.* Retrieved from http://www.guttmacher. org/pubs/fb_contr_use.html

Ha, J.-H., & Ingersoll-Dayton, B. (2008). The effect of widowhood on international ambivalence. *Journals of Gerontology: Social Sciences, 63B*(1), S49–S58.

Ha, J., Yoon, H., Lim, Y. O., & Heo, S. (2016). The effect of widowhood on parent–child relationships in Korea: Do parents' filial expectations and geographic proximity to children matter? *Journal of Cross-Cultural Gerontology, 31*(1), 73–88. doi:10.1007/ s10823-016-9280-6

Habermas, T., Negele, A., & Mayer, F. B. (2010). "Honey, you're jumping about"—Mothers' scaffolding of their children's and adolescents' life narration. *Cognitive Development, 25,* 339–351.

Haga, M., Gísladóttír, T., & Sigmundsson, H. (2015). The relationship between motor competence and physical fitness is weaker in the 15–16 yr. adolescent age group than in younger age groups (4–5 yr. and 11–12 yr.). *Perceptual and Motor Skills, 121*(3), 900–912.

Hagestad, G. O. (1985). Continuity and connectedness. In V. L. Bengtson & J. F. Robertson (Eds.), *Grandparenthood* (pp. 31–48). Thousand Oaks, CA: Sage.

Haines, S. J., Gleeson, J., Kuppens, P., Hollenstein, T., Ciarrochi, J., Labuschagne, I., . . . Koval, P. (2016). The wisdom to know the difference. *Psychological Science, 27*(12), 1651–1659. doi. org/10.1177/0956797616669086

Hakoyama, M., & MaloneBeach, E. E. (2013). Predictors of grandparent–grandchild closeness: An ecological perspective. *Journal of Intergenerational Relationships, 11*(1), 32–49.

Hall, S. (2011). "It's going to stop in this generation": Women with a history of child abuse resolving to raise their children without abuse. *Harvard Educational Review, 81*(1), 24–49.

Hall, S., & Walls, J. (2015). Exploring family-oriented markers of adulthood: Political and personal variations among emerging adults. *Emerging Adulthood, 4*(3), 192–199.

Halperin, J. M., & Healey, D. M. (2011). The influences of environmental enrichment, cognitive enhancement, and physical exercise on brain development: Can we alter the developmental trajectory of ADHD? *Neuroscience and Biobehavioral Reviews, 35,* 621–634.

Halpern, H. P., & Perry-Jenkins, M. (2016). Parents' gender ideology and gendered behavior as predictors of children's gender-role attitudes: A longitudinal exploration. *Sex Roles, 74*(11–12), 527–542. doi:10.1007/ s11199-015-0539-0

Halpern-Meekin, S., Manning, W. D., Giordano, P. C., & Longmore, M. A. (2013). Relationship churning in emerging adulthood: On/off relationships and sex with an ex. *Journal of Adolescent Research, 28*(2), 166–188.

Haltigan, J., Roisman, G., Cauffman, E., & Booth-LaForce, C. (2017). Correlates of childhood vs. adolescence internalizing symptomatology from infancy to young adulthood. *Journal of Youth & Adolescence, 46*(1), 197–212.

Hamlin, J. K. (2013a). Failed attempts to help and harm: Intention versus outcome in preverbal infants' social evaluations. *Cognition, 128*(3), 451–474.

Hamlin, J. K. (2013b). Moral judgment and action in preverbal infants and toddlers: Evidence for an innate moral core. *Current Directions in Psychological Science, 22*(3), 186–193.

Hamlin, J. K., Mahajan, N., Liberman, Z., & Wynn, K. (2013). Not like me = bad: Infants prefer those who harm dissimilar others. *Psychological Science, 24*(4), 589–594.

Hamlin, J. K., & Wynn, K. (2011). Young infants prefer prosocial to antisocial others. *Cognitive Development, 26,* 30–39.

Hampson, S. E., Edmonds, G. W., Goldberg, L. R., Dubanoski, J. P., & Hillier, T. A. (2013). Childhood conscientiousness relates to objectively measured adult physical health four decades later. *Health Psychology, 32*(8), 925–928.

Harbourne, R. T., Lobo, M. A., Karst, G. M., & Galloway, J. C. (2013). Sit happens: Does sitting development perturb reaching development, or vice versa? *Infant Behavior and Development, 36*(3), 438–450.

Hari, A. (2017). Who gets to "work hard, play hard"? Gendering the work–life balance rhetoric in Canadian tech companies. *Gender, Work & Organization, 24*(2), 99–112.

Harley, K., & Reese, E. (1999). Origins of autobiographical memory. *Developmental Psychology, 35,* 1338–1348.

Harlow, C. M. (Ed.). (1986). *From learning to love: The selected papers of H. F. Harlow.* New York, NY: Praeger.

Harlow, H. F. (1958). The nature of love. *American Psychologist, 13,* 673–685.

Harlow, H. F., Harlow, M. K., Dodsworth, R. O., & Arling, G. L. (1966). Maternal behavior of rhesus monkeys deprived of mothering and peer associations in infancy. *Proceedings of the American Philosophical Society, 110,* 58–66.

Harper, G. W., & Wilson, B. M. (2017). Situating sexual orientation and gender identity diversity in context and communities. In M. A. Bond, I. Serrano-Garcia, C. B. Keys, & M. Shinn (Eds.), *APA handbook of community psychology: Theoretical foundations, core concepts, and emerging challenges* (pp. 387–402). Washington, DC, US: American Psychological Association.

Harriger, J. A., Calogero, R. M., Witherington, D. C., & Smith, J. E. (2010). Body size stereotyping and internalization of the thin ideal in preschool girls. *Sex Roles, 63,* 609–620.

Harris, J. R. (1995). Where is the child's environment? A group socialization theory of development. *Psychological Review, 102,* 458–489.

Harris, J. R. (1998). *The nurture assumption: Why children turn out the way they do.* New York, NY: Free Press.

Harris, J. R. (2002). Beyond the nurture assumption: Testing hypotheses about the child's environment. In J. G. Borkowski, S. L. Ramey, & M. Bristol-Power (Eds.), *Parenting and the child's world: Influences on academic, intellectual, and social-emotional development* (pp. 3–20). Mahwah, NJ: Erlbaum.

Harris, J. R. (2006). *No two alike: Human nature and human individuality.* New York, NY: Norton.

Harris, P., Wong, E., Farrington, S., Craig, T. R., Harrold, J. K., Oldanie, B., . . . Casarett, D. J. (2013). Patterns of functional decline in hospice: What can individuals and their families expect? *Journal of the American Geriatrics Society, 61*(3), 413–417.

Harrist, A. W., Thompson, S. D., & Norris, D. J. (2007). Defining quality childcare: Multiple stakeholder perspectives. *Early Education and Development, 18*(2), 305–336.

Hart, H. M., McAdams, D. P., Hirsch, B. J., & Bauer, J. J. (2001). Generativity and social involvement among African Americans and White adults. *Journal of Research in Personality, 35,* 208–230.

Harter, S. (1981). A new self-report scale of intrinsic versus extrinsic orientation in the classroom: Motivational and informational components. *Developmental Psychology, 17,* 300–312.

Harter, S. (1999). *The construction of the self: A developmental perspective.* New York, NY: Guilford Press.

Hartup, W. W., & Stevens, N. (1997). Friendships and adaptation in the life course. *Psychological Bulletin, 121,* 355–370.

Hashimoto-Torii, K., Kawasawa, Y. I., Kuhn, A., & Rakic, P. (2011). Combined transcriptome analysis of fetal human and mouse cerebral cortex exposed to alcohol. *Proceedings of the National Academy of Sciences of the United States of America, 108*(10), 4212–4217.

Hashizume, Y. (2010). Releasing from the oppression: Caregiving for the elderly parents of Japanese working women. *Qualitative Health Research, 20*(6), 830–844.

Haskett, M. E., Neupert, S. D., & Okado, Y. (2014). Factors associated with 3-year stability and change in parenting behavior of abusive parents. *Journal of Child and Family Studies, 23*(2), 263–274.

Hatano, K., Sugimura, K., & Crocetti, E. (2016). Looking at the dark and bright sides of identity formation: New insights from adolescents and emerging adults in Japan. *Journal of Adolescence, 141,* 156–168.

Hayslip, B., Jr., & Patrick, J. H. (Eds.). (2003). *Working with custodial grandparents.* New York, NY: Springer.

Hazan, C., & Shaver, P. (1987). Romantic love conceptualized as an attachment process. *Journal of Personality and Social Psychology, 52,* 511–524.

Healthychildren.org. (n.d.). Retreived from http/www/Healthychildren.org

Healy, E., Reichenberg, A., Nam, K. W., Allin, M. G., Walshe, M., Rifkin, L., . . . Nosarti, C. (2013). Preterm birth and adolescent social functioning—Alterations in emotion-processing brain areas. *Journal of Pediatrics, 163*(6), 1596–1604.

Hearing Loop. (n.d.) Retrieved from http://www.hearingloop.com

Heatherton, T. F. (2011). Neuroscience of self and self-regulation. *Annual Review of Psychology, 62,* 363–390.

Heaven, P. C. L., Ciarrochi, J., & Vialle, W. (2008). Self-nominated peer crowds, school achievement, and psychological adjustment in adolescents: Longitudinal analysis. *Personality and Individual Differences, 44,* 977–988.

Hedley, D., Brewer, N., Nevill, R., Uljarević, M., Butter, E., & Mulick, J. A. (2016). The relationship between clinicians' confidence and accuracy, and the influence of child characteristics, in the screening of autism spectrum disorder. *Journal of Autism and Developmental Disorders, 46*(7), 2340–2348. doi:10.1007/s10803-016-2766-9

Hefner, V., Woodward, K., Figge, L., Bevan, J. L., Santora, N., & Baloch, S. (2014). The influence of television and film viewing on midlife women's body image, disordered eating, and food choice. *Media Psychology, 17*(2), 185–207. doi.org/10.1080/15213269.2013.838903

Hehman, J. A., & Bugental, D. B. (2013). "Life stage-specific" variations in performance in response to age stereotypes. *Developmental Psychology, 49*(7), 1396–1406.

Heilbrun, K., DeMatteo, D., & Goldstein, N. S. (2016). *APA handbook of psychology and juvenile justice.* Washington, DC: American Psychological Association.

Hellerstein, S., Feldman, S., & Duan, T. (2016). Survey of obstetric care and cesarean delivery rates in Shanghai, China. *Birth: Issues in Perinatal Care, 43*(3), 193–199.

Helson, R., & Soto, C. J. (2005). Up and down in middle age: Monotonic and nonmonotonic changes in roles, status, and personality. *Journal of Personality and Social Psychology, 89*(2), 194–204.

Henderson, T. L., Dinh, M., Morgan, K., & Lewis, J. (2017). Alaska native grandparents rearing grandchildren: A rural community story. *Journal of Family Issues, 38*(4), 547–572. doi.org/10.1177/0192513X15597292

Hendry, A., Jones, E. J., & Charman, T. (2016). Executive function in the first three years of life: Precursors, predictors and patterns. *Developmental Review, 42,* 1–33. doi:10.1016/j.dr.2016.06.005

Hendry, L. B., & Kloep, M. (2010). How universal is emerging adulthood? An empirical example. *Journal of Youth Studies, 13*(2), 169–179.

Hengartner, M. P., Muller, M., Rodgers, S., Rossler, W., & Ajdacic-Gross, V. (2013). Can protective factors moderate the detrimental effects of child maltreatment on personality functioning? *Journal of Psychiatric Research, 47*(9), 1180–1186.

Henin, A., & Berman, N. (2016). The promise and peril of emerging adulthood: Introduction to the special issue. *Cognitive and Behavioral Practice, 23*(3), 263–269. doi:10.1016/j.cbpra.2016.05.005

Hennekam, S. (2016). Identity transition during pregnancy: The importance of role models. *Human Relations, 69*(9), 1765. doi:10.1177/0018726716631402

Henning, G., Lindwall, M., & Johansson, B. (2016). Continuity in well-being in the transition to retirement. *Geropsych: The Journal of Gerontopsychology and Geriatric Psychiatry, 29*(4), 225–237. doi:10.1024/1662-9647/a000155

Henretta, J. C., & McCrory, C. (2016). Childhood circumstances and mid-life functional mobility. *Journal of Aging and Health, 28*(3), 440–459.

Henrique, R. S., Alessandro, H. N., Stodden, D. F., Fransen, J., Campos, C. M. C., Queiroz, D. R., & Cattuzzo, M. T. (2016). Association between sports participation, motor competence and weight status: A longitudinal study. *Journal of Science and Medicine in Sport, 19*(10), 825–829.

Henry, L. A., Messer, D. J., & Nash, G. (2012). Executive functioning in children with specific language impairment. *Journal of Child Psychology and Psychiatry, 53*, 37–45.

Hensler, B. S., Schatschneider, C., Taylor, J., & Wagner, R. K. (2010). Behavioral genetic approach to the study of dyslexia. *Journal of Developmental and Behavioral Pediatrics, 31*(7), 525–532.

Hepach, R., Vaish, A., & Tomasello, M. (2013). A new look at children's prosocial motivation. *Infancy, 18*(1), 67–90.

Herbert, A. C., Ramirez, A. M., Lee, G., North, S. J., Askari, M. S., West, R. L., Sommer, M. (2016). Puberty experiences of low-income girls in the United States: A systematic review of qualitative literature from 2000 to 2014. *Journal of Adolescent Health, 60*(4), 363–379.

Herrnstein, R. J., & Murray, C. A. (1994). *The bell curve: Intelligence and class structure in American life.* New York, NY: Free Press.

Hershey, D. A., Henkens, K., & van Dalen, H. P. (2010). What drives retirement income worries in Europe? A multilevel analysis. *European Journal of Ageing, 7*, 301–311.

Herting, M. M., & Sowell, E. R. (2017). Puberty and structural brain development in humans. *Frontiers in Neuroendocrinology, 44*, 122–137.

Hertzog, C. (1996). Research design in studies of aging and cognition. In J. E. Birren, K. W. Schaie, R. P. Abeles, M. Gatz, & T. A. Salthouse (Eds.), *Handbook of the psychology of aging* (4th ed., pp. 24–37). San Diego, CA: Academic Press.

Hesse-Biber, S., Livingstone, S., Ramirez, D., Barko, E. B., & Johnson, A. L. (2010). Racial identity and body image among black female college students attending predominately white colleges. *Sex Roles, 63*, 697–711.

Hetherington, E. M., & Kelly, J. (2002). *For better or for worse: Divorce reconsidered.* New York, NY: Norton.

Hewitt, B., Haynes, M., & Baxter, J. (2013). Relationship dissolution and time on housework. *Journal of Comparative Family Studies, 44*(3), 327–340.

Higher Education Research Institute. (2013). Class of 2012: Findings from the college senior survey. *HERI Research Brief.* Retrieved from http://www.heri.ucla.edu/

Hilmert, C. J., Kvasnicka-Gates, L., Teoh, A. N., Bresin, K., & Fiebiger, S. (2016). Major flood related strains and pregnancy outcomes. *Health Psychology, 35*(11), 1189–1196. doi:10.1037/hea0000386

Hinde, R. A. (2005). Ethology and attachment theory. In K. E. Grossmann, K. Grossmann, & E. Waters (Eds.), *Attachment from infancy to adulthood: The major longitudinal studies* (pp. 1–12). New York, NY: Guilford Press.

Hipwell, A. E., Keenan, K., Loeber, R., & Battista, D. (2010). Early predictors of sexually intimate behaviors in an urban sample of young girls. *Developmental Psychology, 46*(2), 366–378.

Hirschfield, P. J., & Gasper, J. (2011). The relationship between school engagement and delinquency in late childhood and early adolescence. *Journal of Youth and Adolescence, 40*(1), 3–22.

Hoeben, E. M., Meldrum, R. C., Walker, D., & Young, J. T. (2016). The role of peer delinquency and unstructured socializing in explaining delinquency and substance use: A state-of-the-art review. *Journal of Criminal Justice, 47*, 108–122.

Hoff-Ginsberg, E. (1997). *Language development.* Belmont, CA: Brooks/Cole.

Hoffman, M. L. (1994). Discipline and internalization. *Developmental Psychology, 30*, 26–28.

Hoffman, M. L. (2001). Toward a comprehensive empathy-based theory of prosocial moral development. In A. C. Bohart & D. J. Stipek (Eds.), *Constructive and destructive behavior: Implications for family, school, and society* (pp. 61–86). Washington, DC: American Psychological Association.

Hofstede, G. (1981). Cultures and organizations. *International Studies of Management and Organization, 10*(4), 15–41.

Hofstede, G. (2001). *Culture's consequences: Comparing values, behaviors, institutions, and organizations across nations* (2nd ed.). Thousand Oaks, CA: Sage.

Hohman, T. J., Tommet, D., Marks, S., Contreras, J., Jones, R., & Mungas, D. (2017). Evaluating Alzheimer's disease biomarkers as mediators of age-related cognitive decline. *Neurobiology of Aging, 58*, 120–128. doi:10.1016/j.neurobiolaging.2017.06.022

Holland, J. (1997). *Making vocational choices: A theory of vocational personalities and work environments* (3rd ed.). Odessa, FL: Psychological Assessment Resources.

Holland, L. A., Brown, T. A., & Keel, P. K. (2014). Defining features of unhealthy exercise associated with disordered eating and eating disorder diagnoses. *Psychology of Sport and Exercise, 15*(1), 116–123.

Holmes, T. H., & Rahe, R. H. (1967). The social readjustment rating scale. *Journal of Psychosomatic Research, 11*, 213–218.

Hong, O., Chin, D. L., & Kerr, M. J. (2015). Lifelong occupational exposures and hearing loss among elderly Latino Americans aged 65–75 years. *International Journal of Audiology, 54*, S57–64. doi:10.3109/14992027.2014.973541

Hooghe, A., Rosenblatt, P. C., & Rober, P. (2017). "We hardly ever talk about it": Emotional responsive attunement in couples after a child's death. *Family Process, 57*, 226–240. doi:10.1111/famp.12274

Hoogman, M., Onnink, M., Cools, R., Aarts, E., Kan, C., Arias Vasquez, A., . . . Franke, B. (2013). The dopamine transporter haplotype and reward-related striatal responses in adult ADHD. *European Neuropsychopharmacology, 23*(6), 469–478.

Hoover, E. (2011). *The Chronicle of Higher Education: Surveys of the public and presidents.* In *College's value goes deeper than the degree, graduates say.* Retrieved from http://www.chronicle.com/article/Its-More-Than_the/127534

Hoppe, U., Hocke, T., Müller, A., & Hast, A. (2016). Speech perception and information-carrying capacity for hearing aid users of different ages. *Audiology & Neuro-Otology, 21,* 16–20. doi:10.1159/000448349

Horwitz, B. N., Reynolds, C. A., Walum, H., Ganiban, J., Spotts, E. L., Reiss, D., . . . Neiderhiser, J. M. (2016). Understanding the role of mate selection processes in couples' pair-bonding behavior. *Behavior Genetics, 46*(1), 143–149.

House, B. R., Silk, J. B., Henrich, J., Barrett, H. C., Scelza, B. A., Boyette, A. H., . . . Laurence, S. (2013). Ontogeny of prosocial behavior across diverse societies. *Proceedings of the National Academy of Sciences of the United States of America, 110*(36), 14586–14591.

Hrdy, S. B. (1999). *Mother nature: A history of mothers, infants, and natural selection.* New York, NY: Pantheon Books.

Hu, P., Wang, S., & Lee, J. (2017). Socioeconomic gradients of cardiovascular risk factors in China and India: Results from the China health and retirement longitudinal study and longitudinal aging study in India. *International Journal of Public Health, 62*(7), 763–773. doi:10.1007/s00038-017-0968-3

Hu, S., & Kuh, G. D. (2003). Diversity experiences and college student learning and personal development. *Journal of College Student Development, 44,* 320–334.

Huang, H., Coleman, S., Bridge, J. A., Yonkers, K., & Katon, W. (2014). A meta-analysis of the relationship between antidepressant use in pregnancy and the risk of preterm birth and low birth weight. *General Hospital Psychiatry, 36*(1), 13–18.

Huang, P., Fang, R., Li, B. Y., & Chen, S. D. (2016). Exercise-related changes of networks in aging and mild cognitive impairment brain. *Frontiers in Aging Neuroscience, 8*(47). doi.org/10.3389/fnagi.2016.00047

Huddleston, J., & Ge, X. (2003). Boys at puberty: Psychosocial implications. In C. Hayward (Ed.), *Gender differences at puberty* (pp. 113–134). New York, NY: Cambridge University Press.

Hudson, M. B., Nicolas, S. C., Howser, M. E., Lipsett, K. E., Robinson, I. W., Pope, L. J., . . . Friedman, D. R. (2015). Examining how gender and emoticons influence Facebook jealousy. *Cyberpsychology, Behavior & Social Networking, 18*(2), 87–92.

Hughes, C., & Devine, R. T. (2015). Individual differences in theory of mind from preschool to adolescence: Achievements and directions. *Child Development Perspectives, 9*(3), 149–153. doi:10.1111/cdep12124

Hughes, M. L., Geraci, L., & De Forrest, R. L. (2013). Aging 5 years in 5 minutes: The effect of taking a memory test on older adults' subjective age. *Psychological Science, 24*(12), 2481–2488.

Huizink, A. J. (2015). Prenatal maternal substance use and offspring outcomes: Overview of recent findings and possible interventions. *European Psychologist,* Special Issue: Prenatal Adversity: Impact and Potential Interventions, *20*(2), 90–101.

Hülsheger, U. R., Lang, J. B., Depenbrock, F., Fehrmann, C., Zijlstra, F. H., & Alberts, H. M. (2014). The power of presence: The role of mindfulness at work for daily levels and change trajectories of psychological detachment and sleep quality. *Journal of Applied Psychology, 99*(6), 1113–1128.

Humphrey, G. M. & Zimpfer, D. G. (2007). *Counselling for grief and bereavement* (2nd ed.) Los Angeles, CA: Sage.

Hunger and Poverty Facts and Statistics. (2016). Retrieved from http://www.feedingamerica.org/hunger-in-america/impact-of-hunger/hunger-and-poverty/hunger-and-poverty-fact-sheet.html?referrer=https://www.google.com/

Hungerford, T. L. (2003). Is there an American way of aging? Income dynamics of the elderly in the United States and Germany. *Research on Aging, 25,* 435–455.

Hunt, C. K. (2003). Concepts in caregiver research. *Journal of Nursing Scholarship, 35,* 27–32.

Hurt, T. R. (2013). Toward a deeper understanding of the meaning of marriage among Black men. *Journal of Family Issues, 34*(7), 859–884.

Hutteman, R., Hennecke, M., Orth U., Reitz, A. K., & Specht, J. (2014). Developmental tasks as a framework to study personality development in adulthood and old age. *European Journal of Personality, 28*(3), 267–278.

Huttenlocher, P. R. (2002). *Neural plasticity: The effects of environment on the development of the cerebral cortex.* Cambridge, MA: Harvard University Press.

Hvas, L. (2001). Positive aspects of menopause: A qualitative study. *Maturitas, 39,* 11–17.

Hwang, J., Castelli, D. M., & Gonzalez-Lima, F. (2017). The positive cognitive impact of aerobic fitness is associated with peripheral inflammatory and brain-derived neurotrophic biomarkers in young adults. *Physiology and Behavior, 179,* 75–89. doi.org/10.1016/j.physbeh.2017.05.011

Hyde, A., Drennan, J., Butler, M., Howlett, E., Carney, M., & Lohan, M. (2013). Parents' constructions of communication with their children about safer sex. *Journal of Clinical Nursing, 22*(23–24), 3438–3446.

Icenogle, G., Steinberg, L., Olino, T. M., Shulman, E. P., Chein, J., Alampay, L. P., . . . Uribe Tirado, L. M. (2016). Puberty predicts approach but not avoidance on the Iowa gambling task in a multinational sample. *Child Development.* doi:10.1111/cdev.12655

Ilies, R., Zheng, X., Liu, Y., & Liu, X. (2017). Why do employees have better family lives when they are highly engaged at work? *Journal of Applied Psychology, 6,* 956.

Imuta, K., Henry, J. D., Slaughter, V., Selcuk, B., & Ruffman, T. (2016). Theory of mind and prosocial behavior in childhood: A meta-analytic view. *Developmental Psychology, 54*(8), 1192–1205.

Infurna, F. J., Gerstorf, D., & Zarit, S. H. (2013). Substantial changes in mastery perceptions of dementia caregivers with the placement of a care recipient. *Journals of Gerontology Series B: Psychological Sciences and Social Sciences, 68*(2), 202–214.

Infurna, F. J., & Luthar, S. S. (2017). Parents' adjustment following the death of their child: Resilience is multidimensional and differs across outcomes examined. *Journal of Research in Personality, 68,* 38–53. doi:10.1016/j.jrp.2017.04.004

Institute for Women's Policy Research. (2017, March). Pay equity & discrimination. Retrieved from https://iwpr.org/issue/employment-education-economic-change/pay-equity-discrimination/

Ishitani, T. T. (2016). Time-varying effects of academic and social integration on student persistence for first and second year of college. National data approach. *Journal of College Student Retention, 18*(3), 263–286.

Israel, S., Moffitt, T. E., Belsky, D. W., Hancox, R. J., Poulton, R., Roberts, B. W., . . .Caspi, A. (2014). Translating personality psychology to help personalize preventive medicine for young-adult patients. *Journal of Personality and Social Psychology, 106*(3), 484–498.

Issacs, J. B. (2012). Starting school at a disadvantage: The school readiness of poor children. *Center on Children and Families at Brookings (Social Genome Project).* Retrieved from https://www.brookings.edu/wp-content/uploads/2016/06/0319_school_disadvantage_isaacs.pdf

Ito, M., & Sharts-Hopko, N. C. (2002). Japanese women's experience of childbirth in the United States. *Health Care for Women International, 23,* 666–677.

Ito, Y., & Izumi-Taylor, S. (2013). A comparative study of fathers' thoughts about fatherhood in the USA and Japan. *Early Child Development and Care, 183*(11), 1689–1704.

Jach, H. K., Sun, J., Loton, D., Chin, T., & Waters, L. E. (2017). Strengths and subjective well-being in adolescence: Strength-based parenting and the moderating effect of mindset. *Journal of Happiness Studies.*

Jack, C. (2018). Overview of the NIA-AA research framework. Paper delivered at the Alzheimer's Association International Conference. Chicago, Illinois, July 25, 2018.

Jackson, D. B. (2016). Breastfeeding duration and offspring conduct problems: The moderating role of genetic risk. *Social Science & Medicine, 166,* 128–136. doi:10.1016/j.socscimed.2016.08.014

Jackson, T., & Chen, H. (2008). Predicting changes in eating disorder symptoms among Chinese adolescents: A 9-month prospective study. *Journal of Psychosomatic Research, 64,* 87–95.

Jaffe, J., & Diamond, M. O. (2011). *Reproductive trauma: Psychotherapy with infertility and pregnancy loss clients.* Washington, DC: American Psychological Association.

Jaffee, S. R., Bowes, L., Ouellet-Morin, I., Fisher, H. L., Moffitt, T. E., Merrick, M. T., & Arseneault, L. (2013). Safe, stable, nurturing relationships break the intergenerational cycle of abuse: A prospective nationally representative

cohort of children in the United Kingdom. *Journal of Adolescent Health, 53*(4, Suppl.), S4–S10.

Jang, H., Reeve, J., & Deci, E. L. (2010). Engaging students in learning activities: It is not autonomy support or structure but autonomy support and structure. *Journal of Educational Psychology, 102*(3), 588–600.

Jang, H., & Tang, F. (2016). Effects of social support and volunteering on depression among grandparents raising grandchildren. *International Journal of Aging and Human Development, 83*(4), 491–507. doi.org/10.1177/0091415016657561

Jang, Y., Park, N. S., Chiriboga, D. A., Radhakrishnan, K., & Kim, M. T. (2017). The knowing–doing gap in advance directives in Asian Americans: The role of education and acculturation. *American Journal of Hospice & Palliative Medicine, 34*(9), 874–879. doi:10.1177/1049909116668518

Janssen, I. (2015). Hyper-parenting is negatively associated with physical activity among 7- to 12-year-olds. *Preventative Medicine, 73,* 55–59.

Janssen, T. W., Bink, M., Gelade, K., Mourik, R. V., Maras, A., & Oosterlaan, J. (2016). A randomized controlled trial into the effects of neurofeedback, methylphenidate, and physical activity on EEG power spectra in children with ADHD. *Journal of Child Psychology and Psychiatry, 57*(5), 633–644. doi:10.1111/jcpp.12517

Jemaa, B. A., Irato, G., Zanela, A., Brescia, A., Turki, M., & Jaïdane, M. (2017). Congruent auditory display and confusion in sound localization: Case of elderly drivers. Transportation Research Part F: *Psychology and Behaviour.* doi:10.1016/j.trf.2017.06.020.

Jenkins, S., Bhanugopan, R., & Lockhart, P. (2016). A framework for optimizing work–life balance practices in Australia: Perceived options for employee support. *Journal of Employment Counseling, 3,* 112. doi:10.1002/joec.12033

Jennings, W. G., Gonzalez, J. R., Piquero, A. R., Bird, H., Canino, G., & Maldonado-Molina, M. (2016). The nature and relevance of risk and protective factors for violence among Hispanic children and adolescents: Results from the Boricua Youth Study. *Journal of Criminal Justice, 45,* 41–47.

Jensen, C., Steinhausen, H., & Lauritson, M. B. (2014). Time trends over 16 years in incidence rates of autism spectrum disorders across the lifespan based on nationwide Danish register data. In *Journal of Autism Development Disorders, 44*(8), 1808–1818.

Jensen, H., Gron, R., Lidegaard, O., Pedersen, L., Andersen, P., & Kessing, L. (2013). The effects of maternal depression and use of antidepressants during pregnancy on risk of a child small for gestational age. *Psychopharmacology, 228*(2), 199–205.

Jensen, T. M., Shafer, K., & Larson, J. H. (2014). (Step)parenting attitudes and expectations: Implications for stepfamily functioning and clinical intervention. *Families in Society, 95*(3), 213–220.

Jenson, W. R., Olympia, D., Farley, M., & Clark, E. (2004). Positive psychology and externalizing students in a sea of negativity. *Psychology in the Schools, 41,* 67–79.

Jette, A. M., Assmann, S. F., Rooks, D., Harris, B. A., & Crawford, S. (1998). Interrelationships among disablement concepts. *Journals of Gerontology Series A: Biological Sciences and Medical Sciences, 53A,* M395–M404.

Jiang, H., & Men, R. L. (2017). Creating an engaged workforce. *Communication Research, 44*(2), 225. doi:10.1177/0093650215613137

Jiang, Y., Ekono, M., & Skinner, C. (2016). Basic facts about low-income children: Children under 18 years, 2014. National Center for Children in Poverty, 1–8.

John, D., & Lang, F. R. (2015). Subjective acceleration of time experience in everyday life across adulthood. *Developmental Psychology, 51*(12), 1824–1839.

Johns, M. M., Zimmerman, M., & Bauermeister, J. A. (2013). Sexual attraction, sexual identity, and psychosocial well-being in a national sample of young women during emerging adulthood. *Journal of Youth and Adolescence, 42*(1), 82–95.

Johnson, K. M. (2013). Making families: Organizational boundary work in U.S. egg and sperm donation. *Social Science & Medicine, 99,* 64–71.

Johnson, R. A., & Bibbo, J. (2014). Relocation decisions and constructing the meaning of home: A phenomenological study of the transition into a nursing home. *Journal of Aging Studies, 30,* 56–63.

Johnson, R. W. (2009). Employment opportunities at older ages: Introduction to the special issue. *Research on Aging, 31,* 3–16.

Johnston, L. D., Miech, R. A., O'Malley, P. M., Bachman, J. G., & Schulenberg, J. E. (2016). Monitoring the Future, 2016 overview: Key findings on adolescent drug use, p. 10.

Johnston, L. D., O'Malley, P. M., Bachman, J. G., & Schulenberg, J. E. (2011). *Marijuana use continues to rise among U.S. teens, while alcohol use hits historic lows.* In *University of Michigan New Service: Ann Arbor, MI.* Retrieved from http://www.monitoringthefuture.org

Johri, M., Beland, F., & Bergman, H. (2003). International experiments in integrated care for the elderly: A synthesis of the evidence. *International Journal of Geriatric Psychiatry, 18,* 222–235.

Jokhi, R. P., & Whitby, E. H. (2011). Magnetic resonance imaging of the fetus. *Developmental Medicine & Child Neurology, 53,* 18–28.

Jonasson, L. S., Nyberg, L., Kramer, A. F., Lundquist, A., Riklund, K., & Boraxbekk, C. J. (2017). Aerobic exercise intervention, cognitive performance, and brain structure: Results from the Physical Influences on Brain in Aging (PHIBRA) Study. *Frontiers in Aging Neuroscience, 8*(336). doi.org/10.3389/fnagi.2016.00336

Jones, B. K., & McAdams, D. P. (2013). Becoming generative: Socializing influences recalled in life stories in late midlife. *Journal of Adult Development, 20*(3), 158–172.

Jonkmann, K., Thoemmes, F., Lüdtke, O., & Trautwein, U. (2014). Personality traits and living arrangements in young adulthood: Selection and socialization. *Developmental Psychology, 50*(3), 683–698.

Jordan, A. H., & Litz, B. T. (2014). Prolonged grief disorder: Diagnostic, assessment, and treatment considerations. *Professional Psychology: Research and Practice, 45*(3), 180–187.

Jorgensen, B. S., Jamieson, R. D., & Martin, J. F. (2010). Income, sense of community and subjective well-being: Combining economic and psychological variables. *Journal of Economic Psychology, 31*(4), 612–623.

Joyce, B. T., & Lau, D. T. (2013). Hospice experiences and approaches to support and assess family caregivers in managing medications for home hospice patients: A providers survey. *Palliative Medicine, 27*(4), 329–338.

Juarascio, A. S., Shoaib, A., & Timko, C. A. (2010). Pro-eating disorder communities on social networking sites: A content analysis. *Eating Disorders, 18,* 393–407.

Judge, T. A., & Hurst, C. (2007). Capitalizing on one's advantages: Role of core self-evaluations. *Journal of Applied Psychology, 92*(5), 1212–1227.

Julian, M. M. (2013). Age at adoption from institutional care as a window into the lasting effects of early experiences. *Clinical Child and Family Psychology Review, 16*(2), 101–145.

Kagan, J. (1984). *The nature of the child.* New York, NY: Basic Books.

Kagan, J. (1998). *Galen's prophecy: Temperament in human nature.* Boulder, CO: Westview Press.

Källstrand-Eriksson, J., Baigi, A., Buer, N., & Hildingh, C. (2013). Perceived vision-related quality of life and risk of falling among community living elderly people. *Scandinavian Journal of Caring Sciences, 27*(2), 433–439.

Kalmijn, M. (2013). Adult children's relationships with married parents, divorced parents, and stepparents: Biology, marriage, or residence? *Journal of Marriage and Family, 75*(5), 1181–1193.

Kane, R. A., & Cutler, L. J. (2015). Re-imagining long-term services and supports: Towards livable environments, service capacity, and enhanced community integration, choice, and quality of life for seniors. *Gerontologist, 55*(2), 286–295.

Karantzas, G. C., & Gillath, O. (2017). Stress and wellbeing during chronic illness and partner death in later-life: The role of social support. *Current Opinion in Psychology, 75.* doi:10.1016/j.copsyc.2016.05.009

Karen, M., Sachdev, P., Trollor, J., Sachdev, P. S., Lipnicki, D. M., Crawford, J., . . . Brodaty, H. (2013). Factors predicting reversion from mild cognitive impairment to normal cognitive functioning: A population-based study. *Plos One, 8*(3).

Karen, R. (1998). *Becoming attached: First relationships and how they shape our capacity to love.* London, England: Oxford University Press.

Karlamangla, A. S., Miller-Martinez, D., Lachman, M. E., Tun, P. A., Koretz, B. K., & Seeman, T. E. (2014). Biological correlates of adult cognition: Midlife in the United States (MIDUS). *Neurobiology of Aging, 35*(2), 387–394.

Karlsson, C., & Berggren, I. (2011). Dignified end-of-life care in the patients' own homes. *Nursing Ethics, 18*(3), 374–385.

Karni, E., Leshno, M., & Rapaport, S. (2014). Helping patients and physicians reach individualized medical decisions: Theory and application to prenatal diagnostic testing. *Theory and Decision, 76*(4), 451–467.

Karns, J. T. (2001). Health, nutrition, and safety. In G. Bremner & A. Fogel (Eds.), *Blackwell handbook of infant development* (pp. 693–725). Malden, MA: Blackwell.

Kasper, J. D., Pezzin, L. E., & Rice, J. B. (2010). Stability and changes in living arrangements: Relationship to nursing home admission and timing of placement. *Journals of Gerontology: Social Sciences, 65B*(6), 783–791.

Kastenbaum, R. (2004). *On our way: The final passage through life and death.* Berkeley, CA: University of California Press.

Kataoka-Yahiro, M. R., McFarlane, S., Koijane, J., & Li, D. (2017). Culturally competent palliative and hospice care training for ethnically diverse staff in long-term care facilities. *American Journal of Hospice & Palliative Medicine, 34*(4), 335–346.

Kato, K., & Pedersen, N. L. (2005). Personality and coping: A study of twins reared apart and twins reared together. *Behavior Genetics, 35,* 147–158.

Katz, I., Kaplan, A., & Gueta, G. (2010). Students' needs, teachers' support, and motivation for doing homework: A cross-sectional study. *Journal of Experimental Education, 78*(2), 246–267.

Keefe, M. R., Karlsen, K. A., Lobo, M. L., Kotzer, A. M., & Dudley, W. N. (2006). Reducing parenting stress in families with irritable infants. *Nursing Research, 55*(3), 198–205.

Keel, P. K., Baxter, M. G., Heatherton, T. F., & Joiner, T. E. (2007). A 20-year longitudinal study of body weight, dieting, and eating disorder symptoms. *Journal of Abnormal Psychology, 116*(2), 422–432.

Keen, C., Murray, C., & Payne, S. (2013). Sensing the presence of the deceased: A narrative review. *Mental Health, Religion & Culture, 16*(4), 384–402.

Keijsers, L., & Poulin, F. (2013). Developmental changes in parent–child communication throughout adolescence. *Developmental Psychology, 49*(12), 2301–2308.

Kelley, M., Demiris, G., Nguyen, H., Oliver, D. P., & Wittenberg-Lyles, E. (2013). Informal hospice caregiver pain management concerns: A qualitative study. *Palliative Medicine, 27*(7), 673–682.

Kellman, P. J., & Banks, M. S. (1998). Infant visual perception. In W. Damon (Series Ed.) & D. Kuhn & R. S. Siegler (Vol. Eds.), *Handbook of child psychology: Vol. 2, Cognition, perception, and language* (pp. 103–146). Hoboken, NJ: Wiley.

Kelly, T. B., Tolson, D., Day, T., McColgan, G., Thilo, K., & Maclaren, W. (2013). Older people's views on what they need to successfully adjust to life with a hearing aid. *Health and Social Care in the Community, 21*(3), 293–302.

Kemper, S., & Mitzner, T. L. (2001). Language production and comprehension. In J. E. Birren & K. W. Schaie (Eds.), *Handbook of the psychology of aging* (5th ed. pp. 378–398). San Diego, CA: Academic Press.

Kermel-Schiffman, I., & Werner, P. (2017). Review: Knowledge regarding advance care planning: A systematic review. *Archives of Gerontology and Geriatrics, 73*,133–142. doi:10.1016/j.archger.2017.07.012

Keys, C. L. (2007). Promoting and protecting mental health as flourishing: A complementary strategy for improving national mental health. *American Psychologist, 61*, 95–108.

Kiang, L., & Fuligni, A. J. (2009). Ethnic identity and family processes among adolescents from Latin American, Asian, and European backgrounds. *Journal of Youth and Adolescence, 38*, 228–241.

Kids Count Data Center. (n.d.). Retrieved from http://datacenter.kidscount.org/data/tables

Kiefer, S. M., & Wang, J. H. (2016). Associations of coolness and social goals with aggression and engagement during adolescence. *Journal of Applied Developmental Psychology, 44*, 52–62.

Killewald, A. (2013). A reconsideration of the fatherhood premium: Marriage, coresidence, biology, and fathers' wages. *American Sociological Review, 78*(1), 96–116.

Kim, B. K. E., Oesterle, S., Catalano, R. F., & Hawkins, J. D. (2015). Change in protective factors across adolescent development. *Journal of Applied Developmental Psychology, 40*, 31.

Kim, M., & Park, I. J. K. (2011). Testing the moderating effect of parent–adolescent communication on the acculturation gap–distress relation in Korean American families. *Journal of Youth and Adolescence, 40*, 1661–1673.

Kim, S., Yun, I., & Kim, J. (2016). Associations between body weight and bullying among South Korean adolescents. *The Journal of Early Adolescence, 36*(4), 551–574. doi:10.1177/0272431615577204

Kim, S. U., Lee, H. J., & Kim, Y. B. (2013). Neural stem cell-based treatment for neurodegenerative diseases. *Neuropathology, 33*(5), 491–504.

Kim, S. Y., Chen, Q., Wang, Y., Shen, Y., & Orozco-Lapray, D. (2013). Longitudinal linkages among parent–child acculturation discrepancy, parenting, parent–child sense of alienation, and adolescent adjustment in Chinese immigrant families. *Developmental Psychology, 49*(5), 900–912.

Kim, S. Y., Wang, Y., Orozco-Lapray, D., Shen, Y., & Murtuza, M. (2013). Does "tiger parenting" exist? Parenting profiles of Chinese Americans and adolescent developmental outcomes. *Asian American Journal of Psychology, 4*(1), 7–18.

Kimiko, T., Nozomi, O., Masayuki, M., & Norio, K. (2015). Self-reported hearing loss predicts 5-year decline in higher-level functional capacity in high-functioning elderly adults: The Fujiwara–Kyo study. *Journal of the American Geriatrics Society, 63*(11), 2260–2268. doi:10.1111/jgs.13780

King, E. K., Pierro, R. C., Li, J., Porterfield, M. L., & Rucker, L. (2016). Classroom quality in infant and toddler classrooms: Impact of age and programme type. *Early Child Development & Care, 186*(11), 1821–1835. doi:10.1080/03004430.2015.1134521

Kinniburgh-White, R., Cartwright, C., & Seymour, F. (2010). Young adults' narratives of relational development with stepfathers. *Journal of Social and Personal Relationships, 27*(7), 890–907.

Kins, E., & Beyers, W. (2010). Failure to launch, failure to achieve criteria for adulthood. *Journal of Adolescence Research, 25*(5), 743–777.

Kins, E., de Mol, J., & Beyers, W. (2014). "Why should I leave?" Belgian emerging adults' departure from home. *Journal of Adolescent Research, 29*(1), 89–119.

Kinsella, K., & Velkoff, V. A. (2001). *An aging world: 2001* (Series P95/01-1). Washington, DC: U.S. Census Bureau.

Kitahara, M. (1989). Childhood in Japanese culture. *Journal of Psychohistory, 17*, 43–72.

Kitzinger, S. (2000). *Rediscovering birth.* New York, NY: Pocket Books.

Klencklen, G., Banta Lavenex, P., Brandner, C., & Lavenex, P. (2017). Working memory decline in normal aging: Memory load and representational demands affect performance. *Learning and Motivation, 60*, 10–22. doi:10.1016/j.lmot.2017.09.002

Klobucar, N. R. (2016). Transition to parenthood and susceptibility to divorce: Qualitative research of divorced young parents in Slovenia. The person and the challenges. *The Journal of Theology, Education, Canon Law and Social Studies Inspired By Pope John Paul II, 6*(1), 157–177. doi:10.15633/pch.1663

Kloep, M., & Hendry, L. B. (2010). Letting go or holding on? Parents' perceptions of their relationships with their children during emerging adulthood. *British Journal of Developmental Psychology, 28*(4), 817–834.

Klusmann, D. (2002). Sexual motivation and the duration of partnership. *Archives of Sexual Behavior, 31*, 275–287.

Knopik, V. S., Marceau, K., Palmer, R. H., Smith, T. F., & Heath, A. C. (2016). Maternal smoking during pregnancy and offspring birth weight: A genetically informed approach comparing multiple raters. *Behavior Genetics, 46*(3), 353–364.

Knox, M. (2010). On hitting children: A review of corporal punishment in the United States. *Journal of Pediatric Health Care, 24*(2), 103–107.

Kobayashi, M., Cassia, V. M., Kanazawa, S., Yamaguchi, M. K., & Kakigi, R. (2016). Perceptual narrowing towards adult faces is a cross-cultural phenomenon in infancy: A behavioral and near-infrared spectroscopy study with Japanese infants. *Developmental Science.* doi:10.1111/desc.12498

Kobel, S., Kettner, D. K., Erkelenz, N., Drenowatz, C., & Steinacker, J. M. (2015). Correlates of habitual physical activity and organized sports in German primary school children. *Public Health, 129*, 237–243.

Koch, P. B., Mansfield, P. K., Thurau, D., & Carey, M. (2005). "Feeling frumpy": The relationships between body image and sexual response changes in midlife women. *Journal of Sex Research, 42*(3), 215–223. doi.org/10.1080/00224490509552276

Kochanska, G., Aksan, N., Penney, S. J., & Boldt, L. J. (2007). Parental personality as an inner resource that moderates the impact of ecological adversity on parenting. *Journal of Personality and Social Psychology, 92*(1), 136–150.

Kochanska, G., Coy, K. C., & Murray, K. T. (2001). The development of self-regulation in the first four years of life. *Child Development, 72*, 1091–1111.

Kochanska, G., & Kim, S. (2013). Early attachment organization with both parents and future behavior problems: From infancy to middle childhood. *Child Development, 84*(1), 283–296.

Kochanska, G., & Knaack, A. (2003). Effortful control as a personality characteristic of young children: Antecedents, correlates, and consequences. *Journal of Personality, 71,* 1087–1112.

Kochanska, G., Woodard, J., Kim, S., Koenig, J. L., Yoon, J. E., & Barry, R. A. (2010). Positive socialization mechanisms in secure and insecure parent–child dyads: Two longitudinal studies. *Journal of Child Psychology and Psychiatry, 51*(9), 998–1009.

Kocsor, F., Saxton, T. K., Lang, A., & Bereczkei, T. (2016). Preference for faces resembling opposite-sex parents is moderated by emotional closeness in childhood. *Personality and Individual Differences, 93,* 23–29.

Koehn, S., Mahmood, A., & Stott-Eveneshen, S. (2016). Quality of life for diverse older adults in assisted living: The centrality of control. *Journal of Gerontological Social Work, 59*(7–8), 512–536. doi:10.1080/01634372.2016.1254699

Koenig, T. L., Lee, J. H., Macmillan, K. R., Fields, N. L., & Spano, R. (2014). Older adult and family member perspectives of the decision-making process involved in moving to assisted living. *Qualitative Social Work, 13*(3), 335–350.

Kogan, A., Impett, E. A., Oveis, C., Hui, B., Gordon, A. M., & Keltner, D. (2010). When giving feels good: The intrinsic benefits of sacrifice in romantic relationships for the communally motivated. *Psychological Science, 21*(12), 1918–1924.

Kohlberg, L. (1966). Moral education in the schools: A developmental view. *School Review, 74,* 1–30.

Kohlberg, L. (1981). *The meaning and measurement of moral development.* Worcester, MA: Clark University Press.

Kohlberg, L. (1984). *The psychology of moral development: The nature and validity of moral stages.* San Francisco: Harper & Row.

Komarraju, M., Musulkin, S., & Bhattacharya, G. (2010). Role of student–faculty interactions in developing college students' academic self-concept, motivation, and achievement. *Journal of College Student Development, 51*(1), 332–342.

Konner, M. (2010). *The evolution of childhood.* Cambridge, MA: Harvard University Press.

Kooij, D. M., Bal, P. M., & Kanfer, R. (2014). Future time perspective and promotion focus as determinants of intra-individual change in work motivation. *Psychology and Aging, 29*(2), 319–328.

Koolschijn, P. C., & Crone, E. A. (2013). Sex differences and structural brain maturation from childhood to early adulthood. *Developmental Cognitive Neuroscience, 5,* 106–118.

Kopala-Sibley, D. C., Mongrain, M., & Zuroff, D. C. (2013). A lifespan perspective on dependency and self-criticism: Age-related differences from 18 to 59. *Journal of Adult Development, 20*(3), 126–141.

Korunka, C., & Kubicek, B. (2017). Job demands in a changing world of work: Impact on workers' health and performance and implications for research and practice. Cham, Switzerland: Springer International Publishing. doi:10.1007/978-3-319-54678-0

Kover, S. T., Edmunds, S. R., & Weismer, S. E. (2016). Brief report: Ages of language milestones as predictors of developmental trajectories in young children with autism spectrum disorder. *Journal of Autism and Developmental Disorders, 46*(7), 2501–2507. doi:10.1007/s10803-016-2756-y

Kraft, I., Schreiber, J., Cafiero, R., Metere, R., Schaadt, G., Brauer, J., . . . Skeide, M. A. (2016). Predicting early signs of dyslexia at a preliterate age by combining behavioral assessment with structural MRI. *Neuroimage, 143,* 378–386.

Kramer, B. J., & Thompson, E. H. (2002). *Men as caregivers: Theory, research, and service implications.* New York, NY: Springer.

Krampe, R. T., & Baltes, P. B. (2003). Intelligence as adaptive resource development and resource allocation: A new look through the lenses of SOC and expertise. In R. J. Sternberg & E. L. Grigorenko (Eds.), *The psychology of abilities, competencies, and expertise* (pp. 31–68). New York, NY: Cambridge University Press.

Krause, N. (2016). Assessing the relationships among wisdom, humility, and life satisfaction. *Journal of Adult Development, 23*(3), 140–149. doi.org/10.1007/s10804-016-9230-0

Kreicbergs, U., Valdimarsdóttir, U., Onelöv, E., Henter, J.-I., & Steineck, G. (2004). Talking about death with children who have severe malignant disease. *New England Journal of Medicine, 351,* 1175–1186.

Kreppner, J., Rutter, M., Marvin, R., O'Conner, T., & Sonuga-Barke, E. (2011). Assessing the concept of the "insecure-other" category in the Cassidy-Marvin scheme: Changes between 4 and 6 years in the English and Romanian adoptee study. *Social Development, 20*(1), 1–16.

Kretsch, N., & Harden, K. P. (2014). Pubertal development and peer influence on risky decision making. *The Journal of Early Adolescence, 34*(3), 339–359.

Kroger, J. (2000). *Identity development: Adolescence through adulthood.* Thousand Oaks, CA: Sage.

Kronenberg, M. E., Hansel, T. C., Brennan, A. M., Osofsky, H. J., Osofsky, J. D., & Lawrason, B. (2010). Children of Katrina: Lessons learned about post disaster symptoms and recovery patterns. *Child Development, 81*(4), 1241–1259.

Krstev, S., Marinković, J., Simić, S., Kocev, N., & Bondy, S. J. (2013). The influence of maternal smoking and exposure to residential ETS on pregnancy outcomes: A retrospective national study. *Maternal and Child Health Journal, 17*(9), 1591–1598.

Kübler-Ross, E. (1969). *On death and dying.* New York, NY: Macmillan.

Kuhn, D. (1989). Children and adults as intuitive scientists. *Psychological Review, 96,* 674–689.

Kuhnert, R., Begeer, S., Fink, E., & Rosnay, M. D. (2017). Gender-differentiated effects of theory of mind, emotion understanding, and social preference on prosocial behavior development: A longitudinal study. *Journal of Experimental Child Psychology, 154,* 13–27. doi:10.1016/j.jecp.2016.10.001

Kulik, L. (2007). Contemporary midlife grandparenthood. In V. Muhlbauer & J. C. Chrisler (Eds.), *Women over 50: Psychological perspectives* (pp. 131–146). New York, NY: Springer Science + Business Media.

Kunze, F., Boehm, S., & Bruch, H. (2013). Age, resistance to change, and job performance. *Journal of Managerial Psychology, 28*(7-8), 741–760.

Kwon, M., Setoodehnia, M., Baek, J., Luck, S. J., & Oakes, L. M. (2016). The development of visual search in infancy: Attention to faces versus salience. *Developmental Psychology, 52*(4), 537–555.

La Paro, K. M., & Gloeckler, L. (2016). The context of child care for toddlers: The "experience expectable environment." *Early Childhood Education Journal, 44*(2), 147–153. doi:10.1007/s10643-015-0699-0

Labouvie-Vief, G. (1992). A neo-Piagetian perspective on adult cognitive development. In R. J. Sternberg & C. A. Berg (Eds.), *Intellectual development* (pp. 197–228). New York, NY: Cambridge University Press.

Labouvie-Vief, G. (2006). Emerging structures of adult thought. In J. J. Arnett & J. L. Tanner (Eds.), *Emerging adults in America: Coming of age in the 21st century* (pp. 59–84). Washington, DC: American Psychological Association.

Lachman, M. E. (2004). Development in midlife. *Annual Review of Psychology*, 55, 305–331.

Ladis, K., Daniels, N., & Kawachi, I. (2009). Exploring the relationship between absolute and relative position and late-life depression: Evidence from 10 European countries. *The Gerontologist*, 50(1), 48–59.

Laditka, J. N., & Laditka, S. B. (2016). Unemployment, disability and life expectancy in the United States: A life course study. *Disability and Health Journal*, 9(1), 46–54. doi:10.1016/j.dhjo.2015.08.003

Laditka, S. B., & Laditka, J. N. (2017). Moxie matters: Associations of future orientation with active life expectancy. *Aging & Mental Health*, 21(10), 1040–1046. doi:10.1080/13607863.2016.1199011

LaFontana, K. M., & Cillessen, A. H. N. (2010). Developmental changes in the priority of perceived status in childhood and adolescence. *Social Development*, 19(1), 130–147.

Laible, D. J. (2004). Mother–child discourse surrounding a child's past behavior at 30 months: Links to emotional understanding and early conscience development at 36 months. *Merrill-Palmer Quarterly*, 50, 159–180.

Lam, B. P., Cross, S. E., Wu, T., Yeh, K., Wang, Y., & Su, J. C. (2016). What do you want in a marriage? Examining marriage ideals in Taiwan and the United States. *Personality & Social Psychology Bulletin*, 42(6), 703–722. doi:10.1177/0146167216637842

Lamb, M. E. (1997). *The role of the father in child development* (3rd ed.). Hoboken, NJ: Wiley.

Lamela, D., Figueiredo, B., Bastos, A., & Feinberg, M. (2016). Typologies of post-divorce coparenting and parental well-being, parenting quality and children's psychological adjustment. *Child Psychiatry & Human Development*, 47(5), 716–728. doi:10.1007/s10578-015-0604-5

Landerl, K., & Moll, K. (2010). Comorbidity of learning disorders: Prevalence and familial transmission. *Journal of Child Psychology and Psychiatry*, 51(3), 287–294.

Landor, A., Simons, L. G., Simons, R. L., Brody, G. H., & Gibbons, F. X. (2011). The role of religiosity in the relationship between parents, peers, and adolescents in risky sexual behavior. *Journal of Youth and Adolescence*, 40, 296–309.

Lane, B. L., Piercy, C. W., & Carr, C. T. (2016). Making it Facebook official: The warranting value of online relationship status disclosures on relational characteristics. *Computers in Human Behavior*, 56, 561–568.

Lang, F. R., Weiss, D., Gerstorf, D., & Wagner, G. G. (2013). Forecasting life satisfaction across adulthood: Benefits of seeing a dark future? *Psychology and Aging*, 28(1), 249–261.

Lapsley, D., & Woodbury, R. D. (2016). Social cognitive development in emerging adulthood. In J. J. Arnett (Ed.), *The Oxford handbook of emerging adulthood* (pp. 142–159). New York, NY: Oxford University Press.

Larsen, L., Hartmann, P., & Nyborg, H. (2007). The stability of general intelligence from early adulthood to middle age. *Intelligence*, 36(1), 29–34.

Larson, K., & Grisso, T. (2016). Transfer and commitment of youth in the United States: Law, policy, and forensic practice. In K. Heilbrun, D. DeMatteo, & N. S. Goldstein (Eds.), *APA handbook of psychology and juvenile justice* (pp. 445–466). Washington, DC: American Psychological Association.

Larsson, H., Andkarsater, H., Rastam, M., Chang, Z., & Lichtenstein, O. (2012). Childhood attention-deficit hyperactivity disorder as an extreme of a continuous trait: A quantitative genetic study of 8,500 twin pairs. *Journal of Child Psychology and Psychiatry*, 53(1), 73–80.

LaRusso, M. D., Romer, D., & Selman, R. L. (2008). Teachers as builders of respectful school climates: Implications for adolescent drug use norms and depressive symptoms in high school. *Journal of Youth and Adolescence*, 37, 386–398.

Larzelere, R. E., & Knowles, S. J. (2015, August). Toddlers need both positive parenting and consistent consequences from mothers. Paper presented at the American Psychological Association, Toronto, ON.

Larzelere, R. E., & Kuhn, B. R. (2005). Comparing child outcomes of physical punishment and alternative disciplinary tactics: A meta-analysis. *Clinical Child and Family Psychology Review*, 8, 1–37.

Latz, S., Wolf, A. W., & Lozoff, B. (1999). Cosleeping in context: Sleep practices and problems in young children in Japan and the United States. *Archives of Pediatrics & Adolescent Medicine*, 153, 339–346.

Lavadera, A. L., Caravelli, L., & Togliatti, M. M. (2013). Child custody in Italian management of divorce. *Journal of Family Issues*, 34(11), 1536–1562.

Lavender, J. M., Utzinger, L. M., Li, C., Wonderlich, S. A., Engel, S. G., Mitchell, J. E., & Cao, L. (2016). Reciprocal associations between negative affect, binge eating, and purging in the natural environment in women with bulimia nervosa. *Journal of Abnormal Psychology*, 125(3), 381–386. doi:10.1037/abn0000135

Lavezzi, A. M., Corna, M., Mingrone, R., & Matturri, L. (2010). Study of the human hypoglossal nucleus: Normal development and morpho-functional alterations in sudden unexplained late fetal and infant death. *Brain & Development*, 32, 275–284.

Lavezzi, A. M., Matturri, L., Del Corno, G., & Johanson, C. E. (2013). Vulnerability of fourth ventricle choroid plexus in sudden unexplained fetal and infant death syndromes related to smoking mothers. *International Journal of Developmental Neuroscience*, 31(5), 319–327.

Lavner, J. A., & Bradbury, T. N. (2010). Patterns of change in marital satisfaction over the newlywed years. *Journal of Marriage and Family*, 72, 1171–1187.

Lavner, J. A., Karney, B. R., & Bradbury, T. N. (2013). Newlyweds' optimistic forecasts of their marriage: For better or for worse? *Journal of Family Psychology*, 27(4), 531–540.

Lawler, M., & Nixon, E. (2011). Body dissatisfaction among adolescent boys and girls: The effects of body mass, peer appearance culture and internalization of appearance ideals. *Journal of Youth and Adolescence*, 40, 59–71.

Lawn, J. E., Blencowe, H., Pattinson, R., Cousens, S., Kumar, R., Ibiebele, I., . . . Stanton, C. (2011). Stillbirths: Where? When? Why? How to make the data count? *The Lancet*, 377(9775), 1448–1463.

Le Vigouroux, S., Scola, C., Raes, M. E., Mikolajczak, M., & Roskam, I. (2017). The big five personality traits and parental burnout: Protective and risk factors. *Personality and Individual Differences*, 119, 216–219. doi.org/10.1016/j.paid.2017.07.023

Leavitt, J. W. (1986). *Brought to bed: Childbearing in America, 1750 to 1950.* New York, NY: Oxford University Press.

Lecanuet, J. P., Graniere-Deferre, C., Jacquet, A. Y., & DeCasper, A. J. (2000). Fetal discrimination of low-pitched musical notes. *Developmental Psychobiology, 36,* 29–39.

Lee, A. (2016). Implementing character education program through music and integrated activities in early childhood settings in Taiwan. *International Journal of Music Education, 34*(3), 340–351.

Lee, D. M., Nazroo, J., O'Connor, D. B., Blake, M., & Pendleton, N. (2016). Sexual health and well-being among older men and women in England: Findings from the English Longitudinal Study of Ageing. *Archives of Sexual Behavior, 45*(1), 133–144. doi.org/10.1007/s10508-014-0465-1

Lee, E. A. E., & Troop-Gordon, W. (2011). Peer processes and gender role development: Changes in gender atypicality related to negative peer treatment and children's friendships. *Sex Roles, 64,* 90–102.

Lee, J. (2008). "A Kotex and a smile": Mothers and daughters at menarche. *Journal of Family Issues, 29,* 1325–1347.

Lee, S. J., & Altschul, I. (2015). Children: Do immigrant and U.S.-born Hispanic parents differ? *Journal of Interpersonal Violence, 30*(3), 475–498. doi: 10.1177/0886260514535098

Lee, Y., & Blitz, L. V. (2016). We're GRAND: A qualitative design and development pilot project addressing the needs and strengths of grandparents raising grandchildren. *Child and Family Social Work, 21*(4), 381–390. doi.org/10.1111/cfs.12153

Lee, Y., & Styne, D. (2013). Influences on the onset and tempo of puberty in human beings and implications for adolescent psychological development. *Hormones and Behavior, 64*(2), 250–261.

LeFebvre, L., Blackburn, K., & Brody, N. (2015). Navigating romantic relationships on Facebook: Extending the relationship dissolution model to social networking environments. *Journal of Social and Personal Relationships, 32*(1), 78–98.

Leicht, K. T., & Fitzgerald, S. T. (2014). The real reason 60 is the new 30: Consumer debt and income insecurity in late middle age. *The Sociological Quarterly, 55*(2), 236–260.

Lenroot, R. K., & Giedd, J. N. (2010). Sex differences in the adolescent brain. *Brain and Cognition, 72,* 46–55.

Lepp, A., Li, J., & Barkley, J. E. (2016). College students' cell phone use and attachment to parents and peers. *Computers in Human Behavior, 64,* 401–408.

Leppänen, P. H. T., Hämäläinen, J. A., Salminen, H. K., Eklund, K. M., Guttorm, T. K., Lohvansuu, K., . . . Lyytinen, H. (2010). Newborn brain event-related potentials revealing atypical processing of sound frequency and the subsequent association with later literacy skills in children with familial dyslexia. *Cortex, 46,* 1362–1376.

Lepper, M. R., Greene, D., & Nisbett, R. E. (1973). Undermining children's intrinsic interest with extrinsic reward: A test of the "overjustification" hypothesis. *Journal of Personality and Social Psychology, 28,* 129–137.

Lerner, R. M. (1998). Theories of human development: Contemporary perspectives. In W. Damon (Series Ed.) & R. M. Lerner (Vol. Ed.). *Handbook of child psychology: Vol. 1. Theoretical models of human development* (5th ed., pp. 1–24). Hoboken, NJ: Wiley.

Lerner, R. M., Dowling, E. M., & Anderson, P. M. (2003). Positive youth development: Thriving as the basis of personhood and civil society. *Applied Developmental Science, 7,* 172–180.

Lerner, R. M., Dowling, E., & Roth, S. L. (2003). Contributions of life span psychology to the future elaboration of developmental systems theory. In U. M. Staudinger & U. Lindenberger (Eds.), *Understanding human development: Dialogues with lifespan psychology* (pp. 413–422). Dordrecht, Netherlands: Kluwer Academic.

Lerner, R. M., Lerner, J. V., Urban, J. B., & Zaff, J. (2016). Evaluating programs aimed at promoting positive youth development: A relational development systems-based view. *Applied Developmental Science, 20*(3), 175–187.

Lerner, R. M., von Eye, A., Lerner, J. V., Lewin-Bizan, S., & Bowers, E. P. (2010). Special issue introduction: The meaning and measurement of thriving: A view of the issues. *Journal of Youth and Adolescence, 39,* 707–719.

Lerner-Geva, L., Boyko, V., Blumstein, T., & Benyamini, Y. (2010). The impact of education, cultural background, and lifestyle on symptoms of the menopausal transition: The Women's Health at Midlife Study. *Journal of Women's Health, 18*(5), 975–985.

Lessard, G., Flynn, C., Turcotte, P., Damant, D., Vezina, J., Godin, M., & Rondeau-Cantin, S. (2010). Child custody issues and co-occurrence of intimate partner violence and child maltreatment: Controversies and points of agreement amongst practitioners. *Child & Family Social Work, 15*(4), 492–500.

Lester, F., Benfield, N., & Fathalla, M. M. F. (2010). Global women's health in 2010: Facing the challenges. *Journal of Women's Health, 19*(11), 2081–2089.

Leung, A. K., & Chiu, C. (2011). Multicultural experience fosters creative conceptual expansion. In A. K. Leung, C. Chiu, & Y. Y. Hong (Eds.), *Cultural processes: A social psychological perspective* (pp. 263–285). New York, NY: Cambridge University Press.

Leung, K. K., Tsai, J. S., Cheng, S. Y., Liu, W. J., Chiu, T. Y., Wu, C. H., & Chen, C. Y. (2010). Can a good death and quality of life be achieved for patients with terminal cancer in a palliative care unit? *Journal of Palliative Medicine, 13*(12), 1433–1438.

Leve, L. D., Kerr, D. C. R., Shaw, D., Ge, X., Neiderhiser, J. M., Scaramella, L. V., . . . Reiss, D. (2010). Infant pathways to externalizing behavior: Evidence of genotype X environmental interaction. *Child Development, 81*(1), 240–356.

Levenson, A. (2017). Workplace fatigue is a systems problem. *Consulting Psychology Journal: Practice and Research, 69*(2), 130–142. doi:10.1037/cpb0000091

Leventhal, T., & Newman, S. (2010). Housing and child development. *Children and Youth Services Review, 32*(9), 1165–1174.

Levine, A., & Dean, D. (2012). *Generation on a tightrope: A portrait of today's college students.* San Francisco, CA: Jossey-Bass.

Lewin-Bizan, S., Lynch, A. D., Fay, K., Schmid, K., McPherran, C., Lerner, J. V., & Lerner, R. M. (2010). Trajectories of positive and negative behaviors from early- to middle-adolescence. *Journal of Youth and Adolescence, 39,* 751–763.

Lewis, A. D., Huebner, E. S., Malone, P. S., & Valois, R. F. (2011). Life satisfaction and student engagement in adolescents. *Journal of Youth and Adolescence, 40,* 249–262.

Li, A., Bagger, J., & Cropanzano, R. (2017). The impact of stereotypes and supervisor perceptions of employee work–family conflict on job performance ratings. *Human Relations, 70*(1), 119–145. doi:10.1177/0018726716645660

Li, L., Zhong, J. A., Chen, Y., Xie, Y., & Mao, S. (2014). Moderating effects of proactive personality on factors influencing work engagement based on the job demands-resources model. *Social Behavior and Personality, 42*(1), 7–16.

Li, W., Fay, D., Frese, M., Harms, P. D., & Gao, X. Y. (2014). Reciprocal relationship between proactive personality and work characteristics: A latent change score approach. *Journal of Applied Psychology, 99*(5), 948–965.

Li, X., Ling, H., Zhang, J., Si, X., & Ma, X. (2013). Influence of timing of puberty on boys' self-concept and peer relationship. *Chinese Journal of Clinical Psychology, 21*(3), 512–514.

Li, Y., & Lerner, R. M. (2011). Trajectories of school engagement during adolescence: Implications for grades, depression, delinquency, and substance use. *Developmental Psychology, 4*(1), 233–247.

Liben, S., Papadatou, D., & Wolfe, J. (2008). Paediatric palliative care: Challenges and emerging ideas. *The Lancet, 371*, 852–864.

Lickenbrock, D. M., Braungart-Rieker, J. M., Ekas, N. V., Zentall, S. R., Oshio, T., & Planalp, E. M. (2013). Early temperament and attachment security with mothers and fathers as predictors of toddler compliance and noncompliance. *Infant and Child Development, 22*(6), 580–602.

Lieberman, A. F. (1993).*The emotional life of the toddler.* New York, NY: Free Press.

Liebherr, M., Schubert, P., Schiebener, J., Kersten, S., & Haas, C. T. (2016). Dual-tasking and aging—About multiple perspectives and possible implementations in interventions for the elderly. *Cogent Psychology, 3*(1), doi:10.1080/23311908.2016.1261440

Liebschutz, J. M., Crooks, D., Rose-Jacobs, R., Cabral, H. J., Heeren, T. C., Gerteis, J., . . . Frank, D. A. (2015). Prenatal substance exposure: What predicts behavioral resilience by early adolescence? *Psychology of Addictive Behaviors, 29*(2), 329–337. doi:10.1037/adb0000082

Light, R. J. (2001). *Making the most of college: Students speak their minds.* Cambridge, MA: Harvard University Press.

Lightfoot, C. (1997). *The culture of adolescent risk-taking.* New York, NY: Guilford Press.

Lilgendahl, J. P., Helson, R., & John, O. P. (2013). Does ego development increase during midlife? The effects of openness and accommodative processing of difficult events. *Journal of Personality, 81*(4), 403–416.

Lilgendahl, J. P., & McAdams, D. P. (2011). Constructing stories of self-growth: How individual differences in patterns of autobiographical reasonings relate to well-being in midlife. *Journal of Personality, 79*(2), 392–425.

Lim, S. L., Yeh, M., Liang, J., Lau, A. S., & McCabe, K. (2009) Acculturation gap, intergenerational conflict, parenting style, and youth distress in immigrant Chinese American families. *Marriage & Family Review, 45*, 84–106.

Lin, W., Li, T., & Chen, L. (2016). Are "we" good? A longitudinal study of we-talk and stress coping in dual-earner couples. *Journal of Happiness Studies, 17*(2), 757–772. doi:10.1007/s10902-015-9621-0

Lin, Y., Chang, J., Chen, Y., Li, C., & Huang, L. (2017). Health-related quality of life among frail and pre-frail older adults in Taiwan. *International Journal of Gerontology, 11*, 249–252. doi:10.1016/j.ijge.2017.01.003

Lin, Y., Tsai, Y., & Lai, P. (2013). The experience of Taiwanese women achieving post-infertility pregnancy through assisted reproductive treatment. *The Family Journal, 21*, 189–197.

Lin, Y., Xu, J., Huang, J., Jia, Y., Zhang, J., Yan, C., & Zhang, J. (2017). Effects of prenatal and postnatal maternal emotional stress on toddlers' cognitive and temperamental development. *Journal of Affective Disorders, 207*, 9–17. doi:10.1016/j.jad.2016.09.010

Linares, R., Bajo, M. T., & Pelegrina, S. (2016). Age-related differences in working memory updating components. *Journal of Experimental Child Psychology, 147*, 39–52. doi:10.1016/j.jecp.2016.02.009

Lindau, S. T., Schumm, L. P., Laumann, E. O., Levinson, W., O'Muircheartaigh, C. A., & Waite, L. J. (2007). A study of sexuality and health among older adults in the United States. *New England Journal of Medicine, 357*(8), 762–774. doi:10.1056/NEJMoa067423

Lindberg, L. D., Maddow-Zimet, I., & Boonstra, H. (2016). Changes in adolescents' receipt of sex education, 2006–2013. *The Journal of Adolescent Health: Official Publication of the Society for Adolescent Medicine, 58*(6), 621–627. doi:10.1016/j.jadohealth.2016.02.004

Lindberg, L., Kost, K., & Maddow-Zimet, I. (2017). The role of men's childbearing intentions in father involvement. *Journal of Marriage and Family, 79*(1), 44–59. doi:10.1111/jomf.12377

Lindemann, E. (1944). Symptomatology and management of acute grief. *American Journal of Psychiatry, 101*, 141–148.

Lindenberger, U., & Mayr, U. (2014). Cognitive aging: Is there a dark side to environmental support? *Trends in Cognitive Sciences, 18*(1), 7–15.

Lindsey, E. W. (2014). Physical activity play and preschool children's peer acceptance: Distinctions between rough-and-tumble and exercise play. *Early Education and Development, 25*(3), 277–294. doi:10.1080/10409289.2014.890854

Linver, M. R., Roth, J. L., & Brooks-Gunn, J. (2009). Patterns of adolescents' participation in organized activities: Are sports best when combined with other activities? *Developmental Psychology, 45*, 354–367.

Liu, R. T., Cheek, S. M., & Nestor, B. A. (2016). Non-suicidal self-injury and life stress: A systematic meta-analysis and theoretical elaboration. *Clinical Psychology Review, 47*, 1–14.

Liu, X., Lu, B., & Feng, Z. (2017). Intergenerational transfers and informal care for disabled elderly persons in China: Evidence from CHARLS. *Health and Social Care in the Community, 25*(4), 1364–1374. doi.org/10.1111/hsc.12441.

Liu, Y. C., Su, P. Y., Chen, C. H., Chiang, H. H., Wang, K. Y., & Tzeng, W. C. (2011). Facing death, facing self: Nursing students' emotional reactions during an experiential workshop on life-and-death issues. *Journal of Clinical Nursing, 20*(5–6), 856–863.

Liu, Z., Wu, D., Huang, J., Qian, D., Chen, F., Xu, J., . . . Wang, X. (2016). Visual impairment, but not hearing impairment, is independently associated with lower subjective well-being among individuals over 95 years of age: A population-based study. *Archives of Gerontology & Geriatrics, 62*, 30–35. doi:10.1016/j.archger.2015.10.011

Lonardo, R. A., Giordano, P. C., Longmore, M. A., & Manning, W. D. (2009). Parents, friends, and romantic partners: Enmeshment in deviant networks and adolescent delinquency involvement. *Journal of Youth and Adolescence, 38*, 367–383.

Lopes, L., Santos, R., Pereira, B., & Lopes, V. P. (2013). Associations between gross motor coordination and academic achievement in elementary school children. *Human Movement Science, 32*(1), 9–20.

Lopez-Caneda, E., Holguin, S., Rodrigues, C., Cadaveira, F., Corral, M., & Doallo, S. (2014). The impact of alcohol use on inhibitory control (and vice versa) during adolescence and young adulthood: A review. *Alcohol and Alcoholism, 49*(2), 173–184.

López-Guimerà, G., Levine, M. P., Sanchez-Carracedo, D., & Fauquet, J. (2010). Influence of mass media on body image and eating disordered attitudes and behaviors in females: A review of effects and processes. *Media Psychology, 13*(4), 387–416.

Lorber, M. F., Mitnick, D. M., & Slep, A. M. (2016). Parents' experience of flooding in discipline encounters: Associations with discipline and interplay with related factors. *Journal of Family Psychology, 30*(4), 470–479. doi:10.1037/fam0000176

Lorber, M. F., O'Leary, S. G., & Smith Slep, A. M. (2011). An initial evaluation of the role of emotion and impulsivity in explaining racial/ethnic differences in the use of corporal punishment. *Developmental Psychology, 47*(6), 1744–1749.

Lorenz, K. (1935). Der Kumpan in der Umwelt des Vogels. Der Artgenosse als auslosendes Moment sozialer Verhaltungsweisen [The companion in the bird's world. The fellow-member of the species as releasing factor of social behavior]. *Journal für Ornithologie. Beiblatt. (Leipzig), 83,* 137–213.

Lou, V. Q., Lu, N., Xu, L., & Chi, I. (2013). Grandparent–grandchild family capital and self-rated health of older rural Chinese adults: The role of the grandparent–parent relationship. *The Journals of Gerontology Series B: Psychological Sciences and Social Sciences, 68B*(4), 599–608.

Loukas, A., Roalson, L. A., & Herrera, D. E. (2010). School connectedness buffers the effects of negative family relations and poor effortful control on early adolescent conduct problems. *Journal of Research on Adolescence, 20*(1), 13–22.

Lubans, D. R., Morgan, P. J., Cliff, D. P., Barnett, L. M., & Okeley, A. D. (2010). Fundamental movement skills in children and adolescents: Review of associated health benefits. *Sports Medicine, 40*(12), 1019–1035.

Lubold, A. M. (2016). Breastfeeding and employment: A propensity score matching approach. *Sociological Spectrum, 36*(6), 391–405. doi:10.1080/02732173.2016.1227286

Luciana, M. (2010). Adolescent brain development: Current themes and future directions. Introduction to the special issue [Editorial]. *Brain and Cognition, 72,* 1–5.

Luciano, E. C., & Orth, U. (2017). Transitions in romantic relationships and development of self-esteem. *Journal of Personality and Social Psychology, 122*(2), 307–328.

Lui, P. R., & Rollock, D. (2013). Tiger mother: Popular and psychological scientific perspectives on Asian culture and parenting. *American Journal of Orthopsychiatry, 83*(4), 450–456.

Luo, S. (2014). Effects of texting on satisfaction in romantic relationships: The role of attachment. *Computers in Human Behavior, 33,* 145–152.

Luong, G., Charles, S. T., & Fingerman, K. L. (2010). Better with age: Social relationships across adulthood. *Journal of Social and Personal Relationships, 28*(1), 9–23.

Lydecker, J. A., & Grilo, C. M. (2016). Fathers and mothers with eating-disorder psychopathology: Associations with child eating-disorder behaviors. *Journal of Psychosomatic Research, 86,* 63–69. doi:10.1016/j.jpsychores.2016.05.006

Lynch, R. J., Kistner, J. A., Stephens, H. F., & David-Ferdon, C. (2016). Positively biased self-perceptions of peer acceptance and subtypes of aggression in children. *Aggressive Behavior, 42*(1), 82–96. doi:10.1002/ab.21611

Lynne-Landsman, S. D., Graber, J. A., & Andrews, J. A. (2010). Do trajectories of household risk in childhood moderate pubertal timing effects on substance initiation in middle school? *Developmental Psychology, 46*(4), 853–868.

Lytle, M. C., Foley, P. F., & Cotter, E. W. (2015). Career and retirement theories: Relevance for older workers across cultures. *Journal of Career Development, 42*(3), 185–198. doi:10.1177/0894845314547638

Ma, F., Evans, A. D., Liu, Y., Luo, X., & Xu, F. (2015). To lie or not to lie? The influence of parenting and theory of-mind understanding on three-year-old children's honesty. *Journal of Moral Education, 44*(2), 198–212. doi 10.1080/03057240.2015.1023182

Ma, J. (2016). Neighborhood and parenting both matter: The role of neighborhood collective efficacy and maternal spanking in early behavioral problems. *Children and Youth Services Review, 61,* 250–260.

Maccoby, E. E. (1990). Gender and relationships: A developmental account. *American Psychologist, 45,* 513–520.

Maccoby, E. E. (1998). *The two sexes: Growing up apart, coming together.* Cambridge, MA: Belknap Press of Harvard University Press.

Maccoby, E. E. (2002). Gender and group process: A developmental perspective. *Current Directions in Psychological Science, 11,* 54–58.

Macdonald, J. L., & Levy, S. R. (2016). Ageism in the workplace: The role of psychosocial factors in predicting job satisfaction, commitment, and engagement. *Journal of Social Issues, 72*(1), 169–190.

Macek, P., Bejcek, J., & Vanickova, J. (2007). Contemporary Czech emerging adults: Generation growing up in the period of social changes. *Journal of Adolescent Research, 22*(5), 444–474.

Machado, S., de Sá Filho, A. S., Wilbert, M., Barbieri, G., Almeida, V., Gurgel, A., . . . Murillo-Rodriguez, E. (2017). Physical exercise as stabilizer for Alzheimer's disease cognitive decline: Current status. *Clinical Practice and Epidemiology in Mental Health, 13,* 181–184. doi:10.2174/1745017901713010181

Mackinnon, S. P., Nosko, A., Pratt, M. W., & Norris, J. E. (2011). Intimacy in young adults' narratives of romance and friendship predicts Eriksonian generativity: A mixed method analysis. *Journal of Personality, 79*(3), 587–617.

MacMillan, H. L., Tanaka, M., Duku, E., Vaillancourt, T., & Boyle, M. H. (2013). Child physical and sexual abuse in a community sample of young adults: Results from the Ontario Child Health Study. *Child Abuse & Neglect: The International Journal, 37*(1), 14–21.

MacRae, H. (2008). Making the best you can of it: Living with early-stage Alzheimer's disease. *Sociology of Health & Wellness, 30*(3), 396–412.

Maggs, J. L., Patrick, M. E., & Feinstein, L. (2008). Childhood and adolescent predictors of alcohol use and problems in adolescence and adulthood in the National Child Development Study. *Addiction, 103* (Suppl. 1), 7–22.

Mahne, K., & Huxhold, O. (2015). Grandparenthood and subjective well-being: Moderating effects of educational level. *The Journals of Gerontology: Series B, 70*(5), 782–792. doi.org/10.1093/geronb/gbu147

Malacrida, C., & Boulton, T. (2014). The best laid plans? Women's choices, expectations and experiences in childbirth. *Health: An Interdisciplinary Journal for the Social Study of Health, Illness and Medicine, 18*(1), 41–59.

Malin, H., Reilly, T. S., Quinn, B., & Moran, S. (2014). Adolescent purpose development: Exploring empathy, discovering roles, shifting priorities, and creating pathways. *Journal of Research on Adolescence, 24*(1), 186–199.

Malpas, P. J., Wilson, M. R., Rae, N., & Johnson, M. (2014). Why do older people oppose physician-assisted dying? A qualitative study. *Palliative Medicine, 28*(4), 353–359.

Mandler, J. M. (2007). On the origins of the conceptual system. *American Psychologist, 62*(8), 741–751.

Manfra, L., & Winsler, A. (2006). Preschool children's awareness of private speech. *International Journal of Behavioral Development, 30*(6), 537–549.

Manning, W. D., Giordano, P. C., & Longmore, M. A. (2006). Hooking up: The relationship contexts of "nonrelationship" sex. *Journal of Adolescent Research, 21*(5), 459–483.

Manrique-Huarte, R., Calavia, D., Huarte Irujo, A., Girón, L., & Manrique-Rodríguez, M. (2016). Treatment for hearing loss among the elderly: Auditory outcomes and impact on quality of life. *Audiology & Neuro-Otology, 21*, 29–35. doi:10.1159/000448352

Marcia, J. E. (1966). Development and validation of ego-identity status. *Journal of Personality and Social Psychology, 3*, 551–558.

Marcia, J. E. (1987). The identity status approach to the study of ego identity development. In T. Honess & K. Yardley (Eds.), *Self and identity: Perspectives across the lifespan* (pp. 161–171). New York, NY: Routledge.

Mare, R. D. (2016). Educational homogamy in two gilded ages: Evidence from intergenerational social mobility data. *Annals of the American Academy of Political and Social Science, 663*(1), 117–139.

Mares, M., Bartsch, A., & Bonus, J. A. (2016). When meaning matters more: Media preferences across the adult life span. *Psychology & Aging, 31*(5), 513–531. doi:10.1037/pag0000098

Margelisch, K., Schneewind, K. A., Violette, J., & Perrig-Chiello, P. (2017). Marital stability, satisfaction and well-being in old age: Variability and continuity in long-term continuously married older persons. *Aging & Mental Health, 21*(4), 389–398. doi:10.1080/13607863.2015.1102197

Marieb, E. N. (2004). *Human anatomy & physiology* (6th ed.). New York, NY: Pearson Education.

Markey, P. M., & Markey, C. N. (2007). Romantic ideals, romantic obtainment, and relationship experiences: The complementarity of interpersonal traits among romantic partners. *Journal of Social and Personal Relationships, 24*(4), 517–533.

Markin, R. D. (2016). What clinicians miss about miscarriages: Clinical errors in the treatment of early term perinatal loss. *Psychotherapy, 53*(3), Special Issue: Clinical Errors, 347–353.

Marlier, L., Schaal, B., & Soussignan, R. (1998). Neonatal responsiveness to the odor of amniotic and lacteal fluids: A test of perinatal chemosensory continuity. *Child Development, 69*, 611–623.

Marsiglio, W. (2004). When stepfathers claim stepchildren: A conceptual analysis. *Journal of Marriage and Family, 66*, 22–39.

Martin, A. J., Mansour, M., Anderson, M., Gibson, R., Liem, G. D., & Sudmalis, D. (2013). The role of arts participation in students' academic and nonacademic outcomes: A longitudinal study of school, home, and community factors. *Journal of Educational Psychology, 105*(3), 709–727.

Martin, C. L., & Dinella, L. M. (2002). Children's gender cognitions, the social environment, and sex differences in cognitive domains. In A. McGillicuddy-De Lisi & R. De Lisi (Eds.), *Biology, society, and behavior: The development of sex differences in cognition* (pp. 207–239). Westport, CT: Ablex.

Martin, C. L., & Fabes, R. A. (2001). The stability and consequences of young children's same-sex peer interactions. *Developmental Psychology, 37*, 431–446.

Martin, C. L., & Ruble, D. N. (2010). Patterns of gender development. *Annual Review of Psychology, 61*, 353–381.

Martin, K. A. (1996). *Puberty, sexuality, and the self: Boys and girls at adolescence.* New York, NY: Routledge.

Martin, M. A., Garcia, G., Kaplan, H. S., & Gurven, M. D. (2016). Conflict or congruence? Maternal and infant-centric factors associated with shorter exclusive breastfeeding durations among the Tsimane. *Social Science & Medicine, 170*, 9–17. doi:10.1016/j.socscimed.2016.10.003

Martinelli, P., Anssens, A., Sperduti, M., & Piolino, P. (2013). The influence of normal aging and Alzheimer's disease in autobiographical memory highly related to the self. *Neuropsychology, 27*(1), 69–78.

Martín-María, N., Miret, M., Caballero, F. F., Rico-Uribe, L. A., Steptoe, A., Chatterji, S., & Ayuso-Mateos, J. L. (2017). The impact of subjective well-being on mortality: A meta-analysis of longitudinal studies in the general population. *Psychosomatic Medicine, 79*(5), 565–575. doi:10.1097/PSY.0000000000000444

Marysko, M., Finke, P., Wiebel, A., Resch, F., & Moehler, E. (2010). Can mothers predict childhood behavioral inhibition in early infancy? *Child and Adolescent Mental Health, 15*(2), 91–96.

Mason, K., Kim, E., Blake Martin, W., & Gober, R. J. (2017). The moral deliberations of 15 clergy on suicide and assisted death: A qualitative study. *Pastoral Psychology, 66*(3), 335. doi:10.1007/s11089-016-0744-y

Masoro, E. (1999). *Challenges of biological aging.* New York, NY: Springer National Center for Gender Equality. (n.d.). Frequently asked questions about transgender people. Retrieved from https://transequality.org/issues

Masten, A. S. (2004). Regulatory processes, risk, and resilience in adolescent development. In R. E. Dahl & L. P. Spear (Eds.), *Adolescent brain development: Vulnerabilities and opportunities* (Vol. 1021, pp. 310–319). New York, NY: New York Academy of Sciences.

Masters, W. H., & Johnson, V. E. (1966). *Human sexual response.* Boston, MA: Little, Brown.

May, P. A., Hamrick, K. J., Corbin, K. D., Hasken, J. M., Marais, A., Blankenship, J., . . . Gossage, J. P. (2016). Maternal nutritional status as a contributing factor for the risk of fetal alcohol spectrum disorders. *Reproductive Toxicology, 59*, 101–108. doi:10.1016/j.reprotox.2015.11.006

Mayberry, M. L., & Espelage, D. L. (2007). Associations among empathy, social competence, & reactive/proactive aggression subtypes. *Journal of Youth and Adolescence, 36*, 787–798.

Mayeux, L., & Cillessen, A. H. N. (2008). It's not just being popular, it's knowing it, too: The role of self-perceptions of status in the associations between peer status and aggression. *Social Development, 17*, 871–888.

Maynard, A. E., & Greenfield, P. M. (2003). Implicit cognitive development in cultural tools and children: Lessons from Maya Mexico. *Cognitive Development, 18*, 489–510.

Mazzotti, D. R., Tufik, S., & Andersen, M. L. (2013). A step forward in understanding the association between social attainment and health disparities: Evidence from late life telomere length and educational level. *Brain, Behavior, and Immunity, 27*, 13–14.

McAdams, D. P. (2001a). Generativity in midlife. In M. E. Lachman (Ed.), *Handbook of midlife development* (pp. 395–443). Hoboken, NJ: Wiley.

McAdams, D. P. (2006). *The redemptive self: Stories Americans live by*. New York, NY: Oxford University Press.

McAdams, D. P. (2013). The psychological self as actor, agent, and author. *Perspectives on Psychological Science, 8*(3), 272–295.

McAdams, D. P., & Bowman, P. J. (2001). Narrating life's turning points: Redemption and contamination. In D. P. McAdams, R. Josselson, & A. Lieblich (Eds.), *Turns in the road: Narrative studies of lives in transition* (pp. 3–34). Washington, DC: American Psychological Association.

McAdams, D. P., de St. Aubin, E., & Logan, R. L. (1993). Generativity among young, midlife, and older adults. *Psychology and Aging, 8*, 221–230.

McAdams, D. P., Hart, H. M., & Maruna, S. (1998). The anatomy of generativity. In D. P. McAdams & E. de St. Aubin (Eds.), *Generativity and adult development: How and why we care for the next generation* (pp. 7–43). Washington, DC: American Psychological Association.

McAlister, A. R., & Peterson, C. C. (2013). Siblings, theory of mind, and executive functioning in children aged 3–6 years: New longitudinal evidence. *Child Development, 84*(4), 1442–1458.

McAuley, E., Kramer, A. F., & Colcombe, S. J. (2004). Cardiovascular fitness and neurocognitive function in older adults: A brief review. *Brain, Behavior, and Immunity, 18*(3), 214–220. doi. org/10.1016/j.bbi.2003.12.007

McCall, R. B., Muhamedrahimov, R. J., Groark, C. J., Palmov, O. I., Nikiforova, N. V., Salaway, J. L., & Julian, M. M. (2016). The development of children placed into different types of Russian families following an institutional intervention. *International Perspectives in Psychology: Research, Practice, Consultation, 5*(4), 255–270. doi:10.1037/ipp0000060

McCann, R. M., & Keaton, S. A. (2013). A cross cultural investigation of age stereotypes and communication perceptions of older and younger workers in the USA and Thailand. *Educational Gerontology, 39*(5), 326–341.

McCarthy, J. R., & Jessop, J. (2005). *Young people, bereavement and loss: Disruptive transitions?* London, England: National Children's Bureau.

McCarthy, M. C., & Lumley, M. N. (2012). Sources of emotional maltreatment and the differential development of unconditional and conditional schemas. *Cognitive Behavior Therapy, 41*(4), 288–297.

McCarty, A. T., & Teoh, E. R. (2015). Tracking progress in teenage driver crash risk in the United States since the advent of graduated driver licensing programs. *Journal of Safety Research, 53*, 1–9.

McClain, L. L., & Brown, S. (2017). The roles of fathers' involvement and coparenting in relationship quality among cohabiting and married parents. *Sex Roles, 76*(5/6), 334–345.

McClintock, M. K., & Herdt, G. (1996). Rethinking puberty: The development of sexual attraction. *Current Directions in Psychological Science, 5*, 178–183.

McCloskey, L. A. (2013). The intergenerational transfer of mother–daughter risk for gender-based abuse. *Psychodynamic Psychiatry, 41*(2), 303–328.

McCormack, A., & Fortnum, H. (2013). Why do people fitted with hearing aids not wear them? *International Journal of Audiology, 52*(5), 360–368.

McCrae, R. R., & Costa, P. T. (1990). *Personality in adulthood*. New York, NY: Guilford Press.

McCreight, B. S. (2004). A grief ignored: Narratives of pregnancy loss from a male perspective. *Sociology of Health and Illness, 26*, 326–350.

McDaniel, M. A., Binder, E. F., Bugg, J. M., Waldum, E. R., Dufault, C., Meyer, A., . . . Kudelka, C. (2014). Effects of cognitive training with and without aerobic exercise on cognitively demanding everyday activities. *Psychology and Aging, 29*(3), 717–730.

McDonald, K. L., Malti, T., Killen, M., & Rubin, K. H. (2014). Best friends' discussions of social dilemmas. *Journal of Youth and Adolescence, 43*(2), 233–244.

McDonnell, C. G., Valentino, K., Comas, M., & Nuttall, A. K. (2016). Mother–child reminiscing at risk: Maternal attachment, elaboration, and child autobiographical memory specificity. *Journal of Experimental Child Psychology, 143*, 64–84. doi:10.1016/j.jecp.2015.10.012

McElwain, N. L., Booth-LaForce, C., & Wu, X. (2011). Infant–mother attachment and children's friendship quality: Maternal mental-state talk as an intervening mechanism. *Developmental Psychology, 47*(5), 1295–1311.

McGeown, K. (2005). *Life in Ceausescu's institutions*. Retrieved from http://news.bbc.co.uk/2/hi/europe/4630855.stm

McGill, B. S. (2014). Navigating new norms of involved fatherhood: Employment, fathering attitudes, and father involvement. *Journal of Family Issues, 35*(8), 1089–1106.

McGrath, P. (2004). Affirming the connection: Comparative findings on communication issues from hospice patients and hematology survivors. *Death Studies, 28*, 829–848.

McIntosh, H., Metz, E., & Youniss, J. (2005). Community service and identity formation in adolescents. In J. L. Mahoney, R. W. Larson, & J. S. Eccles (Eds.), *Organized activities as contexts of development: Extracurricular activities, after-school and community programs* (pp. 331–351). Mahwah, NJ: Erlbaum.

McKay, A., & Barrett, M. (2010). Trends in teen pregnancy rates from 1996–2006: A comparison of Canada, Sweden, U.S.A., and England/Wales. *Canadian Journal of Human Sexuality, 19*(1–2), 43–52.

McLaughlin, K. A., Fox, N. A., Zeanah, C. H., Sheridan, M. A., Marshall, P., & Nelson, C. A. (2010). Delayed maturation in brain electrical activity partially explains the association between early environmental deprivation and symptoms of attention-deficit/hyperactivity disorder. *Biological Psychiatry, 68*(4), 329–336.

McLaughlin, K. A., Zeanah, C. H., Fox, N. A., & Nelson, C. A. (2012). Attachment security as a mechanism linking foster care placement to improved mental health outcomes in previously institutionalized children. *Journal of Child Psychology and Psychiatry, 53*(1), 46–55.

McLeskey, J., Waldron, N. L., & Redd, L. (2014). A case study of a highly effective, inclusive elementary school. *Journal of Special Education, 48*(1), 59–70.

McMahan, R. D., Knight, S. J., Fried, T. R., & Sudore, R. L. (2013). Advance care planning beyond advance directives: Perspectives from patients and surrogates. *Journal of Pain and Symptom Management, 46*(3), 355.

McNeely, C. A., & Barber, B. K. (2010). How do parents make adolescents feel loved? Perspectives on supportive parenting from adolescents in 12 cultures. *Journal of Adolescent Research, 25*(4), 601–631.

McNiel, M. E., Labbok, M. H., & Abrahams, S. W. (2010). What are the risks associated with formula feeding? A re-analysis and review. *Birth: Issues in Prenatal Care, 37*(1), 50–58.

Meier, M. H., Hall, W., Caspi, A., Belsky, D. W., Cerda, M., Harrington, H. L., . . .Moffitt, T. E. (2016). Which adolescents develop persistent substance dependence in adulthood? Using population-representative longitudinal data to inform universal risk assessment. *Psychological Medicine, 46*(4), 877–889.

Melinder, A., Baugerud, G. A., Ovenstad, K. S., & Goodman, G. S. (2013). Children's memories of removal: A test of attachment theory. *Journal of Traumatic Stress, 26*(1), 125–133.

Mellor, D., Fuller-Tyszkiewicz, M., McCabe, M. P., & Ricciardelli, L. A. (2010). Body image and self-esteem across age and gender: A short-term longitudinal study. *Sex Roles, 63*(9–10), 672–681.

Menard, J. L., & Hakvoort, R. M. (2007). Variations of maternal care alter offspring levels of behavioral defensiveness in adulthood: Evidence for a threshold model. *Behavioral Brain Research, 176*, 302–313.

Mendle, J., Harden, K. P., Brooks-Gunn, J., & Graber, J. A. (2010). Development's tortoise and hare: Pubertal timing, pubertal tempo, and depressive symptoms in boys and girls. *Developmental Psychology, 46*(5), 1341–1353.

Mendle, J., Moore, S. R., Briley, D. A., & Harden, K. P. (2016). Puberty, socioeconomic status, and depression in girls: Evidence for gene × environment interactions. *Clinical Psychological Science, 4*(1), 3–16.

Mendonça, M., & Fontaine, A. M. (2013). Late nest leaving in Portugal: Its effects on individuation and parent–child relationships. *Emerging Adulthood, 1*(3), 233–244.

Mernitz, S. E., & Dush, C. K. (2016). Emotional health across the transition to first and second unions among emerging adults. *Journal of Family Psychology, 30*(2), 233–244.

Merz, E. M., Schulze, H. J., & Schuengel, C. (2010). Consequences of filial support for two generations: A narrative and quantitative review. *Journal of Family Issues, 31*(11), 1530–1554.

Messler, C. F., Holmberg, H., & Sperlich, B. (2016). Multimodal therapy involving high-intensity interval training improves the physical fitness, motor skills, social behavior, and quality of life of boys with ADHD: A randomized controlled study. *Journal of Attention Disorders.* doi:10.1177/1087054716636936

Meuwly, N., Feinstein, B. A., Davila, J., Nunez, D. G., & Bodenmann, G. (2013). Relationship quality among Swiss women in opposite-sex versus same-sex romantic relationships. *Swiss Journal of Psychology, 72*(4), 229–233.

Mikkelsen, A. T., Madsen, S. A., & Humaidan, P. (2013). Psychological aspects of male fertility treatment. *Journal of Advanced Nursing, 69*(9), 1977–1986.

Mikulincer, M., Florian, V., Cowan, P. A., & Cowan, C. P. (2002). Attachment security in couple relationships: A systemic model and its implications for family dynamics. *Family Process, 41*, 405–434.

Miller, D., & Daniel, B. (2007). Competent to cope, worthy of happiness? How the duality of self-esteem can inform a resilience-based classroom environment. *School Psychology International, 28*(5), 605–622.

Miller, W. D., Sadegh-Nobari, T., & Lillie-Blanton, M. (2011). Healthy starts for all: Policy prescriptions. *American Journal of Preventive Medicine, 40*(1), S19–S37.

Miniño, A. M., Arias, E., Kochanek, K. D., Murphy, S. L., & Smith, B. L. (2002, September 16). Deaths: Final data for 2000. *National Vital Statistics Reports, 50*(16).

Minois, G. (1989). *History of old age: From antiquity to the Renaissance* (S. H. Tenison, Trans.). Chicago, IL: University of Chicago Press.

Mintz, S. (2004). *Huck's raft: A history of American childhood.* Cambridge, MA: Belknap Press of Harvard University Press.

Mirecki, R. M., Brimhall, A. S., & Bramesfeld, K. D. (2013). Communication during conflict: Differences between individuals in first and second marriages. *Journal of Divorce & Remarriage, 54*(3), 197–213.

Mirkovic, K. R., Perrine, C. G., & Scanlon, K. S. (2016). Paid maternity leave and breastfeeding outcomes. *Birth, 43*(3), 233–239. doi:10.1111/birt.12230

Modell, J. (1989). *Into one's own: From youth to adulthood in the United States, 1920–1975.* Berkeley, CA: University of California Press.

Moehler, E., Kagan, J., Oelkers-Ax, R., Brunner, R., Poustka, L., Haffner, J., & Resch, F. (2008). Infant predictors of behavioural inhibition. *British Journal of Developmental Psychology, 26*(1), 145–150.

Moffitt, T. E. (1993). Adolescence-limited and life-course-persistent antisocial behavior: A developmental taxonomy. *Psychological Review, 100*, 674–701.

Moilanen, K. L., Crockett, L. J., Raffaelli, M., & Jones, B. L. (2010). Trajectories of sexual risk from middle adolescence to early adulthood. *Journal of Research on Adolescence, 20*(1), 114–139.

Molden, D. C., & Dweck, C. S. (2006). Finding "meaning" in psychology: A lay theories approach to self-regulation, social perception, and social development. *American Psychologist, 61*, 192–203.

Molina, M. F., & Musich, F. M. (2015). Perception of parenting style by children with ADHD and its relation with inattention, hyperactivity/impulsivity and externalizing symptoms. *Journal of Child and Family Studies, 25*(5), 1656–1671. doi:10.1007/s10826-015-0316-2

Molloy, L. E., Gest, S. D., & Rulison, K. L. (2011). Peer influences on academic motivation: Exploring multiple methods of assessing youths' most "influential" peer relationships. *The Journal of Early Adolescence, 31*(1), 13–40.

Monk, C. S., McClure, E. B., Nelson, E. E., Zarahn, E., Bilder, R. M., Leibenluft, E., . . . Pine, D. S. (2003). Adolescent immaturity in attention-related brain engagement to emotional facial expressions. *Neuroimage, 20*(1), 420–428.

Monroe, B., Hansford, P., Payne, M., & Sykes, N. (2008). St. Christopher's and the future. *Omega: Journal of Death and Dying. Special Issue: "Hospice heritage," in memory of Dame Cicely Saunders, 56*, 63–75.

Montemurro, B. (2014). Getting married, breaking up, and making up for lost time: Relationship transitions as turning points in women's sexuality. *Journal of Contemporary Ethnography, 43*(1), 64–93.

Montepare, J. M., Kempler, D., & McLaughlin-Volpe, T. (2014). The voice of wisdom: New insights on social impressions of aging voices. *Journal of Language and Social Psychology, 33*(3), 241–259.

Monteverde, S. (2017). Nursing and assisted dying: Understanding the sounds of silence. *Nursing Ethics, 24*(1), 3–8. doi:10.1177/0969733016684967

Montgomery, K. E., Sawin, K. J., & Hendricks-Ferguson, V. (2017). Communication during palliative care and end of life: Perceptions of experienced pediatric oncology nurses. *Cancer Nursing, 40*(2), E47–E57. doi:10.1097/NCC.0000000000000363

Montoro-Rodriguez, J., Kosloski, K., Kercher, K., & Montgomery, R. J. V. (2009). The impact of social embarrassment on caregiving distress in a multicultural sample of caregivers. *Journal of Applied Gerontology, 28*, 195–217.

Mooney, A., Brannen, J., Wigfall, V., & Parutis, V. (2013). The impact of employment on fatherhood across family generations in White British, Polish and Irish origin families. *Community, Work & Family, 16*(4), 372–389.

Moore, D. S. (2015). *The developing genome: An introduction to behavioral epigenetics.* Oxford, UK: Oxford University Press.

Moreno, M., & Trainor, M. E. (2013). Adolescence extended: Implications of new brain research on medicine and policy. *Acta Paediatrica, 102*(3), 226–232.

Moret-Tatay, C., Lemus-Zúñiga, L., Tortosa, D. A., Gamermann, D., Vázquez-Martínez, A., Navarro-Pardo, E., & Conejero, J. A. (2017). Age slowing down in detection and visual discrimination under varying presentation times. *Scandinavian Journal of Psychology, 58*(4), 304–311. doi:10.1111/sjop.12372

Morgan, E. M. (2013). Contemporary issues in sexual orientation and identity development in emerging adulthood. *Emerging Adulthood, 1*(1), 52–66.

Morgan, E. M., Thorne, A., & Zubriggen, E. L. (2010). A longitudinal study of conversations with parents about sex and dating during college. *Developmental Psychology, 46*(1), 139–150.

Morgan, H. J., & Shaver, P. R. (1999). Attachment processes and commitment to romantic relationships. In J. M. Adams & W. H. Jones (Eds.), *Handbook of interpersonal commitment and relationship stability* (pp. 109–124). Dordrecht, Netherlands: Kluwer Academic.

Mori, A., & Cigala, A. (2016). Perspective taking: Training procedures in developmentally typical preschoolers.

Different intervention methods and their effectiveness. *Educational Psychological Review, 28*(2), 267–294. doi:10.1007/s10648-015-9306-6

Moss, E., Cyr, C., Bureau, J.-F., Tarabulsy, G. M., & Dubois-Comtois, K. (2005). Stability of attachment during the preschool period. *Developmental Psychology, 41*, 773–783.

Motsa, L. F., Ibisomi, L., & Odimegwu, C. (2016). The influence of infant feeding practices on infant mortality in southern Africa. *Maternal and Child Health Journal, 20*(10), 2130–2141. doi:10.1007/s10995-016-2033-x

Mountain, G., Cahill, J., & Thorpe, H. (2017). Sensitivity and attachment interventions in early childhood: A systematic review and meta-analysis. *Infant Behavior and Development, 46*, 14–32. doi:10.1016/j.infbeh.2016.10.006

Muehlenkamp, J. J., Claes, L., Havertape, L., & Plener, P. L. (2012). International prevalence of adolescent non-suicidal self-injury and deliberate self-harm. *Child and Adolescent Psychiatry and Mental Health, 6*, 1–9.

Mueller, C. M., & Dweck, C. S. (1998). Praise for intelligence can undermine children's motivation and performance. *Journal of Personality and Social Psychology, 75*(1), 33–52.

Müller-Oehring, E. M., Schulte, T., Rohlfing, T., Pfefferbaum, A., & Sullivan, E. V. (2013). Visual search and the aging brain: Discerning the effects of age-related brain volume shrinkage on alertness, feature binding, and attentional control. *Neuropsychology, 27*(1), 48–59.

Mulvey, K. L., & Killen, M. (2016). Keeping quiet just wouldn't be right: Children's and adolescents' evaluations of challenges to peer relational and physical aggression. *Journal of Youth and Adolescence, 45*(9), 1824–1835. doi:10.1007/s10964-016-0437-y

Mumford, K. H., & Kita, S. (2016). At 10–12 months, pointing gesture handedness predicts the size of receptive vocabularies. *Infancy, 21*(6), 751–765. doi:10.1111/infa.12138

Munch, A. L., Hunger, C., & Schweitzer, J. (2016). An investigation of the mediating role of personality and family functioning in the association between attachment styles and eating disorder status. *BMC Psychology, 4*(ARTD), 36.

Muñiz-Velázquez, J. A., Gomez-Baya, D., & Lopez-Casquete, M. (2017). Implicit and explicit assessment of materialism: Associations with happiness and depression. *Personality and Individual Differences, 116*, 123–132. doi. org/10.1016/j.paid.2017.04.033

Munroe, R. L. (2010). Following the Whitings: The study of male pregnancy symptoms. *Journal of Cross-Cultural Psychology, 41*(4), 592–604.

Murray, A. L., Scratch, S. E., Thompson, D. K., Inder, T. E., Doyle, L. W., Anderson, J. I., & Anderson, P. J. (2014). Neonatal brain pathology predicts adverse attention and processing speed outcomes in very preterm and/or very low birth weight children. *Neuropsychology, 28*(4), 552–562.

Murray, S. L., Bellavia, G. M., Rose, P., & Griffin, D. W. (2003). Once hurt, twice hurtful: How perceived regard regulates daily marital interactions. *Journal of Personality and Social Psychology, 84*, 126–147.

Murray, S. L., & Holmes, J. G. (1997). A leap of faith? Positive illusions in romantic relationships. *Personality and Social Psychology Bulletin, 23*, 586–604.

Murray, S. L., Holmes, J. G., Bellavia, G., Griffin, D. W., & Dolderman, D. (2002). Kindred spirits? The benefits of egocentrism in close relationships. *Journal of Personality and Social Psychology, 82*, 563–581.

Murray, S. L., Holmes, J. G., Dolderman, D., & Griffin, D. W. (2000). What the motivated mind sees: Comparing friends' perspectives to married partners' views of each other. *Journal of Experimental Social Psychology, 36*, 600–620.

Murstein, B. I. (1999). The relationship of exchange and commitment. In J. M. Adams & W. H. Jones (Eds.), *Handbook of interpersonal commitment and relationship stability* (pp. 205–219). Dordrecht, Netherlands: Kluwer Academic.

Murstein, B. I., Reif, J. A., & Syracuse-Siewert, G. (2002). Comparison of the function of exchange in couples of similar and differing physical attractiveness. *Psychological Reports, 91*, 299–314.

Must, A., Naumova, E. N., Phillips, S. M., Blum, M., Dawson-Hughes, B., & Rand, W. M. (2005). Childhood overweight and maturational timing in the development of adult overweight and fatness: The Newton Girls Study and its follow-up. *Pediatrics, 116*, 620–627.

Must, O., Must, A., & Mikk, J. (2016). Predicting the Flynn effect through word abstractness: Results from the national intelligence tests support Flynn's explanation. *Intelligence, 57*, 7–14. doi:10.1016/j.intell.2016.03.003

Myers, A. J., Williams, L., Gatt, J. M., McAuley-Clark, E., Dobson-Stone, C., Schofield, P. R., & Nemeroff, C. B. (2014). Variation in the oxytocin receptor gene is associated with increased risk for anxiety, stress and depression in individuals with a history of exposure to early life stress. *Journal of Psychiatric Research, 59*, 93–100.

Myers, L. L., & Wiman, A. M. (2014). Binge eating disorder: A review of a new DSM diagnosis. *Research on Social Work Practice, 24*(1), 86–95.

Naldini, M., Pavolini, E., & Solera, C. (2016). Female employment and elderly care: The role of care policies and culture in 21 European countries. *Work, Employment and Society, 30*(4), 607–630. doi.org/10.1177/0950017015625602

Nappi, R. E., & Kokot-Kierepa, M. (2010). Women's voices in the menopause: Results from an international survey on vaginal atrophy. *Maturitas, 67*, 233–238.

National Center for Health Statistics. (2008). *Health, United States, 2007: With chartbook on trends in the health of Americans.* Hyattsville, MD: U.S. Government Printing Office.

National Center for Health Statistics. (2016). *Health, United States, 2016:* Hyattsville, MD: U.S. Government Printing Office. Retrieved from https://www.cdc.gov/nchs/data/hus/hus16.pdf

National Center on Education Statistics, Fast Facts. (n.d.). *Employment rates of college graduates.* Retrieved from http://www.nces.ed.gov/fastfacts

National Down Syndrome Society. (n.d.). Down syndrome facts. Retrieved from http/www.ndss.org

National Hospice and Palliative Care organization. (2011). *Patients served by hospice in the United States, 1984–2009.* In *NHPCO.* Retrieved from http://www.nhpco.org/files/public/Statistics_Research/Graph-of-hospice_1982_2009.pdf

National Hospice and Palliative Care Organization. (2018). Facts and figures: Hospice care in America, www.nhpco.org

Natsuaki, M., Ge, X., & Wenk, E. (2008). Continuity and changes in the developmental trajectories of criminal career: Examining the roles of timing of first arrest and high school graduation. *Journal of Youth and Adolescence, 37*, 431–444.

Natsuaki, M. N., Leve, L. D., Harold, G. T., Neiderhiser, J. M., Shaw, D. S., Ganiban, J., . . . Reiss, D. (2013). Transactions between child social wariness and observed structured parenting: Evidence from a prospective adoption study. *Child Development, 84*(5), 1750–1765.

Naughton, F., Eborall, H., & Sutton, S. (2013). Dissonance and disengagement in pregnant smokers: A qualitative study. *Journal of Smoking Cessation, 8*(1), 24–32. doi:10.1017/jsc.2013.4

Neberich, W., Penke, L., Lehnart, J., & Asendorpf, J. B. (2010). Family of origin, age at menarche, and reproductive strategies: A test of four evolutionary developmental models. *European Journal of Developmental Psychology, 7*(2), 153–177.

Nedjat-Haiem, F. R., Carrion, I. V., Gonzalez, K., Ell, K., Thompson, B., & Mishra, S. I. (2017). Exploring health care providers' views about initiating end-of-life care communication. *American Journal of Hospice & Palliative Medicine, 34*(4), 308–317. doi:10.1177/1049909115627773

Neff, L. A., & Geers, A. L. (2013). Optimistic expectations in early marriage: A resource or vulnerability for adaptive relationship functioning? *Journal of Personality and Social Psychology, 105*(1), 38–60.

Negriff, S., Dorn, L. D., Pabst, S. R., & Susman, E. J. (2011). Morningness/eveningness, pubertal timing, and substance use in adolescent girls. *Psychiatry Research, 185*, 408–413.

Neimeyer, R. A., Klass, D., & Dennis, M. R. (2014). A social constructionist account of grief: Loss and the narration of meaning. *Death Studies, 38*(8), 485–498.

Nelson, K. (1974). Concept, word, and sentence: Interrelations in acquisition and development. *Psychological Review, 81*, 267–285.

Nelson, K., & Fivush, R. (2004). The emergence of autobiographical memory: A social cultural developmental theory. *Psychological Review, 111*, 486–511.

Nelson, L. J., & Luster, S. S. (2016). "Adulthood" by whose definition? The complexity of emerging adults' conceptions of adulthood. In J. J. Arnett (Ed.), *The Oxford handbook of emerging adulthood* (pp. 421–437). New York, NY: Oxford University Press.

Nelson, S. K., Kushlev, K., & Lyubomirsky, S. (2014). The pains and pleasures of parenting: When, why, and how is parenthood associated with more or less well-being? *Psychological Bulletin, 140*(3), 846–895.

Neri, S. R., Cardoso, J. R., Cruz, L., Lima, R. M., de Oliveira, R. J., Iversen, M. D., & Carregaro, R. L. (2017). Do virtual reality games improve mobility skills and balance measurements in community-dwelling older adults? Systematic review and meta-analysis. *Clinical Rehabilitation, 31*(10), 1292–1304. doi:10.1177/0269215517694677

Nerini, A. (2015). Media influence and body dissatisfaction in preadolescent ballet dancers and non-physically active girls. *Psychology of Sport and Exercise, 20*, 76–83. doi:10.1016/j.psychsport.2015.04.011

Neugarten, B. (1972). Personality and the aging process. *The Gerontologist, 12*(1, Pt. 1), 9–15.

Neugarten, B. L. (1979). Time, age, and the life cycle. *American Journal of Psychiatry, 136*, 887–894.

Neumark, D. (2009). The Age Discrimination in Employment Act and the challenge of population aging. *Research on Aging, 31*, 41–68.

Newcomb, A. F., & Bagwell, C. L. (1995). Children's friendship relations: A meta-analytic review. *Psychological Bulletin, 117*, 306–347.

Newland, R. P., Parade, S., Dickstein, S., & Seifer, R. (2016). Goodness of fit between maternal and infant sleep: Associations with maternal depressive symptoms and attachment security. *Infant Behavior and Development, 44*, 179–188.

Newman, K. L. (2011). Sustainable careers: Lifecycle engagement in work. *Organizational Dynamics, 40*, 136–143.

Newson, R. S., & Kemps, E. B. (2008). Relationship between fitness and cognitive performance in younger and older adults. *Psychology and Health, 23*(3), 369–386. doi.org/10.1080/08870440701421545

Newton, N. J., & Baltys, I. H. (2014). Parent status and generativity within the context of race. *International Journal of Aging & Human Development, 78*(2), 171–195.

Newton, N. J., Russell, S. A., & McAdams, D. P. (2017). Body appraisal, weight management goals, and well-being among midlife men and women. *Journal of Adult Development, 24*(1), 31–39. doi.org/10.1007/s10804-016-9244-7

Nicolopoulou, A., Barbosa de Sa, A., Ilgaz, H., & Brockmeyer, C. (2010). Using the transformative power of play to educate hearts and minds: From Vygotsky to Vivian Paley and beyond. *Mind, Culture, and Activity, 17*, 42–58.

Nielsen, L., Knutson, B., & Carstensen, L. L. (2008). Affect dynamics, affective forecasting, and aging. *Emotion, 8*(3), 318–330.

Nmyanzi, L. A. (2016). Combating childhood obesity: Reactions of children aged 10–11 years toward the National Child Measurement Programme. *Journal of Child Health Care, 20*(4), 464–472. doi:10.1177/1367493515604493

Noh, H., Kim, J., Sims, O. T., Ji, S., & Sawyer, P. (2018). Racial differences in associations of perceived health and social and physical activities with advance care planning, end-of-life concerns, and hospice knowledge. *American Journal of Hospice & Palliative Medicine, 35*(1), 34–40.

Nolvi, S., Karlsson, L., Bridgett, D. J., Korja, R., Huizink, A. C., Kataja, E., & Karlsson, H. (2016). Maternal prenatal stress and infant emotional reactivity six months postpartum. *Journal of Affective Disorders, 199*, 163–170. doi:10.1016/j.jad.2016.04.020

Nomaguchi, K., Brown, S., & Leyman, T. M. (2017). Fathers' participation in parenting and maternal parenting stress: Variation by relationship status. *Journal of Family Issues, 8*, 1132.

Nomaguchi, K. M., & DeMaris, A. (2013). Nonmaternal care's association with mother's parenting sensitivity: A case of self-selection bias? *Journal of Marriage and Family, 75*(3), 760–777.

Nomaguchi, K., & House, A. N. (2013). Racial-ethnic disparities in maternal parenting stress: The role of structural disadvantages and parenting values. *Journal of Health and Social Behavior, 54*(3), 386–404.

Nord, C. C. (2013). A day to be lived. Elderly people's possessions for everyday life in assisted living. *Journal of Aging Studies, 27*(2), 135–142.

Normand, S., Schneider, B., Lee, M., Maisonneuve, M., Chupetlovska-Anastasova, A., Kuehn, S., & Robaey, P. (2013). Continuities and changes in the friendships of children with and without ADHD: A longitudinal, observational study. *Journal of Abnormal Child Psychology, 41*(7), 1161–1175.

Norona, J. C., Roberson, P. E., & Welsh, D. P. (2017). I learned things that make me happy, things that bring me down: Lessons from romantic relationships in adolescence and emerging adulthood. *Journal of Adolescent Research, 32*(2), 155–182.

Obradović, J., Burt, K. B., & Masten, A. S. (2010). Testing a dual cascade model linking competence and symptoms over 20 years from childhood to adulthood. *Journal of Clinical Child and Adolescent Psychology, 39*(1), 90–102.

Oddo, S., Lux, S., Weiss, P. H., Schwab, A., Welzer, H., Markowitsch, H. J., & Fink, G. R. (2010). Specific role of medial prefrontal cortex in retrieving recent autobiographical memories: An fMRI study of young female subjects. *Cortex, 46*, 29–39.

OECD. (2014). *Health at a Glance: Europe 2014*. In *OECD Publishing*. Retrieved from http://www.oecd.org/health/health-at-a-glanceeurope-23056088.htm

Ofen, N., & Shing, Y. L. (2013). From perception to memory: Changes in memory systems across the lifespan. *Neuroscience and Biobehavioral Reviews, 37*(9, Part B), 2258–2267.

Ogolsky, B. G., Surra, C. A., & Monk, J. K. (2016). Pathways of commitment to wed: The development and dissolution of romantic relationships. *Journal of Marriage and Family, 78*(2), 293–310.

Oh, S., Kim, D., Lee, S., Jung, S. H., & Lee, S. Y. (2017). Association between exercise type and quality of life in a community-dwelling older people: A cross-sectional study. *Plos One, 12*(12).

Oldehinkel, A. J., & Bouma, E. C. (2011). Sensitivity to the depressogenic effect of stress and HPA-axis reactivity in adolescence: A review of gender differences. *Neuroscience and Biobehavioral Reviews, 35*(8), 1757–1770.

Oliver, D. P., Wittenberg-Lyles, E., Washington, K., Kruse, R. L., Albright, D. L., Baldwin, P. K., . . . Demiris, G. (2013). Hospice caregivers' experiences with pain management: "I'm not a doctor, and I don't know if I helped her go faster or slower." *Journal of Pain and Symptom Management, 46*(6), 846–858.

Olweus, D., Limber, S., & Mihalic, S. F. (1999). *Blueprints for violence prevention, Book 9: Bullying prevention program*. Boulder, CO: Center for the Study and Prevention of Violence, Institute of Behavioral Science, University of Colorado at Boulder.

Omar, H., McElderry, D., & Zakharia, R. (2003). Educating adolescents about puberty: What are we missing? *International Journal of Adolescent Medicine and Health, 15*, 79–83.

Onadja, Y., Atchessi, N., Soura, B. A., Rossier, C., & Zunzunegui, M. (2013). Gender differences in cognitive impairment and mobility disability in old age: A cross-sectional study in Ouagadougou, Burkina Faso. *Archives of Gerontology and Geriatrics, 57*(3), 311–318.

Onrust, S., Willemse, G., VanDenBout, J., & Cuijpers, P. (2010). Effects of a visiting service for older widowed individuals: A randomized clinical trial. *Death Studies, 34*(9), 777–803.

O'Rourke, N., Neufeld, E., Claxton, A., & Smith, J. A. Z. (2010). Knowing me—knowing you: Reported personality and trait discrepancies as predictors of marital idealization between long-wed spouses. *Psychology and Aging, 25*(2), 412–421.

O'Shea Carney, K., & Norris, M. P. (2017). Transforming long-term care: Expanded roles for mental health professionals. Washington, DC: American Psychological Association. doi:10.1037/15970-000

Ostrov, J. M., & Godleski, S. A. (2010). Toward an integrated gender-linked model of aggression subtypes in early and middle childhood. *Psychological Review, 117*(1), 233–242.

Ostrov, J. M., Murray-Close, D., Godleski, S. A., & Hart, E. J. (2013). Prospective associations between forms and functions of aggression and social and affective processes during early childhood. *Journal of Experimental Child Psychology, 116*(1), 19–36.

Ott, M. A., Millstein, S. G., Ofner, S., & Halpern-Felsher, B. L. (2006). Greater expectations: Adolescents' positive motivations for sex. *Perspectives on Sexual and Reproductive Health, 38*, 84–89.

Otterman, G., Lainpelto, K., & Lindblad, F. (2013). Factors influencing the prosecution of child physical abuse cases in a Swedish metropolitan area. *Acta Paediatrica, 102*(12), 1199–1203.

Owens, E. B., & Hinshaw, S. P. (2013). Perinatal problems and psychiatric comorbidity among children with ADHD. *Journal of Clinical Child and Adolescent Psychology, 42*(6), 762–768.

Paikoff, R. L., & Brooks-Gunn, J. (1991). Do parent–child relationships change during puberty? *Psychological Bulletin, 110*, 47–66.

Palkovitz, R. J. (2002). *Involved fathering and men's adult development: Provisional Balances*. Mahwah, NJ: Erlbaum.

Palladino, G. (1996). *Teenagers: An American history*. New York, NY: Basic Books.

Panagiotaki, G., Hopkins, M., Nobes, G., Ward, E., & Griffiths, D. (2018). Children's and adults' understanding of death: Cognitive, parental, and experiential influences. *Journal of Experimental Child Psychology, 166,* 96–115. doi:10.1016/j.jecp.2017.07.014

Pandelaere, M. (2016). Materialism and well-being: The role of consumption. *Current Opinion in Psychology, 10,* 33–38. doi.org/10.1016/j.copsyc.2015.10.027

Panicker, A. S., & Chelliah, A. (2016). Resilience and stress in children and adolescents with specific learning disability. *Journal of the Canadian Academy of Child & Adolescent Psychiatry, 25*(1), 17–23.

Panter-Brick, C., Grimon, M., Kalin, M., & Eggerman, M. (2015). Trauma memories, mental health, and resilience: A prospective study of Afghan youth. *Journal of Child Psychology & Psychiatry, 56*(7), 814–825. doi:10.1111/jcpp.12350

Parackal, S. M., Parackal, M. K., & Harraway, J. A. (2013). Prevalence and correlates of drinking in early pregnancy among women who stopped drinking on pregnancy recognition. *Maternal and Child Health Journal, 17*(3), 520–529.

Paredes, M. F., James, D., Gil-Perotin, S., Kim, H., Cotter, J. A., Ng, C., . . . Alvarez-Buylia, A. (2016). Extensive migration of young neurons into the infant human frontal lobe. *Science, 354*(6308), aaf 7073 1–7.

Parent, A.-S., Teilmann, G., Juul, A., Skakkebaek, N. E., Toppari, J., & Bourguignon, J.-P. (2003). The timing of normal puberty and the age limits of sexual precocity: Variations around the world, secular trends, and changes after migration. *Endocrine Reviews, 24,* 668–693.

Parent, M. C., & Moradi, B. (2011). His biceps become him: A test of objectification theory's application to drive for muscularity and propensity for steroid use in college men. *Journal of Counseling Psychology, 58,* 246–256.

Parham-Payne, W., Dickerson, B. J., & Everette, T. D. (2013). Trading the picket fence: Perceptions of childbirth, marriage, and career. *Journal of Sociology and Social Welfare, 40*(3), 85–104.

Park, D. C., & McDonough, I. M. (2013). The dynamic aging mind: Revelations from functional neuroimaging research. *Perspectives on Psychological Science, 8*(1), 62–67.

Park, Y. S., Kim, B. S. K., Chiang, J., & Ju, C. M. (2010). Acculturation, enculturation, parental adherence to Asian cultural values, parenting styles, and family conflict among Asian American college students. *Asian American Journal of Psychology, 1*(1), 67–79.

Parkes, C. M. (1987). *Bereavement: Studies of grief in adult life* (2nd ed.). Madison, CT: International Universities Press.

Parrish, D. E., von Sternberg, K., Castro, Y., & Velasquez, M. M. (2016). Processes of change in preventing alcohol exposed pregnancy: A mediation analysis. *Journal of Consulting and Clinical Psychology, 84*(9), 803–812.

Pasco Fearon, R., Bakermans-Kranenburg, M. J., van IJzendoorn, M. H., Lapsley, A., & Roisman, G. I. (2010). The significance of insecure attachment and disorganization in the development of children's externalizing behavior: A meta-analytic study. *Child Development, 81*(2), 435–456.

Pasco Fearon, R. M., & Belsky, J. (2011). Infant–mother attachment and the growth of externalizing problems across the primary-school years. *Journal of Child Psychology and Psychiatry, 52*(7), 782–791.

Paškvan, M., & Kubicek, B. (2017). The intensification of work. In C. Korunka & B. Kubicek (Eds.), *Job demands in a changing world of work: Impact on workers' health and performance and implications for research and practice* (pp. 25–43). Cham, Switzerland: Springer International Publishing. doi:10.1007/978-3-319-54678-0_3

Passini, C. M., Pihet, S., & Favez, N. (2014). Assessing specific discipline techniques: A mixed-methods approach. *Journal of Child and Family Studies, 23*(8), 1389–1402. doi:10.1007/s10826-013-9796-0

Pastorelli, C., Lansford, J. E., Luengo Kanacri, B. P., Malone, P. S., DiGiunta, L., Bacchini, D., . . . Sorbring, E. (2016). Positive parenting and children's prosocial behavior in eight countries. *Journal of Child Psychology and Psychiatry, 57*(7), 824–834. doi:10.1111/jcpp.12477

Patall, E. A., Cooper, H., & Robinson, J. C. (2008). The effects of choice on intrinsic motivation and related outcomes: A meta-analysis of research findings. *Psychological Bulletin, 134*(2), 270–300.

Paul, A. M. (2010). *Origins: How the nine months before birth shape our lives.* New York, NY: Free Press.

Paulus, M., & Moore, C. (2014). The development of recipient-dependent sharing behavior and sharing expectations in preschool children. *Developmental Psychology, 50*(3), 914–921.

Paulussen-Hoogeboom, M. C., Stams, G. J. J. M., Hermanns, J. M. A., & Peetsma, T. T. D. (2007). Child negative emotionality and parenting from infancy to preschool: A meta-analytic review. *Developmental Psychology, 43*(2), 438–453.

Peach, H. D., & Gaultney, J. F. (2013). Sleep, impulse control, and sensation-seeking predict delinquent behavior in adolescents, emerging adults, and adults. *Journal of Adolescent Health, 53*(2), 293–299.

Peacock, S., Forbes, D., Markle-Reid, M., Hawranik, P., Morgan, D., Jansen, L., & Henderson, S. R. (2010). The positive aspects of the caregiving journey with dementia: Using a strengths-based perspective to reveal opportunities. *Journal of Applied Gerontology, 29*(5), 640–659.

Peake, S. J., Dishion, T. J., Stormshak, E. A., Moore, W. E., & Pfeifer, J. H. (2013). Risk-taking and social exclusion in adolescence: Neural mechanisms underlying peer influences on decision-making. *Neuroimage, 82,* 23–34.

Peasgood, T., Bhardwaj, A., Biggs, K., Brazier, J. E., Coghill, D., Cooper, C. L., . . . Sonuga-Barke, E. S. (2016). The impact of ADHD on the health and well-being of ADHD children and their siblings. *European Child & Adolescent Psychiatry, 11,* 1217–1231. doi:10.1007/s00787-016-0841-6

Peck, S. C., Vida, M., & Eccles, J. S. (2008). Adolescent pathways to adulthood drinking: Sport activity involvement is not necessarily risky or protective. *Addiction, 103* (Suppl. 1), 69–83.

Pedersen, D. E. (2017). Quantity and quality: A more nuanced look at the association between family work and marital well-being. *Marriage & Family Review, 53*(3), 281. doi:10.1080/0149492 9.2016.1177632

Pedersen, N. L. (1996). Gerontological behavior genetics. In J. E. Birren, K. W. Schaie, R. P. Abeles, M. Gatz, & T. A. Salthouse (Eds.), *Handbook of the psychology of aging* (4th ed., pp. 59–77). San Diego, CA: Academic Press.

Pellegrini, A. D. (2006). The development and function of rough-and-tumble play in childhood and adolescence: A sexual selection theory perspective. In A. Goncu & S. Gaskins (Eds.), *Play and development: Evolutionary, sociocultural, and functional perspectives. The Jean Piaget Symposium Series* (pp. 77–98). Mahwah, NJ: Erlbaum.

Pellegrini, A. D., Long, J. D., Roseth, C. J., Bohn, C. M., & Van Ryzin, M. (2007). A short-term longitudinal study of preschoolers' (*Homo sapiens*) sex segregation: The role of physical activity, sex, and time. *Journal of Comparative Psychology, 121*(3), 282–289.

Pellegrini, A. D., & Smith, P. K. (Eds.). (2005). *The nature of play: Great apes and humans.* New York, NY: Guilford Press.

Penman, E. L., Breen, L. J., Hewitt, L. Y., & Prigerson, H. G. (2014). Public attitudes about normal and pathological grief. *Death Studies, 38*(8), 510–516.

Peper, J. S., & Dahl, R. E. (2013). The teenage brain: Surging hormones—Brain–behavior interactions during puberty. *Current Directions in Psychological Science, 22*(2), 134–139.

Perelli-Harris, B., & Styrc, M. (2018). Mental well-being differences in cohabitation and marriage: The role of childhood selection. *Journal of Marriage and Family, 1,* 239. doi:10.1111/jomf.12431

Pérez-Edgar, K., Bar-Haim, Y., McDermott, J. M., Chronis-Tuscano, A., Pine, D. S., & Fox, N. A. (2010a). Attention biases to threat and behavioral inhibition in early childhood shape adolescent social withdrawal. *Emotion, 10,* 349–357.

Pérez-Edgar, K., McDermott, J. N., Korelitz, K., Degnan, K. A., Curby, T. W., Pine, D. S., & Fox, N. A. (2010b). Patterns of sustained attention in infancy shape the developmental trajectory of social behavior from toddlerhood through adolescence. *Developmental Psychology, 46*(6), 1723–1730.

Perrig-Chiello, P., & Hutchison, S. (2010). Family caregivers of elderly persons: A differential perspective on stressors, resources, and well-being. *GeroPsych, 23*(4), 195–206.

Perrig-Chiello, P., Spahni, S., Höpflinger, F., & Carr, D. (2016). Cohort and gender differences in psychosocial adjustment to later-life widowhood. *The Journals of Gerontology: Series B: Psychological Sciences and Social Sciences, 71*(4), 765–774. doi:10.1093/geronb/gbv004

Persike, M., & Seiffge-Krenke, I. (2014). Is stress perceived differently in relationships with parents and peers? Inter- and intra-regional comparisons on adolescents from 21 nations. *Journal of Adolescence, 37*(4), 493–504.

Peskin, J. (1992). Ruse and representations: On children's ability to conceal information. *Developmental Psychology, 28,* 84–89.

Peters, E., Riksen-Walraven, J. M., Cillessen, A. H., & Weerth, C. D. (2011). Peer rejection and HPA activity in middle childhood: Friendship makes a difference. *Child Development, 82*(6), 1906–1920. doi:10.1111/j.1467-8624.2011.01647.x

Peterson, B. E. (1998). Case studies of midlife generativity: Analyzing motivation and realization. In D. P. McAdams & E. de St. Aubin (Eds.), *Generativity and adult development: How and why we care for the next generation* (pp. 101–131). Washington, DC: American Psychological Association.

Petraglia, F., Serour, G. I., & Chapron, C. (2013). The changing prevalence of infertility. *International Journal of Gynecology Obstetrics, 123* (Suppl. 2), S4–8.

Pettigrew, S., Jongenelis, M., Chikritzhs, T., Pratt, I. S., Slevin, T., & Glance, D. (2016). A comparison of alcohol consumption intentions among pregnant drinkers and their nonpregnant peers of child-bearing age. *Substance Use & Misuse, 51*(11), 1421–1427.

Pew Research Center. (2014). Public Trust in Government: 1958–2014. http://www.people-press.org/2014/11/13/public-trust-in-government/

Pfinder, M., Kunst, A. E., Feldmann, R., van Eijsden, M., & Vrijkotte, T. M. (2014). Educational differences in continuing or restarting drinking in early and late pregnancy: Role of psychological and physical problems. *Journal of Studies on Alcohol and Drugs, 75*(1), 47–55.

Phelan, P., Davidson, A. L., & Yu, H. C. (1998). *Adolescents' worlds: Negotiating family, peers, and school.* New York, NY: Teachers College Press.

Philbrook, L. E., & Teti, D. M. (2016). Associations between bedtime and nighttime parenting and infant cortisol in the first year. *Developmental Psychobiology, 58*(8), 1087–1100. doi:10.1002/dev.21442

Phillips, D. A., & Lowenstein, A. E. (2011). Early care, education and child development. *American Review of Psychology, 62,* 483–500.

Phillips, J. L., Halcomb, E. J., & Davidson, P. M. (2011). End-of-life care pathways in acute and hospice care: An integrative review. *Journal of Pain and Symptom Management, 41*(5), 940–955.

Phinney, J. S. (2006). Acculturation is not an independent variable: Approaches to studying acculturation as a complex process. In M. H. Bornstein & L. R. Cote (Eds.), *Acculturation and parent–child relationships: Measurement and development* (pp. 79–95). Mahwah, NJ: Erlbaum.

Piaget, J. (1950). *The psychology of intelligence.* Oxford, England: Harcourt.

Piaget, J. (1962). *Play, dreams and imitation in childhood.* New York, NY: Norton. (Original work published 1951)

Piaget, J. (1965). *The moral judgment of the child* (Paperback ed.). New York, NY: Free Press.

Piaget, J. (1971). *The psychology of intelligence.* London, England: Routledge & Kegan Paul. (Original work published 1950)

Pieloch, K. A., McCullough, M. B., & Marks, A. K. (2016). Resilience of children with refugee statuses: A research review. *Canadian Psychology, 57*(4), 330–339. doi:10.1037/cap0000073

Pinker, S. (2011). *The better angels of our nature: Why violence has declined.* New York, NY: Viking.

Pinquart, M. (2013). Do the parent–child relationship and parenting behaviors differ between families with a child with and without chronic illness? A meta-analysis. *Journal of Pediatric Psychology, 38*(7), 708–721.

Pinquart, M., Feubner, C., & Ahnert, L. (2013). Meta-analytic evidence for stability in attachments from infancy to early adulthood. *Attachment & Human Development, 15*(2), 189–218.

Pinquart, M., & Schindler, I. (2007). Changes of life satisfaction in the transition to retirement: A latent-class approach. *Psychology and Aging, 22*(3), 442–455.

Pirhonen, J., & Pietilä, I. (2016). Perceived resident–facility fit and sense of control in assisted living. *Journal of Aging Studies, 38,* 47–56. doi:10.1016/j.jaging.2016.04.006

Plant, C. P., Donohue, B., & Holland, J. M. (2016). Examination of life satisfaction, child maltreatment potential and substance use in mothers referred for treatment by child protective services for child neglect and substance abuse: Implications for intervention planning. *Applied Research in Quality of Life, 3,* 805. doi:10.1007/s11482-015-9398-7

Plant, T. M. (2015). The hypothalamo-pituitary-gonadal axis. *Journal of Endocrinology, 226*(2), T41. doi:10.1530/JOE-15-0113

Plomin, R., & Bergeman, C. S. (1991). The nature of nurture: Genetic influence on "environmental" measures. *Behavioral and Brain Sciences, 14,* 373–427.

Plomin, R., DeFries, J. C., Craig, I. W., & McGuffin, P. (2003). Behavioral genomics. In R. Plomin, J. C. DeFries, I. W. Craig, & P. McGuffin (Eds.), *Behavioral genetics in the postgenomic era* (pp. 531–540). Washington, DC: American Psychological Association.

Plomin, R., & Spinath, F. M. (2004). Intelligence: Genetics, genes, and genomics. *Journal of Personality and Social Psychology, 86,* 112–129.

Pnevmatikos, D., & Trikkaliotis, I. (2013). Intra-individual differences in executive functions during childhood: The role of emotions. *Journal of Experimental Child Psychology, 115*(2), 245–261.

Poirier, F. E., & Smith, E. O. (1974). Socializing functions of primate play. *American Zoologist, 14,* 275–287.

Polanco-Roman, L., & Miranda, R. (2013). Culturally related stress, hopelessness, and vulnerability to depressive symptoms and suicidal ideation in emerging adulthood. *Behavior Therapy, 44*(1), 75–87.

Polivka, L., & Baozhen, L. (2013). The future of retirement security around the globe. *Generations, 37*(1), 39–45.

Pölkki, P. L., & Vornanen, R. H. (2016). Role and success of Finnish early childhood education and care in supporting child welfare clients: Perspectives from parents and professionals. *Early Childhood Education Journal, 44*(6), 581–594. doi:10.1007/s10643-015-0746-x

Poortman, A. R., & Seltzer, J. A. (2007). Parents' expectations about childrearing after divorce: Does anticipating difficulty deter divorce? *Journal of Marriage and Family, 69*(1), 254–269.

Pope, N. D. (2013). Views on aging: How caring for an aging parent influences adult daughters' perspectives on later life. *Journal of Adult Development, 20*(1), 46–56.

Porat-Zyman, G., Taubman-Ben-Ari, O., & Spielman, V. (2017). Dyadic transition to parenthood: A longitudinal assessment of personal growth among parents of pre- and full-term infants. *Stress and Health, 1,* 24. doi:10.1002/smi.2669

Porfeli, E. J., & Mortimer, J. T. (2010). Intrinsic work value–reward dissonance and work satisfaction during young adulthood. *Journal of Vocational Behavior, 76,* 507–519.

Posada, G., Trumbell, J., Noblega, M., Plata, S., Pena, P., Carbonell, O. A., & Lu, T. (2016). Maternal sensitivity and child secure base use in early childhood: Studies in different cultural contexts. *Child Development, 87*(1), 297–311. doi:10.1111/cdev.12454

Potocnik, K., Tordera, N., & Peiro, J. (2013). Truly satisfied with your retirement or just resigned? Pathways toward different patterns of retirement satisfaction. *Journal of Applied Gerontology, 32*(2), 164–187.

Potts, M., Prata, N., & Sahin-Hodoglugil, N. N. (2010). Maternal mortality: One death every 7 min. *The Lancet, 375*(9728), 1762–1763.

Poulin, F., & Chan, A. (2010). Friendship stability and change in childhood and adolescence. *Developmental Review, 30*(3), 257–272.

Poulin, M., & Silver, R. (2008). World benevolence beliefs and well-being across the lifespan. *Psychology and Aging, 23,* 19.

Powers, S. M., Bisconti, T. L., & Bergeman, C. S. (2014). Trajectories of social support and well-being across the first two years of widowhood. *Death Studies, 38*(8), 499–509.

Pressler, K. A., & Ferraro, K. F. (2010). Assistive device use as a dynamic acquisition process in later life. *The Gerontologist, 50*(3), 371–381.

Preston, S. H. (1991). *Fatal years: Child mortality in late nineteenth-century America.* Princeton, NJ: Princeton University Press.

Prevost, S. S., & Wallace, J. B. (2009). Dying in institutions. In J. L. Werth & D. Blevins (Eds.), *Decision making near the end-of-life: Issues, developments, and future directions. Series in death, dying and bereavement* (pp. 189–208). New York, NY: Routledge/Taylor & Francis Group.

Prinstein, M. J., & La Greca, A. M. (2002). Peer crowd affiliation and internalizing distress in childhood and adolescence: A longitudinal follow-back study. *Journal of Research on Adolescence, 12,* 325–351.

Prochaska, M. T., Putman, M. S., Tak, H. J., Yoon, J. D., & Curlin, F. A. (2017). U.S. physicians overwhelmingly endorse hospice as the better option for most patients at the end of life. *American Journal of Hospice & Palliative Medicine, 34*(6), 556–558. doi:10.1177/1049909116636344

Pryor, J. H., Hurtado, S., DeAngelo, L., Blake, L. P., & Tran, S. (2011). The American freshman: National norms, Fall 2010. Los Angeles, Higher Education Research Institute, UCLA.

Puhl, R. M., & Latner, J. D. (2007). Stigma, obesity, and the health of the nation's children. *Psychological Bulletin, 133*(4), 557–580.

Punzo, G., Castellano, R., & Buonocore, M. (2017). Job satisfaction in the 'big four' of Europe: Reasoning between feeling and uncertainty through cub models. *Social Indicators Research.* doi:10.1007/s11205-017-1715-0

Pushkar, D., Chaikelson, J., Conway, M., Etezadi, J., Giannopolous, C., Li, K., & Wrosch, C. (2010). Testing continuity and activity variables as predictors of positive and negative affect in retirement. *Journals of Gerontology: Psychological Sciences, 65B*(1), 42–49.

Qu, Y. (2014). The comparative study of household elderly care in China, the Philippines and Japan. *Home Health Care Management and Practice, 26*(3), 175–181.

Quinn, J. F., & Cahill, K. E. (2016). The new world of retirement income security in America. *American Psychologist, 71*(4), 321–333. doi:10.1037/a0040276

Rabin, J. S., Gilboa, A., Stuss, D. T., Mar, R. A., & Rosenbaum, R. S. (2010). Common and unique neural correlates of autobiographical memory and theory of mind. *Journal of Cognitive Neuroscience, 22*(6), 1095–1111.

Rabins, P. V. (2011, April). Memory. *The John Hopkins White Papers, 48.*

Rahman, M. M., Khan, H. A., & Hafford-Letchfield, T. (2016). Correlates of socioeconomic status and the health of older people in the United Kingdom. *Illness, Crisis & Loss, 24*(4), 195–216. doi:10.1177/1054137315608347

Ralph, D. (2016). Who should do the caring? Involved fatherhood and ambivalent gendered moral rationalities among cohabiting/married Irish parents. *Community Work and Family, 19*(1), 63–79.

Ramsay, S. M., & Santella, R. M. (2011). The definition of life: A survey of obstetricians and neonatologists in New York City hospitals regarding extremely premature births. *Maternal and Child Health Journal, 15*, 446–452.

Ramsey, E., Kelly-Vance, L., Allen, J. A., Rosol, O., & Yoerger, M. (2016). Autism spectrum disorder prevalence rates in the United States: Methodologies, challenges, and implications for individual states. *Journal of Developmental and Physical Disabilities, 28*(6), 803–820. doi:10.1007/s10882-016-9510-4

Ratner, N. B. (2013). Why talk with children matters: Clinical implications of infant- and child-directed speech research. *Seminars in Speech and Language, 34*(4), 203–214.

Rauer, A. J., Pettit, G. S., Lansford, J. E., Bates, J. E., & Dodge, K. A. (2013). Romantic relationship patterns in young adulthood and their developmental antecedents. *Developmental Psychology, 49*(11), 2159–2171.

Ravussin, E., Redman, L. M., Rochon, J., Das, S. K., Fontana, L., Kraus, W. E., . . . Roberts, S. B. (2015). A 2-year randomized controlled trial of human caloric restriction: Feasibility and effects on predictors of health span and longevity. *The Journals of Gerontology*, Series A, 70(9), 1097–1105. doi:10.1093/gerona/glv057

Razeghi, N., Nikiju, M., Mujembari, A. K., & Masihi, A. Z. (2011). Relationship between Big Five Personality Factors and marital satisfaction. *Developmental Psychology: Journal of Iranian Psychologists, 7*(27), 269–278.

Reijneveld, S. A., van der Wal, M. F., Brugman, E., Sing, R. A. H., & Verloove-Vanhorick, S. P. (2004). Infant crying and abuse. *Lancet, 364*, 1340–1342.

Reijntjes, A., Vermande, M., Olthof, T., Goossens, F. A., Aleva, L., & Meulen, M. V. (2016). Defending victimized peers: Opposing the bully, supporting the victim, or both? *Aggressive Behavior, 42*(6), 585–597. doi:10.1002/ab.21653

Reimer, J., Paolitto, D. P., & Hersh, R. H. (1983). *Promoting moral growth: From Piaget to Kohlberg* (2nd ed.). New York, NY: Longman.

Reimer, K. (2003). Committed to caring: Transformation in adolescent moral identity. *Applied Developmental Science, 7*, 129–137.

Reindl, M., Gniewosz, B., & Reinders, H. (2016). Socialization of emotion regulation strategies through friends. *Journal of Adolescence, 49*, 146–157. doi:10.1016/j.adolescence.2016.03.008

Reissman, C., Aron, A., & Bergen, M. R. (1993). Shared activities and marital satisfaction: Causal direction and self-expansion versus boredom. *Journal of Social and Personal Relationships, 10*, 243–254.

Ren, R., Guo, F., & Chen, Z. (2015). Early puberty and delinquent behaviors among adolescent girls: Moderating of parenting. *Chinese Journal of Clinical Psychology, 23*(1), 178–181.

Reuter-Lorenz, P. A. (2013). Aging and cognitive neuroimaging: A fertile union. *Perspectives on Psychological Science, 8*(1), 68–71.

Rhodes, R. L., Elwood, B., Lee, S. C., Tiro, J. A., Halm, E. A., & Skinner, C. S. (2017). The desires of their hearts: The multidisciplinary perspectives of African Americans on end-of-life care in the African American community. *American Journal of Hospice & Palliative Medicine, 34*(6), 510–517. doi:10.1177/1049909116631776

Richter, B., Lindahl, K., & Malik, N. (2017). Examining ethnic differences in parental rejection of LGB youth sexual identity. *Journal of Family Psychology, 31*(2), 244–249.

Rigoli, D., Piek, J., Kane, R., Whillier, A., Baxter, C., & Wilson, P. (2013). An 18-month follow-up investigation of motor coordination and working memory in primary school children. *Human Movement Science, 32*(5), 1116–1126.

Rilling, J. K. (2013). The neural and hormonal bases of human parental care. *Neuropsychologia, 51*(4), 731–747.

Rinehart, M. S., & Kiselica, M. S. (2010). Helping men with the trauma of miscarriage. *Psychotherapy: Theory, Research, Practice, Training, 47*(3), 288–295.

Rispoli, K. M., McGoey, K. E., Koziol, N. A., & Schreiber, J. B. (2013). The relation of parenting, child temperament, and attachment security in early childhood to social competence at school entry. *Journal of School Psychology, 51*(5), 643–658.

Rist, P. M., Nguyen, T. T., Whitmer, R. A., & Glymour, M. M. (2016). Modifiable risk factors for nursing home admission among individuals with high and low dementia risk. *Archives of Gerontology and Geriatrics, 65*, 140–145. doi:10.1016/j.archger.2016.03.016

Rizzo, M. T., Elenbaas, L., Cooley, S., & Killen, M. (2016). Children's recognition of fairness and others' welfare in a resource allocation task: Age-related changes. *Developmental Psychology, 52*(8), 1307–1317. doi:10.1037/dev0000134

Roache, R. (2016). Infertility and non-traditional families. *Journal of Medical Ethics: Journal of the Institute of Medical Ethics, 42*(9), 557–558.

Roberts, A. L., Lyall, K., Rich-Edwards, J. W., Ascherio, A., & Weisskopf, M. G. (2013). Association of maternal exposure to childhood abuse with elevated risk for autism in offspring. *JAMA Psychiatry, 70*(5), 508–515.

Roberts, C. (2016). Tanner's puberty scale: Exploring the historical entanglements of children, scientific photography and sex. *Sexualities, 19*(3), 328–346. doi:10.1177/1363460715593477

Robles, T. F., Slatcher, R. B., Trombello, J. M., & McGinn, M. M. (2014). Marital quality and health: A meta-analytic review. *Psychological Bulletin, 140*(1), 140–187.

Rodgers, R. F., & DuBois, R. H. (2016). Cognitive biases to appearance-related stimuli in body dissatisfaction: A systematic review. *Clinical Psychology Review, 46*, 1–11. doi.org/10.1016/j.cpr.2016.04.006

Rodin, J., & Langer, E. J. (1980). Aging labels: The decline of control and the fall of self-esteem. *Journal of Social Issues, 36*, 12–29.

Rodkin, P. C., & Roisman, G. I. (2010). Antecedents and correlates of the popular-aggressive phenomenon in elementary school. *Child Development, 81*(3), 837–850.

Rodkin, P. C., Ryan, A. M., Jamison, R., & Wilson, T. (2013). Social goals, social behavior, and social status in middle childhood. *Developmental Psychology, 49*(6), 1139–1150.

Rodrigues, R., & Schmidt, A. E. (2010). Expenditures for long-term care: At the crossroads between family and state. *GeroPsych, 23*(4), 183–193.

Rodriguez, C. M., & Henderson, R. C. (2010). Who spares the rod? Religious orientation, social conformity, and child abuse potential. *Child Abuse & Neglect, 34,* 84–94.

Roffwarg, H. P., Muzio, J. N., & Dement, W. C. (1966, April 29). Ontogenetic development of the human sleep–dream cycle. *Science, 152,* 604–619.

Rogoff, B., Paradise, R., Arauz, R. M., Correa-Chavez, M., & Angelillo, C. (2003). Firsthand learning through intent participation. *Annual Review of Psychology, 54,* 175–203.

Rohlf, H., Busching, R., & Krahé, B. (2016). The socializing effect of classroom aggression on the development of aggression and social rejection: A two-wave multilevel analysis. *Journal of School Psychology, 58,* 57–72. doi:10.1016/j.jsp.2016.05.002

Rohlfsen, L. S., & Kronenfeld, J. J. (2014). Gender differences in functional health: Latent curve analysis assessing differential exposure. *Journals of Gerontology Series B: Psychological Sciences and Social Sciences, 69*(4), 1.

Rojas-Flores, L., Herrera, S., Currier, J. M., Lin, E. Y., Kulzer, R., & Foy, D. W. (2013). "We are raising our children in fear": War, community violence, and parenting practices in El Salvador. *International Perspectives in Psychology: Research, Practice, Consultation, 2*(4), 269–285.

Romano, E., Babchishin, L., Pagani, L. S., & Kohen, D. (2010). School readiness and later achievement: Replication and extension using a nationwide Canadian survey. *Developmental Psychology, 46*(5), 995–1007.

Romeo, R. D. (2013). The teenage brain: The stress response and the adolescent brain. *Current Directions in Psychological Science, 22*(2), 140–145.

Rorie, M., Gottfredson, D. C., Cross, A., Wilson, D., & Connell, N. M. (2011). Structure and deviancy training in afterschool programs. *Journal of Adolescence, 34,* 105–117.

Rose, A. J., & Asher, S. R. (2000). Children's friendships. In C. Hendrick & S. S. Hendrick (Eds.), *Close relationships: A sourcebook* (pp. 47–57). Thousand Oaks, CA: Sage.

Rose, J., Vassar, R., Cahill-Rowley, K., Guzman, X., Stevenson, D. K., & Barnea-Goraly, N. (2014). Brain microstructural development at near-term age in very-low-birth-weight preterm infants: An atlas-based diffusion imaging study. *Neuroimage, 86,* 244–256.

Rosen, T., Lachs, M. S., Teresi, J., Eimicke, J., Van Haitsma, K., & Pillemer, K. (2016). Staff-reported strategies for prevention and management of resident-to-resident elder mistreatment in long-term care facilities. *Journal of Elder Abuse & Neglect, 28*(1), 1. doi:10.1080/08946566.2015.1029659

Rosenfield, R. L., Lipton, R. B., & Drum, M. L. (2009). The larche, pubarche, and menarche attainment in children with normal and elevated body mass index. *Pediatrics, 123,* 84–88.

Rosenthal, M., Wallace, G. L., Lawson, R., Wills, M. C., Dixon, E., Yerys, B. E., & Kenworthy, L. (2013). Impairments in real-world executive function increase from childhood to adolescence in autism spectrum disorders. *Neuropsychology, 27*(1), 13–18.

Rothenberg, J. Z., & Gardner, D. S. (2011). Protecting older workers: The failure of the Age Discrimination in Employment Act of 1967. *Journal of Sociology & Social Welfare, 38*(1), 9–30.

Rothermund, K., & Brandtstädter, J. (2003). Depression in later life: Cross-sequential patterns and possible determinants. *Psychology and Aging, 18,* 80–90.

Roussotte, F., Soderberg, L., & Sowell, E. (2010). Structural, metabolic and functional brain abnormalities as a result of prenatal exposure to drugs of abuse: Evidence from neuroimaging. *Neuropsychology Review, 20*(4), 376–397.

Rowe, D. C. (2003). Assessing genotype–environment interactions and correlations in the postgenomic era. In R. Plomin, J. C. DeFries, I. W. Craig, & P. McGuffin (Eds.), *Behavioral genetics in the postgenomic era* (pp. 71–86). Washington, DC: American Psychological Association.

Rowe, J. W., & Kahn, R. L. (1998). *Successful aging.* New York, NY: Pantheon Books.

Rowe, M. L., Levine, S. C., Fisher, J. A., & Goldin-Meadow, S. (2009). Does linguistic input play the same role in language learning for children with and without early brain injury? *Developmental Psychology, 45,* 90–102.

Royal College of Obstetricians and Gynaecologists. (1999). *Alcohol consumption in pregnancy.* Retrieved from http://www.rcog.org/uk/index.asp?PageID=509

Royer, N., & Moreau, C. (2016). A survey of Canadian early childhood educators' psychological well-being at work. *Early Childhood Education Journal, 44*(2), 135–146. doi:10.1007/s10643-015-1696-3

Rubin, M. (2013). Grandparents as caregivers: Emerging issues for the profession. *Journal of Human Behavior in the Social Environment, 23*(3), 330–344.

Ruble, D. N., Martin, C., & Berenbaum, S. A. (2006). Gender development. In N. Eisenberg, W. Damon, & R. M. Lerner (Eds.), *Handbook of child psychology: Vol. 3. Social, emotional, and personality development* (6th ed., pp. 858–932). Hoboken, NJ: Wiley.

Runions, K. C. (2013). Toward a conceptual model of motive and self-control in cyber-aggression: Rage, revenge, reward, and recreation. *Journal of Youth and Adolescence, 42*(5), 751–771.

Rusbult, C. E., Kumashiro, M., Kubacka, K. E., & Finkel, E. J. (2009). "The part of me that you bring out": Ideal similarity and the Michelangelo phenomenon. *Journal of Personality and Social Psychology, 96,* 61–82.

Rushing, C., & Sparks, M. (2017). The mother's perspective: Factors considered when choosing to enter a stay-at-home father and working mother relationship. *American Journal of Men's Health, 11*(4), 1260–1268.

Rushton, J. P., & Jensen, A. R. (2005). Thirty years of research on race differences in cognitive ability. *Psychology, Public Policy, and Law, 11,* 235–294.

Ryan, J. J., Glass, L. A., & Bartels, J. M. (2010). Stability of the WISC-IV in a sample of elementary and middle school children. *Applied Neuropsychology, 17*(1), 68–72.

Ryan, R. M., Deci, E. L., Grolnick, W. S., & La Guardia, J. G. (2006). The significance of autonomy and autonomy support in psychological development and psychopathology. In D. Cicchetti & D. J. Cohen (Eds.), *Developmental psychopathology: Vol. 1. Theory and method* (2nd ed., pp. 795–849). Hoboken, NJ: John Wiley & Sons Inc.

Ryan-Krause, P. (2011). Attention deficit hyperactivity disorder: Part III. *Journal of Pediatric Health Care, 25*(1), 50–53.

Rybash, J. M., Hoyer, W. J., & Roodin, P. (1986). *Adult cognition and aging: Developmental changes in processing, knowing, and thinking.* New York, NY: Pergamon Press.

Ryckebosch-Dayez, A., Zech, E., Mac Cord, J., & Taverne, C. (2016). Daily life stressors and coping strategies during widowhood: A diary study after one year of bereavement. *Death Studies, 40*(8), 461–478. doi:10.1080/07481187.2016.1177750

Sabey, A. K., Rauer, A. J., & Jensen, J. F. (2014). Compassionate love as a mechanism linking sacred qualities of marriage to older couples' marital satisfaction. *Journal of Family Psychology, 28*(5), 594–603.

Sabik, N. J., Cole, E. R., & Ward, L. M. (2010). Are all minority women equally buffered from negative body image? Intra-ethnic moderators of the buffering hypothesis. *Psychology of Women Quarterly, 34*(2), 139–151.

Sadeh, A., Jua-Hanael, M., Livne-Karp, E., Kahn, M., Tkotzky, L., Anders, T. F., . . . Silvan, Y. (2016). Low parental tolerance for infant crying: An underlying factor in infant sleep problems? *Journal of Sleep Research, 25,* 501–507.

Saenz, J., & Alexander, G. M. (2013). Postnatal testosterone levels and disorder relevant behavior in the second year of life. *Biological Psychology, 94*(1), 152–159.

Saeteren, B., Lindström, U. Å., & Nåden, D. (2010). Latching onto life: Living in the area of tension between the possibility of life and the necessity of death. *Journal of Clinical Nursing, 20,* 811–818.

Saigal, S., Day, K. L., Lieshout, R. J., Schmidt, L. A., Morrison, K. M., & Boyle, M. H. (2016). Health, wealth, social integration, and sexuality of extremely low-birth-weight prematurely born adults in the fourth decade of life. *JAMA Pediatrics, 170*(7), 678. doi:10.1001/jamapediatrics.2016.0289

Sakyi, K., Surkan, P. J., Fombonne, E., Cholett, A., & Melchior, M. (2016). Childhood friendships and psychological difficulties in young adulthood: An 18-year follow up study. *European Child and Adolescent Psychiatry, 24*(7), 815–826.

Sala, M., & Levinson, C. A. (2016). The longitudinal relationship between worry and disordered eating: Is worry a precursor or consequence of disordered eating? *Eating Behaviors, 23,* 28–32.

Saleh, R. H., & Luppicini, R. (2017). Exploring the challenges of divorce on Saudi women. *Journal of Family History, 42*(2), 184–198. doi:10.1177/0363199017695721

Salmon, K., & Reese, E. (2015). Talking (or not talking) about the past: The influence of parent–child conversation about negative experiences on children's memories. *Applied Cognitive Psychology, 29*(6), 791–801. doi:10.1002/acp.3186

Salvia, E., Petit, C., Champely, S., Chomette, R., Di Rienzo, F., & Collet, C. (2016). Effects of age and task load on drivers' response accuracy and reaction time when responding to traffic lights. *Frontiers in Aging Neuroscience, 8,* 169.

Samimi, P., & Alderson, K. G. (2014). Sexting among undergraduate students. *Computers in Human Behavior, 31,* 230–241.

Sánchez, B., Esparza, P., Cölon, Y., & Davis, K. E. (2010). Tryin' to make it during the transition from high school: The role of family obligation attitudes and economic context for Latino emerging adults. *Journal of Adolescent Research, 25*(6), 858–884.

Sandberg, L. (2013). Just feeling a naked body close to you: Men, sexuality and intimacy in later life. *Sexualities, 16*(3–4), 261–282.

Sandberg, L. (2015). In lust we trust? Masculinity and sexual desire in later life. *Men and Masculinities, 19*(2), 192–208. doi.org/10.1177/1097184X15606948

Sandberg, L. (2016). Being there for my grandchild—Grandparents' responses to their grandchildren's exposure to domestic violence. *Child and Family Social Work, 21*(2), 136–145. doi.org/10.1111/cfs.12123

Sander, J., Schupp, J., & Richter, D. (2017). Getting together: Social contact frequency across the life span. *Developmental Psychology, 53*(8), 1571–1588. doi:10.1037/dev0000349

Sandler, I. N., Wheeler, L. A., & Braver, S. L. (2013). Relations of parenting quality, interparental conflict, and overnights with mental health problems of children in divorcing families with high legal conflict. *Journal of Family Psychology, 27*(6), 915–924.

Sandler, I. N., Wolchik, S. A., & Ayers, T. S. (2008). Resilience rather than recovery: A contextual framework on adaptation following bereavement. *Death Studies, 32,* 59–73.

Santesso, D. L., Schmidt, L. A., & Trainor, L. J. (2007). Frontal brain electrical activity (EEG) and heart rate in response to affective infant directed (ID) speech in 9-month-old infants. *Brain and Cognition, 65,* 14–21.

Santos, C. E., & Collins, M. A. (2016). Ethnic identity, school connectedness, and achievement in standardized tests among Mexican-origin youth. *Cultural Diversity & Ethnic Minority Psychology, 22*(3), 447–452.

Satici, S. A., & Uysal, R. (2015). Well-being and problematic Facebook use. *Computers in Human Behavior, 49,* 185–190.

Sato, K., Oikawa, M., Hiwatashi, M., Sato, M., & Oyamada, N. (2016). Factors relating to the mental health of women who were pregnant at the time of the Great East Japan earthquake: Analysis from month 10 to month 48 after the earthquake. *BioPsycho-Social Medicine, 10*(1). doi:10.1186/s13030-016-0072-6

Sattler, J. M. (2001). *Assessment of children: Cognitive applications* (4th ed.). La Mesa, CA: Sattler.

Savin-Williams, R. C. (2001). *Mom, Dad, I'm gay. How families negotiate coming out.* Washington, DC: American Psychological Association.

Savin-Williams, R. C. (2008). Then and now: Recruitment, definition, diversity, and positive attributes of same-sex populations. *Developmental Psychology, 44*(1), 135–138.

Savishinsky, J. (2004). The volunteer and the Sannyasin: Archetypes of retirement in America and India. *International Journal of Aging & Human Development, 59,* 25–41.

Saxbe, D., Lyden, H., Edelstein, R., Wardecker, B., Chopik, W., & Moors, A. (2017). Fathers' decline in testosterone and synchrony with partner testosterone during pregnancy predicts greater postpartum relationship investment. *Hormones and Behavior, 90,* 39–47. doi:10.1016/j.yhbeh.2016.07.005

Saxon, S. V., Etten, M., & Perkins, E. A. (2010). *Physical change and aging: A guide for the helping professions* (5th ed.). New York, NY: Springer.

Sayer, L. C., Bianchi, S. M., & Robinson, J. P. (2004). Are parents investing less in children? Trends in mothers' and fathers' time with children. *American Journal of Sociology, 110,* 1–43.

Scahill, L., Bearss, K., Lecavalier, L., Smith, T., Swiezy, N., Aman, M. G., . . . Johnson, C. (2016). Effect of parent training on adaptive behavior in children with autism spectrum disorder and disruptive behavior: Results of a randomized trial. *Journal of the American Academy of Child & Adolescent Psychiatry, 55*(7), 602–609. doi:10.1016/j.jaac.2016.05.001

Scarr, S. (1997). Behavior-genetic and socialization theories of intelligence: Truce and reconciliation. In R. J. Sternberg & E. L. Grigorenko (Eds.), *Intelligence, heredity, and environment* (pp. 3–41). New York, NY: Cambridge University Press.

Scarr, S., & Deater-Deckard, K. (1997). Family effects on individual differences in development. In S. S. Luthar, J. A. Burack, D. Cicchetti, & J. R. Weisz (Eds.), *Developmental psychopathology: Perspectives on adjustment, risk, and disorder* (pp. 115–136). New York, NY: Cambridge University Press.

Schafer, M. H. (2013). Structural advantages of good health in old age: Investigating the health-begets-position hypothesis with a full social network. *Research on Aging, 35*(3), 348–370.

Schaie, K. W. (1996). Intellectual development in adulthood. In J. E. Birren, K. W. Schaie, R. P. Abeles, M. Gatz, & T. A. Salthouse (Eds.), *Handbook of the psychology of aging* (4th ed., pp. 266–286). San Diego, CA: Academic Press.

Schaie, K. W., Willis, S. L., & Caskie, G. I. L. (2004). The Seattle Longitudinal Study: Relationship between personality and cognition. *Aging, Neuropsychology, and Cognition, 11,* 304–324.

Schaie, K. W., & Zanjani, F. A. K. (2006). Intellectual development across adulthood. In C. Hoare (Ed.), *Handbook of adult development and learning* (pp. 99–122). New York, NY: Oxford University Press.

Schellinger, K., & Talmi, A. (2013). Off the charts? Considerations for interpreting parent reports of toddler hyperactivity. *Infant Mental Health Journal, 34*(5), 417–419.

Scheres, A., Tontsch, C., & Lee Thoeny, A. (2013). Steep temporal reward discounting in ADHD-Combined type: Acting upon feelings. *Psychiatry Research, 209*(2), 207–213.

Schirduan, V., & Case, K. (2004). Mindful curriculum leadership for students with attention deficit hyperactivity disorder: Leading in elementary schools by using multiple intelligences theory (SUMIT). *Teachers College Record, 106,* 87–95.

Schlegel, A. (1995). The cultural management of adolescent sexuality. In P. R. Abramson & S. D. Pinkerton (Eds.), *Sexual nature, sexual culture* (pp. 177–194). Chicago, IL: University of Chicago Press.

Schlegel, A., & Barry, H., III. (1991). *Adolescence: An anthropological inquiry.* New York, NY: Free Press.

Schlinger, H. D. (2003). The myth of intelligence. *Psychological Record, 53,* 15–32.

Schmid, G., Schreier, A., Meyer, R., & Wolke, D. (2010). A prospective study in the persistence of infant crying, sleeping and feeding problems and preschool behavior. *Acta Pædiatrica, 99,* 286–290.

Schneidman, E. (Ed.). (1976). *Death: Current perspectives.* Palo Alto, CA: Mayfield.

Schnor, C., Pasteels, I., & Van Bavel, J. (2017). Sole physical custody and mother's repartnering after divorce. *Journal of Marriage and Family, 3,* 879. doi:10.1111/jomf.12389

Scholte, R., Sentse, M., & Granic, I. (2010). Do actions speak louder than words? Classroom attitudes and behavior in relation to bullying in early adolescence. *Journal of Clinical Child & Adolescent Psychology, 39*(6), 789–799.

Schooler, C. (1999). The workplace environment: Measurement, psychological effects, and basic issues. In S. L. Friedman & T. D. Wachs (Eds.), *Measuring environment across the life span: Emerging methods and concepts* (pp. 229–246). Washington, DC: American Psychological Association.

Schooler, C. (2001). The intellectual effects of the demands of the work environment. In R. J. Sternberg & E. L. Grigorenko (Eds.), *Environmental effects on cognitive abilities* (pp. 363–380). Mahwah, NJ: Erlbaum.

Schooler, C., Mulatu, M. S., & Oates, G. (2004). Occupational self-direction, intellectual functioning, and self-directed orientation in older workers: Findings and implications for individuals and societies. *American Journal of Sociology, 110,* 161–197.

Schramm, D. G., Harris, S. M., Whiting, J. B., Hawkins, A. J., Brown, M., & Porter, R. (2013). Economic costs and policy implications associated with divorce: Texas as a case study. *Journal of Divorce & Remarriage, 54*(1), 1–24.

Schreiner, L. A., Noel, P., Anderson, E., & Cantwell, L. (2011). The impact of faculty and staff on high-risk college student persistence. *Journal of College Student Development, 52*(3), 321–338.

Schueler, C. M., & Prinz, R. J. (2013). The role of caregiver contingent

responsiveness in promoting compliance in young children. *Child Psychiatry and Human Development, 44*(3), 370–381.

Schulz, V. M., Crombeen, A. M., Marshall, D., Shadd, J., LaDonna, K. A., & Lingard, L. (2017). Beyond simple planning: Existential dimensions of conversations with patients at risk of dying from heart failure. *Journal of Pain and Symptom Management, 54*(5), 637–644.

Schuster, M. A., Reisner, S. L., & Onorato, S. E. (2016). Beyond bathrooms—Meeting the health needs of transgender people. *New England Journal of Medicine, 374,* 101–103.

Schwartz, C. E., Wright, C. I., Shin, L. M., Kagan, J., & Rauch, S. L. (2003, June 20). Inhibited and uninhibited infants "grown up": Adult amygdalar response to novelty. *Science, 300,* 1952–1953.

Schwartz, S. J. (2016). Turning point for a turning point: Advancing emerging adulthood theory and research. *Emerging Adulthood, 4*(5), 307–317.

Schwartz, S. J, Meca, A., Hardy, S., Zamboanga, B., Waterman, A., Picariello, S., . . . Forthun, L. (2015). Identity in young adulthood: Links with mental health and risky behavior. *Journal of Applied Developmental Psychology, 36,* 39–52.

Scrimgeour, M. B., Davis, E. L., & Buss, K. A. (2016). You get what you get and you don't throw a fit!: Emotion socialization and child physiology jointly predict early prosocial development. *Developmental Psychology, 52*(1), 102–116.

Scrimsher, S., & Tudge, J. (2003). The teaching/learning relationship in the first years of school: Some revolutionary implications of Vygotsky's theory. *Early Education and Development, 14,* 293–312.

Seale, C. (2009). Legalisation of euthanasia or physician-assisted suicide: Survey of doctors' attitudes. *Palliative Medicine, 23,* 205–212.

Seals, D. R., Justice, J. N., & LaRocca, T. J. (2016). Physiological geroscience: Targeting function to increase health span and achieve optimal longevity. *The Journal of Physiology, 594*(8), 2001–2024.

Sebastián-Enesco, C., Hernandez-Lloreda, M. V., & Colmenares, F. (2013). Two and a half-year-old children are prosocial even when their partners are not. *Journal of Experimental Child Psychology, 116*(2), 186–198.

Seiffge-Krenke, I. (2010). Predicting the timing of leaving home and related developmental tasks: Parents' and children's perspectives. *Journal of Social and Personal Relationships*, 27(4), 495–518.

Seiffge-Krenke, I. (2013). "She's leaving home . . ." Antecedents, consequences, and cultural patterns in the leaving home process. *Emerging Adulthood*, 1(2), 114–124.

Seiffge-Krenke, I., Persike, M., & Luyckx, K. (2013). Factors contributing to different agency in work and study: A view on the "forgotten half." *Emerging Adulthood*, 1(4), 283–292.

Selcuk, E., Gunaydin, G., Ong, A. D., & Almeida, D. (2016). Does partner responsiveness predict hedonic and eudiamonic well-being? A 10-year longitudinal study. *Journal of Marriage and Family*, 78(2), 311–325.

Self-Brown, S. R., & Mathews, S. (2003). Effects of classroom structure on student achievement goal orientation. *Journal of Educational Research*, 97, 106–111.

Seligman, M. P. (2011). *Flourish: A visionary new understanding of happiness and well-being*. New York, NY: Free Press.

Sengupta, M., Park-Lee, E., Valverde, R., Caffrey, C., & Jones, A. (2014). Trends in length of hospice care from 1996 to 2007 and the factors associated with length of hospice care in 2007: Findings from the National Home and Hospice Care Surveys. *American Journal of Hospice and Palliative Medicine*, 31(4), 356–364.

Settersten, R. A., & Ray, B. (2010). *What's going on with young people today? The long and twisting path to adulthood*. In *The Future of Children*, 20(1), 1–21. Retrieved from www.princeton.edu/futureofchildren/publications/docs/20_01_02.pdf

Shafer, E. F. (2011). Wives' relative wages, husbands' paid work hours, and wives' labor-force exit. *Journal of Marriage and Family*, 73, 250–263.

Shafer, K., & James, S. L. (2013). Gender and socioeconomic status differences in first and second marriage formation. *Journal of Marriage and Family*, 75(3), 544–564.

Shahaeian, A., Peterson, C. C., Slaughter, V., & Wellman, H. M. (2011). Culture and the sequence of steps in theory of mind development. *Developmental Psychology*, 47(5), 1239–1247. doi:10.1037/a0023899

Shao, S., Kong, R., Zou, L., Zhong, R., Lou, J., Zhou, J., . . . Song, R. (2016). The roles of genes in the neuronal migration and neurite outgrowth network in developmental dyslexia: Single- and multiple-risk genetic variants. *Molecular Neurobiology*, 53(6), 3967–3975. doi:10.1007/s12035-015-9334-8

Sharon, T. (2015). Constructing adulthood: Markers of adulthood and well-being among emerging adults. *Emerging Adulthood*, 4(3), 161–167.

Shaywitz, S. E., Morris, R., & Shaywitz, B. A. (2008). The education of dyslexic children from childhood to young adulthood. *Annual Review of Psychology*, 59, 451–475.

Shearer, C. L., Crouter, A. C., & McHale, S. M. (2005). Parents' perceptions of changes in mother–child and father–child relationships during adolescence. *Journal of Adolescent Research*, 20, 662–684.

Sheehan, A., Schmied, V., & Barclay, L. (2013). Exploring the process of women's infant feeding decisions in the early post-birth period. *Qualitative Health Research*, 23(7), 989–998.

Sheridan, A., Murray, L., Cooper, P. J., Evangeli, M., Byram, V., & Halligan, S. I. (2013). A longitudinal study of child sleep in high- and low-risk families: Relationship to early maternal settling strategies and child psychological functioning. *Sleep Medicine*, 14(3), 266–273.

Shih, F., Lin, H., Gau, M., Chen, C., Hsiao, S., Shih, S., & Sheu, S. J. (2009). Spiritual needs of Taiwan's older patients with terminal cancer. *Oncology Nursing Forum*, 36, e31–e38.

Shimada, H., Makizako, H., Tsutsumimoto, K., Hotta, R., Nakakubo, S., & Doi, T. (2016). Driving and incidence of functional limitation in older people: A prospective population-based study. *Gerontology*, 62(6), 636–643.

Shonkoff, J. P., & Phillips, D. A. (2000). Growing up in child care. In J. P. Shonkoff & D. A. Phillips (Eds.), *From neurons to neighborhoods: The science of early childhood development* (pp. 297–327). Washington, DC: National Academy Press.

Shulman, E. P., Harden, K. P., Chein, J. M., & Steinberg, L. (2015). Sex differences in the developmental trajectories of impulse control and sensation seeking from early adolescence to early adulthood. *Journal of Youth and Adolescence*, 44(1), 1–17.

Shulman, E. P., & Steinberg, L. (2016). Human development and juvenile justice. In K. Heilbrun, D. DeMatteo, & N. S. Goldstein (Eds.), *APA handbook of psychology and juvenile justice* (pp. 69–90). Washington, DC: American Psychological Association.

Shulman, S., & Connolly, J. (2013). The challenge of romantic relationships in emerging adulthood: Reconceptualization of the field. *Emerging Adulthood*, 1(1), 27–39.

Sieswerda-Hoogendoorn, T., Bilo, R. A., van Duurling, L. L., Karst, W. A., Maaskant, J. M., van Aalderen, W. M., & van Rijn, R. R. (2013). Abusive head trauma in young children in the Netherlands: Evidence for multiple incidents of abuse. *Acta Paediatrica*, 102(11), e497–501.

Silk, T. J., Genc, S., Anderson, V., Efron, D., Hazell, P., Nicholson, J. M., . . . Sciberras, E. (2016). Developmental brain trajectories in children with ADHD and controls: A longitudinal neuroimaging study. *BMC Psychiatry*, 16(1). doi:10.1186/s12888-016-0770-4

Silva, J. M. (2016). High hopes and hidden inequalities: How social class shapes pathways to adulthood. *Emerging Adulthood*, 4(4), 239–241.

Silventoinen, K., Haukka, J., Dunkel, L., Tynelius, P., & Rasmussen, F. (2008). Genetics of pubertal timing and its associations with relative weight in childhood and adult height: The Swedish young male twins study. *Pediatrics*, 121(4), 885–891.

Silvetti, M., Castellar, E. N., Roger, C., & Verguts, T. (2014). Reward expectation and prediction error in human medial frontal cortex: An EEG study. *Neuroimage*, 84, 376–382.

Simmons, R. G., & Blyth, D. A. (1987). *Moving into adolescence: The impact of pubertal change and school context*. Hawthorne, NY: Aldine.

Simon, T., Suengas, A. G., Ruiz, G. L., & Bandres, J. (2013). Positive bias is a defining characteristic of aging to the same extent as declining performance. *International Journal of Psychology*, 48(4), 704–714.

Simons, D. A., & Wurtele, S. K. (2010). Relationships between parents' use of corporal punishment and their children's endorsement of spanking and hitting other children. *Child Abuse & Neglect*, 34, 639–646.

Simonton, D. K. (1997). Creative productivity: A predictive and explanatory model of career trajectories and landmarks. *Psychological Review, 104*, 66–89.

Simonton, D. K. (2002). Longitudinal changes in creativity. In D. K. Simonton (Ed.), *Great psychologists and their times: Scientific insights into psychology's history* (pp. 67–101). Washington, DC: American Psychological Association.

Simonton, D. K. (2007). Creative life cycles in literature: Poets versus novelists or conceptualists versus experimentalists? *Psychology of Aesthetics, Creativity, and the Arts, 1*(3), 133–139.

Sims, M., & Rofail, M. (2013). The experiences of grandparents who have limited or no contact with their grandchildren. *Journal of Aging Studies, 27*(4), 377–386.

Sinnott, J. D. (2003). Postformal thought and adult development: Living in balance. In J. Demick & C. Andreoletti (Eds.), *Handbook of adult development* (pp. 221–238). New York, NY: Kluwer Academic/Plenum.

Sirgy, J., & Lee, D.-J. (2017). Work–life balance: An integrative review. *Applied Research in Quality of Life*.

Sjörs, G. (2010). Treatment decisions for extremely preterm newborns: Beyond gestational age. *Acta Paediatrica, 99*(12), 1761–1762.

Skinner, B. F. (1960). *The behavior of organisms: An experimental analysis.* New York, NY: Appleton-Century-Crofts.

Skinner, B. F. (1974). *About behaviorism.* New York, NY: Knopf.

Skoog, T., Stattin, H., Ruiselova, Z., & Ozdemir, M. (2013). Female pubertal timing and problem behaviour: The role of culture. *International Journal of Behavioral Development, 37*(4), 357–365.

Slatcher, R. B., & Selcuk, E. (2017). A social psychological perspective on the links between close relationships and health. *Current Directions in Psychological Science, 26*(1), 16–21.

Slater, A. (2001). Visual perception. In G. Bremner & A. Fogel (Eds.), *Blackwell handbook of infant development* (pp. 5–34). Malden, MA: Blackwell.

Slater, A., Quinn, P. C., Kelly, D. J., Lee, K., Longmore, C. A., McDonald, P. R., & Pascalis, O. (2010). The shaping of the face space in early infancy: Becoming a native face processor. *Child Development Perspectives, 4*(5), 201–211.

Slaughter, V., Peterson, C. C., & Moore, C. (2013). I can talk you into it: Theory of mind and persuasion behavior in young children. *Developmental Psychology, 49*(2), 227–231.

Slavin, R. E., Cheung, A., Holmes, G., Madden, N. A., & Chamberlain, A. (2013). Effects of a data-driven district reform model on state assessment outcomes. *American Educational Research Journal, 50*(2), 371–396.

Slobin, D. I. (1972). Children and language: They learn the same way all around the world. *Psychology Today, 6*(2), 71–74, 82.

Smallfield, S., Clem, K., & Myers, A. (2013). Occupational therapy interventions to improve the reading ability of older adults with low vision: A systematic review. *American Journal of Occupational Therapy, 67*(3), 288–295.

Smeaton, D., Barnes, H., & Vegeris, S. (2017). Does retirement offer a "window of opportunity" for lifestyle change? Views from English workers on the cusp of retirement. *Journal of Aging & Health, 29*(1), 25–44. doi:10.1177/0898264315624903

Smetana, J. G., Campione-Barr, N., & Metzger, A. (2006). Adolescent development in interpersonal and societal contexts. *Annual Review of Psychology, 57*, 255–284.

Smetana, J. G., Kochanska, G., & Chuang, S. (2000). Mothers' conceptions of everyday rules for young toddlers: A longitudinal investigation. *Merrill-Palmer Quarterly, 46*, 391–416.

Smith, A. A., Silva, A. O., Rodrigues, R. P., Moreira, M. P., Nogueira, J. A., & Tura, L. R. (2017). Assessment of risk of falls in elderly living at home. *Revista Latino-Americana De Enfermagem, 25*, e2754.

Smith, A. K., Rhee, S. H., Corley, R. P., Friedman, N. P., Hewitt, J. K., & Robinson, J. L. (2012). The magnitude of genetic and environmental influences on parental and observational measures of behavioral inhibition and shyness in toddlerhood. *Behavior Genetics, 42*(5), 764–777.

Smith, A. R., Steinberg, L., Strang, N., & Chein, J. (2015). Age differences in the impact of peers on adolescents' and adults' neural response to reward. *Developmental Cognitive Neuroscience, 11*, 75–82.

Smith, G. R., Williamson, G. M., Miller, L. S., & Schultz, R. (2011). Depression and quality of informal care: A longitudinal investigation of caregiving stressors. *Psychology and Aging, 15*(3), 385–396.

Smith, J. P., & Ellwood, M. (2011). Feeding patterns and emotional care in breastfed infants. *Social Indicators Research, 101*, 227–231.

Smith, K., Colquhoun, D., Ernst, E., Sampson, W., & Jonas, M. (2016). Child health advice and parental obligation: The case of safe sleep recommendations and sudden unexpected death in infancy. *Bioethics, 2*, 129. doi:10.1111/bioe.12174

Smith, L., Gardner, B., Aggio, D., & Hamer, M. (2015). Association between participation in outdoor play and sport at 10 years old with physical activity in adulthood. *Preventive Medicine: An International Journal Devoted to Practice and Theory, 74*, 31–35.

Smith, M. E. (1926). An investigation of the development of the sentence and the extent of vocabulary in young children. *University of Iowa Studies: Child Welfare, 3*, 92.

Smith, R. L., Rose, A. J., & Schwartz-Mette, R. A. (2010). Relational and overt aggression in childhood and adolescence: Clarifying mean-level gender differences and associations with peer acceptance. *Social Development, 19*(2), 243–269.

Smock, P. J., Manning, W. D., & Porter, M. (2005). "Everything's there except money": How money shapes decisions to marry among cohabitors. *Journal of Marriage and Family, 67*, 680–696.

Smolak, L., & Stein, J. A. (2010). A longitudinal investigation of gender role and muscle building in adolescent boys. *Sex Roles, 63*, 738–746.

Smolucha, L., & Smolucha, F. (1998). The social origins of mind: Post-Piagetian perspectives on pretend play. In O. N. Saracho & B. Spodek (Eds.), *Multiple perspectives on play in early childhood education* (pp. 34–58). Albany, NY: State University of New York Press.

Snarey, J. R. (1985). Cross-cultural universality of social-moral development: A critical review of Kohlbergian research. *Psychological Bulletin, 97*, 202–232.

Snyder, L. (1999). *Speaking our minds: Personal reflections from individuals with Alzheimer's.* New York, NY: Freeman.

Soares, C. (2013). Depression in peri- and post-menopausal women: Prevalence, pathophysiology and pharmacological management. *Drugs and Aging, 30*(9), 677–685.

Sobowale, K., Ham, S., Curlin, F., & Yoon, J. (2017). Personality traits are associated with academic achievement in medical school: A nationally representative study. *Academic Psychiatry.* doi.org/10.1007/s40596-017-0766-5

Soenens, B., & Vansteenkiste, M. (2010). A theoretical upgrade of the concept of parental psychological control: Proposing new insights on the basis of self-determination theory. *Developmental Review, 30*(1), 74–99.

Soldan, A., Pettigrew, C., Cai, Q., Wang, J., Wang, M., Moghekar, A., & Albert, M. (2017). Cognitive reserve and long-term change in cognition in aging and preclinical Alzheimer's disease. *Neurobiology of Aging, 60,* 164–172. doi:10.1016/j.neurobiolaging.2017.09.002

Solmeyer, A. R., McHale, S. M., & Crouter, A. C. (2014). Longitudinal associations between sibling relationship qualities and risky behavior across adolescence. *Developmental Psychology, 50*(2), 600–610.

Son, J., Erno, A., Shea, G., Femia, E. E., Zarit, S. H., & Stephens, M. P. (2007). The caregiver stress process and health outcomes. *Journal of Aging and Health, 19,* 871–887.

Song, Y., & Shi, M. (2017). Associations between empathy and big five personality traits among Chinese undergraduate medical students. *PLoS ONE, 12*(2). doi.org/10.1371/journal.pone.0171665

Sonuga-Barke, E. J. S., & Halperin, J. M. (2010). Developmental phenotypes and causal pathways in attention deficit/hyperactivity disorder: Potential targets for early intervention? *Journal of Child Psychology & Psychiatry, 51*(4), 368–389.

Sorić, I., Penezić, Z., & Burić, I. (2017). The Big Five personality traits, goal orientations, and academic achievement. *Learning and Individual Differences, 54,* 126–134. doi.org/10.1016/j.lindif.2017.01.024

Spear, L. P. (2008). The psychology of adolescence. In K. K. Kline (Ed.), *Authoritative communities: The scientific cases for nurturing the whole child* (pp. 263–280). New York, NY: Springer-Verlag.

Specht, J., Bleidorn, W., Denissen, J. A., Hennecke, M., Hutteman, R., Kandler, C., . . . Zimmermann, J. (2014). What drives adult personality development? A comparison of theoretical perspectives and empirical evidence. *European Journal of Personality, 28*(3), 216–230.

Specht, J., Luhmann, M., & Geiser, C. (2014). On the consistency of personality types across adulthood: Latent profile analyses in two large-scale panel studies. *Journal of Personality and Social Psychology, 107*(3), 540–556.

Speller, B., & Stolee, P. (2015). Client safety in assisted living: Perspectives from clients, personal support workers and administrative staff in Toronto, Canada. *Health & Social Care in the Community, 23*(2), 131–140. doi:10.1111/hsc.12120

Spencer, S. V., Bowker, J. C., Rubin, K. H., Booth-LaForce, C., & Laursen, B. (2013). Similarity between friends in social information processing and associations with positive friendship quality and conflict. *Merrill-Palmer Quarterly, 59*(1), 106–131.

Spense, A. (1989). *The biology of human aging.* Englewood Cliffs, NJ: Prentice Hall.

Sperling, R., Donohue, M., Raman, R., Sun, C.-K., Yaari, R., Siemers, E., Johnson, K., & Aisen, P. (2018). The anti-amyloid treatment in asymptomatic Alzheimer's disease (A4) study: Report of screening data results. Paper delivered at the Alzheimer's Association International Conference. Chicago, Illinois, July 22, 2018.

Spinath, B., & Steinmayr, R. (2008). Longitudinal analysis of intrinsic motivation and competence beliefs: Is there a relation over time? *Child Development, 49,* 1555–1569.

Spreitzer, G. M., Cameron, L., & Garrett, L. (2017). Alternative work arrangements: Two images of the new world of work. *Annual Review of Organizational Psychology and Organizational Behavior, 4,* 4473–4499.

Spronk, K. (2004). Good death and bad death in ancient Israel according to biblical lore. *Social Science & Medicine, 58,* 985–995.

Sroufe, L. A. (2000). Early relationships and the development of children. *Infant Mental Health Journal, 21,* 67–74.

Sroufe, L. A., Egeland, B., Carlson, E., & Collins, W. A. (2005). Placing early attachment experiences in developmental context: The Minnesota Longitudinal Study. In K. E. Grossman, K. Grossman, & E. Waters (Eds.), *Attachment from infancy to adulthood: The major longitudinal studies* (pp. 48–70). New York, NY: Guilford Press.

St. James-Roberts, I. (2007). Helping parents to manage infant crying and sleeping: A review of the evidence and its implications for services. *Child Abuse Review, 16,* 47–69.

Stackman, V. R., Reviere, R., & Medley, B. C. (2016). Attitudes toward marriage, partner availability, and interracial dating among black college students from historically black and predominantly white institutions. *Journal of Black Studies, 47*(2), 169–192.

Staikova, E., Gomes, H., Tartter, V., McCabe, A., & Halperin, J. M. (2013). Pragmatic deficits and social impairment in children with ADHD. *Journal of Child Psychology and Psychiatry, 54*(12), 1275–1283.

Stallman, H. M., & Ohan, J. L. (2016). Parenting style, parental adjustment, and co-parental conflict: Differential predictors of child psychosocial adjustment following divorce. *Behaviour Change, 33*(2), 112–126. doi:10.1017/bec.2016.7

Stamatiadis, N. (1996). Gender effect on the accident patterns of elderly drivers. *Journal of Applied Gerontology, 15,* 8–22.

Stark, R., Bauer, E., Merz, C. J., Zimmermann, M., Reuter, M., Plichta, M. M., . . . Herrmann, M. J. (2011). ADHD related behaviors are associated with brain activation in the reward system. *Neuropsychologia, 49,* 426–434.

Start Strong: Futures Without Violence. Robert Wood Johnson Foundation, Executive Summary March 2012, http://startstrong.futureswithoutviolence.org/

Stattin, H., & Magnusson, D. (1990). *Pubertal maturation in female development.* Hillsdale, NJ: Erlbaum.

Steigler, H., & Thaler, L. (2016). Eating disorders, gene–environment interactions and the genome: Roles of stress exposures and nutritional status. *Physiology and Behavior, 162,* 181–185.

Stein, A., Malmberg, L., Leach, P., Barnes, J., & Sylva, K. (2013). The influence of different forms of early childcare on children's emotional and behavioural development at school entry. *Child: Care, Health and Development, 39*(5), 676–687.

Stein, J. H., & Reiser, L. W. (1994). A study of White middle-class adolescent boys' responses to "semenarche" (the first ejaculation). *Journal of Youth and Adolescence, 23,* 373–384.

Steinberg, L. (2001). We know somethings: Parent–adolescent relationships in retrospect and prospect. *Journal of Research on Adolescence, 11,* 1–19.

Steinberg, L. (2005). Cognitive and affective development in adolescence. *Trends in Cognitive Sciences, 9*, 69–74.

Steinberg, L. (2008). A social neuroscience perspective on adolescent risk-taking. *Developmental Review, 28*, 78–106.

Steinberg, L. (2016). Commentary: Commentary on special issue on the adolescent brain: Redefining adolescence. *Neuroscience and Biobehavioral Reviews, 70*, 343–346.

Steinberg, L., & Hill, J. P. (1978). Patterns of family interaction as a function of age, the onset of puberty, and formal thinking. *Developmental Psychology, 14*, 683–684.

Sternberg, R. J. (1984). Toward a triarchic theory of human intelligence. *Behavioral and Brain Sciences, 7*, 269–315.

Sternberg, R. J. (1986). A triangular theory of love. *Psychological Review, 93*, 119–135.

Sternberg, R. J. (1988). Triangulating love. In R. J. Sternberg & M. L. Barnes (Eds.), *The psychology of love* (pp. 119–138). New Haven, CT: Yale University Press.

Sternberg, R. J. (1996). *Successful intelligence: How practical and creative intelligence determine success in life.* New York, NY: Simon & Schuster.

Sternberg, R. J. (1997). The triarchic theory of intelligence. In D. P. Flanagan, J. L. Genshaft, & P. L. Harrison (Eds.), *Contemporary intellectual assessment: Theories, tests, and issues* (pp. 92–104). New York, NY: Guilford Press.

Sternberg, R. J. (2004). A triangular theory of love. In H. T. Reis & C. E. Rusbult (Eds.), *Close relationships: Key readings* (pp. 213–227). Philadelphia, PA: Taylor & Francis.

Sternberg, R. J. (2007). Who are the bright children? The cultural context of being and acting intelligent. *Educational Researcher, 36*(3), 148–155.

Sternberg, R. J. (2010). WICS: A new model for school psychology. *School Psychology International, 31*(6), 599–616.

Sternberg, R. J. (2013). Teaching for wisdom. In Susan A. David, Ilona Boniwell, & Amanda Conley Ayers (Eds.), *The Oxford handbook of happiness* (pp. 631–643). Oxford, United Kingdom: Oxford University Press.

Sternberg, R. J., & Berg, C. A. (1992). *Intellectual development.* New York, NY: Cambridge University Press.

Sternberg, R. J., Grigorenko, E. L., & Bundy, D. A. (2001). The predictive value of IQ. *Merrill-Palmer Quarterly, 47*, 1–41.

Sternberg, R. J., Grigorenko, E. L., & Kidd, K. K. (2005). Intelligence, race, and genetics. *American Psychologist, 60*, 46–59.

Sternberg, R. J., Jarvin, L., Birney, D. P., Naples, A., Stemler, S. E., Newman, T., . . . Grigorenko, E. L. (2014). Testing the theory of successful intelligence in teaching grade 4 language arts, mathematics, and science. *Journal of Educational Psychology, 106*(3), 881–899.

Sticca, F., & Perren, S. (2013). Is cyberbullying worse than traditional bullying? Examining the differential roles of medium, publicity, and anonymity for the perceived severity of bullying. *Journal of Youth and Adolescence, 42*(5), 739–750.

Stiles, J., & Jernigan, T. L. (2010). The basics of brain development. *Neuropsychology Review, 20*(4), 327–348.

Stipek, D. J. (1996). Motivation and instruction. In D. C. Berliner & R. C. Calfee (Eds.), *Handbook of educational psychology* (pp. 85–113). New York, NY: Macmillan.

Stipek, D. J. (1997). Success in school— For a head start in life. In S. S. Luthar, J. A. Burack, D. Cicchetti, & J. R. Weisz (Eds.), *Developmental psychopathology: Perspectives on adjustment, risk, and disorder* (pp. 75–92). New York, NY: University Press.

Stöckel, T., & Hughes, C. M. L. (2016). The relation between measures of cognitive and motor functioning in 5- to 6-year-old children. *Psychological Research, 80*(4), 543–554.

Stoll, G., Rieger, S., Ludtke, O., Nagengast, B., Trautwein, U., & Roberts, B. W. (2017). Vocational interests assessed at the end of high school predict life outcomes assessed 10 years later over and above IQ and Big Five personality traits. *Journal of Personality and Social Psychology, 113*(1), 167–184. doi.org/10.1037/pspp00000117.

Stoltenborgh, M., Bakermans-Kranenburg, M. J., van IJzendoorn, M. H., & Alink, L. A. (2013). Cultural–geographical differences in the occurrence of child physical abuse. A meta-analysis of global prevalence. *International Journal of Psychology, 48*(2), 81–94.

Stone, C., Trisi, D., Sherman, A., & Horton, E. (2017). Center for Budget and Policy Priorities: Policy Futures, A Guide to Statistics on Historical Trends in Income Inequality, pp. 7, 13. Retrieved from https//www.cbpp.org

Strand, B. H., Langballe, E. M., Hjellvik, V., Handal, M., Næss, Ø., Knudsen, G. P., . . . Bjertness, E. (2013). Midlife vascular risk factors and their association with dementia deaths: Results from a Norwegian prospective study followed up for 35 years. *Journal of the Neurological Sciences, 324*(1–2), 124–130.

Strazdins, L., Baxter, J. A., & Li, J. (2017). Long hours and longings: Australian children's views of fathers' work and family time. *Journal of Marriage and Family, 4*, 965. doi:10.1111/jomf.12400

Stremler, R., Hodnett, E., Kenton, L., Lee, K., Weiss, S., Weston, J., & Willan, A. (2013). Effect of behavioural–educational intervention on sleep for primiparous women and their infants in early postpartum: Multisite randomised controlled trial. *BMJ (British Medical Journal)*, 346.

Strickhouser, J. E., Zell, E., & Krizan, Z. (2017). Does personality predict health and well-being? A metasynthesis. *Health Psychology, 36*(8), 797–810. doi.org/10.1037/hea0000475

Striegel-Moore, R. H., & Bulik, C. M. (2007). Risk factors for eating disorders. *American Psychologist, 62*(3), 181–198.

Stroebe, M., Schut, H., & Stroebe, W. (2007). Health outcomes of bereavement. *The Lancet, 370*, 1960–1973.

Strohmeier, D., Kärnä, A., & Salmivalli, C. (2010). Intrapersonal and interpersonal risk factors for peer victimization in immigrant youth in Finland. *Developmental Psychology, 47*, 248–258.

Stutte, K., Hahn, S., Fierz, K., & Zúñiga, F. (2017). Factors associated with aggressive behavior between residents and staff in nursing homes. *Geriatric Nursing, 38*(5), 398–405. doi:10.1016/j.gerinurse.2017.02.001

Suárez-Orozco, C., Gaytán, F. X., Bang, H. J., Pakes, J., O'Connor, E., & Rhodes, J. (2010). Academic trajectories of newcomer immigrant youth. *Developmental Psychology, 46*(3), 602–618.

Subrahmanyam, K., Greenfield, P. M., & Tynes, B. (2004). Constructing sexuality and identity in an online teen chatroom. *Journal of Applied Developmental Psychology. Special Issue: Developing Children, Developing Media: Research from Television to the Internet from the Children's Digital Media Center, 25*, 651–666.

Subramanian, S. V., Elwert, G., & Christakis, N. (2008). Widowhood and mortality among the elderly: The modifying role of neighborhood concentration of widowed individuals. *Social Science & Medicine, 66*(4), 873–884.

Sulaiman, Z., Liamputtong, P., & Amir, L. H. (2016). The enablers and barriers to continue breast milk feeding in women returning to work. *Journal of Advanced Nursing, 72*(4), 825–835. doi:10.1111/jan.12884

Sullivan, A. R., & Fenelon, A. (2014). Patterns of widowhood mortality. *The Journals of Gerontology Series B: Psychological Sciences and Social Sciences, 69B*(1), 53–62.

Sullivan, H. S. (1953). *The interpersonal theory of psychiatry.* New York, NY: Norton.

Sun, S. S., Schubert, C. M., Chumlea, W. C., Roche, A. F., Kulin, H. E., Lee, P. A., . . . Ryan, A. S. (2002). National estimates of the timing of sexual maturation and racial differences among U.S. children. *Pediatrics, 110,* 911–919.

Sung, Y.-K., Li, L., Blake, C., Betz, J., & Lin, F. R. (2016). Association of hearing loss and loneliness in older adults. *Journal of Aging and Health, 28*(6), 979–994.

Sungeun, Y., & Soyeon, P. (2017). A sociocultural approach to children's perceptions of death and loss. *Omega: Journal of Death & Dying, 76*(1), 53–77. doi:10.1177/0030222817693138

Super, C. M., & Harkness, S. (2003). The metaphors of development. *Human Development, 46,* 3–23.

Super, D. E. (1957). *The psychology of careers: An introduction to vocational development.* New York, NY: Harper.

Surra, C. A., & Hughes, D. K. (1997). Commitment processes in accounts of the development of premarital relationships. *Journal of Marriage and Family, 59,* 5–21.

Surra, C. A., Hughes, D. K., & Jacquet, S. E. (1999). The development of commitment to marriage: A phenomenological approach. In J. M. Adams & W. H. Jones (Eds.), *Handbook of interpersonal commitment and relationship stability* (pp. 125–148). Dordrecht, Netherlands: Kluwer Academic.

Sussman, S., Pokhrel, P., Ashmore, R. D., & Brown, B. B. (2007). Adolescent peer group identification and characteristics: A review of the literature. *Addictive Behaviors, 32,* 1602–1627.

Sutin, A. R., Zonderman, A. B., Ferrucci, L., & Terracciano, A. (2013). Personality traits and chronic disease: Implications for adult personality development. *The Journals of Gerontology Series B: Psychological Sciences and Social Sciences, 68B*(6), 912–920.

Švab, A., & Humer, Ž. (2013). "I only have to ask him and he does it . . ." Active fatherhood and (perceptions of) division of family labour in Slovenia. *Journal of Comparative Family Studies, 44*(1), 57–78.

Svensson, B., Bornehag, C.-G., & Janson, S. (2011). Chronic conditions in children increase the risk for physical abuse—but vary with socio-economic circumstances. *Acta Paediatrica, 100,* 407–412.

Swann, W. B., Chang-Schneider, C., & McClarty, K. L. (2007). Do people's self-views matter? *American Psychologist, 62*(2), 84–94.

Swift, H. J., Abrams, D., & Marques, S. (2013). Threat or boost? Social comparison affects older people's performance differently depending on task domain. *Journals of Gerontology Series B: Psychological Sciences and Social Sciences, 68B*(1), 23–30.

Syed, M., & Seiffge-Krenke, I. (2015). Change in ego development, coping, and symptomatology from adolescence to emerging adulthood. *Journal of Applied Developmental Psychology, 41,* 110–119.

Tadmor, C. T., Tetlock, P. E., & Peng, K. (2009). Acculturation strategies and integrative complexity: The cognitive implications of biculturalism. *Journal of Cross-Cultural Psychology, 40,* 105–139.

Tamir, M., Schwartz, S. H., Oishi, S., & Kim, M. Y. (2017). The secret to happiness: Feeling good or feeling right? *Journal of Experimental Psychology: General, 146*(10), 1448–1459. doi.org/10.1037/xge0000303

Tanner, J. L. (2006). Recentering during emerging adulthood: A critical turning point in life span human development. In J. J. Arnett & J. L. Tanner (Eds.), *Emerging adults in America: Coming of age in the 21st century* (pp. 21–55). Washington, DC: American Psychological Association.

Tanner, J. L., & Arnett, J. J. (2010). Presenting "emerging adulthood": What makes it developmentally distinctive. In J. J. Arnett, M. Kloep, L. B. Hendry, & J. L. Tanner (Eds.), *Debating emerging adulthood: Stage or process?* (pp. 13–30). New York, NY: Oxford University Press.

Tanner, J. M. (1955). *Growth at adolescence.* Oxford, England: Blackwell.

Tanner, J. M. (1978). *Foetus into man: Physical growth from conception to maturity.* Cambridge, MA: Harvard University Press.

Tanofsky-Kraff, M., Shomaker, L. B., Young, J. F., & Wilfley, D. E. (2015). Interpersonal psychotherapy for eating disorders and the prevention of excess weight gain. In H. Thompson-Brenner (Ed.), *Casebook of evidence-based therapy for eating disorders* (pp. 195–219). New York, NY: Guilford Press.

Tanuseputro, P., Budhwani, S., Bai, Y. Q., & Wodchis, W. P. (2017). Palliative care delivery across health sectors: A population-level observational study. *Palliative Medicine, 31*(3), 247–257. doi:10.1177/0269216316653524

Tareque, M. I., Begum, S., & Saito, Y. (2013). Gender differences in disability-free life expectancy at old ages in Bangladesh. *Journal of Aging and Health, 25*(8), 1299–1312.

Tarrant, A., Featherstone, B., O'Dell, L., & Fraser, C. (2017). "You try to keep a brave face on but inside you are in bits": Grandparent experiences of engaging with professionals in Children's Services. *Qualitative Social Work, 16*(3), 351–366. doi.org/10.1177/1473325015615397

Tasimi, A., & Young, L. (2016). Memories of good deeds past: The reinforcing power of prosocial behavior in children. *Journal of Experimental Child Psychology, 147,* 159–166. doi:10.1016/j.jecp.2016.03.001

Taveras, E. M. (2016). Childhood obesity risk and prevention: Shining a lens on the first 1000 days. *Childhood Obesity, 12*(3), 159–161. doi:10.1089/chi.2016.0088

Taylor, C. A., Hamvas, L., & Paris, R. (2011). Perceived instrumentality and normativeness of corporal punishment use among black mothers. *Family Relations, 60,* 60–72.

Tebeka, S., Le Strat, Y., & Dubertret, C. (2016). Developmental trajectories of pregnant and postpartum depression in an epidemiologic survey. *Journal of Affective Disorders, 203,* 62–68.

Tedeschi, R. G., & Calhoun, L. G. (2008). Beyond the concept of recovery: Growth and the experience of loss. *Death Studies, 32*(1), 27–39.

Telzer, E. H., Flannery, J., Shapiro, M., Humphreys, K. L., Goff, B., Gabard-Durman, L., . . . Tottenham, N. (2013). Early experience shapes amygdala sensitivity to race: An international adoption design. *Journal of Neuroscience, 33*(33), 13484–13488.

Telzer, E. H., Fuligni, A. J., Lieberman, M. D., & Galvan, A. (2013). The effects of poor quality sleep on brain function and risk taking in adolescence. *Neuroimage, 71,* 275–283.

Telzer, E., Yuen, C., Gonzales, N., & Fuligni, A. (2016). Filling gaps in the acculturation gap-distress model: Heritage cultural maintenance and adjustment in Mexican-American families. *Journal of Youth & Adolescence, 45*(7), 1412–1425. doi:10.1007/s10964-015-0408-8

Teskereci, G., & Oncel, S. (2013). Effect of lifestyle on quality of life of couples receiving infertility treatment. *Journal of Sex & Marital Therapy, 39*(6), 476–492.

Teti, D. M., Kim, B., Mayer, G., & Countermine, M. (2010). Maternal emotional availability at bedtime predicts infant sleep quality. *Journal of Family Psychology, 24,* 307–315.

Teti, D. M., Shimizu, M., Crosby, B., & Kim, B. (2016). Sleep arrangements, parent–infant sleep during the first year, and family functioning. *Developmental Psychology, 52*(8), 1169–1181. doi:10.1037/dev0000148

Thapar, A., & Cooper, M. (2016). Attention deficit hyperactivity disorder. *Lancet, 387*(10024, North American Edition), 1240–1250. doi:10.1016/s0140-6736(15)00238-x

The Equality of Opportunity Project. (n.d.). http://www.equality-of-opportunity.org/, Chart #2.

Theis, W., & Bleiler, L. (2011). Alzheimer's Association report: 2011 Alzheimer's disease facts and figures. *Alzheimer's & Dementia, 7,* 208–244.

Thiessen, E. D., Hill, E. A., & Saffran, J. R. (2005). Infant-directed speech facilitates word segmentation. *Infancy, 7,* 53–71.

Thomaes, S., Stegge, H., & Olthof, T. (2007). Externalizing shame responses in children: The role of fragile-positive self-esteem. *British Journal of Developmental Psychology, 25*(4), 559–577.

Thomas, A., & Chess, S. (1977). *Temperament and development.* Oxford, England: Brunner/Mazel.

Thomas, A., Chess, S., & Birch, H. G. (1968). *Temperament and behavior disorders in children.* New York, NY: New York University Press.

Thomas, J. R., & French, K. E. (1985). Gender differences across age in motor performance: A meta-analysis. *Psychological Bulletin, 98,* 260–282.

Thompson, E. J., & Barnes, K. (2013). Meaning of sexual performance among men with and without erectile dysfunction. *Psychology of Men & Masculinity, 14*(3), 271–280.

Thompson, R., Lee, C., & Adams, J. (2013). Imagining fatherhood: Young Australian men's perspectives on fathering. *International Journal of Men's Health, 12*(2), 150–165.

Thompson, R. A., & Newton, E. K. (2013). Baby altruists? Examining the complexity of prosocial motivation in young children. *Infancy, 18*(1), 120–133.

Thompson-Brenner, H. (2013). The good news about psychotherapy for eating disorders: Comment on Warren, Schafer, Crowley, and Olivardia. *Psychotherapy, 50*(4), 565–567.

Tiedt, A. D., Saito, Y., & Crimmins, E. M. (2016). Depressive symptoms, transitions to widowhood, and informal support from adult children among older women and men in Japan. *Research on Aging, 6,* 619.

Todd, M. A., Shkolnikov, V. M., & Goldman, N. (2016). Why are well-educated Muscovites more likely to survive? Understanding the biological pathways. *Social Science & Medicine, 157,* 138–147. doi:10.1016/j.socscimed.2016.02.041

Tolan, P. (2016). Positive youth development interventions: Advancing evaluation theory and practice. *Applied Developmental Science, 20*(3), 147–149. doi:10.1080/10888691.2015.1014485

Tomlinson, M., Cooper, P., & Murray, L. (2005). The mother–infant relationship and infant attachment in a South African peri-urban settlement. *Child Development, 76,* 1044–1054.

Tompkins, V. (2015). Improving low-income preschoolers' theory of mind: A training study. *Cognitive Development, 36,* 1–19. doi:10.1016/j.cogdev.2015.07.001

Toomey, R. B., Umaña-Taylor, A. J., Updegraff, K. A., & Jahromi, L. B. (2013). Ethnic identity development and ethnic discrimination: Examining longitudinal associations with adjustment for Mexican-origin adolescent mothers. *Journal of Adolescence, 36*(5), 825–833.

Top 10 Best Dating Sites. (2014). *10 best dating sites, dating site reviews of Match. com.* Retrieved from http://www.top10bestdtingsites.com/index

Toril, P., Reales, J. M., & Ballesteros, S. (2014). Video game training enhances cognition of older adults: A meta-analytic study. *Psychology and Aging, 29*(3), 706–716.

Townsend, A., March, A., & Kimball, J. (2017). Can faith and hospice coexist: Is the African American church the key to increased hospice utilization for African Americans? *Journal of Transcultural Nursing, 28*(1), 32–39. doi:10.1177/1043659615600764

Trahan, M. H. (2017). Paternal self-efficacy and father involvement: A bi-directional relationship. *Psychology of Men & Masculinity.* doi:10.1037/men0000130

Trentowska, M., Svaldi, J., & Tuschen-Caffier, B. (2014). Efficacy of body exposure as treatment component for patients with eating disorders. *Journal of Behavior Therapy and Experimental Psychiatry, 45*(1), 178–185.

Triandis, H. C. (1995). *Individualism & collectivism.* Boulder, CO: Westview Press.

Troll, L. E. (1983). Grandparents: The family watchdog. In T. H. Brubaker (Ed.), *Family relationships in later life* (pp. 63–74). Beverly Hills, CA: Sage.

Troop-Gordon, W., Visconti, K. J., & Kuntz, K. J. (2011). Perceived popularity during early adolescence: Links to declining school adjustment among aggressive youth. *The Journal of Early Adolescence, 31*(1), 125–151.

Tulving, E. (1985). How many memory systems are there? *American Psychologist, 40,* 385–398.

Turkheimer, E. (2004). Spinach and ice cream: Why social science is so difficult. In L. F. DiLalla (Ed.) *Behavior genetic principles: Perspectives in development, personality, and psychopathology.* Washington, DC: American Psychological Association Press.

Turkheimer, E., Haley, A., Waldron, M., D'Onofrio, B., & Gottesman, I. I. (2003). Socioeconomic status modifies heritability of IQ in young children. *Psychological Science, 14,* 623–628.

Turkington, C., & Alper, M. M. (2001). *The encyclopedia of fertility and infertility.* New York, NY: Facts on File.

Turkle, S. (2011). *Alone together: Why we expect more from technology and less from each other*. New York, NY: Basic Books.

Twenge, J. M. (2006). *Generation me: Why today's young Americans are more confident, assertive, entitled—and more miserable than ever before*. New York, NY: Free Press.

Twenge, J. M., Sherman, R. Y., & Lyubomirsky, S. (2016). More happiness for young people and less for mature adults: Time period differences in subjective well being in the United States, 1972–2014. *Social, Psychological and Personality Science*, 7(2), 131–141.

U.S. Bureau of Labor Statistics. (n.d.). Retrieved from https://www.bls.gov/

U.S. Department of Agriculture, Food and Nutrition Service. (2014). Retrieved from http://www.fns.usda.gov/snap/supplemental-nutrition-assistanceprogram

U.S. Department of Labor Statistics, Fertility. (2017). Women's Bureau. Retrieved from https://www.dol.gov/wb/stats/Fertility.htm, February 2017.

Ude, P. U., & Njoku, O. C. (2017). Widowhood practices and impacts on women in sub-Saharan Africa: An empowerment perspective. *International Social Work*, 60(6), 1512–1522. doi:10.1177/0020872817695384

Udry, J. R. (1990). Biosocial models of adolescent problem behaviors. *Social Biology*, 37, 1–10.

Udry, J. R. (2000). Biological limits of gender construction. *American Sociological Review*, 65, 443–457.

Udry, J. R., & Campbell, B. C. (1994). Getting started on sexual behavior. In A. S. Rossi (Ed.), *Sexuality across the life course* (pp. 187–207). Chicago, IL: University of Chicago Press.

Uji, M., Sakamoto, A., Adachi, K., & Kitamura, T. (2014). The impact of authoritative, authoritarian, and permissive parenting styles on children's later mental health in Japan: Focusing on parent and child gender. *Journal of Child and Family Studies*, 23(2), 293–302.

Umemura, T., Jacobvitz, D., Messina, S., & Hazen, N. (2013). Do toddlers prefer the primary caregiver or the parent with whom they feel more secure? The role of toddler emotion. *Infant Behavior and Development*, 36(1), 102–114.

UNFPA. (2015). *Emerging evidence, lessons and practice in comprehensive sexuality education, a global review*. Paris, France: UNESCO.

UNICEF (United Nations Children's Fund). (2009). *The state of the world's children: Maternal and newborn health, 2009*. Retrieved from http://www.unicef.org/publications/index_47127.html

United Nations Children's Fund (UNICEF). (2016). *Uprooted: The growing crisis for refugee and migrant children*. Retrieved from https://data.unicef.org/topic/child-migration-and-displacement/migration/. doi:10.18356/f5cc00a0-en

Urban, J. B., Lewin-Bizan, S., & Lerner, R. M. (2010). The role of intentional self-regulation, lower neighborhood ecological assets, and activity involvement in youth developmental outcomes. *Journal of Youth and Adolescence*, 39, 783–800.

Utz, R. L., Swenson, K. L., Caserta, M., Lund, D., & deVries, B. (2014). Feeling lonely versus being alone: Loneliness and social support among recently bereaved persons. *Journals of Gerontology Series B: Psychological Sciences and Social Sciences*, 69B(1), 85–94.

Valentino, K., Nuttall, A. K., Comas, M., McDonnell, C. G., Piper, B., Thomas, T. E., & Fanuele, S. (2014). Mother–child reminiscing and autobiographical memory specificity among preschool-age children. *Developmental Psychology*, 50(4), 1197–1207.

van Aken, C., Junger, M., Verhoeven, M., van Aken, M. A. G., & Deković, M. (2008). The longitudinal relations between parenting and toddlers' attention problems and aggressive behaviors. *Infant Behavior and Development*, 31, 432–446.

van der Fels, I. M. J., te Wierike, S. C. M., Hartman, E., Elferink-Gemser, M. T., Smith, J., & Visscher, C. (2015). The relationship between motor skills and cognitive skills in 4–16 year old typically developing children: A systematic review. *Journal of Science and Medicine in Sport*, 18(6), 697–703.

Van Dijck, J. (2013). *The culture of connectivity: A critical history of social media*. Oxford, England: Oxford University Press.

van Geel, M., & Vedder, P. (2011). The role of family obligations and school adjustment in explaining the immigrant paradox. *Journal of Youth and Adolescence*, 40, 187–196.

van IJzendoorn, M. H., & Sagi, A. (1999). Cross-cultural patterns of attachment: Universal and contextual dimensions. In J. Cassidy & P. R. Shaver (Eds.), *Handbook of attachment: Theory, research, and clinical applications* (pp. 713–734). New York, NY: Guilford Press.

van Lawick, J., & Visser, M. (2015). No kids in the middle: Dialogical and creative work with parents and children in the context of high conflict divorces. *Australian and New Zealand Journal of Family Therapy*, 36(1), 33–50. doi:10.1002/anzf.1091

van Selm, M., & Van der Heijden, B. M. (2013). Communicating employability enhancement throughout the life-span: A national intervention program aimed at combating age-related stereotypes at the workplace. *Educational Gerontology*, 39(4), 259–272.

van Wijmen, M. S., Pasman, H. W., Widdershoven, G. M., & Onwuteaka-Philipsen, B. D. (2014). Motivations, aims and communication around advance directives: A mixed-methods study into the perspective of their owners and the influence of a current illness. *Patient Education and Counseling*, 95(3), 393–399.

Vandell, D. L., Burchinal, M., Vandergrift, N., Belsky, J., & Steinberg, L. (2010). Do effects of early child care extend to age 15 years? Results from the NICHD Study of Early Child Care and Youth Development. *Child Development*, 81(3), 737–756.

Vanderloo, L. M., & Mandich, G. (2013). Battling bullying: Do obese children face the same fight? *Canadian Journal of Mental Health*, 32(4), 85–88.

Vandorpe, B., Vandendriessche, J., Lefevre, J., Pion, J., Vaeyens, R., Matthys, S., Philippaerts, R., & Lenoir, M. (2011). The Korperkoordinations Test fur Kinder: Reference values and suitability for 6- to 12-year-old children in Flanders. *Scandinavian Journal of Medicine and Science in Sports*, 21(3), 378–388.

Varma, V. R., Varma, S., An, Y., Hohman, T. J., Seddighi, S., Casanova, R., . . . Thambisetty, M. (2017). Alpha-2 macroglobulin in Alzheimer's disease: A marker of neuronal injury through the RCAN1 pathway. *Molecular Psychiatry*, 22(1), 13–23. doi:10.1038/mp.2016.206

Vaughn, L. M., Ireton, C., Geraghty, S. R., Diers, T., Nino, V., Falciglia, G. A., . . . Mosbaugh, C. (2010). Sociocultural influences on the determinants of breast-feeding by Latina mothers in the Cincinnati area. *Family & Community Health*, 33(4), 318–328.

Veenstra, R., Huitsing, G., Dijkstra, J., & Lindenberg, S. (2010). Friday on my mind: The relation of partying with antisocial behavior of early adolescents. The TRAILS Study. *Journal of Research on Adolescence, 20*(2), 420–431.

Vega, P., Rivera, M. S., & González, R. (2014). When grief turns into love: Understanding the experience of parents who have revived after losing a child due to cancer. *Journal of Pediatric Oncology Nursing, 31*(3), 166–176.

Velkoff, E. A., Forrest, L. N., Dodd, D. R., & Smith, A. R. (2016). Predicting suicide risk among sexual minority women. *Psychology of Women Quarterly, 40*(2), 261–274.

Vennum, A., Hardy, N., Sibley, D. S., & Fincham, F. D. (2015). Dedication and sliding in emerging adult cyclical and non-cyclical romantic relationships. *Family Relations, 64*(3), 407–419.

Verhaeghe, L., Dereu, M., Warreyn, P., Groote, I. D., Vanhaesebrouck, P., & Roeyers, H. (2016). Extremely preterm born children at very high risk for developing autism spectrum disorder. *Child Psychiatry & Human Development, 47*(5), 729–739. doi:10.1007/s10578-015-0606-3

Verhage, M. L., Schuengel, C., Madigan, S., Fearon, R. M. P., Oosterman, M., Cassibba, R., . . . van IJzendoorn, M. H. (2016). Narrowing the transmission gap: A synthesis of three decades of research on intergenerational transmission of attachment. *Psychological Bulletin, 142*, 337–366.

Versey, H. S., Stewart, A. J., & Duncan, L. E. (2013). Successful aging in late midlife: The role of personality among college-educated women. *Journal of Adult Development, 20*(2), 63–75.

Verweij, E., Oepkes, D., de Vries, M., van den Akker, M., van den Akker, E. S., & de Boer, M. A. (2013). Non-invasive prenatal screening for trisomy 21: What women want and are willing to pay. *Patient Education and Counseling, 93*(3), 641–645.

Vespa, J. (2014). Historical trends in the marital intentions of one-time and serial cohabitors. *Journal of Marriage and Family, 76*, 207–217.

Vianna, E., & Stetsenko, A. (2006). Embracing history through transforming it: Contrasting Piagetian versus Vygotskian (activity) theories of learning and development to expand constructivism within a dialectical view of history. *Theory & Psychology, 16*(1), 81–108.

Viitasalo, N., & Nätti, J. (2015). Perceived age discrimination at work and subsequent long-term sickness absence among Finnish employees. *Journal of Occupational and Environmental Medicine, 57*(7), 801–805. doi:10.1097/JOM.0000000000000468

Virdun, C., Luckett, T., Davidson, P. M., Phillips, J., & Lorenz, K. (2017). Dying in the hospital setting: A meta-synthesis identifying the elements of end-of-life care that patients and their families describe as being important. *Palliative Medicine, 31*(7), 587–601.

Virmani, E. A., & Ontai, L. L. (2010). Supervision and training in childcare: Does reflective supervision foster caregiver insightfulness? *Infant Mental Health Journal, 31*(1), 16–32.

Visconti, K. J., Ladd, G. W., & Kochenderfer-Ladd, B. (2015). The role of moral disengagement in the associations between children's social goals and aggression. *Merrill-Palmer Quarterly, 1*, 101. doi:10.13110/merrpalmquar1982.61.1.0101

Volk, H. E., Lurmann, F., Penfold, B., Hertz-Picciotto, I., & McConnell, R. (2013). Traffic-related air pollution, particulate matter, and autism. *JAMA Psychiatry, 70*(1), 71–77.

Volkmar, F., Siegel, M., Woodbury-Smith, M., King, B., McCracken, J., & State, M. (2014). Practice parameter for the assessment and treatment of children and adolescents with autism spectrum disorder. *Journal of the American Academy of Child & Adolescent Psychiatry, 53*(2), 237–257.

von der Lippe, A., Eilertsen, D. E., Hartmann, E., & Killen, K. (2010). The role of maternal attachment in children's attachment and cognitive executive functioning: A preliminary study. *Attachment & Human Development, 12*(5), 429–444.

von Hippel, W., Henry, J. D., & Matovic, D. (2008). Aging and social satisfaction: Offsetting positive and negative effects. *Psychology and Aging, 23*, 435–439.

Von Raffler-Engel, W. (1994). *The perception of the unborn across the cultures of the world*. Seattle, WA: Hogrefe & Huber.

Voss, P., Wolff, J. K., & Rothermund, K. (2017). Relations between views on ageing and perceived age discrimination: A domain-specific perspective. *European Journal of Ageing, 1*, 5. doi:10.1007/s10433-016-0381-4

Votruba-Drzal, E., Coley, R. L., Koury, A. S., & Miller, P. (2013). Center-based child care and cognitive skills development: Importance of timing and household resources. *Journal of Educational Psychology, 105*(3), 821–838.

Vouloumanos, A., Werker, J. F., Hauser, M. D., & Martin, A. (2010). The tuning of human neonates' preference for speech. *Child Development, 81*(2), 517–527.

Vreeswijk, C. M., Maas, A. M., Rijk, C. M., & van Bakel, H. A. (2014). Fathers' experiences during pregnancy: Paternal prenatal attachment and representations of the fetus. *Psychology of Men & Masculinity, 15*(2), 129–137.

Vygotsky, L. S. (1962). *Thought and language* (E. Hanfmann & G. Vakar, Eds. & Trans.). New York, NY: MIT Press and Wiley. (Original work published 1934)

Vygotsky, L. S. (1978). *Mind in society: The development of higher psychological processes* (M. Cole, V. John-Steiner, S. Scribner, & E. Souberman, Eds.). Cambridge, MA: Harvard University Press. (Original work published 1935)

Waasdorp, T. E., Baker, C. N., Paskewich, B. S., & Leff, S. S. (2013). The association between forms of aggression, leadership, and social status among urban youth. *Journal of Youth and Adolescence, 42*(2), 263–274.

Waasdorp, T. E., Bradshaw, C. P., & Duong, J. (2011). The link between parents' perceptions of the school and their responses to school bullying: Variation by child characteristics and the forms of victimization. *Journal of Educational Psychology, 103*(2), 324–335.

Wadsworth, B. J. (1996). *Piaget's theory of cognitive and affective development: Foundations of constructivism* (5th ed.). White Plains, NY: Longman.

Wagner, J., Ludtke, O., Jonkmann, K., & Trautwein, U. (2013). Cherish yourself: Longitudinal patterns and conditions of self-esteem change in the transition to young adulthood. *Journal of Personality and Social Psychology, 104*(1), 148–163.

Wagner, T. (2000). *How schools change: Lessons from three communities revisited* (2nd ed.). New York, NY: Routledge Falmer.

Wahl, H., Heyl, V., Drapaniotis, P. M., Hörmann, K., Jonas, J. B., Plinkert, P. K., & Rohrschneider, K. (2013). Severe vision and hearing impairment and successful aging: A multidimensional view. *The Gerontologist, 53*(6), 950–962.

Waite, L. J., Iveniuk, J., Laumann, E. O., & McClintock, M. K. (2017). Sexuality in older couples: Individual and dyadic characteristics. *Archives of Sexual Behavior, 46*(2), 605–618. doi.org/10.1007/s10508-015-0651-9

Walsh, J. L. (2008, March). *Magazine reading as a longitudinal predictor of women's sexual norms and behaviors.* Paper presented at 12th Biennial Meeting of Society for Research on Adolescence, Chicago, IL.

Walter, T. (2003, July 24). Historical and cultural variants on the good death. *BMJ (British Medical Journal), 327,* 218–220.

Walton, K. E., Huyen, B. T., Thorpe, K., Doherty, E. R., Juarez, B., D'Accordo, C., & Reina, M. T. (2013). Cross-sectional personality differences from age 16–90 in a Vietnamese sample. *Journal of Research in Personality, 47*(1), 36–40.

Walvoord, E. C. (2010). The timing of puberty: Is it changing? Does it matter? *Journal of Adolescent Health, 47,* 433–439.

Wang, H., & Abbott, D. A. (2013). Waiting for Mr. Right: The meaning of being a single educated Chinese female over 30 in Beijing and Guangzhou. *Women's Studies International Forum, 40,* 222–229.

Wang, M., & Saudino, K. J. (2013). Genetic and environmental influences on individual differences in emotion regulation and its relation to working memory in toddlerhood. *Emotion, 13*(6), 1055–1067.

Wang, M., & Shi, J. (2014). Psychological research on retirement. *Annual Review of Psychology, 65,* 209–233.

Wang, S., Yang, Y., Xing, W., Chen, J., Liu, C., & Luo, X. (2013). Altered neural circuits related to sustained attention and executive control in children with ADHD: An event-related fMRI study. *Clinical Neurophysiology, 124*(11), 2181–2190.

Wang, Z., Devine, R. T., Wong, K. K., & Hughes, C. (2016). Theory of mind and executive function during middle childhood across cultures. *Journal of Experimental Child Psychology, 149,* 6–22. doi:10.1016/j.jecp.2015.09.028

Wängqvist, M., Carlsson, J., van der Lee, M., & Frisén, A. (2016). Identity development and romantic relationships in the late twenties. *Identity: An International Journal of Theory and Research, 16*(1), 124–144.

Wängqvist, M., & Frisén, A. (2016). Swedish emerging adults' sense of identity and perceptions of adulthood. In R. Žukauskienė (Ed.), *Emerging adulthood in a European context* (pp. 154–174). New York, NY: Routledge/Taylor & Francis Group.

Warren, C. S., Schafer, K. J., Crowley, M. J., & Olivardia, R. (2013). Demographic and work-related correlates of job burnout in professional eating disorder treatment providers. *Psychotherapy, 50*(4), 553–564.

Waterman, A. S. (1999). Identity, the identity statuses, and identity status development: A contemporary statement. *Developmental Review, 19,* 591–621.

Watson, J. B. (1930). *Behaviorism* (Revised ed.). New York, NY: Norton.

Watson, J. B. (with the assistance of Watson, R. R.). (1972). *Psychological care of infant and child.* New York, NY: Arno Press. (Original work published 1928)

Weaver, J. M., & Schofield, T. J. (2015). Mediation and moderation of divorce effects on children's behavior problems. *Journal of Family Psychology, 29*(1), 39–48. doi:10.1037/fam0000043

Wedding, D., Kohout, J., Mengel, M. B., Ohlemiller, M., Ulione, M., Cook, K., . . . Braddock, S. (2007). Psychologists' knowledge and attitudes about fetal alcohol syndrome, fetal alcohol spectrum disorders, and alcohol use during pregnancy. *Professional Psychology: Research and Practice, 38*(2), 208–213.

Weibel-Orlando, J. (1999). Powwow princesses and gospelettes: Growing up in grandmother's world. In M. Schweitzer (Ed.), *Indian grandparenthood* (pp. 181–202). Albuquerque, NM: University of New Mexico Press.

Weisfeld, G. (1997). Puberty rites as clues to the nature of human adolescence. *Cross-Cultural Research: The Journal of Comparative Social Science, 31,* 27–54.

Weisgram, E. S., Fulcher, M., & Dinella, L. M. (2014). Pink gives girls permission: Exploring the roles of explicit gender labels and gender-typed colors on preschool children's toy preferences. *Journal of Applied Developmental Psychology, 35*(5), 401–409. doi:10.1016/j.appdev.2014.06.004

Wells-di Gregorio, S. W. (2009). Family end-of-life decision making. In J. Werth & D. Blevins (Eds.), *Decision making near the end of life: Recent developments and future directions* (pp. 247–280). New York, NY: Routledge.

Wender, P. H., Reimherr, F. W., Marchant, B. K., Sanford, M. E., Czajkowski, L. A., & Tomb, D. A. (2011). A one-year trial of methylphenidate in the treatment of ADHD. *Journal of Attention Disorders, 15*(1), 36–45.

Werner, N. E., & Hill, L. G. (2010). Individual and peer group normative beliefs about relational aggression. *Child Development, 81*(3), 826–836.

Werner-Lin, A., McCoyd, J. L. M., & Bernhardt, B. A. (2016). Balancing genetics (science) and counseling (art) in prenatal chromosomal microarray testing. *Journal of Genetic Counseling, 25*(5), 855–867.

Werth, B., & Tsiaras, A. (2002). *From conception to birth: A life unfolds.* New York, NY: Doubleday.

Wertz, R. W., & Wertz, D. C. (1989). *Lying-in: A history of childbirth in America* (expanded ed.). New Haven, CT: Yale University Press.

Wetzel, M., Huxhold, O., & Tesch-Römer, C. (2016). Transition into retirement affects life satisfaction: Short- and long-term development depends on last labor market status and education. *Social Indicators Research, 125*(3), 991–1009. doi:10.1007/s11205-015-0862-4

Whillans, A. V., Dunn, E. W., Smeets, P., Bekkers, R., & Norton, M. I. (2017). Buying time promotes happiness. *Proceedings of the National Academy of Sciences, 114*(32), 8523–8527. doi.org/10.1073/pnas.1706541114

White, B. A., Jarrett, M. A., & Ollendick, T. H. (2013). Self-regulation deficits explain the link between reactive aggression and internalizing and externalizing behavior problems in children. *Journal of Psychopathology and Behavioral Assessment, 35*(1), 1–9.

White, J. (2006). Multiple invalidities. In J. A. Schaler (Ed.), *Howard Gardner under fire: The rebel psychologist faces his critics* (pp. 45–71). Chicago, IL: Open Court.

White, L., & Edwards, J. N. (1990). Emptying the nest and parental well-being: An analysis of national panel data. *American Sociological Review, 55,* 235–242.

Whiteman, S. D., McHale, S. M., & Crouter, A. C. (2007). Longitudinal changes in marital relationships: The role of offspring's pubertal development. *Journal of Marriage and Family, 69*(4), 1005–1020.

Whiting, J. B., Smith, D. R., Barnett, T., & Grafsky, E. L. (2007). Overcoming the Cinderella myth: A mixed methods study of successful stepmothers. *Journal of Divorce & Remarriage*, 47(1-2), 95–109.

Whitson, H. E., Landerman, L. R., Newman, A. B., Fried, L. P., Pieper, C. F., & Cohen, H. J. (2010). Chronic medical conditions and the sex-based disparity in disability: The cardiovascular health study. *Journals of Gerontology: Medical Sciences*, 65A(12), 1325–1331.

Whitton, S. W., Stanley, S. M., Markman, H. J., & Johnson, C. A. (2013). Attitudes toward divorce, commitment, and divorce proneness in first marriages and remarriages. *Journal of Marriage and Family*, 75(2), 276–287.

Wiebe, S. A., Clark, C. A., Jong, D. M., Chevalier, N., Espy, K. A., & Wakschlag, L. (2015). Prenatal tobacco exposure and self-regulation in early childhood: Implications for developmental psychopathology. *Development and Psychopathology*, 27(2), 397–409. doi:10.1017/s095457941500005x

Wiese, B. S., Burk, C. L., & Jaeckel, D. (2016). Transition to grandparenthood and job-related attitudes: Do grandparental sex and lineage matter? *Journal of Marriage and Family*, 78(3), 830–847. doi.org/10.1111/jomf.12307

Wiik, K. L., Loman, M. M., Van Ryzin, M. J., Armstrong, J. M., Essex, M. J., Pollak, S. D., & Gunnar, M. R. (2011). Behavioral and emotional symptoms of post-institutionalized children in middle childhood. *Journal of Child Psychology and Psychiatry*, 52(1), 56–63.

Wilkinson, R., & Pickett, K. (2009). *The spirit level: Why greater equality makes societies stronger.* New York, NY: Bloomsbury Press.

Williams, K. E., Nicholson, J. M., Walker, S., & Berthelsen, D. (2016). Early childhood profiles of sleep problems and self-regulation predict later school adjustment. *British Journal of Educational Psychology*, 86(2), 331–350. doi:10.1111/bjep.12109

Williams, V. J., Hayes, J. P., Forman, D. E., Salat, D. H., Sperling, R. A., Verfaellie, M., & Hayes, S. M. (2017). Cardiorespiratory fitness is differentially associated with cortical thickness in young and older adults. *Neuroimage*, 146, 1084–1092. doi.org/10.1016/j.neuroimage.2016.10.033

Williamson, H. C., Nguyen, T. P., Bradbury, T. N., & Karney, B. R. (2016). Are problems that contribute to divorce present at the start of marriage, or do they emerge over time? *Journal of Social and Personal Relationships*, 33(8), 1120–1134. doi:10.1177/0265407515617705

Willoughby, B., & Hall, S. (2015). Enthusiasts, delayers, and the ambiguous middle: Marital paradigms among emerging adults. *Emerging Adulthood*, 3(2), 123–135.

Willoughby, B., Medaris, M., James, S., & Bartholomew, K. (2015). Changes in marital beliefs among emerging adults: Examining marital paradigms over time. *Emerging Adulthood*, 3(4), 219–228.

Willoughby, T., Good, M., Adachi, P. C., Hamza, C., & Tavernier, R. (2013). Examining the link between adolescent brain development and risk taking from a social–developmental perspective. *Brain and Cognition*, 83(3), 315–323.

Wilson, S. M., Ngige, L. W., & Trollinger, L. J. (2003). Connecting generations: Paths to Maasai and Kamba marriage in Kenya. In R. R. Hamon & B. B. Ingoldsby (Eds.), *Mate selection across cultures* (pp. 95–118). Thousand Oaks, CA: Sage.

Wilson, T., Karimpour, R., & Rodkin, P. C. (2011). African American and European American students' peer groups during early adolescence: Structure, status, and academic achievement. *The Journal of Early Adolescence*, 31(1), 74–98.

Wimmer, H., & Perner, J. (1983). Beliefs about beliefs: Representation and constraining function of wrong beliefs in young children's understanding of deception. *Cognition*, 13, 103–128.

Windsor, T. D., & Anstey, K. J. (2010). Age differences in psychosocial predictors of positive and negative affect: A longitudinal investigation of young, midlife, and older adults. *Psychology and Aging*, 25(3), 641–652.

Windsor, T. D., & Butterworth, P. (2010). Supportive, aversive, ambivalent, and indifferent partner evaluations in midlife and young-old adulthood. *Journals of Gerontology: Psychological Sciences*, 65B(3), 287–295.

Wink, P., & Staudinger, U. M. (2016). Wisdom and psychosocial functioning in later life. *Journal of Personality*, 84(3), 306–318. doi.org/10.1111/jopy.12160

Wöhrmann, A. M., Deller, J., & Wang, M. (2013). Outcome expectations and work design characteristics in post-retirement work planning. *Journal of Vocational Behavior*, 83(3), 219–228.

Wolfe, D. A. (2011). Risk factors for child abuse perpetration. In J. W. White, M. P. Koss, & A. E. Kazdin (Eds.), *Violence against women and children: Vol. 1. Mapping the terrain* (pp. 31–53). Washington, DC: American Psychological Association.

Woltering, S., & Shi, Q. (2016). On the neuroscience of self-regulation in children with disruptive behavior problems: Implications for education. *Review of Educational Research*, 86(4), 1085–1110. doi:10.3102/0034654316673722

Wood, D., Bruner, J. S., & Ross, G. (1976). The role of tutoring in problem solving. *Journal of Child Psychology and Psychiatry*, 17, 89–100.

Wood, W. R., & Williamson, J. B. (2003). Historical changes in the meaning of death in the western tradition. In C. D. Bryant (Ed.), *Handbook of death & dying* (pp. 14–23). Thousand Oaks, CA: Sage.

Wood-Barcalow, N. L., Tylka, T. L., & Augustus-Horvath, C. L. (2010). "But I like my body": Positive body image characteristics and a holistic model for young-adult women. *Body Image*, 7, 106–116.

Woody, M. L., Burkhouse, K. L., & Gibb, B. E. (2015). Overgeneral autobiographical memory in children of depressed mothers. *Cognition and Emotion*, 29(1), 130–137. doi:10.1080/02699931.2014.891972

World Bank. (n.d.). Life expectancy at birth. Retrieved December 2017, from https://data.worldbank.org/indicator/SP.DYN.LE00.IN

World Health Organization. (2003). *Kangaroo mother care: A practical guide*. Geneva, Switzerland: Department of Reproductive Health and Research, World Health Organization.

World Health Organization. (2006). Retrieved from http://www.who.int/childgrowth/standards/mm_windows_graph.pdf?ua=1

World Health Organization. (2016). Media Centre, Maternal Mortality Fact Sheet. Retrieved from http://www.who.int/mediacentre/factsheets/fs348/en/

Wray-Lake, L., Crouter, A. C., & McHale, S. M. (2010). Developmental patterns in decision-making autonomy across middle childhood and adolescence: European American parents' perspectives. *Child Development*, 81(2), 636–651.

Wright, M. O., & Masten, A. S. (2005). Resilience processes in development: Fostering positive adaptation in the context of adversity. In S. Goldstein & R. B. Brooks (Eds.), *Handbook of resilience in children* (pp. 17–37). New York, NY: Kluwer Academic/Plenum.

Wu, C., & Chao, R. K. (2011). Intergenerational cultural dissonance in parent–adolescent relationships among Chinese and European Americans. *Developmental Psychology, 47*(2), 493–508.

Wu, H., & Ouyang, P. (2017). Fall prevalence, time trend and its related risk factors among elderly people in China. *Archives of Gerontology & Geriatrics, 73,* 294–299. doi:10.1016/j.archger.2017.08.009

Wurm, S., Diehl, M., Kornadt, A. E., Westerhof, G. J., & Wahl, H. (2017). How do views on aging affect health outcomes in adulthood and late life? Explanations for an established connection. *Developmental Review, 46,* 27–43. doi:10.1016/j.dr.2017.08.002

Wymbs, B. T., & Pelham, Jr., W. E. (2010). Child effects on communication between parents of youth with and without attention-deficit/hyperactivity disorder. *Journal of Abnormal Psychology, 119*(2), 366–375.

Xia, Y. R., & Zhou, Z. G. (2003). The transition of courtship, mate selection, and marriage in China. In R. R. Hamon & B. B. Ingoldsby (Eds.), *Mate selection across cultures* (pp. 231–246). Thousand Oaks, CA: Sage.

Xie, W. (2014). Social network site use, mobile personal talk and social capital among teenagers. *Computers in Human Behavior, 41,* 228–235.

Xu, H., Wen, L. M., Hardy, L. L., & Rissel, C. (2016). A 5-year longitudinal analysis of modifiable predictors for outdoor play and screen-time of 2- to 5-year-olds. *International Journal of Behavioral Nutrition and Physical Activity, 13*(1). doi:10.1186/s12966-016-0

Yamasoba, T., Lin, F. R., Someya, S., Kashio, A., Sakamoto, T., & Kondo, K. (2013). Current concepts in age-related hearing loss: Epidemiology and mechanistic pathways. *Hearing Research, 303,* 30–38.

Yancey, G. A., & Yancey, S. W. (2002). *Just don't marry one: Interracial dating, marriage, and parenting.* Valley Forge, PA: Judson Press.

Yang, C. K., & Hahn, H. M. (2002). Cosleeping in young Korean children. *Journal of Developmental & Behavioral Pediatrics, 23,* 151–157.

Yang, J., Granja, M. R., & Koball, H. (2017). Basic facts about low-income children. *Children under 18 years, 2015.* National Center for Children in Poverty. http://nccp.org/publications/pub_1170.html

Yang, P., Chen, Y., Yen, C., & Chen, H. (2014). Psychiatric diagnoses, emotional–behavioral symptoms and functional outcomes in adolescents born preterm with very low birth weights. *Child Psychiatry and Human Development, 46,* 358–366.

Yaros, A., Lochman, J. E., & Wells, K. (2015). Parental aggression as a predictor of boys' hostile attribution across the transition to middle school. *International Journal of Behavioral Development, 40*(5), 452–458. doi:10.1177/0165025415607085

Yates, M., & Youniss, J. (1998). Community service and political identity development in adolescence. *Journal of Social Issues, 54,* 495–512.

Yeung, W. J., & Hu, S. (2013). Coming of age in times of change: The transition to adulthood in China. *Annals of the American Academy of Political and Social Science, 646*(1), 149–171.

Ying, L., & Loke, A. Y. (2016). An analysis of the concept of partnership in the couples undergoing infertility treatment. *Journal of Sex & Marital Therapy, 42*(3), 243–256.

Yoon, J. D., Hunt, N. B., Ravella, K. C., Jun, C. S., & Curlin, F. A. (2017). Physician burnout and the calling to care for the dying: A national survey. *American Journal of Hospice & Palliative Medicine, 34*(10), 931–937. doi:10.1177/1049909116661817

You Joung, K., Kim, B., Hoyoung, A., Ki Woong, K., Young Shin, P., Kim, Y. J., . . . Park, Y. S. (2017). An international comparative study on driving regulations on people with dementia. *Journal of Alzheimer's Disease, 56*(3), 1007–1014. doi:10.3233/JAD-160762

You, J., Lin, M., & Leung, F. (2013). Functions of non-suicidal self-injury among Chinese community adolescents. *Journal of Adolescence, 36*(4), 737–745.

Young, K., Koppel, S., & Charlton, J. (2017). Toward best practice in Human Machine Interface design for older drivers: A review of current design guidelines. *Accident Analysis and Prevention, 106,* 460–468. doi:10.1016/j.aap.2016.06.010

Young, S., & Amarasinghe, J. M. (2010). Practitioner review: Non-pharmacological treatments for ADHD: A lifespan approach. *Journal of Child Psychology and Psychiatry, 51*(2), 116–133.

YRBSS. (n.d.). Trends in the prevalence of suicide-related behavior, National YRBS: 1991–2016. Retrieved from www.cdc.gov/yrbss

Zahabi, M., Machado, P., Pankok, C. J., Lau, M. Y., Liao, Y., Hummer, J., & Kaber, D. B. (2017). The role of driver age in performance and attention allocation effects of roadway sign count, format and familiarity. *Applied Ergonomics, 63,* 17–30. doi:10.1016/j.apergo.2017.04.001

Zaichkowsky, L. D., & Larson, G. A. (1995). Physical, motor, and fitness development in children and adolescents. *Journal of Education, 177,* 55–79.

Zaman, S., Inbadas, H., Whitelaw, A., & Clark, D. (2017). Review article: Common or multiple futures for end of life care around the world? Ideas from the 'waiting room of history.' *Social Science & Medicine, 172,* 72–79. doi:10.1016/j.socscimed.2016.11.012

Zantinge, E. M., van den Berg, M., Smit, H. A., & Picavet, H. J. (2014). Retirement and a healthy lifestyle: Opportunity or pitfall? A narrative review of the literature. *European Journal of Public Health, 24*(3), 433–439.

Zayas, V., Mischel, W., Shoda, Y., & Aber, J. L. (2011). Roots of adult attachment: Maternal caregiving at 18 months predicts adult peer and partner attachment. *Social Psychological and Personality Science, 2*(3), 289–297.

Zeanah, C. H., Berlin, L. J., & Boris, N. W. (2011). Practitioner review: Clinical applications of attachment theory and research for infants and young children. *Journal of Child Psychology and Psychiatry, 52*(8), 819–833.

Zerbe, K. (2013). Personal meaning and eating disorder treatment: Comment on Warren et al. *Psychotherapy, 50*(4), 573–575.

Zeskind, P. S., & Lester, B. M. (2001). Analysis of infant crying. In L. T. Singer & P. S. Zeskind (Eds.), *Biobehavioral assessment of the infant* (pp. 149–166). New York, NY: Guilford Press.

Zettergren, P. (2007). Cluster analysis in sociometric research: A pattern-oriented approach to identifying temporally stable peer status groups of girls. *The Journal of Early Adolescence, 27,* 90–114.

Zhang, Z., Liu, H., & Yu, Y. (2016). Marital biography and health in middle and late life. In J. Bookwala & J. Bookwala (Eds.), *Couple relationships in the middle and later years: Their nature, complexity, and role in health and illness* (pp. 199–218). Washington, DC, US: American Psychological Association. doi:10.1037/14897-011

Zhou, J., & Hearst, N. (2016). Health-related quality of life of among elders in rural China: The effect of widowhood. *Quality of Life Research, 25*(12), 3087–3095. doi:10.1007/s11136-016-1338-y

Zhou, N., & Buehler, C. (2016). Family, employment, and individual resource-based antecedents of maternal work–family enrichment from infancy through middle childhood. *Journal of Occupational Health Psychology,* 21(3), 309–321. doi:10.1037/ocp0000016

Ziaei, M., Salami, A., & Persson, J. (2017). Age-related alterations in functional connectivity patterns during working memory encoding of emotional items. *Neuropsychologia, 94*, 1–12. doi:10.1016/j.neuropsychologia.2016.11.012

Zimmer-Gembeck, M. J., & Helfand, M. (2008). Ten years of longitudinal research on U.S. adolescent sexual behavior: Developmental correlates of sexual intercourse, and the importance of age, gender and ethnic background. *Developmental Review, 28*, 153–224.

Zimmermann, P., & Iwanski, A. (2014). Emotion regulation from early adolescence to emerging adulthood and middle adulthood: Age differences, gender differences, and emotion-specific developmental variations. International Journal of Behavioral Development, 38(2), 182–194.

Zucker, A. N., Ostrove, J. M., & Stewart, A. J. (2002). College-educated women's personality development in adulthood: Perceptions and age differences. *Psychology and Aging, 17*, 236–244.

Zúñiga, F., Ausserhofer, D., Hamers, J. P., Engberg, S., Simon, M., & Schwendimann, R. (2015). Original study: Are staffing, work environment, work stressors, and rationing of care related to care workers' perception of quality of care? A cross-sectional study. *Journal of the American Medical Directors Association, 16*, 860–866. doi:10.1016/j.jamda.2015.04.012

Subject Index